The Acts of the Apostles

Translated from the 14th German edition (1965) by permission of Vandenhoeck and Ruprecht, Göttingen, by Bernard Noble and Gerald Shinn, under the supervision of Hugh Anderson, and with the translation revised and brought up to date by R. McL. Wilson.

THE ACTS OF
THE APOSTLES
A Commentary

by ERNST HAENCHEN

THE WESTMINSTER PRESS
Philadelphia

ISBN 0–664–20919–X

Library of Congress Catalog Card No. 78–161218

Published by The Westminster Press
Philadelphia, Pennsylvania   ®

PRINTED IN THE UNITED STATES OF AMERICA

3 4 5 6 7 8 9

To H. J. Cadbury,
in gratitude

PREFACE

Fifty-six years ago, in my first semester, I bought as my first books the Nestle *Novum Testamentum Graece* and Wendt's commentary on Acts, which had just appeared in its 9th edition in the Meyer commentary series. At that time I did not suspect that Acts one day would claim the major part of my time and effort for 20 years on end, and that as author of the 10th edition I was to be Wendt's successor.

Probably neither of these things would have come about had I not had to travel to Switzerland for a cure in 1944. It was then strictly forbidden to take books across the frontier. Only in Davos did I discover that Nestle (thin-paper edition) had made the journey with me in my coat pocket. This was all I had when I began to occupy the time of my convalescence with some serious work. That was a great blessing. For when I now sought to penetrate more deeply into Acts, I was not led astray by any secondary literature which was primarily interested in Luke's sources. So I came quite independently to the question what the author of Acts had wanted to say to his readers through the varied scenes of his book, and I sought myself to become his reader.

In this way there came into being, in 1946, the first brief outline of my work, which before the appearance of the book grew into a comprehensive volume. For now an answer had also to be found for the many other questions which Acts presents to the expositor. By the 15th edition (1968) the commentary had been twice substantially revised, and the English translation also contains many new insights.

So comprehensive a volume does not come into being without many helpers. Joachim Jeremias and Ernst Käsemann read the entire manuscript of the first edition in its various stages with a critical eye, and this I would recall once again with gratitude today. In regard to literature from outside Germany I am particularly indebted to the writings of Dom Jacques Dupont and H. J. Cadbury. The treasures of *The Beginnings of Christianity* have been consulted again and again.

Many hands have worked on the translation into English; Professor R. McL. Wilson has finally brought it to a successful conclusion. Special thanks are due to him, and also to Miss S. Williams of Blackwell's, who with other willing helpers has contributed substantially to the success of the work.

ERNST HAENCHEN

Münster (Westf.),
22 November 1970

NOTE TO THE ENGLISH EDITION

Where foreign books are known to be available in English, the fact has been noted, but no attempt has been made to identify every reference except in the case of the frequently cited *Studies in Acts* by Dibelius. Quotations have been translated direct from the German in most cases, without reference to existing English translations. In the case of books originally published in English, however, quotations have of course been traced and conformed to the original.

In the making of books an important but all too often unacknowledged part is played behind the scenes: by the printer and his readers, and particularly by the editorial supervisor in the publisher's office. In the present case a very special tribute is due to Miss Susan Williams, who not only saw the book through the press, but earlier, when arrangements for the retyping of the heavily-corrected script broke down, gallantly undertook the gigantic task in addition to her other work. Every reader owes her a debt which only the editor can fully appreciate.

R. McL. W.

CONTENTS

Introduction

Commentary

ABBREVIATIONS

1a) Apostolic Fathers

Barn.	= Epistle of Barnabas
I. Clem.	= First Epistle of Clement
II Clem.	= Second Epistle of Clement
Did.	= Didache
Diog.	= Epistle to Diognetus
Herm.	= Shepherd of Hermas
(*Man.*)	= Mandates
(*Sim.*)	= Similitudes
(*Vis.*)	= Visions
Ign.	= Ignatius
Ign. *Eph.*	= Ignatius to the Ephesians
Ign. *Magn.*	= Ignatius to the Magnesians
Ign. *Phil.*	= Ignatius to the Philadelphians
Ign. *Pol.*	= Ignatius to Polycarp
Ign. *Rom.*	= Ignatius to the·Romans
Ign. *Smyrn.*	= Ignatius to the Smyrnaeans
Ign. *Trall.*	= Ignatius to the Thrallians
Mar. Pol.	= Martyrdom of Polycarp
Pol. *Phil.*	= Epistle of Polycarp (to the Philippians)
Pap.	= Papias

1b) Apocrypha and Pseudepigrapha

Asc. Is.	= Ascension of Isaiah
Ass. Mos.	= Assumption of Moses
Bar.	= Baruch
Bar. (Gr.)	= Greek Apocalypse of Baruch
Bar. (Syr.)	= Syriac Apocalypse of Baruch
Eb. Ev.	= Gospel of the Ebionites
3 Es.	= 3rd Book of Esdras
4 Es.	= 4th Book of Esdras
Est.	= Esther
En. (Eth.)	= Ethiopic Enoch
En. (Gr.)	= Greek Enoch
En. (Slav.)	= Slavonic Enoch
Jdt.	= Judith

I Macc.   = I Maccabees
II Macc.   = II Maccabees
III Macc.   = III Maccabees
IV Macc.   = IV Maccabees
Od. Sol.   = Odes of Solomon
Petr. Ev.   = Gospel of Peter
Ps. Sol.   = Psalms of Solomon
Sib.   = Sibylline Oracles
Tob.   = Tobias
Wisd.   = Wisdom of Solomon
Test. XII   = Testament of the Twelve Patriarchs

2. *Periodicals etc.*

AJP   = *American Journal of Philology*
AngThR   = *Anglican Theological Review*
AThANT   = *Abhandlungen zur Theologie des Alten und Neuen
                     Testaments*
BFchTh   = *Beiträge zur Förderung christl. Theologie*
BJRL   = *Bulletin of the John Rylands Library*
BWANT   = *Beiträge zur Wissenschaft vom Alten und Neuen
                     Testaments*
BZ   = *Biblische Zeitschrift*
CBQ   = *Catholic Biblical Quarterly*
CQR   = *Church Quarterly Review*
Con.Neot.   = *Coniectanea Neotestamentica*
DtT   = *Dansk teologisk Tidsskrift*
Eph.Theol.Lou.   = *Ephemerides Theologicae Lovanienses*
Eranos   = *Eranos. Acta philologica Suecana*
Ev.Th.   = *Evangelische Theologie*
Exp.   = *Expositor*
Exp.Tim.   = *Expository Times*
FGLPr   = *Forschungen zur Geschichte u. Lehre des Protes-
                     tantismus*
FRLANT   = *Forschungen zu Religion u. Literatur des Alten u.
                     Neuen Testaments*
HTR   = *Harvard Theological Review*
JAOS   = *Journal of the American Oriental Society*
JBL   = *Journal of Biblical Literature*
JEH   = *Journal of Ecclesiastical History*
JJS   = *Journal of Jewish Studies*
JQR   = *Jewish Quarterly Review*
JRomSt   = *Journal of Roman Studies*
JTS   = *Journal of Theological Studies*
NGG   = *Nachrichten der Gesellschaft der Wissenschaften
                     zu Göttingen*

NkZ	= *Neue kirchliche Zeitschrift*
NovTest	= *Novum Testamentum*
NTA	= *New Testament Abstracts*
NTS	= *New Testament Studies*
NTT	= *Norsk Teologisk Tidsskrift*
Rev.Bibl.	= *Revue Biblique*
RevScR	= *Revue de Science religieuse*
RHEcclés.	= *Revue d'Histoire ecclésiastique*
RHPhr	= *Revue d'Histoire et de philosophie religieuses*
RScR	= *Recherches de Science religieuse*
RSPT	= *Revue de Sciences philosophiques et théologiques*
RThPh	= *Revue de Théologie et de philosophie*
SAB	= *Sitzungsberichte der Deutschen Akademie der Wissenschaften zu Berlin* (philosophical-historical category)
SAH	= *Sitzungsberichte der Akademie der Wissenschaften zu Heidelberg*
SEÅ	= *Svensk Exegetisk Årsbok*
StKr	= *Studien und Kritiken*
SvTKv	= *Svensk Teologisk Kvartalskrift*
TAPA	= *Transactions of the American Philological Association*
ThBl	= *Theologische Blätter*
ThR	= *Theologische Rundschau*
ThQ	= *Theologische Quartalschrift*
ThStKr	= *Theologische Studien und Kritiken*
ThZ	= *Theologische Zeitschrift* (Basel)
TLZ	= *Theologische Literaturzeitung*
TU	= *Texte und Untersuchungen zur Geschichte der altchristlichen Literatur*
VuF	= *Verkündigung und Forschung*
ZAW	= *Zeitschrift für die alttestamentliche Wissenschaft*
ZKG	= *Zeitschrift für Kirchengeschichte*
ZkTh	= *Zeitschrift für katholische Theologie*
ZNW	= *Zeitschrift für die neutestamentliche Wissenschaft*
ZsyTh	= *Zeitschrift für systematische Theologie*
ZThK	= *Zeitschrift für Theologie und Kirche*
ZwTh	= *Zeitschrift für wissenschaftliche Theologie*

3. Commentaries

Bauernfeind	= Otto Bauernfeind, *Die Apostelgeschichte. Theologischer Handkommentar zum Neuen Testament*, V, Leipzig 1939.
Beg. IV	= *The Beginnings of Christianity*, Vol. IV: English Translation and Commentary, edited by Kirsopp Lake and Henry J. Cadbury, London 1933.

Beg. V = *The Beginnings of Christianity*, Vol. V: *Additional Notes to the Commentary*, edited by Kirsopp Lake and Henry J. Cadbury, London 1933.

Beyer = Hermann Wolfgang Beyer, *Die Apostelgeschichte. Translated and explained. Das Neue Testament Deutsch.* Vol. 2, part 5, Göttingen 1933, 4th ed. 1947.

Bruce = *The Acts of the Apostles.* The Greek Text with Introduction and Commentary by F. F. Bruce, 2nd ed., London 1951.

Dupont = *Les Actes des Apôtres.* Introduction de M. le Chanoine L. Cerfaux, Professeur à l'Université de Louvain, Traduction et notes de Dom J. Dupont, O.S.B., Professeur à l'Abbaye de Saint-André. (*La Sainte Bible*, traduite en français sous la direction de l'École Biblique de Jérusalem) Les Éditions du Cerf, 2nd ed., Paris 1954.

Holtzmann = Heinrich Julius Holtzmann, *Die Apostelgeschichte. Hand-Kommentar zum Neuen Testament*, vol. I, part 2, 3rd ed., Tübingen/Leipzig 1901.

Jacquier = E. Jacquier, *Les Actes des Apôtres. Études Bibliques*, Paris 1926.

Knopf = Rudolf Knopf, *Die Apostelgeschichte.* Die Schriften des Neuen Testaments neu übersetzt und für die Gegenwart erklärt. Vol. I, Göttingen 1907, pp. 526–667.

Loisy = Alfred Loisy, *Les Actes des Apôtres*, Paris 1920.

Michaelis = Wilhelm Michaelis, *Das Neue Testament verdeutscht und erläutert.* Vol. 2: *Taten der Apostel* (pp. 1–115), *Briefe, Offenbarung* (= Kröners Taschenausgabe, vol. 121), Leipzig 1935.

Overbeck = *Kurze Erklärung der Apostelgeschichte* by Dr. W. M. L. de Wette, 4th ed., revised and enlarged by Franz Overbeck. *Kurzgefaßtes exegetisches Handbuch zum Neuen Testament.* Vol. I, part 4, Leipzig 1870.

Preuschen = Erwin Preuschen, *Die Apostelgeschichte.* Handbuch zum Neuen Testament, vol. 4, part 1, Tübingen 1913.

Rieu = *The Acts of the Apostles*, by Saint Luke. Translated with an Introduction and Notes by C. V. Rieu. Baltimore, Penguin Books Inc. 1957.

Schlatter = Adolf Schlatter, *Die Apostelgeschichte.* Erläuterungen zum Neuen Testament, part 4, Calwer Verlag, Stuttgart 1948.

Wendt	= Hans Hinrich Wendt, *Die Apostelgeschichte*, Kritisch-exegetischer Kommentar über das Neue Testament, begründet von H. A. W. Meyer, part 3, 9th ed., Göttingen 1913.
Williams	= C. S. C. Williams, *A Commentary on the Acts of the Apostles* (Black's New Testament Commentaries), London 1957.
Wikenh. Apg.	= *Die Apostelgeschichte* übersetzt und erklärt von Alfred Wikenhauser. (Regensburger Neues Testament, vol. 5.) 3rd revised ed., Regensburg 1956.
Zahn	= Theodor Zahn, *Die Apostelgeschichte des Lucas.* (*Kommentar zum Neuen Testament*. vol. 5.) Leipzig/Erlangen, part 1 1919, part 2 1921.

4. *Other Works*

Beg.	= *The Beginnings of Christianity*. Part I: *The Acts of the Apostles*. Edited by F. J. Foakes Jackson and Kirsopp Lake.
Beg. I	= Vol. I: *Prolegomena I. The Jewish, Gentile and Christian Backgrounds* 1920. Reprinted 1942.
Beg. II	= Vol. II: *Prolegomena II. Criticism.* 1922.
Beg. III	= Vol. III: *The Text of Acts*, by James Hardy Ropes, 1926.
Beg. IV, V	= See List of Commentaries.
Cadbury	= Henry J. Cadbury, *The Book of Acts in History*, London 1955.
Conzelmann	= Hans Conzelmann, *Die Mitte der Zeit*. Studien zur Theologie des Lukas (Beiträge zur historischen Theologie 17), 4th ed., Tübingen 1963. (ET: *The Theology of St. Luke.* London and New York 1960.)
Conzelmann, Hdb	= Hans Conzelmann, *Die Apostelgeschichte* (Handbuch zum NT 7, Tübingen 1963).
Dibelius	= Martin Dibelius, *Aufsätze zur Apostelgeschichte*, edited by Heinrich Greeven (FRLANT N.F. 42), Göttingen 1951. (ET: *Studies in the Acts of the Apostles*, London 1956. (1) Style Criticism of the Book of Acts, 1923, pp. 1–25. (2) Paul on the Areopagus, 1939, pp. 26–77. (3) Paul in Athens, 1939, pp. 78–83. (4) The Text of Acts, 1941, pp. 84–92. (5) The Apostolic Council, 1947, pp. 93–101. (6) The Acts of the Apostles as an Historical Source, 1947, pp. 102–108. (7) The Conversion of Cornelius, 1947, pp. 109–122. (8) The First Christian Historian, 1948, pp. 123–37. (9) The Speeches in Acts and Ancient Historiography, 1949, pp.

Trocmé	= Etienne Trocmé, *Le 'Livre des Actes' et l'histoire*, Paris 1957.
J. Weiß	= Johannes Weiß, *Über die Absicht und den literarischen Charakter der Apostelgeschichte*, Göttingen 1897.
Wellhausen	= Julius Wellhausen, *Kritische Analyse der Apostelgeschichte*, AAG, vol. 15, 2, Berlin 1914.
Wikenhauser	= Alfred Wikenhauser, *Die Apostelgeschichte und ihr Geschichtswert (Ntl. Abhandlungen* 8, 3–5), Münster 1921.

5. Texts, dictionaries, grammars, etc.

Nestle	= Novum Testamentum Graece, cum apparatu critico curavit D. Eberhard Nestle, novis curis elabocaverunt D. Dr. Erwin Nestle et D. Kurt Aland D.D. Edition vicesima quinta, Stuttgart 1963.
von Soden	= Hermann von Soden, *Die Schriften des Neuen Testaments in ihrer ältesten erreichbaren Textgestalt.*
	I. *Untersuchungen.*
	1. Die Textzeugen. Göttingen 1911².
	2. Die Textformen. A. Die Evangelien. Göttingen 1911².
	3. Die Textformen. B. Der Apostolos mit Apokalypse. Göttingen 1911².
	II. *Text und Apparat.* Göttingen 1913.
LXX	= Septuaginta, id est Vetus Testamentum Graece iuxta LXX interpretes edidit Alfred Rahlfs. Stuttgart 1935.
Hebr	= Biblia Hebraica, edidit Rudolf Kittel. Editio septima. Stuttgart 1951.
Bauer, *Wb*	= Walter Bauer, *Griechisch-deutsches Wörterbuch zu den Schriften des Neuen Testaments und der übrigen urchristlichen Literatur.* 5th revised and enlarged edition, Berlin 1958. English edition by W. F. Arndt and F. W. Gingrich, *A Greek-English Lexicon of the NT*, Chicago and Cambridge 1957.
ThWb	= Gerhard Kittel, *Theologisches Wörterbuch zum Neuen Testament*, vol. 1 1933 (α–γ), vol. 2 1935 (δ–η), vol. 3 1938 (ν–χ), vol. 4 1942 (λ–ν), vol. 5 1954 (ξ–πα), vol. 6 1959 (πε–ρ), vol. 7 1966 (σ), vol. 8 1969 (τ–υ) ET (Vols. 1–6): *Theological Dictionary of the NT*, tr. G. W. Bromiley, 1964–.

Liddell-Scott = *A Greek-English Lexicon*, compiled by H. G. Liddell and R. Scott, a new edition, reprinted 1953.

Bl.-Debr. = Friedrich Blaß, *Grammatik des neutestamentlichen Griechisch*, bearbeitet von Dr. Phil. Alb. Debrunner, 11th ed. 1963. ET: *A Greek Grammar of the NT*, ed. R. W. Funk, Cambridge and Chicago 1961.

Radermacher = Ludwig Radermacher, *Neutestamentliche Grammatik*. 2nd enlarged ed., Tübingen 1925 (*Handbuch zum Neuen Testament*).

Moulton = J. H. Moulton, *A Grammar of NT Greek*, Vol. I: *Prolegomena*, London 1906.

Bauer, *Einf.* = Walter Bauer, *Zur Einführung in das Wörterbuch zum Neuen Testament*. Lund 1955 (Coniectanea Neotestamentica XV).

B. Weiß, *Einl.* = Bernhard Weiß, *Einleitung in das Neue Testament*, 1886.

Zahn, *Einl.* = Theodor Zahn, *Einleitung in das Neue Testament*, 2. ³1907. (ET: *Introduction to the New Testament*, 3 vols., 1909.)

Zahn, *Gesch. ntl.*
Kanons = Theodor Zahn, *Geschichte des neutestamentlichen Kanons*, 1888–92.

Zahn, *Forsch. z. Gesch.*
des ntl. Kanons = Theodor Zahn, *Forschung zur Geschichte des neutestamentlichen Kanons*, Vol. IX, 1916.

Schürer, *GJV* = Emil Schürer, *Geschichte des jüdischen Volkes im Zeitalter Christi*. Vol. 1 1901³ ⁴, vol. 2 1907⁴, vol. 3 1909⁴. (ET: *History of the Jewish People in the Time of Jesus*, New York 1961.)

Billerbeck = Hermann L. Strack and Paul Billerbeck, *Kommentar zum Neuen Testament aus Talmud und Midrasch*. 6 vols., Munich 1922–61.

Leitzmann = Hans Leitzmann, *Geschichte der Alten Kirche*. I. *Die Anfänge* 1932¹ 1953³. ET: *The Beginnings of the Christian Church*, tr. B. L. Woolf, London 1937.

CIG = *Corpus Inscriptionum Graecarum*, edited by E. Curtius, A. Kirchhoff and others, 1825–77.

CIL = *Corpus Inscriptionum Latinarum*, Berlin 1862–.

CSEL = *Corpus Scriptorum Ecclesiastiorum Latinorum*, Vienna 1866–.

GCS = *Die griechisch-christliche Schriftsteller der ersten drei Jahrhunderte*, Leipzig, Berlin 1897–.

OGis = *Orientis Graeci inscriptiones selectae*, ed. W. Dittenberger, 2 vols., 1903–1905.

RAC   = *Reallexikon für Antike und Christentum*, ed. T. Klauser, 1950–.

RGG   = *Die Religion in Geschichte und Gegenwart.* 2nd ed., Tübingen 1927–31, 3rd ed. 1957 ff.

INTRODUCTION

1. THE CHURCH'S OLDEST WITNESSES FOR ACTS AND ITS AUTHOR

When is Acts first mentioned, either by the naming of its author or through a verbal citation? It was once thought possible to show in this way that by the end of the first century Acts was already an authoritative document of the Church. Its composition would then lie considerably earlier. We shall first consider such 'quotations' and then discuss the explicit references to Acts and its author.

I. The earliest document said to make use of Acts is the *First Epistle of Clement*[1]:

(a) First there are two passages which are linked by their use of the word *place* (τόπος) with Acts **1**.25: 'that he might go to his own place.' These are I Clem. **5**.4: 'Peter, who . . . , having borne witness, has gone to the place of glory which befits him', and **5**.7: 'After he [Paul] had borne witness before the governors, he departed this world and was received into the holy place.' But in fact Acts was not the model here. It is simply a matter of a familiar image of edifying language, which can be used in various connections, as in the following related passages: Ignatius *Magn.* **5**.1: 'and since each man will go to his own place'; Polycarp *Phil.* **9**.2: 'all these are in their rightful place beside the Lord'; Hermas *Sim.* IX 27.3: 'their place is with the angels'.

(b) At I Clem. **2**.2: 'and there was a full outpouring of the Holy Spirit upon all', K. Bihlmeyer[2] recalls Acts **2**.17: 'I shall pour forth of my spirit on all flesh' (quoted from Joel **3**.1). This peculiar expression is however too far removed from the Lucan thought and wording to justify the assertion of a use of Acts.

(c) There is a strikingly exact coincidence between I Clem. **18**.1: 'God said, I have found a man after my heart, David the son of Jesse; him I have anointed with eternal mercy,' and Acts **13**.22: 'I have found David the son of Jesse, a man after my heart.' Both link up Psalm **89**.21 ('I have found David'), I Samuel **13**.14 ('a man after his heart')[3] and II Samuel **23**.1 ('David the son of Jesse'; so also Psalm **72**.20). However, we need not think

---

[1] Harnack dates it between 93 and 95, Knopf to 95 or 96, Molland to 96, Kümmel between 80 and 90. See Harnack, *Chronologie der altchristlichen Literatur bis Euseb.*, I, 255; R. Knopf, *Hdb. z. NT*, Suppl. 1920, 43; E. Molland, *RGG*[3] I, 1837; W. G. Kümmel, *Einleitung in das NT* 1965[2], 125 (ET 1966, 304).

[2] Karl Bihlmeyer, *Die apostolischen Väter*, Part I 1924, 156.

[3] Here LXX renders the word אִישׁ by ἄνθρωπος.

of a borrowing from Acts. Luke continues with the words 'who shall do all I will', from Isaiah **44**.28 LXX, while Clement completes the sentence with words from Psalm **89**.21: 'him I have anointed with eternal mercy'[1]. Moreover the composite quotation stands in each case in a quite different and self-contained context. Acts brings out God's pleasure in David, but Clement emphasizes that even the pious David was a sinner who had to sue for mercy. Finally it is unlikely that Clement waited until the moment of writing to the Corinthians before assembling in his mind the men who had won God's approbation (μεμαρτυρημένοι). More probably, in this list, as elsewhere, he was taking over an item of tradition, in which the same composite quotation as in Acts appeared. According to A. Loisy and L. Cerfaux this is explained by the use of a 'book of testimonies'.[2]

(d) One might claim I Clem. **2**.1: 'rather giving than taking', as a quotation of Acts **20**.35: 'It is more blessed to give than to receive.' However, as shown in the commentary on this passage, both texts simply make independent use of the same Greek proverb. Luke regards it as a saying of Jesus, but no such claim appears in I Clem. **2**.1.

(e) Bihlmeyer[3] has drawn attention to the similarity between I Clem. **59**.2: 'who has called us from darkness into light', and Acts **26**.18: 'that they may turn from darkness to light' (cf. Isaiah **42**.7, 16). The position of this expression in Clement's great final prayer shows that what we have here is a liturgical formula. Luke uses it as part of the utterance of the exalted Lord.

II. The next Christian writer we have to consider is IGNATIUS OF ANTIOCH[4]:

(a) We have already dealt, under I(a) above, with the relation between Ignatius *Magn.* **5**.1 and Acts **1**.25.

(b) Ignatius *Smyrn.* **3**.3: 'after the Resurrection he ate and drank with them as a man of flesh', corresponds with Acts **10**.41: 'we who did eat and drink with him after he rose from the dead.' As Loisy rightly remarks (op. cit., 8), this correspondence nevertheless does not prove any dependence of Ignatius on Acts, especially as he quotes immediately before, in **3**.2, an extra-canonical gospel. All we can say is that both Ignatius and Acts are here following a relatively recent tradition (produced in opposition to Docetism).

(c) Still less convincing is the supposed link (through the use of the 'wolf'-idea) between Ignatius *Phil.* **2**.2: 'for many wolves, who feign trust-

---

[1] Here LXX, in accordance with the Hebrew, reads, 'with holy oil' (ἐλαίῳ). Only MS B offers the spiritualizing ἐλέει.

[2] Alfred Loisy, *Les Actes des Apôtres*, 1920, 7; Lucien Cerfaux, 'Citations scripturaires et tradition textuelle dans le Livre des Actes', in *Aux sources de la Tradition chrétienne. Mélanges offerts à M. Maurice Goguel*, 1950, 43–51 (references to testimony books, 46, 48f.).

[3] Bihlmeyer, op. cit., 156.

[4] Harnack (op. cit. 406) dates his letters 110–17 but adds 'perhaps . . . 117–25'. H. W. Bartsch (*RGG*[3] III, 665) sets the martyrdom of Ignatius soon after 110.

worthiness', and Acts **20.29**: 'I know that after my departing grievous wolves shall enter in among you.' Metaphors of the shepherd, wolf and flock are standard components of early Christian edificatory language (cf. Matt. **7.15** and John **10.11ff.!**).

III. Perhaps the third place should be allotted to the author of the *Second Epistle to Timothy*[1]: the sufferings and persecutions mentioned in **3.11** as endured by Paul 'at Antioch, Iconium and Lystra' seem to refer to Acts **13.50** and **14.5,19**. But the mention of Timothy's mother Lois and grandmother Eunice in II Tim. **1.5**, and of Onesiphorus in **1.16** (quite apart from the persons named in **4.10–21!**), suggests that the author is probably making use of a legendary tradition concerning Paul.[2] But another opinion is held by Conzelmann, *Hdb. z. NT*, 13³, 4.

IV. Neither can the *Epistle of Barnabas*[3] vouch with certainty for the use of Acts:

(a) The beginning of **5.9**: 'but as he was choosing his apostles who were to declare his message', certainly recalls the text of D (not simply the 'Western' text) in Acts **1.2**. But the resemblance is not close enough to prove dependence. The word ἐκέλευσεν is lacking in Barnabas, and no form or variant of the Western text (see the commentary on this verse) has the μου, following 'message', which would correspond with the text of Barnabas. Moreover it can be shown that D here offers a secondary reading within the Western text.

(b) By calling the Son of God him 'who will judge the quick and the dead', Barnabas **7.2** recalls Acts **10.42**: 'judge of the quick and the dead'. But what we see here is two different forms of a very old kerygmatic formula: the verb-form in Barnabas (as also in II Tim. **4.1**, I Peter **4.5**, Hegesippus *apud* Euseb. *H.E.* III 20.4, and in the Apostles' Creed) and the substantive in Acts—as in Polycarp *Phil.* **2.1** and II Clem. **1.1**.

(c) Barnabas **16.2** quotes Isaiah **66.1**, 'Heaven is my throne', also found in Acts **7.49**. But the concordant idea—the rejection of the Temple—is differently motivated and linked with different OT verses: in Barnabas with Isaiah **40.12** ('Who hath ... meted out heaven?'), in Acts with Isaiah **66.2** ('What manner of house will ye build unto me?'). Windisch convincingly argues that Barnabas was quoting 'in substance from a testimony book' (*Hdb. z. NT*, Suppl., 314f.).

(d) As for Barnabas **19.8**, see V(b) below.

---

[1] According to W. Schmithals (*RGG*³ V, 147) to be dated about 150. The older dating in Jülicher-Fascher, *Einleitung in das NT*, 7th ed., 1931, 186 (ET *An Introduction to the New Testament*, 1904): about 115.

[2] Dibelius, *Hdb. z. NT* Vol. 3, II 1913, 196: 'in a genuine epistle of Paul we would be suspicious to find ... no mention of the vicissitudes shared by Paul and Timothy (Acts 16 & 17).' Similarly *Hdb.* 13³, 89.

[3] Written in 130 or 131 (so Harnack, op. cit., 427); R. Schütz (*RGG*³ I, 880): second century; Kümmel (*Einleitung* 355; ET 340): soon after the middle of the second century.

V. The *Didache*[1] reminds us of Acts in two places:

(a) Didache **9**.2 and **10**.2 call Jesus παῖς θεοῦ, as in Acts **3**.13,26 & **4**.27, 30. This is an application of an old tradition[2] corresponding to the 'liturgical formula of late Judaism',[3] 'David thy servant'. The formula 'through thy servant Jesus' has nothing to do in the Didache with the idea of the suffering Messiah.

(b) Didache **4**.8: 'thou shouldst have everything in common with thy brother and not say that it is thine own', derives, as the parallel in Barnabas **19**.8 shows ('thou shouldst have community with thy neighbour in everything and not say it is thine own'), from a source on which both writings have drawn, an earlier version of the doctrine of the two ways. The reasoning which follows in both Barnabas and the Didache pertains likewise to this origin. Acts **4**.32: 'no one said that any of the things he possessed was his own', is connected with these passages only inasmuch as it depicts the fulfilment of the injunction and can therefore lay no claim to priority.

VI. We now come to the '*Shepherd of Hermas*'[4]:

(a) Hermas *Sim.* IX 27.3 has already been discussed under I(a) above.

(b) Hermas *Sim.* IX 28.2 employs the formula 'suffer for the name of the Son of God' (as a variant of which we have 'on account of the name' in IX 28.3, 5, 6). Thereby it recalls Acts **5**.41: 'to suffer dishonour for the Name'; **9**.16: 'for my name's sake'; **15**.26: 'hazarded their lives for the name'; and **21**.13: 'to die for the name'. But this is no borrowing; it is simply a common Christian figure of speech.

VII. There are many correspondences of detail between Acts and the *Epistle of Polycarp to the Philippians*[5]:

(a) There is a strikingly close resemblance between Polycarp *Phil.* **1**.2: 'whom God hath awakened, loosing the pangs of Hades', and Acts **2**.24: 'whom God raised up, having loosed the pangs of death'. Both are variants of an old kerygmatic formula, liturgically amplified. This is evident from the variations in detail.

(b) We have already discussed, under IV(b) above, the formula 'judge of the quick and the dead', which appears in Polycarp *Phil.* **2**.1 and Acts **10**.42.

(c) With its introductory formula, 'mindful of what the Lord has said, teaching . . .', Polycarp *Phil.* **2**.3 recalls Acts **20**.35: 'to remember the words of the Lord Jesus', but also II Clem. **17**.3: 'let us remember the commandments of the Lord'. But the content of the injunctions of Jesus, introduced by

---

[1] Harnack (op. cit. 438) dates it broadly 131–160; E. Molland (*RGG*³ III, 242) 'about the middle of the second century'.

[2] J. Jeremias, *ThWb* V, 705, lines 11ff. (ET 707, lines 15f.).

[3] Id., 698f. (ET 700f.).

[4] Dates proposed: Harnack (op. cit. 266f.):–110–140; Dibelius (*Hdb. z. NT*, Suppl., 423f.):–120–130, but in *RGG*² II, 1822, between 120 and 140.

[5] Dates proposed: Harnack (op. cit. 388):–110–154; von Campenhausen (*RGG*³ V, 449): chapters 13f. about 110, chapters 1–12 'a much later second letter'.

this flexible formula, is very different in Polycarp *Phil.* **2**.3 and Acts **20**.35. On the other hand, the continuation in Polycarp is in much closer agreement with I Clem. **13**.1f.[1] In R. Knopf's judgment[2], both Polycarp and Clement are perhaps dependent on some 'lost apocryphal collection'.

(d) As the parallel I Clem. **17**.1 (the prophets 'announcing the coming of Christ') makes clear, the agreement between Polycarp *Phil.* **6**.3: 'the prophets, who announced beforehand (προκηρύξαντες) the coming of our Lord', and Acts **7**.52: 'the prophets which shewed before (προκαταγγείλαντας) of the coming of the righteous one', is explained by the fact that here we have a τόπος, which can be variously formulated, of the first coming of Christ.

(e) We have already dealt, under I(a) above, with Polycarp *Phil.* **9**.2 and its connection with Acts **1**.25.

(f) Polycarp *Phil.* **12**.2 includes the clause 'who are under heaven', which has its counterparts in Acts **2**.5 and **4**.12. The expression is also found in Col. **1**.23. It derives from LXX Eccles. **1**.13 and **3**.1. It is therefore very improbable that Polycarp is here quoting Acts.

(g) In the same section, **12**.2, appears the expression 'lot and part'. It is a positive counterpart to the negative 'neither part nor lot' in Acts **8**.21 (cf. Col. **1**.12), which is formed on the model of Deut. **12**.12 and **14**.27,29— so there can be no question of quotation here.

(h) Finally **12**.2 ('*det vobis . . . partem inter sanctos suos*') recalls Acts **20**.32: 'to give the inheritance among all them that are sanctified', and **26**.18: 'to receive . . . inheritance among them that are sanctified'. One may say that here we have a variable formula (also present in Col. **1**.12) for which Deut. **33**.3f. supplied the material: 'all the saints . . . an inheritance for the assembly of Jacob'.

The conclusion therefore is that Polycarp, despite the numerous echoes, did not use Acts as a source, but that both he and the author of Acts were working with a stock of contemporary formulae held largely in common.

VIII. *The Second Epistle of Clement*[3] offers four passages which Bihlmeyer[4] connects with Acts:

(a) **1**.1 has 'judge of the quick and the dead', as has Acts **10**.42. See IV(b) above.

(b) II Clem. **4**.4: 'and we must not fear men, but rather God', certainly resembles Acts **4**.19: 'whether it be right in the sight of God to hearken unto you rather than unto God', and, still more closely, **5**.29: 'We must obey God rather than men'. But 'the idea that one must obey God rather

---

[1] W. Bauer, *Hdb. z. NT*, Suppl., 286.

[2] R. Knopf, *Hdb. z. NT*, Suppl., 64.

[3] Dates proposed: Harnack (op. cit. 448f.):–130–170; Knopf (*Hdb. z. NT*, Suppl., 152):–120–50; E. Molland (*RGG*[3] I, 1838): 'from the middle of the second century'.

[4] Bihlmeyer, op. cit. 158.

than men is a widespread commonplace'[1]—cf., for example, I Clem. **14**.1. The present verse is at least as strongly influenced by the idea expressed in Matt. **10**.28, i.e. 'fear not men, but fear God'. We may not therefore assert a quotation from Acts.

(c) II Clem. **13**.1 is too far removed from Acts **3**.19: Clement speaks of our throwing off our sins by our own efforts: in Acts it is God who blots them out.

(d) In the words σωτῆρα καὶ ἀρχηγὸν τῆς ἀφθαρσίας II Clem. **20**.5 seems linked with Acts **3**.15: ἀρχηγὸν τῆς ζωῆς and **5**.31: ἀρχηγὸν καὶ σωτῆρα. As Heb. **2**.10: ἀρχηγὸν τῆς σωτηρίας shows, we are here dealing with an elastic figure of speech characteristic of sub-apostolic, Hellenistic edificatory language. It cannot therefore be proved that Clement's second epistle actually quotes Acts.

IX. Eusebius has not transmitted to us any sayings of PAPIAS[2] alluding to Luke's Gospel and Acts. According to Jülicher, he probably withheld the judgment of Papias from us because 'it offended his feeling for the Church' (Jülicher–Fascher, 312). But there remains the other possibility, that Papias said nothing about the two documents because he knew nothing of them. Certainly Papias mentioned persons who appear in Acts, e.g. Judas, Justus Barsabbas[3]. But it is clear that he was reaching back to other traditions than those offered in Acts. In any case, his silence on the subject precludes his recognition of Luke's work.

X. Not until JUSTIN MARTYR[4] can a knowledge and use of Luke's two works be established.

(a) *Apol.* I 39.3, speaking of the twelve Apostles as ἰδιῶται, λαλεῖν μὴ δυνάμενοι is strongly reminiscent of Acts **4**.13: ἄνθρωποι ἀγράμματοι . . . καὶ ἰδιῶται. But this coincidence does not offer convincing proof when taken by itself.

(b) Similarly, *Apol.* I 49.5, where the Gentiles, hearing the gospel from the Apostles, are said to be 'filled with gladness', seems to allude to Acts **13**.48: 'And as the gentiles heard this they were glad.'

(c) But the first decisive reference is *Apol.* I 50.12. This first quotes the substance of Luke **23**.49a in recapitulating the story of the Passion, next makes clear use of Luke **24**.25, 44f. as the account continues, and finally narrates the Ascension and the conferring of the Holy Spirit with a verbal echo of Acts **1**.8: δύναμιν . . . λαβόντες corresponding to λήμψεσθε δύναμιν in Acts.

---

[1] Knopf, *Hdb. z. NT*, Suppl., 65.
[2] Dates proposed: Harnack (op. cit. 357):–140 (145)–160; E. Bammel (*RGG*[3] V, 47): 'about 130/140 A.D.'; second third of second century; Jülicher-Fascher (256):–about 150.
[3] As we are told by Eusebius, *H.E.* III 39.9; on Judas, see 160 below.
[4] Harnack (op. cit. 284) dates the *Apology* and the *Dialogue with Trypho* between 150 and 160; C. Andresen (*RGG*[3] III, 891): about 180.

(d) Consequently we may perhaps attribute the mention of θεὸς ἄγνωστος (*Apol.* II 10.6) to the influence of Acts **17**.23.

This survey shows two things. First, until the middle of the second century Acts was not yet considered an authoritative book to which one might appeal.[1] But to this negative conclusion a positive one must be added: the supposed borrowings from Acts in writers from Clement of Rome to Polycarp demonstrate that the edificatory language of the sub-apostolic period was familiar to the writer of Acts and readily employed by him. Acts breathes the very spirit of this age. But why then was this work not earlier acknowledged as a book of the Church? The only answer is that, unlike the gospel, it had no 'life-situation' in the Church at all. In Acts the Christian reader encountered a book unlike any he had previously known, and one which was neither necessary nor customarily used in preaching or instruction. Only because of its connection with the third gospel, then, was Acts allowed to cross the threshold of the Canon.[2]

XI. This step was taken a generation after Justin. In the struggle waged by IRENAEUS[3] against gnosticism, Acts proved immediately useful: from it one could demonstrate the unity of the apostolic message—and for this purpose it was copiously quoted by Irenaeus (*Adv. haer.* III, 12.1–15). Now we are even presented with statements, eagerly repeated in years to come, about the author of Acts:—Luke was a '*sectator Pauli*' and 'wrote into a book the gospel Paul preached.' (*Adv. haer.* III, 1.1). Irenaeus offered no backing for this assertion; we may suppose it derives from those Pauline passages where the Apostle speaks of 'his gospel'[4]. That Luke was Paul's inseparable collaborator in spreading the Gospel, Irenaeus proves from the 'we' passages in Acts. The fact that Luke there withholds his own name shows only that he was modest. In II Tim. **4**.10f. and Col. **4**.14, Paul himself affirms that Luke was 'always associated with him and inseparable from him' (*Adv. haer.* III, 14.1). Finally, Irenaeus took the idea that Luke had been the 'disciple and companion of the Apostles' from Luke **1**.2: 'eyewitnesses . . . have delivered unto us.' (*Adv. haer.* III, 10.1; 14.2).

The tradition about Luke which Irenaeus outlined in this way contains nothing which he could not have read out of Luke's two-volume work. There is no trace of any knowledge of Luke from independent sources.

[1] Cf. M. Dibelius, *Aufsätze zur Apostelgeschichte*, ed. H. Greeven, 1951, 127f., 80 (ET *Studies in the Acts of the Apostles*, 1956, 147f., 89. Future references will be given to the English translation only.) Harnack's judgment is in fact even more sweeping: '. . . so far as we know, the Acts of the Apostles was hidden in obscurity up to the time of Irenaeus (even taking into account the writings of Justin and the Gnostics) . . .' (*TLZ* 53 (1928) 126). In our opinion, Harnack has undervalued Justin's quotations.

[2] Wendt, *Die Apostelgeschichte*, 9th ed. 1913, 48.

[3] W. Eltester locates his main work c. 180 (*RGG*³ III, 891). The relevant references here are *Adv. haer.* III, 1.1; 10.1; 14.1–4.

[4] E.g. Rom. 2.16. Eusebius (*H.E.* III, 4.6) was of course the first to discuss Paul's 'gospel' at any length.

B

The so-called Anti-Marcionite Prologues are neither an organic unity nor in fact anti-Marcionite in character.[1]

[1] A word is needed here on the so-called Anti-Marcionite Prologues. In 1928 Dom Donatien de Bruyne made the assertion that three Latin gospel-prologues were anti-Marcionite ('Les plus anciens prologues latins des Évangiles', *Revue Bénédictine* 40, 195–214). When, save for a few points of difference, A. von Harnack allied himself to this view ('Die ältesten Evangelienprologe und die Bildung des NTs', in *SBA* 1928, 320–41), even scholars like Jülicher and Lietzmann considered the theory as good as proved. Opposition was not however entirely lacking: refutations were offered by M.-J. Lagrange (*Rev. Bibl.* 38 (1929), 115–21) and B. W. Bacon (*JBL* 49 (1930), 43–64; cf. his article in *JTS* 23 (1922), 134–60), while among others who demurred were W. F. Howard ('The Anti-Marcionite Prologues to the Gospels', *Exp. Tim.* 47 (1936), 534–8), R. M. Grant (*AngThR* 23 (1941), 231–45) and R. G. Heard (*JTS* 56 (1955), 1–16). Jürgen Regul's recently published Bonn dissertation, *Die antimarcion. Evangelienprologe* (Herder, Freiburg 1969), has confirmed and expanded our results (p. 269).

The theory's point of outset is anything but brilliant. After twenty years of research de Bruyne had found in 31 Latin manuscripts ranging from the fifth to the fourteenth century, prologues to Mark, Luke and John which he considered anti-Marcionite. Only six of the manuscripts included all three prologues; 21 others (among them the oldest) included only the prologue to Luke. De Bruyne does not mention what other prologues appear in these 31 manuscripts—it is certainly not unknown for a gospel to be introduced by more than one.

De Bruyne assumed that Marcion had issued his version of the NT (i.e. Luke plus ten Pauline epistles) with prologues for the epistles, which prologues were therefore of his own making. Thereupon the Roman community riposted with a Catholic edition of the NT containing four gospels and ten 'or probably thirteen' Pauline epistles. In doing so—without noticing the fact—it simply took over Marcion's prologues to the epistles, and supplied further prologues for the gospels (also the Pastoral Epistles). This is the alleged origin of the 'anti-Marcionite' gospel-prologues.

Now this thesis is untenable. If Rome did publish such a counter-edition, the editors must have had the loathed heretic's work (his NT or his *Antitheses*, which according to Jülicher contained the Pauline prologues) under their eyes, and they could not have transcribed the prologues without noticing where they came from. It is moreover highly unlikely that Marcion himself wrote *Romani sunt in partibus Italiae* or *Galati sunt Graeci*—in either case his information was somewhat less vague!

As for the allegedly anti-Marcionite gospel-prologues, these three (for de Bruyne did not find one to fit Matthew) appear only in Latin manuscripts; only one Greek manuscript of the twelfth century (see Von Soden, Vol. 1, 327) also contains the prologue to Luke, and *Cod.Bodl.Misc.Graec.* 141 (eleventh century) the first sentence of it. Now do these three prologues form one literary unit? Are they all modelled on similar lines? Is each written with the others in mind, so that they neither overlap nor contradict each other and could have been written by the same hand? Lastly, were they levelled at Marcion? The answer to all these questions must be—No!

The *Prologue to Mark* is short and contains nothing directly or indirectly anti-Marcionite. De Bruyne considers it to be genuinely old-Roman because Mark is called *colobodactylus* and 'that is not the kind of thing that anyone would invent' (201). But the prologue's innocuous explanation of the word (that Mark's fingers were too short in relation to his body) does not really offer a very competent gloss on the epithet 'stumpyfingers'—which could have been borrowed from Hippolytus. De Bruyne points to 'Justus the flat-footed' in the apocryphal Acts of Paul, but this leads in another direction: such traits are survivals of popular phantasy.

The *Prologue to Luke* is by far the most extensive. It answers among others the question why Luke wrote his gospel *in partibus Achaiae*: Judaea had already been provided for by Matthew, and Italy by Mark! To the discussion of Luke's gospel (see below) are joined the following remarks: 'And afterwards this same Luke wrote the Acts of the

Apostles. But later the Apostle John wrote the Revelation on the island of Patmos, and afterwards the gospel in Asia Minor' (yet the Prologue to John says that he dictated it!). Thus the writer expands his introduction to the third gospel into a general view over the whole non-epistolary half of the NT. This is not a prologue intended to accompany others, but an independent unit.

But can we at least say that it is directed against Marcion? Indirectly, yes, says de Bruyne, for the prologue dwells on the story of the Baptist's birth, which Marcion had suppressed. Yet Marcion had also deleted the account of Jesus' own birth, while he did not on the other hand contest the precursory status of the Baptist. Any anti-Marcionite polemic would therefore have to wear a different complexion. In reality the prologue here simply explains what distinguishes Luke from the other three gospels: the infancy narrative and the peculiar parallelism between John and Jesus. The prologue ends with a reference to Malachi, who has already thought of ταύτης τῆς οἰκονομίας (='this divine dispensation'). The term οἰκονομία is here used in the same way as in e.g. Theodore of Mopsuestia's prologue to John (see Von Soden, op. cit. 326), where the overall sense of the word (='divine plan of redemption'; cf. O. Michel, *ThWb* V, 154f., ET 151f.) is particularized, as in the ταύτης τῆς οἰκονομίας at the end of our prologue to Luke, to mean a special dispensation of God (so that Theodore can speak, line 11, of διαφόροις οἰκονομίαις). So here there is no evidence of the anti-Marcionite polemic that Strobel professes to discern. On the contrary, the prologue contains something which would have brought water to Marcion's mill, for it is specially mentioned that Luke remained unmarried and childless, and therefore served the Lord without distraction: this is precisely the virginity which Marcion demanded of his '*electi*'! However, there is something even stranger: the Latin text of this prologue to Luke describes the primary purpose of the gospel in these incomprehensible words: '*ne Iudaicis fabulis desiderio tenerentur*'. Only the variant makes sense: '*ne Iudaicis fabulis adtenti in solo legis desiderio tenerentur*'. But this variant, according to de Bruyne, derives from the Monarchian revision of the prologue to Luke. Yet this is the only place where such a Marcionite tendency is discernible in any Monarchian prologue! The question therefore remains open whether its text 'ne Judaicis fabulis intenti in solo legis desiderio tenerentur' does not simply reproduce the wording of the so-called anti-Marcionite Prologue to Luke—which in that event would be anything but anti-Marcionite. But even ignoring all this, it is very striking that the 'anti-Marcionite' prologue to Luke contains, alongside its anti-gnostic bias, an 'anti-Judaic' tendency of the third gospel: as Lagrange has already noted, the expression '*Iudaicis fabulis*' distinctly echoes I Tim. 1.4-6. One cannot, with de Bruyne (205), dismiss this as a commonplace. Again, de Bruyne takes the 84 years of age which Luke enjoyed, according to the prologue, as valuable evidence of old tradition. But would not Luke 2.37 have provided the model for this detail? De Bruyne himself, moreover, is astonished that the Roman community, which knew so little of Mark, should have possessed this exact information about Luke.

In sum, there is no polemic against Marcion here, neither direct or indirect.

On the other hand, the *Prologue to John* does mention Marcion—but in what terms? Marcion is said to have been repudiated by John! De Bruyne (208) and Harnack only circumvented this difficulty by striking out the words '*ab Johanne*'. But de Bruyne played fair enough not to hush up the difficulty which still remains: 'Why speak of Marcion at all in a prologue to John, when John was not involved in the affair?' He found no answer to this question. Our own surmise is that the writer had only a vague notion of the relationships in the apostolic and sub-apostolic ages. It was thus he could arrive at his fantastic assertions that Papias was 'one of John's cherished disciples' and that John had dictated his gospel to Papias! This is certainly no prologue written in the latter half of the second century (so de Bruyne 210) and used by Irenaeus. It is a later production. Furthermore, it is not this one which is used in the Monarchian prologue to John, but the 'anti-Marcionite' prologue to Luke!

Strobel (*ZNW* 49 (1958) 132 n. 5) claims that the words of Irenaeus, '*Lucas autem sector et discipulus apostolorum*', were copied from the 'anti-Marcionite' prologue to Luke. But if Irenaeus had made use of the latter, he would also have taken over the detail '*Lucas Antiochenus Syrus*'. In reality, Irenaeus took his information about Luke from the NT itself. Since he did not yet read, in his text of Acts, the 'we' of Acts 11.28, Codex D

XII. The case of the *Muratorian Canon*[1] is not very different. Here too we see how the tradition concerning Luke is inferred from what one finds—or does not find—in Luke's writings themselves. From the lack of reference to Peter's martyrdom and Paul's voyage to Spain (accepted without question on account of Rom. **15**.24 and perhaps I Clem. **5**.7), it was concluded that Luke confined himself in Acts to his own experiences.[2] If the Muratorian Canon affirms that Luke narrated the 'deeds of all Apostles'[3], it appears we should ascribe this to the kind of optical illusion which lets one see what one really wants to see (cf. Loisy, *Les Actes des Apôtres*, 10).

The received text of the Muratorian Canon describes Luke as '*iuris studiosus*'[4]. This would certainly be a new tradition concerning Luke. But this reading is untenable. Zahn's suggested amendment '*itineris studiosum*' would only be possible if one took *itineris* as the equivalent of ὁδοῦ in the sense of Acts **9**.2 and similar passages, and *studiosum* as a translation of σπουδαστήν—cf. the description of Luke as σπουδαστὴς Παύλου in the Βίος of Sophronius (Von Soden, 309), and *De vir. ill.* 7, Migne P.L. 23, Col. 652A. Hort has conjectured '*itineris sui socium*'.[5]

XIII. The succeeding Fathers add little new to this information about Luke. According to CLEMENT OF ALEXANDRIA,[6] Luke translated the Epistle to the Hebrews into Greek for Paul—evidently a learned hypothesis intended to explain the un-Pauline style of this allegedly Pauline letter.

XIV. TERTULLIAN[7] shows what his age in fact demanded of a canonical gospel: '*Constituimus evangelicum instrumentum apostolos auctores habere*'. Considering the traditional status of Mark and Luke, this stipulation must

---

(see *Adv. haer.* III **14**.1), he had no reason to describe Luke as a man of Antioch. It was from Luke **1**.3, where he misconstrued πᾶσιν as masculine, that he inferred Luke to have been '*sectator et discipulus apostolorum*'.

Thus the three so-called anti-Marcionite gospel-prologues do not form a single literary unit and are not levelled at Marcion. The words in the prologue to Luke, '*Lucas Antiochenus Syrus*', do not come down to us from the time before Irenaeus.

[1] See Hans Lietzmann, *Kleine Texte* Vol. 1, 4th ed., 1933, and Preuschen, *Analecta* II, 2nd ed. 1910. Zahn, *Gesch. d. ntl. Kanons* II, 1890, 1–143, offers text and commentary. English trans. in Hennecke-Schneemelcher *NT Apocrypha* i, 42ff. According to G. Strecker (*RGG*[3] IV, 1191), 'towards the end of the second century.'

[2] *Can. Mur.* line 36 read '*quae*' for '*quia*', line 37 '*semota passione*', line 38 '*profectione*'. In *ZNW* 14 (1913), 216–21, Friedrich Pfister ascribed the extant text '*semote passionem*' and '*profectionem*' to the *Actus Vercellenses*, which begin with Paul's departure for Spain and go on to Peter's martyrdom: the suggestion is that the end of Luke's *Acts* was cut in order to join on these two highly-treasured apostolic acts. But the end of *Acts* is not in fact removed. On M. R. James's explanation, which is reminiscent of Pfister's, see Cadbury, *Beg.* V, 495.

[3] Muratorian Canon, line 34.   [4] Muratorian Canon, line 4.

[5] Zahn's suggestion of an implied contrast here between Luke and the reluctant traveller John Mark (Acts **13**.13) is a mere bow drawn at a venture. E. Klostermann suggested '*melioris studiosum*' (*ZNW* 22 (1923), 308f.).

[6] Clem. Alex., *Adumbr. in I Petr.* (*GCS*, Vol. 17, 206), quoted in *Beg.* II, 222.

[7] Tertullian, *Adv. Marcionem* IV 2 (*CSEL*, Vol. 47, 426ff.), quoted *Beg.* II, 222ff.

of course be widened to include (direct) disciples of the Apostles. In this way the '*sectator Pauli*' is reprieved.

XV. According to ORIGEN (*apud* Euseb. *H.E.* VI 25.6), Luke wrote down for the Gentiles the gospel preached by Paul. II Cor. 8.18 also is now referred to Luke: he is the brother '*cuius laus in Evangelio est per omnes Ecclesias*'.[1]

XVI. EUSEBIUS[2] has something new to add—Luke came from Antioch. He does not betray the source of his knowledge.[3] His other relevant statements tell us only what we already know—that Luke was a physician, was generally in Paul's company and had also close relations with the other Apostles. It was apparently from taking πᾶσιν in Luke 1.3 as a masculine that Eusebius inferred Luke to have been the follower of them all.

XVII. JEROME indeed reiterated the traditional data, but in *De viris illustribus* 7 he had new details to add: Acts with Paul's two-year imprisonment in Rome extends as far as the fourth year of Nero's reign.[4] '*Ex quo intelligimus, in eadem urbe librum esse compositum*'—thus once again we see how the tradition about Luke is augmented by the evaluation of his work. The preamble of Jerome's Commentary on Matthew[5] asserts that Luke wrote the gospel in Achaea and Boeotia: this agrees with Jerome's later statement that Luke died in Thebes. The origin of this late tradition we do not know.

Jerome exhibits a particular interest in Lucan style: Luke wrote the best Greek of all the Evangelists, not surprisingly, since he had studied and indeed had also penned the gospel among Greeks.[6] Accordingly he preferred to omit words if they could not be precisely translated into Greek. Both in the gospel and in Acts his language is more elegant and betrays a secular eloquence (Commentary on Isaiah 6.9, Migne P. L. 24, 100D).

But for Jerome another problem is linked with the question of Luke's Greek: his use of the Septuagint, even in cases where the Greek text does not correspond with the Hebrew. Jerome offers two explanations. According to the first, Luke, like the Apostles and apostolic workers in general, used mostly the form of text already well-regarded by Gentile Christians: the

---

[1] *Hom. in Luc.*, trans. Jerome; Migne P. L. 26, 234.

[2] *H.E.* III 4, 6.

[3] Perhaps he took this information from Julius Africanus, but more probably it was already part of his (lost) *Quaestiones evangelicae* (see *Beg.* II, 247f.).

It is a reasonable conjecture that this tradition is connected with the 'we'-reading of D sy^hmg sy^p gig p in Acts 11.28. Nevertheless, this reading is not one of the original constituents of the Western text. For Irenaeus, who read the NT in a Western version (as is especially clear from his quotation of Gal. 2.5 in *Adv. haer.* III, 13.3), speaks of Luke as Paul's companion only from the 'we'-reference in Acts 16.8ff. onwards (III, 14.1). We may confidently assume, from the exactitude with which he made use of Acts, that a 'we' in 11.28 would not have escaped him. But this means we have no grounds for supposing that the tradition of Luke's Antiochian origin was already current in the days of Irenaeus.

[4] The year 58, says Jerome, without revealing how he computed that date.

[5] Migne P. L. 26, 18.

[6] *Epist.* 20 *ad Damasum* (CSEL, Vol. 54, 108): '*inter omnes evangelistas Graeci sermonis eruditissimus fuit, quippe ut medicus et qui in Graecis Evangelium scripserit*'.

Septuagint possessed great authority, whereas Luke did not.[1] At the same time, Jerome repeatedly alludes to the reputed weakness of Luke's accomplishment in Hebrew[2]—indeed he quotes the assertion that as a proselyte Luke was entirely ignorant of that language.[3]

XVIII. In the Dialogue of ADAMANTIUS called *De recta in Deum fide*,[4] Megethios maintains that neither Mark nor Luke was a disciple of Christ— why then were these two gospels written by non-disciples? But Adamantius knows better: Mark and Luke were in fact two of the seventy-two disciples ...

XIX. Let us conclude with the *Monarchian Prologues*[5]; whether they are Priscillian's work or not, they give us a tradition about Luke advocated in the fourth century and add (as demanded by the piety of the age) the following: Luke was *serviens Deo sine crimine. Nam neque uxorem unquam habens neque filios LXXIV annorum obiit in Bithynia plenus spiritu sancto.* Despite the precedent set by Zahn, it would be naive to deduce the authenticity of these data from the fact that they are unmatched in the NT. The mention of 'seventy-four years' could have arisen from the inadvertent dropping of an 'X' from the older tradition of LXXXIV (cf. Luke 2.37!). Likewise 'Bithynia' and 'Bethany'—which is also a possibility—could result from misreadings of the older 'Boeotia'.

Cadbury's argument on this matter[6] holds: whatever information we glean from the earliest tradition about Luke could have been taken, although not necessarily so, from the Lucan writings themselves. Quite possibly, but not necessarily, it was a process of elimination, for which II Tim. 4.11 ('Only Luke is with me') would have provided the starting-signal, that led to the name of Luke. Whenever the 'internal evidence' of the Lucan writings demonstrates Luke's authorship, this is worth more than all the traditions put together. But it is only in recent times that the traditions have come to be regarded thus critically. For centuries they remained undisputed and were taken for granted.

2. SURVEY OF HISTORICAL AND CRITICAL RESEARCH INTO THE ACTS OF THE APOSTLES[7]

Towards the end of the eighteenth century the traditional view of Acts began to weaken. Until then it had been customary to see the book as the 'history of all the Apostles', as the first history of the Church, composed by Luke the

---

[1] *Lib. heb. quaest. in Genes.*, Migne P. L. 23, 1053B.
[2] Commentary on Isaiah 6.9, Migne P. L. 24, 100D, 101A.
[3] *Lib. heb. quaest. in Genes.*, Migne P. L. 23, 1053B.
[4] *GCS*, Vol. 4 (1901) 8ff., quoted *Beg.* II, 240ff.
[5] For text see p. 12 n. 1 above; Preuschen, op. cit., 91f.
[6] *Beg.* II, 260ff.
[7] For Acts, unfortunately, we possess no real counterpart to Albert Schweitzer's *Quest of the Historical Jesus*—or, for that matter, his less successful history of Pauline

companion of Paul. Now the reader began to look at the work with his own eyes, and he noticed to his astonishment that the traditional picture did not accord with what he saw. At first Luke's authorship remained undoubted. But it was discovered that, far from telling the history of all the Apostles, he had been writing only of Peter and Paul. Moreover the Lucan account was not even complete in that respect, for Luke is silent about many things we learn from the Epistles of Paul.

As Schwanbeck[1] saw, this situation could be explained in one of two ways: either the author of Acts was *unwilling*, or he was *unable*, to say more. The latter possibility led to source-criticism, the former—with which we begin our survey—to so-called 'tendency-criticism'.

A. The Age of Tendency-Criticism

If Luke deliberately omitted much of what he must have known, he must have made a selection. What interest guided him in his selection? What aim, what 'tendency', was he pursuing? It was no longer possible for scholarly criticism to understand Acts as a simple reproduction of what had happened. For Acts to be comprehensible, one first had to appreciate the impulse which drove the author's pen.

Now the guess-work began. The scholars of the day—Michaelis, Griesbach, Eckermann, Hänlein, Eichhorn, Frisch, Mayerhoff, Credner, Hug—differed widely, each according to the individual point of view from which he determined the purpose of Acts.[2] It was Schrader[3] who took up the most advanced position. He was not only struck by the degree to which

---

research. However, there are three works which provide some kind of substitute. The principal is A. C. McGiffert's contribution to *Beg.* II 1922 (363–95), 'The historical criticism of Acts in Germany', which is outstanding in its copious use of literature and excellent choice of quotations, but nevertheless presents, in effect, no more than the age of 'tendency-criticism'. We have gratefully made use of McGiffert's quotations from inaccessible works. To this survey we must add § 2, 'Le travail critique sur le livre des Actes' (17–50) from A. Loisy's great commentary, *Les Actes des Apôtres* (Paris 1920), which is more concerned with source-criticism, and finally the 'Histoire de la critique des Actes des Apôtres' (XV–LV) from E. Jacquier's voluminous Catholic commentary *Les Actes des Apôtres* (Paris 1926), admittedly more an anthology than a true history.

[1] Schwanbeck, *Über die Quellen der Schriften des Lukas*, 1847, 74: quoted in *Beg.* II, 364.

[2] J. D. Michaelis, *Einleitung in die göttlichen Schriften des Neuen Bundes*, 3rd ed. 1777, Vol. II § 154 (ET *Introduction to the NT*, 1793) (quoted *Beg.* II, 364):—There are two intentions behind Acts, firstly to give a trustworthy report on the first outpouring of the Holy Spirit and the first miracles corroborating the truth of the Christian religion; secondly to recount the circumstances which proved the validity of the Gentile mission over against the Jews. Luke is said to have written during Paul's Roman captivity.

J. J. Griesbach, the Jena Easter-programme for 1798: '*De consilio, quo scriptor in Actibus Apostolicis concinnandis ductus fuerit*' (quoted *Beg.* II, 364):—Acts is intended to defend Paul against the attacks of Jewish Christians. This aim was also suggested by

the Paul of Acts was dependent on the original Apostles and the miracles of this Paul ran parallel with those of Peter, but he also saw that the Paul of the Epistles was another Paul. He therefore ventured to assert that the apologetic purpose of Acts had compromised its historical reliability.[1] What is striking about this conclusion is not only the discrediting of a canonical document, for Schrader also begins to link together the questions of Acts and of the Pauline epistles. Nevertheless one should refrain from naming him, as McGiffert does, in the same breath as F. C. Baur.[2]

H. E. G. Paulus in pages 281ff. of his *Introductionis in Novum Testamentum capita selectiora* (1799), and Lechler (see pp. 19f. below) indeed attributed '*De consilio*' to him.

Eckermann, *Erklärung aller dunklen Stellen des Neuen Testaments*, 1807, Vol. II, 164ff. (quoted *Beg.* II, 365):—Luke selected only those events which most clearly demonstrate the wonderful workings of God in the setting up of his kingdom on earth.

Hänlein, *Einleitung in die Schriften des Neuen Testaments*, 2nd ed. 1809, Part 3, 156f. (quoted *Beg.* II, 365):—Acts is intended to show God's help in the propagation of Christianity, enhance the Apostles' reputation by reporting their miracles, and urge the equal right of gentiles as well as Jews to the blessings of the faith.

J. G. Eichhorn, *Einleitung in das Neue Testament*, 1810, Vol. II § 147 (quoted *Beg.* II, 365):—Acts is intended to give a history not of the Church nor of the Apostles, but of the Christian mission.

S. G. Frisch, Dissertation '*Utrumque Lucae commentarium de vita, dictis factisque Jesu et apostolorum non tam historicae simplicitatis, quam artificiosae tractationis indolem habere*', 1817, 53 (quoted *Beg.* II, 365f.):—In Acts, Luke was attempting to convince Jews and Jewish Christians that the worth and standing of the Messiah Jesus was greater than that of Moses, and that it was the will of God and of his Messiah Jesus that all men should share in the Christian salvation.

Mayerhoff, *Einleitung in die petrinischen Schriften, nebst einer Abhandlung über den Verfasser der Apostelgeschichte*, 1835, 5 (quoted *Beg.* II, 366):—It was the aim of Acts to set down 1. the spread of Christianity from Jerusalem, the centre of Judaism, to Rome, the centre of paganism, 2. the reaction against this (which nevertheless always served the further propagation of the Church) and 3. the Church's internal consolidation.

K. A. Credner, *Einleitung in das Neue Testament*, 1836, Vol. I, Pt. 1, 269 (quoted *Beg.* II, 366f.):—As a disciple of Paul, the author of Acts selected only what was important for Pauline doctrine. The whole work is a historical commentary on the following verses in Romans: 1.16, 3.9, 10.12. The author intended to write yet a third book (279); that is why he gives no account of Paul's death.

J. L. Hug, *Einleitung in das Neue Testament*, 1st ed. 1808, 4th ed. 1847 (quoted *Beg.* II, 367):—Acts is a historical work; its author exercised selection in accordance with the special needs of Theophilus.

[3] Karl Schrader, *Der Apostel Paulus*, Vol. V, 1836 (exposition of the Epistles).

[1] Op. cit., 537f., quoted *Beg.* II, pp. 367f.

[2] Ferdinand Christian Baur, 'Die Christuspartei in der korinthischen Gemeinde; der Gegensatz des petrinischen und paulinischen Christentums in der ältesten Kirche', in the *Tübinger Zeitschrift für Theologie*, 1831, No. 4. In 1836, in the same periodical (No. 3, 100ff.), Baur published 'Über Zweck und Veranlassung des Römerbriefs und die damit zusammenhängenden Verhältnisse der römischen Gemeinde'; here Acts is characterized as the work of a Paulinist wishing to defend the Apostle against the attacks of Jewish Christians. In 1838 (No. 3, 142ff. 'Über den Ursprung des Episkopats') Baur gave a reasoned account of his fundamental views on Acts. His *magnum opus*, entitled *Paulus, der Apostel Jesu Christi*, 1845 (ET *Paul, the Apostle of Jesus Christ*, 2 vols., 1873–6), is of particular importance; the second edition, edited by Zeller, appeared posthumously in 1866/7.

BAUR's contribution unites three important theses. The first does not concern Acts at all, but deals with the Epistles. Paul, says Baur, preached a different gospel from that of the original Apostles (the gospel of freedom from the law, as against that of circumcision), and the outcome of this antithesis was a struggle between two Christianities in early Christendom—the Pauline and the Petrine. On this basis Baur arrived at his second thesis, which deals with Acts and maintains that the book was an attempt to reconcile the hostile parties of the Paulinists and the Judaists. But the significance of this second thesis became clear only with the enunciation of the third: that an age is not really understood—and this includes the age of the New Testament—until it is viewed from the standpoint of its central problem. In every age, that is to say, there is a struggle between two great powers, the old and the new, until they are at length reconciled in some higher unity.[1] Every document has to be located in the context of this process. Only when this has been done is the document historically understood.

The vital question of the New Testament age, i.e. the apostolic and sub-apostolic, was the question of the legitimacy of the mission to the Gentiles. Acts seeks to reconcile the opposing parties; it therefore belongs to the closing stage of the process, is unhistorical and not the work of Luke.

Thus took shape, in all its strength and weakness, the picture of early Christianity advocated by the Tübingen school. Its strength lay in the elevated vantage point from which it was drawn—permitting a broad survey of the development of Christianity as far as the early Catholic Church. But its weakness is none the less patent: it makes an unwarranted simplification of history, rigidly differentiating 'Gentile Christianity' from 'Jewish Christianity,' and turns a problem of the initial stages into the driving force behind an epoch which had long since been moved by other questions and forces. From the beginning, therefore, Baur's solution bears within itself the seed of its demise.

The master's views were developed, enlarged and intensified by his disciples Schwegler and Zeller. Baur had thought it possible that the author of Acts had used certain sketches or diaries of Luke.[2] Acts thus remained, even if it would take a most rigorous criticism to sift out the true historical picture, a highly important source for the Apostolic age (op. cit., 17). SCHWEGLER,[3] on the other hand, explained Acts as a peace-offering and attempt at reconciliation 'in the form of a history.' He maintains that the author treated tradition as arbitrarily and high-handedly as it was treated in

---

[1] Of course, this unity immediately becomes the power of the old, provoking the rise of a new in opposition. That is the Hegelian dialectic of history which Baur used to teach. On this point, see Emmanuel Hirsch, *Geschichte der neueren evangelischen Theologie*, Vol. V, 1954, 518–552, and, among older presentations, Albert Schweitzer, *Geschichte der paulinischen Forschung*, 1911, 10–17 (ET *Paul and his Interpreters*, London 1912, 12ff.).

[2] *Der Apostel Paulus*, 2nd ed., 16.

[3] Albert Schwegler, *Das nachapostolische Zeitalter*, 1846, Vol. II, 73ff.

the Clementine homilies. Taken as a whole, Acts has the value of a historical document only for the time, the circumstances and the situation in which it arose. The period in question, according to Schwegler, was 110–50, when, he says, the Jewish form of Christianity was still dominant.[1]

ZELLER[2] arrived at a similar conclusion. The Peter-Paul parallelism is a scheme devised by the writer himself. He had no intention whatever of presenting a historical account,[3] but was striving to influence the conflicting parties of the Paulinists and Judaists.[4] Acts has a 'conciliatory tendency'.[5] Seeing that Acts scarcely touches on the antithesis of faith and works, and that only the practical question of the law's validity plays a part, Zeller placed Acts in a period when 'the significance of the dogmatic antithesis . . . had already receded'.[6] In this way he came to choose the first decades of the second century.

Although such respected scholars as Hausrath[7] and Hilgenfeld,[8] together with the rising stars Ritschl[9] and Holtzmann,[10] confessed their allegiance to Baur, his view of early Christian history did not carry the day. This was not surprising. Very few theologians were ready to admit that the New Testament could be contradictory in a central doctrine, and it was obvious that Baur's historical picture had points of weakness. The opposition was most diversified in form and content. Such a man as NEANDER[11] could indeed describe Baur's essay on the Christ-party as 'ingenious'—but remained wholly unconvinced. In his *Paulus*, Baur sharply but not unjustly censures Neander for passing off as perfectly innocuous certain parts of Acts which gave Baur himself real difficulty;[12] nevertheless it was this way of proceeding which rendered Neander and others like him immune against infection from Baur's thought. Schneckenburger[13] ventured deeper into the dangerous jungle of criticism.

---

[1] Op. cit., 113.

[2] Eduard Zeller, *Die Apostelgeschichte nach ihrem Inhalt und Ursprung kritisch untersucht*, 1854.

[3] Op. cit., 357.   [4] Op. cit., 344.

[5] Op. cit., 358.   [6] Op. cit., 474.

[7] Adolf Hausrath, *Neutestamentliche Zeitgeschichte*, 1868. (ET *History of New Testament Times*, 4 vols.)

[8] Adolf Hilgenfeld, *ZwTh* 1858, 54–140, 377–440, 562–602 ('Das Urchristentum und seine neuesten Bearbeitungen von Lechler und Ritschl'), and *Historisch-kritische Einleitung in das Neue Testament*, 1874.

[9] Albrecht Ritschl, *Das Evangelium Marcions und das kanonische Evangelium des Lucas*, 1846.

[10] H. J. Holtzmann, *ZwTh* 1882/3, quoted *Beg.* II, 376.

[11] August Neander, *Geschichte der Pflanzung und Leitung der christlichen Kirche durch die Apostel*, 2nd enlarged ed., 2 vols., Hamburg 1838. The comment here reproduced is in Vol. I, p. 302 n. 1, and further references to Baur—purely mere polite rejections—are to be found in the notes to pages 307, 308, 310, 311, 325, 341, 361, 363, 366, 367, 373, 379, 389 and 421.

[12] Baur, *Paulus, der Apostel Jesu Christi*, 2nd ed., 26 n. 1 and 29ff. (ET *Paul, the Apostle of Jesus Christ*).

[13] Matthias Schneckenburger, *Über den Zweck der Apostelgeschichte*, Berne 1841.

He saw the apologetic character of Acts. In spite of this, he did not abandon the idea of its Lucan origin; the apologetics did no harm to the book's credibility. Undeniably, Paul appears other in Acts than he is in the Epistles.[1] Luke has presented him in such a light that Judaist recriminations are powerless against him. Yet Luke achieved this result not by distortion of history, but by the choice of what he adduces.[2]

Baur had little difficulty in showing the untenability of Schneckenburger's position.[3] But there were doughtier opponents than Schneckenburger (whose services in demonstrating the apologetic element in Acts were, by the way, readily acknowledged by Baur). In connection with a prize-competition, the Teyler Theological Society of the Netherlands spoke openly, as of something generally known, about the Tübingen school's 'hostility to Christianity'.[4] The prize was won by G. V. LECHLER.[5] He had no objection, to be sure, against 'striving to get a satisfying insight into the positive historical and genuinely human evolution of primitive Christianity.'[6] He goes indeed so far as to recognize that the Tübingen school had opened access to a development 'which as a historical process embraces both uniformity and also differences.' But this is the very point of departure for his censure. Instead of a peaceful evolution the Tübingen school insist on an absolute contradiction between Paul and the Jerusalem Apostles regarding 'that which forms the very essence of Christianity'; thereby they are contributing to the 'overthrow' of Christianity. The historical picture which Lechler opposed to Baur's was governed by his idea of such a peaceful evolution. Paul was no 'assailant of the law'.[7] He used to observe the Jewish feasts and the Mosaic law.[8] Acts—whose author is Luke—portrays him correctly.

The Tübingen school could dispose of this objection without much trouble. The second thrust was, however, more difficult to parry, for it struck at a most vulnerable place in Baur's edifice. Lechler maintained that Jewish

---

[1] Op. cit., 150.　　　　　　　　　　[2] Op. cit., 58, 92.

[3] Baur, *Paulus, der Apostel Jesu Christi*, 2nd ed., 8–17. On page 13 we read, 'Any person who intentionally suppresses so much, and who thereby has already placed the objects in another light, will not scruple, if necessary, to proceed more unhistorically still.' And on page 14: 'It is probable that the author altered the actual history not only in a negative sense, through the suppression of essential facts, but also in a positive.' Finally, 13f.: 'The fact remains that the Peter-Paul parallelism was not achieved purely by selection of material!'

[4] To quote from *ZwTh* I, 1858, 56: 'It is well known that the so-called school of Tübingen seeks to base its hostility to Christianity on its own assumption of an absolute discrepancy between Paul's doctrine and tendency and those of the other Apostles, as well as on its alleged ability to prove the rise of a conflict between the two consequent parties, who are supposed to have achieved at length a reconciliation and a settlement of differences.'

[5] Gotthold Viktor Lechler, *Das apostolische und das nachapostolische Zeitalter mit Rücksicht auf Unterschied und Einheit zwischen Paulus und den übrigen Aposteln, zwischen Heidenchristen und Judenchristen*, 1st ed., Haarlem 1851 (the prize-winning work); 2nd rev. ed., Stuttgart 1857.

[6] Op. cit., 2nd ed., 2.　　　　　　　[7] Op. cit., 524.

[8] Op. cit., 418f.

Christianity had rapidly lost its authority after the destruction of Jerusalem and the death of most of the Apostles. For that reason it would have been completely unable to play the part assigned to it by the Tübingen school for the second century. It follows, however, that the advance to the early Catholic Church must have taken place within Gentile Christianity itself. 'As in the case of the general idea of the Church, it was in Pauline circles that her self-contained organization took definite shape.' By the end of the second century, the Gentile Christian majority 'without either borrowing from Jewish Christianity . . . or coming to terms with it' had been led 'by the implicit evolution of its being' and by its opposition to gnosticism, 'to a legal and hierarchical standpoint intimately related to the theocracy of the Old Testament'.[1]

This point was also raised by ALBRECHT RITSCHL, who specifically made his final break with Baur's theories in the second edition of his work on the rise of the early Catholic Church.[2] He objected to Baur that Catholic Christianity is not a reconciliation of Paulinism and Jewish Christianity, or at least not one resulting from a blurring of antitheses, but a stage in Gentile Christianity alone, which had never been under the overall domination of Paul's peculiar doctrinal emphases.[3] Furthermore, Ritschl saw the insufficiency of Baur's Pauline-Judaist dichotomy: 'It is necessary to make many more distinctions before we can make proper combinations.'[4] Finally he posed the troublesome question of the common ground which, despite everything, Paul and the Jewish Christians must have shared.[5]

Baur found a reckless, ruthless and at all events highly unwelcome comrade-in-arms and at the same time antagonist in the former *Privatdozent* BRUNO BAUER.[6] Basically, the ideas which Bauer tossed into the debate were three in number. In the first place he insisted passionately and without restraint on the transformation undergone in Acts by the Paul of the epistles:

---

[1] Op. cit., 523.

[2] A. Ritschl, *Die Entstehung der altkatholischen Kirche: eine kirchen- und dogmen- geschichtliche Monographie*, 2nd, thoroughly revised, edition, Bonn 1857.

[3] Op. cit., 271.   [4] Op. cit., 22.

[5] Op. cit., 15.

[6] Cf. Emanuel Hirsch's acute character-sketch in his *Geschichte der neueren evange- lischen Theologie*, Vol. V, 601. In his *Geschichte der Leben-Jesu-Forschung*, 2nd ed., 141–61 (ET *The Quest of the Historical Jesus*, London 1910, 137ff.), Schweitzer presents a moving portrait of this man, whose genius failed to save him from an obduracy of negation and whose radical criticism of the gospels (*Kritik der evangelischen Geschichte des Johannes*, Bremen 1840; *Kritik der evangelischen Geschichte der Synoptiker*, 3 vols., Leipzig 1841/42) had cost him the *venia legendi*. His work of most present relevance is *Die Apostelgeschichte, eine Ausgleichung des Paulinismus und des Judenthums innerhalb der Kirche*, which appeared in 1852 immediately after his *Kritik der paulinischen Briefe*, Parts 1–3, 1850/2. See also Schweitzer's *Geschichte der paulinischen Forschung*, 94–7 (ET 120ff.), and Martin Kegel's *Bruno Bauer und seine Theorie über die Entstehung des Christentums*, 1908, as well as Karl Löwith's *Von Hegel zu Nietzsche*, 142ff., 411ff., 467ff. (ET *From Hegel to Nietzsche*, London 1965.)

the religious dialectician, accustomed to fight only with words, is supplanted by the 'wizard' who 'dazzles his opponents'.[1] The Apostle, 'who fulfils his historical work through sufferings, struggles and trials,' becomes the 'miracle-worker'.[2] The author of Acts is out to convey the 'godlike impression' made by Peter and Paul alike.[3]

But Acts effects a second transformation: it takes away from Paul the honour of the mission to the Gentiles and gives it to Peter, who then 'legitimates and sanctions' Paul's activity.[4] Paul has in the end to give the assurance 'that he is a strict servant of the law, who could never have dreamed of abandoning the basis of the Law'.[5] 'Thereby the contrast with the Epistles reaches its peak'.[6]

Nevertheless—and this is where Bruno Bauer attacked the master from Tübingen—this was no late attempt at reconciliation. F. C. Baur's working-hypothesis, the opposition between Paulinism and Jewish Christianity, was simply no longer present.[7] Inasmuch as the Church recognized in Acts the canonical expression of her own consciousness, the victor was 'Judaism', i.e. the power which will brook no individual reshaping and immediately brings the new 'to the level of the established'.[8] 'It was no single-handed revolution—this is the basic thesis of Acts—when Paul brought salvation to the Gentiles.' 'The revolutionary is absorbed into the holy chain of tradition'.[9]

If it at first appeared that Bruno Bauer was trying to uphold the *theologia crucis* of Paul's Epistles against a *theologia gloriae* in Acts, it becomes clear here that, under the impress of his own experiences, he conceives the Apostle, in the romantic, idealist way, as the free, creative individual, who is kept down by the 'existing' order: Paul is the 'hero strong in his own powers,' 'who draws resolve and power to act from the spring of his inner being.'[10]

But Bruno Bauer, in whose sceptical hands all texts crumbled, could not even hold together the great Pauline documents which had been his base for the assault upon Acts. Even they became for him the 'works of free reflexion',[11] and in the end he considered Acts a necessary precursor of Galatians![12]

This thesis was advanced afresh in 1882 by A. D. LOMAN,[13] independently of Bauer. The Paul of the great Epistles is, he says, an idealization(!) of the

---

[1] Bauer, *Apostelgeschichte*, 7–9.
[2] *Apostelgeschichte*, 8: 'The wizard has nothing in common with the religious dialectician; the miracle-worker contradicts the spiritual hero.'
[3] Op. cit., 21f.   [4] Op. cit., 53.
[5] Op. cit., 91.   [6] Op. cit., 92.
[7] Op. cit., 121.   [8] Op. cit., 124.
[9] Op. cit., 125.   [10] Op. cit., 124.
[11] Bauer, *Kritik der paulinischen Briefe*, Part 1, 'Der Ursprung des Galaterbriefes', 1850, III.
[12] Idem, VI.
[13] Loman, '*Quaestiones Paulinae*' in the *Theol. Tijdschrift* for 1882, 141ff., 302ff., and 452ff.; also 1883, 14ff. and 241ff., and 1886, 42ff., and 387ff. Cf. 98 of Schweitzer's *Geschichte der paulinischen Forschung* (ET *Paul and his Interpreters*, 1956) and Rudolf Steck, *Der Galaterbrief*, 1888, 12–14.

historical figure of the Apostle. The Paul-figures of the 'we'-narrative, of the rest of Acts and of the main Epistles are 'the progressive evolutionary stages of a legend of Paul'.[1] After long examination, RUDOLF STECK,[2] Professor at Berne, decided in 1888 that Loman was right—the Pauline Epistles were the work of a school.[3] ('We shall have to get used to the idea that no Apostle wrote anything, any more than Jesus himself did.'[4]) The report which Acts represents is the fundamental datum for the historical situation.[5]

Thus we come to the grotesque spectacle of 'ultra-radicals' transformed into champions of Acts. But there is nothing new under the sun. As long before as 1792, an English divine, EDWARD EVANSON,[6] had denied the authenticity of the Epistle to the Romans on the grounds of its being at variance with Acts.

The only followers that F. C. Baur found in England, where the great scholar J. B. LIGHTFOOT opposed the Tübingen theories (see *Beg.* II, 419f.), were SAMUEL DAVIDSON and W. R. CASSELS.[7]

Neither was Baur a success in France. ERNEST RENAN[8] believed Acts to be a very carefully planned work, written by Luke about the year 80 (later Renan went as far as 100). It is Luke who speaks in the 'we'.[9] The book is well-disposed to the Romans (hence breaks off before Nero's persecutions[10]) and delights in miracles: 'a dogmatic quasi-history, designed to support the orthodox doctrines of the time or to impress on readers' minds the ideas *qui souriaient le plus à la piété de l'auteur*'. Why not? 'It is only from the writings of the faithful that we know about the origins of any religion. Only the sceptic writes *ad narrandum*'[11] (a truth often overlooked in Harnack's generation of source-critics!). Luke was less concerned, says Renan, with stating historical facts or satisfying the demands of logic than with edifying the pious reader. His work belongs to those semi-historical, semi-legendary

---

[1] As summarized by Steck, from whose work we borrow our representation of Loman's ideas.

[2] Steck, *Der Galaterbrief nach seiner Echtheit untersucht nebst kritischen Bemerkungen zu den paulinischen Hauptbriefen*, Berlin 1888. In this context we should also mention the Dutch critic Van Manen, the first volume (1890) of whose *Paulus* is entitled *De Handelingen der Apostelen*. See Schweitzer, *Geschichte der paulinischen Forschung*, 98ff. (ET 125ff.).

[3] Op. cit., 363.   [4] Op. cit., 353.

[5] Op. cit., 357.

[6] According to J. W. Hunkin, 'British Work on the Acts' (*Beg.* II, 396–433), 417f. Evanson's work was entitled *The Dissonance of the Four generally received Evangelists, and the Evidence of their respective Authenticity examined*.

[7] Davidson, *An Introduction to the Study of the New Testament*, London 1894, Vol. II, 76–175; E. Jacquier, op. cit., XXIf.

Cassels, *Supernatural Religion: an Inquiry into the Reality of Divine Revelation*, 1874 (see Hunkin, *Beg.* II, 419).

[8] Renan, *Les Apôtres*, 1866. (ET *History of the Origins of Christianity*, Vol. II, *The Apostles*, 1890.)

[9] *Les Apôtres*, Xf.   [10] Op. cit., XXII.

[11] Op. cit., XXIX.

documents which one can take neither as history nor as legend. Though nearly every detail is false, such works enshrine valuable truths which are there for the finding.[1]

In his commentary on Acts, Nietzsche's friend FRANZ OVERBECK[2] assembled the body of evidence so far gathered against Baur's historical synthesis. Acts does not stand midway between the earliest Christian parties: 'its Gentile Christianity is not the Pauline one, still less is its Judaism that of the first Apostles.' Rather is the Judaistic element already a constituent of its own peculiar Gentile Christianity, which—itself strongly influenced by the original Christian Judaism—can be seen trying 'to come to terms with its own genesis and with its founder Paul'. Save for the universalism, the specifically Pauline is laid aside, not as a concession to an alien party, but only because Paul is no longer understood.[3] On the other hand, Acts is concerned to win the favour of the Roman authorities[4]: the intention of averting political discredit from Christianity is obvious.[5] Gentile Christianity is not justified from the theology of Paul: the universal mission is for the Christian community already established from the very first (cf. Acts 1.8!). Far from being presupposed, the gospel according to Paul is effaced.[6] The antagonists of Paul as of the earliest community are the *unbelieving* Jews; his conflict with the 'Judaists' is in Acts not only without trace, but inconceivable.[7] Where the author's share predominates (he is not Luke), historical details can scarcely be established; at most in the accounts relating to Peter, and in certain individual references.[8] It is 'particularly the fact that Paul is the hero of Acts', and that nonetheless his portrait is already so distorted, which makes it probable that the work was composed in the second or third decade of the second century.[9] The external and internal detachment from Judaism, together with the implication of conflicts with the Roman authorities, suggests the time of Trajan: Acts is a direct precursor of the apologetic literature.[10] Probably it originated in Asia Minor, perhaps Ephesus.[11]

JOHANNES WEISS's work of 1897, *Absicht und literarischer Charakter der Apostelgeschichte*, gives the impression of being a late straggler of 'tendency-

---

[1] Op. cit., XLI.

[2] Overbeck was the editor of the fourth edition (1870) of W. M. L. de Wette's *Kurzgefasstes exegetisches Handbuch zum Neuen Testament* I, 4, where he inserted his own glosses, indicated by half-brackets, within De Wette's text. This makes him wearisome to read, but the effort is well rewarded. McGiffert (1922) considered Overbeck's commentary to be in many respects the best we possess (see *Beg.* II, 381).

[3] Op. cit., XXXIf.   [4] Op. cit., XXXII.
[5] Op. cit., XXXIII.   [6] Op. cit., XXXVI.
[7] Op. cit., XXXVI.   [8] Op. cit., LXII.
[9] Op. cit., LXIV.   [10] Op. cit., LXV.

[11] Op. cit., LXIX. In *Der Paulinismus*, 1873, 495 (ET London 1877, vol. II, 228), Otto Pfleiderer concurs with Overbeck (XXXI) in the following judgement: 'The Acts of the Apostles bears witness to late Paulinism's awareness of its own past.' The author has, in all good faith, transferred the relationships of his own time into that of the Apostles (497).

criticism' who has fallen in with a strange column.[1] He defines the spiritual climate of Acts exactly like Overbeck: it stands materially nearer to the Apologists than to Paul,[2] being 'an apology for the Christian religion before the Gentiles in the face of Jewish indictment, one which demonstrates how it has come about that Christianity has taken over and fulfils the worldwide mission of Judaism'.[3] Two ideas constantly recur: 1. The Christians are guiltless of any transgression within the competence of the Roman authorities, who have therefore no cause for taking steps against them;[4] 2. Christianity is a Judaism teaching the fulfilment of Jewish hopes. Thereby it replaces Judaism proper.[5]

After this work of Weiss's, 'tendency-criticism' fell silent.

B. The Age of Source-Criticism

'Tendency-criticism' had ascribed the fragmentary character of Acts to the author's *unwillingness* to say more.[6] The other possibility, his *inability* to say more, would imply that he was restricted by the incompleteness of his sources. This idea played a big part at the beginning of the nineteenth century. One hundred years later the question of sources again became a burning topic. On both occasions a spate of writings promptly poured forth. But soon the flow dwindled, and at length it ceased altogether.

The first epoch of source-criticism stretched from its advent to the triumph of Baur's 'tendency-criticism'. McGiffert (*Beg.* II, 385ff.) has given a very thorough account of the now mostly forgotten scholars of that age, and we shall make grateful use of his information.

It was the Flensburg Rector BERNHARD L. KÖNIGSMANN who set the ball rolling in 1798 with a seminar-programme, '*De fontibus commentariorum sacrorum, qui Lucae nomen praeferunt, deque eorum consilio et aetate*'[7]. He inferred from the prologue of Luke that the author of the work did not claim to be an eye-witness and ought therefore to be distinguished from the writer of the 'we'-passages. He concluded the presence of further sources (which, however, he did not seek to define more closely) from the variety and unevenness of the style and from contradictions in the matter presented.

---

[1] In this connexion we do not enter into the valuable researches on the composition of Acts, which Weiss carried out in order 'to elicit the ultimate intention of the book and therewith its literary character' (2).

[2] *Absicht*, 56.   [3] Op. cit., 57.

[4] Op. cit., 58. Likewise Carl Weizsäcker, *Das apostolische Zeitalter der christlichen Kirche*, 1886, 459 (ET *The Apostolic Age* II, 123): The author was trying 'to show that Christianity held absolutely no danger for the Roman state and embodied no crime deserving of punishment by the law'.

[5] Op. cit., 59.

[6] See the quotation from Schwanbeck, p. 15 above.

[7] Reprinted in Potts, *Sylloge Commentationum Theologicarum*, Vol. 3, 1802, 215–39; see *Beg.* II, 385.

In a work which appeared in 1799, J. A. BOLTEN showed by the very title—*Die Geschichte der Apostel von Lukas übersetzt und mit Anmerkungen versehen*—that he held quite a different opinion on the origin of Acts: Luke is said to have translated and annotated one, or even several, Aramaic sources. This raises the problem of the Lucan semitisms. Bolten's solution foreshadowed Torrey's.

An article published by W. K. L. ZIEGLER[1] in 1801 pointed in yet another direction. The accounts concerning Peter reminded him of the Acts and Kerygma of Peter which are mentioned by the early Fathers. At the same time he conjectured written accounts of Stephen's martyrdom and Paul's conversion as sources for the first part of Acts, which played a special rôle in these investigations.

J. G. EICHHORN[2] found in Acts a 'self-consistent original historical narrative' and for this reason wished to attribute to Luke even the speeches of Acts, 'which all take place under circumstances where no one could have written them down'.

The Dutchman J. C. RIEHM[3] dealt exhaustively with the source-question in 1821 in his *Dissertatio critico-theologica de fontibus actuum apostolicorum*. Since Luke, as a friend of Paul and of other participants as well as an eye-witness (the 'I' of the 'we'-passages!), was himself the principal authority for the second part of Acts, he had little need of sources there, but on the other hand he used many minor, fragmentary sources for the first part.

In 1831/2, FRIEDRICH SCHLEIERMACHER[4] devoted his §§ 85–90 (pp. 344–79) to the Acts of the Apostles. Acts formed one dual work with the third gospel, but had an independent and peculiar genesis. Whereas the separate stories underlying the gospels were a necessary complement of apostolic preaching (which—Schleiermacher does not think like Dibelius!—did not publicly proclaim anything of the sort), it was only the Christians' historical sense which could have aroused interest in the tales of the Apostles. Both documents were intended to present a coherent account *de rebus christianis*. The prologue in Luke applied to both—which meant one must presuppose guarantors and sources for Acts too! The author was not the 'I' who speaks in the 'we'-parts: rather do these represent a source. The fact that there are three separate accounts of Paul's conversion, and two of Peter's vision, likewise suggests multiple sources. On several occasions it is clear that a new report is beginning, hence with it a new source. The author compiled Acts

---

[1] Ziegler, 'Über den Zweck, die Quellen und die Interpolationen der Apostelgeschichte' in *Gablers Neuestes Theologisches Journal*, Vol. VII, 1801, 125ff.; *Beg.* II, 385.

[2] Eichhorn, *Einleitung in das Neue Testament*, 1810, Vol. II, 149; discussed by Schleiermacher, *Einleitung*, 371—see note 4.

[3] Our account is taken from *Beg.* II, 386.

[4] Schleiermacher's Collected Works, Division I: *Zur Theologie*, Vol. VIII, *Einleitung ins Neue Testament*, ed. G. Wolde, Berlin 1845.

from already assembled written sources, probably opuscules from the communities at Jerusalem, Antioch and Ephesus, as well as a travel-diary. The Lucan work, composed after the sack of Jerusalem, remained incomplete. Its author was unacquainted with Paul's Epistles. Through a misunderstanding he recorded, in 11.30, a journey which never took place. The speeches were already present in one or other of the separate accounts comprising the author's source-material. Yet they employ the Septuagint, while Aramaic was the language of Jerusalem. Schleiermacher's way out of this difficulty is the hypothesis that the Aramaic tradition had been adopted and revised by Hellenistic Christians.

So here we have an astonishing variety of observations and points of view. Which makes all the more astonishing the patent inability to combine the idea of a use of sources with that of a comprehensive revision and presentation. But did not form-criticism also regard the Evangelists—including Luke—at first as essentially transcribers and editors?

MAYERHOFF (see p. 15 n. 2 above) rose to protest against Schleiermacher's distinction between Luke and the 'I' in the 'we,' and proceeded to demonstrate the stylistic accord between the 'we'-passages and the rest of Acts. Actually, the author of both Acts and the third gospel was—Timothy. Whereupon FRIEDRICH BLEEK and M. ULRICH rose up in their turn to expostulate.[1] Both saw in Timothy the 'I' of the 'we'-passages, and ascribed to Luke the penning of Acts. A. F. GFRÖRER's solution, in his *Geschichte des Urchristentums* (1838), was different again.[2] Chapters 1 to 12 (highly legendary, with few and incomplete sources) are the work of one author, whereas 13 to 28 are the work of another—Luke, the eyewitness and the companion of Paul. The two parts were united by an unknown hand towards the end of the first century.

With EUGEN SCHWANBECK's book, *Über die Quellen der Apostelgeschichte,* 1847, the first age of source-criticism came to an end. He detected as sources not only a biography of Paul but also a supposed life of Barnabas and memoirs of Silas, these last forming the basis of Chapters 15–28.

This age undoubtedly produced an abundance of important observations. But their evaluation was a matter of disagreement, and often the scholar's imagination ran away with him. Nevertheless, the viewpoints which have arisen in source-criticism were, almost without exception, established in this first epoch, when the explorers of the subject were still venturing into uncharted regions.

---

[1] Bleek's discussion of Mayerhoff in *Studien und Kritik*, 1836, pp. 1021ff.; see *Beg.* II, 387.

Ulrich, 'Kommt Lukas wirklich in der Apostelgeschichte vor?' in *Stud. u. Krit.*, 1837, 369ff., and 'Lukas kommt nicht in der Apostelgeschichte vor' in *Stud. u. Krit.*, 1840, 1003; see *Beg.* II, 387.

[2] According to *Beg.* II, 387 n. 2.

It was only in 1885 that JACOBSEN's work, *Die Quellen der Apostel-geschichte*, showed that interest in the problem was not yet extinct. Jacobsen believed that in Acts 1–12 the author offered 'in the main more or less happy combinations, chiefly with reference to notices' in Pauline Epistles(!).[1] He assumed that some document about Barnabas was the source for Chapters 13 to 15.

The following year, in the first edition of his introduction to the New Testament, BERNHARD WEISS presented an exhaustive source-criticism of Acts (570–84), which made a strong impression. Acts, he said, is the work of Paul's companion Luke, from whom the whole of the second part derives; here he was reshaping his own travel-notes.[2] For the first part he made use of an account by a Jewish Christian eyewitness.[3] Luke is therefore responsible for everything unhistorical between Acts **1**.1 and **15**.31.[4] Weiss attributed the following sections[5] to communications made to Luke by word of mouth: **9**.1–30; **11**.19–30; **12**.25; Chapters **13** and **14**.

The weakness of this division of sources is, once again, not hard to discern. Anything discordant with the hypothetical eyewitness is said to be a later addition. But this begs the question, for it presupposes that a merely conjectural eyewitness record is already a proven fact. On the other hand, there is no denying the value of many separate observations presented by Weiss in the notes to these few pages of introduction.

Though VAN MANEN's ultra-radical position stands undisguised, his analysis of Acts,[6] published in 1890, calls Wendt to mind, where it touches on the question of sources. He assumes the basic source to be certain *Acta Pauli*, into which a Lucan travel-diary (from the first meeting in Troas to the arrival in Rome) had already been interwoven. The editor responsible for Acts, writing between 125 and 150, further employed an analogous Acts of Peter (an imitation of minimal historical value), which plays roughly the same rôle as Weiss's Jewish Christian source, and to it he added traditions current in the community of Damascus on the subjects of Stephen, Paul's conversion and the foundation of the community in Antioch.

---

[1] See *Beg.* II, 388. The formulation quoted is in H. J. Holtzmann, 'Forschungen über die Apostelgeschichte', *ZwTh* 1885, cited by Heitmüller, *ThR* 2 (1899) 52.

[2] Weiss, *Lehrbuch der Einleitung in das Neue Testament*, 2nd ed. 1889, 584.

[3] Op. cit., 574.

[4] E.g. the Pentecostal gift of tongues, the session of the council in Ch. 4 (op. cit., 572), the earthquake of **4**.31 (573), the delivering angel and the reference to Theudas in Ch. 5 (574), everything postulating an orderly trial in the story of Stephen (574 n. 5), the references to Paul in **8**.3 & **9**.1 (577), the dispersal of the community (574 n. 5), the aside of **10**.41 (575) and the remarks about the growth of the Church (574) and the community of goods (573 n. 3).

[5] Op. cit., 576.

[6] Van Manen, *Paulus*, Vol. I: *De Handelingen der Apostelen*, Leyden 1890. Our account rests on Heitmüller's report in *ThR* 2 (1889) 86ff.

Here we may recognize two methods of looking for sources. Either there is a person round whom the sources revolve (hence the supposition of Acts of Paul or Peter), or a community in which they are handed down—here it is Antioch, but we saw that Schleiermacher would add Ephesus and Jerusalem.

In the same year there appeared the work of MARTIN SOROF, *Die Entstehung der Apostelgeschichte*. According to Sorof, the basis of Acts was the document destined for Theophilus by Luke, who had already, for Chapters 13 and 14, made use of a source relating to Barnabas. Considerably later Timothy added legends glorifying Peter and generally acted as editor, making a large number of interpolations. With this theory, Sorof is Loisy's forerunner: there is an authentic foundation to Acts, later extensively built upon by the redactor. Like many another student of Acts in this period, Sorof lived in the naive assurance that all revisions consisted simply of the addition of new material, so that it must be possible to name the origin of every verse.[1] Moreover, underlying his entire scheme is the primitive impression that certain parts to the scholar are historically possible and probable, while others are not: the first constitute the Lucan substratum, the rest the additions unfortunately inserted by Timothy. For the scholars of the time (as also, however, for Emanuel Hirsch in later days) it was an overwhelming temptation to attribute sources as far as possible to known persons of the apostolic age.

The year 1891 brought two works on the sources of Acts. PAUL FEINE, with his *Eine vorkanonische Überlieferung des Lukas in Evangelium und Apostelgeschichte*, threw a wholly new idea into the debate[2]: the special source of the third gospel, he says, runs beyond Luke 24 and appears in Acts **1**.4,5,(8),9–17 etc.; its use even extends to Acts **12**.24[3]! This source, a Jewish Christian document composed before the year 70 and mainly con-

---

[1] Two examples must suffice: (1) Acts **1**.1,2 are ascribed to Luke, **1**.3–**2**.42 to the legend of Peter inserted by Timothy (this 'explains' in terms of source-criticism the difficult transition from **1**.2 to **1**.3); **2**.43–5 were added from Timothy's own ideas; **2**.46 represents the resumption of the Lucan document. (2) Chapter 15 is divided as follows: 1–7a are by Luke, Timothy inserted 7b–18, while Luke's text is resumed with 19–34; James is thus cast adrift.

[2] Feine had already made his idea public in 1890 through the article, 'Die alte Quelle in der ersten Hälfte der Apostelgeschichte' (*Jahrb. für prot. Theologie* XVI, 84. 133). Later Emanuel Hirsch was to advocate the notion that the special source of Luke extends into Acts (*Frühgeschichte des Evangeliums*, vol. 1: *Das Werden des Markusevangeliums*, XXX–XXXIX of the 2nd enlarged edition, 1951). In support of this case, Hirsch dismissed Acts **1**.3 from the text of the old source and made two conjectures: in **1**.4, συναλιζομένοις for συναλιζόμενος and ἤκουσάς μου (just as Hemsterhuis had suggested before him). The original account continues with Acts **1**.12, 15a, 16–17, 20–6. καὶ ἐξῆλθεν should be deleted in **1**.21, and everything in **1**.22 before μάρτυρα: instead of τούτων read τῶν δύο. Thus, in Hirsch's reading, one of the two disciples of Emmaus was designated as the new Apostle. The whole conjectural edifice exemplifies the strength and weakness of the kind of source-reconstruction, in the spirit of H. J. Holtzmann's age, which proceeds with the aid of rash hypotheses.

[3] *Überlieferung* 156–212.

cerned with Peter and Jerusalem, is according to Feine of unusual historical value. But in Chapters 6 and 7 he detects traces of a second source. Whereas one source in the story of Stephen develops the theme that 'the Jewish people has always ungratefully striven against God',[1] the other deals with the idea that God's saving presence is not bound to any particular place.[2] At other points also the story of Stephen shows the use of two sources; **9**.1–30 and **11**.15–31, and perhaps **8**.25–40, should be referred to the second source,[3] which portrays Stephen as the precursor of Paul.[4]

How it should be intrinsically possible for a Jewish Christian, before the year 70, to break the established mould of the gospel by prolonging it into a history of the Church—that is a question which Feine neglected to ask. Admittedly, it has remained largely disregarded even later.

The second work on Acts of the year 1891 was by FRIEDRICH SPITTA: *Die Apostelgeschichte, ihre Quellen und deren geschichtlicher Wert*. Spitta too is convinced that Acts 1 is a continuation of Luke **24**.53[5]: this source he calls *A*. As an eyewitness-report[6], it has higher historical value than the second source, *B*,[7] which is of an artless, popular character.[8] These two sources are interwoven throughout Acts; the German translation of the sources which Spitta supplies in his appendix[9] conveys an impression of how ingeniously the whole of Acts has been dismembered into these two sources without leaving too much of a surplus to be attributed to the editor.[10] While *A* probably derives from Luke himself (p. 312), *B* was not written until after the sack of Jerusalem (p. 317). The (unknown) editor combined the two documents as early as the first century. As for the third book, concerned with the remaining history of the Apostles, either he was no longer able to compile it, or it has been lost.[11]

Spitta's skill in dissection is as astounding as his trust in the editor's skill in combination.

After this high tide of source-hypotheses there followed a perceptible slackening of output in research on the subject. In his *Chronologie der paulinischen Briefe*, 1893,[12] C. CLEMEN developed a somewhat complicated

---

[1] Acts **6**.9–11, 15; **7**.22–8, 35–43, 51–6, 59f.; **8**.1, from ἐγένετο, **8**.2 (*Überlieferung*, 193).

[2] Acts **6**.13f., **7**.2–21, 29–34, 44–50, 57–8a; **8**.1, up to ἀναιρέσει αὐτοῦ (op. cit., 190f.).

[3] This source according to Feine begins with Acts **6**.1ff. (193).

[4] Op. cit., 192f.

[5] Specifically in verses 15–26.

[6] Spitta, 303.

[7] To which belong, in Chapter 1, verses 4–7, 9–14, 18 and 19.

[8] Op. cit., 291.   [9] Op. cit., 321–80.

[10] E.g. **1**.18f. (op. cit., 14), 21b & 22a (13f.). In Chapter 15, he inserted verses 5–12 into *B*, which alone reports the Apostolic Council (186ff.). On the other hand, **11**.27–32 & **12**.25 come from *A*.

[11] Op. cit., 319.

[12] Supplemented by his article in *Stud. u. Krit.*, 1895, 'Der Zusammenhang von Apostelgeschichte 1–5'.

story concerning the genesis of Acts: a Life of Peter, already embodying half a dozen minor sources, was united by a Judaistic editor with a Life of Paul based on Luke's travel-journal; the whole was revised and emended by an *anti*-Judaist.[1]

The ground-plan of the 'good' source *A* (stemming from Luke[2]) and the 'legendary' (Jewish Christian) source *B* was once more put to the test by JOHANNES JÜNGST in his *Die Quellen der Apostelgeschichte* (1895). A 'redactor' of Trajan's or even Hadrian's time, one who already tended toward the ideas of the Apologists and wished to secure for Christianity the character of a *religio licita*, wove *A* and *B* together, adding much material of his own,[3] especially in the second part of Acts. *B* continues the special source of the Third Gospel. But Jüngst also takes into account the very strong probability of editorial transpositions.[4]

The last work of this kind came from ADOLF HILGENFELD.[5] He assumes three sources: 1. Judaistic *Acta Petri*, 2. Hellenistic 'Acts of the Seven', 3. Lucan *Acta Pauli*. To these three sources the 'redactor', who wished to show Paul and the Gentile Christians on good terms with the original Church, occasionally made considerable additions.

'Since 1896 ... high tide has suddenly yielded to the ebb. Has the problem been solved? Has it been recognized as insoluble? Or has that vigorous *Quos ego!* which in his well-known thesis on the text of Acts a "master of the lower criticism", Friedrich Blass, hurled at the "higher critics" while they still sailed aloft in Icarian flight made so strong an impression that in shame and horror people abandoned the outlawed venture?' Such was Heitmüller's question in 1899.[6]

The philologist FRIEDRICH BLASS had put forward the thesis that Luke drafted Acts at Rome between 57 and 59 A.D. Copies of the draft were circulated, and so arose the 'Western' text of Acts. Once back in the Levant, Luke recast the book with prunings and improvements for Theophilus, the 'most excellent citizen of Antioch', and thus he made the 'Eastern' text.[7]

---

[1] Clemen retracted this hypothesis in his *Paulus* of 1904 (VII).

[2] See Jüngst, 201.

[3] E.g. Acts 14.8–21a, **15**.5–13a, 21–9, **16**.23a, b, c–34.

[4] Thus in *A* **15**.1–4, 30a, 32, 35 are said to have followed immediately after **11**.19–23, 25f., while **11**.27–28a, 30 & **12**.25ab followed **14**.1f., 6f., 21b–27ab, 28; to this latter sequence **15**.36 & **16**.1, 3a, 6a, 7–23a were attached.

[5] Hilgenfeld, 'Die Apostelgeschichte nach ihren Quellen untersucht', *ZwTh* 1895/6. Our account of Hilgenfeld's views is based on Heitmüller's review in *ThR* 2 (1899) 133f. Later Hilgenfeld published, in *ZwTh* for 1899, two articles: 'Das Aposteldekret nach seinem ursprünglichen Wortlaut' (138ff.) and 'Nachwort zu *Acta apostolorum graece et latine*' (382ff.).

[6] *ThR* 2 (1899) 48.

[7] Blass, 'Die Textüberlieferung in der Apostelgeschichte', in *Stud. u. Krit.*, 1894, 86–119. Also, *Acta Apostolorum sive Lucae ad Theophilum liber alter* (*editio philologica*) 1895; *Acta Apostolorum secundum formam quae videtur romanam*, 1896.

Zahn, who along with others adopted this hypothesis, altered it at the same time: Luke, he suggested, sent his draft to Theophilus as a mark of personal regard. Copies of this draft produced the 'Western' text. When the question of regular publication presented itself to Luke later on, he revised the book, deleting personal details, and thus arose the 'Eastern' form of text, as in B ℵ etc.[1]

Most scholars—rightly—rejected Blass's theory, because the two texts are to some extent mutually exclusive (Zahn avoided this admission only by rejecting from the 'Western' text the 'Western' form of the Apostolic Decree) and because it is in fact the 'Western' text which seeks to remove tensions and disagreements. This apart, the hypothesis in no way renders the source-question redundant: it merely, as Loisy saw,[2] puts it back behind the textual problem.

A final attempt to clarify the problem of sources—and not only this, but the problem of Acts in general—was made by ADOLF HARNACK in the first years of the new century. In his *Lucas der Arzt* (1906),[3] he took up again the researches of W. K. Hobart[4] and endeavoured to demonstrate from the language of the twin 'Lucan' works that a physician must have been their author—Luke the 'beloved physician' of Col. 4.14.[5] Two years later, his book *Die Apostelgeschichte* dealt among other things with the question of sources.[6] 'If Luke the physician is the author of Acts, the source-question is simply and quickly settled for the whole second half of the book' (p. 131): for one part of the events recounted Luke was himself an eyewitness, for the remainder he possessed the reports of eyewitnesses. As for the first half of the book, it is impossible to ascertain its sources through stylistic analysis. Accordingly Harnack first turns his inquiry to the scenes and persons recounted.[7] The story of Stephen must have a documentary source,[8] to which belong 6.1–8.4, 11.19–30 and 12.25 (13.1)–15.35. This 'Antioch-Jerusalem source', perhaps as a whole to be considered documentary,[9] derives its authority from Silas. We may call it *C*. Harnack distinguishes it from a 'Jerusalem-Caesarea source *A*,' from which come 3.1–5.16, 8.5–40, 9.31–11.18 and 12.1–23: here Luke received partly oral, partly written information from Philip—or from him and his prophetess daughters, whence the predilection for the enthusiastic![10] Finally, running parallel with the historically

[1] Theodor Zahn, 'Die Urausgabe der Apostelgeschichte des Lucas', *Forsch. z. Gesch. des ntl. Kanons* IX, 1916, 2–6.

[2] *Les Actes*, p. 41.

[3] ET *Luke the Physician* (1907).

[4] Hobart, *The Medical Language of St. Luke*, 1882; cf. Zahn, *Einleitung in das NT*, 3rd ed., Vol. 2, 433f. & 442f. (ET *Introduction to the NT*, Edinburgh, 1909).

[5] See p. 73 n. 2.

[6] *Beiträge zur Einleitung in das NT* III (1908); ET *The Acts of the Apostles* (1909).

[7] Op. cit., 132ff.   [8] Op. cit., 138.

[9] Op. cit., 187.

[10] Op. cit., 151 and 185.

respectable source A there is a legendary source B (Chapter 2 and 5.17–42) with which Harnack refuses to saddle any member of the apostolic circle. Thus it remains as anonymous as it is worthless.[1]

To make a really sound case for the parallelism of *A* and *B* Harnack simply described the coming of the Spirit with the gift of tongues in 4.31ff. as the 'real historical Pentecost', to which Chapter 2 is the legendary counterpart.[2] It goes without saying that the two arrests of Chapters 4 and 5 were likewise interpreted as parallel accounts.[3] Finally, in his *Neue Untersuchungen zur Apostelgeschichte*,[4] Harnack demonstrated the stylistic accord of the 'we'-passages with the rest of Acts, hastening somewhat rashly to infer the identity of their author with the writer of the whole. Originally,[5] by the way, Harnack had placed Acts c. 80 A.D. In the last-mentioned work, however, he opted for composition at Rome some time before the outcome of Paul's trial.[6]

At a meeting of the Royal Göttingen Scientific Society on 12 January 1907, JULIUS WELLHAUSEN read a paper on Acts[7] in which he dealt with a number of selected passages. His general conclusion, in criticism of research up to that time, runs: 'Of late we have seen an endeavour to apportion the Acts of the Apostles by source-criticism in such a way that very little remains for Luke, who yet was certainly no mere compiler ... Yet the fact remains that often enough the documentary information used by Luke floats like *croûtons* in the soup..., joints and seams are discernible at many points,... and in Chapters 16 to 21 in particular there comes to light a travel-journal, which of course has been revised and enriched with episodes'.[8]

A similar view is found in perhaps the best thing written on Acts before the first World War: § XII, 'Apostelgeschichten', of PAUL WENDLAND's 'Urchristliche Literaturformen'.[9] Wendland does not engage in a source-theory of the kind favoured so far. With regard to the history of the primitive Church and the earliest spread of Christianity, he says, 'the writer possessed only separate traditions, whose sequence and interconnection lie open to strong suspicion.'[10] The inadequacy of many references is to be explained not by Luke's exercise of selection but by 'the fragmentary character of the

---

[1] 'The latest and least trustworthy' portions of the book (op. cit., 184).
[2] Op. cit., 146.   [3] Op. cit., 143f.
[4] *Beiträge zur Einleitung in das NT* IV (1911); ET *The Date of the Acts* ..., 1911.
[5] Harnack, *Die Chronologie der altchristlichen Literatur bis Eusebius*, Vol. I, 1897, 246–50; see 248: '... the indication is, therefore, that the book ... may be dated roughly as far back as the year 80.'
[6] Beiträge IV, 63–114.
[7] 1–21 of the Proceedings of the *Kgl. Gesellschaft der Wissenschaften zu Göttingen, Phil.-Hist. Klasse*, 1907. 263–99 contain the extremely important article by Eduard Schwartz, 'Zur Chronologie des Paulus', in which he dates the council of the Apostles in the winter of 43/44 (p. 269).
[8] Wellhausen, 21.
[9] *Hdb. z. NT* Vol. I, Part 3, 2nd & 3rd edd., 1912.
[10] Op. cit., 315.

traditions known to him'.[1] His 'presentation, eschewing tensions and controversy, is not the ingenious product of a would-be conciliator, but the natural expression of more developed church conditions and the changed historical outlook they brought'.[2] 'The special vocation of Paul to be an Apostle to the Gentiles' is no longer evident. The theory which dominates the presentation in **13**.46, **18**.6, **19**.9, and **28**.25ff. lifts 'the events described out of their limits to the level of images having a universal and typical significance'; it thus illustrates the replacing of God's revelation to the Jews by its communication to the Gentiles.[3] The Jews (the Judaists being as good as forgotten) are the Apostle's enemy, although he is presented as a law-abiding Jew in a way irreconcilable with his own statements.[4] Joins and contradictions show that a diversity of presumably documentary sources has been used. The author is acquainted with secular literature; the gospel begins with a stylish exordium in the traditional manner.[5] But the whole is not a genuine history; like the Books of the Maccabees, it hovers between history and epic. Its lineal descendants are the Lives of the Saints and Martyrs. Its loose composition, its absorption in anecdote, are akin to the embroidered or panegyric presentation of great historical persons or religious miracle-workers.[6] The technique of such models is more familiar to the author than the style of (rhetorical) history. The many repetitions betray the carelessness of the popular story-teller,[7] whose habit is to present scene after scene without making sure that each is wholly in harmony with what has gone before.[8] 'In the formulation of the speeches', the author 'stands on a level with John'[9]; as in the fourth gospel, the speeches often do not suit the situation, but express his religious opinions. Luke, however, is not the author: the prologue is far removed from the time of the Apostles.[10] His medical knowledge does not exceed that of an educated layman.[11]

And so Wendland's study opened the way for a new view of Acts, one which abandons the various biases of 'tendency'- and source-criticism, thereby allowing the problem of literary form to come into focus. Wendland's observations form a transition to the method of style and form criticism practised by Dibelius.

In 1913 *Agnostos Theos*, a work by the great Berlin philologist EDUARD NORDEN,[12] caused quite a stir among the experts on Acts. Even today Norden's historical investigations into the style of liturgical and preaching formulae,[13] and his Appendices IV to VIII on stylistic questions, have not lost their

---

[1] Op. cit., 316.
[2] Op. cit., 321.
[3] Op. cit., 322.
[4] Op. cit., 323.
[5] Op. cit., 324.
[6] Op. cit., 325.
[7] Op. cit., 328.
[8] Op. cit., 329.
[9] Op. cit., 331.
[10] Op. cit., 334.
[11] Op. cit., 335.
[12] The book has the sub-title *Untersuchungen zur Formengeschichte religiöser Rede*.
[13] Op. cit., 143–308.

validity or value. His demonstration that in the Areopagus speech a Jewish-Christian basic theme goes hand in hand with a Stoic secondary theme[1] has likewise been gratefully accepted. On the other hand we have abandoned his thesis that Luke borrowed the altar-inscription to the unknown god from the work of Apollonius of Tyana, περὶ θυσιῶν.[2] Moreover, to identify the 'unknown god' with the supreme, unknowable God of the gnostics seems inappropriate.[3] Luke was hardly anxious to maintain that this was the God whom Christianity proclaimed! However, Norden did in fact assume that the 'unknown Father' was an item of doctrine in the community at Jerusalem.[4]

The commentary on Acts which THEODOR ZAHN completed in 1920 represented an unbroken traditionalism unembarrassed by source-problems. The great scholar sacrificed all too large a part of his 884 pages to proving that even the 'Western' text derived from Luke. Zahn hardly examined dissenting opinions with any degree of thoroughness, nor did he lay bare Luke's particular theological bent.

It is scarcely possible to imagine a greater contrast to Zahn's work than ALFRED LOISY's commentary, *Les Actes des Apôtres,* which appeared in the same year. Stimulated by the writings of Wellhausen and Schwartz,[5] he represents the resurgence of a bygone age of research, a straggler like Johannes Weiss before him in 1897 (see p. 23f. above). But just as Weiss already faced the problems of form in Acts, which were not to come into their own until the rise of Form-criticism, so Loisy in fact left all previous research behind. True, he still believed that Luke did at one time write a genuinely historical—in the modern sense—Acts of the Apostles. But, he said, the extant work represents an editor's rewriting of the whole to suit the taste of a later age! If, however, we substitute the actual author of Acts for this supposed 'redactor', we are confronting the real problem of Acts, a problem for whose solution Loisy paved the way with innumerable flashes of insight. To this extent Loisy's commentary, which, with its 980 pages of close print, stands like a giant among its brothers, is not merely in outward appearance an imposing production.

C. Criticism up to 1945. The First Phase of Form-Criticism

The Smaller Units

In 1923 a short essay of only 23 pages by Martin Dibelius ushered in a new era of research on Acts: 'Stilkritisches zur Apostelgeschichte'[6]. The

---

[1] Op. cit., 1–30.
[2] Op. cit., 31–55 & 333–46.   [3] Op. cit., 56ff.
[4] Op. cit., 77. Admittedly the saying stood in Q. But this merely indicates that even Q is not synonymous with 'oldest tradition.' Q has more recent elements also, of which the logion Matt. 11.27 or Luke 10.22 is probably the latest.
[5] Notably those mentioned in note 7, page 32 above.
[6] Εὐχαριστήριον *für Hermann Gunkel* II, 27–49; translation in Martin Dibelius, *Studies,* 1–25.

characteristic of the new era is that interest in reconstructing the early history of Christianity recedes, and its place is taken by an uncovering of new possibilities in the field of Christian *literary* history. The real instigator of this change was Hermann Gunkel. His predecessors had been accustomed to think in terms of great source-documents, e.g., in the case of the Old Testament, those of the Yahwist and the Elohist. Now Gunkel drew attention to the smaller units and their types. These smaller units stand at the beginning of the tradition (for instance separate accounts later woven into a legendary anthology). They are far older than the supposed source documents, not to mention the canonical books themselves. One is therefore justified in investigating them first and for their own sake.

In 1919 Dibelius applied this 'Form-critical' method to the Synoptic Gospels.[1] In 1923 he used it for the first time on Acts. Thereby he brought to an end, to use his own words, the 'one-sided attention to the source-question' and the 'one-sided interpretation, which only inquired about the historical reliability of the material'.[2] His initiative produced an astounding result, whose consequences Dibelius himself did not at first grasp: the smaller units which he had demonstrated to exist in the Synoptic Gospels can only be found in one part of Acts. 'The examples intended for preaching' (i.e. the paradigms) 'one seeks in Acts . . . in vain, for so far there has not been any preaching about the Apostles in the early Church.'[3] This is an extremely important statement. It shows that for Acts we cannot presume the extensive mass of separate stories which Luke was able to use in his gospel. This very fact shows how questionable was the assumption, hitherto prevalent, that Luke used the same working-method in Acts as in the third gospel. The preconditions in each case were far too different for this to be so. In the composition of Acts Luke neither possessed the great mass of material at his command for the gospel, nor was he able to lean on a predecessor who had already marshalled the available material and offered a prototype.[4] For, seeing that the first Christians lived in expectation of the imminent end of the world, they felt no call to write down for posterity 'how it all really happened'—they had actually stopped thinking in terms of a future generation. As unlettered people, moreover, they were inclined neither to write nor to read works of history. In addition, the lack of traditional material and the need to supplement or supply deficiencies with original composition, giving the whole a suitable form, compelled the author of Acts to adopt a new method of work.

[1] *Die Formgeschichte des Evangeliums* (=*FRLANT*, New Series 42), 2nd ed. 1933 (ET *From Tradition to Gospel* 1934).
[2] Dibelius, 'Zur Formgeschichte des Neuen Testaments' (*ThR*, New Series 3 (1931) 207–42) 211. See now Klaus Koch, *Was ist Formgeschichte?*, Neukirchen 1964 (ET *The Growth of the Biblical Tradition* 1969).
[3] Ib., 236.
[4] *Studies*, 3, 124, 148, 192, 196.

These observations and considerations are borne out by Dibelius' findings. Apart from the 'travel-journal', he finds in Acts no substantial, coherent sources, but rather a number of smaller, self-contained accounts. For the most part the 'heroes' of these smaller units, which Dibelius often calls 'legends', are Peter and Paul. But on the other hand it is a 'travel-journal' which in the middle part of Acts governs the structure of the narrative.[1] The journal does not however coincide with the 'we'-passages, for the 'we' 'may equally well indicate an old source or a new literary work'.[2] Further, lists of names (**6.5, 13**.1) and details like **11**.20,26 can be singled out as data woven in by Luke.

If this represents all the existing material incorporated by Luke, a very much larger part of Acts must be laid to the account of the author himself, including 1. the so-called summaries—'little cross-sectional descriptions of a general kind', at which Luke arrived by generalizing particular events;[3] 2. Lucan reworkings and expansions of legends—of which the story of Cornelius, **10**.1–**11**.18, offers a specially clear example;[4] 3. Lucan links of various kinds between items from the tradition; and 4. the speeches composed by Luke. These last, numbering 24 according to Dibelius, comprise nearly one third of the book. They are intended to bear witness to the gospel. This is especially true of the Apostles' missionary addresses, which probably correspond to Christian preaching of about the year 90: 'So does one preach —and so should one preach!'[5] On the other hand, by the apologetic speeches of Paul in the later chapters, 'the author wishes . . . to advise the Christians of his time to employ these ideas in self-vindication'.[6] Paul's Miletus address shows the portrait Luke wished to present of the Apostle, and is at the same time an admonition to the whole Church.[7]

At the end of his essay Dibelius stresses that such style-criticism in no way serves to determine the historical authenticity or inauthenticity of the individual stories. The question of historicity must be decided differently for each different part (obviously it is the journal which receives the most favourable verdict). Nevertheless, this judgment can only ensue once style-criticism has done its work. Instead of prematurely asking them historical questions, one should first 'listen to what the stories have to say' (p. 25).

This essay had scarcely any effect. This is not surprising, for Dibelius had robbed Acts-research of its source-documents and replaced them with a mere handful of separate stories of varying historical value, plus a few *faits divers*. The further implications of his findings were only made apparent in his own later work on Acts. If, however, scholars had examined the essay

---

[1] *Studies*, esp. 5f., 69f., 73–6, 86, 105, 129f., 196–201.
[2] Ib., 204.   [3] Ib., 127.
[4] Ib., 13f., 94f., 109–22.
[5] Ib., 165.   [6] Ib., 213.
[7] Ib., 158.

more closely, they could already have asked Dibelius whether he had not in fact demonstrated the inapplicability of Form-criticism to Acts. After all, Dibelius himself had let slip (p. 4) that in Acts—where Luke had not, as for the gospel, a ready-made tradition to hand—it was a question 'not of any Form-critical approach, but only of style-criticism'.

Since Dibelius' further work on Acts became known only after the second World War, research at first went its way, to all intents and purposes, completely uninfluenced by him. Let us now turn, then, to the *Anglo-Saxon* field of study. The five volumes appearing between 1920 and 1933 of the gigantic work entitled *The Beginnings of Christianity*, for which Jackson, Lake and Cadbury were chiefly responsible, remained close in essentials to the outlook of Harnack's time.[1] In the chronology, and hence in the historical outline, one may trace the influence of Eduard Schwartz. The theology of Acts remains rather in the background, but so do its qualities of composition. As against this, the rich abundance of linguistic, historical and archaeological details renders the work, now as then, indispensable to the scholar, and ensures its value even on the Continent.

At the same time as the fifth volume there appeared in Oxford an edition of Acts by A. C. CLARK,[2] provided with an introduction and notes, which is still important as a study of the 'Western' text. In 1936 B. S. EASTON[3] published his Reinicke Lectures on 'The Purpose of Acts', which anticipate Dibelius—even 'late' Dibelius—to an astonishing extent: Luke, according to Easton, was not writing for only *one* public but wished both to edify the Christians and to present an apology for the attention of pagan Rome. The first aim caused him to simplify the story: geographically (Jerusalem—Rome), biographically (Peter—Paul) and chronologically through abandonment of strict chronology.[4] The speeches show the nature of Christianity, as Luke understood it, and already constitute part of the apologetic attempt to make Christianity a *religio licita*.[5] Clark had tried to prove through a word-count that Luke and Acts are not by the same writer.[6] This thesis was refuted in 1948 by W. L. KNOX,[7] whose book on Acts, derived from summer-school

---

[1] Part I, *The Acts of the Apostles*, ed. F. J. Foakes Jackson and Kirsopp Lake. Vol. 1 (1920): *Prolegomena* I—the Jewish, Gentile, Christian Background. Vol. 2 (1922): *Prolegomena* II—Composition and Authorship of Acts; History of Criticism. Vol. 3 (1926)—Text of Acts, by J. H. Ropes. Vol. 4 (1933)—English translation and commentary by Lake and H. J. Cadbury. Vol. 5 (1933)—Appendices. In all, 2450 pages.

[2] Albert Curtis Clark, *The Acts of the Apostles*, critical edition 1933. Discussed with important corrections by K. and S. Lake in *JBL* 53 (1934) 34–52.

[3] Burton Scott Easton, *Early Christianity*: 'The Purpose of Acts' and other papers; ed. F. C. Grant, London SPCK, 1955.

[4] Op. cit., 33–5.   [5] Op. cit., 36f., 41–56.

[6] Clark, op. cit., 394–408: Appendix III—Authorship of Luke and Acts; sample statistics: τε Luke 8 times, Acts 158; μὲν οὖν Luke 1, Acts 27; μετά Luke 52, Acts 32; σύν Luke 26, Acts 51; ἐγένετο + finite vb., Luke 22, Acts 0; ἐγένετο + inf. Luke 5, Acts 16; ἵνα Luke 38, Acts 12; ὅπως Luke 7, Acts 15.

[7] Wilfred L. Knox, *The Acts of the Apostles*. See especially pp. 100–9 and 3–15.

lectures, retains the freshness of its first oral delivery, and to that extent may readily be excused for a certain lack of co-ordination in the material of its five chapters.[1] Stimulated by Torrey, this ingenious author detected, in 1.4–5.16, Aramaic material which had been incorrectly translated (KNOX, p. 18); for the rest, he thought in terms of oral sources available to Paul's travelling-companion Luke, whom he declared to be no historian in the proper sense. Luke was casting the advance of Christianity from Jerusalem to Rome into the forms of a traveller's tale. 'Such stories, whether true or fictitious, appealed to the popular taste by providing a variety of scenes and adventures, with plenty of marvels thrown in' (p. 55).

Turning to *French* research, let us first mention the investigation of Acts undertaken by MAURICE GOGUEL in 1922 as the third volume, *Le Livre des Actes*, of his *Introduction au Nouveau Testament*. It deals with the traditions (pp. 15–36), the history of criticism (pp. 36–72), the text—the 'Western' form being secondary—(pp. 73–104), literary connections with Luke, the Pauline epistles and Josephus (pp. 105–29), the style and language (pp. 130–46) and the book's literary character (pp. 147–71); under this last head the book is said to have no exact plan, even if the second part is relatively coherent: the prologue and the story of the Ascension are the work of an interpolator, and the 'we'-passages are parts of an extensive report on Paul and his mission by a temporary companion. Goguel continues with a critical analysis of the first half (pp. 172–257) and the second (pp. 258–341). The author, says Goguel, had planned a third book. The strictly historical Acts which Loisy thought Luke to have written is a figment of wishful thinking: Luke did in fact write the travel-diary, which was used by the *auctor ad Theophilum*. He wrote around the year 80—where, it is impossible to say. He does not offer a complete theology. The book contains, alongside parts of minimal historical value, material which is essential to the history of primitive Christianity. Its place in literary history?—The gospels had shown how faith rests on the person and work of Jesus. It was now necessary to go further and show how 'the principle created by the gospels'(!) had been realized in practice (p. 368); here Goguel is brushing aside a serious problem. The work, he goes on to say, falls into a new category, foreshadowing the Lives of the Martyrs and apocryphal Acts of Apostles (pp. 342–70). The picture of early Christianity which thus results was later outlined by Goguel in *La Naissance du christianisme*[2]: the Church's year of destiny was the year 44, during which

[1] Authorship, 1–15; Sources, 16–39; Galatians and Acts, 40–53; Acts and History, 54–68; Theology, 69–99.
[2] *La Naissance du christianisme*, 2nd ed. 1946 (ET *The Birth of Christianity*, 1953); it is the second volume of his survey *Jésus et les origines du christianisme*, which recalls Eduard Meyer's three-volume *Ursprung und Anfänge des Christentums* (1921–3). Vol. 3 treats of Acts. Like Goguel, Meyer considers Luke, the companion of Paul, to be the author, and locates the 'Apostolic Council' before the year 44.

the recognition of Paul's apostolate unleashed persecution, eliminated the Apostles, and brought James to the leadership.[1]

On the other side the Catholic exegete E. JACQUIER[2] defended the traditional points of view. The product of a truly beaver-like industry, his enormous volume of over 1000 pages frankly assembles the material rather than masters it. In 1949 J. RENIÉ translated the Vulgate text of Acts into French, providing a conservative but knowledgeable commentary.[3]

Even in *Germany*, for the time being, research by-passed the work of Dibelius. The commentary of H. W. BEYER[4] pressed psychology into the service of pious exegesis, seeking thereby to open Acts to a wider public. Only on occasion does he take up critical questions, including, as it happens, the concession that Luke was the author only of the 'we'-passages, not of Acts as a whole.

In 1925 H. H. WENDT, who from 1880 to 1913 had dealt with Acts in Meyer's Commentaries, from the fifth to the ninth edition, re-opened the source-question.[5] Independently Joachim Jeremias in 1937 developed almost the same hypothesis.[6] Both attempted to isolate an Antiochian source beginning with Chapter 6. At the same time Jeremias disputed Harnack's source-theory whereby Acts 4 and 5 represent the same trial as seen in two parallel traditions.

OTTO BAUERNFEIND[7] wrote the only German commentary of any size during this period (1939). Writing in the menacing atmosphere of National-Socialism, to which he makes constant allusions, he sought to reconcile the exigencies of scientific criticism with the desire for moral comfort evinced by pastors and their flocks. Only the thorough reader notices that critical questions are not merely recognized but thoughtfully considered.

D. Criticism after 1945. The Second Phase of Form-Criticism: The Composition

Meanwhile MARTIN DIBELIUS had forged ahead with the problems of Acts in his history of early Christian literature (1926)[8] and his interim survey of 1931, 'Formgeschichte des Neuen Testaments'[9]. The various papers on Acts which Dibelius had produced up to his untimely death in 1947 were

---

[1] *Naissance*, 124–7. ET 106ff.

[2] *Les Actes des Apôtres: Études bibliques*, Paris 1926.

[3] *La Sainte Bible*, tome XI, Paris, Letouzey & Ané, 368 pages.

[4] *Das Neue Testament Deutsch*, 5. Die Apostelgeschichte übersetzt und erklärt von Hermann Wolfgang Beyer, Göttingen 1933, 4th ed. 1947.

[5] 'Die Hauptquelle der Apostelgeschichte', *ZNW* 24 (1925) 293–305.

[6] 'Untersuchungen zum Quellenproblem der Apostelgeschichte', *ZNW* 36 (1937) 205–21.

[7] *Die Apostelgeschichte, Theol. Handkommentar zum NT*, V, 1939.

[8] *Geschichte der altchristlichen Literatur* II, Göschen Collection No. 935, 95–106 (ET *A Fresh Approach to the NT and Early Christian Literature* 1936).

[9] *ThR*, N.F. 3, 207–42.

collected together in 1951 and published by H. Greeven under the title of *Aufsätze zur Apostelgeschichte*. An English edition appeared in 1956.[1]

Now for the first time the picture of the writer Luke which was faintly delineated in the 1923 essay becomes plainly visible. Luke, the companion of Paul, wrote Acts: the Lucan writings cannot have appeared anonymously. But that is still no reason for supposing that Acts is historically reliable in its rendering of events. For Luke, whose literary plans are most probably the product of later years, does not stand as a mere reporter vis-à-vis Paul.[2] Above all, it must be remembered that he was a historian in the ancient, not the modern sense. As such he wanted 'to present and illuminate the typical. And this penchant for the typical and significant led even the author of Acts partly to omit, alter or generalize what really happened'.[3] 'In order to bring out the communal ideal . . ., he overdoes the communism; in order to make effective the Apostolic ideal, he minimizes the differences between one Apostle and another. For the sake of intellectual symbolism, Athens has to be the place of encounter between Antiquity and Christianity, even though the historical centre of the mission was Corinth.'[4] But Luke is not only an ancient historian: he is a preacher, inasmuch as he 'expounds the destination of events'.[5] He shows that events do not take place by chance but move in a definite direction, and that these directed events have a meaning: they are realizing God's plan of salvation.

We can see nowadays that in this conception of Acts the doubtful and the promising lay side by side. For it is highly improbable that the ancient historians' striving for the typical should have brought a companion of Paul to the point of suppressing his own experiences in Paul's company (Chapter 27!) and substituting a fictional story of travel and adventure (*Studies*, 205f., 213f.). It is even more improbable that for the same reason he should allow the Apostle's portrait to disappear in favour of an apostolic stereotype. It is much more likely that Luke in fact knew only the uniform Apostle figure of his time, and that consequently he did not himself accompany Paul on his wanderings at all. According to Dibelius, the apologies of Paul are intended to show the Christians what ideas they should employ in self-defence[6]—this too seems

---

[1] *Studies in the Acts of the Apostles*, tr. M. Ling, 1956.

[2] *Studies*, 98 n. 11. Zahn disagrees (813f.): 'What stood in the way of the natural desire . . . to obtain exact information from Paul as to his latest experiences and to satisfy curiosity by interjecting questions? Moreover, Luke would not have omitted, as was his . . . habit, to write down what he heard, without delay, in his diary.' Here Zahn is obviously confusing Paul and Luke with Goethe and Eckermann. Unfortunately Zahn did not pause to consider what Acts must have looked like if Luke had really followed this procedure.

[3] *Studies*, 136f.

[4] Thus Dibelius in a letter to the present writer, 10 February, 1947.

[5] *Studies*, 129, also 134, 163.

[6] *Studies*, 213: 'They should stress the fact that they have transgressed neither against Caesar, nor against the Temple, nor against the Law . . .' What have the Christians of Luke's time to do with the Temple that was destroyed in the year 70?

very dubious. For these addresses contain far too much biographical matter: Christians about the year 90 were no longer, for the most part, people like Paul, who had had their origins in Jewry or had been Pharisees. Dibelius maintains that these speeches stand loosely in their surroundings; if Luke had composed them, we should have expected otherwise. But in reality they are not so loosely inserted; in other words, the problem of the speeches has here clearly not yet been fully solved. The same is true of the travel-journal. For it is not a really satisfying conclusion that it noted routes and places to spend the night for the sake of later missionary travellers.[1] As soon as the Pauline mission had got a foothold and Paul was in correspondence by letter and emissary with the various communities such travel-guides became superfluous.

What was promising in Dibelius' work was that now at last it gave due prominence to the New Testament author. No longer was Luke a mere 'compiler or transmitter,' but a writer with his own positive characteristics— and a theologian. For the first time the deeply-rooted tendency to regard Acts as no more than a quarry to furnish material for the reconstruction of primitive Christianity was overcome. For the first time the question could be faced of what this biblical author was trying to tell his readers. In this way Dibelius was the instigator of a trend which has ever since become increasingly pronounced in New Testament research. Investigations, that is to say, have turned from the question of historical reliability to that of the message of the New Testament writings.

Beyond a doubt, however, Dibelius and his followers must expect to encounter strong resistance. Although Catholic research now handles New Testament problems with far greater freedom than before, the kind of liberty which Dibelius claims for the writer Luke is hard to stomach—and not only for Catholic scholars. Wherever, as in England, scholarship is governed by the spirit of conservatism, Dibelius' interpretation of Acts is bound to seem a revival of that radicalism which chronically afflicts the Continent. But it is not only a question of overcoming the reverence attaching to a Biblical commission's decision, scholarly tradition or the desires of congregations: it is a question of disappointing the longing for historical information, which it had been customary to lift from every part of Acts. The purely historical outlook, after a reign of two hundred years, could scarcely be dethroned overnight.

English theologians have remained almost wholly uninfluenced by Dibelius (perhaps the English translation of his Essays will change this). As far back as 1942 F. F. BRUCE published a study of *The Speeches in the Acts of the Apostles*, which, he claims, reproduce more or less verbatim the text of sources that Luke may well have held to be authentic renderings of the

---

[1] *Studies*, 199: '. . . so that on retracing the journey one might rediscover the routes and the former hosts'. Cf. G. Schille, *TLZ* 84 (1959) 165ff.

original addresses. In 1951 appeared Bruce's commentary on Acts,[1] which goes carefully into philological and historical questions; the theological problems are dealt with in his *New International Commentary* volume (1954, 1956[2]).

In 1953 C. S. C. Williams issued the second, revised edition of A. H. MᶜNᴇɪʟᴇ's *Introduction to the Study of the New Testament*. This assembles practically everything which with any shadow of justification can be brought against Dibelius: 1. literary forms are arbitrarily ascribed to certain sections; 2. the 'community myth,' i.e. that of the collective production of the Gospels, is unwarrantably created; 3. a false analogy is drawn with folklore ('a ballad is written by only one poet')—moreover the time between Jesus' death and Mark is too short for the development of a tradition; 4. I Cor. 7.25 shows how exactly the words of Jesus were handed down; 5. the form of a miracle-story has nothing to do with its historical value; 6. the gospels say nothing at all about the questions which later exercised the Church; 7. the Marcan framework is historically authentic(!). Dibelius is not of course refuted by these arguments. But the objections are well worth thinking over.

In the same year, 1953, appeared the posthumous work of DOM GREGORY DIX, *Jew and Greek, A Study in the Primitive Church*. The author wanted to call it 'the problem of the sub-Apostolic Church', and it was this which really interested him.[2] It was only by dethroning Paul that he was able to justify the sub-apostolic Church: Paul was, according to Dix, only one of the missionaries from the Jewish Christian(!) mission in the diaspora who accepted Gentiles in the years 40 to 50,[3] and Jerusalem did not pronounce any veto against the practice. This is how the 'leap' was made from the Syrian into the Greek world (Toynbee!). The full form of the Syrian gospel was however first developed by the Palestinian John. The Pauline doctrine of justification was the basis of the whole Jewish Christian Church[4]—which surely makes it utterly incomprehensible why Paul should have had to put up such a stiff fight on its behalf against both Jews and Jewish Christians.

In *The Interpreter's Bible*, an interesting commentary on Acts appeared in 1954. G. H. C. MACGREGOR contributed an introduction and scholarly exegesis of a mildly critical order,[5] while Theodore P. Ferris provided the

---

[1] *The Acts of the Apostles*, Oxford 1951, 2nd ed. 1952. Bruce explains in the preface to the second edition, VIII: 'it is not a theological commentary'.

[2] Dix: 'The problem of the following discussion will . . . be the problem of the legitimacy of the sub-Apostolic Church . . .'

[3] Op. cit., 30ff.

[4] Op. cit., 45.

[5] Macgregor says a 'cautious Yes' to Luke's authorship (p. 20). The 'travel-journal' contained parts in the first and third persons (p. 16).—In vol. 5 of the Moffatt commentary series, 1931, Foakes-Jackson worked with Moffatt's translation: 'This commentary is critical in places, but it is frankly an appreciation of the work of Luke' (p. XX).

devotional exposition. Over the two commentaries is printed the English text to which they refer (King James and RSV).

In 1957 C. S. C. WILLIAMS issued his commentary on Acts.[1] His conclusions were that Luke the companion of Paul wrote Acts between 66 and 70, though perhaps he did not publish until much later. The discrepancies between Acts and the Pauline epistles are not so important as to cast doubt on this authorship. Galatians could have been written before the Apostolic council. Paul did not meet the Apostles in the course of the events of Acts 11, and therefore did not need to mention this visit in Galatians. The speeches are not free compositions of Luke. Peter's speeches in the first chapters show Christianity still as a reformed Judaism. Since Williams simply fails to see many of the historical and literary problems, they do not disturb him and he has no occasion to avail himself of Dibelius' ideas.

In the same year N. B. STONEHOUSE[2] also crossed swords with Dibelius. He denied that Luke made free with historical facts. It is true that the Areopagus address is condensed, but it has real individuality and is no mere adapted formula. To suppose, however, that a writer could not endow his adaptations with individuality is a deplorable misunderstanding. In general, moreover, Stonehouse tends to minimize difficulties in his polemic against Dibelius. When he reproaches Dibelius and Eduard Schweizer for failing to observe that according to I Thess. 1.9 conversion is a turning from idols to God, that does not yet prove Acts 17.30f. a Pauline sermon!

The doyen of Anglo-Saxon research on Acts is H. J. CADBURY. To him we owe the investigation of Luke's style and literary method[3] which among other things put an end to the myth of Luke's medical language; also *The Making of Luke-Acts* (1927, reprinted 1958), described by Dibelius as 'excellent', which at that time provided the profoundest introduction to Luke's creative mind, and the linguistic and literary part of Vols. 4 and 5 of *The Beginnings of Christianity* (1933). Subsequently, in 1955, he produced a further book entitled *The Book of Acts in History*.[4] Here he discusses the place of Acts in its historical setting, first in general terms, then with respect to its Greek, Roman, Jewish and Christian environment, and finally the book's subsequent destiny. The connections of Acts with all the elements of its time have probably never been so illuminatingly and convincingly presented as here, through the medium of Cadbury's sovereign command of the primary and

---

[1] *The Acts of the Apostles*, Black's NT Commentaries, 1957.
[2] *Paul before the Areopagus, and other NT Studies*, London, 1957, III + 197: 1–40—'The Areopagus Address'; 151–85—'Martin Dibelius and the relation of History and Faith'. Earlier Stonehouse had published *The Witness of Luke to Christ*, Michigan, 1951—an expanded version of lectures delivered in Edinburgh in April 1949.
[3] Henry Joel Cadbury, 'The Style and Literary Method of Luke' in *Harvard Theological Studies* 6, 1919–20. His proofs are consolidated in articles *JBL* 45 (1926) 190–209, and 52 (1933) 55–65.
[4] In addition there are important articles.

secondary literature involved. The problem of authorship is set aside as inessential.

In French-speaking circles research into Acts has become more lively. The edition of Acts in *La Sainte Bible de Jérusalem*[1] includes a well-balanced introduction by LUCIEN CERFAUX, who already had to his credit a series of separate papers on Acts, while the translation and notes are by JACQUES DUPONT. The latter had published in 1950 a praiseworthy survey of recent literature on Acts, and has since made a number of valuable contributions to individual problems.[2]

1957 saw the publication in Paris of ETIENNE TROCMÉ's interesting study, *Le "Livre des Actes" et l'histoire,* dedicated to the memory of Goguel and gratefully indebted—though with no cession of independence—to Ph.-H. Menoud (from whom, after his important articles,[3] we expect also a commentary on Acts). As indicated by the fifty-three references in the index, a running controversy is sustained against Dibelius, but indeed the whole range of research is touched upon. The theme brings the source-question once more to the fore. The author of Acts is said to have written between 80 and 85 and to have been an eyewitness of many of the incidents, as attested by his 'we'. But Chapters 16 to 28 are not simply an eyewitness-report: the author used sources. Not a ὑπόμνημα (that would have been a literary work!), but a '*diaire personnel*' (Trocmé, p. 135) which Paul from time to time had one of his fellow-workers keep and which in the end passed into Luke's possession. It was to this that he resorted when, twenty years later, he wrote a 'gospel' in which Paul played a leading rôle in the sacred history. For, like Sahlin and Menoud, Trocmé assumes that Luke 24.50–3 and Acts 1.1–3 were inserted when Luke's work was divided 'on its acceptance into the canon.'

---

[1] *Les Actes des Apôtres*, by Canon L. Cerfaux and Dom J. Dupont, OSB; Editions du Cerf, Paris 1954, 3rd ed. 1964.

[2] Jacques Dupont, *Les Problèmes du Livre des Actes. État de question,* Bruges 1950; id. *Les Sources du Livre des Actes,* Bruges 1960 (ET *The Sources of Acts,* 1964); 'L'Utilisation apologétique de l'Ancien Testament dans les discours des Actes', *Eph. Theol. Lov.* 26 (1953) 289–327. 'Notes sur les Actes des Apôtres', *Rev.Bibl.* 62 (1955) 45–59. 'Pierre et Paul dans les Actes', *Rev.Bibl.* 64 (1957) 35–47. 'La Mission de Paul "à Jérusalem" (Actes 12.25)', *NovTest.* I (1956) 275–303. 'Pierre et Paul à Antioche et à Jérusalem', *RScR* 45 (1957) 42–60 and 225–39. ΛΑΟΣ 'ΕΞ 'ΕΘΝΩΝ (Acts 15.14)', *NTS* 4 (1957) 47–50. *Paulus und die Seelsorger,* Patmos Verlag 1966.

[3] 'La Mort d'Ananias et Saphira (Actes 5.1–11)' in *Mélanges Goguel,* 1950, 146–52. 'The Western Text and the Theology of Acts' in *Stud. Novi Test. Soc. Bulletin* Vol. 2, 1951, 19–32. 'Remarques sur les textes de l'Ascension dans Luc-Actes' in *Neutestamentliche Studien für Rudolf Bultmann,* 1954, 148–56. 'Les Actes des Apôtres et l'Eucharistie' in *RHPhR* 33 (1953) 21–36. 'Le Plan des Actes des Apôtres' in *NTS* II (1954) 44–51. 'Les Additions au groupe des douze apôtres d'après le Livre des Actes' in *RHPhR* 37 (1957) 71–80: a reply to Charles Masson's 'La reconstitution du collège des Douze d'après Actes 1.15–26'.

On the basis of Trocmé's book, JEAN-PAUL BENOÎT has produced an exposition of Acts intended for a wide circle of readers.[1] It is written with breathtaking verve and is marvellous to read, but could scarcely be translated. None of the more popular German presentations of Acts—not even Otto Dibelius' *Die werdende Kirche*—comes near its blend of edification and scholarship.

In 1958 appeared MARCEL SIMON's *St. Stephen and the Hellenists in the Primitive Church*.[2] It puts forward the view that the Hellenists were a group of Jewish reformists. Jesus' saying about the Temple had brought this anti-Temple, anti-sacrificial group into alliance with the Christians. Driven from Jerusalem, they began the mission in Samaria and Antioch. Simon does not consider the contribution of Lucan composition very great.

To Dutch scholarship we owe D. PLOOIJ's fundamental work on Pauline chronology and a number of special investigations such as A. F. J. KLIJN's critical survey of work on the 'Western' text and W. C. VAN UNNIK's fine study on the question whether Paul spent his youth in Tarsus or Jerusalem.[3] The commentary on Acts by F. W. GROSHEIDE[4] considers it impossible that Luke the companion of Paul should have made use of a written source. This conservative scholar pursues his thesis with such consistent rigour that he will not even hear of any use of Mark in the Third Gospel.

The *Scandinavian* countries also have made a considerable contribution to research on Acts in recent years. We must therefore mention the work of three Norwegians: F. BIRKELI, who treats the historical problems of Acts **15**, R. LEIVESTAD, writing of Luke as the 'pietist among the Evangelists', and A. KRAGERUD, who discusses the travel-journal (from **13.4** to **21.16!**).[5]

---

[1] *Combats d'Apôtres pour une humanité nouvelle: traduction et commentaire du Livre des Actes des Apôtres*; SCE 1957.

[2] Simon had previously published the excellent *Verus Israel*, Paris 1948 (ET in preparation); 'Retour du Christ et Reconstruction du Temple dans la pensée chrétienne primitive' in *Mélanges Goguel*, 1950, 247–57; 'St. Stephen and the Jerusalem Temple' in *JEH* 2 (1951) 127–42; and 'La Prophétie de Nathan et le Temple' in *RHPhR*, 1952, 41–58.

[3] D. Plooij. *De Chronologie van het Leven van Paulus*, Leyden 1918; Albert Frederik Johannes Klijn, *A Survey of the Researches into the Western Text of the Gospels and Acts*, Utrecht 1949, and 'Stephen's Speech, Acts 7.2–53' in *NTS* 4 (1957) 25–31; W. C. van Unnik, *Tarsus of Jerusalem?*, Amsterdam 1952 (ET *Tarsus or Jerusalem*, London 1962); 'Opmerkingen over het doel van Lucas' Geschiedwerk (Luc. **1**.4)' in *Ned. Teol. Tijdschr.* 9 (1955) 323–31; and 'De Achtergrond en Betekenis van Handelingen **10**.4 en 35' in *Ned. Teol. Tijdschr.* 3 (1948–9) 260–84 & 336–54.

[4] *De Handelingen der Apostelen*: Kommentaar op het Nieuwe Testament V, Amsterdam 1942–9.

[5] Fridtjov Birkeli, 'De historiske problemer som knytter sig til beretningen om Apostelkonsilet i Apostlenes gjerninger Kapitel 15' in *Norsk Teol. Tidsskr.* 54 (1953) 144–64; Ragnar Leivestad, 'Pietisten bland evangelistene' in *Norsk Teol. Tidsskr.* 55 (1954) 185–200; Alf Kragerud, 'Itinerariet i Apostlenes gjerninger' in *Norsk Teol. Tidsskr.* 56 (1955) 249–72.

To the Swedish scholar GUNNAR RUDBERG we owe a lively book on Hellas and the New Testament, as well as a number of weighty essays.[1] ALBERT WIFSTRAND has corrected our conception of Lucan language in several articles packed with information.[2] HARALD SAHLIN's work on the 'Messiah and the People of God'[3] includes a source-theory, inspired by Torrey, for Luke's writings. In one of those solid and learned dissertations that Swedish scholarship is wont to produce, BERTIL GÄRTNER[4] has undertaken to demonstrate the compatibility of the Areopagus address with Pauline theology: in his view the Stoic element of the speech recedes in favour of the Old Testament. BO REICKE[5] has sought to represent the 'faith and life of the primitive Church' in accordance with Acts 1 to 8 and without lapsing into a 'destruction of the portrayal' (Reicke, p. 8), i.e. without allowing contradictions to open up between Lucan and Pauline theology.

In an essay on primitive Christianity in Acts, the Danish scholar JOHANNES MUNCK revealed a part of the individualistic historical picture which he later developed in his book *Paul and the Salvation of Mankind*.[6] Munck fights a lone battle against the picture hitherto accepted: he says that the Judaists were Galatian Gentile Christians who had misunderstood Paul's respectful references to the Jerusalem Apostles—Luke wrongly transplanted them to Jerusalem. The 'hellenists', including the 'Seven', were not a splinter-group; but the whole Jerusalem community was banished, only to return later without anyone taking exception to it. Peter had no other standpoint than that of the Hellenists. The 'thousands' of Jewish Christians in Acts 21.20 should be changed into Jews by striking out the words τῶν πεπιστευμένων—

---

[1] *Hellas och Nya Testamentet*, 1929; 'Hellenistisk litteraturforskning och Nya Testamentet: Några Synpunkter' in *Eranos* 23 (1925) 193–205; 'Ad usum circumscribentem praepositionum graecarum adnotationes' in *Eranos* 19 (1919–20) 173–206 (Acts: p. 180); 'Parentesen i Nya Testamentet' in *SEÅ* V, 1940, 126–37; and 'Concerning Codex Cantabrigiensis' in *SEÅ* XII, 1947, 287–92.

[2] 'Lukas och den grekiska klassicismen' in *SEÅ* V, 1940, 139–51; 'Lukas och Septuaginta' in *SvTKv* 16 (1940) 243–62; 'A Problem concerning the Word Order in the New Testament' in *Stud. Theol.* III, 1950–1, 172–84; and 'Det grekiska prosaspråket: en historisk oversikt' in *Eranos* 50 (1952) 149–63.

[3] *Der Messias und das Gottesvolk*. Studien zur protolukanischen Theologie (*Acta Sem. Neotest. Upsal.* XII, 1945), p. 9 & passim; and 'Pingstberättelsens teologiska innebord' in *SvTKv* 25 (1949) 185–200.

[4] *The Areopagus Speech and Natural Revelation* (*Acta Sem. Neotest. Upsal.* XXI), 1955; and 'Missionspredikan i Apostlagärningarna' in *SEÅ* XV, 1950, 34–54.

[5] *Glaube und Leben der Urgemeinde* (*AThANT* 32), 1957; 'Der historische Hintergrund des Apostelkonzils und der antiochenischen Episode Gal. 2.1–14' in *Studia Paulina* 1953, 172–87; and 'Die Mahlzeit des Paulus auf den Wellen des Mittelmeeres Act. 27.33–8' in *ThZ* 4 (1948) 401–10.

[6] 'Den aeldste Kristendom i Apostlenes Gerninger' in *Dansk Teol. Tidsskrift* 16 (1953) 129–64, and *Paulus und die Heilsgeschichte* (*Acta Jutlandica* 26: 1), Aarhus-Copenhagen 1954, *ET* London 1959. Cf. also 'Paulus og Apostelbegrebet' by the same author, in *Dansk Teol. Tidsskrift* 11 (1948) 141–57, as well as Holger Mosbech's 'Apostolos in the New Testament', *Studia Theol.* Vol. II, Lund 1949–50, 165–200, and Mosbech's commentary, *Apostlenes Gerninger inledet og forklaret*, Copenhagen 1929.

the community at Jerusalem welcomed Paul joyfully, etc. What is useful for scholarship here lies in Munck's observations, not in the conclusions he draws from them.

The same is true—and here we return to the literature on Acts in *German* —of PAUL GÄCHTER, S.J. His articles[1] discuss the stumbling-blocks which he encounters in the text of Acts and overcomes in his own way. 'The uproar against St. Stephen was to a large extent a fraud', provoked by Annas. Peter appointed not only the Hellenist Seven but also a Hebraic Seven, namely the presbyters. Both groups obtained, though perhaps not both immediately, full power of consecration and jurisdiction: it followed that the circle of the Twelve came eventually to appreciate the redundancy of their own empirical existence, since those whom they had consecrated had consecrated others in their turn. The election of Matthias, together with the mode of election, must derive from an instruction of Jesus ('if there were none such, we would come up against insoluble difficulties'). Gächter presumes that Jesus gave this instruction after John 21.19. Another of his conclusions is that Jerusalem owed its central position only to Peter's residence there; as soon as he leaves the city, the 'Rome-feeling' of the communities towards Jerusalem dies away ('Jerusalem und Antiochia', p. 36). Incomparably more valuable is the commentary of ALFRED WIKENHAUSER[2] who, with his work on the historical value of Acts,[3] had shown his merits as far back as 1921.

In 1949 the Swiss ROBERT MORGENTHALER[4] threw a new idea into the debate: the Lucan writings are a work of art! Unfortunately this fruitful idea was reduced to the simple implication that Luke deliberately followed the 'rule of duality' ('duality' here being understood in very various ways). This 'Lucan' method is justified by the strange contention that double utterance lends breadth and assurance to the narrative. In 1958 Morgenthaler published a statistical analysis of NT vocabulary (*Statistik des neutestamentlichen Wortschatzes*): this immensely industrious work is a useful tool for

---

[1] 'The Hatred of the House of Annas' in *Theological Studies*, Vol. 8, 1947, 3ff.; 'Jerusalem und Antiochia: ein Beitrag zur urkirchlichen Rechtsentwicklung' in *ZkTh* 70 (1948) 1–48; 'Die Wahl des Matthias (Apg 1.17–26)' in *ZkTh* 71 (1949) 318–46; and 'Die Sieben' in *ZkTh* 74 (1952) 129–66.

[2] *Die Apostelgeschichte übersetzt und erklärt (Regensburger Neues Testament* No. 5), 3rd ed. 1956. (The commentary on Acts by Joseph Kürzinger in the *Echter-Bibel*, 1951, is intended for wider circles).

[3] 'Die Apostelgeschichte und ihre Geschichtswert' (*Neutestamentliche Abhandlungen* 8, 3–5), Münster 1921; 'Die Traumgesichte des Neuen Testaments in religionsgeschichtlicher Sicht' in *Pisciculi . . . Dölger . . . dargeboten*, Münster 1939, 320–33; 'Doppelträume' in *Biblica* 29 (1948) 100–11; 'Die Belehrung der Apostel durch den Auferstandenen', *Meinertz Festschrift*, Münster 1951, 105–13; and 'Die Wirkung der Christophanie vor Damaskus auf Paulus und seine Begleiter nach den Berichten der Apostelgeschichte' in *Biblica* 33 (1952) 313–23.

[4] *Die lukanische Geschichtsschreibung als Zeugnis: Gestalt und Gehalt der Kunst des Lukas* (*AThANT* 14), Zürich 1948. See the reviews by W. G. Kümmel ('Das Urchristentum' in *ThR* 22 (1954) 197f.) and E. Käsemann (*VuF* 1947–8, Münich 1950, 210).

the scholar to range beside the dictionary, grammar and concordance for work on the linguistic questions of Acts.

Dibelius had shown that, being an author as well as a historian, Luke was capable of reproducing reality in an altered form in order to illuminate its meaning. In the 1950's, Protestant research on Acts in Germany focussed its attention on this unexpected phenomenon of a Luke with independent ideas of authorship, because it was Luke the *theologian*—not the historian—who became important. The new development became apparent in 1950 when an article by PHILIPP VIELHAUER,[1] in which he compared Luke's theology with Paul's, attracted considerable notice. He found that Luke, the supposed companion of Paul, is everywhere at odds with the Apostle: he lends a positive tendency to the *theologia naturalis*, plays down the redemptive significance of the Cross and abandons expectation of the End. Vielhauer found an ally in HANS CONZELMANN, whose studies in Lucan theology[2] demonstrated that Luke replaces primitive Christian doctrine, obsessed with the imminent End, by a theology of saving history with three successive periods: 1. the law and the prophets (including the Baptist); 2. the time of salvation corresponding to Jesus' life on earth—the middle of history (p. 146); and 3. the period stretching thenceforward up to the Parousia; a period which, to use an expression not yet employed by Luke, may be called the time of the Church. On the other hand, ERNST KÄSEMANN[3] was of the opinion that Luke's real theme was to represent the hour of the Church as the middle

---

[1] 'Zum "Paulinismus" der Apostelgeschichte' in *Ev. Th.* 10, New Series No. 5, 1950–51, 1–15; 'Franz Overbeck und die neutestamentliche Wissenschaft', ibid. 193–207; and 'Urchristentum und Christentum in der Sicht W. Kamlahs' in *Ev. Th.* 1955, 307–32. The first-named article gave rise to the following: Götz Harbsmeier, 'Unsere Predigt im Spiegel der Apostelgeschichte' in *Ev. Th.* 1950–51, 352–68; Wilhelm Andersen, 'Die Autorität der apostolischen Zeugnisse' in *Ev. Th.* 1952–3, 467–81; Vielhauer, 'Zu W. Andersen', ibid. 482–4; Bauernfeind, 'Vom historischen zum lukanischen Paulus' in *Ev. Th.* 1953, 347–53, and 'Zur Frage nach der Entscheidung zwischen Lukas und Paulus' in *ZsyTh* 23 (1954) 59–88; lastly Willi Marxsen, 'Exegese und Verkündigung' in *Theol. Existenz heute*, New Series 59, 1957: 'Exegese im NT' 5–30 and 'Der Beitrag der wissenschaftlichen Exegese des NTs für die Verkündigung', 31–36.

[2] *Die Mitte der Zeit: Studien zur Theologie des Lukas* (*Beiträge zur historischen Theologie* 17), Tübingen 1954, 3rd ed. 1960 (ET *The Theology of St. Luke*, London 1960). Also 'Zur Lukasanalyse' in *ZThK* 49 (1952) 16–33, and 'Die Rede des Paulus auf dem Areopag' in *Gymnasium Helveticum* 12 (1958) 18–32.

[3] 'Aus der neutestamentlichen Arbeit der letzten Jahre' in *VuF: Theologischer Jahresbericht* 1947–8, Munich 1949–50, 196–223, esp. 219ff.; 'Ein neutestamentlicher Überblick' in *VuF: Theol. Jahresb.* 1949–50, Munich 1950, 191–218, esp. 208f.; 'Probleme neutestamentlicher Arbeit in Deutschland' in *Beiträge zur evangelischen Theologie*, Vol. 15, Munich 1952, 133–52, esp. 141f.; 'Die Johannesjünger von Ephesus' in *ZThK* 49 (1952) 144–54; 'Begründet der neutestamentliche Kanon die Einheit der Kirche?' in *Ev. Th.* 1951–2, 13–22; 'Eine Apologie der urchristlichen Eschatologie' in *ZThK* 49 (1952) 272–96, esp. 279; 'Das Problem des historischen Jesus' in *ZThK* 51 (1954) 125–53, esp. 136–8; lastly, 'Neutestamentliche Fragen von heute' in *ZThK* 54 (1957) 1–21, esp. 20f. (The article from *Ev. Th.* 1951–2, the two articles from *ZThK* 49 and that from *ZThK* 51 are available in English in *Essays on NT Themes* 1964, that from *ZThK* 54 in *NT Questions of Today* 1969.)

of time: 'Luke is . . . the first representative of evolving early Catholicism' (*ZThK* (1957) 20). The problem of his theology can be reduced to the formula that he replaces the *theologia crucis* with the *theologia gloriae*.

The Tenth Edition of the present commentary[1] joined the chorus of these voices, albeit with some moderation. There were two reasons for this. Firstly, it did not treat the theology of Acts as the only theme of this book, because its immediate concern was to expound the composition of the writer Luke both as a whole and in detail, a composition which at times appears almost to create *ex nihilo*. It is only by virtue of this astounding freedom that Luke's historical narrative can become the trusty tool of Lucan theology. Secondly—and at this point, in order not to anticipate the argument of §7 below, we are content simply to notice the fact—the following must be considered: Luke does not yet present, like the Ignatian letters, a theology of the episcopal office, he outlines no theory of all-embracing ecclesiastical organization (only in 9.31 does ἐκκλησία mean anything more than the individual community), nor does he develop any sacramentalism such as may furnish a φάρμακον ἀθανασίας. No, the real subject of Acts is the λόγος τοῦ θεοῦ and its growth. It is certainly proclaimed by men and authenticated by God through signs and miracles. This theology is no steep tumble from the Pauline heights—for on those heights Luke never stood. His teaching is one of the many variants of Gentile Christian theology which—more or less independent of the great Apostle to the gentiles—grew up alongside and after the theology of Paul. The germs of what then evolved into early catholicism may well have lain, even before Luke's time, in this gentile theology, which bore in itself a tendency to law and observances even where it was not influenced by Jerusalem. Recognition of this fact does not preclude us from finding the *vera vox evangelii* in Paul's *theologia crucis*.

Bibliography

H. Mosbech, *Apostlenes gerninger, indledet og forklaret*, Copenhagen 1938; J. A. Findlay, *The Acts of the Apostles. A Commentary*, London: 3rd ed. 1946; F. J. Foakes Jackson, *The Acts of the Apostles* (Moffatt Commentary), London: 8th ed. 1951; J. Keulers, *De Handelingen der Apostelen* (De boeken van het NT IV), Roermond-Maaseik, 2nd ed. 1952; C. F. Dessain, The Acts of the Apostles, in *A Catholic Commentary on Holy Scripture*, 1953;

---

[1] Ernst Haenchen, *Die Apostelgeschichte* (*Kritisch-exegetischer Kommentar über das Neue Testament*, Division 3), 10th ed. 1956, 15th revised ed. 1968. See also Haenchen, 'Schriftzitate und Textüberlieferung in der Apostelgeschichte' in *ZThK* 51 (1954) 153–67; 'Tradition und Komposition in der Apostelgeschichte' in *ZThK* 52 (1955) 205–25; 'Zum Text der Apostelgeschichte' in *ZThK* 54 (1957) 22–55. 12th revised ed., 1959; 'The Book of Acts as Source Material for the History of Early Christianity' (*Studies in Luke-Acts.* Essays presented in honour of Paul Schubert, 1966, 258–78); and 'Judentum und Christentum in der Apostelgeschichte' (*Die Bibel und Wir*, 1967, 338–74).

R. R. Williams, *The Acts of the Apostles* (Torch Bible Commentaries), London 1953; H. A. Guy, *The Acts of the Apostles*, London (Macmillan) 1953; F. F. Bruce, *Commentary on the Book of Acts*. The English Text with Introduction, Exposition and Notes (The New London Commentary on the New Testament), 2nd ed. 1956; W. Barclay, *The Acts of the Apostles* Philadelphia (Westminster Press) 1957; A. C. Winn, *The Acts of the Apostles*, Richmond 1960.

3. THE TEXT OF ACTS

For the textual problem of Acts[1] the least ancient, Byzantine version (Von Soden: Koine text—siglum $\mathfrak{K}$ taken over by Nestle) and the so-called Caesarea text[2] are of little significance. The only two important forms are the text once called 'neutral' or 'Egyptian' (Von Soden's Hesychius text—siglum $\mathfrak{H}$ adopted by Nestle) and the so-called 'Western' text.

In the case of Acts the chief witnesses for $\mathfrak{H}$ are the manuscripts B $\aleph$ A C 81[3] and the Sahidic and the Bohairic—i.e. Upper (South) and Lower (North) Egyptian—Coptic translations.[4] A similar text is attested by Egyptian papyrus discoveries for a date as early as the second century.[5]

[1] Eberhard Nestle's *Einführung in das griechische Neue Testament*, 4th ed. thoroughly revised by Ernst von Dobschütz, Göttingen 1933 (out of print; ET *Introduction to the Textual Criticism of the Greek New Testament*, tr. from 2nd ed., 1901), was not able to handle the overflowing wealth of material in a lucid manner. To some extent F. G. Kenyon's *Text of the Greek Bible* (1937) offers a substitute; see further H. Vogels, *Handbuch der Textkritik des Neuen Testaments*, 2nd ed. 1955, B. M. Metzger, *The Text of the NT*, 2nd ed. Oxford 1968.
[2] This text is dealt with in detail by A. F. J. Klijn, *A Survey of the Researches into the Western Text of the Gospels and Acts*, Utrecht 1949, 110–28. It may be that we possess evidence for the Caesarea text of Acts in Codex 1739 (K. and S. Lake published a collation in 1932 in 'Six Collations of New Testament Manuscripts', *Harvard Theological Studies* XVII, 142ff.; cf. by the same, 'The Scribe Ephraim' in *JBL* 62 (1943) 263–8.) On this see, as also in connection with what follows, E. Haenchen, 'Zum Text der Apostelgeschichte' in *ZThK* 54 (1957) 22–55, and the earlier article 'Schriftzitate und Textüberlieferung in der Apostelgeschichte', *ZThK* 51 (1954) 153–67. In Vol. III of *Beg.* 1926, J. H. Ropes compared the Acts texts of *B* and *D* and appended the translation of *d* (frequently also of *h* and *Iren. lat.*); the exhaustive introduction to this volume is also highly valuable.
[3] Ropes CCL–CCLXXV.
[4] Ropes CXLIII–CXLVI; 317–71; Kenyon 129ff.
[5] The discovery of Papyrus 66, dated c. 200 (v. Papyrus Bodmer II, Bibliotheca Bodmeriana V, Cologny-Genève 1956) has shown in respect of John that the *B* text in Egypt is as old as the 'Western' text; see A. F. J. Klijn in *New Testament Studies* III, 1956–57, 327–34. In *BZ*, New Series 2, 1958, 214–43, Heinrich Zimmermann demonstrated that the text of $\mathfrak{P}^{66}$, like that of Sinaiticus only to a far less marked degree, was subsequently exposed to the influence of the 'Western' text. $\mathfrak{P}^{75}$ (Bodmer XIV–XV, 1961; written about 200) agrees astonishingly closely with the B text (see below, pp. 56f.).

Evidence for the 'Western' text is found above all in the Uncial D,[1] old Latin translations[2] and the variants of the Syrian Harklensis.[3] But such early figures as Marcion,[4] Tatian[5] and Irenaeus[6] already used a similar text, whose existence in Egypt also is attested by papyri.[7]

In Acts the two text-forms show such wide divergences that Blass and Zahn supposed Luke to have issued two different editions.[8] This hypothesis comes to grief, however, from the very fact that the texts often contradict each other, e.g. in the case of the 'Apostolic Decree' (see p. 449 n.6 below).

What is then the relationship of the 'Western' to the $\mathfrak{H}$ text in Acts?

1. As in the gospels and the Pauline epistles, the 'Western' text in Acts shows a mass of small alterations intended to clarify and smooth. For example, they expressly name subject or object, improve this or that expression, introduce pious turns of phrase: 'Jesus' becomes 'the Lord Jesus Christ'. As an instance of such changes, let us take the variations in 12.1–7.

In verse 1 the 'Western' text adds the clarification 'in Judaea' to the word 'Church'. In the $\mathfrak{H}$ text verse 3 reads: 'when he saw that it pleased the Jews'—the reader having to deduce the exact sense of 'it', which the Greek does not express at all; D and sy[hmg], however, specify: 'his proceeding against the faithful'. In verse 4 the phrase ὃν καὶ πιάσας is one of those quasi-relative clauses to which Luke was addicted and which seem to us to contain a redundant καί. D and gig offer normal Greek, substituting τοῦτον for ὃν καί. Verse 5 is stylistically improved. In verse 7 an explanatory 'to Peter' is inserted, and the verb πατάσσω, which generally means 'strike', is replaced by νύσσω, meaning 'nudge', so as to obviate misunderstanding. In all these emendations the 'Western' text of Acts shows no difference in spirit from the 'Western' text of Matthew or Mark.

2. Variants of another kind are peculiar to the 'Western' text of Acts. Quite often, where the author of Acts has worked small details in, the seam

---

[1] Von Soden, esp. 1720–7 & 1814–36; Ropes LVI–LXXXIV; Kenyon 89ff

[2] Von Soden 1544–72, 1824 (Gigas); Ropes CVI–CXXVII; Kenyon 135ff.

[3] Von Soden 1824; Ropes CLV–CLXXX; Kenyon 125; Klijn 78–82. In 616 Thomas of Harkel, at Enaton Monastery near Alexandria, collated the text translated from Greek in 506 by Philoxenus with three old MSS in the case of the Gospels and, in the case of Acts, with one, which contained a Western text.

[4] Von Soden 1624–9; see also Harnack, *Marcion: das Evangelium vom fremden Gott*, 2nd ed. 1924, 65–123 & 165–220.

[5] Von Soden 1632–48.

[6] Von Soden 1838–48; Ropes CLXXXVIIf.

[7] On the Pierpont Morgan Coptic text of Acts see Haenchen-Weigandt. *NTS* 14 (1968) 469ff.

[8] See 30 n.7 and 31 n.1 above. While differing in details, the Catholic scholar Johannes Belser allowed himself on the whole to be persuaded by Blass, as shown by his *Beiträge zur Erklärung der Apostelgeschichte auf Grund des Codex D und seiner Genossen*, Freiburg/Br. 1897. Provided this work is read in a critical spirit, it furnishes a useful comparative study of the 'Western' variants and their characteristics. In 1896 Eberhard Nestle published a short but exemplary collation of the Codex Cantabrigiensis in his *Novi Testamenti Supplementum*, 7–66. See also Kenyon 232.

remains visible. Thus for example, in **3.8**, Peter and John go into the ἱερόν with the healed cripple, and in **3.11** the people come running up to them 'in Solomon's Portico'. But this did not lie within the ἱερόν. For this reason the 'Western' redactor has the Apostles and the healed man 'go out' again in verse 11 before the crowd gathers in the Portico. The first thing this alteration shows is that the redactor knew his Temple better than the author. But at the same time it shows how attentively he had read the text. Thirdly it reveals that he did not yet consider Acts to be 'holy writ' which no one was allowed to alter. These observations are corroborated time after time. The alterations made by this redactor of the 'Western' text reveal a meticulous, alert and erudite man, anxious to remove the faults in a book which strikes him as potentially valuable. A few examples will vouch for this.

Reading **16.35**, the redactor said to himself, 'We have just had an account of an earthquake which shattered the prison and freed the prisoners, but we learn nothing more about it. Moreover, why do the authorities suddenly change their attitude and release Paul and Silas?' Thinking the matter over, he thought he saw the solution: it was the thought of the earthquake that made the magistrates change their mind! He therefore recast verse 35 as follows: 'But when it was day the praetors came together in the forum, and when they remembered the earthquake which had taken place, they were afraid and sent the lictors . . .' As we can see, the redactor of course believes in the miracle narrated. But he is also a realist and wants a clear sequence of events. Once he is persuaded that he has found the link, he makes no bones about altering the Lucan text. Admittedly, his limitations as a critical reader are also clear. The *reader* knows that the earthquake appears to ensue from the hymns sung by Paul and Silas: but how could the authorities suspect the connection?

A further emendation, in verse 30, reveals more of this redactor's characteristics. According to the ℌ text, the jailer had eyes only for Paul and Silas. About the other prisoners—though they too were now free!—he does not trouble himself at all. That is no way for a jailer to behave! And so the redactor inserts the words: 'after he had secured the rest'. A miracle and a conversion are all very fine—but people must continue to behave as they normally do in everyday life.

Acts **20.4** contains a list of Paul's travelling-companions. According to the ℌ text these include one Gaius from Derbe. But the 'Western' redactor had noted that in **19.29** the Ephesian mob had dragged two companions of Paul into the theatre, Γάϊον καὶ Ἀρίσταρχον Μακεδόνας. He therefore took this Gaius to be the same as that in **20.4**. It followed, however, that the latter could not come from Derbe, which is in Asia Minor, not Macedonia. Δερβαῖος was therefore a scribal error, and a similar Macedonian place-name had to be found which could feasibly have been confused with the better-known Derbe. The redactor actually came up with such a name—that of the little Macedonian township Doberus, otherwise practically unknown—and in **20**.4 conjectured Δουβέριος for Δερβαῖος. Clark and other scholars[1] have taken this to be the original reading. Like the redactor himself, they have overlooked the fact that the seven companions of **20**.4 are named in a systematic order. First comes Sopater of Beroea, then two Thessalonians (Secundus and the aforementioned Aristarchus), next Gaius of Derbe and Timothy from Lystra, which lies near Derbe, and finally two men from Asia Minor, Tychicus and Trophimus. Thus the last six are paired according to their home-region, and accordingly Gaius must come from Derbe, not Doberus! Either, therefore, the Gaius of **19**.29 is another person—and after all the name was then as common as Smith today—or the final sigma of Μακεδόνα derives from an old dittography of the initial sigma of the following συνεκδήμους.[2]

The 'Western' text treats **20**.15 in similar fashion, adding 'and stayed in Trogylion' after 'we passed over to Samos'. Since the redactor held it unlikely that the ship spent the night in the roads instead of putting in at the nearest harbour, he emended accordingly.

Likewise, in **21**.1, the phrase 'and from there to Patara' is completed with 'and Myra'. Myra—cf. **27**.5—was the normal trans-shipping port which the redactor here found wanting and supplied. It did not strike him, however, that the distance was now much too long for one day's sailing. Even as the crow flies, from Patara to Myra makes fifty miles. And so what we have here is no better and older text, but the old conjecture of Acts' earliest commentator.

It follows that the famous 'seven steps' which the 'Western' text adds in **12**.10 are only a local tradition of the redactor's time, not a remnant of an original Lucan text.

3. Other variants do not belong to the 'Western' text as such, nor to the redactor we have been discussing, but to a particular codex, the famous Codex Bezae. This was written about the year 500 and is a bilingual manuscript with the Greek text (D) on the left and the Latin (d) on the right. It was evidently the custom in services of that time (and indeed somewhat earlier, already in the model for our manuscript) to read out still from the Greek, in each case a short sense-line—but immediately to follow up, for the hearers' benefit, with the Latin translation. It is plain that the congregations of that locality, which we cannot exactly identify, understood practically no Greek. Hence it is also conceivable that the scribe's own accomplishment in Greek was likewise limited. This is the only way in which we can explain the influence which the Latin text has in many places exercised upon the Greek. When for example in **5**.32 D reads τὸ πνεῦμα τὸ ἅγιον ὃν ἔδωκεν, it is the

[1] A. C. Clark, *The Acts of the Apostles*, 1933, XLIX–XL & 374–6; Kenyon 234 n. 1.
[2] Nestle/Dobschütz, *Einführung* (see 50 n.1) 4, line 22 up.

Latin *spiritum sanctum quem dedit* which has led the scribe. Likewise in 4.12 D's reading, ὄνομα . . . ὃ δεδόμενον, shows the influence of the Latin *nomen . . . quod datum est*. In 2.30 D gives καρποῦ τῆς καρδίας, a mistranslation of *fructum de praecordia*: d had rendered the κοιλία of the Greek source as *praecordia*, which means 'loins' but may also signify 'heart'.

However, D also exhibits quite other kinds of scribal error. It is true that such mistakes were more likely in uncial writing, with neither accents nor separation of words, but they go beyond anything one would *a priori* expect. In 4.34 the 𝕾 text reads ἔφερον τὰς (τιμάς). The D scribe pronounced αι like ε; he therefore often wrote αι for ε. Thus here he wrote αιφερον. But that is not all—he misread the article τας as the participial suffix τες and produced the non-existent participle αιφεροντες[1]!

Likewise in 15.4 the scribe turned ἀνήγγειλάν τε into an aorist participle ἀπηγγείλαντες.

In 8.2 we find a further instance, and it is only because of it that we have mentioned the two foregoing errors. Here B reads συνεκόμισαν δὲ . . . καὶ ἐποίησαν, but D: συνκομίσαντες . . . καὶ ἐποίησαν.[2] In his well-known work, *An Aramaic Approach to the Gospels and Acts*,[3] Matthew Black interprets this connection of the participle to a finite verb by 'and' as an Aramaism and concludes from these instances that D, with such Aramaisms, stands closer than B to the original text. When we consider what pains Luke took to improve the Greek, when recapitulating Mark, then it is as a matter of course improbable that in Acts he tolerated such Aramaisms, impossible in the Greek of his time. This last example has in fact quite a different explanation, one similar to those preceding. The Latin text d reads *comportaveruntque*, to which would correspond συνεκόμισάν τε, and this the scribe has drawn together and expanded into one of the above-mentioned participle-forms: συνκομίσαντες.

Other instances of D's following a participle by 'and' with a finite verb have a different origin. Latin has no counterpart to the aorist participle active. For that reason the Latin translation often transforms such a participle into a main verb, linking it to the original main verb by means of *et*. If the

---

[1] Ropes (p. 45) makes things worse by correcting αιφεροντες to [κ]αι φεροντες.

[2] There are two ways of explaining this carelessness. First of all, it looks as if the transcriber scarcely took in more than three words of the text at a time. Secondly one should not forget that for the century in which he wrote Radermacher's remark is fully valid: 'To a great extent in that age καί presents itself as a particle which shatters the firm structure of the sentence' (*Ntl. Grammatik*[2], 218). In John Malalas a genitive absolute attached by καί to the main verb occurs twenty times (A. Werner, 'Die Syntax des einfachen Satzes bei Genesios' in *Byzant. Zeitschr*. 31 (1931) 258–323: see 322).

[3] 2nd ed. Oxford 1956, 50. Black names a string of forerunners in the field. The most important are J. Wellhausen (*Einleitung in die ersten drei Evangelien*, 2nd ed. 1911, 4–32) and A. J. Wensinck ('The Semitisms of Codex Bezae and their relation to the non-Western text of the Gospel of Saint Luke', *Bulletin of the Bezan Club* No. XII, Leyden 1937, 11–48). Chapters 3 to 5 of Black's work are chiefly relevant for us here (third edition: Oxford 1967).

Latin and Greek texts were placed in sense-lines side by side, it would seem that where such an *et* appeared, a corresponding καί was missing. The scribe accordingly made bold to supply the 'deficiency' in the bilingual manuscript, without troubling about the construction. We find a case of this kind in 7.4, where the 𝔖 reading is ἐξελθών . . . κατῴκησεν. This the Latin d renders *exivit . . . et habitavit*, which in turn produces ἐξελθών . . . καὶ κατῴκησεν in D. The same phenomenon[1] recurs in D 5.23, 12.16, 13.29, 14.6 & 14, 16.17, 19.19 and 20.10. There is no question of an Aramaism in any of these cases.

Black also thinks to detect[2] a trace of the Aramaic particle ᵊ (which may equal ἵνα, ὥστε, ὅτι and the relative pronoun) in d 1.17, where the Latin translates ὅτι κατηριθμημένος ἦν by *qui adnumeratus erat*. Has the translator really reproduced an Aramaic ᵊ here? Not in the least! This is just one of the haplographies to which *scriptio continua* is highly conducive—*quiadnumeratus* stands for *quia adnumeratus*. We have likewise in 5.9 *efferente* for *efferent te*, and in 5.19, with in addition the miswriting of *u* as *i*, *cumquedixisset* for *cumque eduxisset*. Black's second example of ᵊ is in 7.39. Here, with gratifying unanimity, B, d, gig and Iren. lat. give the relative pronoun ᾧ. But D in fact reads ὅτι! This, however, in the context does not make the slightest sense, and simply represents a misreading of a smudged or faint ω.

As examples of the Aramaic anticipation of the pronoun Black cites D's version of 3.2 and 7.52. Yet in the first case he himself admits that it probably originated only through a scribal oversight. But this is an error the scribe often commits, and Bernhard Weiss[3] saw long ago how it came about: the copyist wrote down the word he expected, and then when he saw that his model offered something else he simply wrote that down too. It has to be

---

[1] Cf. 41f. of Haenchen's article 'Zum Text . . .' (see p. 50 h.2 above). The inverse phenomenon is found in 19.29: 𝔖 text ὥρμησαν . . . συναρπάσαντες; d—*impetumque fecerunt . . . et rapuerunt*; D—ὥρμησαν . . . καὶ συναρπάσαντες.

[2] Black op. cit., 56. The instances of *casus pendens* and hyperbaton (an anticipated subject or object later resumed by a personal pronoun) which Black considers Aramaisms (p. 38) occur in 2.22f., 3.6, 4.10, 7.35ff., 13.32f.In all of them, however, we find only the repetition, customary in Greek rhetoric, of concepts which have been moved to the front for emphasis: see pp. 43f. of 'Zum Text . . .' Of the 33 cases of asyndeton (Black 38 [2nd ed.], 59 [3rd ed.]), 7 do not come into question, because the text in reality is not asyndetic. A further 17 are the product of rhetorical considerations (see 'Zum Text . . .' 44f.). The remaining nine stand in D, but only one is also covered by d, and they derive from the negligence of our notorious scribe. There is certainly a preponderance of parataxis in D as against the 𝔖 text (Black 44–51), but that only shows D to have been formulated according to a more popular style. The expression αὐτῇ τῇ ὥρᾳ in Acts 16.18 & 22.23 is not, as Black thinks (pp. 78–81), an Aramaism (this had already been established by J. Jeremias in *ZNW* 42 (1949), 217 n. 6) but a borrowing from the Septuagint. As for Black's other alleged Aramaisms, see 'Zum Text . . .' 49–51 and the commentary below on 2.47, 4.19, 5.32, 12.10. An 'Aramaic approach' to Acts has not yet been found.

[3] Weiss, *Der Codex D in der Apostelgeschichte: Textkritische Untersuchung*, Leipzig 1897 (=*TU* XII, New Series II, 1899), 7–16.

understood that he only read one small part of the text at a time and transcribed in a purely mechanical fashion. Let us illustrate this fault with a few examples:

In 3.2 the scribe expects παραυτων, and in fact he is nearly right, for the text has παρατων (one must bear in mind the *scriptio continua*). Having written παραυτων, however, he sees that after των the text continues with εισπορευομενων, and so he placidly writes this word down. Similarly in 7.52 he wrote απεκτειναναυτους in accordance with his expectation (he noted only the τους, and thought it was the accusative object αυτους). But then he noticed that the text continues with προκαταγγειλαντας and transcribed this word with no hesitation. This has nothing to do with the Aramaic use of a proleptic pronoun, as other instances make very clear. In 14.2 the scribe expected επηγαγον αυτοις διωγμον ('they brought up a persecution against them') and duly wrote that down. But when he found that the text designates the object with κατα των δικαιων, he had no qualms in putting that too. Likewise with 15.2 and 16.38. The latter instance is particularly glaring: the scribe expected, and wrote, a dative 'to them' after the verb 'reported' which opens the sentence, then he began to add the subject, 'the lictors' (or police). Thus he had already 'committed' αυτοις οι to paper when he noticed that the text expressly said 'to the praetors' (magistrates). Thinking that he had just written the article τοις, he merely added στρατηγοις.

And so we see that our original question—'What is then the relationship of the "Western" to the 𝔥 text in Acts?'—is in reality ambiguous, because the expression '"Western" text' does not have one clear and invariable meaning. It may denote 1. the text which we already encounter in Marcion, Tatian and Irenaeus, and which is clearly everywhere, in East and West, the product, albeit by no means uniform, of elucidations and of explanatory or occasionally pious interpolations and expansions; there is no reason to call this a 'recension'—this text is not and never was a unity. But '"Western" text' may also denote 2. the revision to which a thoughtful, painstaking and erudite reader—already using a 'Western' text in the first sense—subjected our book, removing seams and gaps and inserting a detail here and there. Finally 3. it may denote those variants which sometimes resemble Aramaisms but are no more nor less than the careless mistakes of a scribe (or two successive scribes), working *ca.* 500, mistakes which have added a special flavour to one particular codex based on the 'Western' text in the first two senses.

In none of these three cases does the 'Western' text of Acts provide us with the 'original' text: that is the lesson we have been in gradual process of learning.

The highly meritorious publication of the Lucan text of Pap. 75 (which appeared in 1961 as No. XIV of the Bibliotheca Bodmeriana, with the Johannine text of the same Papyrus codex as No. XV) seems to us to suggest that the situation for the third gospel was similar to that for Acts, and thereby indirectly corroborates the observations on the text of Acts. Not that the Lucan text of Pap. 75 was a 'Western' text! It looks rather, over considerable stretches, like an anticipation of the Nestle Text and contains only a very few readings from the first group of the 'Western' text; as the editors Victor Martin and Rodolphe Kasser note (p. 29), it stands nearest to Vaticanus.

This oldest (at least to the present) extant Lucan text poses the question: Do the famous 'Western non-interpolations'—which are supported mostly by D, it, sy^{cs}, Marcion or some of them—not belong in the final analysis to those emendations which were created by an astute and extraordinarily precise reader of the Lucan work and up till the present have enjoyed the honour of standing 'above' in the Nestle Text, while the corresponding 'neutral' readings had to be content with a miserable existence below in the apparatus? How does the situation stand, for example, in Chap. 24?

Let us begin with Lk. 24.1. D it sy^{cs} sa omit the word αρωματα here, and probably not as an oversight but as a carefully considered correction. In 23.56 it had been related that the women had prepared not only αρωματα but also μυρα. In 24.1, in the 'neutral' and here probably also original text, only the αρωματα are mentioned. This contradiction is removed by the omission of αρωματα in the 'Western' text of Lk. 24.1. Now the women bring 'what they had prepared'. This alteration corresponds exactly to those corrections by which the 'Western' text of Acts removed tensions and contradictions.

Now we turn to Lk. 24.53. Luke had (see below, p. 79) the characteristic of promptly repeating a word just used. In Lk. 24.51 he had employed the word ευλογειν for that blessing with which the ascending Christ departed from his disciples. He uses the same word afresh in 24.53, although ευλογουντες τον θεον here means 'praising God'. D and it read instead the synonym αινουντες τον θεον. This does away with the offence that ευλογειν is applied to the disciples immediately after it has been ascribed to the ascending Lord.

Even more of an offence was the fact that the ascension itself was recounted twice, and on quite different days: in Lk. 24.51 it happened on Easter Sunday, in Acts 1.9–11, on the other hand, forty days later. On account of this discrepancy—so we may think—D it sy^{cs} have omitted the words και ανεφερετο εις τον ουρανον in Lk. 24.51, as Joachim Jeremias (see below, p. 138 n.8) long ago assumed. As has been seen even more clearly in recent years, the ascension actually possesses a somewhat different meaning at the conclusion of Luke than at the beginning of Acts: it triumphantly closes the existence of the Lord on earth. In the context of Acts, on the other hand, it links the instruction of the disciples by the risen Lord—and thus the Church's instruction by him—with the further history of the Christian proclamation and the growing congregation. The correction which the 'Western' text achieves by deleting και ... ουρανον has only perceived the conflict, but has not grasped the freedom with which Luke by the use of two different traditions had expressed the different aspects of the ascension.

Pap. 75 reads αρωματα in Lk. **24**.1 with the 'neutral' text, in Lk. **24**.53 ευλογουντες and in **24**.51 και ανεφερετο εις τον ουρανον. These readings of the oldest Lucan text yet found suggest that we should no longer describe them bluntly as 'interpolations,' or call them more politely 'Western non-interpolations,' but that we should see in them the original text.

The same may hold also for a fourth passage in Lk. **24**. D it sy[cs] have omitted the words προσκυνησαντες αυτον in v. **52**. In their view with good reason: as soon as Jesus at the end of Luke was no longer understood to be taking final leave of the disciples, the expression for the behaviour of the disciples corresponding to this final departure also lost its meaning, and became superfluous.

We are then faced with the question: Has the verse Lk. **24**.12, missing in D it and Marcion, been correctly relegated by the Nestle Text to the apparatus, although it is contained in the $-text and now also Pap. 75? This question is not so easily answered as the previous one concerning the so-called Western non-interpolations. For Lk. **24**.13–43 is indeed so constructed that the proclamation of the reality of the Resurrection again and again meets with incredulity among the disciples, and thereby elicits ever new, clearer and more convincing evidences of the risen Lord. So far v. 12 seems to contradict the direction which the Lucan composition is here following. But this objection against the authenticity of the verse is not unshakeable. The Lucan composition of Lk. **24**.13–43 is not an entirely self-contained unity. This is shown by the episode of the Emmaus disciples: it derives from another tradition than the stories of the empty grave and the appearances before Peter and the Twelve, and 'all the Apostles'. This episode ends not with disbelief, but rather with recognition and belief. It is, therefore, very possible that v. 12 also—which does not lead to belief but only to wonder!— is an organic part of the Lucan account (see now K. Aland, *Stud. z. Überl. d. NTs* II, 1967, 155–72, especially 168f.).

It has, of course, been pointed out against the verse that it makes use of John 20.8–10. It does in fact contain all sorts of similarities, even to the wording. But it is very questionable whether in this case also, as in many others, the fourth gospel does not presuppose a tradition which is very closely related to the Lucan and reported Peter's visit to the empty grave.

Finally objection has been taken to v. 12 on the basis that if it were original then there must be a reason for its omission, and there is nothing of the sort. But the situation may be different: actually v. 12 contradicts v. 24, according to which *several* disciples went to the grave and found it empty. The expression 'some of those with us' moreover seems actually to exclude a primary disciple such as Peter. It is, therefore, thoroughly possible that the early reader who searched out and deleted the contradictions has removed the apparently inaccurate and contradictory v. 12. We must therefore consider very seriously—in spite of D, it and Marcion—whether we should not release v. 12 from its exile in the apparatus and accept it into the text of the gospel, as Pap. 75 suggests.

But the importance of this papyrus is not yet exhausted. The distinguished Dutch textual scholar A. F. J. Klijn wrote in 1959 (*Nov. Test.* 3, 18) on the basis of his studies on Pap. 66 (*NTS* 3 (1956–7) 327–34): 'a neutral text existed, but it certainly is not palpable in a MS. or in any one type of text. The neutral text was manifest in numerous readings which were strewn over a great number of MSS. Only by a long purifying process did the readings come together in the present so-called neutral text.' This judgement could at that time appeal to the findings which Pap. 45 and Pap. 66 had revealed. But Pap. 75, it seems to us, has made this judgement obsolete. For in this MS., which may have been written around 200 A.D., the 'neutral' readings are already practically all present, without any need for a long process of purification to bring them together *miro quodam modo* out of a multitude of manuscripts. For the reference to a long continuing eclecticism, in which probably Origen unconsciously played a role (Klijn, *ibid.*), does not show us the magnet which gradually brought the 'neutral' readings together. Pap. 75 allows us rather to see the 'neutral' text already as good as finished, before that slow development could have started at all; it allows us the conclusion that such manuscripts as lay behind Vaticanus—even if not in all New Testament books—already existed for centuries alongside all the confusion into which Papyri 45 and (although not so clearly) 66 afford us an insight. The 'neutral' text of the Lucan work (about which we are here speaking) is no scholarly construction, but rather a text which was not, or at any rate only a little, affected by the adaptation to contemporary taste which set in in the second century or by the arbitrary procedure of the scribes. This is not to say that a specific individual manuscript[1]—such as Pap. 75—contains the Lucan text word for word as the author wrote it down. It is, however, probable that the original text of the Lucan work is not far different from the text of B and Pap. 75. In so far as Pap. 75 leads us to this picture of the development of the Lucan text, it is—although it permits only indirect conclusions about the text of Acts—more important than Pap. 74, which itself contains a text of Acts.

---

[1] What the editors report (p. 22) about the writing of the names Johannes and Bethsaida arouses the suspicion that the writer of the manuscript (or of his model?) united the text of Luke and John from two independent individual gospel manuscripts into one large papyrus codex. Very probably there existed beside this—as Kurt Aland at once remarked in conversation—a second volume with the gospels of Matthew and Mark.

Bibliography

A. Pott, *Der abendländische Text der Apg. und die Wir-Quelle*, Leipzig, Hinrichs, 1900; A. Jülicher, 'Kritische Analyse d. lateinischen Übersetzungen der Apg.', *ZNW* 15 (1916), 163–88; H. A. Sanders, 'The Egyptian Text of the Four Gospels and Acts', *HTR* 26 (1933), 77–89; B. H. Streeter, 'The Primitive Text of Acts', *JTS* 34 (1933), 232–41; P. L. Hedley, 'The Egyptian Text of the Gospels and Acts', *CQR* 118 (1934), 188–230; J. A. Montgomery, 'The Ethiopic Text of Acts', *HTR* 27 (1934), 169–206; R. P. Langrange, 'Le Papyrus Beatty des Actes des Apôtres', *Rev. Bibl.* 43 (1934), 161–71; J. M. Creed, 'The Collations of the Text of Acts in Codex 876 etc.', *JTS* 38 (1937), 395–9; R. V. G. Tasker, 'The Nature of the Text of the Chester Beatty Papyrus in Acts', *JTS* 38 (1937), 383–94; W. G. Kümmel, 'Textkritik und Textgeschichte des N.T. 1914–1937', *Th. R.* 11 (1939), 84–107; G. D. Kilpatrick, 'Western Text and Original Text in the Gospels and Acts', *JTS* 44 (1943), 24–36; R. C. Stone, *The Language of the Latin Text of Codex Bezae*, Illinois Studies in Language and Literature, vol. 30, University of Illinois, Urbana, Illinois, 1946; W. B. Sedgwick, 'St. Paul and the D-Text', *Exp. Tim.* 59 (1947–8), 222f; B. K. Soper, 'St. Luke and the Western Text (Luke 24³⁴)', *Exp. Tim.* 60 (1948–9), 63; C. S. C. Williams, 'St. Luke and the "Western" Text', *Exp. Tim.* 60 (1948–9), 25f; Ph.-H. Menoud, 'The Western Text and the Theology of Acts', *Studiorum Novi Testamenti Bulletin* II (1951), 19–34; J. Heuschen, 'De oudste texten van de Handelingen in verband met de verrijzenis', *Rev. Ecclés. de Liège* 38 (1951), 33–42; C. S. C. Williams, *Alterations to the Text of the Synoptic Gospels and Acts*, Oxford (Blackwell), 1951; A. F. J. Klijn, 'A Mediaeval Dutch Text of Acts', *NTS* 1 (1954–5), 51–6; J. D. Yoder, *The Language of the Variants of Codex Cantabrigiensis*, Princeton Library, 1958; J. N. Birdsall, *The Bodmer Papyrus of the Gospel of John*, London (The Tyndale New Testament Lecture 1958), 1958; A. F. J. Klijn, 'A Survey of the Researches into the Western Text of the Gospels and Acts (1949–59), *Novum Testamentum* 3 (1959), 1–27; Papyrus Bodmer XIV–XV, Evangiles de Luc et Jean, Tom. I, XIV, Luc chap. 3–24, 1961; Papyrus Bodmer XVII, Actes des Apôtres etc., Cologny-Genève, 1961; A. F. J. Klijn, *A Survey of the Researches into the Western Text of the Gospels and Acts* (Part Two, 1949–1969), Leiden 1969.

4. THE CHRONOLOGY OF ACTS

There are few details in Acts which may be turned to chronological account. The readers did not look for them, neither did Luke have much material for them.[1]

---

[1] In 'A Tentative Synthetic Chronology of the Apostolic Age' (*JBL* 56 (1937), 177–91) C. J. Cadoux interpreted the statements at 2.47b, 6.7, 9.31, 12.24, 16.5, 19.20 and 28.31 as references to Pentecostal feasts recurring at five-yearly intervals from the year 30 to 60. But no reader would have noticed such recondite chronological clues, and Cadoux passes in silence over similar places, such as 4.4 and 5.14.

1. Chapters 1 to 8 contribute nothing to chronology. According to the parallel II Cor. **11**.32f., Paul's flight from Damascus, described in **9**.23–5, took place during the lifetime of the Nabataean king Aretas (Harithat IV), who died in the year 40. The date of the flight cannot be more closely determined.[1]

2. Acts **11**.27–**12**.25 admit of chronological evaluation. Here, of course, five questions overlap: (a) When did Herod Agrippa die? (b) When did he persecute the Christians? (c) When was there a famine? (d) When was it prophesied? (e) When was the collection delivered?

(a) Herod's death fell in the year 44.[2] The games[3] at which he was taken ill in Caesarea must have been the *ludi pro salute Caesaris.*[4] According to Eusebius, these took place on 5 March. Herod died five days later, thus on 10 March 44 (by Schwartz's reckoning[5]).

[1] In *Arethas IV, König der Nabatäer*, Freiburg/Br. 1909, Alfons Steinmann puts it in the year 37, it being in this year that Caligula presented Damascus to the Nabataeans (Steinmann thence infers that Paul was converted between 35 and 37). This contention is based solely on the fact that no Roman coins for the period 37 to 54 have yet been unearthed at Damascus. However, Aretas' ethnarch, in II Cor. **11**.32f., lies in wait for Paul not *in* but *before* the city (see below p. 332 n.2). Eduard Schwartz disputes the alleged gift of the city in *NGG* 1907, 275 n. 3.

[2] According to Josephus, *Ant.* XVIII 236f., 'a few days' after the death of Tiberius (16 March 37) Herod Agrippa received from Caligula, with his freedom and the diadem, the tetrarchies of Philip and Lysanias. It is therefore possible that his reign had begun by 1 April 37. In the fourth year of his reign (Spring 40 to Spring 41) he received from Caligula Galilee also, which had been taken from Antipas (*Ant.* XVIII 252). In January 41 the new emperor, Claudius, gave him Judaea and Samaria as a reward for services rendered in connection with the Senate's recognition of Claudius (*Ant.* XIX 236–44; 274). Over the thus restored kingdom of Herod the Great, Agrippa had reigned three full years when he died (*Ant.* XIX 343, recapitulated 19, 351). Accordingly Agrippa must have died early in 44 after a reign of seven years. This fits in with Claudius' missive to the Jews of Summer 45 (*Ant.* XX 11–14; see *Beg.* V, 452f.). Doubt was cast on this reckoning by two coins which have since disappeared, to be dated, according to Madden (*The Coins of the Jews*, London 1881, 129ff.), from the eighth and ninth years of Agrippa's reign.

[3] In Vol. I, 4th ed., of his *Geschichte des jüdischen Volkes* (ET *History of the Jewish People in the Time of Jesus*), 560 n. 40, Schürer writes in terms of special games which 'were organized in Rome to celebrate the return of Claudius from Britain in the year 44 . . . and were afterwards probably copied in the provinces'. This was also Zahn's interpretation of the celebrations (*Einl.* II³ 641), based upon Dio Cassius LX 23, Suetonius (*Claudius* 17) and Eusebius (*Chron.* ed. Helm, 179). But all these speak only of the emperor's triumph in Rome, not of celebrations in the provinces. Schürer and Zahn were trying to overcome the incompatibility between the date of the Passover and that of Agrippa's death if the games were identified with the *ludi pro salute Caesaris* of 5 March 44—an equation which Schürer moreover rejected owing to his own error of calculation (see next note). Unfortunately the as yet unpublished Habilitationsschrift by Dr. Alfred Suhl, 'Paulus und seine Briefe. Ein Beitrag zur paulinischen Chronologie', could not be taken into account.

[4] In the same footnote Schürer contended that these games would yield the year 43, not 44; Plooij (pp. 13f.) followed him in this. But, as Lake shows in *Beg.* V, 451, Josephus (*Ant.* XV 354) places the journey of Augustus to Syria (Dio Cassius LIV 7), which can be dated in the summer of 20 B.C., in the seventeenth year of Herod's reign. The twenty-eighth year of this reign, the year in which the games were founded in honour of the emperor, was therefore 9 B.C., and their quinquennial recurrence brings us to 44 A.D.

[5] Eduard Schwartz, 'Zur Chronologie des Paulus' in *NGG*, 1907, 265f.

(b) According to Acts **12**.3f., the persecution took place about the time of the Passover before the king's death. In 44 the fifteenth day of Nisan fell on the first of April[1]—thus nearly three weeks *after* the king's death! This[2] means that he must already have persecuted the Christians during the Passover[3] of 43, but many months would then have lain between the Passover and his death. Or it may be that the connection of the persecution with the Passover is merely a secondary assimilation to the Passion of Jesus. It is already clear that these Lucan dates do not admit of any exact chronological evaluation. The only thing one may say with certainty is that Herod Agrippa persecuted the Apostles at some time during the last years of his life.

(c) According to Luke,[4] famine spread over the whole world during the reign of Claudius. But there never was such a world-famine. On the other hand the whole reign of Claudius was afflicted by local famines.[5] Palestine was particularly hard-hit, according to Josephus (*Ant.* 20, 101), in the term of office of Tiberius Alexander, i.e. in the years 46 to 48.[6] Now, as Joachim

---

[1] See Plooij, 15.

[2] Since in Acts **12**.3f., as in Luke **22**.1, Luke equates the Passover with the seven-day feast of unleavened bread (so—rightly—*Beg.* IV, 134 against Zahn, 385 n. 36), the end of the feast would in 44 have been as much as four weeks after the king's death. To obviate this contradiction, Lake assumed (*Beg.* V, 452) that during the first century the games at Caesarea began not on 5 March, as in the time of Eusebius, but, as at Lyons (Suetonius, *Claudius* 2), on the first of August. In this case Agrippa would have died on 6 August. Had this been so, however, the news of his death would not have reached Rome before the end of September, and by the time a decision had been taken it would have been too late for the new procurator to complete his journey in 44. The latter (Fadus) was nevertheless already in office in 44. Lake retrieves himself by having Agrippa die on 6 August 43, but thereby contradicts Josephus on the length of the king's reign.

[3] The fact that Passover was considered especially as a time of salvation (August Strobel, Erlangen) prompts a double interpretation of the case before us: (a) here once again the Passover confirmed its character as the special time of God's saving help (so Strobel); (b) Peter's rescue was assigned to Passover as the special time of 'saving' (see Strobel, *ZNW* 49 (1958) 157ff.).

[4] Acts **11**.28. The interpretation of οἰκουμένη as restricted to Palestine is a mere apologetic artifice.

[5] In 'The Universal Famine under Claudius' (*HTR* 28 (1935), 258–65), K. S. Gapp points out that the Teptunis papyri testify to a record high price for wheat in Autumn 45 (an exceptionally high Nile flood had been catastrophic for the harvest). This had for result not only famine in Judaea but a steep rise in the cost of living in the West, while an African campaign of Galba's in 45 had perhaps reduced corn-supplies from Mauretania. But since Queen Helen of Adiabene had corn brought from Egypt during the famine in Judaea, the failure of the Egyptian harvest must have been overcome by the time famine was reaching its peak in Jerusalem in 47/48. There were shortages of corn in Rome in 41, 42 and 50/51 (Tacitus, *Ann.* 12, 43, says 51; Orosius, *Hist.c.pag.* VII 6. 17 says 50). Against all good nautical precedents Claudius had the big grain-ships bring corn in winter from Egypt (as well as Africa), himself underwriting both vessels and cargoes. The gamble succeeded, as the winter storms held off. All this is recounted by Suetonius (*Claudius* 18), but without dates. One may not speak of a famine covering the whole Roman Empire.

[6] In *Ant.* XX 101, Josephus dates the Judaean famine with the words ἐπὶ τούτοις δὲ καὶ τὸν μέγαν λιμὸν κατὰ τὴν Ἰουδαίαν συνέβη γενέσθαι. In the expression of dates 'on which' Josephus correctly uses ἐπὶ with the genitive (e.g. *Ant.* XX 14, 144 or 228; *Vita* 37: places where—according to H. St. John Thackeray, *Josephus, the Man and the Historian,*

Jeremias has pointed out, the year 47/48 (the Jewish year beginning and ending in autumn) was a sabbatical year, in which the land remained untilled and there was no harvest. Jeremias says, 'In the summer of 47 the harvest failed, the sabbatical year 47/48 intensified the famine and prolonged it until the next harvest in early 49.' This catastrophe, therefore, did not occur until several years after the death of Herod Agrippa.

(d) The prophecy of this famine must surely have been uttered before 46. Zahn[1] inferred from the words 'and this came to pass in the days of Claudius' that the famine was prophesied under his predecessor Caligula (d. 24 January 41). But Luke could not have possessed any exact information here—he does not even specify any particular year. He intended that the phrase should not so much provide a date as emphasize the fulfilment of the prophecy.

(e) Zahn and Ramsay contend that several years elapsed between the decision to collect relief (verse 29) and its actual delivery (verse 30).[2] But no

---

1929, 100ff.—Josephus' Greek assistants have not made stylistic revisions). ἐπί with the dative, on the other hand, he uses to denote 'to', 'on (grounds of)', 'in addition to'—thus for example *Ant.* XX 10 ('in addition to this reply') or 120 ('the baseness additional to the offence'). By extension, ἐπί + dative sometimes assumes the meaning of 'then' or 'next', as in *Ant.* XX 267: 'and then I intend to make an end of archaeology'. ἐπὶ τούτοις means 'in these circumstances' neither in Josephus nor in Eusebius, where it always means 'in addition to this' (e.g. *H.E.* I 1. 2; I 8. 15; II 6. 8; III 9. 1; III 32. 7). In Josephus the word συνέβη corresponds to the Lucan ἐγένετο and marks the advent of some new occurrence. Accordingly the words ἐπὶ τούτοις συνέβη κτλ. imply 'it next happened that famine appeared', hence under Tiberius Alexander, the successor of Fadus.

Fadus will have landed in Caesarea in the summer of 44 (the news of Agrippa's death having reached Rome at the end of April, and the decision having been taken, after some hesitation, to send out a Roman governor in view of the extreme youth of Agrippa the Younger, his son and heir). After taking punitive measures against the inhabitants of Caesarea (for on the news of the king's death they had dragged the statues of his daughters into the brothels—a sign of how unpopular Agrippa had become: *Ant.* XIX 364–6), after suppressing unrest in Peraea and removing the partisan-leader Ptolemy (*Ant.* XX 2–5), Fadus joined forces with the legate of Syria, Cassius Longinus, marched on Jerusalem and compelled the surrender of the high-priestly vestments—which had been kept by the Jews themselves during their independence. The Jewish politicians were obliged to yield, but obtained permission to send a deputation to the emperor. We must suppose that it was by then too late in 44 to undertake the voyage. If it ensued in March 45, the deputation could have arrived in Rome at some time during April or May. The emperor's favourable reply to their petitions (*Ant.* XX 11–14) bears the date 28 (month missing) 45—only manuscripts of the Latin translation give 'June' (*Beg.* V, 453). But even if this document dates from the earliest possible *terminus a quo*, i.e. the end of May, it would still imply that Fadus's tenure of office was extended. For, in accordance with an ordinance made by Claudius in 43, any successor of Fadus would already have taken ship for Palestine in the middle of April. It follows that Fadus held office for a διετία, from 44 to 46. His successor, Tiberius Alexander, seems also to have held office for a διετία, since Cumanus relieved him in 48.

[1] *Einl.*[3] II, 643 (ET *Introduction to the NT*, 1909).

[2] Here Zahn takes the Pauline collection as model. But Luke's aim is not to present what is usual in a rational and realistic manner but to present what is unusual and edifying. Hardly has the Church at Antioch heard of the threat of famine when it thinks, not of itself, but of Jerusalem, decides on a collection, carries it out—everyone giving what he can—and lo! Paul and Barnabas are already on the road to Jerusalem. That they happen

reader understands Luke's words in this sense. He speaks of the delivery of the relief in **11**.30 and **12**.25, i.e. before the account of the persecution begins and after the end of the Herod story. This gives the impression that Paul and Barnabas stayed in Jerusalem throughout the most critical period and that it was on this account that they entrusted their gift to the elders, not to the Apostles, who were being persecuted and were on the run. This is not of course expressed in plain words: Luke is telling his story for the sake of edification, and does not go into chronological details. Doubt has been thrown on his report—not without reason—by the fact that Paul does not mention this relief-mission in Gal. **1**.18–**2**.10. It remains, however, possible that Barnabas alone, without Paul, did at one time carry relief from Antioch to Jerusalem (see our commentary on **11**.30 below).

3. In Acts **13**.7ff., Sergius Paulus is named as the proconsul of Cyprus. So far the hope of finding his year of office mentioned in an inscription has been disappointed.[1]

4. Acts **15**.1ff. shows such striking similarities to Gal. **2**.1–10 that most scholars consider the two accounts, both telling of a journey by Paul and Barnabas from Antioch to Jerusalem on account of the circumcision question, to refer to one and the same episode. It likewise appears that both Acts **9**.26–9 and Gal. **1**.18–20 describe Paul's first visit to Jerusalem after his conversion.

The fact that between these two journeys Luke relates, in Acts **11**.30, another journey of Paul's (with Barnabas) to Jerusalem, the relief-expedition discussed above, may perhaps be ascribed to Luke's misconstruing some less worthy tradition (see commentary on **11**.30 below). A number of scholars[2]

---

to arrive in the midst of the persecution serves but to heighten edification: could anything show better the close bonds of affection between the two communities?

[1] In *CIL* VI 4, II, 3116 (No. 31545) a certain Lucius Sergius Paullus is named as a member of the Roman authority the *curatores riparum*—but without a date. The manuscripts of Pliny's *Nat. hist.* mention in Book 1, as source for Book 2, one Sergius Plautus, and in the source-list for Book 18 sometimes Sergius Plautus, sometimes Sergius Paulus (*Beg.* V, 457f.). The first name is right without a doubt. An inscription from Soli in Cyprus (in 1889 D. G. Hogarth published the full text in *Devia Cypria*, p. 114) shows at the end two lines, apparently added later, to the effect that the erector of the memorial worked as a censor under the pro-consul Paulus. The body of the inscription is dated 'in the thirteenth year.' If this meant the thirteenth year of Claudius' reign (53 A.D.), Paulus must have become proconsul after this year, which would rule out any encounter with the Apostle. Other possibilities for the dating (e.g. the thirteenth year since Cyprus became a Roman province) give 42 B.C. or 14 B.C.: neither of these would have anything to do with the Apostle's travels. The inscription may perhaps refer to Paullus Fabius Maximus, who was consul in 11 B.C. (Mommsen in *ZNW* 2 (1901), 83; cf. Plooij, 25f.). Bibliography: Zahn in *NkZ*, 1904, 189–95, & *Einl.*[3] II, 645; W. Ramsay, *The Bearing of Recent Discoveries . . .*, 1915, 150–72; Harnack, *Mission und Ausbreitung*, 4th ed., 676ff. (ET *The Mission and Expansion of Christianity*); Wikenhauser, 338–41; Lake, *Beg.* V, 455–9.

[2] Holtzmann (p. 82), Emanuel Hirsch (*ZNW* 29 (1930), 64f.), H. W. Beyer (*NT deutsch, Apg.*, 1933, 89ff.), H. Lietzmann (*Hdb. z. NT, Brief an die Gal.*, 2nd ed., 1932, 9), J. Jeremias (*ZNW* 36 (1937), 205ff.), A. Oepke (*Der Brief des Paulus an die Galater*, 1937, 39) and G. Hölscher (*SAH*, 1939–40, 25f.). Lake too (*Beg.* V, 202–4) may be included here.

have seen in **11**.30 an inferior parallel tradition to Acts **15**, but believe that **11**.30 correctly gives the time of the journey to the 'Apostolic council': Herod Agrippa persecuted the 'pillars' (Gal. **2**.9)—at the instigation of the Pharisees—precisely because, in their negotiations with Barnabas and Paul, they consented to the mission to the gentiles without circumcision.[1] But this hypothesis comes up against difficulties which in our opinion are insurmountable: the meeting of the Apostles would have taken place in the winter of 43/44 (if not indeed a year earlier—see 2(b) above), and Paul would then have been converted 'fourteen years' before—i.e. almost immediately after the death of Jesus in the year 30. Even if Jesus' death is dated back to 29, the interval is insufficient to accommodate all the events implied in Acts 6. It is more plausible to date the 'Apostolic council' about the year 48.

5. The chronological value of Acts 18.1f. is a matter of debate. Aquila and Priscilla are here said to have come recently from Italy to Corinth 'because Claudius had commanded all the Jews to leave Rome'. This recalls a famous sentence in Suetonius: *Judaeos impulsore Chresto assidue tumultuantes Roma expulit* (*Claudius* 25). Evidence that the uncomprehended name χριστός was construed as the common proper name χρηστός, both words being pronounced alike,[2] is forthcoming *inter alia* in the pun of Tacitus, *Ann.* XV 44: *quos per flagitia invisos vulgus Chrestianos appellabat.* Admittedly the historian, as a man of education, adds: *Auctor nominis eius, Christus.* . . . According to Orosius, writing about the year 400 (*Historia contra paganos* VII 6, 15f.), this expulsion took place in the ninth year of Claudius' reign (49 A.D.). We should then have to assume that at some time in the forties Christians (whose names we do not know) brought the gospel to Rome and that this messianic preaching led to violent upheavals in Roman Jewry. Unfortunately Orosius appeals to Josephus as his authority, and in the latter's extant writings no such statement has been found. Moreover Dio Cassius raises doubt with his assertion that Claudius did not indeed drive out the Jews (which on account of their great number would not have been possible without serious disturbances), but denied them the right of association[3] (at least, this is the most likely interpretation of LX 6, 6f.). In view of this we cannot reject out of hand the conjecture that only the more factious Jews and Jewish Christians were expelled from Rome—but a conjecture it remains.

---

[1] J. Wellhausen (*NGG*, 1907, 7f.; *Kritische Analyse der Apostelgeschichte*, 1914, 30), Eduard Schwartz (*NGG*, 1907, 267ff.), P. Wendland (*Urchristliche Literaturformen*, 3rd ed., 1912, 317–21), E. Preuschen (*Hdb. z. NT, Apg.*, 1912, 75f. & 91ff.), W. Bousset (*ZNW* 15 (1914), 157ff.), A. Loisy (pp. 474 & 509), Eduard Meyer (III, 165ff.), R. Bultmann (*ZKG*, New Series 12 (1930), 91), M. Goguel (*La Naissance du christianisme*, 1946, 322ff. ET *The Birth of Christianity*, London 1953) and now A. Suhl (see above, p. 61 n.3).

[2] Similarly even ℵ* reads χρηστιανους for χριστιανους in Acts 11.26.

[3] This is perhaps why the individual Jewish communities shown by inscriptions to have existed in Rome did not combine in one large colony. In view of Claudius' general Jewish policy, the prohibition of synagogue-services suggested by Bruce (p. 342) is unlikely.

6. The most important chronological datum—moreover supporting this interpretation of **18.1**—is furnished by an inscription found at Delphi which mentions the proconsul Gallio referred to in Acts **18.12–17**.[1] The inscription says among other things that Claudius has been acclaimed Imperator twenty-six times. This acclamation must have taken place between 25 January and 1 August 52, and within this period Gallio's proconsular year must have either begun or ended: in other words, his term of office ran either from 1 May[2] 52 to 1 May 53 or from 1 May 51 to 1 May 52. A careful analysis of the possibilities lends support to the second hypothesis[3]: Gallio must have taken office in Corinth (the seat of government for Achaea) about the first

---

[1] The four fragments *Delphi* 2178, 2271, 3883 and 4001 permit the following reconstruction: 'Tiberius Claudius Caesar Augustus Germanicus, *pontifex maximus*, in the twelfth year of office as tribune, for the twenty-sixth time acclaimed emperor, father of the fatherland, for the fifth time consul, censor, greets the city of Delphi. I have long been devoted to the city of Delphi and it has from the beginning stood in my favour: I have ever revered Pythian Apollo. But now the common rumour, and that strife among citizens of which my friend Lucius Junius Gallio, proconsul of Achaea, has sent me word . . .' (see C. K. Barrett, *The New Testament Background* (London, 1956) p. 48f.)

Of the numbers involved, only the number '26' has been preserved: the others have been inferred. The emperor used to be acclaimed as *imperator* not at regular intervals but on the occasion of major successes of the Roman troops (though by the time of Claudius the requirements for the fulfilment of this condition had become quite modest). The 22nd, 23rd and 24th acclamations took place during the eleventh year of Claudius' reign (see *CIL* III, 467 and 1977), thus by 25 January 52 at the latest. Since Claudius was never acclaimed more than three times in any one year (*Beg.* V, 463), the unidentified twenty-fifth acclamation must belong to the twelfth year of his reign and have taken place some time after 25 January 52. Of the twenty-sixth acclamation we know first of all that it occurred in the year 52 (see G. Cousin and G. Deschamps, 'Emplacements des ruines de la ville de Küç en Carie' in the *Bulletin de Correspondance hellénique* IX, 1887, 305ff.). But the inscription *CIL* 1256, whose date has been fixed (*via* Frontinus, *De Aquis* I, 13) as 1 August 52, already mentions the 27th acclamation. It follows that the twenty-sixth acclamation took place some time between 25 January and 1 August 52.

[2] According to Dio Cassius LX 17. 3, Claudius had decreed in 43 that newly-appointed governors should leave for their provinces before the middle of April. Gallio will accordingly have arrived in Corinth about 1 May. Remoter provinces were reached later: for Judaea, 1 July, which Mommsen (*Römisches Staatsrecht* II, 2nd ed., 255f.) called the 'normal terminus', may be considered an average date of arrival. Pliny the Younger did not get to Bithynia until 17 September (Zahn, *Einl.*, 655).

[3] The inscription records the imperial decision in a Delphic controversy reported by Gallio. Supposing that Gallio had reached Corinth on 1 May 52 and had heard the parties that very month, he would still have had to order the drafting of a report and send it by courier to Rome, where it would have been caught up in the bureaucratic machine. Yet the answer was forthcoming before the emperor's 27th acclamation, hence before 1 August 52. How long before, we do not know—perhaps in July, but it may have been even in June. But in that case, there would not have been sufficient time for Gallio's investigation, the drafting of the report, the courier's journey to Rome, and the document's progress through the organs of State. If, on the other hand, Gallio had taken office on 1 May 51, these chronological difficulties vanish. The 26th acclamation could have occurred in March 52 (for the 25th must, as we have shown, be placed after 25 January 52, say in February), and the imperial reply, which postulates that Gallio is still in office, would then have been composed in March or April.

At all events, the year 52 brought no great victories. Ummidius Quadratus (see p. 69 below) pacified Palestine, Antiochus III of Commagene subdued the Clites (Tacitus,

of May 51. It is probable that the Jews sought—even perhaps as early as that same May—to lay their complaint against Paul before the new governor. Paul would in that case have left Corinth in the early summer of 51. Since, according to Acts **18**.11, he had stayed there for eighteen months, he would have come to Corinth in the winter of 49/50. This fits the statement that Aquila and Priscilla had 'lately come from Italy', in conjunction with Orosius' dating of the expulsion to 49.

7. According to the chronology devised by John Knox,[1] the obscure verse **18**.22 alludes to Paul's journey to the Apostolic Council! The starting-point here, for Knox and a number of other scholars, is the references to 'fourteen years' in Gal. **2**.1 and II Cor. **12**.2, and the identification of the 'catching-up into the third heaven' with Paul's call on the road to Damascus. Hence they deduce the following chronology: conversion 37; first journey to Jerusalem 40; mission in Syria, Cilicia, Galatia, Macedonia, Greece and Asia Minor 40–51; second journey to Jerusalem (to the Apostolic council = Acts **18**.22) 51; thereupon preparation of the fund and further mission in Greece and Asia Minor 51/52; last journey to Jerusalem (the relief-expedition) and arrest 53. The journey of Acts **11**.30 never took place, and—since he was already in Corinth in 45—Paul never came up before Gallio! But it is already very doubtful whether Acts **18**.22 refers to a journey to Jerusalem at all, and whether Paul was really in Jerusalem about that time. Presumably Paul went from Caesarea direct to Antioch, then in the early summer of 52 made his way over the Taurus passes and across Asia Minor to Ephesus. The dates in Acts **19**.8 & 10 contain the exact details, while the τριετία of Acts **20**.31 represents a round total counting in full the year of commencement, in accordance with the inclusive reckoning of the ancients. This sojourn in Ephesus came to an end in the autumn of 54: Paul then reached Corinth via Troas and spent there three months of the winter of 54/55. In the spring of 55 he journeyed over Macedonia on the way to Jerusalem, conveying the fund. He had no sooner arrived, about the time of Pentecost, than he was arrested.

Ann. XII 55) and in Britain the Siluri were finally vanquished (Tacitus, *Ann.* XII 40): Plooij, 37.

    Bibl.: Plooij, 28 lists a bibliography for 1912–17; his own chronological estimates appear in *Hoofdstuck* IV, 27–45. He regards F. Prat, 'La chronologie de l'âge apostolique' in *RScR*, 1912, 374ff., as particularly important. Zahn 867 recommends Wohlenberg's article, 'Die Claudiusinschrift von Delphi in ihrer Bedeutung für die paulinische Chronologie' in *NkZ* 23 (1912), 380–96. Cf. Lake, 'The Chronology of Acts', *Beg.* V, 460–4.

[1] Knox, '"Fourteen Years Later": a note on the Pauline chronology' in *Journal of Religion* 16 (1936) 341–9; 'The Pauline Chronology' in *JBL* 58 (1939), 15–40; *Chapters in a Life of Paul* 1950, 54ff. P. S. Minear, 'The Jerusalem Fund and Pauline Chronology' in *AngThR* 25 (1943), 389–96. D. T. Rowlingson, 'The Jerusalem-Conference and Jesus' Nazareth Visit' in *JBL* 71 (1952), 69–74. George Ogg, 'A New Chronology of St. Paul's Life' in *Exp. Tim.* 67 (1955/56), 120–3. Dieter Georgi, *Die Geschichte der Kollekte des Paulus für Jerusalem* (Theol. Forschung 38 Hamburg-Bergstedt 1965).

8. Shortly after, according to Acts **23**.23ff., Paul was brought to the procurator Felix in Caesarea, where (**24**.27) he remained in custody for two years. It is possible however that in **24**.27 Luke has mistakenly applied to Paul, instead of to Felix, his source's mention of the διετία: 'But when the διετία was fulfilled, Felix was succeeded by Porcius Festus.' Evidence for this is not wanting.

Our extra-biblical sources, Tacitus and Josephus, are admittedly at variance here. Tacitus, who is often ill-informed about provincial affairs and shows little appreciation of military matters, maintains in his presentation of the year 52 (*Ann*. XII 54) that Felix had already been governor of Judaea 'for a long time' and had arranged with Cumanus that he, Felix, should rule Samaria, and Cumanus Galilee. The Galileans and the Samaritans had been fighting each other, the situation being tolerated by the governors—who had their share in the booty. But when civil war threatened to flare up in the province and military measures were imperative, Quadratus, the legate of Syria, intervened and executed the Jews responsible for the death of Roman soldiers. Felix he accepted into the college of judges (for he had been empowered by the emperor to try the governors), Cumanus he condemned.

Now all this is extremely improbable, for the following reasons: 1. That in 52 Felix was *iam pridem Iudaeae impositus* conflicts with Josephus' precise indications (*Bell*. II 233 & *Ant*. XX 103) as to the succession of Tiberius Alexander. 2. Such a partition of Judaea is unparalleled. 3. Both Judaea and Jerusalem are disregarded. 4. Tacitus speaks only of guerilla-warfare between Galileans and Samaritans. Of their more exact relationships he knows nothing. The only concrete detail, namely that Quadratus had Cumanus' Jewish captives executed, fits only the account given by Josephus, who specifically mentions hostilities engaged by Cumanus against the Jews. 5. If Quadratus had pronounced judgment on the two governors, the proceedings in Rome, which are circumstantially reported by Josephus, would not have ensued.

Possibly Tacitus misconstrued a source that ran like this: under the procurators Cumanus and Felix there were troubles in Palestine. The conflicts between Galileans and Samaritans even reached the point where the legate Quadratus intervened, sending Cumanus to Rome for trial.

An account of this kind could easily have been misinterpreted to imply that Cumanus and Felix were procurators in Palestine at the same time. It only remained to apportion them the areas of the respective dissidents, and there was the broad outline of Tacitus' version! Such an account as we suggest as Tacitus' source would also, however, correspond in all points with Josephus.

By and large, there is no disagreement between the version of Josephus in the *Bellum Iudaicum* and his version in the *Antiquities*: In 48 Cumanus took over the province of Judaea. In the autumn of 51, one of the Galilean pilgrims to the Feast of Tabernacles, making their way through Samaria to Jerusalem, was set upon and killed in a Samaritan village.[1] The 'first men among the Galileans' demanded in vain that Cumanus should punish those guilty.[2] Whereupon Jews from Jerusalem and Galilean pilgrims, reinforced by partisans and commanded by two rebel leaders,[3] undertook a punitive expedition. They burned Samaritan border-villages and massacred the entire population. At this juncture Cumanus at last made haste with his men from Caesarea. He inflicted heavy losses on the plundering rabble, who were forced to disperse.[4] The Samaritans now complained to the legate Quadratus of the destruction of their villages, but the Jews also sought his ear: the Samaritans, they claimed, had begun the fight, and had bribed Cumanus to stay his hand until the clash could no longer be averted.[5]

Quadratus had all the Jews captured by Cumanus executed after trials at Caesarea[6] and Lydda,[7] and sent the former high-priest Jonathan and the reigning high-priest Ananias, together with the latter's son (the captain of the Temple Ananos) and a number of other Jews, as prisoners to Rome.[8] Evidently he had no faith in the innocence of the Jewish authorities, upon which Josephus insists. But he also sent the leaders of the Samaritans, as well as Cumanus and a tribune named Celer, to answer for their actions in Rome.[9] The Jews were saved by the intercession of Agrippa the Younger (the 'King Agrippa' of Acts 25.13): Claudius declared the Samaritans guilty, executed three of them, exiled Cumanus and delivered Celer to the Jews for execution.[10] At Jonathan's request[11] he appointed Felix, the brother of his favourite, Pallas, to be governor over Judaea, Samaria, Galilee and Peraea.[12]

This convincingly reveals the clever strategy which enabled the Jewish politicians to outwit and checkmate Cumanus and his backers. Agrippa acted as broker for a 'gentlemen's agreement' between Pallas and Jonathan: if Pallas could get the empress—politically and otherwise in his debt[13]—to secure the Jews' triumph and release, Jonathan would ask that the brother of

---

[1] *Bell.* II 232, 234, 237; *Ant.* XX 118.
[2] *Bell.* II 233; *Ant.* XX 121.
[3] *Bell.* II 235; *Ant.* XX 121.
[4] *Bell.* II 236f.; *Ant.* XX 122ff.
[5] *Bell.* II 239f.; *Ant.* XX 125–7.
[6] *Bell.* II 241.
[7] *Bell.* II 242; *Ant.* XX 130f.
[8] *Bell.* II 243; *Ant.* XX 131f.
[9] *Bell.* II 243; *Ant.* XX 131f.
[10] *Bell.* II 245; *Ant.* XX 134–6.
[11] *Ant.* XX 162.
[12] *Bell.* II 247; *Ant.* XX 137.
[13] Pallas had helped secure Agrippina's marriage to Claudius (Tacitus, *Ann.* XII 1ff.) and expedited the latter's adoption of her son Domitius, later called Nero (*Ann.* XII 25): *C. Antistio M. Suillio consulibus* (i.e. in the year 50) *adoptio in Domitium auctoritate Pallantis festinatur, qui obstrictus Agrippinae ut conciliator nuptiarum et mox stupro eius inligatus, stimulabat Claudium, consuleret rei publicae . . .*

Pallas be appointed procurator of Palestine. It was at that time novel, unheard-of, that a freed slave, such as was Felix, should obtain the high and lucrative office of a provincial governor. Such an innovation would however be facilitated if the representative of the people affected should himself request it. Not only was Cumanus powerless against such a combination— he actually had to lose his post so that Felix could get it.

Comparison of the two versions shows: Tacitus once again draws his recurrent portrait of the man who stops at no iniquity when driven by avarice, self-interest and the lust for power. Felix and Cumanus are made into exemplary specimens of such depravity. But even the man of still higher standing, the legate who finally intervenes to restore order, is swayed by self-seeking partiality: he spares Felix because he is the brother of the all-powerful Pallas! Politically and militarily, on the other hand, Tacitus' version of these events is wellnigh worthless. It is true that Josephus—especially in the *Antiquities*—seeks to exonerate the Jews. Nevertheless he allows the reader a penetrating look behind the scenes of the political game which, developing out of that scuffle between Galilean pilgrims and Samaritan peasants, found its catastrophic conclusion in the great revolt. For it was the sending of such procurators as Felix that finally provoked the Jewish uprising.

When did Felix take office in Palestine? The captive Jews, whose journey to Rome began about the Passover of 52, must have arrived in the early summer.[1] The trials did not begin at once: the parties were given time to prepare their case.[2] Moreover the trials did not take place before Pallas and Jonathan had made their compact and the empress had persuaded her husband to recognize the innocence of the Jews. We must further suppose that Jonathan waited a little before asking that Felix be appointed, otherwise his game would have been all too blatant. Felix would thus have received his new commission in the autumn of 52, and it is questionable whether he did not land in Caesarea only in the spring of 53, after the resumption of shipping.

When was he recalled? According to Josephus (*Ant*. XX 182), the Jews of Caesarea sent complaints about him to Nero, 'and he would certainly have had to pay for his crimes against the Jews if Nero had not yielded to the entreaties of his brother Pallas, then in the emperor's highest esteem'. Now the date of Pallas' downfall can be inferred with fair accuracy.[3] He

---

[1] In 52 the Passover fell either on 4 April or 3 May (Plooij, 85). This means that the captives would have arrived in Rome about the middle of May or June.

[2] *Ant*. XX 134.

[3] In *Ann*. XIII 14, Tacitus relates the downfall of Pallas immediately before the murder of Britannicus. According to *Ann*. XIII 15, Nero decided during the Saturnalia (17–19 Dec.) that Britannicus should be forthwith dispatched by poison 'as the day was near whereon Britannicus would have completed his 14th year'. When would this fourteenth birthday have fallen? Suetonius (*Claudius* 27) says: *Britannicum vicesimo die inque secundo consulatu natum sibi*. Plooij (p. 66 n. 7), like others, has noted a discrepancy here: the 20th day of

lost his position towards the end of 55. It was therefore still possible, if Felix came to Rome in the summer of 55, for him to be saved by Pallas. His διετία, then, mentioned in Acts 24.27, ran from 53 to 55.

It was mostly assumed earlier that Felix was not relieved until the year 60, and that Festus died after only one year. This supposition was largely based upon an *argumentum e silentio*: Josephus has little to say about Festus. But Festus seems to have been an honest man whose conduct did not give rise to such scandals as Josephus recorded. Other scholars conclude from the minting of new Palestinian coins in 59 that there had been a change of procurator. Yet Pilate took office in 26 and issued no new coins until 29/30.

Under the circumstances one should seriously consider whether Felix might not have been replaced as early as 55, and Paul have already reached Rome in early 56. In that case, the last two verses of Acts would take us to 58 A.D.

We therefore propose, as a basis for discussion, the following Pauline chronology: conversion around 35, then a stay in Nabataean Arabia. About 37/38, first journey to Jerusalem. Activity in Syria, Cilicia, Antioch. About 48, the Apostolic Council. Stay in Corinth: winter 49/50–summer 51. Journey to Antioch via Caesarea. Early 52, through Asia Minor to Ephesus, thence in 54 to Macedonia. Winter 54/55: three months in Corinth. Pentecost 55 in Jerusalem. Arrest. Transfer to Caesarea. Late summer 55, departure for Rome. Malta. Early 56, arrival in Rome. End of Acts—58. Cf. H. Braun (*RGG*³ I, 1964) on the chronological problems.

Bibliography

C. H. Turner, 'Eusebius' Chronology of Felix and Festus', *JTS* 3 (1901), 120–3; J. Knox, 'Fourteen Years Later', *Journal of Religion* 16 (1936), 341–9; Id., 'The Pauline Chronology', *JBL* 58 (1939), 15–29; C. King, 'The Outline of New Testament Chronology', *CQR* 139 (1945), 129–53; G. S. Duncan, 'Chronological Table to illustrate Paul's Ministry in Asia', *NTS* 5 (1959), 43–5.

---

the *imperium Claudii* fell on 13 Feb. 41, but the second consulate in 42. Yet so flagrant a contradiction would surely have been noticed by Suetonius himself. Actually it is merely the *day* which he denotes with the first part of his twofold expression: the *imperium Claudii* was renewed every 25 Jan., therefore the 20th day was always a 13 Feb. The second part gives the *year*—42. Hence 13 February 56 was Britannicus' 14th birthday, and he was murdered at the end of December 55. If Pallas was removed from office immediately before, this must have happened in November or at the beginning of December 55.

5. THE LANGUAGE AND STYLE OF ACTS

A. Luke's Vocabulary

A rich vocabulary is a sign that an author is well-educated. For this reason counts have been made of the different words with which Luke operates. But since the calculations have been based on different editions of the text and different ways of reckoning, there have been fairly wide divergences in results.[1] Yet this much has become clear: of NT writers, only Paul has a comparably exhaustive vocabulary at his command. Luke and he surpass the rest of the New Testament writers in the number of words peculiar to each of them.[2]

Even when compared with other writers, Luke acquits himself well in this respect. In his *Memorabilia*, a work comparable in scope with Luke-Acts, Xenophon used a somewhat smaller vocabulary; in *Anabasis*, Books 1 to 4, one slightly larger. In contrast, Luke's vocabulary far surpasses that of such orators as Aeschines or Antiphon.

Nine-tenths of this vocabulary is also found in the Septuagint.[3] This does not of course mean that Luke took all these words from that source. This becomes clear from the very fact that 85 per cent of the Lucan vocabulary coincides with Plutarch's, but only 70 per cent with the rest of the New Testament, while 70 per cent again may be found in the satirist Lucian of

---

[1] In *The Style and Literary Method of Luke*, Harvard Theological Studies VI (Part I, 1919, Part II, 1920), H. J. Cadbury gives the counts of previous writers: according to Goodspeed (*JBL* 31 (1912), 92ff.), Acts contains 2054 different words, Luke and Acts together 3120. J. R. Smith (*Presbyterian and Reformed Review* 2 (1891), 647ff.) counted 2697 in Luke and Acts, while F. Blass (*Acta Apostolorum*, editio philologica, 1895, 334) found 1787 in Acts, excluding proper nouns.

[2] Cadbury, op. cit. 2ff.: the words peculiar to Luke's work number according to Thayer between 750 and 851, to Smith 715, and to Hawkins 732 (Thayer's count for Paul gives between 593 and 627). But Cadbury, in *The Making of Luke-Acts*, 214, rightly warns against considering a word as 'peculiar to Luke' because it happens to occur only, or more frequently, in his work. If their subject-matter had so required, Matthew or Paul would also have employed words like 'tanner', 'eyewitness' or 'fathom'. *Hapax legomena* 'indicate not so much the limitation of their currency as that of our knowledge': the 'hapax' αἰτίωμα of Acts 25.7 suddenly came to light in an indictment dating from the end of Domitian's reign, brought against a muleteer for running over two pigeons.

[3] As might be expected, the 90 per cent must be reduced to 80 if the Apocrypha are excluded. Luke has most in common with the historical books—Judges, Samuel, Kings—and then with II Maccabees. On his relation to LXX, see W. K. L. Clarke, 'The Use of the Septuagint in Acts' (*Beg.* II, 66–105), A. Wifstrand, 'Lukas och Septuaginta' (*SvTKv* 16 (1940), 243–62) and H. F. D. Sparks, 'The Semitisms of Acts' (*JTS*, New Series I (1950), 16–28). See Max Wilcox, *The Semitisms of Acts*, Oxford 1965, with my review, *TLZ* 91 (1966), 355ff.

Samosata (second century A.D.), 67 in Greek comedy and 65 in the Papyri.[1] This shows that Luke's vocabulary is flavoured both by the spoken vernacular (the *koine* in the narrower sense) and by the Hellenistic written language— as yet untouched by Atticism, though containing a good deal of Attic material (see § B. ii below).[2]

B. The Peculiarities of Luke's Language

It is impossible here to discuss every detail of these peculiarities. We shall therefore confine ourselves to two questions: (i) Does the language of the first half of Acts (Chapters 1 to 15.35), or of the greater part of it, represent a 'translation Greek' which renders the Aramaic text of one or more source-documents? and (ii) How does Luke's language stand in relation to the *koine* and to Atticism?

(i) According to C. C. Torrey,[3] Acts 1.11–15.35 is Luke's translation of an Aramaic document written by a Palestinian Christian at the end of 49 or the beginning of 50, shortly after the Apostolic Council (p. 68), one which entered Luke's possession after he had come to Rome in 62 (p. 67): 'The book of Acts . . . was not a work of research, nor of any considerable labor. It was merely the translation of a single document—a lucky find—supplemented by a very brief outline of Paul's missionary labors, enlivened by miscellaneous personal reminiscences' (p. 68 n. 1). On pages 23–41 Torrey adduces fifty-two 'minor slips' of the translator (including over-literal renderings). He relies above all, however, on the conclusiveness of six especially striking examples of mistranslation[4] (pp. 10–22), where translation back into Aramaic allows the fault to be easily traced and put right.

[1] See Cadbury, *The Style* . . ., p. 5.
[2] In *The Style* . . ., pp. 39–72 (cf. also *JBL* 14 (1926), 190–209), Cadbury disproved the thesis supported by W. K. Hobart (*The Medical Language of St. Luke*, 1882), Zahn (*Einl.* III, 3rd ed., 160ff.) and Harnack (*Lucas der Arzt*, 1906; ET *Luke the Physician*, 1907), namely that Luke's use of words betrays 'Luke the physician': by the same criterion Lucian of Samosata would also have been a doctor. On p. 335 of *Urchristliche Literaturformen* (2nd & 3rd edd. 1912) Paul Wendland says that Luke's medical knowledge 'does not go beyond what is to be expected in educated laymen . . . Philo's knowledge in this field goes considerably farther than our author's, yet he was no doctor': cf. Cadbury, *The Making* . . ., pp. 118f., 178, 196, 219 & 358. Against the special plea that Luke's very interest in healings is proof enough that he was a physician, Cadbury objects: 'It is doubtful whether his interest in disease and healing exceeds that of his fellow-evangelists, or other contemporaries who were not doctors . . .' (*The Making* . . ., p. 358).
[3] Charles Cutler Torrey, *The Composition and Date of Acts*, Harvard Theological Studies I, 1916. By the same author: 'Facts and Fancy in Theories concerning Acts' in *American Journal of Theology* 23 (1919), 61ff. & 189ff.; *Our Translated Gospels: Some of the Evidence*, London and New York 1936; *Documents of the Primitive Church*, 1941.
[4] Acts 2.47, 3.16, 4.24f., 8.10, 11.28 and 15.7: see Commentary on these verses.

De Zwaan[1] only holds it likely that Acts **1**.1b–**5**.16 and **9**.31–**11**.18 derive from an Aramaic source, while W. Knox[2] demands an Aramaic original solely for **1**.1b–**5**.16.

Unfortunately Torrey neglected to compare the Septuagint usage in every case where he wanted to demonstrate an Aramaic substratum.[3] His contention that as a Hellenist Luke systematically reproduced the LXX wording for every OT quotation occurring in the Aramaic source (p. 58) overlooks the fact that in Chapters 2 and 15 the argument depends on the LXX text, and that the Hebrew text would have been useless for the purpose. Furthermore Torrey has enlisted, in support of his 'Aramaic' hypothesis, certain expressions which were perfectly admissible in the Greek of that time.[4] Again, Torrey, taking his stand on the *koine* (p. 7), denies that an Aramaic original was used in the second half of Acts, though the presumable semitisms in these later chapters are in no way distinct from those of the first half. Finally, Torrey did not fail to remark the correspondence in thought between the two sections of Acts (p. 65), but he did fail to notice the difficulty produced thereby: that the original author of the first part must have been 'a veritable *âme sœur* of Luke' (De Zwaan, op. cit., 55). All this—quite apart from the fact that his six stock examples of Lucan mistranslation are anything but convincing—goes to show that Torrey's thesis is untenable.

The phenomena claimed by Torrey as Aramaisms are, as H. F. D. Sparks[5] already saw, 'Septuagintisms'. It was to the Greek Old Testament, his own Holy Scripture, that Luke turned for the linguistic means of presenting the holy apostolic age, especially in Palestine: he had the Apostles speak a 'sacred tongue'.[6] But even apart from their speeches (in which he also used the liturgical heritage of the Christian community[7]), we encounter Septuagint words and phrases over and over again. Luke employed this medium in a most scrupulous and deliberate manner. For example, he calls Peter by that name, but in **15**.14 he makes the Lord's brother speak not of Peter but of Συμεών. By this periphrasis Luke shows the reader that James

---

[1] 'The Use of the Greek Language in Acts' in *Beg.* II, 30–65.
[2] *The Acts of the Apostles*, Cambridge 1948, 18.
[3] Of the alleged Aramaisms the expressions which Torrey criticizes in **11**.22a, **12**.3, **14**.2b and **15**.7, for example, derive from LXX.
[4] ῥύμην μίαν is for example 'sound *koine*' (De Zwaan, 59); ἐκπλησσόμενος ἐπί in **13**.12 is also 'good *koine* after verbs of emotion' (ibid) and οὐκ ἐγώ εἰμι in **13**.25 is 'quite sound vernacular Greek' (idem, 60).
[5] *JTS*, NS 1 (1950), 16–28.
[6] Jacquier, CXCII: 'He wrote what one might call "sacred prose", in imitation of LXX style.' But De Zwaan also (p. 53) warns against confusing 'sacred prose' and translation Greek.
[7] Acts **3**.16 & 26 and **4**.27 & 30. Jeremias says (*ThWb*, V, 700f.): 'This simple liturgical formula is very old . . . The title survived in the gentile Church . . . as a liturgical formula which crystallized at an early date and was anchored in the eucharistic prayer, the doxology and the general confession.'

is employing the Semitic form שָׁעֹין and is therefore speaking ἑβραΐδι διαλέκτῳ, i.e. in Aramaic.[1] There is the same implication when the exalted Lord addresses Paul as Σαούλ on the road to Damascus: in 26.14 it is expressly stated that Christ spoke in Aramaic. Here we have already met with one of those passages in the second half of Acts where Luke felt obliged to use 'biblical' utterance. That is why here too alleged 'semitisms' occur. Acts 26.14–18 is in fact splendid evidence of the forethought with which Luke went to work: Paul is speaking to a mixed audience of Jews and educated gentiles; Luke takes both parties into account, and this determines his rendering of Christ's words: alongside biblical phrases stands the Greek proverb of the goads.[2]

And so no case can be made out for 'translation Greek'.

(ii) We now come to the second linguistic problem which we propose to discuss: the relationship of Acts to the *koine* and 'Atticism'. Albert Wifstrand[3] has shown that Luke is uninfluenced by Atticism. He employs the educated written language of Hellenism, which in his time was as yet untouched by classicism and Atticism. If there are nevertheless quite a few Attic elements, it is because the written language of the Hellenistic age had preserved a certain continuity with the Attic literary language of the fourth century B.C. Spoken *koine* Greek, on the other hand, diverged far more sharply from the everyday Attic of that time. It is to the Attic heritage of the Hellenistic written language that we may attach, in Acts, the use of the optative (whether in a potential clause, as in 5.24 or 10.17, or in a conditional clause, as in 17.27, 24.19, 25.20 or 27.12), of the future participle and infinitive and of the occasional negation of the participle by οὐ (Wifstrand. 141f.). Wifstrand also points, quite rightly, to the LXX style from which are derived many of the details held to be classicisms by Eduard Norden.

Luke is at his most 'literary', from the viewpoint of Hellenistic written language, in the four scenes where the subject matter demands it: 17.16–34, 19.21–40, 24.1–23 and Chapter 26. But the first part of Acts also contains such 'literary' passages, e.g. Gamaliel's speech, 5.35–9, and others are to be found in the second half apart from the four scenes mentioned, e.g. Paul's

---

[1] Grotesque misconceptions of the situation are to be found in two articles: Donald W. Riddle, 'The Cephas-Peter Problem and a possible Solution' in *JBL* 59 (1940), 169–80, and Donald Fay Robinson, 'Where and When did Peter die?' in *JBL* 64 (1945), 255–67: Simon and Peter are supposed to have been two different early Christian leaders whose identities were only merged by later tradition. Robinson says the Symeon of 15.14 was the Symeon Niger of 13.1, while Peter was executed in 44: 'he went to another place' (Acts 12.17) (!)

[2] Acts 26.14, σκληρόν σοι κτλ. beside Ezek. 2.1 & 3, Jer. 1.7 and Isaiah 33.5, 42.7 & 16 and 61.1.

[3] 'Lukas och den grekiska klassicismen' in *SEÅ* V (1940), 139–51, and 'Det grekiska prosaspråket: en historisk översikt' in *Eranos* 50 (1952), 149–63. Cf. also a dissertation by Wifstrand's pupil, Jonas Palm, 'Über Sprache und Stil des Diodoros von Sizilien: ein Beitrag zur Beleuchtung der hellenistischen Prosa', Lund 1955, and A. Debrunner's review of it in *Gnomon* 28 (1956) esp. 588.

words to the tribune, **21**.39. Yet even in the four renowned scenes—on the Areopagus, in Ephesus, before Felix, before Agrippa—Luke's stylistic prowess leaves something to be desired. Codex D finds the threefold ἐν of **17**.31 troublesome, and therefore discards ἐν ᾗ μέλλει. The town-clerk's great speech in **19**.35–40 ends in obscurity, for no interpreter is sure what he should do with the three περί-expressions (D already offers a forceful correction). But even the elegant utterances of Tertullus (**24**.2–8) tail off into three parallel relative clauses, and it has long been recognized that Paul's speech before Agrippa departs from exemplary Greek with ὧν . . . μελλόντων. Small wonder that textual corruption has been suspected in such cases, since we hardly expect such lapses from the *auctor ad Theophilum*. In using this familiar description we are usually thinking of Luke **1**.1–4 and assuming that a writer capable of so beautiful a period must also have written elegant Greek elsewhere, especially where the subject matter called for it. But at that time a zealously cultivated technique, which anyone could learn, facilitated the composition of such prologues.[1] Moreover, there were plenty of writings whose prologues could serve as models. We may not therefore draw any conclusions from the special case of Luke's prologue.

Furthermore, Blass and Cadbury[2] have demonstrated that even this prologue is not linguistically unimpeachable. Luke begins with ἐπειδήπερ— in normal usage this word would be preceded by the main clause. But Luke uses it as he does because it is weightier and sounds loftier than mere ἐπειδή. Probably πεπληροφορημένων is another case in point—Luke 'might have written πληρωθέντων' for this grandiloquent word, and it would have been clearer (Blass, op. cit., 8). καθώς being frowned upon by the Atticists, D substitutes the 'correct' καθά.

In Acts **26**.4, where Luke is particularly anxious to use high literary style, he writes the form ἴσασι—elsewhere he employs the vulgar οἴδασι, as in Luke **11**.44. The number of *koine* forms in verbs and nouns is far from negligible, beginning with such forms as εἶπαν and χάριτα (**24**.27). It is particularly striking that Luke puts εἰς for ἐν—Wendt took great pains to demonstrate, in these cases of allegedly 'pregnant' usage, the after-effect of an earlier movement reflected in the εἰς. No less Hellenistic is the replacement of ἐκεῖ by ἐκεῖσε in **21**.3 and **22**.5, the use of reinforced expressions such as ἕως ἐπί in **17**.14 and ἕως εἰς in **26**.11, or the intrusion of ὅστις in the rôle of the simple relative, so that it no longer means 'everyone who' or 'every such'. πρότερος is replaced by the Hellenistic πρῶτος, which puts paid to

---

[1] Cadbury, *The Making* . . ., pp. 194f.: 'Neither the ancient Greek writers nor the Semitic authors used prefaces. They came into vogue in the Hellenistic age.' In LXX they are used only by Jesus Sirach and the author of II Maccabees—'The contents of the preface were prescribed by rhetorical rulebooks, largely on the basis of the technique of the orator's exordium.'

[2] F. Blass, *Philology of the Gospels*, London 1898, 7–20; Cadbury, *Beg.* II, 489–510.

Zahn's thesis that Luke intended to write a third book (see Commentary on 1.1). In **19**.16 ἀμφότεροι must simply mean 'all', even though the examples we have of this vulgar usage are rare and late.[1] But we should not forget that for everyday spoken Greek we have nothing like the mass of evidence we possess for literary Greek.

If we take into account all the linguistic observations made by scholars, we can hardly reject Radermacher's judgment: 'Luke possesses the determining characteristics of a *koine*-writer. He writes the language of the people with a slight varnish, inasmuch as he has appropriated, perhaps from school, perhaps from reading, individual words and expressions which were no longer current in popular speech.'[2]

With good reason De Zwaan had pointed out that, especially in the first half of Acts, Luke did not make things easy for his Greek readers.[3] Certainly even in those days people appreciated the fascination of the oriental, and could put a positive value on the 'barbarous', when it promised to impart religious mysteries. But any reader not to some extent familiar with the Septuagint, the holy book of the Gentile Christians, must at times have shaken his head sadly over the Greek of Acts. The book was not written for strangers to whom things Christian were *terra incognita*.

C. The Peculiarities of Lucan Style

It is not easy to define the individuality of Lucan style. We cannot speak of a Lucan style in the sense in which we speak of the style of Tacitus, which stamps every sentence of the *Annals*. We may indeed point to certain words, expressions, turns of phrase, for which Luke appears to have a special liking. But here we must ask ourselves to what extent Luke thereby distinguishes himself from contemporary writers of similar cultural background. For example, he likes to use ἱκανός in the sense of 'great' or 'much.' The word can be seen gradually acquiring this sense in the later books of LXX—μέγας and πολύς are so hackneyed! What is 'Lucan,' therefore, is probably only the frequency of his use of the word.

It is perhaps the same with relative clauses, which are frequently main clauses introduced by a relative. Acts **11**.23, for example, ὃς παραγενόμενος ... ἐχάρη κτλ, is a regular main clause whose introduction by a relative looks like a Latinism. But a contemporary of Luke's, Diodorus Siculus, has 53 sentences introduced by a relative in each of Books XIII and XIX, while Agatharchides, in the second century B.C., seems to have employed the relative connection even more frequently.[4] Luke therefore was not the only

---

[1] See *Beg.* IV, 241f.
[2] Radermacher, 25.
[3] *Beg.* II, 65.
[4] Palm, op. cit. p. 75 n.3 above, p. 69.

writer of his time to favour this construction. Nevertheless, it belongs among the peculiarities of his style.

Worthy of special note is the quite frequent use of καί after a relative pronoun. The καί should be omitted in translation. When, for example, it is said of the two men in white raiment, in **1**.11, οἳ καὶ εἶπαν, this is not to be explained, with Bernhard Weiss,[1] in the sense that they let themselves be *not only* seen *but also* heard. The meaning is simply 'These said'. Likewise, in **28**.28, αὐτοὶ καὶ ἀκούσονται does not mean 'They will also hear' but stresses 'They will hear.' This καί also is not *in itself* a characteristic of Lucan style, but only by virtue of its frequency, for Justin and Eusebius also employ it.

In order to enliven the narrative, Luke occasionally resorts to the same stylistic device: omission of the verb '(he) said,' as in **2**.38: Πέτρος δὲ πρὸς αὐτούς. Most MSS. naturally insert ἔφη or φησιν. But instances such as **5**.9, **9**.11 or **26**.27 show that Luke really intended to ensure the vitality of the scene by this means.

Similarly with the transition from indirect to direct speech.[2] Some have supposed Luke simply incapable of sustaining indirect speech.[3] But this is to underrate his ability and individuality as a writer. This transition occurs frequently between Acts **1**.4 and **25**.5 and is intended to avert stiffness in the presentation. The converse transition to indirect speech is to be found in **23**.24.

Litotes—e.g. the famous 'no mean city'—offers a further example of Lucan style, again revealing his attachment to his age. 'In Hellenistic times,' writes Wifstrand's pupil Jonas Palm,[4] 'litotes was clearly a feature of studied language.' He goes on to note the following instances in Acts: **12**.18, **14**.28, **17**.4 & 12, **19**.11 & 23f., **20**.12, **21**.39, **27**.20 and **28**.2, then has this remark: litotes 'is at times rather pointless here; it is evidently regarded as no more than a refinement, as is perhaps also the word ἱκανός, similar to litotes. All the examples are very stereotyped'.

Even the occasional freedom of word-order which we encounter in Acts is not exclusive to Luke but widespread in Hellenistic literature. It should however be acknowledged that Luke has made discreet and meaningful use of this freedom. Sometimes he displaces the words because he meets with specific difficulties of formulation. Thus in **11**.22 the expression ἠκούσθη εἰς τὰ ὦτα (cf. Isaiah **5**.9 LXX) could not be too widely pulled apart; hence περὶ αὐτῶν had to go to the end. In **20**.3 the author was in direr straits: the genitive absolute after ποιήσας was an unhappy start, and now this genitive, γενομένης ἐπιβουλῆς, could not very well be separated from αὐτῷ; on the

---

[1] *Die Apostelgeschichte*, Textkritische Untersuchungen und Textherstellung, Leipzig 1893 (=TU IX 3/4), 74.
[2] Luke **5**.14; Acts **1**.4, **14**.22, **17**.3, **23**.22 and **25**.5.
[3] Bl.-Debr. § 470, 2.
[4] Op. cit., p. 75 n.3 above, 155.

other hand, τῶν Ἰουδαίων could not be held back for the μέλλοντι ... Συρίαν which is the logical continuation of αὐτῷ. Thus the tangle of words here betokens a difficulty the writer could not quite work out. Considerations of rhythm must have determined the division of τοῦτο τὸ μέρος in **19**.27 and the strange word-order of ἀνὴρ ἀδύνατος κτλ in **14**.8. But in the majority of cases Luke displaces words in order to bring what is being stressed into the emphatic positions, i.e. the beginning and the end. In **10**.28 he wishes to emphasize that Peter has learned to call no man unclean, whoever he may be. He achieves this emphasis by putting μηδένα at the beginning of the clause and ἄνθρωπον at the end, with κοινὸν ἢ ἀκάθαρτον λέγειν in the middle. Similarly in the case of **13**.23: 'of his seed' is to be stressed, consequently τούτου goes to the beginning and σπέρματος to the end. We have doubtless another case of this kind in **21**.20, where τῶν πεπιστευκότων does not immediately follow πόσαι μυριάδες. Likewise the purpose of the inversion is clear at **19**.26, where the opening words οὐ μόνον Ἐφέσου ... Ἀσίας depend on the final ἱκανὸν ὄχλον. Once one is familiar with this Lucan stylistic artifice, even the text of **12**.25 is no longer a problem: εἰς Ἱερουσαλὴμ πληρώσαντες τὴν διακονίαν belong together, and show the accentuated ideas at the beginning and the end.[1] Probably the most striking inversion occurs in **4**.33. At first glance the text appears to refer to 'Apostles of the Lord Jesus'. But in fact Luke is speaking of 'witness of the resurrection of the Lord Jesus', and because he wishes to emphasize both the Apostles' attestation and the overwhelming fact of the Resurrection he places τὸ μαρτύριον at the beginning and τῆς ἀναστάσεως at the end of the whole. Most manuscripts have 'normalized' the word-order in one way or another,[2] thus destroying the verse's distinct Lucan flavour; B in contrast here stands vindicated once again.

'Like the rest of us (Luke) has the habit of soon repeating a word when he has used it.[3] Hence certain words and expressions occur in one part of his writings and others in another part. It is unwise to attribute these phenomena to his sources,[4] for his Greek sources at least are largely recast in his copying of them.' Here[5] as usual Cadbury is correct in his observations.

---

[1] See Commentary on this verse.

[2] אA: τῆς ἀναστάσεως Ἰησοῦ Χριστοῦ τοῦ κυρίου; Pap.[8] D: τῆς ἀναστάσεως τοῦ κυρίου Ἰησοῦ Χριστοῦ: ℜ τῆς ἀναστάσεως τοῦ κυρίου Ἰησοῦ.

[3] Examples: **19**.35f. καταστέλλω; **19**.38 & 40 ἐγκαλέω; **20**.1f. παρακαλέσας. Theodor Vogel (*Zur Charakteristik des Lukas nach Sprache und Stil*, 2nd ed., Leipzig 1899, 17) had already drawn attention to the matter (**9**.13, 32, 41 ἅγιοι; **13**.46 & 48 ζωὴ αἰώνιος; **15**.32 & 41 ἐπιστηρίζω; **5**.29 & 32 πειθαρχέω; **2**.42 & 46 προσκαρτεροῦντες).

[4] As did H. Waitz in respect of the repetitions of **8**.6 & 10 ('Die Quellen der Philippusgeschichte in der Apostelgeschichte **8**.5–40' in *ZNW* 7 (1906), 340–55). But μαγεύων καὶ ἐξιστάνων (**8**.9) is repeated by μαγείαις ἐξεστακέναι (**8**.11), and here Waitz does not speak in terms of source-differences.

[5] *The Making of Luke-Acts*, 218f.

Cadbury has also pointed out[1] the versatility of Lucan style. It was taken for granted by Luke that Apostles should speak with dignified biblical expressions, especially on solemn occasions. Thus came into being those speeches which to our ears have a remarkably stilted, not to say artificial ring: those speeches of Paul (**13.10f.**), Peter (**15.7–11**) and James (**15.14–21**) that have so troubled the exegetes. But when Luke does not feel compelled by the occasion to employ these solemn tones, he is capable of painting a scene easily and expansively, dwelling lovingly on details, in almost conversational tones, as in the visit of Paul's nephew to the tribune, **23.17ff.** Luke may have found the story of the rescue of Peter (Ch. 12), with its popular bluntness, in tradition—left to himself, he would probably have had the angel treat Peter with a little more courtesy!—but he left this down-to-earth style untouched because it renders so credible the reality of this miraculous incident. In **25.22** Luke puts in the mouth of the Procurator Festus a phrase which in its Roman curtness ('*cras audies eum*') recalls the more famous *quod scripsi scripsi* of Pilate (John **19.22**). He can provide the orator Tertullus with a set-piece of rhetoric (**24.2–8**), let Demetrius incite the workers (**19.25–7**), and again portray the Christians as they fall weeping on the neck of Paul, who is marked for death (**20.37**). He varies his style according to the tone required and the situation he is depicting, and the stylistic contrast in the alternation of dry log-book and exciting 'legends' does much to heighten the effect.

At first this stylistic versatility is less impressive than the monumental monotony we find in Tacitus. But Luke's readers must have been grateful for a variety which did not drill life into the uniform grey of pessimism. Similarly they will not have felt it a defect, as modern critics do, that Luke, although he had all the necessary stylistic capabilities, painted no individual portraits of the Apostles.[2] Peter and Paul are figures drawn from the same model: they embody the apostolic ideal as seen through the eyes of Luke's age. That they preached the same doctrine Luke would not have doubted for a moment. What difference, then, remained to be indicated, save that the Paul of the later chapters should appear more Hellenistic than the man who preached in Pisidian Antioch and the orator of Pentecost?

Bibliography

V. H. Stanton, 'Style and Authorship in the Acts of the Apostles', *JTS* 24 (1922–3), 362–81; W. G. Letham, 'Luke's Literary Method as a Controlling Factor in the Composition of Acts' (diss.), Divinity School, University of Chicago, 1926; D. W. Riddle, 'The Logic of the Theory of Translation

---

[1] Op. cit., 221ff.
[2] Dibelius judges somewhat differently: *Studies*, 182.

Greek', *JBL* 51 (1932), 13–30; G. A. Barton, 'Prof. Torrey's Theory of the Aramaic Origin of the Gospels and the First Half of the Acts of the Apostles', *JTS* 36 (1935), 357–73; H. F. D. Sparks, 'Some Observations on the Semitic Background of the N.T.' in *Novi Test. Soc. Bulletin* II, 1951, 33–42; N. Turner, 'The Relation of Luke I and II to Hebraic Sources and to the Rest of Luke-Acts', *NTS* 2 (1955–6), 100–9.

6. THE SOURCE-QUESTION

Scholars have long been in suspense over the question of sources in Acts.[1] Even today it has not been finally answered. Form-criticism, with its interest in the smaller units[2] and in the literary and theological composition,[3] pushed the source-problem into the background. This was not unjustified: during the long period of preoccupation with 'What really happened?'— and this question was the motive force behind source-research— scholars had failed to do justice to the aim and intentions of the biblical writings. Nevertheless, Form-criticism by no means 'disposed' of the source-question once and for all—certainly not in so difficult a case as that of Acts. No more than the third gospel can this voluminous work have arisen without 'sources.'

But—and this is what makes the source-problem in Acts so difficult— comparison with Luke's Gospel is full of risk. For the situation in Acts is utterly different. We are in possession of one of the sources for Luke: the Gospel of Mark. Another—Q—can to a large extent be inferred. In the case of Acts we are not in the happy position of possessing one of its sources. This is the more regrettable since Luke, as we have learned from comparing him with Mark, subjects his sources to a stylistic revision which renders their reconstitution impossible from his text alone.[4] We may assume that he did not treat the underlying sources of Acts any differently. No sources can therefore be discerned in Acts by stylistic criteria.[5]

On the other hand it is highly improbable that Luke had so many and varied sources at his command for Acts as for his gospel. The Apostles and

---

[1] See 24–34 above.
[2] See 34–39 above.
[3] See 39–50 above.
[4] This is the real significance of Harnack's finding that the 'we'-passages are not stylistically distinct from the rest of the book. Cf. F. C. Burkitt's outstanding investigation, 'The Use of Mark in the Gospel according to Luke' in *Beg.* II, 106–20. It is only when we place Mark and Luke side by side that we can see the style of the second Evangelist 'shining through' that of the third (so C. S. C. Williams, *The Acts of the Apostles*, 1957, 6).
[5] It has occasionally been held as a pointer to Aramaic sources that the first half of Acts sounds so much more Semitic than the second (see pp. 28f. & 73ff. above). But this phenomenon is simply due, in fact, to a more intensive use of 'biblical' language (see pp. 74f. above).

other Christian missionaries did not proclaim their own words and deeds, but those of the Lord Jesus. Hence no tradition corresponding to the Synoptic had formed with reference to Paul and the Apostles.[1] Certainly we encounter miracle-stories in Acts—mostly concerning Peter—which resemble those in the Synoptic Gospels and are probably not uninfluenced by them.[2] But the *speeches*[3] do not in Acts, as in the Synoptic Gospels, consist of individual logia which gradually grew together, but are literary compositions thought out to the last detail. Admittedly they did not come to the author out of the blue: the kerygma of Jesus and scriptural warrant are behind the missionary sermons of Acts[4] as the biography of Paul and the story of his conversion stand behind his great apologetic discourses. Those who naively believe that Luke went to work with Acts in exactly the same way as with his gospel[5] fail to notice that their opinion rests on an untenable assumption: there just were no 'histories of the Apostles' which Luke could have woven together as, in the case of the third gospel, he wove together Mark, Q, and that other gospel from which he derived his special material.

This is not to deny that in some sections of Acts Luke was able to make use of written 'sources'. Two such hypothetical sources deserve serious consideration: the 'Antiochene source' and the 'travel-journal'. But precisely here we encounter peculiarly difficult problems. To see these clearly, we shall do well to look first at the *story of Stephen*.

Here the account of the martyrdom is broken off in the middle of the description of the stoning (Acts 7.58b), and the author inserts the detail that the witnesses laid their garments at the feet of a young man—he was to guard them, as 22.20 will add. In this way Paul is drawn into the sombre affair. But here is the astounding thing: the martyrdom of Stephen did not mention Paul at all! Luke however knew (like probably every Christian of his time) that 'Paul persecuted the Church' (cf. Acts 9.21 and Gal. 1.13). But for Luke there was in those early days only one Church: that of Jerusalem. He must

---

[1] See Dibelius, 'Zur Formgeschichte des Neuen Testaments' (*ThR*, New Series 3, 1931, 207–42), 236; *Studies*, 2f., 124, 146, 196.

[2] The awakening of Tabitha especially is reminiscent of the awakening of Jairus' daughter with '*Talitha qum*' in Mark 5.41. But Δορκάς was already in the source. Wellhausen (p. 20) was of the opinion that 'The captain of Capernaum has probably rightly been considered the model of Captain Cornelius.'

[3] See Cadbury, *The Making of Luke-Acts*, London 1927 (reprinted 1958) 61; Dibelius, *Studies*, 138–85; and Ulrich Wilckens, *Die Missionsreden der Apostelgeschichte*, Neukirchen 2nd edn. 1967.

[4] Dibelius, *Formgeschichte des Evangeliums*, 2nd ed., 15f. (ET *From Tradition to Gospel*), and *Studies*, 165; C. H. Dodd, *The Apostolic Preaching and its Developments*, 2nd ed., 1951.

[5] Certainly fragments of different provenance succeed one another in Acts too, but there is no question of a blocklike juxtaposition of sources. Moreover Dom Jacques Dupont has shown, with specific reference to the Beatitudes (in *Les deux versions du Sermon sur la montagne et des Béatitudes*, Louvain 1958), what freedom Luke allowed himself, even in the Gospel, in expounding and interpreting his material.

necessarily conclude that this was the Church which Paul persecuted. If now the source maintained a puzzling silence on the fact, what was missing had to be supplied and inserted. Hence the sentence about the 'witnesses', which told the reader that Saul/Paul was present in person at the stoning and—as is added expressly in **8.1**—approved of it. Only, even this did not amount to showing that 'Paul persecuted the Church'. For this reason Luke dared the bold leap of **8.3**: he suddenly turns the approving onlooker[1] Saul into the only persecutor who is even so much as named, and no sooner is he converted than the Church has peace (**9.31**). Later (**26.10ff.**) Luke gives us in detail his idea of this persecution: Saul was one of the judges at the many trials of Christians, and he always voted for the death-penalty! The old tradition knew indeed of only a single victim, Stephen. Luke, however, conceived of the situation differently—otherwise there would have been no Pauline persecution of Christians in Jerusalem! Stephen's trial marked the beginning of a long series of similar incidents. Yet not content with this, so Luke inferred, Saul carried his persecutions into the 'cities without' Jerusalem, hence as far afield as Damascus.[2] In this way Luke neatly dovetails the story of Stephen with his next item of tradition: the account current among the communities of Paul's conversion before Damascus.[3]

We see, then, that here Luke had no continuous source at his disposal (the same holds for chapters 1 to 5)[4]. He seeks to supply this deficiency by drawing conclusions from the information available and adding complementary details. In this he is guided by certain preconceptions as to the course and the coherence of the history of the primitive Church.

To this extent the source-question and the author's procedure are relatively clear. But the question now arises: did Luke use only an isolated account of a martyrdom[5] or was this account already part of a larger whole, an 'Antiochene source'? The latter answer is suggested by Luke's mention, in the introduction to the Stephen episode (**6.1ff.**), of a dispute between 'Hellenists' and 'Hebrews', hence a conflict between groups within the primitive Church. This is scarcely in harmony with the ideal picture of this

---

[1] Cf. Dibelius, *Studies*, 208. When Albert Schweitzer maintains (*Die Mystik des Apostels Paulus*, Tübingen 1930, 154 n. 1. ET *The Mysticism of Paul the Apostle*, 2nd ed., London 1956.) that the witnesses' laying of their garments at the feet of Saul 'makes him recognizable as the leader of the action,' he is disregarding **22.20**. When he goes on to find in the mention of witnesses proof of a 'regular execution as described in the Mishnah tractate Sanhedrin', he is overlooking the fact that in this very tractate a wholly different method of stoning is described, which would rule out any kneeling-down on the part of Stephen. The traditional view of the scene is so powerful that it distorts the better judgment even in a book so rich in inspired insights as this one.

[2] Luke has caused his interpreters much trouble with this historical reconstruction. He was unaware that the High Priest enjoyed no right of arrest in Damascus. See p. 320 n.2 below.

[3] Cf. § 7 below, pp. 107–110.

[4] This is now fairly generally admitted.

[5] So Dibelius, *Studies*, 176 n. 68.

community which Luke otherwise paints for the reader. It follows that he did not invent it but received it from some tradition. Moreover, in **6.5** he presents us with a list of the 'Seven' which almost certainly did not flutter down on to his desk as an isolated note. But Luke's information about the preaching to the Gentiles in Antioch (**11.**19f.), the Antiochian origin of the name 'Christian' (**11.**26), the prophecy of Agabus and the 'Jerusalem fund' (**11.**27–30) has also been regarded as drawn from such an Antiochene source, to which might also have belonged in some form the account of the so-called first missionary journey (**13.**1ff.).

We can therefore understand why in 'Zur Frage nach den Quellen der Apostelgeschichte' (*New Testament Essays*, edited by A. J. B. Higgins, Manchester 1959, 68–80) Rudolf Bultmann should have opted for a hypothetical Antiochene source, a chronicle of this community which the author of Acts unearthed from the archives of Antioch (Wendt and Jeremias[1] had already postulated an Antiochene source, without, however, indicating how Luke came to know of it).

But there are two problems which damp our enthusiasm for this suggestion. We have in the first place the riddle of how this chronicle could have come into being: a generation which thinks itself the last does not write for posterity.[2] What could then have moved the Christians of Antioch to record the events leading to the foundation of their community, together with its subsequent deeds and experiences?[3] In the second place it seems inconceivable that the author of Acts should have twisted what he read in this old chronicle into its very opposite, as must have happened in his account of the election of the Seven.[4] After all, he was not simply dealing with any mere rumour that could and must be corrected, but with the truth as set down by the eyewitnesses of the actual events!

So we need not be surprised that Etienne Trocmé—and in this he too is the heir of a worthy tradition—should advocate another view of the source on which Luke drew for his knowledge of the past: it was an itinerary— *un diaire*—which Luke had at his disposal.[5] Paul, on his missionary travels,

---

[1] H. H. Wendt, 'Die Hauptquelle der Apostelgeschichte' in *ZNW* 24 (1925), 293–305, and Joachim Jeremias, 'Die antiochenische Quelle und die Datierung der ersten Missionsreise' in 'Untersuchungen zum Quellenproblem der Apostelgeschichte' (*ZNW* 36 (1937), 205–21) 213–20. See below, literature to § 34.

[2] Cf. Dibelius, *Studies* 103.

[3] At most it might have been a question of an account of their history in self-vindication over against Jerusalem. But when the dispute with the Jerusalem community arose—for the latter apparently did not at first concern itself with the distant and essentially gentile community—it was about the concrete question of circumcision.

[4] See Commentary on **6.**1–7, pp. 264ff. below.

[5] Trocmé (*Le Livre des Actes et l'histoire*, 1957) 134–40. Trocmé indeed admits (p. 135) that we possess no document of this kind from antiquity, but he asserts that the analogy of later times is evidence enough. He is here, however, in a more favourable position than he suspects; A. D. Nock (*Gnomon* 25 (1953), 500) draws attention to examples

from time to time got an assistant to record the day's events with a few brief notes, or even set pen to paper himself when the occasion required. Eventually it was Luke who kept this journal, and much later he made use of it when he set about the composition of Acts (Trocmé, 138). Here then is another very plausible theory although, on closer examination, it too leaves room for doubt.

Evidently the brief notices of the day's events in **16.**11f. and **20.**5–**21.**18 have been thought to imply such a hypothesis as this. For it is only in these two sections that we find, at one and the same time, both the 'we' implying that the writer was Paul's companion[1] and the day-by-day description of the journey. One is naturally tempted to assume the same source for every travel-report in Acts. But Dibelius has already drawn attention to the fact that the 'we' may just as well represent the author's last-minute embellishment as an original component of an old source (*Studies*, 104f., 205f.). In **16.**16f., for example, it occurs in an episode which is not part of a travel-journal but a separate, self-contained story. It has obviously been taken over as a link from the preceding journal-entries. If **27.**1–6 is examined closely, it will be seen that the 'we' is by no means entirely appropriate: it has been inserted in order to lend the narrative of the voyage the appearance of a fellow-traveller's account. This points to the conclusion that the 'we' was in fact used here as a stylistic device.

Trocmé believes that the author of the book was Luke the companion of Paul. If we should conclude (see Intro. § 8 below) that this assumption is unacceptable, we are immediately faced with the problem of how this travel-journal could have come into the hands of the author. But that is not all: it is also a question whether the extremely meagre and obscure details (Barjesus—Elymas!) have been taken from a travel-diary at all. It is no less questionable whether Paul really kept a diary on the long journey from Ephesus to Caesarea and Antioch, then back again to Ephesus across the whole of Asia Minor. What exactly would have been the use to him of this '*diaire*', of which his epistles give no hint? After his separation from Barnabas, Paul carried on his mission in independence of any local congregation, at his own risk and answerable to no earthly master. If in Antioch he related his missionary travels (**18.**22), he did not need to enumerate every stage of the journey. Finally, who can believe that when in Cenchreae Paul would have confided to such a diary that he had had his hair cut (**18.**18)—quite apart from the facts that a Nazirite vow could only be absolved by having

---

of such journals. According to Trocmé, Paul used the '*diaire*' as an '*aide-mémoire*'. This is doubtless preferable to Dibelius' explanation of it as 'a catalogue of resting-places such as it was probably the custom to draw up on such journeys, for the practical purpose of being able to rediscover the route and the former hosts should the journey be repeated' (*Studies*, 199).

[1] In the 'Western' text's 'we' at **11.**28 this is simply not the case.

the hair cut in Jerusalem and that the 'quasi-Nazirite private vow' has been invented by the commentators to suit only this passage and no other)?

But have we in fact only the choice between a travel-journal[1] and the chronicle of Antioch? Not at all. When, years after Paul had run his course, Luke set about the task of describing the era of primitive Christianity, various possibilities of collecting the required material lay open to him.[2] He could himself, for example, look up the most important Pauline communities— say Philippi, Corinth, Ephesus, Antioch. He might even visit Jerusalem. But it was also possible for him to ask other Christians travelling to these places to glean for him whatever was still known of the old times (if he was preparing Acts about the year 75, twenty years would not yet have elapsed since Paul's death, and perhaps forty from the foundation of the community in Antioch). Lastly, he could have written to the congregations in question and asked them for information. Yet in each of these cases, whether the author himself listened to the reminiscences of older members of the congregations and then wrote them up, or received the reports of his informants or replies to letters, he had before him a collection of reports which may well have included some of the

---

[1] In his article, 'Die Fragwürdigkeit eines Itinerars der Paulusreisen' (*TLZ* 84 (1959), 165–74), G. Schille has demonstrated that Dibelius' arguments in favour of the use of an itinerary in Acts 13 to 21 do not hold water. His own solution is indicated by his closing sentences: The itinerary-hypothesis 'is perhaps no more than a last vestige of those source-theories which M. Dibelius so severely castigated. His reference to Luke's literary capacity throws light upon more things than even Dibelius himself assumed.' Luke's literary capacity is thus to explain what was previously accounted for by the assumption of an itinerary. Yet one should not overwork the discovery that at times (e.g. Acts 25.13–22) Luke was capable of entirely independent composition. Schille takes his picture of Paul's missionary proceedings from Didache 11.4–6: the Apostle was not allowed to spend more than two days in one place. 'Presumably, then, Paul's so-called travelling-companions were independent fellow-workers who followed in the footprints of the founder of communities. One must therefore be prepared to find a great part of the "Pauline mission" was Pauline at most in that Paul led the way' (p. 174). Other considerations apart, Schille is here misapplying to Paul a rule designed for an entirely different age—two generations later— and an entirely different situation, when it was a question of regulating the activity of wandering preachers among congregations already organized under monarchic bishops. Paul was after all a founder of congregations where nothing existed, whereas the 'apostles and prophets' in the Didache, already become suspect, were active in Christian communities of long standing and had to be prevented from becoming a burden upon them. The rule for the early Christian mission in Mark 6.10 *Par.* presupposes a fairly long stay by the mission-aries in one place: this is clear precisely from the prohibition against changing hosts during this period. A community cannot be founded overnight, and the Didache does not justify our dismissing all references to Paul's staying longer in one place. Our examination above of the possible ways in which Luke could have obtained his material on the Pauline mission, and to a large extent its arrangement, shows that we are not reduced to the mere choice between a weak itinerary-hypothesis and Luke's 'story-telling' capacity.

[2] This is no modernization! We can see from the third gospel what pains Luke took over sources: it can by no means be taken for granted that Mark's gospel was available in his congregation, and in addition he procured the gospel from which he derived his special material, and further also 'Q'. For Acts, the material was not easier but harder to come by, and only one who considered the task highly important would have undertaken the toil involved.

episodes which we now find woven into the descriptions of travel.[1] It is entirely possible that from Philippi Luke received the diary of one of those men who, as representatives of that community, had accompanied Paul from there to Jerusalem with the large fund that had been collected, and gladly incorporated it, with only a slight amount of editing, in his book. It would be wholly understandable that least should be known about the very first missionary journey (Chapters 13 and 14) and that the remembrance of what took place at the court of Sergius Paulus should have become somewhat dim; it is hard to say whether—apart from the names of the Seven and the later venerated teachers—people in Antioch would have retained exact knowledge of the conflict over the widows. At all events, in this way we can quite well understand the greater part of the material which Luke introduces into Acts as tradition that has undergone a literary revision at his hands. The fact that the description of the journey to Rome shows these signs of literary revision in special measure impelled Dibelius (*Studies*, 205) to assume that Luke was here using 'a "secular" representation of voyaging and shipwreck as example, model or source'. The correct view will be that here there was no travel-diary (the papyrus-scroll—or would it have been a codex?—would scarcely have survived the shipwreck[2]), but a tale told from memory which Luke then enriched with interpolations.

Of course this still does not answer the historian's question as to the real events underlying the stories of Acts: we have done no more than indicate certain possible ways in which Luke may have come by his material. The historical value of the single item of information will have to be weighed more exactly where appropriate in the Commentary. Here we can only discuss a few individual cases by way of example.

(a) That Luke in general used written sources is suggested by **18**.18–22 (see pp. 542–8 below). The somewhat meaningless text 'and he left them there' (in Ephesus) 'but he himself entered into the synagogue'—which also was in Ephesus (moreover it is hard to see why the pious couple, whom we actually meet in the synagogue in **18**.26, did not accompany him)—can only be understood properly on the assumption that the text before Luke ran 'and he left them there, but he himself sailed away from Ephesus' (cf. verse 21). Luke would then have added the rest in order to secure for Paul the first preaching of Christ in Ephesus and thereby make him the real founder of the Church there. We learn however from **18**.27 and **19**.9 (see p. 559 below) that a Jewish Christian community already existed within the fold of the synagogue. Paul however later, after three months' activity, formed the

---

[1] This may explain the interpolations which appear to be present in **14**.8–20, **18**.18–21, **20**.16–**21**.1 etc., and also helps one understand the insertions in Chapter 27 (see commentary on these passages).

[2] A. D. Nock, *Gnomon* 25 (1953) 499 n. 3: but 'authentic transcription of the recollections of an eyewitness'.

Christians into a congregation independent of the synagogue. To that extent he is in fact the founder of the self-contained Christian community of Ephesus. Hence Luke intended by his interpolation to underline and magnify Paul's importance for the Ephesian community.

(b) If Luke gathered his sources in the manner indicated above (p. 86f.), he probably received accounts not only of journeys but of striking incidents that had lodged in the memory—even legends that had grown up in the meantime might thus have come to his notice. The episode in **16**.25–34 may for instance be explained in this way: it is entirely possible that Paul's erstwhile jailer later became a Christian, and that it was then even said that Paul himself had baptized him. Luke would then have recounted this conversion with all the resources of Hellenistic narrative art (see p. 501 below). Similarly in the case of **14**.8–18 (see pp. 430–4 below): the healing of the unnamed cripple—it is typical of old healing stories not to give the name of the person healed—may have been handed down through the congregation at Lystra; but Luke must then have placed this material in a setting which his own culture (a visit from the gods, as in the legend of Philemon and Baucis—see p. 426f. below) made incomparably more impressive. It is however clear that in such hypotheses the line between tradition and literary embellishment cannot always be sharply drawn: we are moving in the realm of the possible, at most the probable, in no sense the rigorously demonstrable.

(c) Another point to be considered is that information about a given community need not derive from that community itself. How, for example, did the author come to learn the background to the Stephen episode and the subsequent persecution, as it is sketched in **6**.1ff.? From Jerusalem, or from Hellenists driven out (say) to Antioch? The unexpected light thrown on the state of the Jerusalem congregation by the mention of the two groups, the Hebrews and the Hellenists, and the crisis over the widows, betrays such an intimate knowledge of the situation as one expects only from participants. On the other hand, the conflict in **6**.1ff. has been minimized—by whom? Is Luke simply transmitting, without important alterations, the view of things bequeathed him by former members of the Jerusalem congregation? Has he himself rubbed down the most jagged points of a 'Hellenistic' recollection? Or had the original tradition mellowed, even in gentile circles, into a harmonious overall picture?[1] Here we come to a further problem.

(d) How tangled the strands of tradition may have become is shown by a fact to which Olof Linton[2] has drawn attention, namely that Acts

---

[1] Generally speaking, this means: Should we lay the discrepancies of Acts from the picture arising out of our historical reconstruction at the door of tradition or of the author? If the former, we have still to answer the further question: Where lie the reasons for such a transformation within the tradition?

[2] Olof Linton, 'The Third Aspect—a neglected point of view: a study in Gal. I–II and Acts IX and XV' (*Studia Theologica*, Vol. III, Lund 1950/51, 79–95).

contains traditions against which Paul already had sought to defend himself!
In Gal. **1**.15–20 he is evidently combating the calumny that immediately
after his conversion he went to Jerusalem and was initiated into the gospel
by the Twelve. He was thus not an Apostle in his own right, and when—as
on the circumcision question—he departed from Judaistic doctrine (which
rightly or wrongly appealed to Jerusalem), he was speaking without authority.[1]
Against this, Paul points out that he did not visit Jerusalem for three years,
and then only for a fortnight, also that of the Apostles he saw only Peter
(apart from James 'the Lord's brother'). For all this he calls God to witness
(Gal. **1**.20)—a sure sign that he is warding off assertions to the contrary.
However, Luke also knows nothing of those three years or of Paul's journey
into Arabia: he has Paul, after a time (ἡμέραι ἱκαναί—**9**.23), go straight
from Damascus to Jerusalem, where he becomes inseparable from the
Apostles (**9**.28). This does not of course mean that Luke wanted to challenge
Paul's claim (Gal. **2**.7) to occupy a place equivalent to Peter's, for Luke was
totally unaware of such a claim. Rather was he glad to be able in this way
to associate Paul with the original congregation and with the front of Church
unity whose existence he was everywhere anxious to demonstrate. But where
did he get his version of this chapter of Paul's life? Or let us take Gal. **5**.11.
Here Paul defends himself with bitter irony against the assertion of the
Judaists that he still occasionally preached circumcision. Once again we find
that the version in Acts is astonishingly near the Judaistic: Paul circumcises
Timothy 'because of the Jews in those parts' (**16**.3). Here—in all innocence—
Luke ascribes to Paul the very thing which in Gal. **5**.11 he passionately
declares a falsehood, that from time to time he practised circumcision in
order to avoid untoward consequences. Once again, Luke is not seeking to
bring Paul into discredit. On the contrary, he is pleased to be able to show
what a pious Jew Paul always was. And where did he get this version of
affairs—a version, moreover, to which otherwise highly perceptive scholars
have bowed assent? Perhaps we may infer that the Judaistic image of Paul
was not merely current among Jewish Christians (cf. **21**.21) but had insinuated
itself into Gentile Christianity too. There, however, it was toned down and
lost its polemic accent—Paul becomes a missionary recognized and recommended by the Twelve (cf. **15**.25!). This portrait Luke gladly adopted,
presumably 'improving' it in his own way: by baptizing Cornelius, Peter
relieves Paul of the odium of the Gentile mission, and thus the much-maligned
'innovator' is exonerated. This could be an exploitation, brilliant in its own
way, of the Caesarean community's legend of its own origin.

   That the source-question has not come to a standstill is shown by works
by Dom Jacques Dupont, A. J. Mattill Jun., and Walter Eltester. We discuss

----

[1] So J. Jeremias also interprets Gal. **1**.10–12 ('Chiasmus in den Paulusbriefen' in
ZNW 49 (1958), 153). This takes into account the concern of W. Schmithals, *The Office
of Apostle in the Early Church*, 1969, 182ff.

these below in § 9, 'The Work Continues'; the Paul Schubert Festschrift (*Studies in Luke-Acts*, ed. I.. E. Keck and J. L. Martyn, Nashville 1966, 258ff.) contains an essay by the present writer on ' Acts as Source-Material for the History of Early Christianity'.

Bibliography

G. A. van den Bergh van Eysinga, 'Iets over bronnenscheiding in de Handelingen der Apostelen', *Nieuw Theol. Tijdschr.* 12 (1923), 274–98; Id.: 'Nog iets over bronnenscheiding in Handelingen', ibid. 18 (1929), 146–64; Id.: 'Bronnenscheiding in Handelingen 17–28', ibid. 19 (1930), 124–38; P. L. Couchoud and R. Stahl, 'Les deux auteurs des Actes des Apôtres', *Revue de l'histoire des religions* 97 (1928), 6–52; M. H. Shepherd, 'A Venture of Source Analysis of Acts' in *Munera Studiosa*, Cambridge, Mass. (1946), 92–103; R. Bultmann, 'Zur Frage nach den Quellen der Apostelgeschichte' in *New Testament Essays in Memory of T. W. Manson* (1959), 68–80; E. Haenchen, 'Quellenanalyse und Kompositionsanalyse in Apg. 15', *Festschrift für Joachim Jeremias* (Berlin 2nd. edn. 1964), 153–64; Dom J. Dupont, *Les sources du Livre des Actes, État de la question*, Bruges, 1960 (ET London 1964); E. Haenchen, 'Das "Wir" in der Apostelgeschichte und das Itinerar', *ZThK* 1961 (ET in *Journal for Theology and the Church*, Vol. I: *The Bultmann School of Biblical Interpretation*: *New Directions*, New York 1965).

7. LUKE AS THEOLOGIAN, HISTORIAN AND WRITER[1]

There is an uncommonly close tie in Luke between theology, historiography and literary prowess. One cannot avoid treating the three separately, but that remains an expedient. Scholars of past generations regarded Luke as above all a historian (see pp. 12–34 above). More recently the worthy labours

---

[1] Prompted by the *Christusbilder* of Ernst von Dobschütz (*TU* XVIII, Leipzig 1899), Dorothee Klein went into the question how 'Luke the physician' became a painter and patron of the painters' guild, in her Hamburg dissertation *St Lukas als Maler der Madonna: Ikonographie der Lukas-Madonna*, Berlin 1933 (cf. review by Dobschütz, *TLZ* 59 (1934) 278). The first known mention of paintings by St. Luke occurred in the 'image controversy' of the eighth century (Klein, 8). Dobschütz had surmised that even earlier, in Rome, wonderworking images had been attributed to Luke the evangelist (p. 10). But just as the first testimony to Luke's painting appears in the East, so the oldest representation of him as a painter originates there (p. 18). The motif of the painting evangelist had evolved in Byzantine art by the ninth or eleventh—at the latest the thirteenth—century (p. 22). But the image has a long pre-history: first the portrayal of the reading philosopher (gravestone, fifth cent. B.C.) evolved into that of the writer (Augustan period), which served as model for the writing evangelist; then the substitution of a painting-board for the codex converted the figure into the painter-saint (pp. 24f.). However, it remains obscure just why Luke, in particular, should have been transformed from a writing to a painting evangelist.

of Vielhauer and especially Conzelmann (p. 48 above) have done much to bring his theology to light. It is the art of the writer[1] which now stands most in need of evaluation.

I. Lucan Theology in Acts

Luke is no systematic theologian. He does not seek to develop any unified doctrine, the product of thorough reflection. Nevertheless he has a theology of his own; he sets out from definite theological premises and treats the immediate theological questions of his age. But he does not proceed by the systematic discussion of dogmatic themes: these are rather, directly or indirectly, suggested to the reader in his historical presentation by means of vivid scenes.

A. The Theological Premises

Upon occasion Luke has been praised for presenting so faithful a picture of the primitive theology of early Christian times.[2] But it is his own simple theology (which he shared with his community) which he everywhere presupposes and which should be understood behind the sermons, prayers, liturgical expressions and occasional pertinent remarks in Acts.

It is *God* (the Father) who occupies the dominant place[3]; Luke would joyfully have subscribed to the words of Paul in I Cor. 8.6: 'We have one God, the Father, of whom are all things, . . . and one Lord, Jesus Christ. . . .' Everywhere God appears placed over Christ. He is the Creator,[4] but in the work of salvation also the real direction of events is in his hands: the plan of salvation was his design, and he has reserved for himself the moment of redemption.[5] It is also he who causes miracles to happen through Jesus[6] and the Christians.[7] He raised Jesus from the dead.[8]

Luke does not mention any pre-existence of Jesus. In 2.22 he describes *Jesus* as a man whom God has legitimated by mighty works, wonders and signs, which he has done through him. Jesus made his way doing good and

---

[1] In which field Dibelius has hitherto made the most valuable contribution—see pp. 34ff. and 39ff. above.

[2] Foakes-Jackson, *The Acts of the Apostles*, 1931, XVI: 'Luke seems to have been able to give us an extraordinarily accurate picture of the undeveloped theology of the earliest Christians . . .'

[3] See Conzelmann, *Die Mitte der Zeit*, 149 (ET *The Theology of St. Luke*, London and New York 1960, 173). Conzelmann has also done the decisive spadework for the further statements in Section A—cf. further Acts 2.36, 3.15 & 26, 5.31, 10.40 and 13.30.

[4] Acts 4.24, 14.15 and 17.24; Conzelmann 173.

[5] Acts 1.7; 2.33; 8.26 & 29; 10.4, 13 & 38; 11.5ff.; 12.7; 17.31; Conzelmann 174.

[6] Acts 2.22 & 10.38.

[7] 3.13, 4.30, 19.11 and 21.30.

[8] 2.24, 3.15, 4.10, 5.30, 13.37, 17.30 and 26.8; Conzelmann 175.

performing miracles through the country of the Jews, and healed all those who were oppressed by the devil.[1] The title of 'Son'[2] recedes almost out of sight behind those of 'Lord' and 'Anointed'.[3] Jesus sends the Spirit, true— but he received the Spirit from the Father. Luke thus clearly advocates a subordinationist Christology: God bestowed the Spirit on Jesus at his baptism, making him the Lord and the Anointed.[4] By his resurrection he became the 'Leader of Life'[5]: i.e. he was the first to rise from the dead, therefore the first to receive the new life on the farther side of death and mortality. Through his resurrection he is our hope; on the other hand, Acts does not contain a doctrine of vicarious atonement[6]—not even in the book's one quotation from Isaiah 53.[7] God has taken Jesus to sit at his right hand on his throne,[8] and to him he has confided the judgment of the world.[9] That is why it is so imperative to have Jesus as one's Lord and to belong to the community which calls upon his name.[10] For while Jesus himself dwells in heaven until the Parousia,[11] his Name is present and active among us here and now[12]; it performs miracles and is the channel of salvation. Luke takes pains to distinguish this calling on the Name of Jesus from the magic conjurations of antiquity: it is God who acts when the name of Jesus is invoked, and who thereby glorifies his παῖς.[13] Herein is seen at once the bond between God and Jesus and the supremacy of God.

In his teaching concerning the *Holy Spirit*,[14] likewise, Luke does not yet show the balance attained by later theology in the doctrine of the Trinity. He links together three predicates of different provenance. Firstly, he presents the Spirit as the gift which every Christian receives at baptism;[15] its

---

[1] Acts **10**.38f.; cf. Conzelmann pp. 146ff.

[2] Acts **9**.20, **13**.33; Conzelmann, 147 n. 2.

[3] Jesus as Kyrios: Acts **1**.21; **2**.21, 25 & 36; **4**.33; **5**.14; **7**.60; **8**.16; **9**.1, 5, 10f., **13**, 15, 17 & 27f.; **10**.36; **11**.16f. & 20; **13**.12; **14**.23; **15**.11 & 26; **16**.15 & 31; **18**.9; **19**.5, 13 & 17; **20**.19, 21, 24 & 35; **21**.13; **22**.8, 10, 16 & 19; **23**.11; **26**.15; **28**.31: since God also is called 'Kyrios' there are many places where it is hard to tell whether he or Jesus is meant.—Jesus as Christos: **2**.31 & 36; **3**.6, 18 & 20; **4**.10, 26 & 33; **5**.42; **8**.5 & 12, **9**.22 & 34; **10**.36 & 48; **11**.7; **15**.11 (*var*.); **16**.18 & 31; **17**.3; **18**.5 & 28; **20**.21 & 24; **26**.23; **28**.31: this list also includes the verses containing the title Jesus Christ. Cf. Conzelmann, 174 n. 3.

[4] Acts **2**.33, cf. **5**.32: it is God who bestows the Spirit!—see Conzelmann, 174.

[5] Acts **3**.15, cf. **5**.31; Conzelmann, 205f.

[6] Though there is an echo of this in the formula of **20**.28, with which I Peter **5**.2 should be compared.

[7] Acts **8**.32f.

[8] **2**.25 & 33f.; **5**.31; **7**.55f.

[9] **10**.42 and **17**.31.

[10] **2**.21; **9**.14 & 21; **22**.16.

[11] **3**.21.

[12] **3**.16; **4**.10, 12 & 30; **8**.12; **9**.16 & 27; **10**.43; **15**.26; **19**.13; **21**.13; Conzelmann, 177f.

[13] Acts **3**.13.

[14] Conzelmann, 179ff.

[15] Acts **1**.5 & 8; **2**.4 & 38.

ecstatic effects afford Luke the welcome opportunity of making the reality
of the gift visible.[1] Secondly, Luke describes the Spirit as the equipment
possessed by individual Christians for a given task at a particular moment[2];
it was already possible for Judaism to speak of the Spirit in this manner.
Thirdly, according to Acts, the Spirit gives specific directions for the Christian
mission at important junctures[3]—like a *bath qol* in Jewish tradition; but in
such cases the Spirit could as well be replaced by 'the angel of the Lord'[4]
or a 'vision'[5].

Luke elaborates no doctrine of the *Church*—only once (9.31) does the
word ἐκκλησία have a meaning beyond 'local congregation' and it then
simply covers the Church in Judaea, Galilee and Samaria. We have once
again to fall back upon scattered clues in the historical narrative. The first
vehicles of the 'Word of God'[6] are the twelve Apostles. They are witnesses
of Jesus' life and resurrection[7]; to this extent the whole of Christian missionary
preaching goes back to them. At the same time it is they—mostly represented
by Peter—who inaugurate the principal stages of the Christian mission. Peter
preaches the first missionary sermon in Jerusalem[8]; he and John successfully
complete the mission to the Samaritans[9]; with the baptism of Cornelius Peter
opens the mission to the Gentiles, which of course is then endorsed by the
other Apostles and the whole of the community in Jerusalem.[10] From that point
the Twelve fade out of Acts—they are actually mentioned for the last time
in **16.4**—without any declaration of an apostolic succession: Luke does not
indicate whether they installed the Lord's brother James and the presbyters, who
succeeded them in the leadership of the Jerusalem community.[11] According
to Luke it was in essentials Paul who carried out the mission to the diaspora
—Paul, whom Jesus called in a special appearance,[12] and to whom time and
again he revealed his instructions through visions.[13] In newly-founded communities Paul and Silas appointed elders, but here again we cannot speak

[1] **2.33 & 38; 8.15f. & 18f.; 10.44 & 47; 11.15; 15.8; 19.6.**
[2] **4.8 & 31; 7.55; 11.28; 13.2, 4 & 9; 15.28.**
[3] **8.29; 10.19; 11.12; 16.6f.; 21.4 & 11; 23.9f.**
[4] **8.26; 10.3; 23.9; 27.23.**
[5] **7.31; 9.10 & 12; 10.3; 11.5; 16.9f.; 18.9.**
[6] **2.41; 4.4, 29 & 31; 6.2, 4 & 7; 8.4, 14 & 25; 10.36 & 44; 11.1 & 19; 12.24;
13.5, 7, 26, 44, 46 & 48f.; 14.4, 12 & 25; 15.7 & 35f.; 16.6 & 32; 17.11 & 13; 18.11;
19.19f.** Mark already employs ὁ λόγος for the delivery of the message: 'he spoke the
word to them' (**2.2** and elsewhere).
[7] Acts **1.21f.**
[8] **2.14f.**
[9] **8.14f.**
[10] **10.1–11.18.**
[11] The elders first appear in **11.30**; in **15.6, 22** and **16.4** they are mentioned together
with the Apostles; in **21.18** they are evidently, with James, the leaders of the community
at Jerusalem.
[12] Acts **9.1–19a; 22.6–21; 26.12–18.**
[13] **16.9; 18.9; 22.17–21; 23.11; (27.23).**

of an 'apostolic succession': the elders are regarded rather as holding their authority from the Holy Spirit, and as entrusted by the Spirit with the leadership of the congregation.

Nor does Luke provide any systematic teaching on how one becomes a *Christian*; we can only gather certain essentials from a mass of scenes and separate statements. First, μετάνοια is required, both from Jewish and from gentile listeners. This word may embrace the whole 'conversion'-process[1]; it may however signify merely the 'negative' aspect: the turning-away from the former, perverted life. In the latter case it is completed by the positive 'turning to' God[2] and faith in Christ.[3] These form the preconditions for baptism,[4] and in baptism the Spirit is bestowed. It is the Spirit which is the essence of Christian baptism and distinguishes it from John's.[5]

For 'conversion' in the inclusive sense Luke also favours the term πιστεῦσαι. It may be translated simply as 'to become a Christian': οἱ πιστεύοντες or πιστεύσαντες are 'the Christians'. What they 'believe' may be 'the Word'[6] which they have 'heard'[7] or 'received',[8] but believing may also signify 'trust in'[9] or 'believing *on* the Lord'.[10] That God 'cleanses hearts' by faith[11] shows the high value which Luke attaches to the moral effects of faith.

Of baptism we have already spoken. The *breaking of bread*, performed in private Christian houses,[12] appears as a Christian custom whose practice is everywhere a matter of course: in 2.46 it is performed 'with gladness'. But of a sacramental piety which saw in the Lord's Supper the φάρμακον ἀθανασίας there is as little mention in Acts as of a monarchical episcopate. Among other things, this shows how carefully one should handle the label 'early Catholicism'.

B. Theological Questions of the Day

Two theological questions of the day appear to receive special attention in Acts: the expectation of the imminent end of the world, and the mission to the Gentiles without the law. It was only the position which Luke adopted with regard to the eschatological problem that made his writing of history intrinsically possible; it may therefore aptly be treated here and now. The question of the mission to the Gentiles and freedom from the law is on the other hand so inextricable from the course of the historical narrative that we must hold it back until the next section, on Luke the historian.

[1] 2.38; 17.30; 5.31; 11.18; 20.21.
[2] 3.19; 8.22; 26.20.
[3] 20.21.
[4] 8.13 & 18.8.
[5] 1.22; 10.37; 13.24; 18.25; 19.3f.
[6] 4.4.
[7] 10.44.
[8] 2.41.
[9] 5.14.
[10] 9.42f.
[11] 15.9.
[12] 2.46 and 20.7.

(1) *How the first generation saw history*

The Christians of the first generation were convinced that they stood amid the decisive revolution of the ages; this world, the present era, was passing away,[1] and the era to come was upon them.[2] John the Baptist had been the Elijah foretold,[3] but Jesus himself was the Messiah[4]; his resurrection would soon[5] be followed by his second coming and the general resurrection of the dead[6]; the short interval before the Parousia must be used by his disciples to spread the glad tidings as wide as possible: believe in Jesus, the judge of the world, and you will be saved in the judgment shortly to come! The powers of the coming reign of God were already at work in the healings and exorcisms performed by Jesus and his disciples.[7] In the teachings of Paul the ferment of the new is even more clearly all-pervading—whoever possesses the Spirit (=is in Christ) has already died to the old,[8] and at the coming of Christ will also receive the 'body of glory' which the Lord exalted already enjoys.[9]

(2) *How the view of history changed*

This expectation of the imminent end was not fulfilled. When Luke wrote Acts, Paul had been executed and James the brother of the Lord had died a martyr; Christians had burned as living torches in the gardens of Nero; the Holy City and its Temple lay in rubble. Yet the world went on. By this many Christians recognized that the imminent expectation of the end was false. If, however, the end was not to come soon, when would it come?

Here two possibilities presented themselves. One might see the last things happening here and now, in the present, or one might expect their realization only in a remote, indefinite future. Both courses were followed.

(a) The Fourth Evangelist sought to show his readers that they had, or could have, the resurrection and the life here and now. Whenever the word of Jesus—which is none other than God's own Word!—issues from the mouth of Jesus or is uttered in Christian preaching by one of his disciples, its hearers are confronted with the eternal decision, and then is the moment of resurrection—or damnation.[10] Whoever believed this affirmation of the evangelist need no longer gaze anxiously to the skies in longing for the Son

---

[1] I Cor. 7.31. On what follows, cf. R. Bultmann, *Theologie des Neuen Testaments*, § 6 (ET *Theology of the New Testament*, London 1952).
[2] Luke 11.20.
[3] Mark 9.13; Matt. 11.14.
[4] Mark 8.29. [5] Rom. 13.11.
[6] I Thess. 4.15. [7] Luke 11.20.
[8] Rom. 6.2 & 8; II Cor. 5.14f.; Gal. 2.19.
[9] I Cor. 15.44; Phil. 3.21.
[10] John 5.24f. and 11.25.

of Man descending with clouds, for to him the Son, with the Father, had already come, and they had taken their dwelling with him. This fulfilment in the here-and-now developed to its highest pitch what Paul had expressed in his doctrine of being 'in Christ.' This was only possible, however, by virtue of the confluence in the hearer's 'now' of all those elements which had been chronologically divergent in the teaching of the earliest Christians: the preaching of Jesus in Galilee and Jerusalem, the proclamation of the gospel by his disciples, and the last day.

(b) The Third Evangelist also denied the imminent expectation. It seemed to him to claim a knowledge which God has reserved for himself alone.[1] Christian life should no longer be governed by speculation as to whether this world would soon come to an end.[2] Christians must reckon with the world's survival.

But in rejecting the imminent expectation Luke did not take the same course as the Fourth Evangelist. Instead, he took the chronological dimension, rendered meaningless in John, into serious consideration, and asked himself where and how God's work of salvation proceeds in time. He saw the history of salvation as a great unity which ended in the parousia.

In this history we may distinguish[3] three periods. The first was that of the law and the prophets.[4] This came to an end with John the Baptist, who no longer belonged to it. The second—hence the 'middle of time'[5]—was the earthly life of Jesus, up to his Ascension. This has with the forty days of the risen Lord among his disciples passed over into a new, third era. Luke has as yet no name for it, but we may call it the age (or period) of the Church. And this will one day end with the return of the Lord in judgment.[6] But the time is not yet ripe. First must run its course a period in which the 'Word of God' spreads far and wide,[7] the period of the mission 'to the ends of the earth'.[8]

(3) *Luke's first book to Theophilus*[9]

Luke accepted the reality of time, with its threefold division into past, present and future. He did not shrink from treating the earthly life of Jesus as something belonging to the past.[10] But if it really lay in the past, he had to

[1] Acts 1.7.
[2] Acts 1.11—despite 2.20!
[3] Conzelmann, 128f.
[4] Luke 16.16.
[5] Conzelmann, 129 and 146ff.
[6] Acts 1.11.
[7] Acts 6.7; 12.24; 13.49; 19.20.
[8] 1.8 and 13.47.
[9] It is quite possible that the two books bore no title; cf. commentary on 1.1 below.
[10] Luke 4.18; cf. Conzelmann, 144f.

seek to grasp it as one seeks to lay hold on anything from the past: as a historian. This meant that he was obliged to gather and sift the 'sources' of the biography, arrange the events of that life in their proper chronological order, distinguish and relate causes and effects, and finally immerse himself in the psychological climate of past history. He had, in short, to overcome the historical remoteness of this bygone life with the methods of the historian. All this Luke did in fact accomplish, and so it is that his gospel is the first 'Life of Jesus'.[1]

Two things helped him in this work. One was that he found a rich store of traditions regarding Jesus ready to hand; the other, that he had predecessors who had already formed this material into a definite shape. Yet this help was at the same time a hindrance: it meant that his own initiative was frequently reduced to the stylistic re-working which he imposed on the mass of collected material. However, as a result of this re-working we can only recognize his sources when they have come down to us along with his own work.[2]

(4) *Luke's second book to Theophilus*

Now if the earthly life of Jesus, brought to a close by his Ascension, represents an epoch in chronologically regarded history, one is drawn to the highly important inference that it had a chronological sequel. With bold logic Luke considers this sequel also a historical event, and presents it as the continuation of his gospel! This was a daring enterprise which none of his predecessors had thought to execute,[3] and in which he found no successors.[4] We need not be surprised at this, since what was important for salvation was knowledge of the history of Jesus—could the same be said of the history of the Church? To Luke the question appeared in a rather different form: what was the inner link between the previous epoch, the life of Jesus, and what followed? Some scholars have credited Luke with a very simple answer: the first book depicts what Jesus himself did, the second represents what he accomplished through his Spirit in the Apostles.[5] But Luke knows no counterpart to Paul's 'being in Christ'. Jesus is dwelling in heaven, which

---

[1] E. Käsemann, 'Problem des historischen Jesus' in *ZThK* (1954), 137 (ET *Essays on NT Themes*, 1964. p. 29): 'His Gospel is indeed the first 'life of Jesus'. In it, consideration is given to the points of view of causality and teleology; and psychological insight, the composition of the historian and the particular slant of the writer who aims at edification are all equally discernible.'

[2] C. S. C. Williams, *A Commentary on the Acts of the Apostles*, London 1957, 7: '. . . if Mark's Gospel did not exist, it would be impossible to reconstruct it accurately from Luke's . . .; so any reconstruction of the sources behind Acts must be tentative.'

[3] Dibelius, *Studies*, 3.

[4] The apocryphal Acts of Apostles are not intended to continue a gospel; see W. Michaelis, *Das Neue Testament verdeutscht und erläutert*, 1935, Vol. II, 1.

[5] Cf. Harnack, *Beitr.* III, 4 (ET): 'A historical presentation of the power of the Spirit of Jesus in the Apostles.'

must receive him until the Parousia.[1] Only on exceptional occasions (above all at the call of Paul) does he interfere, through 'visions' and appearances, in earthly happenings. It is only in **16**.7 that Luke speaks of the 'Spirit of Jesus', and even here the effect is no different from that of 'the angel of the Lord' or 'the Spirit (of God)', namely to give a direction at a specific juncture of the mission. In reality it is God himself—the supreme authority—who governs and prescribes, in accordance with his plan, the course to be followed by the 'Word of God'.

It is this '*Word of God*' which fills the time after Pentecost; this Word is furthermore the message concerning Jesus, belief in whom brings forgiveness of sins and deliverance in the judgment. Here then is the clamp which fastens the two eras together and justifies, indeed demands, the continuation of the first book (depicting the life of Jesus as a time of salvation) in a second; for the salvation which has appeared must be preached to all peoples, and the very portrayal of this mission will serve the awakening of belief, and hence the attainment of that salvation.

But at what point should this portrayal stop? Of course its proper end would be the return of Jesus, but this is hidden from us in an unknown future. And so the historian, who can only report what has already actually happened, is obliged to call a halt somewhere before his true conclusion. The presumption that Luke brought his account up to his own time falls to the ground from the fact that Paul (as is hinted to the alert reader in **20**.25 & 38 and **27**.24) bore witness before the emperor and did not return to his congregations; thus he suffered martyrdom. Luke did not take this event into his story but concluded with a picture of Paul at work unhindered in Rome. The path of the gospel from Jerusalem to Rome formed a complete story, a rounded whole, in itself. It brought comfort and reassurance to the faithful, for it showed them how God's ways continued even after the departure of Jesus. The interval of time thus represented by the second book roughly corresponds to what we call 'the apostolic age'. For to Luke Paul is a kind of typical substitute for the twelve Apostles, the last representative of the 'heroic age'[2] when the Church was as yet undefiled by heresy (which did not break out until after Paul's death) and exemplary in its way of life.

II. Luke the Historian in Acts

It was his familiarity with the theological situation, and his understanding of what it required, that led Luke to turn historian and write a

---

[1] Acts **3**.21.
[2] So styled by A. D. Nock, *Gnomon* 25 (1953), 498. Cf. A. Schweitzer, *Mess. u. Leid.-Geh.* 109.

historical work in two volumes.[1] The picture which he there sketched of the history of primitive Christianity is marked by astonishing uniformity and simplicity. Everything that might interfere with its straightforward movement is smoothed out or omitted.

In the earliest times[2] the Christian community was entirely confined to Jerusalem, though here it registered extraordinary missionary successes: among the first converts were Jews from the whole Eastern half of the Empire and beyond, as far as the Parthians and Elamites.[3]

The persecution consequent upon the Stephen episode—and above all the work of Paul!—temporarily drove the whole community out of Jerusalem (only the twelve Apostles uphold the continuity of the mother Church!) and gave rise to the mission in Samaria, Galilee and the coastal reaches from Gaza to Caesarea.[4] All these communities were won or taken over by Peter (and John) and were thus incorporated in the apostolic Church.[5] With the baptism of the Gentile Cornelius, Peter legalized the subsequent mission to the Gentiles in Antioch,[6] which was moreover approved and taken over by Barnabas, the delegate from Jerusalem.[7]

The execution of James son of Zebedee,[8] then Peter's escape and flight,[9] brought James the Lord's brother into the foreground. He first appears, together with the elders,[10] at the Apostles' side,[11] and later supersedes them in Jerusalem.[12]

From Chapter 13 onwards, Syrian Antioch occupies the centre of the missionary scene. It is from here that Barnabas and Paul set out on the mission to Cyprus and to found congregations in Pisidia and Lycaonia.[13]

---

[1] Many (e.g. Torrey, Sahlin, Menoud, Trocmé) have surmised that Luke's work was once a single book, which was only divided 'when it was taken into the canon,' on which occasion the conclusion of Luke (24.50–3) and the beginning of Acts (1.1–5) were added. Many things led to this hypothesis: the contradiction in the dating of the Ascension, real or apparent stumbling-blocks in Acts 1.1–5, the 'biblical' tone of the first half of Acts, which fits with the gospel so well, and the interpretation of Luke 1.1–4 as a prologue to the whole work. Yet a careful examination destroys the cogency of these reasons (see commentary to 1.1ff.). Here we would only point to two things. First, the works were not taken into the canon by an ecclesiastical authority able to ensure the simultaneous alteration of all existing copies: their acceptance was, rather, a long drawn-out process. Nowhere have any traces come to light of the hypothetical older book. Second, it was daring enough to provide the gospel with a sequel in the shape of a book on the apostolic age, but it is downright unthinkable that, instead of closing the gospel with the Resurrection and Ascension, Luke should prolong it until Paul's arrival in Rome; for him the life of Jesus was a self-contained epoch in the history of salvation, one distinct from the period which followed.

[2] Acts 1 to 5.

[3] Acts 2.9. Here belong also the other references to the growth of the Jerusalem community: 2.41, 2.47, 4.4, 5.14, 6.7 and finally 21.20.

[4] Chapters 6 to 8.
[5] 8.14–25; 9.32–42.
[6] 10.1–11.18.
[7] 11.22–4.
[8] 12.2.
[9] 12.3–17.
[10] See p. 93 n.11 above.
[11] 12.17; 15.13.
[12] 21.18.
[13] Chapters 13 and 14.

Since this mission is sanctioned by Jerusalem, nothing more stands in the way of Barnabas' further mission to Cyprus, and more especially, the mission of Paul.[1]

And so Paul carries on the mission, from Chapter 16, pressing on through Asia Minor[2] and Macedonia to Corinth.[3] His next base is Ephesus, from where his influence radiates over all the province of Asia.[4]

His captivity in Jerusalem[5] and Caesarea[6] affords him repeated opportunities to defend the Christian mission to the Gentiles,[7] in the face of Jewish accusations, before the Roman authorities. His appeal to Caesar[8] finally brings Paul to the goal for which he has striven so long: Rome.[9] The book closes with his unhampered missionary activity in the capital of the world.[10]

This presentation gives the impression of a problem-free, victorious progress on the part of the Christian mission. But in reality Luke the historian is wrestling, from the first page to the last, with the problem of the *mission to the Gentiles without the law*.[11] His entire presentation is influenced by this. It is a problem with two aspects: a theological and a political. By forsaking observance of the Jewish law Christianity parts company with Judaism; does this not break the continuity of the history of salvation? That is the theological aspect. But in cutting adrift from Judaism Christianity also loses the toleration which the Jewish religion enjoys.[12] Denounced by the Jews as hostile to the state, it becomes the object of suspicion to Rome. That is the political aspect. Acts takes both constantly into account.

According to Luke, the problem's true solution, which he supports with a number of auxiliary ideas, lies in demonstrating that the instigators and leaders of the Christian mission, far from falling away from their Jewish faith, in fact held fast to it, but that God unmistakably and irresistibly steered them into the mission to the Gentiles.

Accordingly Acts opens in Jerusalem. The traditional Galilean appearances of the Lord are set aside: there was of course no denying the Galilean origins of the Apostles,[13] but the community arose in Jerusalem[14] and there remained. The Apostles, with Peter to the fore, are devout temple-goers[15] and keepers of the law who refrain from entering any Gentile Christian house and rigorously observe the regulations concerning clean and unclean food.[16]

---

[1] Chapter 15.
[2] 16.6ff.
[3] Chapters 16 to 18.
[4] 19.10 & 16.
[5] 21.1–23.30.
[6] 23.31–27.1.
[7] 22.1–21; 23.6; 24.10–21; 26.2–29.
[8] 25.11.
[9] 28.14 & 16.
[10] 28.31.
[11] This problem is heralded as early as 1.8 and remains a burning question right up to 28.28.
[12] See B. S. Easton, *Early Christianity*, 1955, §II 'Religio licita', 41–57.
[13] Acts 2.7.
[14] 1.12ff.
[15] 3.1 & 5.12.
[16] 10.14f. & 11.3.

The only way in which such men can be led to the Gentile mission is that God should constrain them against their will. This much becomes evident in the Cornelius episode,[1] so far as Peter and the original community are concerned, and in the conversion[2] and apologies[3] with regard to Paul. If God has endowed Gentile audiences with the Spirit, who can deny them baptism?[4] In the same way Paul, the Jewish missionary who was brought up in Jerusalem,[5] must bow to the irresistible will of God: it is no use his kicking against the pricks![6]

Yet the Christian mission need not have become the purely Gentile mission which in fact it was in Luke's day: it was to the Jews that salvation was first offered, and offered again and again. It was not until they refused it by their vilification of Jesus that the emissaries of Christianity turned to the Gentiles.[7]

There is, finally, along with the foregoing, a third line of thought which justifies the Gentile mission, namely that God has no partisan prejudice in favour of one particular people. If he were to admit only Israel to salvation, that would be an unfair preference such as one may not ascribe to God.[8] In this, the thought of Gentile Christians in Luke's time is particularly discernible.

But over and above all these considerations, Luke was also anxious to disprove the accusation that the Gentile Christians did not care for the law. Not only does he stress the fact that Paul continued to live and feel as a Pharisee, but he indicates that even the Gentile Christians kept the law so far as they were bidden by the Old Testament.[9]

Nevertheless this defence of the Gentile Christian attitude to the law is still inadequate to present, as Luke would like, the complete resolution of the conflict between Jew and Christian. There are two further points here: firstly, the thoroughly developed scriptural proofs[10] attest the resurrection whereby Jesus has become the pioneer of the new life beyond the grave, the Lord and the Anointed. When Paul asserts that he says nothing other than what Moses and the prophets foretold he is referring to the death and resurrection of the Messiah.[11] Thus Israel's own holy writ bears witness to Jesus' resurrection, hence to the focal point of Christian doctrine. But—and this is the second point—this very centrepiece of the kerygma, the doctrine of the resurrection, already had adherents in Israel itself: the Pharisees![12] Accordingly, the strictest tendency in Judaism was properly speaking on the side of the Christians—if they refused to recognize the resurrection of Jesus, it was out of mere inconsistency. Correspondingly Luke represents the Pharisees, whom the tradition which lay before him depicted as the explicit enemies

[1] 10.1–11.18.   [2] 9.1–19a.
[3] 22.1–21.   [4] 10.47 & 11.17.
[5] 22.3 & 26.4.   [6] 26.14.
[7] 13.46, 18.6 & 28.28.   [8] 10.34f.
[9] 15.21 & 21.25.
[10] In Chapters 2, 3, 7, 8, 10, 13, 15 & 26, to mention only the principal references.
[11] 26.22f.; cf. 23.6 26.6 & 28.20.   [12] 23.8.

of Jesus and the young Church, to be as pro-Christian as he could possibly make them: Gamaliel takes it upon himself to plead the Apostles' case,[1] and before the High Council the Pharisees take Paul's part against the Sadducees, who alone remain as opponents of the Christians.[2]

Yet these efforts on Luke's part to minimize the distance between Jews and Christians will be seen in a false perspective unless one bears in mind from the outset that, unlike Paul, Luke has abandoned hope of converting Israel. It is in Rome itself that stubborn Israel is subjected to one last appeal—and dismissed; 'this salvation of God is sent unto the Gentiles, and they will hear!'—such are Paul's last word in Acts.[3] In the circumstances, the book's manifold attempts to throw a bridge between Jews and Christians no longer represent a missionary wooing of Israel: by Luke's time the Christian mission was directed solely to the Gentiles, whose readiness for the word and willingness to listen were the current experience. No, what the demonstration of the links with Israel is intended to make plain is the implicit unity which confirms the continuity of the history of salvation in the divine will.

In this way Luke as a historian solved as best he could the theological problem posed by the mission to the Gentiles without the law. But he had also at the same time done most of the work necessary for the solution of the political problem. As a religion of the resurrection, Christianity was in the direct line of succession to Judaism. And one cannot, indeed one should not, expect the Roman State to trouble itself with theological niceties alien to its concern.[4] On the other hand Christianity does not imply any transgression of Roman laws. Consequently the intelligent representatives of Rome always took a benevolent view of the Christian mission: the procurator Sergius Paulus lets himself be converted;[5] the procurator Gallio dismisses a Jewish complaint against Paul;[6] some of the Asiarchs (whose office it was to promote the cult of the emperor) are friendly with Paul;[7] the town-clerk of Ephesus defends the Christians against the charge of profanation;[8] the tribune of Jerusalem, Claudius Lysias,[9] likewise the governors Felix[10] and Festus,[11] refuse to condemn Paul out of hand; and as a prisoner in Rome Paul is allowed to carry on his missionary work unhindered[12]—indeed that very word, ἀκωλύτως, is the last word in the book, standing as the summation of past experience and a recommendation in respect of future policy.

But for such a simplification of the course of history, for thus mastering the problem of the mission, Luke the historian was obliged to pay a heavy price—one heavier than he suspected. Two instances make this clear. Luke

---

[1] 5.35–9.
[2] 23.9.
[3] 28.28.
[4] 25.19 & 26; 26.14.
[5] 13.12.
[6] 18.15.
[7] 19.31.
[8] 19.37.
[9] 23.29.
[10] 24.22.
[11] 25.4, 16 & 25; cf. 26.32.
[12] 28.31.

himself could not entirely sustain his thesis that the persecution beginning with Stephen drove the entire Jerusalem congregation out on the missionary road,[1] for by **9.31** the community is already back in Jerusalem and thriving in peace, whereas **11.19ff.** shows the victims of persecution still scattered over the face of the land. The natural inference is that it was not the Church at Jerusalem (nor Peter himself) that began the mission to the Gentiles without the law, but Hellenists from the expelled splinter-group of the 'Seven'.[2] This means that Luke's attempt to reduce the tension between 'Hellenists' and 'Hebrews' to the minimal issue of the widows[3] has not succeeded. Moreover Paul's conflict with the Judaists[4] would be incomprehensible if Peter had already lifted from his shoulders the responsibility for the mission to the Gentiles.

Even the uplifting picture with which Acts closes is not entirely above suspicion. To make such a picture possible, Luke had to suppress the fact that long before Paul ever reached Rome the Christian mission had got a foothold and created a community there. But for the moment we must hold over to the next section (§ 8) the question of the unhistorical character of Luke's presentation of Paul.

The spread of Christianity was no such simple uniform process as the reader of Acts must at first impression be given to believe. The congregations at Damascus, Antioch, Ephesus and Rome were founded by unknown Christians. It is not the oft-broken line of the mission's actual evolution that Luke traces —but its ideal curve.

III. Luke the Writer and Edifier

The elegant exordium of the third gospel has left many scholars with the impression that Luke would have been capable of writing the history of the dawn of Christianity in the style of a Xenophon, if not a Thucydides. However, he lacked at least two requisites for such an undertaking: an adequate historical foundation—and the right readers. Any book he might conceivably offer his readers—especially as a sequel to the third gospel— had to be a work of *edification*. Of course Luke firmly believed that the history of Christian beginnings was edifying in itself, but to present it as such he had to employ a special technique and offer his readers history in the guise of stories. Everything he knew concerning apostolic times, or thought himself entitled to infer, he had to translate into the language of vivid and dramatic scenes. Let us illustrate:

At the beginning of Acts Luke could merely have told his readers: Since the treason of Judas had left a vacancy in the circle of the Twelve, a

---

[1] 8.4.

[2] Cf. **11.19f.**

[3] 6.1ff.

[4] See especially Galatians.

new Apostle had to be chosen to replace him; Matthias was the man. But such a sentence would not have conveyed much significance to the readers. So Luke the writer sets about it another way: he causes a living scene to rise before their eyes. Peter stands up among the brethren and begins a speech[1]: the scripture concerning the death of Judas has been fulfilled and Peter reveals with what manner of death he has been punished. He goes on to cite the psalm-verse which has thus been fulfilled, and that other to whose fulfilment the disciples must now contribute: another must now take the office of Judas. This gives an opportunity for Peter to inform—the readers!— of the qualifications which an Apostle must possess: he must have been a companion of Jesus from the latter's baptism to the Ascension and therefore be able to bear witness to the Resurrection. Lots are cast between two disciples possessing this qualification—for the Holy Spirit capable of deciding the issue has not yet been poured forth—and when the assembly has prayed God to guide them to the man of his choice, the lot falls on Matthias.

This example serves to show Luke's ability to transform a simple report into action and to weave a speech into the course of such an action. That he himself composed the speech is evident from the fact that only the Septuagint text of Psalms 69 and 109 gives the meanings required.

Hand in hand with this gift of enlivening bare facts goes Luke's ability to condense events ranging over a long period and encompass them within

---

[1] The speeches in Acts—Dibelius (*Studies*, 150) has counted 24, of which 8 belong to Peter, 9 to Paul—occupy, in round figures, 300 of the book's 1000 verses. In his valuable essay, 'Hebreisk berättarstil' (*SvTKv* 25 (1949), 81–90), Gillis Gerleman has pointed out that the OT narrators did not interpose themselves between the event and the reader, and therefore allow the reader to 'hear' the direct speech (indirect speech has always passed through the reflection of the narrator, and shows the fact). Luke follows this OT narrative style when, putting words in his characters' mouths with the freedom of an ancient historian, he practically always uses direct speech. There was a schematic preaching-method, much favoured in Luke's time, which has been investigated by Dibelius (*Studies*, 165ff.) and C. H. Dodd (*The Apostolic Preaching and its Developments*, 2nd ed. 1944, 7–36), and it is on this that Luke rings the changes in the missionary speeches of Acts (Chapters 2–4, 7, 8, 10 & 13). Dibelius describes the paradigm in these words: 'An introduction suggested by the actual situation is normally followed by the kerygma of Jesus' life, passion and resurrection, usually with emphasis on the disciples' witness; to this is subjoined a scriptural proof and an exhortation to repentance' (165). Stephen (7.2ff.) and Paul in Antioch (13.15ff.) open with a survey of the history of Israel, as must have been frequent in synagogue homilies. On the other hand, the Areopagus address (17.22ff.), with which we may link the speech at Lystra (14.15–17), gives the model sermon as addressed to Gentiles (Dibelius, *Studies*, 71f.): here the reference to pagan poets is a kind of substitute for the scriptural proof. Paul's Miletus address (20.19–35) is a testament, as it were, portraying the Apostle as the exemplary missionary and leader of the flock whose necessity to the Church will be all the more urgent in the face of the gnostic seduction to come. In Paul's later speeches, relevance to his own trial steadily recedes in favour of the real business in hand, which is to prove Christianity itself innocent of all crimes against Roman law: at bottom it is the one true Judaic religion, and is thus entitled to the tolerance which the State extends to Judaism itself.

a single scene.[1] In his gospel he tells of the two disciples at Emmaus who are joined by the risen Jesus, fail to recognize him, invite him to supper, then realize his identity when he breaks the bread and vanishes (Luke 24.13–35). It goes without saying that Luke is here using a tradition. But one feature of the story does not breathe the air of popular tradition, namely that in the course of conversation the strange fellow-traveller should expound to the two disciples the whole of the scriptures concerning himself (Luke 24.25–7, though we must note that the preceding conversation is also moving up to this point). In reality the Church was not presented with its scriptural proofs complete in one single moment—certainly not in the peculiar manner we find in Luke.[2] On the contrary, they were a gradually accumulated treasure, built up piece by piece as each new teacher or prophet came to grasp the hitherto concealed but actually intended testimonies to Christ in the Old Testament scripture. Such recognitions were the gift of the Lord, indeed, but of the exalted Lord. And it is this whole process whereby the Church acquired its scriptural proofs that Luke draws together in a single scene where the risen Christ gives the disciples at Emmaus the entire scriptural proof from Moses and the prophets for the passion and resurrection of the Messiah.

In Acts, too, Luke employs this device of condensation. In the Palestine of the Apostles there had been much unrest and frequent insurrection. Often in the jostling and turmoil of the great feasts, the daggers of the *sicarii* had struck down suspected collaborators of the Roman occupier. Fired by some 'prophet's' message, great trains of pilgrims had set off into the wilderness, with the hope that there the Messiah would manifest himself. And an Egyptian Jew had led his followers up the Mount of Olives, expecting that now the walls of Jerusalem would fall down before them. But Luke fuses all this in one. 'Aren't you the Egyptian,' says the tribune at 21.38, 'who stirred up a revolt some time ago and led four thousand sicarii into the desert?' In this way Luke makes the point that the Christian message has nothing to do with any political revolution. It would be an error of method to interpret

---

[1] Luke learned another way of representing long periods from Mark—the résumé or 'summary,' as we call it. The longest and most important are to be found in Acts 2.42–5, 4.32–5 and 5.12–16. Luke obtained them largely by generalizing individual incidents. If they contain repetitions, that is no oversight on the writer's part: it is Luke's way of imprinting on the reader's mind his image of the ideal apostolic community. The structural problems of each summary are treated below in the general commentaries on the passages mentioned. With the summaries may also be counted the statements about the growth of the Christian mission. In the article 'Chronology' of the *Hastings Dictionary of the Bible*, C. H. Turner calls six of these (6.7, 9.31, 12.24, 16.5, 19.20 and 28.31) 'panels' separating one important period of the mission from another; but the summaries of 2.47 and 11.21 are at least as significant.

[2] The essential content of the Lucan scriptural proof is the death and resurrection of the Messiah.

E

such a 'condensed' sentence as historical information and hence, say, identify the unarmed pilgrims of the wilderness with the dagger-men of Jerusalem.[1]

Luke was most anxious to impress upon his readers that the Roman authorities treated the Christian missionaries with benevolence and acknowledged them to be politically harmless. Put in the form of a general contention, the idea would scarcely have carried weight: after all, the fate finally suffered by both Peter and Paul spoke clearly against it. Luke was therefore obliged to show in concrete stories how friendly and correct had been the behaviour of Roman officials towards Paul. He found suitable material in the anecdotes of the conversion of Sergius Paulus (**13**.7–12) and Gallio's attitude in Corinth (**18**.12–17). But this was insufficient. Matter was especially lacking for the last period of the captivity in Caesarea. Why did the new and efficient governor Festus not release Paul but send him to Rome? Did this not speak against Paul's innocence, or at least the justness of the Roman? Luke had to prove the contrary by the use of dramatic scenes: a disquisition on legal technicalities would have meant nothing to his readers. Consequently, like a dramatist, he produces a rapid succession of vivid and lively scenes (**25**.14–**26**.32):

Scene 1: in the palace of the Roman governor; Festus and King Agrippa in close conversation. The governor is concerned about a prisoner on a serious charge: the Jews have demanded his condemnation, but Rome lives by the rule of law and condemns no-one unheard. Festus has satisfied himself that Paul has not broken the laws of Rome. But then, there are these intricate questions of Jewish religion, with which Festus is not wholly familiar: the Jews maintain that a certain Jesus is dead, and the prisoner Paul says 'He lives!' (In this way the Christian reader is indirectly shown that poor pagan Festus has not understood the resurrection-message in the slightest. He is not an exception, though, but a typical Roman official, hence this is no case for Roman justice!) Now Festus has to make his report to Rome. What should he write? His Jewish guest shows interest: 'I should like to see this man.' 'You'll hear him tomorrow,' promises Festus.

Scene 2: next day; the audience-chamber is filling; the Caesarean authorities and the officer-corps are already here, and the governor too. Enter King Agrippa with his sister Berenice and an imposing retinue. But the real centre of interest is Paul, who is now brought in by a legionary. Festus recapitulates the case; can Agrippa, the expert *in rebus Iudaicis*, advise him what to do?

---

[1] One cannot help wondering whether a similar 'condensation' is not present in **19**.35. It is never said that the statue of Ephesian Artemis fell from the sky, although it is said of other images. Probably Luke here is making the town-clerk superimpose different features drawn from the cult in order to characterize the veneration in which the local goddess was held.

Scene 3: Paul—in close-up, as it were—speaks. It is of course the readers of the book who are his real public. They hear the story of his life for the second time from his own lips. What is already known is therefore lightly touched upon: he, Paul, who from his earliest youth had lived a Pharisee in Jerusalem, now stands accused by virtue of his adherence to that very hope of resurrection which is Jewish through and through (and has been fulfilled in Jesus!). He did indeed once grievously persecute the followers of this Jesus—here is a rapid flashback to Paul the persecutor, the judge who always voted for the death-penalty. But then came Damascus. A man cannot pit himself against God (the image of the goads!), therefore Paul must be obedient to the commands of Christ. Then comes dramatic by-play between Paul and Festus (who can again make neither head nor tail of the resurrection-message), then Paul and the king, who, however non-committally, expresses his appreciation to the Christian. The final scene is a short consultation in an adjoining room, Agrippa summing up in these words: Paul could have gone free had he not appealed to the emperor.

Thus we may clearly discern Luke's dramatic technique of scene-writing[1] in an episode where, untrammelled by tradition, he enjoyed freedom of movement. Scholars like Zahn, who thought to see in this episode an eyewitness-report by a companion of Paul, have completely overlooked this technique. In reality, once Paul had appealed to the emperor, the case was out of Festus' hands. It no longer mattered whether he thought Paul guilty or not.

But even where a given tradition lay before Luke, he did not by any means feel himself slavishly bound to it. Tradition is not petrified but still molten lava, and the conjuncture of circumstances may permit its transformation, the realization of its many latent possibilities.[2] The clearest

---

[1] In the style of these dramatic episodes De Zwaan (*Beg.* II, 64f.) detects the Alexandrine influence also present in Virgil. Dramatic scenes replace the even flow of narrative. What Wilhelm Kroll, in 'Die Originalität Vergils' (*Neue Jahrbücher für das klassische Altertum*, Leipzig 1908, 521ff.), says about Virgil sounds to a large extent like a description of Luke's procedure: 'his goal is everywhere dramatic and solemn effects, and he heedlessly casts aside everything which does not serve this end; . . . renouncing all broad expansions or digressions, his narrative strives onward to given climaxes, which always possess a strong emotional value' etc. But it was probably the Greek OT and the tradition of the gospels which were Luke's real models for the style of Acts. Whatever reminded a Greek reader of Plutarch, or a Roman of Virgil, appeared to the Christian as the heritage of the sacred past.

[2] This has been most convincingly expressed by Dom Jacques Dupont in his work, *Les Béatitudes*, 2nd ed. 1958: 'It was not the ambition of Matthew, Mark and Luke to preserve for posterity the minutes of Jesus' speeches or any kind of authentic account of the minutiae of his behaviour. An "evangelist," as the name shows, takes it upon himself to declare the good news; whether he does this by speaking or by writing, he performs the work of a preacher. This preaching, being in the direct line of a still vital tradition, bears the impress of eye-witness recollections. But the preacher's purpose in recapitulating these is not simply historiographic: he aims at the same time to consolidate the incidence of Jesus' words and deeds on the life of the Christians he is addressing. Thus the things recounted do not merely belong to a past that is over and done with: what Jesus says and does remains "topical", full of lessons for everyday life' (pp. 10f.).

illustration of this lies in Luke's recounting one and the same event, namely Paul's conversion, in three different ways. Even earlier scholars had noticed the differences. It did not however occur to them to ascribe this diversity to internal causes, the changing necessities of the literary situation. Only an external reason was given, that Luke had differing sources before him and reproduced now this one, now that. This interpretation is at its most triumphant in Emanuel Hirsch,[1] according to whom Luke in Chapter 9 reproduces the account of the Damascene congregation and in Chapter 26 that of Paul himself, whereas in Chapter 22 he shows, as a good historian, how he imagines the two traditions can be reconciled. But for Luke 'the conversion of Paul' was an event which had to be told differently according to the context. Of course certain elements always recur—Paul on the road to Damascus; the light from heaven; the voice crying 'Saul, Saul, why are you persecuting me?'; the question, 'Lord, who are you?' and the answer: 'I am Jesus, whom you are persecuting!' But every other feature of the story may be changed if necessary. And it is necessary.

It is in Chapter 9 that the story is first told, as a report of the writer referring to Paul in the third person. The reader is not yet acquainted with the incident and its consequences, therefore must be made aware of the significance of the episode. For this purpose, a present-day narrator would, having described the event, break into the account with an observation of his own: 'Now consider what an unprecedented transformation we have here—the persecutor becoming the missionary of the persecuted' etc. But Luke goes to work another way. He does not break off the description, but puts everything he wishes to say to the reader in the mouths of the protagonists themselves. He does the same thing elsewhere in Acts: thus in **1**.18f. it is Peter who announces the fate of Judas, in **2**.8–11 it is the actual witnesses of the events of Pentecost who enumerate the peoples, and in **21**.21 the elders in Jerusalem who inform Paul of the Jews' accusations against him. Here, in the conversion episode, the reader must have everything from the lips of Ananias or of the Lord himself. Luke to begin with resorts to a device belonging to Hellenistic narrative technique: the 'double dream.' This enables him to show at one and the same time how Paul behaved during the three days in question, and how it came about that Ananias rescued him. Next Luke employs a dialogue, in which Ananias portrays Saul as the dreaded persecutor who has come with full authority to launch a reign of terror. With this Christ contrasts what Saul is henceforth—no longer a persecutor of the name of Christ, but one who will carry that name before the Gentiles, the kings and the sons of Israel: no longer one who brings suffering to the Christians, but one who himself suffers for the sake of Christ.

---

[1] *ZNW* 28 (1929), 305–12; see our commentary below on **9**.1–19a.

But all this is already known to the reader of Chapter 22. Here it is a
question of vindicating the gentile mission in the teeth of the fanatical Jews,
and this is achieved by a Pauline autobiography: he who carried the mission
to the Gentiles recounts his life and his vocation. Like every speech of
antiquity, this one begins, however unobtrusively, with a *captatio benevolentiae*, inasmuch as Paul first (verses 3f.) dwells on what he has in common
with the listeners: he first came to Jerusalem as a little child (hence is
practically a born Jerusalemite), and there Gamaliel instilled in him the strict
observance of the law. He was therefore as zealous for the law as his present
audience—more zealous, even, for he had hounded Christians to their deaths.
But now is told again, with certain discrepancies of detail, the incident of
the Damascus road, up to the moment where he had to wait in that city for
further guidance. This time, however, the dialogue between Christ and
Ananias is left out. For with this the readers are already acquainted—and
before this fanatical audience Jesus must be mentioned as little as possible.
Instead, Ananias is represented as a pious Jew whom the Damascus Jewish
community holds in high esteem: thus to become a Christian, it is implied,
does not mean cutting oneself off from one's people as a renegade. But so
pious a Jew cannot very well disclose to Paul his missionary vocation towards
the Gentiles. A second scene is therefore necessary, and on this Paul embarks
immediately: praying on the holy ground of the Temple, he, whose only
desire was to be a witness of Christ to the Jews, fell into a trance and heard
Christ commanding him to go forth from Jerusalem, since his witness would
be rejected: 'I send you afar to the Gentiles!' At this the anger of the
people flares up anew, and Paul's speech is brought to an abrupt end. Yet
Luke has made his point: that Christ made Paul a missionary to the Gentiles
against Paul's own wish and on account of Jewish unbelief.

In Chapter 26 it is once again a question of justifying the Christian
mission to the Gentiles, as symbolized by Paul, but this time in the presence
of the Roman authorities and the expert in Jewish affairs, King Agrippa II.
Thus Paul's speech is constructed somewhat differently. It is unnecessary to
recapitulate in detail what is already familiar to the reader, Paul's childhood
and the instruction of Gamaliel. Paul needs only to represent himself as a
man of Jerusalem and a strict Pharisee. On the other hand, his persecution
of the Christians in Jerusalem is more vividly depicted so as to intensify the
contrast with the vision before Damascus. Paul (and Luke), for the sake of
the Greek listeners (and readers), explains the necessity of obeying Christ's
command by the Greek proverb of the goads: Greek paganism, too, knew
well enough that fate was irresistible. For the Jewish listeners however (and
readers who knew their Bible), the directive of Christ is presented in an
elaborate tissue of OT quotations: Old Testament prophecies find their
fulfilment in Paul's call to the Gentile mission. Paul cannot disobey this direct
command of God. But since it is direct, Ananias the intermediary has to

disappear, and with him also the healing of the blindness, and the blinding itself. All, both Paul and his travelling-companions, now see the light and fall to the ground (**26**.13), but nobody is blinded. Thus, when the situation demands, the narrator has even to renounce the feature of the blinding of Paul, which quite certainly was part and parcel of the conversion-story current in the Church.

That a writer should thus make free with tradition[1] must at first strike us as irresponsible, as an unwarranted licence. But evidently Luke has a conception of the narrator's calling that is different from ours. For him, a narration should not describe an event with the precision of a police-report, but must make the listener or reader aware of the inner significance of what happened, and impress upon him, unforgettably, the truth of the power of God made manifest in it. The writer's obedience is indeed fulfilled in the very freedom of his rendering.

Bibliography

H. J. Cadbury, 'Luke Translator or Author?', *American Journal of Theology* 34 (1920), 436–50; J. de Zwaan, 'Was the Book of Acts a Posthumous Edition?', *HTR* 17, 95–153; M. A. Reinke, 'The Church in Acts' (diss.), The Divinity School, University of Chicago, 1926; W. G. Letham, 'Luke's Literary Method as a Controlling Factor in the Composition of Acts' (diss.), The Divinity School, University of Chicago, 1926; W. Bartlett, 'St. Paul and the Twelve', *Exp. Tim.* 39 (1927–8), 39–44; J. R. Smith, 'The Purpose of Luke-Acts' (diss.), The Divinity School, University of Chicago, 1929; E. Barnikol, *Der nichtpaulin. Ursprung des Parallelismus d. Apostel Petrus u. Paulus* (Gal. 2^{7-8}), 1931 (=*Forsch. z. Gesch. d. Urchrtms. u. d. Kirche*, V); L. B. Radford, 'St. Peter and St. Paul', *Exp. Tim.* 35 (1933–4) 300–5; K. Lake and S. Lake, 'The Acts of the Apostles', *JBL* 53 (1934) 34–45; M. Riddle, 'The Admission of the Gentiles in St. Luke's Gospel and Acts', *JTS* 36 (1935), 160–73; J. Renié, 'Valeur historique des Actes des Apôtres', *Rev. Apologétique* 61 (1935), 24–37; Id., 'L'enseignement doctrinal des Actes des Apôtres', *La nouvelle revue théologique* 62 (1935), 268–77; E. M. Schofield, 'Luke's Interest in Medical Terms' (diss.), Southern Baptist Theol. Seminary, 1937; K. Karner, 'Die Stellung d. Apostels Paulus i. Urchristentum', *ZsystTh.* 14 (1937), 142–93; O. Bauernfeind, 'Die Geschichtsauffassung d. Urchristentums', *ZsystTh.* 15 (1938), 347–78; M. S. Enslin, '"Luke" and "Paul"', *JAOS* 58 (1938), 81–91; S. E. Johnson, 'A Proposed Form-Critical Treatment of Acts', *AngThR* 21 (1939), 22–31; W. Grundmann, 'Das Problem des hellenist. Christentums innerhalb d. Jerusalemer Urgemeinde', *ZNW* 38 (1939), 45–73; Id., 'Die Apostel zwisch. Jerusalem u. Antiochia', *ZNW* 39 (1940), 110–37; W. G. Kümmel, 'Das Urchristentum', *ThR* 14

---

[1] See Haenchen, 'Tradition und Komposition in der Apostelgeschichte' in *ZThK* 52 (1955), 205–25.

(1942), 81–95, 155–73; S. H. Price, 'The Authorship of Luke-Acts', *Exp. Tim.* 55 (1943–4), 194; T. W. Manson, 'The Work of St. Luke', *BJRL* 28 (1944), 382–403; B. Katzenmayer, 'Die Beziehungen des Petrus zur Urkirche v. Jerusalem u. Antiochia', *Intern. kirchl. Zeitschrift* 35 (1945), 116–30; H. Sahlin, 'Kyrkotanken på apostlarnas tid. En studie av Apostlagärningarnas förra hälft', *Ny kyrkl. Tidskr.* 16 (1947), 81–98; R. Leija, 'Prédication des Apôtres', *La nouvelle rev. théol.* 69 (1947), 605–18; V. Jacques, 'L'expansion chrétienne à partir de la Pentecôte', *Rev. diocésaine de Namur* 2 (1947), 73–89; Id., 'L'apostolat de Saint Pierre auprès des Juifs', ibid. 153–60; W. G. Kümmel, 'Das Urchristentum', *ThR* 17 (1948–9), 3–50, 103–42; M. Goguel, *Les premiers temps de l'église*, Paris 1949; W. G. Kümmel, 'Das Urchristentum', *ThR* 18 (1950), 1–53; A. Rétif, 'Témoignage et prédication missionnaires dans les Actes des Apôtres', *La nouvelle revue théol.* 83 (1951), 152–65; C. F. D. Moule, *Christ's Messengers. Studies in the Acts of the Apostles*, New York 1954 (World Christian Books, Association Press); C. S. C. Williams, 'The Date of Luke-Acts', *Exp. Tim.* 64 (1952–3), 283f; A. Rétif, *Foi au Christ et mission d'après les Actes des Apôtres*, Paris 1953; W. G. Kümmel, 'Das Urchristentum', *ThR* 22 (1954), 138–70, 191–211; Ph.-H. Menoud, 'Le plan des Actes des Apôtres', *NTS* 1 (1954–5), 44–51; G. W. H. Lampe, 'The Holy Spirit in the Writings of Luke' in *Studies in the Gospels. Essays in Memory of R. H. Lightfoot*, ed. Nineham, Oxford 1955, 159–200; W. C. van Unnik, 'Opmerkingen over het doel van Lucas' Geschiedwerk (Luc. 1[1–4])' *Nederl. Theol. Tijdschr.* 9 (1955), 323–31; F. Stagg, *The Book of Acts; The Early Struggle for an Unhindered Gospel*, Nashville, Broadman Press, 1955; H. M. Féret, *Pierre et Paul à Antioch et à Jérusalem* Paris, 1955; C. P. M. Jones, 'The Epistle to the Hebrews and the Lucan Writings' in *Studies in the Gospels. Essays in Memory of R. H. Lightfoot*, ed. D. E. Nineham, Oxford 1955, 113–43; E. Molland, 'La circoncision, le baptême et l'autorité du décret apostolique dans les milieux judéochrétiens des Pseudo-Clémentines', *Stud. Theol.* 9 (1955), 1–39; W. C. van Unnik, 'Christendom en nationalisme in de eerste ecuwen der kerkgeschiedenis' in *Christendom en nationalisme*, 's Gravenhage 1956, 38–54; C. F. Evans, 'The Kerygma', *JTS* 7 (1956), 25–41; J. Baker, 'Luke the Critical Evangelist', *Exp. Tim.* 68 (1956–7) 123–5; J. Dupont, 'Pierre et Paul dans les Actes', *Rev. Bibl.* 64 (1957), 35–47; E. Haenchen, 'Apostelgeschichte' in RGG[3] I, Tübingen 1957, 501–7; W. Hillmann, 'Grundzüge d. urkirchliche Glaubensverkündigung', *Wissensch. u. Weisheit* 20 (1957), 163–80; G. Heuthorst, 'The Apologetic Aspect of Acts 2:1–13', *Scripture* 9 (1957), 33–43; J. Hamaide and P. Guilbert, 'Résonances pastorales du plan des Actes des Apôtres', *Église vivante* 9 (1957), 95–113; W. Baird, 'What is the Kerygma? A Study of I Cor. 15:3–8 and Gal. 1:15–17', *JBL* 76 (1957), 181–91; R. G. Nikolainen, 'Till frågan om Apostlagärningarnas komposition', *Sv. Exeg. Årsskr.* 22–3 (1957–8), 119–26; A. Ehrhardt, 'The Construction and Purpose of Acts' in *Stud. Theol.* 12 (1958), 45–79; W. G. Kümmel, 'Futurische u. präsent. Eschatologie im ältesten Urchristentum', *NTS* 5 (1959), 113–26; A. C. Winn, 'Elusive Mystery. The Purpose of Acts' in *Interpretation* 13 (1959), 144–56;

J. Munck, 'Jewish Christianity in Post-Apostolic Times', *NTS* 6 (1960), 103–16; W. C. van Unnik, 'The "Book of Acts" the Confirmation of the Gospel', *Nov. Test.* 4 (1960), 26–59; G. Klein, 'Galater 2:6–9 u. d. Geschichte der Jerusalemer Urgemeinde', *ZThK* 57 (1960), 275–95; Id., *Die zwölf Apostel. Ursprung und Gehalt einer Idee*, Göttingen 1961; U. Wilckens, *Die Missionsreden der Apostelgeschichte*, Neukirchen Kreis Moers 1961 (= *Wiss. Monographien z. A. u. N.T.*, vol. 5); C. K. Barrett, *Luke the Historian in Recent Study*, London, Epworth Press 1961 (A. S. Peake Memorial Lecture No. 6); W. Eltester, 'Lukas und Paulus' in *Eranion. Festschr. f. H. Hommel*, Tübingen 1961, 1–17; W. Schmithals, *Das kirchliche Apostelamt. Eine historische Untersuchung*, Göttingen 1961 (ET *The Office of Apostle in the Early Church*, 1969); E. Haenchen, 'Das "Wir" in der Apostelgeschichte und das Itinerar', *ZThK* 58 (1961); Id., 'Acta 27' in *Zeit u. Geschichte* (Bultmann Festschr.), Tübingen 1964, 235–54; Id., 'The Book of Acts as Source Material for the History of the Early Church', *Stud. in Luke/Acts* ed. by L. E. Keck and J. L. Martin, 1966, 258–78.

8. LUKE AND PAUL

It was a tradition from the second half of the second century[1] which first identified the author of Acts with 'Luke, the beloved physician.'[2] For the sake of simplicity we have up to now likewise denoted the author as 'Luke,' and shall continue to do so. But we have to ask ourselves whether this writer was really that companion of Paul, or any companion of his at all. To prepare for an answer to this question, let us recall three things:

1. For both 'Luke' and Paul, the overriding problem was that of the *mission to the Gentiles without the law*. But 'Luke' is *unaware of Paul's solution*. Paul was able to justify the mission without the law on *internal* evidence: the law leads not to God, but into sin.[3] For it causes man to put his trust not in God, but in his own righteousness.[4] Even so, admittedly, it still has served the purposes of God, who has shut up all under unbelief.[5] But Christ is the end of the law for all who believe.[6] For when the sinner places his trust in Christ, the son of God, he thereby enters into the right

---

[1] Irenaeus, *Adv. haer.* III 1.1; 10, 1; 12.1–15; 14, 1. *Canon Muratori* (ed. Lietzmann) *fol.* 10r, lines 2ff.; 10v, lines 34ff.

[2] Col. 4.14. Irenaeus and the theologian author of the *Canon Muratori* both obviously derived their evidence of Luke's authorship from an appraisal of NT data.

[3] Gal. 3.19; cf. Bultmann, *Theologie des Neuen Testaments*, 261ff. (ET *Theology of the New Testament* I, 259ff.), and see also Rom. 4.13–16, II Cor. 3.6 and I Cor. 15.56.

[4] Rom. 10.3.

[5] Gal. 3.21f.

[6] Rom. 10.4.

relationship to God. Of this view of the law, with its simultaneous affirmation and negation, there is no trace in Acts. When in **15**.10 Peter says of the law that 'neither we nor our fathers could bear' this 'yoke,' something quite different is meant: here the Judaic law is regarded as through the eyes of a Gentile Christian, who would see in it a mass of commands and prohibitions such as no-one could unravel or master.

Luke has no doubt whatever of the legitimacy of the Gentile mission; on the contrary he takes it for granted. Yet he is incapable of justifying it, like Paul, 'from within'. He must therefore seize on a justification 'from without' —God willed the mission, and that was sufficient. One can speak here of a majestic divine will that will brook no discussion; nevertheless, inasmuch as men cannot grasp it on its inward side, it smacks of that ineluctable destiny known to pagan belief.[1] Be that as it may, Luke was not greatly helped by the bare reference to the will of God: how could he persuade his *readers* that God really willed *this* and no other thing? It is here that the miracle, the 'sign,' attains its full significance for Luke—and, we may be sure, for the community in which he lived. The miracles and signs form the visible, demonstrable, reliable legitimation. That is why they play so dominant a role in the work of Luke. They are the accompaniment of the beginning and development of the mission in general, from **2**.1ff. onwards, but more especially of the Gentile mission.[2] The miracles give to the Gentile mission the good conscience that 'it is God's will.'

2. On this basis we can understand a further fact: there is a *discrepancy between the 'Lucan' Paul and the Paul of the epistles.*

(a) Luke portrays in Paul (as in Peter before him) the great *miracle-worker*. Paul blinds Elymas (**13**.6–12), gives the cripple at Lystra the power to walk (**14**.8–10) and, when apparently killed by stoning, rises up and continues his mission (**14**.19f.). In healings and exorcisms, moreover, the touch of his hand is superfluous: his very body-linen, his handkerchiefs, are so full of his miraculous power, that they quell disease and drive out evil spirits (**19**.12). In such a context it is not surprising that a serpent's venom should leave him unscathed (**28**.3–6) or that Eutychus should return to life (**20**.7–12) when Paul lies upon his corpse, as Elijah and Elisha lay on the dead boys (I Kings **17**.21 & II Kings **4**.34). Now it is true that the real Paul did on one occasion lay claim to the 'signs of an Apostle' (II Cor. **12**.12), but the exploits in question were so little out of the ordinary that his opponents flatly denied his ability to perform miracles.[3] The important fact is

---

[1] This is why Luke is able to employ the proverb of the goads with reference to Paul's vocation (**26**.14). Of course Paul himself speaks (in I Cor. **9**.16) of a necessity which is laid upon him, but here it represents his being subjectively conquered by his recognition of the glory of God in the countenance of Christ: II Cor. **4**.6.

[2] Acts **10**.1–**11**.18; cf. also **9**.1–19a *Par.* & **13**.1–4 and see the commentary on these passages.

[3] Cf. E. Käsemann, 'Die Legitimität des Apostels' in *ZNW* (1942/43) 35.

that Paul did not see the essential of his apostolate in such feats; far from overcoming all obstacles by miraculous means, an Apostle must plunge into the depths of suffering and *there* experience the help of Christ (II Cor. **12**.10).[1]

(b) The same state of affairs may be demonstrated from a second point of difference: the 'Lucan' Paul is an *outstanding orator*. His enemies are obliged to engage an advocate—Paul defends himself with convincing eloquence (Acts **24**.1ff., 10ff.). Hardly snatched from the rough handling of the raging mob, he steps forward once again with the orator's raised hand, and the turbulent throng is hushed (**21**.40, **22**.1f.). Whether he speaks before Jews[2] or Gentiles,[3] governors[4] or philosophers (**17**.22–31), he is never at a loss for the right word. He is a born orator, imposing himself with the eloquence of a Demosthenes. Alas, the real Paul, as he himself admits, was anything but a master of the improvised speech. He has found, in dictating his letters, words which have echoed down the centuries: as a speaker he was feeble, unimpressive (II Cor. **10**.10). When Luke paints so different a portrait of him, it is not the alchemy of remembrance which is at work, but the presumption, so tempting for the later generation, that Paul the great missionary must also have been Paul the great orator.

(c) It is not until we thus see the splendour in which Luke has bathed the figure **of Paul** that we can properly appreciate the remarkable fact that *he did not affirm Paul's real claim*. When Paul embarked upon his European mission, he demanded of the communities he founded that they should recognize him as an Apostle in the highest sense, with as good a title to the name as the Twelve, nay Peter himself (Gal. **2**.8). In the kerygma proclaimed to the Church it is reported: 'Christ appeared to Cephas ... then he appeared to James,' and from there Paul continues with his own, 'he appeared also to me' (I Cor. **15**.5–8). And Paul had furthermore received—from no man, not even from any of the Twelve—a unique commission: to bring the gospel to the Gentiles (Gal. **2**.7).

Acts takes another view. In Acts only the Twelve are Apostles.[5] They were called by the Lord himself and lived in community with him from his baptism to the Ascension (Acts **1**.21f.). They had eaten and drunk with the risen Christ (**10**.41). They alone, therefore, could fulfil the conditions of apostolic witness. Paul, like any other Christian missionary, must appeal to their authority (**13**.31). Not only is the place thereby assigned to him completely at variance with his own claim, but also the underlying notion of events. For Paul, Jesus was no longer 'flesh and blood' (I Cor. **15**.50) after

---

[1] Cf. E, Käsemann, 'Die Legitimität des Apostels' in *ZNW* (1942/43) 69–71.
[2] Acts **13**.16–41; **22**.1–21; **23**.1ff.; **26**.2–23, 27; **28**.17–20, 26–8.
[3] **14**.15–17; **17**.22–31.
[4] **13**.9–11; **24**.10–21; **25**.10f.; **26**.2–26.
[5] It makes no difference that in **14**.4 & 14 Paul and Barnabas, as envoys from Antioch, are called 'Apostles'.

his resurrection—he and Peter had been allowed to *see* the transfigured Lord (I Cor. **9**.1), and the idea that the risen Christ had eaten and drunk with the disciples would have rung like a blasphemy in Paul's ears. Luke, however, oblivious of difficulties, takes for granted the more down-to-earth representation that had grown up as almost a practical necessity in a later generation, when all those witnesses had died and the reality of Jesus' resurrection had to be defended against gnostic docetism and Jewish or pagan scepticism at one and the same time.

3. Finally, Acts draws a *picture of relations between Jews and Christians which contradicts that of the Pauline epistles.* From beginning to end, according to Acts, the Jewish hostility to the Christians was kindled by the latter's preaching of the Resurrection (Acts **4**.2, **28**.23). In Acts it is no special doctrine of his which brings Jewish persecution down on Paul's head, but the general Christian message of the resurrection. This exactly matches the overall view of Acts, according to which all Christian missionaries taught the same doctrine (**7**.52, 55f. & **18**.24–8). Since Luke is moreover convinced that this very teaching corresponds to the hope of the Jews,[1] we necessarily arrive at the astounding contention that Paul was expressly persecuted by the Jews for disseminating an age-old Jewish doctrine. There is clearly something amiss in this contention, and indeed one has only to examine the matter closely to discover two points in which Luke has distorted the position:

In the first place, the Pharisaic doctrine of resurrection is by no means congruent with the Christian. The Pharisees expect the resurrection of the dead at the *end* of this aeon; a resurrection in the *middle* of this aeon—and such, according to Luke, was that of Jesus—has nothing in common with the Pharisaic expectation.[2] But—and here we come to the second point—it was not the message that Christ had risen which set the Jews against Paul and the Gentile Christians. Even in Acts itself, at certain places, a quite different situation may be glimpsed: in **15**.5 Christian Pharisees demand the circumcision of the Gentile Christians; in **21**.21 the Jews declare that Paul is teaching men to forsake the law; in **21**.28 the Ephesian Jews on pilgrimage in Jerusalem fall upon Paul in the Temple because he everywhere teaches against the law!

In fact, any fellow-worker of Paul's must have known that what brought him everywhere into conflict with the Jews was his teaching with regard to the law and his corresponding missionary practice.[3] If any of Paul's fellow-workers had maintained that the stumbling-block was not his view of the law but his message of resurrection (an ostensibly Jewish message at that!), he

---

[1] Acts **23**.6; **24**.15, 21; **26**.6f., 27; **28**.20.

[2] Still less has the Christian doctrine of the death and resurrection of the Messiah anything to do with the Pharisaic doctrine of resurrection.

[3] Cf. I Thess. **2**.15: the Jews who 'hinder us from speaking to the Gentiles that they may be saved.'

could only have been speaking against his better knowledge. On the other hand this contradiction is easily resolved if here, in Acts, we are listening to the voice of a man of the sub-apostolic age. For such a person, Christianity and Judaism had already drifted apart: they still spoke against each other, but no longer listened to each other. Only a Christian of the sub-apostolic period could have entertained the 'Lucan' viewpoint, according to which Christianity and Judaism were at bottom, in their resurrection faith, really one, and it was only an unfortunate misunderstanding on the part of the Jews which caused the conflict to break out just at this point. This argument could no longer, of course, be expected to convince a Jew. But then, it was not designed to win Jews to the fold; it was designed to win over the Roman authorities.

The time has come to strike the balance: the representation of Paul in Acts—not to mention the overall picture of missionary beginnings—shows that here we have no collaborator of Paul telling his story, but someone of a later generation trying in his own way to give an account of things that can no longer be viewed in their true perspective. That this writer venerated Paul and sought in every way to bring his achievements to light, to make them 'tell,' that much is evident from every line he devotes to the Apostle—and quite half of Acts is concerned with Paul. Yet it is no less evident that the real Paul, as known to his followers and opponents alike, has been replaced by a Paul seen through the eyes of a later age, and that the primitive age of Christianity is not described here by one who lived through the greater part of it. We need have no qualms about letting this truth be the last word, for without detracting from Luke's real merit, it ensures that the gospel according to Paul will not be robbed of its due.

Bibliography

See on § 7, p. 110ff. above.

9. THE WORK CONTINUES

Research into Acts in recent years has made rapid progress. For long it had been at a standstill, because scholars disagreed on the one question in which they were interested, namely that of the sources. Only when it was recognized how important are the questions of Lucan composition and theology did the picture change. Acts became a favourite theme for NT research. But the more clearly the uniqueness of the Lucan theology appeared, the livelier became the opposition. Acts was accused of replacing the Pauline *theologia crucis* with the *theologia gloriae* and thereby introducing early Catholicism.

In recent years the traditional questions concerning the author of Acts and his sources have not been silenced, but rather have become even more lively. At the same time it has been shown that there are various ways of explaining why Luke portrays Paul as such a law-abiding Jew. The portrait of Paul in Acts becomes an especially attractive problem. The big surprise is, however, something else: Lucan theology has found fervent supporters who maintain that it is precisely the Lucan doctrine of salvation history that permits a deeper understanding of revelation. We shall briefly discuss the most important literature according to this sequence of problems: 'author and sources,' 'the meaning of the Lucan portrait of Paul', and 'the significance of the Lucan theology of history'.

I

The question of sources had already been considered in some detail in 1959 in the 12th edition of the present commentary (see above § 6, pp. 81–90). A year later appeared the learned book of DOM JACQUES DUPONT: *Les sources du Livre des Actes. État de la question* (ET London 1964). Dupont, appealing especially to J. Jeremias, M. Dibelius and H. J. Cadbury, came out in favour of authorship by Paul's companion Luke, the physician, who had made use of an itinerary. The arguments of the 12th edition against this authorship (see above § 8, pp. 112–116) he rejected: 'We must admit that these massive objections impress us very little' (ET, 127 n. 52); in another place (141 n. 10) he even states: 'Such antitheses seem to us very superficial.' Yet Dupont admitted in the summary at the end of his investigation: 'The predominant impression is certainly very negative . . . it has not been possible to define any of the sources . . . in a way which will meet with widespread agreement among the critics' (166).

In this admission of problems which remain unsolved, Dupont is very close to ANDREW JACOB MATTILL, Jr., at that time Assistant Professor, who in 1959 in his work *Luke as a Historian in Criticism since 1840* recognized at the conclusion of his presentation: 'Many problems remain unsolved, perhaps unsolvable, and many ghosts refuse to be laid' (383). Mattill's work— it earned him the degree of Doctor of Philosophy in Religion at Vanderbilt University in Nashville, Tennessee—did not only deal with the source problem. The author reviewed for the reader the different epochs of research since Schneckenburger and the Tübingen school, and questioned each one about what they thought of Luke as a historian. Mattill has withheld his own opinion as much as possible, making reference to the words of William Sanday: 'Opinions are always less important than the presentation of the data' (p. 8). Yet he came to the concluding judgement: every objective investigation will see in Luke one of those true historians whom Polybius (I, 14) characterized as writing 'for the truth and the good of mankind' (p. 383). One might formulate the conception of a good historian that is presupposed here as follows: He presents the events as they actually happened. But what does one do, then, with the discrepancy between the Lucan picture of Paul and the Pauline epistles? Mattill does not deny it, but thinks he can smooth it away by the following statement: 'Paul was less "Pauline" and more Jewish than "hyperpaulinists" have allowed. . . . Whatever disagreement there was between Paul and Jewish Christians in principle, there was inevitably accommodation in practice on both sides.' (p. 322)

WALTER ELTESTER ('Lukas and Paulus' in *Eranion*, Festschrift für H. Hommel, Tübingen 1961, 1–17) also sees the differences between the Paulines and the picture of Paul in Acts. They do not however preclude Lucan authorship, but rather can be explained: 'In view of the extraordinary value for Luke of the tradition "from the beginning", he had to give special distinction to the disciples, who were now the guarantors of the gospel tradition, by recognizing them alone as Apostles' (10). The fact that Luke depicts Paul and the other disciples as devout Jews and men of the law is explained by the fact that Luke saw 'in the Church the Israel of Promise' (15). He had to make the Gentile Christians certain of this, that they were really the people of promise. 'It is simply the will to self-assertion of a Church which has usurped the documents of its faith that finds expression in Luke' (*ibid.*). Finally: Luke was 'not a Jew, but a Greek' (16). Hence the inner problems of the OT were to him a closed book. He could not therefore appropriate the Pauline doctrine of the law.

Three different solutions to the question of authorship have thus been offered, each of which assumes that Luke the physician wrote Acts. But the first solution says that there was no difference at all between Luke and Paul. The second admits the difference, but considers it purely theoretical. Finally, the third seeks to explain why Luke did not understand Paul although he was his pupil. In our opinion none of these solutions is very happy.

DUPONT's three authorities leave him in the lurch. The arguments of the preceding commentary against Jeremias (see below, p. 255) have still not been refuted. If they sound weak in Dupont's reproduction, it is only because they are not accurately quoted. Dibelius had only one reason for considering Luke the author of Acts, as we have shown in the article 'Das "Wir" in der Apg. und das Itinerar' which appeared in *ZThK* 58 (1961) 329–66 (ET 1965): an ancient writing with a dedication was intended for the bookmarket. It could not however appear without an author's name. A. D. Nock has shown (*Gnomon* 25 (1953) 501) that Dibelius misunderstood the ancient dedication and the ancient method of book publication. There were anonymous books; they were cited according to the name of the person to whom they were dedicated (Dupont in mentioning Nock's objections against Dibelius names among others the 'Letter to Diognetus' and the four books on rhetoric 'ad Herennium': ET p. 138 n. 3); the books were disseminated mostly by private copyists. Dibelius is thereby excluded as a primary authority. Cadbury finally had inferred the Lucan composition of Acts from the prologue to the third gospel. We believe we have shown in the above-mentioned article on the 'we' in Acts that Cadbury's explanation of the prologue to Luke is not possible. Luke 1.1 speaks of the events which have occurred 'among us' (the Christians). These events have been reported by 'many', scil. in gospels. This already indicates that this prologue says nothing about Acts. For at that time there were several gospels but not several Acts. Luke 1.2 indicates the presupposition of these gospels: the eyewitnesses have reported the events (of the life of Jesus) as 'servants of the Word'. Luke apparently knows of no gospel written by an Apostle. He clearly differentiates himself and the 'many' from the 'eyewitnesses'. Luke 1.3 describes his own work: '(Since many have composed "gospels"), I also have decided . . . to write for I have carefully followed everything from the beginning.' According to Cadbury παρακολουθεῖν here means 'to have participated directly in the events' and not to have received the information second-hand. This meaning παρακολουθεῖν cannot possess here because of its connection with ἀκριβῶς. I can obtain accurate information, but not participate accurately in the mission. Moreover, 'everything' does not fit Cadbury's proposed meaning: Luke would indeed have been present only during a part of the Pauline mission. If none the less we wished with Cadbury to assume that the sentence 'for I have followed everything carefully for a long time' refers to Luke's participation in the Pauline mission in the second half of Acts, then the entire prologue to the third gospel would lose its meaning; for Luke then in this prologue to the gospel would only be demonstrating his qualifications as a writer of the *historia Pauli*, but would say not a word of his qualification as a writer of the *historia Jesu*. In other words, the prologue to the third gospel says nothing about Acts.

Dupont has further appealed to the 'we' in Acts. It need not however by any means indicate that the author writes as an eyewitness. Dibelius himself in 1923 (*Studies*, 7 n. 15) had described it as possible that Luke 'obtained a short report of the events from some other place (and affirmed his informant's part as a witness in the "we") . . .'

We have decided in favour of just this possibility for good reasons. However, BARRETT also writes in his recent book, *Luke the Historian in Recent Study* (London 1961, 22) concerning the 'we' in Acts: 'This means, not necessarily that the author was an eye-witness but that he had some sort of access to some sort of eye-witness material for this part of the narrative.' Thus this argument for the composition of Acts by an eyewitness also fails. It is indeed very noteworthy that the author does not, like Josephus in the

'Jewish War,' refer to his having seen the events personally. Rather he indicates indirectly that he has utilized written sources for his gospel.

MATTILL's work (kindly made available to me on microfilm) is valuable not only for its very perceptive and lively account of the history of scholarship on Acts, which is supplemented by numerous 'Appendices' (384–468), but also for its almost exhaustive bibliography (469–634), to which we are obliged for many otherwise unattainable accounts. But Mattill's conception of correct historiography makes him consider the form-critical view of the Lucan composition of Acts as an evasion of the historical question (315), indeed as historical scepticism. Thus he can derive from the present commentary, to the tenth edition of which he devoted a chapter of its own ('The Revaluation of Acts by Haenchen': 297–314) the conception that Acts is only a historical novel. In reality the passage cited for this (*ZThK* 52 (1955) 210) only affirms that Luke as a historian enjoyed a freedom which we today grant only to the historical novel; it thus by no means affirms that Acts as such is 'a historical novel'.

The way in which Mattill interprets the 'disagreements' between Paul and the Jewish-Christians, namely as an opposition only in principle but not sustained in practice, does not seem to us commendable, although Alf Kragerud ('Itinerariet i Apostlenes gjerninger', in: *Norsk teologisk tidsskrift* 56 (1955), 249–72; see p. 268) differentiates in a similar manner Paul's 'theory and transcendental perspective' on one hand and his 'actual practice and immanent level' on the other hand. For Gal. 2.11ff. shows all too clearly that for Paul his theology was just not simply theory, but determined his practice. The distinction drawn by Mattill and Kragerud means only, strictly speaking, that one decides against the Pauline self-attestation (as a purely 'theoretical' speculation!) in order to be able to consider the statements in Acts as historically reliable.

ELTESTER's article contains important insights and observations to which we shall return later. But his attempt to secure the ecclesiastical tradition concerning the composition of Acts by the physician Luke encounters insurmountable difficulties. This companion of Paul, according to tradition—this one may not forget—was with Paul not only during the short journey from Troas to Philippi and the longer one from Philippi to Jerusalem, but also (if for the moment we disregard the period of Paul's imprisonment in Caesarea) during the journey to Rome and the two years of the Roman imprisonment, of which Acts 28.30 speaks. Such a fellow worker of Paul would have known exactly how energetically Paul laid claim to the title of Apostle and how tenaciously he defended it—for to reject his apostleship was to deny his gospel. When Eltester refers to the extraordinary value of the tradition of the life of Jesus, authenticated by the Twelve, which allowed only the Twelve to be considered Apostles, then he ought to ascribe to Luke a second conversion: from the Pauline proclamation of Christ to the apostolic

Church of the Twelve. In other words: this Luke must have taken a mental leap out of the apostolic age, in which he had very actively participated, into the post-apostolic generation and its view of things, if he had written Acts. Eltester's second explanation leads to difficulties just as deep. That to this fellow worker of Paul's the Old Testament should appear as an usurped document of faith, and that to conceal this usurpation he presented Paul, against his better knowledge, as a man of the law, certainly cannot be maintained. And finally: even if Luke as a 'Greek' did not understand the 'inner problematics' of the Old Testament, this would not in the least explain why—again against better judgment—he should have suppressed the fact that the Jews persecuted Paul because of his attitude to the law. That Paul, to whom his one-time Pharisaism was 'dung' (σκύβαλα, Phil. **3**.8!), from which he had turned away in order to win Christ; that this Paul before the council should recall his unbroken association with the Pharisees and therefore was to a large extent shielded by them (Acts **23**.6,9), is an idea so grotesque that it is only comprehensible in a member of the post-apostolic generation who no longer had any notion of Paul's real conflicts. He who, like Eltester, has eaten of the tree of historical criticism cannot remain in the paradise of naive tradition.

II

The portrait of Paul in Acts has occasioned much discussion on account of its differences from the Pauline epistles. In spite of this it is questionable whether one may consider it 'the' problem of Acts, or whether it ought not rather to be classified in a larger context. It is further in dispute whether there is only one such comprehensive problem, or whether we have to reckon with a number of questions which cannot be traced back one after another.

Barrett's excellent book already mentioned, *Luke the Historian in Recent Study*, briefly discusses, pp. 8–26, half a dozen questions: the original text of Acts, the position of Luke within Hellenistic historical writing, his relationship to the religious authors of Hellenism, to the Old Testament and to the Christian tradition, and the image of the Church which he projects in Acts. But finally (26) he names—over against 'such naive questions' as that of authorship—as 'vital questions': What did Luke intend to do and what did he in fact achieve? What made him embark on religious history? What does he reveal to us, consciously or unconsciously, about the life of the Church before and in his time? On p. 50 Barrett then takes up his questions again: To what category do the Lucan writings belong? He answers: Luke himself would not have understood at all the distinction between Church History and proclamation. Hence for Barrett also it plays no further role. Instead, two basic problems now emerge. First: Luke was the first (?) NT writer who consciously sought by his two-fold work to combine two different epochs. While Paul begins where Mark ends (54), Luke allows his two books to overlap in order to build a bridge from the life of Jesus to that of the Church (55). The ascension thus takes on a double aspect: on the one hand it closes 'the story of Jesus, who works cures, perishes in Jerusalem and on the third day is perfected'; on the other hand it begins the history of the Church (56). It closes the first and opens the second period. That means, however, that in Luke's thought the end of the story of Jesus is the Church, and the story of Jesus is the beginning of the Church (57). Luke recounts the story of Jesus as that of the founder of a religion. The stress is laid upon the acts of Jesus and not upon his death. Barrett cites (23 and 59) the words of J. M. Creed that in Luke there is no *theologia crucis*, beyond the affirmation that the Christ must suffer because it was so foretold. Barrett considers this statement to be overdrawn; but in the speeches of Acts the death of Christ 'tends to be treated negatively, as an unfortunate event which nevertheless, in view of the resurrection, need not be an obstacle to faith' (59). The cross is not an atoning sacrifice but a temporary reverse, not unforeseen, and speedily retrieved (60). The relationship of Jesus to the Church determines that of Acts to the gospel: 'The story of the Church was not an independent or spontaneous movement, but the outcome of the life of Jesus.' Luke simplifies and smoothes over the story of the Church, partly because he did not have more accurate knowledge and partly because otherwise the connection between the story of Jesus and the story of the Church would have been obscured. Luke 'found it necessary to show that those who had been with Jesus in his ministry took the lead in the gentile mission, because only in this way could he visibly connect the gentile mission with Jesus (61)'. This accounts for the way in which Luke writes history.

But what made Luke—toward the end of the first century—present this connection of the life of Jesus with the Church in his two-volume work? Here we come to the second fundamental question with which Barrett deals. Luke avoids gnostic thought and language. Acts is 'an apology addressed to the Church' which demonstrates 'Paul's anti-Gnostic orthodoxy, and his practical and doctrinal solidarity with the church at Jerusalem.' Out of the eschatological expectation is evolved the *Heilsgeschichte* described by Conzelmann (although the expectation of the return of Jesus is retained). If one wishes to call this defence against the Gnostics and transformation of eschatology 'early Catholicism', the expression is justified. If, however, 'early Catholicism' means something more, namely the Church as an institution of salvation as with Clement and Ignatius, then Luke does not belong to 'early Catholicism'. For the Church of Luke lives by and for the Word (76).

Günther Klein's book *Die zwölf Apostel. Ursprung und Gehalt einer Idee*

(Göttingen 1961; cf. also his articles 'Gal. 2:6–9 und die Geschichte der Jerusalemer Urgemeinde', *ZThK* 57 (1960) 275–95 and 'Die Verleugnung des Petrus', *ZThK* 58 (1961) 285–328, together with his review of the 13th edition of the present commentary, *ZKG* 1962, 358–63) deals fundamentally with Barrett's second question. Klein also finds the key to the Lucan presentation of the early Church and of Paul in the conflict with Gnosticism. Nevertheless an entirely different picture emerges here. Luke—he writes according to Klein (*ZKG* 1960, 371) in the second century—knows the Pauline epistles, but he does not utilize them. For Paul, so Klein conjectures, was at that time under suspicion as a Gnostic in orthodox eyes. He can only be rescued if he is brought as a subordinate member into the Church of the 'twelve Apostles'. Luke's great achievement was his identification of 'the Twelve', who in the early days of eschatological expectation were temporarily an authoritative council for the earliest community of all (215), with 'the Apostles'. The circle thus created he projected back into the story of Jesus. In this way 'the truly irreplaceable role of Paul in the development of the Church is preserved,' but on the other hand he is subordinated to 'the guarantors of the *historia Jesu* which was set in opposition to incipient Gnostic thought.' By this 'domestication' Luke preserved Paul for the Church (215f.).

How consciously Luke carried through this undertaking Klein seeks to show from Acts **14**.4, 14 (212). Here Barnabas and Paul are called 'Apostles'. Why? So that the reader (who meanwhile has already learned that only the Twelve are 'Apostles') does not notice that Acts withholds from Paul the title of apostle! That Luke here uses the word 'apostle' can only be explained as 'a part of that mimicry under cover of which he accomplished the portentous modification of the traditional conception of the Apostle.' Luke accepts 'with the greatest composure (or should one say: with the utmost cunning?) serious flaws in the objectivity of his presentation, so long as his primary intentions remain undisturbed.'

Thus: since Paul had become the great Gnostic authority Luke, according to Klein, consciously rewrote the history of early Christianity—and indeed with the utmost cunning!—in order to preserve Paul for the Church. Of an unrestricted cult of Paul (215) there is frankly not a trace, either in the writings of Paul himself or in the Deutero-Paulines, and that Luke intends to show that 'this man too was a human being with normal characteristics and weaknesses' is in view of Acts as far from the mark as possible. Paul according to Luke's presentation is a chosen instrument of Christ, and this is evident also, indeed precisely, in the fact that he never loses heart or surrenders, that in every situation he finds the right word, and wins one missionary success after another. But Paul for Luke is also not a man with average shortcomings: he is rather the great persecutor of the infant Church, and as soon as he is called by Christ the persecution at one stroke is at an end. As an enemy of the Christians he is of demonic stature; but as the emissary of Jesus he more and more takes over the apostolic task alone and unaided. To speak of normality here (215) is to close one's eyes to the fact that in Acts Paul is actually presented as a man out of the ordinary.

Klein's construction however cannot rest content with introducing Paul into the non-Gnostic Church as a subordinate member; rather must it go further and ascribe to Luke the creation also of that authoritative circle which represents this Church. In order to exclude Paul from this new-formed church leadership, Luke has first of all to invent this body, by identifying 'the Twelve' with 'the Apostles'. The major part of Klein's book is therefore concerned with 'the twelve Apostles', and only the last three pages (213–16) raise the question of the reason for the new conception of the apostolate, and answer it by the theory of preserving Paul for orthodoxy.

A substantial part of the space devoted to the Lucan concept of the apostle is claimed by discussion of those New Testament passages outside the Lucan writings in which the 'twelve Apostles' also appear. For they threaten to prove that Luke's 'inspired plan'—this very identification of the 'twelve' and the 'Apostles'—was already taken over by Luke.

The chief stumbling-block is Rev. **21**.14, for here in the description of the new Jerusalem it is said: 'The wall of the city has twelve foundation stones, and on these stand (the) twelve names of the twelve Apostles of the Lamb.' These 'twelve Apostles' are not to be removed by the aid of textual criticism, so the only recourse is the bold statement: 'It is not because the author knows of twelve original apostles that the number twelve is relevant for him; but because it is relevant, then where he is concerned about the relation between the ideal 'twelve tribes' and the apostolic faith he has to postulate an ideal 'twelve apostles'—without regard to the number there may have been on the level of empirical fact' (78). The sense of the text is missed when 'the singular combination(!) of the number twelve and the noun is treated in isolation and its special significance ignored—this significance lies specifically in the uniform functional dependence of the variable nouns upon the constant number' (78). But however we interpret the number in Rev. **7**.4ff., **21**.16ff. or **21**.12—that here in **21**.14 the names of the twelve Apostles are written on the foundation stones is only possible if the author knew of twelve Apostles who were known by name, but not if the number of the Apostles was in the mind of the author and his readers quite indefinite. It is only because the number of the names of the twelve Apostles was for the author (and his readers) a given fact that he could fit the twelve Apostles into a description of the New Jerusalem structured on the number twelve. This presupposes that co-ordination of the twelve disciples and the twelve tribes of Israel which is already attested in Matt. **19**.28 and Luke **22**.30 (i.e. Q), save that here in **21**.14 the twelve disciples are already identical with the twelve Apostles known by name.

But it is not a question of Rev. **21**.14 alone; rather must we also consider Mark and Matthew. In Mk **3**.14, B ℵ (W) Θ sy^hmg sa read, after καὶ ἐποίησεν δώδεκα, the words οὓς καὶ ἀποστόλους ὠνόμασεν. ℵ D pl omit them. Nestle and other editors omit, because they see here the influence of Lk **6**.13, where the same text occurs. This seems to have in its favour the fact that here we find the expansion of the relative by καί, frequent in Luke (it simply gives a stronger emphasis to the relative; see above, p. 139 n.8). In our view however the situation is different. In Luke **6**.16 it is said of Judas: ὃς ἐγένετο προδότης, while Mk **3**.19 has ὃς καὶ παρέδωκεν αὐτόν. Matthew reproduces the statement as ὁ καὶ παραδοὺς αὐτόν. It is thus by no means stated that D and the Koine manuscripts present the original text in Mk **3**.14, while the longer text is expanded from Luke. Rather may Luke have taken over the phrase from Mark, but—like Matthew—made stylistic improvements.

The situation is different again with Mk **6**.7 and **6**.30. In **6**.7 it is said of Jesus: 'and he called the twelve and began to send them out (ἀποστέλλειν) two by two' (D 565 al it offer a clear stylistic improvement: 'summoning the twelve disciples he sent them'). Here the noun 'apostle' is missing, certainly not without reason: Mark wishes to explain how the designation 'apostle' was arrived at, and he then uses it in **6**.30: 'and the apostles came together.' But these according to **6**.7 are the twelve. The result is, then, that Mark firstly knows of the sending out of the twelve during the earthly life of Jesus, and secondly understands the designation ἀπόστολος on the basis of this sending.

Basically the situation is no different in Matthew. In **10**.1 he speaks first of Jesus calling the twelve disciples and endowing them with authority over the demons and for healing. Then he continues in v. 2: 'The names of the twelve Apostles are these'. V. 5 repeats: 'These twelve Jesus sent out (ἀπέστειλεν), saying . . .'

The outcome is thus: the sending out of the twelve, described by the verb ἀποστέλλειν, and the explanation of the designation ἀπόστολος on the basis of this verb, are already found in Mark and Matthew. When therefore Klein writes (214): 'The creation by Luke of the apostolate of the twelve is the most inspired plan . . . ,' it must be answered that Luke found ready to hand not only the designation 'the twelve' in the sense of 'the twelve disciples' (during the earthly life of Jesus!) but also their sending out, from which according to Mark and Matthew they derived the designation 'apostles.' 'The twelve Apostles' are therefore not a group first created by Luke, but a circle which he already found before him in the tradition. For the view that this circle played a special role after Easter Mark and Matthew yield as little evidence as does Luke.

For Luke's knowledge of the Pauline epistles, and hence also of I Cor. **15**.5, no proof can be offered. That Paul's persecuting activity is described in Gal. **1**.13 and Acts **9**.21 by the verb πορθέω cannot be taken to show that Luke knew the Pauline letters.

Thoroughly questionable, finally, in our opinion is Klein's conjecture that Luke had to rescue Paul from Gnosticism. We do indeed occasionally hear (Clem. Alex. *Strom.* VII 106.4) that Valentinus (or his disciples?) appealed to a disciple of Paul named Theodas. But in the same way Basilides allegedly appealed to Peter, with Glaucias, an interpreter of the apostle's, as intermediary. In that they claimed to possess such apostolic traditions, certain Gnostic circles evidently wanted to prove their orthodoxy at a time when Peter and Paul already ranked as the chief Apostles. It would therefore be completely mistaken to conclude from these Gnostic efforts that Peter and Paul counted as Gnostics; and this Klein has not maintained.

According to the Revelation of John there had been Gnostic groups in some churches of Asia Minor, but only in Pergamum and Thyatira had they held their own within Christian congregations; in Ephesus they had been excluded. That apart from the seven churches no others are named in the missive is certainly connected with the sacred number seven, chosen for reasons of composition; the 'letters from heaven' are not intended to give a comprehensive survey. Hence we cannot draw any conclusions from the silence about the churches in Colossae and Hierapolis. That the churches in Asia Minor were submerged in the Gnostic flood would be a hasty judgment. But this means that the conjecture that Paul as a Gnostic was suspect in the eyes of the Great Church now itself becomes questionable. That II Peter **3**.15 says of 'our dear brother Paul' that 'according to the wisdom given to him' he has written some things hard to understand, which the ἀμαθεῖς καὶ ἀστήρικτοι distort as they do the other Scriptures, is not enough to provide a foundation for Klein's conjecture.

A further word on the new interpretation of the Lucan prologue which Klein has put forward (*Zeit und Geschichte. Dankesgabe an Rudolf Bultmann zum 80. Geburtstag*, Tübingen 1964, 193–216). Klein would relate the word παρέδοσαν in Lk. **1**.2 not to the immediately preceding πραγμάτων but to the more distant διήγησιν: the eye-witnesses had already proclaimed a connected narrative of the words and works of Jesus; the 'many' had only repeated this oral report in writing (ἀνατάξασθαι); Luke himself on the other hand was not thinking of the line of tradition but of its relation to the facts themselves, and he endeavoured to break through the *traditionsgeschichtlich* gap between the διήγησις and facts preserved in it (206). In our opinion the Lucan prologue does not admit of this interpretation. It describes the eye-witnesses as 'servants of the Word', which means for Luke: as preaching missionaries. Such missionaries however do not give any—oral— διήγησις in the sense of a connected presentation of the works and words of Jesus. Rather was it first the 'many' who undertook to compose a διήγησις out of the material handed down, and because *they* did so Luke also resolved to present in sequence 'what has happened among us Christians', after investigating everything from the beginning. Certainly the word δοκεῖ is like the same word in Acts **15**.28, but it does not follow that this 'I have resolved' possesses the same quality as 'we and the Holy Spirit have resolved'. We cannot therefore impute to the ordinary phrase δοκεῖ μοι the idea that in its author's mind a fundamental importance attaches to Luke's work (215); it is not this phrase which indicates the authority in **15**.28, but the accompanying 'and the Holy Spirit'. To claim the Spirit as co-author for his work, however, did not occur to Luke.

That Luke found his superiority over his predecessors in the fact that he was concerned with the facts and they only with the tradition is said to be reflected also in the word ἐπιχειρεῖν, with which Luke describes their undertaking (195). Klein feels something derogatory here. But the negative tone, where it is present, comes in only through the context, and not through the word ἐπιχειρεῖν. Klein indeed affirms that its use *in malam partem* is the rule elsewhere in Luke. Disregarding for the moment the disputed passage in the prologue, only two passages in Luke call for consideration: Acts **9**.29 and **19**.13. In Acts **9**.29 the negative tone is brought about only by the following 'to kill him'; in **19**.13 it is not the attempt at exorcism as such that is censured, but the attempt by 'unqualified' people! Klein further appeals to Hermas *Sim.* IX.2.6, the only other early Christian passage which comes into question. But here again we see the same spectacle: the 'derogatory' sense is not due to the ἐπιχειρεῖν, but to the accompanying ὡς συνετὸς ὤν; one ought instead to enquire of the Lord. There can therefore be no question of ἐπιχειρεῖν having a 'negative touch' in Luke.

Finally Klein's interpretation of καθεξῆς in the Lucan prologue is untenable (210ff.). It is intended not to refer to arrangement of the material, but to be 'chronologically structured', i.e. to indicate the connection of several phases of the history; it is to mark 'the succession of *historia Jesu* and time of the Church', to bring to expression the continuation of Luke by Acts. Here also the wish appears to be the father of the thought. What reader would really guess from Luke's intimation that he intends to write in sequence —an intimation, be it noted, contained in the prologue to the *gospel*—that Luke thereby is alluding to a coming sequel in a book of Acts?

In short, the attempt to ascribe to Luke a consciously manipulated method—distinct from that of the 'many'—appears to us unsuccessful. We do not dispute that Luke's presentation does not coincide with that of Mark, however much he has taken over from Mark. Nor do we deny that Luke's Acts was something new; rather do we hope ourselves to have made that clear. What we are resisting is simply the attempt to look for the meaning of Luke in a passage where his text does not allow it.

We should however like here to go further into the questions of the Lucan picture of the early Church and of Paul, quite independently of Klein's theses. Acts contains a remarkable contradiction not always noticed: on the one hand it is not only related that Peter converts 3,000 Jews with his preaching on Pentecost (Acts **2**.41), and that after the next Petrine sermon the number of these Jewish Christians mounts to 5,000 (Acts **4**.2), but finally we even hear, at **21**.20, that there are many tens of thousands of Jewish Christians who are all ζηλωταὶ τοῦ νόμου. On the other hand Luke develops in the speech of Stephen (which is even more important for the recognition of his own theology than we have indicated on pp. 289–90) a picture of the Jewish people which shows the Jews as already rebellious and unbelieving over against Moses (Acts **7**.35ff.). During the sojourn in the wilderness the Jews, according to Acts **7**.42f., brought sacrifices to strange gods, and on their arrival in Canaan they built the temple against God's will. They have murdered the prophets (**7**.52) and killed Jesus himself. Stubborn and uncircumcised in heart and ears, they always resist the Holy Spirit. Already in Peter's second speech (**3**.23!), but especially in Paul's first speech (**13**.40f.!), the possibility looms threateningly up that the Jewish listeners have missed their chance and refused the salvation offered to them in Jesus. And then three times over—before the Jews of Asia Minor (**13**.46), Greece (**18**.6) and Rome (**28**.28)—it is explained that the Jewish people (λαός **28**.26!) has forfeited its salvation. For Luke the Jews are 'written off'. Acts **28**.28 is not only a very effective conclusion of the book but also the expression of a conviction which already resounds in the Lucan account of the first sermon of Jesus at Nazareth: in the days of Elijah there were many widows in Israel, but the prophet was sent to a widow in Zarephath, hence into pagan country. And at the time of Elisha there were many lepers in Israel, but only the pagan Naaman was healed (Lk. **4**.25–27).

If this however is the case, if for Luke the Jews have finally excluded themselves from salvation, why does he portray the men of the early Church and Paul as devout and law-abiding Jews? It is to Eltester's credit that he has not allowed this question to rest. We do not of course seek the answer, like Barrett and Klein, in the fact that Luke in this manner conducted an apologetic against Gnosticism. But Luke shows it is not the fault of early Christianity if the Jews reject the proffered salvation, if they 'consider themselves unworthy of eternal life' (**13**.46). Hence Luke grasps eagerly at all traditions which depict Paul as a law-abiding Jew; hence he reports the circumcision of Timothy; hence he has Paul come to Jerusalem already as a small child and return there as often as possible; hence he was happy to have discovered in the resurrection faith a bond between the Pharisees and the Christians. These were not the tricks of a skilful propagandist—Luke was himself convinced, precisely on the basis of such traditions, that this was actually the situation. In this context the statements about the mass conversions of Palestinian Jews at the beginning of the Church and the zeal for the law of the myriads of Jewish Christians take on particular meaning. They prove—just like the reference back to the apostolic decree at **21.25**—that the Christians were in no way guilty if the Jews hardened themselves against the Christian message of salvation.

That Luke depicts the Jewish people as a whole as in such a way abandoned is the negative side of that view of history whose positive aspect Dom J. Dupont has presented in his important and fruitful article 'Le salut des gentils et la signification théologique du Livre des Actes' (*NTS* 6 (1960) 132–55). The Gentile mission belongs from the beginning to the theme of Luke's two-fold work! It is not for nothing that Luke—alone among the evangelists!—quotes Is. **40**.3–5 in full, including the words 'and all flesh will see the salvation of God' (Lk. **3**.4f.). It is of this very salvation—and with the same Greek expression τὸ σωτήριον τοῦ θεοῦ—that Acts **28**.28 also speaks: 'This salvation of God was sent to the Gentiles; they will listen!' Between these two passages, however, thus between the beginning of the actual story of Jesus in the third gospel and the end of Acts, Luke emphasizes again and again the fact that the Gentile mission belongs to God's promises which will find their fulfilment through Christ. This makes it more comprehensible than in the commentary why Luke could let Acts follow upon his gospel: it describes an event which belongs to the *Heilsgeschichte* planned by God and proclaimed. In that the gospel is made accessible to the Gentiles, a salvation promised in the Old Testament is realized, and the story of Jesus is thus continued. In this connection one may perhaps also refer expressly to the fact that Simeon's song of praise (Lk. **2**.30) already speaks of this σωτήριον and then dies away in the words: φῶς εἰς ἀποκάλυψιν ἐθνῶν—the child Jesus is the light which is to be revealed to the Gentiles (cf. Acts **13**.47).

Christianity for Luke is not (as Eltester thinks) the Israel of Promise, but from the beginning salvation was promised to both: the Jews and the Gentiles. The early Church consisted of devout Jews, but Judaism in the Roman Empire did not want to know anything about the proclamation of Christ, and so now the mission goes only to the Gentiles. Luke did not have a bad conscience because of the usurping of documents of the faith: the Old Testament itself warned the Jews and promised salvation to the Gentiles. What became of the myriads of believing Jewish Christians mentioned at **21**.20, Luke tells us just as little as he does the fate of the Apostles. We learn only that one of these was executed by Herod Antipas. But he is not replaced: the 'Twelve Apostles' are not a permanent institution. They bore witness to the life and teaching, death and resurrection of Jesus and directed the congregation of Jerusalem until it was time for the Gentile mission. The apostolic decree is at the same time the last word of the Apostles.

III

Ulrich Wilckens in his work *Die Missionsreden der Apostelgeschichte* (Neukirchen 1961[1], 1963[2]) has proved against Dibelius and Dodd that

Peter's speeches in the first part of Acts do not contain any old pattern of Jewish-Christian missionary preaching. Rather Luke is here using his pattern of the Gentile Christian missionary preaching to present the early Jewish mission. This demonstration is well worthy of recognition; for it makes still clearer the manner and the extent of the Lucan composition. More important for our present purpose however is the final section of the work, the third chapter: 'Results and Outlook', and above all its second section: 'On the problem of the theological evaluation of the Lucan outline' (pp. 193–218). Beside other differences from Paul, Wilckens singles out the fact that 'the problem of the historical time of Christianity, the theological problem of Church History, and hence the historicity of the Christian faith as such' had forced itself upon the Third Evangelist. Luke's concern is thus not merely with the delay of the Parousia. This 'negative experience of the non-arrival of the events of the end' led Luke alone among the Evangelists to the 'positive discovery of the reality of history as such, which as a whole became intelligible to him as a sequence of events controlled by God and directed toward an end' (p. 201). 'The stance of the Lucan theology is . . . accordingly positively to be described as an "inclusive horizon of Christian theology" ' (ibid.).

This formulation, taken over from Pannenberg's essay 'Heilsgeschehen und Geschichte' (*Kerygma und Dogma* 5 (1959) 218), shows like other things that Wilckens belongs to the group of younger theologians (Pannenberg, R. Rendtorff, D. Rössler *et al.*) who ultimately wanted to correct the follies of the older generation—that of Barth, Bultmann, Gogarten and their pupils —by setting themselves to replace the 'theology of the Word' by a 'theology of history'. In this the Lucan design, taken over from H. Conzelmann (*Die Mitte der Zeit*, ET *The Theology of St Luke*), plays an important role. True, it differs from that in Käsemann ('Das Problem des historischen Jesus', *ZThK* 51 (1954) esp. 136–9, ET in *Essays on NT Themes*, 15–47), who had likewise adopted Conzelmann's view (esp. p. 137, ET 28f.). Käsemann saw in the recession of eschatology the reason for the Lucan picture of history. According to Käsemann the Lucan period of the Apostles directly continues the *historia Jesu*, unrealistically combines the life of Jesus and the apostolic age, and sets between the latter and all post-apostolic Church History a clear caesura, because fundamentally the later Church has to live from the apostolic tradition. If the time of Jesus and the apostolic age were actually set together as a 'holy past' over against the post-apostolic Church, then Acts would in fact not offer any historical theological conception, but the time of Jesus and that of the Apostles would be set outside the limits of the normal course of history, and the *initium Christianismi* would be mythologized. This Wilckens admits (p. 208). But he declares: Paul—and with him the second half of Acts—does not represent the Apostles, but the Church as such: Paul's work already belongs to Luke's Gentile-Christian post-apostolic present. Acts does not portray a 'holy past,' but 'the real connection of the time of Jesus, the apostolic age and post-apostolic Gentile Christianity' (p. 210).

This Lucan outline is according to Wilckens theologically legitimate. To Käsemann's critical question 'How can Jesus possess saving power for present believers . . . if Jesus himself does not continually encounter them in the present as the exalted Lord?' (*ZThK* 51 (1954) 139), Wilckens answers: 'What happens if not only do the historical Jesus and the *Christus praesens* draw apart with the progress of historical time, but at the same time also the presence of the exalted Lord detaches itself more and more from his eschatological coming?' (p. 212). If the past is to have only exemplary significance, then 'every present experience of the exalted Lord becomes of necessity a mythical *Nunc* of mythological religiosity' (213). 'That Luke consistently blocked this way to the solution of the problems of his time . . . should not be brought as a reproach against him, but rather only assessed as theologically legitimate' (213). Luke set the Jesus-event as 'the middle of time' 'at the same time in the context of a universal history understood as *Heilsgeschichte*' (ibid.). In so doing—Wilckens thinks—Luke did not imprison the saving event as a 'brutum factum' in a 'causal relationship' (which Jewish and primitive Christian antiquity did not know). Rather—and this in Pannenberg is a central idea—in Jesus all promises are fulfilled: 'In the life of Jesus that is *completely anticipated* which tradition described as the eschatological time of salvation . . .' (214). 'What will happen in the Parousia is thus basically the return of the exalted Lord in the *heilsgeschichtlich* function of the immediately present locus of salvation. . . .' 'The soteriological importance which pre-Lucan Christianity attributed to the eschatological coming of Christ Luke has thus consistently transferred to the past epoch of the earthly time of Jesus' (ibid.). The salvation which the Parousia 'will inaugurate for the elect' is 'in no respect different from the salvation which was already fully present in the earthly life of Jesus' (p. 216).

Did Luke really—as Pannenberg and Wilckens affirm—understand the past life of Jesus as proleptic, an anticipation of the future time of salvation, and thus point Christian faith back from the expectation of a mythical Parousia to the past history of Jesus of Nazareth? Wilckens admits that in the process Jesus' significance as judge of the living and the dead at the Parousia is left out of consideration (216). Luke still expects—although for an indeterminate date (Acts 3.19ff.)—the 'mythical' Parousia, after which no more sick will be healed, no more sinners converted. To that extent the earthly work of Jesus is for Luke *not* an anticipation of the consummation of all history at the Parousia. But over and above that there remains to be considered (as Wilckens himself, p. 216f., recalls to the reader's memory by spacing the type): 'The death of Jesus has' (for Luke) 'no redemptive significance, and hence the Lucan Christology in general lacks any substantial soteriology.' But what then has the (alleged) anticipation of the consummation of the divine saving activity in the earthly life of Jesus to say to Luke's reader—and to us?

Käsemann thinks to detect a deep caesura in Luke between the time of Jesus and the Apostles and the time of the Church. Wilckens on the other hand saw such a caesura between the time of Jesus and the time which follows; only so does the time of Jesus take on for him its proleptic character. Perhaps both have read too much theory of history into Luke's work. For Luke a mighty arch stretches from Abraham to the Parousia; Luke knows that he himself—even if Jesus now dwells in heaven until his coming again, and only his name is here miraculously present—he himself is in the same time and under the same saving plan of God as the disciples in Galilee. In that Luke has Jesus meet with the Apostles for forty days before his Ascension, there is no deep caesura between the time of Jesus and that which follows. Our time (Luke does not yet use the word 'Church' in its present-day sense) in which the 'Word of God', the Christian proclamation, spreads victorious over all the earth, belongs for Luke to the saving plan of God just as much as the time of Jesus.

Admittedly we must confess: the fact that Luke thus levelled out the difference between the times did not remain without its consequences. The risen Jesus—in contrast to the Pauline doctrine—has flesh and bones again. Earth and heaven are not so far apart that a cloud cannot provide transport from here to there and back again. This massive theology (in which now and then 'direct experiences of transcendence', i.e. of God, occur) is not a positive appraisal of history. Luke is just as little an anticipation of Hegel as a Kierkegaard before his time. He seeks for his Church a way which will preserve it against the worst evil in this world; he shows his Church a meaning for its life during this time, in the victorious proclamation of the message of Christ. He no longer watches passionately, like Paul, for the imminent turn of the ages, but he lives in the certainty that even in this our time God's goodness is new every morning.

COMMENTARY

1
ACTS 1: 1–8
RETROSPECT AND A FAREWELL SPEECH

[1] The first book I wrote, O Theophilus, concerning all that Jesus did and taught, [2] up to the day on which, after giving instructions to the Apostles whom he had chosen through the Holy Spirit, he was taken up. [3] To them he presented himself alive after his passion by many proofs, appearing to them during the space of forty days, and speaking of the kingdom of God. [4] And as he was eating with them, he charged them not to depart from Jerusalem, but to wait for the promise of the Father, 'which you have heard from me. [5] For John baptized with water; but you will be baptized with the Holy Spirit not many days hence.' [6] The assembled group, then, asked him, 'Lord, do you at this time restore the kingdom to Israel?' [7] He said to them: 'It is not for you to know times or seasons which the Father has established in his own authority, [8] but you will receive power, when the Holy Spirit comes upon you; and you will be my witnesses in Jerusalem, and in all Judaea and Samaria, and even to the end of the earth.'

Bibliography:

Alfred Gerke, 'Der δεύτερος λόγος und die Apostelgeschichte des Lukas', *Hermes* 29 (1894), 377–92 (on **1**.1ff.); Roland Schütz, ''Ιερουσαλήμ and 'Ιεροσόλυμα im NT', *ZNW* 11 (1910), 179–87 (on **1**.4); E. Norden, *Agnostos Theos: Untersuchungen zur Formengeschichte religiöser Rede*, 1913 (on **1**.1f.); T. Zahn, 'Das dritte Buch des Lukas', *NkZ* (1917), 373–95 (on **1**.1); Emil Donckel, 'Sale sumpto', *Ephem. Liturg. N.R.* 7, Rome 1933, 101–12 (on **1**.4); J. M. Creed, 'The Text and Interpretation of Acts **1**.1–2', *JTS* 35 (1934), 176–82; Victoriano Larrañaga, 'El Proemio-Transición de Act. **1**.1–3 en los methodos literarios de la historiographia Griega', *Miscellanea Biblica*, Vol. II, Rome 1934, 311–74; Franz Dornseiff, 'Lukas der Schriftsteller', *ZNW* 35 (1936), 129–54 (esp. 135 on **1**.3); E. Günther, ΜΑΡΤΥΣ: *die Geschichte eines Wortes*, Gütersloh 1941 (on **1**.8), and 'Zeuge und Märtyrer', *ZNW* 47 (1956), 145–61; Lucien Cerfaux, 'Témoins du Christ d'après le Livre des Actes', *Angelicum* 20 (1943), 166–83 (= *Recueil Cerfaux* 1954, II, 157–74); W. Michaelis, *Herkunft und Bedeutung des Ausdrucks 'Leiden und Sterben Jesu Christi'*, Berne 1945 (on **1**.3); Bent Noack, 'Das Gottesreich bei Lukas', *Symb. Bibl. Upsal.*, suppl. to *SEÅ* 10, Lund 1948 (on **1**.3); José Ramón García

C.M.F., 'La restauración de Israel', *Estudios Biblicos*, Vol. VIII, 2nd series, Madrid 1949, 75–133 (on **1**.6); André Rétif, S.J., 'Témoignage et Prédication missionnaire dans les Actes des Apôtres', *Nouv. rev. théol.* 73 (1951), 152–65 (on **1**.8); A. Wikenhauser, 'Die Belehrung der Apostel durch den Auferstandenen nach Apg **1**.3', *Festschrift Meinertz*, Münster 1951, 105–13; J. W. Doeve, *Jewish Hermeneutics in the Gospels and Acts*, Assen 1953 (on **1**.4, 9–11, 16); Johannes Munck, 'Den aeldste Kristendom i Apostlenes Gerninger', *Dansk Teol. Tidsskrift* 16 (1953), 129–64 (esp. 130ff. on **1**.4); E. J. Goodspeed, 'Some Greek Notes', *JBL* 73 (1954), 84 (on **1**.1); P. A. van Stempvoort, 'De Betekenis van λέγων τὰ περὶ τῆς βασιλείας τοῦ θεοῦ in Hand. **1**.3', *Ned. Th. Tijdsch.* 9 (1954/5), 349–55; H. J. Cadbury, '"We" and "I"-passages in Luke-Acts', *NTS* 3 (1956/7), 128–32 (on **1**.1); Reicke, 1957, 9–18.

E. J. Goodspeed, 'Was Theophilus Luke's Publisher?', *JBL* 73 (1954), 84 (on **1**.1); H. Braun, 'Zur Terminologie der Acta v. d. Auferstehung Jesu', *TLZ* 77 (1952), 633–7; A. J. C. Burke, 'The Resurrection in the Acts of the Apostles', Princeton Theol. Seminary Diss. 1952 (on **1**.3); E. Stauffer, 'Abschiedsreden und -szenen' in *Theologie d. NT*, 4th edn. 1948, 327–30 (on **1**.3ff.) (ET *NT Theology*, 1956); A. van Veldhuizen, 'συναλιζόμενος', *Nieuwe Theol. Studien* 4 (1921), 135 (on **1**.4).

VERSE 1: Acts,[1] as the second book of a large[2] historical work, begins in accordance with literary forms with a renewed dedication[3] (to Theophilus[4])

---

[1] In antiquity πράξεις denotes outstanding deeds, especially those of rulers. It thus becomes the title of historical works (Wikenhauser, *Geschichtswerk* 94–104). If Luke's two books had appeared simultaneously as one whole on one scroll, they would not have borne individual titles. It has been conjectured that the superscriptions were only added when they came to occupy different positions in the canon. Tertullian and Cyprian render πράξεις correctly as *acta*, but the Italic and Vulgate later introduced *actus*, which is less acceptable. The *Canon Muratori* with its 'acta omnium apostolorum' shows what people hoped to find in the book. The singular πράξις, found in D and elsewhere, may have originated in an itacism.

[2] Together Luke's two works make up over a quarter of the New Testament.

[3] Cf. Luke **1** 1–4. The prologue to Luke applies only to the third gospel (against Cadbury, *Beg.* II, 489–510). An ancient book was not specially written for the person to whom it is dedicated. The dedication honours him as a patron (who in certain cases undertook to finance or disseminate the book) and (despite Zahn 9f.) attests the author's desire for publicity. See now Haenchen, *ZThK* 58 (1961), 362–5.

[4] We do not know who Theophilus was (even Jews bore the name, e.g. a high priest mentioned in Josephus, *Antiquities* XVIII 123); perhaps it was a pseudonym (for Flavius Clemens?). The identification with the Theophilus of *Clem. Rec.* X. 1 or that of Seneca's 7th Epistle (a Christian forgery) is worthless. It was considered preferable, when repeating a dedication, not to repeat the title κράτιστε (in prologues this was generally not a high title of honour, corresponding to *egregius*, but was simply the equivalent of *optimus*). In the case of ancient books, dedication constituted the act of publication. The picture of the book-market painted by Theodor Birt (*Das antike Buchwesen*, Berlin 1882), who speaks of editions running into 500 or 1000 copies, was long ago toned down by Karl Diatsko (*Untersuchungen über ausgewählte Kapitel des antiken Buchwesens*, Leipzig 1900, 149–78) and finally corrected by II. I. Marrou in 'La Technique de l'édition à l'époque patristique',

and a backward glance to the first book,[1] the Gospel according to Luke. This had given an account of everything that[2] Jesus[3] did and taught[4]: thus it was Luke's intention[5] to gather up the whole tradition. This opening verse of Acts shows that firstly: Christianity is adopting the literary forms. It is therefore on the point of leaving the milieu of 'ordinary folk'[6] and entering the world of literature, the cultural world of antiquity.[7] Thus its aloofness from the 'world' in which it grew up, expecting the end of this aeon, is diminishing. The first stirrings can be sensed of the transition from a

---

Vigil. Christianae III (1949), 208–24. The person to whom the book was dedicated would give permission for copies to be made and see to its dissemination. In this connection a letter of Augustine's is of particular interest. He asks the priest Firmus, to whom he is sending, in 22 fascicles, the 22 books of *De Civitate Dei*, if he would kindly authorize one or two master copies from which other copies might be made (C. Lambot, *Revue Béné-dictine* 51 (1939), 109–21: Augustine's letter is on pp. 112ff.). The Lucan writings will not have appeared on the 'book market' at all; reviewing Dibelius's *Aufsätze*, A. D. Nock already showed that Dibelius's ideas about ancient practice in dedication and publishing were misconceptions (*Gnomon* 25 (1953), 501). There was therefore no need for these writings to bear the name of the author (cf. *Studies*, 89); also there is now even less reason to speak of a double public, since Acts was incomprehensible to an educated Gentile, if he was not familiar with the synagogues or the Christian church. This does not of course exclude the possibility that Acts might, and was intended to, influence a patron acquainted with and well-disposed to Christianity.

[1] This is the meaning of πρῶτος λόγος here (see p. 76f. above and cf. Dupont p. 35). At 7.12 and 12.10 Luke Hellenistically employs πρῶτον and πρῶτος for πρότερος, without implying a τρίτος. This removes all basis for the supposition of Ramsay (pp. 27f.) and Zahn (pp. 16–18) that Luke planned a third book. The μέν alone (without a following δέ) also appears in 3.21, 27.21, and 28.22 (as well as eight times in μὲν οὖν: 1.18, 2.41, 5.41, 13 4, 17.30, 23.22 and 26.4 & 9), and hence does not betray any revision supplanting the Lucan text.

[2] ὧν for ἅ: such 'attraction of the relative' (Bl.-Debr. § 294) occurs eleven times in Luke, 22 times in Acts.

[3] In B D the article is missing before Ἰησοῦς, probably through haplography.

[4] ἤρξατο is a periphrasis for the finite verb. It is in this way that LXX renders the Hebrew הֵחֵל. But in everyday popular Latin also *coepi* was in those days used to render the tenses of the normal verb (W. Süss, *Gnomon* (1951) 314). To translate 'everything which Jesus from the beginning . . .' (as e.g. *Beg.* IV 3, Loisy 135, Dupont 35) is to do violence to the language. The use of this periphrasis enabled Luke, in his very nicely balanced opening sentence, to achieve a rhythmically impeccable sequence of words, which could not have been attained with a simple imperfect or aorist. ποιεῖν τε καὶ διδάσκειν denotes Jesus' miracles and teaching (cf. 7.22 ἐν λόγοις καὶ ἔργοις). ποιεῖν of Jesus' miracles also occurs at Acts 10.39: πάντων ὧν ἐποίησεν. διδάσκειν is the normal expression in Luke's Gospel for Jesus' teaching. There is thus no reason here to deny (with Menoud, *NT Studien für R. Bultmann* (1954) 153) Luke's authorship of this verse.

[5] Jacquier (p. 4) disputes this intention, referring to John 21.25. But this hyperbolical conclusion cannot be taken as a measure of Luke's aspirations. Matthew also (probably not far removed in time from Luke) appears to be striving for something similar, though without explicitly saying so. Towards the end of the first century the necessity of collecting the valuable tradition must have become pressing. And what Matthew and Luke offer must represent very nearly the whole of the old tradition still available.

[6] Dibelius, *Studies*, 2.

[7] Ibid., 4.

F

Palestinian sect[1] to a world religion.[2] And this provokes the question: In this transition from aloofness to contact with the 'world', will the Christian faith remain true to itself and find a new form compatible with its original essence? Secondly the determination to collect the whole of the Jesus-tradition indicates a desire not to lose any fragment of the precious heritage on which the Church is founded. But there is a parallel endeavour to fix the form of the Jesus-tradition for all time: the canonical gospel looms in prospect,[3] and with it the end of the first, the foundation-laying era of the Church. Even now a time is beginning, an age of transformation, in which the very forces which have conserved the Old are pressing forward to something New. This is evident from the fact that, probably for the first time,[4] a writer is daring to continue the Gospel with a second book—a book of Acts.[5]

VERSE 2: ἄχρι[6] ἧς ἡμέρας[7] ἀνελήμφθη[8] refers to the point at which

[1] Acts 24.14 and especially 28.22 show that the Jews then regarded Christianity as a sect of dubious character.

[2] That we are not reading too much into the words is confirmed by ἕως ἐσχάτου τῆς γῆς in verse 8 and by εἰς πάντα τὰ ἔθνη in Luke 24.47.

[3] This end admittedly was not achieved, because for various reasons four separate gospels were vying for universal recognition. Tatian's attempt to unite them in a gospel harmony did not succeed—whether he also used a fifth, apocryphal gospel is a question we must put aside.

[4] Pre-Lucan comprehensive accounts of the original Christian mission have not been shown to exist.

[5] See pp. 34f. and 97 above. The linking of the two books in a composite historical work was only possible because Luke saw a *heilsgeschichtlich* continuity between the earthly life of Jesus and the apostolic age. But at the same time this conferred on the age of Jesus the character of a historical epoch.

[6] The suggestion (Michaelis, 7) that ἄχρι means 'up to, but not including' is an apologetic expedient which leads to a dead-end. Luke is after all referring to a day of which he gave some account, not one which he failed to mention in his gospel.

[7] ἄχρι ἧς ἡμέρας = ἄχρι τῆς ἡμέρας, (ἐν) ᾗ: see Bl.-Debr. § 294, 2 & 5.

[8] ἀνελήμφθη proves that διέστη ἀπ' αὐτῶν in Luke 24.51 refers to the Ascension, even if καὶ ἀνεφέρετο εἰς τὸν οὐρανόν (absent from D, which changes διέστη into ἀπέστη, and from the 'Western' text) should be a later addition (according to Jeremias, *Die Abend-mahlsworte Jesu*, 4th ed., 144f. [ET *The Eucharistic Words of Jesus* 1966, 151], the shorter 'Western' text 'eliminates the ascension on Easter evening for harmonising purposes'). If 'he parted from them' implied merely that Jesus left his disciples for a while, the whole pathos of the Lucan ending would be meaningless. Why should Jesus take them to Bethany (on ἕως πρός see p. 76 above), if his absence from them was to be merely temporary? This detail is in itself evidence that Luke was reproducing an Ascension-tradition. Moreover Luke 24.53 ('they were continually in the Temple') describes a fairly permanent situation. It need scarcely be added that the Ascension of Jesus also represents the most fitting conclusion to the gospel from the literary point of view.

In this way, of course, arose that discordance between the end of Luke and the beginning of Acts which impelled the 'Western' witnesses to alter the text transmitted by B ℵ A C 81. It was not enough to leave out καὶ ἀνεφέρετο εἰς τὸν οὐρανόν in Luke 24.51: ἀνελήμφθη in Acts 1.2 had also to disappear. This however made a new main verb necessary, hence—1: Gig and t chose ἐντειλάμενος: *usque in diem quo praecepit apostolis per spiritum sanctum* etc.; but *praecepit* demanded some such complement as *praedicare evangelium* (recalling Luke 24.47 and Acts 1.8), which entailed the clumsy postponement of *quos elegerat*. 2: The Old Latin text in Augustine's *De cons. evang.* 4.8, and in the pseudo-Augustinian *De unitate eccles.* 11 (27), makes ἐξελέξατο the main verb: *usque in diem quo*

Luke's gospel ends,[1] and ἐντειλάμενος to the words of Jesus in Luke 24·44–9.[2] διὰ πνεύματος ἁγίου relates to the succeeding phrase, the choice of the Apostles.[3] This is Luke's way of making the Apostles' authority plain to the reader: Jesus chose them through the Holy Spirit and commissioned them before his departure. The most important part of the charge he laid upon them is repeated, and partly reformulated, in verses 4f. and 7f. Basically, of course, the action recounted in Acts is a divine one,[4] but as witnesses of Jesus the Apostles (and their helpers) are the human instruments[5] through which that action is performed.[6]

VERSE 3: With οἷς[7] καί[8] Luke passes directly from the content of the earlier book into the presentation of the new action, as was certainly

---

apostolos elegit per spiritum sanctum, mandans eis etc.; but this text is ridiculous—the gospel does not end with the choosing of the Apostles (Luke 6.13ff.)! 3: Nor does the variant *in die quo (qua) apostolos elegit* (Augustine, *Contra Felicem* 1.4; *Contra epist. Fundamenti* 9, similarly the treatise *Contra Varimodum* 1.31 & 3.71) escape the same charge. D and d are eclectic. It is easy to see why ἀνελήμφθη was deleted and *praedicare evangelium* inserted as a supplement; but at the same time the resulting text is so meaningless that one cannot follow Ropes (*Beg.* III, 256–61) in regarding it as the original, and ἀνελήμφθη as a later addition which found its way into every Greek MS.

[1] After P. Feine, C. C. Torrey and H. Sahlin had thought to detect in Acts 1–15.35 a Jewish Christian or Aramaic source which had already served the third gospel (see pp. 28f., 72ff. & 46 above), P. H. Menoud put forward the thesis that Luke's two books had originally been one ('Remarques sur les textes de l'Ascension dans Luc-Actes', *NT Studien für R. Bultmann* (1954) 148–56); in this he was followed by Trocmé (pp. 32f.). Luke 24.50–3 and Acts 1.1–5, it is suggested, were not added until on admittance to the canon the whole was divided into two. But it is highly unlikely that Luke would have broken the already hardened mould of the gospel in this way; moreover Acts 1.6 would be incomprehensible directly after Luke 24.47, the catalogue of Apostles in Acts 1.13 implies the reader's unfamiliarity with that of Luke 6.14–16, and Jesus would scarcely have risen heavenwards from the house in Jerusalem which is the scene of Luke 24.36–49. The stylistic reasons which led to Menoud's thesis are dealt with in our detailed comments and the general discussion.

[2] There is no reason why F. J. A. Hort should have complained (*The Christian Ecclesia* (1897) 39, quoted *Ned. Th. Tijds.* 9 (1954/5) 349), that we do not know what ἐντειλάμενος refers to.

[3] For Luke (despite 14.4, 14) only the Twelve are Apostles (or here the Eleven— see below on 1.21f.). They represent the legitimate Church in his eyes, which is why he stresses the part played by the Spirit in their election (διὰ πνεύματος ἁγίου belongs with οὓς ἐξελέξατο: Luke readily shifts stressed words forward, e.g. Luke 24.7, Acts 1.10, 3.19, 4.33, 5.13, 7.35, 9.14, 12.25, 16.14, 19.4, 20—cf. p. 79f. above and Dupont, 'La Mission de Paul "à Jérusalem"', Actes 12.25' in *NovTest.* I, 1956, 275–303).

[4] The λόγος τοῦ θεοῦ is in a sense the subject of Acts.

[5] Cf. Acts 9.15.   [6] See below on 1.8.

[7] This is the first of those ostensibly relative, but in reality main clauses to which Luke is addicted: 1.3, 11; 2 24; 3.2, 3, 21; 5.36; 6.6; 7.20, 39, 45, 46; 8.15; 9.39; 10.38, 40; 11.6, 23, 30; 12.4, 31, 43; 14.9, 16; 16.2, 14, 24; 17.10; 18.27; 19.25; 21.4, 32; 22 4, 5; 23 14, 29, 33; 24.18, 19; 25.16, 18, 26; 26.7, 10, 12, 19; 27.17; 28.8, 10, 14, 15, 18, 23. In *Gnomon* 28 (1956) 588, A. Debrunner describes Acts 25.16 as a Latinism, from which he distinguishes the 'characterizing' use of the relative clause found as far back as Homer; with this one might perhaps classify such a passage as Acts 7.53. In other cases, again, e.g. 3.15 and 4.10, the model seems to be a Semitic use of the relative clause in description of God. D. Tabachowitz has pointed out (*Eranos* 30, Göteborg 1932, 99ff.)

permissible in ancient historiography.[1] The only striking thing is that Luke goes back beyond the final point just mentioned, the Ascension,[2] and speaks of the many 'convincing proofs'[3] by which Jesus showed himself to be alive after his death.[4] These are the 'appearances',[5] which ensued

---

that conjunction with the relative is very frequent in Byzantine Greek. A. Werner (*Byzant. Zeitschr.* 31 (1931) 275) suspects a development within Greek itself, while W. Fritz, H. Christensen and L. Thurnayr (ibid.) think it a Latinism.

[8] καί after a relative occurs in Acts 1.3, 11; 7.45; 10.39; 11.30; 12.4; 13.22; 17.34; 22.5; 24.6 (twice!); 26.10, 26, 29; 27.23; 28.10. Other NT instances: Mark 3.19; Luke 6.13, 16; 7.49; 10.30, 39; 23.51 (*v.l.*); John 8.25(?); Rom. 4.22 (*v.l.*); 5.2; 8.34; 9.24: I Cor. 1.8; 2.13; 4.5; 11.23; 15.1, 2, 3, 29f.; II Cor. 1.22; 3.6; 5.5 (*v.l.*); Gal. 2.10; Eph. 1.11, 13 (twice); 2.22; Phil. 2.5; 3.12, 20; 4.9; Col. 1.29; 2.11f.; 3.15; I Thess. 1.5, 11; Hebr. 1.2; 6.7; 7.2, 4; I Peter 2.8; 3.19, 21 (list completed after Zerwick, who rightly draws attention also to the expression διὰ τοῦτο καί, e.g. Luke 11.49; I Thess. 2.13 & 3.5). In all these cases the καί ought to be left untransiated. A. J. Wensinck's attempt ('The Semitisms of Codex Bezae', *Bulletin of the Bezan Club* No. XII, Leyden 1937, 11–48) to derive it from the Semitic is not successful: it belongs to the Greek koine (used by Justin and Eusebius), and has a counterpart in Latin (cf. Gösta Thörnell, 'De usu particulae "et",' *Studia Tertullianea* II, Uppsala 1920, 74–9).

[1] This is shown by the prologues to Books 2–5 & 7 of Xenophon's *Anabasis*, 8 & 13 of Josephus' *Antiquities*, and 3–8 of Herodian's histories (see V. Larrañaga, *L'Ascension de Notre Seigneur dans le NT*, Rome 1938, 270–325). Most historians used to follow their review of the preceding book with a preview of the one in hand.

[2] This was one of Gerke's main reasons for advancing the hypothesis that the prologue has been retouched. The author 'had no intention of dealing once again with the Ascension, for he expressly states that he has dealt with it in the first book . . . The δεύτερος λόγος was only meant to cover the history of the succeeding period, from the moment when Jesus parted from his disciples (up to, say, the death of Paul?).' Gerke conjectures as the original continuation of verse 2: νῦν δὲ δεύτερόν σοι γράψαι λόγον ἔδοξέ μοι περὶ κτλ (op. cit., 390). Norden (*Agnostos Theos*, 315f.) similarly supplied: 'But now I will try to relate what followed, as I myself was present to see it or learned from trustworthy witnesses, up to Paul's arrival in Rome.' Loisy (p. 138) already wondered why the reviser should have suppressed so harmless a sentence. He could indeed have gone on, without more ado: 'Now Jesus presented himself alive' etc. What neither Gerke nor Norden nor Preuschen (p. 4) nor Meyer (III, p. 12) noticed was that verse 3 is one of those typically Lucan relative sentences discussed on pp. 77 & 139 (n.7) above. It is scarcely to be assumed that a reviser would have imitated this peculiarity, and the καί after the relative into the bargain.

[3] The fact that τεκμήριον is a *hapax legomenon* does not entitle us (with Menoud, op. cit., 153) to ascribe it to a reviser.

[4] In *ThWb* V, 910–23, Michaelis has demonstrated that in Luke 24.26, 46; Acts 1.3; 3.18; 17.3 & 26.23 (or παθητός) signifies not 'suffer' but 'die' (antonym: 'rise' or 'be awakened'). This usage occurs also in Hebr. 9.26 & 13.11 and I Peter 3.18 (B); other places cited by Michaelis are open to question, especially Luke 22.15, the opening words of Christ at the Last Supper. The formula πολλὰ παθεῖν (adopted from Mark 8.31 in Luke 9.22, and repeated in Luke 17.25) refers to the many pains that Jesus had to undergo during the Passion, and should not be confused with the absolute use of παθεῖν. This cannot be derived from the לָבַס ('to bear') of Isaiah 53.4 (against Michaelis, 914f.), which no Greek translation renders by παθεῖν. The absolute use appears to derive from Hellenism.

[5] The Hellenistic ὀπτάνομαι (cognate with ὀπτασία) means 'appear', 'show oneself', but not in the sense of a 'vision'. In I Kings 8.8 LXX it means 'be visible', while in the Papyri οὐκ ὀπτάνομαι is said of missing persons (*Beg.* IV, 4). The word does not indicate anything visionary (against Wendt, 67): Luke does not regard the appearances of the risen Christ as visions! Tobit 12.19 (in the longer text) is probably already influenced by Acts.

within the sacred space of forty days.[1] The gospel of Luke had left the reader with the impression that the Lord's final parting from his disciples took place on the very night of Easter Sunday. Now we learn that during the following forty days Jesus was repeatedly in their company and spoke to them of the 'kingdom of God'.[2] This not only gives the content of the conversation but prepares for the disciples' question about the kingdom (v. 6).

VERSE 4: Having thus summarized the forty days, Luke now presents an individual scene; not until verse 9 is the reader aware that this is Jesus' last conversation with his disciples. At table with them,[3] Jesus enjoins them not to leave[4] Jerusalem[5] but to wait here for the promised coming of the

[1] δι' ἡμερῶν τεσσεράκοντα is Hellenistic for 'within forty days.' According to 1 Cor. 15.3–7 the appearances of Jesus to Peter, the Twelve, over 500 brethren, James and all the Apostles seem to follow one another fairly rapidly. This space of time was then probably denoted by the 'sacred' number of 40 days (cf. Dornseiff, op. cit., 135). Later came an attempt to secure the reality of these appearances, against gnostic docetism, by accounts of communal meals (Acts 10.41, cf. Luke 24.43). Tradition preserved the number of five appearances mentioned by Paul just as little as it did the original account of them.

[2] The βασιλεία τοῦ θεοῦ is mentioned in Acts 1.3 & 6, 8.12, 14.22, 19.8, 20 25, 28.23 & 31. Acts 1.6 and 14.22 obviously refer to the kingdom of God which will begin with the Parousia. This is not contradicted by Luke 17.21, for as Luke understands it Jesus is not declaring that the kingdom is in the unbelieving Pharisees, but that in his own person it is in the midst of them; hence it will return with his second coming (cf. Luke 22.30). An *imminent* expectation of the kingdom Luke admittedly rejects (see on 1.7 below), but he does not for that reason give up the expectation as such. Since the kingdom of God is the state of perfection towards which the Christians are advancing, Luke can describe it simply in 1.3, 19.8, 20.25 and 28.23 as the content of the Christian proclamation. The significance of the 'name of Jesus' (8.12) in this connection is evident from 4.12. Acts lends no support to Dodd's thesis of 'realized eschatology' (*Apostolic Preaching*, 46f., *History and the Gospel*, 113ff.) namely that the kingdom 'came' in Jesus' life, death and resurrection. Wikenhauser rightly stresses (*NT Abhandlungen*, Suppl. vol. 1, 1951, 108) that Acts strictly separates the concepts of God's kingdom and the Church. Van Stempvoort (op. cit., 353) misses Luke's meaning in saying that the kingdom is 'everything God does in Christ to gather the Church out of the world': see rather Conzelmann *Theology of St. Luke*, 113–119.

[3] Assuming that συναλίζομαι means 'to eat (salt) together with someone.' In *Clem. Rec.* 7.2 and *Clem. Hom.* 13.4 the word denotes the evening meal (here consisting of bread and salt); see E. Donckel, 'Sale Sumpto', *Ephem. Liturg.* 47 (1933), 101–12, and cf. Hanssen, ibid. 42 (1928) 551–60. Luke speaks of the risen Jesus eating in Luke 24.43 and Acts 10.41, also in the latter verse of the communal meal with the disciples: cf. Bowen, *ZNW* 13 (1912), 247ff. Other interpretations: a variant spelling of συναυλίζομαι (the reading of many minuscules): *Beg.* IV, 5, appealing to Euseb., *Suppl. quaest. ad Marinum*, Migne PG 22, 1005, suggests 'lie together' or 'be together' (Bauer s.v.). The meaning 'be together with' has been conjectured but not proved. In Josephus (e.g. *Ant.* VIII 105), the active denotes 'to gather' (trans.) and the middle voice (e.g. *Bell.* III 162) 'to gather' (intrans.). Hemsterhuis' much-favoured conjecture συναλιζομένοις presupposes the latter sense.

[4] In classical grammar (see Moulton, 122ff.) μὴ χωρίζεσθαι implies 'to stop moving away' as against μὴ χωρισθῆναι = 'not to begin moving away'. But Luke's constructions are not to be measured with classical yardsticks. Here, as in Luke 24.49, he means 'to stay in Jerusalem'. Loisy conjectures (p. 152) that in the original version of Acts Jesus ordered the disciples to wait in Jerusalem for the Parousia (='the promise of the Father'). But the version offered by Luke seems rather intended to preclude the tradition of the disciples' return to Galilee.

[5] Here Ἱεροσολύμων breaks R. Schütz's rule that the Hebraic form Ἱερουσαλήμ (occurring 39 times in Acts) is employed in the speeches of Aramaic-speakers.

Spirit. Luke was certainly acquainted with the tradition that Jesus had directed the disciples to Galilee (Mark **14**.28, **16**.7), but this he had corrected in Luke **24**.6. The tradition of the forty days was the more welcome to him in that it attested the unbroken continuity of the early church community. Here in Jerusalem, at Pentecost, the Father's promise,[1] which the disciples have heard from Jesus himself,[2] will be fulfilled. Not until **2**.17, however, is there any reference to the OT passage in which that promise is enshrined.[3] Up to that point the reader learns merely that Jesus has communicated some such word of promise to his disciples.[4]

VERSE 5: Luke gives the reason for the instruction to wait in a saying of Jesus which he will recall in **11**.16. In contrast to the mere water-baptism of John, the disciples are to be baptized with the Holy Spirit, and that before long.[5] The only occasion in the synoptic gospels when Jesus speaks of the Spirit is in the logion Mark **13**.11 *par*. The saying quoted in the present verse seems to have developed in the course of tradition from a saying of the Baptist (Matt. **3**.11, Luke **3**.16) into a saying of Jesus. It well suited Luke's purpose, in that it ascribes to John a mere water-baptism, while reserving the Spirit for the baptism of Christ and his Church. This is in accordance with what Luke teaches in Acts **19**.1–6.

VERSE 6: is slightly set apart from what precedes by the μὲν οὖν.[6] Those gathered—Luke chooses the indefinite expression because **1**.21 implies that

---

[1] 'The promise of the Father' means in the first place 'what the Father had promised', i.e. the Spirit (as also in Luke 24.49 and Acts 2.33): with this περιμένειν fits. But also it is 'the word of promise', and with this alone is ἠκούσατε appropriate. Cf. Eph. 1.13.

[2] As in Luke 5.14 and Acts 14.22, 17.3, 23.22 & 25.5, the transition to direct speech (marked by ἠκούσατέ μου) is a device—also known to classical Greek—for loosening the stiffness of the presentation; the converse is found in 23.24. Thus there is no justification for the reproofs administered by many commentators over this stylistic error. D smoothes the transition by interpolating: φησιν, διὰ τοῦ στόματός μου.

[3] Joel 3.1–5 (so e.g. Wendt, 68). Holtzmann (p. 24) and others relate the end of v. 4 to Luke 24.49. But this saying is in substance identical with our passage. Jesus would thus 'be referring his hearers to the words he is on the point of uttering' (Loisy, 151f.).

[4] ὅτι is understood as 'because' by e.g. Overbeck (3), Knopf (531) and Bauernfeind (17). Others, including Zahn (28 n. 47), Preuschen (5), Wellhausen (2) and Jacquier (13), take it as ὅτι *recitativum* (Bl.-Debr. § 397, 5), in which case v. 5 would itself become the 'promise of the Father'.

[5] The words οὐ μετὰ πολλὰς ταύτας ἡμέρας are definitely part of Jesus' speech. They are not a Latinism, as has persistently been maintained ever since Blass: *non post multos hos dies* would be bad Latin (*Beg*. IV, 7, with reference to LXX Ex. 2.23 & 4.19: μετὰ δὲ τὰς ἡμέρας τὰς πολλὰς ἐκείνας). On the position of negatives in Luke, see Bl.-Debr. § 433, 3: 'In classical style there is a tendency to place before the preposition any negative ... modifying a participle or adjective governed by a preposition; the same practice is occasionally found in the NT.' Luke's meaning is 'within the next few days'.

[6] μὲν οὖν is 'a favourite formula of Acts in opening a new story which is nevertheless connected with what goes before' (*Beg*. IV, 7). It occurs in Acts 1.6, 18; 2.41; 5.41; 8.4, 25; 9.31; 11.19; 12.5; 13.4; 14.3; 15.3, 30; 16.5; 17.12, 17, 30; 19.32, 38; 23.18, 22, 31; 25.4, 11; 26.4, 9; 28.5. According to Overbeck (p. 4) it indicates here that the following scene is no longer in the house.

not only the Apostles were present—ask whether[1] Jesus will now restore[2] the kingdom to Israel. The question is not meant to show the disciples' ignorance, but provides an opportunity to clarify a problem of the highest significance. The earliest Christians regarded the outpouring of the Spirit as a sign that the end of the world was at hand.[3] With this in mind it is easy to understand why they should ask, 'Is the kingdom coming now,[4] at the same time as the Spirit?' The question thus brings up the problem of the eschatological near-expectation, which is however linked with a second problem: 'Is the kingdom restricted to Israel?' Here we have the first mention of the problem of the Gentile mission, which will make itself felt again and again in Acts, right up to 28.28.

VERSE 7: The asyndetic[5] 'He said to them: It is not for you . . .' makes clear to the reader that Jesus is expressing a stern injunction which must be obeyed. But at the same time the Christian is relieved of the painful disappointment brought on by non-fulfilment of the imminent expectation (cf. II Peter 3.3ff.). For this purpose Luke makes use of a logion which he had not taken from Mark into his own gospel but had saved for this passage (cf. Mark 13.32 = Matt. 24.36). In its Lucan form,[6] it forbids the asking of any questions about the hour of the Parousia. It is evident from this that Luke is the spokesman of a new age. He has decisively renounced all expectation of an imminent end. Consequently the task has arisen of finding a new relationship to this world in which, by God's inscrutable will, the Christians must continue to live.

VERSE 8: After it has been made clear what the Christians must renounce, they learn what they are to be given: the disciples will receive the Holy Spirit[7] and then be Jesus' witnesses[8] to the ends of the earth.[9] This

---

[1] εἰ is a Hellenistic way of introducing direct questions also (Bl.-Debr. § 440, 3).

[2] From Malachi 3.23 LXX onwards, ἀποκαθίστημι is a technical term in eschatology: the establishment of the right order by God (here, Jesus) at the end of time (cf. *ThWb* I, 386ff.).

[3] So Zeller (78), Schneckenburger (198) and Overbeck (5).

[4] 'At this time' = οὐ μετὰ πολλὰς ταύτας ἡμέρας.

[5] ℵ A and 𝔊 remove the asyndeton by the insertion of δέ; D it by καί.

[6] Luke omits 'not even the Son knows that day and hour,' which had now become a stumbling-block.

[7] Here the Holy Spirit appears as the mediator of the marvellous power (δύναμις) which works miracles (δυνάμεις). Since these were regarded in primitive Christianity as the decisive sign of legitimation (Acts 2.22, cf. II Cor. 12.12), the Spirit which conferred miraculous power was a *sine qua non* for the mission (*Beg.* IV, 8).

[8] The term 'Jesus' witnesses' is applied to the Apostles in Acts 1.8, 22; 2.32; 3.15; 5.32; 10.39, 41 & 13.31, to Paul in 22.15 & 26.16, and to Stephen in 22.20. The subject of their witness is Jesus' resurrection, and it is before Israel and the Gentile authorities that they testify. Isaiah 43.10 LXX offers an instance of μάρτυς in the OT: γένεσθέ μοι μάρτυρες κτλ.

[9] Verse 8bc contains the groundplan of Acts: Chapters 1 to 7—Jerusalem; 8 & 9— Judaea and Samaria; 10 to 28—the mission 'to the ends of the earth.' This last expression is borrowed from Isaiah 49.6, which Acts 13.47 interprets as a charge laid upon the

utterance is command and promise in one. It defines for the Church the terms of its commission (the Apostles are only the Church's representatives, hence they may stay quietly in Jerusalem and allow Paul to carry on the main mission).[1] As Acts presents it, the Christian Church is a *missionary* Church.[2] Hence the other problem posed by the disciples' question of verse 6 is also resolved: the world-mission here decreed presupposes that salvation is not restricted to Israel.[3]

The words of Jesus however have yet another implication. In laying down the course of the Christian mission from Jerusalem to the 'end of the earth,' they also prescribe the content of Acts: the progress of the gospel from Jerusalem to Rome. Thus what any normal statement of contents would have mentioned in verse 3 is here brought home to the community by the Lord himself as a God-willed sequence of events. In this way the story which Luke's second book relates receives the divine seal: it was the Lord himself who pointed the way for the Church. The story of the Church is the history of divine salvation.

This word of Jesus, containing at once gift and obligation, is the last word he speaks on earth. It is final and conclusive.

At the hands of modern scholarship the proem of Acts has received undeservedly rough treatment. Even conservative scholars like Beyer (p. 10) and Bauernfeind (p. 18) deny it to Luke and charge it to a redactor. Why? Because it is not constructed in the habitual way for classical times. The typical proem begins by reminding the reader of what he learned from the previous book, then tells him what he is about to learn. This antithesis of past and future between which the proem is balanced is normally accentuated by the use of μέν and δέ. With this procedure the present example is somewhat inconsistent. There is no δέ after the μέν. The events of the previous book, Luke's Gospel, are indeed recalled, but there is no rehearsal of those to come. Instead, the author harks back beyond the Ascension story which brought

---

Christian mission. By ἔσχατα LXX here means simply 'distant lands': in Ps. Sol. **8**.15 it applies to Rome; correspondingly, Rome is in Acts the farthest place perceptible and attained by the mission. Luke **2**.32 attaches Isaiah **49**.6 to Jesus, and it is from the will of God there expressed that Luke takes the injunction of Acts **1**.8.

[1] The Twelve do no missionary work apart from the activity of Peter and John in Samaria (**8**.25). As Acts presents it, the rest of the mission falls essentially to Paul's share. I Clem. **42**.3f. offers quite another picture of the Apostles' missionary activity. 'Now when they had received their charges . . ., they went forth . . . to declare the glad tidings that the kingdom of God was at hand. They preached in town and village . . .' (Knopf, *Hdb. z. NT*, Suppl. 1920, 116). So do Justin, *Apol.* I 39.3: 'men twelve in number set forth from . . . Jerusalem into the world . . .', and Hermas *Sim.* IX 25.2: 'Apostles and teachers who preached in all the world.' Cf. E. Lohse, *ThZ* (1953), 263–5.

[2] Cf. Thomas Ohm, *ZfMWuRW* 37 (1953) 8.

[3] There is no suggestion in Acts of any mission west of Rome, say in Spain.

Luke to a close, and tells of appearances of the risen Christ during the forty days before the Ascension. The train of the narrative pulls out of the terminus *a quo* and—after a longish journey—pulls in at the same platform! It takes a redactor to produce such a muddle. . . .

Moreover these philological and literary considerations[1] are not the only ones: there are also the theological. Two Ascensions—one on Easter Day (Luke **24**.51), the other forty days after (Acts **1**.9)—are one too many. Unless, like Michaelis (*Die Erscheinungen des Auferstandenen*, 1944, 84–6), one adopts the simple expedient that Jesus came down from heaven for every one of these appearances—Acts **1**.9 recounting merely the last of them— it is tempting to strike out the end of Luke (24.50–3) and the beginning of Acts, to verse 5. As *inter alios* Sahlin, Menoud and Trocmé believe, the two works were originally a single book, an outsize gospel containing the Acts not only of Jesus but of the Apostles. It was not until the question arose of taking the work into the canon, which admitted only gospels with the customary contents, that the work was cut in two at the appropriate place and the first part furnished with a conclusion, the second with an introduction for which the late legend of the forty days was pressed into service. Thus at one blow these scholars have eliminated the dual ascension and exonerated Luke from the alleged stylistic clumsiness of Acts' opening verses.

But if we want to judge the proem's difficulties correctly, we must separate the real from the apparent. To the latter category belongs the solitary μέν, for instance, which is followed by no δέ: this is a frequent feature in Acts. Again, it is wrongly assumed that in **1**.5 a redactor lapsed into direct speech out of sheer incompetence; on the contrary, the passage from indirect to direct speech is a stylistic device often used by Luke in Acts in the interest of flexibility. The author has unjustly been reproached with showing Jesus as taking his departure, in Luke **24**.50, with the gesture of the Benediction; this is however one of the many traits which Luke drew from his own Bible, the Old Testament (Ecclesiasticus 50.20). If Acts **1**.1–5 contains several expressions not to be found in the rest of the book, there are on the other hand a number of peculiarly Lucan expressions: 1. παθεῖν in the sense of 'to die,' 2. καί after the relative and 3. the ostensible relative clause which is in fact a main clause introduced by a relative; these are not exactly things that catch the eye and spur a redactor to imitation. Still less should Luke be criticised for omitting the normal statement of contents in respect of the book now under way. For one thing, it was quite possible for a writer of those days to plunge straight into the matter of the new book after reviewing the contents of the old; for another, Luke has in fact described the contents of Acts through the words of Jesus in verse 8. He has done so, moreover, in a way incomparably superior to the classical scheme, for now the whole action

---

[1] Forcefully expressed by Eduard Norden on pp. 315f. of *Agnostos Theos*.

of Acts becomes the fulfilment of Jesus' word, and this is much more than a mere table of contents: it is a promise!

It must be admitted that the two-fold account of the Ascension constitutes a greater stumbling-block. Here we must remind ourselves that Luke does not set as much store as we upon consistency in the story. This is for example evident from the freedom with which he tells three differing stories of Paul's conversion, each answering the needs of the moment. The present case is no different. To Luke it is of the utmost importance that Acts should begin not with the disciples left to their own devices, but with the Lord, who visits and instructs them for forty days more. In this way the Christian mission on which they then embark becomes not a merely human enterprise but a process which the Lord himself has guided on its way. (The modern reader, who imagines the Apostles and other leading figures of the Early Church as completely self-sufficient human beings, must again and again in Acts be struck by the way in which such 'mythical powers' as the Lord, the Spirit, an angel, the 'vision', decisively intervene in the action!) This Ascension after forty days is however suitable only for Acts, not for the end of Luke. There the normal gospel version is appropriate, according to which Jesus took his leave on the night of Easter Sunday. And, of course, in ceremonial fashion: hence the gesture of benediction, which makes a peculiarly deep impression on the reader because of its very singularity. Exception to the variance of the two versions—this the alterations in D already show—has been taken only by those scholars who hold the writer to account for each stroke of the pen and are not satisfied until each tiny stone exactly fits its neighbours. It is thus by no means necessary to assume that Luke only heard about the forty days after his first book had appeared.

Once we visualize this attitude on the part of early Christian writer Luke, we need no longer raise a hue and cry about the Acts proem or speculate on what happened at the juncture of 'admittance to the canon'. This 'admittance' was in any case not decided by some central Bible Commission, which, having split the text, could have completed the halves in a consistent way! A document's 'admittance to the canon' came about simply because large and important congregations loved and used it in their services; from this grew its general recognition—and canonicity. So it is probable that first Luke's gospel became 'canonical', and only later (because Luke was now one of the 'four Evangelists') his second book also, our 'Acts'.

Its name is not entirely justified. For in reality the author has detailed knowledge only of Peter and Paul; moreover Paul is not even one of the Twelve, who in Luke's eyes are the only Apostles in the real sense. Of James the son of Zebedee the reader learns no more than that he was executed by the sword; his brother John is never more than Peter's shadowy companion. The remaining nine Apostles are mere names. On the other hand there appears, alongside the two leading rôles, an extensive cast of characters, sacred and profane, from the girl in the doorway to the emperor (over eighty are actually named!). With them comes thronging in the motley life which fills Acts to the brim. For it deals not with isolated Apostles, but with the whole world of the Levantine seaboard, a soil in which the Christian Church grows and multiplies like the wonderful seed of the parable, which bore fruit thirty-, sixty- and a hundredfold.

But then again, the book's title is not wholly a misnomer. For one thing the Twelve are for Luke the first rulers of the Early Church, for another, Paul is their representative: a suffragan Apostle, as it were. With him (as **20**.29 quietly suggests) there draws to its close a time, a special time, when the Church was still pure. It was because, as Luke saw it, the 'apostolic' age comprehended the ideal existence of the Church that he could dare, in this second book, to place its history beside the earthly life of the Lord.

2
ACTS 1: 9–12
THE ASCENSION

[9] And when he had said this, he was taken up as they were looking; and a cloud received him out of their sight. [10] And while they were looking steadfastly as he went into heaven, behold, two men stood by them in white apparel. [11] These said: 'Men of Galilee, why do you stand looking into heaven? This Jesus, who was received up from you, shall come in the same manner as you have seen him go into heaven.' [12] Then they returned to Jerusalem from the mountain, called the Mount of Olives, which lies near Jerusalem, a sabbath day's journey off.

Bibliography:

E. Nestle, 'Zu Acta **1**.12', *ZNW* 3 (1902), 247–9; B. W. Bacon, 'The Ascension in Luke and Acts', *Exp.* (1909) 154–61; W. Michaelis, 'Zur Überlieferung der Himmelfahrtsgeschichte', *ThBl* 4 (1925), 101–9; Lyder Brun, *Die Auferstehung Christi in der urchr. Überlieferung*, Oslo 1925 (esp. Appendix 3, 'Die Himmelfahrt', 90–7); Erich Fascher, 'Die Auferstehung Jesu und ihr Verhältnis zur urchristlichen Verkündigung', *ZNW* 27 (1926), 1–26; Anton Fridrichsen, 'Die Himmelfahrt bei Lukas', *ThBl* 6 (1927), 337–41; M. S. Enslin, 'The Ascension Story', *JBL* 47 (1928), 60–73; V. Larrañaga, *L'Ascension de Notre Seigneur dans le Nouveau Testament* (IPB), Rome and Paris 1938; Amos Wilder, 'Variant Traditions of the Resurrection in Acts', *JBL* 62 (1943), 307–18; P. H. Menoud, 'Remarques sur textes de l'Ascension dans Luc-Actes' in *NT Studien für R. Bultmann* (*ZNW* Suppl. No. 21), Berlin 1954, 148–56; Georg Kretschmar, 'Himmelfahrt und Pfingsten' *ZKG* 66 (1954/5), 209–53; A. W. Argyle, 'The Ascension', *Exp. Tim.* 66 (1955), 240–2; G. M. Young, 'A Parallel to Acts **1**.9', *JTS* N.S. 1/2 (1950/1), 156; K. Lake, 'The Ascension', *Beg.* V, 16–22; id., 'The Mount of Olives and Bethany', *Beg.* V, 475f.

F. Ogara, 'De ascensionis Christi spectatoribus', *Gregorianum* 14 (1933), 37–61 (on **1**.10f.); P. Benoit, 'L'Ascension', *Rev. Bibl.* 56 (1949), 161–203; M. D. H. Willinck, 'A Cloud received Him (Acts **1**.9)', *Theology* 14 (1927), 297–9; C. F. D. Moule, 'The Ascension—Acts **1**.9', *Exp. Tim.* 68 (1956–7), 205–9; P. A. van Stempvoort, 'The Interpretation of the Ascension in Luke and Acts', *NTS* 5 (1959), 30–42; J. E. Howard, 'Acts **1**.11', *Exp. Tim.* 39 (1927–8), 92.

VERSE 9: The tale moves seamlessly[1] on. After the 'last word' of Jesus, the command to mission, he is lifted up[2] before the gaze of the disciples (who thus become the eyewitnesses of the Ascension), enveloped by a cloud,[3] and withdrawn from their sight,[4] so that the report cannot further describe his entry into heaven itself. Luke's account differs from pagan[5] or Jewish[6] representations of similar ascents by the fact that no earthly element (a whirlwind or the cloud itself) bears the exalted one aloft.

VERSE 10: The disciples look on[7] intently as Jesus goes up to heaven.[8]

---

[1] When E. Schwartz (*NGG* (1907), 278f. n. 1) and Preuschen (p. 6) had the impression of a sudden abruptness which they could only explain by the commencement of a new source, what they really missed was a 'personal' farewell, such as one might find if need be in the blessing of Luke **24**.50.

[2] D sa have the cloud enfold Jesus while he is yet on the ground. Doubtless they had in mind the cloud which envelops Jesus in the transfiguration story of Mark **9**.7.

[3] NT parallels are Rev. **11**.12, where the two witnesses rise to heaven ἐν τῇ νεφέλῃ, and I Thess. **4**.17, according to which the surviving Christians will be ravished skywards ἐν νεφέλαις to meet the Lord. See also Bauer, *Einf.* p. 22.

[4] So Bauer translates, *Wb.* 1672; ὑπολαμβάνω here covers the moment of both concealment and separation, either of which may be expressed by ἀπό (Bauer, 171). There is no need, *pace* Torrey, to think of a translation from Aramaic.

[5] Livy, *Ab urbe cond.* I 16, 1: Romulus is enveloped by a cloud and swept up to heaven by a whirlwind. Livy himself adopts a sceptical attitude to the story, but it shows how the people of his time imagined the taking-up to heaven (of a *living* being), and that they considered it possible.

[6] Especially noteworthy here is Enoch **39**.3: 'At that time did a cloud and a whirlwind snatch me from off the earth and set me down at the end of heaven.'

[7] ἀτενίζοντες ἦσαν. In "Ἧν διδάσκων: die periphrastischen Konstruktionen im Griechischen' (*Skrifter utg. av Kgl. Humanist. Vetenskaps-Samfundet i Uppsala*, 32, 2, 1940), Gudmund Björck showed that: 1. the so-called adjectival periphrasis (e.g. Acts **19**.36: δέον ἐστίν for δεῖ) employs a participle like an adjective if either the duration of the attribute is to be indicated or a hiatus avoided (cf. Acts **2**.29, **9**.9 and **13**.11); 2. what Björck calls the 'progressive' periphrasis of the verb by a present participle with εἶναι indicates the time-context within which something takes place (p. 42). Often a periphrastic conjugation at the beginning of a pericope depicts the setting for the action proper, which is then rendered with simple tenses (e.g. Acts **8**.28, **10**.30, **12**.20 & **22**.19), and it is in this light that **8**.1 also should be seen (pp. 44f.). Within the narrative, periphrasis appears whenever reference is made to the background against which the action proper is taking place, e.g. in Acts **1**.10, **10**.24, **12**.4f., **14**.6 & **16**.12 (p. 46). In some instances the periphrasis occurs in an incidental remark referring to the 'context': Acts **1**.14, **2**.2, **12**.12 & **21**.3. Lastly it may come at the end of an episode in order to convey the situation resulting from the action: **1**.14, **2**.41, **8**.13 & **9**.28 (p. 47). On the other hand, in **5**.25 and **11**.5 εἶναι has an independent significance: 'they are in the Temple, standing there and teaching,' 'I was in the city of Joppa and was praying' (p. 51). Periphrasis with the aorist participle (Luke **23**.19: ἦν βληθείς = 'he had been thrown into prison') replaces the pluperfect and has nothing to do with the above-cited cases. Lucan predilection for periphrasis does not, as might be thought, betray the rendering of Aramaic sources (pp. 67ff.) but corresponds to the outlook of the author, 'who took equal pleasure in the portrayal of the concrete background situation and in the picturesque coinage of the individual expression' (p. 67). Here the use of periphrasis in Acts stands clarified over and above what Radermacher (p. 102) and Bl.-Debr. (§ 353) have to say.—ἀτενίζειν, a favourite word of Luke's, occurs ten times in Acts.—Temporal ὡς = 'as', 'when', as often in LXX.

[8] εἰς τὸν οὐρανόν is here placed before the πορευομένου αὐτοῦ with which it belongs (see above on **1**.2).

Suddenly,[1] as in the story of the empty tomb (Luke 24.4), there stand before them two men in white (i.e. shining[2]) raiment[3]—*angeli interpretes*,[4] 'who also'[5] speak to them.

VERSE 11: Just as in Luke 24, the mortals are rebuked for their human reaction[6]: 'Why do you stand looking into heaven?'[7] The Jesus who has been received up from the disciples into heaven[8] will return[9] thence in like fashion as they have seen him go—there is not a word as to the 'when'. Their looking skywards is not forbidden for the reason which Loisy suggests (p. 162): 'C'est temps perdu. Le Christ est parti, bien parti,' but because it expresses the imminent expectation, which Luke does not mention but only describes by this attitude.

VERSE 12: Bowing to the angels' words, the disciples return to Jerusalem. As a postscript we learn that the Ascension took place on the Mount of Olives,[10] on which, according to the interpretation of Zech. 14.4 LXX, the Messiah (=κύριος) will one day descend from heaven. The statement that the Mount of Olives is a sabbath day's journey[11] from Jerusalem does not

---

[1] Luke borrows καὶ ἰδού from LXX, using it 24 times in his gospel, and eight times in Acts (1.10, 5.28, 8.27, 10.30, 11.11, 12.7, 16.1 & 27.24). It lends an OT, Palestinian colour. Cf. καὶ νῦν ἰδού in 13.11 and 20.22 & 25: also a LXX turn of phrase.

[2] The shining garments of heavenly beings are mentioned in II Macc. 11.8; Mark 9.3 *par.*, 16.5 *par.*; John 20.12; Hermas *Vis.* IV 2. 1; 3. 5; *Sim.* VIII 2.3 (*Beg.* IV, 9).

[3] ἐσθήσεσι: dative plural of ἐσθής (Bauer, 617).

[4] Their only function here is to help the men to a proper understanding of the situation. Wellhausen's conjecture (p. 2) that they may be identified with Moses and Elijah is purely gratuitous.

[5] The καί in οἳ καὶ εἶπαν should not be translated (see above on 1.3). This relative clause too is really a principal clause introduced by a relative.

[6] Renan, in *Les Apôtres*, 1866, 103, takes the angels' words as a consolation; but then one would expect to find some explicit word of consolation in their message.

[7] According to Preuschen (p. 6), the address ἄνδρες Γαλιλαῖοι is not Semitic, but Greek 'polished rhetoric'. Later this passage was used to confute the star-gazing disciples of Galileo—*Viri Galilaei, quid statis aspicientes in caelum?* (Holtzmann, 25).

[8] The second εἰς τὸν οὐρανόν is missing in D d gig Aug (*sermo* 277)—'probably rightly omitted' is the verdict of Ropes in *Beg.* III, 6. But Luke probably wished to stress this aspect by including εἰς τὸν οὐρανόν four times in rapid succession.

[9] Daniel 7.13, adduced in Mark 13.26 (=Matt. 24.30, Luke 21.27), 14.62 (=Matt. 26.64) and Rev. 1.7 as a description of the Parousia, originally says nothing about a descent to earth of the 'Son of Man', but was enlisted as a reference to this by Christian exegesis. The two variants (G: ἐπὶ τῶν νεφελῶν; Θ: μετὰ τῶν νεφελῶν) recur in Mark 14.62, Matt. and Rev. 1.7; the form ἐν (τῇ) νεφέλῃ used in Luke 21.27, Acts 1.9 and Rev. 11.12, is further removed from that text.

[10] Ἐλαιών, as in Luke 19.29 & 21.37, Josephus *Ant.* VII 202 (and probably XX, 169) and *Bell.* V 70 (Billerbeck I, 870; Bl.-Debr. § 143 Appendix).

[11] A sabbath day's journey (the distance a Jew might travel on the sabbath without breaking the commandment of Ex. 16.29) comprised 2000 ells = 960 yds. (Billerbeck II, 590–4). According to Josephus, *Ant.* XX 169, the Mount of Olives was five stadia distant from Jerusalem. John 11.18 puts Bethany (whose position is uncertain: *Beg.* V, 475f.) fifteen stadia away from Jerusalem. 'Luke,' says *Beg.* V, 475, 'seems to treat "Mount of Olives" and Bethany (Luke 24.50!) as interchangeable.' It seems as if he did not possess any exact notion of the topography of Jerusalem: see on 3.11 below.—ἔχον is Hellenistic for ἀπέχον: *Beg.* IV, 10.

imply that Luke thought the Ascension took place on a Sabbath (so Chrysostom); the expression belongs to the biblical language in which his story is clothed.[1]

The peculiarity of this account lies in the fact that all embroidery of the action (think of the description of the Ascension in the Gospel of Peter!) and all dwelling on the sensations of the participants, so dear to legend, are entirely lacking: the story is unsentimental, almost uncannily austere. There is no vestige of popular tradition, though Luke cannot surely have been the first to tell the story of the Ascension; probably the narrative of the empty tomb (cf. especially Luke **24**.4) served as his model. Attention is entirely concentrated on the fact of the Ascension itself (note the fourfold 'into heaven' of verses 9ff.) and on the message of the angels. It does not really explain the Ascension, as one might at first expect, but corrects the attitude which the disciples adopt towards it. Furthermore, one should not seek a psychological explanation of this attitude—here, as in **1**.6, the psychology of the Apostles is a matter of indifference to Luke—or cudgel one's brains to know why Jesus did not prepare them for his departure or, if he did, why they did not behave accordingly. As in **1**.6, Luke here takes the disciples as the model, so to speak, of a particular attitude which in his time—one need only think of Revelation!—was still dominant in many Christian communities: belief in the imminence of the last days.

Once alive to this peculiarity of Luke's account, one realizes that it was in no way his purpose to compose (or pass on) a vivid and exceptionally impressive picture of the Ascension. It was not Luke the historian who moulded this episode, nor yet the pious story-teller, but (if one may for once so pointedly express it) the conscientious Christian wanting to help his brothers understand their existence as God willed they should. That is why he says nothing of the disciples' feelings when their Lord is taken away, nothing of the impression made on mortals by the envoys from the heavenly world (cf. Luke **24**.4!), nothing of any farewell gesture of blessing such as Jesus makes in Luke **24**.51. The disciples are not presented, here, in their private relationship with Jesus; they are rather the representatives of the Church, which must learn its right relationship to the Ascension and the Parousia.

Yet even if, from now on, no term is set for the return of Jesus, no doubt is thrown on the belief that he will eventually return. Far from it!—the concrete fact narrated, that Jesus went to heaven *before the eyes of* his disciples, led the reader not merely to believe, but almost to *see* that he would return in like manner, as the angels foretell. This vividness seemed to guarantee the reality of what had happened, and was yet to happen. But

---

[1] 'Sacred measurement'—Bauernfeind, 23.

in this respect the modern situation, and hence our reaction to this story, is somewhat different. It was in forms belonging to the ancient view of the world that Luke represented, first to himself, then to the faithful, how Jesus went to God, and only those who do not understand will take exception to the fact. For no matter what this or that dogmatist may decree, Christian preaching in the first century no more moved in a vacuum than it does in the twentieth. Luke himself affords proof of this in yet another sense. The first generation was dominated by the expectation of the imminent end. Luke replaces this view—with the utmost discretion, as must be said both here and in **1**.6—by a new form of the Christian hope, which renounces all dating of the Parousia and, to that extent, no longer 'walks by sight' but contents itself with the not yet visible. We ourselves must go a stage farther and realize that we cannot even visualize that which Luke did not indeed describe with elaborate embroidery but yet briefly depicted: Jesus' way to the Father.

With **1**.12 the first section of Acts, its introduction, so to speak, draws to a close. In it the Lord who walked on earth was once more in person the protagonist. Henceforth, unless God miraculously intervenes, it is of the disciples that the story will tell.

3

ACTS 1:13–14
THE DISCIPLES RETURN TO JERUSALEM, WHERE THEY FORM THE FIRST CONGREGATION

¹³ And when they had come in, they went up into the upper room where they were staying: Peter and John and James and Andrew; Philip and Thomas; Bartholomew and Matthew; James the son of Alphaeus, and Simon the Zealot, and Judas the son of James. ¹⁴ These all with one accord continued steadfastly in prayer, with the women and Mary the mother of Jesus, and with his brethren.

Bibliography:

H. J. Cadbury, 'The Summaries in Acts', *Beg.* V, 392–402; Ethelbert Stauffer, 'Jüdisches Erbe im urchristl. Kirchenrecht', *TLZ* 77 (1952), 201–6; E. Bickermann, 'Viri Magnae Congregationis', *Rev. Bibl.* 55 (1948), 397–402; Reicke 20f.; Trocmé 183.

VERSE 13: This verse sketches the disciples' new situation in a few concise strokes: 'when they had come' into the city¹, 'they went up into the'(hitherto unmentioned) 'upper room,² where they were staying.'³ Upper rooms of this kind, according to Billerbeck II, 594, used to 'serve the learned as place of assembly, study and prayer,' but were sometimes also let as dwellings. The life of the disciples and their circle during this period is accordingly characterized as devoted to the assemblies, prayer and contemplation which, judging by **9.11** and **13.2**, are thought of as a preparation for the expected revelation of the Spirit, even if (**6.4**) this is not the only purpose of the Apostles' prayer.

Had the third gospel and Acts appeared simultaneously as one book, the new list of Apostles would have been superfluous after Luke **6.14–16**. It

---

¹ 'Into the city' should be understood after εἰσῆλθον.

² In Hebrew, עֲלִיָּה. According to *Beg.* IV, 10, the ὑπερῷον was perhaps identical with the ἀνάγαιον of Luke **22.12**, which Zahn's conjecture (44f.) places in the house of Mary the mother of John Mark (Acts **12.12**). Holtzmann (p. 26) and others, however, have thought to locate it in the Temple, on the strength of a false equation of Acts **1.13** with Luke **24.52f.**: Loisy (p. 65) is here undecided. In fact Luke **24.53** would seem to correspond with Acts **2.46** (Wendt p. 72).

³ ἦσαν καταμένοντες implies permanent residence; see above on **1.10**.

acquaints the reader of Acts with the now incomplete circle of Apostles, the guiding council of the later congregation, which here at the same time appears as its nucleus. Peter and John stand at the head; they will appear together in **3**.1 and **8**.14. Then follows James, whose death will be reported in **12**.2. That, as opposed to Luke **6**.14f., Thomas is named before Bartholomew and Matthew does not necessarily prove the use of a new tradition. Σίμων ὁ ζηλωτής was evidently a member of the Zealot liberation-movement who had gone over to Jesus (see Bauer, *Einf.* 25).

Influenced by what he takes to be the practice of the Qumran community, Stauffer (op. cit., 201) interprets the roll of names as a list of members arranged in order of 'length of ecclesiastical service'. But neither was the order of sitting at Qumran determined by length of service (it appears to have been based on the yearly spiritual review), nor have we any reason to regard the earliest Christian community as analogous with the quasi-monastic sect of Qumran, whose extreme legalism, to mention but one feature, was utterly alien to the Christian outlook.

VERSE 14: We now learn that the Eleven, according to Luke, did not form the whole of the germ-cell of the primitive Church: in one accord,[1] leading with them a life steadfastly[2] devoted to prayer, there were also 'the women',[3] the witnesses of the empty grave, as well as the mother of Jesus and his brothers. Thus at least eight other persons,[4] forming two distinct groups, must be added to the Eleven: 'the women' are well-to-do followers of Jesus, some of high position; Jesus' relatives comprise not one but several families, since we must picture his brothers as married (nothing is known of their trades or professions).

Most exegetes have, not entirely without reason, attached verse 12 to verses 13f.; in fact it is a transitional verse leading to the following scene.

In this we have the first of those instances where Luke interrupts the progress of the action to describe some situation which prevailed for a more or less lengthy period; it is not surprising that here he uses the *coniugatio periphrastica* (see note on **1**.10 above). Cadbury in his note on 'The Summaries

---

[1] In Acts **1**.14, **2**.46, **4**.24, **5**.12 and **8**.6 on the one hand, and **7**.57, **18**.12 and **19**.29 on the other, Luke uses ὁμοθυμαδόν to depict respectively the Christians' exemplary unity and the unanimity of a hostile group. The word (=יַחַד, יַחְדָּו) occurs 36 times in LXX.

[2] προσκαρτερέω, implying assiduity, also occurs in descriptions of Christian conduct in **2**.42, **2**.46 and **6**.4.

[3] D turns them into the 'wives and children'—presumably of the Apostles (the phrase σὺν γυναιξὶν καὶ τέκνοις occurs also in Acts **21**.5): from this verse and **18**.26 we may perhaps conclude that D expresses a very hesitant attitude towards the independent activity of women in the congregation.

[4] These are Mary Magdalene, Joanna the wife of Chuza (a high officer under Herod), Susanna ('and many others', Luke **8**.3); Mary the mother of Jesus, and his brothers James, Joses, Judas and Simon (Mark **6**.3).

in Acts' (*Beg*. V, 392) mentions the suggestion that these summaries divide the book into six 'panels'. They do not only divide, however: they also *link* the separate incidents reported by tradition. Popular tradition has a predilection for what is striking, individual, the vivid concrete event which imprints itself on the memory, and the writer whose object is to edify also relies on the arresting, self-contained episode. Luke as a historian, however, wishes also to fill in gaps between such elements of tradition, and to say something about those times which are not distinguished by special incidents. In everyday routine as such Luke had admittedly no more interest than the rest of his community. When he inserts a general summary, it must likewise serve for edification and present an exemplary situation. To a limited extent Luke can also indicate something like a development by his summaries: thus the growth of the community is described in summary statements like 2.47b, 5.14 and similar verses. Popular tradition affords the author but little help in such descriptions. He must therefore find his own material by generalizing particular cases or by other methods (cf. Introduction § 7, p. 105 n.1).

Luke is here trying to throw light on the history of the very earliest congregation. He begins by naming the Eleven. At first sight, they appear to have been the sole witnesses of Jesus' Ascension (but see 1.21f.!) and to have gathered afterwards in the upper room in Jerusalem. But Luke now adds that 'the women' were present. Since he shows no interest in the wives of the Apostles or of Jesus' brothers (cf. I Cor. 9.5), but rather in the women who supported Jesus (Luke 8.2f., 23.49, 55 and 24.10), it is to the latter that he here refers. With their generosity and loyalty they are in Luke's eyes shining examples as well as being the highly important witnesses for the empty tomb. Finally Luke mentions Jesus' mother and brothers. From Mark 3.21 and 31ff. it can still be recognised that they regarded Jesus as possessed by a devil and hence wanted to take him home; John 7.5 also presupposes that his brothers did not believe in him. Paul, however, recounts in I Cor. 15.7 an appearance of the risen Christ to James (which also appears with legendary additions in the Gospel of the Hebrews: Jerome *De vir. ill.* 2). The natural inference is that as a result of this appearance not only James but also Jesus' mother and brothers attached themselves to the congregation. The transformation of this older tradition into Luke's version is wholly understandable. To the later Church the rejection of Jesus by his own family was inconceivable; even in Mark this tradition had been softened, and Luke 8.19 replaces it with a more recent one. From Psalms 38.11 (37.12 LXX: οἱ ἔγγιστά μου ἀπὸ μακρόθεν ἔστησαν) and 88.8 (87.9 LXX: ἐμάκρυνας τοὺς γνωστούς μου ἀπ᾽ ἐμοῦ), read in the light of the Passion, the Christians gathered that Jesus' family had accompanied him to Jerusalem and witnessed his agony as distant spectators. It seemed automatically to follow that they afterwards remained in the city with the Eleven and the women. Bauernfeind (p. 24) passes a more favourable verdict on the historical value of this text:

because in verse 14 persons are named who are of no interest from the viewpoints of piety or doctrine, it must have been the insistence of remembered facts, plus a certain will to be historically accurate, that led Luke to mention them here. But in reality an edifying interest does attach to this motif: that Jesus' family belonged to his community from the beginning is precisely a feature of the pious image of these early days that was subsequently developed.

4
ACTS 1:15–26
THE COMPLETION OF THE APOSTOLIC CIRCLE

[15] And in these days Peter stood up in the midst of the brethren and said (and the company of persons gathered together was about a hundred and twenty), [16] 'Brethren, the scripture had to be fulfilled which the Holy Spirit spoke before by the mouth of David concerning Judas, who was guide to those who arrested Jesus; [17] for he was numbered among us and had received his portion in this ministry. [18] Now this man obtained a property with the reward of his iniquity; and falling headlong he burst asunder in the midst, and all his bowels gushed out. [19] And it became known to all the inhabitants of Jerusalem, so that in their language that field was called Akeldama, that is: the field of blood. [20] For it is written in the book of Psalms: 'Let his farmstead become desolate, and let no man dwell therein' and 'His overseership let another take.' [21] Of the men therefore who have accompanied us all the time that the Lord Jesus went in and out among us, [22] beginning from the baptism of John until the day when he was taken up from us, of these must one become a witness of his resurrection together with us.' [23] And they put forward two, Joseph called Barsabbas, who was surnamed Justus, and Matthias. [24] And they prayed and said, 'Thou, Lord, who knowest the hearts of all men, show which of these two thou hast chosen, [25] to take the place in this ministry and apostleship from which Judas fell away, to go to his own place'. [26] And they gave lots to them, and the lot fell upon Matthias; and he was numbered with the eleven Apostles.

Bibliography:

J. Renié, 'L'Élection de Matthias: authenticité du récit', *Rev. Bibl.* 53 (1948), 43–53; P. Gaechter S. J., 'Die Wahl des Matthias', *ZkTh* 71 (1949), 318–46; E. Stauffer, 'Jüdisches Erbe im urchristl. Kirchenrecht', *TLZ* 77 (1952) 201–6; Bo Reicke, 'Die Verfassung der Urgemeinde im Lichte jüdischer Dokumente', *ThZ* 10 (1954), 95–112; Ch. Masson, 'La Reconstitution du collège des Douze', *RThPh* 3e série t. 5 (1955), 193–201; P.H. Menoud, 'Les Additions au groupe des 12 apôtres d'après le Livre des

Actes', *RHPhR* 37 (1957), 71–80; Reicke 21–6; Trocmé 68 and 198–200; E. Schweizer, 'Zu Apg. **1**.16–22', *ThZ* 14 (1958), 46; K. H. Rengstorf, 'Die Zuwahl d. Matthias', *Stud. Theol.* XI. 1 (1962), 35–67; E. Haenchen, *ZNW* 54 (1963), 161f.; J. Roloff, *Apostolat* ... , 1965, 172–7.

On **1**.16: Donatus Haugg, *Judas Iskarioth in den ntl. Berichten*, Freiburg im Breisgau 1930; Kurt Lüthi, 'Das Problem des Judas Iskariot neu untersucht', *Ev.Th.* 16 (1956), 98–114.

On **1**.21: W. Mundle, 'Das Apostelbild der Apostelgeschichte', *ZNW* 27 (1928), 1–10; K. H. Rengstorf, art. ἀπόστολος in *ThWb* I, 1933, 406–46; K. Lake, 'The Twelve and the Apostles', *Beg.* V, 37–59; G. Sass, *Apostelamt und Kirche* (FGLPr. 2), Munich 1939; Marcus Barth, *Der Augenzeuge*, Zollikon-Zürich 1946; A. Fridrichsen, *The Apostle and his Message*, Uppsala 1947; H. von Campenhausen, 'Der urchristl. Apostelbegriff', *Stud. Theol.* I, Lund 1948, 96–130; H. Mosbech, 'Apostolos in the NT', *Stud. Theol.* II, Lund 1949/50, 165–200; J. Munck, 'Paul, the Apostles and the Twelve', *Stud. Theol.* III, Lund 1950, 96–110; H. von Campenhausen, *Kirchl. Amt und geistl. Vollmacht in den ersten drei Jahrhunderten*, Tübingen 1953 (esp. 15–31 and 82–8; ET *Ecclesiastical Authority and Spiritual Power in the Church of the First 3 Centuries*, 1969); E. Lohse, 'Ursprung und Prägung des chr. Apostolates', *ThZ* 9 (1953), 259–75; E. M. Kredel, 'Der Apostelbegriff in der neueren Exegese', *ZkTh* 78 (1956), 169–93 and 257–305; J. Schmitt, *Rech. Bib.* 4 (1959), 224ff.; J. Dupont, 'La destinée de Judas prophetisée par David', *CBQ* 1961, 41ff.; P. Benoit, *Exégèse et théologie* I, 340ff.; Günter Klein, *Die zwölf Apostel*, Göttingen 1961; Walter Schmithals, *Das kirchl. Apostelamt*, Göttingen 1961 (ET *The Office of Apostle in the Early Church*, 1969).

On **1**.23: Cadbury, *Amicitiae Corolla*, London 1933, 49f.

On **1**.26: S. E. Johnson, 'The Dead Sea Manual of Discipline and the Jerusalem Church of Acts', *ZAW* 66 (1954), 106–20; O. Cullmann, 'The Significance of the Qumran Texts for Research into the Beginning of Christianity', *JBL* 74 (1955), 213–26; M. Burrows, *The Dead Sea Scrolls*, 1955; J. T. Milik, *Dix ans de découvertes dans le désert de Juda* (Paris 1957; ET *Ten Years of Discovery in the Wilderness of Judaea*, London 1959); K. Schubert, *Die Gemeinde vom Toten Meer*, Basel-Munich 1958 (ET *The Dead Sea Community*, 1959).

A. D. Knox, 'The death of Judas (Acts **1**.18)', *JTS* 25 (1923–4), 289f; J. Herber, 'La mort de Judas', *Rev. d'hist. des Rel.* 129 (1945), 45f; J. Sickenberger, 'Judas als Stifter des Blutackers', *BZ* 18 (1928), 69–71; J. Crehan, 'Peter according to the D-Text of Acts', *Theol. Studies* 18 (1957), 596–603 (on **1**.23); H. Bruston, 'La notion d'apostolat dans l'église primitive', *Rev. de Théol. et d'Action évangélique* (1943), 177-92; A. Verheul, 'De moderne exegese over ἀπόστολος', *Sacris Erudiri* 1 (1948), 380-96; J. W. Harbin, 'The Significance of the Twelve Apostles in the Ministry of Jesus and Primitive Christianity' (diss.), Southern Baptist Theol. Seminary 1952; W. K. L. Clarke, 'The Election of St. Matthias', *Theology* 30 (1935), 230–2; A. Tricot, 'Sur Actes **1**.15 et 26', *RScR* 15 (1925), 164–7; U. Holzmeister, 'St. Matthias Apostolus (Act. **1**.23, 26)', *Verb. Domini* 29 (1944), 7–14; L. S. Thornton, 'The Choice of Matthias', *JTS* 46 (1945), 51–9.

VERSE 15: 'In these days'[1]—hence between the Ascension and Pentecost —Peter rose[2] in the midst of the brethren to make a speech: thus Luke introduces his account of the election of Matthias. Nearly every turn of phrase in this sentence can be traced back to the Septuagint, which means that it sounded to Luke's readers like the beginning of a biblical story. As the assembly is said to number one hundred and twenty[3] 'names',[4] this represents the complement with which the community embarked on its history.

VERSE 16: Luke has the Apostle address the men[5] with the compound Greek-OT expression ἄνδρες ἀδελφοί.[6] He first speaks of the fatal end[7] which inevitably[8] befell Judas because the Holy Spirit had foretold it in the passage[9]

---

[1] The LXX expression 'in these (those) days' occurs in Luke 1.39, 2.1, 4.6, 6.12, 9.36, 21.23 and 23.7; Acts 1.15, 2.18, 7.41, 9.37 and 11.27.

[2] ἀναστάς (18 times in Acts) also derives from LXX, introducing a movement (e.g. 'he rose up and went'); here, as in 13.16 and 15.17, it refers to an orator's getting to his feet. Again, ἐν μέσῳ is frequent in LXX, as is also the name of brother which, feeling themselves one great fraternity, the Christians gave each other (*ThWb* I, 145f.; *Beg.* V, 378f.)—in Acts 6.3; 9.17, 30; 10.23; 11.1, 12, 29; 12.17; 14.2; 15.1, 3, 13, 22f., 32f., 36, 40; 16.2, 40; 17.6, 10, 14; 18.18, 27; 21.7, 17, 20; 22.13 and 28.14f. (D replaces 'brethren' by 'disciples' in order to obviate confusion with the brothers of Jesus, 1.14.)

[3] Stauffer (p. 202) infers from Jewish tradition that the 'community' of 120 regarded itself as the *Ecclesia Magna* at the beginning of the history of the Church. E. Bickermann, however, discovered, 'not without astonishment, that the Great Synagogue is a pure and simple invention of the commentators. The talmudic authorities mention only "anshe keneset haggedolah".' (p. 393): what is meant by this is the generation which returned from captivity (401). The name comes from the prophetic terminology of Ezek. 34.13 and 36.24, Isa. 60.4 and Jer. 31.8; in Ezek. 39.27f. the second sentence has the verb *kanas* used to express the gathering-in of the scattered (402).

[4] The use of ὄνομα in the sense of 'person' is borrowed from LXX (cf. Bauer *Wb* s.v. III, col. 1136), as is also ἐπὶ τὸ αὐτό (see p. 192 n. 4 below).

[5] Though the women are probably thought of as present, they have no part in the proceedings.

[6] Recurring in 2.29, 37; 7.2; 13.15, 26, 38; 15.7, 13; 22.1; 23.1, 6; 28.17.

[7] The psalm cited does not refer to the betrayal: this was taken to be foretold in Ps. 41.9.

[8] ἔδει: in Luke δεῖ implies that God wills something and that it therefore must happen. Such instances of the divine will can be recognized from the fact that they are prophetically expressed by the Spirit in holy scripture. The fated necessity embodied in the δεῖ of Hellenism appears here (since God is personal will) transformed into the unconditional and inexorable supremacy of the Lord, in whose mercy the Christian may put his trust. As even the betrayal is encompassed in this almighty will, it loses, in Luke's eyes, all character of scandalous outrage, though Judas' guilt is not thereby removed. The element of human free will which is thus combined, in a manner which Luke has not explicitly thought out, with the divine will that imposes itself in the teeth of all resistance, also finds expression in the fact that δεῖ, as in verse 21, may denote the will of God which stands as a commandment to men and may be learned from the scriptures. Cf. Grundmann, *ThWb* II, 21–5, and Fascher, 'Theologische Beobachtungen zu δεῖ', *NT Studien für R. Bultmann* (1954), 228–54. (D failed to understand that two themes are involved here, the death of Judas, which already belongs to the past (ἔδει), and the election of a successor, which the congregation is to undertake in accordance with God's will (δεῖ, verse 21). Hence D replaces ἔδει with δεῖ and reduces both themes to the second.

[9] γραφή means the particular locus; 'scripture' =αἱ γραφαί. The two psalm verses 69.26 LXX (death of Judas) and 109.8 (election) are treated as one citation, though this point is obscured in Nestle by the way in which the καί is printed between them. It was really the Spirit that spoke in the psalm, David being merely his human mouthpiece.

from the Psalms later cited in verse 20. So that the reader shall know which Judas is meant, he is designated as the man 'who was guide to those who arrested Jesus'.

VERSE 17: With the conjunction ὅτι evidence is adduced that the Holy Spirit really spoke of Judas[1]: the scripture speaks of the ἐπισκοπή which is taken to denote the office of Apostle—and Judas had truly been an Apostle: κατηριθμημένος ἦν ἐν ἡμῖν resembles Luke **22**.3 to the very wording. Judas had 'received his portion' (or *lot*) 'in this (apostolic) ministry'[2]; to which corresponds, in verses 25f., that the lot should fall upon Matthias, who now receives the apostolic office and ministry.

VERSE 18: Now that[3] Judas has been presented to the reader[4], Peter comes to speak of his fate, which is here described in accordance with a different tradition from that employed in Matt. **27**.3–10[5]: with the 'reward of unrighteousness'[6] the traitor had bought a small farm,[7] but falling headlong (from the roof of the house)[8] he was split open and his bowels gushed out. On ἐκχέω in this sense, see Bauer, *Einf.* 22; λακάω—*Wb* 915. Cf. also II Sam. **10**.10 LXX.

VERSE 19: This verse shows very clearly that it is really Luke himself who is speaking (he did not have the device of a footnote at his command). For Peter, who spoke Aramaic like his listeners, would not have told them

---

[1] Preuschen disagrees: 'ὅτι states the reason . . . for the idea that the traitor must be replaced' (7). But this subject is not raised until verse 21. Beyer (11) finds in the ὅτι-clause Peter's grief at the fact that 'after all, he was one of us.' But Judas to the first Christians was an object of horror and loathing. Wendt (74), Loisy (175) and Bauernfeind (28) offer similar explanations to the one above.

[2] Every office in the congregation, from the service at table to the teaching mission of the Apostles, can be called διακονία, because it means serving God in the community (cf. Acts **6**.1–4). The play on the words 'lot' and 'office' belongs to the special rhetoric with which Luke embroiders the Apostle's speech.

[3] On μὲν οὖν see above on **1**.6.

[4] It is fairly evident that these words are not really meant for Peter's hearers (who must have known of Judas' end for some weeks) but for the readers of the book; the next verse makes this even clearer.

[5] There are various Christian accounts of the end of Judas: according to Matthew he hanged himself in despair, but according to Papias—quoted by Apollinaris of Laodicea and preserved in Cramer's *Catena* (see Lake, *Beg.* V, 22–30)—he swelled to such monstrous proportions that he could no longer pass where a horse and cart could easily drive through! As E. Schweizer has shown (*ThZ* 14 (1958), 46), this version is influenced by Num. **5**.21f., 27 (water of the curse: cf. Ps. **109**.18) and Ps. **69**.24, whereas Matthew is influenced by Zech. **11**.12 as well as Jer. **18**.2f., **19**.1f., and **32**.6–15 (see P. Benoît, 'La Mort de Judas' in *Synoptische Studien* offered to A. Wikenhauser, Munich 1953, 1–19). 'As against C. H. Dodd (*According to the Scriptures*, 1952, 61ff., 107f. and 126) this means that the OT passages were in the first place interpreted without regard to the context . . . , but that further passages from the context were attached at a secondary stage' (Schweizer, loc. cit.).

[6] LXX expression: cf. II Sam. **3**.34, I Kings **2**.32 etc., and Luke **16**.8f. and **18**.6.

[7] χωρίον ='small farm' (Bauer *Wb* 1760), not 'field' like ἀγρός, Matt. **27**.7f.

[8] Cf. Bill. II, 595: Ḥullin 56b—'A gentile saw how a man fell from the roof to the ground, so that his belly burst and his bowels came out.'

(who had moreover lived through all the events recounted)[1] that the inhabitants of Jerusalem called the field where Judas met his end Akeldama 'in their language'[2], nor would he have translated this Aramaic name.

VERSE 20: Now we have the Psalm-verses in which early Hellenistic Christian biblical scholars saw an adumbration of the fate of Judas. Hellenistic, because the interpretation presupposes the LXX text[3]—which Peter would not have used before his audience. Many exegetes[4] have referred verse 20a[5] ('Let his farmstead become empty, and let there be no man dwelling therein') to Judas' apostolic office, but this must be wrong, for the verse would then expressly forbid the election of a successor (Wendt, 74 n.2). Rather, according to the interpretation of the early Christians, verse 20a speaks of Judas' death and implies merely that he possessed a farmstead, rather than a field. Verse 20b, on the other hand, is understood as an injunction: 'His overseership let another take.'[6]

VERSES 21 and 22: The conclusion is now drawn from the command in verse 20b: 'Of the men who were together with us[7] all the time that the Lord went in and out among us[8]—from the baptism of John to the day he was taken up from us—one must become a witness with us of his resurrection.' This makes plain the condition which, by the standards of Acts, a man must fulfil to qualify as an Apostle: he must have been a witness of Jesus' life from the baptism of John to the Ascension. If this condition is to be capable of fulfilment, not only the Eleven but other disciples also must have been with Jesus during the forty days and at the Ascension.

---

[1] This was less than two months after Good Friday, and Judas' death had taken place even more recently! (On γνωστόν see note on 4.16.)

[2] א could be transliterated into Greek as χ: cf. Σίραχ for סִירָא (Bill. I, 1029). So we get the Aramaic חֲקֵל דְּמָא.

[3] The Hebrew text, which Rabbinic exegesis did not alter, did not give this sense.

[4] Zeller 474f., Feine 165, Spitta 14f. and J. Weiss, *StKr* (1893) 487.

[5] Verse 20a (Ps. **69**.25 [26 LXX]) in the original text curses the enemies of the suffering righteous one. αὐτῶν has been changed to αὐτοῦ, while ἐν τοῖς σκηνώμασιν αὐτῶν has been omitted and replaced by ἐν αὐτῇ, referring back to ἔπαυλις. Verse 20b (Ps. **109**.8) is also a suppliant's curse in the original (according to Athanasius Miller, 'Fluchpsalmen und israelitisches Recht', *Angelicum* 20 (Rome 1943), 92–101, the curse-psalm corresponds 'perfectly to the normal sentiments of the average devout Jew'!). This human wish is turned into a divine command by the substitution of the imperative λαβέτω for λάβοι. Such interpretations presuppose that the OT is a book of divine mysteries in which the spirit unveils particular passages in the meaning relating to the Christians (*pace* Dodd, *According to the Scriptures*, 126).

[6] ἐπισκοπή here means the apostolic office.

[7] συνελθόντων cf. οἱ συνελθόντες in **1**.6 above.

[8] Without verse 22a (ἀρξάμενος . . . ἡμῶν), this would refer only to the forty days during which the risen Jesus 'went in and out' (LXX locution) among the disciples. But since Luke seeks also to enlist the Apostles as witnesses for the activity of the earthly Jesus, he has intercalated ἀρξάμενος . . . ἡμῶν, without noticing that Jesus' goings-out and comings-in among the Apostles are now no longer quite appropriate.

VERSE 23: Peter's suggestion is acted upon: 'they'—whether the Apostles or the brethren in general (cf. 6.4)[1]—put forward two men[2] who satisfy the precondition: Joseph called Barsabbas,[3] surnamed Justus,[4] and Matthias.[5]

VERSES 24 and 25: The prayer is uttered[6] with marvellous unanimity by the whole congregation[7]: May God, who knows all hearts—a favourite expression of post-apostolic Christendom[8]—show which of these two he has chosen to take the place[9] in the 'ministry and apostleship'[10] which Judas has abandoned in order to go to his own place (in hell)[11].

VERSE 26: It is not clear who gives the lots to whom—perhaps the two candidates to the Apostles. But one should not—on the basis of the Latin rendering, *dederunt sortes suas*—imagine that the disciples proceeded to a vote (this is considered possible in *Beg.* IV, 15); in this election the human factor is excluded: it is God who is choosing. The rare word συγκαταψηφίζω (like συμψηφίζω in Acts 19.19) must signify 'number together,' 'count in.'[12]

---

[1] By using ἔστησεν D d gig Aug make Peter the performer of the action: a glimpse of the monarchic episcopate of later times.

[2] According to Beyer (p. 12) only two satisfied the requirements; but τῶν συνελθόντων κτλ shows that a larger number came into consideration.

[3] *Clem. Rec.* I. 60, in the Syriac text, states that the choice fell on Barabbas (a scribal error for Barsabbas)!

[4] On Greek and Latin names among the Jews, see Bill. II, 712.

[5] Matthias is a contraction of Mattathias. Clem. Alex., *Strom.* IV 6.33, identifies him with Zacchaeus. According to Church tradition the remains of Matthias, sent by Constantine to Trèves and lost under débris at the time of the Norman onslaught, were miraculously rediscovered and buried afresh. Matthias is the only Apostle whose remains (without the skull, preserved in Italy) lie in Germany. The monograph by Joachim Jeremias, *Heiligengräber in Jesu Umwelt* (*Matt.* 23.29, *Luke* 11.47): *eine Untersuchung zur Volksreligion der Zeit Jesu*, Göttingen 1958, throws light on the following places in Acts: 1.23 (88), 2.29 (royal graves, 57, 114 and 129), 6.9 (synagogue of Greek-speaking Jews, 60) and 7.15f. (patriarchal graves, 32, 37, 95ff. and 114. Here, says Jeremias, we have a late tradition preserved only among the Samaritans.).

[6] προσευξάμενοι εἶπαν (cf. LXX locution ἀποκριθεὶς εἶπεν, occurring 38 times in Luke and 7 in Acts): here the aorist participle does not express chronological precedence but its action is simultaneous with that of the main verb (Bl.-Debr. § 339, 1).

[7] In *Contra Felicem* 1. 4f. and *Contra epist. Fund.* 9 Augustine reads *et praedicatus dixit*, which makes Peter the speaker (cf. n. 1 above).

[8] Hermas *Mand.* IV 3.4; *Acta Pauli et Theclae* 24; *Apost. Const.* II 24.6; III 7.8; IV 6.8; VI 12.4; VIII 5.6; Clem. Alex. *Strom.* V 14.96 (*Beg.* IV, 15).

[9] The relative clause introduced by ὅν depends on ἕνα τούτων, which depends in turn on ἀνάδειξον, while λαβεῖν is governed by ἐξελέξω. δύο and ἕνα are juxtaposed for contrast. On τόπος see Introd., p. 3 above. Stauffer (p. 203) detects the influence of the Qumran τόπος-theme in I Cor. 10.14ff. and elsewhere—but the Corinthian 'pneumatics' were not a strictly organized group that sat facing the 'unspiritual' (=ἰδιῶται) in reserved seats! Qumran influence is no more real here than in Clement, Ignatius or Polycarp.

[10] The two expressions, resuming verse 17, mean the apostolic office.

[11] From Lightfoot's 'Horae hebr. in Acta Apost. 15' Jacquier quotes (41) the following rabbinical gloss on Num. 24.25: *Balaam ivit in locum suum, id est in Gehennam*. Cf. Bill. IV, 2, 1097f.

[12] Here μετά stands for σύν. D, however, understanding it in the sense of 'among' (*Bl.-Debr.* § 227), substitutes δώδεκα for ἕνδεκα.

Beyer (pp. 11f.) still found in this narrative a sound tradition concerning Matthias' election and the speech Peter made on that occasion. He was, it is true, obliged to admit (p. 12): 'It is quite impossible . . . that, addressing Aramaic-speaking Jews in Jerusalem, Peter should term that very language 'the tongue of the inhabitants' and explain the word *Akeldama* in Greek'. He was thus constrained to eliminate verse 19 as an 'interpolation'. But he was not able to retain verse 18 either, for 'it would have been utterly meaningless to tell this story to Peter's audience, for whom this' (the end that befell Judas) 'could not have been anything new' (p. 11). Criticism cannot, however, stop even at this point, for neither could Peter have produced before these Jews any scriptural proof from the Septuagint which the Hebrew text did not admit. This means striking out verse 20 also; but it carries with it verse 16, which also refers to this γραφή. Finally, verses 21f. exhibit an Apostle-concept of later date: all twelve Apostles, together with a few other disciples (at least Matthias and Barsabbas), had remained constantly in Jesus' company from his baptism onwards; yet the accounts of their call in Mark 1.16–20 clearly reflect an older and divergent tradition. All of which must put paid to any attempt to see verses 16–22 as reproducing a speech made by Peter at this juncture.

Not that Luke freely invented everything! He was certainly not the first to tell of the punishment God meted out to Judas: here he is echoing Palestinian traditions. The interpretation of the Psalms passages he also took over, no doubt from Hellenistic Christianity; and finally the information that Matthias and not Barsabbas was chosen by lot to be an Apostle must also derive from some tradition.

Luke however—and this shows his talent as an author—did not use these traditions for a dry historical record, but created from them a living scene. At the centre is Peter, whose figure dominates the first half of Acts. He speaks to the congregation about Judas' death (of which the reader of Luke's works learns only now, through the mouth of the Apostle) and the choice, willed by God, of a successor to his office. Luke uses this opportunity to bring into prominence, indirectly, the significance of the twelve Apostles. In the first place they are the witnesses of Jesus' Resurrection. This for Luke is specially important: his theology has its centre of gravity in the Resurrection. At the same time he considers belief in the Resurrection as the binding link between Christianity and Judaism. In the light of this the opening verses of Acts may be more readily understood: by presenting the life of the risen Lord among his disciples, Luke the historian certifies to his readers the factor which is decisive for faith—the Resurrection.

In the second place (as in verses 21f., but more explicitly still in 10.39) the Apostles are the witnesses of the earthly life of Jesus, from the baptism of John to the end, and thereby they are guarantors of the gospel tradition, the ἀπ' ἀρχῆς αὐτόπται of Luke 1.2, and as ὑπηρέται τοῦ λόγου they have handed down that knowledge of events which the 'many' evangelists of Luke **1**.1 have recorded. Luke knows of no gospel written by an actual Apostle.

In Luke **22**.30 he had mentioned the eschatological role of the Apostles; here he says nothing of it, and it recedes behind their historical task. The Church, whose view of the apostolate Luke here reproduces, has a long way before it on earth, and needs for its present purposes authentic guarantors of its message.

It is striking that Jesus himself should not have appointed the new Apostle during the forty days. Instead, it is God who now carries out the 'election,' inasmuch as it is he who picks Matthias through the casting of lots. Thus the sacred number of twelve Apostles is reconstituted, and the group is ready for the miracle of Pentecost.

These few verses already show Luke's literary skill: from the comparatively meagre material he possesses he fashions scenes of great vividness and vitality, skilfully articulating and relating them together. On the other hand Luke had no thought, when writing this story, of what one nowadays seeks in part to learn from it: information as to the constitution of the primitive Church.

Thus Bo Reicke (p. 25) asks whether it was governed in a monarchic-episcopal, oligarchic-presbyterian or democratic-congregational manner. But to do so is to force modern notions on the text, and, more especially, to forget that we are handling a Lucan composition intended to deal with quite other matters, not a historical reference-book on constitutional questions.

Other scholars are reminded of Qumran by the constitution they find outlined in Acts. The twelve Apostles remind them of the Qumran community Council, which according to the Rule of the sect (1 QS 8, 1) consisted of twelve laymen and three priests. But Luke's account does not reproduce a historical reality in the same sense as the sect's Rule. The kerygma of the primitive Church (I Cor. **15**.5) did certainly name the Twelve as witnesses of the Resurrection. But this by no means implied that all twelve were now governors of the congregation. In Gal. **2**.9 Paul describes James the brother of Jesus, Cephas and John as the three men looked up to as 'pillars' in Jerusalem. From this may be deduced that these three guided the fortunes of the congregation there in the second half of the 'forties.' When Luke presents the 'twelve Apostles' as the leaders of the congregation in the earliest times, he is reproducing the picture of the primitive Church which he himself—and most probably the rest of the Christian community—had before his eyes about the year 80. Admittedly, the evolution of the Apostle-concept is a hotly contested subject, as witness the literature listed above. This much may however be stated with certainty: what Luke offers is the late form of the tradition about 'the Apostles'.

Trocmé, following a suggestion by J. Schmitt, thinks to discover a further connection between the early Church and Qumran (Trocmé, pp. 198–200).

In Acts **5**.6 νεώτεροι are mentioned. Both Schmitt and Trocmé see these as novices *à la* Qumran, which leads to the supposition that the 120 of Acts **1**.15 were 'perfects'. But this is ignoring that the νεώτεροι (varied as νεανίσκοι in **5**.10) correspond to those in I Tim. **5**.1, Titus **2**.6 and especially I Peter **5**.5. Luke's account of the conversions of the chamberlain (Ch. 8), Cornelius (Ch. 10) and the janitor (Ch. 16) shows very clearly that he does not imagine the primitive Church to have imposed any novitiate (or catechumenate): it would at all events have been unnecessary in view of the simplicity of the original kerygma. With the 'monastic order' of Qumran the situation was wholly different: there painfully scrupulous observance of the Law, frequently interpreted entirely afresh, was combined with an ascetic discipline to which the candidate could prove himself equal only through a long period of probation. One should therefore refrain from matching isolated details of primitive Christian life with similar features of Qumran, but rather take into account the whole circumstantial context. Only so can one learn what the primitive Church on the one hand had in common with contemporaneous phenomena, and what particularly marked it out on the other.

5
ACTS 2:1–13
THE MIRACLE OF PENTECOST

[1] And when the day of Pentecost was fulfilled, they were all together in one place. [2] And suddenly there came from heaven a sound as of a rushing mighty wind, and it filled all the house where they were sitting. [3] And there appeared to them tongues forking out, as of fire; and it sat upon each one of them. [4] And they were all filled with the Holy Spirit, and began to speak with other tongues, as the Spirit gave them utterance. [5] Now there were dwelling at Jerusalem Jews, devout men, from every nation under heaven. [6] And when this sound came, the crowd gathered and were bewildered, because every man heard them speaking in his own language. [7] And they were all amazed and marvelled, saying, 'Behold, are not all these who speak Galileans? [8] And how do we hear, every man in our own language wherein we were born? [9] Parthians and Medes and Elamites, and the inhabitants of Mesopotamia, Judaea and Cappadocia, Pontus and Asia, [10] Phrygia and Pamphylia, Egypt and the region of Libyan Cyrenaica, and sojourners from Rome, [11] both Jews and proselytes, Cretans and Arabians, we hear them speaking in our tongues the mighty works of God!' [12] And they were all amazed and were perplexed, saying one to another, 'What can this mean?' [13] But others mocking said, 'They are filled with new wine!'

Bibliography:

W. Hadorn, 'Der Zweck der Apostelgeschichte', *Festschrift Orelli*, Basel 1898, 281–320, esp. 310ff. (on 2.9–11); K. L. Schmidt, *Die Pfingsterzählung und das Pfingstereignis*, Leipzig 1919; F. Cumont, 'La plus ancienne géographie astrologique', *Klio* 9 (1909), 263–73 (on 2.9–01); H. J. Cadbury, 'The Odor of the Spirit at Pentecost', *JBL* 47 (1928), 237–56 (on 2.1–3); K. Lake, 'The Gift of the Spirit on the Day of Pentecost' in *Beg.* V, 111–21; M. S. Enslin, 'A Notable Contribution to Acts', *JBL* 52 (1933), 230–8, esp. 235 (on 2.5); L. Cerfaux, 'Le symbolisme attaché au miracle des langues', *Eph. Theol. Lov.* 13 (1936), 256–9 = *Recueil Cerfaux* II, 183–7 (on 2.4ff.); N. Adler, *Das erste christliche Pfingstfest: Sinn und Bedeutung des Pfingstberichtes Apg.* 2.1–13, NTA 18–1, 1938; A. Causse, 'Le pèlerinage à Jérusalem et la première Pentecôte', *RHPhR* 20 (1940), 120–41; L. Cerfaux, *Témoins du Christ*, 1943, see Commentary, §1 bibl.; S. Weinstock in *JRS* 38 (1948), 43–6 (on **2**.9–11); H. Fuchs in *ThZ* 5 (1949), 233f. (on **2**.9–11); H. Sahlin, 'Pingstberättelsens teologisk innebörd', *SvTKv* 25, Lund 1949, 185–200; J. G. Davies, 'Pentecost and Glossolalia', *JTS* N.S. 3 (1952), 228–31; E. Lohse, 'Die Bedeutung des Pfingstberichtes in Rahmen des lukanischen Geschichtswerkes', *Ev.Th.* 1953, 422–36; G. Kretschmar, 'Himmelfahrt und Pfingsten', *ZKG* 66 (1954/5), 209–53; E. Kutsch, 'Das Herbstfest in Israel', dissertation, Mainz 1955, esp. 146–58; Reicke 27–37; Trocmé 201ff.; Conzelmann, *Handbuch* 7, 26f.

W. S. Thomson, 'Tongues at Pentecost', *Exp. Tim.* 38 (1926–7), 284–6; H. E. Edwards, 'The Tongues at Pentecost. A Suggestion', *Theology* 16 (1928), 248–52; R. O. P. Taylor, 'The Tongues of Pentecost', *Exp.Tim.* 40 (1928–9), 300–3; S. Lyonnet, 'De glossolalia eiusque significatione', *Verb. Domini* 24 (1944), 65–75; I. J. Martin, 'Glossolalia in the Apostolic Church', *JBL* 63 (1944), 123–30; U. Holzmeister, 'Colloquium testium Pentecostes (Act. **2**.7–11)', *Verb. Domini* 21 (1941), 123–8; N. H. Snaith, 'Pentecost the Day of Power', *Exp.Tim.* 43 (1931–2), 379f.; W. Moock, 'Die Bedeutung d. ersten Pfingstfestes', *Theol. u. Glaube* 28 (1936), 429–37; R. E. Ker, 'Acts **2**.1–13', *Exp.Tim.* 54 (1942–3), 250; R. F. Stoll, 'The First Christian Pentecost', *Eccles. Rev.* 108 (1943), 337–47; E. Lohse, Πεντεκοστή, *ThWb* Vol. VI (1954), 44–53; J. A. M. Weterman, 'Het Pinksterverhaal naar Hand. **2**', *Nederl. Kathol. Stemmen* 52 (1956), 97–108.

VERSE 1: ἐν[1] τῷ κτλ.—at the dawning[2] of the day of Pentecost,[3] the Christians, i.e. the one hundred and twenty persons[4] of **1**.15, were all gathered together.[5] There is a biblical ring about this beginning: cf. Jer. **25**.12 LXX (ἐν τῷ συμπληρωθῆναι τὰ ἑβδομήκοντα ἔτη) and Luke **9**.51.

VERSE 2 describes an at first enigmatic[6] phenomenon: a sound[7] as of a rushing wind (for Greek-speakers πνοή and πνεῦμα were thoroughly related

---

[1] ἐν with substantival infinitive (Bl.-Debr. § 404, 2): five times in Acts, over thirty in Luke.

[2] συμπληροῦσθαι =completion of an interval. An ending of a period is as such a fixed term. Hence the linguistic development leads via hybrid forms like Gen. **25**.24 LXX (imitated in Luke **1**.57 and **2**.6, 21f.) to cases where πληροῦσθαι signifies the actual coming of the appointed day, as in Lev. **8**.33 LXX (cf. *ThWb* VI, 307, 18–25), Luke **9**.51 and here. The revision alleged by Spitta (pp. 52f.) and Bauernfeind (p. 37) is not in evidence, nor does this LXX locution allude to the Father's promise, as Lohse believes (op. cit., 422f. and 430).

[3] πεντηκοστή (ἡμέρα understood) is the Jewish חַג שָׁבֻעוֹת, which according to Lev. **23**.15f. (cf. Num. **28**.16, Deut. **16**.9–12 and Josephus *Ant.* III 252) was to be celebrated seven weeks, hence on the fiftieth day, after 'the morrow after the sabbath' of the Passover. Lit. in Lohse, art. πεντηκοστή in *ThWb* VI, 44–53; rabbinical references in Bill. II, 597–602; liturgical and iconographic aspects in Kretschmar, op. cit. See also general discussion.

[4] It is not only the Apostles who receive the Spirit: while they stand forward (verse 14), the ecstatic event further extends to the others—cf. verse 33.

[5] On ἦσαν . . . ὁμοῦ (−D) ἐπὶ τὸ αὐτό see note on **1**.15.

[6] The reader does not learn until verse 4 that the Spirit is the cause of the phenomenon.

[7] Philo *Decal.* 33: God caused an ἦχος to arise on Sinai, and it changed into a πῦρ which all could perceive as a διάλεκτος.

ideas) comes out of heaven. The celestial irruption directs itself towards the disciples, and the house[1] in which they are sitting is pervaded by this ἦχος.

VERSE 3: The still unnamed heavenly visitation now mysteriously passes from the audible to the visible, to fiery tongues[2] which fork in such a way as to light on each Christian—and provide visual evidence that the Spirit is given them as individuals.

VERSE 4: Only now, when the effects of the gift are described, is the name 'Holy Spirit' mentioned. The Spirit causes the Christians it pervades to discourse[3] in 'other[4] tongues'. The equation of 'tongue' and διάλεκτος in verse 8 shows that speech in different languages is meant:[5] which languages, we shall shortly learn.

VERSE 5: The scene now changes from inside to outside the house, from the speakers to the hearers. In[6] Jerusalem were dwelling[7] Jews,[8] devout men,[9] from every nation under heaven;[10] these are now seized with wonder at the miracle.

VERSE 6: Is this φωνή the ἦχος of verse 2 (in which case the crowd would first have been attracted by the rushing onset of the Spirit) or the speech of the Christians (when the crowd would have been drawn by their loud, ecstatic

---

[1] Attempting to visualise and reconstruct the crowd-scene which follows, Zahn (77) and Holtzmann (31) have taken the 'house' to be the Temple. But this Luke always (22 times) calls τὸ ἱερόν. If Josephus on one occasion (*Ant*. VIII. 65ff.) gives the name of οἶκος to the Temple which he elsewhere styles ναός, the context still shows unmistakably what he means, as is also true of Isa. 6.4. Here that is not the case. Above all, we ought not to treat the story as a documentary film.

[2] Enoch 14.8–15 mentions a wall encircled with 'fiery tongues' and a house built of 'fiery tongues' in heaven; 71.5 refers to a building of crystal stones interspersed with 'tongues of living fire'. These denote the element of divinity but have nothing to do with languages.

[3] ἀποφθέγγομαι: to speak in a solemn or inspired way, but not ecstatic speech (see *ThWb* I, 448).

[4] On ἕτερος see *ThWb* II, 700; Lake draws attention to Isa. 28.11f. (cited in I Cor. 14.21).

[5] Wendt surmised that the Christians spoke in an ecstatic spirit-language which each hearer understood as if it were his mother tongue, even if he noticed it was not (!). This thesis, taken over by Wikenhauser (*Apg*. 34), comes to grief on the present verse; moreover the hearers, who have not yet attained to faith, are not endowed with ἑρμηνεία.

[6] As frequently (e.g. in 9.21), εἰς is Hellenistic for ἐν (Bl.-Debr. §205).

[7] ἦσαν . . . κατοικοῦντες: on the periphrastic conjugation see p. 149 n. 7 above. D draws both together into the normal word-order. C produces by transposition the formula ἄνδρες Ἰουδαῖοι. None of which means that either κατοικοῦντες or Ἰουδαῖοι is a late addition. The Jews in question have become residents of Jerusalem; Luke is *not* thinking of pilgrims at the feast (against Bill. II, 604, and others).

[8] ℵ omits Ἰουδαῖοι. Lake (*Beg*. V, 111–21) misconstrued 'Jews and proselytes' as a separate group and inferred that the other groups were not Jews, hence that Ἰουδαῖοι should here be struck out.

[9] εὐλαβεῖς is missing in Augustine *Contra Felicem* 1. 4f. and *Contra epist. fund*. 9, but is not therefore suspect. Neither here nor elsewhere does the word have the sense of φοβούμενοι or σεβόμενοι (*Beg*. IV, 18): it means 'pious'.

[10] LXX locution: cf. e.g. Deut. 2.25.

utterance) or the voice of the Spirit itself? This question is submerged in the mysterious chiaroscuro of the scene. At all events, the assembled pious Jews of the diaspora are thunderstruck,[1] since each hears Christians speaking in his own native tongue. Luke expresses this in few words, as verse 4 has made it clear that the Christians are speaking several different languages;[2] it is of little consequence how many Christians speak Parthian etc. The ἤκουον of A D K (a construction according to the sense; ἤκουσεν in B ℵ E =came to hear) describes a hearing of some duration.

VERSE 7: Thus the people stand amazed and bewildered. Luke makes them tell his reader why: as Galileans the disciples could not have learned these foreign tongues in any natural way.[3] This shows that the listeners do not think they are hearing a 'spirit' language, for such a language a Galilean could speak as well as any other person.

VERSE 8: This point is clarified in a further question. Since the words of the foreign Jews are given in direct speech, they can only thus describe the miracle: 'Each one of us is hearing the language proper to the country in which he was born.'

VERSES 9—11: Instead of interrupting the scene with an historical report, Luke makes the diaspora Jews themselves enumerate the long series of countries and peoples which represent 'every nation under heaven'. The countries named possessed a considerable Jewish minority[4]. Broadly speaking, the list[5] moves from east to west, naming in its middle section first

---

[1] συνεχύθη (reinforced by ἐξίσταντο in verses 7 and 12 and by διηποροῦντο in verse 12) expresses the surprise caused by the miracle.

[2] As in 1.19, διάλεκτος means the vernacular of a country. W. L. Knox (p. 83) observes: 'In reality it is most unlikely that any Jew of the Dispersion would have understood such native dialects as survived in the remoter regions of the Middle East, since the Jews of the Dispersion were almost entirely city-dwellers.' The Jews in the regions enumerated did *in fact* speak either Aramaic or Greek. But Luke has quite another picture in mind, and this ought not to be explained away.

[3] How does the crowd know that? According to Beyer (14) the information 'quickly spreads from mouth to mouth,' while Loisy (190) ironically observes: 'These people know everything.' In reality Luke puts something into the mouth of the speakers in order not to interrupt the scene with an explanation of his own. Reicke is wrong when he says (36) 'that the emphasis lies on the overcoming of the linguistic barriers between the Galilean Apostles and the other people present'; the stressing of the Christians' Galilean origins is only meant to guarantee that they have not learned the different languages as their mother tongues. (On the Christianization of Galilee, see comments on 9.31 below.)

[4] References in Bill. II, 606–14.

[5] Cumont (*Klio* 1909, 263–73) investigated the list of the twelve signs of the zodiac and the countries subordinated to them, given in 378 A.D. by Paul of Alexandria in his introduction to astrology entitled Εἰσαγωγὴ εἰς τὴν Ἀποτελεσματικήν (sc. τέχνην), ed. Schato, Wittenberg 1585: 1. Aries =Persia. 2. Taurus =Babylon. 3. Gemini =Cappadocia. 4. Cancer =Armenia. 5. Leo =Asia. 6. Virgo =Hellas and Ionia. 7. Libra =Libya and Cyrene. 8. Scorpio =Italy. 9. Sagittarius =Cilicia and Crete. 10. Capricorn =Syria. 11. Aquarius =Egypt. 12. Pisces =Red Sea and Indian lands. Cumont deduces Paul's source, the work of an Egyptian in the Persian epoch, from two passages previously incorporated by Vettius Valens (2nd cent. A.D.) in his work on the zodiac (ed. Kroll, I, 2, 12, lines 15–21 and 13, lines 15–22); the astronomical system itself was Babylonian in origin (see now Eckhard

G

the northern and then the southern lands. In those days the Parthians were known particularly through their raids on the eastern boundaries of the Roman Empire. Luke may have taken the Medes and Elamites from the Bible (cf. Ἐλαμῖται in Isaiah 21.2 LXX), for the name 'Medes' had long been past history, as had also the country of 'Elam'[1], north of the Persian Gulf. Nevertheless, these names convey to the reader the impression that the Christian mission is already reaching out 'to the ends of the earth'! Judaea has long been acknowledged a late insertion[2], as is *a priori* obvious from the fact that its vernacular is not foreign to Jerusalem. Instead of Pontus, perhaps Armenia stood in Luke's model for this list, but Pontus was the homeland of Aquila and Priscilla (18.2), as was Egypt that of Apollos (18.24), likewise Cyrene was that of Lucius (13.1) and the unnamed ἄνδρες Κυρηναῖοι of 11.20. 'Romans', i.e. Rome-born Jews now living as foreigners in Jerusalem

---

Unger, 'Fata Morgana als geisteswissenschaftliches Phänomen im alten Orient' in *Rivista degli Studii Orientali*, Rome, 33 (1958), § 3, 'Das babylonische Weltsystem zur Hammura-bizeit'). F. C. Burkitt had already drawn Cumont's attention to the fact that the symbols employed in Dan. 8.20f. (Persian king =ram, Seleucid ruler =goat) agree with the above list. A later marginal note of Burkitt's on this article served as a basis for S. Weinstock (op. cit.), who attempted to demonstrate the relation of this astrological list to Acts 2.9–11. Harald Fuchs (op. cit.) soon chimed in approvingly. This stimulated Reicke (pp. 34–6) to advance the hypothesis that around the year 50 the community at Antioch had, for the training of future missionaries, drawn up a table of its main missionary areas, using the astrological list; this compilation was later used by Luke. In this form this hypothesis is untenable. It should not be assumed either that missionary-training at Antioch was run on the lines of a modern mission society or that the Antiochian community at that time planned missions in all these areas. Nor may one seriously maintain that the Medes and Elamites (mere historical names by then) were more feasible missionary objectives than the Greeks. Yet Reicke has the merit of having drawn attention to the problem posed by the peculiar 'horizon' of the list. W. L. Knox (p. 84 n. 1) had thought that Luke was using an enumeration of the territories subject to Rome (as did Philo *Legat. ad Gaium*, §§ 281ff.). This alone would not however explain the particular choice and arrangement of the list. In its original form it must have contained twelve names: 1. Parthians. 2. Medes. 3. Elamites. 4. Mesopotamia. 5. Cappadocia. 6. Pontus. 7. Asia. 8. Phrygia. 9. Pamphylia. 10. Egypt. 11. Libya Cyrenaica. 12. Rome. It is no accident that the list ends, like Acts itself, with Rome, for Luke did not just write the list down 'anyhow', but adapted it to his purposes. In place of the Persians he introduces the Parthians, whose name was at that time on everyone's lips. It is likely, on the other hand, that he took the Medes and Elamites, those erstwhile Great Powers, from LXX, in order to name the remotest possible peoples 'from the ends of the earth'. But all the twelve peoples must speak *foreign* languages: thus the Greeks and the Jews themselves (hence Hellas, Palestine and Syria) were ruled out as usable names. Further supposed alterations are discussed in the text. We do not know where Luke found this list; presumably his source contained names only of countries, not of signs of the zodiac. It is therefore advisable, when seeking to understand Luke's list, not to think exclusively in terms of a tradition but to make due allowance for a theological writer's sense of effective 'composition'.

[1] See Bauer *Wb* 492. In ancient Babylonian cosmography (see Unger, op. cit.) Elam formed with Akkad and Amurru the three countries of the world.

[2] Harnack (*Beitr*. III, 65ff.; ET), Preuschen (12), Wellhausen (4), Wendt (83) and Loisy (190) are among those who have recognized that 'Judaea' is a late addition. It has no place between Mesopotamia and Cappadocia, and Reicke's contention (36) that seen from Antioch its location is logical may be refuted by a glance at the map. Moreover,

(ἐπιδημοῦντες, Bauer, *Wb*, 577f.) and considered to have Latin as their mother-tongue, form the last group—just as Rome itself brings Acts to a close in Chapter 28. The phrase 'Jews and proselytes' does not refer to any specific national group with its own language (proselytes—see Philo!—were not obliged to learn Hebrew or Aramaic), but covers *all* the preceding groups with respect to religious affiliation: these are no pagans, for the gentile mission did not (according to Luke) begin until Peter baptized Cornelius (Chapter 10). Such a general description has meaning only at the end of the list, which shows that the 'Cretans and Arabians' are a later addition[1]. When these two and Judaea have been set aside, there remain exactly twelve different peoples. In verse 11, ἀκούομεν resumes, after the long list, the verb of verse 8. The 'mighty works of God'[2] are left in the abstract because the specific objects of praise—the sending and exaltation of Jesus—are reserved as matter for Peter's forthcoming speech.

VERSE 12 parallels verse 7 in the tone of perplexity it lends to the hearers' amazement. The pious Jews' question as to the meaning of the incident permits a formal transition to Peter's speech (Bauernfeind, 42), though this does not in fact dwell overmuch on the meaning of the miracle itself. On the question why the miracle arouses only astonishment, not belief, see the general discussion of this section below.

VERSE 13: The 'others' (ἕτεροι = ἄλλοι) seems remarkable after the 'all' of verse 12. One may think of Jerusalem Jews who did not know the foreign languages. As in 5.34ff., 14.4, 17.18ff., 23.6ff. and 28.24, Luke introduces two opposing groups, one defending or tolerating, the other hostile to the

---

according to the present text, Judaea and Cappadocia are linked by the direct succession of τε καί, which Luke only employs when he wishes to make an especially close connection between two units, as in Acts 1.1; 2.10f.; 4.27; 5.14; 8.12; 9.2, 15, 24, 29; 14.1, 5; 15.9, 32; 19.10, 17; 20.21; 21.12; 22.4; 24.3, 15; 26.3, 20, 22. If Judaea is omitted however, the two neighbouring lands of Mesopotamia and Cappadocia become closely connected; what is more, Cappadocia then falls into third place (corresponding to Gemini in the zodiac-list), exactly as in Paul of Alexandria. Pontus would then replace Armenia, and Asia have fifth place, again as in Paul's list.

[1] Presumably a scribe, who wrongly took 'Jews and proselytes' as a national group like the others, wanted in this way to find a place for Paul's missions in Arabia (Gal. 1.17) and Crete (Tit. 1.5) (see Knox p. 82 n. 2). Otto Eissfeldt's explanation (*TLZ* 1947, 207–12), which finds here named the seafarers of the West and desert-dwellers of the East, is a mere stopgap, while Reicke, in distributing this group over Paul of Alexandria's list, has wholly overlooked its intrinsic unsuitability. If, however, the Jews were once understood as a national group in their own right, it was natural to introduce Judaea among the other countries. Strictly speaking it was illogical, for thus Jews are mentioned twice, in verses 5 and 11. The addition must have been made early, since every MS has it. But the use in the Peshitta of the name of the people for that of the country shows that the problem had been seen and some attempt made to remove it.

[2] The expression λαλεῖν κτλ (=μεγαλύνειν τὸν θεὸν 10.46) was in common use among Jews and Christians; LXX rendered נִדְלֹת by μεγαλεῖα (a late Hellenistic formation from μέγας).

Christians. γλεύχους χτλ.[1]: to the 'others' the speakers with tongues give the impression of drunkards.

How have scholars set about these various difficulties? The first method of attack was the differentiation of sources, for which Spitta (see § 2 of Introduction, p. 29 above) may serve as an example: whatever is consistent with the 'speaking with tongues' of I Cor. 14 derives from the 'historical source *A*' (verses 1a, 4 and 11–36). The rest comes from the 'legendary source *B*' (the Jewish theme of the voice of God which speaks to all peoples). Verses 3b and 7f. were inserted by the redactor, who thus inserted the *human* linguistic miracle.

Then for a while it became the fashion to psychologize. Thus Beyer was of the opinion (p. 17) that remembrance of the first missionary sermon must over the years have grown ever more rich and radiant. This is a very doubtful supposition, considering that the memory of so basic an incident as the first Christophany to Peter, far from increasing in radiance, grew dim to the point of being mentioned only once—and in passing, at that (Luke **24**.24).

W. L. Knox started out from the religious parallels in Judaism: there Pentecost has become the day of the giving of the law, among the Christians it is the day of the giving of the Spirit. A Jew of the diaspora, living in Jerusalem, represented Pentecost as a proclamation of the new Torah to the proselytes of the whole world, and Luke recast his work. Unfortunately, not the slightest trace of any 'new Torah' tradition is to be found in Luke's text, and the dating at Pentecost is itself by no means an old tradition.

This was recognized by Bauernfeind: the dating at Pentecost is bound up with the late tradition of the forty days, and offers no basis for any hypothesis regarding more ancient tradition. Therefore Bauernfeind ascribes to Luke's source only the nature-miracle of the Spirit's descent (though is this not just where an author's hand is discernible?) and the miracle of the languages (p. 55). This latter, he claims, evolved from the experience of ecstatic speech and its interpretation: 'it is no long step from miraculous understanding on the part of a single διερμηνευτής to miraculous understanding on the part of a whole company, or at least many of them' (p. 56).

Some, however, will find the step quite a long one, the more so since it merely leads to Wendt's solution (see p. 168 n. 5 above). For that reason Lohse postulates that Luke used only one tradition, an oral tradition about the first occurrence of pneumatic speech in Jerusalem, and that he was responsible for the γλῶσσαι becoming languages. Thus it would not have been pre-Lucan tradition (so Bauernfeind), but Luke himself who transformed the 'speaking with tongues' into the miracle of the languages.

---

[1] As there is no new wine by Pentecost in Palestine, Bill. II, 614 thinks of wine sweetened with honey; *Beg*. IV, 20 recalls that new wine could be kept from going sour. But these are not considerations which are likely to have troubled Luke.

Williams conjectured an (Aramaic?) source in which the twelve Apostles were equipped with the Spirit and sent forth into twelve different parts of the world. Luke altered this, because he wanted to present a gradual progress of the mission (pp. 61–5). But if such a tradition had become known to Luke, would he not have seized on it with joy? Moreover, that Williams should prefer to Luke the late legend of the going-forth of the Apostles into the wide world contravenes the principle which holds good here as elsewhere: *lectio difficilior placet*. For the exodus of the Apostles to the ends of the earth would have fulfilled Acts **1.**8 far more completely than the mission described by Luke ever could.

According to Trocmé (pp. 202–6), Luke took the narrative of verses 1–6 and 12f. from a source which reported how divine grace had finally removed the confusion of languages that resulted from the Tower of Babel (Gen. **11.**1–9): as an eschatological gift, the men of every nation at Pentecost received a new language in which they could henceforth praise God with one voice: the miraculous features accompanying this 'supernatural Esperanto' were taken from a midrash on Ex. 19, from which Philo also could already have drawn material. Wanting to show the universality of the Christian mission, and knowing that ecstatic speeches are not a useful propaganda weapon, Luke resorted to a list of some synagogues drawn up by Jews of Antioch and introduced the idea of foreign languages. Verses 7f. and 11 comprise his interpretation of the episode. The words ἑτέραις γλώσσαις in verse 4 and Ἰουδαῖοι in verse 5 may derive from his pen.

Nearly all these exegetes identify sources very quickly and, to some extent, even the events which lie behind them. It is however very salutary that Bauernfeind and Lohse should remind us to begin with the question, 'What was Luke trying to do?' (Bauernfeind pp. 31ff.) The quickest way to find the answer is to look at his story of Pentecost from the standpoint of its composition. In so doing, of course, we will not understand it properly unless, as Bauernfeind and Lohse insist, we constantly bear in mind Luke's theological attitude.

When he came to the Pentecost episode, Luke found himself confronted with a difficult task. He wanted to present one of the most important incidents since the departure of Jesus: the coming of the Spirit. He had to depict it vividly so that it would rise unforgettably before the eyes of his readers. But this was not enough: he would not have succeeded in his task unless at the same time the *meaning* of this incident was plain to them. He could not count on much help from sources: there was no ancient or uniform tradition. This we know from the sole relevant report to be found in the Gospels—John **20.**22 —which tells that on the evening of Easter Day the risen Christ breathed (ἐνεφύσησεν) on his disciples and thereby transmitted to them the Holy Spirit. The implication of this account is clear: as God at the Creation breathed breath into man, so now the inbreathing of the Holy Spirit creates the new man. Here we have a profound application of an Old Testament idea, but not a primitive tradition from the dawn of the Church. And we may surely rule out the possibility of any other ancient tradition putting the investiture with the Spirit at so late a date as Luke (fifty days, remember, after Easter!). Luke fixed on this date because he had adopted the tradition of the forty days (Bauernfeind). The advent of the Spirit was simply dated to coincide with the next feast. Originally the tradition of the forty days had nothing to do with Pentecost. How Luke nevertheless came to combine the two will suggest itself from the following.

It was first a question of making plain that the Spirit came from God, from heaven. There is of course nothing sensory about the Spirit. But for Greek-speakers πνεῦμα (spirit) and πνοή (breath of wind) were certainly related concepts. Hence Luke was able to describe the descent of the Spirit as the rushing of a mighty wind that comes whirling down. It is thus clear *whence* it comes. But how best could Luke show *whither* it is going? How could he make clear to the reader that this irruption of the heavenly into the earthly has the disciples as its goal? Of course the house in which they sat could be shown to be pervaded by such a gale from the eternal. Luke had to make quite plain, however, that it is on the disciples as individuals that the Spirit fastens, and this task he could only perform with the aid of the Jewish Pentecost tradition, which allowed him the bold, mysterious transition to the tongues of fire appearing in the story of Sinai. That story is associated with the date of Pentecost, which thus becomes a factor of Luke's story too. Even if evidence for this Jewish tradition has not been found earlier than the middle of the second century, the one-time feast of the corn-harvest had doubtless already been transformed in people's minds into the feast of the lawgiving. At the same time (as Philo relates) the tongues of fire had become tongues of speech, and here we have another tradition still closer to Acts: when God spoke on Sinai his word divided into seventy tongues—corresponding to the seventy nations of the world—so that each people could hear the Law in its own language (though of course only Israel accepted it!). If Luke, however, was—as we may assume—acquainted with this or a similar tradition, he did not adopt it mechanically, for he says nothing of a new law and the Spirit is represented as an individual gift to each Christian (not only the Twelve but the whole congregation receive it). Each tongue corresponds to and bestows one particular language. This goes far beyond the Jewish Pentecost tradition. Yet insofar as he adopts the feast of Pentecost as the date of his episode, Luke is beholden to the Jewish heritage.

It was open to him to interpret the coming of the Spirit in the manner favoured by pious hermeneutics, as the occasion when the confusion of Babel was abolished: the Spirit of Christ healing the divisions of mankind. But in Luke's eyes the history of the Christian mission precluded this interpretation. At Pentecost, the time was not yet ripe for the ἔθνη, the Gentile peoples, to be seized by the Spirit: it was to the Jews that the mission first turned. As

Luke will describe at length in Chapters 10, 11 and 15, God brought about the mission to the Gentiles in his own good time—the course of history. This first Pentecost in Jerusalem may only reveal his power to Jews.

Nor does Luke think of the crowd gathered at Pentecost as pilgrims in Jerusalem for the feast. No, he is speaking of diaspora Jews who have taken *residence* in Jerusalem, and for this he has his reason: he can hardly have the mission's first 3,000 converts, the nucleus of the community secured from among them, streaming off to the four corners of the world within a week of conversion!

He therefore supposes (and there is nothing unlikely in it) that Jews from all over the world have settled in Jerusalem. Lured by the ἦχος, the sound which the Spirit made as it rushed down from heaven into the house of the Christians, these Jews gather in front of the dwelling. The catalogue of peoples (even if it only contains twelve names) shows that the Jewry of all nations is represented. Luke was too good a storyteller to break the spell with historical asides, so without more ado he places this catalogue in the very mouths of the people concerned. They can all hear the mighty works of God being praised in their own languages. In this way the reality of the bestowal of the Spirit and its effect is, as it were, objectively established.

But why is more not said about the content of this inspired utterance?— Because these 120 Christians could not preach in chorus the first sermon, which won the first 3,000 Jews for Christ. Luke wishes to give this sermon *in extenso*, however, so he reserves it for Peter as the official spokesman. But in order not to rob Peter of his material he has to make a clear distinction between the pneumatic speech, on the one hand, and Peter's discourse on the other. For that purpose Luke resorts to the phenomenon, with which he was also acquainted, of ecstatic speech. This brought a new motif into the story: ecstatic speech is incomprehensible to most listeners, but so far the languages bestowed by the Spirit have been represented as comprehensible. To avoid self-contradiction Luke therefore introduces at this point a new group of listeners, the 'others' (ἕτεροι, verse 13), who consider that the Christians under the Spirit's influence are drunk. Luke thereby employs one of his favourite devices: opposing two parties, one of which is more or less well-disposed to the Christians, while the other is hostile. At the same time this new factor, the accusation of drunkenness, serves as a bridge to Peter's address.

We now see why only the essential minimum was said about the content of the pneumatic speech ('the mighty works of God') and why this speech did not induce faith, but only amazement, bewilderment, puzzlement: it must neither anticipate nor detract from the effect of Peter's sermon—the conversion of the multitude. The advantage gained by Luke in return for this sacrifice is that the ecstatic pneumatic speech and the non-ecstatic discourse of Peter are intimately linked, making the story of Pentecost one great unity.

6
ACTS 2:14–41
PETER'S SPEECH AT PENTECOST

¹⁴ But Peter, standing up with the eleven, lifted up his voice and spoke solemnly to them, 'Men of Judaea, and all you that dwell in Jerusalem, be this known to you, and give ear to my words. ¹⁵ For these are not drunk, as you imagine, for it is only the third hour of the day; ¹⁶ but this is what was spoken by the prophet Joel: ¹⁷ "And it shall be thereafter, says God, I will pour out my Spirit upon all flesh; and your sons and your daughters shall prophesy, and your young men shall see visions, and your old men shall dream dreams. ¹⁸ And on my servants and on my handmaidens in those days will I pour out my Spirit, and they shall prophesy. ¹⁹ And I will work wonders in the heavens above, and signs on the earth beneath, blood, and fire, and vapour of smoke. ²⁰ The sun shall be turned into darkness, and moon into blood, before the great and glorious day of the Lord comes. ²¹ And it shall be, that everyone who calls on the name of the Lord shall be saved." ²² Men of Israel, hear these words: Jesus of Nazareth, a man approved of God to you by mighty works and wonders and signs, which God did by him among you, as you yourselves know, ²³ this man, who was delivered up by the determinate counsel and foreknowledge of God, you by the hand of lawless men did crucify and slay. ²⁴ Him God raised up, loosing the pangs of death, because it was not possible that he should be held in its power. ²⁵ For David says concerning him, "I saw the Lord always before me; for he is on my right hand, that I may not be shaken. ²⁶ Therefore my heart was glad, and my tongue rejoiced; moreover my flesh also shall dwell in hope, ²⁷ because thou wilt not leave my soul in Hades, neither wilt thou give thy Holy One to see corruption. ²⁸ Thou hast made known unto me the ways of life; thou wilt fill me with gladness by thy presence." ²⁹ Brethren, I may speak to you freely of the patriarch David, that he both died and was buried, and his tomb is with us to this day. ³⁰ Because he was a prophet, and knew that God had sworn an oath to him, that (someone) of the fruit of his loins should sit on his throne, ³¹ he foreseeing this spoke of the resurrection of the Christ, that neither was he abandoned to Hades, nor did his flesh see corruption. ³² This Jesus did God raise up; of which we all are witnesses. ³³ Being therefore exalted to the right hand of God, and having received of the Father the promise of the Holy Spirit, he has poured forth this, which you see and hear.

[34] For David did not ascend into the heavens: but he says himself, "The Lord said to my Lord, Sit thou on my right hand, [35] until I set thine enemies as a footstool under thy feet." [36] Let all the house of Israel therefore know assuredly, that God hath made him both Lord and Christ, this Jesus whom you crucified.' [37] Now when they heard this, it cut them to the heart, and they said to Peter and the rest of the Apostles, 'Brethren, what shall we do?' [38] And Peter said to them, 'Repent, and be baptized every one of you in the name of Jesus Christ for the forgiveness of sins; and you shall receive the gift of the Holy Spirit. [39] For to you is the promise, and to your children, and to all that are far away, every one whom the Lord our God shall call to him.' [40] And with many other words he testified and exhorted them, saying, 'Save yourselves from this crooked generation.' [41] They then that received his word were baptized: and there were added in that day about three thousand souls.

Bibliography:

Goro Mayeda, *Le langage et l'Évangile*, Geneva 1948; C. H. Dodd, *The Apostolic Preaching and its Developments*, 2nd edn., London 1951; H. Riesenfeld, 'Kristen gudstjänst i ljuset av Nya Testamentet', SEÅ 17 (1952), 32–65; J. W. Doeve, *Jewish Hermeneutics* (see § 1, bibl.); A. W. Argyle, 'The Theory of an Aramaic Source in Acts **2**.14–40', *JTS*, N.S. 4 (1953), 213ff.; C. H. Dodd, *According to the Scriptures: the Substructure of NT Theology*, London 1952; M. Black, *An Aramaic Approach to the Gospels and Acts*, 3rd edn., London 1967; Reicke, 38–54; Trocmé, 64–6, 192, 201, 204, 207f., 210; U. Wilckens, *Die Missionsreden d. Apg.*, 1961, 32–4, 56–9; A. Kerrigan, 'The "*sensus plenior*" of Joel **3**.1–5 in Acts **2**.14–16', *Sacra Pagina* 11, 295ff.
    R. G. Bratcher, 'Having loosed the pangs of death', *Bibl. Transl.* 10 (1959), 18–20; W. H. Bass, 'Acts **2**.28 and Ps. **16**.11', *Exp. Tim.* 29 (1917–8), 523; J. R. Harris, 'A Lacuna in the Text of the Apostles (**2**.32)', *Exp. Tim.* 36 (1924–5), 173–5; A. Vitti, 'Et Dominum et Christum fecit Deus (Act. **2**.36)', *Verb. Domini* 20 (1940), 193–200; M. Jonghe, 'Le baptême au nom de Jésus d'après les Actes des Apôtres', *Eph. Theol. Lov.* 10 (1933), 647–53; G. Lund, 'Pentecost Converts', *Exp.Tim.* 66 (1954–5), 372; P. de Ambroggi, 'I discorsi di S. Pietro negli Atti. Realità storica o finzione letteraria?', *Scuola Cattol.* Ser VI, Vol. XI (1928), 81–97, 161–86, 243–264; A. W. Arbez, 'Notes on the Teaching of the Acts of the Apostles', *Eccles. Rev.* 94 (1936), 519–523, 624–8; 95 (1936), 79–90, 182–6; J. Hamaide, 'The Message of Salvation in the Acts of the Apostles: Composition and Structure', *Lumen Vitae* 12 (1957), 406–17; U. Wilckens (see § 9), 32–7, 56–61, 121–6, 150.

VERSE 14: At this moment, as the tension reaches its height, Peter stands up[1] with[2] the eleven and begins[3] a solemn[4] address. Hellenistic and Septuagintal styles are united both in this introductory sentence and in the address to the multitude at Jerusalem[5]: the *parallelismus membrorum* is particularly clear.[6] On γνωστόν cf. note on 4.16 below; ἐνωτίζομαι is frequent in LXX, and the whole expression occurs in Job 32.11 LXX.

VERSE 15: Peter takes up the accusation of drunkenness in verse 13[7] and dismisses it with a reference to the early time of day (=9 a.m.[8]), when even drunkards and wassailers have not yet begun to imbibe.[9]

VERSE 16: Now comes the positive explanation: far from representing insobriety, the ecstatic behaviour of the Christians[10] is the fulfilment[11] of the prophecy[12] of Joel.[13]

---

[1] σταθείς, to take up the stance of a (Greek) orator, as likewise in 5.20, 11.13, 17.22, 25.18 and 27.21.

[2] σὺν κτλ. does not mean, as in classical Greek, 'with the eleven inclusively', which would disregard the election of Matthias (so Preuschen, p. 13), but is Hellenistic for μετά, as is usual in Luke (Bl.-Debr. § 221).

[3] ἐπῆρεν τὴν φωνήν: as in Luke 11.27, Acts 14.11 and 22.22, this is a LXX idiom rendering Hebrew נָשָׂא קוֹל, 'to begin to speak'.

[4] ἀποφθέγγομαι, to speak in inspired or solemn fashion (but not glossolalia): cf. 26.25 (*Beg.* IV, 21). 'Ici nous sommes à l'inauguration solennelle du Christianisme' (Loisy, p. 196).

[5] On ἄνδρες 'Ιουδαῖοι see on 1.16 above.

[6] 'Men of Judaea' and 'you that dwell at Jerusalem' do not refer to two distinct groups (cf. Morgenthaler, *Die luk. Geschichtsschreibung*, Part 2, 27 and 37).

[7] For the sake of simplicity Luke has Peter speak as if all the hearers cherished this suspicion. It is pointless to inquire how Peter knew of it, for Luke is only making clear to his readers through the mouth of Peter that the 'natural' explanation for the phenomenon of ecstasy does not apply.

[8] This was not, as many commentators maintain, a time of prayer for the Jews. Judaism never laid down definite hours for the prayers that were to be offered three times a day (Bill. II, 696ff.). For the most part people prayed at sunrise, in the afternoon and at sunset. The Christians themselves adopted the thrice-daily custom: according to Didache 8.3 the Lord's prayer was to be recited three times a day. By the time of Tertullian (*De orat.* 25, *De jejun.* 10) the third hour was the first of the daily times for prayer.

[9] Cicero, *Philosophical Discourses* II 41, 104: ... *ab hora tertia bibebatur, ludebatur.*

[10] As in verse 33, τοῦτό ἐστιν shows that the Christians—apart from the Twelve— are imagined as still given over to ecstasy, though somewhat in the background of the scene.

[11] Joel does not mention speech in foreign languages, which is reason enough why Peter's discourse cannot refer to the miracle of the languages. Ecstatic utterance, on the other hand, is covered by the προφητεύειν of the quotation.

[12] According to Bauernfeind (p. 34) Joel 3.1ff.(Eng.version 2.28ff.) is part of the apologetic armament against anti-pneumatic polemic. However, the taunt of drunkenness is countered not with this passage but with the reference to the time of day.

[13] The name Joel is lacking in D d Ir Aug (*epist.* 199.23) Hil (*Beg.* III 16). *Beg.* IV 21 explains this as a 'western non-interpolation'—a passage which the Western text alone has refrained from expanding—on the ground that subsequent quotations from the minor prophets (7.42f., 13.40f. and 15.16) omit the prophet's name.

VERSE 17: The text of B, μετὰ ταῦτα, is the original[1]: in Lucan theology the last days do not begin as soon as the Spirit has been outpoured! The authoritative 'says God' is interpolated into the LXX text. By ἀπὸ τοῦ πνεύματός μου LXX already indicates that the fulness of the Spirit remains with God and that man only partakes of it. In the original text πᾶσαν σάρκα[2] does not mean man in general, but Luke also does not yet intend Peter to proclaim the gift of the Spirit to all men, for that would be anticipating the decisive turning-point of the Cornelius episode (10.44f., 11.18). Prophecy, elsewhere distinguished from the gift of tongues, is here identified with it to facilitate the scriptural proof. The exceptional position of the prophet, his direct contact with God, becomes the portion of all. When writing ὁράσεις and ἐνύπνια Luke may have had in mind such phenomena as in 9.10, 10.10, 11.5, 16.9, 22.17f., 27.23. With regard to ἐνυπνίοις κτλ. cf. Gen. 37.5 LXX.

VERSE 18: The μου added to δούλους and δούλας, against the Hebrew and LXX, turns the slaves of the Jews into servants and handmaids of God:[3] it is not, therefore, a new group that is introduced here. The first καί should strictly speaking be omitted in translation. καὶ προφητεύσουσιν follows the pattern of verse 17.[4]

VERSES 19–21: The addition of ἄνω, σημεῖα and κάτω turns the bipartite Hebrew sentence into a tripartite one. The cosmic events describe the terrible end which threatens, when only he who calls on the name of the Lord (=Jesus!)[5] shall be saved.

VERSE 22: As in verse 29, the mode of address, growing more intimate, shows that Peter is resuming his own words after the OT quotation.[6] But neither the mode of address nor the call to listen is inserted for mere schematic reasons. In the forefront of the Christian message stands the name of Jesus, here further identified as ὁ Ναζωραῖος,[7] which Luke takes to mean 'from

---

[1] See my 'Schriftzitate und Textüberlieferung in der Apg.', *ZThK* 51 (1954), 162.

[2] D alters to πάσας σάρκας, so as to express the universality of the Christian mission which turns to all men.

[3] See *ZThK* 51 (1954), 161.

[4] It is missing in the Hebrew and LXX, and may go back to an old scribal error.

[5] Since both the Hebrew text and the Targum of the prophets read 'Yahweh' here, it follows that it was only in Hellenistic Christianity that Joel 3.1ff. became available as a scriptural proof! Likewise ἐπιφανῆ ('manifest') must be laid at the door of LXX, which wrongly derived נוֹרָא ('terrible') from רָאָה ('to see') instead of יָרֵא ('to fear').

[6] This disposes of Preuschen's contention (p. 13) that the triple address destroys the unity of the sermon. The ancient writer had no quotation-marks at his disposal.

[7] Likewise in 3.6, 4.10, 6.14, 22.8 and 26.9, and already in Luke 18.37. In 24.5 Tertullus describes the Christians as Nazoraeans, a name which adhered to the Jewish Christians and with them grew alien to the Church. Cf. *ThWb* IV, 879–84: '. . . the interpretation of Ναζωραῖος as rendering Aramaic nāṣrājā, derived from the name of the town Nazareth . . . is linguistically and objectively unimpeachable' (Schaeder).

Nazareth'.[1] Jesus is vouched for[2] to the Jews[3] by[4] God through wonders of all kinds[5] which[6] God[7] has done by him in their midst.[8]

VERSE 23: Jesus' death on the Cross seems to contradict his divine legitimation through the miracles (Wendt, p. 92). For Luke and his community this σκάνδαλον of the Cross is overcome by the fact that God's own will, as revealed in the scriptures, is fulfilled therein.[9] 'Thus human freedom' (ἀνείλατε, did slay[10]) 'and divine necessity' (ἔκδοτον, delivered up) 'here go hand in hand: the simplest and probably the oldest way of reconciling oneself to the paradoxical fate of the Messiah' (Holtzmann, p. 35). It is the Jews who were really responsible for the death of Jesus; the Gentiles were merely[11] instruments.[12]

VERSE 24: ὅν ὁ θεὸς ἀνέστησεν (ἤγειρεν) is a Lucan formation,[13] which crudely contrasts 'you slew' and 'God raised up'. ὅν (see above, p. 139 n. 7) betrays the hand of Luke. τὰς ὠδῖνας τοῦ θανάτου: LXX in II Sam. 22.6, Ps. 17.6 and 114.3 wrongly derives חֶבְלִי from חֵבֶל, 'birthpang,' instead of חֶבֶל, 'cord.' These 'deathpangs' (cf. the parallel images 'the snares of death came upon me,' 'the dangers of Hades encompassed me,' 'the crushings of death encompassed me') were regarded as a mysterious expression for the power of death.[14] In this sense the expression entered into liturgical use and

---

[1] In Luke 4.16 the place is called Ναζαρά (Luke 4.34 and 24.19 have the derivative Ναζαρηνός). The village is not mentioned in OT, nor by the Talmud, Mishnah or Josephus, but appears (c. 800?) in the Elegy of Eleazer ben Qalir (Bill. I, 92).

[2] ἀποδεδειγμένος =accredited or legitimated. Here an old phrase is used: cf. Dibelius, *Studies* 165.

[3] D changes ὑμᾶς to ἡμᾶς, because only the disciples, not the men of Jerusalem, have experienced these miracles.

[4] ἀπό Hellenistic for ὑπό (Bl.-Debr. § 210, 2). Preuschen (p. 14) found the juxtaposition of 'by God' and the relative clause 'intolerable'. But Luke wishes precisely to throw into relief the divine action in and through Jesus.

[5] δυνάμεσι κτλ. is meant to indicate the whole wealth of Jesus' miracles, hence the completeness of his credentials.

[6] οἷς for ἅ by relative attraction (Bl.-Debr. § 294).

[7] That God is the true author of the miracles corresponds to the Jewish outlook.

[8] 'As you yourselves know' shows that the Galilean miracles of Jesus are generally known.

[9] Cf. Luke 24.26f., 44ff.; Acts 3.18, 13.27 and 26.23. Luke has nothing corresponding to the Pauline doctrine of the σκάνδαλον τοῦ σταυροῦ (see Wendt, p. 92 n. 1).

[10] Overbeck (p. 39) finds here, and in 2.36, 3.13ff., 4.10, 4.27f. and 5.30, an anti-Jewish bias characteristic of Acts. It would be more correct to discover an exoneration of the Romans.

[11] ἄνομος is the Gentile, who cannot but sin, because he does not know the will of God. The Romans especially are so called in Jewish writings; cf. *ThWb* IV, 1079f.

[12] διὰ χειρός (LXX style) =instrumental 'by', with reference to προσπήξαντες 'having pinned' (on the Cross).

[13] Cf. 2.32, 3.15, 4.10, 5.30, 10.40, 13.30, 13.33f. and 17.31.

[14] Holtzmann (p. 36), Wendt (p. 92) and others find here implied the metaphor of death in labour bringing forth (=delivering) Jesus when God looses (=puts an end to) the 'sorrows of death' (cf. Job 39.2 LXX). Col. 1.18, to which Bauernfeind (p. 47) also refers, does not support this interpretation. If one asks, concerning the formula πρωτότοκος

probably from there into Acts.[1] λύσας relates to death's power to bind man fast.

VERSE 25: The pious author of the sixteenth psalm[2] is sure that God will not let him die before his time: early death is a punishment for the godless. The Christians found something else in the Greek text: the psalmist foretells the resurrection of the Messiah, inasmuch as he speaks in the person of the Anointed.[3] Probably verses 25f. refer to Jesus' earthly life in general, but include the hour of death on the Cross so that—on this interpretation of the psalm—Jesus did not feel forsaken of God.[4] It should be remembered that Luke omitted from his gospel the cry from the Cross, 'My God, my God, why hast thou forsaken me?' προορώμην does not have a chronological sense (so *Beg.* IV, 24), but means 'to have before one's eyes' (see Bauer *Wb*, 1406). If Ps. 16.8ff. is taken seriously as an utterance of Christ, he saw God before him on the Cross and also throughout the 'three days.' Luke can hardly mean that God also was in Hades, as Bauernfeind p. 47 seems to understand; he wishes, rather, to say the same as in Luke 23.43: 'Today thou wilt be with me in Paradise.'

VERSE 26: LXX renders כְּבוֹדִי[5] very freely as ἡ γλῶσσα,[6] and לָבֶטַח (in safety) as ἐπ' ἐλπίδι. This alone enabled the Christians to hear at this point an echo of the hope of resurrection: the psalmist was merely repeating his assurance of preservation from (untimely) death.

VERSE 27: It was the older Christian conception that every soul entered the realm of death (cf. Jeremias, *ThWb* I, 146–50). Luke, however, seems to believe that the souls of the righteous go straight to Paradise (verse 25). Whereas the early Christians probably understood εἰς ᾅδην as meaning ἐν ᾅδῃ—the soul of Jesus enters Hades but does not stay there—Luke sees an indication in the

---

(ἐκ νεκρῶν), who the mother or the begetter is, the answer can only be God. II. Esdras 4.41f., to which appeal is similarly made, says only that the as yet unborn souls of the righteous must first enter the world before this aeon expires. Torrey (pp. 28f.) detects Aramaic here, supposing Luke to have translated שדא חבליא די מותא. But LXX is quite adequate to explain the passage; that Luke knew no Aramaic is evident from his explanation of 'Barnabas' as υἱὸς παρακλήσεως in Acts 4.36.

[1] See Introduction §1, VIIa p. 6 above.

[2] Also cited as a proof-text in Acts 13.35.

[3] εἰς αὐτόν ='concerning him'.

[4] The 'Elijah' theology suggested by Mark 15.34ff. had of course no place in Luke's scheme.

[5] Probably a corruption of כְּבֵדִי, 'my liver', the liver being regarded as the seat of the emotions. The Rabbis later linked כְּבוֹדִי with 'the king, the Messiah'. Later still the psalm was interpreted even in Judaism as a reference to resurrection, though not in the same way as in Acts: e.g. midrash on Ps. 16, §10 (62a), 'even my flesh shall dwell in safety'—that is, after death. Rabbi Yitzhaq (c. 300) said: 'This shows that neither worm nor corruption has power over his flesh' (Bill. II 618).

[6] According to Holtzmann (p. 36), there is an allusion to the glossolalia. Most unlikely! (On ἐλπίς see *ThWb* II, 518, 16ff.)

psalm that the soul of Jesus was not delivered into Hades (cf. Ps. Sol. 2.7) and that he did not 'see', i.e. experience, corruption;[1] cf. Luke 2.26.

VERSE 28: אֹרַח חַיִּים in the Hebrew meant the life well-pleasing to God, which preserved the devout from untimely death. The ὁδοὶ ζωῆς, on the other hand, are the way which leads from death into the life of the Resurrection (Wendt, p. 93). While, as the early Christians understood it, verse 27 implied that the body of the Messiah was saved from decomposition, verse 28 speaks positively of the Resurrection. Once again, the Christological interpretation can only have arisen in Hellenistic Christianity.

VERSE 29: On the address, see remarks on 1.16 and 2.22. Now the contention of verse 25, that the psalm spoke of Jesus, is to be proved: David died and was buried,[2] so he cannot have meant himself by 'I', but only the Messiah of his line. ἐξόν = ἔξεστιν (Bl.-Debr. § 353, 5). μετὰ παρρησίας means freely or frankly (*ThWb* V, 880). Peter's bestowing on David the honourable title of patriarch shows that he is not without respect, even if he—indirectly—maintains that David's body has decomposed: for he implies no less by saying that David is dead and buried and his tomb still in evidence.[3]

VERSE 30: προφήτης ὑπάρχων (= ὤν)—God grants the prophet an insight into the future; hence προιδὼν κτλ. in v. 31f. ought properly to follow here. But another thought intervenes: God had solemnly sworn to David that one[4] of his descendants[5] should sit upon his—God's—throne.

VERSE 31: Now comes the proposition expected after προφήτης ὑπάρχων: with his prophetic foreknowledge David spoke of the resurrection of the Christ, saying namely (ὅτι) that he was not abandoned to Hades,[6] and that his flesh did not see corruption. These aorists make sense, because for the speaker, Peter, the prophecy has already been fulfilled (Wendt, p. 94).

VERSE 32: The scriptural proof for the sake of which the kerygma was interrupted in verse 24 is now complete, and the message is resumed from the point of digression. What the scripture foretold, 'we all' (the twelve Apostles) attest as having really come to pass.

---

[1] διαφθορά, meaning deterioration or putrefaction, is a mistranslation taken from LXX, which made an erroneous derivation of שַׁחַת (a pit) from שָׁחַת (to spoil). The Hebrew spoke only of preservation from death, the Greek of preservation from decomposition: only the latter permitted the Christological interpretation.

[2] Von Campenhausen, *Der Ablauf der Osterereignisse* (1952), 19: '"dead and buried" underlines the reality of the death.'(ET *Tradition and Life in the Early Church*, 1968).

[3] Josephus speaks of David's grave in *Ant.* VII 392–4, XIII 249, and *Bell.* I 61.

[4] Ps. 132.11 is the only place mentioning a single scion of David; even so, the very next verse shows that what is meant is merely David's descendants occupying his throne.

[5] The Western text (except D) replaces ὀσφύος with the κοιλίας of LXX. This contradicts Lucan usage, in which κοιλία means 'womb'. D's reading, καρδίας, goes back to a wrong retranslation of the Latin *praecordia* (='belly' and 'heart') in d: see *ZThK* 1954, 164f., where however the third line from the foot of p. 164 should read 'Ps. 131.11 LXX' instead of 'Ps. 131 und B'.

[6] D offers the classical εἰς ᾅδου, which passed into most MSS.

VERSE 33: With οὖν we are led imperceptibly from the Resurrection to the Exaltation 'to[1] the right hand of God' (corresponding to καθίσαι ἐπὶ τὸν θρόνον αὐτοῦ in verse 30: Jesus, sitting on God's right, shares his throne). This expression, like 'promise of the Holy Spirit' (cf. 1.4 and Luke 24.49), is a traditional formula employed by Luke. It was not part of the oldest view that the exalted Lord only acquired the Spirit in order to share it abroad: that much is clear from I Tim. 3.16 and the pre-Pauline formula found in Rom. 1.4. Here Luke is effecting a reconciliation between the received view and his own (Luke 3.21f.). The Spirit bestowed on the Exalted was not an endowment of which he had need: it was given him only for distribution! That Jesus has poured forth this Spirit can be seen and heard in the Christians who are still under its influence (Bauernfeind, p. 49). Hence the ecstatic speaking with tongues is still going on in the background.

VERSES 34 and 35: Another indirect scriptural proof is now provided for the expression 'exalted to the right hand of God': David cannot have been speaking of himself in Psalm 110,[2] for he did not ascend into heaven. He therefore who shall sit on the right hand of God can only be the Messiah, who is identified in the psalm by τῷ κυρίῳ μου. Thus the citation entails the consequence declared in the following verse.[3]

VERSE 36: This scriptural testimony, joined with that of the eyewitnesses, the Apostles, brings the 'house of Israel' (another LXX locution) the certain knowledge that God has made Jesus the κύριος (Ps. 110.1) and Messiah.[4] Here the guilt of the Jews is brought explicitly to the fore: they slew this Jesus![5] That specifically the pious diaspora Jews (2.5!) are charged with this guilt is from a literary point of view inept.

VERSE 37: Recognition of this guilt pierces the hearers' hearts.[6] They are seized with remorse, and they beg Peter and the other Apostles[7] to tell them what to do. The very form of address they use, ἄνδρες ἀδελφοί, shows

---

[1] We could also translate 'exalted by God's right hand' (cf. Bauer *Wb* 316, 2a); but it is entirely possible to assume, both here and in 5.31, the dative of place (Bl.-Debr. §199 prefer this explanation). See also on verses 34f.

[2] According to its basic meaning, this psalm promises a Jewish king that God will not desert him in the face of his enemies. On the interpretation of Ps. 110 in the old rabbinic literature, see the excursus in Billerbeck IV 1, 452ff.

[3] One can scarcely resist the impression that τῇ δεξιᾷ was inserted in verse 33 with ἐκ δεξιῶν μου already in mind. Cf. Heitmüller, *Im Namen Jesu*, 88ff.

[4] The same psalm is cited in Mark 12.35–7, I Cor. 15.25 and Heb. 1.13. It underlay the belief that Jesus, as God's protégé and deputy (Loisy 211), sits at his right hand. For a long time Judaism did not give the psalm a Messianic interpretation—probably out of opposition to Christianity.

[5] No anti-Judaism here, but an attempt to show the man who is to come to faith in Jesus that he is guilty of Jesus' death. The next verse shows that this interpretation is correct.

[6] Ps. 109 (108).16: κατανενυγμένον τῇ καρδίᾳ. The verb can express emotional stress of various kinds.

[7] They are not mentioned without reason: Peter has not been brought to the fore as an individual, but only as the spokesman of the Twelve. It is the apostolic, not the Petrine, which Luke considers the true Church.

that their hearts are already won over.[1] (This is one of the few occasions in Acts where Luke weaves in a short dialogue.)

VERSE 38: In answer follows the exhortation to repent (which already in Judaism included confession of sins) and be baptized. Luke presupposes the form of baptism practised in his own community: the name 'Jesus Christ' is pronounced over the candidate. Thereby he comes under the power of Jesus, his sins are in consequence remitted,[2] and he 'receives the Holy Spirit'. The few cases in Acts when reception of the Spirit is separated from baptism are justified exceptions.[3] By the time of Luke, it was not every Christian (if it ever had been) who received the *ecstatic* Spirit at baptism.[4] Rather was the Spirit now regarded as a gift no longer bound to any outward sign. Cf. Heitmüller, *Im Namen Jesu*, 88ff.

VERSE 39: Peter can promise to his hearers forgiveness and the Holy Spirit because Joel's promise[5] is assured to them and to their children—'all that are afar off'. Acts **22**.21, not to mention Ecclesiasticus **24**.32, corroborates the spatial interpretation of this expression. The listeners cannot take it as a reference to the Gentile mission, though there is nothing in the text to preclude this idea.

VERSE 40: By ἑτέροις λόγοις πλείοσιν the writer implies that Peter said more than the words reported,[6] and that in this continuation he reinforced his exhortations[7] to conversion.[8] The expression γενεὰ σκολιά derives from Deut. **32**.5 and Ps. **78**.8.

VERSE 41: Here we are made to see the success of the first Christian sermon: 'They then that received his word were baptized.' The question whether such a mass-baptism was at that time possible in Jerusalem—without,

---

[1] Since the whole multitude cannot address the Apostles, D says: 'and some of them spoke . . .' The further emendations of D are clearly secondary: τῇ καρδίᾳ, as in LXX, for τὴν καρδίαν, and the expansion: 'show us!'

[2] According to Luke **3**.3 John the Baptist preached the baptism of forgiveness. However, when Bauernfeind (53) maintains that in verse 38 Luke is prompting his readers to reflect on the relation of Christian to Johannine baptism, he is raising a point which is extraneous to the text.

[3] Cf. the remarks in the commentary on Acts **8**.16, **10**.44 and **19**.2–6.

[4] Luke also says nothing, in v. 41, of the newly baptized speaking in tongues, although according to v. 38 they have received the Holy Spirit.

[5] There is a clear echo of Joel **2**.32b (**3**.5b LXX), οὓς κύριος προσκέκληται, in ὅσους ἂν προσκαλέσηται κύριος . . .

[6] Dibelius, *Studies* 178: 'A . . . technical device which is also common in "grand-style" literature . . . It is an artifice which allows the writer freedom to put whatever suits his plan in the speaker's mouth, but at the same time to give the reader to understand that this does not exhaust what the speaker said.'

[7] The aorist διεμαρτύρατο refers to the whole address, whereas the imperfect παρεκάλει expresses the repeated exhortations. It is not the Christians (so Beyer, p. 28) who are imagined as speaking, but Peter.

[8] Finding that σώθητε κτλ. contains nothing specially appropriate to the situation, as regards either form or content, Bauernfeind (p. 54) jumps to the conclusion that this word is specially connected with the person of Peter. In fact Luke is simply placing a current missionary word suggested by σωθήσεται in verse 21.

above all, alerting the authorities—is alien to the nature of the presentation. ψυχαί ='persons' (LXX).[1]

Our detailed examination has demonstrated again and again that the scriptural evidence adduced by Peter presupposes the Septuagint text: it has no earlier origin, therefore, than Hellenistic Christianity. It follows that Dodd is in error when he holds that Peter's speeches in the first part of Acts 'represent the kerygma of the Church at Jerusalem at an early period' (*Apostolic Preaching*, 21), and the older view that we have here, if not Peter's actual expressions, at least his original train of thought, is even more discredited. Rather is Martin Dibelius' thesis confirmed, that Peter's speeches go back to Luke himself. And so we come to the question: how, exactly, did Luke construct this speech?

The scriptural proofs which make up so large a proportion of it would not be very appropriate as the content of a speech 'with other tongues' and in the mysterious context of a miracle. For scriptural proof appeals to the hearers' reason, which to be sure must not struggle against the recognition of the truth; the method is to demonstrate the truth of the kerygma from already accepted scriptural passages. That is why Luke connected this sermon not to the miracle of the *languages*—which could not moreover be suitably linked with the Joel citation—but to the mockery in verse 13, hence to the idea of the *ecstatic speech* (whose content he nevertheless omits to reveal!). It is in the situation created by the listeners' taunts that the first part of the sermon (verses 16–21) opens: this is the link with the situation, which in this case contains at the same time part of the scriptural proof. The second part (verses 22–36) introduces the kerygma proper, presented in close association with the scriptural proof. The last part (from verse 38 on) draws the practical moral: exhortation to repentance and baptism.

Dibelius (*Studies* 165) draws attention to the fact that Luke is here following a pattern recurrent in Acts: an introduction adapted to the situation leads to the 'kerygma of Jesus' life, passion and resurrection (2.22–4; 3.13–5; 5.30f.; 10.36–42; 13.23–5), usually stressing the witnessing function of the disciples (2.32; 3.15; 5.32; 10.39, 41; 13.31), and to this are joined a scriptural proof (2.25–31; 3.22–6; 10.43; 13.32–7) and an exhortation to repentance (2.38f.; 3.17–20; 5.31; 10.42f.; 13.38–41)'. Like Bauernfeind

---

[1] In 'Das Fehlen der Taufe in der Quellenschrift der Apostelgeschichte und in den Urgemeinden der Hebräer und Hellenisten' (*Wissensch. Zeitschr. der M.-Luther-Universität Halle-Wittenberg* VI 4 (1956/7), 1–18) Ernst Barnikol contends that only the baptism of the Spirit was known to apostolic times: 'The ritualistic *religio* of man in his Church' (p. 18) was not added until the second century. Barnikol argues this thesis by adopting A. C. Clark's view that the (secondary!) Western text is the original (p. 3: cf. my 'Zum Text . . .' in *ZThK* 54 (1957), esp. 23–9) and by striking out all references to water-baptism as late additions of the author, writing *c.* 135 (p. 4). The various problems of the text, of the tradition and its historical reliability, of the composition and theological plan in relation to the evolution of dogma, are here lumped indistinguishably together, while the phantasm of a cultless, non-ecclesiastical pneumatic faith holds undisputed sway.

before him (p. 46), Dibelius makes the point that Luke was following typical practice in the preaching of his age (according to Dibelius, 'about A.D. 90').

There is no proof here that older texts have been employed: there was no stenographer to write down the sermons of the Apostles. But it is quite likely that Luke combined some expressions from the tradition of his Church with his own formulations. Not that Luke had any conscious desire to write in an archaic manner: the only intention we may in this respect ascribe to Luke as teacher and writer is that of making the Apostles speak *solemnly* (ἀπεφθέγξατο, verse 14). But this led him to copious use of the Bible—that is to say, the Greek Old Testament. With this Luke was remarkably familiar, and he had far more frequent recourse to it than would appear from the marginal references in Nestle.

The introduction had to take the situation of the 'speaking with tongues' as its point of departure (the contention of many scholars that Luke knew nothing more about it is completely wide of the mark). Luke chose Joel 3.1–5 (Eng. versions 2.28–32) for this purpose. The problem was to find the phenomenon of the ecstasy—which must have come as a complete surprise to the community—foretold and explained in the Bible. Of course, Joel was speaking not of ecstasy but of prophecy. But for the sake of appropriating his text Luke took the two related but not identical phenomena as one and the same. He felt more deeply justified in so doing by his conviction that the Spirit had determined the whole life of the first community, but especially its most important decisions, and that a position had thereby arisen which corresponded to the prophecy of Joel. To be sure, Luke could not directly link the cosmic omens of the last days with the context of the sermon; for him there lay between the coming of the Spirit and those heavenly signs (cf. Introduction § 7, pp. 94ff. above) a lengthy interval. But there was no need for him to go into that question here. The disadvantage was outweighed by the opportunity offered by Joel 3.5a of continuing at once with the kerygma: 'whosoever shall call on the name of the Lord' Jesus 'shall be saved'.

Jesus is described as a man for whom God has vouched to the Jews by wonders of all kinds. That miracles were regarded as divine legitimation is clear from John 2.18 and 3.2. But in the passage under discussion the σημεῖον is not, as in John 3.3, declined as a credential: it is accepted. The guilt of the Jews indeed consists in their having rejected Jesus in spite of it.

Jesus' death on the Cross appeared to contradict this divine legitimation. It is explained with reference to God and the Jews, as an event willed and foreseen by the former and a deed whereby the latter incurred guilt. Thus understood, the shame of the death falls not upon Jesus but upon his murderers. But God has released Jesus from the bonds of death and raised him up.

So far these things have been merely asserted. Now they are corroborated by reference to Ps. 16. This presupposes the belief that David, as author of the psalm, spoke the truth. Given that David did not refer to himself in the 'I' of the psalm, the text must bear upon another in whose person David was speaking: his Messianic successor, whom he not only foresaw with prophetic vision but had been promised by an oath of God. Concerning him the psalm says: God did not abandon his soul to Hades nor give his flesh to corruption. Thereby Luke proved—and it was for his age a strict proof—that death could not hold Jesus in its power: his resurrection had been guaranteed by God from the beginning. To use a modern expression, it is no 'chance fact of history' but a necessity founded in the will of God. The demonstration of this is reinforced in verse 32 by the testimony of the eyewitnesses to the effect that what had to come to pass did come to pass.

Luke employs an aside to clarify the connection between Jesus and the Spirit of Pentecost. This Spirit Jesus received from the Father and poured forth on the Christians, as is proved by their ecstatic utterance (verse 33). Generally—one has only to examine the 62 occurrences of πνεῦμα in Acts— Luke sees the Spirit in another context: 1. the Spirit belongs to Christian baptism, which it fails to accompany only in exceptional cases; 2. beside belief in the Spirit associated with baptism there stands belief (of Judaic origin: cf. Bultmann, *Theologie des NTs*, 1948, 155; ET *Theology of the New Testament*, 1952, 157) in the Spirit bestowed on one particular Christian or congregation for the performance of some special task (**4.**8, 31; **7.**55; **13.**9, 52); 3. closely related to these passages are those in which the Spirit—rather like an angel elsewhere—imparts some particular directive or advice (**8.**29; **10.**19, 44; **11.**28; **13.**2, 4; **16.**6f.; **20.**23; **21.**11); 4. probably the latest— certainly a Hellenistic—Christian view is enshrined in those verses which attribute the possession of the Spirit as a permanent property to men such as Stephen (**6.**5) or Barnabas (**11.**24). Luke connects the pentecostal gift of the Spirit with the first group: the pouring-out of the Spirit is a baptism with the Spirit, as is expressly said in Acts **1.**5.

The Ascension of Jesus is also verified from scripture (verses 34f.): Ps. **110.**1 renders possible the proof—again indirect. It brings the assurance that God has made the Jesus whom the Jews crucified both κύριος and χριστός. The expressions, taken from older tradition, with which the speech is brought to a provisional end use formulae that are at odds with Lucan Christology: Luke assumes that Jesus during his earthly life already possessed both his dignity as Son of God and the endowment of the Holy Spirit (cf. Luke **2.**40ff.; **3.**22; **4.**18; **9.**35). For that reason the description of Jesus in verse 22 also (ἄνδρα ἀποδεδειγμένον κτλ.) does not wholly agree with Lucan Christology. Yet Luke had no intention, in verses 22, 33 and 36, of outlining an older Christology (Luke is seen in much too modern terms when he is credited with the intention, in a book designed for edification, of making such a Christological anomaly apparent!). Far from it: on the one hand, just as is our own practice with liturgical texts, he understood traditional statements in terms of contemporary doctrine; on the other, he strove to reconcile divergences whenever he thought it necessary and feasible (thus the Exalted One receives the Spirit—but only in order to pour it out!).

Prefacing it with a short question from the listeners, Luke now comes to the third part, verses 38f. This is the summons to repentance and baptism, which is to be followed by the forgiveness of sins and the bestowal of the Holy Spirit. For the promise is to all Jews near and far. Even if Luke's formulation does not exclude the mission to the Gentiles, this mission is yet not brought into view for Peter's audience.

As a narrator, Luke had to place the broad lines of the incident in vivid images before his readers. Such a method already made it difficult enough to present the development of the primitive community, quite apart from the dearth of sources. But there was this other factor, that the very idea of an internal evolution within Christianity was as alien to Luke himself as to the community of which he was a member (as he viewed it, the beginning of the Gentile mission was *not* an internal development). If followed that, fundamentally, the Church had existed from the outset in the form in which Luke found it: from the beginning its scriptural credentials had lain ready and waiting—had not the risen Lord, according to Luke **24**.25ff., 44f., himself revealed them to his disciples on the very day of Easter? That much searching of the scriptures had been necessary, much reflection and many a happy illumination, to create over the lapse of many years the Church's imposing body of scriptural proof, that is something of which Luke has lost all notion: no, this precious possession has always been there, for so long as there has been a Christian community. It is the same with baptism: Jesus himself neither baptized nor caused his disciples to baptize. The command to baptize in Matt. **28**.19 emanates from the risen Lord and betrays its late origin by its very form, which is trinitarian. How different the synoptic tradition would appear if the primitive community had known something, after the style of the later tradition in John **3**.22 and **4**.2, of the baptismal activities of Jesus and his disciples! Baptism did indeed very early gain access into the Church. There must have been baptist influences which paved the way; probably some of the first disciples, like Jesus himself, were baptized by his forerunner John.

And now we must come to speak not only of the inward but also of the outward evolution of the community. This, according to Acts, proceeded as it were by leaps and bounds, by means of such mass-conversion as we see in Chapter 2. Needless to say, the critics have objected that the figure of 3,000 in verse 41 is much too high (people should realise how hard it is—without a microphone!—to make one's voice carry to 3,000 men in the open, and it is impossible to speak in solemn cadences under such conditions . . .), and certain criticisms have also been levelled against the manner in which verse 6 declares the scene to have been set for the preaching (see p. 168f. above). But on the whole they have had no objection against the crowd scene as such—what better proof of the power of conviction which radiates from Luke's account?

Yet it is far more probable that the little flock of Christians led 'a quiet, even in the Jewish sense "devout" life in Jerusalem. It was a modest existence, and nothing but the triumphant conviction of the faithful betrayed that from this flock was to go forth a movement which would transform the world' (Dibelius, *Studies* 124). When Luke speaks here and later of multitudes, he is bowing to the same persuasion which causes him to make the Sanhedrin, or the Proconsul and his staff, or a king, or even the illustrious company on the Areopagus, an audience for the Apostles—i.e., 'These things were not done in a corner' (Acts **26**.26). It is on the basis of this conviction that he draws his picture of the first mission. This is not to deny that other motives are at work: Luke loves the multitudes of converts, the mass-successes. Not that he was unduly impressed by sheer numbers. But the crowds streaming into the fold of Christ are for him the visible expression of the divine blessing resting on the Church. Even so, the danger admittedly remains that what is great and imposing by merely worldly standards may pass for a revelation of God's power. It is likely, however, that in reality the Christians sought adherents for their Lord, in the earliest days, without attracting much attention: I Corinthians is there to tell us that the ecstatic experience of the Spirit, to which modern presentations give so great a role in psychological reconstructions of Pentecost, does not impel people to preach in the streets but rather makes them cling together in a narrow circle; it was the 'Hellenists' (see on Ch. 6) who first broke out from this reserve of the Jewish sect that believed in Jesus.

And so we misuse Luke's account of Pentecost when we make believe that it offers us a documentary film of the beginnings of the Christian mission, instead of confining ourselves to the essential theological pronouncements which it embodies: that the Spirit which indwells, drives and directs the Christian community is not generated by that community's own inwardness, but comes from God, is mediated to us through Jesus Christ, and transcends all boundaries of countries and peoples.

7
ACTS 2:42-47
THE WAY OF LIFE OF THE FIRST COMMUNITY

[42] And they continued steadfastly in the Apostles' teaching and in the fellowship, the breaking of bread and the prayers. [43] And fear came upon every soul: and many wonders and signs were done through the Apostles. [44] And all those who believed, one and all, had all things in common. [45] They sold their property and (other) possessions, and distributed them to all, according as any man had need. [46] Day by day, continuing steadfastly with one accord in the Temple, and breaking bread in private houses, they shared their meals with unaffected joy, [47] praising God, and enjoying the favour of the whole people. And day by day the Lord added to their number those who were being saved.

Bibliography:

Cadbury, 'The Summaries in Acts', *Beg.* V, 392–402; Cerfaux, 'La Composition de la première partie du Livre des Actes', *Eph. Theol. Lov.* 13 (1936), 667–91 (esp. 671–80) = *Recueil Cerfaux* II, 63–91; Jeremias, 'Untersuchungen zum Quellenproblem der Apg.', *ZNW* 36 (1937), 205–21; L. S. Thornton, *The Common Life in the Body of Christ* (1942), 1–33 (on **2**.42); Dodd, *Apostolic Preaching* (see § 6, bibl.); P. Benoit, 'Remarques sur les "sommaires" des Actes: **2**.42 à 5', *Mélanges Goguel*, 1950, 1–10; Reicke 53–62; Trocmé 71, 88 and 120; Conzelmann 31f.

E. Barnikol, 'Sie blieben aber beständig i. d. Apostel Lehre: Gott hat Jesum auferweckt', *Theol. Jahrbuch* 7 (1939), 48–60 (on **2**.42); L. Cerfaux, 'La première communauté chrétienne à Jérusalem', *Eph. Theol Lov.* 16 (1939), 5–31; W. A. Dord, 'Breaking Bread (Acts **2**.46)', *CBQ* I (1939), 358–62; J. Heuschen, 'Het godsdienstig leven in de erste kerkgemeente te Jerusalem', *Rev. ecclés. de Liège* 35 (1948), 95–102, 172–80; E. L. Hicks, 'The Communistic Experiment of Acts 2 and 4', *Expos. Ser.* VII, Vol. I (1906), 21–32; S. Lyonnet, 'La κοινωνία de l'église primitive et la sainte église (Act. **2**.42-7)', *35 Congresso Eucharist. Internat., Sess. de estud.* I, Barcelona (1954), 511–15; Ph.-H. Menoud, 'Les Actes des Apôtres et l'Eucharistie', *RHPhr* 33 (1953), 21–36; J. Mircea, 'L'organisation de l'église et la vie des premiers chrétiens d'après les Actes des Apôtres', *Stud. Theol.* VII (1955), 64–92.

VERSE 42 leads to the following description of the situation which does indeed still speak of the new converts, but at the same time describes the life of all the faithful. According to Jeremias[1] and Bauernfeind, the original ritual of the Christian daily service is here depicted: 1. instruction by the Apostles, 2. contribution of offerings (cf. Acts 6.1), 3. solemn partaking of food together and 4. prayers; here the 'breaking of bread', an entirely novel manner of speaking,[2] denotes the whole of the Christians' communal meal: 'the non-Christian is not *meant* to understand what this is about.'

In our opinion the following considerations militate against this explanation: a) prayers do not constitute merely the conclusion of Christian worship; b) according to Acts 3.1 prayers are said by the Christians together with the Jewish congregation in the Temple; c) the summaries of Acts attempt to depict the whole of the Christians' way of life, hence the activities paired with καί probably represent detached and self-contained units: 1. the teaching of the Apostles[3] which, according to 4.48 and 5.21, 33, was not confined to the ritual meal but was also given in the Temple; 2. the κοινωνία was not limited to the offering of gifts in worship but embraced at least the entire collection and distribution of gifts in money and kind (see on 6.1ff.); 3. the κλάσις τοῦ ἄρτου[4] is the name for the Christians' communal meal. We scarcely have the beginnings of the *disciplina arcani* here—a community which transmits expressions which sound so thoroughly suspect to outsiders as 'This is my body' and 'This cup is the new covenant in my blood' (Luke 22.19f.), phrases which have aroused the suspicion of Thyestean banquets, does not yet show any inclination towards the *disciplina arcani*. Considering the simplicity of the ritual meal, consisting essentially of bread (and wine), it is not hard to imagine that its opening action might come to stand for the whole (Catholic exegesis finds here the *communio sub una*); 4. the prayers are above all those offered together with the Jewish congregation. This by no means precludes the possibility that the Christians also had their own prayers and set times for devotion; cf. Reicke, *Diakonie, Festfreude und Zelos*, 1951, 25–8.

VERSE 43: While verse 41 is slightly detached from the preceding narrative by μὲν οὖν, it is here that the first comprehensive summary[5] begins: its matter is taken from the summaries of Chapters 4 and 5.[6] πᾶσα ψυχή (i.e. 'everyone'),

---

[1] *Jesus als Weltvollender* (Beitr. zur Förd. chr. Theol. 33, no. 4), 1930, p. 78; *Die Abendmahlsworte Jesu*, 3rd edn. 1960, 60f. and 114ff. (ET *The Eucharistic Words of Jesus*, 1966, 66 and 118ff.) Similarly Wikenhauser, *Apg.* 45.

[2] *Eucharistic Words*, ²1966, 120 n. 1: 'the constantly repeated assertion that "breaking of bread" is an expression used in Jewish sources meaning "to have a meal" is an error that it seems to be impossible to eradicate'. But, as Jeremias himself admits (2nd edn., 64 n. 6), the opening ritual of the meal (blessing, breaking and distribution) may well be denoted by 'breaking of bread'.

[3] There was at first not yet a special order of διδάσκαλοι.

[4] κλάσις τοῦ ἄρτου also in Luke 24.35, the verb in Luke 24.30, Acts 20.7, 11 and 27.35.

[5] See Introduction § 7, p. 105 n. 1 above.

[6] The evidence is adduced in the general discussion, p. 193ff.

the LXX rendering of כָּל־בָּשָׂר, means here the surrounding non-Christians. φόβος: here, religious awe at the self-manifestation of the divine. The expression[1] 'many wonders and signs'[2] gives the reader the impression that the whole life of the primitive Church was filled with miracles.[3]

VERSES 44f. speak of the congregation as a whole: 'all those who believed, one and all'.[4] This sharing of property presupposes that possessions were *not* disposed of. κτήματα denotes property,[5] with or without buildings (see note on 4.34); ὑπάρξεις =goods and chattels. ἄν with the imperfect expresses habitual past action (Bl.-Debr. § 367). Whenever there is need of money for the poor of the congregation, one of the property-owners sells his piece of land or valuables, and the proceeds are given to the needy.[6]

VERSE 46: With one accord the Christians make daily attendance at the Temple, thus demonstrating that they have not forsaken the religion of their fathers[7] (Wendt, p. 101). On ὁμοθυμαδόν see note to 1.14. καθ' ἡμέραν applies also to κλῶντες: the implication here (as is borne out by the διακονία καθημερινή of 6.1) is that the Christian meals took place 'at home'—or in a number of houses. They are described as substantial repasts (τροφῆς) of which the Christians partook with simple piety and gladness.[8] The fact that this is

---

[1] This expression appears only in the first part of Acts: 2.19, 22, 43; 4.30; 5.12; 6.8; 7.36; 14.3; 15.2.

[2] The concrete miracles known to Luke are reported in 3.1–10; 5.1–11, 15; 9.32–11.18.

[3] After the second ἐγίνετο, ℵ A C vg pesh read; ἐν Ἰερουσαλήμ, φόβος τε ἦν μέγας ἐπὶ πάντας. This according to *Beg.* III, 24 is original, but may be rather a smoothing of the transition to verse 44, continued by an introductory καί.

[4] Here as in verse 47 (see p. 193 n. 4 below) Luke employs, as edifyingly 'biblical', the phrase ἐπὶ τὸ αὐτό, which recurrently renders יַחַד or יַחְדָּו in the Greek Psalter, viz. Psalms 2.2, 4.9(8), 19.10(9), 34.4(3), 37.38, 48.5(4), 49.11(10), 55.15(14), 71.10, 74.6, 74.8, 98.8, 102.23(22), 122.3 and 133.1.

[5] κτῆμα in 5.1 in interchangeable with χωρίον in 5.3 and 8.

[6] Since the text seems to suggest that every Christian was a property-owner, D alters verse 45 to run: καὶ ὅσοι κτήματα εἶχον . . .

[7] Certainly not merely, as Calvin and even Preuschen (p. 17) maintained, because the Temple offered the best opportunity for missionary work. See on 5.12b below.

[8] In *Die Abendmahlsworte Jesu* (2nd edn., 65 n. 4; this is lacking in the 3rd edn. ET) Jeremias suggests putting the comma after τροφῆς instead of after καρδίας: 'It was not the eating, but the praise of God, which proceeded with "gladness and singleness of heart".' This interpretation seems dubious in view of the resulting quasi-pleonasm, 'breaking bread . . . they partook of food', not to mention the following phrase, 'with rejoicing . . . praising God', which is no less tautological. Apart from that, the general construction suggests the usual punctuation: two co-ordinate participles preceding a main clause are balanced by two succeeding co-ordinate participles. The first pair establish time, place and circumstances; the second, relations with God and men. The main clause describes the way the believers took their communal meal—'with gladness and singleness of heart.' (The more sonorous ἐν ἀφελότητι καρδίας stands for the more usual ἐν ἁπλότητι καρδίας—*Beg.* IV, 30. Elsewhere too, Luke preferred longer to shorter expressions, even when they were not fully synonymous with what was meant: cf. Reicke, *Diakonie, Festfreude und Zelos,* Uppsala Universitets Årsskrift 1951, no. 5, 202ff.). Cf. Eklund, *D. Auge d. Einfalt,* 83ff.

emphasised leads one to suppose that by Luke's time these Christian communal meals had already incurred grave suspicion.[1]

VERSE 47: Other places in Luke's two books which mention the αἰνεῖν τὸν θεόν (Luke 2.13, 20; 19.37; Acts 3.8) are associated with the experience of God's helpful loving-kindness and saving grace, which may also therefore be assumed here. After the attitude towards God, the relation with men is described: the Christians are liked by the whole (Jewish) people.[2] Meanwhile God's favour is manifested in his daily addition[3] to the number of the saved.[4]

Research into the summaries has passed through two stages. During the first, which can be put roughly between 1890 and 1910, these reports had not yet been recognized as separate literary units. As with the speeches and narrative episodes, it was much more a question of deciding whether they derived from a historically reliable source (which, as reporting on the earliest congregation in Jerusalem, would necessarily be Jewish Christian) or from a worthless legendary source—or whether indeed the redactor had given himself free rein, for good or ill. In the absence of an accepted criterion for deciding what might have historical worth, judgments varied considerably. Harnack (*Beitr.* III, 144; ET) thought 2.41–7 belonged to the unreliable source B, whereas Sorof (p. 53) laid verses 43–7 at the door of the redactor, detecting only in verse 46 an item of genuine history. Others generally mistrusted verse 43 (miracles either belong to a legendary source or were inserted by the redactor!), while verse 46 invariably met a favourable reception. It was universally assumed of this passage, unless one agreed with Feine (pp. 171ff.) in ascribing it wholly to a Jewish Christian source, that it had been assembled from clearly distinguishable source-components, between which, likewise clearly delimited, stand the additions of the redactor.

[1] See also our comments on 20.8, p. 585 n. 3 below.

[2] 'The Jews' show no enmity to the Christians until 12.3. (D goes farther: the Christians find favour not only with the whole Jewish people but with all the world!)

[3] We find in σωζομένους yet another echo of the σωθήσεται of Joel 2.32 (Acts 2.21).

[4] Once again Luke has added, from the Greek Psalter (see p. 192 n. 4 above), the pious biblical reinforcement of ἐπὶ τὸ αὐτό ='all at once,' 'all together,' 'one and all.' The variants show that it was not long before readers failed to understand this phrase. In *The Composition and Date of Acts*, 10ff., Torrey develops the hypothesis that Luke misconstrued the Aramaic לחדא, which could mean 'together' but also, in South-Palestinian Aramaic, 'very', 'in high degree'. Thus Luke should have written: ὁ δὲ κύριος προσετίθει τοῖς σωζομένοις καθ᾽ ἡμέραν σφόδρα. This anything but illuminating text has made a curiously strong impression on scholars and is listed by De Zwaan (*Beg.* II, 50) among the 'decisive points.' On the other hand *Beg.* IV, 30 suggests that Luke had not yet made his final revision and had forgotten to add the number which should follow ἐπὶ τὸ αὐτό! But he is talking about the daily growth of the community, not some determinate total reached on a given date and expressible with a figure! What finally condemns Torrey's speculation is the pronouncement of M. Black in *An Aramaic Approach* . . . , 3rd edn., 10: 'The Aramaic adverb *lahda* could never be represented in Greek by ἐπὶ τὸ αὐτό; the Aramaic for Luke's Greek adverbial phrase is *kahda*'. Luke set ἐπὶ τὸ αὐτό at the end for reasons of rhythm, as the Septuagint also often does.

But in 1923 Dibelius inaugurated a new way of looking at these passages (prepared for by Schwartz in *NGG*, 1907, 282 n. 1) by recognizing that the writer Luke—like Mk **3**.10–12 already—generalized individual incidents and in this way introduced narrative episodes. This technique enabled Luke to indicate the general line of development even when he possessed no coherent tradition about it (*Studies* 7ff.).

Cadbury took this up in 1933 (*Beg.* V, 392–402) and demonstrated by exact analysis that Matthew and Luke boldly use the same Marcan summary more than once—the Chronicler once did the same with reports in the books of Kings. Cadbury saw that the summaries in Acts are interposed with both linking and separating effect between the individual stories, that they are later than the stories, and that they mostly turn on the generalization of some concrete detail of information. When they resemble one another, this can be attributed to Luke's well-known tendency to repeat with a difference; if however two similar summaries derive from the one written source, the second gives the place where the original stood in the source. From this standpoint Cadbury goes on to examine the relationship between **2**.42ff. and the summaries in Chapters 4 and 5.

Cadbury reaches no final conclusion as to whether Luke took over the summaries as part of his sources, or what is their historical worth. Each case must be taken on its merits.

At this point Jeremias and Cerfaux took up the problem almost simultaneously. Both claimed to have solved the riddle of the summaries. According to Jeremias (*ZNW* 36 (1937), 206f.) verses 41f. belong to the older body of material, verses 43–6 being a later expansion; a similar process was at work in the summaries of Chapters 4 and 5—in fact all three summaries underwent the same history. Though Cerfaux does not contradict this general conclusion, he interprets verses 41f. as Lucan redaction and sees the older material in verses 46 and 47a; on Chapters **4** and **5** he is broadly in accord with Jeremias (see *Eph. Theol. Lov.* 13 (1936), 673–80 and 16 (1939), 5ff.).

In 1950 Pierre Benoit criticized both these predecessors in his 'Remarques sur les "sommaires"' (cited in § 7, bibl., above). He too believes that the three summaries were subjected to the same process, but this he defines in a different way: a redactor, finding the summaries already attached to their respective contexts, has expanded each one in the light of the other two. So as not to endanger the connection, however, he made his interpolations in the middle. Thus **2**.43–5 was inserted in an older substratum (p. 4). The redactor responsible for this cannot have been Luke himself, who would not have impaired the passage, with its wholly Lucan stamp, by such an interpolation: the very language of it is alien to Luke—πᾶσα ψυχή occurs otherwise only in **3**.23, and there only as a Septuagint quotation; Luke constructs φόβος with ἐπί (Luke **1**.12, 65; Acts **5**.5, 11; **19**.17), prefers τὰ ὑπάρχοντα to the rarer ὑπάρξεις in Acts **4**.32 and eight times in his gospel, and employs διὰ χειρός or χειρῶν in **5**.12, **14**.3 and **19**.11 instead of the simple διά.

On closer inspection these arguments are less convincing than they at first appear. If one imagines verse 46 directly following verse 42, it is not a proper continuation but (with προσκαρτεροῦντες and κλῶντες … ἄρτον) a stylistically inadmissible repetition; it is therefore not feasible to excise verses 43–5 as editorial interpolation. Nor do the linguistic observations hold water. Luke was content to use the simple διά in Acts **2**.22 and **4**.16. Considering how characteristic of Acts is the exploitation of the Septuagint, it does not speak against but *for* Lucan authorship that πᾶσα ψυχή should derive from that source. τὰ ὑπάρχοντα in the Lucan *Sondergut* means property as a whole; hence here, harnessed to τὰ κτήματα, when it is a question of separate private possessions, it would have been out of place. Again, the Septuagint usually constructs φόβος with ἐπί, but also (and precisely in later writings), with a simple dative; it follows that πάσῃ ψυχῇ is still adequately explained by Luke's use of the Septuagint.

For these reasons we cannot follow Benoit but prefer to take another road. To us the summaries appear to flow entirely from the pen of Luke. At present we are concerned only with that in Chapter 2. Now Luke was too good a writer to allow Peter's second speech to tread on the heels of the first. He appears, however, to have been at a loss for an incident which occurred or might be presented as occurring in the interval. This circumstance suggested the idea of separating them with a representation of the life of the Christian community. The idea was the more attractive in the light of his wish not to deal with the Apostles alone, but to focus attention again and again on the community. Moreover an interim report of this kind served to inform the reader that between the first speech and the second there was a certain lapse of time—Luke scarcely ever specifies chronology with any greater exactitude.

The findings of Cadbury and Jeremias show that Luke possessed no special material for the passage under discussion. In content and form, verse 41a is related to (**4**.4), **8**.12 and **18**.8; verse 41b to **2**.47b, **4**.4, **5**.14, **6**.7, **11**.24b, **12**.24 and **16**.5; verse 42 to **1**.14 and **2**.46; verse 43a to **5**.5b and **5**.11; verse 43b to **5**.12a; verses 44f. to **4**.32 and **4**.34f.; verse 46a to **1**.14a and **5**.12b; verse 46b to **2**.42; verse 47a to (**4**.33?), **5**.13b; verse 47b to **5**.14. In other words, the material was furnished in essentials by the summary in Chapter 5; only verses 44f. were supplied from Chapter 4. Luke did not slavishly transcribe his own work, but at least slightly recast his formulations.

It is obvious that blocks acquired in this fashion cannot be built in without joints appearing. Yet Luke has succeeded in imposing a certain order. First he speaks of religious activities within the congregation (verse 42). Next he relates the religious awe which that awakens among outsiders, and this leads him to the miracles performed by the Apostles (verse 43). In verses 44f. he describes the religiously inspired social activity of the Christians.

Finally in verses 46f. he stresses their attendance in the Temple, their innocent ritual meals and the favourable impression they made on the Jewish people. The growth of the communion reflects the divine blessing that rests upon it.

We must wait until we come to Chapters 4 and 5 before discussing the historical value of the separate items of information, for from these chapters they derive.

8

ACTS 3:1–10
PETER HEALS A CRIPPLE

[1] Now Peter and John went up to the Temple at the hour of prayer, the ninth hour. [2] And a man lame from his mother's womb was carried, whom they laid daily at the gate of the Temple which is called Beautiful, to ask alms from those who were going into the Temple. [3] When he saw Peter and John about to go into the Temple, he asked for alms. [4] But Peter looked steadily at him, with John, and said, 'Look at us!' [5] And he fixed his attention upon them, expecting to receive something from them. [6] But Peter said, 'Silver and gold have I none; but what I have, that I give you. In the name of Jesus Christ of Nazareth, walk!' [7] And he took him by the right hand and raised him up. And immediately his feet and ankles grew strong, [8] and springing up he stood, and began to walk; and he entered with them into the Temple, walking and leaping and praising God. [9] And all the people saw him walking and praising God. [10] And they recognized him, that it was he who sat for alms at the Beautiful Gate of the Temple: and they were filled with wonder and amazement at what had happened to him.

Bibliography:

Lake, 'Localities in and near Jerusalem, 6: The Beautiful Gate', in *Beg.* V, 479–86; G. Schrenk, *ThWb* III (1938), 235f.: Jeremias, *ThWb* III, 173 n. 5 (with bibl.); E. Wiesenberg, 'The Nicanor Gate', *JJS* 3 (1952), 14–29; E. Stauffer, 'Das Tor des Nikanor' in *ZNW* 44 (1952/3), 44–66; Reicke 63–6; Trocmé 194f.; Conzelmann 32f.

T. W. Crafer, *The Healing Miracles in the Book of Acts*, London 1939; J. A. Hardon, 'The Miracle Narratives in the Acts of the Apostles', *CBQ* 16 (1954), 303–18.

VERSE 1: The story begins without any connective,[1] as if it were originally told separately and for its own sake. Peter and John are named, but John

---

[1] D felt that the absence of a connective was a defect and therefore added 'in these days.'

keeps silent.[1] The two disciples were going up[2] to the Temple[3] at the time of prayer, about three in the afternoon.[4] There the evening Tamid sacrifice was being offered up.

VERSE 2: 'And [5] a man, being[6] lame[7] from[8] his[9] mother's womb,[10] was being[11] carried by, whom they laid at the Beautiful Gate[12] of the Temple,

[1] Originally John must have been absent (Bauernfeind (p. 59); see on verse 4). According to Morgenthaler (*Die lukanische Geschichtsschreibung* I, 36) this pair of names represents a peculiarity of Lucan style, which follows a rule of two (on this point see Introduction § 2, p. 47 n. 4 above). Harnack roundly asserts that Luke 'smuggles' John 'in as a stowaway' (*Lukas der Arzt*, 107; ET *Luke the Physician*, 1907). Wellhausen's comments are even more disrespectful.

[2] 'The imperfect . . . ἀνέβαινον . . . conveys . . . a vivid impression' (Radermacher[2], 153): the process is unrolling before our eyes. 'They were on their way up,' as Wendt (102) would render it, is something different and would probably read ἦσαν ἀναβαίνοντες in Lucan Greek.

[3] In Exodus 29.39 the evening Tamid sacrifice is designated τὸ δειλινόν 'the afternoon one.' This probably accounts for D's addition here of the adverbial τὸ δειλινόν ='in the afternoon.'

[4] According to Daniel 6.10 and 9.21, one of the three hours of prayer coincided with the evening Tamid sacrifice, which was offered up at about the third hour after noon (Billerbeck II, 696–8). One may regard this time (the 'ninth hour') as in general the usual second time of prayer: it is admittedly a question only of custom, not of a binding prescription.

[5] Semitic narrative style, familiar to Luke from LXX. Do the words here show a trace of an ultimately Palestinian source, or has Luke chosen LXX style to relate events in Jerusalem?

[6] In Acts Luke twenty-five times prefers the more sonorous ὑπάρχειν to εἶναι.

[7] Cf. Acts 14.8.

[8] Healing stories readily stress that the suffering has lasted a long time or is inborn, as this goes to show the greatness of the miraculous power (cf. Bultmann, *Geschichte der synoptischen Tradition*[2], 236; ET *History of the Synoptic Tradition*[2], Oxford 1968, 221).

[9] The addition of the personal possessive, superfluous by Greek ideas, is once again Semitic and regular in LXX.

[10] In classical and medical Greek κοιλία denotes the digestive tract (*Beg.* IV, 31). Luke uses it for the womb, following LXX which thus renders בֶּטֶן.

[11] On the significance of the imperfect see n. on 3.1 above. The beggar would not be brought to the Temple only in the afternoon. Here again we detect that the note of time in verse 1 does not belong to the original story.

[12] Neither Josephus, who gives a detailed description of the Temple in *Ant.* XV 410–25 and *Bell.* V 190–221, nor the Mishnah (Middoth 1, 3f.; see Billerbeck II 260–5) mentions the 'Beautiful Gate'. Tradition has identified it since the fifth century with the Shushan Gate, which led on the east side into the Temple precincts, and remained standing after the sack of Jerusalem (*Beg.* V, 480 and 484f.). That would have been a poor pitch for a beggar. From all that Josephus and the Mishnah have to say, Nicanor's Gate is far more likely, but on its position there is no agreement among scholars. In his article τὸ ἱερόν, B (*ThWb* III, 230ff.), Schrenk advocates the opinion now customary, that the Beautiful Gate was the gate of Corinthian bronze (Josephus *Bell.* II 411, V 198 and 201–6, VI 293 =Nicanor's Gate) which led from the east from the Court of the Gentiles into the Court of the Women (whereas the Mishnah wrongly places this gate between the Court of the Women and that of the Men). Stauffer, on the other hand (*ZNW* 44 (1952/3), 44–66), has advanced the thesis that Josephus and the Mishnah can be reconciled, and Nicanor's Gate located on the east of the Court of the Men. If by τὸ ἱερόν Luke understood the Temple-complex exclusive of the Court of the Gentiles, he would imply that the Beautiful Gate lay

to ask alms[1] of those who were going into the Temple.' After the real 'protagonist' of the story has appeared in the person of Peter (basically of course it is the name of Christ which plays the principal role), his 'antagonist' is now introduced. Luke scarcely ever brings more than two persons or groups into confrontation: he makes do with quite a small scenario.

VERSE 3: Peter and John intend to enter the sanctuary[2] at the gate of which the beggar is sitting—Luke seems to imagine the Beautiful Gate at the entrance to the Court of the Women. The beggar sees the two coming and begins to ask alms.[3]

VERSE 4: Peter looks the beggar in the eye[4]—the way 'with John' is tacked on shows that this name was added subsequently—and invites him to look at them.[5]

VERSE 5: ἐπεῖχε,[6] to focus one's eyes upon (Bauer, *Wb* 565, 2a). The beggar has no suspicion of what is in store for him: he hopes to receive a valuable gift, at whose givers he is to look in order to call down God's blessing on them.

VERSE 6: Peter's words at first disappoint him: 'silver and gold'—just what a beggar hopes for—'have I none;[7] but what I have, that I give you!' Luke does not make Peter speak in the plural (nor does the act of healing itself have a plural subject): this once more goes to show that John is a late

---

between this court and that of the women. But it is by no means certain that we may assume in Luke our own knowledge of the Temple, let alone a better. Cf. also Billerbeck II, 620–5 and Lake (§ 8 bibl. above). Jeremias supports Stauffer's view: the Beautiful Gate lay on the east of the Court of the Men): see *Jerusalem zur Zeit Jesu*[2], Göttingen 1962, 185f. (ET *Jerusalem in the Time of Jesus*, 1969, 23 n., 117f.).

[1] To give alms was regarded as meritorious work: cf. Billerbeck I, 387f., and the excursus 'Die altjüdische Privatwohltätigkeit', No. 4.

[2] Billerbeck I, 150f.: τὸ ἱερόν =בֵּית הַמִּקְדָּשׁ designates the whole complex of buildings belonging to the sanctuary on the mount of the Temple; ὁ ναός =הֵיכָל is the Temple proper, comprising porch (אוּלָם), sanctum and holy of holies (דְּבִיר).' But Luke's text cannot be reconciled with this terminology.

[3] The infinitive after ἠρώτα (the imperfect probably indicates here the incompleteness of the action: Bl.-Debr. § 328) instead of ἵνα or ὅπως: Bl.-Debr. § 392, 1. Cf. Luke 5.3 and 8.37; Acts 10.48, 16.39, 18.20 and 23.18.

[4] Here, as in Acts 13.9, the looking is meant to establish the inner contact necessary for the miracle. ἀτενίζειν often appears in this sense in miracle-stories (*Beg.* IV, 33). This may perhaps have some connection with the fact that, from verse 3 onward, D switches the verbs of seeing in such a way that ἀτενίζειν has the beggar as its subject.

[5] Bauernfeind, p. 59: 'It is impossible to look fixedly in this way at two men at once. One must suppose that originally the story spoke of only *one* miracle-worker.'

[6] Understand τὸν νοῦν or τοὺς ὀφθαλμούς: the imperfect once again serves the purpose of vivid narration (see Bl.-Debr. § 327).

[7] According to Wendt (103) and Bauernfeind (60), Peter's saying here corresponds to 2.44f. on the Christians' lack of property. But the opposite is the case: Peter, be it remembered, had at his disposal the money set aside for the poor (Loisy, 224). Of course Luke might have assumed that this fund was reserved for the support of needy Christians. Probably, however, he did not consider the point with great exactitude.

addition. What then does Peter 'have'?—the plenary power to heal in the name of Jesus. That one should pronounce the miraculous ὄνομα in healings and conjurations was taken for granted by ancient thought[1] and is therefore part and parcel of the technique in accounts of healing miracles.[2] The ὄνομα (=proper name) is no chance attribute of the person, but expresses his very essence. Hence the power of the person named, be he human or divine, is itself present and available in the ὄνομα. Peter does not beg the exalted Jesus for healing, but releases the very power of healing through utterance of the name of Jesus Christ (whose identity is further defined by ὁ Ναζωραῖος). Cf. *ThWb* V, 242–81, with literature. Luke refers back to this utterance of Jesus' name in Acts **3**.16 and **4**.10. (Cf. also Matt. **10**.9.)

VERSE 7: The touch (πιάσας)[3] is added to the word; this is the channel through which the miraculous powers of the healer stream forth over the sick man.[4] βάσις is not a medical *terminus technicus*;[5] in Acts **14**.8–10, a parallel account, its place is taken by πούς. σφυδρόν[6] =ankles: not an exclusively medical term.

VERSE 8: ἐξαλλόμενος ἔστη καὶ περιεπάτει: 'springing up, he set foot firmly to the ground' (Bauer, *Wb* 755, II 1e) 'and walked about' (imperfect). Thus is the reality of the healing confirmed. The following words 'and he entered with them into the Temple', exhibit the un-Jewish use of ἱερόν and must be attributed to Luke, as must the subsequent phrase: περιπατῶν καὶ ἀλλόμενος κτλ. Here ἄλλεσθαι no longer refers to the initial springing-up of the lame man: it means that he 'leapt like a hart', thus fulfilling the prophecy of Isaiah **35**.6: ἀλεῖται ὡς ἔλαφος ὁ χωλός. The point of his passing through the gate is shown in the sequel (v. 11).

VERSES 9f.: These two verses contain the closing formula normal in such stories of healing: all the people acknowledge in amazement the reality of the miracle, which is thereby raised beyond all doubt. All see the man that was lame pass into the Temple, and hear him praising God. Because they recognize that he truly is the beggar who used to sit for alms at the Beautiful Gate, they are overcome with θάμβος, the awe felt in the presence of divine activity (cf. *ThWb* III 5–7), and ἔκστασις: man is lifted out of his habitual life and

---

[1] Cf. Mark **9**.38f. and Luke **10**.17, and see Billerbeck I, 36.

[2] Cf. Bietenhard's article ὄνομα in *ThWb* V, 242–81 (with bibl.) esp. 276f. We may add that, in cases like the present, the ὄνομα Ἰησοῦ offers a parallel to the יהרה שֵׁם. If no name is invoked in the case of Jesus' own healings, this is unusual but understandable: the healer here possesses divine powers in himself.

[3] Physical contact is also frequently mentioned in the miracle stories in the Gospels: see Bauernfeind, p. 60, and Bultmann, *Geschichte der synoptischen Tradition*, 2nd ed., 237f. (ET *History of the Synoptic Tradition*[2], 1968).

[4] Cf. Mark **5**.27f., 30; Acts **5**.15 and **19**.12.

[5] Originally the word meant 'step' or 'pace', then—at first in tragedy, later in such writers of 'poetic' prose as Apollodorus and Philostratus—'foot' (*Beg*. IV 33f.).

[6] Later MSS. replace it by the more usual form σφυρά. Cf. Cadbury, *The Making of Luke-Acts*, 119 and *Beg*. IV, 33f.

thought by encountering the power of God (see Bauer, *Wb* 485). Thus not merely the healing itself, but also the human reaction to it—in both the man healed and the spectators—belong to the realm of such accounts (cf. Dibelius, *Die Formgeschichte des Evangeliums,* 2nd edn., 54f.; ET *From Tradition to Gospel,* 1937).

Long before Luke appeared on the scene, the Christians must have recounted to each other the story of Peter's healing of the lame man. What kind of story did Luke find to hand? What alterations did he make? He gave Peter a silent companion in John—it must be two witnesses of Jesus who later stand before the High Council (4.20); Peter and John also appear together in Luke 22.8 and Acts 8.14ff. Similarly the exact note of time in verse 1 hardly belongs to the original story. That the beggar, having seen the two Apostles coming (verse 3), should nevertheless be invited to 'Look at us!' (verse 4) also suggests a re-working of the material. Again, since verses 3 and 5 both end with the word λαβεῖν, verses 4f. have the effect of an intercalation using the well-known technique whereby the insertion closes on the same word as the older text. But if σὺν τῷ Ἰωάννῃ (verse 4) derives from Luke, may we not infer that the rest of verse 4 (and hence also verse 5) already lay before him? The argument is not irresistible: Luke could not very well have the Apostles address the beggar in unison, especially as Peter remained the real miracle-worker; the necessity of clearly bringing out his position as such was enough to suggest and account for the present form of words. Bauernfeind (p. 60) considers it possible that Luke himself inserted in verse 6 the words, 'Silver and gold have I none; but what I have, that I give you.' The slight conflict between this verse and 2.44f. (see n. 7 on v. 6) by no means precludes Luke's having himself conceived this impressive antithesis. These words indeed introduce a theme wholly extraneous to the healing story. Here the original account would simply have reported that Peter took the cripple by the hand and said to him: 'In the name of Jesus Christ of Nazareth, walk!' Many scholars have felt verse 8 to be overloaded. Feine (p. 174) looked on 8b-10 as an editorial addition. Spitta (p. 77) considered verses 8a and 9f. as secondary. Jüngst, finally, (pp. 38ff.) regarded as editorial expansion not only the words from ἠρώτα in verse 3 to ὁ δέ in verse 5, but also those from περιπατῶν (verse 8) to συμβεβηκότι αὐτῷ. In both cases he correctly sensed the difficulty, but attempted to remedy it by too drastic an operation. In verse 8 it is rather καὶ εἰσῆλθεν . . . τὸν θεόν which should be laid at the author's door. Verse 10 as the typical conclusion to a healing story belongs to the ancient miracle-story.

If, then, we have correctly assessed the various clues to Lucan revision, the story available to Luke recounted a miracle of healing which is very similar to that in Acts 9.32–5 and, like it, depicts the healing power of the saviour Jesus as a means of awakening faith.

H

Luke's contribution was to present the two arch-Apostles appearing together, even if Peter remains the real protagonist. Luke also takes pains to represent the inner contact resulting from the exchange of fixed regards between Peter and the beggar. The contrast between the silver and gold which Peter lacks and the gift in his power makes clear the surpassing value of what is peculiarly the Christians' possession: the healing power of the name of Jesus Christ. But for Luke this theme forms part of a wider context, which is precisely why he has introduced the story at this point: it paves the way not only for the following speech by Peter, linked to the healing, but also for the consequent arrest and inquisition. For at the trial Peter, by referring to the healed cripple, will be able to declare impressively that only in the name of Jesus is σωτηρία given to men (4.12).

Finally it is not impossible that, over and above the foregoing considerations, Luke already had in mind the charges against the *nomen Christianum* which we find discussed at official level in Pliny's correspondence with Trajan. In this case Luke's ends as an apologist would also be served.

According to Bauernfeind (p. 60) the present story in no way differs basically from Jewish and pagan miracle-stories, except that it is Jesus' name, and no other, which stands at its centre. But before we may discuss the theological problem here raised, we shall have to see the use which Luke makes of the story in Chapters 3 and 4.

9

ACTS 3:11–26
PETER'S SPEECH BEFORE THE TEMPLE

[11] As he clung to Peter and John, all the people ran together to them in the portico called Solomon's, greatly wondering. [12] When Peter saw it, he began to speak to the people: 'Men of Israel, why do you marvel at this man? or why do you fasten your eyes on us, as if by our own power or godliness we had made him walk? [13] The God of Abraham and Isaac and Jacob, the God of our fathers, has glorified his Son Jesus, whom you delivered up and denied before the face of Pilate, when he had decided to release him. [14] But you denied the holy and righteous one, and asked that a murderer be granted to you. [15] The author of life you killed, whom God raised from the dead; whereof we are witnesses. [16] And on the ground of faith in his name this man, whom you see and know, his name has made strong; and the faith awakened through it (the name) has given him this perfect soundness in the presence of you all. [17] And now, brethren, I know that you did it in ignorance, as did also your rulers. [18] But what God proclaimed beforehand by the mouth of all the prophets, that his Anointed should suffer, he thus fulfilled. [19] Repent therefore, and turn again, that your sins may be blotted out, [20] that so there may come seasons of refreshing from the presence of the Lord; and that he may send the Christ appointed for you, that is, Jesus: [21] whom the heaven must receive until the time when everything will be established which God spoke by the mouth of his holy prophets from of old. [22] Moses indeed said, "A prophet shall the Lord God raise up for you from among your brethren, like unto me; to him shall you listen in everything that he may say to you. [23] And it shall be, that every soul which does not listen to that prophet shall be utterly destroyed from among the people." [24] And all the prophets from Samuel and those who followed, as many as have spoken, they also proclaimed these days. [25] You are the sons of the prophets, and of the covenant which God made with your fathers, saying to Abraham, "And in thy seed shall all the families of the earth be blessed." [26] To you first God sent his Son when he caused him to arise, blessing you, if you turn each one of you away from his sins'.

Bibliography:

Silva New, 'The Name, Baptism and Laying-on of Hands', *Beg.* V, 121–40 (on 3.16); Jeremias, *ThWb* IV, 862–4 (on 3.22f.); W. D. Davies, *Paul and*

Rabbinic Judaism (1948), 276–84 (on **3**.13); Dodd, *According to the Scriptures* (1952), 52–6 (on **3**.22f.); J. Schmitt, 'L'Eglise de Jérusalem ou la "Restauration" d'Israël', *RevScR* 27 (1953), 209–18, esp. 212ff. (on **3**.11–26); J. Dupont, 'L'utilisation apologétique de l'Ancien Testament dans les discours des Actes', *Anal. Lov. Bibl. & Orient.*, Sér. II, fasc. 40, esp. 292ff. and 321ff. (on **3**.22f.); C. F. D. Moule, *Exp.Tim.* 65 (1953/4), 220 (on **3**.16); E. Schweizer, *Erniedrigung und Erhöhung* (1955), 81–6 (on **3**.13) (ET *Lordship and Discipleship*, SBT 28); Reicke 66–71; Trocmé 110f., 192 and 270f.

J. A. Duplacy, 'A propos d'une variante "occidentale" des Actes des Apôtres (**3**.11)', *Rev. des Etud. Augustiniennes* 2 (1956), 231–42; J. A. T. Robinson, 'The most primitive Christology of all? (Acts **3**.12–26)', *JTS* 7 (1956), 177–89; J. E. Ménard, '"Pais Theou" as a Messianic Title in The Book of Acts', *CBQ* 19 (1957), 83–92; U. Wilckens, *Die Missionsreden der Apg.*², Neukirchen 1963, 37–44, 60f., 127–31, 153–6, 163–70, 189–93; U. Holzmeister, 'Num et quomodo docente S. Petro (Act. **3**.19a; II Petr. **3**.12) parusiam accelerare possimus', *Verb. Domini* 20 (1940), 129–38; J. W. Doeve, 'Apokatastasis in Act. **3**.21, een voorbereiding?', *Vox Theol.* 18 (1947–8), 165–9; M. Jonghe, 'De Apokatastasis Pantoon in Handelingen **3**.21', *Vox Theol.* 18 (1947–8), 68–71; J. Dupont, 'La conversion dans les Actes des Apôtres', *Lumière et Vie* 47 (1960), 48–70; Id., 'Repentir et conversion d'après les Actes des Apôtres', *Sciences ecclés.* 12 (Montréal 1960), 137–73; H. Sahlin, 'Tillförståelsen av två ställen i Apostlagärningarna (**3**.20; **8**.23)', *SEÅ* 22–3 (1957–8), 127–36; Ménard, *Sacra Pagina* 11, 314ff.

VERSE 11: The healed man clutches the Apostles with a firm grasp, thus informing the crowd running from all sides, who have not of course seen the actual working of the miracle before the gate, to whom he owes his cure.[1] The setting in 'Solomon's portico'—it was there, according to **5**.12, that the Christians used to foregather—is intended to heighten the local colour. But this portico lay on the outer side of Nicanor's Gate.[2] Luke evidently enjoyed no direct personal knowledge of the Temple; his topology is therefore incompatible with Josephus and the Mishnah. Luke has taken ἔκθαμβοι (the plural refers, κατὰ σύνεσιν, to λαός) from θάμβος in verse 10.

VERSE 12: Seeing the people's astonishment, Peter grasps the opportunity to address them. ἀπεκρίνατο (LXX uses it for עָנָה) means 'to launch into speech'. ἄνδρες Ἰσραηλῖται: see on **2**.22 above. Whether ἐπὶ τούτῳ is taken to be neuter or, what is probably more correct, masculine (for the ex-cripple is mentioned immediately before and after), it is the healing which in either case

---

[1] We can see from the style the trouble it gave Luke to connect the sermon with the transmitted healing story. According to Bauernfeind (p. 62), the speech in Luke's source was perhaps only loosely attached and without any fresh indication of setting. But what Bauernfeind regards as a survival of older material will prove in fact to be Lucan composition.

[2] Hence D, with good local knowledge at his disposal, has the beggar and the Apostles pass out again through the gate (Dibelius, *Studies* 85). According to Bruce (p. 106) the Western text, though not original, yet describes what really happened!

is the object of the amazement. In itself such amazement is thoroughly justifiable; it is to be deprecated only when it means no more than the following parallel statement: 'Why do you look on us as if by our own power or godliness we had made him walk?' But that the 'multitude should imagine that a miracle . . . had been performed unaided by the extraordinary powers of a human being,' says Bauernfeind, (p. 63) 'is most unlikely'. Luke must have introduced the idea 'by our own power' simply as a contrast to the act of God which he really wished to stress.[1] The implication of ἢ εὐσεβείᾳ[2] is probably that the Apostles have not influenced the deity by their own piety either, and thus caused the healing indirectly.

VERSE 13: The thought is: 'It is not we who have made this man well, but God through Jesus, who has thereby been glorified.' Peter expresses this in biblical terms. The designation of God derives from Exodus 3.6, 15. ἐδόξασεν τὸν παῖδα αὐτοῦ refers to Isaiah 52.13 LXX: ὁ παῖς μου δοξασθήσεται. The glorification which Luke has in mind is not that of the resurrection but that of the miracle performed in Jesus' name.[3] It was from Jewish prayers, in which great men of God, especially David, were called God's παῖς (= עֶבֶד), that the Christians adopted the term for application to Jesus (see above, 186); Luke treats it as a formal expression for 'Son of God'.[4] Peter goes on to speak of Jesus in a series of antitheses of Lucan rhetoric. ὃν ὑμεῖς μὲν παρεδώκατε: the matching δέ and the clause 'but God has raised him up'

---

[1] Bauernfeind asks (p. 63) whether Luke has not here transplanted the scene of 14.11 into a Jewish context. It was of course out of the question for him to attribute to the Jews the opinion that the Apostles were divine beings. Thus (the suggestion goes) he hit upon the attenuating phrase 'by our own powers,' without noticing that this drew him into new difficulties. Gewiess, *Die urapostolische Heilsverkündigung nach der Apostelgeschichte* (Breslau 1939), 48 offers a different interpretation: 'It is not a question whether God or the Apostles have caused the miracle, but whether it has been mediated through the Apostles or through Jesus.' But the marvelling crowd do not of course yet know that the miracle was accomplished through the name of Jesus: they know only that it was performed by the Apostles. That the act of God was mediated in the first place through the name of Jesus, and in the second by the Apostles, Luke understandably does not here explain: he is not writing dogmatics.

[2] Bauer, *Wb* 645, cites I Clem. 32.4: 'We are not justified by our wisdom or insight or εὐσεβείᾳ.' In h vg codd pesh arm this difficult word is replaced by ἐξουσίᾳ (*potestate*); Irenaeus left it out (*Beg.* III, 28).

[3] The resurrection is not mentioned until verse 15; it would in any case be nonsense for the statement 'It is not we who have healed this man' to be followed by 'but God raised Jesus.'

[4] On the problem of παῖς θεοῦ see Jeremias, *ThWb* V, 676–713 (ET *Servant of God*, *SBT*). He sees in Acts 3 and 4 'a stratum of tradition marked at other points also by its antiquity' (p. 699). Cf. Martin Rese, 'Nachprüfung einiger Thesen von Joachim Jeremias zum Thema des Gottesknechts in Judentum,' *ZThK* 60 (1963), 21–41, and E. Haenchen, 'Die frühe Christologie,' *ZThK* 63 (1966), 132 n. 16. For the disignation of Jesus as παῖς, see the eucharistic prayer in Didache 9.2f. and 10.2f., the great prayer in I Clem. 59.2–4, the prayer of Mart. Polycarp 14.1, the doxology *ibid.* 20.2, and Barnabas 6.1 and 9.2. Here παῖς κυρίου or τοῦ παιδός μου is added to citations from Isaiah 50.8f. or Jer. 7.27f., Ps. 33.13 and Exodus 15.26.

do not follow as expected. παραδιδόναι is an old technical term of the primitive kerygma: I Cor. **11.**23 (where it means 'delivered over by God'); for Luke it signifies 'delivery into the hands of men', the Romans. ἀρνέομαι ='refuse', 'reject' (see *ThWb* I, 468–71); its opposite is ἐξομολογοῦμαι. The Jews, in the presence of Pilate and in contrast to him, refused to Jesus the acknowledgement they owed, although the governor had decided to release him.[1]

VERSE 14: This is an allusion to the Barabbas episode (Luke **23.**18ff.), as is proved by the new ἀρνεῖσθαι-clause; here the messianic epithets of 'holy' and 'righteous' one[2] are attached to Jesus. In antithesis to the holy and righteous man whom the Jews rejected stands the murderer[3] whose release they entreated and obtained.

VERSE 15: To this murderer is now opposed the ἀρχηγὸς τῆς ζωῆς,[4] who as the first raised up assures his own of resurrection, and consequently 'life'.[5] That the Jews killed this man contrasts again with the statement, which properly must bear the strongest emphasis, that 'God raised him from the dead'.[6] This time the statement is corroborated not, as in Peter's first sermon, by scriptural proof, but by the testimony of the eyewitnesses, the Apostles: 'whereof we are witnesses'. With this the sermon has returned again to the kerygma.

---

[1] Here Luke takes up again the later tradition presented in Luke **23.**4, 14f., 20 and 23, according to which Pilate found Jesus innocent and wished to release him, so that the guilt was thrown entirely on the Jews. Did the primitive community interpret Isaiah **53.**8, ἡ κρίσις αὐτοῦ ἤρθη, in the sense that Pilate acquitted Jesus?

[2] According to Acts **7.**52, the prophets foretold the coming of 'the righteous one'. In the Similitudes of Ethiopic Enoch, **38.**2 and **53.**6 (**47.**1 and 4 are of doubtful value), the Messiah is named 'the righteous,' though generally he is here called 'the chosen one.' The messianic community is constantly described as 'the chosen righteous' or 'the righteous,' or 'the community of the holy and chosen.' In Matt. **10.**41, is δίκαιος a title for the ordinary Christian believer? For ἅγιος as a predicate of the Messiah, cf. ὁ ἅγιος τοῦ θεοῦ in Mark **1.**24, Luke **4.**34 and John **6.**69.

[3] Cf. Luke **23.**19, 25, also Luke **5.**8 (ἀνὴρ ἁμαρτωλός) and **24.**19 (ἀνὴρ προφήτης).

[4] While Bruce (109) understands ἀρχηγὸς τῆς ζωῆς as 'author of life,' Wendt (104) and Loisy (231) take ἀρχηγὸς to mean 'leader.' Since however 'leader (or commander) *of* life' makes little sense, they assume with Bauernfeind (63) the meaning 'leader *to* life'. Delling, *ThWb* V, 485f., understands ἀρχηγὸς in the Greek sense of the patron-hero of a city or other community; Christ is the eponymous hero of the Christians, who share the destiny of their saviour-hero, i.e. his resurrection. Since ἀνάστασις ζωῆς (John **5.**29) is equivalent to ἀνάστασις εἰς ζωήν (II Macc. **7.**14 LXX), it is also possible to find in the present phrase the genitive of direction (Bl.-Debr. §166).

[5] Outside the NT, the association of Jesus and 'life' is to be found in Didache **9.**3 (linked with the παῖς-formula), Barnabas **1.**4 and **12.**5, Ignatius *Magn.* **9.**2 and *Trall.* **9.**2. (cited Bultmann, *ThWb* II, 866, n. 291). That we have a liturgical formula before us in this verse 15 is shown by σωτῆρα καὶ ἀρχηγὸν τῆς ἀφθαρσίας in the closing prayer of II Clem. **20.**5, and ἀρχηγὸν τῆς σωτηρίας in Hebr. **2.**10 (see Introduction § 1, VIII above). It is this kind of ἀρχηγὸς τῆς ζωῆς that Jesus proved to be himself in the healing of the lame man.

[6] On this early traditional formula, see on **2.**24 above.

VERSE 16: 'On the ground of faith in his name his name has made this man strong[1] ... and the faith awakened through it' (the name) 'has given him this perfect soundness': here the healing is solemnly described in a dual statement, comprising a *parallelismus membrorum*, which brings into prominence the importance of faith, *scil.* on the part of the sick man. The name is ineffective unless faith in it is present, but on the other hand it is the name preached by Peter which enables the faith to come into being. The significance of faith is stressed, of course, because the context is that of an 'appeal preached with missionary intent' (Bauernfeind, p. 64). There is no reason to assume the activity of a redactor.[2]

VERSE 17: With 'and now, brethren' begins a new section in a new tone: Peter addresses his audience as 'brothers', as if they were already Christians. There is no need for any religious barrier to arise; it is not too late for everything to be put right. For the grave guilt of the Jews underlined in verses 13f. is—in modern terms—subjectively speaking not so great: it is a sin of ignorance. The Jews did not know what they did.[3] This assertion admittedly comes as something of a surprise after 2.22: Jesus through his miracles had been sufficiently marked out by God—how can one still speak of ἄγνοια?[4] By way of answer one may refer to the fact that Luke took up traditions of various kinds which were not always devoid of contradictions; but of that he was not sensible. Basically, the situation is no different in the congregation of today. If behind a statement we sense an empirical truth, we do not allow ourselves to be distracted by its incongruity with another similarly justified statement. In sum, then, the ἄγνοια here counts as an exculpation.

VERSE 18: Without any ostensible connection, this exculpation is joined by another, framed with evident caution: 'So by God's will it had to come to

---

[1] ἐστερέωσεν refers back to ἐστερεώθησαν αἱ βάσεις αὐτοῦ in verse 7. Torrey's assumption (op. cit., 14ff.) that Luke made a mistake in translation, having read תָּקְף שָׁמֵה for שָׁמֵה תָּקְף (ὑγιῆ ἐποίησεν αὐτόν), is therefore out of place.

[2] Preuschen (p. 20) wanted to exclude verse 16b as an expansion. Loisy assumed as Lucan only 'Him, whom ye see and know, has his name set upon his feet.'

[3] The logion contained in many MSS of the third gospel, 'Father, forgive them, for they know not what they do' (23.24), already asserts this point of view. The thought will return in Acts 13.27 and 17.30. Wendt (p. 105) points to its OT basis in Lev. 22.14 and Num. 15.22–31 (unwitting sins). Bauernfeind (p. 63) supposes that the indictment and exoneration of the Jews expressed respectively in verses 15 and 17 were given to Christian missionaries as an aid in their work, and that Luke was here transposing such material into *oratio recta*. However that may be, it is doubtless correct to suggest that Luke was not the first to develop the thought but received it from tradition.

[4] Here the σκάνδαλον τοῦ σταυροῦ is threatening to vanish. In truth, of course, the real guilt lies precisely in the ἄγνοια: if men had not hardened their heart against God, they would have recognised Jesus. Only so does it become plain that in the Cross our guilt is revealed. The stressing of the fact that even the Jewish ἄρχοντες shared the ἄγνοια has nothing in common with I Cor. 2.8. According to Paul it was the blinded spiritual powers who did not recognize Jesus. The Jewish authorities of whom Luke is speaking are not the ἄρχοντες τοῦ αἰῶνος τούτου, and Luke certainly does not intend to call them blinded here.

pass.' For God had declared through the mouth[1] of all the prophets[2] that the Messiah would die (on παθεῖν see on **1**.3). This prophecy and the eternal will manifest in it have now been fulfilled.

VERSE 19: Both concepts, μετανοέω[3] and ἐπιστρέφω, whether separately or combined, can express the 'turning'[4] which leads a Gentile[5] or Jew[6] to God and to faith in the κύριος Ἰησοῦς. Since God offers the possibility of such a change of heart,[7] Peter and John can call on men to return. Where, as in the present verse, the two concepts are found together, μετανοεῖν will express more the turning away from evil, ἐπιστρέφειν on the other hand the positive new direction, the turning to God and his κύριος (cf. **20**.21), and the new way of life (**26**.20). This conversion leads to 'life' (**5**.31), to the forgiveness of sins (**3**.19, **5**.31). This last ensues, like the bestowing of the Holy Spirit, in baptism (**2**.38). (For πρὸς τό with the infinitive, cf. Luke **18**.1 and see Moulton, p. 218.)

VERSE 20: But the 'turning' also has a significance beyond the individual's relationship with God. If the Jews turn from their old ways, there will come 'seasons of refreshing'[8] from the presence of the Lord'[9] (i.e. God), and God will send the Messiah Jesus forechosen[10] for the Jews. Thus the conversion will also hasten the Parousia—cf. II Peter **3**.12.[11]

VERSE 21: Until then heaven must be the home of Jesus. The text does not mean that Jesus is in heaven 'only temporarily' (so Preuschen, p. 21), but accounts for the delay of the Parousia, which is attributed to the will of God. In place of the Parousia concept we find another eschatological term: that of the 'restitution', the realisation of all prophetic promises, which is at the same time a restoration of the original order of creation (see Oepke, *ThWb* I, 390f.). The χρόνοι ἀποκαταστάσεως πάντων will descend upon the faithful as καιροὶ ἀναψύξεως. ὧν refers not to χρόνων (so Bauernfeind p. 69) but to πάντων (Oepke, loc. cit.). ἐλάλησεν κτλ. is a nearly verbatim repetition

---

[1] Another LXX locution.

[2] The Christians saw the prophets as one great company united in foretelling the 'sufferings of the Messiah' in accordance with the will of God (Wendt 105, Bauernfeind 65). Loisy (233) refers to Luke **24**.44 and Acts **10**.43.

[3] See Behm-Würthwein, *ThWb* V, 972–1004; for Acts, p. 999.

[4] שוב: see also Billerbeck I, 165–72.

[5] See Acts **11**.18, 21, **14**.15 and **17**.30.

[6] See Acts **2**.38, **5**.31, **9**.35, **20**.21 and **28**.27. Both terms appear together in **3**.19 and **26**.20.

[7] **5**.31 and **11**.18 must be understood in this sense.

[8] Bauernfeind (p. 68) sees them as moments of relief in the distress of the Messianic Woes. But the two promises are complementary statements about one and the same event. ἀνάψυξις derives from Exodus **8**.11 LXX.

[9] Not a 'marked Semitism' (so Bauernfeind, p. 68) but a locution frequent in LXX: cf. Acts **5**.41 and **7**.45.

[10] Contrary to etymology, Luke doubtless took the word in a temporal sense: see προκαταγγέλλειν (**3**.18), προορίζειν (**4**.28) and προχειροτονεῖν (**10**.41) (*Beg.* IV. 37f.).

[11] δεῖ ὑπάρχειν ἐν ἁγίαις ἀναστροφαῖς καὶ εὐσεβείαις προσδοκῶντας καὶ σπεύδοντας τὴν παρουσίαν.

of Luke **1**.70: the expression is therefore one which made a special appeal to Luke;[1] cf. Tobit **4**.12 LXX.

VERSE 22: The difficulty of this verse consists in the fact that although certain prophecies are specified, they refer not to the second but to the first coming of Jesus. The verse makes its connection not with verse 21 but with verse 19a, resuming the exhortation to repentance by establishing its biblical authority. Thus Deut. **18**.15, 18[2] is explained as referring to Jesus, who is the 'prophet like Moses' foretold. Everything he says must be heeded—and he is now speaking through his Apostles ...

VERSE 23: Every person who does not heed this prophet will be 'destroyed from among the people': the Jew who does not turn to Christ is no longer a member of God's people! Hereby the listeners are confronted with what is at stake for them. The idea that the Christians are the true Israel is here brought into sharp relief, though formulated in other, biblical terms (Lev. **23**.29).

VERSE 24: Now that Moses' prophecy of the Messiah has been adduced, the later prophets are summarily mentioned. But two ideas are telescoped and thereby create a *crux interpretum*: 1. all the prophets from Samuel onwards, and 2. all the prophets, Samuel and those that followed (Wendt, p. 108). All the prophets that have spoken[3] (even these apparently redundant words belong to the solemn style for which Luke is here striving) have also announced this day. Which does not imply that the Christians must have found a Messianic passage to hand in every single prophet.

VERSE 25: The listeners are the sons of the prophets and of the covenant of Abraham,[4] which is described with expressions from Gen. **12**.3 and **22**.18. πάντα τὰ ἔθνη (Gen. **22**.18), however, was something that Luke could not say without anticipating the story of Cornelius. πᾶσαι αἱ πατριαί[5] τῆς γῆς can be understood in the sense of 'all the tribes of the country'; they will all be blessed in the σπέρμα Ἀβραάμ (=Christ).[6] υἱοὶ τῆς διαθήκης echoes Ezek. **30**.5.

VERSE 26: If ἀναστῆσαι here meant 'to resuscitate', one could translate: 'to you God has raised his Son from the dead as the first so raised'.[7] But

---

[1] ἀπ' αἰῶνος (Gen. **6**.4 LXX and elsewhere) is as hyperbolical as ἀφ' ἡμερῶν ἀρχαίων in Acts **15**.7; cf. Acts **15**.18, and Méhat, *Vig. Chr.* 10 (1956) 196ff.

[2] On the interpretation of this passage, see Jeremias, *ThWb* IV, 862–4.

[3] The peculiar reading of D, ὃ ἐλάλησαν, arose through the influence of the Latin text d, *quodquod locuti sunt*, which itself results from the misunderstanding of *quotquot locuti sunt* (as in h) (see *Beg.* III, 32f.).

[4] Here the word 'sons' hovers between two meanings: the Jews are the descendants of those with whom God made the covenant of grace, and therefore also 'belong' to the covenant as 'sons of the covenant'. (On ἧς for ἥν, see notes to 1.2.)

[5] LXX rendering of מִשְׁפְּחוֹת.

[6] Originally Gen. **12**.3 and **22**.18 meant by this expression that the peoples outside the law would come to regard the blessing of the 'seed,' i.e. of Abraham's descendants, as the highest and would bless themselves by it—'Be thou blessed as Abraham is blessed!'

[7] Cf. Acts **26**.23: πρῶτος ἐξ ἀναστάσεως νεκρῶν.

here in fact, echoing verse 22,[1] ἀναστῆσαι designates the sending of Jesus to the earth. Hence we must translate: 'Unto you God has first caused his Son[2] to arise, blessing[3] you, if every one of you turn from his sins (πονηριῶν)' (see verse 19).[4]

With this appeal to the hearers and invitation to conversion, this missionary sermon comes to its intrinsic close.

Once again, the primitive Christian kerygma is the basis of the speech. But it is combined with other ideas: 1. a consideration of the occasion of the speech, the miracle (verses 12 and 13a); 2. an exposition of the significance of faith (verse 16); 3. expansion of the scriptural proof (verses 22f. and 25b). The Apostle speaks throughout in solemn terms (especially in verses 16, 20f. and 24), whose elevated tone is not always, for us, united with the utmost clarity. Hence the immediate effect of the speech is somewhat opaque.

It exhibits a style quite different from that of the Pentecost sermon. This is partly due to the reduction of scriptural quotation. But verses 13b to 15 bring, in a manner hitherto unencountered in Acts, a number of reiterated antitheses which do not contain any Semitic relative clauses, but rather confront the reader with Greek rhetoric.

To the striking peculiarities of style are added singularities of content, such as the idea of the hastening of the second advent through the conversion of the Jews and the conception, elsewhere absent, of the καιροὶ ἀναψύξεως.

For all these difficulties Bauernfeind (pp. 66f.) has suggested a radical solution: in connection with Jewish eschatological expectations there developed a word of admonition and comfort that spoke of Elijah as the Messianic person and ran, more or less, as follows: 'Times of relief are coming; God will be sending Elijah who is waiting ready to do his work; as the scripture says, he is now in heaven (i.e. in no lesser place) until he comes to accomplish his task; it is he who will come as the prophet like Moses who has been foretold; thus shall be fulfilled all that the prophets have spoken from of old; thus shall be fulfilled the promise made to Abraham' (p. 67). This text, according to Bauernfeind, was appropriated by disciples of Jesus who identified their master with Elijah; the Messianic community of Jesus inherited this Christianized text, and 'long before Luke ... it had been transformed' as a matter of course from an Elijah-text into a 'Χριστὸς' Ἰησοῦς-text'. Finally Luke made use of it to expand Peter's sermon in verses 20–25.

Bauernfeind can appeal to two facts in support of his bold construction. One is that verse 21 mentions the ἀποκατάστασις πάντων which Malachi

---

[1] Bauernfeind, p. 71. ἀπέστειλεν decides the matter.
[2] παῖς αὐτοῦ refers back to verse 13.
[3] εὐλογοῦντα echoes ἐνευλογηθήσονται in verse 25.
[4] Despite the word-order, ἕκαστος and ὑμῶν belong together. There is no means of telling whether B's omission of the troublesome word ὑμῶν is intentional or due to a scribal error. Cf. p. 78f. above.

4.5f. ascribes to Elijah. The other is that there was in Judaism an expectation of Elijah which had manifold ramifications and has left traces even in the New Testament (see Jeremias, *ThWb* II, 930–43). But in Acts **1.**6 Luke has already attributed the ἀποκαθιστάνειν to Jesus, and here probably nobody will assume an underlying Jewish document on the subject of Elijah. For verse 21 the hypothesis offers only the very forced explanation that the consolatory document relating to Elijah must have argued polemically against the belief that he was irrevocably in Paradise. Neither is the difficulty of verse 24 removed. The reference to the covenant of Abraham has absolutely nothing to do with Elijah: certainly the Jews who pinned their faith to this prophet did not speak of him as the 'seed of Abraham' mentioned in Gen. **12.**3. On the other hand, as our commentary sought to show, verses 20–25, taken in context, can easily be conceived as Lucan composition without our having to resort to the by no means simple assumption of a self-transmuting yet—be it noted!—*written* text, and a mere broadsheet at that.

Yet this is still insufficient for an understanding of the speech within its context. Why did Luke, after reporting a long speech by Peter in Chapter 2, introduce here again a Petrine sermon? The assumption of a source (which according to Bauernfeind, p. 62, is indeed recognizable only in verse 16) is precluded by the situation at verse 11: we can see exactly what difficulty Luke had here in attaching the speech to the traditional healing story. Why did Luke introduce this new speech?

We may discover the answer by observing the dramatic structure of the composition. Luke did not want to have the great holy day of Pentecost end with an arrest of the Apostles. Moreover he possessed a fine artistic sense of climax, that mysterious capacity for heightening tension. And so he connected the Apostles' initial skirmish with the Sanhedrin, soon to intensify, to a second Petrine discourse, for which the traditional πρᾶξις Πέτρου of the healing of the cripple seemed to offer him a good point of departure. There was no lack of matter for this new speech. Indeed, here was an opportunity to bring home the significance of the 'name of Jesus,' not as an abstract dogmatic proposition but in living illustration. Furthermore, Luke could now correct or supplement the traditional healing story in one important point: he could make Peter indicate the significance which faith possesses for σωτηρία—both earthly and eternal. Again, it was now possible to give all its due weight to a significant aspect which the first sermon, in **2.**36, had merely touched upon. This was the guilt of Israel, incurred by the rejection and killing of the Messiah. As Bauernfeind has rightly noticed (pp. 64f.), Luke expounds the two ideas which the Christian mission had to assert in this connection. First comes emphasis on the guilt, which might make conversion of the Jews appear a hopeless prospect, and therefore called for the exoneration which Luke goes on to provide: not only did Israel sin unwittingly, but this was also the will of God. Luke might have concluded with the exhortation to repentance which develops naturally at this point, if he had not wished to add a word on the theme of the Parousia, its hastening and retardation, a word which would give scope and encouragement to human activity—conversion hastens the end!—while at the same time ascribing the suspension of the Parousia to the δεῖ of the divine will (cf. Acts **1**.7). But then he returns, by way of a transitional 'cue' (the prophets of old—Moses), to the call to conversion, and clarifies the significance of this decision: a Jew who does not become a Christian will no longer be regarded as a Jew by God in judgement. The Jews are the first candidates for the blessing of Abraham which Christ is making a reality—in ὑμῖν πρῶτον Luke ventures to hint at what will be openly declared in Acts **13**.46. With this appeal the sermon has reached its goal—no speech in Acts is brought to a premature end.

In this way Luke created the opening which enabled him to go ahead with his historical presentation: now he can show how the Christian mission aroused the opposition of the Sadducees—which meant practically, as he saw it, the High Council—an opposition which will ultimately lead to the great persecution of the faithful in Chapters 7 and 8.

And so this second sermon of Peter proves to be an essential element in the succession of the events which Luke uses to depict the historical taking-shape of early Christianity, while at the same time it is full of Christian teaching for the reader. Here we come to one final point.

Let Acts be read in continuity, but omitting the speeches. Then the reader will notice to how great an extent these speeches give the book its intellectual and spiritual weight. Without them Acts would be like a gospel consisting only of miracle-stories, without any sayings of Jesus. The speeches in Acts, different as they are in provenance and value, correspond in some way to the discourse material in the gospels. In this the greatness of Luke's talent becomes clear, even if we entirely discount such a masterpiece as the sermon on the Areopagus. They are not merely accounts of Christian proclamation but themselves offer Christian proclamation, and that even though, with the exception of Stephen's speech, they are but speeches 'in miniature' (Dibelius), which can be read in two or three minutes. That they nevertheless have the effect of real speeches, not mere outlines, should never cease to waken our astonishment and admiration.

10
ACTS 4:1–22
PETER AND JOHN BEFORE THE HIGH COUNCIL

[1] As they spoke to the people, the priests and the captain of the Temple and the Sadducees came upon them, [2] vexed because they taught the people and proclaimed in Jesus the resurrection from the dead. [3] And they laid hands on them, and put them in custody until the next day: for it was already evening. [4] But many of those who heard the word believed; and the number of the men came to be about five thousand.

[5] And it came to pass on the following day, that their rulers and elders and scribes assembled in Jerusalem; [6] and Annas the High Priest, and Caiaphas and John and Alexander, and all who were of high-priestly family. [7] And when they had set them in the midst, they enquired, 'By what power, or in what name, have you done this?' [8] Then Peter, filled with the Holy Spirit, said to them, 'Rulers of the people and elders, [9] if we this day are examined concerning a good deed done to a sick man, by what means this man was cured; [10] be it known to you all, and to all the people of Israel, that by the name of Jesus Christ of Nazareth, whom you crucified, whom God raised from the dead, by this name does this man stand here before you healed. [11] This is the stone which was rejected by you, the builders, which has become the head of the corner. [12] And in none other is there salvation: for there is no other name under heaven which is given to men by which we must be saved.' [13] Now when they saw the boldness of Peter and John, and perceived that they were unlearned and ignorant men, they marvelled; and they recognized them, that they had been with Jesus. [14] And seeing the man who was healed standing with them, they could say nothing in contradiction. [15] But they commanded them to go aside out of the Council, and conferred among themselves, [16] saying, 'What shall we do with these men? For that a notable miracle has been done through them is manifest to all that dwell in Jerusalem; and we cannot deny it. [17] But that it may not spread further among the people, let us forbid them with threats ever to speak again to any man in this name.' [18] And they called them, and charged them not to speak at all or teach in the name of Jesus. [19] But Peter and John answered and said to them, 'Whether it is right in the sight of God to listen to you rather than to God, you must judge: [20] for we cannot but speak of what we have seen and heard.' [21] And when

they had further threatened them, they let them go, finding no way to punish them, because of the people; for all men were glorifying God for what had happened. [22] For the man was more than forty years old on whom this sign of healing had been wrought.

Bibliography:

Harnack, *Die Apostelgeschichte* (1908), 166–9 and 173–6 (ET *The Acts of the Apostles*, NT Studies III) (on **4**.1–22); Jeremias, *Untersuchungen* (§ 7, bibl.) (on **4**.1–22); Dodd, *According to the Scriptures* (1952), 37f. (on **4**.9f.); Reicke 71–80 (on **4**.1–22); Trocmé 102f.; Conzelmann 35–7.

P. de Ambroggi, 'Petri loquentis ΠΑΡΡΗΣΙΑ', *Verb. Domini* IX (1929), 269–76; U. Wilckens (see § 9), 44f., 61f., 109ff., 131ff., 163ff.

VERSE 1. λαλούντων κτλ.: The speech now broken off is retrospectively attributed to both Apostles. ἐπέστησαν as in Luke **20**.1[1] and Acts **6**.12. The στρατηγὸς τοῦ ἱεροῦ[2] would be the officer commanding the Temple-police, which consisted of Levites; he came immediately after the High Priest in rank. The ἱερεῖς must be those serving in the Temple. οἱ Σαδδουκαῖοι[3]: 'The Sadducees formed, properly speaking, no party. They were the circles, constituted especially from the nobility and high-caste priests, which had consciously kept aloof from the Pharisees' movement of repentance and renewal' (W. Foerster, *Neutestamentliche Zeitgeschichte* I, 2nd edn., 65; ET *Palestinian Judaism in NT Times* (1964), 162); they were chiefly represented among the lay nobility (Jeremias, *Jerusalem zur Zeit Jesu* II, 95ff.; ET *Jerusalem in the time of Jesus*, 1969, 288ff.). In the present verse they play the role of an authority, but this in fact they were not.

VERSE 2: διαπονούμενοι[4] κτλ. ('distressed, because . . .')—according to this account the Apostles were arrested for teaching that the resurrection which the Sadducees denied (Acts **23**.8) had come to pass in the person of Jesus.[5] This is of crucial importance in the historical picture painted by Luke:

---

[1] According to Wikenhauser, *Apg.* 51, the priests are the Temple-police. But in **5**.26 Luke calls the police ὑπηρέται.

[2] He is also mentioned in Acts **5**.24 and 26; the Mishnah calls him סגן הכהנים. The plural στρατηγοί (Luke **22**.52) reminds one that there were other officers placed under him in the Temple-police, of whom the איש הר הבית, who was in charge of the outer forecourt (and is perhaps mentioned in Josephus *Bell.* VI, 294), could here be meant (S. Zeitlin, *JQR* 31 (1941) 117 n. 120; Billerbeck II, 628ff.). The identification is difficult because Luke himself, as is shown by his representation of the Sadducees as an authority, possessed no thorough knowledge of these relationships.

[3] Schürer, *GJV*[4] II, 320ff.; RGG V, 27ff.; Foerster, op. cit., 62–6, 149 and 159–64.

[4] Ecclesiastes **10**.9 LXX; II Macc. **2**.28.

[5] Preuschen (p. 22) declares this translation impossible, since it would presuppose τὴν ἐν τῷ Ἰησοῦ γεγενημένην. But the condensed expression is one of which Luke is certainly capable. μαρτύρομαι ἐν κυρίῳ in Eph. **4**.17, to which Preuschen refers, cannot be considered a parallel.

opposition to Christianity is voiced only by one group (αἵρεσις τῶν Σαδδου-καίων, 5.17) among the Jewish people, but not by the strictest rigorists, the Pharisees (ἀκριβεστάτη αἵρεσις 26.5). (For causal διὰ τό plus infinitive, see Bl.-Debr. §402, 1.)

VERSE 3: ἐπέβαλον αὐτοῖς τὰς χεῖρας as in 12.1,[1] 'to lay hands violently on a person': here begins the formation of distinctive terminology, to be used in the chronicles of Christian martyrs and confessors. Here, as in 5.18 (τήρησις δημοσία), τήρησις must mean prison. 'It was already evening': Preuschen (p. 22) calculates that 'a space of three hours remains for all the happenings mentioned antecedent to the speech.' But Luke is not intending to give an indirect indication of time; the Council cannot in the evening be immediately on the spot.

VERSE 4: Luke had no other place at his disposal for giving the result of Peter's speech, which increased the membership of the community to five thousand: Peter must therefore once again have spoken to thousands. On the question of the growth of the community, see p. 188f. above.[2]

VERSE 5: On the next day assembles the High Council,[3] of whose composition Luke gives a detailed account. First among the seventy-one members come the ἄρχοντες or (the more usual term) ἀρχιερεῖς[4] (senior priests with the presiding High Priest at their head). From them are distinguished the elders (זְקֵנִים, originally the heads of the principal tribes) and the scribes or men of law, γραμματεῖς (סוֹפְרִים, in post-Christian times חֲכָמִים). Whereas the πρεσβύτεροι represented above all the Sadducean element, the Pharisees—who *de facto* laid down the law—were especially to be found among the γραμματεῖς. All the most powerful opponents of the Christians in Jerusalem

---

[1] This phrase occurs in LXX and later Hellenism (Bauer, *Wb* 573). D (καὶ ἐπιβαλόντες καὶ ἔθεντο) has overlooked that after the change of ἐπέβαλον into a participle the following καί should be omitted: this is not a case of Aramaism.

[2] At that time, on Jeremias' reckoning (*Zeitschr. d. dtsch. Palästinavereins*, 1943, 24–31), Jerusalem had between twenty-five and thirty thousand inhabitants and included very many non-Jews: accordingly after Peter's second sermon one-fifth or one-sixth of them would have become Christians. This shows that the figure of five thousand possesses not statistical but symbolic value.

[3] The older literature, above all Schürer, op. cit., II⁴, 320ff., and Billerbeck I, 78–82 and II, 568–71 and 631, is partly superseded by Jeremias, *Jerusalem zur Zeit Jesu* II, 1929, 3–59 (ET *Jerusalem in the time of Jesus*, 1969, 222–70); these corrections were adopted by Schrenk, *ThWb* III, 1936, art. ἱερός, 221–84, esp. 270–2. (As in Acts 9.3, 32, 37; 14.1; 19.1; 21.1, 5; 27.44; 28.8, 17, ἐγένετο plus acc. and infin. corresponds to OT וַיְהִי: Bl.-Debr. § 408. αὐτῶν is placed before the three nouns to which it belongs.)

[4] 'A tight-knit college' with power over the 'conduct of worship, the running and policing of the Temple, the disposal of Temple funds and the discipline of the priesthood' (*ThWb* III, 270). It consisted of the High Priest in office, the Chief Constable of the Temple (στρατηγὸς τοῦ ἱεροῦ), the heads of the serving officers of the week, the 'leaders of the serving officers of the day, the στρατηγοί—i.e. Temple Wardens—numbering at least seven, and the treasurers, of whom there were at least three' (idem, 271). Perhaps former High Priests should be added to the number. Thus it was an influential group of no mean size.

are gathered together: all the greater therefore does the Apostles' fearlessness appear, the more pusillanimous their enemies' irresolution.

VERSE 6: With a neglect of construction (D removes this defect by its version of verse 5), mention is now made of certain individuals in the first group. The text conveys the impression that Annas (חָנָן) was the High Priest then in office. In fact he held the office from the year 6 to the year 15, though to be sure he still possessed very great influence. *Circa* 17 to 36 it was Joseph, called Caiaphas, who officiated (according to John **18**.13 a son-in-law of Annas). Both John[1] and Alexander are unknown to us. If Luke possessed exact historical information, the words 'and all who were of high-priestly family' must be a way of referring to the persons mentioned in verse 5 above.[2]

VERSE 7: The subject is the men who have just been named. According to the Mishnah, the members of the Sanhedrin sat in a semi-circle, in the middle of which we may imagine the accused standing. At present the preaching of the Resurrection is not made into a count of indictment (cf. verse 2); it is not even clear whether the question 'By[3] what power or in what name[4] have you done this?' embodies an accusation or merely opens an inquiry. 'The author is not interested in the judicial aspect,' says Preuschen (22). On the other hand it is clear that the High Priest's question provides the Apostle with exactly the right cue for his speech (Wellhausen, 8; Preuschen, 23).

VERSE 8: In accordance with the promise of Luke **12**.11f., Peter—once again the spokesman, John remaining silent—is filled with the Holy Spirit. The gift of the Spirit here is not given with the fact of being a Christian, but is bestowed on special occasions.[5]

VERSE 9: Peter solemnly addresses the members of the highest Jewish authority, whom he treats respectfully yet with frankness. 'We are being tried,'[6] he declares, 'for a good deed to a sick man, by what means[7] he has been saved.' This is in itself sufficient to show the senselessness of the situation created by the High Council: is a healing a reason for arraigning

---

[1] D substitutes Ἰωνάθας, who succeeded Caiaphas in 36, only to be replaced in 37. In Paul's time he still played an important political role (see Introduction § 4, p. 69f. above).

[2] See *ThWb* III, 270: at the time in question these comprised the four families of Boethus, Annas, Camith and Ishmael ben Phiabi. The expression γένος ἀρχιερατικόν is to be found in Josephus *Ant.* XV 40, and in *CIG* 4363.

[3] 'By', or 'with the aid of' best renders the sense of ἐν.

[4] Bauernfeind's thesis, shared with Wikenhauser (*Apg.* 52), that 'black magic' had been suspected, is dealt with in the general discussion.

[5] See general discussion of **2**.14–41, 187 above. The Early Church maintained this view: 'For a long time to come, the Confessors were regarded . . . as persons filled with the Spirit' (Preuschen, 23).

[6] In Attic Greek ἀνακρίνομαι is indeed used of a preliminary enquiry, but Acts **12**.19, **24**.8 and **28**.18 show that in Luke's work it means 'to be put on trial'.

[7] ἐν τίνι, referring to ὀνόματι, is neuter (Wendt 112, Bauernfeind 76). σέσωται in ℵ A pc is an old scribal error.

the healer? Peter now uses the occasion to make a missionary address; the double sense of σωθῆναι enables him to use the healing as a proof that Jesus also brings deliverance in the Last Judgement.

VERSE 10: Now that the question has been reiterated with renewed emphasis on 'by what means (or name) this man is delivered', there follows the answer, which basically is directed not only at Peter's audience but also at Luke's readers: Peter himself states that he is not speaking to the judges alone. From ὅτι onward formulae of Lucan rhetoric[1] again appear. It is the name of Jesus which has healed the sick man, who stands before them in person.[2] So much for the Sanhedrin's question, but Peter continues his witness for Jesus with a short scriptural proof.

VERSE 11: οὗτος refers to ἐν τούτῳ in verse 10.[3] Ps. **118** (117).22 is already quoted, from LXX,[4] in Mark **12**.10 (=Luke **20**.71), but Luke is here following another tradition. Scripture foretold that men would reject Jesus, but God appoint him to the highest place.

VERSE 12: σωτηρία embraces both 'healing' and 'salvation' (Preuschen, 24). There is no distinction between the ὄνομα which saves from God's judgement and the ὄνομα which dispenses healing and is employed by the Christian exorcists.[5] Here the expression, elaborated in the reiteration οὐδὲ γὰρ ὄνομα κτλ., of the point that we can be saved by no other name[6] (Luke's way of asserting that Christianity is absolute) has a close affinity with Hermas *Vis.* IV 2.4, δι' οὐδενὸς δύνῃ σωθῆναι εἰ μὴ διὰ τοῦ μεγάλου καὶ ἐνδόξου ὀνόματος[7], hence stands revealed as a turning to account of a Jewish formula

---

[1] Cf. **2**.23f. and **3**.13ff. For the relative clauses see above, p. 139 n. 7 and below p. 282 n. 3. Otherwise it would not be a subordinate clause which proclaims the resurrection of Jesus. Preuschen (23) speaks of the roots of symbol-formation which become visible here.

[2] Not because the scene of a police-trial in the Temple precincts has been transferred to the Sanhedrin (Loisy 243, Bauernfeind 73), nor because he has been called as a witness, but because he serves the writer as a living testimony against the judges (see verse 14). Similarly with the six Christians from Joppa in **11**.12.

[3] If the words from ἐν τούτῳ (verse 10) to ὑγιής be omitted, the citation makes an excellent connection with verse 10. But that does not justify the assumption of a revision. Moreover the broader style corresponds exactly to Luke's way of writing, especially in a passage such as this, which calls for measured solemnity.

[4] The passage is important for the problem raised by Kahle as to whether other 'Greek Targums' existed alongside LXX. Another question also raises its head, that of the testimony book which Rendel Harris suggested Luke employed (cf. Cadbury, *The Making of Luke-Acts*, 56f.).—According to Jeremias, *ThWb* I, 792f., the κεφαλὴ γωνίας is the finishing-stone of the building, i.e. the keystone above the portal.

[5] For Luke (see Luke **4**.39) there is no sharp dividing line between healing and the expulsion of demons.

[6] There is here no distinction between ἄλλος and ἕτερος (Radermacher[2], 77, Bl.-Debr. § 306, 2). τὸ δεδομένον: the participle with article plays the role of a relative clause (Bl.-Debr. § 412, 4). As frequently in LXX, ἐν replaces the simple dative. ὑπὸ τὸν οὐρανόν: cf. Eccles. **1**.13 and **3**.1. There is no reason to assume a translation from Aramaic (Torrey, op. cit. 30, followed by Bauernfeind, 76). D's ὃ δεδόμενον is influenced by d: *quod datum est*.

[7] That is, God's name: see Dibelius, *Handb. z. NT*, Supplement, 464 (on *Vis.* III 3, 5: τοῦ παντοκράτορος καὶ ἐνδόξου ὀνόματος) and 487.

concerned with the שֵׁם יהוה. Luke adopted the formula as it lay to hand, and was not the first to lend it a Christian significance.

VERSE 13: This answer amazes the judges. They can see Peter's fearless confidence, yet at the same time recognize that the defendants are quite ordinary men,[1] whose assurance thus cannot be explained by membership of the educated class. On the basis of this speech they are recognized as former companions and disciples of Jesus.[2] The High Council has reached the point where it must decide its position towards the movement centred on Jesus. καταλαβόμενοι: the middle voice designates mental perception—Moulton, p. 158.

VERSE 14: As in John 5 and 9, the healed man is a living proof which the adversaries are unable to circumvent. οὐδὲν εἶχον ἀντειπεῖν fulfils the prophecy of Luke 21.15[3] that Jesus would bestow wisdom and eloquence on his disciples: ᾗ οὐ δυνήσονται ἀντιστῆναι ἢ ἀντειπεῖν . . . οἱ ἀντικείμενοι.

VERSE 15: With this the first part of the action is concluded: the court 'adjourns to consider its findings,' sending the accused out of the συνέδριον, the room where the authority holds session.[4] The author reports the closed deliberations[5] as if he had been present.

VERSE 16: The Council's question[6] betrays at once its helplessness and its anxiety to extricate itself from the dilemma. The ensuing ὅτι-clause[7] gives the reason for its accepting defeat: a γνωστὸν[8] σημεῖον is a fact manifest[9] to all the inhabitants of Jerusalem. The words 'we cannot deny it' emphasize the reality of the miracle and show that if they had the least

---

[1] ἀγράμματος denotes, according to the Papyri, anyone incapable of writing; ἰδιώτης may either designate the layman as distinct from the expert or be synonymous with ἀγράμματος in the sense of 'unlearned', 'man of the people'. It is very doubtful that Luke is here thinking of lack of legal knowledge: see commentary on 5.17–42 below.

[2] That the disciple John according to John 18.15 (assuming that he is meant by the 'other disciple') was γνωστὸς τῷ ἀρχιερεῖ cannot in any way be reconciled with the present passage.

[3] Cf. Acts 6.10: οὐκ ἴσχυον ἀντιστῆναι.

[4] We do not know where the High Council met at that time (see Billerbeck I, 997f.; *Beg.* V, 477f.) nor where Luke himself locates the scene in his imagination.

[5] After συνέβαλλον understand λόγους; cf. 17.18, where the word is construed with the dative. The text of verses 13–15 in h, which *Beg.* III, 38 considers to render the original text, is clearly secondary.

[6] The reading ποιήσομεν to be inferred from *faciemus* (in h vg) is due to faulty hearing: in the first two centuries A.D. the quantitative difference between ω and ο disappeared (Bl.-Debr. § 22); this is important for Rom. 5.1.

[7] The subordination is scarcely noticeable, hence ὅτι is to be translated 'for' (cf. Bl.-Debr. § 456, 1).

[8] γνωστός: Acts 1.19, 2.14, 4.10, 4.16, 9.42, 13.38, 15.18, 19.17, 28.22 and 28.28, evidently one of Luke's favourite words. It is not an Aramaism (so Bauernfeind, 77) but taken over from LXX, where also the formula γνωστὸν ἔστω frequently occurs.

[9] Instead of γέγονεν D reads γεγονέναι. Probably the explanation is not a dittography of the following δι' (mentioned as a possibility in *Beg.* III, 38), but the D-scribe began with ὅτι and then continued γνωστὸν σημεῖον γεγονέναι φανερότερόν ἐστιν without erasing the ὅτι. On the subject of the comparative φανερότερον, cf. below on 17.21.

prospect of success the authorities would deny all. That they do not allow themselves to be convinced by the miracle is evidence of their hardness of heart.

VERSE 17: 'But[1] that it[2] may spread[3] no further[4] among the people, let us threaten them,[5] that they speak henceforth to no man in this name.[6]' The formula ἐπὶ τῷ ὀνόματι allows the author to pass from the miracle effected by the utterance of Jesus' name to the ban on any preaching of Jesus (cf. also **5**.28).

VERSE 18: This verse, expanded in the Western text,[7] contains the strict command not in any circumstances[8] to speak[9] or teach in this name,[10] and thereby paves the way for the Apostles' famous reply.

VERSE 19: In the most decided manner possible the Apostles declare they will defy the interdict: the Sanhedrin may judge for itself whether it is right in the sight of God to heed them rather than *him*.[11] Luke thus makes the attitude of the Apostles comprehensible to his readers by using a phrase familiar to them.

VERSE 20: What the Apostles have seen and heard is the words and deeds of Jesus (cf. **10**.39), but above all the Resurrection, which is in question here.

[1] ἀλλά corresponds to the μέν in verse 16.

[2] Grammatically the subject is τὸ σημεῖον, but what is meant is probably knowledge of the miracle, and beyond that knowledge of Jesus.

[3] διανέμω strictly means 'distribute' or 'share out,' as in Deut. **29**.25 LXX.

[4] Taken in a spatial sense, μὴ ἐπὶ πλεῖον would imply 'not outside Jerusalem'. In Acts **24**.4 we find the connotation of duration, which is preferable here also. The difficulty is that the author on the one hand stresses that the miracle is already common knowledge, yet on the other seeks to motivate the Council's repressive measures, which only make sense if there are still people who have not yet heard of Jesus and his miracle.

[5] Later MSS add ἀπειλῇ, under the influence, supposes Wendt (114 n.), of παραγγελίᾳ παρηγγείλαμεν in **5**.28. But cf. also such passages as Exodus **22**.15, 22f.

[6] Cf. Heitmüller, *Im Namen Jesu* 61: 'If the Council orders the Apostles μὴ λαλεῖν ἐπὶ τῷ ὀνόματι, it is scarcely troubled over the reason for or basis of the preaching; what distresses them is the content: they wish to prevent the hated name from being constantly repeated and made known.'

[7] D d (gig) h sy^hmg smooth the transition with ' and as they were now of one mind in their decision . . .'

[8] (τὸ) καθόλου is a strong negation, as in Exodus **22**.10 *var.*, Amos **3**.3f., Ezek. **13**.3, 22 and **17**.14, and Dan. **3**.50: once again, LXX terminology.

[9] φθέγγομαι: 'to call aloud,' 'proclaim' (Wis. Sol. **1**.8), hence yet another expression, not unknown to LXX, whose later writings Luke seems to have known particularly well.

[10] Wellhausen, p. 7: ' The Name (absolute and without a following genitive, as הַשֵּׁם among the Jews for God) takes the place of Jesus himself and appears a hypostasis comparable in power with the Spirit.' In *ThWb* V, 272f. it is not clear that the use of ὄνομα in Acts 4 corresponds to OT usage inasmuch as Jesus (like Yahweh) is in heaven and only his name (when trustfully invoked) present on earth.

[11] Preuschen maintains (25) that ever since Plato (*Apology* 29D) the answer given by the Apostles had been a commonplace, but this *Beg.* IV denies—' The idea is common, though not commonplace' (45)—while nevertheless accepting, on account of Acts **17**.29, that Luke was acquainted with the story of Socrates. That Luke consciously used Greek thought-forms in order to make himself understood to his readers becomes especially clear from **26**.14. And so here.—ἀποκριθέντες εἶπαν is frequent in LXX.

VERSE 21 : It is not surprising that the Council refrains from any discussion as to who here represents God. Two reasons are given why (though with renewed threats) it releases the Apostles, despite their steadfast defiance: 1. the Council sees no possibility of punishment,[1] 2. it is afraid of the people. The first reason is not intended to indicate a latent sense of justice on the part of the High Council, but to make clear to the reader that there was no legal case against the Apostles. τὸ πῶς κτλ.: Bl.-Debr. § 267, 2; cf. Bruce, p. 125.

VERSE 22: The stressing of the duration of the disease, frequent in stories of healing because it makes the healing appear so much the more miraculous, is here used to explain and justify the feelings of the people: the healed man had been lame all his life, more than[2] forty years! On γεγόνει see Bl.-Debr. § 66, 1.

The present section contains many kinds of difficulties. That becomes clear from the attitude of the critics. Wendt (111) and Bauernfeind (74) feel obliged to understand ἀνδρῶν in verse 4 as 'human beings' in order to include the women and avoid increasing the number of converts even further. Harnack (*Beitr.* III, 143 n. 1; ET) boldly cuts the five thousand to a tenth of that number. Like Beyer (35) he is inclined to discover here the 'more than five hundred brethren' of I Cor. 15.6. But this stands or falls with Harnack's erroneous source-theory, of which we shall have more to say in connection with 5.17–42. Sorof (55), Jüngst (48), Clemen (*St.Kr.* 1895, 331) and Hilgenfeld (*ZwTh* 1895, 198f.) see verse 4 as an editorial addition, since the statement stands at an inappropriate point. On the names in verse 6 Beyer (35) declares, 'These exact details must rest on a precise and knowledgeable tradition,' but Preuschen (23) thinks, 'The names of members of the High Priest's family are meant to create the impression of scrupulous exactitude.' Loisy (242f.) considers that John and Alexander were names chosen at random.

But taken as wholes the scenes of the arrest and the trial are truly remarkable. The Sadducees did not constitute an authority, therefore could arrest nobody. However, if one overcomes this difficulty by identifying them with the authoritative priestly nobility (in the teeth of Jeremias' conclusive demonstration[3] that they had their adherents chiefly among the πρεσβύτεροι

---

[1] μηδὲν εὑρίσκοντες κτλ. gives the reason for releasing the prisoners (Moulton, 230). But διὰ τὸν λαόν also depends on ἀπέλυσαν. Loisy (250) points out that fear of the people is out of place here, because the people quietly permitted the arrest of the Apostles. He seeks to explain this by supposing that the original story mentioned a mere intervention of the Temple-police, such as would not excite the crowd (Bauernfeind, 73 and 77, follows him in this). But in fact Luke likes to sound the theme of the Apostles' popularity (cf. 5.26!), without strictly integrating it with the context.

[2] 'When πλείων ... precedes numerical expressions, "than" is omitted ...' (Bl.-Debr. § 185, 4). ἄνθρωπος ἦν ἐτῶν is *gen. qualitatis* (Bl.-Debr. § 165).

[3] *Jerusalem zur Zeit Jesu* II, 95 (ET *Jerusalem in the time of Jesus*, 1969, 228).

or lay nobility), a further difficulty remains: the fact that someone proposes a theology different from their own is not in itself sufficient to justify an arrest, and if the Sadducees had wished to proceed against all believers in resurrection they would have had to throw every Pharisee into jail. In reality, despite the Sadducees' tenure of the highest offices, the character of the Sanhedrin was largely determined by the resurrectionist Pharisees; and behind the Pharisees stood the people.

At all events, the accusation of having preached resurrection is not raised during the hearing. Instead, the Apostles are interrogated as to the power or name by which they have healed the cripple. Hence, for the moment, our difficulty is removed. But, alas, there are others to take its place. Properly, the personal identification of the accused ought first to be established, but this formality is missing. Only the contents of Peter's plea tell the High Council that it is in the presence of former companions of Jesus: this despite the fact that the name of Jesus had been the centre of both the healing and the sermon it occasioned. Neither is it first established whether the case ought to be brought before the highest court at all; Luke plunges into the proceedings without any such formal preliminaries.

The miracle—authenticated by the man restored to health—is undeniable: the whole city knows about it. Notwithstanding, the Apostles are forbidden all reference, whether in speaking or teaching, to this salutary name. The Apostles' energetic refusal of the interdict only produces threats: they are set free, above all because the Sanhedrin fears the people. But, the critics object, the thousands did not lift a finger when the Apostles were arrested before their very eyes. Why is the Council now so anxious, when it has the Apostles in its power?

To make a clean sweep of all these difficulties, Dauernfeind (73)—like B. Weiss before him—assumes that in the source the scene was played on the public square of the Temple. The Temple-police arrested the Apostles out of hand, on the supposition that 'black magic' had its part in the miracle. Hence the question—now ascribed to the High Priest—concerning the ὄνομα by which the miracle was effected. Luke transposed the scene into the Council Chamber because he possessed information from another source that the Apostles had been arraigned before the Council. In this transformation of the story, all these difficulties inevitably resulted.

Jacquier (who does not share the transposition hypothesis) conjectures (125) that Peter was suspected of having called on the name of Beelzebub, and appeals to Luke **11**.15 and John **8**.48. A most unlikely hypothesis! For if this accusation had formerly been brought against Jesus, this was in order to discredit the undeniable successes of a hated opponent. In the present case, however, the identity of the miracle-workers is still unknown, and there is therefore no reason for besmirching their success or attributing it to Beelzebub.

Bauernfeind offers no closer indication of what we should understand here under the heading of 'black magic,' of which he moreover adduces not one instance. At bottom, his entire construction is based on the question in verse 7 as to the miracle-working name. Yet this question does not embody an accusation of 'black magic', and it is highly improbable that such an idea would have occurred to any Temple-policeman confronted with a miraculous healing. Indeed many are the legends of Judaism concerning the miracles which could be done through 'the Name'—Yahweh's. But here there is no suggestion even of an unauthorised use of God's name. Nor does the text say that the use of Jesus' name is prohibited as blasphemous. In fact no reason for the ban is given, apart from that in verse 17: 'that it spread no further among the people'—and this points back to the hostility against the proclamation of Jesus because of the resurrection doctrine (verse 2).

In sum, then, the 'black magic' theory is a dead end. Which is hardly surprising, for it revives the approach current in Harnack's day: the assumption of and search for a source-report that Luke has retouched. Hitherto none such has come to light, neither do we find traces here. The employment of archaic ideas (such as Bauernfeind considers 'the Name'—but why should this not have been live, spontaneous usage in Luke's own day and community?) by no means guarantees the existence of an ancient written source. Let us rather, therefore, attempt an analysis of the text which will permit the exploitation of knowledge already acquired (see on 3.11 above).

We must, first, not overlook that the Apostles are arrested only after Peter's sermon, not immediately after the healing. Since, as we saw from 3.11, the attachment of sermon to story gave the writer trouble, one might suppose that the account of the arrest was once joined directly to that of the miracle. But this is not the case: the story of the healing of the cripple forms a self-contained unit, like those of the healing of Aeneas and the raising of Tabitha (9.32–42). It is an ancient πρᾶξις Πέτρου, circulated among the communities for its own sake. Luke did not link the arrest with it immediately, but with the Apostle's preaching of the Risen Jesus as the ἀρχηγὸς τῆς ζωῆς. Whether we find this connection plausible is neither here nor there: we must not move precipitately from examination of the literary material to historical reconstruction of the incidents narrated. This 'teaching of the people and proclamation in Jesus of the resurrection from the dead' (4.2) returns to the foreground at the end of the trial-scene (4.17f.), when the preaching of Christ is prohibited.

Between them stands that other piece which begins with the High Priest's question. There can be no denying that this question provides Peter with the point of departure for his new speech. But this speech—whose Lucan origin, despite or because of the Septuagint style, admits of no doubt—conflicts with 4.2 by postulating that the healing, not the preaching, was the occasion of the trial. Does this mean that a new source begins here? Not at all! Luke has merely not let slip the opportunity of bringing forward the irrefutable healing in the name of Jesus as proof that in Jesus' name, in that name *alone*, lies σωτηρία. The enemy is defenceless against this proof—and utters not one syllable of protest that the healing was 'not procured by proper means' (Bauernfeind 71). Once the miracle has served Luke's purpose as a proof, he uses the double meaning of ἐπὶ τῷ ὀνόματι τούτῳ λαλεῖν to steer back from it to the preaching of Christ in general, which is left in sole command of the field (verses 18–20). Thus one may judge how adroitly the author has used the theme of the miracle-working name to establish the overriding and truly crucial theme of the Apostles' right and duty to *preach* it.

Now that the literary analysis has helped elucidate the features of the text, we may enquire into the historical authenticity of Luke's conception here. It must first be recognized that the Sadducees' hostility to the Christian preaching of the resurrection was of the highest importance to Luke, even if we disregard its later consequences for the Christians' position vis-à-vis the State. According to Luke, it is not Judaism and Christianity which confront each other as enemies, but only Sadducees and Christians. For Pharisee and Christian are at one where belief in resurrection, the nucleus of Christianity, is concerned (even if the Pharisees fail to draw the necessary conclusions in respect of Jesus' resurrection). Christianity is not a falling-away from Judaism; on the contrary, its doctrine of resurrection is the basic teaching of Israel, which only the αἵρεσις τῶν Σαδδουκαίων disputes.

Within this impressive scheme a profound appreciation lies mingled with incorrect assumptions. Luke correctly saw that the primitive Christian congregation was closely bound up with the Jewish community, that it had no thought of proclaiming a new religion but only the Jewish hope which came to fulfilment in the Messiah Jesus. It is also true that, unlike the Sadducees, the Pharisees believed in a resurrection at the end of this world. However, it was not the Sadducees who dominated the High Council, but the Pharisees, and *these* it was who adopted an unfriendly attitude towards the Christians. This is shown by the Christian polemic against the 'scribes and Pharisees' (Matt. **23**.13ff.; Luke **11**.39–53 and **20**.45–7), by Herod Agrippa's persecution in A.D. 44, probably the result of Pharisee pressure, and finally by the persecution of Christians by the Pharisee Saul. It is only because, in Acts, Luke keeps the question of the law so firmly in the background that this hostility of the Pharisees is not evident here. Admittedly—and this can be adduced in his favour—it was more especially directed against Hellenistic Christianity (cf. Acts **15**.5).

Nevertheless, this does not imply that the trial before the Sanhedrin related in Chapter 4 was in reality brought about by the Pharisees. This story of the trial is rather one of those lively tableaux or dramatic scenes which Luke prefers to unadorned dogmatic exposition for the purpose of bringing home to the reader the justice and obligation of preaching Christ, and showing from the example of the Apostles, those ἄνθρωποι ἀγράμματοι καὶ ἰδιῶται, how the Christian, certain of divine assistance, should fearlessly bear witness for his Lord, unquelled by police, arrest or official interdiction.

Luke was naturally convinced that, in essentials, the scene he depicted corresponded to events: he knew from Mark **13**.9 (cf. Luke **12**.11f.) that Christians had been summoned before the High Council. We cannot blame the author for not allowing the opportunity to pass of creating this great scene for himself and his readers. But Luke the historian also laid store by this scene, for only so could he present the intensification of the conflict up to the dispersion of the community (Chapter 8) as a historical process.

11
ACTS 4:23-31
THE CONGREGATION PRAYS AND IS HEARD

[23] On being released, they came to their friends, and told them all that the chief priests and elders had said. [24] And when they heard it, they lifted up their voice to God together, and said, 'O Lord, who made heaven and earth and sea, and all that in them is: [25] who by the mouth of thy servant David (our father) didst say (by the Holy Spirit), "Why did the gentiles rage, and the peoples plot in vain? [26] The kings of the earth set themselves in array, and the rulers were gathered together, against the Lord and against his Anointed." [27] For truly they were gathered together in this city against thy holy Son Jesus, whom thou didst anoint, Herod and Pontius Pilate, with the gentiles and the peoples of Israel, [28] to do whatsoever thy hand and thy counsel foreordained to come to pass. [29] And now, Lord, look upon their threatenings, and grant to thy servants to speak thy word with all boldness, [30] while thou stretchest forth thy hand that healing and signs and wonders may be done through the name of thy holy Son Jesus.' [31] And when they had prayed, the place in which they were gathered together was shaken: and they were all filled with the Holy Spirit, and they spoke the word of God with boldness.

Bibliography:

E. von der Goltz, *Das Gebet in der ältesten Christenheit*, 1901, 235; M. S. Enslin, 'An Additional Step toward the Understanding of Jesus', *JR* 9 (1929), 419–35, esp. 431f. (on **4.8** and 31); D. W. Riddle, 'Die Verfolgungslogien in formgeschichtlicher und soziologischer Bedeutung', *JBL* 52 (1934), 271–89 (on **4.24–30**); H. W. Moule, *Exp.Tim.* 51 (1939/40), 396 (on **4.25**); A. E. Haefner, 'The Earliest Christian Prayer', *JBL* 61 (1942), XI (on **4.24–30**); J. Dupont, 'Les Problèmes du Livre des Actes', *Anal. Lov. Bibl. et Or.* II, 17 (1950), 110 (on **4.26**); Dodd, *According to the Scriptures*, 1952, 31f. and 104–6 (on **4.26**); A. Hamman, 'La Nouvelle Pentecôte (Actes **4.24–30**)', *Bible et vie chrétienne* 14 (1956), 82–90; Reicke 80–4; Trocmé 95f., 103, 115 and 192 (on **4.24–31**); Conzelmann, 37f.

C. F. D. Moule, 'H. W. Moule on Acts **4.25**', *Exp. Tim.* 65 (1953–4), 220f; R. Rimaud, 'La première prière liturgique dans le livre des Actes (Actes **4.23-31**)', *Maison Dieu* 51 (1957), 99–115, Dibelius, *Botschaft* I (1953), 289ff.

VERSE 23: ἀπολυθέντες corresponds to ἀπέλυσαν in verse 21: 'on being released they came to their friends', i.e., the members of the congregation imagined as gathered together. When Luke speaks of the community assembled for worship or deliberation, he sees in his mind's eye not the great numbers he used in 2.41 and 4.4 to illustrate the divine blessing that lay on the community, but the band of believers gathered in one room which he was accustomed to see around him in the services of his own congregation. We may therefore not infer from a story like the present that it comes to us from a very early period, when the whole community could find a place in one room. —The opponents are not described in detail as before: only the πρεσβύτεροι are mentioned along with the ἀρχιερεῖς. ὅσα εἶπαν, an allusion to the 'threatenings' in vv. 17 and 21, links up with what follows.

VERSE 24: The prayer uttered with one accord demonstrates the unity of the Spirit. The forms of worship of Luke's own day must have acquainted him with prayers spoken aloud by the whole congregation. Isaiah 37.16–20 LXX is generally acknowledged to offer at least an analogy with this prayer;[1] the apostrophic κύριε there employed was inadvisable here, however, as it could ambiguously refer to Christ: the δέσποτα which replaces it (cf. also Luke 2.29) occurs some twenty-five times in LXX. ὁ ποιήσας[2]: the fact that God is the Creator gives the congregation the assurance that he is also the Lord of history and holds our fate in his hand.

VERSES 25f.: The text offered by Nestle (supported by 𝕭) is the most ancient attested in manuscripts, even though grammatically impossible.[3] 'Of our father' and 'by the Holy Spirit' are later additions. God does not speak through the Spirit, but through the mouths of the prophets (Loisy, 253). The 𝕶 reading, 'who by the mouth of David thy servant didst say', for once restores the correct text (Preuschen 25).[4]

VERSES 27f. interpret the Psalm quotation, which exactly follows LXX, as a prophecy fulfilled in the events leading to the Passion: Jesus is the Messiah

---

[1] κύριε, σὺ ἐποίησας τὸν οὐρανὸν καὶ τὴν γῆν (+ καὶ τὴν θάλασσαν καὶ πάντα ἐν αὐτοῖς: Psalm 146 (145).6) . . . ἴδε τοὺς λόγους, οὓς ἀπέστειλεν Σενναχεριμ ὀνειδίζειν θεὸν ζῶντα. ἐπ' ἀληθείας γὰρ . . . σὺ δὲ κύριε, σῶσον ἡμᾶς ἐκ χειρὸς αὐτῶν . . . (the parallel II Kings 19.19 has καὶ νῦν, κύριε κτλ.).

[2] Dibelius in *ZNW* 16 (1915), 124: 'We need no longer hestitate over the participial predication ὁ ποιήσας κτλ. after Norden's exposition of the matter in *Agnostos Theos*, 201ff., thanks to which we have no qualms in affirming, not as the mere verdict of flair or taste, but as an assured literary thesis, that it is a "literary formula".'

[3] See *ZThK* 51 (1954), 156f. The verse has been overloaded with two interpolations: τοῦ πατρὸς ἡμῶν was added to Δαυιδ παιδός σου but now stands in the wrong place; διὰ πνεύματος ἁγίου was inserted before διὰ στόματος, but at the same time the second διὰ dropped out.

[4] Torrey, op. cit., 17f., reconstructs the following Aramaic original: 'that which our father, thy servant David, spoke through the mouth of the Holy Spirit'! No writer, Aramaic or otherwise, has ever maintained that David spoke through the mouth of the Holy Spirit. Nevertheless Bruce (p. 127) considers this 'a very attractive solution'.

of whom the Psalm speaks.[1] Herod Antipas represents 'the kings of the earth', Pilate 'the rulers', the Roman soldiers the ἔθνη, and the tribes of Israel the λαοί.[2] ἐπ' ἀληθείας occurs also in Luke 4.25, 20.21 and 22.59 and in Acts 10.34; in LXX in Deut. 22.20, Tobit 8.7, Job 9.2, 19.4, 36.4, Isa. 37.18, Dan. 2.5, 8f., 47 and 8.26. God's hand—an image of his power—and his counsel guided the course of the Passion. In itself προώρισεν only applies to βουλή (Preuschen, 26), but both, the omnipotence and the wisdom, form one indissoluble unit (Loisy, 295). On τὸν ἅγιον παῖδα κτλ. see on 3.13 above.

VERSE 29, which is introduced by a Lucan καὶ τὰ νῦν,[3] leads to the present time and thus to the petition. In point of substance, ἔπιδε corresponds to ἴδε κτλ in Isa. 37.17 (see p. 226 n. 1 above). Grammatically αὐτῶν refers to Herod and Pilate, but it is the present enemies who are meant: the seam between verses 28 and 29 is obvious.[4] ἀπειλάς echoes verses 17 and 21. 'Servants' corresponds to δέσποτα in verse 24: as God's servants the Christians have the right to beg their master's help. The language corresponds to that of LXX. λαλεῖν τὸν λόγον[5] is a technical term of the primitive mission and designates missionary preaching. 'Thy word,' the 'word of God,' is the glad tidings of Jesus which God has the Apostles proclaim.

VERSE 30: May the preaching—this is the sense of the prayer—be accompanied[6] by healings[7] and signs and wonders[8] performed by[9] God, 'done through the name of thy holy Son Jesus'; this expression combines the formula διὰ Ἰησοῦ, τοῦ παιδός σου[10] (or the like) with the other, ἐν (ἐπὶ) τῷ ὀνόματι Ἰησοῦ Χριστοῦ, which has played so important a part in Chapters 3 and 4. With these solemn cadences the prayer comes to an end.

---

[1] ὃν ἔχρισας ='whom thou hast made Messiah': Luke 3.22, 4.1 and 4.14 and Acts 10.38 link this with the baptism of Jesus (Wendt 116; Loisy 254). ἔχρισας, i.e. at baptism.

[2] In OT לְאֻמִּים? never refers to Israel, hence we have here not Palestinian but Hellenistic interpretation.

[3] Found in NT only in Acts 5.38, (17.30), 20.32 and 27.22: cf. καὶ νῦν, κύριε in II Kings 19.19.

[4] Dibelius, op. cit., 124: 'τὰς ἀπειλὰς αὐτῶν—these are not the threats of the potentates just named, but of the members of the Sanhedrin who at the time of the story are out to make trouble for the congregation.'

[5] Acts 4.29, 31; 8.25; 11.19f.; 13.46 (+τοῦ θεοῦ); 14.1 (without τὸν λόγον), 25; 16.6, 32. With these should be associated 6.2, 7; 8.4, 14, 25 (τοῦ κυρίου); 10.44; 11.1; 12.24; 13.5, 7, 44, 48 (τοῦ κυρίου), 49 (ditto); 14.3, 15.7 (λόγος τοῦ εὐαγγελίου), 36; 17.13; 18.5 (without τοῦ θεοῦ), 11; 19.10, 20; 20.7 (without τοῦ θεοῦ).

[6] Expressed here by ἐν.

[7] ἴασις recalls the healing of the beggar which sparked off the persecution.

[8] Acts 2.43, 5.12, 6.8, 7.36, 14.3 and 15.12. One should not look for any essential difference between the two (Bauernfeind, 80). It is a locution taken from LXX.

[9] ἐκτείνειν τὴν χεῖρα occurs some eighty times in LXX.

[10] See on 3.13 above.

VERSE 31: ἐσαλεύθη ὁ τόπος[1]: to the ancient[2] mind, the trembling of the place signified that the prayer had been 'heard.' Once again ἐλάλουν τὸν λόγον denotes the missionary preaching and not a 'ritual, cultic declamation of the divine word within the narrower circle.'[3] It is the Holy Spirit which bestows the fearlessness with which the Christian message is proclaimed in the face of danger. Luke is not referring to a pneumatic 'possession' given vent in ecstatic utterance; when Harnack saw this episode as the 'real historical Pentecost' (*Beitr.* III, 146; ET), he was chasing a will-o'-the-wisp.

Bauernfeind (79) thought to discover in this section Luke's adaptation of an old 'prayer in time of distress'[4]—old, though not necessarily belonging to the earliest stratum of Christian communal prayer. In that case the close affinity with the prayer of Isa. 37 would mean that the original prayer itself leaned on the OT model. However, the end of the OT prayer is missing here, and verse 29, which is not only closely related to Isa. 37 but exactly and exclusively fits the situation of Chapter 4, is of obvious Lucan stamp. One would therefore rather suppose, pursuing a suggestion of Dibelius, that with the Isaiah prayer as model Luke has cunningly recast in prayer-form an early Christian exegesis of Psalm 2.1f. LXX, weaving in at the same time the prophetic predicates of Christ he had already adopted (3.13, τὸν παῖδα αὐτοῦ Ἰησοῦν; 3.14, τὸν ἅγιον). It is true that in itself the verdict passed on Pilate by the psalm-exegesis was at odds with his own theology, which (as we have seen in connection with 3.13) sought to exculpate the governor—but then Luke was elastic enough in outlook to accept a representation of Herod as hostile to Christ (Luke 23.11ff.) while in the next breath (23.15) claiming him as a witness of Jesus' innocence. Again, Luke has to make the best of the fact that the Passion-situation of verse 27 was somewhat incongruous with the threatening of the Apostles: the word αὐτῶν—which every reader will at first sight refer to Pilate and Herod, but means the members of the Sanhedrin —cannot wholly paper over the rift between verses 27 and 29, even though both have a general bearing on hostility to Christ. That verses 29f. depart from the Isaiah prayer in not asking for the averting of external dangers is connected with the fact that in the sequel Luke must of course report the

---

[1] σαλεύω is a favourite word of LXX, where it occurs over seventy-five times. The nearest equivalent to the present phrase is the oft-encountered ἐσαλεύθη ἡ γῆ. Luke does not indicate where the Christians are assembled; they are not in the Temple.

[2] The OT references given by *Beg.* IV, 47, viz. Exodus 19.18, Isa. 6.4, II Esdras 6.14 and 29, are not real parallels: they speak of an earth-tremor occurring at the approach of God or the sound of his voice. The trembling of a place in answer to a prayer is described, on the other hand, by Ovid (*Metam.* XV. 669–72) and Virgil (*Aen.* III. 88–91).

[3] A possibility mentioned by Bauernfeind (p. 80). D shows, by the addition of παντὶ τῷ θέλοντι πιστεύειν, a correct grasp of the situation (Wendt, 117; Loisy, 257).

[4] Cf. H. Schütz, *Entstehung und Bedeutung des urchristlichen Gemeindegebets*, dissertation 1925, 151ff.

continuation of the persecution. Lastly, verse 31 betrays the use of pagan, Hellenistic ideas.

Such an analysis, however, still fails to inform us what Luke wished to tell his readers by this prayer. The prayer shows the reader how Christians behave when the threat of persecution rears its head: they turn to God, their almighty Lord, who created heaven and earth and sea and all that is therein, and who therefore has all things in his power. *He himself* foretold the Passion of Jesus, preordained by his own hand and counsel: suffering does not take us out of his hand. The present passage cannot contain a prayer for preservation from such suffering—Chapters 5 to 7 will describe the intensification of the Christians' distress. Hence the prayer is limited to 'look upon their threatenings'—in the present episode a concrete expression—and it is left to God to do what he will with them. But further petitions are uttered for unfaltering courage in the face of all danger and for miracles to accredit the preaching of Christ—of both Acts will yet have much to say. For the benefit of his Hellenistic audience, Luke illustrates God's hearing of the prayer with a vivid device which he dared to borrow from pagan religion. He was encouraged to such licence by the consideration that the Christian message was now invading the milieu of Hellenistic culture and piety. But if one compares Luke's work with later (apocryphal) Acts of the Apostles, one has to admit that he made but sparing use of such liberties. The end of the episode shows that the Christians have thus with God's help defeated the attempt to stifle their mission. At the same time, however, the way is paved for the coming narrative of the new persecution.

12
ACTS 4: 32–37
COMMUNITY OF GOODS IN THE
PRIMITIVE CHURCH

[32] The multitude of those who believed were of one heart and soul: and not one said that any of the things which he possessed was his own; but they had all things common. [33] And with great power the Apostles gave their witness of the resurrection of the Lord Jesus: and great grace was upon them all. [34] For there was no needy person among them: for as many as were possessors of lands or houses sold them, and brought the price of the things that were sold, [35] and laid it at the Apostles' feet: and distribution was made to each according to his need. [36] And Joseph, who was surnamed by the Apostles Barnabas (which is, being interpreted, 'Son of consolation'), a Levite, a man of Cyprus by race, [37] sold a field which he owned, and brought the money and laid it at the Apostles' feet.

Bibliography:

Cadbury, Cerfaux, Jeremias, Benoit—see § 7 bibl. above; A. Deissmann, *ZNW* 7 (1906), 91f. (on Barnabas, **4**.36); E. Schwartz, *NGG* (1907), 282 n. 1; Cadbury, 'Some Semitic Personal Names in Luke-Acts', *Amicitiae Corolla*, ed. Wood, 1933, 45–56 (47f. on Barnabas, **4**.36); R. O. P. Taylor, 'What was Barnabas?', *CQR* 136 (1943), 59–79; Reicke, 85–7; Trocmé, 30, 120 and 195f.

E. Hicks, see § 7; L. Cerfaux, 'St. Barnabé, apôtre des gentiles', *Coll. dioec. Thorn.* 23 (1927–8), 209–217; Id., 'Le "Supernomen" dans le Livre des Actes', *Eph. Theol. Lov.* 15 (1938), 74–80; J. D. Burger, 'L'énigme de Barnabé', *Museum Helveticum* 3 (1946), 180–193.

VERSE 32: πλῆθος[1] τῶν πιστευσάντων means the whole congregation. 'Heart' and 'soul' are often juxtaposed in the OT, above all in the familiar

---

[1] πλῆθος has essentially two meanings in Acts. In **2**.6, **14**.1, **17**.4 and **28**.3 it means the 'multitude' or 'crowd' (the plural in **5**.14 = 'masses'); in **5**.16 and **14**.4 this sense is enlarged to signify the whole 'population'; in **25**.24, ἅπαν τὸ πλῆθος κτλ. on the one hand implies 'the Jewish people', but on the other enables the writer to conjure up a picture of the crowd demonstrating in front of the governor's palace; **23**.7—with the tumultuous assembly of the Sanhedrin—really belongs here too. The second basic meaning is 'the congregation', as in **4**.32, **6**.2, **6**.5, **15**.12, **15**.30, **19**.9 (the Jewish/Christian congregation!) and **21**.22 (variant). Luke usually makes this sense clear by such additions as τῶν μαθητῶν or πᾶν (τὸ πλῆθος). Cf. *Beg.* IV, 47f.

expression in Deut. 'with all thy heart and with all thy soul';[1] together they denote the innermost seat of man's personality, from which his conduct is determined. The expression ψυχή μία is found in I Chr. **12**.39 LXX as a translation of בֵּל אֶחָד. On the other hand μία ψυχή and κοινά τά τῶν φίλων are mentioned as παροιμίαι in the Nicomachean Ethics (IX 8, 1168b). Hence Luke has here completely fused his OT heritage, transmitted via LXX, with Greek material.—The verse implies that private property as such still subsisted, for owners only gave up their property-rights vis-à-vis their brethren in the faith.[2]

VERSE 33: From the condition of the community the report passes to the Apostles' preaching of Jesus' resurrection.[3] Loisy (259) and *Beg.* IV 48 rightly identify the δύναμις with the power to work miracles: miracles which answer the prayer of the congregation in verse 30. The divine grace is not however restricted to the Apostles; it spreads over them all.[4] ἀπεδίδουν—Bl.-Debr. § 94.

VERSES 34f.: It is part and parcel of this divine blessing that the community should receive the fulfilment of the promise made in Deut. **15**.4: οὐκ ἔσται ἐν σοὶ ἐνδεής. How this came about is immediately explained: when necessary (this is the force of the imperfect), owners of land or houses sold their property and laid the proceeds at the feet of the Apostles;[5] from this source each needy member received what he needed. Luke does not say who undertook this distribution, but it is natural to think of the Apostles. ἐτίθουν is Hellenistic —Bl.-Debr. § 94.

VERSES 36f.: Barnabas' deed serves Luke as a concrete example of this spirit of sacrifice, and at the same time brings this important man before the readers (Wellhausen, 9). Luke uses the by-name Barnabas, bestowed by the Apostles,[6] to distinguish this Joseph, as he should rightly be called, from his

---

[1] See Deut. **6**.5; **10**.12; **11**.13; **13**.4; **26**.16; **30**.2, 6, 10 and elsewhere.

[2] Cf. H. von Schubert, 'Der Kommunismus der Wiedertäufer in Münster und seine Quellen', *SAH* 1919, Abh. 11: Acts 4 and the ancient ideal of true community worked together in Münster when the endeavour was made to realise the 'apostolic' ideal of poverty in apocalyptic expectation. On p. 38 an Essene influence on the primitive Church is conjectured.

[3] One should not follow Wendt (118) in linking 'the Apostles' with 'of the Lord Jesus': Luke treats 'the Apostles' as a fixed title and never links it with a genitive. The unusual word-order is explained by Luke's predilection for placing ideas he wishes to stress in a forward position (cf. on **1**.3 above).

[4] The parallel Luke **2**.40 shows (as Joachim Jeremias has remarked in conversation) that Luke is not here referring to the favour found by the Christians with the people.

[5] παρά τούς πόδας: Acts **4**.35, 37; **5**.2; **7**.58; **22**.3; Luke **7**.38, **8**.35, 41, **17**.16. Preuschen (27), referring to Ps. **8**.7 LXX πάντα ὑπέταξας ὑποκάτω τῶν ποδῶν αὐτοῦ, recalls an old custom whereby one setting his foot on a person or object acquired rights of property and free disposal over the same. Wetstein offers the following parallel from Cicero *Pro Flacco* 68: *ante pedes praetoris in foro expensum est auri pondo*. On καθότι ἄν τις χρείαν εἶχεν, see **2**.45.

[6] According to Preuschen (28), ἀπό τῶν ἀποστόλων means not 'by' but 'of the Apostles' and is used as a title. But Preuschen translates: 'Joseph, who was named Barnabas by the Apostles'. 'Barnabas of the Apostles' (= one of the Apostles) is not a possible title.

many namesakes, and explains it as 'Son of encouragement' or 'consolation'.[1] Bar-nabas would presumably, however, mean 'Son of Nebo'.[2] His family[3] comes from Cyprus.[4] E. Schwartz conjectured (*NGG*, 1907, 282 n. 1) that the precise report about Barnabas was contained in Luke's source for Acts **13**.1ff. and transposed to this place by Luke; in so doing he must have misapplied to Barnabas a note concerning Manaen (=Menahem, 'the comforter'). This is at all events more plausible than the attempts to derive 'son of consolation' from Barnabas. If Barnabas came from a family settled in Cyprus, he could have acquired land in Palestine through inheritance or purchase (Wendt, 199, recalls Jer. **32**.7ff.), but he might equally have sold a property in Cyprus and given the money to the brethren in Jerusalem (Jacquier, 149).

Earlier scholars mostly excluded verses 34f. as an editorial insertion (Wendt, 117 n. 1). Jeremias, Cerfaux and Benoit, however (see p. 194f. above), sensed an intruder in verse 33. According to Cerfaux it once stood between **5**.12a and **5**.12b (but how then did it get here?): according to Benoit it was inserted on the basis of **2**.47a (but there is no report there of the Apostles' witness to the Resurrection!). All three scholars however agree that verse 34 joins up with verse 32.

This does not spare us the necessity of making our own analysis. The summary properly begins with the imperfect ἐλάλουν in verse 31, the verse which describes the crucial event: they were all filled with the Holy Spirit, which allowed the Christian proclamation to go its way in joy and fearlessness. But Luke saw also another effect of the Spirit in the fact that the throng[5] of believers were of one heart and soul, that (as D E h Cypr rightly gloss) there was no division among them. This general characterization is now expanded by the special feature that no Christian regarded his possessions as his personal property: 'they had all things common'. Luke does not show how this worked in practice; there was something else which appeared to

---

[1] A. Klostermann (*Probleme im Aposteltexte*, 8ff.) explains Barnabas as rendering בַּר־נְוָחָא ('son of soothing'), but that would not have produced the Greek form Βαρνάβας. Wendt (119) suggests בַּר־נְבוּאָה ('son of prophecy'); but this is simply not υἱὸς τῆς παρακλήσεως (Loisy, 263).

[2] So Dalman, *Worte Jesu* I, 32, (ET *The Words of Jesus*); Deissmann, *Bibelstudien*, 177f. and *Neue Bibelstudien*, 15f. (ET *Bible Studies*, 1901); also Torrey, 31. According to Preuschen (28), 'Bar-Nebo' appears on inscriptions at Palmyra. As the bearer of the name of a pagan divinity, however, Barnabas could not have been a Levite. Luke, of course, does not mean that the Apostles called him "son of Nebo"; Billerbeck II, 634, confuses in his argumentation two wholly different standpoints.

[3] This according to *Beg*. IV, 49 is probably the best rendering of γένος: cf. Acts **18**.2, 24. τῷ γένει is a 'dative of reference' (Moulton, 75; Bl.-Debr. § 197).

[4] Cf. Acts **11**.20 (ἄνδρες Κύπριοι!) and **13**.4ff., **15**.39.

[5] Here πλῆθος means not only the 'congregation' but also the 'multitude'.

him more important than such details. For in depicting the heartfelt unity of the believers he had chosen such OT concepts as would simultaneously remind the cultivated reader of Aristotle's παροιμίαι in the Nicomachean Ethics. This Greek element was reinforced by πάντα κοινά, reminiscent of κοινὰ τὰ τῶν φίλων, which occurs not only in the same Aristotelian context but many times in Plato. In short, Luke is here suggesting that the primitive Church also realized the *Greek* communal ideal!

From the πλῆθος Luke now passes to its leaders, the Apostles; the transition is not so abrupt as is often maintained. This statement about the Apostles is linked with the prayer of the congregation and the bestowal of the Spirit (verses 30f.)—the miracles are of course tantamount to divine endorsement of the apostolic preaching. The latter part of the verse (firmly subjoined with τε) is Luke's bridge to verse 34: the blessing of God lay upon all, not only the Apostles. It was manifest also in the fact that the promise of Deut. 15.4 was here fulfilled: in this community no one suffered want. How this came about is explained by the sentence beginning with ὅσοι: whenever the community needed money, those who had valuable assets (houses or pieces of land) realized them and remitted the proceeds to the Apostles. From this fund every person in want received what he needed. Luke relates Barnabas' act of sacrifice as an example of such selfless behaviour. But the next story also, 5.1-11, is only comprehensible when there likewise it is a case of such an extraordinary deed as that of Barnabas.

Verses 32 and 34 thus do not speak of one and the same attitude towards property: in verse 32 it is retained, in 34f. sold. Verse 32 portrays the realization of the Greek communal ideal, 34f. the fulfilment of the OT promise. Luke has separated the one from the other by the statement about the Apostles.

In all likelihood Luke obtained verses 34f. by generalizing from the instances known to him involving Barnabas and Ananias. The traditional concepts regarding wealth and property included in the third gospel show plainly how dangerous he considered that bondage to the world which is the fruit of 'unrighteous Mammon'.

In reality, no doubt, the good deed of Barnabas only survived in memory because it was something out of the ordinary, not the rule. That being so, however, Troeltsch's picture of the 'primitive Christian love-communism' which prevailed at the beginning in the Jerusalem congregation (and whose collapse is said to have led to its later financial crisis) fades out of existence. Of course, such expedients as Luke describes in verses 34f. would not have covered the long-term financial needs of the community: only a few Christians can have possessed houses or real estate. But in reality even these few did not sell all their property—Acts 12.12 implies that Mary, the mother of John Mark, retained her house. That was entirely appropriate: the community needed houses in which to assemble.

On the other hand the Dead Sea scrolls, above all the 'Rule of the Community', seem to support the assumption that the Christians of the primitive community really did renounce private property. But on closer inspection this proves to be a deceptive appearance. The Essenes—it now seems virtually certain that in the Qumran 'Monastery' we have the ruins of their centre—did not form one uniform society, but various groups who lived side by side and in chronological succession. In the 'Monastery' no individual was allowed private property: whoever entered had to deposit his worldly possessions with the 'Overseer' at the end of the first year of novitiate, and make them over to the 'Order' when he was finally received (1 QS I, 11f.; Josephus *Bell.* II 122). From the fund thus created the needs of each were satisfied in equal fashion. Pliny the Elder (who died 79 A.D. in the eruption of Vesuvius) was also aware of this, as he describes the 'Esseni' living on the west bank of the Dead Sea as a community 'without money' (*h.n.* V 17, 13). The celibacy of the order is also mentioned in his account. Philo would appear to be saying the same thing when he calls the Ἐσσαῖοι[1] 'moneyless and propertyless' (*Quod omnis probus liber*, C.-W. VI § 77). Nevertheless, Philo differs in his picture of their way of life. It is true that his Ἐσσαῖοι are also unmarried, but instead of living in a kind of monastery in the wilderness, they dwell in the villages as γεωπονοῦντες or artisans (like Josephus, Philo numbers them at over 4,000). Each group lives under an 'overseer', to whom each member hands over his earnings, receiving clothing and food—i.e. a share of the communal meal—in return. The 'Damascus document' (*CDC* VI 15; VIII.5; XIX.17) opens up a third possibility: here only unjustified property is forbidden; the existence of the family is implicitly accepted, therefore only the earnings for two (?) working-days per month are deducted for poor-relief (XIV.12f.). From this one may see that the demands made on the individual correspond to the prevailing way of life, and that the total sacrifice of personal property is only called for when a celibate community is leading a monastic or semi-monastic existence.

There was no question of this in the Christian community at Jerusalem. The Apostles and the brothers of Jesus were married (I Cor. 9.5), as doubtless were most of the other Christians. Family life and monastic life are however incompatible. Furthermore these Christians did not form a closed and self-sufficient society like the men of Qumran. Some of them came from Galilee, where they had led the lives of small farmers or fishermen. This existence they could not continue in Jerusalem. Even if they had not simply abandoned their property there, in order to wait in Jerusalem for the coming of the Messiah Jesus, even if they had sold or leased out their house, land or boat, they could not have brought much with them on which to live. In Jerusalem they scarcely had any choice but to earn their own and their families' keep

---

[1] Like Ἐσσηνοί in Josephus, this is evidently a Greek rendering of an Aramaic designation.

as day-labourers or servants. Christians already resident in Jerusalem were more favourably placed (among them were the Hellenists—see § 16 below): they had their calling and income in the city before becoming Christians, and these would not have been unduly affected by membership of the new community. A not wholly negligible charge on the community, who had to support them, were the families of the Apostles and of Jesus' brothers. To these must be added the widows—many Jews came to Jerusalem to die and be buried in the Holy City, and their widows had no families to look after them. Hence the relief-work of the Christian community had begun even before the persecution of the year 44—indeed before the controversy with the Hellenists (Acts 6.1ff.). But the situation was precarious, and it is easy to understand why, at the 'Apostolic Council', the three 'pillars' of the community at Jerusalem should have begged Barnabas and Paul, representing the community at Antioch, to collect for the poor of the parent congregation (Gal. 2.10). And if we further remember that (see Jeremias, *Jerusalem zur Zeit Jesu* I, 59ff., ET *Jerusalem in the Time of Jesus*, 1969, 121f.) the economic state of Palestine was all the time steadily deteriorating through famine and continued unrest, we cannot but assume that the early community lived in increasingly straitened circumstances and was constantly driven back on the spirit of sacrifice of its members and their brethren in other congregations. True, this does not wholly match the sunlit picture given in the Lucan text. But it is nevertheless consistent with it in the same way as a historical situation with the transfigured portrait which later generations developed in the course of tradition.

13
ACTS 5: 1–11
ANANIAS AND SAPPHIRA

[1] But a man named Ananias, with his wife Sapphira, sold a property, [2] and kept back part of the price, with his wife's connivance, and part he brought and laid it at the Apostles' feet. [3] But Peter said, 'Ananias, why has Satan filled your heart to lie to the Holy Spirit, and to keep back part of the price of the land? [4] While it remained (unsold), did it not remain your own? and after it was sold, was it not in your power? Why have you conceived this thing in your heart? You have not lied to men, but to God!' [5] When Ananias heard these words he fell down and expired. And great fear came upon all who heard it. [6] And the younger men arose and wrapped him up, and carried him out and buried him. [7] And there was an interval of about three hours, and his wife came in, not knowing anything of what had happened. [8] And Peter addressed her, 'Tell me, did you sell the land for so much?' And she said, 'Yes, for so much.' [9] But Peter (said) to her: 'Why have you agreed together to tempt the Spirit of the Lord? Behold, the feet of those who buried your husband are at the door, and they shall carry you out!' [10] And she fell down immediately at his feet, and expired: and the young men came in and found her dead, and they carried her out and buried her by her husband. [11] And great fear came upon the whole congregation, and upon all who heard these things.

Bibliography:

A. d'Alès, 'Act. **5**.3', *RScR* 24 (1934), 194f.; P.-H. Menoud, 'La Mort d'Ananias et de Saphira', *Mélanges Goguel* (1950), 146–54 (on **5**.1–11); H. Cunliffe-Jones, *Congr. Quart.* 27 (1949), 116–21 (on **5**.1–11); Reicke, 89–96; Trocmé, 196ff. and 217; J. Schmitt, *Les Manuscrits de la Mer Morte*, 1957, 93–109; Conzelmann 39f.

    E. Becker, 'Ananias u. Sapphira', *Röm. Quartalschr. für christl. Altertumskunde usw.* (1909), 183–94; P. Joüon et A. d'Alès, 'Actes **5**.3', *RScR* 24 (1934), 199f.; F. Scheidweiler, 'Zu Acta **5**.4', *ZNW* 49 (1958), 136f.

VERSE 1 presents the *dramatis personae*: a Jewish Christian called Ananias[1] and his wife Sapphira,[2] names doubtless originating in pre-Lucan tradition. Ananias sells his κτῆμα =parcel of land.[3]

VERSE 2: ἐνοσφίσατο[4] recalls Joshua 7.1–26 LXX (Achan misappropriated =ἐνοσφίσατο part of the spoils consecrated to Yahweh and was stoned to death for it) and implies that Ananias had no right to withold any part of the proceeds. Luke will have found the expression 'laid at the Apostles' feet' here in the tradition, and used it in 4.35 and 37 also (Bauernfeind, 85).

VERSE 3: Peter appears as spokesman for the community. As not uncommonly in Luke (see above on 1.4: 'the promise of the Father'), two ideas are telescoped in his question: 1. Why have you done this? and 2. Satan has filled your heart.[5] Ananias has lied to the Holy Spirit, inasmuch as the Spirit is present in Peter (and in the community). Hence in the last resort it is not simply two men who confront one another, but in them the Holy Spirit and Satan, whose instruments they are.

VERSE 4 is in tension with 4.32 and 34. Luke must have reasoned that the spontaneity with which all devoted their property to the common cause should, in itself, have permitted Ananias to keep his. 'Why[6] have you conceived this thing[7] in your heart[8]?' Ananias thought he was dealing only with men, but in reality he was offending against God, who through his Spirit is present in the community.

Verses 4f., especially, have called down the wrath of the critics on this story. Wendt asks (121), 'Did this first sordid offence deserve . . . an immediate capital punishment which allowed no time for repentance?' and W. L. Knox remarks: 'We may hope that Ananias and Sapphira are legendary' (63).

VERSE 5: 'While Ananias was listening to these words,[9] he fell down and

---

[1] Probably =חֲנַנְיָה, 'Jahweh is merciful', as in Tobit 5.13, Judith 8.1, IV Macc. 16.21. Another possibility is however עֲנָנְיָה, 'Jahweh hears', as in Neh. 3.23. The name Ananias also appears in Acts 9.10, 22.12 and 23.2.

[2] The πφ corresponds to a Hebrew פ; what is meant is the Aramaic name שַׁפִּירָא, 'the beautiful'. In 1923 this name was found on an ossuary at Jerusalem (Bruce, 152).

[3] In Hellenistic times κτῆμα meant only landed property, a field or parcel (it renders שָׂדֶה in Prov. 23.10 LXX), hence it may be varied with χωρίον in verses 3 and 8.

[4] *Beg.* IV, 50, gives many precedents and literary references for this word, which in Hellenism always implies: (a) that the theft was secret, (b) its object was part of a larger sum, (c) which was the property of a community. But 'Acts certainly describes the offence as not against men but God'.

[5] A scribal error turned ἐπλήρωσεν into ἐπήρωσεν (א), which under the influence of πειράσαι (verse 9) was wrongly emended into ἐπείρασεν (*Beg.* IV, 50).

[6] τί ὅτι: properly τί γέγονεν, ὅτι (John 14.22)—Bl.-Debr. § 299, 4.

[7] In *Beg.* IV, 51, πρᾶγμα is translated 'business'.

[8] Cf. Luke 21.14. τίθεμαι ἐν τῇ καρδίᾳ: LXX I Sam. 21.13 and 29.10; in Jer. 12.11 for שִׂים עַל־לֵב, but not unGreek—cf. Homer's θέσθαι ἐπὶ φρέσιν, to which of course τίθεσθαι ἐπὶ τὴν καρδίαν (שִׂים עַל־לֵב) elsewhere in LXX is still closer.

[9] According to Wendt (120) the present participle expresses simultaneity: while still listening, he abruptly collapses, as if struck by lightning.

expired.'[1] Luke surely felt that ἐκψύχω was an expression well-suited to the fearful solemnity of the scene. The meaning is wholly missed when attempts are made to translate the incident in terms of modern psychology, e.g. 'As a result of the shock treatment Ananias suffered a fatal collapse.' God, who speaks by the mouth of the Apostles, is executing judgment! Thus the 'great fear' which 'came upon all that heard it' also becomes understandable. As De Wette says (*Apg.*[4], 70), 'οἱ ἀκούοντες are not those present, who of course not merely heard but saw'.[2]

VERSE 6: νεώτεροι (in verse 10 νεανίσκοι) is a term denoting age, not office[3] (Preuschen, 29). συστέλλω must here mean 'cover up'.[4] The narrative keeps to essentials, but these bare indications are striking enough: a shroud is thrown over the corpse, which is carried out (on a bier) to the burial-place and immediately interred.

VERSE 7: According to Bl.-Debr. § 144 (appendix), Luke has here combined two usages: ἐγένετο . . . καί (a phrase with which LXX renders וַיְהִי) and 'the use of the asyndetically prefixed nominative absolute to express chronology.' Thus διάστημα[5] is nominative: 'It came to pass—(there being) about three hours' interval—and his wife came in all unsuspecting.' Loisy misses the point by asking the purpose of her visit: the unsuspecting Sapphira has to come in to make the next scene possible. Ancient listeners were ready to pass over such secondary questions, which interfered with the edifying effect.

VERSE 8: ἀπεκρίθη[6]: Peter's words are not meant to give Sapphira a 'last chance' of confessing the truth,[7] but to make her complicity plain to

---

[1] In LXX ἐκψύχω is used of the dying of Sisera, Judges 4.21A. In Acts 5.5, 10 and 12.23 it is applied to the death of one struck by divine punishment. The word probably entered neo-Greek from vulgar Greek, where it had replaced the classical ἀποψύχω. To suppose it here used as a medical term (Hobart, 37) is to ignore the demands of style (see Introduction, p. 73 n. 2 above).

[2] De Wette explains this expression as 'a prolepsis'. Overbeck adds: 'The author hastens, as it were, to impress the thing on the reader's mind.' Such explanations seem called for only because the story runs on after verse 5. Originally, however, it will have ended with this typical conclusion of a miracle-story.

[3] Since the νεώτεροι are here introduced as if they required no explaining, Bauernfeind (86f.) holds it possible that Luke found some expression denoting an office in his source and has made it unrecognizable, as in his belief the only office which existed at this early stage was that of Apostle.

[4] In medicine the term was used of bandaging. But the corpse would not be swathed in winding-sheets in the very room where the Apostles sit enthroned!

[5] Ecclesiasticus Prologue 32 ἐν τῷ διαστήματι τοῦ χρόνου and III Macc. 4.17 τοῦ χρόνου διάστημα; otherwise LXX uses διάστημα only in the spatial sense. It is wrong, *pace* Bauernfeind (86), to speak of a 'Semitism'.

[6] In LXX ἀποκρίνομαι is used in the sense of 'to begin (to speak)', which gave rise to the frequent ἀποκριθεὶς εἶπεν. Here Luke simplifies and enlivens by the omission of εἶπεν.

[7] Despite Chrysostom's 'Peter wants to save her', quoted with approval by Jacquier (154).

the reader. She is given no time to repent (Loisy, 269). τοσούτου[1]: the sum
of money still lies at the Apostles' feet, just as Ananias had laid it.

VERSE 9: 'Why did you arrange together[2] to tempt the Spirit of the
Lord?' As in verse 3, Peter's question fuses two ideas: 1. Why did you plot
this deceit? and 2. You have tempted the Spirit of the Lord. They have unwittingly provoked God, as did rebellious Israel in the wilderness. Peter's
declaration introduced by ἰδού is not only a prophecy (so Bauernfeind, 84)
but a pronouncement of the divine judgment and its immediate execution.[3]

VERSE 10: In exactly the same way as Ananias, Sapphira falls dead as if
struck by lightning. The entry of the 'young men', their finding her dead,
carrying her out and burying her beside her husband—all this is handled
without pity, for we are in the presence of the divine punishment which should
be witnessed in fear and trembling, but not with Aristotelian fear and pity.

VERSE 11 describes the effect on 'the whole congregation'—the word
ἐκκλησία here appears for the first time in Acts—'and upon all who heard
these things' (cf. ἀκούοντας in verse 5): i.e. the non-Christian world, which
learned of the incident with shuddering awe. Here the tale ends.

This story seems an exact parallel of Achan's (Joshua, Ch. 7); like him
Ananias has misappropriated something which belongs to God (part of the
promised money) and is punished with death for it. Here, however, it is not
a question of booty consecrated to Yahweh, but of a voluntary gift of money
to the community, and Ananias is not stoned by the community but Peter's
accusation causes him to fall dead. The end of his wife Sapphira resembles
Achan's more closely: Peter *kills* her by announcing her husband's demise
and her own imminent death. The way in which Paul consigns a guilty man
to Satan (I Cor. 5.1–5) does not offer an exact parallel, for Ananias and his
wife are not killed in order that their πνεῦμα may be saved in the Last Judgment! How little a modern psychological interpretation meets the case is
evident in Reicke's thesis, for Sapphira does not, as he says (p. 89), die of
shame, but collapses at the news that her husband has already been buried
and that it is now her own turn. But Bauernfeind also (p. 84) gets into difficulties: Peter does not merely prophesy Sapphira's death but, as Rieu rightly
asserts (p. 124), wants to kill—and succeeds. Here we pass from the *quaestio
facti* to the *quaestio iuris*. Wendt had already asked (p. 121) why Peter did
not give the couple a chance (after all, according to Matt. **18**.15 one first
talks to the sinner in private: the questions *coram publico* in verses 3 and
8 are anything but a 'last-chance' offer!). Rieu accordingly accuses Peter

---

[1] Genitive of price (Bl.-Debr. § 179).

[2] Bl.-Debr. § 202, § 409, 3 appendix.—D's συνεφώνησεν ὑμῖν is a verbatim translation
of d's *convenit*!

[3] The mention of 'feet' corresponds to OT usage; cf. e.g. Isaiah **52**.7 and especially
59.7.

outright: what he did was a sin, at least by the standard of Jesus, who did not kill Judas at the Last Supper! Menoud therefore (p. 153f.) takes this story to be a legend: Ananias and Sapphira were the first persons to die in the primitive community; people had forgotten the cause of their death, but legend insisted on knowing, and Luke connected it with the communal-property system. However, by the time Ananias and Sapphira were remembered as mere names, the shock of Christians' dying before the Parousia—if indeed such a shock (cf. I Thess. **4**.13ff.) had ever been felt in Jerusalem—had long been overcome. People had learned that even Christians die, and had therefore no need to invent a legend to explain Ananias' death. For this reason Schmitt expresses approval of Menoud's general thesis (p. 101) but alters his explanation, tackling the story from the viewpoint of form criticism: the passage combines a first theme, 'the sinner shall be destroyed' (cf. **3**.23), with a second, namely that the others are deterred from sin by holy fear (Rieu says frankly 'terror'!). In this way Schmitt finds the *Sitz im Leben*: it was a cautionary tale told to the newly-baptized for catechetic purposes, to make it clear that God watches over the purity of the community and exacts vengeance for its violation. It is not wholly clear whether Schmitt sees in this merely an instructive fiction (Pfleiderer, 559, had previously spoken of an 'allegorical fable') or an incident which had really occurred. At all events, Trocmé took up his idea in terms of the latter (198f.), suggesting that the couple had wanted to use the ostensibly total sacrifice of their wealth to buy entry into the circle of the τέλειοι, who might perhaps be identified with the 120 of Acts **1**.15. Both Schmitt and Trocmé refer to the requirement of community of goods in force at Qumran (see pp. 234–5 above), where the member who lied about his possessions was severely punished (I QS VI.24f.). Both also venture to interpret the νεώτεροι of verse 6 as novices, while according to Schmitt (104) Peter's role corresponds to the disciplinary function in Qumran of the Mebaqqer, or 'Overseer'.

The observations of Menoud, Schmitt and Trocmé are valuable and open up new paths of investigation. Menoud recognizes that the story has only a secondary connection with Luke's general community of goods: verse 4 indeed emphasizes that the surrender of property was entirely voluntary; and if we imagine that all the other Christians made this sacrifice freely, but Ananias—under moral obligation—did not want to be left out, yet at the same time privately sought to ensure his security, that certainly makes him a moral weakling whom we can understand all too well (what doesn't a modern man do, because 'one' must act thus and thus?)—but not a transgressor worthy of death. Trocmé is absolutely right: the story is only comprehensible if Ananias and Sapphira wanted to enjoy the glory of the exceptional without making the corresponding sacrifice. But there were not 120 wealthy members in the Jerusalem congregation, and of the few who did have property only a handful sold their χωρίον and donated the proceeds to the community—at all events, Barnabas and Ananias were the only names handed down!

The misguided attempt to ascribe the surrender of property to a large but strictly circumscribed group of 'perfects' must be blamed on the—at present—inapposite concentration on Qumran, where certainly such a circle of 'men of exceptional holiness' did exist (1 QS VIII.20ff.). It is quite wrong to say that Peter acts like a Mebaqqer of Qumran: the Overseer did not execute judgments of God but 'shall have mercy on them as a father on his sons, and shall bring back all their erring ones as a shepherd does with his flock' (CDC XIII.7ff.; translation by Millar Burrows, *The Dead Sea Scrolls*, 1955, 362). If a member tells a lie about his property, Qumran punishes him not with death, but with one year's reduction to the rank of novice and the curtailment of one part in four of his food (1 QS VI.24f.). Verse 10 shows that Luke saw the νεώτεροι simply as νεανίσκοι 'youths', and there is nothing to justify the assumption that the early Christians were subjected to a lengthy novitiate (cf. the immediate succession of baptism upon conversion in Acts 2.38, 41; 8.36; 9.18 and 10.48). What was there for them to learn apart from the one essential that Jesus was the Messiah?

Schmitt too is right in detecting a cautionary tale in this episode. Whatever did occur, it could not have developed in the way reported by verses 6–11. That after three hours the Apostles should still be sitting as before, with the money at their feet, is the least objection to be made. But that the Christians should simply have buried the corpse of Ananias, without a word to his wife—even if this is indispensable to Sapphira's own story—sins against all objective and subjective plausibility.

The story of Ananias himself is another matter: it presupposes that a Christian filled with the Spirit has the power of looking into the heart of a sinner (cf. I Cor. 14.24f.) and that a deceiver so convicted simply collapses at the exposure of his guilt. Why should the traditions of the Jerusalem community not have contained such a story? If they did, however, there is no denying that Luke must have reworked an already expanded version, bringing the theme of 'not men, but God' to the fore. The original story probably closed with the judgment which befell the sinner and its effect on those who heard of it. It was not concerned with what became of the corpse. All that mattered has been said: God visits a dreadful vengeance on deceivers. With that the narrative has reached its goal.

14
ACTS 5:12–16
THE MIRACLES OF THE APOSTLES

[12] By the hands of the Apostles many signs and wonders were wrought among the people; and they were all with one accord in Solomon's Portico. [13] But of the rest no man dared join himself to them: but the people magnified them; [14] and more were added as believers to the Lord, multitudes both of men and women; [15] so that they even carried out the sick into the streets, and laid them on beds and couches, that as Peter came by at least his shadow might fall on one of them. [16] And there also came together the multitude from the cities round about Jerusalem, bringing the sick and those afflicted with unclean spirits, who were healed every one.

Bibliography:

Reicke, 89–96; Trocmé, 30, 81, 183 and 195f.; Williams (1957), 89; Conzelmann, 41.

VERSE 12 begins a new 'summary'. It is not only Peter but 'the Apostles'[1] who perform many 'signs and wonders'[2] among the people. They and the other Christians gather with one accord[3] in Solomon's Portico (cf. on **3.11** above).

VERSE 13: 'The rest',[4] i.e. the non-Christians, do not dare to consort[5] with the Christians in Solomon's Portico (actual entry into the community is not meant at this point). Thus the Christians form a self-contained group from which the others keep their distance—not, as the continuation makes clear, out of enmity, for the people sang their praises, but in reverent awe.

[1] διὰ χειρὸς τῶν: LXX style.
[2] See on **4.30** above. The fulfilment of the congregation's prayer continues.
[3] In Hellenism ὁμοθυμαδόν gradually weakened to mean simply 'together' (as in Acts **15.25**)—*Beg*. IV, 54. Here, however, it doubtless retains its full meaning.
[4] In Luke **8.10**, reproducing Mark **4.11**, Luke replaced the term οἱ ἔξω with οἱ λοιποί. Wendt's distinction (122) between λαός as the narrower term (the people favourable to the Christians) and οἱ λοιποί as the wider, including also those hostile (!), betrays the exegete's utter helplessness at this point. Dibelius' conjecture, ἀρχόντων (*Studies* 91), was just a makeshift.
[5] In Acts **8.29** also κολλᾶσθαι has the sense of spatial proximity. But in **10.28**, **17.34** and—more especially—**9.26** it also at the same time suggests the alliance of hearts and minds. In LXX κολλάω is used to translate various Hebrew verbs, whose meanings vary from physical sticking to subjective adherence.

VERSE 14: Luke does not mean by this that the community won no new members at all; on the contrary, masses of men and women,[1] in even greater numbers than before,[2] were brought as believers to the Lord.[3]—This verse is generally conceived as a parenthesis.

VERSE 15: As Bauernfeind rightly saw, the clause introduced by ὥστε relates to the whole preceding account of the esteem in which the Christians were held. The subject of ἐκφέρειν is the indefinite 'they'—here referring not to the new converts but to the non-Christian Jews of Jerusalem. It is peculiar that the rare κ'ἄν (='even only': Bl.-Debr. § 18) occurs in the close parallel Mark 6.56, which Luke did not accept into his gospel. Loisy (274) thinks that Luke renounced using this passage in his gospel in order to place it here. That in Luke's opinion Peter's shadow possessed healing power ought not to be disputed; that such healings were merely expected, without actually occurring, would have had to be stated.

VERSE 16: The fame of the Christian miracles spreads outside Jerusalem, and from the 'cities' round about—though there are of course no real πόλεις in the vicinity[4]—the sick and bedevilled are brought in and cured, every one.[5] But it is precisely this extraordinary success within and without Jerusalem which causes the Sadducees to take counter-action.

This third important summary (see above on 2.42-7 and 4.32-7) has been a battlefield of the critics for the past sixty years, though at first sight a free-for-all is raging, rather than a battle. But a closer look reveals certain alliances. More important, however, than the hypotheses erected by this or that scholar are the observations from which they derive. Basically these are two in number, the first being that there is no proper connection between verses 14 and 15, the second that 15 would link up convincingly with 12a.

---

[1] Does this specific mention of women imply that Luke has hitherto reported only conversions of men?

[2] Bauer, *Wb* 966.

[3] As Acts **11**.24 unequivocally exhibits the phrase 'to add to the Lord', we may assume its correctness here, though Bauernfeind (89), appealing to Acts **16**.34 and **18**.8, wishes to connect πιστεύοντες τῷ κυρίῳ together.

[4] Wendt (123) falls back on the supposition that here πόλεις refers to mere townships. Loisy (274) points to Luke **6**.17 (which is similar even in wording) and correspondingly interprets the πόλεις as the towns in Judaea.—Luke had no exact ideas of the geography of Palestine.

[5] οἵτινες (cf. **7**.53, **8**.15, **9**.35, **10**.41, **10**.47, **11**.20, **11**.28, **12**.10, **13**.31, **13**.43, **16**.12, **16**.16f., **17**.10f., **21**.4, **23**.14, **23**.21, **23**.33, **24**.1 and **28**.18): in Hellenism there is no longer any sharp distinction between ὅς, the relative pronoun with definite reference, and ὅστις = 'whosoever' (*quicumque*); ὅστις remains prized by men of letters for its fuller sonority (Radermacher², 75; Bl.-Debr. § 293, esp. appendix). While (apart from the formula ἕως ὅτου) the word scarcely appears in LXX save in the nominatives ὅστις, ἥτις, οἵτινες, αἵτινες, Luke uses the pronouns ἥτις, οἵτινες, αἵτινες in Acts as definite relatives, not only in such cases as **8**.15, where the simple οἵ would have been confused with the article, but systematically.

This led Harnack and Sorof to remove verse 14, B. Weiss verse 16 also, and Hilgenfeld verses 15 and 16. This was contradicted by Spitta and J. Weiss: since verse 15 fitted so well with 12a, it was 12b–14 which must be eliminated. Spitta's work on Acts appeared in 1891—but Benoit arrived at exactly the same conclusion in 1950! Jeremias also saw the connection between 12a and 15, but made a different inference: that verses 15 and 16 were an addition related to 12a.

It is Benoit's thesis that makes the most immediate impact: the redactor, he says, has once again, as in the cases of 2.43 and 4.33, deposited a cuckoo's egg—verses 12b–14—in the middle of a cohesive summary. He expanded each summary with ideas taken from the other two, and placed the expansion in the middle so as not to harm the summary's continuity with the surrounding context.

Nevertheless, before making so free, as used to be common practice, with the idea of a redactor, it is worthwhile giving a moment's consideration to the position of the author Luke. In 5.1–11 he had just depicted a miraculous punishment brought about by Peter. He now intends to relate new persecution which the Sadducees set afoot against the Christians because of their success. 5.17ff. thus could not attach directly to 5.11; before 5.17 Luke had to report the great success of the Christians. The story of Ananias, however, demanded a quite different continuation: after the great φόβος aroused by the punishing of the couple, one would expect the Jews to sense the *mysterium tremendum* and apprehensively keep their distance. (This is not to say that Luke followed this line of conscious reasoning; a good narrator senses, even without reflection, what the continuation of his story demands.) Thus a contradiction inevitably arose: on the one hand an awestruck reserve, on the other great missionary successes. This contradiction lay in the material itself, and we need no blundering redactor to explain it. Let us rather see how Luke tried to overcome the difficulty.

He begins by 'generalizing' (verse 12a) the Petrine miracle just reported: it is not only Peter but 'the Apostles' in general who perform many signs and wonders. Peter's prominence in the first part of Acts has given rise to the mistaken notion that Luke meant to present him as the Prince of Apostles. There is no question of this. He is the Twelve's representative (alone or with John) and their spokesman. But he has to render an account of what he does in that capacity (see 11.1–17). As has already been remarked, Luke knows no Petrine, only an Apostolic Church. Hence it is no 'mere' generalization if, despite the almost total absence from his tradition of feats other than Peter's, Luke now ascribes the signs and wonders to all the Apostles. In this 'generalization' lies embedded a piece of his theology.

From the Apostles Luke turns to the congregation (πάντες, verse 13). They, naturally including the Apostles, were all gathered 'with one accord' in the *stoa* of Solomon. At the time when Luke wrote, the Temple had been destroyed for a decade. By mentioning this building, Luke is seeking to implant a vivid image in the minds of his readers, most of whom had never seen the Temple. Each might now summon up a vision of a colonnaded hall in which the Apostles were teaching like the ancient philosophers. Round this group of Christians holy awe draws its protective circle: none of the 'rest', the non-Christians, dare mix with the listening believers (here, as in 8.29, the word κολλᾶσθαι does not mean joining the congregation, but simply physical approach). So that the reader may not misunderstand this reserve on the part of the λοιποί, Luke adds that the people praised the Christians: it was not hostility but reverent awe which made them keep their distance from the circle in Solomon's Portico. However, this explanation was not enough: it would now appear as if no one dared join the congregation. To remove this impression Luke continues by intimating, in verse 14, that the influx of new members became still greater than before.

Luke's negotiation of a dangerous reef is in this way fairly successful. He plots his course from holy φόβος to μεγαλύνειν, thence to προστίθεσθαι, and—unless one reads more into κολλᾶσθαι than it implies—the way is not so hard to follow.

Yet with the end in sight Luke fetches up against another, not inconsiderable hazard. Among the traditions that had come down to him was a story of the healing shadow of Peter. We may well imagine that he was not minded to forgo so striking a proof of Christian thaumaturgy. But it made rather a lame connection with the mass-conversions just reported. So Luke ties it very loosely, by means of ὥστε καί, to all the details with which he has sought to convey the impression made by the Christians on the Jewish people, viz. 'the result was that the people even carried the sick into the streets', etc. Even this singular story of the healing shadow is capped by verse 16, inasmuch as this shows the effects of Christianity rippling out beyond Jerusalem: the sick and the possessed are brought in even from 'the cities round about Jerusalem' (a scene with a strong appeal to the reader's imagination)—to whom is not stated, but one may conclude from verse 18 that Luke has the Apostles in mind—'and they were healed every one'.

Thus the healing of the cripple, which first provoked the Sadducees' intervention by commending Christ and his followers to the people, has now been repeated ten, a hundred times over; so it is not to be wondered at if the jealous ζῆλος of the Sadducees erupts anew . . .

It should be clear from the foregoing that there is no necessity to bring in a redactor. The passage is completely intelligible in terms of the difficulties faced at this juncture by the author Luke. Nobody will pretend that he mastered them all; but others would have done no better.

The only serious difficulty which this summary offers—for reformed theology, that is—lies in the story of Peter's healing shadow. To say that Luke merely wished to depict the people's great expectations, not the Apostle's real miracles, or that Peter did not approve the people's action, is to fall back on apologetic devices which, however well-meant, are useless. For it is not only the sick from outside who are 'all' (verse 16) healed in Jerusalem, but the sick in Jerusalem too, and Acts **19**.12 shows that Luke has nothing against this popular conception of miracles. It was present in the community long before Luke: the Corinthians who in II Cor. **12**.12 find the σημεῖα τοῦ ἀποστόλου missing in Paul obviously imagine a true Apostle as a heavenly visitant imbued with miraculous powers. In the summary before us, it must be confessed, this idea of the Apostle is so heightened as to be fantastic: Peter need not so much as touch a sick person to cure him—it is enough for his shadow to fall on him. If this is so, however, the Apostle can no longer be distinguished from the θεῖος ἄνθρωπος dear to paganism. We see here the danger threatening the popular tradition of the apostolic miracles: it transforms the μάρτυς 'Ιησοῦ Χριστοῦ into a man filled to his very shadow with miraculous power, by the aid of which he directly manifests the divine omnipotence. It cannot well be denied that the Pauline understanding of the apostolate (cf. E. Käsemann, 'Die Legitimität des Apostels', *ZNW* 41 (1942), 33–71) is here being abandoned.

15

ACTS 5: 17–42
THE APOSTLES BEFORE THE COUNCIL

[17] But the High Priest rose up, and all who were with him, the party of the Sadducees, and they were filled with jealousy, [18] and laid hands on the Apostles, and put them in public custody. [19] But an angel of the Lord by night opened the prison doors, and brought them out, and said: [20] 'Go and stand in the Temple and speak to the people all the words of this life!' [21] And when they heard this, they entered into the Temple about daybreak, and taught. But the High Priest came, and those who were with him, and called the Council together, and all the senate of the children of Israel, and sent to the prison to have them brought. [22] But when the officers came they did not find them in the prison; and they returned and reported, [23] saying: 'The prison we found shut with all security, and the keepers standing at the doors; but when we opened, we found no one inside.' [24] Now when the captain of the Temple and the chief priests heard these words, they were much perplexed concerning them, (wondering) what this would lead to. [25] And someone came and told them: 'Look, the men whom you put in the prison are standing in the Temple and teaching the people.' [26] Then the captain went with the officers and brought them, without violence, for they feared the people, lest they should be stoned. [27] And when they had brought them, they set them before the Council. And the High Priest asked them, [28] saying: 'We strictly charged you not to teach in this name, and behold, you have filled Jerusalem with your teaching, and intend to bring this man's blood upon us.' [29] But Peter and the Apostles answered and said: 'One must obey God rather than men. [30] The God of our fathers raised up Jesus, whom you slew, hanging him on a tree. [31] Him did God exalt to his right hand as a Prince and a Saviour, to give repentance to Israel and remission of sins. [32] And we are witnesses of these things, and the Holy Spirit, whom God has given to those who obey him.' [33] But when they heard this, they were furious, and wanted to slay them. [34] But there stood up in the Council a Pharisee named Gamaliel, a doctor of the law held in honour by all the people, and commanded that the men be taken out a little while. [35] And he said to them: 'Men of Israel, take care what you are about to do concerning these men. [36] For before these days rose up Theudas, giving himself out to be somebody; to whom a number of men, about four hundred, attached themselves. He was slain, and all who obeyed

him were dispersed and came to nothing. [37] After him rose up Judas the Galilean in the days of the census, and led people away after him. He also perished, and all who obeyed him were scattered. [38] And now I say to you, Stand away from these men, and let them alone: for if this counsel or this work is of men, it will be overthrown, [39] but if it is of God, you will not be able to overthrow them; that you may not be found even fighting against God.' They took his advice, [40] and when they had called in the Apostles, they had them flogged and charged them not to speak in the name of Jesus, and let them go. [41] So they went from the presence of the Council, rejoicing that they were counted worthy to suffer dishonour for the Name. [42] And all day long, in the Temple and at home, they did not cease to teach and preach Jesus the Christ.

Bibliography:

F. Büchsel, 'Zur Blutsgerichtsbarkeit des Synhedriums', *ZNW* 30 (1931), 202–10 and 33 (1934), 84–7 (on **5**.33); E. Fascher, 'Die Auferstehung Jesu und ihr Verhältnis zur urchristlichen Verkündigung', *ZNW* 26 (1927), 1–25; L. Campeau, 'Theudas le faux prophète et Judas le Galiléen', *Sc. Eccl.* 5 (1953), Montreal, 235–45 (on **5**.34ff.); H. Lietzmann, 'Bemerkungen zum Prozess Jesu', *ZNW* 30 (1931), 211–5 and 31 (1932), 78–84 (on **5**.33); Goguel, 'A propos du procès de Jésus', *ZNW* 31 (1932), 289–301 (on **5**.33); V. Ryssel, 'Materialien zur Geschichte der Kreuzauffindungslegende in der syrischen Literatur', *ZKG* 15 (1895), 222–43, esp. 233–40 (on **5**.34); M. S. Enslin, 'Paul and Gamaliel', *JRel.* 7 (1927) no. 1; Reicke, 96–108; Trocmé 82, 102ff. and 208–10; Williams, 91–5; Wilckens, *Missionsreden*[2] 45–62; Conzelmann 40–3.

J. W. Swain, 'Gamaliel's Speech and Caligula's Statue (Acts **5**.34–39)', *HTR* 37 (1944), 341–9; P. Winter, 'Miszellen zu Apg. **5**.26 (Theudas), **15**.14 und die lukanische Kompositionstechnik', *Ev. Th.* 17 (1957), 348–406.

VERSE 17: ἀναστάς,[1] like παραγενόμενος in verse 21, relates to the word immediately following. The parade of antagonists seen in **4**.6 is not repeated; simply the High Priest and the αἵρεσις[2] of the Sadducees are once again named as enemies of the Christians (see on **4**.1 above). As later in **13**.45, 'they are filled with[3] jealousy' over the Christians' mounting influence.

[1] Blass wanted (with *perp*) to read Ἅννας. His suggestion was well received by Preuschen (31), Wellhausen (10), Loisy (275) and Dibelius (*Studies* 91: 'worth considering'). However, Luke uses the anticipatory ἀναστάς in Luke 23.1 and Acts 5.34 and 23.9 also. The expression, derived from LXX, has at all events more force than *Beg.* IV (56: 'little more than a copula') grants to it. '*Annas autem* [*perp*]: an early corruption'—Bruce, 140.

[2] See *ThWb* I, 181. The word has not yet acquired any 'heretical' taint or connotation. Here, as in Acts 13.1, 14.13 (D) and 28.17, the preceding οὖσα may be regarded as 'a mannerism peculiarly characteristic of Hellenistic officialese yet also (as evidenced even in NT) of a popular nature' (E. Mayser, *Grammatik der griechischen Papyri* II 1, 347ff.). While, according to Mayser, the addition of this word makes no difference to the sense, it here appears to lend a more official, and at the same time more menacing sound to the whole. *Beg.* IV, 57 contains a survey of the various interpretations put forward.

[3] πλησθῆναι + partitive genitive (Bl.-Debr. § 172)—common in LXX.

VERSE 18: ἐπιβαλεῖν τὰς χεῖρας: see on **4**.3 above (other instances: Luke **20**.19 and **21**.12; Acts **12**.1 and **21**.27). The Apostles are thrown into gaol.[1] This provides the occasion for the angel's intervention in the night. D completes the picture by adding, 'and they went home, every one'—not, as Fascher misconstrues (*Textgeschichte als hermeneutisches Problem*, 1953, 28), 'and each went into his individual cell'. Cf. verse 21.

VERSE 19: ἄγγελος κυρίου, an expression found *passim* in LXX, recurs in **7**.30 (D ℜ); **8**.26; **12**.7, 11; (**27**.23). διὰ νυκτός, like the classical νυκτός, =‘by night’ (Bl-Debr. § 223, 1). 'From the threefold occurrence in Acts of the theme of prison doors miraculously opened, and its equal allocation to the Apostles (**5**.19), Peter (**12**.6–11) and Paul (**16**.26f.), not to mention the coincidence in numerous details with ancient parallels, . . . one would hazard a guess that Luke is at least modelling his text on some established τόπος' (Jeremias, *ThWb* III, 175f.).

VERSE 20: ἵστασθαι =‘stand up to make a speech’ (see notes on **2**.14 and cf. verse 25).[2] The peculiar expression τῆς ζωῆς ταύτης doubtless means the same as τῆς σωτηρίας ταύτης in **13**.26: the ‘life’ and ‘salvation’ brought by Jesus.[3]

VERSE 21: According to Josephus *Ant.* XVIII.29, the gates of the Temple were opened at midnight. But the worshippers—hence also the Apostles— came only at dawn. Now the scene changes. The High Priest, whose name is not mentioned,[4] appears with his train (cf. verse 17). πᾶσαν τὴν γερουσίαν κτλ. is a verbatim quotation of Exod. **12**.21 LXX (πᾶσαν γερουσίαν υἱῶν Ἰσραήλ). As the συνέδριον is none other than this same γερουσία Luke's text can only be defended as an epexegetical gloss: ‘that is, the Senate’. But, as Bauernfeind (91) rightly asks, what reader would construe in this sense unprompted? According to Preuschen (31), Luke imagined the college of elders

---

[1] In Acts **16**.37, **18**.28 and **20**.20, II Macc. **6**.10 and III Macc. **2**.27, δημοσία, used as an adverb, signifies ‘publicly’. So also here, according to *Beg.* IV, 57. On the other hand, Preuschen (31), Bauernfeind (92) and Bauer (*Wb* 355) take it in conjunction with τηρήσει to mean ‘State prison’, ‘close arrest’, *custodia publica*. In verse 21 it is replaced by δεσμωτήριον. The word δημόσιον, in the form of דימוֹס, passed into Rabbinic Hebrew with the sense of ‘common jail’: Billerbeck II, 635. On this scene cf. O. Weinreich, *Gebet und Wunder*, 1929, 315f. and 326ff.

[2] In *Die Probleme des paläst. Spätjudentums*, 48 n. 3, G. Kittel draws attention to Schlatter, *Der Evangelist Johannes*, 108: ‘The Palestinian would no more neglect to say that an action took place standing up than he would fail to mention the sitting-down if it took place sitting.’ But σταθέντες is not the same as ἑστηκότες (see John **3**.29)!

[3] ζωή stands for a word which may be rendered either by ζωή or σωτηρία, just as in Syriac the word for ‘life’ is used to render σωτηρία (*Beg* IV, 57). ‘Speak the words of this life’ and (in verse 21) ‘they taught’ are obviously one and the same. Hence in our opinion Dodd's conception of διδαχή as the dissemination of a moral ideal (*History and the Gospel*, 1938, 51) breaks down here.

[4] Caiaphas was a Sadducee; whether Annas was we do not know. That the (later) High Priest Ἄνανος adhered to the sect is specifically stated by Josephus, *Ant.* XX.199, which is strong evidence against the view that all High Priests were Sadducees.

as analogous to the *Roman* Senate and distinct from the college of titular judges. However that may be, it here becomes obvious that, for want of adequate information, Luke had no accurate notion of Jerusalem's institutional structure. The grandiose enumeration of the antagonists in v. 21 stands in intentional contrast to the pitiful fiasco in store for them.—D d have an expansion similar to that of verse 18: ἐγερθέντες τὸ πρωΐ.[1]

VERSES 22-24 depict the consternation of the persecutors, who are 'ludicrously embarrassed' (Bauernfeind 92) when they find the prison empty. As commander-in-chief of the police, the Captain of the Temple is particularly affected by the prisoners' disappearance. τί ἂν γένοιτο τοῦτο is a literary turn of phrase (Preuschen 32): Moulton translates it, 'What *will* this come to?' (198).

VERSE 25: Loisy (279) asks who here breaks so boldly into the Council Chamber. But how is the scene to continue unless the Council learns the whereabouts of the accused?

VERSE 26: No violence is used to bring the Apostles to the Council, out of respect for the temper of the people (no allusion is made, either here or later, to the miracle).[2] The fear of the crowd shows how popular the Christians are.[3]

VERSE 27: The Captain and the 'officers' (Luke was probably unaware that the Temple-police consisted of Levites) bring the Apostles and set them before the assembled Council (cf. **4**.7). Even in a literal sense, the Apostles occupy the centre of the stage. Without any mention of their disappearance from prison, the High Priest[4] opens the trial by referring to the ban of **4**.18 which has gone unheeded, and the Christians' allegations against the High Council itself.

VERSE 28: Though only Peter and John have so far been 'strictly charged'[5] not to teach 'in this name'—the High Priest again avoids uttering the actual name of Jesus—the prohibition applied to all. It is here implied that only the

---

[1] The text of D (παραγενόμενος . . . καὶ ἐγερθέντες; . . . καὶ συγκαλεσάμενοι . . . καὶ ἀπέστειλαν) arose from the fact that B's συνεκάλεσαν was changed into a participle without the scribe's striking out the now superfluous καὶ before ἀπέστειλαν. The addition ἐγερθέντες τὸ πρωΐ corresponds exactly to that in verse 18: καὶ ἐπορεύθη εἰς ἕκαστος εἰς τὰ ἴδια.

[2] D, probably following d (*cum vim*), omits the οὐ. D's impossible φοβούμενοι γὰρ τὸν λαόν derives from some such Latin text as h: *metuens enim*.

[3] According to Bauernfeind (93) this verse is a Lucan introduction to the trial-scene. The story originally ended with the newly-won freedom to teach and the gladness of the persecuted. If the story of the freeing of the Apostles was, as Bauernfeind admits, an—inferior—variant of the narrative in Chapter 12, it must have mentioned the Apostles' flight from Jerusalem.

[4] 'D ἱερεύς is probably due to the influence of the Latin (cf. *gig Lucif*), the oldest form of which often translated ἀρχιερεύς by *sacerdos*; see Zahn, *Urausgabe* 177': Ropes, *Beg*. III 50.

[5] παραγγέλλω occurs over twenty times in LXX, but not παραγγελία (in the papyri, as a legal technical term, it means a summons: *Beg*. IV, 58). The expression παραγγελίᾳ παρηγγείλαμεν imitates the emphatic manner of LXX, as e.g. in Gen. **43**.3; cf. Bauer, *Einf*. 21f., Bruce 142.

Apostles teach and that their teaching has penetrated into the remotest corners of Jerusalem (Loisy 281). Peter had said of Jesus in his sermon: 'whom you crucified' (4.10). This accusation, naturally recurring in every Christian missionary sermon, is taken by the High Priest to mean that the Christians seek divine retribution for the killing of Jesus.[1] Formally the High Priest's speech contains no question,[2] but rather serves to throw the Apostles' disobedience into sharp relief against his earlier command.

VERSE 29: ἀποκριθεὶς Πέτρος[3] . . . εἶπαν: they all speak, with divinely inspired unanimity. 'One must obey God rather than men' is even more succinct than **4.19**, and even closer to the dictum of Socrates in Plato's *Apology* (29D), πείσομαι δὲ μᾶλλον τῷ θεῷ ἢ ὑμῖν, which Luke as an educated man knew, and probably used as a model (*Beg.* IV, 45).

VERSES 30–32: The ensuing testimony to Jesus is not, as Preuschen considers (32), unmotivated, but despite the homiletic style (Loisy 282) thoroughly apposite: it stands as an example to all readers of how the Apostles bear witness before the authorities, whose guilt in the death of Jesus they fearlessly expose. The OT expression κρεμάσαντες ἐπὶ ξύλου alludes to Deut. **21.22f.** LXX, which the Christians applied to the crucifixion of Jesus.[4] ἀρχηγὸν καὶ σωτῆρα corresponds to ἀρχηγὸν τῆς ζωῆς in **3.15** and ἄρχοντα καὶ λυτρωτὴν in **7.35**. τοῦ δοῦναι: no thought is here given to the question whether it is Christ's work of salvation or the preaching of the Apostles which leads to repentance and remission of sins (Wendt 125): either way, Israel now has the opportunity to repent and win forgiveness. This point is part and parcel of the kerygma (cf. **2.38** and **3.19**). The witnesses to these 'things' (ῥήματα) are the Apostles and the Holy Spirit, whom[5] God bestows on every one who obeys him =every believer. On σωτήρ, see Conzelmann in *Hdb. zum NT*, vol. 13[4], 74ff.

VERSE 33: As in **7.54**, the effect of this testimony is described by the word διεπρίοντο: they were furious (Bauer, *Wb* 373).[6] They therefore wanted to kill the Apostles, who were near to suffering the fate of Stephen.[7] Luke imagines the Sanhedrin as an assembly swept away by an irresistible passion —cf. **23.10**!

---

[1] The frequent ἐπάγω of LXX is mostly said of God bringing on man the punishment for his sin.

[2] D and later MSS have sought to remedy this presumable deficiency by inserting οὐ and turning the whole into an interrogative sentence.

[3] Despite the presence of the same construction in **5.17** and **5.21**, Bauernfeind (91) wrongly thinks of revision of a source in which only Peter appeared. D and d offer a confused composite text deriving from B and a Latin text (cf. h), which by way of expansion introduced a dialogue between Peter and the High Priest (cf. *Beg.* III, 50.f).

[4] As Gal. **3.13** and Acts **10.39** also attest.

[5] ὅ is omitted in B through scribal error. ὅν in D is the slavish reproduction of (*spiritum*) *quem*—so d h Iren.

[6] Strictly 'they were sawn up'. The word is used in this sense in I Chron. **20.3** LXX.

[7] D's reading ἐβουλεύοντο (= *cogitabant* in d h) has in mind a judicial verdict.

VERSE 34: In these dire straits, with martyrdom all but certain, the Apostles are saved by the intervention of Gamaliel. It is enough for this universally revered jurist to rise to his feet for all the storming councillors to be brought to their senses—this is how Luke wishes the scene understood.[1] Gamaliel[2] here appears to do no less than assume the leadership of the house, even ordering that the accused be withdrawn for a time. Luke sees verses 35–39 as the report of a session *in camera*.

VERSE 35: It is probably only for emphasis that ἐπὶ τοῖς ἀνθρώποις τούτοις is placed before the τί μέλλετε κτλ. to which it belongs (see above on 1.2).[3] The councillors should consider before doing anything to these men. The risk they may run in persecuting the Apostles remains to be specified in verse 39.

VERSE 36: As the next verse shows, 'before these days' means the time before the census of Quirinius. In reality Theudas promised his followers under the Procurator Fadus, between 44 and 46 A.D.—hence some ten years after the presumptive date of Gamaliel's speech—that he would lead them dry-shod across the Jordan, thus repeating Joshua's miracle.[4] Luke's designation of him as λέγων εἶναί τινα ἑαυτόν recalls the description of Simon Magus in 8.9. The figure of 400[5] may derive from some historical writing. διελύθησαν: 'they scattered' (Bauer, *Wb* 370).[6]

VERSE 37: 'After Theudas rose up Judas the Galilean in the days of the census'.[7] The indication given of his success, ἀπέστησεν λαὸν ὀπίσω αὐτοῦ[8],

---

[1] Loisy fails to understand this; his scorn (284) is wholly unjustified.

[2] On Gamaliel, see Billerbeck II, 636–9. From the few surviving words we have of Gamaliel it cannot, despite Billerbeck's confident affirmative, be deduced with certainty whether he was in fact a Pharisee, as the aphorism attributed to him may really be that of his grandson, Gamaliel II (see Bill. II, 638 under d).

[3] The usual expression for 'beware of doing something' is προσέχειν ἑαυτὸν ἀπό.

[4] Josephus, *Ant.* XX 97: γόης τις . . . προφήτης γὰρ ἔλεγεν εἶναι. According to Preuschen (33), Loisy (287), *Beg.* IV (61) and Jeremias (*ThWb* IV, 863), he was the instigator of a Messianic movement. See on 21.38 below. Bruce (147) assumes the existence of two Theudases (cf. Wikenhauser, *Apg.* 61).

[5] Josephus says merely πολλοὺς ἠπάτησεν.—On ὡς see notes to 19.7 below.

[6] According to *Ant.* XX 98, a large proportion of them was cut down by the cavalry of Fadus.

[7] See *Ant.* XVIII 4–10, 23–5 and XX 102; *Bell.* II 118, 433 and VII 253. Wendt (43f.), *Beg.* II (356) and others conjecture that Luke's inaccurate recollection of Josephus is responsible for his error, whereas Dibelius (*Studies* 186f.) contests any such connection: 'Luke is more likely, on the evidence, to have freely invented these examples, like the whole speech.' A bibliography on the census is given under ἀπογραφή in Bauer *Wb* 176f.

Horst Braunert (Bonn) in his essay 'Der römische Provinzialzensus und der Schätzungsbericht des Lukas-Evangeliums' (*Historia* (1957), 192–214) has established the following: in linking the revolt of Judas with the census effected by Quirinius in AD 6/7, Luke is following a tradition found also in Josephus but incorrect. In fact this revolt broke out on the death of Herod the Great. No survey of Judaea took place either in the lifetime of Herod or in connection with his death; not until after the deposition of Archelaus was one to be carried out. Then and only then did Judaea (as an annex of the imperial province of Syria, but with a Procurator of her own) come under Roman government, hence Roman taxation. This survey took the form of a census of the provincials (not the *cives Romani*!) in Syria and is reminiscent of *Ant.* XX 102: 'Moreover the sons of Judas the Galilean were killed τοῦ τὸν λαὸν ἀπὸ 'Ρωμαίων ἀποστήσαντος Κυρινίου τῆς 'Ιουδαίας τιμη-τεύοντος.' Josephus says nothing about the end of Judas; the Zealot movement unleashed by him was not in fact suppressed but grew to greater dimensions (*Beg.* IV 61f.).—The census took place in A.D. 6.

VERSES 38f.: καὶ τὰ νῦν (cf. **4**.29): a typically Lucan phrase. The outcome of the speech, 'Do not molest the Christians!', is expressed with a *parallelismus membrorum*—Gamaliel too employs the traditional Jewish style of the Old Testament! And this is his reasoning: any movement of purely human inspiration[1] must fail of its own accord, but one which comes from God cannot be overthrown.[2] The loosely attached μήποτε κτλ.[3] is only meaningful

---

Judaea. Under Augustus there was never any census of provincials covering the whole empire: Luke's mention of such a census rests on an error (205). This corrects the arguments of L. R. Taylor ('Quirinius and the Census of Judaea', *AJP* 54 (1933) 120ff.) and T. Corbishley ('Quirinius and the Census: a re-study of the evidence', *Klio* 29 (1936) 81ff.) (203). On the other hand Braunert fails to see that his attempts to explain the journey of Joseph and Mary to Bethlehem in terms of census-procedures (on the questionable model of the Egyptian provincial census) are doomed from the outset on his own premises: if, like him, one is convinced that Jesus was born under Herod and that the only census of Judaea took place in AD 6/7, one has no right to make Joseph and Mary journey to Bethlehem for census purposes in the time of Herod. Apparently Luke had heard something about the provincial census and the way it was carried out (reporting in person to the authorities at the place of domicile or wherever the family possessions were located) and combined this with the descent of Jesus' family from David (Bethlehem!). Whether Augustus' census of Roman *citizens* in AD 8 and 14 (194f.) caused Luke or his source to confuse the provincial census with a census of all the empire, we do not know. At all events, the information at his disposal gave him no clearer picture of the census than of the chronology of Theudas and Judas. It is commendable that Braunert refrains from the inference that Quirinius carried out another census of the provincials of Judaea under Herod. On the other hand, we must scout the conjecture that Luke's information derived from Zealot sources (203ff.). We see from Josephus that it was in those days difficult even for a historian to fix the moment when the rising of Judas the Galilean broke out. There is all the less reason for reproaching Luke that he did not find his way through the tangle of traditions.

[8] In LXX ὀπίσω + genitive after a verb of motion is extremely common. Luke combines the Greek turn of phrase 'bring a people to its downfall' with the biblical 'lead a people after one'.

[1] In Luke **23**.51 βουλή and πρᾶξις are combined in the same way as βουλή and ἔργον here.

[2] This argument is reminiscent of the words of Rabbi Johanan the Sandalmaker (*ca.* 140): 'Any gathering which takes place by the will of God will finally endure, but any which does not take place by the will of God will not endure' (Billerbeck II, 640). By changing from ἐάν to εἰ Luke must have wished to indicate that the work of the Christians was really from God. According to classical grammar, the indicative in conditional clauses implies that the connection of 'if *x*, then *y*' is a real one, but not that the condition mentioned in the if-clause is a fact. On the other hand the classical subjunctive suggests that the speaker regards the possibility mentioned in the conditional clause as a likely eventuality. As a Hellenistic writer Luke is unaware of classical grammatical nuances. In **5**.38 he has Gamaliel use the subjunctive to express the possibility that the Christians' work is of men, not God; for the opposite possibility he employs the indicative. This shows that he uses the subjunctive to express mere possibility and the indicative to express actual fact.

[3] According to Wendt (129) μήποτε introduces a clause dependent on ἄφετε, but according to *Beg.* IV (62) the clause is independent. The whole passage has undergone a

if the cause of the Christians is really ἐκ θεοῦ. The καί only intensifies θεομάχοι (cf. **1**.3).—ἐπείσθησαν αὐτῷ: Luke's meaning is, insofar as they give up the idea of putting the Apostles to death.

VERSE 40: δείραντες: the flogging, consisting of 'forty strokes less one' (so II Cor. **11**.24; cf. also Acts **22**.19 and Mark **13**.9), which in fact any synagogue was in certain circumstances authorized to inflict on its members. παρήγγειλαν κτλ.: and so the ban on the preaching of Jesus remains.[1]

VERSE 41: The LXX expression ἀπὸ προσώπου lends the text a solemn, biblical ring. χαίροντες κτλ. corresponds to Luke **6**.23 and recurs constantly in the Acts of the martyrs (Preuschen 34). What is dishonour in the eyes of the world becomes an honour for the Apostles, since they suffer 'for the sake of the Name' (cf. **9**.16, **15**.26 and **21**.13).[2]

VERSE 42: The conclusion takes the form of yet another miniature summary: the Apostles teach and preach[3] the Messiah Jesus the whole day long in the Temple and in home gatherings.

The trial-scene of Chapter 5 strikingly resembles that of Chapter 4. Older scholarship explained both the similarities and the divergences in terms of sources. But what was genuine tradition, what Lucan addition? B. Weiss (*Einleitung* 574, ET *Introduction*) and Feine (181ff.) attributed the court-proceedings and the speech of Gamaliel to an older source, and the

---

mass of corrections in the 'Western' text. D's reading in verse 37, διελύθη αὐτὸς δι' αὐτοῦ, has Theudas end in suicide. In verse 38 D d h replace καὶ ἄφετε αὐτούς by καὶ ἐάσατε αὐτούς μὴ μιαίναντες τὰς χεῖρας. After καταλῦσαι αὐτούς in verse 39, D d h sy^hms add οὔτε βασιλεῖς οὔτε τύραννοι. To this is subjoined, by way of recapitulation, ἀπέχεσθε οὖν ἀπὸ τῶν ἀνθρώπων τούτων μήποτε κτλ.; in this way μήποτε acquires a clear reference. It is evident that all these alterations are secondary. The theme of θεομαχεῖν recalls the *Bacchae* of Euripides; nevertheless, as A. Vögeli appears to have established once and for all ('Lukas und Euripides', *ThZ* 9 (1953), 415–38), this only signifies a 'convergence of theme' and the adoption by Luke of expressions that had become proverbial.

[1] Bornhäuser (65f.) concludes, from the fact that at **8**.1 the Apostles are not included in the persecution, and that the Sanhedrin did not inflict any more death-penalties on Christians until the killing of James the brother of Jesus, that Gamaliel's advice first took effect in favour of the Apostles, and was subsequently extended to the whole Christian community. But this construction agrees neither with Luke's general line (according to which the Sanhedrin's action against the Christians was intensified in the persecution of Stephen, as now the whole community was affected) nor with reality, in which the Gamaliel scene is devoid of historical basis.

[2] According to *Beg.* IV, 62f., the absolute use of τὸ ὄνομα does not derive from Jewish Aramaic, but is Christian Greek: cf. III John 7, ὑπὲρ τοῦ ὀνόματος ἐξῆλθαν; Barnabas **16**.8, ἐλπίσαντες ἐπὶ τὸ ὄνομα; Ign. *Eph.* 3.1, δέδεμαι ἐν ὀνόματι; Ign. *Phil.* 10.1, δοξάσαι τὸ ὄνομα (*ThWb* V, 277, lines 23ff. and n. 205).

[3] Though syntactically co-ordinate, εὐαγγελιζόμενοι is from the point of view of meaning (according to Wendt 129) a closer definition of διδάσκοντες. But Luke is fond of such double expressions (Morgenthaler, op. cit., I 26): see **5**.42, **15**.35, **16**.35 and Luke **20**.1.

story of the Apostles' liberation to Luke himself. In contrast, Spitta (85ff.) and Jüngst (58) saw in the latter story the use of a source in which it was immediately followed by Gamaliel's speech! Harnack, however, did not stop at such distinctions: 5.17–42 was simply a doublet (arising from the bad source B!) of 3.15–5.16. The belief that the same episode had been rendered by tradition in different ways was also expressed by Preuschen (31), Wellhausen (10), Wendt (109 n. 3) and—with reserve—*Beg.* IV 59.

In the opposite camp, K. Bornhäuser and Jeremias sought to demonstrate, with the aid of rabbinic law, that the two trials must have been successive. The law laid down that the culprit must receive, in the presence of at least two witnesses, so clear a caution that he 'understands the reason of the case'. A caution of this kind was also necessary before a flogging could be ordered. Jeremias attempted to prove from I Tim. 1.10 that such warnings were demanded as far back as the middle of the first century (cf. Bill. I, 810ff.), which however implies considerable optimism over the dating of I Tim. According to Bornhäuser and Jeremias, Acts 4.1–22 describes the cautioning of the Apostles, regarded as uneducated laymen (4.13), for blasphemy. The ἀπειλή is the warning, and 5.28 refers to it: now condemnation to death for blasphemy becomes possible!

But, Reicke objected (105f.), appealing to the tractates Sanhedrin and Makkot, the cautioning only applied to capital trials, and must be carried out by two witnesses *privatim et in flagranti*. Here, on the other hand, where an arrest and a trial ensue, such a warning has no place.

Quite apart, moreover, from these considerations, one must take account of the fact that Luke places the arrest and the trial in quite another light than Bornhäuser and Jeremias: Peter and John are not arrested for blasphemy but because they have aroused the anger of the Sadducees, who are hostile to all preaching of resurrection (4.2). The two Apostles' lack of learning is stressed to make their παρρησία the more astonishing. Nowhere is there any question of a blasphemy punishable with death: it is the dissemination of the name of Jesus which is the issue. The word ἀπειλή has no more the technical sense of a 'caution' here than in 9.1; it simply means 'threat'. Luke wishes to show the intensification of the conflict, and that is why actual punishment must be postponed and the High Council limit itself to menaces (Ch. 4: it would be meaningless to suppose that προσαπειλησάμενοι in 4.21 had the sense of 'cautioning further').

As Reicke has done away with the connection Bornhäuser and Jeremias sought to establish between the two trial-scenes, he is free to return to Harnack's 'doublet' theory. It seems to us, however, that Bornhäuser and Jeremias were at least right on this point, that Chapters 4 and 5 do not represent two strands from different sources, as Harnack maintained. On the other hand, Harnack was undoubtedly right in contending that in Chapter 5 a legendary feature crops up which is absent from Chapter 4, i.e. the angel's freeing of the Apostles. It is the consensus of expert opinion that Luke has here adopted a tradition representing an inferior variant of the liberation episode in **12.**3ff. This he reproduces in the baldest way, and from an author's viewpoint his instinct is right, for if he had depicted an angel's liberation of all the Apostles in as lively and colourful a manner as later that of Peter, he would have destroyed in advance the effect of Chapter 12. Commentators like Loisy have found fault with Luke for having the angel send the Apostles to preach in the Temple, where they are promptly re-arrested. But how could the story have continued if the Apostles (like Peter, later, when he has gone to 'another place') were nowhere to be found? Be that as it may, the preaching, taken in itself, certainly makes sense: even this transient freedom shows the reader how God can at any time intervene on behalf of his own and put their judges in a ludicrously embarrassing position (Bauernfeind 92). In what follows, Luke makes play with this embarrassment on a scale which this scene alone permitted (whereas in **12.**18 he contents himself with a brief indication). At length the messenger's news enables the Apostles to be brought before the Sanhedrin. During the proceedings Luke must of course avoid all reference to the miracle of liberation (even the Apostles do not mention it), otherwise —as a γνωστὸν σημεῖον—it would as much preclude severe punishment as did the healing of the cripple at the time of the first trial.

This, admittedly, only explains the author's manner of proceeding; the conduct of the authorities—assuming the reality of the miracle—remains incomprehensible. They have every interest in learning who released the Apostles. That they make no enquiry in this sense is clear evidence that the miracle-story is a foreign body in the rest of this account. Peter's answer could not well be different from the first time (apart from the fact that now all twelve utter it at once). The kerygma attached to it serves to motivate the fury of the Councillors, who would put the Apostles—like Stephen, later—to death there and then. This detail, too, has its own special meaning in the Lucan context: the reader sees that, even if Stephen was the first to die for witnessing to his Lord, the shadow—and glory!—of martyrdom had already fallen across the Apostles too.

Yet, as the shadow must not become reality, the great figure of Gamaliel with his eloquence stills the raging magistrates and saves the lives of the Apostles. According to Luke indeed, the Pharisees—of whom, without known corroborative evidence, he makes Gamaliel one—stand on the side of the Christians. Moreover the intervention stresses to the reader that the most highly esteemed doctor-at-law of his time, a man whose name was known to all who moved in Jewish or Jewish-Christian circles, warned that the Christians should not be persecuted, for fear of fighting against God— perhaps history itself will prove the Christians to be in the right? At the time of Luke they had already successfully weathered a harsh persecution and were more numerous than before: had history, then, not already proved them ἐκ θεοῦ? It has long been remarked that Gamaliel's advice to 'leave the Christians alone' represents Luke's own demand, which he expresses yet again in the very last word of Acts: ἀκωλύτως.

Let us now turn to Gamaliel's speech itself. We have already mentioned that Theudas did not appear on the scene until long after the point (about the mid-thirties) at which the speech must be located. Bruce (147) is now the only commentator to suggest the existence of another Theudas who undertook the same operations as the first, only some decades earlier. There is little more to be said for the special pleading that Josephus' account of Fadus' governorship is one mass of errors. Even Schlatter ascribes the error to Luke (*Das Evangelium des Lukas*, 1931, 185). But this error has greater significance than Schlatter realized. That Luke should have been capable of transposing Theudas' march to the Jordan—which took place perhaps forty years before the composition of Acts—to the time preceding the census of Quirinius, some *eighty* years distant from Acts, proves that the traditions reaching him had left him in utter confusion where chronology was concerned. This is also true for the account of the ἀπογραφή given in the Gospel itself (Luke **2**.1f.): only *one* census is known to him, that of Quirinius (see p. 252 n. 7 above), and this he represents both as the first census of the empire and as taking place under Herod. Even the indefatigable Zahn and Ramsay have been unable to dispose entirely of this contradiction.

It is untenable that the instances adduced by Gamaliel derive from an older source (*pace* Bauernfeind 91). For what do they prove? At the most, that when its leader has met violent death, a purely human movement collapses. Hence they could only exemplify the first part of the thesis (ἐξ ἀνθρώπων . . . καταλυθήσεται). But even here they only serve the purpose because certain parts of the story have been omitted. As it happens, Theudas' movement did not dissolve of its own accord after his death; his followers had to be put down by the cavalry of Fadus, some of them being taken prisoner and others killed. Nor, likewise, did the Zealot movement unleashed by Judas merely fade away; it survived and steadily grew right up to the desperate last struggle of the Jewish War. So it cannot be some older source, standing nearer to the events, which glimmers through the text of Gamaliel's speech: this must be rather the expression of Luke himself, betraying the inadequacy of his information gleaned from more recent accounts. It is recognisably from his own linguistic resources that the word θεομαχεῖν also derives (cf. note on **26**.14). Altogether, we have no reason to dissent from the conclusion reached by Dibelius in his essay 'Die Reden der Apostelgeschichte und die antike Geschichtsschreibung' (1949 = *Studies* 187): Luke, 'it is plain, freely composed these examples, as also the entire speech; the cultivated man's desire to employ such references, the error of one ill-informed about Theudas' rebellious life and times—both must be ascribed to the author himself'.

But then there is no reason to ascribe the speech as a whole to Luke, and yet to maintain that Gamaliel did nevertheless intervene at that time on the Christians' behalf. On the contrary, the conclusion of the story shows that, like the freeing by the angel, the whole Gamaliel interlude fits badly enough into the trial-scene. Gamaliel warns the Sanhedrin to leave the Christians strictly alone, lest they find themselves fighting against God; the others allow themselves to be persuaded—and sentence the Apostles to the thirty-nine lashes under which (as Jeremias rightly reminds us) many a prisoner had been known to die!

Still less admissible is Ramsay's attempt to deduce from Gamaliel's intervention the veritable Magna Charta of Christian preaching. We must make the converse inference: if the Apostolic community remained essentially unmolested up to the year 44 (for, as we shall shortly see, the Stephen episode is another matter), we must acknowledge that the picture drawn by Dibelius in his article 'Der erste christliche Historiker' (1948 = *Studies* 124) is most probably accurate: 'A group of men and women had come together in faith in Jesus Christ and in the expectation of his return, and they led in Jerusalem a quiet and even in the Jewish sense "devout" life. It was a modest existence, and nothing other than the believers' conviction of victory betrayed that from this group would go out a movement to transform the world, that this congregation was the nucleus of the Church.' In the quiet life of the primitive community there were no mass assemblies such as Luke places at the outset of the Christian mission, therefore no conflicts with the Sadducees arising from them. The end of this secluded situation, in which the winning of souls for the Lord went on in the quiet personal encounter of man with man, is foreshadowed in the next Chapter. The 'Hellenists' brought it about.

16
ACTS 6: 1–7
THE ELECTION OF THE SEVEN

[1] In these days, when the disciples were increasing in numbers, there arose a murmuring of the Hellenists against the Hebrews because their widows were being overlooked in the daily ministration. [2] And the Twelve called the whole community of the disciples together and said, 'It is not pleasing (to God) that we should neglect the word of God and serve tables. [3] Select from among you, brethren, seven men of good reputation, full of the Spirit and of wisdom, whom we shall appoint for this task. [4] But we will continue in prayer and in the ministry of the Word.' [5] And the saying pleased the whole community: and they chose Stephen, a man full of faith and of the Holy Spirit, and Philip, and Prochorus, and Nicanor, and Timon, and Parmenas, and Nicolaos a proselyte of Antioch, [6] whom they set before the Apostles. And when they had prayed, they laid their hands on them. [7] And the word of God increased; and the number of the disciples in Jerusalem multiplied greatly; and a great many of the priests were obedient to the faith.

Bibliography:

J. Behm, *Die Handauflegung im Urchristentum*, Leipzig 1911 (on **6**.6): W. Grundmann, 'Die Apostel zwischen Jerusalem und Antiochia', *ZNW* 39 (1940), 110–36; P. Gaechter, S. J., 'The hatred of the house of Annas', *Theol. St.* 8 (1947), 3ff. and 'Die Sieben', *ZkTh* 74 (1952), 129–66; N. Adler, *Taufe und Handauflegung* (=*NT Abhandl.* 19,3), Münster 1951; J. Munck, see § 1 bibl., 137–46, and *Paulus und die Heilsgeschichte* (=*Acta Jutlandica* 26, 1954, 213–222 (ET *Paul and the Salvation of Mankind*, 1959); O. Cullmann, 'The significance of the Qumran texts for research into the Beginning of Christianity', *JBL* 74 (1955), 213–26 (=Krister Stendahl, *The Scrolls and the NT*, New York, 1957, 18–32); M. Simon, 'Les sectes juives d'après les témoignages patristiques', *Studia Patristica* I part 1, 1957, and *St. Stephen and the Hellenists in the Primitive Church*, London, 1958, 130 pp.; J. L. Teicher, 'The Essenes', *Stud. Patr.* I, 540–5; S. Giet, 'Traditions chronologiques légendaires ou historiques', *Stud. Patr.* I, 607–20; Reicke 115–28; Trocmé 188ff.; Conzelmann 43ff.
E. C. Blackman, 'The Hellenists of Acts **6**.1', *Exp.Tim.* 48 (1936–7), 524f.; C. F. D. Moule, 'Once more, Who were the Hellenists?' *Exp. Tim.*

70 (1959), 100–102; W. C. van Unnik, 'Kruising van enzamheid en gemeen-
schap in het N.T. (Hand. **6**.4; **11**.19)', *Vox Theol.* 28 (1957–8), 81–6; J.
Viteau, 'L'institution des diacres et des veuves', *RHEcclés.* 22 (1926), 513–63;
S. Bihel, 'De septem diaconis (Acta **6**.1–7)', *Antonianum* 3 (1928), 129–50;
E. Barnikol, 'Die ersten Diakonen, die Zwölf nach Apg. **1**.25', *Theol.
Jahrbuch* 1941, 88f.

VERSE 1: 'In these days' serves to bind two episodes closely together, as
in **1**.15 (q.v.), **7**.41, **9**.37 and **11**.27. 'When the disciples[1] were increasing in
numbers':[2] an attendant circumstance which explains the developments about
to be described. It is understandable that the size of the community should
now create difficulties as regards the διακονία; Luke spends no time in
examining who was at fault. Here 'Hellenists' means Greek-speaking Jews,
as opposed to the 'Hebrews' or Aramaic-speaking Jews.[3] Many such Hellenistic Jews, born abroad, lived in Jerusalem, where they possessed several

[1] μαθητής, appearing here for the first time in Acts (see Rengstorf, *ThWb*, 417–65,
esp. 462f.), corresponds to תַּלְמִיד. In LXX it appears only as a translation of אַלּוּף in
Jeremiah; on the other hand it occurs in Philo. It goes back to a self-designation of Jewish
Christians in Palestine, but is not found in the Pauline epistles or sub-apostolic literature.
In Acts μαθητής is used absolutely in **6**.1f., 7; **9**.10, 19, 26, 38; **11**.26, 29; **13**.52; **14**.20, 22,
28; **15**.10; **16**.1; **18**.23, 27; **19**.1, 9, 30; **20**.1, 30; **21**.4, 16. In **9**.1 it is expanded with τοῦ
Κυρίου, whereas in **9**.25 it appears to refer solely to disciples of Paul (see comments thereon). The use of the word in Acts is fully comprehensible on the assumption that Luke took
it over together with a given body of tradition, and then made occasional use of it himself
in the same sense (e.g. **15**.10).
[2] On its frequent appearances in LXX, πληθύνω usually means 'to fill (something) up',
though such passages as Exod. **1**.20, ἐπλήθυνεν ὁ λαός, also occur. In the NT it is used
intransitively only here.
[3] So most commentaries. The following confirmations may be adduced: 1. Chrysostom (*hom.* 14 on Acts 6.1), 'I believe that by "Hellenists" he refers to those who spoke
Greek'; 2. Philo (*de conf. ling.* § 129) ἔστι δὲ ὡς μὲν Ἑβραῖοι λέγουσι Φανουήλ, ὡς δὲ
ἡμεῖς ἀποστροφὴ θεοῦ) makes a distinction between Ἑβραῖοι and 'us', the Greek-
speaking Jews; 3. Billerbeck II, 448 instances such usage in Palestine also. As the contrast
of Greek and Aramaic-speaking Jews rarely comes up in literature, the references are few.
In *Beg.* IV, 64 and V, 59–74, Cadbury explains the Hellenists as Ἕλληνες, hence as Gentiles,
and presents linguistic arguments. In our general comments, however, (p. 266f.) we demonstrate the greater probability that Luke's reference is to Greek-speaking Jews of the diaspora.
Lohmeyer's fantastic theory ['Das Abendmahl in der Urgemeinde' (*JBL* 56 (1937), 217–52)]
is no longer taken seriously, that the seven baskets of Mark **8**.6 have an occult reference to a
communion of the Hellenists (= Gentiles), and the twelve baskets of Mark **6**.43 to one of
the Hebrews (= full Christians). According to W. Grundmann ('Die Apostel zwischen
Jerusalem und Antiochia', ZNW 39 (1940), 110–36) there were in Jerusalem originally
three groups: Galileans (twelve Apostles), Hellenists (Stephen) and Judaists (James). This is
not how Acts sees it. Moreover James was himself a Galilean.
In several publications, including 'The significance of the Qumran texts . . .' (see bibl.
above) and 'Secte de Qumran, Hellénistes des Actes et 4e Evangile' in *Les Manuscrits de la
Mer Morte*, Paris 1957, 61–74, Oscar Cullmann defends the thesis that the Hellenists of
Acts were Jews of syncretistic tendency, forming a bridge between Qumran and the primitive
Church. His main arguments are: 1. ἑλληνίζω means 'to live à la grecque', not 'to speak
Greek'; 2. 'the name "Hellenists" was chosen because there was no other name for the
representatives of what we call Hellenistic Syncretism' (Stendahl, 30); 3. they were at one

synagogues (see note on **6**.9) from whose members the Christians had won supporters. αἱ χῆραι: perhaps the number of Hellenistic widows was relatively large, for many pious Jews in the evening of their days settled in Jerusalem so as to be buried near the Holy City;[1] the widows of such men had no relatives at hand to look after them and tended to become dependent on public charity. διακονία καθημερινή: Jewry (according to Billerbeck II, 643ff., and Jeremias, *Jerusalem zur Zeit Jesu* II, 45–8, ET *Jerusalem in the Time of Jesus*, 1969, 130ff.) practised two kinds of poor-relief: (a) every Friday the local poor would be given, by three relief officers, enough money for fourteen meals— money first collected in the 'box' (קוּפָּה), by two relief officers, from the local residents; (b) poor strangers, i.e. those whose presence was only transitory, received daily offerings of food and drink from the 'tray' (תַּמְחוּי), which had been filled by three officers going from house to house. The διακονία καθημερινή[2]

---

with Qumran in opposition to the Temple worship; 4. Acts **6**.7 mentions the conversion of many priests, and at Qumran priests were members of the community, and 5. John **4**.38 acknowledges the success of Philip's Hellenistic missionary activity in Samaria (Acts Ch. 8) —cf. Cullmann's article in *École Pratique des Hautes Études* Yearbook 1953–4, Paris, 2–12. But these arguments by no means overcome the difficulties which beset this thesis: 1. Acts does not speak of ἑλληνίζειν but of 'Hellenists" as opposed to 'Hebrews'—K. G. Kuhn, in the same book (*Les Manuscrits* . . . , 135), demonstrates that the expression 'means those who speak Greek', and we ourselves show below that Luke himself understands the term to cover Greek-speaking diaspora Jews from Egypt, Cilicia and Asia Minor who have taken residence in Jerusalem. 2. The suggestion that 'Hellenists' denotes 'Jews of syncretistic tendency who deviated from official Judaism' is clearly question-begging: Cullmann himself adds 'bien que je reconnaisse que cette appellation pose un problème que mon hypothèse ne résout pas entièrement . . .' (ibid., 73). But the real difficulty lies in the implicit contradiction at the heart of Cullmann's picture—on the one hand the Hellenists must be 'syncretistic' to the extent of beginning the mission to the Gentiles, on the other they must be closely connected with Qumran, which is more legalistic than the legalists. The theory of the 'two spirits' incorporated in Qumran's monotheism offers inadequate grounds for styling Qumran itself 'syncretistic', and Kuhn has rightly abandoned his original theory that Qumran was gnostic, since adequate sources became available. 3. The opposition to the Temple in Acts (Cullmann did not trouble himself with the composition problem of Acts Ch. 7—where of course Luke propounds the same theology as in Ch. 17!) is utterly different from Qumran's objection to Temple-service: Luke rejects any temple or temple-worship, Qumran only the way in which this service was carried out in Jerusalem by unworthy priests and in accordance with a false calendar. 4. We demonstrate below (p. 269) that the priests of Qumran formed only a very small fraction of the Jewish priesthood. There is absolutely no reason to suppose that precisely this priestly élite of Qumran went over to Christianity. 5. Of John **4**.38 we can only say that the Fourth Gospel nowhere mentions the Twelve or the twelve Apostles, nor therefore does it oppose them to another Christian group; furthermore, according to John **4**.35 and 42 it was Jesus himself who began the mission in Samaria: **4**.38 does not imply that Jesus sent out the disciples to *Samaria*—he himself, in this story, remains the only missionary of Samaria. John **4**.36–8 deals rather quite generally with the Christian mission, 'within which every missionary has already predecessors to look back to' (Bultmann, *Johannesevangelium*, 148; ET *The Gospel of John*, 1971). For further discussions of the Qumran problem see 'Qumran' in the index.

[1] Personal communication from K. H. Rengstorf.

[2] καθημερινός LXX Judith **12**.15; διακονία Ezra **6**.3, 5 A = server's office, as also in I Macc. **11**.58. Cf. Bo Reicke, 'Diakonie, Festfreude und Zelos', *Uppsala Universitets Årsskrift* 1951, 25–31, 75 and 85–9.

corresponds to neither, as it applied to local poor, like (a), but was daily, like (b). Hence the Christians presumably had already introduced a system of poor-relief distinct from the Jewish. This could only have been necessary if they were no longer supported by the relief-arrangements of the Jewish community. In other words, it presupposes a lengthy evolution and an estrangement from the synagogue.

VERSE 2: This is the only place in Acts where the Twelve are directly named, though they are indirectly mentioned in **1**.26 and **2**.14. The idea occurs already in the old tradition cited in I Cor. **15**.3–5,[1] but the influence of an old source here is uncertain, since both **1**.26 and **2**.14 were formulated by Luke without recourse to anything of the sort. On πλῆθος see above on **4**.32. The Twelve call an assembly of the whole community (see above on **4**.23). οὐκ ἀρεστόν ἐστιν is not the equivalent of *non placet* (Preuschen 35): the Apostles are not stipulating but suggesting; it is the community which decides. Luke took the expression ἀρεστόν ἐστιν (or ἀρέσκειν) from LXX: 'it is not proper' (understand 'in the sight of God'). These words do not mean that the Apostles gave up this service because they were overworked; καταλείψαντας does not express past action: the Apostles are not reproaching themselves with having taken over the serving of tables[2] (with unhappy results, at that) and therefore neglected their preaching. Luke is rather explaining to the reader why the Apostles did not themselves assume this responsibility. He does not ask: 'Who was really to blame for the situation?', but 'What did the Apostles do to remedy the injustice?' Answer: 'They took immediate steps to remove it by having the Seven elected and installing them in office.'

VERSE 3: ἐπισκέπτομαι[3] recalls Num. **27**.16ff. LXX, which probably served as model: 'Let the Lord . . . appoint a man over the congregation . . . (18) . . . a man in whom is the spirit.' Here not only πνεῦμα but also σοφία is demanded. Luke is certainly fond of such resonant double expressions (cf. Morgenthaler, op. cit. I, 23, and see verses 8 and 10 below);[4] but Wendt may be right in thinking that σοφία here means worldly prudence (132). This would at all events fit the implication of μαρτυρούμενοι: men who will be handling the community's money and offerings must possess a good reputation. The passage recalls the qualities demanded of bishops and deacons in I Tim. **3**.7ff. Luke avoids using the title διάκονος, even though verses 1 and 4 speak of διακονία and verse 2 of διακονεῖν. Nevertheless his readers may

---

[1] Cf. Rengstorf, *ThWb*, II, 321–8.

[2] According to *Beg.* IV, 64, τράπεζα also denotes the money-changer's table. Nevertheless what is meant by τραπέζαις διακονεῖν is not the 'general financial administration of the community', but the care of the poor.

[3] Beyer, *ThWb* II, 600.37ff.

[4] LXX also however couples σοφία with σύνεσις, φρόνησις, δύναμις etc., and offers the expression πνεῦμα σοφίας in Exod. **31**.3 and **35**.31; Wis. **1**.4f.

have seen the Seven as deacons. In Hellenistic usage χρεία means 'function' and 'office', not 'requirement'.

ἐπτά[1]: in **21**.8 Philip the Evangelist is designated as ἐκ τῶν ἐπτά, hence these men bore the title of οἱ ἐπτά. There is possibly some connection here with a Jewish institution, for in Jewish communities the local council usually consisted of seven men known as the 'Seven of the Town' or 'Seven Best of the Town' (Bill. II, 641). From οὓς καταστήσομεν we see that their election devolves on the congregation, their installation on the Apostles. But as Luke will have depicted the scene in accordance with the uses of his own congregation, it would be rash to draw conclusions about the conceptions of office in the Jerusalem Church. Wikenhauser (*Apg.* 64): the first stages towards the diaconate.

VERSE 4: In **1**.14 already it was said of the Apostles that they 'continued steadfastly in prayer'. That means not only observance of Jewish times of prayer (**3**.1); from Matt. **6**.5f.[2] it is clear that—provided its motive is not to impress other men—prayer was regarded by Christians also as a meritorious work of piety. According to this high estimate of prayer, inherited from Judaism, the Apostles are represented as great men of prayer. We may understand Luke to mean that the Apostles through their prayers are active for the well-being (*Heil*) of the whole community.[3] In addition they devote themselves to the διακονία[4] τοῦ λόγου,[5] the ministry of teaching.

VERSE 5: ἤρεσεν ἐνώπιον is LXX-style, not a rendering of *placet*. Luke describes the scene with an OT turn of phrase.[6] πᾶν τὸ πλῆθος also can be found in the same sense ('the whole community') in LXX.[7] Stephen is full[8] (of the Spirit and) of πίστις: perhaps this means (cf. I Cor. **13**.2b) the

---

[1] Cf. Rengstorf, *ThWb* II, 630, where other and, in our opinion, erroneous conclusions are drawn from this text.

[2] This is not to deny that an authentic logion of Jesus may lie behind this Jewish Christian tradition.

[3] Loisy analyses προσευχή as 'exercices communs auxquels ils président dans la réunion des fidèles' (300). The text offers nothing to warrant this interpretation.

[4] The word διακονία did not find its way into NT via LXX, where on its few occurrences it denotes non-Jewish institutions. The original meaning of διακονεῖν was 'serve at table', but it gradually extended to 'feed and clothe' and 'serve' in general, until the care of the poor and ailing came to be covered (*ThWb* II, 81–93; see esp. 90, lines 35–45 and 84, lines 30–41).

[5] This designates teaching and preaching, for which according to Luke the Apostles were solely responsible. Billerbeck II, 647, draws attention to a formal parallel in Judaism, the 'service of the Torah'; but this meant only the learning of tradition by frequenting the company of the Rabbis.

[6] E.g. II Sam. **3**.36 LXX ἤρεσεν ἐνώπιον αὐτῶν πάντα; Jer. **18**.4 ἤρεσεν ἐνώπιον αὐτοῦ. ἐνώπιον may also be replaced by ἐναντίον. The addition of τῶν μαθητῶν in D and h shows that the scribes took the expression in the sense of 'the whole congregation'.

[7] II Chron. **31**.18 εἰς πᾶν τὸ πλῆθος (לְכָל־קְהַל?); I Ezra **9**.10; Exod. **12**.6.

[8] The indeclinable πλήρης found in א A C D will be original, and B's πλήρη a correction: Ropes, *Beg.* III, 56 and Moulton, 50.

faith which confers the power to work miracles (cf. verse 8). Since Irenaeus,[1] Nicolaos has been identified with the founder of the Nicolaitans, but only the similarity of name seems to underlie this conclusion. Since Nicolaos was born a Gentile (a proselyte of Antioch), we may infer that the others were born Jews.

VERSE 6: The laying-on of hands was a Judaic practice taken over by the Christians.[2] It did not merely symbolize the conferring of the qualities demanded of the office (so Wendt 133): there was real conviction that it directly transmitted blessing and power.[3]

VERSE 7 supplies a conclusion and a transition. The Word of God here appears as a living reality; we should probably say 'Christianity spread'. The congregation at Jerusalem continues its powerful growth—a sign of God's blessing—and (a concrete point with which Luke enlivens an otherwise colourless résumé) many priests now give their allegiance. In *Jerusalem zur Zeit Jesu* (II, (1924) 66; ET *Jerusalem in the Time of Jesus*, 1969, 204) Jeremias estimates that in Jesus' time the Jews included some 18,000 priests and Levites, of whom 10,000 fell into the latter category. The eight thousand or so priests had livings so exiguous that they were obliged to follow a trade during the ten or eleven months in which their service of the Temple left them free to do so (op. cit., 206). There was a deep social gulf between them and the ἀρχιερεῖς (op. cit., 180). In *Ant.* XX 181, Josephus reports that the ἀρχιερεῖς sent their servants to the threshing-floors of the priests to take the tithe away, 'and it came about that the priests without means died of want'. That shows what kind of income these priests enjoyed, but it also enables us to glimpse the tension which existed between them and the ἀρχιερεῖς.—On ὑπήκουον τῇ πίστει cf. II Thess. **1**.8: Bruce, *Acts*, 154.

Criticism has only gradually mastered this passage. In 1913 Wendt did not quite know what to make of the opposition of Hellenists and Hebrews; on the other hand it struck him (130f.) that the congregation was still small (the πλῆθος could still assemble in one place) and had its poor—therefore no community of goods! But in the same year Preuschen, following up a suggestion made by E. Schwartz (*NGG*, 1907, 280ff.), argued that the Seven were to care for the spiritual needs of the proselytes, while the Twelve did the same for the Jews (36). In 1914 Wellhausen (p. 11) penetrated more deeply: the Seven were the leaders of the Hellenists, and we can see signs of an incipient schism (such as F. C. Baur had already conjectured). Loisy

---

[1] *Adv. haer.* i.26.3; contrast Clem. Alex. *Strom.* ii.118.3ff., and iii. 25.5–26.2.

[2] OT precedents: the calling of Joshua to be Moses' successor, Num. **27**.18, 23 and the consecration of the Levites, Num. **8**.10. The laying on of hands in NT forms part of baptism (Acts **8**.17 and **19**.6), ordination (**6**.6 and **13**.3; I Tim. **4**.14 and **5**.22; II Tim. **1**.6) and healing (Acts **9**.17 and **28**.8, probably also **5**.12, **14**.3 and **19**.11).

[3] Cf. *Beg.* V, 137f. ('The Laying-on of Hands'), Billerbeck II, 647–61, and our comments on **13**.3.

(1920) suggested that the election of the Seven signified the organization of the Hellenistic group, but their final separation (on account of the widows dispute) was still not a schism. Lake (in *Beg.* V, 1933) endeavoured to keep more closely in touch with the realities of the Lucan text: the communistic experiment of Chapter 4 must have failed, because the subsidized fell out among themselves and the dispensers of relief were killed or hounded into exile (140–51). Beyer, also in 1933, considered there had been two groups, which however united, the Twelve acknowledging the Seven but seeking to subordinate them (44). According to Bauernfeind (1939), the Twelve—with that faith which moves mountains—entrusted the leaders of the Hellenistic group with the charitable work of the whole congregation; the two groups did not, however, entirely amalgamate—for only one of them was persecuted (105). In the opinion of P. Gaechter, S.J. (1952), the Apostles ordained the Seven with full powers for the cure of souls among the Hellenists and correspondingly ordained seven 'Presbyters' for the Hebrews (150ff.). J. Munck (1953) throws all criticism to the winds—the persecution, he contends, affected the whole community (143), and why should Stephen not have been a Hebrew, entirely at one with the primitive congregation (144)? Trocmé (1957) makes a distinction between the sense of the present text and that of the 'original': the former shows the Twelve losing control of the arrangements made for the community's material subsistence; according to the latter—although the name 'Hellenists' is Luke's invention (!)—there had always been a Greek-speaking group in the Jerusalem community, which played off its official recognition by the Twelve against the James party (188–91). Finally, C. S. C. Williams, likewise in 1957, offered a threefold choice from the views of C. Gore (the Seven were the prototype of the deacons), W. K. L. Clarke (they were presbyters) and A. M. Farrer (the Seven are elders, and their sending is parallel to that of the Apostles, but does not carry the same commission) (96f.).

As always, we must here distinguish between what Luke himself wished to say and what may be inferred from his account. Luke wishes only to explain how Stephen (whose martyrdom he is planning to relate) came to occupy so prominent a position in the community. The expansion of this community had led to a certain tension between so-called Hellenists and Hebrews, as the widows among the former were being overlooked in the daily dispensation of relief. But as soon as this came to their attention the Apostles, themselves wholly claimed by prayer and the 'ministry of the Word', had seven men chosen from the assembled community to 'serve tables'. At the head of these men came Stephen.

At first sight this story seems entirely plausible: a critical state of affairs in the community—unrest—summoning of a general assembly—a proposal of the governing body accepted by the plenary session—creation of a new office. But even if Luke makes repeated mention of διαχονεῖν or διαχονία, he does *not* say that the Seven were made deacons, and for good reason. For the

K

little we learn about these 'relief officers' in Acts shows them much rather as Christian preachers and missionaries. The collection from Antioch was received in Jerusalem not by deacons but by the presbyters (**11**.30). No wonder the exegetes so steadily endeavour to turn the Seven into elders!

But the tangle may not be so easily unravelled. One must begin at the other end, and this means looking beyond the passage under discussion. We are told in **8**.1 that the whole primitive community, apart from the Apostles, was persecuted and dispersed. But in **9**.31 it is once more peacefully united; yet in **11**.19ff. those 'that were scattered' continue to go preaching through various countries. It follows it was not the whole community which was persecuted (if it had been, the first move would surely have been an attempt to arrest its leaders, the Apostles—cf. **12**.1ff.), but a particular group including diaspora Jews from Cyrene (and Cyprus). This inference, once admitted, sets off a chain-reaction: at the moment of the persecution the primitive community embodied two groups which were already so clearly distinct even to outsiders that the one was persecuted, the other left unharmed. It is no wonder that Luke could find no place for so profound a cleavage in his ideal picture of the primitive community—always ὁμοθυμαδόν and ἐπὶ τὸ αὐτό! Once convinced, however, that this cleavage really existed, we may make further deductions concerning the two groups, which Luke chooses to style the 'Hellenists' and the 'Hebrew'.

It is highly unlikely that the 'Hellenists' were either Gentiles (Cadbury) or a group akin to the Qumran sect: the primitive community did not accept Gentiles (else why the struggles of Paul?), nor would Qumran's extreme legalism—its essential feature—have been compatible with the way in which Stephen's erstwhile associates went over to preaching to Gentiles (**11**.20). On the other hand Luke himself has left a pointer to what he meant by 'Hellenists' and 'Hebrews'. In **6**.9 he provides a closer description of the opponents with whom Stephen successfully debated. These are Hellenistic Jews (resident in Jerusalem) from the diaspora (Libya (?), Cyrene and Alexandria on the one hand, Cilicia and Asia Minor on the other.) There is no intrinsic reason in Luke's narrative for presenting the adversaries of Stephen (and—for Luke— of the whole congregation) as Jews born outside Palestine. If Luke does so— and in such detail at that—he must have taken this information from a tradition. But this datum we may now link with another item of tradition: Luke reports in **11**.20 that Stephen's followers included men of Cyrene, i.e. compatriots of certain of his opponents. This debate now takes on an intelligible meaning. For it remains truly remarkable that precisely Hellenistic diaspora Jews—and only they—joined issue with Stephen because he worked miracles (of healing, perhaps). But the whole story becomes transparently clear if Stephen had *led a mission* among his compatriots and erstwhile companions of the synagogue, the more so if that mission had been crowned with great success. Luke, however, could not bring Stephen in as a missionary, because he imagined the teaching and preaching to be still the prerogative of the twelve Apostles. Consequently he did his best for Stephen and the Seven by creating for them an honourable place as guardians of the poor.

We may surely conclude that Stephen and the 'Hellenists' were in fact Hellenistic Jews of the diaspora who had taken up residence in Jerusalem. That we are on the right lines here is evidenced not only by the names of the Seven, which are Greek without exception, but by the scene at 9.29f., which shows Paul campaigning among the 'Hellenists' in Jerusalem and offers a certain analogy with the story of Stephen. Luke can scarcely have thought of Gentiles there, for Gentiles would not actually have plotted to kill a Christian missionary who claimed their attention— plots to assassinate Paul are, in Acts, hatched exclusively by Jews. In this connection it is not a question whether this adventure of Paul's is historical or not: all that matters is what Luke meant by 'Hellenists'. Since among the Hellenistic diaspora Jews dwelling in Jerusalem, according to 6.9, there were men of Cilicia, Paul's homeland, it was natural for Luke to assume that Paul attempted a mission among his compatriots. It follows that both in 6.1 and in 9.29 'Hellenists' means 'Hellenistic diaspora Jews' whose mother-tongue was Greek, and that conversely Luke uses 'Hebrews' (cf. Ἑβραΐδι διαλέκτῳ, 21.40) to refer to the Aramaic-speaking Jews born in Palestine.

Naturally, this linguistic difference cannot have been the reason why Stephen's group was persecuted. This persecution can have had but *one* possible cause: that the teaching which this group attempted to disseminate by its mission contained some element which to many Jews went beyond the bounds of the tolerable. (The 'Hebrews' probably forbore to publicize their views in the same open way, preferring to bear witness in quiet seclusion: the great crowd-scenes were doubtless invented by Luke to condense the mission in a few impressive tableaux.) Now the stumbling-block could not have been the preaching of Jesus as Messiah, for James the brother of the Lord was able to maintain this doctrine in Jerusalem right up to the year 60. We cannot offhand deduce, from what Luke tells us concerning the charge brought against Stephen and his reply to it, the actual contents of the message proclaimed by Stephen and his followers. The previous version of the present Commentary too was in this respect over-hasty—to that extent Günter Klein was perfectly right in his criticism (*ZKG* 68 (1957), 368). But Klein's own conjecture, that the Hellenists had already in Jerusalem begun baptizing uncircumcised Gentiles, is itself none too convincing, for then the 'Hebrews' must have rejected such a baptism, and it would be scarcely conceivable that they could yet concede it later to Paul and Barnabas. No, Luke's own presentation, on which Stephen's followers first began accepting uncircumcised Gentiles outside Judaea, namely in Syrian Antioch, has an incomparably more plausible ring. But in that case what provoked the wrath of the Jews in Jerusalem against Stephen and his group can only have been the exercise of great freedom in relation to the law. Jesus himself both used and taught such freedom in questions of such practical importance as the Sabbath and ritual purity (cf. Mark **2**.27 and **7**.15). It is entirely possible that the Hellenists were more ready than the 'Hebrews' to interpret the law in Jesus' sense: to that extent the accusation of **6**.14 indirectly expresses a truth.

Be that as it may, this element in the preaching of the Hellenists must have estranged and repelled not only the Jews but also the 'Hebrews': at all events, their immunity from the persecution shows that they did not adopt it. If so, this would explain the shabby treatment of the Hellenistic widows. For here Luke's account contains a puzzle: a 'daily ministration' existed before the widows' dispute, so someone must have done the ministering—Wendt suggested this was the work of private benefactors. Yet either the offerings were distributed from a central store, in which case the office which ostensibly is only now created must already have existed; or the private benefactors from time to time distributed their offerings personally to the families and individuals befriended, in which case one fails to see why they should suddenly have ceased giving to the Hellenistic widows. The D scribe had already pondered this question and his solution appears in his addition: ἐν τῇ διακονίᾳ τῶν Ἑβραίων (**6**.1): the daily distribution must have been in the hands of the 'Hebrews'. That these distributors began to 'overlook' the Hellenistic widows (note the imperfect παρεθεωροῦντο!) accords with the hypothesis that the Hellenistic Christians had become suspect to the others and began to sense the fact on some such tell-tale occasion as—precisely—the distribution of poor-relief. If matters had thus come to a head, the 'Hebrews' would presumably have had no objection to the Hellenists' forming a community of their own under the leadership of the Seven. This would explain all the more easily why the 'Hebrews' were not touched by the persecution.

Bauernfeind has raised the question whether such an organized group headed by the Seven could have subsisted alongside the community of the twelve Apostles. However, the problem is not whether it could have subsisted, but that it could have arisen—and this Bauernfeind concedes. Let us remember that the contemporaries of the Twelve by no means saw them as Düreresque figures surpassing average men; they were the twelve witnesses to the Resurrection, who were neither the first nor yet the last to have seen the risen Lord. Nothing rules out the possibility that the 'above five hundred brethren' of I Cor. **15**.6 included many a so-called Hellenist—perhaps Stephen himself among them. Then again, Gal. **2**.9 shows that when Paul came to Jerusalem for the second time it was not 'the twelve Apostles' who formed the real leadership of the community, but Cephas, John and the Lord's brother. Gal. **1**.18f. prompts one to ask whether the situation was so very different at the time of Paul's first visit. Even then two or three years had elapsed since the persecution of **8**.1, yet the Jerusalem community still seems to consist only of the 'Hebrews' with their leaders.

Luke rounds off the episode with a transitional note on the adherence of many priests to the Christian community. It has recently been suggested that these reinforcements came from the Qumran community, which had a strong priestly element. But the ratio of priests to laity there was at most one to ten, and the 'Essenes' themselves, of whom the Qumran sect is now generally believed to have formed part, did not, according to Philo and Josephus, number much above four thousand. This implies a maximum of about four hundred Essene priests. On the other hand, Jeremias reckons the number of Jewish priests in Palestine at around eight thousand. The probability that it was precisely the priestly élite of Qumran which went over to the Christians is thus infinitesimally small. On the other hand the Jewish priests in the country formed a poor and depressed class, and there is nothing against the view that many of them opened their hearts to the gospel.

17
ACTS 6: 8–7: 1
THE ARREST OF STEPHEN

[8] But Stephen, full of grace and power, wrought great wonders and signs among the people. [9] But there arose some of those who were of the so-called synagogue of the Libertines and Cyrenians and Alexandrians, and of those from Cilicia and Asia, disputing with Stephen. [10] And they were not able to withstand the wisdom and the Spirit with which he spoke. [11] Then they suborned men, who said: 'We have heard him speak blasphemous words against Moses and God.' [12] And they stirred up the people and the elders and the scribes, and came upon him and seized him, and brought him into the High Council, [13] and set up false witnesses, who said: 'This man never ceases to speak words against this holy place and the law: [14] for we have heard him say that this Jesus of Nazareth will destroy this place, and change the customs which Moses delivered to us.' [15] And all who sat in the High Council, fastening their eyes on him, saw his face like the face of an angel. [7] And the High Priest said, 'Are these things so?'

Bibliography: See § 16.

J. R. Harris, 'A new Witness for a famous Western Reading (Acts 6.15)', *Exp.Tim.* 39 (1927–8), 380f.; R. P. C. Hanson, 'Studies in Texts (Acts 6.13–14)', *Theology* 50 (1947), 142–5; J. Bihler, 'Der Stephanusbericht (Apg. 6.8–15 und 7.54–8.2)', *BZ* NF 3 (1959), 252–70, and *Die Stephanusgeschichte*, Münchener Theol. Stud. I, 16 (1963), 9–29.

VERSE 8: The δύναμις here coupled with χάρις corresponds to the πίστις of verse 5: it is the miraculous power which enables Stephen to perform the great wonders and signs[1] among the 'people', i.e. the Jews. By these he attracts the special attention of the Jews. Arguing from Luke's text, Zahn (241) contests the supposition that Stephen actually preached, but concedes that he 'did not refrain from uttering the name of Jesus . . . and probably used other words also to refer the sick to this saviour from all ill'.[2]

---

[1] D adds, in accordance with the taste of a later age, 'through the Name of the Lord Jesus Christ'.

[2] Zahn failed to notice that this was merely to reintroduce Stephen's preaching in all but name.

VERSE 9: ἀνέστησαν (see on **5**.17) expresses a moving into action. Luke emphasizes the great number of enemies over whom Stephen triumphs. From the purely syntactical point of view these fall into two groups: 1. members of a synagogue of freedmen, and Cyrenians and Alexandrians (τινες τῶν ἐκ . . .);[1] 2. Jews from Cilicia and Asia Minor (τινες τῶν ἀπό . . .). We do not know where Stephen himself came from. It is important to note that not 'Hebrews' but Hellenistic Jews rise up against Stephen—whom Luke has not introduced as a 'Hellenist'. According to Luke, it is *they*, not Stephen, who start the conflict, by involving him in disputation.

VERSE 10: 'They were not able[2] to withstand' fulfils the promise of Luke **21**.15, where the gift of σοφία (coupled with στόμα) is also mentioned. Here it signifies not, as in verse 3, shrewdness in practical matters, but religious wisdom and the capacity to express it persuasively.

VERSE 11: 'They secretly suborned men who said': Stephen's opponents thus do not themselves come forward with these allegations. 'Blasphemous words against Moses and God': according to Loisy (309) 'Moses' in this unusual expression stands for the law and 'God' for the Temple.

VERSE 12: Are the 'τινες' working behind the scenes the subject, or their hired calumniators? Who are the people who then 'come upon and seize'[3] Stephen, as if they had powers of arrest, and drag him before the (ready and waiting?)[4] Council? Neither point is clear. This is the first time 'the people' appear hostile to the Christians.

VERSE 13: The opponents—probably the 'τινες'—now produce 'false witnesses'. Here we have yet another OT idea: both in the Psalms (**27**.12, **35**.11) and in Proverbs (**14**.5, **24**.28) the pious complain of μάρτυρες ἄδικοι or ψευδεῖς.[5] Stephen is alleged to have spoken incessantly against 'this' holy place[6] and the law.

---

[1] Schürer (II⁴, 87), Zahn (241f.) and Strathmann (*ThWb* IV, 269) take the Λιβερτῖνοι to have been the Jews brought to Rome by Pompey, and probably soon liberated, together with their descendants. But why such people should have joined forces with two semi-national groups in one synagogue in Jerusalem, no one can say. Dibelius therefore suggested that Λιβερτίνων was a corruption of Λιβύων (*Studies* 91). And in fact the Armenian version, based on an old Greek text, does read *Libyorum*. Billerbeck (II, 663f.) instances a synagogue of Alexandrians in Jerusalem. Acts **24**.12 presupposes the existence of several Hellenistic (?) synagogues there. Up to five may be inferred from the present verse: B. Weiss and Lietzmann count five, Wendt (135) and Zahn (141) two, Jeremias (in conversation) one. Luke seems to us to be thinking only of one.

[2] ἰσχύω + inf. ('be capable of') is not a Semitism (Preuschen, 37), but is attested in papyri and in Plutarch (Bauer, *Wb* 758).

[3] συναρπάζω also in **19**.29, **27**.15 and Luke **8**.29, likewise the martyrdoms of II Macc. **3**.27 and **4**.41 and IV Macc. **5**.4; similarly Prov. **6**.25 LXX. On ἐπιστάντες see note to **4**.1 above.

[4] Zahn (243) arbitrarily interpolates a lapse of 24 hours to win sufficient time for the convening of the High Council.

[5] Cf. Exod. **20**.16 and **23**.1 and Deut. **19**.16, 18.

[6] From the τούτου of B C, Wendt (136) infers that Luke's source must had the proceedings take place in the courtyard of the Temple—otherwise the demonstrative

VERSE 14: Here Luke introduces, as though it were a word of Stephen's concerning Jesus, a saying which according to the other Evangelists played a part in the trial of Jesus himself.[1] As regards the second half of the verse, Bauernfeind (110) correctly points to such antecedents as Mark **2**.23ff., **3**.2ff., **7**.14f. and **10**.5f., and Matt. **5**.21f.[2]

VERSE 15: ἀτενίσαντες: see on **1**.10. This exact focussing of the eyes makes it impossible to dismiss the following experience (εἶδον κτλ.) as illusion or imagination. 'Like the face of an angel': this transfiguration signifies for Luke that Stephen is filled with the Holy Spirit, and thereby enabled to make the speech which now follows. At the same time God is accrediting Stephen before the Sanhedrin.[3]

CHAPTER 7

VERSE 1: For εἰ in direct questions see Bl.-Debr. § 440, 3. The accused is called upon to answer the charge.

Luke here shows how Stephen came to stand accused: his (healing) miracles made an impression and aroused the opposition of Hellenistic Jews, who forced him into expressing his opinions; that is the gist of **6**.8f. But he got the better of his opponents, who therefore turned to other means, i.e. a smear-campaign which set the people and certain members of the High Council (elders and scribes are mentioned) against him. Stephen was seized,

---

could not have been used! For the same reasons τόπος is interpreted by Zahn (244f.) as 'Jerusalem' and by Jacquier (199) as the council-chamber. Naturally it is the Temple which is meant. In addition we have to take into account the influence on this verse of Mark **14**.57ff.
  [1] According to Mark **14**.58 and Matt. **26**.61 (cf. Mark **15**.29 and Matt. **27**.40) the saying is attributed to Jesus by false witnesses; according to John **2**.19, 21, on the other hand, it was misunderstood. Matthew tones it down with 'I *can* destroy', John by changing it to 'the temple of my body'. The antithesis of ναὸν χειροποίητον and ἀχειροποίητον is only found in Mark **14**.58 (cf. Philo, *De vita Mos.* II § 88, ἱερὸν χειροποίητον and Isa. **16**.12 LXX): here an eschatological event appears to be prophesied—the earthly Temple is to be destroyed, and replaced at the Parousia (three days later?) by the heavenly Temple of which it is the mere prefiguration. According to Enoch **90**.20 the Lord of the sheep will bring them a new house, larger and taller than the old. Rev. **21**.22 denies the existence of any Temple in the new Jerusalem.
  [2] An alleged saying of Jesus against the law seems also (indirectly) attested by Matt. **5**.17, a Jewish Christian logion refuting the assertion current among the Jews that Jesus was out to abolish the law. Even more than Luke **16**.17, Matt. **5**.18 poses the question whether the law is inoperative in the new era.
  [3] It was frequently said in Judaism that devout or holy men resembled angels (Bill. II, 665f.). Of the transfiguration of a martyr Loisy says (317f.): 'This feature, which we meet in the martyr stories of every age, must often have corresponded to reality. Here however it is out of place as preface to a lecture on the history of Israel, and belongs rather at the end of **7**.56 . . .' Whether Luke's material contained this feature, but in another place, must be dealt with separately (see general discussion). Zahn says, 'Stephen . . . betrays by his radiant countenance that he is enthusiastically ready . . . to bear witness to the truth of Jesus' words' (246); such psychologizing is quite beside the point.

dragged before the Council, and accused of continually blaspheming Moses and God. The proof?—false witnesses quote him as saying that Jesus would destroy the Temple and change the customs handed down from Moses. But the transfiguration of Stephen, visible to all the Council, testifies that God has in this hour filled him with his Holy Spirit.

Critical scholarship sensed here from an early date a conflict between lynch law and orderly trial proceedings. Source-research suggested three solutions: (a) the source spoke of an act of terrorism, but the reviser introduced a court-trial (thus e.g. Weiss, *Einl.*, 2nd edn. 1889, 574 n. 5; Wendt, 134 n. 2); (b) the source spoke of a regular trial, but the reviser introduced features of 'popular' justice (Loisy, 308); (c) two sources were worked together, one speaking of a trial, the other of a lynching (Feine, 186f., 190ff.; Spitta, 96ff.; J. Weiss, 498f.; Jüngst, 67ff.).

But these conclusions as to sources have no solid foundation. Luke did not imagine the High Council as a worthy body keeping strictly within the letter of legality, but as an assembly capable of any act of violence and carried away, unchecked, by its passion (5.33, 23.10). Hence he could portray the behaviour of the authorities as exhibiting both juridical and anarchic features. In view of this it is important that certain facts nevertheless betray the use of a tradition. For one thing, it is Stephen who here stands in the centre of the trial and persecution. This does not correspond to Luke's normal conception or scheme: hitherto it has been the Apostles who, as alone entitled to expound the doctrine (6.4), have occupied the focus of attention. If they here have no role to play and are not even persecuted (8.1), the author must be following a line imposed on him by a tradition concerning Stephen. Secondly, it has hitherto been the Christians' real enemies, the Sadducees, who have seized the initiative (4.1ff., 5.17ff.), but here it is Hellenistic Jews of the diaspora (6.9). There was nothing to oblige Luke to introduce these men, unless there was a tradition he could not ignore. Finally, Luke's explanation of why Stephen was accused and done to death remains unsatisfactory: 'great wonders and signs' on the part of a Christian welfare-officer are in themselves no occasion for diaspora Jews to draw him into debate. These miracles are furthermore represented in so abstract a manner that (*pace* Bauernfeind, 108) no tradition of the Hellenists can surely be discerned in them. More probably, Luke himself found Stephen's disputation with Hellenistic diaspora Jews uncongenial, and did his best to explain it in terms of the miracles. Needless to say, he was debarred from depicting Stephen as a teacher and preacher since he had represented prayer and the ministry of the Word (in 6.4) as a preserve claimed by the Apostles themselves.

Luke introduced the High Council because he wished as a historian to present the action in logical continuity with the earlier persecutions of the Christians. At the same time this produced an ostensibly natural climax: the first trial had ended in mere threatenings (4.17, 21), the second (though the intention to kill became evident in **5**.33) with scourging (**5**.40). But the third will culminate in the sentence of death and the scattering of the congregation. However, it was not only the historian in Luke who welcomed a Sanhedrin trial-scene at this point, but also the author. Here alone—not before any howling mob!—was there scope for the great speech which would enable Luke to make the Christian position vis-à-vis Judaism plain. It goes without saying that in the circumstances the moderating Gamaliel and the Pharisees who (according to Luke!) to some extent sympathized with the Christians do not make themselves heard—Luke possessed the happy gift of forgetting people when they might interfere with his literary designs.

On the other hand Luke here brings in the false witnesses whom he did not mention in connection with the trial of Jesus (cf. Mark **14**.55–60 and Luke **22**.66f.). He further cites the alleged saying of Jesus concerning the destruction of the Temple, which gave so much trouble to the other Evangelists (cf. Mark **14**.58, Matt. **26**.61 and John **2**.19). Luke felt no need to tone it down or get around it, so the concept of χειροποίητος, the proclamation of the Temple built anew, the allegory of the Temple as the body of Jesus—all are absent. As the statement of false witnesses about what Stephen reported as a word attributed to Jesus, the saying is now so far removed from Jesus that these expedients are superfluous. (On the other hand Luke adds the 'changing of the customs delivered by Moses', which does not appear in the other forms of the logion. The concrete sense of this is not stated. But from **21**.21 we may gather that it refers to dispensing with circumcision.) Thus in relating the trial of the first martyr, Luke had the trial of Jesus in mind and used material which might have been dangerous if applied to the earlier occasion. It would therefore be methodologically wrong to try to deduce something of Stephen's real history from the details of **6**.13f. How little, at bottom, the saying of Jesus fits the Lucan context is evident from these same verses: Luke has the accusers maintain that Stephen incessantly speaks against the Temple and the law, and as an instance of this allegedly continual criticism he adduces one isolated logion which they claim to have heard him say. But this logion represents the only concrete material Luke could find on which to base both the accusation and Stephen's defence-speech. In fact Luke here followed very bold tactics, using the logion as a stepping-stone for his own polemic against the Temple (and the Temple cult). However, we must wait until the next section to discuss this polemic, for it is there that it finds expression.

18

ACTS 7: 2–53
STEPHEN'S SPEECH

[2] But he said: 'Brethren and fathers, listen. The God of glory appeared to our father Abraham when he was in Mesopotamia, before he settled in Haran, [3] and said to him: "Go out from your land and from your kindred, and come into the land which I will show you." [4] Then he went out of the land of the Chaldaeans and settled in Haran: and from there, after his father's death, He removed him into this land wherein you now dwell: [5] and He gave him no inheritance in it, not even a foot's breadth; and He promised to give it to him in possession, and to his seed after him, although he had no child. [6] But God spoke in this way: that his seed would sojourn in a strange land, and that they would enslave them, and ill-treat them for four hundred years. [7] "And the nation to which they shall be in bondage I will judge," said God: "and after that they will come forth, and serve me in this place." [8] And He gave him the covenant of circumcision: and so he begat Isaac, and circumcised him the eighth day; and Isaac Jacob, and Jacob the twelve patriarchs. [9] And the patriarchs, moved with jealousy, sold Joseph into Egypt; and God was with him, [10] and delivered him out of all his afflictions, and gave him favour and wisdom before Pharaoh king of Egypt; and he made him governor over Egypt and all his house. [11] Now there came a famine over all Egypt and Canaan, and great affliction: and our fathers found no sustenance. [12] But when Jacob heard that there was corn in Egypt, he sent our fathers a first time. [13] And at the second time Joseph made himself known to his brethren; and Joseph's lineage was made known to Pharaoh. [14] And Joseph sent, and called to him Jacob his father and all his kindred, amounting to seventy-five souls. [15] And Jacob went down into Egypt; and he died, himself, and our fathers; [16] and they were carried over to Shechem, and laid in the tomb that Abraham bought for a price in silver from the sons of Hamor in Shechem.

[17] But as the time of the promise drew near, which God pledged to Abraham, the people grew and multiplied in Egypt, [18] till there arose another king over Egypt who knew not Joseph. [19] This king, full of cunning against our race, ill-treated our fathers to make them cast out their babes, that they might not be kept alive. [20] At this season Moses was born, and he was fair in God's eyes; and he was nurtured three months in his father's

house. ²¹ But when he was cast out, Pharaoh's daughter took him up, and nurtured him for her own son. ²² And Moses was instructed in all the wisdom of the Egyptians; and he was mighty in his words and works. ²³ But when he was well-nigh forty years old, it came into his heart to visit his brethren the children of Israel. ²⁴ And seeing one suffer wrong, he defended him, and avenged him who was oppressed, smiting the Egyptian. ²⁵ But he thought that his brethren would understand that God by his hand was giving them salvation; but they did not understand. ²⁶ And the next day he appeared to them as they fought, and tried to reconcile them peacefully, saying: " Men, you are brethren: why do you wrong one another?" ²⁷ But he who did his neighbour wrong thrust him away, saying: "Who made you a ruler and a judge over us? ²⁸ Would you kill me, as you killed the Egyptian yesterday?" ²⁹ And Moses fled at this saying, and became a sojourner in the land of Midian, where he begat two sons. ³⁰ And when forty years were fulfilled, an angel appreared to him in the wilderness of Mount Sinai, in a flame of fire in a bush. ³¹ And when Moses saw it he wondered at the sight: and as he drew near to look closely, there came the voice of the Lord: "I am the God of your fathers, the God of Abraham and Isaac and Jacob." And Moses trembled, and dared not look closely. ³³ And the Lord said to him: "Loose the shoes from your feet, for the place on which you are standing is holy ground. ³⁴ I have indeed seen the affliction of my people in Egypt, and have heard their groaning, and I have come down to deliver them: and now come, I will send you into Egypt."

³⁵ This Moses, whom they disowned, saying, "Who made you a ruler and a judge?", him did God send, both a ruler and a redeemer, by the hand of the angel who appeared to him in the bush. ³⁶ This man led them out, having wrought wonders and signs in Egypt and in the Red Sea and in the wilderness forty years. ³⁷ This Moses it is who said to the children of Israel: "A prophet shall God raise up to you from among your brethren, like me." ³⁸ This is he who in the assembly in the wilderness was mediator between the angel who spoke to him on Mount Sinai and our fathers: who received living sayings to give to you; ³⁹ to whom our fathers would not be obedient, but thrust him from them, and turned back in their hearts to Egypt, ⁴⁰ saying to Aaron: "Make us gods which shall go before us, for as for this Moses, who led us out of the land of Egypt, we know not what has become of him." ⁴¹ And they made a calf in those days, and brought a sacrifice to the idol, and rejoiced in the works of their hands. ⁴² But God turned, and gave them up to serve the host of heaven, as it is written in the book of the prophets: "Did you offer to me slain beasts and sacrifices forty years in the wilderness, O House of Israel? ⁴³ And you took up the tent of Moloch, and the star of the god Rephan, the idols which you made to worship them: and I will carry you away beyond Babylon."

[44] Our fathers had the tent of witness in the wilderness, just as He who spoke to Moses commanded, that he should make it according to the pattern which he had seen. [45] This our fathers in their turn brought in with Joshua, when they entered on the possession of (the land of) the nations whom God drove out before our fathers, down to the days of David. [46] He found favour in the sight of God, and asked to find a habitation for the God of Jacob. [47] But Solomon built Him a house. [48] Nevertheless the Most High does not dwell in that made with hands: as the prophet says: [49] "'The heaven is my throne, and the earth the footstool of my feet: what manner of house would you build me?' says the Lord, 'or what is the place of my rest? [50] Did not my hand make all these things?'"

[51] You stiffnecked and uncircumcised in heart and ears, you always resist the Holy Spirit. As your fathers did, so do you. [52] Which of the prophets did your fathers not persecute? And they killed those who proclaimed beforehand the coming of the Righteous One; of whom you have now become betrayers and murderers, [53] you who received the law by ordinances of angels, and did not keep it.'

Bibliography:

II. Kranichfeld, 'Der Gedankengang in der Rede des Stephanus' (containing earlier bibl.), *StKr* 1900, 541–62; B. W. Bacon, 'Stephen's speech: its argument and doctrinal relationship', *Biblical and Semitic Studies* (Yale Bicentenary Publication) 1901, 213–76; C. A. Bugge, 'Das Gesetz und Christus', *ZNW* 4 (1903), 89–110; W. Mundle, 'Die Stephanusrede Apg. 7: eine Märtyrerapologie', *ZNW* 20 (1921), 133–47; F. J. Foakes Jackson, 'Stephen's speech in Acts', *JBL* 49 (1930), 283–6; D. W. Riddle, see § 11 bibl.; H. W. Surkau, *Martyrien in jüdischer und fruhchr. Zeit* (FRLANT 54), Göttingen 1938, 105–19; H. J. Schoeps, 'Die jüdischen Prophetenmorde', *Symb. Bibl. Upps.* 2, Uppsala 1943; G. D. Kilpatrick, *JTS* 46 (1945), 136–45 (on 7.52); P. Gaechter, see § 16 bibl.; R. P. C. Hanson, *Theology* 50 (1947), 142–5 (on Stephen's speech); H. J. Schoeps, *Theologie und Geschichte des Judenchristentums* 1949; M. Simon, 'Retour du Christ et reconstruction du Temple dans la pensée chrétienne primitive', *Mélanges Goguel*, 1950, 247–57; 'St. Stephen and the Jerusalem Temple', *JEH* 2 (1951), 127–41; 'La prophétie de Nathan et le Temple', *RHPhR* 1952, 41–58; *St. Stephen and the Hellenists*, London, 1958; *Verus Israel*, Paris 1948, 57f. (ET in preparation); *Les sectes juives au temps de Jésus*, Paris 1960, 74f. (ET *Jewish Sects in the Time of Jesus*, 1967); Dom Célestin Charlier, 'De la communauté de Jérusalem aux églises Pauliniennes (Acta 1–12), *Bible et Vie chrétienne* 1 (1953), 72–93; J. Munck, *Paulus und die Heilsgeschichte* (1954), 214–22 (ET *Paul and the Salvation of Mankind*, 1959); A. F. J. Klijn, 'Stephen's speech', *NTS* 2 (1957), 25–31; Reicke, 127–52; Trocmé, 66, 109, 111, 185 and 207f.; Williams, 108–12. On the legend of Stephen see Ryssel, § 15 bibl.; J. Bihler, *Die Stephanusgeschichte =* Münchener Theol. Studien I, 260ff. (cf. *TLZ* 91 (1966) 435f.); Conzelmann 52f.;

E. Haenchen, *ZNW* 54 (1963), 164–6; R. Storch, 'Die Stephanusrede usw.', Diss. Göttingen 1967; Conzelmann 44–51 (lit.);
J. H. Ropes, 'Bemerkungen z.d. Rede des Stephanus und der Vision des Petrus', *ThStKr* 102 (1930), 307–15; A. Fridrichsen, 'Zur Stephanusrede', *Monde Oriental* 25 (1931), 44–52; H. Wenschkewitz, 'Die Spiritualisierung der Kultusbegriffe Tempel, Priester und Opfer im N.T.', *Angelos* 4 (1932) (see esp. 170–4); G. Duterme, 'Le vocabulaire du discours d'Etienne, Act. 7.2–53' (Diss. Univ. Cathol. de Louvain, 1950); O. Cullmann, 'L'opposition contre le temple de Jérusalem, motif commun de la théologie johannique et du monde ambiant', *NTS* 5 (1959), 157–73.

VERSE 2: ἄνδρες ἀδελφοὶ καὶ πατέρες: Paul too addresses the Jews in this way in 22.1; the formulation has a Greek ring. 'The God of glory' (Ps. 29 (28).3) opens the long series of OT citations and expressions which is a feature of this speech. 'Appeared to Abraham' corresponds to Gen. 12.7 LXX, and 'when he was in Mesopotamia' to Gen. 12.1. But the author wrongly relates Gen. 12 to Abraham's first departure instead of the second.[1] Verses 2 to 8 are devoted to Abraham's story.

VERSE 3: Accordingly Gen. 12.1 is here understood as referring to the exodus from Ur in Chaldaea. The words 'from your father's house' are omitted, for of course Abraham journeyed from Ur in the company of his father Terah.

VERSE 4: The reader of Gen. 11.27–12.4 is left with the impression that Abraham departed from Haran after the death of his father. And here Luke was no more an exception than Philo, who in *De migr. Abr.* § 177 also places this departure after Terah's death. People 'with an unusual instinct for mental arithmetic' (*Beg.* IV, 70) will calculate as follows: when Abraham was born Terah was seventy years old (Gen. 11.26); since Abraham when he left Haran was seventy-five (Gen. 12.4) and Terah attained the age of 205 (Gen. 11.32), Terah must have survived Abraham's departure by sixty years. 'The land in which you now live' is striking: Stephen himself lives there too. With κἀκεῖθεν God suddenly replaces Abraham as the subject.

VERSE 5 makes use of God's words in Deut. 2.5 as a suitably 'biblical' expression (they really refer to Mount Seir, which is to remain in the hands of

---

[1] Abraham journeyed from Ur in Chaldaea (called χώρα τῶν Χαλδαίων in Gen. 11.28, 31 and 15.7 LXX) to Haran. There he received (Gen. 12.1 ff.) God's command to set out for Canaan. The present verse, however, attaches this command to the first migration, from Mesopotamia to Haran, not the second, from Haran to Canaan. Philo can occasionally explain the significance of Abraham's migration by reference to Gen. 12.1 (*De Abr.* 62–7), even though he knows well enough (as proved by *De migr. Abr.* 176) that Gen. 12.4f. relates to the departure from Haran. There is therefore no need to suppose a 'scholastic tradition' here followed by Luke (*Beg.* IV, 70). Josephus, also cited in this connection, combines the two migrations in a single exodus 'from Chaldaea to Canaan' (*Ant.* I, 154). Though the origin of the 'scholastic tradition' has been seen in Gen. 15.7, neither Philo nor Josephus mentions that verse in this connection.

the Edomites). Next Gen. **17**.8 is pressed into service ('I will give to you and your seed the land . . .'). That Abraham had as yet no son could have been an occasion for speaking of his faith; but the opportunity is not taken.[1] The negation of ὄντος by οὐκ rather than μή arises from the feeling that οὐ is 'the proper negative for a statement of a downright fact' (Moulton 232).

VERSE 6: Gen. **15**.13 LXX is now quoted by way of explanation: the descendants of Abraham will have to spend four hundred[2] years as πάροικοι in slavery (to the Egyptians).

VERSE 7: The first half is an exact quotation of Gen. **15**.14 LXX: Egypt will be punished for this oppression. The second half quotes Exod. **3**.12, replacing 'on this mountain' (Horeb) by 'in this place' (Canaan or Jerusalem).

VERSE 8 enlists Gen. **17**.10 to make the transition to the story of the patriarchs. The 'covenant of circumcision' here appears as a divine gift. Then mentions of Isaac's circumcision (Gen. **21**.4) and of Jacob are used as stepping-stones to the twelve patriarchs and the story of Joseph, which extends from verse 9 to verse 16.

VERSE 9 contains echoes of Gen. **37**.11 ('his brothers became envious of him') and **37**.28 ('and sold Joseph to the Ishmaelites . . . and they brought Joseph down to Egypt'). The term 'patriarchs' for the sons of Jacob is a late usage (*Beg.* IV, 72).[3]

VERSE 10: Gen. **39**.21 runs: 'and the Lord was with Joseph'. Gen. **41**.41 contributes 'I have set you over all Egypt'. The verse also alludes to Ps. **105** (104).21: 'He made him lord of his house'.[4] χάριν is expanded—as in Acts **4**.33 and **6**.8—by the addition of καὶ σοφίαν, which admittedly does not fit 'before Pharaoh' so well as χάριν. The reference is to Joseph's divinely inspired skill in the reading of dreams.

VERSE 11: The χορτάσματα are indeed mentioned in Gen. **42**.27, but here the influence is that of Ps. **37**(36).19 (Preuschen, 39). But the essential contributions are those of Gen. **41**.54, 56 ('there arose a great famine over all the land') and **42**.5 ('there was a famine in the land of Canaan').

VERSE 12 presents Gen. **42**.1f. simplified. πρῶτον is Hellenistic for πρότερον and εἰς Hellenistic for ἐν. D following LXX reads ἐν (Bruce, *Acts* 165).

VERSE: 13: ἐγνωρίσθη (B A) = Gen. **45**.1.[5] Even if Joseph were a τύπος of the redeeming Messiah, the twofold coming of the brothers would still

---

[1] No reference is made to Abraham's purchase of the cave of Machpelah near Hebron (Gen. 23). According to verse 16 it was in Shechem (= Samaria), not in Hebron, that Abraham bought a burial-ground.

[2] Exod. 12.40 says 430 years: the present verse retains the round figure of Gen. 15.13.

[3] Where reference is made to the title 'The Testaments of the Twelve Patriarchs', as well as to IV Macc. 7.19 and 16.25.

[4] This psalm is important as exemplifying the edification drawn by the Jews from their history between Abraham and Moses. Many of the themes of verses 2 to 9 can be traced to it. The subject of κατάστησας in verse 10 is not Pharaoh but God.

[5] Most MSS of Acts, influenced by the ἀνεγνωρίζετο of LXX, have ἀνεγνωρίσθη.

not justify our thinking of the first and second advent of Jesus (*pace Beg.* IV, 73). γένος: Joseph's family (Gen. **45**.16). For according to Gen. **41**.12 Pharaoh already knew that Joseph was a παῖς Ἑβραῖος.

VERSE 14: According to Gen. **46**.26, Jacob came to Egypt with sixty-six 'souls'. If Jacob himself, Joseph and the latter's two sons are added, this gives a round total of seventy (Gen. **46**.27). LXX does not include Jacob and Joseph, but does include *nine* sons of Joseph in the reckoning, thus arriving (Gen. **46**.27 LXX) at the 'seventy-five souls' of Acts.[1] ἐν = 'amounting to', 'in all'; Moulton, 103.

VERSE 15: Cf. Deut. **10**.22 ('The fathers went down into Egypt') and Exod. **1**.6 ('And Joseph died, and all his brethren'). αὐτός seems to refer to Jacob, to whom then the statement of verse 16 also applies.

VERSE 16: Jacob and his twelve sons are laid to rest in the tomb which Abraham had purchased at Shechem. Here Abraham's purchase (Gen. 23) is confused with Jacob's (Gen. **33**.19)—the text is cited from memory.[2] See J. Jeremias, *Heiligengräber*, 31–8, 95f.

VERSE 17: Here we find καθώς in the rare temporal connotation—'as', 'when' (Bauer, *Wb* 773). ὁ χρόνος τῆς ἐπαγγελίας: the time of the promise's fulfilment.[3] Use is made of Exod. **1**.7.

VERSE 18 quotes Exod. **1**.8 LXX verbatim.

VERSE 19 makes freer use of Exod. **1**.10f. κατασοφίζομαι, 'to outwit' (only here in NT), renders the Hithpa'el form of חכם; κακόω means to "ill-treat' or 'torment'—the prophecy of **7**.6 fulfilled.[4]

VERSE 20 begins the section dealing with Moses, which extends to verse 44. In Ex. **2**.2 the child is called no more than טוב ('goodly'), which LXX (cf. also Hebr. **11**.23) translates by ἀστεῖος[5]; τῷ θεῷ is added as an intensive, as

---

[1] Since Joseph and his sons did not now come from Canaan, this number is in any case wrong (Loisy, 326). Exod. **1**.5 'from Jacob descended 75 souls" is on the other hand incontrovertible.

[2] There are no grounds for Bauernfeind's conjecture that we may here possess 'the remains of a thoroughly authentic report' (115). There is nothing in OT on the burial of Joseph's brothers. According to Josephus *Ant.* II, 198f., Jubilees 46.8 and the 'Testaments of the Twelve Patriarchs' (see thereon, and on the Rabbinic tradition, Bill. II, 672–8) they were laid to rest with Abraham, Isaac and Jacob in the double cave near Hebron. This later tradition imagined the bones of all the patriarchs together in one grave. This may have resulted from a generalization of the report of the burial of Joseph in Shechem in Joshua **24**.32.

[3] ὁμολογέω, which was later felt to mean 'make a confession', is replaced by ἐπαγγέλλομαι in 𝔓45 D E, and by ὀμνύναι in ℵ.

[4] On the loosely subjoined infinitive see Bl.-Debr. § 400, 8; but a final sense may be intended here: 'he tormented our fathers to make them expose their babies'. Though the proper meaning of ζωογονέω is 'bring to life', it is used here and in other places of LXX and Luke in the sense of 'keep alive' (cf. Exod. **1**.18).

[5] According to Bill. II, 678, the Targum Jerusalem I interprets: 'The woman ... bore a son at the end of six months, and when she saw that it was a viable child she hid it for three months ...'

in Jonah 3.2: Nineveh was a city μεγάλη τῷ θεῷ, a great and powerful city (Moulton, 104, speaks of the 'dative of the person judging'; see also Bruce 167).

VERSE 21: In Exod. 2.5 Pharaoh's daughter ἀνείλατο the little 'ark' and in Exod. 2.10 ἐγενήθη αὐτῇ εἰς υἱόν. On ἐγεννήθη, ἀνετράφη and ἐπαιδεύθη, see comments on 22.3 below.

VERSE 22: According to Exod. 4.10–16, Aaron becomes spokesman because Moses is devoid of eloquence; Exod. 4.10 LXX depicts him as even ἰσχνόφωνος, 'stammering'. This did not prevent later legend (Josephus *Ant.* II 272; III 13ff.) from turning him into a great orator.[1]

VERSE 23: The 120-year span of Moses' life was occasionally, on the cue of the forty years in the wilderness, dissected into three equal parts (Billerbeck II. 679f.). For ἀνέβη ἐπὶ τὴν καρδίαν see e.g. Isa. 65.16 (LXX), and Jer. 3.16, 51 (44 M).21 and 28 (51 M).50. The end of the verse alludes to Exod. 2.11 but replaces ἐξῆλθεν πρός by ἐπισκέπτομαι, which is especially frequent in LXX (e.g. Exod. 3.16 and 4.31), 'to look someone up', with the subsidiary sense of concern for his welfare.

VERSE 24: πατάξας τὸν Αἰγύπτιον—Exod. 2.12. The usual meaning of ἀμύνομαι is 'defend', but Isa. 59.16 LXX admits the translation 'he helped him'. As in Luke 18.7, ποιεῖν τὴν ἐκδίκησιν means 'to exact retribution'; Judges 11.36 LXX uses the phrase with the same meaning.[2]

VERSE 25: Philo, *Vita Mos.* I, § 44, exculpates Moses' deed by labelling the Egyptian overseer a 'beast in human form'. But here the killing is understood as an act of God, of which Moses is merely the agent. For the first time in the speech we hear the theme of the people's incomprehension and their failure to recognize the saviour sent by God.

VERSE 26 offers a free rendering of Exod. 2.13.[3] Loisy (331) suggests that ὤφθη represents the appearance of God's envoy. συνήλλασσεν is a conative imperfect (Moulton, 129).

VERSES 27f.: From a purely logical point of view, ὁ ἀδικῶν κτλ. (modelled on λέγει τῷ ἀδικοῦντι in Exod. 2.13 LXX) contradicts the preceding 'one another'. But here (it is different in Exodus) Moses is addressing not the guilty man but both contestants, who represent the whole of strife-torn Israel. The words ἀπώσατο αὐτόν, characterizing the attitude of Israel to the man sent by God, are an addition to the OT text; verses 35 and 39 refer back to them.

---

[1] The starting-point of this tradition may perhaps be seen in Ecclesiasticus 45.3. According to Philo, *Vita Mos.* I § 23, Moses was also an adept of the mysteries of Egypt. Luke 24.19 styles Jesus δυνατὸς ἐν ἔργῳ καὶ λόγῳ, probably not by chance but because Moses is the τύπος here.

[2] The Western text adds, in accordance with Exod. 2.12, 'and hid him in the sand'.

[3] Bill. II, 680, prefers to translate: 'You are men who are brothers'. But ἄνδρες is the normal form of address, hence 'Men, you are brothers!' The Western text 'corrects' to: 'What are you doing, ἄνδρες ἀδελφοί?'

VERSE 29: According to Exod. **2**.15 Moses flees because Pharaoh seeks to kill him; here his own people are the cause of his flight ('at this saying'). There are echoes of Exod. **2**.22 and **18**.3.[1]

VERSE 30: 'Forty years'—see on verse 23 above. The wording corresponds to Exod. **3**.1f., except that there the place of revelation is situated ὑπὸ τὸν ἔρημον, 'down behind the wilderness'.[2]

VERSE 31 freely renders Exod. **3**.3f. Hitherto only the angel of the Lord had appeared, but now we hear the voice of God himself.

VERSE 32: While the words of God are quoted exactly enough from Exod. **3**.6, the reaction of the man is freely paraphrased. The revelation of the name of God is not related; only the continuity of the revelation is indicated.

VERSE 33 corresponds to Exod. **3**.5: in OT the prohibition to come near precedes the revelation. It is an ancient Oriental custom that shoes must not be worn in a holy place. That here 'the main idea of the speech, that God once revealed himself in a strange land and made a place there holy . . . comes once again clearly to the fore' (Wendt, 144) is a bold assertion. The emphasis lies on verse 34.

VERSE 34: almost literal quotations from Exod. **3**.7f. and 10. In δεῦρο ἀποστείλω we have an example of the 'conjunctive of exhortation', 'come, then; let me send you' (Bl.-Debr. § 364, 1; Radermacher[3], 169): this sending of Moses is the culmination of the extract from his history given here.

VERSE 35: Now we have an abrupt change of style.[3] The placid flow of historical narrative gives way to passionate, rhetorically heightened indictment. The Jews—for, as with Barnabas' deed (**4**.36f.), the isolated case of verse 27 is generalized as a typical occurrence—'denied' Moses and behaved then towards him as now towards Jesus (cf. **3**.13f.!). But the correspondence does not end here: ἄρχοντα matches ἀρχηγός in **3**.15 and **5**.31, and λυτρωτήν has its counterpart in Luke **24**.21.[4] The leader and redeemer sent by God is rejected by the Jews: this applies both to Moses and to Jesus, though the speaker does not come to the theme of Jesus until verse 52.[5] ἀπέσταλκεν: the sending is an action of a continuous nature (Moulton, 144).

[1] Loisy (332) interprets the details symbolically: the flight to Midian = carrying of the gospel to the Gentiles (!); birth of two sons = fruitfulness of the gospel among the Gentiles. But in reality the text treats the persons and events as τύπος, not allegorically. The details which are not 'typical' (e.g. the two sons) preserve the narrative from becoming pale and colourless.

[2] The Rabbis wondered why God should have chosen to speak from a thornbush. An attractive answer was 'To teach men that there is no place, however desolate, not even a thornbush, without the Shekinah' (Bill. II, 680).

[3] A sign of this is the heavily stressed, repeated τοῦτον, taken up again in verses 36–8 by the threefold οὗτος. Cf. Norden, *Agnostos Theos*, 164f. and 222ff. Luke employs the style of the encomium, originally devised for the praise of a god, for the eulogy of Moses, the man of God, as did Philo for the emperor (*Leg. ad Gaium*, C.-W. VI, 145ff.).

[4] λυτρωτής is applied to the κύριος in Ps. **19**.14 (**18**.15 LXX) and to God in Ps. **79**(78).35.

[5] Wendt (145) glosses σὺν χειρὶ ἀγγέλου 'escorted by the angel'. Lake lists ἐν χειρί, σὺν χειρί and διὰ χειρός all as rendering בְּיַד = instrumental 'through' (*Beg.* IV, 77).

VERSE 36: Apart from οὗτος, which preserves the style of verse 35, this verse carries on the story of Moses. It bears a striking resemblance to *Assumptio Mosis* 3.11 (*Beg.* IV, 77f.).[1] Such an aggregation was clearly popular. According to Exod. 7.3 it was God himself who promised to perform 'many wonders and signs in the land of Egypt'.

VERSE 37: Again οὗτός ἐστιν. Here the theme of Deut. 18.15 once more emerges: see on 3.22 above.

VERSE 38: οὗτός ἐστιν for a third time. ἐκκλησία: in Deut. 4.10, 9.10 and 18.16 ἡμέρα τῆς ἐκκλησίας is the day on which the people gather to receive the law, hence ἐκκλησία here signifies the 'gathering' or 'assembly'. As in Acts 9.19 and 20.18, γίγνομαι μετά means 'to be together with'.[2] Moses received λόγια[3] ζῶντα to transmit to the people—cf. Deut. 32.45–7: originally this implies that those who observed the law would live long, whence these sayings were called 'your life', i.e. 'lifegiving'; but Luke has in mind that ζωή which is participation in the Kingdom of God.

VERSE 39: According to Wendt (146) this verse is based on Ezek. 20. ἀπώσαντο certainly occurs there in verses 13, 16 and 24 (with reference to God's commandments), but ἐστράφησαν εἰς Αἴγυπτον reflects Num. 14.3 ('Now it is better for us to return into Egypt'). Of course, the present verse 'spiritualizes' this return: 'they became once more Egyptian in their hearts', i.e. fell into the idolatry which prevailed in Egypt. The disobedience of godless Israel is dramatically emphasized by the use of the three verbs.

VERSE 40 is taken almost word for word from Ex. 32.1. The speaker sees this as expressing a worship of various idols.[4] The *nominativus pendens* is not un-Greek (Moulton 69).

VERSE 41: Cf. Exod. 32.4 (ἐποίησαν . . . μόσχον) and 32.6 (προσήνεγκαν θυσίαν). In 1 Kings 3.15 LXX ἀνάγειν is used for the bringing-up of the sacrifice to the altar. The whole guilt is placed on the shoulders of the people, Aaron being relegated to the background. The idolater's veneration of what he himself has made ranks as the special mark of the blind infatuation in all idolatry.

VERSES 42f.: Like ἀναστρέφω in 5.22 and 15.16, ἔστρεψεν is here reflexive: God turns away and gives them over to idolatry. παρέδωκεν recalls Rom.

---

[1] *Moyses . . . qui multa passus est in Aegypto et in mari rubro et in heremo annis quadraginta.*

[2] According to *Beg.* IV, 78, μετὰ τοῦ ἀγγέλου καὶ τῶν πατέρων could render the Hebrew וּבֵין . . . בֵּין: Moses would thus be the mediator between the angel and Israel. P. Schmiedel wanted to place ἐν τῇ ἐκκλησίᾳ before τῶν πατέρων. There is nothing disparaging in the representation of God by an angel here; cf. Josephus, *Ant.* XV 136: 'We have learned the best teachings and holiest commands from God through angels.'

[3] According to *Beg.* IV, 78, λόγια means 'oracles', just like χρησμός; see *ThWb* IV, 141.

[4] θεούς here originally translated אלהים. The effect of this is that the golden calf is designated as 'the gods' which are to go before Israel. τί ἐγένετο αὐτῷ renders מֶה הָיָה לֹו.

1.24, 26 and 28; but the idea is different: according to Paul, God *punishes* idolaters by 'giving them up' to moral ruin, whereas here the 'giving-up' to serve the host of heaven is understood as the *consequence* of the worship of the calf. Such service of the stars is held against Israel in Deut. 4.19 and other places, though apart from the λατρεύειν to be found there the wording is not reminiscent of the present verse. On the other hand, Jer. 7.18 and 19.13 LXX mention the 'host of heaven', which in LXX is never named in conjunction with λατρεύω. But, above all, verses 42f. cite Amos 5.25–7 LXX. The original implication of this text was: 'In the exemplary times in the wilderness Israel offered no sacrifices; this proves that God desires no sacrifices.' Here, however, the following meaning is extracted: 'Israel offered sacrifices in the wilderness not to Yahweh but to graven images—for forty years!' Thus the wilderness period no longer ranks as exemplary. Whereas verse 42 ends with a rhetorical question (expecting the answer No!, as is shown by μή), verse 43 opens with a direct statement.[1] The speaker finds in Amos a statement about the wilderness period in which the Israelites took up the 'tent of Moloch' and the 'star of the god Rephan'. Since the Exile in reality stretched beyond the limits threatened by the prophets, 'beyond Damascus' is altered into 'beyond Babylon', which again prompted D to the 'improvement' of ἐπὶ τὰ μέρη Βαβυλῶνος.

VERSE 44: It is astonishing that the fathers nevertheless, during their time in the wilderness, possessed the σκηνὴ τοῦ μαρτυρίου,[2] made in conformity with the ordinance of God.[3] The style makes a striking contrast with the preceding verses and recalls verses 2–34.

[1] According to the Hebrew text, Amos announces to his contemporaries that they will go into captivity 'beyond Damascus', together with their idols, the star-gods Saccuth (to be read for Sikkuth; it is the Assyro-Babylonian deity Nin-Ib) and Kaiwan (the Hebrew *kijjun* will originally have been pronounced *kewan*, which corresponded to an Assyrian designation for the planet Saturn: Wendt, 147f., and *Beg.* IV, 79). LXX misreads *sukkath* for *Sakkuth* and consequently translates: σκηνή. Out of מלככם, 'your king', LXX extracts 'Moloch', its rendering of מַלְכְּ? in II Kings 23.10 and Jer. 32.35. This was the text inherited by our author. Probably LXX at first still read Καιφαν, but extant MSS have the corruption Ραιφαν. Of Acts MSS, A אᶜ have Ραιφαν, C Ρεφαν (spoken αι=ε), likewise *bo* and *sa.* Most 'Western' MSS show Ρεμφαν (or Ρεμφαμ), the intrusive μ appearing also in the Ρομφα of B and the Ρομφαν of א³ (see *Beg.* III, 70f.)—The ὑμῶν after θεοῦ is missing in B D gig Ir; perhaps a pagan god was not to be described as the God of Israel. Ropes on the other hand holds that א³ A C have added ὑμῶν after LXX.—The Damascus document (CDC VII, 14ff.) uses the same Amos verses, but already quotes freely: 'I will send into captivity Sikkuth, your king, and Kiyyun your image, the star of your god, ... even beyond Damascus.' This is then interpreted thus: Sikkuth = the books of the Torah; the 'king' = the community; Kiyyun = the books of the prophets; the 'star' = the true teacher of the Torah. There is here no relationship of any sort with Acts.

[2] LXX translation of both אֹהֶל עֵדוּת and אֹהֶל מוֹעֵד (tent of the assembly).

[3] The idea seen here by Wendt (148), that this tabernacle was a direct replica of the heavenly original, whereas the Temple was merely a copy of the copy, goes too far outside the text. Even the 'tabernacle of witness' must properly fall under the head of what is 'made by the hands of men'; cf. Philo, *De vita Mos.* II, § 88: ἱερὸν χειροποίητον κατασκευάζοντας τῷ πατρὶ καὶ ἡγεμόνι τοῦ παντός. But the author does not think of this either.

VERSE 45: Joshua **3**.14 recounts how the ark of the covenant was carried over into Canaan, and Joshua **18**.1 the erection of the tabernacle at Shiloh. διαδεξάμενοι refers not only to Joshua's generation (note its position after εἰσήγαγον) but each generation took over the ark from the earlier ones down to the days of David. ἦν . . . εἰσήγαγον is to be linked with ἐν (=εἰς) τῇ κατασχέσει τῶν ἐθνῶν:[1] the speaker is thinking above all of the use of the tabernacle, not of the expulsion of the heathen, which is only incidentally mentioned. On ὧν see Bl.-Debr. § 294. ἐξῶσεν is an unaugmented aorist (Bl.-Debr. § 66.2, *Appendix*).

VERSE 46 carries the story smoothly on, the second half using Psalm **132** (**131**).5. The best MSS replace θεῷ by οἴκῳ, probably inserted for an illegible θεῷ by an early copyist, on the analogy of the recurrent οἶκος Ἰακώβ. A C ℜ restore the θεῷ of the Psalm. The speaker understands σκήνωμα in the sense that the pious David wanted to 'find' God only a tented dwelling, i.e. the tabernacle, not build him a solid house. But Klijn, pp. 30f., thinks otherwise.[2]

VERSE 47: αὐτῷ—i.e. θεῷ. Cf. I Kings **8**.20 and **6**.2 LXX for the wording. The speaker sees in the building of the Temple an apostasy from the true service of God, though in itself the text merely brings to a close the account of the tabernacle and the Temple. On οἰκοδόμησεν see Bl.-Debr. § 67, 1.

VERSE 48: ὕψιστος = עֶלְיוֹן in LXX. Wendt thinks (149) that the author wished to 'demonstrate the merely relative value of the Temple building', and Bauernfeind (118) that he sought to express the supra-spatial exaltation of God. But these interpretations do not do justice to the words: the Most High does not inhabit *temples of human construction*[3] (cf. Acts **17**.24). In fact Judaism did not represent Yahweh himself as dwelling in the Temple, but only his 'Name'. Stephen's words would have had a blasphemous ring for Jews.

VERSE 49f.: Here we have Isa. **66**.1 as in LXX, with the sole difference (as in Barn. **16**.2)[4] that τίς replaces ποῖος and turns an exclamation into a

---

[1] The original meaning of κατάσχεσις is the 'taking of possession', hence Preuschen (43) and Wendt (148) see in the text ('on taking possession of' the land of 'the heathen' or 'nations') a fulfilment of verse 5; but the fulfilment of the prophecy is already described by verse 17. In LXX the word means 'possession': cf. e.g. Gen. **17**.8 εἰς κατάσχεσιν αἰώνιον (*Beg.* IV, 80f.) and esp. II Chron. **11**.14.

[2] Klijn finds here (analogously to I QS IX, 3–6) an allusion to a tabernacle or house within the 'house of Jacob', in which God is served in a purely spiritual sense (cf. John **4**.38, I Peter **2**.5 and Eph. **2**.21f.). The original text means that while David wanted to build the Temple, it was Solomon who carried out the project. Luke (who nowhere brings forward the idea of a spiritual house) would not have been understood by any reader in the sense proposed by Klijn.

[3] It is not correct that LXX employs χειροποίητος only of idols (Dibelius, *Studies* 41f.); Isa. **16**.12 LXX εἰσελεύσεται εἰς τὰ χειροποίητα αὐτῆς (a rendering of מִקְדָּשׁ, 'sanctuary').

[4] Does this, as *Beg.* IV (82) suggests, point to the use by Luke and 'Barnabas' of a 'testimony book'? Lake finds it significant that Justin (*Dial.* **22**.2–5, 11) also links Amos **5**.25f. and Isa. **66**.1f. together. But Justin does not cite these verses in immediate succession, and he gives in each case the exact source of the quotation.

rhetorical question. Again as in Barnabas, the fact that I Kings **6**.11f. already meets the objection is ignored.

VERSES 51f.: The swift passage to the string of charges in verses 51-3 which goad the audience into fury can only be explained if the preceding verses form a radical denunciation of the Temple worship. The various counts of the indictment coincide either with OT texts (Exod. **33**.3 and 5; Lev. **26**.41; Jer. **6**.10; Num. **27**.14; Isa. **63**.10) or with late-Jewish convictions (verse 52).[1] According to Blass, Stephen must have been interrupted after verse 50, and verse 51 presents his reaction. But Luke always informs the reader of such interruptions—which, moreover, never occur until the speaker has said everything that Luke wants said.

VERSE 53: The speech ends with a stinging accusation: the Jews have received the law in ordinances of angels (εἰς = ἐν!), *yet* they have not observed it (the meaning is thus exactly opposite to Gal. **3**.19).[2]

Stephen's speech offers three main difficulties about which the experts have cudgelled their brains. Let us dwell on the first before embarking on the others: Stephen is supposed to be answering the question whether he is guilty of the charge, but a very large part of his speech has no bearing on this at all!

Faced with this situation, exegetes have sought either to show that he does really answer the charge, or to explain why he does not. Some maintain that the speech has one consistent theme related to the accusation. According to F. C. Baur (*Vorlesungen über NT Theologie*, 1864, 337) this was the antithesis between the wondrous works of God and Israel's constant ingratitude. But this is a theme—very general at that—which the listener must first discover for himself and apply to the speech; even then it does not entirely fit! Hence Spitta suggested another theme: Moses as the type of the Messiah. Yet only a few verses speak of this, and what has it to do with the concrete accusation? Accordingly Wendt (138) hit upon a third theme: the idea that God's saving presence is not limited to the Temple. Unfortunately this allegedly principal idea is nowhere actually expressed, and Wendt was driven to concede a secondary theme in the Moses-Jesus analogy. Williams, in his

---

[1] Cf. Matt. **5**.12 and **23**.30f., 37; Justin, *Dial.* **16**.4. According to Billerbeck (I.943) rabbinic writings mention the killing of Isaiah, Uriah (Jer. **26**.20ff.) and Zechariah (II Chron. **24**.20f.). Jer. **2**.30 may well have appeared to represent being murdered as the normal lot of a prophet. On the Jewish origin of the idea, see *Beg.* IV, 82; on the whole problem, H. J. Schoeps, *Aus frühchristlicher Zeit: religionsgeschichtliche Untersuchungen*, Tübingen 1950, V: 'Die jüdischen Prophetenmorde', 126–43.

[2] In *Theologie u. Geschichte des Judenchristentums*, 1949 (66 and 440), H. J. Schoeps takes seriously the allegation of the pseudo-Clementines that Paul tried to murder James the Lord's brother, and on the strength of it conjectures that to exonerate Paul Luke invented the figure of Stephen and put into his mouth, with certain alterations, a speech in reality delivered by James (of which he possessed the written text). This should serve as a warning of what happens when the late pseudo-Clementine romance is uncritically enlisted as a historical source.

survey (100ff.), also reports the theses of R. P. C. Hanson and B. S. Easton, the first of whom mentions three themes, the second two. But this means that the speech has no consistent theme.

At this point there appeared two ways out of the impasse. Wendt followed one: the present text must be distinguished from the original speech. The latter 'naturally' dealt with the accusation. But the 'source' did not make this connection clear; the 'reviser' therefore introduced instead the Moses-Jesus antithesis. On this reading, the 'authenticity' of the speech goes by the board, and the 'tradition-or-composition' problem looms ahead. To this W. Foerster offered the following solution in 1953: only the part concerning Moses certainly goes back to Stephen; for the rest, Luke reproduces certain ideas of Stephen's circle which he had learned from Philip the Evangelist (27). This conjecture is based on the consideration that the polemical anti-thesis of Moses and Jesus is germane to the charge and appropriate to a militant speech; the rest Luke accepted because historically it had to do with Stephen's movement. But that Luke for this reason only filled up so important an exposition with irrelevant material is at variance with all we know of his manner of proceeding.

The second way out is that the speech has one consistent theme, indeed, but offers no defence against the indictment! Thus Beyer (1933): Stephen 'says nothing about himself or the charges against him' (49). Lake (also in 1933) seconds this: '. . . religious or political pioneers when brought to court never attempt to rebut the accusations brought against them, but use the opportunity for making a partisan address' (*Beg.* IV, 70). This is perhaps too sweeping. But even if it is not, what has the first half of the speech to do with Stephen's cause? In the upshot, Bauernfeind decided, in 1939, that 'the historical right of the speech to bear the concrete name of Stephen' was 'purely relative' (131). As long ago as 1913, however, Wellhausen had said the same thing in clearer terms: 'The speech is . . . an erudite disquisition based on the Septuagint' (13). In the same year Preuschen—taking his cue from Overbeck, p. 94—had maintained that the author was using the demon-stration of Israel's constant ingratitude to open up the way for the mission to the Gentiles (39). Loisy took the argument a stage further in 1920: the redactor is explaining to Gentile readers that God's people is not Israel, but the Christians (318ff.). Thus all these scholars see the speech no longer in terms of Stephen's historical situation (hence from the viewpoint of *tradition*) but in terms of the situation of the author of Acts (hence from the viewpoint of its *composition*).

Dibelius now donned the mantle of succession, roundly declaring: 'The speech was inserted . . . by Luke in the . . . Martyrdom of Stephen which lay before him.' If so, why does it not deal more strongly with the accusation? Beyer had already (49) called the speech a sermon of the kind used to inter-pret the history of God's people in the synagogue on feast-days. Dibelius supposes that Luke employed a text of this kind in the narrative part of the speech, but he supplied the polemical sections himself and, of course, revised the whole. 'In substance'—once again there is an echo of Overbeck—'the speech prepares for the separation of the Christians from the synagogue. It is no typical martyr's speech, for neither the benefits nor the dangers of martyrdom find expression' (*Studies* 168f.). H. W. Surkau (1938) reaches the same conclusion: the speech does not belong to the Martyrdom: it is not the speech of a martyr, but a sermon (109). Trocmé also shares this view (1957): Stephen's long speech has little connection with the turbulent scene in which it has been inserted; the survey of Israel's history belongs to the Christian kerygma (212); the Martyrdom of Stephen could not have contained such a speech (208).

There we have, spread before us, the long road travelled by criticism up to the present. From Riehm's staunch conviction that Saul noted down Stephen's words in the very courtroom (Zahn, 246, still has Paul attend the sitting as an *auscultator*!) it leads to the thesis that Luke revised for his own ends the historical survey contained in a Hellenistic synagogue sermon.

But what does *analysis* tell us? With few exceptions, verses 2–46 merely offer a didactic recapitulation of Israel's relations with God. Ps. 105 proves that such a historical survey was no isolated case (cf. also Acts **13**.15ff.). No relevance to the immediate situation can yet be glimpsed in the story of Abraham (verses 2–7). Abraham's departure from his homeland, the baldly stated promise coupled with the intimation of the Egyptian servitude, the circumcision on which the 'covenant' depends, these momentous events are named. But that is all. How could the Council have understood from this that the Temple should not be overrated because God's revelation had begun in heathen lands long before its construction? No: this is simply sacred history told for its own sake and with no other theme. There is no trace here of Lake's 'religious pioneer' employing his last hours in a public appeal for his cause. Zahn was quite right!—it is incomprehensible that the judges did not interrupt Stephen after the first few sentences and order him to keep to the point (247). But his suggestion for coming to terms with what even he finds incomprehensible, namely that the judges 'were held spellbound' and therefore listened in silence to 'the lecture', might be credible of some lectures, but certainly not of *this* one.

The story of Joseph (verses 8–16) mentions the selling of Joseph. But this is not in itself polemical—Ps. **105**.17 also does not pass it by. The same reverent tone of historical narration is maintained throughout the story of Moses (verses 17–44). Nevertheless the style and syntax now show that single or grouped verses lending the account a more tendentious significance have been inserted into a 'neutral' presentation (Dibelius) of sacred history. It is verse 25 which introduces this new element: 'you did not recognize the saviour sent by God', whereas verse 26 continues verse 24 in the old style. With verse 35 the simple narrative is transformed into a rhetorically passionate indictment, taking verse 27 as a 'type' of all Jews: it is not individual Jews of a remote past but 'they', *the Jews,* who denied and rejected the man appointed by God to be their ἄρχων and λυτρωτής. And now Israel's treatment of Moses and treatment of Jesus appear as parallels: verse 37 explicitly stresses the similarity between Moses and the 'prophet like me'. Verses 39–43 accuse Israel of idol-worship, *citing a LXX text.* Nobody will maintain that Stephen sought to persuade the High Council with a LXX text which diverges widely from the Hebrew. In sum, then, verses 35, 37, 39–43 and 48–53 appear to be Lucan additions. Verses 44–7 narrate, in themselves without polemic, how the fathers first had the tabernacle, and how the Temple came to be built later. There are visible seams between verses 43 and 44 (Overbeck, 108) and 47 and 48. These testify that Luke has taken over a 'history-sermon' *en bloc* and tailored it for his purposes with additions (and perhaps also abbreviations). So much for the problem of tradition as regards this part. As for verses 51–3, it is plain that they did not form part of the 'history-sermon' but come from the hand of Luke—by no means an inexperienced rhetorician.

And now we come to the *second problem* posed by the speech. This problem is not visible so long as one assumes that Luke was simply representing, out of pure historical interest, the preaching of Stephen and his circle. It can be summed up in the question: why did Luke take over a long historical narrative of which he could really assimilate only a part through his revision? We can only understand our author if we remember that as a historian he saw in the first martyrdom no isolated incident but one link in a long chain, one stone in a great edifice. This the reader now learns from the mouth of the hero himself. (Whether Stephen really made a speech at the time is beside the point; the educated reader certainly did not expect to be regaled with a verbatim original.) Stephen had vanquished his Hellenistic opponents with irresistible wisdom and spirit (6.10). He was therefore particularly suited for the task of disclosing in a great speech the 'suprahistorical significance' of this 'historical moment' (Dibelius). He will owe his death to a state of mind which has long been a recurrent feature in the history of Israel. His speech must therefore deal with this history and show that the Jews have 'always resisted the Holy Spirit' (7.51).

But here we are already in the thick of the *third problem.* Luke has always hitherto (5.13, 26) stressed the great popularity enjoyed by the Christians among the Jewish people. He has shown in the speech of the Pharisee Gamaliel, and will reiterate in 23.9, that the Pharisees are on their side and that strictly only the Sadducees harbour hostility against them. How can all this be reconciled with the grim portrayal of the Jewish people in Stephen's speech? Is it not possible that Luke is here reproducing, with historical fidelity, a line of thought alien to his own conceptions? Not in the least. What Luke is here depicting is the constant experience of his own community, of which Acts indeed tells a long enough tale: it is the Jews who unleash

persecution upon persecution against the Christians; it is they who drive
Paul from town to town and blasphemously reject the gospel again and again.
At the time when Luke wrote, the Jews were the Christians' mighty and
irreconcilable enemies; Jewry humbly open to receive the Word had become
the dwindling exception, a merely theoretical possibility. And so these two
images of Israel stand confronted, without any systematic comment on the
part of Luke: on the one hand Israel with its task in salvation-history, the
people of the patriarchs, of Moses and the prophets; on the other Israel, a
people forever bent on the worship of idols and athirst for the blood of the
prophets.

What strikes us most, perhaps, in the anti-Jewish diatribe which Luke
has put in the mouth of Stephen, is the rejection of the Temple and the
Temple-cult. This has not the slightest connection with Qumran's formal
rejection of the Temple worship at Jerusalem, which was based on the belief
that the services were celebrated by unworthy priests and—according to the
Qumran calendar—at the wrong times. Luke rejects the Temple and its cult
with an argument which Hellenistic Judaism had borrowed from Hellenistic
rationalism. He does not, however, develop any such doctrine as the Fourth
Evangelist's 'spiritual service of God' or Paul's 'body of Christ'. The Gentile
Christianity in whose name Luke speaks has a very sober outlook, not given
to any 'pneumatic mysticism'. It contents itself with the knowledge that the
world's Creator cannot be confined in a house raised by men, and hence
understands that it is not without God's will that, in the year 70, the Temple
of Jerusalem went up in flames and became a place of ruin.

19

ACTS 7:54–8:3

STEPHEN IS MARTYRED AND THE CHRISTIANS PERSECUTED

[54] Now when they heard this, they were enraged in their hearts and gnashed with their teeth against him. [55] But he, full of the Holy Spirit, looked up into heaven, and saw the glory of God, and Jesus standing on the right hand of God, [56] and said: 'Look, I see the heavens opened, and the Son of Man standing on the right hand of God.' [57] But crying out with a loud voice they stopped their ears, and rushed upon him with one accord; [58] and cast him out of the city, and stoned him. And the witnesses laid down their garments at the feet of a young man named Saul. [59] And they stoned Stephen and he called out saying: 'Lord Jesus, receive my spirit'. And kneeling down he cried with a loud voice: 'Lord, lay not this sin to their charge!' And when he had said this, he fell asleep. [1] But Saul was approving of his death. And there arose on that day a great persecution against the community in Jerusalem; and they were all scattered abroad throughout the regions of Judaea and Samaria, except the Apostles. [2] And devout men buried Stephen, and made great lamentation over him. [3] But Saul sought to destroy the community; for he entered house after house, dragging out men and women, and sending them to prison.

Bibliography:

See under § 18. Also F. C. Conybeare, 'The Stoning of St. Stephen', *Expositor* Ser. 8, vol. 6 (1913), 466–70; K. Bornhäuser, 'Zur Erzählung von der Steinigung des Stephanus (Apg. 7.54–8.3)', *Beth-El* 22 (1930), 313–21; F. X. Porporato, 'De S. Stephano Protomartyre', *Verb. Domini* 16 (1936), 81–8; J. Mehlmann, 'De S. Stephano Protomartyre', *Verb. Domini* 21 (1941), 22–9, 33–9; G. D. Kilpatrick, 'Acts 7.52, ELEUSIS', *JTS* 46 (1945), 136–45; H. P. Owen, 'Stephen's Vision in Acts 7.55–6', *NTS* 1 (1955), 224–6; M. H. Scharlemann, 'Stephen, A Singular Saint', *Analecta Biblica* 34, Rome, 1968.

VERSE 54: As in 5.33, διεπρίοντο describes the seething rage of the councillors. The picture is completed with the OT expression 'they gnashed on him with their teeth'.[1] But the storm had yet to break.

[1] Job 16.9; Pss. 35.16, 37.12 and 112.10; Lam. 2.16.

VERSE 55: Full of the Holy Spirit,[1] Stephen looks up to heaven[2] and sees the glory of God[3] and Jesus standing on the right hand of God.[4] This explanation enables even the non-Christian reader to understand the description of his vision which Stephen goes on to give.

VERSE 56: 'I see the heavens opened'—God of course is in the highest heaven[5]—'and the Son of Man standing on the right hand of God.' The writer presumes that those listening grasp the reference to Jesus and regard the exclamation as a blasphemy.

VERSE 57: At all events the Councillors behave in accordance with that presumption. They shout or stop their ears[6] so as to be spared listening to the blasphemy, and rush ὁμοθυμαδόν[7] on Stephen without the formality of spoken judgment—Luke represents them as acting out of blind passion.

VERSE 58: It is in conformity with Jewish law that Stephen is not put to death within the walls of the Holy City.[8] The context of the Lucan description would imply that the members of the Sanhedrin themselves carried out the stoning. Otherwise one must suppose an indefinite 'they' as the subject of ἐκβαλόντες and ἐλιθοβόλουν. The 'witnesses' (already mentioned in Deut. 17.1–7) recall the official procedure laid down for stoning in the Mishnah.[9] But according to Sanh. 6.3 (Billerbeck II, 685) it is not the

---

[1] Cf. 6.3 and 11.24. ὑπάρχω is a Hellenistic substitute for εἰμί, but, like ἀτενίζω also (see note to 1.10), is especially frequent in Luke's work (see note to 3.4). Here the being filled with the Holy Spirit is not thought of as permanent but as a special gift that enables Stephen, at this moment, to look into heaven.

[2] The singular corresponds with Lucan usage: we find the plural only in the borrowed formula of Luke 10.20 (but see note to verse 56 below). Commentators have concluded from Stephen's heavenward glance that the scene originally took place in the open air.

[3] See *ThWb* II, 247–51.

[4] The standard formula, deriving from Ps. 110.1, runs: '*sitting* at the right hand of God'. The following suggestions have been made to explain the variant: 1. Jesus was standing up to welcome Stephen (who thus, like the repentant criminal of Luke 23.43, goes to heaven the moment he dies: *Beg.* IV, 84); so the majority of exegetes, ever since Bengel's '*quasi obvium Stephano*'; 2. Jesus had stood up in order to enter upon his Messianic office on earth: Loisy 349, Surkau, *Martyrien* 117, and finally H. P. Owen, 'Stephen's Vision in Acts 7.55–56' in *NTS* 1, 1955, 224–6 ('Stephen's vision is proleptic. He sees forward to the glory of the Parousia'—225); 3. Originally, Jesus (like the angels) was imagined as standing in the presence of God: the Son of Man described in Dan. 7.13 must also be thought of in this manner. According to Bauernfeind (120) the departure from the normal vouches for the authenticity of the account of the vision. Martyrs' visions are frequently described in the Acts of the Martyrs: Preuschen 45.

[5] The plural could admittedly also correspond to a שָׁמַיִם in the tradition used by Luke.

[6] 'If a man hear an unseemly word he shall put his fingers in his ears' (Billerbeck II, 684): this piece of evidence admittedly comes only from the third century A.D., but the custom is ancient.

[7] A favourite word of Luke's (see note to 1.14), but literary tradition may also be involved, e.g. Job 16.10 LXX ὁμοθυμαδόν . . . κατέδραμον ἐπ' ἐμοί.

[8] Lev. 24.11ff., Num. 15.35; Sanh. 6.1 (Bill. II, 684).

[9] Sanh. 6.1ff.; Bill. II, 685f. The first witness pushes the condemned down from the place of execution (about twelve feet high). Should the victim survive the fall, the second witness must drop a boulder aimed at his heart, so that his ribs will be smashed.

witnesses who lay aside their garments, but the condemned who is stripped.[1] Here the clothes are laid at the feet of a youth[2] for him to guard;[3] his name is Saul. Thus Luke introduces the Paul of later chapters into his story.

VERSE 59: The description of the stoning is resumed.[4] In the face of death Stephen—in a manner corresponding to an ancient Jewish evening-prayer (Ps. 31.5)[5]—commends his spirit to the Lord Jesus, who here takes the place of God (cf. Luke 23.46).[6]

VERSE 60: Stephen, who up to now had been standing, kneels[7] and prays aloud[8] for his enemies[9] before 'falling asleep': 'Death has become a sleeping.' But paganism too used κοιμηθῆναι in the sense of 'to die' (Bauer *Wb* 865).

CHAPTER 8

VERSE 1: ἦν συνευδοκῶν depicts an attitude of some duration, not a momentary reaction. διωγμὸς μέγας corresponds to the account which follows, whereas 11.19 speaks only of θλῖψις, 'troubles'. Since Luke thinks of the Jerusalem community only as a single united congregation, he is sure that the persecution is directed against it as a whole: 'all were scattered throughout Judaea and Samaria' (this paves the way for the story of Philip in 8.4ff.)—'except the Apostles'. By remaining, these preserve the continuity of the community.

VERSE 2: According to Sanh. 6.6 (Billerbeck II, 686) it was forbidden to hold a lamentation over one executed by stoning. The fact that a great

---

[1] Sanh. 6.3. The suggestion (*Beg.* IV, 85) that the garments were laid merely by chance at Saul's feet is inconsistent with Acts 22.20.

[2] νεανίας (a 'distinguished' word, according to De Zwaan, *Beg.* II, 35) means in Luke 'youth': in Acts 20.9 it equals the παῖς of 20.12; in 23.17 the νεανίσκος of 23.22.

[3] Acts 22.20.

[4] The second ἐλιθοβόλουν is necessary since Luke has inserted the statement that the witnesses laid their clothes at the feet of Saul (Wendt 251).

[5] Bill. II, 269. Surkau (110) links up the last words of verse 60 with verse 59.

[6] Bauernfeind (121) thinks it possible that we have here an older version of Luke 23.46. But probably it was not thought desirable to put Jesus' prayer from the Cross, word for word, in the mouth of Stephen.

[7] Hence this is not a description of a stoning in accordance with the treatise Sanhedrin (see 294 n. 2 below). Reicke sees the discrepancy, but takes refuge in the argument that the mortally wounded Stephen could have raised himself to his knees! But τιθέναι τὰ γόνατα does not bear this meaning either elsewhere or in Acts 7.60, 9.40, 20.36 and 21.5, where, as in Luke 22.41, it signifies 'to kneel down'.

[8] Cf. the φωνῇ μεγάλη of Luke 23.46. Such a cry would be unthinkable at a Mishnah lapidation.

[9] Luke 23.34a is missing in BD syr^sin sa and will not belong to the original text. Dornseiff (*ZNW* 35 (1936) 136) has pointed out that Stephen's last three utterances correspond to three logia of Jesus: 7.56 = Luke 22.69; 7.59 = Luke 23.46; 7.60 = Luke 23.34. In *Beg.* II 40 De Zwaan explains μὴ στήσῃς in accordance with the classical rules of grammar: 'Do not begin to reckon . . .'; but Luke 7.13 and Acts 9.38, 16.28 and 23.12 show that Luke did not bind himself by these rules. Luke will have borrowed ἵστημι in the sense of 'ascribe' from LXX: the fact that it is there associated with sums of money (Wendt 152) is no disproof.

mourning did take place supports the suggestion that Stephen met his end through lynch law. Since according to Luke all the Christians have fled, it can only be 'devout' non-Christian Jews who now bury Stephen.[1] A victim of judicial stoning was not permitted an individual grave: Sanh. **6.5** stipulates burial in the common grave for those stoned or burned. So here we have further evidence against a legal stoning. 'The presence of such details in the sort of account Acts gives here is explicable solely on the assumption that these represent the conclusion of the older Martyrdom' (Dibelius in *ThR*, N S 3 (1931) 234).

VERSE 3: The transformation in the picture of Saul is breathtaking, to say the least. A moment ago he was a youth looking on with approval at the execution. Now he is the arch-persecutor, invading Christian homes to seize men and women and fling them into gaol. Luke sees only the dread figure of the Christian-baiter, and therefore forgets all critical problems . . . Why, for instance, did Saul not arrest the Apostles? With the contents of **26.10ff.** already at the back of his mind, Luke probably imagined the progress of the terror thus: first Saul purged Jerusalem of Christians, hunting them out of every synagogue, so that they scattered and fled before the storm of his zeal; next he proceeded to comb out the ἔξω πόλεις in ever-widening circles, until finally he came to Damascus. Cf. comments on **22.3f.** and **26.10f.** below.[2]

[1] Originally the Christians must have been mentioned here (see general discussion).

[2] According to Zahn, Paul was 'at that time no longer an immature youth' but 'a rabbinic student who had already reached the age of manhood' (246), who 'had in all probability taken part as an observer in the session of the Sanhedrin' and 'was unlikely to have been under 30' (264). That the witnesses laid their clothes at his feet (Zahn continues) does not mean that they 'picked some mere bystander or other to watch that nobody made off with them' (Zahn writes this in the teeth of Paul's statement in Acts **22.20**) 'but identifies' him 'as the leader of the execution or, at least, one of the leading participants' (!). In 1934 K. Bornhäuser (*Studien zur Apg.*, 71–88) developed the thesis that Stephen was executed in accordance with the prescriptions of the tractate Sanhedrin: Paul, as one of the two assessors prescribed, accompanied the procession to the city walls in order to bring Stephen back again, should anything of moment still arise in his favour; any man under the age of sixty could be accounted a νεανίας, and συνευδοχεῖν (according to II Macc. **11.35**) means to assent as a judge. But even in the Maccabees verse, συνευδοχέω signifies merely 'to be consenting'; for the rest, Bornhäuser imports all the Mishnah features into a text which struggles against them. Above all it is to be observed that according to Sanhedrin VI 1c (S. Krauss, 185 n.8): 'If he' (the condemned, who even on the way to execution has declared himself able to adduce some essential ground for his reprieve) 'is unable to adduce anything essential, he is brought back once and even twice, for terror may have confused his wits; further than that he is not brought back, yet he is given to accompany him two doctors of the law who, should he thereafter be able to adduce anything essential, immediately bring him back, even a fourth and a fifth time (*Bar* and *b* 43a, also T IX 4).' Thus the two rabbis do not in every case accompany the condemned to the place of execution, but only in the exceptional event of his having already twice on the way there claimed some ground of exculpation of which he has not, however, been able to convince the judges. Surely no one will maintain that this was so in the case of Stephen. Hence there is no justification for declaring that Paul must have accompanied the execution-party as one of the two rabbis, and the whole attempt to render plausible his participation in the trial falls to the ground. Not even in Acts 22,

The integrity of this story has been contested by B. Weiss (*Einl.* 574 n. 5), Sorof (62f.), Hilgenfeld (*ZwTh*, 1895, 403), Harnack [*Beitr.* III, 171 (ET)], Wellhausen (12f.), Wendt (150 n. 1) and Loisy (349ff.): Harnack, recently followed by Bauernfeind, sees two sources interwoven, while Dibelius with B. Weiss decides that Luke worked up a single source. But it is not only 7.58-8.1 which offer difficulty, as they think.

In 7.51-3 Stephen so goads the Councillors that they ought really to have flung themselves on him in fury. But they remain quietly seated and only gnash their teeth until the reference to the Son of Man. Luke sets great store by this reference and therefore first in verse 55 makes it plain to every reader that the allusion is to Jesus (incidentally, this detail also shows that the third gospel and Acts appeared as two separate books). Not until verse 56 does Stephen make his exclamation, which originally was not connected with this preceding speech. The speech had, with great scriptural erudition, depicted Israel's disobedience to God over many centuries of a hallowed yet also unholy past, and by way of peroration had unrolled the whole record of the sins of that people. But now something totally different occurs: the Holy Spirit opens the eyes of Stephen—and therewith of the reader—to the heavenly Reality so infinitely raised above all earthly polemics. It is, however, precisely what can there be seen that the Sanhedrin cannot bear to hear related. For if Jesus stands on the right hand of God, this must show that the Christians are right in the sight of God and that the High Council is virtually God's enemy. And so the opposition breaks loose—now the witness's tongue will be stilled. To this extent Luke's presentation has a profound significance, if it is seen not as a court record (with Paul as the reporter, according to Zahn) but as a vision of the ultimate decision which shatters the frame of earthly events. As a witness to the exalted and victorious Jesus, Stephen earns his Passion. Now the storm may and must break loose which Luke has hitherto held in check, for now what is crucial in his eyes, hence intolerably scandalous to the Jews, has been uttered. This technique of presentation must be appreciated not from the standpoint of modern empirical psychology but from that of Luke's own theological conceptions.

Now the pack is unleashed to hunt Stephen out of the city and stone him. Probably here a part of the older Martyrdom emerges, and it threatens

---

where the whole context would prompt such an assertion, if anything of the kind were possible, does Luke himself state that Paul was a judge or official participant in Stephen's trial. Actually (let us not lose sight of this) Luke could find no better way of associating Paul with the Stephen story than having him guard the clothes of the 'witnesses': a detail explicitly stressed in 22.20. On the other hand he made no bones about Paul's role of judge in subsequent trials of Christians (26.10), despite the fact, which he overlooks, that the Sanhedrin was in no way empowered to pass capital sentences (nor does tradition contain any record of its having done so). But, as is shown in the text above, the 'trial' of Stephen was in any case a piece of lynch law, which Luke himself first brought into connection with the Council.

to destroy the framework which Luke has so ingeniously, painstakingly constructed: that of ostensibly legal proceedings before the High Council. From the fact that this one man is hounded through the streets by the raging mob and stoned at the gates, the lynch-justice becomes obvious. Hence Luke, by mentioning the witnesses (of whom he knew from Deut. 17), attempts to steer his account back into the paths of judicial procedure. He had no idea how judicial stonings were carried out—we know the details from the Mishnah tractate *Sanhedrin*: the condemned man (who probably has his hands tied behind his back) is pushed by the first witness off the brink of a steep drop; if this does not finish him the second witness lets fall a boulder on his chest, which smashes his ribs, damaging the heart and lungs. Luke has in mind quite a different kind of stoning, one in which heavy stones are picked up and hurled at a standing—or fleeing—victim. That was the kind of thing which happened in the East when a man was stoned by a riotous mob, and this is probably how the story was told in the original Martyrdom (though we no longer have any means of restoring its text). And this was the point where Luke could introduce Paul, of whom the Martyrdom knew and said nothing (see p. 82f. above). In the official procedure it was the condemned man who was stripped; but Luke assumes that the witnesses would have to remove their outer garments, the better to throw the stones at Stephen. This enabled him to associate Saul with the killing, as the minder of the clothes (**22**.20). Then in verse 59 he simply picks up the ἐλιθοβόλουν again.

For the present, however, we have a more important point to consider. In themselves, Stephen's words in verse 59b appear modelled on a short Jewish evening-prayer taken from Ps. 31.5. Here, though, we find it addressed not to God but to the 'Lord Jesus'. Thus we encounter a specifically Christian devotion which is already so centred on Jesus that it is *his* name which is invoked in the hour of death. In the present context this detail signifies that Stephen is commending himself to the Lord of whom he has just had a vision.

Then comes the end, piously stylized (the collapse becomes a kneeling). But one last word (this martyrdom has gone through development, just like the Passion of Jesus)—a parallel, in LXX language, to the word from the Cross added at Luke 23.34: the plea that the enemies be forgiven. Now all has been said and done, and Stephen 'falls asleep'.

The original Martyrdom probably concluded with the report of the great lamentation. Such a mourning among his followers is entirely possible, for when the populace has done a man to death it tends to keep quiet and has a guilty conscience. But this lamentation proves that no judicial stoning occurred, as mourning was strictly forbidden in the case of persons so executed.

If it was a fomented mob which brought about Stephen's death, we need no longer wonder why the Roman cohorts from the citadel of Antonia did not intervene, as later in the case of Paul. The pursuit began somewhere in the warren of alleys which Roman military police were powerless to penetrate (cf. **23**.21). It is then also unnecessary to date the incident during the interim following Pilate's recall, i.e. in the year 37, on the ground that under the Roman governors the Sanhedrin scarcely possessed the power of life and death.

The second theme of this section is the *persecution of the community*. We have already seen (cf. 82f. and 293 above) how Luke mistakenly supposed that the whole Jerusalem community (with the exception of the Apostles) was driven out of the town. As he could not conceive that it fell into two distinct groups, he was obliged to think of a dispersion of the whole community. On the other hand, tradition said nothing about a persecution of the Apostles—so they must have held out and thereby ensured the continuity of the primitive Church! Luke failed to realize that this construction was doomed to collapse by the contradiction between **9**.31 and **11**.19. Actually it was probably not even the whole Hellenistic group but only its leaders who left the city of murderers and who continued the mission outside Judaea with unabated zeal. And by beginning, in Syrian Antioch, the acceptance of uncircumcised Gentiles into the fold, these men opened a new chapter in the history of the Church—a chapter of unprecedented importance. Christianity is, once and for all time, preserved from the fate of becoming just another Jewish messianic sect.

Luke now proceeds somewhat laboriously to associate Paul with the persecution in Jerusalem—for him there was at that time only this one Christian community, and Paul did after all persecute 'the community'. At first Saul appears merely as an approving onlooker. Zahn's assertion (264) that Saul 'is the leader of the expedition' or at any rate 'one of the leading figures' is in open contradiction to the text. But here Zahn is only one of several commentators bent on improving Luke. Among them there is Bornhäuser, who tries to make an ordained Rabbi out of Paul. If this had been so, Paul would not have refrained from mentioning it in the list of his Jewish credentials in Phil. **3**.5. But we are not reduced to this *argumentum e silentio*. That Paul did not take part as a Rabbi in this persecution is fully evident from his own words in Gal. **1**.22f.: 'And I was still unknown by sight to the communities of Judaea'—the context shows that this includes Jerusalem —'. . ., but they only heard say: "Our former persecutor is now preaching the faith of which he once made havoc."' Now these are *not* the words of the Judaean communities themselves (so that here Paul's persecution of them would be attested), but the words they have heard spoken by Paul's former victims. According to Acts **8**.3 Paul in Jerusalem dragged Christian men and women out of their houses and flung them into gaol. According to **26**.11 he extended this persecution to the towns outside Jerusalem. But anyone whom a persecutor has thus dragged out of his home knows him 'by sight'. Moreover it is in this very verse 3 that the break in the narrative, the transition

L

from the report of Stephen's martyrdom to the legend of Paul, becomes very clear: the Hellenistic Jews who have hitherto been the persecutors vanish at one stroke, and Saul singlehanded assumes their role. But the lack of numbers is compensated by Saul's rabid activity: he bursts into the Christians' dwellings and hales them off to prison. He compels them to blaspheme (26.11); he is always present when the Christians are tried by the authorities—who can be no other than the Sanhedrin—and inexorably votes for their death. Bauernfeind (121) bestows on him an 'executive body' to carry out the more brutal measures. But this is to misunderstand the frightfulness of the persecutor-figure Saul. The later Church saw him as a veritable demon (a legend reflected in the pseudo-Clementines) and sent up awed thanks for the miracle of grace whereby God transformed this fearful enemy into a servant of Jesus Christ. The darker the period of his persecuting zeal, the brighter shone his apostolate. Hence it is of no interest to this legend that Paul headed for Damascus with a squad of police—this was in any case impossible from both legal and political standpoints. Paul is not the commander of a striking-force, an *Einsatz-Kommando*: he *is* the persecution *in person*. It follows that his conversion brings immediate peace to the churches in Judaea, Galilee and Samaria (9.31). Whoever attaches real historical value to these features of the legendary portrait taken over by Luke (Saul was a judge, hence a regular Rabbi, hence at least forty, hence married though perhaps a widower) simply cannot explain the sudden jump in Luke's description between 7.58 and 8.3. In reality, the extension of Christianity did not await this alleged dispersal of the entire Jerusalem community; it had already, before Stephen was put to death and his followers persecuted, spread as far as Damascus, nearly two hundred miles away. And it was in or near Damascus that Paul 'persecuted the community', with the means commanded by the Jewish synagogue over its members, means whose effect he was later to feel in his own body (II Cor. 11.24).

Any reader who reflects on the course of events in the story of Stephen, and their divine meaning, apparently so clear, cannot but wonder why certain inevitable conclusions are not actually stated or indicated. For example, Luke demonstrates in the speech that Israel has for a long time been going astray, and the murder of Stephen proves afresh that Israel will not be converted but is defiantly entrenched in its rejection of God. What could now be more apposite than to indicate that it was the very expulsion of the primitive community by this same faithless Israel which instigated and justified the Gentile mission? This reasoning—as we shall shortly see—was by no means alien to the mind of our author. But it was not enough for him. It remained on the human plane. If the Gentile mission was to be really legitimate, it must depend entirely and solely on the *will of God*. But this will not be definitely demonstrated until the story of Cornelius in Chapter 10, and this means that Luke must postpone the most important consequence of the dispersion of the primitive Church (actually, the Stephenites) until 11.18.

A further point is that Luke associated the Gentile mission almost exclusively with the figure of Paul. Paul is 'the' missionary to the Gentiles. In reality the Pauline mission was preceded by an 'anonymous' stage unconnected with names of particular renown, one which moreover continued alongside the Pauline, for it was not Paul in fact who initiated Christian congregations in Damascus, Antioch, Ephesus or Rome. But the popular writer Luke needed a well-known name and figure to discharge in person the great tasks of the mission, and indeed he himself saw history in this guise: as the work of a particular and celebrated instrument of God. This is why the other Christian missionaries are so overshadowed by Paul, even his intimate collaborators. Today we see the evolution of early Christianity differently from Luke in many points, and know that it was richer in successful missionaries. On the other hand, the restriction of Luke's narrative to the great names—above all that of Paul—does at least present us with a picture of that Pauline activity which, all in all, was the most important and effective in the dawn of the mission.

Luke ascribes the beginning of the mission outside Judaea to Philip, one of the Seven. But since Luke knows no expulsion of the Hellenist leaders as such, Philip does not appear as their representative but simply as a member of the scattered primitive community. The historical facts of the case do not indeed here stand revealed with complete clarity. That we can nevertheless to some extent guess them, however, is above all due to Luke's work. It remains a matter for astonishment that a man of the sub-apostolic generation can have sensed so much of the true state of affairs: he has left us a priceless gift.

20

ACTS 8: 4–25

PHILIP AND PETER CONVERT THE SAMARITANS

[4] Now those who were scattered abroad went about preaching the Word. [5] And Philip went down to the city of Samaria, and proclaimed to them the Messiah. [6] And the multitude gave heed with one accord to the things that were said by Philip, when they heard and saw the signs which he did. [7] For many of those who had unclean spirits—they came out, crying with a loud voice; and many who were crippled and lame were healed. [8] And there was much joy in that city.

[9] But a man named Simon had previously practised magic in the city, and amazed the people of Samaria, saying that he was someone great. [10] To him they all gave heed, great and small, saying: 'This man is that power of God which is called great.' [11] And they gave heed to him, because for a long time he had amazed them with his sorceries. [12] But when they believed Philip, who preached good news about the kingdom of God and the name of Jesus Christ, they were baptized, both men and women. [13] And Simon himself also believed: and being baptized he continued with Philip; and seeing great signs and wonders done, he was amazed.

[14] Now when the Apostles in Jerusalem heard that Samaria had received the Word of God, they sent to them Peter and John: [15] who went down and prayed for them, that they might receive the Holy Spirit: [16] for it had not yet fallen on any of them: they had only been baptized in the name of the Lord Jesus. [17] Then they laid their hands on them, and they received the Holy Spirit. [18] Now when Simon saw that through the laying-on of the Apostles' hands the Spirit was given, he offered them money, [19] saying, 'Give me also this power, that whoever I lay my hands on may receive the Holy Spirit.' [20] But Peter said to him: 'Your silver perish with you, because you have thought to obtain the gift of God with money. [21] You have neither part nor lot in this word, for your heart is not right before God. [22] Repent therefore of this your wickedness, and pray the Lord, if perhaps the thought of your heart may be forgiven. [23] For I see that you are in the gall of bitterness and in the bond of iniquity.' [24] And Simon answered and said: 'Pray for me to the Lord, that none of the things which you have spoken come upon me!' [25] So after they had testified and spoken the Word of the Lord, they returned to Jerusalem, and preached the gospel in many villages of the Samaritans.

Bibliography:

H. Waitz, 'Die Quellen der Philippusgeschichten i. d. Apg. **8**.5–40', *ZNW* 7 (1906), 340–55; J. Boehmer, 'Studien z. Geographie Palästinas, bes. im NT', *ZNW* 9 (1908), 216–29 (on **8**.5); K. Pieper, *Die Simon-Magus-Perikope* (*NT-Abhdl.* 3, 5), Münster 1911; J. Behm, see Bibl. on § 16 (on **8**.17); L. Cerfaux, 'La Gnose simonienne', *RScR* 15 (1925), 489–511 and 'Simon le magicien à Samarie', *RScR* 27 (1937), 615–7; E. Fascher, 'Die Auferstehung Jesu und ihr Verhältnis zur urchristlichen Verkündigung', *ZNW* 26 (1927), 1–25; R. P. Casey, 'Simon Magus', *Beg.* V, 151–63; N. Adler, *Taufe und Handauflegung* (*NT-Abhdl.* 19, 3), Münster 1951 (on **8**.14); G. Quispel, *Gnosis als Weltreligion*, Zürich 1951, and 'Simon en Helena' in *Ned. Theol. Tijdschr.* (1952), 339–45; E. Haenchen, 'Gab es eine vorchristl. Gnosis?', *ZThK* 49 (1952), 316–49; J. E. L. Oulton, 'The Holy Spirit, baptism and laying-on of hands in Acts', *Exp. Tim.* 66 (1954/5), 236–40 (on **8**.14); R. McL. Wilson, 'Simon, Dositheus and the Dead Sea Scrolls', *ZRGG* 9 (1957), 21–30; 'Gnostic Origins Again', *Vigil. Christ.* 11 (1957), 93–110; *The Gnostic Problem: A Study of the Relations between Hellenistic Judaism and the Gnostic Heresy*, London 1958; E. Haenchen, 'Neutestamentliche u. gnostische Evangelien' in W. Eltester, *Christentum und Gnosis* (Beiheft 37 der *ZNW*), Berlin 1969, 19–45.

VERSE 4: μὲν οὖν marks a change of scene (see on **1**.6 above). οἱ διασπαρέντες points back to **8**.1 and onwards to **11**.19. διῆλθον: they travelled over the provinces (not 'country districts'; the action takes place in a town!) of Judaea and Samaria (**8**.1).[1] The scene of the first of the following stories is laid in Samaria, that of the second in Judaea. Thus the verse constitutes both a summary resumption of events and a superscription for what follows. Here, as in **15**.35, εὐαγγελίζομαι means simply 'to preach' and may therefore do duty for the customary λαλεῖν (τὸν λόγον—see on **4**.29 above). Thus the scattered Christians transform their flight into a missionary tour.

VERSE 5: Φίλιππος: the second of the Seven enumerated in **6**.5 (see **21**.8). 'According to John 12 it was he who brought the Hellenists to Jesus; that as an Apostle he became one of the Twelve . . . is nothing surprising' (Wellhausen 14). The introductory verse 4 makes his mission part of the preaching of the dispersed Hellenists. 'Went down' (κατελθών) i.e. from highlying Jerusalem. τὴν πόλιν τῆς Σαμαρείας (so B ℵ A) can according to Wendt (154) refer only to Sebaste (the old Samaria), but Wellhausen (14), Zahn

---

[1] Acts employs διέρχομαι after the model of LXX, which uses it to render various Hebrew verbs, construing either with the accusative of the space traversed (**12**.10, **13**.6, **14**.24, **15**.3, **15**.41, **16**.6, **18**.23, **19**.1, **19**.21 and **20**.2) or with ἕως + terminus of journey (**8**.40, **9**.38 and **11**.19). Used absolutely (**8**.4, **10**.38 and **17**.23) the verb implies an unexpressed accusative (e.g. 'the land'). The ἐν οἷς of **20**.25 is also to be found in LXX (II Kings 20.14; II Chron. 17.9) in the sense of 'go around', while the ἀπό of **13**.14 reminds one that the word may simply mean 'go'—διά having here, and in the construction with ἕως, lost all its force.

(273) and E. Meyer (III 277) are just as insistent that Shechem must be meant, as Sebaste had become wholly pagan.[1] The legitimacy of the Christian mission in Samaria is certified by the words of Jesus in **1**.8.

VERSE 6: οἱ ὄχλοι[2]—the people listen to him[3] (here and in verse 11 προσέχω has the same sense as in LXX, e.g. Isa. **49**.1) gathered attentively together (see **1**.14 above). ἐν with the articular infinitive (Bl.-Debr. § 404) gives the reason: they hear and see his miracles.

VERSE 7 explains that. The parallelism shows what is really meant—many[4] unclean spirits are exorcised and many a cripple walks. The first are heard, the second seen. The first part of the sentence is confused, since the identification of the sick with their devils is in conflict with the distinction between them (the sick man has the unclean spirit). Hence the anacoluthon:[5] 'for many of those who had unclean spirits—crying with a loud voice they came out'. These are the audible miracles. Luke prefers παραλελυμένος to the vulgar παραλυτικός (not 'paralytic' but 'crippled').

VERSE 8: Great joy reigns in the city on account of the numerous healings. This verse looks like the end of a miracle-story, but was probably modelled on such endings by Luke in order to round off the first part of the story.

VERSE 9 gives a flashback. 'Before then'[6] a certain Simon[7] had been practising magic in that city and leaving the Samaritans open-mouthed with wonder. λέγων κτλ. does not indicate what formula he used to create that effect, but merely adds a complementary detail that he 'gave himself out to be a "great one"'. In this way Luke assimilates the saying about Simon in verse 10—which even he found difficult—to the formula used in **5**.36 (and

---

[1] D and the later MSS omit the article and relate the story to a town unnamed; so also Bauernfeind (122), detecting an echo of Matt. **10**.5 εἰς πόλιν Σαμαριτῶν μὴ εἰσέλθητε, which was more important than geographical exactitude.

[2] So also Luke **3**.7, 10; **4**.42; **5**.3, 15; **7**.24; **8**.42, 45; **9**.11, 18; **11**.14, 29; **12**.54; **14**.25 and **23**.4, 48 and Acts **14**.11, 13, 18f. and **17**.13.

[3] *Pace Beg.* IV 89, we cannot equate this with the πιστεῦσαι of verse 12: it describes a situation, not the act of faith.

[4] From πολλοὶ τῶν ἐχόντων Jacquier (253) and Bauernfeind (125) conclude that not all were healed. But the genitive here is no longer felt as partitive: a story emphasizing Philip's mighty miracles (verse 12) cannot speak of merely partial success.

[5] Wellhausen (15; also *Einl. in die drei ersten Evangelien*, 2nd edn. 11) draws attention to Mk. **1**.34 D: τοὺς δαιμόνια ἔχοντας — ἐξέβαλεν αὐτὰ ἀπ' αὐτῶν. Zahn (277) unwarrantably assumes that an ἐκ has been lost after ἐποίει and that the next word should read πολλῶν.

[6] As in Luke **23**.12, προυπάρχω means 'to be prior'. Here also ὑπάρχω replaces εἰμί.

[7] See Haenchen, 'Gab es eine vorchristliche Gnosis?', *ZThK* 49 (1952), 316–49, which traces the Simonian movement from Hippolytus back to Luke. Older bibl. may be found in R. P. Casey's 'Simon Magus' (*Beg.* V, 151–63). See also E. Meyer III, 217ff. Zahn's exposition (277ff.) has been superseded. On 'Simon Magus in der Haggada?' see H. J. Schoeps, *Aus frühchristlicher Zeit. Religionsgeschichtliche Untersuchungen*, Tübingen 1950, 239–54. O. Cullmann deals with Acts **8**.4–25 in his *Peter. Disciple, Apostle, Martyr*, London 1962, 36ff., and in 'Samaria and the Origins of the Christian Mission', *The Early Church*, 1956, 185–94. Cf. also L. Goppelt, *Christentum u. Judentum im 1. und 2. Jahrh.*, 1954, 132ff. (ET *Jesus, Paul and Judaism*, New York, 1964, 176ff.)

summarily restored here by Blass). ἐξιστάνω is a Hellenistic equivalent of ἐξίστημι.

VERSE 10: ᾧ προσεῖχον¹ κτλ.—Justin, himself a Samaritan, reports in I *Apol.* 26.3, *Dial.* 120.6 that nearly all his countrymen revered Simon as the highest god. It is clear from the history of his movement that 'the great power' was a Samaritan designation for the supreme deity. Simon declared that this deity had come to earth in his person for the redemption of men. The word καλουμένη, despite its poor reception from the commentators, shows that Luke rightly recognized in μεγάλη a title, whereas τοῦ θεοῦ (cf. Luke 22.69) is a mere gloss, and misleading at that: the 'great power' is not *a* power of God, but the highest divinity itself.² Simon was thus not just a pseudo-Messiah (Knox, 25; Wikenhauser, *Apg.* 77): he claimed to be far more. This however is not discernible in the present episode. ἀπὸ μικροῦ κτλ., i.e. from children to the aged.

VERSE 11: Luke cannot say that the Samaritans actually 'believed in' Simon, since for him Simon is a mere wizard. He must therefore confine himself to the colourless προσέχειν—they were 'all eyes and ears' for Simon (as later—verse 6—for Philip) over the long³ period during which he gave evidence of his magical powers.

VERSE 12: The narrative steers back from the past to the present. Philip has come preaching in Samaria—preaching, we now learn, of God's (coming) kingdom⁴ and Jesus' (all-powerful) name—, the people have believed⁵ him, and now they come to be baptized, both men and women.

VERSE 13: Even Simon, although his faith is not of the soundest, believes and is baptized. He remains closely at Philip's side (ἦν προσκαρτερῶν—see on 1.10 above) and is amazed at the wonders he sees . . . Here the narrative comes to a sudden and disappointing end.⁶ If even this great magician was so overwhelmed by Philip's miracles, they must have been extraordinary indeed. Yet we hear no more of them, and Philip himself suddenly disappears.

---

¹ The conjecture (*Beg.* IV, 90) that Simon used the Pythagorean formula τὸ μικρὸν μέγα ἔσται, possibly in recommending special sacraments, and that his distorted saying strayed into the present context, may be noted as a curiosity. On the meaning of that saying in the Μεγάλη 'Απόφασις see Haenchen, op. cit., 327.

² This disposes of Klostermann's endeavour (*Probleme im Aposteltexte*, 15ff.) to show that μεγάλη translates the Samaritan מְגַלְּיָ or מְגַלְיָא ('revealer' or 'revealing'), likewise Knox's suggestion (25) that 'The Greatness' had been formed as a title for Simon on the analogy of the rabbinic use of גְּבוּרָה to designate God.

³ ἱκανός, in the sense of 'large' or 'many', is a favourite word of Luke's: Acts 8.11; 9.23, 43; 11.24, 26; 12.12; 14.3, 21; 18.18; 19.19; 20.8, 11, 37; 22.6 and 27.7, 9.

⁴ Without adequate reason *Beg.* IV 91 thinks of the Church.

⁵ The accession to faith is described in the aorist, whereas the imperfect (προσεῖχον) was used in verses 6 and 10 for the preliminary circumstances.

⁶ Preuschen (50) conjectures that in the 'source' Simon was amazed at the increase of his own thaumaturgical powers after baptism. According to Zahn (286) Simon became a Christian because Philip's preaching had robbed him of adherents and income. Did becoming a Christian restore these?

VERSE 14: The thread of narration is connected anew; the Apostles in Jerusalem hear that 'Samaria'[1] has been converted and send Peter and John[2] to investigate. Persecution no longer seems to be in the air.

VERSE 15: It is *Peter and John* who put the seal on the conversion, by praying for the descent of the Holy Spirit. So, in retrospect, Philip's success in the mission is minimized: the most important factor was beyond his powers.

VERSE 16: Exegetes (see *Beg.* IV, 93) have been much exercised by this failure of the (enthusiastic) Spirit to descend on any of the new converts. The Spirit makes itself known in Acts by the gift of speaking in tongues (so also Zahn, 287); as this was not in evidence, the Spirit must have been absent.

VERSE 17: Now the Spirit is imparted by the Apostles' prayer and laying-on of hands. The Didache and Justin do not mention the laying-on of hands as part of baptism, but Tertullian does (*De baptismo* 8). Later it was dissociated from baptism and continued to exist as *confirmatio* (*Beg.* IV, 93). In Luke's community baptism and the laying-on of hands must still have been associated (Bauernfeind, 126).

VERSE 18: Simon notes that the Apostles' action bestows the Spirit—which (*pace* Loisy, 369) is here imagined, as Wendt (157) rightly observed, to be recognizable by the sign of glossolalia.[3] But Simon's reaction is incomprehensible. There is no indication that he was excluded from the laying-on of hands, and there was presumably no reason to exclude him. On the other hand, his subsequent behaviour is incompatible with possession of the Spirit. There is a bad seam in the narrative here.

VERSE 19: Simon does not wish to buy the gift of the Spirit, but the capacity to confer it through the laying-on of hands. As Luke must have imagined the situation, Simon regarded the bestowal of the Spirit as a specially effective piece of magic.

VERSE 20: 'Peter gives the magician an answer which itself is—unintentionally on the part of Luke—almost reminiscent of magic formulae' (Bauernfeind, 127).[4] But the expression is biblical: cf. Dan. **2**.5 Theodotion εἰς ἀπώλειαν ἔσεσθε! and **3**.29 εἰς ἀπώλειαν ἔσονται. Peter's meaning is 'To hell with you and your money!' This makes clear to the reader that the divine Spirit is not for human trafficking.

---

[1] Early-Christian usage (cf. Rom. **15**.26, II Cor. **9**.2) called a country Christian if Christian communities had been established there. Wikenhauser (*Apg.* 78) describes this as popular overstatement.

[2] *Beg.* IV, 92 considers it possible that John Mark may be meant here. But this is wholly excluded in view of **3**.1 and **4**.13, not to mention **12**.25.

[3] According to Bauernfeind (124) Simon correctly recognized the Holy Spirit as the prime source of all individual miracles. But did the Samaritans who received the Spirit perform concrete miracles?

[4] Citing παραδίδωμί σε τὸ μέλαν χάος ἐν ταῖς ἀπωλείαις from Magic Papyrus IV, 1248.

VERSE 21: The λόγος in which Simon is refused a share is Christianity, from which he is here solemnly excluded; the wording is a form of excommunication (οὐκ μερὶς οὐδε κλῆρος comes from LXX, e.g. Deut. **12**.12 and **14**.27). The justification given in the second half of the verse corresponds, though not quite literally, to Ps. **77**.37 LXX.

VERSE 22: We now learn, however, that—contrary to the teaching of the Epistle to the Hebrews—a possibility of repentance for this grave post-baptismal sin is still open to Simon. Yet it remains uncertain whether the wicked 'thought of his heart'—this is the seat of sin!—will indeed be forgiven him. Jacquier indeed explains (263) that Peter doubts, not of God's forgiveness, but of Simon's ability to repent; but this is not stated.

VERSE 23: εἰς again for ἐν; D even corrects accordingly. Deut. **29**.17 (LXX) warns against idolatry: 'let there not be a root which bears the fruit of bitterness and wormwood'; Isa. **58**.6 demands that the bonds of wickedness be loosed. However, we cannot speak of actual citation of these verses; for Luke, 'bitter gall' and 'bonds of iniquity' alike are just metaphors of the state of sin.

VERSE 24: Simon answers humbly,[1] pleading for the Apostles' intercession to avert the fulfilment of their threats. In fact, there has been no such warning of multiple disasters as would justify the wording μηδὲν ὧν (=τούτων ἅ) εἰρήκατε; this is not, however, intended to illustrate the confusion in Simon's mind, but is a harmless Lucan formulation (cf. Loisy, 373) which underlines the dangerous power of the apostolic words. The plural εἰρήκατε retrospectively suggests that John had also contributed to the dialogue.

VERSE 25: With its μὲν οὖν, this is strictly a transitional verse. Peter and John[2] return to Jerusalem, themselves preaching in many Samaritan villages on the way.

This pericope offers a first-class example of the way in which the methods of NT interpretation have changed. The Tübingen school—F. C. Baur, Zeller and the rest (see Intro. § 2, pp. 17ff.)—took the pseudo-Clementines as their starting-point. In this late fabrication, which certainly contains *some* ancient material in however distorted a form, Simon Magus has some traits characteristic of Paul. The Tübingers therefore concluded that Luke intended to protect Paul from such disparaging associations by here depicting Simon as an entirely different person! The 'source-criticism' which followed this 'tendency-criticism' advocated, in its least extravagant form [i.e. in Harnack, *Beitr.* III, 142 (ET)], the view that Philip had himself recounted to Luke his experiences in Samaria! In so doing the aged pneumatic—he had obviously transmitted his characteristics to his four prophetic daughters

---

[1] D accentuates the penitent aspect of Simon's reply by adding: 'who ceased not to weep copious tears'.

[2] And Philip too, according to *Beg.* IV 95!

(151)—gave special prominence to the ecstatic element in the reception of the Spirit. Here it is clear how—in all innocence—modern psychology and theories of heredity have been pressed into service as guarantors of Lucan authenticity.

It is a long way from such speculation to Bauernfeind's recognition (124) of how difficult it must be to disentangle in this passage the strands of tradition and composition. Luke, he says, has woven together a tradition regarding Philip's missionary successes in Samaria (even Simon was converted!) and another about 'Simon Peter and Simon Magus'. Bauernfeind also suggests (125) that in an earlier version of the story Simon wished to buy the gift of healing, not that of imparting the Spirit. At all events, these very carefully and cautiously formulated considerations help the reflective reader to appreciate that, to avoid jumping to false conclusions, one must scrupulously keep separate in one's mind the writer's intention and action, the contents and history of his 'sources', and finally the events themselves.

Let us ourselves begin by asking what Luke wished to tell his readers in this story, and why he arranged his data in this and no other way. He starts with the later happening, Philip's mission in Samaria (verses 4–8), thus causing this activity to appear the direct consequence of the persecution levelled at the Stephenites. The Jews' rejection of the gospel drives Philip to the Samaritans and brings about the fulfilment of the promise of **1**.8: 'You shall be my witnesses . . . in Samaria.' It is not until he has established this point that Luke gives us his 'flashback' to earlier events: a magician called Simon had been getting the Samaritans under his spell (verses 9–11). In verse 12 Luke resumes the Philip theme and brings it to its provisional close: the Samaritans are baptized, while even Simon becomes a Christian (verse 13) and marvels at Philip's mighty deeds. Verses 14ff. narrate a new turn of events, which Luke regarded as the essential complement of Philip's mission: the Apostles Peter and John come down from Jerusalem and it is their prayer and their laying-on of hands which mediate the (ecstatic) Spirit the converts have hitherto lacked. Thus the mission to the Samaritans was not completed by any subordinate outsider, but was carried out in due form by the legal heads of the Church in person—that is, so far as acts of men had any part in the matter. But now (verses 18–24) Luke makes plain in his continuation of the Simon story that the bestowal of the Spirit is a *divine* gift: when Simon attempts to buy it from the Apostles he deservedly reaps a harsh refusal and an excommunication which he humbly seeks to avert. The seventh and final scene of this little cycle depicts the Apostles preaching their way home to Jerusalem (verse 25).

The whole story has such a simple ring, yet raises so many questions . . . Take Samaria, which 'received the Word of God' (verse 14). The population of Samaria was heterogeneous: side by side with the Samaritans proper —who could be roughly classified as (from Jerusalem's point of view) Jews not wholly unexceptionable either racially or dogmatically speaking—there lived many Gentiles, especially in the recently-founded Sebaste. The Samaritans' main centre was Shechem. Now where did the Hellenists (in the person of Philip) conduct their mission: among the Gentiles, or among the genuine Samaritans, with whom their common opposition to Jerusalem gave them an affinity? Evidently the latter possibility is the more likely. Then where had Simon Magus—for quite some time past, according to verse 11—been active, among the Jews or the Gentiles of Samaria? The belief, much favoured nowadays, that Gnosticism was an offshoot of unorthodox Judaism has given rise to the untested assumption that Simon was a 'Samaritan Jew'. But here there is an intermediate question, whether he was in fact already a gnostic. Luke after all, as Cerfaux and R. McL. Wilson emphasize, portrays him as no more than a successful conjuror. Here one must take care not to overlook the difference between Luke's characterization of this man and the tradition about him which Luke quotes. The word καλουμένη in verse 10 shows clearly that 'the great power' is an established formula, which Luke, patently considering it to require explanation, glosses (wrongly) by appending 'of God'. This has nothing to do with the 'power of God' mentioned in I Cor. 1.24, no more than with the *Ta'eb* expected, according to later sources, by the Samaritans. No, 'the great power' is rather the Simonian designation for that supreme divinity which is opposed and superior to the daemonic rulers of this world. If Simon did lay claim to this title, then he gave himself out to be the highest god made man—and this some considerable time, according to our text, before the Christian mission in Samaria. But where— we now resume the question—where did Simon make his appearance, and so hugely successful an appearance, with this message: among the Samaritan Jews, or among the Gentiles in Samaria? Surely among the latter, and the name Simon—pure Greek—says nothing to the contrary. The fact is that the earliest form of Simonian doctrine contains nothing to suggest Judaic provenance. As Justin reports (see comments on verse 10 above), about the year 150 nearly all the Samaritans revered Simon as the highest deity. The Christian mission's habit of calling a region or province Christian once a mission-centre had arisen there is obviously at work in verse 14, from which we may certainly not deduce that the whole of Samaria was converted by Philip (and the two Apostles). It may on the other hand be taken as a kernel of historical truth that Philip's Christian mission effected a breach in Samaritan Jewry.

The net conclusion—already pointed out by Dibelius (*Studies*, 17) and Bauernfeind (122)—is that there was no initial connection between the stories of Simon and Philip. Later however, to illustrate Philip's great success, it was said that he even converted Simon Magus! In the process, of course, Simon had to be downgraded from the rank of an incarnate god to that of mere magician. But even in this comparatively modest station he was too notorious for his baptism to be felt as the correct expression for his total defeat. Rather the original version (as Wellhausen and Dibelius have suggested) seems to have been that he offered to buy the miraculous powers of that great wonder-worker Philip. If Simon is thought of as a wizard, such a gesture completely accords with his role: obviously the magician would put Philip's *tours de force* down to secret magic formulae more potent than his own, which he therefore wanted to buy. But Luke could do little with such a tradition while recounting the Apostles' completion of the mission in Samaria, for they were not performing miracles in the style of Philip's. The only miracle they were in fact performing—though of course, in Christian eyes, the most miraculous of all—was the bestowing of the Spirit. Thus it was that Luke had Simon offer his money not to Philip but to the Apostles, and ask not for the power of healing but for the ἐξουσία of imparting the Spirit. This seemed to bring the old tradition into line. But in reality the difficulties are not removed, only covered up. Philip performs the greatest miracles, heals and exorcises. Then he suddenly vanishes, and we discover that his baptism lacked the most essential element, that which could have distinguished it from the baptism of John—the Spirit! Luke has done no less than to take the combination of baptism, laying-on of hands and reception of the Spirit, which in the belief and custom of his time formed one indissoluble whole, and divide it among Philip and the Apostles in such a way that the former got the beginning and the latter the end. Luke presupposes neither the laying-on of Philip's hands nor the Apostles' re-baptism of the converts. What moved Luke to incorporate the—Christianized—Simon tradition in his narrative was probably the possibility here offered, as later in the cases of Elymas and the sons of Sceva (**13**. 6ff. and **19**. 13ff.), of vividly illustrating the superiority of Christian miracles over the magical practices current in the area and of demonstrating the antithesis between the power of God and demonic wizardry. It is not the healings and exorcisms which are the supreme endowment constituting the Church superior to pagan religions. No: its highest gift consists in its power to confer, to mediate God's holy Spirit. But since this Spirit has to be represented as a demonstrable phenomenon (Simon must 'see' it if he is to covet it), it can only take the form of the ecstatic Spirit—not the Spirit of ἀγάπη of which I Cor. 13 speaks.

21

ACTS 8: 26–40
PHILIP CONVERTS A CHAMBERLAIN

[26] But an angel of the Lord spoke to Philip, saying: 'Arise, and go southwards to the road that goes down from Jerusalem to Gaza—this is desert.' [27] And he arose and went. And behold, a man of Ethiopia, a eunuch, a chamberlain of Candace, queen of the Ethiopians, who was over all her treasure, had come to Jerusalem in order to worship; [28] and he was returning and sitting in his chariot, and was reading the prophet Isaiah. [29] And the Spirit said to Philip: 'Go near, and join yourself to this chariot.' [30] And Philip ran to him, and heard him reading the prophet Isaiah, and said: 'Do you understand what you are reading?' [31] And he said: 'How can I, unless someone shall guide me?' And he besought Philip to come up and sit with him. [32] Now the text of the scripture passage which he was reading was this: 'As a sheep is led to the slaughter, and as a lamb before its shearer is dumb, so he opened not his mouth. [33] In his humiliation his judgment was taken away. His generation who shall declare? For his life is taken from earth.' [34] And the eunuch answered Philip, and said: 'I pray you, of whom does the prophet speak this: of himself, or of some other?' [35] And Philip opened his mouth, and beginning from this scripture declared to him the good news of Jesus. [36] And as they went on the way, they came to some water, and the eunuch said: 'Look, water! what is to hinder me from being baptized?' [[37] And Philip said: 'If you believe with all your heart, you may'. And he answered and said: 'I believe that Jesus Christ is the Son of God.'] [38] And he commanded the chariot to stand still, and they both went down into the water, both Philip and the eunuch; and he baptized him. [39] And when they came up out of the water, the Spirit of the Lord caught away Philip, and the eunuch saw him no more; for he went on his way rejoicing. [40] But Philip was found at Ashdod: and passing through he preached the gospel to all the cities, till he came to Caesarea.

Bibliography

H. Waitz, see § 20 bibl.; S. Lösch, 'Der Kämmerer der Königin Kandace', *Theol. Quart.* 111 (1930), 477–516; O. Cullmann, *Die Tauflehre des neuen Testaments,* Zürich 1948, 65–73 (ET *Baptism in the NT* (1950), 71ff.); A. W. Argyle, 'O. Cullmann's theory concerning κωλύειν', *Exp. Tim.* 67 (1955/6), 17; Conzelmann 54–7.

M. van Wanroy, 'Eunuchus Aetiops a diacono Philippo conversus (Act. 8.26–40)', *Verb. Domini* 20 (1940), 287–93; E. F. F. Bishop, 'Which Philip?', *AngThR* 28 (1946), 154–9; T. Riise-Hanssen, 'Etiopierens Messiasbillede og vårt. En Studie over Acta 8.32–33', *NTT* 44 (1946), 175–80; W. C. van Unnik, 'Der Befehl an Philippus (Apg. 8.26–27a)', *ZNW* 47 (1956), 181–91; E. Ullendorff, 'Candace (Acts 8.27) and the Queen of Sheba', *NTS* 2 (1956), 53–6.

VERSE 26: Here it is an angel, in verse 29 the Spirit, who speaks to Philip; in both cases this is the narrator's way of presenting the supernatural guidance ruling Philip's actions. We are not told where Philip is at the outset of the episode.[1] κατὰ μεσημβρίαν: literally 'against midday', but most probably in a topographical sense—'southwards'.[2] Gaza is the last settlement before the desert waste stretching away to Egypt.[3] αὕτη ἐστὶν ἔρημος is used in geographical descriptions of cities that have been laid waste.[4] ἄγγελος κυρίου, ἐλάλησεν λέγων and ἀνάστηθι καὶ πορεύου are all LXX locutions.

VERSE 27: ἀνὴρ Αἰθίοψ[5]—one of the Nubians whose kingdom between Aswan and Khartoum was always ruled by a queen mother entitled the Candace (Zahn 314f.). The promise of Ps. 68.31 is now fulfilled (Loisy 377). εὐνοῦχος—*Beg.* IV 96 cites Plutarch, *Demetrios* 25,5: 'They were accustomed . . . to have mostly eunuchs as treasurers.' But 'the εὐνοῦχος of LXX, like both εὐνοῦχος and סָרִיס elsewhere, frequently denotes high political or military officers; it does not necessarily indicate castration' (*ThWb* II, 764).[6] δυνάστης may denote a court official.[7] *Beg.* IV 96 translates προσκυ-

---

[1] In Sebaste or even Caesarea Philippi, according to Preuschen (47), in Jerusalem according to *Beg.* IV 95.

[2] According to Bl.-Debr. § 253, 5 (Appendix) no article is used before the points of the compass. Nestle (*StKr* 65 (1892) 335–7) urged the chronological reading 'at noon' on the ground that in LXX μεσημβρία always denotes the time of day; yet in Dan. 8.4, 9 LXX it denotes the direction. It is moreover usual to avoid travelling at noon if possible.

[3] Two roads led there from Jerusalem. Whether Luke knew this is doubtful; that the reader does not need to know is certain.

[4] αὕτη can be related to Γάζα, which (see Preuschen, 52) had several times been destroyed. But in that case the remark would add nothing to the designation of the road. Hence Jacquier (269) and others attach αὕτη to ὁδός: the road is deserted, which facilitates the playing-out of the scene to come. Zahn (311) regards the words as Luke's explanation to the reader. That would not however preclude Luke's putting them in the mouth of the angel: he was not familiar with footnotes in the modern sense.

[5] See Wikenhauser, 361f. Being an Ethiopian he was not, as has sometimes been suggested, a son of Jews carried off by the celebrated one-eyed Candace in 22 B.C. after an incursion into the Thebaid (see Preuschen, 53).

[6] Deut. 23.1 ruled out the acceptance of the castrated into the Jewish racial or religious community. Hence the eunuch is usually considered σεβόμενος. But would such a person have access to a scroll of the prophet Isaiah (*ThWb* II, 766 n. 26)? K. Bornhäuser assumes (*Studien zur Apg.* 94 and 96) that with the coming of the Messiah Isa. 56.3ff. was fulfilled, and the Christian community therefore justified in accepting eunuchs. But this passage is not mentioned.

[7] LXX uses δυνάστης to translate סָרִיס in Jer. 34.19—probably indeed simply because a eunuch, according to Deut. 23.1f., could not take part in the cult (thus Schneider, *ThWb* loc. cit.).

νήσων (also said of Paul in Acts **24**.11) as 'on a pilgrimage'; according to De Zwaan (*Beg.* II, 33) the future participle as a substitute for a final clause is literary Greek. LXX expressions are καὶ ἀναστὰς ἐπορεύθη and καὶ ἰδού.

VERSE 28: ἦν ὑποστρέφων = 'he was travelling back'.[1] ἄρμα: here a travelling-carriage; perhaps the word was used because of the relation to II Kings 2 (see comments on verse 39 below). The eunuch is reading aloud, as was usual in antiquity.[2] The carriage travels slowly, so that reading is possible.

VERSE 29: The first divine directive has brought Philip to the right spot. The second causes him to run alongside the carriage, with which a person on foot might keep abreast for a while. All Philip's actions are determined by the miraculous intervention of God.

VERSE 30: Philip not only understands the words read aloud, but recognizes that they provide him with an opening to deliver his message. Here for the first time in Acts a passage from Isaiah 53 is explicitly related to the Passion of Jesus.[3] Philip's question is so phrased that it leads directly to instruction concerning Christ; γινώσκεις ἃ ἀναγινώσκεις is a pointed play on words (Bl.-Debr. § 488, 1b).

VERSE 31: The potential optative +ἄν does not occur in vulgar Greek (Bl.-Debr. § 385, 1). ἐὰν ... ὁδηγήσει: 'a familiar case of future condition with the less vivid form in the apodosis' (Moulton 198f., cf. Bl.-Debr. § 373, 2 *Appendix*). Luke makes this high official (a finance minister!) speak in a very educated fashion. The eunuch is not at all 'touchy': he immediately admits his inability, and begs the stranger to sit beside him so that he may hear from him.

VERSE 32: περιοχὴ τῆς γραφῆς could be translated 'the passage of scripture', but since γραφή in verse 35 means 'the scriptural passage', the meaning here is probably 'the wording of the scripture'.[4] The quotation from Isaiah 53 LXX begins in the middle of verse 7 and ends in the middle of verse 8. Bauernfeind (127) translates: 'Like a sheep was he brought to the slaughter-bench', but Preuschen (53): 'As a sheep is brought to the slaughter-bench'. If Lake (see n. 3 below) is right, Preuschen's rendering must be preferred.

[1] A piece of general scene-setting employing periphrastic conjugation (see first footnote to **1**.10 above). Against this background the special feature that 'he was reading' stands out. These transitory circumstances are in the imperfect. The aorist εἶπεν describes the real action, which now begins.

[2] This affirmation of Norden's (*Antike Kunstprosa*, 1898, 6), based on Augustine's *Confessions* VI.3, is wrongly contested by *Beg.* IV 96f. Billerbeck tells us (II, 687) that silent reading was forbidden among the Jews. The commentators who provided the eunuch with a companion to read to him were as yet unacquainted with Norden's discovery.

[3] And only verses 7ff. at that. If in Luke's day the whole chapter had been Christologically interpreted, it would have been used somewhere in Luke's scriptural proof. According to Lake (*Beg.* IV, 97) there is also a dogmatic reason for this selection: the quotation avoids the connection between sin and the death of the sacrifice, which Luke also shuns elsewhere.

[4] Whether the passage was a synagogue lection in Judaism is of no consequence here.

VERSE 33: Luke does not give us the Christological significance of the verses quoted, but he probably saw the ταπείνωσις as the death and the 'taking-away of the judgment' as the Resurrection. The meaning of γενεά is not 'life-span' but 'those who are contemporaries', hence 'generation' (see *ThWb* I, 661; Bauer *Wb* 305). Perhaps it is here understood as 'race' in the sense of spiritual descendants. Then the sentence means: 'The number of his disciples will grow incalculably, because he has become the Exalted.'

VERSE 34: ἀποκριθείς is LXX style, in the sense of 'beginning to speak'. δέομαί σου ='please' before a request—the eunuch displays exemplary courtesy and modesty. That he thought Isaiah could have been speaking of himself was formerly taken as a sign of his complete lack of understanding. But the narrator makes him put the question in this way because this either/or immediately makes the Christian proclamation possible, without preliminary discussion of the content of the text.[1]

VERSE 35: 'Beginning from this scripture'—Philip's witness to Christ is not limited to Isaiah 53.7f., which is here added to the passages adduced as Christological proofs. Understandably enough, Luke accommodates most of these in the first chapters of Acts, but in the rest of Acts also new *dicta probantia* again and again appear.

VERSE 36: The attempts to identify the ὕδωρ with a particular water-course[2] are as touching as they are vain. The narrator certainly set no store by exact location. The question τί κωλύει . . . presupposes that Philip had

---

[1] The chamberlain's question is not meant to show him as slow-witted or far from the truth: soon to be a Christian, he stands on quite another level from those Greeks or Romans to whom the ἀνάστασις appears meaningless (Acts 17.18, 32; 25.19; 26.24). In *Die Verkündung vom leidenden Gottesknecht aus Jesaja 53 in der griechischen Bibel*, 1934, K. F. Euler attempted to show that a Hellenistic Jew must have seen Isa. 53 as primarily the prophet's foretelling of his own fate. Euler's proof relies above all on the conjectural Jewish document underlying the *Ascensio Jesaiae*. But the edifice he builds is more than so exiguous a foundation can bear. It is only in the Christian-gnostic part of the book that any gnosis or glorification and exaltation of Isaiah may be found: the delineation of the prophet in the Jewish source is incongruent with the servant-of-God image, so that we cannot read off any Jewish interpretation of Isaiah 53 from it. In his *Jesaja 53 im Urchristentum*, 3rd edn. 1952 (cf. the reviews by E. Käsemann in *Verkündigung und Forschung: Theol. Jahresbericht* 1949/50, Munich 1950, 200-3, and W. G. Kümmel in *ThR* N.S. 22, 1954, 164f.), H. W. Wolff notes that Isa. 53 is, 'with the solitary exception of Luke 22.37, never unequivocally cited of Jesus'. Nevertheless he thinks that 'from the form of outstanding logia we can see that Isa. 53 played a special part in the personal decisions' of Jesus 'as in the instruction of the disciples' (69). 'The Peter of Acts was among the first who understood Jesus' instruction of his disciples' (88f.). Since however it is Luke himself who speaks in the Peter of Acts 3 and 4, Wolff's pronouncement takes on a meaning he would scarcely find desirable. He also writes concerning Acts: 'We note how the prophecy itself grips the Church with primal force precisely where it is not adduced in citations. This abstinence from quotation is the reticence of awe'—but such an *argumentum e silentio* cannot be used as a scientific proof.

[2] 'The Wadi el-Hasi north of Gaza has found advocates' (*Beg.* IV, 98). So also Bruce (194). Wikenhauser (*Apg* 86) suggests 'Ain Dirweh, near Bethsura (now Beit Sur).

mentioned baptism, but perhaps also (like **10.47**?) contains the problem of a hindrance to baptism.[1]

VERSE 37 appears only in part of the 'Western' tradition: E e gig perp sy[hmg], and in part in Irenaeus and Cyprian (*Beg.* III, 83). The missing baptismal confession was subsequently added—not, be it remarked, in Trinitarian form. Zahn's premises oblige him to declare the verse authentic (317f.).

VERSE 38: Philip's acquiescence is presumed, and so the baptism may follow immediately. Baptizer and the one to be baptized enter the water, where the rite, of which no details are given, is duly performed.

VERSE 39: The carrying off by the Spirit is thought of in real, spatial terms.[2] The eunuch does not behave like the sons of the prophets, who in II Kings 2.16–18 spend three days looking for Elijah, but continues joyfully on his way. This explains why he 'saw him no more'—the words taken from II Kings 2.12 have here a quite different sense. The emphasis laid on joy is a special Lucan characteristic [Harnack, *Beitr.* III, 207–10 (ET)].

VERSE 40: εὑρέθη (see n. 2): the Spirit deposits Philip at Ashdod. From there he travels preaching through the coastal towns until he comes to Caesarea (see on **21.8f.** below).[3] This might prompt one to credit him with the founding of the communities in Lydda, Joppa and Caesarea (see below on **9.32** and **36**, and **10.48**), but Luke does not expressly say so.

Up to and even including Bauernfeind, Harnack's influence has dominated exposition of this passage. He ascribed the story to Philip in person, from whom Luke took it over [*Beitr.* III, 149–51 (ET)]: Philip's 'pneumato-scientific' disposition, which was passed on to his prophetess daughters, accounted for the 'enthusiastic historiography'. E. Meyer bolstered this 'psychological' interpretation with the fruits of his studies of Paul, Muhammad and the Mormons, not to mention his intercourse with modern spiritualists: since Philip had four prophetess daughters, he could himself have been no stranger to the visionary state—'In his mind the borderline between truth and fancy must have been even more blurred than in the minds of more prosaic men' (III, 276). Lake joined in the 'psychological' chorus: 'The

---

[1] See O. Cullmann, *Baptism in the NT*, London 1950, 71–78, Jeremias, *Infant Baptism in the First Four Centuries*, 1961; K. Aland, *Did the Early Church baptise Infants?* London 1963.

[2] Cf. especially II Kings 2.16–18, also I Kings 18.12, Ezek. 3.14, 8.3, 11.1 and 11.24 and II Cor. 12.2: ἁρπαγέντα εἴτε ἐν σώματι . . .; Gospel of the Hebrews (Origen, *in Johannem* 2.6; Jerome, *in Mich.* 7.6). II Kings 2 has several points of similarity with the passage under discussion, e.g. 1) its verse 11 speaks of a ἅρμα; 2) its οὐκ εἶδεν αὐτὸν ἔτι (v. 12) corresponds verbatim to our **8.39**; 3) εὑρέθη (**8.40**) recalls οὐκ εὗρον αὐτόν (v. 17); 4) cf. ἦρεν αὐτὸν πνεῦμα κυρίου (v. 16) and πνεῦμα κυρίου ἥρπασεν τὸν Φίλιππον (**8.39**).

[3] According to Beyer (1933, 58) 'Philip takes leave of the new Christian in a mood of excitement which he senses as possession by the Spirit'. The physical snatching-away by the Spirit is thus psychologized out of existence. Beyer's fourth edition uses more cautious terms at this point.

Christian preacher (Philip) moves about in a state of ecstasy and hardly knows how he goes from place to place' (*Beg.* IV, 99). Bauernfeind himself was making his own niche in this expository tradition when he wrote: 'The carrying-away should not be regarded as proving a gulf between the historical process and the legend before us: this very ending may well have been recounted by Philip himself' (129).

But before taking this leap from the narrative to what once actually happened, we ought first to consider the position of this story in Acts: it is situated between the conversion of the Samaritans and that—in Chapter 10 —of the Gentiles. At first sight, indeed, the eunuch himself seems presented as a Gentile: the conversion of a Jew (be he Jewish by birth or by full acceptance of the law) would be of no special consequence for the progress of the mission. The bar against a eunuch's becoming a Jew (Deut. **23**.1) is not conclusive here: 'eunuch' may be a mere title of office, and Luke was also free to believe that Deut. **23**.1 had been superseded by Isa. **56**.3–5. But however that may be—and neither passage is cited—Luke cannot and did not say that the eunuch was a Gentile; otherwise Philip would have forestalled Peter, the legitimate founder of the Gentile mission! For that reason Luke leaves the eunuch's status in a doubtful light. The Candace's finance minister has been on a pilgrimage from the far land of Cush to Jerusalem. He possesses a scroll of the Book of Isaiah and studies it in his carriage on the way home. For a merely 'God-fearing' man that would be unusual, and in fact the description φοβούμενος, with which Cornelius is introduced in **10**.2, is not mentioned. On the other hand, he is presented to the reader as a 'man of Ethiopia' and a eunuch—which immediately conjures up a Gentile. And so it remains uncertain what the eunuch really is; but it is precisely this screen of secrecy about his person which is best suited to the stage now reached in the history of the mission. Without permitting the emergence of all the problems which an explicit baptism of a Gentile must bring in its wake, Luke here leaves the reader with the feeling that with this new convert the mission has taken a step beyond the conversion of Jews and Samaritans. This eunuch will not be returning to Jerusalem, to place Christians in the embarrassment later provoked by the baptism of Cornelius. Nothing more is heard of him, and since the adequacy of his baptism is not contested, even the gift of the Spirit need not be mentioned—the reader would otherwise wonder why the Spirit should descend more readily on eunuchs than on Samaritans. So much for the significance of the eunuch's conversion, in the context of Luke's history of the mission, as a stepping-stone between those of the Samaritans and the Gentiles.

Now for the story itself . . . It may be called a miracle-story. But its peculiar nature requires closer definition. Notice how exceptionally high an incidence of divine intervenings and directives is needed, what extra-special providence must do its work, for the accomplishment of this one conversion and baptism. Thus Philip is not in the right place—an angel must first send him to the spot where he is to encounter the eunuch. Yet of this he is unaware: God's design is not at once revealed to him. Then God's second intervention —the prompting of the Spirit to approach the carriage—gives him no notice of what will ensue. This may be felt as the mere technique of a talented story-teller, holding his audience in suspense by letting out no more than is strictly necessary. But though we may be sure that the original audience for this story hung on the lips of its narrator, the real reason for this procedure is different. This is clear from the third circumstance which furthers the action: at the very moment when Philip comes up to the carriage, the eunuch is reading aloud the passage from Isaiah! This time, it is true, neither an angel nor the Spirit is at work. But this coincidence is nevertheless an astounding marvel. That the eunuch should at exactly this moment be reading just these two verses, that Philip should hear him reading them—and only if all this coincides can the rapid conversion ensue!—is only explicable in terms of a special dispensation of God. A fourth circumstance, indeed, ought properly to be added: that the chamberlain has progressed so far in his understanding of scripture that he needs only to learn the identity of the person referred to by Isaiah **53**.7f. This alone enables his baptism (for which even the water is to hand according to God's plan) to take place there and then, and bring the story to its happy ending.

Acts contains but one other story distinguished—indeed to an even greater degree—by this same feature of divine direction determining the course of events at every turn: the story of Cornelius. The conversion of that first Gentile is not the work of men; it is brought about solely by the action of God. This is, however, scarcely less true of the present conversion: if the chamberlain returns home a Christian, it is not the persuasiveness of human missionary zeal which has made him so, but the power of God who orders all things in his infinite wisdom. This makes it clear that here no ordinary con-version is being depicted, nor even just any Gentile-conversion, but one which has a quite overwhelming significance. In the context of Luke's history of the mission it has admittedly lost this character. But then, it is not at home in this environment. Luke took it over from a tradition and, since the human protagonist is 'Philip the evangelist, one of the Seven' (**21**.8), this tradition must derive from Hellenistic Christian circles, from the communities founded by the Seven (Bauernfeind 128f.). There our story would have possessed all the importance for which it appears designed: this was the account which the *Hellenists* handed down of the first conversion of a Gentile —and the name of the first missionary to effect such a conversion was not Peter, but Philip! In other words, the story of the eunuch is the Hellenistic parallel to Luke's account of the first Gentile-conversion by Peter: its parallel—and rival. As such, of course, Luke could not accept it, in view of the importance of the twelve Apostles in his eyes. But he could incorporate it in his work as an edifying story—albeit more suggestive than explicit—illustrating the progress of the mission (Bruce, 195, sees the position likewise).

Now that both the Philip episodes have been reviewed, we can add a word of comparison. They are extraordinarily different. The first takes place in Samaria, the second somewhere to the south-west of Jerusalem. The first deals with the conversion of 'Samaria', an area previously sworn to Simon. The second recounts the conversion of an individual and is the first story of its kind in Acts. The first portrays Philip as the great worker of miracles: no other story in the New Testament is so exclusively devoted to celebrating the exploits of a Christian wonder worker. In the second, Philip does not perform a single miracle. At bottom, here, he scarcely acts at all, and is rather presented as the guided instrument of God. Whether he is addressed by the Spirit or an angel, or is whirled away, he is in one way or another divinely controlled. However, the one instance where the second story speaks of his independent activity reveals him as a preacher wielding scriptural proof with uncommon persuasiveness.

Once these differences are clearly seen, Harnack's primitive explanation can no longer satisfy. It cannot be true that Luke is repeating what he learned from Philip himself. A longer, heterogeneous tradition lies behind both narratives. As Luke certainly revised them, at least stylistically, it is hard to estimate the age of these traditions or the extent to which they have been altered. But one thing is certain: the portrait of Simon in the first story does not derive from an eyewitness. It was sketched by a Christian who knew about Simon—or about Philip, for that matter—only from hearsay. Next the Simon story was recast, probably by Luke himself, who introduced the Apostles and turned Simon into the—admittedly dubious—Christian penitent.

Luke's part in the second story is less easy to assess. His hand may be traced in the linguistic elegance deployed to establish the eunuch as a cultivated man: Luke's educated readers must have relished the potential optative with ἄν—the Greeks had an ear for such things. One might ask whether Luke did not also introduce the angel: Philip had somehow to be directed to the right place from Samaria. But wherever this isolated story (for we may presume that it was originally told for its own sake) presupposed Philip to be at the outset, it could scarcely have been on the actual road from Jerusalem to Gaza—which means that he had first to be brought to the scene of the action in *any* version of the story. On the other hand Luke's own touch may be detected in the way Philip is 'found at Ashdod' (verse 40—OT locution from II Kings 2.16f.). Here the legend whereby Philip was carried away at the end of the episode is pressed into the service of history. This story too is not the personal account of a prophet wandering as in a trance from place to place, but a skilfully condensed tradition from quite another stratum than the popular amazement over Philip's miracles which we see in

8.4–25. The two stories, then, did not spring from the same soil, but here they fulfil the same function, namely to place before the reader's eyes, in vivid, arresting images, the progress of the mission beyond Jerusalem.

22
ACTS 9: 1–19a
THE CONVERSION OF SAUL

¹ But Saul, still breathing threats and murder against the disciples of the Lord, went to the High Priest, ² and asked of him letters to the synagogues in Damascus, that if he found any who were of the Way, whether men or women, he might bring them bound to Jerusalem. ³ And as he journeyed, it came about that he was drawing near Damascus; and suddenly there shone round about him a light from heaven, ⁴ and falling on the ground he heard a voice saying to him: 'Saul, Saul, why do you persecute me?' ⁵ And he said, 'Who are you, Lord?' And he said: 'I am Jesus, whom you are persecuting. ⁶ But rise, and go into the city, and it shall be told you what you must do.' ⁷ And the men who journeyed with him stood speechless, hearing the voice indeed but seeing no one. ⁸ And Saul was lifted from the ground; and when he opened his eyes, he saw nothing. Leading him by the hand, they brought him into Damascus. ⁹ And he was three days without sight, and neither ate nor drank. ¹⁰ Now there was a disciple in Damascus, named Ananias; and the Lord said to him in a vision: 'Ananias!' And he said, 'Here I am, Lord!' ¹¹ And the Lord said to him: 'Arise, and go to the street which is called Straight, and inquire in the house of Judas for a man of Tarsus named Saul. ¹¹/¹² For behold, he is praying; ¹² and he has seen in a vision a man named Ananias coming in, and laying his hands on him, that he may recover his sight.' ¹³ But Ananias answered: 'Lord, I have heard from many about this man, how much evil he has done to your saints in Jerusalem: ¹⁴ and here he has authority from the chief priests to bind all who call upon your name.' ¹⁵ But the Lord said to him, 'Go your way, for he is a chosen instrument to me, to bear my name before peoples and kings and the children of Israel: ¹⁶ for I will show him how much he must suffer for my name's sake.' ¹⁷ And Ananias departed, and went into the house, and laying his hands on him said: 'Brother Saul, the Lord has sent me, Jesus who appeared to you on the road by which you came, that you may recover your sight, and be filled with the Holy Spirit.' ¹⁸ And straightway there fell from his eyes as it were scales, and he recovered his sight; and he arose and was baptized. ¹⁹ᵃ And he took food and was strengthened.

Bibliography:

J. Behm, see § 16 bibl.; G. P. Wetter, 'Die Damaskusvision u. d. paulin. Evangelium', *Festgabe Jülicher*, Tübingen 1927, 80–92; E. Hirsch, 'Die drei Berichte d. Apg. über d. Bekehrung d. Paulus', *ZNW* 28 (1929), 62–9; E. von Dobschütz, 'Die Berichte über d. Bekehrung d. Paulus', *ZNW* 29 (1930), 144–7; H. Windisch, 'Die Christophanien v. Damaskus (Acta 9.22 u. 26) u. ihre religionsgesch. Parallelen', *ZNW* 31 (1932), 1–23; K. Lake, 'The Conversion of Paul and the Events immediately following it', *Beg.* V, 1933, 188–95; F. Dornseiff, see § 1 bibl. (on 9.4); J. Munck, 'La vocation de l'apôtre Paul', *Stud. Theol.* I, Lund 1948, 131–45; A. Wikenhauser, 'Doppelträume', *Biblica* 29 (1948), 100–11, and 'Die Wirkung d. Christophanie vor Damaskus auf Paulus u. s. Begleiter', *Biblica* 33 (1952), 313–23; O. Linton, 'The third Aspect', *Stud. Theol.* III, Lund 1950/1, 79–95; G. Wingren, '"Weg", "Wanderung" und verwandte Begriffe', ibid. (on 9.2); D. M. Stanley, 'Why the Three Accounts?', *CBQ* 15 (1953), 315–38; H. P. Owen, 'Resurrection and Apostolate in St. Paul', *Exp. Tim.* 65 (1953/4), 321–8; H. G. Wood, 'The Conversion of St. Paul: its Nature, Antecedents and Consequences', *NTS* 1 (1954/5), 176–89; H. J. Cadbury, *The Book of Acts in History*, 1955, 19–21 (on 9.23–5); G. Lohfink, *Paulus vor Damaskus* (Stuttg. Bib. Stud. 4), 1965, 101f.; Conzelmann 57–9.

W. K. L. Clarke, 'Acts 9.5', *Theology* 6 (1923), 100f.; F. A. Schilling, 'Why did Paul go to Damascus?' *AngThR* 16 (1934), 199–201; H. E. Dana, 'Where did Paul persecute the Church?', ibid. 20 (1938), 16–26; W. Prentice, 'St. Paul's Journey to Damascus', *ZNW* 46 (1955), 250–4; R. Baracaldo, 'Christofania de Damasco', *Virtud y Letras* 13 (1954), 3–11; J. L. Lilly, 'The Conversion of Paul', *CBQ* 6 (1944), 180–204; E. Fascher, 'Zur Taufe des Paulus', *TLZ* 80 (1955), 643–8; S. V. McCasland, 'The Way', *JBL* 77 (1958), 222–30; U. Wilckens, 'Die Bekehrung des Paulus als religionsgesch. Problem', *ZThK* 56 (1959), 273–93; E. Repo, *Der 'Weg' als Selbstbezeichnung des Urchristentums*, Helsinki 1964 (= Ann. Acad. Scient. Fennicae, Ser. B 132, 2; cf. review in *Gnomon* (1966), 51–3).

VERSE 1: ἔτι, i.e. even after the close of the persecution in Jerusalem. ἐμπνέων κτλ.: 'breathing threatening[1] and murder' (the classical phrase would be φόνον πνεῖν: see Bl-Debr. § 174); the first is illustrated by 26.11, the second by 26.10. *Pace* R. Schütz, (*Apostel und Jünger*, 1921, esp. p. 19), μαθηταὶ τοῦ κυρίου is no proof of a separate source here: Luke is always changing the designation for 'Christians'.[2] Note that Saul himself, not the

---

[1] It would be grotesque to accept Bornhäuser's reading of ἀπειλή as 'warning' ('breathing warning and murder . . .'!) Nor is the phrase a hendiadys ('threatening with murder', Loisy, 387): according to Luke, Paul really did murder (cf. 26.10). Bruce (196) refers to Ps. 18 (17). 16b.

[2] Thus in the present chapter we have the following variations: μαθηταί (v. 1), τῆς ὁδοῦ εἶναι (v. 2), μαθητής (v. 10), ἅγιοι (v. 13), ἐπικαλούμενοι τὸ ὄνομα κυρίου (v. 14), ἀδελφός (v. 17), μαθηταί (vv. 19 and 25), ἀδελφοί (v. 30), ἅγιοι (v. 32), μαθήτρια (v. 36), μαθηταί (v. 38) and ἅγιοι (v. 41). See Cadbury's Note 30: 'Names for Christians and Christianity in Acts' (*Beg.* V, 375–92).

unnamed High Priest (Caiaphas, up to the year 36), is the driving spirit of the persecution.

VERSE 2: As we see from 9.14, 22.5 and 26.12, the 'letters' addressed to the synagogues are mandates empowering Saul to root out adherents of 'the Way',[1] i.e. Christians, and place them under arrest.[2] According to 26.10 Saul had already carried out the Jerusalem persecution on the basis of such

---

[1] See W. Michaelis, *ThWb* V, 93–5. We do not know for certain—despite Repo's fine study—the origin of the absolute use of ὁδός for Christianity in Acts 9.2, 19.9, 23, 22.4, 24.14 and 24.22. The primary sense of 'the way of the Lord' and 'the way of God' in 18.25f. is 'the saving action of God'; it is of course possible that τοῦ κυρίου or τοῦ θεοῦ, like τοῦ θεοῦ in 8.10, represents a (mistaken) gloss on the part of Luke. It is clear from 24.14 that ἡ ὁδός was a designation applied to the Church by the Christians themselves whereas their opponents spoke of a αἵρεσις. It is hard to see why, as Michaelis maintains (op. cit. 93), the term ὁδός should not here refer to the Christians as a community. The translation 'teaching' is surely too narrow. The passages cited by Billerbeck (II, 680), where ὁδοί (τῶν ἐθνῶν) is equivalent to 'manners and customs', 'way of life' or 'morals', are not real parallels.

[2] The statements about the ἐπιστολαί have unleashed a great debate over the powers of jurisdiction enjoyed at that time by the High Priest (and the Sanhedrin). Luke seems to assume that they had powers of life and death over all the Jews in the Roman Empire. In defence of this assumption the following points have been adduced:

1. According to I Macc. 15.15–21 the 'consul' Lucius (or Λεύκιος) bade Ptolemy deliver the λοιμοί who had fled from Judaea into the hands of Simon the High Priest for punishment under Jewish law, similar injunctions having gone out to the other 'kings and countries'. But, as Wellhausen rightly saw (*Isr. und Jüd. Geschichte*, 2nd edn., 257 n. 3), this is an interpolation; I Macc. 15.26 is the natural continuation of 15.14. J. C. Dancy, indeed, on p. 6 of his *Commentary on I Maccabees* (Oxford, 1954), admits there is something suspect about every passage concerning the Jews' relations with Rome or Sparta: Ch. 8, 12.1–33, 14.16–24 and 15.15–24 can all be excised not merely without harm to the text but even to its advantage. Nevertheless Dancy does not believe in later interpolations, for an interpolator would have adapted his insertions to fit the text; it is more likely that the author died before the final completion of his work. The author must then have inserted these alleged documents subsequently into the finished work. But Dancy does not observe that there are good and bad interpolators, and here one of the latter sort seems to have been at work. This is much more probable than that the author himself only later had the idea of inserting documents, and wedged them in as best he might. See also Laqueur, *Historische Zeitschrift*, 1927, 241ff.

2. According to Josephus (*Ant.* XIV, 190–5), Caesar in a letter to Sidon enacted certain provisions regarding the status and powers of Hyrcanus, in which he (together with his successors) was confirmed as ethnarch, High Priest and one of the φίλοι of the Roman nation. This text contains nothing, however, which would justify the procedure of the High Priest in Acts 9.2.

3. According to Josephus (*Bell.* I, 474) Caesar conceded to Herod a right withheld from every other king, namely—τὸν ἀπ' αὐτοῦ φυγόντα καὶ μὴ προσηκούσης πόλεως ἐξαγαγεῖν. On the one hand, however, supposing the report to be true at all, this applied solely to the Herod who had deserved so well of Caesar as to earn the title of *socius et amicus populi Romani*; on the other hand, it does not imply that even Herod was empowered to make arrests on Roman territory. As for the enjoyment of such a right by the High Priest in the time of Saul, nothing warrants the deduction.

Generally speaking, Schürer's attitude towards the data of Acts was uncritical—the more so that they were for the most part his only source of material. He did not notice that Luke, who knew the books of the Maccabees, has generalized from the information regarding Simon in I Macc. 15.15–21, extended the authority to all High Priests and linked it with something quite distinct, i.e. the letters which the Sanhedrin could address to synagogues in

authority; **26**.11 sees him pursuing his task in the ἔξω πόλεις,[1] among which may also be numbered Damascus, the great trading-city at the foot of the Anti-Lebanon range, with its large Jewish colony. At that time it was incorporated in the province of Syria; some scholars assume that it was temporarily in Nabataean hands (see on verses 24f.). ἐάν κτλ. seems to imply for Luke (cf. **5**.38) that it was not certain whether Christians were to be found in Damascus. According to **9**.14 and **26**.10, 12, it was the ἀρχιερεῖς who issued the letters of authority, according to **22**.5 πᾶν τὸ πρεσβυτέριον, i.e. the whole of the High Council.

VERSE 3: In biblical language (on ἐν + articular infinitive see **2**.1; on ἐγένετο with acc. + inf. see **4**.5) Luke describes Saul's approach to Damascus. At this point[2] a 'light from heaven'[3] shone about[4] him[5]—Windisch (see bibl.) points out the resemblance to the legend of Heliodorus (II Macc. 3).[6]

VERSE 4: This light causes Saul to fall to the ground (γῇ in **9**.4 and **26**.14, ἔδαφος in **22**.7). **26**.13 shows that Luke understands this as the effect of 'being dazed and dazzled'.[7] From verse 7 (μηδένα θεωροῦντες), **26**.13 ('I saw a light') and **22**.14 (Paul was appointed 'to see the Righteous One'), taken in conjunction with **26**.16 ('a witness' that 'you have seen me'), it seems to follow that Saul saw Jesus only inasmuch as he beheld this tremendous

---

the diaspora. It is through this conflation that the Council is credited with the right —which it certainly did not have—to secure the arrest of Jews in foreign States and their extradition to Judaea. Only so, however, could Luke link up Paul's (unhistorical!) persecution of the Christians in Jerusalem with his (inferential) pursuit of them to Damascus.

[1] It is not clear whether cities outside Judaea or even Palestine are meant here. As the persecution had so far been limited to Jerusalem, and the author, moreover, assumes the presence of 'cities' round Jerusalem (**5**.16), it is better to think of all the towns of Judaea and beyond.

[2] In the sixth century it was common knowledge that the event took place at the second milestone before Damascus (Preuschen 55).

[3] In **22**.6 it is called a 'great light' (φῶς ἱκανόν); in **26**.13 Paul even says that it was brighter than the noonday sun: it is open to a narrator to counter the lulling effect of repetition by reinforcing the emphasis of a salient feature.

[4] Here περιαστράπτω is constructed with the accusative, in **22**.6 with περί; Luke does not repeat himself schematically; in **26**.13 περιαστράπτω is replaced by the περιλάμπω familiar from Luke **2**.9, where it similarly describes the heavenly splendour. In other respects Ch. 9 and Ch. 26 often agree in their formulation against Ch. 22.

[5] According to **9**.3 and **22**.6 the light shines only round Paul. **26**.13 has it shine round his companions too.

[6] The verbal echoes are found in verse 27: πεσόντα πρὸς γῆν; more as regards content καὶ πολλῷ σκότει περιχυθέντα ἔφερον ἀβοήθητον ἑαυτῷ καθεστῶτα. The antithesis of power and impotence is broadly developed in the story of Heliodorus. Cf. also F. Smend in *Angelos* (1925) I, 1/2, 34ff.

[7] In Ch. 26 the absence of Ananias entails the omission of the healing effected through him, hence also of the blinding effect of the light. Luke compensates this diminution in the light's effect by making it flash round the heads of Paul's companions, so that they too fall to the ground. This was only possible because here the light no longer blinds. As against this, 'they that were with me beheld the light' (**22**.9) shows a certain thoughtlessness on the writer's part.

blaze of light. Presumably, however, Luke imagined the occurrence in such a way that Saul's companions saw only a formless glare where he himself saw in it the figure of Jesus. This would make it more understandable that Saul should apostrophize the being addressing him with κύριε. Saul, then, hears a voice[1] speaking to him. The first words it utters are the same in all three accounts: 'Saul, Saul, why do you persecute me?'[2] This does not however imply that Paul himself used to recount his call in this way—his reticent manner in Gal. 1.15 and II Cor. 4.6 makes it very unlikely.—The double calling of the name is also found in Luke 8.24, 10.41 and 22.31.

VERSE 5: The short dialogue which follows is also virtually the same in all three accounts (see 22.8 and 26.15), and must likewise have formed part of the story of Paul's call underlying Luke's words. Saul would grasp from the experience he has just undergone that his interlocutor is some otherwordly figure, a κύριος. The identity of this κύριος he learns from the exalted Lord himself. Whoever persecutes the Christians persecutes Christ: cf. Luke 10.16.

VERSE 6: ἀλλά introduces the imperative.[3] Saul learns only what he must do at once. The future otherwise remains concealed from him.[4] This manner of presentation stresses how completely Saul is now thrown on the (direct or indirect) guidance of the Lord. He who a moment ago was so powerful has now become utterly powerless. But it is not of course the weakness of Saul so much as the power of Christ that Luke is concerned to show.

VERSE 7: οἱ συνοδεύοντες, i.e. the other members of the 'caravan',[5] hear the voice without seeing the speaker, therefore stand speechless with astonishment.[6] This detail guarantees the objectivity of the phenomenon. On the other hand, the witnesses may not participate in the revelation. When in 22.9 Luke writes that Saul's companions saw the light but heard nothing, it is only the means of expression which are changed, not the sense of the statement. Needless to say, such cases show how little documentary,

---

[1] Once again, ἤκουσεν φωνήν (here and 26.14) compared with ἤκουσα φωνῆς (22.7) shows Luke's avoidance of schematic repetition. The two constructions—one with the accusative, the other with a classical genitive (Bl.-Debr. § 173)—are interchangeable without any difference of meaning.

[2] The form Σαούλ (in Ch. 9.22 and 26) indicates that Jesus is speaking Aramaic; in 26.14 this is expressly stated. τί με διώκεις can be rendered by לְמָא תִּרְדְּפַנִי? or something similar (see Windisch, op. cit., 20).

[3] As the imperative always demands something supplementary to what has gone before, the adversative particle has a good sense.

[4] 22.10 interpolates at this point a short dialogue. This led some representatives of the 'Western' text (see *Beg.* III, 84) to spin out the dialogue in 9.6 (incorporating the saying of 'the goad'). This obviously suited the taste of their age.

[5] Wendt 163f., *Beg.* IV, 101. Zahn (321) identifies them as Paul's police escort. To imagine Paul roving outside Judaea with a squad of Jerusalem temple-police is enough to place this hypothesis in the realm of fantasy.

[6] Perhaps Deut. 4.12 served as a model here: 'you heard the voice of words, but you saw no form'.

historical reliance may be placed on auxiliary details of this kind. Similarly, Luke is not troubled by the contradiction that the companions here remain standing, but in **26**.14 fall to the ground with Saul. Both statements make sense in their context. Bruce, p. 199, interprets φωνῆς of the voice of Saul!

VERSE 8: The Christophany is over, the earthly action proceeds.[1] Saul is lifted to his feet, being incapable of rising by himself, and it is discovered that, blinded by the light from heaven, he can no longer see. He has to be led by the hand[2] to Damascus. Such is the pitiful state in which the terror of the Christians makes his entry.

VERSE 9: His blindness lasts three days (οn ἦν μὴ βλέπων see **1**.10). It would be wrong to construe it as a punishment: it is simply the natural consequence of his beholding the heavenly light (cf. **22**.11).[3] More, it is concrete proof of the vision. Meanwhile the three-day fast—best understood as a penance—demonstrates his inward transformation.

VERSE 10 inaugurates a new scene, extending to verse 16. Its characters are Christ and Ananias. A μαθητής, hence a Christian—and, as shown by verse 13 and **22**.12, a 'Hebrew' already settled in Damascus—named Ananias (concerning his name, see note on **5**.1), is called[4] by the Lord in a ὅραμα,[5] and at once reports himself present and attentive.[6]

VERSE 11: As in **9**.5, Luke enlivens the dialogue by dropping εἶπεν. ἀναστὰς πορεύθητι—an LXX locution. As Ananias cannot well intrude into a strange house at night, the scene must be supposed to take place in the daytime. Ananias is given Saul's exact address, which shows how, in these instructions, a *providentia specialissima* is at work in the smallest detail. καλουμένη makes the following εὐθεῖαν part of a name.[7]

---

[1] Another short dialogue is here interpolated by h (*Beg.* III, 85).

[2] On χειραγωγοῦντες cf. ἐζήτει χειραγωγούς (**13**.11): the need of a guide is a typical touch for characterizing the blind as such.

[3] Luke has overlooked the fact that according to **22**.9 the others also saw the light.

[4] Commentators have recalled Samuel's vocation (I Sam. **3**.1ff.), which may well have served as model for this very feature (cf. Samuel's ἰδοὺ ἐγώ, v.4). Ananias however, unlike Samuel, knows at once that it is his Lord, Christ, who calls.—Cf. Wikenhauser, *Biblica* (1948), 100–11.

[5] It is not stated that the ὅραμα took place at night. The ἀναστάς of verse 11 is merely part of an OT expression which Luke puts in the Lord's mouth. ὅραμα (*ThWb* V, 372ff.) here denotes a condition in which the man, in his waking consciousness, is open to receive the voice or messenger from the celestial world (**10**.3!). In **16**.9 and **18**.9 it is explicitly stated that Paul has the 'vision' at night.

[6] The virtual sense of ἰδοὺ ἐγώ here: cf. last footnote but one, above.

[7] 'Straight Street' traversed Damascus from East to West, and had colonnaded halls on both sides and imposing gates at each end (*Beg.* IV, 102). It was presumably as well known in antiquity as Regent Street in London today, and like it was a highly fashionable street. That Saul's host lived here is scarcely old tradition; the narrator is using a name familiar to every reader. The house that sheltered Paul is nowadays pointed out at the western end of the street, but this is to overlook the fact that in antiquity the course of the street ran considerably farther to the South: Preuschen, 58.

VERSE 12: To this address Ananias must go, for the Lord has already shown the praying[1] Saul in a ὅραμα[2] the Ananias who will heal him. Saul's praying demonstrates the sincerity of his conversion. There is no mention here of communication of the Holy Spirit by the laying-on of hands (verse 17 speaks of it); the narrator is not bound to repeat every detail of recurring features.

VERSE 13: Ananias does not know Saul personally. If he were a refugee from the Jerusalem persecution, he would not need to call on the testimony of others. Here, as in 22.12, he is presented as a member of a Jewish-Christian group in Damascus.[3] How this group came into being remains obscure. On the other hand the 'many' from whom Ananias has learned of Saul's evil deeds appear to have come from Jerusalem. A certain time has therefore elapsed since the persecution there. The hesitations evinced by Ananias are meant to show the reader yet again what a menace Saul but a while ago represented for the ἅγιοι,[4] and thereby to impress on him the astounding magnitude of the change undergone. Luke has no thought of portraying the devout Jewish Christian Ananias[5] as refractory to God's command!

VERSE 14: Ananias now turns to the present. He shows himself extremely well-informed as to Saul's intentions and the extent of his authority (at least, as Luke imagined them), although it is then certainly strange that he apparently knows nothing of Saul's collapse three days before, —and yet in the following conversation with Saul he has knowledge of it. In reality the narrator makes Ananias express first the one and then the other, because in the relevant context it serves to draw the reader's attention to particular circumstances. The whole dialogue between Christ and Ananias thus proves to be of Lucan composition. Saul, then, is ostensibly in Damascus with full authority from the chief priests to arrest the Christians—now described by the formula 'those who call on the Name of the Lord'.

VERSE 15: After this further reminder of the menace embodied by Saul, the reader cannot fail to appreciate the unprecedented transformation which Christ is bringing about and in which the errand of Ananias, now commanded forth, will also be instrumental. Has Saul come to persecute those who call

---

[1] Prayer and visions are often associated in Luke's work: Luke 1.10, 3.21, 9.28 (and 22.43) and Acts 10.3, 10.30 and 22.17.

[2] The placing of ἐν ὁράματι varies, but this does not imply that the words are a late addition. The (original) word-order in B C is unusual (though not unheard-of in Luke— see Acts 14.8!) and has therefore been 'emended' by later MSS.

[3] It is improbable that the sect of the 'Damascus document' had any connection with the Christian community here presupposed.

[4] The Christians are called ἅγιοι here and in verses 32 and 41 (also the parallel 26.10). This does not reflect the usage of a particular source; Luke once again shows his aversion to any schematization (*Beg.* IV, 103).

[5] He speaks Aramaic to Saul, as witness the vocative Σαούλ of verse 17; 22.12 makes him a devout man under the law, and held in high esteem by all the Jews of Damascus.

on the Name of the Lord? Quite the reverse! He is a chosen instrument,[1] destined to bear the Lord's Name[2] before the Gentiles and kings and the children of Israel.

VERSE 16: Ananias had averred that Saul would make those suffer who call on the Name of Christ. Quite the reverse! Christ will show him how much he must suffer for the Name! Thus the words of Christ exactly counter those of Ananias. As may be seen from Wendt, p. 165, expositors have not always noticed this.

VERSE 17: Ananias hesitates no more, but hastens away into the house where Saul is staying.[3] All at once the action gains rapid momentum: already Ananias lays his hands on Saul—who forthwith receives the Christian title 'brother'—and declares himself sent by Jesus that Saul may be healed and be filled with the Holy Spirit.

VERSE 18: The healing is instantaneous. Luke adds no medical report—λεπίδες in medical literature are scaly crusts forming on the skin; ancient medicine knew of none falling from the eyes (*Beg.* IV, 104). Evidently the verse reflects a popular conception prompted, most likely, by Tobit **11**.12 καὶ ἐλεπίσθη ἀπὸ τῶν κανθῶν τῶν ὀφθαλμῶν αὐτοῦ τὰ λευκώματα (B A). Saul is immediately baptized—by Ananias, seeing that no other Christian is with him. *Pace* Zahn (327 n. 15), Luke can scarcely have supposed that this baptism took place in Judas' conveniently adjoining bathroom; we may rather presume that he did not worry his head over this detail.

VERSE 19a: Now, and only now, does Paul take food and regain his strength. We may well suppose that baptisands in Luke's community observed a period of prior fasting devoted mainly to prayer; cf. Didache 7.4: κελεύσεις δὲ νηστεῦσαι τὸν βαπτιζόμενον πρὸ μιᾶς ἢ δύο.

Seldom is the difference between our chosen method and that of source criticism so clearly visible as in this episode. Three characteristic arguments may here stand as typifying the 'source-hunter's' manner of proceeding:

1. Spitta's fantasy (270ff.) deduced from the words 'on the road' of **9**.17 (and **9**.27) that in the one source Jesus met Saul in the guise of a wayfarer, analogous to the gospel appearances of the risen Lord, which take place on earth. This must be the better source A, which does not have Saul taken to Damascus but Ananias brought to Saul, who is still at the spot where Jesus met him. It is this good source A which must lie behind Chapters 22 and 26, whereas the story of the call in Chapter 9 derives from the legendary source B. The verbal coincidences were first brought about by the redactor

---

[1] σκεῦος signifies not only 'vessel' but also 'instrument' or 'tool' (*Beg.* IV, 103).

[2] This formulation combines, not very happily, LXX expressions on the one hand (Ps. 7.14 [13] σκεύη θανάτου; Jer. 50 [27].25 σκεύη ὀργῆς) and the association of βαστάζω ('carry') with the idea of the ὄνομα on the other, but the sense is still clear.

[3] The scene takes place in the daytime (see on verse 11).

who combined the two. He imported from B into Chapter 22 verses 4, 10 and 11b, and in Chapter 9 incorporated verses 4f. from A with corresponding modification of verse 3.

2. In view of the arbitrary manner in which the sources were thus differentiated, Spitta's thesis met with little approval (except from Jüngst, 86ff.). Wendt (166ff.) took a less extravagant line: the version of Chapter 22 is a brief reproduction of Chapter 9, but Chapter 26 must be based on Paul's own story, for the mediator Ananias is missing and Paul—as in his own account—receives his call directly from Christ. In addition, the words of 26.14 (σκληρόν κτλ.) point to a vain resistance 'against some force impelling him to Christianity', in which Wendt sees a key to the psychological understanding of Paul's conversion.

3. Emanuel Hirsch adopted and modified this two-source hypothesis (*ZNW* 28 (1929), 305–12). In Chapter 9 he finds the tradition of the community at Damascus: 'The Christians in Damascus' regard the incident 'as purely a judgement on Paul, or better a preserving of the congregation from imminent persecution'. 'A Christian-baiter is laid low by Jesus, then the Spirit and baptism are vouchsafed to him within the Christian fold: that is all there is to the story.' In other words, the Damascus tradition spoke only of a crushing judgement, saying nothing of election by grace. In Chapter 26—here Hirsch is at one with Wendt—the Pauline account makes itself heard. On the other hand Hirsch takes a different view of Chapter 22: here Luke shows how he thought the two sources may be reconciled.

Thus this method attributes the repetitions of the story of the call to the plurality of sources confronting the writer, enlisting modern psychology to account for the divergent attitudes of the conjectural original sources. This method is found at its purest—hence most questionable—in Hirsch: he basically represents Luke as a modern historian who, possessing two respectable sources and unwilling to forgo either, incorporates both but also informs the reader how he himself would reconstruct the historical events lying behind them. But this version of things makes no allowance whatsoever for the fact that Luke was an early Christian, writing for purposes of edification, who had not the slightest interest in drawing the attention of members of his community to discrepancies in the tradition.

Alongside Hirsch's attempt to make the stories of Paul's conversion comprehensible by ascription to differing sources, there is the effort of the historians of religion to explain them from parallels in *Religionsgeschichte*. Arthur Drews went farthest: in his *Entstehung des Christentums aus dem Gnostizismus* (1924) he roundly asserted that 'the whole account of Paul's conversion is modelled on that of Heliodorus, II Macc. 3'. It was likewise in the story of Heliodorus that Friedrich Smend found a model for Chapter 9 (see his 'Untersuchungen zu den Acta-Darstellungen von der Bekehrung des Paulus' in *Angelos* I (1925), 34–45, produced independently of Drews). Hans

Windisch, in 1932 (see bibl.), was more cautious: perhaps Luke knew the Heliodorus legend, but it was not a source, only a parallel tale. On the other hand, Windisch conjectured a deliberate literary relation to the *Bacchae* of Euripides—on this we shall have more to say in connection with Chapter 26. All the other comparable stories that have been unearthed—in the Iliad (XXII.8ff.: a persecuted god reveals his identity) or OT (I Sam. 24.14 and 26.18: Saul persecutes David; also the story of Balaam)—are of no significance.

Shortly before Windisch wrote, Ernst von Dobschütz (*ZNW* 29 (1930), 144–7) put a question independent of all source-theories: why does Luke recount the conversion of Paul three times? Dobschütz conjectures that here a stylistic rule of ancient historiography comes into play.

Careful exegesis shows that Hirsch's description of the account in Chapter 9 is wide of the mark. Here the story of the call is related for the first time. Not yet acquainted with the story, the reader is kept in suspense: all he learns at first is that Saul was instructed to go to Damascus (we have seen how this touch also serves to demonstrate Saul's utter dependence on the Lord's direction). Then he is made to feel how Ananias balks at his mission of healing: thus even the dimmest wit will appreciate the unprecedented nature of the call. Now all is ready for the breathtakingly swift dénouement: Ananias goes to Saul, heals and baptizes him. Saul recovers his strength and embarks on his missionary career. Nothing here justifies the assumption of a source which spoke only of a crushing judgement and omitted all reference to election by grace. On the contrary: Saul is expressly designated σκεῦος ἐκλογῆς, and that this dread persecutor should be commissioned to bear the Name of Christ before the Gentiles, the kings (Luke must have had Agrippa II and Nero in mind) and the children of Israel—what else can this be but election by grace? One should not allow the succeeding words about the suffering to which Paul is called to overshadow all the rest. But above all, the hesitations of Ananias do not reflect the quaking Damascene congregation which has had 'yet another providential escape' but portray the unutterable past, now superseded by the incredibly wonderful present: the persecutor of Christ has become his Name's confessor, and his enemy his witness!

As Dibelius has already shown (*Studies*, 158 n. 47), the omission of Ananias does not suffice to make a Pauline reminiscence of Chapter 26. Here Luke put the Greek proverb of kicking against the pricks into the mouth of Jesus because Paul is addressing a mixed audience of Greeks and Jews, and he certainly did not give it that psychological connotation which modern scholars have read into it (see on 26.14 below).

Why did Luke recount Paul's conversion three times? Luke employs such repetitions only when he considers something to be extraordinarily important and wishes to impress it unforgettably on the reader. That is the case here. Let us not be misled by the various accusations against Paul which

Acts mentions: Luke—and quite rightly!—felt that the one real problem was the Pauline mission to the Gentiles. Here, in the last resort, lay the ground of indictment—indictment, indeed, not only of Paul but of Christianity in general. Why did the Christians not content themselves with the mission to the Jews? Had they done so, they would have been spared the conflict both with Israel and with Rome. Against this, Luke constantly drives home the idea that *Christ himself* brought about this change of front. Paul did not want to become a Christian or a missionary, but he had no option! The idea that Luke wanted to suggest a psychological explanation such as modern psychology would offer is completely wrong: on the contrary, Luke wishes to show that *no* human evolution is responsible for the change, but an act of God—and that alone! That—along with the many other things he has to say in this connection—is Luke's real argument, and here he cannot be said to conflict with Paul.

None of this is incompatible with Luke's having used a community tradition about Paul's call—the same in all three cases. We cannot reconstruct its wording. Nor may we assume that it contained the two curious corresponding ὁράματα: they may rather be literary devices, as in the tale of Cornelius. But at all events Paul, having seen Christ in or near Damascus, was baptized by some member of the congregation there—and why should this Christian not have been called Ananias? Again, the blinding and healing of Paul fit well into popular tradition: it loves concrete, vivid incidents. The figure of Ananias therefore cannot be completely erased from this tradition. That Ananias should confer the Spirit on Paul goes without saying, given the belief that baptism and reception of the Spirit are intimately connected. As for his informing Paul (**22**.14) of his call to high office, there is no need to take exception: it is one of the forms in which Luke instructs the reader through the mouth of a participant in the action. It is not of course impossible that in Gal. **1**.1 Paul alluded by δι' ἀνθρώπου to a Jewish Christian distortion of Ananias' role, but he was more probably referring to a contention that his Apostolate depended not on Damascus but on Jerusalem.

In Luke's hands the popular tale of the calling of Paul has become a piece of history—not, admittedly, a strict Thucydidean chronicle, but something rather in the story-telling manner of a Herodotus. What was available to Luke in the way of edifying material—the blinding and conversion of Paul —now describes an event of crucial significance for the Christian mission: through the Stephen-persecution, which he ostensibly carried out, Paul provided the stimulus for the rise of the Hellenistic communities; through his conversion he now gives the Church its needed respite, and turns from a 'commissar' ('*le commissaire général*' is Loisy's epithet, *La Naissance du christianisme*, 1933, 160; *ET Birth of the Christian Religion* 1948) into a suffragan Apostle. With the best will in the world Luke cannot rank him among the Twelve, and outside that holy circle there is no room for another full Apostle. So Luke contents himself with having Paul's authority at least sanctioned by that circle. But with this we are straying into the subject of the following verses...

23
ACTS 9: 19b-31
PAUL IN DAMASCUS AND JERUSALEM

[19b] And he was with the disciples in Damascus some days: [20] and immediately in the synagogues he proclaimed Jesus, that he is the Son of God. [21] And all who heard him were amazed, and said: 'Is not this the man who in Jerusalem made havoc of those who called on this name, and has come here for this purpose, that he might bring them bound before the chief priests?' [22] But Saul increased the more in strength, and confounded the Jews who lived in Damascus, proving that this is the Messiah.

[23] And when many days were fulfilled, the Jews determined to kill him; [24] but their plot became known to Saul. And they were watching the gates also day and night, that they might kill him: [25] but [his] disciples took him, and let him down by night through the wall, lowering him in a basket. [26] And when he came to Jerusalem, he attempted to join the disciples; and they were all afraid of him, since they did not believe that he was a disciple. [27] But Barnabas took him and brought him to the Apostles, and declared to them how he had seen the Lord on the road, and that he had spoken to him, and how in Damascus he had preached boldly in the name of Jesus. [28] And he was with them going in and out in Jerusalem, preaching boldly in the name of the Lord: [29] and he spoke and disputed against the Hellenists; but they were seeking to kill him. [30] And when the brethren got to know of it, they brought him down to Caesarea, and sent him off to Tarsus. [31] So the Church in all Judaea and Galilee and Samaria now had peace, being edified and walking in the fear of the Lord, and it was multiplied by the comfort of the Holy Spirit.

Bibliography:

A. Steinmann, *Arethas IV, König der Nabatäer*, Freiburg-im-Breisgau, 1909; G. Rudberg, see § 46f., bibl. (on 9.24); O. Linton, see § 22, bibl.; S. Giet, 'Les trois premiers voyages de Saint Paul à Jérusalem' in *RScR* 41 (1953), 321–7.

    S. Greydanus, *Is Hand. 9 (met 22 en 26) en 15 in tegenspraak met Galaten 1 en 2? Eine verglijkende exegetisch studie, Kampen* 1935; A. Kappeler, 'S. Barnabas in vita S. Pauli', *Verb. Domini* 22 (1942), 129–35; R. Lichtenhahn, 'Die beiden ersten Besuche des Paulus in Jerusalem', *Harnack-Ehrung*, Leipzig, 1921, 51–67; F. W. Beare, 'A Note on Paul's First Two Visits to

Jerusalem', *JBL* 63 (1944), 407–9; S. Giet, 'Nouvelles remarques sur les voyages de St. Paul à Jérusalem', *RevScR* 31 (1957), 329–42.

VERSE 19b: Paul—let us henceforth use this name, which (see note on 13.9) he always bore along with the Hebrew שָׁאוּל—remains a number of days[1] in the company[2] of the Christians of Damascus.

VERSE 20: Immediately after this he preaches in the synagogues of Damascus (the imperfect serves to indicate the numerous occasions). υἱὸς θεοῦ occurs only here in Acts, though Ps. 2.7, whence the title derives, is cited in Paul's sermon, 13.33; nevertheless Bousset goes too far when he maintains (*Kyrios Christos*,[2] 56) that Luke intended the expression to characterize the Pauline preaching: he needed a title synonymous with the Messianic epithet of verse 22 and this was the most natural one.

VERSE 21: The amazement of Paul's audiences expresses at the same time their recoil from his message. By describing this reaction of incredulity in exactly the same way as verses 13f., this verse (also reminiscent of Luke 4.22) impresses still further on the reader the unprecedented *volte-face* that has occurred in Paul: 'Can this really be the man who persecuted[3] the Christians in[4] Jerusalem and purposed to do the same here?'

VERSE 22: ἐνδυναμέω, συμβιβάζω and also συγχέω occur in LXX.[5] Paul's (spiritual) strength is still more increased as he preaches the Messiahship of Jesus. Luke has taken pains to create the impression of an intensification relative to verses 20f., so as to provide a motive for the Jewish plot against Paul.[6]

VERSE 23: The stubborn, fearless preaching of Christ with which Paul demonstrates the authenticity of his conversion (cf. verse 27) drives the Jews to plot his assassination. According to Paul himself, however (II Cor. 11.32f.), it was the ethnarch of King Aretas who was behind it. Christian tradition soon forgot that Paul had become suspect to Aretas through his activity in 'Arabia' (cf. the general discussion). Luke uses a later tradition in which Jews appear as Paul's (customary) enemies.

VERSE 24: Though Paul learns what is afoot, flight is difficult because the

---

[1] 𝔓⁴⁵ reads ἡμέρας ἱκανάς, which is presumably what h means by *plurimos*. This Western variant wrongly supposes that the days mentioned in verses 19b and 23 are identical.

[2] γίνομαι μετά as in 7.38.

[3] Here and in Gal. 1.13 and 23 the word πορθέω is used (originally 'to lay waste' a city or 'wipe out' a community). Loisy (416) infers that the author knew the Paulines, but deliberately discounted them. Paul alternates πορθέω and διώκω in Gal. 1. The πορθέω coincidence is not enough to show that Luke knew Galatians (Wendt 173).

[4] א A have εἰς Hellenistically for the ἐν of B C and the bulk of later MSS. This is not to say that א A offer the original reading.

[5] ἐνδυναμέω Judges 6.34, I Chron. 12.19(18), Ps. 52.7(51.9); συμβιβάζω Exodus 4.12, 15; 8.16; Lev. 10.11; Deut. 4.9 etc. (='teach'); συγχύ(ν)νω is a Hellenistic form of συγχέω ('confound', 'overthrow'), as in Gen. 11.7, 9 and often.

[6] Verses 21f. are erroneously struck out as an interpolation by E. Schwarz, *NGG* 1907, 275 n. 1, and Preuschen (60).

gates are watched day and night by the murderous Jews. It is usually[1] assumed, on account of II Cor. **11**.32f., that Damascus was at the time in Nabataean hands and that the Jews had alerted the governor.[2]

VERSE 25: Wherever μαθηταί occurs in this section it means simply 'Christians'; μαθηταὶ αὐτοῦ must be an early corruption.[3] The escape takes place as in II Cor. **11**.33.[4]

VERSE 26: As in **13**.14, παραγίνομαι εἰς ='arrive in'; πειράζω (also **16**.7, **24**.6) and πειράω (**26**.21) ='tried'; κολλᾶσθαι τοῖς μαθηταῖς implies that the Jerusalem community still subsisted (or had been reconstituted).

VERSE 27: How Barnabas happens to be better informed than the Apostles is not explained. Luke has Barnabas and Paul enter into close association. Wikenhauser (*Apg.* 91) suggests that the subject of διηγήσατο may be Paul!

VERSE 28: Paul now lives in intimate companionship with the Apostles— that is the Lucan sense of 'to go in and go out with someone' (cf. **1**.21); ἦν + participle expresses duration (cf. **1**.10).[5] 'By the very fact that he— known to many in Jerusalem as the Christian-baiter—allowed himself to be seen walking arm-in-arm, as it were, in the streets and lanes of that city with the leaders of the Nazarene sect (themselves familiar as such throughout Jerusalem), Saul made open confession of his faith in Jesus' (Zahn, 331). This largely corresponds, no doubt, with the meaning of Acts, but it cannot be reconciled with Gal. **1**.18f.[6] Besides, to Luke this public association has a further significance, for it attests the seal of approval placed by the Twelve upon Paul as a Christian missionary.

VERSE 29: Paul repeatedly (*imperfect*) engages in debate with the Jewish

---

[1] E.g. by H. Schlier, *Der Galaterbrief* (*Krit.-Exeg. Kommentar über das NT*), 1939, p. 29.

[2] φρουρέω can indeed also mean 'to occupy' or 'garrison'. But that the ethnarch should occupy 'the city of the Damascenes' in order to seize Paul does not make sense. Hence Loisy and Lake here interpret II Cor. **11**.32 in accordance with the usual sense of φρουρέω: 'to camp round and seal the issues' (references in Zahn, *NkZ* (1904), 40 n. 1, and *Apg.* 329). Thus the ethnarch should be regarded as either the headman of the Arab suburbs (*Beg.* V, 193) or the sheikh of the local Nabataean tribe (Loisy) who at his king's command watches over Damascus proper ('the city of the Damascenes') by posting sentries or watchers at the gates.

[3] Here ΑΥΤΟΝ has been misread as ΑΥΤΟΥ, just as in certain Western MSS at Acts **14**.20 (D d E e). The reading αὐτόν in the later MSS is thus a correction which—for once—is correct; the omission of αὐτοῦ by other scribes simply mitigates a difficulty. Cf. *Beg.* III, 88f. The interpretation of οἱ μαθηταὶ αὐτοῦ as 'companions of Paul on the road to Damascus who through his guidance and testimony have themselves come to the faith and now help him out of his mortal danger' (*ThWb* IV, 464) is impossible. The text does not indicate either that Paul's fellow-travellers (**9**.7) had anything to do with him or that he made conversions in Damascus (Loisy 420).

[4] The σαργάνη of II Cor. **11**.33 denotes a woven basket suitable for carrying hay, straw or bales of wool (*Beg.* IV, 106). σπυρίς (cf. Mark **8**.8) indicates something similar but probably smaller. W. L. Knox (29) thinks Luke put σπυρίς because it was more classical.

[5] There is no thought of activity outside Jerusalem; εἰς is again Hellenistic for ἐν.

[6] 'For πρὸς τοὺς ἀποστόλους indicates that in any case more than the two named by Paul were involved' (Overbeck, 145).

'Hellenists'—like Stephen before him.[1] They react against him in the same way: with a threat against his life.

VERSE 30: The text differs from Gal. 1.21 in suggesting a land journey to Caesarea followed by a voyage. The writer assumes that Paul now remains quietly for a while in his home town of Tarsus.

VERSE 31: μὲν οὖν—see 1.6. A new period of the history is now beginning. Paul's call brings the persecution to an end. The community is no longer confined to Jerusalem but exists also in Galilee, on whose Christianization Luke apparently possessed no material,[2] and in Samaria (see Chapter 8). ἐκκλησία here takes on the sense of 'the Church'.[3] Its being 'edified'—consolidated —strikes no longer an apocalyptic or Messianic, but an ecclesiastical note (Michel, *ThWb* V, 141.41). God it is, who is setting about building the Church; the answering human behaviour is described in πορευομένη κτλ.: the fear of the Lord (fear of God) determines the Christians' way of life. The concluding words imply that the community continued to enjoy the sense of the Holy Spirit's protection when the persecution was over.

Harnack made lighter work of this passage than any other critic: Luke had heard of these events from Paul's own lips; incorrect or conflicting details might be laid at the door of his style [*Beitr.* III, 139 and 173 (ET)]! B. Weiss (*Einl.* 116ff., ET *Introd.*) conceded that, before visiting Jerusalem, Paul spent three years in 'Arabia' (i.e. the Hauran) 'in order to digest his experiences by prayer and meditation in the solitude of the desert'. Of these years Acts admittedly knew nothing but is otherwise correct, even in making the Jews in Damascus the persecutors: 'It is inconceivable that the ethnarch could have reached this pitch of enmity against Paul if the Jews . . . had not denounced him to the governor as a disturber of the peace.'

H. J. Holtzmann (72f.) saw that this solution was too facile: it was 'unthinkable' that 'after a lapse of three years' (Gal. 1.18) the Christians in Jerusalem should still be ignorant of what had happened in Damascus (9.26f.), and 'this automatically eliminates the intermediary role of Barnabas'. Paul did not seek any contact with the Jerusalem community: the 'Apostles' of 9.27 'boil down to one person—Peter'. In Holtzmann's opinion Luke had

---

[1] *Beg.* IV, 106 sees the 'Hellenists' as Gentiles. That is indeed the implication of the weakly attested Ἕλληνας (A). But Gentiles would not have plotted the murder of a Jewish missionary in Jerusalem, and Luke cannot have meant to relate anything of the kind.

[2] Luke thus assumed that only now did Christian communities come into being in Galilee. Cf. Loisy (*La Naissance du christianisme*, 1933, 149 n. 1 (ET *Birth of the Christian Religion*, 1948, p. 121): 'The invective against the Galilean towns (Mathew 11.20–4, Luke 10.12–15) and the symbolic check to the preaching of Jesus at Nazareth (Mark 6.1–6; Matthew 13.53–8; Luke 4.15–30) would rather invite the conclusion that there were no groups of believers in Galilee in apostolic times'.

[3] Cf. *ThWb* III, 506. D is defective, but later Western-influenced witnesses read the plural, which according to *Beg.* IV, 107 could be the genuine text. But the attestation is weak, and an alteration to the singular seems improbable.

only two data: Paul's flight from Damascus and his brief stay in Jerusalem. Not surprisingly, such radical critics as Wellhausen (17f.), Preuschen (61) and Loisy (414ff.) take similar views, but so, at bottom, do Beyer and Bauernfeind. A mere fortnight's secret visit, in which Paul saw only Peter and James, is the reality which Beyer (62) opposes to the Acts account. He nevertheless detects 'traces of sound reminiscence' in the occurrence of the word 'Hellenist': since Paul was himself a Hellenist (on which Acts admittedly keeps silent), his attempt to create a *rapport* with Peter and James must have been an effort to bridge the rift between Hellenists and Hebrews, hence Paul's first great historical initiative . . .

Wisely, Bauernfeind (136f.) refrains from such venturesome flights. In his view, the material available to Luke contained no mention of any official commissioning of Paul by the leaders in Jerusalem. There was only 'a small, colourful, certainly oft-told tale of the flight from Damascus (verses 23ff.) and general reminiscences of doings in Damascus and Jerusalem.' Bauernfeind thinks it possible that Luke may have felt it incumbent upon him to rectify in his own sense—whereby the Jews were the enemies—some tradition corresponding to II Cor. 11.32f. On this view, Barnabas did not at that time come into contact with Paul, but his position as mediator between Paul and the Apostles is correctly seen.

Closer examination of this criticism leads one to conclude that where the tradition used by Luke was really deficient was in its total ignorance of Paul's sojourn in 'Arabia'. It can easily be understood that Christian tradition contained nothing about it. *Pace* B. Weiss, Paul did not of course spend all his time in the Nabataean kingdom praying and meditating (incidentally, as Wellhausen, p. 18, observes, *Arabia provincia* was by no means a desert): he was also essaying the first steps of his missionary career—'When it pleased God to reveal his Son to me, that I might preach him to the Gentiles, . . . I went forth into Arabia' (Gal. 1.15–17). However, this activity bore no fruit (at least, Paul nowhere mentions having founded any congregations in these regions), and this was doubtless why no record of it was handed down.

The events following his call were now inevitably seen in a false light. Once the 'Arabian' period had fallen into oblivion, only a trifling interval appeared to separate Paul's journey to Jerusalem from his call. What is more, the circumstances of the flight from Damascus now became obscure: the ethnarch no longer came plausibly into the picture. If, on the other hand, Paul had been conducting a mission in Nabataean territory, it is perfectly understandable that he should have fallen foul of Aretas: this Jew with his preaching of the κύριος ᾽Ιησοῦς and the imminent end of the world became suspect to the authorities, and Paul finally thought it better to leave Arabia and return to Damascus. But even there he was not out of danger; the ethnarch of Aretas sought to lay hands on him. (Here we can leave on one side the question, which cannot in the present state of our knowledge be answered with certainty, of whether the ethnarch was, as generally assumed, the Nabataean commander of the city or, as Lake [*Beg.* V, 193] and Loisy suggest, the sheikh of some Nabataean tribe which controlled the country round Damascus.) But once the motives of this mysterious person had become a source of puzzlement, it is not surprising that his role of persecutor should have been transferred to Paul's eternal enemies, the Jews. It seemed to Luke that it must have been their hostile scheming which provoked Paul's flight to Jerusalem.

It is highly important to understand how Luke extracted concrete scenes from this material. He took it for granted that Paul after his conversion immediately began his missionary career. Here his judgement of Paul was in itself entirely correct. Only, he committed the error— in the circumstances probably unavoidable—of having him begin it not in Arabia but among the Damascene Jews. And this début he describes most vividly. From this we learn that concrete scenes in Acts, however vividly narrated, do not necessarily, as such, possess any historical value . . . they may be Lucan compositions which overshoot reality.

The same applies to verses 26–30. According to Luke, Paul wanted to join the Jerusalem congregation, but was mistrusted until Barnabas introduced him to the Apostles. At first sight this all seems very plausible. But the story only makes sense if, as Luke of course erroneously assumes, Paul went to Jerusalem very shortly after his call. Only with such a brief interval could people there still not be informed of his conversion. In fact, however, Paul did not get to Jerusalem until three years later, by which time everybody there knew what had happened in Damascus. Apart from that, it is inconceivable that the truth about Paul should be known to Barnabas, but not to the Apostles. In other words, the ground on which this entire Lucan edifice is erected will bear no weight, and all must come toppling down. One need scarcely point out that Paul's public appearances with 'the Apostles' are, furthermore, excluded by Gal. **1**.18f. Even apart from this, it is clear enough that Luke has developed everything from erroneous premises. Needless to add, Paul's public disputes with the 'Hellenists' and the new Jewish plot against him must also be discounted.

This passage helps us to appreciate the extraordinary difficulties with which Luke had to struggle in the composition of Acts. Earlier scholars (e.g. Harnack) presumed that he was able to work under almost ideal conditions, with a multiplicity of sources, some deriving from eyewitnesses, plus the possibility of interviewing persons who had played decisive parts in the events. Zahn even grandly opened for him the Roman archives, in which the reports of Claudius Lysias to Felix—copies or originals—naturally reposed. We here learn to see, instead of this ideal situation, the real world in which Luke was not blessed with a mass of reports and personal accounts but had often to be content with very little, a little which by no means always consisted of the sort of thing his readers expected, and he wanted to give to them: impressive, gripping scenes. Thus he had perforce to make such heavy call on the 'divination' without which no historian can fulfil his task, i.e. the intuitive grasp of situations and their significance, and on the imagination which alone can clothe the historical skeleton with flesh and blood, that errors became inevitable; not least because he had to work within the horizon of an age divorced by a generation from the problems of the apostolic era. Hence (to return to the detail of our text) his conviction that Paul must have lost no time in seeking out the Twelve, the fount of all legitimacy. This is certainly not intended to 'downgrade' Paul—on the contrary, Luke hopes to accredit him! By having Paul show himself in Jerusalem (as Zahn nicely puts it) 'arm in arm with the leaders of the Nazarene sect' he incorporates Paul into the recognized hierarchy of the Church; though not indeed among the Twelve, whose number is complete and admits of no thirteenth. Yet 'arm in arm' with them Paul nonetheless publicly appears, and this is tantamount to an official endorsement of his mission before it has properly begun. Let us not forget that these verses showing Paul and the Twelve together in Jerusalem are the last in which the Twelve alone constitute the whole of the Christian high command. Afterwards the elders and James the Lord's brother share the direction of the community—why, we do not rightly know—and at length the Apostles actually vanish: a problem that we (and, it may be, Luke before us!) find one of the most distressing in Acts. But they do not vanish before, here in Chapter 9, signifying their acceptance of Paul (for the time being still called Saul). Thus he has now been not only called by Christ but acknowledged by the Apostles, and is therefore in all respects—*rite vocatus.*

24

ACTS 9: 32–43
PETER HEALS AENEAS AND RAISES TABITHA

[32] And it came to pass, as Peter went throughout all parts, he came down also to the saints who dwelt at Lydda. [33] And there he found a man named Aeneas, who had kept his bed eight years, for he was paralysed. [34] And Peter said to him: 'Aeneas, Jesus Christ heals you: get up, and make your bed!' And immediately he arose. [35] And all who dwelt at Lydda and in Sharon saw him, and they turned to the Lord.

[36] Now there was at Joppa a disciple named Tabitha, which translated means Gazelle [Dorcas]: this woman was full of good works and almsdeeds which she did. [37] And it came to pass in those days that she fell sick and died; and when they had washed her, they laid her in an upper chamber. [38] And as Lydda is near Joppa, the disciples, hearing that Peter was there, sent two men to him, with the request: 'Do not delay to come on to us!' [39] And Peter arose and went with them. And when he had come, they brought him into the upper chamber: and all the widows stood by him weeping, and showing the coats and garments which the 'Gazelle' made while she was with them. [40] But Peter sent them all out, and knelt down and prayed; and turning to the body, he said: 'Tabitha, arise!' And she opened her eyes; and when she saw Peter, she sat up. [41] And he gave her his hand, and raised her up; and calling the saints and widows, he presented her alive. [42] And it became known throughout all Joppa; and many believed on the Lord. [43] And it came to pass that he remained many days in Joppa, with one Simon, a tanner.

Bibliography:

J. Kreyenbühl, 'Ursprung und Stammbaum eines biblischen Wunders', *ZNW* 10 (1909), 265–76; Williams, 128–30; Rieu, 135ff.

    H. J. Cadbury, 'A possible Perfect in Acts **9**.34', *JTS* 49 (1948), 57–8; J. McConnachie, 'Simon a Tanner (Acts **9**.43; **10**.6, 32)', *Exp.Tim.* 36 (1924/5), 90.

VERSE 32: In OT tones[1] Luke tells how Peter, on a kind of tour of inspection,[2] came down to the plain from high-lying Jerusalem and visited the Christians[3] living in Lydda—nowadays Ludd—about twenty-five miles north-west of the Holy City. A transitional and introductory verse.

VERSE 33: As the scene apparently takes place indoors and Peter speaks the name of Jesus, ἐχεῖ doubtless refers not so much to Lydda in general as to the Christian community there.[4] Peter finds there a sick man (who despite his thoroughly Greek name[5] is thought of as a Jewish Christian) who for eight years (ἐξ ἐτῶν ὀχτώ)[6] has been lying paralysed on his bed.[7]

VERSE 34: The words 'Aeneas, Jesus is healing[8] you! Get up and make your bed!'[9] effect an immediate cure.

VERSE 35: That *all* the inhabitants of the plain of Sharon[10] saw[11] the cured Aeneas is no less hyperbolical than that they were all converted. Here Jews are the subject; in the case of the Gentiles it would be 'turned to God' (cf. **14**.15, **15**.19 and **26**.20). In any case, conversion of Gentiles would at this juncture radically conflict with the viewpoint of Acts.

VERSE 36: The second story begins with a clean break. In Joppa (modern Jaffa) there lived a Christian woman by the name of Tabitha (טְבִיתָא) or in Greek Δορχάς = 'gazelle'.[12] Here we have the only NT example of the

---

[1] On ἐγένετο + acc. & inf. see **4.**5; on διέρχομαι see **8.**4. The διὰ πάντων refers to the regions named in verse 31.

[2] 'Peter ... came ... in fulfilment ... of the injunction to feed the flock, the young sheep as well as the old' (Zahn, 335).

[3] ἅγιοι (see note to 9.1). Luke interchanges the ancient styles μαθηταί and ἅγιοι, with other designations; the terms should not be regarded as a clue to sources.

[4] Cf. verse 34. Of course, Peter could enter Gentile houses. But it seems more likely that he was visiting his own community. We are also not informed that the healed man became a Christian—which tells against *Beg.* IV, 108f.: 'apparently Aeneas was not a Christian'.

[5] In the synoptic healing-stories the names of the persons healed are not reported (even 'Jairus' is probably an interpolation); interest in the names seems to be a later feature.

[6] According to *Beg.* IV, 109 one might also translate: 'since he was eight years old'.

[7] χράβατος probably comes from Luke's source-material, for in Luke **5.**19, 24 he replaces the χράβατος of Mark **2.**4, 9 by χλινίδιον; Acts **5.**15 mentions χλινίδια and χράβατοι in the same breath.

[8] ἰᾶσθαι is a favourite word of Luke's: Luke **5.**17; **6.**19; **9.**2, 11, 42; **14.**4; **22.**51; Acts **10.**38; **28.**8. ἰᾶται is an 'aoristic' present—'this instant Jesus is healing you' (cf. Bl.-Debr. § 320).

[9] The scene clearly presupposes that Peter is with Aeneas in his house; an injunction to go out with the bed (as in the Synoptics) would then be meaningless. The translation 'lay the table for yourself' (corresponding to the expression χλίνην στρώννυμι), suggested by *Beg.* IV, 109, is misconceived: the χλίνην to be supplied with στρῶσαι can indeed also mean the cushion used at mealtimes, but in the case of an invalid his sick-bed is surely meant.

[10] Only in Isa. 33.9 does LXX render the name in this way.

[11] εἶδαν Hellenistic for εἶδον: Bl.-Debr. § 80 and 81, 3.

[12] The form 'Tabea' in the present Luther text stands in no Greek MS, but only in the corrupt text of e in Mk. 5.41: tabea acultha cumhi! See E. Nestle, *ZNW* 11 (1910), 240.

feminine μαθήτρια.[1] The expression praising her conflates two ideas: 'full of good works' and 'she did good works'. The second (with attraction of the relative ἅ) was added to obviate the impression that she *received* alms. Jacquier (p. 307) inclines to read the καί before ἐλεημοσυνῶν epexegetically as 'and indeed', for the 'good works' might also have consisted of prayer and fasting. But the reference is to her donations—cf. verse 39.

VERSE 37: ἐγένετο as in verse 32—'And it came to pass in those days' (when Peter was in Lydda) 'that she fell sick and died.' The body is washed, but not—as was normal—anointed: in anticipation of the hoped-for restoration to life? Then it is carried into the ὑπερῷον, probably not merely because of the greater ventilation—but following the OT models to this story, I Kings 17.17ff. and II Kings 4.32ff.

VERSE 38: ἐγγύς—in fact, three hours away on foot; perhaps Luke took the distance to be smaller. The Joppa Christians, who had heard[2] of Peter's presence in Lydda, sent two men to ask him if he would be so kind[3] as to come without delay. It is part of the subtle art with which the tale is told that the plea for the raising of Tabitha goes unexpressed.

VERSE 39: On ἀναστάς see 1.15. Even when Peter has arrived and been shown into the upper room, no explicit statement is made of what is desired. Instead, the widows supported by Tabitha's charity (who are possibly there as mourners) come up to him and show him the coats and undergarments she had made them:[4] her works of mercy are to move the Apostle to perform the miracle.

VERSE 40 verbally echoes II Kings 4.33 (καὶ προσηύξατο) and Mark 5.40.[5] As Loisy remarks (430), it is out of the question for Peter to proceed with a woman as Elijah and Elisha with a dead boy. He sends out all those present,[6] kneels in prayer, and speaks to the prone figure words virtually identical with those of Jesus in Mk. 5—translation back into Aramaic gives a difference of only one letter.[7] This accounts for the fact that the name of

---

[1] Although μαθήτρια occurs here and μαθηταί in verse 38, and ἀπόστολος is missing, R. Schütz (*Apostel und Jünger*, 1921, 33) has to assign this section to the 'Apostle' source. This shows how little we can rely on such words for distinguishing sources. μαθήτρια is a Hellenistic word: Bauer, *Wb* 961.

[2] ἀκούσαντες must be understood as a pluperfect.

[3] The formal μὴ ὀκνήσῃς replaces the imperative. De Zwaan (*Beg.* II, 40) would interpret according to the classical rule: 'Do not begin to hesitate!' In reality it is a customary Greek expression, which already occurs at Num. 22.16 LXX.

[4] Preuschen (62f.) advances the idea that Peter was shown Tabitha's own clothing as a sign of her wealth—which to primitive Christian and especially Lucan sentiment would be no less than a slap in the face.

[5] The parallel Luke 8.51ff. does not contain this clause; it therefore stood in Luke's source.

[6] ἐκβάλλειν should not be translated 'drive out'; the verb in Hellenism has largely lost its force. Cf. Bauer, *Wb* 471, s.v. 2.

[7] Mk. 5.41: ταλιθα κουμ—here ταβιθα κουμ. But Luke 8.54 translates ἡ παῖς ἔγειρε. The detail derives from his source, which had already translated the Aramaic words into Greek. It will also have supplied the translation of Tabitha by δορκάς.

Jesus is not mentioned. 'She opened her eyes': cf. the last words of II Kings 4.35. ἀνεκάθισεν—like the youth of Nain in Luke 7.15.

VERSE 41: 'He gave her his hand': cf. Mark 5.41 (=Luke 8.54)— κρατήσας τῆς χειρός (Jesus admittedly grasps the hand before the resuscitation). Now Peter calls back the Christians (ἅγιοι) and the widows: for the latter the restoration to life of their benefactress is especially important. παρέστησεν αὐτὴν ζῶσαν is a Lucan construction: cf. Acts 1.3, παρέστησεν ἑαυτὸν ζῶντα.

VERSE 42: On γνωστὸν ἐγένετο see 1.19. As in Lydda, the miracle moves many to faith in Christ; as before, these are Jews.

VERSE 43: ἐγένετο + infin.: see Bl-Debr. § 393, 1. ἡμέρας ἱκανάς: a long succession of days (on ἱκανός see 8.11). This verse makes a link with the next story: instead of returning to Lydda, which he had left so hastily, Peter stays on in Joppa, where the messengers of Cornelius will find him. Peter lodges with a tanner called Simon.[1] Would this be a local tradition? At all events, some address must be named to which Cornelius may send his messengers. Loisy was sceptical: 'Simon the tanner, Peter's host, is no more likely to belong to the category of men who really lived than Judas of Straight Street, Damascus' (431).

Practically all the questions raised by this passage were heralded long ago by critics of the old school. B. Weiss (*Einl.*,[2] 575, *ET Introd.*) was convinced that, as 'this introduction is absolutely irrelevant from the pragmatical standpoint of the narrator', these two *acta Petri* already formed the introduction to the Cornelius episode in the Jewish Christian source employed by Luke. J. Weiss was also persuaded of this: 'The only explanation for their incorporation is that the writer found them in the tradition before him and did not care to discard them, especially as they at least showed how Peter came to Joppa.' Sorof (75) and Feine (199) also regard a Jewish Christian source as probable. Spitta (157ff.), on account of the piece's miraculous character, could only assign it to source B. Harnack was opposed to derivation from any written source: Luke had the story told to him 'when he stayed with Philip in Caesarea' [*Beiträge* III, 125 (*ET*)]. In this form it is a legend, yet Peter may himself have believed that he had 'called a dead woman back to life' (124). Holtzmann, on the other hand, allowed Pfleiderer to persuade him that 'the whole resuscitation forms no more than the legendary parallel to the historical account in 20.9–12' (74)! Wellhausen (18f.), while not denying that Peter conducted a mission outside Jerusalem, felt it odd that in so

---

[1] Attempts have been made to find here a psychological preparation for his relationship with Cornelius (so e.g. Billerbeck II, 695, referring to the contempt of the rabbis for the tanner's trade). But Luke is not in the least interested in such a preparation; on the contrary, he presents Peter as guided only by the heavenly power.

doing he should 'retrace the footsteps of Philip': he finds communities already present and 'does not baptize but performs miracles on both the living and the dead'; these miracle-stories differ from older ones in that names are mentioned; the 'Tabitha' story is dependent on the 'talitha' story; 'in verse 39 the χῆραι appear only as a knot of women mourners, but in verse 41 they represent a social class in their own right.'

More recent research has brought little fresh. Beyer comes to the conclusion that Peter frequently travelled round the communities in Palestine: 'We can see what care the Apostles took to keep the communities together in one great Church' (63). Bauernfeind harbours the cautiously expressed suspicion that perhaps 'in both cases the story was built entirely on the word of power, which circulated independently in . . . different forms' (139f.).

Now, what was Luke trying to tell his readers with these two stories? The answer must differ according to whether one enquires as to the meaning of the individual stories or their significance in context. The first relates the lesser miracle. Luke, who does not readily waste time or space on incidentals and is in addition bent on attaining a climax, has dispensed with everything superfluous and recounted it entirely in his own words, bringing out (in verse 34) the point that the real performer of the miracle is Jesus. The second story he has left relatively untouched. It showed the reader that where miracles were concerned the Apostles could stand comparison with the great prophets of the Old Testament—indeed, as was foreseen in John 14.12, could do the same mighty works as their Master, if not mightier still!

In addition to this edifying and theological significance we must consider what the two miracle-stories meant to Luke the historian. These πράξεις Πέτρου give Luke, the first to link the local legends in this way, the opportunity of bringing Peter down from Jerusalem in the direction of Caesarea, which was no small distance away. Secondly, they show how Christianity spread: Luke develops the first story's 'choral finale' into a mass conversion similar to that in 4.4, though without the sermon: Peter's actions speak louder for his cause than words. In the process, existing local congregations (founded by Philip?) are incorporated into the Jerusalem fold. The first miracle having converted the entire plain of Sharon, there remains for the second, though it is a far greater miracle, only its effect on the citizens of Joppa. And so, if we put the data together, the whole of the country west of the Jordan, from Ashdod northward almost as far as Caesarea, has now become Christian. Congregations have been established in Judaea, Samaria and Galilee (there are no reports about the country east of Jordan). The task in Palestine proper has been accomplished, and it is time for the Christian mission to seek goals farther afield. Phoenicia, Cyprus and Antioch are the nearest prospects; and they will be taken in hand . . . as soon as, through the conversion of Cornelius, Peter has legalized the mission to the Gentiles.

Now we can see with what thorough deliberation Luke has ordered his material. It is a feat of which not every writer would have been capable. For history does not write itself, as the source-critics have often thought.

25
ACTS 10:1–11:18
FIRST CONVERSION OF A GENTILE

[1] Now a man in Caesarea named Cornelius, a centurion of the cohort called the Italian, [2] —he was a pious man and worshipped God with all his house; he gave liberal alms to the (Jewish) people and prayed incessantly to God, [3] —saw clearly in a vision, about the ninth hour of the day, an angel of God coming in to him and saying to him, 'Cornelius!' [4] But he fixed his eyes upon him and, struck with fear, said, 'What is it, Lord?' And he said unto him: 'Your prayers and your alms have gone up for a memorial before God. [5] And now send men to Joppa, and fetch one Simon, who is also named Peter. [6] He is lodging with a tanner, Simon, whose house is by the sea.' [7] And when the angel who spoke to him had departed, he called two of his servants and a devout soldier from among those who waited on him; [8] and having recounted everything to them, he sent them to Joppa. [9] Now on the following day, as they were on their journey and drew near to the city, Peter went up on the housetop to pray, about the sixth hour. [10] And he became hungry and desired to eat. But while they made ready he fell into a trance; [11] and he saw the heaven opened, and a vessel like a great sheet descending, let down by four corners upon the earth; [12] in which were every kind of fourfooted and crawling beast of the earth and birds of the air. [13] And there came a voice to him: 'Rise, Peter: kill and eat!' [14] But Peter said, 'Not so, Lord; for I have never eaten anything common and unclean.' [15] And a voice came to him again the second time: 'What God has declared clean, declare not common!' [16] And this happened three times; and immediately the vessel was taken up into heaven. [17] Now while Peter was perplexed as to what the vision which he had seen might mean, behold, the men sent by Cornelius, having made enquiry for Simon's house, stood before the door, [18] and called and asked whether Simon, also called Peter, were lodging there. [19] And while Peter thought on the vision, the Spirit said to him, 'Behold, two men are seeking you. [20] Now arise, and get down and go with them, nothing doubting; for I have sent them.' [21] And Peter went down to the men and said, 'Behold, I am he whom you seek; what is the reason for which you have come?' [22] And they said: 'The centurion Cornelius, a righteous and God-fearing man, and well reported-of by all the nation of the Jews, was directed by a holy angel to have you brought to his house and to hear words

from you.' ²³ So he called them in and lodged them. And on the following day he arose and went off with them, and some of the brethren from Joppa accompanied him. ²⁴ And on the following day he entered into Caesarea. And Cornelius was waiting for them, and had called together his kinsmen and his close friends. ²⁵ And when it came to pass that Peter entered, Cornelius met him, and fell down at his feet and worshipped him. ²⁶ But Peter lifted him up, saying 'Stand up: I too am a man!' ²⁷ Still talking with him, he went in, and found many come together; ²⁸ and he said unto them: 'You yourselves know how unlawful it is for a Jew to associate with or visit one of another race; yet to me has God shown that we may call no man common or unclean. ²⁹ Therefore I came without gainsaying when I was sent for. Hence I ask with what intent you sent for me.' ³⁰ And Cornelius said: 'Four days ago about this hour, I was praying during the ninth hour in my house; and behold, a man stood before me in bright clothes, ³¹ and said: "Cornelius, your prayer has been heard, and your alms remembered before God. ³² Send therefore to Joppa, and summon Simon also named Peter: he is lodging in the house of Simon the tanner by the sea." ³³ So immediately I sent to you; and you have been so kind as to come. Now therefore we are all here present in the sight of God, to hear all that has been commanded you by the Lord.' ³⁴ And Peter opened his mouth and said: 'Truly I perceive that God has no favourites, ³⁵ but in every nation he who fears him and works righteousness is acceptable to him. ³⁶ The word he sent to the children of Israel, declaring good tidings of peace through Jesus Christ: he is Lord of all. ³⁷ You know what happened throughout all Judaea, beginning from Galilee after the baptism which John preached: ³⁸ Jesus of Nazareth, how God anointed him with the Holy Spirit and with power, who went about doing good, and healing all who were oppressed by the devil, for God was with him. ³⁹ And we are witnesses of all that he did both in the country of the Jews and in Jerusalem. Him they slew, hanging him on a tree. ⁴⁰ Him God raised up the third day, and gave him to be manifested, ⁴¹ not to all the people, but to witnesses chosen beforehand by God, to us who ate and drank with him after he rose from the dead. ⁴² And he charged us to preach to the people, and to testify that he is the judge of the living and the dead, ordained of God. ⁴³ To him all the prophets bear witness, that through his name everyone who believes on him shall receive forgiveness of sins.' ⁴⁴ While Peter was still speaking these words, the Holy Spirit fell on all who heard the word. ⁴⁵ And those of the circumcision who believed, who had come with Peter, were amazed that the gift of the Holy Spirit was poured out on the Gentiles also. ⁴⁶ For they heard them speak with tongues and magnify God. Then Peter answered: ⁴⁷ 'Can any man prohibit the water, so that these should not be baptized, who have received the Holy Spirit as well as we?' ⁴⁸ And he commanded them to be baptized in the name of Jesus Christ. Then they asked him to remain for some days.

CHAPTER 11

[1] Now the Apostles and the brethren who were in Judaea heard that the Gentiles also had received the word of God. [2] And when Peter came up to Jerusalem, those who were of the circumcision contended with him, [3] saying, 'You went in to men uncircumcised and ate with them'. [4] But Peter began and explained to them in order, saying: [5] 'I was in the city of Joppa praying, and in a trance I saw a vision: a vessel descending—like a great sheet let down by the four corners—from heaven, and it came even to me. [6] Looking closely at it, I observed and saw the fourfooted beasts of the earth, and the wild and the crawling beasts, and the birds of the air. [7] And I heard also a voice saying to me: "Rise, Peter: kill and eat!" [8] But I said, "Not so, Lord; for nothing common or unclean has ever entered my mouth." [9] But a voice answered the second time out of heaven: "What God has declared clean, declare not common!" [10] And this happened three times, and all was drawn up again into heaven. [11] And behold, immediately three men stood before the house in which we were, sent to me from Caesarea. [12] And the Spirit bade me go with them without demur. And these six brethren also accompanied me; and we entered into the man's house. [13] And he told us how he had seen the angel standing in his house and saying: "Send to Joppa, and fetch Simon, also called Peter, [14] who will speak to you words by which you shall be saved, you and all your house." [15] And as I began to speak, the Holy Spirit fell on them, even as on us at the beginning. [16] And I remembered the word of the Lord, how he said: "John indeed baptized with water, but you shall be baptized with the Holy Spirit." [17] If then God gave to them the same gift as also to us, when we believed on the Lord Jesus Christ, who was I, that I could withstand God?' [18] And when they heard this, they were silent, and glorified God, saying: 'Then to the Gentiles also has God granted repentance unto life!'

Bibliography:

T. R. S. Broughton, 'The Roman Army', *Beg.* V, 427–45 (on **10**.1); F. Dornseiff, see § 1 bibl.; W. C. van Unnik, 'De Achtergrond en Betekenis van Hand. **10**.4 en 35', *Ned. Theol. Tijdschr.* 3 (1948/9), 260–83 and 336–54; L. H. Feldmann, 'Jewish "Sympathizers" in Classical Literature and Inscriptions', *TAPA* (see § 65 bibl.), 1950, 200–8; J. Maiworm, 'Fremde Gestalten des Verklärten', *Bibel und Kirche*, 1954, 100–22; J. Munck, see § 22 bibl.; A. W. Argyle, see § 21 bibl.; H. J. Cadbury, *The Book of Acts in History*, 1955, 16, 59, 69, 76, 151, and 160; U. Wilckens, *Die Missionsreden der Apg.*, 1963², 46–50 and 63–70; Conzelmann 61–7.

F. W. Dillistone, 'πρόσπεινος (Acts **10**.10)', *Exp.Tim.* 46 (1934–5), 380;
J. Sint, 'Schlachten und Opfern (Acta **10**.13;**11**.7)', *ZkTh* 78 (1956), 194–205;
E. F. F. Bishop, 'Acts **10**.25', *Exp.Tim* 61 (1949–50), 31; H. Schürmann, 'Es
tut Not, der Worte des Herrn zu gedenken (Acta **10**.35)', *Katech. Blätter*
79 (1954), 254–61; H. Schlier, 'Die Entscheidung für die Heidenmission in
der Urchristenheit', *Evg. Missionzeitsch.* 3 (1942), 166–82 and 208–12; U.
Wilckens, 'Kerygma und Evangelium bei Lukas (Apg. **10**.24–43)', *ZNW*
49 (1958), 223–37.

VERSE 1: Herod the Great named the rebuilt 'Straton's Tower' Καισάρεια
Σεβαστή in honour of the emperor.[1] The city with its excellent harbour was
the seat of the Roman proconsul and the station of a Roman garrison.
Cornelius was a very common name, since thousands of slaves freed by Sulla
had taken his *nomen*. A centurion (ἑκατοντάρχης) was an officer, risen from
the ranks, with a hundred men under his command. The σπεῖρα Ἰταλική was
probably the *Cohors II Miliaria Italica Civium Romanorum Voluntariorum*.[2]

VERSE 2: εὐσεβής, 'pious', denotes a personal quality: φοβούμενος τὸν
θεόν can mean the same (see verse 35), but may also (like σεβόμενος τὸν θεόν)
imply membership of the group of Gentiles who took part in synagogue
services without, by adopting the whole of the law, becoming really προσήλυτοι
i.e., fully-entitled members of the Jewish religious community. Because
they were uncircumcised, such 'God-fearers' were looked on by the Jews as
Gentiles, and therefore unclean.[3] The piety of Cornelius is described in terms
reminiscent, in the association of prayer and alms, of Matt. **6**.2–6, I Peter
4.7f., II Clem. **16**.4 and Didache **15**.4. ὁ λαός: here the Jewish community
(cf. Luke **7**.4f.). 'Constantly praying' is hyperbolical—needless to say, Cornelius must see to his military duties too.

VERSE 3: ὅραμα: see **9**.10. The mention of the ninth hour (see **3**.1)
shows not merely Cornelius' piety but at the same time (like φανερῶς) the
reality of the occurrence; it takes place in broad daylight.

VERSE 4: On ἀτενίσας see **1**.10. In the presence of heavenly messengers,
mortals feel terror; here instead of the customary 'Fear not!' there follows

---

[1] See Bauer, *Wb* 782 s.v. 2, with references and literature.

[2] This battalion of archers (*miliaria* indicates a nominal strength of 1,000 men) was
probably an auxiliary unit formed originally in Italy from freedmen, on whom Roman
citizenship was conferred. It was later transferred to Syria, and is known to have been
there from shortly before A.D. 69 down into the second century. In the East its numbers will
have been supplemented by native Syrians. As a centurion, Cornelius possessed Roman
citizenship. These details from T. R. S. Broughton, 'The Roman Army' (Note 33 in *Beg.*
V, 427–45) esp. pp. 429f. and 441–3. In the years before Herod Agrippa's death, Roman
troops cannot have been quartered in Caesarea. Presumably Luke has transferred the situation of his own time to the earlier period. Bauernfeind also (144) considers it possible that
the author here has slipped into an anachronism. Bruce (215) dates the event before 41.

[3] Cf. Bauer, *Wb* 469 s.v. ἑκατοντάρχης, with bibliography; 1478 s.v. σέβω 1a; 1707 s.v.
φοβέω 2a; K. Lake, 'Proselytes and God-fearers', Note 8 in *Beg.* V, 74–96; Billerbeck II,
715–23; only there are no 'half-proselytes'.

in biblical terms[1] the comforting assurance that Cornelius' prayers and alms have commended him to God.[2]

VERSE 5: We now see the point of 9.43. Σίμωνά τινα: Peter is unknown to Cornelius. We are not meant to imagine that Cornelius has been praying urgently for admittance to the Christian community—of which, despite verse 37 (see notes there), he does not even know. This community also has not so far admitted any Gentile.

VERSE 6: The 'surname' Peter serves to distinguish this Simon from his host the tanner (see notes on 9.43), who lives by the sea on account of his trade (Holtzmann, 75). It is not said what God had in store for Cornelius or why Peter should be sent for. This of course keeps the reader in suspense but, what is more important, also shows that both Peter and Cornelius act in blind obedience to God, the sole governor of all the action.

VERSE 7: The departure of the angel is depicted as just as real a process as the commissioning and sending of the messengers. The 'devout' soldier—the narrator doubtless thought of him too as φοβούμενος—was probably one of Cornelius' orderlies (*Beg.* IV, 114).

VERSE 8: Caesarea is about thirty miles from Joppa. Leaving in the afternoon, the messengers walk throughout the night (with, of course, pauses for rest) and reach Joppa about noon the next day. This ends the first scene, which we may call 'The Vision of Cornelius'. The second—'The Vision of Peter'—extends from verse 9 to verse 16.—Bruce (217) has the messengers ride.

VERSE 9: The sixth hour (noon) was not a fixed time of prayer.[3] The flat roof, with its parapet (Deut. 22.8) and awning, offered rest and a cool breeze.

VERSE 10: πρόσπεινος, 'hungry'; the narrator is paving the way for the ensuing vision.[4]

VERSE 11: Peter sees[5] the sky open and a kind of receptacle resembling a large sheet lowered to earth by the four corners.[6]

---

[1] For ἀνέβησαν see Ex. 2.23 LXX; for μνημόσυνον Ex. 17.14 LXX; also Matt. 26.13, Mk. 14.9.

[2] Verse 31 reproduces ἀνέβησαν εἰς μνημόσυνον κτλ. simply by 'are remembered before God'. The connection with μνημόσυνον = אַזְכָּרָה Lev. 2.1f. (the burnt part of the meal-offering, which is to make God attentive; so Wendt) is too remote.

[3] Billerbeck (II, 693f.) ponders whether Peter's prayer was a belated morning prayer or an early Minhah-prayer (see above on 3.1). But Luke is not striving for antiquarian accuracy; ὅραμα and prayer for him belong together.

[4] In Greece and Rome the *prandium* (=ἄριστον) was taken about noon. Among the Jews (Billerbeck II, 204ff.) breakfast was eaten in the forenoon and the main meal in the late afternoon. The text does not suggest that it was a case of one of the usual mealtimes here.

[5] θεωρεῖ here and εὑρίσκει in v. 27 are among the few cases of a historic present in Luke: *Beg.* IV, 115.

[6] The Western text, for which only a few witnesses are available (*Beg.* III, pp. CXCII and 93), seems to have read 'a vessel bound at the four corners and lowered'—the sheet lowered from heaven seemed inconceivable.

VERSE 12: This enumeration recalls Gen. **1**.24, even to its omission of fish (hard to contain live in a sheet!).[1] Rom. **1**.23 shows that such lists were customary.

VERSE 13: It remains mysteriously uncertain whose voice resounds. ἀναστάς has roughly the sense of 'Come on, then!' (see **1**.15). θύω means 'slaughter', not 'sacrifice'.[2]

VERSE 14: As in Ezek. **4**.14, the refusal is expressed in the words μηδαμῶς, κύριε. Peter has always adhered strictly to the food-laws and never eaten anything 'unclean or common'—a hendiadys. The possible presence of clean animals in the sheet is disregarded.[3]

VERSE 15: *Pace* Torrey (7), πάλιν ἐκ δευτέρου is not a Semitism, but a locution found seven times in LXX and also in the Papyri. 'What God has declared clean (hence also made clean) declare not unclean!'[4] This declaration of purity is promulgated here and now.[5]

VERSE 16: The double repetition[6] of invitation, refusal and rejection of this refusal shows that while Peter staunchly resists, the heavenly voice stands by its verdict. It is only the dialogue which is repeated; the 'sheet' is then finally drawn back aloft. And there ends the scene, leaving the reader, no less than Peter, with a riddle on his mind.

VERSES 17f. open a new scene, 'Peter receives the Messengers', which lasts until verse 23a. Peter is sorely embarrassed over the meaning of the vision—the narrator seems to discount any question of taking it literally.[7] Thus, though lost in meditation, he has returned to normal consciousness from the state of ἔκστασις when the messengers of Cornelius appear at Simon's door,[8] to which they have asked their way (διερωτήσαντες).

---

[1] τετράποδα καὶ ἑρπετὰ καὶ θηρία τῆς γῆς. Correspondingly the θηρία also, in the present verse too weakly supported, are introduced at **11**.6. The birds are mentioned at Gen. **6**.20.

[2] According to Billerbeck (II, 708) θύω corresponds to the Hebrew שָׁחַט: kill ritually. Unclean animals admittedly cannot be ritually slaughtered. But here in fact the distinction of clean and unclean is done away!

[3] Wendt (180) adopts as an expedient the idea that Peter thought indiscriminate eating was expected of him. This is highly artificial.—The suggestion that the clean animals through their association with the unclean would themselves become unclean misses fire: beasts are clean or unclean by nature. Clean animals therefore do not lose their purity through contact with unclean—otherwise one could never be certain of the ritual purity of any clean beast.

[4] καθαρίζω = to declare clean, e.g. Lev. **13**.13 LXX.

[5] *Beg.* IV, 115 conjectures an allusion to Mk. **7**.14ff., while the words there καθαρίζων πάντα τὰ βρώματα could be an allusion to Peter's vision!—But our text in reality does not speak of clean foods.

[6] ἐπὶ τρίς: Hellenistic for τρίς = three times: Preuschen, 65.

[7] In Barn. **10**.1ff. the animals listed in the Mosaic food-laws are allegorically interpreted of men, but not declared clean.

[8] A tanner does not possess an imposing house, separated from the street by gatehouse (πυλών) and courtyard. We must therefore translate here: 'They came to the door and asked, shouting aloud: Is Simon, also called Peter, lodging here?'

VERSE 19: That Peter, lost in thought, does not hear their call, enables the narrator to substitute heavenly for earthly motivation: it is the Spirit which tells Peter, 'Two[1] men are looking for you!'

VERSE 20: The Spirit does not explain the vision (which Peter himself comprehends in verse 28), but directs Peter to go down[2] and, without hesitation, follow the men whom 'I have sent'—Spirit and angel (verses 4f.) both represent the same divine power.

VERSE 21: No one having heard the messengers call, it is Peter himself who opens to them: the writer is concerned to show that he, and no other Jew, lets the Gentiles in. Luke is not aiming at realism, but wishes to present the Spirit-moved actions of Peter, who now enquires what the messengers want of him.[3]

VERSE 22 briefly recapitulates the contents of verses 1 to 5. What is new is that Cornelius wishes to 'hear words from' Peter. But the general expression also maintains the tension unresolved. The author does not feel it extravagant to say that Cornelius enjoys a high reputation[4] with the whole Jewish nation.[5]

VERSE 23a: Peter no longer recoils from entertaining Gentiles. He acts rather as a host than as a lodger, but this simplifies the narrative and concentrates the interest on the Apostle's actions, which alone are important.

VERSE 23b leads to the next scene, 'Peter comes to Cornelius' (verses 23b–33). The tired messengers rest before returning with Peter to Caesarea, accompanied by some Jewish Christians from Joppa, who later (**11**.12) serve as witnesses. —ἀναστὰς ἐξῆλθεν is a LXX locution (see **1**.15).

VERSE 24: Cornelius is expecting Peter's arrival[6] and, prompted by the angel (**11**.14), has invited together his relatives and closest[7] friends. So the

---

[1] So B. D and the late MSS omit the number; A C e gig sa bo read: three men. Ropes (*Beg.* III, 94f.) considers the number 2 correct; the soldier sent as escort is not a messenger. Wendt (181 n. 1) and also Zahn, Loisy and Bauernfeind hold that δύο arose from mechanical reference to verse 7 (two servants); Holtzmann, Preuschen and Beyer read 'two'. Luke's source will have spoken of two messengers, since it did not regard the soldier as one. This does not prevent the summary mention of three men in **11**.11.

[2] In verse 20 the classical ἀλλά before the imperative is combined with the LXX usage of ἀναστάς and the imperative (cf. Bl.-Debr. § 448, 3).

[3] D syʰ have him speak even more formally: 'What do you wish, or what is the reason . . .' We can see what the second century considered edifying.

[4] In the same general terms it is said of the centurion at Capernaum (Lk. **7**.1): 'he loves our nation' (ἔθνος).

[5] Non-Jews speak of the ἔθνος τῶν Ἰουδαίων instead of the λαός.—χρηματίζομαι means in Hellenistic paganism also 'to receive a divine instruction'; it thus fits well in the mouth of a Gentile: *Beg.* IV, 117. —μαρτυροῦμαι ὑπό = to stand in good repute with, has been documented by Deissmann in an inscription from the second half of the first century A.D. (*Neue Bibelstudien*, n. 95; ET *Bible Studies*, 1901).

[6] εἰσελθεῖν here means entry into the house.

[7] ἀναγκαῖος (see Bauer, *Wb* 104), like *necessarius*, of the natural bonds of kinship and friendship: cf. Jos. *Ant.* VII, 350.

audience is set for Peter's speech and, at the same time, the founding of the congregation in Caesarea is prepared for.

VERSE 25: ἐγένετο τοῦ εἰσελθεῖν[1] is 'on the model of the LXX (=Hebr. לְ)': Bl.-Debr. § 400, 7. 'As Peter was in the act of entering' (the gateway or 'pylon'), 'Cornelius, who had come to meet him, threw himself at his feet' —as if he were a heavenly visitant.

VERSE 26: Peter makes him rise with the words, 'I too am only a man'— Luke's way of illustrating his exemplary humility.

VERSE 27: 'And talking to him,[2] Peter went in'—i.e. from the 'gateway' to the house itself, where the gathering awaited him.

VERSE 28: Peter begins by impressing on his audience (and the reader!) how unprecedented is his coming: it is unlawful[3] for any Jew to mix with members of another race[4]—the word 'Gentile' is avoided. But God has shown him that one should call no man unclean[5]—the reference is without any doubt to the hitherto enigmatic vision.—Bruce (222) renders ἀθέμιτον as 'tabu'.

VERSE 29: In making God's guidance responsible for Peter's not resisting the invitation, it is primarily on his readers that Luke seeks to impress the point. The same motive is ultimately behind his exhaustive treatment of what follows. Why[6] Cornelius sent for the Apostle is only very gradually made clear.

VERSE 30: The meaning strictly can only be: 'Four days ago at this hour I was "saying nones" in my home'.[7] But the extant text implies 'From the fourth day up to this hour' etc. Apparently the ἀπό, which may denote an interval of time (Bauer *Wb*, 171, s.v. II 2a), misled an early copyist into inserting a μέχρι before ταύτης ὥρας, the indication of 'time at which', possibly under the influence of the idea of the constantly praying Cornelius

---

[1] The idea of purpose (Wendt, 181) is not present here. Cf. the apocryphal Acts of Barnabas 7: ὡς δὲ ἐγένετο τοῦ τελέσαι αὐτοὺς διδάσκοντας (*Beg*. IV, 117). D understood εἰσελθεῖν of entrance into the city, and expanded the text accordingly: 'As Peter drew near Caesarea, one of the servants (of Cornelius, stationed at the city boundary to give warning) ran ahead and reported that he had come. Cornelius sprang up and going to meet him . . .'.

[2] Wellhausen (20) finds no place for this conversation. Luke however does not want to draw a realistic picture, but to show Peter's affability.

[3] ἀθέμιτος: Hellenistic for ἀθέμιστος; D βέλτιον ἐπίστασθε='you know well'; the comparative in Hellenistic Greek often stands for the positive.

[4] This too is not a realistic description of the situation: diaspora Jews were not hermetically sealed off from dealings with the Gentiles: Overbeck (159) recalls Jos. *Ant*. XX, 34ff. But here the intention is to make it plain that God has utterly demolished the barrier which existed for the Jews. ἀλλόφυλος: often in LXX.

[5] The author thus shows how Peter's vision is to be understood: it is not a question of food, but of people. So also Wikenhauser (*Apg*. 97).

[6] τίνι λόγῳ: *dativus causae*, Jacquier 325, referring to Eurip. *Iph. Taur*. 1358: τίνι λόγῳ πορθμεύετε.—μεταπεμφθείς (μεταπέμπομαι in passive only here) is contemporaneous with ἦλθον.

[7] This translation, which of course contains an anachronism, is taken from *Beg*. IV, 118. The mention of the ninth hour is not meant to give the exact time, but to emphasize the time of prayer.

(verse 2: διὰ παντός).[1] The following description of the angel draws upon LXX: καὶ ἰδού, ἐνώπιόν σου; the angel coming to the rescue of the Jews in II Macc. **11**.8 appears ἐν λευκῇ ἐσθῆτι (cf. Acts **1**.10).

VERSE 31 repeats more simply (and thus elucidates) what was expressed with fitting solemnity in verse 4b.

VERSE 32 summarizes verse 6.

VERSE 33: ἐξαυτῆς (understand τῆς ὥρας) = 'at once'. καλῶς ἐποίησας παραγενόμενος[2] = 'you were good enough to come'; an expression of gratitude often encountered in the Papyri (*Beg*. IV, 118f.). ἐνώπιον τοῦ θεοῦ —another solemn LXX locution: Luke has the devout Cornelius too speak and think 'biblically'; wherever the Apostle appears and speaks, his hearers are in the presence of God.[3]

VERSE 34: Peter must now speak (verses 34–43). However, Luke may not yet have him proclaim the baptism of Gentiles, especially as Cornelius still knows nothing at all of Christ. He therefore inserts a sermon corresponding in outline to the speeches of Chapter 1: link with the situation, vv. 34f.; kerygma, vv. 36–41; scriptural proof, v. 43a; summons to repentance, vv. 42 and 43b (Dibelius, *Studies*, 110f.). As in **8**.35, ἀνοίξας τὸ στόμα expresses the solemnity of this decisive moment; the same applies to ἐπ' ἀληθείας (Dan. Θ2.8: ἐπ' ἀληθείας οἶδα ἐγώ). God is not προσωπολήμπτης:[4] he makes no unfair discriminations in admitting to Christian salvation. See Wilckens, *ZNW* 49 (1958), 223–37.

VERSE 35: 'Whoever fears God and does right is acceptable to him' (δεκτός is frequent in LXX): there is no racial barrier to Christian salvation. The author is not thinking of Israel's past, but of the challenge now posed by the gospel.

VERSE 36: Paul's speech in Pisidian Antioch provides an excellent parallel to the section of this sermon which now begins. Both are addressed to the same kind of audience: Paul's speech to Jews and 'Godfearing men', into which latter category fall Cornelius and, as Luke must have seen it, the centurion's friends and relatives. **13**.26 helps to unravel the complicated

---

[1] D once again has recognized the difficulty of the transmitted text and attempted to improve it: 'From the third day to this hour I fasted (again the three-day fast before baptism; see 9.6) and as I was praying about this hour . . .'. This does not remove the defect, but instead introduces the fasting. Zahn (346) adopts this text, but tones down the νηστεύειν to a 'half-fasting'.

[2] D (which here constantly expands) has this coming too already foretold in the angel's speech, and makes Cornelius expressly request it; to καλῶς ἐποίησας it adds ἐν τάχει: in D's view, that Peter should come is a matter of course, but that he came immediately is a special kindness.

[3] D was puzzled by this 'before God', and replaced it by 'before thee.' Loisy (443) would much prefer this, if it were better attested.

[4] Deut. **10**.17 כָּנִים אִשָּׂא: to be partisan (as a judge, to prefer unjustly). Cf. Rom. **2**.11, Eph. **6**.9, Col. **3**.25, I Pet. **1**.17, James **2**.1, 9, I Clem. **1**.3, Barn. **4**.12, Polyc. *Phil*. **6**.1.

syntax: 'to us is the word of this salvation sent forth' corresponds to the clause 'He sent the word to the children of Israel'. The λόγος is in both contexts the Christian message of salvation, not the 'Word' of John 1.1. In sending this message (through the Apostles) God declares peace between himself and man: a peace established by Jesus Christ. The 'aside' concerning 'Jesus Christ' ('he is Lord of all') seeks to reconcile the restriction of God's announcements to Israel with the universality of salvation. This difficult sentence is therefore to be rendered: 'God sent the word[1] to the children of Israel, "bringing the good tidings"[2] of peace through Jesus Christ;[3] he is Lord of all.'[4] —So also Bruce, 225.

VERSE 37: While in 13.23ff. the proclamation of Jesus precedes the statement about the destination of the redemption he has brought, here it follows. It is presupposed that even every 'Godfearing' person in Palestine knows of the events[5] involving Jesus, which had taken place throughout Judaea,[6] beginning with[7] Galilee, after the baptism preached by John the Baptist.[8] What is assumed to be known is thus an account which like Mark begins with the preaching of the Baptist, not with the nativity stories.

VERSE 38: These events are now more closely described. Luke[9] lifts Ἰησοῦν τὸν ἀπὸ Ναζαρέθ from the ensuing ὡς-clause in order to place it in the emphatic first position,[10] picking it up again later by αὐτόν. God anointed Jesus (at baptism) with the Holy Spirit and miraculous power (Isa. 61.1, already quoted *in extenso* at Luke 4.18), thus making him the Χριστός.

---

[1] Here Ps. 107 (106).20 is used: ἀπέστειλεν τὸν λόγον αὐτοῦ καὶ ἰάσατο αὐτοὺς καὶ ἐρρύσατο αὐτοὺς ἐκ τῶν διαφθορῶν αὐτῶν. The intrusive ὅν will have originated through dittography of the preceding (λόγ)ον in an early copy. B A 81 do not have it; in ℵ* it appears to have been immediately cancelled, according to Ropes probably even before the codex left the scriptorium (*Beg.* III, 98 n. 36).

[2] Isa. 52.7.

[3] 'Through Jesus Christ' belongs not to εὐαγγελιζόμενος but to εἰρήνην. Peter sees in Jesus not a proclaimer of salvation (=εἰρήνη = peace between God and man), but the one through whom it is brought about.

[4] Properly a pagan predicate of God: κύριος τῶν ὅλων or πάντων, 'Lord of all'; see Cadbury, 'The Titles of Jesus in Acts' (Note 29 in *Beg.* V, 354–74) 361f., with abundant references. Here πάντων is meant personally. Jesus is Lord of all, both Jews and Gentiles. Cf. Rom. 10.12.

[5] As in Lk. 2.15, ῥῆμα = 'event', not 'word'; *Beg.* IV, 120.

[6] Galilee, mentioned later, is included in 'all Judaea' and Preuschen (68) considers it an interpolation.

[7] ἀρξάμενος = 'from . . . to' is already classical usage: Bl.-Debr. § 419, 3. The inconsistency ῥῆμα . . . ἀρξάμενος, corrected by 𝔓⁴⁶ L P, arose according to Bl.-Debr. § 137, 3 through the adoption of ἀρξάμενος ἀπὸ τῆς Γαλιλαίας from Lk. 23.5. Similarly Wendt (184 n.1). But the nominative absolute ἀρξάμενος appears in Hellenistic Greek to have acquired a quasi-adverbial significance: *Beg.* IV, 14 on 1.27 and 120 on 10.36ff.

[8] The parallel in 13.24: προκηρύξαντος Ἰωάννου . . . βάπτισμα μετανοίας παντὶ τῷ λαῷ Ἰσραήλ.

[9] See e.g. 1.2, 4.33, 5.35, 9.20, 11.29, 12.25, 19.4. In the present passage Ἰησοῦν is picked up again by αὐτόν.

[10] Wendt (183) and others take it in apposition to ῥῆμα.

With εὐεργετῶν Luke perhaps plays on the predicate of Hellenistic rulers, εὐεργέτης (Luke **22**.25): *Beg.* IV, 121. ἰώμενος (see note on **9**.34) and καταδυναστεύω also probably betray the hand of Luke: the reference is to such healings and exorcisms as are found in Mark; they prove that God was with Jesus (Acts **2**.22). Passages like the present help us to understand why the Synoptists place such emphasis on Jesus' miracles.

VERSE 39: The twelve Apostles, in whose name Peter is speaking, are eyewitnesses of the 'life of Jesus' from his baptism onwards, and thereby the guarantors of the one true tradition of the Church. Galilee is included in 'the country of the Jews': Luke has no interest in bringing out at this point the originally Galilean character of the Christian movement. On ὃν καί see **1**.11. Once again we have one of those apparent relative clauses which are really main clauses introduced by a relative: 'him they killed, hanging him on a tree' (cf. Deut. **21**.22). This passage also belongs to early Christian scriptural proof (see **5**.30).

VERSES 40f.: The Lucan-formulated kerygma is continued: God raised Jesus on the third day[1] and 'gave[2] him to be manifested' to 'witnesses chosen by God' (cf. Luke **24**.48 and Acts **1**.8), namely, the Apostles, who ate and drank with him (cf. Luke **24**.30 and Acts **1**.4).

VERSE 42: τῷ λαῷ = to the Jews. 'This[3] is he who is ordained of God to be the judge of the living and the dead' (cf. Acts **17**.31 and Intro. § 1, IVb, p. 5 above). This is the function of the 'Son of Man' in the earliest 'Son of Man' passages in the Synoptics. Up to this point the sermon has reckoned almost solely with the mission to the Jews, which of course according to Acts is the only one so far existing. But Luke did not see this as conflicting with **1**.8.

VERSE 43: The πάντα τὸν πιστεύοντα crashes through the barrier which is still intact in the preceding verse. The similar passages in **3**.23 and **5**.31 were still addressed to Jews. For 'all the prophets', see Luke **24**.27. For 'remission of sins through his name', see Luke **24**.47 (*Beg.* IV, 122). So ends this section of the speech.

VERSE 44: Peter's address is really at an end. The alleged interruption (by the coming of the Spirit) is a device on the part of the author (cf. Dibelius, *Studies*, 57 and 178), though one here fraught with quite special significance (see **11**.15). τὸν λόγον evidently means the missionary sermon just delivered by Peter. The Spirit falls on all 'the hearers', i.e. Cornelius, his relatives and his friends—not Peter and the Joppa Christians, who are rather the witnesses to attest this event (*pace* Wendt, 185).

---

[1] D d sy^hms read 'after the third day', and add to v. 41 καὶ συνεστράφημεν μετὰ τὸ ἀναστῆναι ἐκ νεκρῶν ἡμέρας μ. The addition '40 days' is also found in E e perp gig t sa: *Beg.* III, 100 n. 41.

[2] Cf. Ps. **16**.8-11 in Acts **2**.27; δώσεις τὸν ὅσιον . . . ἰδεῖν, and Acts **14**.3.

[3] Cf. Acts **9**.20, 22 and **17**.3.

VERSE 45: 'The believers of the circumcision'—the Christians from Joppa, who are thus Jewish Christians and here characterize the attitude of such. 'On the Gentiles also': the incident is not taken as an isolated phenomenon of little importance, but as a decision of God affecting the whole of the pagan world (see comments on **11**.18 and **15**.7).

VERSE 46: There is no question of 'foreign languages' here; as in **19**.6, only ecstatic utterance is in the writer's mind.

VERSE 47: The question is addressed to the six Jewish Christians, but at the same time to the reader: '*Can* anyone deny these water and[1] make them go without baptism . . .?' On κωλύω see **8**.36. μήτι expects the answer 'No!'

VERSE 48: Peter does not himself baptize; Luke is no doubt reproducing here the position obtaining in his own day. *Pace* Wendt 186, this has nothing to do with I Cor. **1**.17. No trinitarian baptismal formula is yet employed (cf. **8**.16 and **19**.5). Peter's staying 'for some days' with the Christians of Caesarea (his acceding to their request is implicit in the context) demonstrates that he regards them as Christians in the full sense and as 'clean'.

CHAPTER 11

VERSE 1: Here begins the final episode, 'Peter's self-justification in Jerusalem'. It ends with **11**.18. Not only the Jerusalem congregation with the Apostles but the Christians in all Judaea hear—cf. **8**.14 and **11**.22—that 'the Gentiles have received God's word too!' This formula shows (like **10**.45 already) that Luke is presenting this conversion not as an unimportant isolated case, but as a fundamental turning-point (Loisy, 453).

VERSE 2: Jerusalem's high-lying site produced the technical terms ἀναβαίνειν ('come up') and καταβαίνειν ('go down') in respect of journeys to or from Jerusalem. διακρίνομαι πρός τινα: as in Ezek. **20**.35f. (translation of עִם Niph'al) = 'contend' in the sense of 'litigate', 'remonstrate' with someone. οἱ ἐκ περιτομῆς: this appellation (cf. **10**.45) explains the attitude of the primitive congregation towards the 'uncircumcised' mentioned in verse 3.[2] The Western text has a pious expansion of this verse.

VERSE 3: On ὅτι before direct speech see Bl.-Debr. § 397, 6 and § 470, 1. The accusation is directed only against table-fellowship: Luke does not make the Jerusalem congregation protest openly against the baptism of the Gentiles.

VERSE 4: This speech of Peter's too is introduced with solemnity. It is not stated that Peter is defending himself. It is enough for him to tell his audience what happened to open up for them the right decision.

---

[1] 'The genitive of the articular infinitive ... belongs to a higher level of the *koine* (often in LXX ...)': Bl.-Debr. § 400 (and appendix). Here we have not the final but the consecutive significance. Cf. Lk. **4**.42, **24**.16; Acts **14**.18, **20**.20, 27.

[2] Wikenhauser, *Apg.* 101: 'those of the circumcision' means the narrow-minded members of the community. But the text does not yield this.

VERSES 5–16: The report does not schematically repeat all that has been said before; this would only weary the reader. Bauernfeind (142) rightly points to the narrator's licence used by Luke in Acts: 'He prefers a sizeable self-contradiction to a dreary self-repetition.' We find such a self-contradiction, for example, in the implication of verses 11f. that the six Jewish Christians (their number is here mentioned for the first time) were already in Peter's lodgings at Joppa when the messengers arrived.[1] Again, as the readers now know why Cornelius sent for Peter, 11.14 makes the angel already disclose to the former that Peter will speak words by which he and his house will be saved. This presupposes a finished speech from Peter, and with 10.34–43 is somewhat contradicted by the statement of 11.15 that the Spirit fell on the hearers the moment Peter *began* to speak. Luke presents it in this way because then the coming of the Spirit has even more unexpected and decisive effect. The speech in Chapter 11 is comprehensible only to the readers of the book, not to Peter's audience in Jerusalem. Luke makes Peter (like Paul in 20.35) end with a (reputed) logion of Jesus.[2]

VERSE 17: If God has given the same gift of the Spirit to the new Christians as to the old,[3] how could Peter stand in his way?[4] The reference of course is not to the Spirit-baptism which has already taken place, but to the water-baptism clearly willed by God. This reproduces 10.47 in a different form.

VERSE 18: Peter's opponents (that they are the eleven other Apostles together with the primitive community is not stated, as too shocking) hold their peace and recognize that God has now admitted the Gentiles to the community—and hence to the way of salvation implied in μετάνοια εἰς ζωήν—without their first having to become Jews. Once again, the formulation (τοῖς ἔθνεσιν—cf. 10.45 and 11.1) shows that what is happening is no negligible special case but a revolution of principle.

The Tübingen critics already found in Chapter 10 an important point of attack. According to ZELLER, 'the essential content of this story is . . .

---

[1] While B ℵ A D read ἦμεν, the versions and thus the MSS they used read ἤμην: *Beg.* III, 104. This avoids the contradiction.

[2] *Beg.* IV, 126 and 263 refer to Lk. 22.61 and 24.6ff.; I Clem. 13.1, 46.7; Polyc. *Phil.* 2.3.

[3] 'πιστεύσασιν seems to relate both to the newly converted Christians and to those won earlier': Bauernfeind 152. Here as there faith is the presupposition of endowment with the Spirit.

[4] Two ideas here flow together: 1. Who was I, to prevent God? 2. How was I in a position to prevent God? D (with some other witnesses) has misjudged the context in its alteration τοῦ μὴ δοῦναι αὐτοῖς πνεῦμα ἅγιον πιστεύσασιν ἐπ' αὐτῷ. Zahn (365 n. 90) finds in this reading, treated as genuine, confirmation that 'it is not the transitory possession by the . . . Spirit, but . . . baptism' which is 'the form and presupposition for the bestowal of the Spirit for permanent indwelling'. The 'understanding reader', to whom Zahn appeals at this point, will nevertheless say to himself that Luke here as in Chapter 2 is describing the ecstatic Spirit and not an invisible permanent indwelling of the baptismal Spirit such as Zahn's dogmatic position requires.

unhistorical, whether what lies behind it be the insignificant baptism of a proselyte or no fact of history at all' (190). In 1852 Bruno BAUER accused Acts of giving to Peter the glory of the Gentile mission (see Intro. § 2, p. 21 above), and in 1870 OVERBECK repeated the assertion that the author of Acts shows Paul's mission 'prepared and legitimized' by the precedent set by Peter (150). But the less radical critics were very slow and reluctant to acknowledge the truth of this.

B. WEISS vehemently resisted the contention that in the Cornelius story the author of Acts designed to 'make Peter the Apostle to the Gentiles': according to Acts **15**.7 the episode occurred even before the Stephen affair (*Einl.*[2], 129 n. 2 and 567 n. 2; ET). 'In fact the story in no way settles the issue of whether the mission to the Gentiles is lawful or, for that matter, obligatory, as it was an absolutely exceptional divine intervention that compelled Peter to preach the Gospel to Cornelius. Nor does it even settle the question of whether believing Gentiles should be baptized, as in Cornelius' case baptism was preceded by the pouring-out of the Spirit. What is more, it was on neither of these issues that the primitive community took exception, but solely on the point that Peter had consorted and eaten with the uncircumcised, as a law-abiding Jew must not, and we further see from this why the original Apostles at first simply could not think of a mission to the Gentiles.' Accordingly B. Weiss ascribed Chapter 10 to his Jewish Christian source (while conceding **11**.1–18 to the compiler). Needless to say, SPITTA assigned the whole section to his legendary source B (153–7). HILGENFELD, still more critical, laid the whole at the door of the editor (*ZwTh* (1895) 486ff.).

Unlike B. Weiss, WENDT saw in **11**.1–18 the 'foundation of tradition' and attributed Chapter 10 to the author of Acts (177f. n. 1). WELLHAUSEN rejected this: 'Baur is right to consider the story of Captain Cornelius an unhistorical fabrication. Only the view ... that the Gentiles ... with whose reception it is chiefly concerned are σεβόμενοι is certainly correct ... It is probably right to see in the captain of Capernaum the model of Captain Cornelius' (20). PREUSCHEN, agreeing, added: 'The conversion of Cornelius is a pendant to the baptism of the Ethiopian treasurer and the fundamental justification of the Gentile mission' (63). In **11**.1–18 Preuschen found a parallel narrative to **15**.1–29, by which 'the author or redactor has made Chapter 15 utterly incomprehensible' (69). BEYER's judgment was uncommonly trenchant: 'At the turning-point in the history of the Christian mission stands one man alone: Peter. Admittedly, he stands there wholly as a tool in the hands of God, who alone is really active. That is the historical picture presented by Acts. We must however say—it is false' (69). The author has indeed 'a lively sense ... of the dangers to be overcome', but on the other hand the Church was even at that early time inclined 'to regard its own history as a frictionless, God-willed, logical process'.

BAUERNFEIND is more mild in his verdict. According to him, Luke's conclusion is 'that, though perhaps not the first nor yet the second to do so (see comments on **11**.19), the Apostles did in due course open the way to the Gentiles' (141). In **11**.15 Bauernfeind traces a 'remnant of pre-Lucan tradition, which instead of the speech **10**.34ff. contained just a brief maxim: "Whoever fears God is acceptable to him"—a slogan, perhaps, of Peter himself . . .' (149). The vision must originally have been recounted with reference to food: 'You may—indeed must, if necessary—set aside all the commandments to do with meats when your service of the Gospel requires it' (145).

DIBELIUS shares Bauernfeind's conjecture as to the original meaning of the vision (*Studies*, 111f.) but, for the rest, goes his own way. At one time Peter 'incidentally and not on principle' converted a God-fearing Gentile by the name of Cornelius. Out of this incident the Christians made a 'simple conversion-legend'. 'Evidently the congregations commemorated the conversions of persons of social standing in the form of such "pious" tales' (120). In the controversy over table-fellowship at Antioch, 'Peter may... have appealed to the vision of clean and unclean animals'. Luke over-exploited the Cornelius story: 'he wants to resolve the conflict over the Pauline mission by the recollection of the conversion of Cornelius' (117). He 'elevated the story of Cornelius into a principle . . . Here, as elsewhere, Luke sacrificed the exact reproduction of the tradition for the sake of a higher historical truth . . .: the idea' of the Gentile mission 'came neither from Paul nor from Peter—but from God!' (122).

If we wish to gain firm ground in this jostling throng of opinions, we must first set aside all questions of historical authenticity or sources and seek to understand Luke's concern in reproducing the story of Cornelius. He has told it in such a way that it can be understood only from the standpoint of its theological meaning. Thus viewed, even those parts which otherwise appear odd and fragmentary lose their strangeness, and the effect of the whole is marvellously rounded and self-contained.

Scene One (**10**.1–8) introduces Cornelius, a captain and company-commander in a provincial regiment, who with his entire household (family and domestic staff) is 'devout and God-fearing'—and, we may take it, a friendly visitor at the synagogue, where on account of his alms he is held in high regard. Yet at the same time Cornelius is more than an individual: he is the type of the φοβούμενος τὸν θεὸν καὶ ἐργαζόμενος δικαιοσύνην who in every nation is acceptable to God and may therefore be accepted into the Church. He is reminiscent of the 'captain of Capernaum' in Luke 7.5, and his piety merits that his prayers be heard. Of this piety verses 2,4, 22 and 30 speak. This technique of repetition is one to which Luke always resorts when he wants to impress something specially upon the reader. Here the idea is this, that the community does not accept just *any* Gentile, but only Gentiles of such piety that even a Jew must approve—and prayer and alms are (with fasting) *the* good works of Jewry. That an angel should come to such a man is perfectly comprehensible: God has taken note of his pious acts, and now instructs him to send for Simon Peter. The latter is unknown to Cornelius, who is likewise unaware what he may expect from him. The notion that man must submit to guidance at every step pervades the whole story, lending an air of passivity to Cornelius—even, indeed, to Peter himself. But what is uppermost in Luke's mind is obedience to the guidance offered: what more could Cornelius do than send the messengers to Peter?

Scene Two (**10**.9–16) is skilfully linked to the first and the third. As the messengers draw near to Joppa, the hungry Peter is praying on the roof. He falls into a trance, and from the opened heavens there descends a receptacle crowded with all kinds of animals, while a voice cries, 'Come, Peter, kill and eat!' Scandalized, the pious Jew rebuts the imputation that he could eat any-thing unclean. But *is* the food offered unclean? 'What God has declared clean, declare thou not unclean!' retorts the heavenly voice. Three times this invitation, refusal and admonition occur. Then the receptacle vanishes into heaven and Peter is left baffled.

But God sends him guidance. In *Scene Three*, that is (**10**.17–23a), the Spirit commands him to follow, without misgiving, the men whom *he*—the Holy Spirit—has sent. Once more we encounter the technique of reiteration: the angel's visit is narrated a second time in **10**.22, and later (**10**.30 and **11**.13) twice more. By the end of the story the reader will no longer forget that it was *God* who brought about the whole of these events: and thereby instituted the mission to the Gentiles. But we anticipate. For the moment, Peter (like the reader!) still does not know why he is to go to Cornelius: Cornelius is to 'hear words' from him. The very vagueness of this expression has its own good meaning: a Peter thus groping in the dark cannot conceivably be acting on his own initiative, but must abandon himself unreservedly to the guidance of God. If it were here stated that Peter is to baptize Cornelius, the miracle of the outpouring of the Spirit would fall away, yet it is this which eventually justifies the baptism of Gentiles.

Even *Scene Four* (**10**.23b–33) does not yet bring the decisive point. It describes the journey to Caesarea in the company of Christians from Joppa, and broadly depicts the meeting with Cornelius. The centurion has, at the angel's bidding, summoned his friends and relatives, so the Apostle finds 'many' awaiting him. Cornelius throws himself at his feet as if he were a being of some higher order, but Peter at once lifts him up: 'I am only a man, like you!' Nevertheless, the impression of majesty, grandeur and power remains, matched only by the gracious kindness conveyed in that very συνομιλῶν which so troubles the exegetes. To them such 'chatting' seems out of place. But they miss the point: Luke is not aiming at realistic detail, but at illustrating the astonishing amiability with which this sublime man comes to the Gentiles even though such conduct is in the eyes of the devout Jew a breach of the law. God himself, however, has now shown Peter, in the vision of the clean and unclean animals, that no man—by the mere fact of his race, be it understood—is unclean. There is no real reason why the speech of **10.34ff.** should not now follow. But Luke prolongs the scene, making Cornelius respond to Peter's question by once more relating the appearance of the angel. Thereby he incontrovertibly establishes that God's will is being done. It is against this background that Peter begins his sermon.

Scene Five consists of Peter's missionary sermon (**10.34–43**), the premise of which is the Apostle's new-found understanding that 'God is no respecter of persons', i.e. that in the question of salvation he does not unjustly prefer one nation to another. Luke is thinking here not of Israel's election in the past but only of the question who *now* may enter the Messianic communion of salvation. To a Jew it would be blasphemy to say 'A preferring of Israel would be προσωπολημψία on the part of God', but this Luke totally ignores. In any case, the accent for him falls on the positive: 'In every nation, whoever fears God and does what is righteous is acceptable to God.' Though this applies in the first place to the φοβούμενοι, it does not exclude other men. From acceptance into the communion the thought next turns to the message of election. This 'word' God addressed to the Jews, indeed. In this development of the kerygma Luke is wrestling with the difficulty that strictly it was formulated in terms of Israel. He overcomes the obstacle with the declaration that through Jesus Christ peace is established (between God and man), that Jesus is Lord of all, and that *any* person who believes in him will have his sins forgiven.

Scene Six (**10.44–8**) brings the great surprise. Even while Peter is speaking, the Spirit falls on the assembled Gentiles and makes them speak with tongues. This event settles the question of Gentile baptism. How can anyone refuse water-baptism to those on whom God has already bestowed the baptism of the Spirit? Faced with this miracle, at which the Jewish Christians present are filled with amazement, Peter needs must allow and ordain the baptism of Cornelius and his companions.

Peter is first among the Apostles. But the whole apostolic Church is greater than he. Hence *Scene Seven* (**11.1–18**), in which the resistance of this body is overcome. Luke shrinks from having the Church protest in so many words against the baptism just effected, though that is what is really meant. Instead he represents the accusation as levelled against table-fellowship with the uncircumcised. In this way he blunts the wounding sharpness of the primitive Church's opposition to the will of God. By way of justification Peter simply relates how the baptism of Cornelius came about. The whole long story cannot be repeated; Luke merely indicates enough for the readers to understand what it is all about. The accusers then tacitly concede the issue, praising God for giving to the Gentiles also 'repentance unto life'. This final word of the narrative (like **11.1** already) shows that the apostolic Church also sees here no mere special case, but the fundamental affirmative to the admission of the Gentiles.

There we have Luke's conception of the matter. Its general sense may be gathered from the repetitions. These fall into two groups. The first shows that the Christians resisted the admission of Gentiles (**10**.14, 28, 47; **11**.2, 8, 17). The second demonstrates that God himself introduced the Gentiles into the Church (**10**.3, 11–16, 22, 30; **11**.5–10, 13).

Still, that is not yet all. It was Peter who first baptized a Gentile, and the Jerusalem congregation subsequently endorsed this decision and adopted it for its own. It was in other words no 'freelance' who began the mission to the Gentiles, but the legitimate, apostolic Church. Hence the baptism of Gentiles is legitimate also insofar as the actions of men had to do with its inception.

Another peculiarity of the story is that the first Gentile to become a Christian should have been a Roman citizen, indeed a Roman officer. This circumstance is not expressly stressed, but we learn as much from the mention of the σπεῖρα ᾽Ιταλική, and it fits admirably with all those passages in Acts which show the Christian Church on good terms with the Roman authorities.

This passage amply illustrates the deep interpenetration in Luke's mind of a theological concern—the attempt to secure for the Church the toleration of the Roman State—and the concern of the historian, namely to describe the 'hero' and his milieu as accurately as possible. On the other hand it shows us that such a 'historical' account does not have to be absolutely reliable. No Roman troops can have been stationed in Caesarea while that city was still under the jurisdiction of Herod Agrippa I, i.e. up to the year 44. So far as can be established, moreover, the σπεῖρα ᾽Ιταλική was not sent East until considerably later. It follows that Luke has calmly generalized from the circumstances of his own day in order to draw a concrete picture of the centurion. The tradition about the centurion, which was not influenced by the historian's concern, will have spoken only of a centurion Cornelius, and it is by no means certain that it originally gave a name: the centurion of Capernaum (Luke **7**.2ff.) is anonymous.

So now we come to the question of the tradition Luke used. Of what could it have consisted? By eliminating every part of the story which clearly derives from Luke himself (**10**.9–16, 27–9, 34–43; **11**.1–18), Dibelius reached the conclusion that tradition only contributed the 'simple conversion-legend' to which we have alluded (357 above). But the premises on which his argument rests are dubious. For one thing, it is improbable that the early Church collected and handed down, for purposes of edification, the conversion-stories of men of rank or consequence. People who believe that the end of the world is near, and who confidently expect to be transfigured into angelic beings, have no interest in retailing the conversion of a centurion. For another, Dibelius, like many another scholar, assumes that in the days of the primitive community a Gentile could have been accepted into the fold without such a singular event exciting remark (but Acts makes it excite remark!). This presupposition too is extremely unlikely. It was precisely in the earliest days that the admission of Gentiles must have been most unthinkable to the community. By such a step it would have forfeited all toleration in Jerusalem. Furthermore, had there been isolated instances of this kind, Paul would have been in a position to make a successful appeal to them against the attacks of the Judaists. To maintain that Paul knew nothing of them is to deny the existence of the very tradition to which appeal is made. The position would be quite different if Peter, at the time when he had already left Jerusalem, had converted and baptized a centurion in Caesarea.

Research has however thrown up another conjecture as to the nature of the tradition (in the circumstances, conjectures are all that is possible). W. L. Knox (*The Acts of the Apostles*, 33) suggests that we may here possess the Caesarean community's tradition of its foundation, which it held to be the work of the Apostle Peter. As a matter of fact, in the Cornelius story it is not only one person who is converted, but an entire (Gentile!) congregation is founded; the relatives and friends of Cornelius also—'many'—receive the Spirit. Luke could employ such a feature of the tradition only to the extent that it enabled him to provide Peter with an audience commensurate with his apostolic dignity. Had he reported that Peter founded a Gentile community in Caesarea, then the objections of the Judaists against the Antiochene mission would have become totally inconceivable.

In addition to the 'simple conversion-legend' Dibelius detected a second tradition in the story of Cornelius: the vision of Peter. This too he derives from some incident in the life of Peter: at the time of the controversy over eating with Gentiles, kindled by the events in Antioch (Gal. 2.11ff.), Peter supposedly had this vision and took his stand upon it. But here again we must express serious reservations. The vision shows Peter 'all kinds of quadrupeds and creeping animals of the earth and birds of the air'. This must include *both* clean and unclean animals. Peter's objection, that he had never eaten anything unclean, does not therefore meet the case: what is to prevent him from killing a clean animal? (Jacquier makes the same point, 318.) Dibelius dismisses this objection as rationalistic. It may however have been this very thought which moved Augustine, in *Contra Faustum* 31.3 to paraphrase the text in these words: 'Peter, kill everything you see in the receptacle and eat it!' (Dibelius, *Studies* 112 n. 6). If the vision refers to clean and unclean men, the juxtaposition of clean and unclean animals is comprehensible. But however that may be (we will return to the point), a second objection remains: if the vision is taken to refer to meats and interpreted accordingly, it must imply that there are no unclean foods. As Overbeck (157) rightly saw, this would be tantamount to abolishing the food commandments of the Old Testament. Now this standpoint was never recognized by the Jerusalem

N

community, and we have no evidence that Peter ever adopted it. That it is foreign to Acts itself is clear from the so-called Apostolic Decree.

Expositors would not have thought of interpreting the vision in terms of food (the actual text sees it only in terms of men!) if **11**.3 had not emboldened them to do so. But here, *pace* Preuschen (70), no 'later proceedings' are 'anticipated'. It is rather the case, as already said, that Luke avoids presenting the apostolic Church as bluntly objecting to the baptism of the uncircumcised; the Apostles and disciples would otherwise too plainly have shared the outlook of those unauthorized men of **15**.24, who troubled the minds of the Christians at Antioch. In fact, of course, the objection of the primitive congregation, including Peter's fellow-Apostles, does coincide with the 'Judaistic' position. However, Luke could scarcely make this explicit, so he clothes the protest in a form which concealed the extreme sharpness of the opposition.

Yet if the vision refers to men, one difficulty nevertheless remains (not counting the difficulty of imagining how even a visionary could have seen 'all kinds of quadrupeds and crawling beasts of the earth and birds of the air' in that one mysterious 'vessel'): Peter's answer does not really make sense unless only unclean things were placed before him. This suggests that the writer himself devised this vision for the sake of illustrating the lesson of **10**.28. It clearly has this sense, too, in Chapter 11, where the men of Jerusalem similarly do not infer 'So now we can eat unclean food as well', but 'So God has given repentance unto life to the Gentiles also'.

Whether or not one believes in the possibility of such licence on the part of the narrator, one thing is certain from our text: here Luke was pressing history into the service of the Christian message. He is not directly chronicling real events, but dressing up a conviction of faith—namely that God instigated the mission to the Gentiles—in the garments of history. Here stands revealed a peculiarity of Lucan theology which can scarcely be claimed as a point in its favour: in endeavouring to make the hand of God visible in the history of the Church, Luke virtually excludes all human decision. Instead of the realization of the divine will *in* human decisions, *through* human decisions, he shows us a series of supernatural interventions in the dealings of men: the appearance of the angel, the vision of the animals, the prompting of the Spirit, the pouring out of the ecstatic πνεῦμα. As Luke presents them, these divine incursions have such compelling force that all doubt in the face of them *must* be stilled. They compellingly prove that God, not man, is at work. The presence of God may be directly ascertained. But here faith loses its true character of decision, and the obedience from faith which Luke would have liked to portray turns into something utterly different: very nearly the twitching of human puppets. Even those who are at one with Luke in the conviction that God willed the mission to the Gentiles will scarcely be able to hide from themselves the suspicion aroused by Luke's version of events. To the extent that he has removed the decision as far as possible from the hands of men to place it in those of God, Luke has forsaken the dimension of reality in which the genuine decisions of faith are taken, and instead of enabling us to trace the acts of God, substituted a string of 'miracles'. This admittedly was not his intention, nor was he aware of it. He simply, in all innocence, gave allegiance to the outlook of his time. This would not be so dangerous if such a manner of thinking had been confined to that age. But in all of us there exists a longing to have the weight of personal decision lifted from our shoulders by abandonment to the choices of God. It is the more important, therefore, that we should resist the temptation inherent in this particular aspect of Lucan theology.

26
ACTS 11:19–26
THE FIRST GENTILE CONGREGATION COMES INTO BEING AT ANTIOCH

[19] Now those who were scattered abroad because of the persecution which arose over Stephen travelled as far as Phoenicia and Cyprus and Antioch, speaking the word to none except Jews only. [20] But some of them were men of Cyprus and Cyrene, who on coming to Antioch spoke to the Greeks also, preaching the Lord Jesus. [21] And the hand of the Lord was with them, and a great number who believed turned to the Lord. [22] And the word concerning them came to the ears of the congregation of Jerusalem, and they sent Barnabas to Antioch. [23] When he had come and seen the grace of God, he was glad and exhorted them all to adhere to the Lord with firm purpose; [24] for he was a good man, and full of the Holy Spirit and of faith. [25] And a great crowd was added to the Lord. [26] And he went off to Tarsus to seek for Saul, and when he had found him, he brought him to Antioch. And it came to pass that for a whole year they were associated together in the community, and taught many people. And the disciples were first called Christians in Antioch.

Bibliography:

W. Michaelis, 'Judaistische Heidenchristen', *ZNW* 30 (1931), 83ff.; C. H. Kraeling, 'The Jewish community at Antioch', *JBL* 51 (1932), 130–60; H. J. Cadbury, 'Names for Christians in Acts', *Beg.* V, 375–92 (on **11**.26); B. M. Metzger, *Antioch on the Orontes* II, Princeton 1938, 1949/50, 70–88; and *Bibl. Archaeologist* 11 (1948), 69–88; F. W. Beare, 'The Sequence of Events in Acts 9–15 and the Career of Peter', *JBL* 62 (1943), 295–306; E. Peterson, 'Christianus', *Studi e Testi* 121, Vatican 1946, 355–72; P. Gaechter, 'Jerusalem und Antiochia', *ZkTh* 70 (1948), 1–48. See also 365 n. 3.

D. R. Fotheringham, 'Acts 11:20', *Exp.Tim.* 45 (1933–4), 430; J. Moreau, 'Le nom des Chrétiens (Actes **11**.26)', *Nouvelle Clio* 1 (1949–50), 190–2; H. B. Mattingly; 'The Origin of the Name "Christiani"', *JTS* 9 (1958), 26–37; B. S. Easton, *Early Christianity*, London 1955 (41–57: religio licita; cf. Tertullian, Apol. 21); A. J. Festugière, *Antioche païenne et chrétienne*, Paris 1959.

VERSE 19: μὲν οὖν introduces a new scene—see note to **1.6**. οἱ διασπαρέντες κτλ. links up with **8.1** but contradicts it: the allegedly scattered community of Jerusalem was already reunited at **9.26**; the dispersed were in reality leaders of the Stephenite splinter-group (cf. comments on **8.1**), if not members of the 'Seven'. On διῆλθον ἕως see note to **8.4**. μηδενὶ λαλοῦντες κτλ refers to the whole of their missionary activity. Phoenicia: the coastal strip, at most 7½ miles wide and about 75 miles long, from Cape Carmel northward to the river Eleutheros (Jacquier 345).[1] The congregations of Tyre and Sidon are mentioned respectively in **21.4** and **27.3**, that of Ptolemais (Acre) in **21.7**. Cyprus[2] had since 22 B.C. been a senatorial province, Paphos being the seat of the proconsul. Whether Christianity first came there with Barnabas and Paul (**13.4**) or 'had already been brought there by refugees from Jerusalem' (so Bauer, *Wb* 829f.) depends on whether our text is a Lucan summary or the direct reproduction of a tradition in its own right. Antioch on the Orontes,[3] the third largest city of the Roman empire, with a population of half a million, lay 22 miles up-river from the Mediterranean, was the seat of the legate of Syria, and possessed a large Jewish colony with many σεβόμενοι (Josephus *Bell.* VII.43).

VERSE 20: ἄνδρες Κύπριοι—according to **4.36** Barnabas came from Cyprus. ἄνδρες Κυρηναῖοι—according to **13.1** Lucius[4] (perhaps also Symeon Niger) hailed from Cyrene. In Antioch these anonymous τινες preach also to the Greeks, i.e. Gentiles,[5] but without insisting on circumcision.[6] Thus

[1] See Pauly-Wissowa XX (1950), cols. 350–380 (Otto Eissfeldt).
[2] See Pauly-Wissowa XII (1924), cols. 59–117; E. Power, *Dictionnaire de la Bible*, Supp. II (1934), 1–23.
[3] V. Schultze, *Altchr. Städte und Landschaften* III (1930). —*Antioch on the Orontes* (Publications of the Committee for the Excavations of Antioch I-IV), Princeton, 1934–52. —J. Jeremias, *ZNW* 40 (1941), 254. —*R.A.C.* I (1950) 461–9.
[4] See H. J. Cadbury, 'Lucius of Cyrene', *Beg.* V, 489–95.
[5] For Ἕλληνας (A D ℵ°), B 81 read Ἑλληνιστάς, which also lies concealed in the scribal error Εὐαγγελιστάς in ℵ* (due to the following εὐαγγελιζόμενοι). Ropes (*Beg.* III, 106) advocates this reading: 'Greek-speaking people' are introduced in contrast to 'Jews'. But those Jews among whom Stephen's group carried on their mission according to verse 19 were also 'Greek-speaking people'. The contrast to 'Jews' requires rather 'Gentiles' = Ἕλληνας; despite *Beg.* IV, 128 and Cadbury's statements in his essay 'The Hellenists' (*Beg.* V, 59–74) Ἑλληνιστής does not have this meaning. In our view B's reading is a correction intended to avoid the supposed contrast to verse 19, or to reserve the Gentile mission proper for Paul.
[6] So the *communis opinio*. Michaelis on the other hand, in his article 'Judaistische Heidenchristen' (*ZNW* 30 (1931), 83–9; cf. also *Das NT* (Kroners Taschenausgabe Bd. 121, 1935), 50; *Einleitung*[2] (1954), 138), has put forward the thesis that the advance described in **11.20** consisted in the fact that the missionaries turned to Gentiles who were not yet σεβόμενοι; but they demanded of them acceptance of circumcision. 'Barnabas and Paul too at first preached circumcision. Only in the course of the first missionary journey were they led to a different policy, which thereafter found entrance into the community of Antioch also' (88). That Barnabas and Paul first preached circumcision—which must have taken place over a whole decade!—is nowhere indicated by Luke, and cannot be reconciled with the Pauline letters. Renunciation of circumcision involved not merely 'a different missionary

opens a new chapter—and in a sense the most important—in the history of the Christian mission.

VERSE 21: 'The hand of the Lord was with them'[1]: Luke reports their success in biblical style—the growth of the community demonstrates that the activity of these men has the approval of God, who is thus authenticating the Antiochian mission to the Gentiles. The use of ἀριθμός in this connection is Lucan (cf. Acts **4**.4, **6**.7, **16**.5). ἐπέστρεψεν = were converted, see **3**.19. πιστεύσας[2]—pious writing is fond of such dual expressions as 'believed and were converted'. Though the κύριον which terminates the verse refers to Jesus, it is God's hand which is meant, as in **13**.11, by the OT formula 'hand of the Lord'.

VERSE 22: ἠκούσθη εἰς τὰ ὦτα (cf. Isa. **5**.9 LXX)—Luke remains true to the biblical way of speaking. ὁ λόγος: the news or rumour. τῆς οὔσης (B ℵ 81) —see n. on **5**.17 above: an example of choice language. ἐξαπέστειλαν: 'they despatched' (not 'they made their Apostle'; so *Beg.* IV, 129); with what instructions is not said. But Barnabas should probably be considered as a plenipotentiary whose assent will legalize the Gentile mission in Antioch. ἕως 'Αντιοχείας: according to Loisy (467), emphatic—'all the way to that far-off city'.[3]

VERSE 23: ὅς: again one of those Lucan relative clauses which are in reality main clauses introduced by a relative. For the sense of the 'grace of God' cf. verse 21. The pun of χάριν-ἐχάρη is intentional: the combination of biblical manner of speaking and rhetoric is characteristic of Luke. παρεκάλει: as Barnabas is called υἱὸς παρακλήσεως in **4**.36, Wendt (190) thought this a play upon it. Edifying language is resumed in 'he exhorted them all to adhere to the Lord with purpose of heart'.[4]

VERSE 24: ἀνὴρ ἀγαθὸς κτλ.—Joseph of Arimathea is called ἀνὴρ ἀγαθός in Luke **23**.50, Stephen in Acts **6**.5 ἀνὴρ πλήρης πίστεως καὶ πνεύματος ἁγίου: a stock terminology of pious language is in process of crystallizing.

---

method' but a change of theological presuppositions which went right to the utmost depths.—Luke does not set Jews and σεβόμενοι on the one side over against Gentiles on the other in verses 19f., but Jews over against Gentiles—just as in **13**.46, the first of those three passages in which he makes Paul turn to the Gentiles because of Jewish obduracy (cf. **18**.6, **28**.28). Michaelis in our view did not sufficiently separate the problems of the Lucan presentation from those of the historical event.

[1] II Sam. **3**.12 LXX corresponds exactly to the present passage.

[2] The stock expression πιστεῦσαι = become faithful does not admit of any inferences as to a Pauline theology of Luke. On this problem see P. Vielhauer's article 'Zum "Paulinismus" der Apostelgeschichte', *Ev. Th.* (1950), 1–15.

[3] D E gig insert διελθεῖν before it and thus restore a usual expression. But perhaps ἕως 'Αντιοχείας also means that Barnabas on his visitation travelled over the whole missionary route of the διασπαρέντες.

[4] LXX uses πρόθεσις in II and III Macc. for 'intention', 'plan'; πρόθεσις τῆς καρδίας Symmachus at Ps. **10**.17 (=LXX **9**.38) instead of ἑτοιμασία τῆς καρδίας of LXX.

Overbeck: 'The author uses the opportunity for one of those general commendations which, here as elsewhere' (allusion to **15**.22 and **22**.12) 'he is anxious to attach to the name of the mediator between Paul and the primitive Church' (174). But Luke has a reason for this commendation: it shows that Barnabas' assent to the Antiochian mission was more than a human decision; it was prompted by the Holy Spirit. On προσετέθη[1] see **2**.41, 47; on ἱκανός, note to **8**.11.

VERSE 25: Luke presupposes that Paul has remained in Tarsus[2] ever since his withdrawal there (9.30). He did not suspect that this involves a period of at least ten years (Gal. **1**.18 and **2**.1!). Possibly he inferred Barnabas' journey to Tarsus from the fact that the tradition used in **13**.1 shows both men together in Antioch.

VERSE 26: Even the statement that Barnabas and Paul worked together for one year in Antioch does not prove that Luke had an exact tradition at his disposal: in the context of his history of the mission, a 'whole year' is in Luke's eyes a long time. Usually, in the Lucan account, Paul stays only a relatively short time in one place—Corinth and Ephesus are exceptions. The sentence introduced by ἐγένετο (though the construction recurs in **22**.6) is oddly clumsy or stilted in effect—this is shown by the impossible translation in *Beg.* IV, 130: 'they were taken as guests' into the community. What might be meant is: 'And it so happened that they joined forces even (καί) for a whole year in the congregation there, and taught a large number of people'. The statement that the disciples were first called Christians in Antioch is then loosely attached by τε, and depends only on ἐγένετο.[3]

---

[1] According to Preuschen (73), the growth of the community is intended to show the influence of Barnabas. In any case, the divine blessing which rests on the Antiochian congregation and its activity is thereby made more evident.

[2] Tarsus, situated on an important road through the mountains, was the chief town of Cilicia and important for trade, but also as a centre of Hellenistic culture. Cf. Ramsay, *The Cities of St. Paul*, 1907, 85–244; H. Böhlig, *Die Geisteskultur von Tarsus*, 1913; H. Steinmann, *Zum Werdegang des Paulus. Die Jugendzeit in Tarsus*, 1928. The picture sketched in these works has been called in question by van Unnik's work *Tarsus or Jerusalem. The City of Paul's Youth* (ET London 1962); see on **22**.3.

[3] D gig sy^hms sy^p offer a quite different text (unfortunately corrupt); see Nestle. d also gives no help: *et cum invenissent* (sic!), *depraecabantur* (sic!) *venire antiochiam; contigit vero eis annum totum commiscere ecclesiam*. Evidently in these Western authorities, as Zahn already conjectured, the words ἐν τῇ ἐκκλησίᾳ καὶ ἐδίδασκον have been omitted.

Χριστιανοί, formed like 'Ασιανοί or 'Ηρωδιανοί, shows that χριστός was understood not as a title but as a proper name (in Paul too it already often appears as part of the name). Tacitus (*Ann.* XV.44) with his two statements *quos per flagitia invisos vulgus Chrestianos appellabat* and *auctor huius nominis Christus* presupposes that in Rome in the sixties the people called the disciples χρηστιανοί, while the educated knew that it was really a case of followers of a certain χριστός. Since the people cannot make anything of this, they understand χριστός as χρηστός and derive the name of the sect from it (both words were at the time pronounced the same).

In recent years **11**.26 has been given a different interpretation. E. Peterson ('Christianus', *Studi e Testi* 121. Miscellanea Giovanni Mercati, vol. I, 1946, 355–72) deduced from it (363) that the Roman authorities in Antioch designated the Christians by the name χριστιανοί

Critical scholarship has singled out three main problems in this passage. In earlier days the *source*-question, needless to say, stood to the fore, and it was Harnack who had the most influential idea (*Beitr.* III, 157; ET): as our text deals with the relations between Antioch and Jerusalem, there lies behind it a source of combined Jerusalem-Antiochian provenance. The διασπαρέντες of **11**.19 point back to those of **8**.4, where Luke had 'already made a start' at recounting what follows in **11**.19. This to Harnack raised his guess to a certainty. The authority behind the source, he thought, could be named without much trouble—it must be the prophet Silas, who came down from Jerusalem to Antioch, Acts **15**.32 (157 and 186f.)! This source, from which sprang **6**.1–**8**.4, **11**.19–30 and **12**.25 (**13**.1)–**15**.35, was perhaps partly, perhaps even wholly available to Luke in written form.

'as adherents of a movement standing under the guidance of the Χριστός and regarded by Herod Antipas as hostile' (doesn't P. really mean Herod Agrippa?) 'When about 44 the appellation χριστιανοί was given to the disciples of Jesus in Antioch, it was . . . as people thought, the designation of a political group within Judaism' (367).

Against this interpretation (we cannot here enter into this explanation of the word χριστιανοί, which seems thoroughly artificial), one thing is decisive: if Luke had here reported that about 44 the Roman authorities had already marked out the Christians as political conspirators (367), then he would by so doing have destroyed everything he further says about the goodwill of the Roman authorities and their friendly treatment of the Christians.

E. J. Bickermann ('The Name of Christians', *HTR* 42 (1949), 109–24, earlier already in *Rev.Bibl.* 47 (1938), 184–97) in contrast expounds **11**.26 to the effect that the Christians of Antioch over against the authorities described themselves as χριστιανοί, in order thus to indicate that 'in the new age' they would be 'officers' or 'agents' of the anointed King, and obtain special positions and tasks in the messianic hierarchy. —This thesis has been taken over by J. Moreau, 'Le nom des Chrétiens', *Nouvelle Clio*, Brussels 1950, 190–2.

But even if the sons of Zebedee (Mk. **10**.37) expected special places of honour, this does not mean that the Christians of Antioch intended by their name to suggest any such expectation to the pagan authorities—no Gentile would have caught the implication.

The word χρηματίζω admittedly (here P. and B. are perfectly correct) can mean 'bear a name (title)'. But this meaning easily passes over into the other: 'be named'. So Philo (*Quod deus sit immutabilis* 121) says that Joseph's brothers, born of other wives, ἀπὸ τοῦ χείρονος γένους (that of the women) χρηματίζουσιν, and this is explained in the words: υἱοὶ γὰρ τῶν γυναικῶν . . . καλοῦνται. It is clear that here χρηματίζουσιν passes over into the meaning καλοῦνται, 'they are called'. Another example is Jos. *Ant.* VIII 157: the Roman emperors, who from birth bear other names (ἀπ᾽ ἄλλων χρηματίσαντες ὀνομάτων), are called Caesars (Καίσαρες καλοῦνται) when they ascend the throne. But Rom. **7**.3 also belongs here: the adulterous wife does not call herself an adulteress, and does not lay claim to this title, but is so called, and such she is. And when Eusebius (*Laud. Const.* **17**.14) mentions κυριακὴν χρηματίζουσαν ἡμέραν, he means 'the day which is named or called after the Lord'.

It is therefore well to adhere to the interpretation hitherto generally maintained. The disciples were first called 'Christians', 'Christ-people', in Antioch, and that by the Gentile population, because it was here for the first time that they clearly stood out as a separate sect from the Jews. That precisely here, where for the first time uncircumcised Gentiles were accepted into the community, a specially Jewish way of thinking was dominant (so Bickermann, 124), is in any case highly improbable.

The subsequent influence of this hastily sketched hypothesis was considerable. It is still evident in Beyer (71f.) and Knox (35). The theory was taken up and modified by Wendt (see Introduction § 2, p. 39 n. 5 above) and Jeremias; according to Jeremias, 9.1–30 also belongs to this source, but not 15.1–33 (a parallel report to 11.27ff.). It seemed to speak in favour of this theory that, if it were right, Luke followed the same process in Acts as in his gospel: in his main source—this very Antiochian source, which extended to 15.35 and beyond—he incorporated his special material in a series of insertions (8.5–40, 9.31–11.18, 12.1–24, 15.1–33), just as he did in his gospel in the Marcan material.

The *second* problem lay in the fact that these 'accounts of the beginnings of the Antiochian congregation' were 'so defective and imprecise'. Noting this, B. Weiss explained it on the view that Luke probably built them on hearsay (*Einl. zum NT*, 576; ET). A quite different conclusion was drawn by J. Weiss (18f.), who was struck by the fact that this 'colourless tale' leaves an impression of anticlimax after the Cornelius story. This could be understood only if Luke closely adhered to an existing account. Properly, in Weiss's view, one should 'expect a much greater array of resources'. Knopf expressed a similar opinion (581).

A *third* problem lay in the fact that 11.19ff. begins abruptly, without connection to the preceding episode. Struck by this, J. Weiss and Bauernfeind reached basically the same solution: Luke was leaving open, or even drawing attention to, the possibility that 11.19ff. in part ran parallel with Chapters 8 to 10 instead of succeeding the events in them. 'Luke cannot maintain, and does not wish to maintain, that the conversion of Cornelius historically preceded all other conversions of Gentiles' (Bauernfeind, 154). 'But with this he frustrated his own arrangement', as J. Weiss affirms (19).

In reality these three problems are inseparable. This becomes very clear in Bauernfeind, who makes a new—and decisive—observation: the wording and form of presentation go back to Luke himself (153)! It is Luke who once again narrates the story in biblical language, employing such favourite expressions as λαλοῦντες τὸν λόγον, πολὺς ἀριθμός, ἀνὴρ ἀγαθός κτλ., προσετέθη ὄχλος ἱκανός. One must only say more explicitly than Bauernfeind (who merely indicates it) that verses 19ff. have entirely the character of a Lucan summary worked up from concrete details. But that means—and Bauernfeind does not hesitate to draw the conclusion—that Luke is not reproducing the wording of an ancient source: 'There are no solid grounds for believing that reports on the early Christian mission were ever presented before Luke in this digested form; he was himself the first to do so' (153). Thus fades Harnack's pipe dream of an Antiochian source ('the oldest missionary history of the Christian Church'—Jeremias, 220). In compensation, however, our three problems become really soluble; though it is not source-criticism which produces the solution, but attention to Luke's methods of composition.

J. Weiss had rightly felt that this 'colourless tale' had the effect of an anticlimax. But Luke had a reason for this. It was precisely not the foundation of the community at Antioch by the διασπαρέντες that he sought to present as the epoch-making event, but the preceding conversion and baptism of Cornelius by Peter! So it would be wrong to expect in 11.19ff. 'a much greater array of resources'. Luke only pulls out every stop at points he considers decisive. By the way in which he recounts the mission of the διασπαρέντες, he gives it the character of the secondary following in the wake of the primary. It is obvious why he could not develop the pragmatic relationship between the conversion of Cornelius and the conversion of Gentiles in Antioch: if he had explicitly presented the latter as the legitimate outcome of the former, the opposition to the Gentile mission in Chapter 15 would have become incomprehensible. But this at the same time implies that to Luke's mind the chronological relationship of the Cornelius story and the Antioch mission may not be inverted. Luke had no thought of 'frustrating his own arrangement'—this concern on the part of J. Weiss was unfounded. It sprang from the fact that the modern scholar read into the Lucan text his own perception that the Stephenites had been the first to begin the Gentile mission, entirely of their own accord. But to do this is to destroy for Luke the very justification he wished to give this mission.

Now what concrete material did Luke possess for this section? He says that men from Cyprus and Cyrene had begun the mission to the Gentiles in Antioch. The list in 13.1, doubtless founded on tradition, mentions among the leading men there one Lucius of Cyrene. We can hardly be wrong in assuming that his companion, Symeon Niger, also came from Cyrene. In all probability, these two are the men of Cyrene of whom 11.20 speaks. And the men of Cyprus? Wellhausen (21) recalls, without wholly adopting, Schwartz's thesis that 'included among the ἄνδρες Κύπριοι is Barnabas himself, who came out as a missionary, not as an agent of Jerusalem'. This surmise, which not only Loisy (466f.) but even the cautious Wendt (189) shared, is not so fanciful as at first appears. In 9.27 we saw with what freedom Luke conjured a Barnabas scene out of the historical picture before him. In the present passage such boldness was quite unnecessary. Luke presumably possessed three pieces of information about Barnabas, which are all to be found in Acts. Firstly, he was celebrated for having sold a piece of land and presented the proceeds to the primitive church in Jerusalem (4.36f.). This showed Luke that Barnabas was in Jerusalem from the earliest times, which for him amounted to proof that Barnabas was a highly-respected member of the apostolic community. But that is by no means certain. It is just as likely that the Cypriot with the Gentile-sounding name was (as his subsequent activities might suggest) a prominent member of Stephen's group—which of course did not exist for Luke.

The second datum about Barnabas available to Luke may be seen in
13.1, where he heads the list of prophets and teachers at Antioch. Since Luke
regarded Barnabas as a loyal follower of the Twelve (9.27f.), he must have
assumed that Barnabas owed this position in Antioch to the fact that the
congregation of Jerusalem had sent him there. But in fact we must reckon
with the probability (already suggested in his cautious way by Bauernfeind,
155) that Barnabas was one of the διασπαρέντες and launched the Antiochian
mission to the Gentiles along with Lucius of Cyrene and one or two others.
This, considering he could lean on no apostolic directive from the Twelve,
was an extraordinary thing to do. It was anything but a matter of course that
a man like Barnabas should waive the demand for circumcision. We cannot
explain this renunciation simply from the impression made upon him by
the readiness and responsiveness of the Gentiles. In Paul's case, his letters
show the theological grounds on which his Gentile mission was founded. It
is only fair—this must be conceded to Loisy—that we should regard Barnabas
also not as a missionary like others, induced to moderate his demands by the
course of events, but as a man who knew what he was doing: one who deliberately took the decisive step to the Gentile mission in virtue of his Christian insight. What reasons he offered—for example, that the last times had
broken in and therefore the time had come for the Gentile mission—we do
not know. Later in Antioch Barnabas admittedly followed Peter's example,
and at the Lord's Supper separated himself, with the other Jewish Christians,
from the Gentile congregation. But this does not mean that he regarded them
as subject to the law: his intervention for their freedom from the law at the
'Apostolic Council' is proof of it. Paul of course in the long run proved the
stronger. But this should not mislead us into seeing Barnabas as a mere extra
on the stage of the history of the mission.

The third datum Luke possessed concerning Barnabas was that he went
with Paul to Jerusalem. This we will discuss in our next section.

Luke's observation that the name 'Christians' originated in Antioch
merits our special attention. The Gentile judgement implicit in this sobriquet
anticipates an insight which the Christians themselves were to reach only
later and reluctantly: that Christianity is no mere variant of Judaism. Once
this impression was entrenched among their contemporaries, the position of
the Christian community must have become critical, and that in two respects.
For one thing they risked losing the protection accorded a *religio licita* (so
B. S. Easton, *Early Christianity*, 41–57), which they had initially enjoyed as a
Jewish αἵρεσις (we shall see that Luke in Acts strives with all his might to
avert this danger). But internally also—and this brings us to the second point—
this development faced them with a very difficult problem: how could the
Church understand itself as still in the continuity of the *Heilsgeschichte* when
its continuity with the Jewish community was broken? Paul was not the only
Christian to wrestle with this question. Others sought the solution on other

paths than he. Luke also offers such an answer, ostensibly simpler, in that he thinks to have found in the doctrine of resurrection the clamp which unites Pharisaic Judaism with the Christian Church. Paul's various ἀπολογίαι in the second half of Acts will lead us to this theme.

27
ACTS 11:27-30
THE COLLECTION AT ANTIOCH

²⁷ Now in these days prophets came down from Jerusalem to Antioch. ²⁸ And one of them named Agabus stood up, and signified by the Spirit that a great famine was about to come over all the world: which came about under Claudius. ²⁹ And the disciples determined that each of them according to his means should send for the relief of the brethren who lived in Judaea: ³⁰ This they did, sending to the elders by the hand of Barnabas and Saul.

Bibliography:

O. Holtzmann, 'Die Jerusalemreisen d. Paulus u. d. Kollekte', *ZNW* 6 (1905), 102–4; J. Jeremias, 'Sabbatjahr u. ntl. Chronologie', *ZNW* 27 (1928), 98–103; K. Lake, 'The Famine in the Time of Claudius', *Beg*. V, 452–5; K. S. Gapp, 'The Universal Famine under Claudius', *HTR* 28 (1935), 258–65; Jeremias, 'Untersuchungen z. Quellenproblem d. Apg.', *ZNW* 36 (1937), 215–9; Cardinal Schuster, 'Actus Apostolorum', *La Scuola Catholica* 81 (1953), 371–4; W. Michaelis, *Das Ältestenamt i. d. chr. Kirche i. Licht d. hl. Schrift*, Berne 1923; R. W. Funk, 'The Enigma of the Famine Visit', *JBL* 75 (1956), 130–6.

J. Dupont, 'La famine sous Claude, Actes **11**.28', *Rev. Bibl.* 62 (1955), 52–5; D. F. Robinson, 'A Note on Acts **11**.27–30', *JBL* 63 (1944), 169–72, 411–2; P. Benoit, 'La deuxième visite de Saint Paul à Jérusalem', *Biblica* 40 (1959), 778–96.

VERSE 27: 'In these days' (see **1**.15), i.e. in the year mentioned by verse 26 or soon after (Knopf 581). κατῆλθον κτλ: see **11**.2. προφῆται: 'One wonders whether Acts also does not already share the view which early became dominant in the Church, that the uncovering of the future was the characteristic function of prophecy' (Overbeck, 176).[1] The account of Agabus given in **21**.10ff. would suggest this—but see **15**.32. Acts has nothing

---

[1] Overbeck refers to Justin, *Apol.* I 31, 1 προφῆται δι' ὧν τὸ προφητικὸν πνεῦμα προεκήρυξε τὰ γενήσεσθαι μέλλοντα πρὶν ἢ γενέσθαι. The Didache (**11**.7–12) speaks of (wandering? see **13**.1!) prophets; Hermas (Mand. XI, 9–15) of true and false prophets.

to say of the prophet's ability to read the secrets of hearts (I Cor. **14**.24f.).[1] On the other hand, the directive of the Spirit in **13**.2 must have been imagined as declared by a prophet.[2]

VERSE 28: ἀναστάς: see **1**.15. Ἄγαβος: according to Wendt (193) this is a rendering of חָגָב = 'locust' (cf. Ezra **2**.46).[3] σημαίνω here indicates a prophecy prompted by the Spirit.[4] Agabus foretold a great famine for the whole οἰκουμένη.[5] The primary intention of the note 'which came about under Claudius' is not to fix a historical date but to establish the fulfilment of the prophecy.[6] There was indeed in the days of Claudius (A.D. 41–54) a series of famines in separate lands (among them an especially severe one in Palestine between 46 and 48; see Introduction § 4, 2c), but none of these was universal. The Western text here introduces the first 'we'.[7]

VERSE 29: τῶν μαθητῶν has been lifted out of the καθώς-clause and set

---

[1] Cf. Harnack, *Die Lehre der 12 Apostel*, 1884, 93ff. and 119ff.; *Mission und Ausbreitung*,[4] 1923, 344ff., 362ff. (ET *Mission and Expansion of Christianity in the First Three Centuries*,[2] 1908; Reitzenstein, *Die hellenist. Mysterienreligionen*[3], 1927, 238–40. That the prophet 'knows all secrets' is also presupposed in I Cor. **13**.2. Fascher, Προφήτης, 1927, 184: 'Agabus has the gift of clairvoyance'.

[2] Cf. on the whole subject Fascher, Προφήτης. *Eine sprach- und religions-geschicht. Untersuchung*, 1927; E. Käsemann, 'Sätze heiligen Rechts im NT', *NTS* 1 (1955), 248ff., ET in *NT Questions of Today* (1969), 66ff.

[3] Zahn (377 n. 17, after A. Klostermann, *Probleme im Aposteltexte*, 10) wanted to find in Agabus the old Greek name Ἀγαυός (Homer: 'shining', 'illustrious'); not a likely name for a Jerusalem prophet! On the other hand the feminine name עגבא has been found on a Palmyrene inscription (*Répertoire d'épigraphie sémitique* II, 1914, No. 1086).

[4] σημαίνω admittedly can also indicate the allusive utterance of an oracle (so Bauer *Wb.* 1482). But here neither this nor a symbolic action as at **21**.11 is in place.

[5] On οἰκουμένη cf. *ThWb* V, 159–61. Michel there conjectures as equivalents for our passage עולם or עלמא; Torrey (*Composition*, 21) suspects a misunderstanding of כל-ארעא, by which Palestine was meant. De Zwaan (*Beg.* II, 59) rightly objects that anyone who did not know the different meanings of ארעא could not translate any Aramaic text at all.— There is no reason for assuming the use of a Semitic source.

[6] On the question of chronology see Introduction § 4, 2a, pp. 61ff.

[7] The famous Western reading συνεστραμμένων ἡμῶν (D d p w Aug. [*serm. dom. in monte* II, 37]: Beg. III 108) shows that the scribe imagined the author as present in Antioch. The later tradition in Eusebius (see Introd. § 1), according to which Luke was an Antiochian, need not yet lie behind this, but only an identification with the Lucius of Acts **13**.1. That this identification was made is proved not only by the 'Prophetiae ex omnibus libris collectae' (see on **13**.1), but also by the Armenian text of Ephraem Syrus' commentary on Acts, preserved in Cod. 571. In this it is said on Acts **12**.25–**13**.3 (the Latin version derives from F. C. Conybeare, see Beg. III, 373–453): *Shavul autem et Barnabas . . . reversi sunt cum Johanne qui vocatus est Marcus, et Lucas Cyrenaicus. Hi autem ambo Evangelistae sunt* (op. cit. 416).

That the later insertion of an 'I' (or 'we') into the text of Acts is not inconceivable is proved already by the Armenian catena to Ephraem on Acts **20**.13, quoted by Preuschen (VI and 121). It read here 'But Luke and those with me . . .'. Preuschen already conjectures that between 'isk' (but) and 'Lovkas' the word 'es' (I) had dropped out. The Armenian text of Ephraem's commentary, published in 1921 (a translation from the Syriac, made in the fifth century: Beg. V, 376), which we have just mentioned, now actually reads: 'But I, Luke, and those with me . . .' (op. cit., 442). This text becomes intelligible as the result of an attempt to explain the 'we' of **20**.13.

at the beginning (cf. **10**.38); the subject of ὥρισαν is 'the disciples'.[1] The text does not speak of a lengthy collecting, such as Zahn and others assume on the analogy of the great Pauline collection, although it does not exclude this. It sounds rather as if every Christian in Antioch hastened to contribute whatever he could, so that the relief might be quickly despatched. It would not occur to any reader of Acts that verses 29 and 30 are separated by an interval of years (Ramsay, *St. Paul*, 49ff., argues for the period from winter 43/44 to 46). Paul also calls the collection διακονία.[2]

VERSE 30: 'Which also they did, sending it to the elders[3] by the hand[4] of Barnabas and Saul.' It is curious that the elders should be thus abruptly thrust forward, and not a word be said of the Apostles. Wellhausen (22) and Wendt (194) include the Apostles among the 'elders'; but in **15**.6 and 22 they stand beside them. Luke seems to have possessed no exact tradition of how the office of elder came into being. The present verse gives the reader to understand that it was created in the interval to perform certain 'welfare' and supervisory functions. He is thus prepared for the elders' prominent role in Chapter 15.[5]

What can the reader learn from these verses when he considers them in the context of Luke's work? First Luke shows how closely the young Gentile congregation at Antioch is linked with the mother community. We have just learned that the highly respected Barnabas was sent to the new foundation. Now prophets from Jerusalem journey to the distant metropolis and allow these Gentile believers to share their gifts of the Spirit. But this leads to an unexpected deepening of the fellowship: the future is unfolded to the prophets, and so the daughter community, with love prompt to help, is able to take active steps to avert the harm threatening the brethren in Jerusalem. Yet the

---

[1] The construction is unusual. It shows that Luke here is concerned for a specially elegant style.

[2] I Cor. **16**.15; II Cor. **8**.4; **9**.1, 13; Rom. **15**.31.

[3] The latest book on the presbyterate, *Das Ältestenamt* by W. Michaelis (1954), uses Acts without misgiving as a reliable historical source. Thus M. assumes that Paul already appointed elders in his congregations; for the Jerusalem elders he conjectures that they were a parallel organization to the Hellenist Seven, and **11**.30 shows a stage in the development of this office.—On the question of the presbyters in the Pauline congregations see the Excursus on I Tim. **3**.7 and **5**.17 in Dibelius-Conzelmann, *Hdb.z.N.T.* 13³, 1955, 44ff., 60f.—When the eldership grew up alongside the Twelve in Jerusalem we do not know. Perhaps its introduction is connected with the assumption of authority by James the Lord's brother.

[4] διὰ χειρός is a favourite LXX expression, which does not mean 'through the mediation' (so Barnikol, *Forschungen* III 14; contrast Bauernfeind, 158), but simply 'through'.—Wikenhauser, *Apg.* 112: perhaps Luke concluded there were messengers.

[5] According to R. Eisler, 'The Meeting of Paul and the "Pillars" in Galatians and in the Acts of the Apostles' (*Bull. Bezan Club* No. 12, Dec. 1937, 58–64), the uncompleted work of Luke (cf. De Zwaan, 'Was the Book of Acts a Posthumous Edition?', *HTR* 17 (1924), 99) consisted of loose leaves, which were in part misplaced. Originally Acts **11**.25f., **13**.1–**15**.2, **11**.27–30, **15**.2–34 (D!), **12**.25, **12**.1–2, **15**.35–41 followed in sequence. This conjecture has rightly met with no approval.

Gentile Christians share not only in the material want of the Jerusalem congregation, but also in its danger, for their delegates, Barnabas and Paul, are
going to remain in Jerusalem during a time of persecution. Here we see this
pair emerging into the foreground, and especially Paul. He is active for
scarcely a year in Antioch, and already he is selected to go with Barnabas on
the mission of relief. The reader will not be surprised when in Chapter 13 he
finds just these two men setting off on a common missionary errand.

So long as the reader simply accepts the passage gratefully, and is edified
by the meaningful and gracious dispensation of history, all is well. But the
moment we attempt to understand this picture historically, then everything
becomes problematic—as the history of research shows.

Why exactly did the prophets come down from Jerusalem to the Syrian
capital? Admittedly there probably still were itinerant Christian prophets
at the turn of the first century, but they appeared singly, not in groups as
here. Moreover they are not here described as itinerant prophets; they are
normally resident in Jerusalem. On the other hand Antioch did not actually
need any such visitation: the congregation there had its own prophets (Loisy,
472). Admittedly, the Jerusalemites come 'as guests' (Bauernfeind, 156), but
this does not explain their journeying to the sink of iniquity that Antioch then
was. Zahn's solution, that they were following 'an impulse of the prophetic
spirit and the footsteps of Barnabas' (377), is not very helpful either: they do
not appear as superintendents like Barnabas! The conjecture that they
'wanted to enrol' Antioch 'in the Jewish front set up to resist Caligula's
attempt to erect a statue to himself in the Temple at Jerusalem' (Knox, 35)
shows how utterly the historians are embarrassed by that simple question.

It is not, however, simply a matter of stating for what purpose the
prophets came (that Agabus would make that prophecy neither he nor his
companions knew in advance; there is thus no motive here for their coming).
What exactly did Agabus prophesy? The text answers: a universal famine,
which came under Claudius. Since no famine so widespread is known to
have happened under Claudius or otherwise, the exegetes have taken all
conceivable pains to interpret the text in such a way as to reconcile it with
reality. Zahn maintains that 'what non-Christian historians report of bad
harvests in the reign of Claudius, with the consequent price-rises and food-
shortages, especially in the large towns', constitutes a 'fully' adequate confirmation of the prophecy (379). In other words, Zahn reduces the universal
famine to a run of bad harvests.

Jeremias takes an entirely different line in 'Sabbatjahr und NT Chronologie' (see bibl.). He deliberately distinguishes the prophetic statement from
the real occurrence: Agabus was prophesying an eschatological event (famines
are listed among the terrors of the last days in Mark **13**.8 *par.*). Knopf had
already written: 'Certainly such violent calamities were often announced by
primitive Christian prophets as portents of the last day' (581). But if the λιμὸς

μεγάλη represents 'an established τόπος of eschatological preaching', how could this τόπος, on this one occasion only, have instigated a specific rescue-operation for Jerusalem? Could Barnabas have been unfamiliar with it? The text frankly says nothing at all about an eschatological catastrophe (even in Lk. 21.11 Luke only speaks of famine 'in divers places'), but foretells a worldwide famine which allegedly, but not in reality, took place under Claudius. 'This,' Knopf freely confesses, 'like many another early-Christian prophecy, has not so far been fulfilled.'

This is not, however, the last of the difficulties. What was there in Agabus' prophecy to prompt the men of Antioch to make a collection for *Judaea*? Bauernfeind replies: the Christians had the Apostles in the forefront of their concern—'If I forget thee, O Jerusalem!' (157). That the Antiochians 'in true-hearted readiness to help' send off 'there and then their modest contribution to meet the coming emergency' is indeed in full accord with Luke's intended picture of the early times. But we know (as Luke did not) that the Antiochian congregation had been founded by Hellenist fugitives from Jerusalem—which bloodthirsty city they would scarcely have recalled with the sentiments of Psalm 137! Bauernfeind even entertains the possibility that serious tension may have existed between the two communities.

The text says finally that Barnabas and Saul brought this relief-fund. Galatians speaks of a single journey which Paul made, in company with Barnabas, from Antioch to Jerusalem, not of two such as Acts reports. Scholars have tried various ways of removing this discrepancy. Zahn's view (382) is that Paul omitted the journey of Acts 11.30 from Galatians because he did not meet the Apostles in Jerusalem, whence they had fled to escape the persecution. Jacquier thinks he did so because 'l'affaire était toute d'ordre matériel' (357) and in no way concerned the Apostles. Both these explanations are inadequate. Whether or no his sojourn was short, or led to a meeting with the Apostles, if Paul in the attempt to demonstrate his independence of Jerusalem had suppressed mention of a journey there, he would have played into the hands of his Judaistic adversaries. This is nowadays more or less generally admitted. Correspondingly, Paul in Gal. 1.18f. expressly mentions the fourteen days' visit, even though on that occasion he saw only Peter and James.

Ramsay (*St. Paul*, 46f.) and Plooij (19f.) have maintained that Gal. 2.1–10 deals with the same journey as Acts 11.30, while Acts 15.1ff. speaks of an event which did not take place until after Galatians was penned. This hypothesis stands or falls with Ramsay's interpretation of Gal. 2.10, ὃ καὶ ἐσπούδασα αὐτὸ τοῦτο ποιῆσαι, as 'a duty which as a matter of fact I at that time made it my special object to perform' (*St. Paul*, 56f.). But these words, lacking precisely a τότε, just cannot have that meaning. All they say is that Paul took pains to perform the duty undertaken in 2.9. Moreover Ramsay can only vindicate his reading of ἐσπούδασα by making an assumption

foreign to the text: that instead of handing over a sum of money to the elders
(the natural implication of Acts **11**.30), Paul and Barnabas had bought
provisions, conveyed them to Jerusalem by sea and overland, and there
personally seen to their distribution among those in need (51f.). No less
artificial is Ramsay's explanation of the silence of Acts regarding the contention over circumcision (Gal. **2**.1–10): the question, he suggests, never came
to an open discussion; Paul just made sure, by private soundings, that the
leaders of the Jerusalem congregation shared his views. Ramsay also divorces
his theory from the Acts account by placing the journey in the year 46. In
sum, his entire construction is an apologetic venture doomed from the start.

Jeremias has striven to retain as correct the report about a relief expedition, without falling into Ramsay's errors. He assumes that Acts **11**.27f. deals
with the same journey as the parallel tradition in **15**.1ff. Barnabas and Paul
thus brought the proceeds of a collection with them to the Apostolic Council,
especially as the famine in Palestine was then at its worst. Hence Jeremias
detaches the relief-journey from the context in which it appears in Acts and
moves it to the year 48. But if we are to find in Gal. **2**.10 reference to a collection brought to the 'Council', then to get any meaning for ἐσπούδασα we
must take over the unhappy legacy of Ramsay's thesis, which we consider
inacceptable.

We will therefore do better to acknowledge the anomalies in **11**.27ff.
This in no way implies that we are dealing, as Overbeck maintains (179), with
a 'tendentious fiction'. Here as elsewhere, Luke is making the best of the
traditions available. One may have concerned the prophet Agabus. There
were personal legends—understanding the word as a literary designation, not
as a historical evaluation—such as popular religious tradition likes to relate
about great men of God. So it was reported of Agabus that he forewarned
Paul of his imprisonment (Acts **21**.10f.) and prophesied the great famine.
This second prophecy Luke has here developed into a vivid scene, and by the
statement 'this came to pass under Claudius' has at once provided historical
confirmation and stamped it as fulfilled.

A second tradition which can be recognized here concerns the relief-
expedition of Paul and Barnabas to Jerusalem. Like many a scholar before
him, Bauernfeind rightly assumes that here Luke had in front of him 'a
tradition which on this point had somewhat strayed from the historical'
(157). For, strangely enough, Luke does not describe in Acts the great collection on which Paul spent so much trouble and exertion and which he mentions
in his epistles to the Corinthians and the Romans. Only in **24**.17 does he have
Paul say that he has come to Jerusalem to bring offerings and alms for his
people. That these alms consisted of a substantial fund collected among his
congregations Luke does not indicate, and no reader could guess it from Acts
if he did not know the Pauline letters. Instead, Luke tells of a collection taken
at Antioch. This is most readily comprehensible if in the course of oral

tradition Paul's journey with the fund was fused with his other journey to Jerusalem, on which he was accompanied by Barnabas, until the story went that both men had made a common journey bearing a fund.

Of course, these two traditions ('Agabus prophesied the great famine' and 'Barnabas and Paul brought a relief-fund from Antioch to Jerusalem') demanded of Luke the historian that they should in some way be connected. The link was not hard to find. Barnabas and Paul came with a collection from Antioch; so the community there had collected for Jerusalem. Why? The Agabus tradition supplied the answer: Agabus had forecast the famine— naturally in Antioch, otherwise that congregation would not have decided on a collection. It followed that Agabus must have been visiting Antioch: it was not unknown even in Luke's time for itinerant prophets to go the rounds of the communities. Old Testament models, which showed prophets going about in bands, may have inspired Luke with the plural 'prophets'. Lastly, Luke knew nothing of the deep rift between the Stephenite and the apostolic congregations in Jerusalem (or if any report reached him he considered it unreliable). It was therefore for him a matter of course that Antioch should hasten to succour Jerusalem. How little he shared the hesitations of modern historians is clear from the fact that he has Barnabas and Paul live unper-turbed in Jerusalem during the persecution. As he saw in Barnabas the com-missioner of the Jerusalem community, such an attitude was for him precisely to be expected. In everything he was guided by his conviction of the intimate, harmonious relations between the primitive community and Antioch. In reality, the Antiochian community had for some considerable time, without seeking any close relationship with Jerusalem, been developing independently and even pushing ahead with the mission to the Gentiles in Syria and Cilicia. Acts **15**.23 proves that Luke has heard of this; but since he had no concrete stories of an edifying character from this area it actually finds no place in his presentation.

Finally, with this journey Luke has also forged the link with what is to follow. When Barnabas and Saul had completed their mission in Jerusalem (**12**.25), they returned, taking John Mark with them. Thus his participation in the first missionary journey is prepared beforehand, and yet another member of the Jerusalem congregation is brought into close association with the Gentile Christians of Antioch.

28

ACTS 12:1–25
PERSECUTION OF THE CHRISTIANS. DELIVERANCE OF PETER

[1] Now about that time Herod the king stretched out his hand to afflict some of those who belonged to the community. [2] He killed James the brother of John with the sword. [3] And when he saw that it pleased the Jews, he proceeded to seize Peter also—now those were the days of unleavened bread. [4] When he had taken him, he put him in prison, and delivered him to four squads of four men each to guard him, intending after the Passover to bring him out to the people. [5] So Peter was under guard in the prison: but prayer was earnestly made to God for him by the community. [6] And when Herod was about to bring him out, in that night Peter was sleeping between two soldiers, bound with two chains; and guards before the door kept watch on the prison. [7] And behold, an angel of the Lord stood by him, and a light shone in the cell; and he struck Peter on the side and awoke him, saying, 'Rise up quickly!' And his chains fell off from his hands. [8] And the angel said, 'Dress, and put on your sandals.' And he did so. And he said to him: 'Put on your cloak, and follow me.' [9] And he went out, and followed; and he did not know that what was done through the angel was real, but thought he was seeing a vision. [10] And passing the first guard and the second, they came to the iron gate leading into the city, which opened to them of its own accord; and they went out, and passed on through one street, and immediately the angel departed from him. [11] And when Peter had come to himself, he said: 'Now I know for certain that the Lord has sent his angel and delivered me out of the hand of Herod, and from all the expectation of the people of the Jews!' [12] When he realized this, he went to the house of Mary the mother of John whose surname was Mark, where many were gathered together and praying. [13] And when he knocked at the door of the gate, a maid named Rhoda came to answer. [14] Recognizing Peter's voice she did not open the gate for joy, but running in announced that Peter stood before the gate. [15] And they said to her: 'You are mad!' But she confidently affirmed that it was so. And they said, 'It is his angel.' [16] But Peter continued knocking; and when they had opened, they saw him and were amazed. [17] But he motioned to them with his hand to be silent and told them how the Lord had brought him out of the prison. And he said: 'Tell these things to James and to the brethren.' And going out he went to another place. [18] When day came, there was no small stir among

the soldiers: What had become of Peter? [19] And when Herod had sought him and not found him, he questioned the guards and commanded that they be led away. Then he went down from Judaea to Caesarea, and remained there. [20] Now he was passionately enraged with the Tyrians and Sidonians. They came to him in a body and, having won over Blastus the king's chamberlain, sued for peace, because their country was supplied with food from the king's country. [21] And on an appointed day Herod arrayed himself in royal apparel, took his seat on the throne, and made them an oration. [22] And the people shouted: 'A god's voice and not a man's!' [23] And at once an angel of the Lord smote him, because he did not give the glory to God. And he was eaten by worms, and expired. [24] But the word of the Lord grew and multiplied. [25] And Barnabas and Saul returned, when they had fulfilled their relief mission in Jerusalem, taking with them John whose surname was Mark.

Bibliography:

W. M. Ramsay, *The Bearing of Recent Discoveries* ..., 1915, 212–5 (on 12.6ff.); G. Kittel, 'Die Stellung d. Jakobus z. Judentum u. Heidenchristentum', *ZNW* 30 (1931), 145–57; K. Lake, 'The Death of Agrippa I', *Beg.* V, 446–52; A. van Feldhuizen, *Markus: de Nef van Barnabas*, Kampen 1933; D. F. Robinson, 'Where and When did Peter die?', *JBL* 64 (1945), 255–67; A. Strobel, 'Passa-Symbolik u. Passa-Wunder in Act. 12.3ff.', *NTS* 4 (1958), 210–5.

B. S. Easton, 'James', *The Interpreter's Bible* 12, 3–74; C. D. Chambers, 'On a Use of the Aorist Participle in Some Hellenistic Writers (Acts 12.25, 25.13)', *JTS* 24 (1922–3), 183–7; S. J. Case, 'John Mark', *Exp.Tim.* 26 (1914–5), 372–6.

VERSE 1: 'About that time'[1] King Herod[2] took it in hand to do evil[3] to some members of the community.'[4] This curious formulation does not betray a correction by the author (or 'redactor', Loisy 478) to a received text, but corresponds exactly to I Esdras 9.20: ἐπέβαλον τὰς χεῖρας ἐκβαλεῖν τὰς γυναῖκας αὐτῶν. It cannot be determined whether τινες represents a Lucan generalization or whether other leaders of the primitive community, of whom we are told nothing, were also arrested. The parallel tradition of 5.18f. also does not answer this question.

[1] κατ' ἐκεῖνον τὸν καιρόν: II Macc. 3.5. Acts 11.30 and 12.25 show that in this note, in itself indefinite, Luke has in view the days when Barnabas and Saul were staying in Jerusalem because of the collection. The objection of many commentators springs in part from misapplied historical considerations and in part from a misunderstanding of 12.25; see there.

[2] Herod Agrippa I is meant, the grandson of Herod the Great (born 10 B.C., died A.D. 44); see Introduction § 4, 2a, p. 61f. For the Christian reader the very title 'King Herod' supplied the prince's motive for persecution: 'King Herod' had to be an enemy of the Christians!

[3] κακόω: a favourite LXX word, used over 60 times.

[4] ἀπό: Hellenistic for the partitive genitive: Bl.-Debr. § 164.

VERSE 2: The wording conveys the impression of a summary execution,[1] as in Mark 6.17ff. The king had powers of life and death. On execution by the sword see Sanh. VII 3a: 'His head is cut off with the sword, as is done by the (Roman) governors.' According to Sanh. IX 1, people to be put to death (by beheading) are 'murderers and the people of a dissident town'.[2] On the theory that John the son of Zebedee was also executed at that time, see Wellhausen 21f. and now A. Suhl (see p. 61 n. 3).

VERSE 3: Hitherto Acts has presented the Jewish people as well-disposed to the Christians, and only the Sadducean leaders as hostile. ἀρεστόν ἐστιν and προστίθημι + inf. are both frequent in LXX: Luke's narrative has an OT ring here. 'This was in the days of the unleavened bread': a parenthetic note.[3]

VERSE 4: ὃν καὶ πιάσας: see note to 1.3;[4] the καὶ need not be translated. On ἔθετο εἰς φυλακήν cf. 4.3 and 5.18[5]—this too is LXX style. παραδοὺς κτλ: four men share each watch and are relieved, in accordance with Roman army regulations,[6] after three hours: see Preuschen, 76, with references.[7] ἀναγαγεῖν[8] τῷ λαῷ: the people had no voice in any regular legal process. In this detail the description probably follows the model of the Passion story (Loisy 484); the Passover here as in Lk. 22.1 is identified with the days of unleavened bread, and thus used for the Passover week.

VERSE 5: Now begins, marked off from the preceding verses by μὲν οὖν (see note on 1.6), the real story of Peter: it opens with the Apostle under strong

---

[1] According to Schwartz (*ZNW* 1910, pp. 89ff.) and Loisy (pp. 480ff.) the king, obliging the Pharisees, persecuted the community because at the Apostolic Council it had agreed to the Pauline mission. Against this is the fact that James the Lord's brother, who according to Gal. 2.9 shared in the agreement with Paul and Barnabas just as much as Peter and John, remained undisturbed (on James see G. Kittel, 'Die Stellung des Jakobus zum Judentum und Heidenchristentum', *ZNW* 30 (1931), 145–57).

[2] Cf. Bill. II 706. Thus according to the Mishnaic law the execution of the son of Zebedee was illegal. Why it occurred we do not know.

[3] Passover is celebrated on 14th Nisan; then follow, to 21st Nisan, the days of unleavened bread: Ex. 12.6–15.—On the addition in D d sy^hmg see Introduction § 3, p. 51; Preuschen (76) overlooks the LXX style!

[4] D gig have replaced ὃν καί, to them incomprehensible, by τοῦτον; see Introd. § 3, p. 51.

[5] Cf. τίθεσθαι ἐν φυλακῇ Gen. 40.3, 42.17, 30 and often.

[6] According to Zahn (386) this was not however the full complement of the guard: see on verse 5. —Jacquier on the other hand (361) thinks these extraordinary measures were taken because Peter had already twice escaped (5.19ff. and 8.1 (?)).

[7] Vegetius, *de re militari* 3,8: '... *et quia impossibile videbatur in speculis* (on sentry duty) *per totam noctem vigilantes singulos permanere, ideo in quattuor partes ... sunt divisae vigiliae, ut non amplius quam tribus horis nocturnis necesse sit vigilare*'. —Preuschen refers also to Philo, *in Flacc.* II, 111: Bassus meets a soldier τῶν ἐν τοῖς τετραδίοις φυλάκων.

[8] ἀνάγειν: 'bring forward'. Bauer, *Wb* 105, lists ἀναχθέντα εἰς δῆμον from the papyri. —Zahn (387 n. 37): 'to set on a widely visible place in front of the building'; this however is not a translation, but an interpretation in terms of the scene he envisages.

guard[1] in the prison, while the community fervently[2] prays God to help him.

VERSE 6: 'And when Herod was about to bring him out, in that night' (i.e. the last of Passover Week)[3] 'Peter was sleeping[4] between two soldiers, bound with two chains, and guards[5] before the door kept watch on his cell'—in other words, all possibility of escape seems precluded.

VERSE 7: Now comes a direct heavenly intervention. The whole of the succeeding action is credited to the angel who so suddenly appears[6]: the liberation of Peter was in no way due to his own efforts but must be ascribed entirely to God. The narrative style is here determined both by that of the Hellenistic miracle stories and by that of LXX.[7] καὶ ἰδού is LXX—see note on 1.10. ἄγγελος κυρίου is common in LXX (cf. verse 11: 'his angel'). φῶς: the heavenly splendour radiating from the visitant. οἴκημα is a euphemism for 'prison-cell'. πατάσσω (see Introd. § 3, above) here amounts to 'prod': the angel is not particularly gentle with Peter. Bauernfeind (163) sees in ἐξέπεσαν κτλ. a direct influence of the *Bacchae* of Euripides, but this surely represents no more than literary convention in the rendering of detail.

VERSE 8: The angel even directs the stages by which Peter gets dressed. The Apostle simply does as he is told.

---

[1] p sy^{hmg} add to ἐτηρεῖτο: *a cohorte regis*, and so indicate the troops from which the guard was mounted. Zahn (386) on the other hand thinks Peter was guarded by the whole σπεῖρα!

[2] ἐκτενῶς does not indicate only the duration of the prayer; the community prays earnestly in the (to human eyes) hopeless situation. D intensifies still further, recalling Judith 4.9 (Preuschen, 76).

[3] Ephraem Syrus already, under the influence of the story of the Passion of Jesus, understood Luke's description to mean that Herod intended to execute Peter on the very morning after his arrest ('. . . *deprehendit, inclusit Schmavona* (Simon) *in vinculis, ita ut mane occideret*'). Zahn renews this misunderstanding: 'In essentials there was to be an exact repetition of what had happened 14 years earlier under the Roman governor Pilate, cf. John 19.4–8, 13–16' (385). But according to Luke the king, who professed to be pious, does not intend to execute Peter on a feast-day. Hence Peter remains a week in custody—and the reader in suspense.

[4] Bauernfeind's suggestion that 'Peter—a few hours before his execution—slept like a child' betrays the modern interest in pious subjectivity, of which Luke here has nothing at all to say. On the other hand B.'s note is very judicious: 'of any kind of initiative to secure his own freedom there is no question' (163).

[5] Usually a prisoner was chained to one guard only: Seneca, *ep.* V 7: 'The same chain united the prisoner and the soldier'; Jos. *Ant.* XVIII, 196. Here however this precautionary measure was duplicated. In addition, between the cell door and the great iron door which shut off the prison from the outside world, and required no guard, sentries were posted at two separate points (v. 10).

[6] ἐπέστη of the angel as in Lk. 2.9, 24.4; of the Lord himself, Acts 23.11. Correspondingly ἀπέστη in v. 10. Pagan writers also use the word for appearances of angels and demons: *Beg.* IV, 135.

[7] Bauernfeind refers to O. Weinreich, *Gebet und Wunder* (Tübinger Beiträge z. Altertumswiss. 5, 1929, 333). Verses 447f. of the *Bacchae* already struck Celsus as a parallel (Orig. *c. Cels.* II 34): αὐτόματα δ᾽αὐταῖς δέσμα διελύθη ποδῶν κλῇδες δ᾽ἀνῆκαν θύρετρ᾽ ἄνευ θνητῆς χερός. Cf. Ovid, *Met.* III 669f.: '. . . *sponte sua patuisse fores lapsasque lacertis sponte sua fama est nullo solvente catenas*'. See R. Reitzenstein, *Hellenistische Wundererzählungen*, 1906, 121.

VERSE 9: Peter thinks he must be dreaming (ὅραμα).[1] See *ThWb* VI, 372.

VERSE 10: The first and second φυλακή are the two guards patrolling the prison-corridor,[2] the third and fourth soldiers of the squad on duty. The narrator does not waste time explaining how it came about that the soldiers did not bar the path of Peter and the angel,[3] but mentions only the great miracle: the heavy iron gate leading to[4] the city opens—and later closes—of its own accord,[5] and allows the two[6] to go out to the street,[7] where the angel takes silent leave of the Apostle.

VERSE 11: 'Only now does Peter fully come to his senses'[8]—'Now I know for certain that the Lord' (= God) 'has sent his angel and delivered me out of the hand of Herod,[9] and from all the expectation[10] of the Jews.'

VERSE 12: συνοράω = 'to get things clear in one's mind' needs no object (cf. **14**.6: 'became aware'). 'The house[11] of Mary the mother of John'[12]

---

[1] In contrast to the ὅραμα stands on the one hand the ἀληθὲς γινόμενον, the real occurrence, on the other ἐν ἑαυτῷ γενόμενος, the realization of the reality of the experience.

[2] That each guarded a door (Zahn, 387) is not said, and need not be assumed.

[3] He will have thought of a deep sleep; cf. Artapanus, *De Judaeis* (the story is preserved in Euseb. *PE* IX 27, 23): 'when night came on, all the doors of the prison opened of themselves, and of the guards some died, but the others were overpowered by sleep . . .'

[4] φέρουσαν: leading to: Bauer, *Wb* 1692 s.v. 4c.

[5] Doors opening of themselves are mentioned by Josephus, *Bell.* VI 293ff.: ἡ δ'ἀνατολικὴ πύλη τοῦ ἐνδοτέρω ναοῦ ... ὤφθη κατὰ νυκτὸς ... ὥραν ἕκτην αὐτομάτως ἠνοιγμένη. Tacitus (*Hist.* V 13), bab. Talmud Joma 39b, jerus. Talmud Joma 43c likewise mention the Temple gates opening of their own accord. But in this case it is an evil omen, such as among others Dio Cassius (60. 35. 1) also reports before the death of Claudius (Weinreich, *Gebet und Wunder*, 1929, 263, 271f., 274). But in Acts **12**.10 the miracle of the doors opening αὐτομάτως is linked with the miracle of the liberation, as in the pagan Hellenistic liberation stories: Weinreich, op. cit., 329–31, 326ff.

[6] Ð d p (*Beg.* III, 41) interpolate κατέβησαν τοὺς ἑπτὰ σταθμούς (see Introd. § 3, p. 53). Zahn (387) is convinced that these words betray local knowledge, 'but a reviser too can possess topological knowledge' (Bauernfeind, 161). In Zahn's view Peter was held captive in Herod's palace, in the west end of the upper city (386), but most expositors opt for the fortress of Antonia, from which steps led to the city and to the Temple (*Beg.* IV, 136). Actually we do not know the place of captivity, nor whether there were really seven steps there.

[7] μίαν is Hellenistic for τινα: 'they went along a street'.

[8] Zahn, 387 n. 43, comparing Rev. 4.1 ἐγενόμην ἐν πνεύματι and Acts **22**.17 γενέσθαι ἐν ἐκστάσει; Jacquier (365) adds 'a classical expression'.

[9] ἐξαιρεῖσθαι ἐκ χειρός is frequent in LXX; but ἐκ τῶν χειρῶν ἐξελέσθαι τῶν Φιλίππου may also be found in Aeschines (III, 256): Jacquier 365. A closer parallel, however, is offered by Dan. 3.15 *Theod.* ὃς ἀπέστειλεν τὸν ἄγγελον αὐτοῦ καὶ ἐξείλατο (ἔσωσε) τοὺς παῖδας αὐτοῦ.

[10] Preuschen unwarrantably seeks to read προσδοκία as 'fear of . . .' (77); the Jews *expected* Peter to be condemned and put to death (Wendt 197)—cf. verse 3. λαὸς τῶν Ἰουδαίων rings very strangely in Peter's mouth, especially after the ἐμεγάλυνεν αὐτοὺς ὁ λαός of 5.13.

[11] The tradition that the Last Supper and the outpouring of the Spirit took place in this house first appears about 300 years after these events (*Beg.* IV, 136f.). It was not the 'headquarters' of James and the brethren. But it is a question whether we can draw any conclusion at all from these Lucan notes about organization.

[12] The rare instance of a person's being identified from his or her offspring occurs when the latter are better-known to the hearer or reader (cf. Mark 15.21, 40). John Mark

prepares for **12**.25 and **13**.5. ἱκανοί—see note to **8**.11 above. προσευχόμενοι: the mention of the continued praying (periphrastic conjugation—see **1**.10 above) reminds the reader that these prayers have now been heard.

VERSE 13: It is a house of some size, with a gateway (πυλών) on the street, from which the house proper was separated by the intervening courtyard. The doorkeeper[1] on the night in question was a slave-girl by the name, frequent among her kind, of ʽΡόδη.[2]

VERSE 14: Losing her wits for very joy,[3] the girl does not open the door, but rushes inside the house to announce the visitor—who is left waiting in the street. In this scene we readily detect a comic element, but through it the narrator brings home the inconceivable greatness of the miracle.

VERSE 15: Though the Christians have been praying for Peter's deliverance, they refuse to believe he has actually been saved! The miracle of that deliverance, in other words, is so great as to be inconceivable. μαίνῃ (ʽYou're crazy!') is most realistic. As in Luke **22**.29 and Acts **15**.2 D, διισχυρίζομαι means 'stubbornly maintain'. ὁ ἄγγελός ἐστιν αὐτοῦ: an expression of the belief that each man has a guardian angel, imagined as his celestial double.[4]

VERSE 16: ʽPeter continued knocking'[5]: see the note on verse 14 about the comic element. For the ancient reader it was a scene of extraordinary suspense—if Peter is not admitted, his knocking will sooner or later rouse the neighbours. But it does not come to that; the Christians open, and are beside themselves with surprise.

VERSE 17: κατασείσας τῇ χειρί: the orator's gesture for silence (also **13**.16 and **21**.40; cf. **26**.1). This was no time for whoops of joy (these are demonstrative Levantines, remember). Peter must now quit Jerusalem with no loss of time, so—without entering the house itself—he shortly recounts his liberation, asks that ʽJames and the brethren' be told, and leaves the town[6]

(if it is always the same Mark) is further mentioned in the NT at Col. **4**.10, Philemon 24, II Tim. **4**.11 and I Peter **5**.14.

[1] ὑπακούω is the technical term for a janitor's work: 'open up'.

[2] Contracted form of ῥοδέα, 'rosebud', 'little rose' (Jacquier, 366).

[3] ἀπὸ τῆς χαρᾶς Luke **24**.41—Lucan psychology? For the construction with ἀπό (= ʽon account of') see Bl.-Debr. § 210, 1.

[4] There are Rabbinic references in Billerbeck II. See also M. Dibelius, *Der Hirt des Hermas*, 1923, 494f.; W. Bousset, *Religion des Judentums*[3], 1926, 324; *ThWb* II, 1935, εἰκών, 378ff.; H. Wilms, Εἰκών I, 1935; J. Jervel, *Imago Dei;* 1960.

[5] ἐπιμένω + participle: Bl.-Debr. § 414, 1; cf. John **8**.7.

[6] D, not content with this brief scene, makes Peter enter the house and tell his story, which means that the ἐξελθών refers to his leaving the house. Jacquier (368) infers from ἀδελφοῖς that there was no other Apostle in Jerusalem, and equates the 'brethren' with the presbyters; this the text does not warrant: the reference is merely to Christians in general. Dibelius (*Studies*, 22) concludes from verse 17 (and verse 12) that the allusion to the praying community derives from Luke; it is clear here that the whole congregation is not assembled. But the Jerusalem congregation was by that time fairly certainly much too large to gather in a single house.

for 'another place'.[1] Thus Peter's story proper comes to an end.

VERSE 18: Here begins a sequel which indirectly attests the 'world's' acknowledgement of the miracle. The next morning (the narrator has not bothered to calculate whether the watch must meantime have been changed) there is a great[2] commotion among the soldiers: 'What has become of Peter?' This scene also (it has a parallel at 5.21ff., where the enemy's help-lessness is depicted at greater length) verges on the comic, but at the same time shows the grim seriousness of the situation.

VERSE 19: The 'sought and not found' corresponds to 5.21b–24. Herod orders the soldiers to be 'led away', probably not merely to prison,[3] but to execution (so, e.g., Wendt 198). On κατελθών κτλ. see 11.27. Luke's account gives the reader the impression that Herod left 'Judaea' (again = 'Jerusalem') for Caesarea very shortly after Passover Week.

VERSE 20: θυμομαχέω (Hellenistic) = rage violently (Bauer, *Wb* 722): Blass notes on this verb that Luke is occasionally fond of rare words. Luke does not draw a very clear picture of the situation. Herod cannot, despite the 'suing for peace', have been waging an actual war on cities of the Roman province of Syria (Wendt 199; Loisy 493). Knopf (584) and Beyer (77) opt for an economic 'war', possibly motivated by the competition offered Caesarea by the Phoenician ports: Herod may have banned grain-exports to Tyre and Sidon. ὁμοθυμαδόν can only refer to a joint delegation,[4] which—probably in the language of baksheesh—'talked' Chamberlain Blastus into being their go-between.

VERSE 21: The τακτὴ ἡμέρα is the day appointed for the formal conclusion of 'peace'. Herod sits on the throne in his kingly raiment[5] and holds forth to the Phoenician envoys.

VERSE 22: It is not clear why the people shouted 'A god's voice, not a man's!' That the (pagan) mob should have been overjoyed at the happy ending of the economic war is a modern conjecture. In Josephus (*Ant.* XIX. 356ff.) we are told that the population of Caesarea reviled the late king,

---

[1] Since Wellhausen (1907) this is usually identified as Antioch, though Catholic exegesis has thought of Rome (cf. Jacquier, 369). Those who, like Dibelius, find here the use of a Peter legend will not be too concerned by the absence of a name: a legend has other ends in view than a historical record (*Studies*, 96 n. 8). There is then no need for such suggestions as that the name of the place was not given because Peter had no permanent domicile (Bauernfeind, 162; Wikenhauser, *Apg.* 114).

[2] οὐκ ὀλίγος—Luke's favourite litotes: cf. Acts 14.28; 15.2; 17.4, 12; 19.23f.; 27.20.

[3] So E. Nestle in 'Bemerkungen über die Urgestalt der Evangelien und Apostel-geschichte', *Philologia Sacra*, Berlin 1896, 53. appealing to Gen. 39.20, 40.3 and 42.16. Linguistically this interpretation is entirely possible, but the sense is against it.

[4] παρῆσαν κτλ: πρός + acc. is frequent with εἶναι also in Hellenistic Greek (replacing classical παρά τινι: Bl-Debr. § 239, 1): 'they came in a body to the king and, having won over his chamberlain Blastus, petitioned for peace, as their country was economically dependent on the king's.'

[5] In Josephus *Ant.* XIX 344, it is described as a garment made entirely of silver.

removed statues of his daughters to brothels, and made merry on the grand scale when his death was known.

VERSE 23: The angel of the Lord smites him because[1] he did not give God the glory,[2] and he dies eaten by worms.[3] This is the typical fate of persecutors of God's Church. D thought it necessary to be even more explicit, and stresses that he was eaten *alive* by worms.

VERSE 24: A miniature summary, corresponding to 6.7 and 19.20. The 'Word of the Lord' (B as against ℵ 81) means exactly the same as the 'Word of God' elsewhere, i.e. the Christian missionary kerygma and the community living by and for it.

VERSE 25: The εἰς of (B and) ℵ is to be preferred here, as against the 'emendations' ἐξ (A 33 sy) and ἀπό (D): Luke has placed εἰς 'Ιερουσαλήμ[4] ahead of the participial phrase in which it belongs (so already Wendt 199f.). In this way Luke makes both retrospective (11.30 and 12.12) and prospective (13.5) connections, bringing one more member of the Jerusalem community into intimate contact with Antioch. Far from striking him as improbable, the continued presence of the Antiochian delegation in Jerusalem throughout the persecution served Luke as a demonstration of the heartfelt communion between the mother church and the daughter congregation.[5]

Scholars of the age of source criticism showed a rare unanimity in ascribing this twelfth chapter to a Jewish Christian source. Only the derivation of the last two verses was contested, and B. Weiss also had reservations about verses 3, 5, 12b and 18–22. With Wendt began the gradual recognition that Chapter 12 forms an independent unit which does not belong to any comprehensive source-document, and Beyer began discriminating, within this unit, between one component and another (verses 1f., 3–19, 20–24).

What such a source-critical approach does not take into account is only observed when we investigate the composition of the chapter. If we think of the persons active in each episode, the chapter appears to be constructed in perfect symmetry. The outer frame is provided by two statements about journeys to or from Jerusalem by Barnabas and Paul. Between these stand two Herod stories (1. how he persecuted, 2. how he died), which themselves

---

[1] ἀνθ' ὧν: Luke 1.20 and 19.44.

[2] Cf. Luke 17.18; LXX Jos. 7.19 *et passim*.

[3] Cf. II Sam. 24.16, II Kings 19.35, II Macc. 9.5–9 (Antiochus Epiphanes), Josephus, *Ant*. XVII 168ff. (Herod the Great), Tertullian, *ad Scap*. 3 (Claudius Lucius Herminianus) and Eusebius, *H. E.* VIII, 16 (Emperor Galerius). Cf. also Isaiah 66.24, Judith 16.17, Apoc. Peter § 27, Papias, Fragm. 3 (Judas). Complete list of passages in Wikenhauser, *Die Apg. u. ihre Geschichtswert*, 1921, 398ff. As the papyri show, σκωληκόβρωτος is neither a word invented by Luke (so Blass) nor a technical medical term, but an unscientific word (*Beg*. IV, 140).

[4] εἰς Hellenistic for ἐν (see Introd. § 5, p. 78f.).

[5] Somewhat differently J. Dupont, 'La mission de Paul à Jérusalem', *NT* 1 (1956), 275f.

frame the kernel of the chapter, devoted to Peter. But this centrepiece is itself twofold: 1. the freeing of Peter (verses 5–11), 2. his reunion with the community (12–17).

Yet this analysis—implying, it would seem, the triumph of Morgenthaler's rule-of-two theory—does not reveal the real structure. This we cannot see until we ask 'What are the climactic points of the narrative?' The first Herod scene (**12**.1–4) is nothing but a prelude. It makes plain what fate awaits Peter unless—by a miracle—he is rescued. But the miracle happens. An angel delivers him from prison in the nick of time. This scene of deliverance forms the first climax. The second part of the Peter section corresponds, so to speak, to the choral finale in miracle stories, which reflects the reality, the greatness of the wonder; this part indirectly proves how inexpressibly great the miracle was—even the Christians, engaged in prayer for this very deliverance, do not believe it has really happened! However, the help of God is incomplete so long as the persecuting tyrant remains alive. And so we have the second Herod story. With it comes a new climax. But this is what Luke wanted. In its absence, the deliverance by the angel, retrospectively summarized in verse 11, would be the culminating point, leaving everything else in the shade. If we keep these two real climaxes in view—the rescue of Peter, the death of Herod—then these two men stand out as adversaries in the Lucan composition.

Where did Luke find his material for this composition? This question is soonest answered in the case of verses 20–23: the story of Herod's guilt and punishment. He died in Caesarea after a few days' painful sickness. This sudden end led the Jews to wonder why God so swiftly snatched away the king. It must have been, they reasoned, as a punishment for his 'not giving God the glory'. Details of this story varied in the telling. The version Luke used is not in all respects superior to that of Josephus; only in Josephus does the mention of the robes make real sense, and the flattery of courtiers is more probable than the unmotivated shout of the (pagan) populace. The fact that Josephus presents Herod's death without any miraculous element (his account makes one think of appendicitis) may be due to his employment of a source which did not wish to show an allegedly popular king as the object of divine wrath. This would explain the substitution, for the 'angel of the Lord' who was certainly contained in the Jewish tradition, of the legendary bird of fate which plays the role of ἄγγελος κακῶν, or harbinger of ill (*Ant.* XIX 346; see XVIII 195ff.); however baleful, this messenger had not the same connotations of vengeance for sin. —It goes without saying that the games in honour of the emperor and the negotiations with the Phoenicians are not mutually exclusive.

The origin of the first Herod story, on the other hand, cannot be precisely settled. Its very extent is questionable, for it merges almost imperceptibly into the Peter story. Luke does indeed mark an incision in verse 5, with μὲν οὖν. But the Peter story certainly began not with his captivity but

with his arrest. Thus the material of verse 4 already belongs to it. Are verses
1 to 3, then, the remains of an extensive narrative shorn of all but the essential
fact, the killing of the son of Zebedee? Does τινες conceal other Apostles,
as might well be inferred from the parallel 5.18? Or is Luke in verse 1 merely
generalizing to make the persecution appear even more dangerous? Did Herod
—B. Weiss raised this point—really wait for the popular reaction to the first
measure before having Peter arrested? If the leaders of a movement are to be
seized, action is usually taken against all at one time. It is not of course
impossible that Peter succeeded in escaping and that the legend of his deliverance developed out of this. At all events, it is generally assumed that Luke
knew more about the death of James than the seven words he devotes to it
—James was after all the first of the Twelve to become a martyr.

However that may be, it is from a literary point of view perfectly intelligible why Luke allowed the martyrdom of James to be overshadowed.
Peter now stands at the midpoint of the whole, even if his role is purely
passive (his liberation is an act of God alone!). His deliverance by God's
miraculous intervention from a—humanly— unavoidable death is the story
Luke wants to relate for the community's edification. Had James's martyrdom
loomed overlarge at this point, the Peter story would have been ousted from
its dominant place in favour of a—for Acts—strictly minor figure. The
deliverance of the one Apostle, so uplifting in its affirmative, its overwhelming triumph, would have been counterbalanced by the harsh death of
the other whom, incomprehensibly, no angel protected from the executioner's
blade. Now if Luke had been intent on portraying the action of God's mercy
against the background of his inscrutable dispensations, on making the
reader feel the whole tension between the *deus revelatus* and the *deus abscon-
ditus*, an extensive account of James's martyrdom would have been in order.
But the illustration of *that* theological dilemma was very far from Luke's
mind. His concern was to bring home to readers the total victory, the triumph
of the good cause. He does not wholly conceal the Cross which throws its
shadow in James's execution. But the light falls not on it but on the palpable
evidence of God's power and saving help.

A further point must be observed. If Luke wanted to satisfy the demands
of what he and his generation found edifying, he could give James's death
extensive treatment only in such a way as to make the Apostle become the
accuser at the trial instead of the accused, and appear the true victor of the
day. These possibilities however Luke had utterly exhausted in his handling
of the Stephen episode. So even in this regard it was advisable to play down
the martyrdom of James. Hence it is wholly understandable that the persecution of the Christians, together with the killing of the son of Zebedee, should
serve only as a foil to the miracle which saved Peter.

This miracle-story falls into two sharply differentiated parts. In the first,
relating the deliverance of the Apostle, God intervenes directly through the

angel. But this episode itself falls into two scenes: the events in the cell and the flight into freedom. The first scene (verses 7f.) has not a word to spare for the two soldiers, who yet are also in the cell; from verse 19 we may conclude that in Luke's view they were not dead—like many of the sentries in Artapanus—but sunk in spellbound slumber. Peter appears to be sleeping very soundly, but this is no reason to gloss 'as calmly as a child' (Bauernfeind). Peter's sleep is not meant to suggest his mental condition, his peace of mind: not by the sleeping Peter will the faithful be edified—but by the angel! Peter's behaviour is completely passive: not only does he make no (hopeless!) attempt to free himself by force, he does not even pray and sing, like Paul and Silas in similar straits (16.25). He just sleeps, and would have slept his last night through, had the angel not awakened him. How soundly he is sleeping may be gauged from the fact that the taciturn angel has to prod him in the ribs (with his foot?) to waken him. 'Get up, quick!' he says. Now this shows that the account did not originate with Luke, who always has heavenly beings use dignified and, as far as possible, biblical language (cf. the angel's words to Cornelius in 10.4). As has been demonstrated by Eric Auerbach in his excellent book *Mimesis,* ancient historians resorted to realism only for the production of comic (or idyllic) effects (ET 1957, 27 and 39). But such intentions are far removed from the mind of our narrator, whether here or in what follows. He makes the angel, at this critical moment, confine himself to doing and saying the essential. There can be no question of a conversation with Peter. Fuddled with sleep, and not even knowing whether he is awake or dreaming, Peter has to be directed into dressing, stage by stage . . . 'Now put on your sandals. Put on your cloak and follow me!' That Peter must be bidden at each step makes plain to the reader that his role throughout the deliverance is merely passive: it is in no sense his own work, but exclusively God's.

The same is true of the second scene (verses 9f.). The narrator wastes no words describing how the two got past the first and second sentinels. The reader will himself supply the answer that they too were sunk in sleep. As is only fitting—for when heavenly powers come into action the laws of physics are, or may be, suspended—the heavy iron gate opens of its own accord in the path of the angel. The inclusion of the self-opening door shows that the narrator was acquainted with Hellenistic escape-legends. The angel escorts the Apostle as far as the street; then, with his protégé safe at last, goes his own way without a word of farewell.

Only now, after everything has taken place without his aid, does Peter come to his senses; and now at last we hear, too, the authentic voice of Luke, for verse 11 with its biblical overtones is in typical Lucan style. Luke lets the reader know exactly the significance of what he has just read.

Necessarily, the second part (verses 12–17) is of quite another kind than the first. Peter is now left to his own resources. He has not been told what to do. He first takes stock of his situation (συνιδών), then goes to a house where he is sure to find Christians. But as he knocks at the gate, he comes up against an unexpected obstacle: the slave-girl who has run to answer is so overjoyed when she recognizes his voice that she loses her presence of mind, leaves him standing outside, and rushes back indoors to announce 'Peter is at the gate!' This allows the narrator to spin out the scene and show the reader how little even the Christians—though they were actually praying for his safety—could believe in the possibility of Peter's escape. And so the girl is met with cries of 'You're crazy!' The realism which we already noted in verse 7 is continued in this verse. Even when the slave-girl stoutly insists that Peter is there, they do not hasten to the gate but fall back on the explanation 'It must be his angel'—perhaps with the tacit corollary: 'coming to notify us of his death . . .'

Meanwhile Peter, still outside, goes on knocking. The moment is one of great tension: will they let him in before the neighbours are alerted and endeavour to capture the fugitive? At last they do open the door to him, and fall back amazed. Peter silences their cries of joy with a gesture, and tells them how the Lord brought him out of prison. So now the miracle stands attested and accredited, and Peter can depart for 'another place' where he will be safe from Herod.

The exegetes are all agreed that Luke took this story over without making any major alterations—its style is wholly alien to him, and he was right not to touch it. For the telling is masterly: there is not a word too many, and from beginning to end the tale is charged with suspense.

Only in two places, which we have left out of our résumé, has the hand of Luke the historian been detected. One is the words tacked on to verse 17, 'And he said: "Tell these things to James and the brethren"'. Such specific reference to a person who plays no part is foreign to the legend. Here Luke the historian is advising us that—in the interim, at least—James has taken over the leadership of the congregation. It would be a mistake to try and learn from these words whether the other Apostles were still in Jerusalem. Luke is simply paving the way for a transition to be pursued in Chapter 15: the replacement of Peter by James.

But we might also ascribe to Luke the statement that Peter went to the house of John Mark's mother, Mary. In itself, this precise detail does not necessarily point to Luke. But in verse 25 Luke reports that it was this very man whom Barnabas and Paul took back with them to Antioch. If one reviews Luke's way of leading up to the relations between his *dramatis personae* (9.27 is a case in point), then another such preparation here—a fairly adroit one at that—seems by no means improbable.

Finally, it is most likely that verses 18f. also derive from Luke. They produce new witnesses to God's deliverance of Peter: the guards realize, with horrified bewilderment, that he has escaped. They are put on trial, all the searching comes to nothing, and at length they are led away. It is they now, not Peter, who must die—a soldier's responsibility for the prisoner in his charge is on his own head. Of pity for the guards (Beyer deeply felt the omission) Luke shows not the slightest trace: whoever stands in God's way must pay the price—this will very soon be exemplified in the case of Herod himself. He is brought back into the picture in these verses—that is their second function—and the narrative may smoothly continue with his journey to Caesarea and his death there.

Verses 24f. show Luke rounding off the narrative by linking the end firmly to the beginning. In this way he endows the whole composition with its remarkably self-contained character.

29

ACTS 13:1-12
FIRST MISSIONARY JOURNEY; CHOOSING
OF PAUL AND BARNABAS; CYPRUS

[1] Now there were in the congregation at Antioch prophets and teachers: Barnabas, and Symeon who was called Niger, and Lucius of Cyrene, and Manaen, a close associate of Herod the tetrarch; and Saul. [2] And as they served the Lord and fasted, the Holy Spirit said: 'Separate me Barnabas and Saul for the work to which I have called them.' [3] Then they fasted and prayed, and laid their hands on them and sent them off. [4] So, sent out by the Holy Spirit, they went down to Seleucia; and from there they sailed to Cyprus. [5] And when they arrived at Salamis, they proclaimed the Word of God in the synagogues of the Jews: and they had also John as their attendant. [6] And when they had gone through the whole island as far as Paphos, they found a certain sorcerer, a Jewish false prophet, whose name was Bar-Jesus; [7] who was with the proconsul Sergius Paulus, a man of understanding. He had Barnabas and Saul summoned, and sought to hear the Word of God. [8] But Elymas the sorcerer (for so is his name translated) opposed them, seeking to turn aside the proconsul from the faith. [9] But Saul, who is also Paul, filled with the Holy Spirit, fastened his eyes on him, [10] and said: 'O full of all guile and all villainy, you son of the devil, you enemy of all righteousness, will you not stop perverting the right ways of the Lord? [11] And now, behold, the hand of the Lord is upon you, and you will be blind, not seeing the sun for a season!' And immediately there fell on him a mist and a darkness; and he went about seeking people to lead him by the hand. [12] Then the proconsul when he saw what happened believed, being astonished at the teaching of the Lord.

Bibliography:

O. Weinreich, *Antike Heilungswunder*, 1909, esp. 189ff. (on verse 11); Behm, see § 16 bibl. (on verse 1); Cadbury, see § 4 bibl. (on verse 1), esp. 53; A. D. Nock, 'Paul and the Magus', *Beg.* V, 164-88; Lake, 'The Proconsulship of Sergius Paulus', *Beg.* V, 455-60; B. T. Holmes, 'Luke's Description of John Mark', *JBL* 54 (1935), 63-72 (on verse 5); G. A. Harrer, 'Saul who is also called Paul', *HTR* 33 (1940), 19-34; F. V. Filson, 'The Christian Teacher in the First Century', *JBL* 60 (1941), 317-28 (on verse 1); E. Peterson, 'La λειτουργία des prophètes et des didascales à Antioche', *RScR* 36 (1949), 577–9; G. Sevenster, 'De wijding van Paulus en Barnabas', *Stud. Paul. in hon. J. de Zwaan*, 1953, 188–201; A. Kragerud, 'Itinerariet i Apostlenes Gjerninger', *Norsk Teol. Tidsskr.* 56 (Oslo 1955), 249–72, esp. 251.

E. A. Thorne, 'The Earlier Missionary Journeys in the Acts of the Apostles', *CQR* 121 (1935–6), 109–17; R. O. P. Taylor, 'The Ministry of Mark', *Exp.Tim.* 54 (1942–3), 136–8; F. C. Burkitt, 'The Interpretation of Bar-Jesus', *JTS* 4 (1903), 127–9; H. Grimme, 'Elym, der Astrolog', *OLZ* 12 (1909), 207–11; B. M. Metzger, 'St. Paul and the Magicians', *Princeton Seminary Bulletin* 38 (1944), 27–30; R. Hughes, 'Acts **13**.11', *Exp.Tim.* 45 (1933–4), 44f.; J. Foster, 'Was Sergius Paulus Converted? (Acts **13**.12)', *Exp.Tim.* 60 (1948–9), 359–62; G. Klein, *ZThK* 64 (1967), 281–7.

VERSE 1: Luke has probably already made use of this tradition[1] about the leading men of the Antiochian congregation[2] in 4.36[3]—see also on **11**.19. Symeon[4] and Lucius (see next note) are unknown; Manaen[5] (=מְנַחֵם) is

---

[1] Dibelius (*Studies*, 11 n. 20) speaks of a list handed down; Bauernfeind also assumes that the narrator had the list of names ready to hand (168). None of the five belongs to the 'Seven'; the Stephenite circle disposed of a fairly large number of outstanding personalities.

[2] On κατὰ τὴν οὖσαν ἐκκλησίαν see second note to 5.17.

[3] E. Schwartz, *NGG* (1907), 282 n. 1; so also Wendt 201.

[4] In 'Did Peter die in Jerusalem?' (*JBL* 71 (1952), 211–6). W. M. Smaltz maintains that Symeon Niger is the Symeon mentioned by Acts 15.14. The latter's identity with Peter is also doubted by S. Giet in his 'L'Assemblée apostolique et le décret de Jérusalem' (*RScR* 39/40, 203–20), where he maintains that the scene of 15.7–12 is not directly connected with that of 15.13–21. Neither scholar advances any proof.

[5] In *Ant.* XV, 373–9, Josephus speaks of an Essene called Manaen who had prophesied to the young Herod (later the Great) that he would accede to the throne. Wellhausen (*NGG* 1907, 13) assumed that our author confused this Herod with the tetrarch, and that his allusion was to the same Manaen. Jacquier (378) is more cautious: perhaps, in recognition of the fulfilment of the prophecy, Herod the Great had given a son or nephew of the Essene Manaen to be the companion of his own son Antipas. Zahn on the other hand (403 n. 18) makes the Essene the grandfather of our Manaen, in whom he sees the unknown βασιλικός of John 4.43ff. —There can be no taxing the great scholar with lack of ingenuity. —Zahn also referred to the *Prophetiae ex omnibus libris collectae* contained in the St Gall Codex 133 ('Kompendium der bibl. Prophetie aus der afrik. Kirche um 305–25' in *Gesch. St. A. Hauck dargeb.*, Leipzig 1916, 52–63; *Forsch. zur Gesch. des ntl Kanons* IX, 20, 145–8 and 350; *Die Apg.* 399ff.), in which Acts **13**.1ff. is rendered as follows: *erant autem in ecclesia prophetae et doctores Barnabas et Saulus, quibus imposuerunt manus prophetae: Symeon qui appellatus est Niger et Lucius Cirinensis, qui manet usque adhuc, et Ticius conlactaneus, qui acceperant responsum a spiritu sancto, unde dixerunt: Segregate* etc.; *hoc est prophetiae.* According to Zahn the words '*Antiocensis Manaenque Herodis tetrarchae*' are missing after 'Titus' (sic!). This would represent the authentic text written by Luke *ca* A.D. 80, in which he imparted to Theophilus certain information regarding Lucius of Cyrene (*Die Apg.*, 400f.). Cadbury, in 'Lucius of Cyrene' (*Beg.* V, 489–95), finds the omission likely but conjectures that *qui manet usque adhuc* is modelled on I Cor. **15**.6 (Vulgate: *manent usque adhuc*) and the scribe intended in this way to identify Lucius of Cyrene with the author of Acts. Ropes (*Beg.* III, 115) judges that this text is a free rendering of Acts **13**.1–3, probably based on the African Latin text; the strange phrase *qui manet usque adhuc et Ticius* arose probably from a corruption of the Latin text (perp. *manaen etiam herodis tetrarchae*; vulg. *et manaen qui erat herodis tetrarchae*): '*Manaen*' explains '*manet*' and

identified as a σύντροφος,[1] i.e. an intimate, of the tetrarch Herod Antipas: hence he was a courtier of some note. 'Prophets and teachers'[2]: it does not emerge from the text that some of the five were prophets and the rest teachers, hence that there were different 'offices' in existence.

VERSES 2f.: With these two verses Luke describes two distinct scenes, in which the presence of the congregation is not mentioned, but probably presupposed. The first scene leads to the selection of the missionaries. Barnabas and Paul are not mentioned together in verse 1, in order that their future association may appear founded solely on the direction of the Spirit. LXX uses λειτουργεῖν of the Temple-service of the priests and Levites (*ThWb* IV, 225-32), Didache **15**.1f. of the regular conduct of the Christian services. Here the thought is of a gathering for communal prayer at which the circle of prophets and teachers is moved to a decision. In 'ministered to the Lord' Luke has borrowed an expression of special solemnity from LXX[3] as an allusion, above all, to prayer.[4] By fasting one withdraws in the highest

---

'*tetrarchae*' accounts for '*ticius*'. —D reads Μαναήν τε Ἡρώδου καὶ τετράρχου σύντροφος: if the καὶ (matched in d) is not a mere slip of the pen, Manaen, the tetrarch's 'foster-brother', becomes a son of Herod the Great. —The text of Ephraem Syrus, who also identifies Luke and Lucius, is quoted above, p. 374 n. 7 to **11**.28.

[1] σύντροφος (see Deissmann, *Bibelstudien* 173 and 178-81; ET *Bible Studies*, 1901) was a title of honour bestowed at court on certain youths brought up as a prince's companions; as grown men they retained the title (*Beg.* IV, 142).

[2] Among those endowed with charismata I Cor. **12**.28f. lists first of all 'apostles, prophets and teachers' (cf. Rom. **12**.6ff., I Cor. **14**.26, 29 and Did. **15**.1f.). It cannot be disputed, in the light of the epistles, that in the Pauline churches the 'offices' of prophet and teacher were of a charismatic order. The Didache passage shows the gradual disappearance of these charismatics and the rise of the episcopate and diaconate in their place. Peterson, however (bibl.), attempts to free the Antiochian congregation of its charismatic character. He dissociates the prophets from it by identifying them with those who came down from Jerusalem (**11**.27). The testimony of the Didache he discredits through the suspicion that it is itself dependent on Acts **13**.1f. Appealing to Hermas, *Sim.* V 3.8, he interprets λειτουργεῖν as meaning a 'special fast'. Since in Judaism only rabbis and leaders of the synagogue might hold a special fast, the implication according to Peterson is that Barnabas and Paul were regarded in Antioch as Christian rabbis, and that in this community a Jewish custom was perpetuated. But the identification of the Jerusalem prophets of **11**.27 with those named much later, who belonged to the congregation of Antioch (κατὰ τὴν οὖσαν ἐκκλησίαν), is completely at variance with the text of Acts **13**.1f. Did. **15**.1f. shows that the dwindling charismatic prophets and teachers were still held in higher esteem than the ἐπίσκοποι and διάκονοι who now took over the cult. The fact that both in Didache **15**.1f. and in Acts **13**.1 (charismatic) prophets and teachers are mentioned together does not justify our discounting the Didache as influenced by Acts. Moreover it is not, in Hermas, the fast as such which is styled λειτουργία but the offering of the money so saved to the poor. The passage thus gives us no right to explain λειτουρεῖν τῷ κυρίῳ καὶ νηστεύειν as a special fast alongside a fast of the congregation. Rather do the passages adduced in *ThWb* IV, 232 for λειτουργεῖν = 'pray' come into the reckoning for Acts **13**.2 also. Luke chose this solemn expression from LXX (see n. 3 on v. 2) to set off this scene from the one immediately following, with its νηστεύσαντες καὶ προσευξάμενοι.—διδάσκαλοι occurs only here in Acts.

[3] II Chron. **5**.14, **13**.10 and **35**.3; Judith **4**.14; Joel **1**.13 and **2**.17; Ezek. **40**.46, **44**.16 and **45**.4; Dan. Θ **7**.10.

[4] So also Strathmann, *ThWb* IV, 233, 15ff.

degree from the influence of the world and makes oneself receptive to commands from heaven.[1] The 'Shepherd of Hermas' offers examples.[2] Naturally it was one of the 'prophets' who gave utterance to the Spirit's direction, but Luke says nothing of this human agency in order to allow as direct an effect as possible to the Spirit's command. The missionaries' task is described in a pious expression of portentous vagueness. ὃ (= εἰς ὃ) προσκέκλημαι: the divine decision has already been taken before it is made manifest.

Then follows a second scene, to be imagined as separated from the first by a lapse of time: a new period of preparation through fasting and prayer. Thus strengthened with spiritual power, the three prophets who will remain in Antioch lay their hands on the two departing, and send them forth.[3]

VERSE 4: αὐτοί[4] as a personal pronoun here carries no special emphasis (cf. **13**.14). μὲν οὖν introduces a new episode—see note to **1**.6. ἐκπεμφθέντες κτλ. is surprising after ἀπέλυσαν, but Luke wants to make it quite clear that properly it is not these men but the Holy Spirit who brings about this mission —it is indeed fundamentally the mission to the Gentiles (**14**.26f!). 'They went down to Seleucia'—i.e. the port,[5] about 16 miles west of Antioch, from which one could take ship to Cyprus.[6]

VERSE 5: γενόμενοι ἐν[7] Σαλαμῖνι[8] = 'having arrived at Salamis'. Philo[9] and Josephus[10] both give accounts of the Jews in Cyprus. Only now does Luke

---

[1] See J. Schümmer, *Die altchristliche Fastenpraxis*, Münster 1933, 212–4.

[2] Hermas, *Vis*. II 2.1; III 1.2; 10.6f. OT instances: *ThWb* IV, 928, 25ff.; on fasting in the early Church see 934f. ('Throughout, fasting appears as a reinforcing accompaniment to prayer or as preparation for the reception of divine revelation'). So also Billerbeck II, 241–4 and excursus 'Fastenfeier'.

[3] It is not a question of 'a gift of grace bestowed for a life-long ministry' (so A. J. Mason in H. B. Swete, *Essays on the Early History of the Church and the Ministry*, 1918, 31), nor of 'power and authority for the ministry' (Steinmann): Lucius, Symeon and Manaen have no higher rank than Barnabas and Paul (Sevenster, bibl.).

[4] Bl.-Debr. § 277, 3, also appendix. D substitutes οἱ (μὲν οὖν).

[5] The city was founded by Seleucus Nicator *ca* 300 B.C.; its harbour (now silted up) welcomed the big ships of Egypt, Phoenicia, Cyprus, Asia Minor, Greece and Italy (Jacquier 381).

[6] From the mouth of the Orontes to Cyprus is a distance of some sixty miles. The island measures, from N.E. to S.W., about 132 miles. Between the two mountain ranges which run the whole length in this direction lies the plain watered by the Pediacos, which in antiquity was very fruitful, producing wine, oil and grain (Jacquier 382). Augustus had given Herod the Great half the yield of the rich copper-mines (Josephus *Ant*. XVI, 28). Zahn (405 n. 22) cites late reports—to which he gladly lends credence—according to which the resurrected Lazarus preached in Cyprus.

[7] ἐν Hellenistic for εἰς (Bl.-Debr. § 218).

[8] Salamis, the island's largest town, was its nearest port to Seleucia. A strong Jewish community there, with several synagogues, is presupposed.

[9] *Leg. ad Gaium* 282 C.-W.; 'and not only the mainlands are full of Jewish colonies, but also the most important islands: Euboea, Cyprus, Crete.'

[10] *Ant*. XIII, 284: 'At this period things were going well not only for the Jews in Jerusalem and the country, but also for those living in Alexandria, Egypt and Cyprus'; 287: 'While the other troops sent to Cyprus by Cleopatra immediately went over to her son Ptolemy, only

weave in his note about John Mark: since he parts from Barnabas and Paul on the way (13.13), he would thereby be sinning against the Spirit if he too had been sent out by the Spirit! Luke says nothing of the results of the preaching, nor can any trace be detected of an earlier mission (11.19). John Mark's position as ὑπηρέτης has created difficulties for the exegetes: 'he was too distinguished to be a mere ministrant' (Preuschen 81). Jacquier (383) ascribes to him the instruction of new converts. But perhaps Luke assigned him only a subordinate function[1]—as the D variant ὑπηρετοῦντα suggests—because then his later failure appeared less serious.

VERSE 6: διελθόντες ... Πάφου[2]: it does not sound as if further attempts at missionary work were undertaken between Salamis and Paphos. Luke apparently possessed only one real tradition about the Cyprus mission, the story of Bar-Jesus. So with 'they found' etc., he launches without more ado on the only theme that really interests him. Bar-Jesus[3] is first described as a sorcerer. Now to Luke this did not imply that he was a charlatan,[4] though this *can* be a connotation of μάγος[5] and it is one brought out by Zahn (116: 'wizard and mountebank'). For Luke the powers which a μάγος has at his

---

the Jews from Onias' army remained true to her, because things went well for their compatriots under the queen.' Schürer and Preuschen adduce I Macc. 15.23 (Jewish offenders fleeing to Cyprus must be delivered to the High Priest Simon), but the verse is spurious (see p. 320 n. 2 above).

[1] According to B. T. Holmes ('Luke's Description of John Mark', *JBL* 54 (1935), 63–72) ὑπηρέτης signified, in the language of the time, a person whose function involved looking after documents. From which Holmes finally comes to affirm that John Mark took a gospel document with him on the journey ...

[2] New Paphos, in the S.W. corner of the island, was the official capital and the seat of the proconsul. D by reading καὶ περιελθόντων δὲ αὐτῶν seems to wish to explain why no further towns in Cyprus are named: the missionaries sail southward from Salamis round the coast to Paphos. Zahn, of course, has them travel overland from one port to the other, thus making Luke's reticence over this alleged mission more enigmatic still (409). Wikenhauser, *Apg* 121: 'they sailed along the southern coast.'

[3] βαριησου: gig perp^vid (the old-Latin text of this codex breaks off with this verse, only resuming with 28.16–31) vg bo; nominative βαριησους B C E e sa. The accusative βαριησουν of A 81 must come from the reading ὀνόματι (+καλούμενον) in D min. The Latin forms *barieu* and *bariheu* derive from the abbreviation βαριηυ and *barihu*. D's βαριησουα (d: *bariesuam*, acc. ending) seems intended to render the Hebrew form בַּר־יֵשׁוּעַ and testifies to the scribe's erudition. From this form arose *bariesuban* (Lucifer) and *varisuas* (*Opus imperf.* in Matt. 24.3)—Ropes, *Beg.* III, 116f. Klostermann, *Probleme im Aposteltext*, 1883, 21ff.: '*bar-yishwan*'; Clemen, *Paulus* I, 1904, 222: '*baryishwah*'.

[4] γόης would express this sense.

[5] In 'Paul and the Magus' (*Beg.* V, 164–88) Nock traces the changing connotations of the Persian loanword μάγος from 'member of the priestly caste of the Medes' (firepriest) down to the late sense of 'wizard' and 'charlatan' (181–4 deal with the present verse). Jews were forbidden to practise magic (see Billerbeck I, 76); the (probably Jewish) list of prohibitions in Did. 2.2 contains οὐ μαγεύσεις οὐ φαρμακεύσεις. Yet Jewish magicians are presupposed by Luke 11.19 (=Matt. 12.27) and Acts 19.13. 'Jewish magic is part of the whole interesting phenomenon of heretical Judaism in Antiquity' (Nock, *Beg.* V, 182 n. 2, with reference to his *Early Gentile Christianity*, 54f.)

command are far too real for him to dismiss the matter so lightly (see comments on **19**.13–16). But these powers are the false powers with which man should have no truck: powers opposed to God yet subordinate to God. And so Luke's proof of the superiority of Christianity over magic lies in his demonstrating that the former with its invocation of the Name of Christ is more powerful. Secondly, Bar-Jesus is called a 'false prophet'.[1] A prophet who speaks against the Christian kerygma is *ipso facto* a ψευδοπροφήτης. As the decisive sign of a prophet is in Luke's eyes knowledge of the future, he must have imagined Bar-Jesus as the proconsul's court-astrologer, who at the same time claimed to know the magic formulae by which the bonds of fate can be broken.

VERSE 7: σύν = in the retinue of Sergius Paulus (see Intro. § 4, 3, above). The latter is called 'a man of understanding', because he proves receptive to the Christian message. He sends for the missionaries (who must therefore already have aroused interest by their preaching) and desires them to tell him that message (λόγος τοῦ θεοῦ).

VERSE 8: But now Bar-Jesus obstructs them. This time he is called Elymas, which name is explained as μάγος.[2] He strives to turn the proconsul aside

---

[1] ψευδοπροφήτης: Matt. **7**.15, 24.11, 24.24; Mark **13**.22; Luke **6**.26; II Peter **2**.1; I John **4**.1; Rev. **16**.13, 19.20, 20.10. In Did. **11**.5, 8–10. it signifies anyone who pretends to speak in the name of Christ but this is quite another meaning of the word.

[2] Or so the word-order suggests. Zahn admittedly develops an entirely different line of reasoning, which may be roughly summarized as follows: 1. Greek-readers required a translation and explanation of the magician's Aramaic name. 2. Hence the second name, introduced as a translation, can only be Greek. 3. 'Ελυμας does not answer this requirement, so the 'Ετοιμας of D and other authorities should be preferred. 4. The Aramaic name *Bar* (בר־) *Jesus* must conceal some meaning that could be translated as ἕτοιμος: Zahn decided for בַּר־יְשָׁוָה (416f.). 5. The proper name יְשָׁוָה occurs in Gen. **46**.17 and I Chron. **7**.30: in the first instance LXX has 'Ιεσουα and (A) 'Ιεσσαι, in the second 'Ισουα and (A) 'Ιεσουα. 6. שָׁוָה means 'be level, smooth, adequate, worthy' (418) or in the Pi'el 'make level, smooth, ready'. 'Thus בַּר־יְשָׁוָה might very well be translated by ἕτοιμος.' 7. D has ἑτοιμᾶς; d, *etoemas*; Ambrosiaster, *quaest*. **102**.2, *etimas*; Pacianus, *ep*. II 6, *hetymam*; Lucifer, *etoemus* (and also in verse 6, *quod interpretatur: paratus*). 8. ἕτοιμος (or ἑτοιμᾶς) also serves to denote that a person has 'that dexterity and rapidity of speech and action which are acquired by practice, qualities indispensable to a sorcerer or conjuror' (416). And so Zahn takes it as proved that the magician rendered his name בַּר־יְשָׁוָה by ἕτοιμος (or ἑτοιμᾶς).

Against this theory, however, it may be said: 1. If 'Bar-Jesus' was to be explained with a Greek word for Greek readers, the Greek explanation ought to have been placed immediately after the Aramaic name. This is not the case, and Luke had every reason not to explain the name: otherwise he would have drawn Greek readers' attention to the fact that this wizard was called 'Son of Jesus'! 2. Luke obviously regarded the name Elymas as foreign, and therefore added ὁ μάγος, οὕτως γὰρ μεθερμηνεύεται τὸ ὄνομα αὐτοῦ. 3. If the OT name יְשָׁוָה is to be derived from שׁוה, then it means 'he is flat, smooth'; from this there is no bridge to ἕτοιμος—the Pi'el, which is of course not present here, means not 'make ready', as Zahn maintains, but 'make level' (W. Rudolph orally). 4. None of the LXX renderings of יְשָׁוָה contains an η; this struck Zahn himself (417 n. 49), but instead of

from the faith—here πίστις, as in **6.7**, seems to mean not 'belief' in the subjective sense but the objective 'faith', i.e. the Christian religion (*Beg.* IV, 144; Bauernfeind, 171 takes a different view).

VERSE 9: With the expression 'Saul who is also Paul'[1] the author completes the transition from one name to the other. The text neither implies that Paul hitherto called himself Saul nor suggests that he adopted the name of the proconsul—the change of name is noted before the governor has been

---

doubting his interpretation he doubted the correctness of the η in D's Βαριησουα!
5. "Ετοιμος in the sense in which Zahn conceives it would not have been a suitable name for Bar-Jesus: a magician in a music-hall may call himself Dr. Fix, but a magician on the staff of a governor may not bear a name suggestive of sleight of hand. 6. The commentaries usually explain 'Elymas' with the Arabic word *elim*, meaning 'the wise': this would have been a thoroughly suitable title for Bar-Jesus, even if one wonders how a Jew in Cyprus came by it; to render *elim* by ὁ μάγος would be free but not wrong.

How the "Ετοιμος of D and other Western witnesses arose is a problem by itself. Zahn himself has drawn attention to an allusion in Josephus, *Ant.* XX, 142, to a Cypriot Jew called Atomos who posed as a magician and was in the service of the proconsul Felix. Long ago (*Exp.* 1902, 183ff.) Rendel Harris conjectured that *Hetoimos* should be read for *Atomos*, which is unknown as a proper name. Zahn (419) identifies this Atomos-Hetoimos with Bar-Jesus: 'As the judgement which Paul brought down on him was to remain effective for only a short time, he may very well have practised his trade again in Palestine some eight years later'. It is more likely that the learned reviser of D substituted this Hetoimos for an unknown Elymas. —In an interesting but controversial essay, 'Der älteste Text der geschichtlichen Bücher des NTs' (*ZNW* 45 (1954), 90–108), Paul Glaue describes ἑτοίμως (='quick') as the original text and 'Ελύμας as a conjecture of the other MSS, though how they hit upon it remains obscure (98). In Luke's work ἑτοίμως in the sense of 'quick' does not appear; in Acts **21.13** it means 'ready'. Liddell-Scott, 704, gives no instance for this meaning.

[1] G. A. Harrer shed considerable light on the problems bound up with this change of name in 'Saul who also is called Paul', *HTR* 33 (1940), 19–34. Paul was a Roman citizen. Such a man had three names, the *praenomen*, e.g. Lucius, the *nomen* (*gentilicium*), e.g. Sergius, and the *cognomen*, e.g. Paul(l)us. If Paul's father had been a freed slave, he would have taken over the *praenomen* and *nomen* of his ex-master and made his slave-name his *cognomen* (cf. e.g. Marcus Tullius Tiro; a free foreigner awarded Roman citizenship would have acted likewise). The son of such a man could alter the (*praenomen* and) *cognomen*, but this rarely happened (20). It was in the Egypt of the Macedonian period that a fourth name, with which one was addressed by intimates, was introduced: the so-called *signum* or *supernomen*. It is usually conveyed by the formula ὁ καί (*qui et*), but occasionally by ὁ ἐπικαλούμενος or ὁ λεγόμενος (21). Thus Acts **13.9** presents such a *signum* (others occur in **1.23**, **4.36**, **12.12**, **12.25** and **13.1**). Since the Apostle was a Roman citizen, 'Paulus' must have been his *cognomen* (22). The *cognomen* may be mentioned before or after ὁ καί. Thus 'Saul' is to be regarded as a *signum*, which his father probably gave him at birth—for, like King Saul, the family was of the tribe of Benjamin (Phil. **3.5**) (23). Acts transcribes שָׁאוּל as Σαῦλος (except for the vocative, where it is Σαούλ as in LXX: **9.4**, 17; **22.7**, 13; **26.14**. In **13.21** King Σαούλ is also named). But 𝔓⁴⁵ (third century) never offers Σαῦλος (not found in either LXX or Josephus: perhaps it established itself under the influence of Παῦλος some time in the third or fourth century) but always Σαούλ (24f.). The indeclinable Σαούλ, then, was the *signum*, and 'Paul' the *cognomen* (26). The name Paul is not the token of a distinct 'Paul' source (27), nor (*pace* H. Dessau, E. Meyer and E. Groag: see Pauly-Wissowa *s.v.* Sergius Paulus) was it adopted after the proconsul. Though in the main we may agree with Harrer, his explanation (32) must be rejected: 'The apostle now assumes (the author of Acts seems to say) the regular use of his regular *cognomen* Paul, because of

converted! Luke goes over to the new name, however, at the very moment when Paul through a miracle proves himself the missionary filled with the Holy Spirit, who is now the real head of the Christian group.[1] ἀτενίσας does not mean that Paul possessed the withering glance that Jewish legend attributed to the rabbis.[2]

VERSE 10: With the exception of ῥαδιούργημα, every word of this verse may be found in LXX.[3] While Paul is full of the Holy Spirit, his opponent is full of every guile and villainy, a son of the devil (i.e. the devil's creature) and an enemy of all righteousness. The 'right'—i.e. straight—way of the Lord leads to the governor's conversion, but this 'way' Bar-Jesus would divert or 'pervert'. οὐ παύσῃ = 'will you not stop?'

VERSE 11: The biblical language continues.[4] For ἄχρι καιροῦ cf. Luke 4.13; the blindness is not to be permanent. ἀχλύς ('darkness'): as a medical term (so Harnack, *Beitr.* I, 34; ET) it does not come into question here.[5] It would be more than unstylish if in a solemn curse a technical medical term was used, e.g.: 'And now will God send upon you acute conjunctivitis'!

VERSE 12: The teaching proves able to work miracles, hence compels belief. πιστεύω can denote confidence in the wonder-worker, but may also mean to become a Christian (cf. John 4.50, 53). The readers must have taken it in the latter sense, which is therefore what Luke intended. The idea of *Beg.* IV, 147, that Paul and Barnabas mistook mere courtesy on the governor's part for a conversion, deserves mention only as a curiosity.

Around the turn of the century, the source-critics mostly traced chapters 13 and 14 back to Luke, even if particular verses aroused suspicion.[6] More

---

the association with the governor and possibly because of the increasingly frequent contact with Greeks and Romans, which he saw must be ahead of him.' Luke has hitherto designated Paul as Saul because he has been striving as far as possible to present him as a full and strict Jew (see comments on 22.3). But now, at the point where Paul is donning the mantle of the great missionary well known to every Christian, Luke has to switch over to the Roman *cognomen* which alone Paul employed in his epistles and which alone is familiar to later Christendom. There are no grounds for supposing that Paul also adopted *praenomen* and *nomen* from Lucius Sergius Paulus—a possibility which Harrer still retains in his conclusion—and was thus in reality named L. Aemilius Paulus *qui et* Saul.

[1] So also Cadbury, *The Making of Luke-Acts*, 225; *Beg.* IV, 145, disagrees.

[2] Belief in the 'evil eye' played an important part among the Jews: 'Ninety-nine die of the evil eye and one of a natural death' (Billerbeck, II, 713).

[3] πλήρης δόλου—Ecclus. 1.30, 19.26; Jer. 5.27. πᾶσα δικαιοσύνη—Gen. 32.11; I Sam. 12.7. In διαστρέφων κτλ we find a blend of Prov. 10.9 ὁ δὲ (the evil one) διαστρέφων τὰς ὁδοὺς αὐτοῦ and Hosea 14.10 εὐθαῖαι αἱ ὁδοὶ τοῦ κυρίου.

[4] καὶ νῦν ἰδού occurs in LXX Gen. 12.19 *et passim*, χεὶρ κυρίου ἐπὶ σέ in LXX I Sam. 7.13 *et passim*.

[5] The author wishes to describe an immediate blinding; ἀχλύς as a technical medical expression denotes an inflammation which causes a clouding in the eye (*Beg.* IV, 146). Luke is not describing different stages of going blind (so Hobart, 45).

[6] B. Weiss: 6–12; Hilgenfeld: 25, 27, 31, 38f., 42, 45–7, 50f.; Jüngst: 8–12, 24f., 27b, 29, 34–7, 39–41, 42, 44–9, 52; Sorof: 27–31, 34–7; Spitta: 6–12, 44–9, 52.

significant was the unfavourable overall impression made on B. Weiss and Harnack. The latter thought that **13**.4–**14**.38 was less convincing and reliable than most of the second half of the work (*Beitr.* III, 155; ET), and to this B. Weiss assented (576). This travel-report was so stereotyped and so failed to give a clear picture of chronology or results that it could only have been concocted from hearsay. Only **13**.6–12 and **14**.8–18 gave real details. The great speech of **13**.16–41 was an attempt by Luke to present Paul's way of preaching in the synagogues, and **13**.42–52, as well as **14**.1–7 and 19f., could not come from any source. This closely coincides with Bauernfeind's verdict, forty years later: the whole section shows Luke's skill, which guides the reader through this period of preparation. The details of the itinerary should not be placed on the same level as the fluent geographical references of the later chapters (e.g. 20): 'Most of them came into being simultaneously with Acts.' Even the mentions of John Mark and the accounts of the opposition to Paul, especially **13**.50–2 and **14**.19f., go back to Luke. As for Paul's sermon, it was a mixture of old material and the author's own ideas (Bauernfeind 167ff.).

These observations are the more significant for being those of scholars in eager quest of historical results, scholars for whom the discrimination of sources represented their most valuable tool. The inadequacy of their method can be unusually well illustrated from the beginning of the passage. With **13**.1 begins a new scene sharply divided from the preceding one. Those who believe Luke's method was the assembly of fragments from different sources will thus be inclined, like *Beg.* IV, 145, to conjecture the beginning of a new source. Wendt (200 n. 1) concedes that it could be a source already used which had not so far mentioned Barnabas and Paul. But as soon as one reflects on the task of *composition* facing Luke at this juncture, the situation looks entirely different. He wanted to depict a new, extremely important episode in the history of the mission: the work, begun by the congregation of Syrian Antioch, which finally evolved—in Pisidian Antioch—into a mission directed purely to the Gentiles. As in the case of the Cornelius story, it had to be made perfectly clear that this development sprang not from human impulse but from the divine will. To achieve that result, Luke begins by ceremoniously presenting the circle of prophets and teachers in Syrian Antioch, from which the two messengers of the gospel then emerge. Since they are first chosen through the pronouncement of the Spirit, Luke does not set them side by side in this list, but separates them as widely as possible: Barnabas begins the list, Paul ends it. In so doing he secures the advantage, from a literary point of view, that (as always in such cases) the first and last names make a special impression on the reader. After thus naming his candidates, Luke describes the first scene: the five prepare themselves with fasting and earnest prayer— the biblical λειτουργεῖν τῷ κυρίῳ should be noted—for the reception of a divine command. The Spirit speaks—through which prophet we are not told, but we hear the Spirit's words. These do not go into detail (*minima non curat praetor*) but in general terms order the sending out of Barnabas and Paul to the work for which they have already long been called: God's will plans far ahead of events. The vagueness offers the author the advantage of keeping the reader in suspense. Now Luke begins a second scene: the men of Antioch do not accomplish even the sending-forth of their own unaided will. They prepare themselves by further prayer and fasting, and thus gather the strength which by laying on of hands they bestow upon the two.

But as if even this left too great a part to human initiative, verse 4 expressly emphasizes that it is the Holy Spirit which really sends the two men forth. They go down (half a day's march) to the port of Seleucia and take ship to Cyprus. Having arrived at the port of Salamis, they preach the Christian message in 'the synagogue of the Jews', as is emphatically stated: it is still a case of the kerygma to the Jews! We learn nothing of the success of these efforts, and there is nothing to suggest that (as has—probably erroneously— been inferred from **11**.19) any Christians have been active here before. All these points Luke could have made without enlisting the help of any tradition: indeed he seems to possess no concrete tradition of this journey but the Bar-Jesus episode, which he hastens to recount. First, however, he mentions that John Mark was taken along as an assistant by Paul and Barnabas. It was not lack of literary skill that made Luke append this here: in **13**.13 John Mark will be forsaking the missionaries and going home to Jerusalem. Had Luke shown him as also sent forth by the Spirit, this self-willed return would be a grave disobedience to the Spirit, and Barnabas could never have countenanced taking him **as a** companion once again (**15**.37). Thus even in apparently insignificant details the planning hand of the writer can be seen.

Without mentioning any further missionary efforts, Luke takes the Christian preachers right across the island—a week's journey in the best of circumstances—to New Paphos, where they encounter the Jewish magician and 'false prophet' Bar-Jesus, the man of whom Luke really wishes to speak. Now anybody with the faintest knowledge of Aramaic knew that Bar-Jesus meant 'son of Jesus', and Luke carefully refrains from alerting other readers also to the fact that this rascal bore the sacred name of Jesus as part of his own. If Luke had invented the story himself, he would never have hit upon *this* name: we have thus here a proof that Luke is following a tradition. This Bar-Jesus, then (we should perhaps say: as court astrologer and theologian), was in the retinue of Sergius Paulus—a perspicacious man, for he has the Christian missionaries summoned; thus he has heard of their activities. Luke takes care not to say that they have attracted attention through signs and wonders, for this would depreciate the miracle he is about to relate. The Jewish court theologian senses a threat to his influence and vigorously opposes what the Christians preach (note the forward position of ἀνθίστατο). Luke here takes the opportunity of emphasizing his character as a magician by reference to a second epithet which Bar-Jesus bore. This does not mean 'juggler', as Zahn understood it; the magi for Luke had to do with real powers, even if they were demons hostile to God. The Christians, however, stand on God's side; this is expressed in the fact that their power is greater than that of the magi. So when Elymas—the second name of Bar-Jesus, somewhat clumsily introduced—endeavours to divert the governor from the faith, Saul rivets his eyes upon him—and here, where he steps into the foreground and will convert his first Gentile, Luke passes over to the second name, which his hero indeed already always bore but with which he is now for the first time (and henceforth always) named—Paul rivets his eyes upon him and in the biblical language of a messenger of God proclaims the divine judgement, which immediately takes effect: Elymas is struck blind and gropes around for someone to guide him—a proof that Paul's word has actually been fulfilled. There is an unexpected leniency in that the punishment is to last only for a certain time. But this judgement is sufficient to bring the governor to the faith.

The historical value of this story has been repeatedly called into question. Earlier scholars simply took objection to the miracle. Zeller, for example, considered it to follow 'automatically that the narrative, as it lies before us, is unhistorical; the only question is whether it is based on any actual fact' or is symbolic in character (212). This feature of the older criticism also, its belief that symbolism could be found in Luke's presentation, was later to be revived: in Loisy. He roundly contested the historicity of the whole: 'Sergius Paulus, the proconsul of Cyprus, was never converted by Paul, for the simple reason that he never met him.' Bar-Jesus symbolizes the blind Jewish people, Sergius Paulus the Gentiles converted by Paul (518). Unfortunately Loisy fails to tell us *why* Luke brings such symbols into play. The absence of reference to any baptism (contrast the Chamberlain and Cornelius episodes) admittedly militates, as Zahn also stresses (421), against the view that the proconsul really became a Christian. Moreover, the conversion of so high an official as Sergius Paulus certainly could not have been without consequences, and would have led at least to the founding of a house-church. It may be conjectured, and given the ambiguities of ἐπίστευσεν it is very possible, that already within the tradition the success was magnified.

Luke's story, as Nock has already demonstrated (*Beg.* V, 188), serves several purposes. First, it shows that at the outset of the Pauline mission the highest Roman authority of a province, the proconsul, 'came to the faith'. What better ἀπολογία for Christianity could there be? There are many passages ahead which will confirm that Luke, especially in the second half of Acts, wanted to present such an apologia. But we could also refer back to the story of Cornelius: the first Gentile convert was actually a Roman officer. Second—and this is especially important in the Lucan design—Paul's feat enables the real hero, to whom only a modest role has hitherto been assigned, to step forward into the first place. From now on 'Paul does the talking . . .,

Barnabas, at the most, chiming in *unisono*' (Wellhausen, 24). There is no reason to maintain, however, that Luke was here striving to establish an exact parallel between Paul and Peter (magician Simon = magician Bar-Jesus); the coincidences are merely due to the very limited variety of miracle-stories. Third, the story illustrates the antithesis of Christianity and magic, which Luke also makes plain in **8**.9ff. and **19**.18f. On his own presuppositions, Luke could only bring home this antithesis by having the agent of Christianity demonstrate his superiority over the sorcerer. Since the Christians are in the service of God, and God is superior to the demons, this demonstration—according to Luke's conviction—could only take one form: the utter defeat, judgement and punishment of the Magus.

30

ACTS 13 : 13–52

FOUNDING OF A CONGREGATION IN PISIDIA; EXPULSION OF THE MISSIONARIES

[13] Setting sail from Paphos, Paul and his companions came to Perga in Pamphylia: but John departed from them and returned to Jerusalem. [14] They passed through from Perga and came to Pisidian Antioch. On the Sabbath they went into the synagogue, and took their seats. [15] And after the reading of the law and the prophets the officials of the synagogue sent to them, saying: 'Brethren, if you have any word of exhortation for the people, speak!' [16] And Paul stood up, motioned with his hand, and said: 'Men of Israel and God-fearers, listen to me! [17] The God of this people of Israel chose our fathers, and made the people great during their stay in the land of Egypt, and with upraised arm he led them out of it, [18] and for about forty years he sustained them in the wilderness. [19] And when he had destroyed seven nations in the land of Canaan, he gave their land to them as an inheritance [20] for about four hundred and fifty years. And after these things he gave judges until Samuel the prophet. [21] And afterward they asked for a king: and God gave them Saul the son of Kish, a man of the tribe of Benjamin, for forty years. [22] And when he had removed him, he raised up David to be their king; to whom he bore witness, and said: "I have found David the son of Jesse, a man after my heart, who shall do all my will." [23] Of this man's seed God according to promise has brought Israel a saviour, Jesus, [24] after John before his coming had first preached a baptism of repentance for all the people of Israel. [25] And as John was fulfilling his course, he said: "What you suppose I am, that I am not. But behold, after me there comes one, the shoes of whose feet I am not worthy to loose." [26] Brethren, sons of the stock of Abraham and the God-fearers among you, to us the Word of this salvation has been sent. [27] For the inhabitants of Jerusalem and their rulers, knowing neither him nor the voices of the prophets read out every sabbath, fulfilled them by condemning him. [28] And though they found no ground of death, they asked Pilate that he should be slain. [29] And when they had fulfilled all that was written about him, they took him down from the tree and laid him in a tomb. [30] But God raised him from the dead. [31] He appeared during many days to those who came up with him from Galilee to Jerusalem, who are his witnesses to the people. [32] And we bring you good tidings of

the promise made to the fathers: [33] that God has fulfilled this for us, the children, in that he raised up Jesus, as also it is written in the second psalm: "You are my son: this day have I begotten you." [34] And that he raised him up from the dead as one who will no more return to corruption, he has thus expressed: "I will give you the faithful blessings of David." [35] Hence he also says in another place: "You will not let your holy one see corruption." [36] For David, after he had served his own generation, fell asleep by the will of God, and was laid beside his fathers, and saw corruption. [37] But he whom God raised up did not see corruption. [38] Be it known to you therefore, brethren, that through this man forgiveness of sins is proclaimed to you: and from all the things of which you could not by the law of Moses be exonerated, [39] by this man every believer is exonerated. [40] Beware therefore, that what was said in the prophets may not come upon you: [41] "Behold, despisers, and marvel, and perish; for I work a work in your days, a work which you will not believe, if one declare it to you."' [42] And as they went out, people asked that these things might be spoken about to them the next sabbath. [43] Now when the synagogue broke up, many of the Jews and the God-fearing proselytes followed Paul and Barnabas, who spoke with them and sought to persuade them to continue in the grace of God. [44] On the following sabbath almost the whole city gathered together to hear the Word of God. [45] But when the Jews saw the multitudes, they were filled with jealousy, and contradicted the things spoken by Paul, and blasphemed. [46] And Paul and Barnabas spoke out boldly, and said: 'It was necessary that the Word of God be spoken first to you. Since you reject it, and judge yourselves unworthy of eternal life, lo! we turn to the Gentiles. [47] For so the Lord has commanded us: "I have set you as a light for the Gentiles, that you may bring salvation to the uttermost part of the earth."' [48] And when the Gentiles heard this, they rejoiced and glorified the Word of the Lord: and as many as were ordained to eternal life believed. [49] And the Word of the Lord was spread abroad throughout all the region. [50] But the Jews incited the God-fearing women of honourable estate, and the chief men of the city, and stirred up a persecution against Paul and Barnabas, and drove them out of their district. [51] But they shook off the dust of their feet against them, and came to Iconium. [52] And the disciples were filled with joy and with the Holy Spirit.

Bibliography:

K. Lake, 'Paul's Route in Asia Minor', *Beg.* V, 224–40; H. J. Cadbury, 'Dust and Garments', *Beg.* V, 269–77; J. W. Doeve, 1953, see § 1 bibl. (esp. 172ff.); Kragerud, see § 29 bibl.; Williams, 1957, 160–8; U. Wilckens, *Die Missionsreden*[2], 1963, 50–5 and 70f.

T. J. Pennell, 'Acts **13**.13', *Exp.Tim.* 44 (1932–3), 476; J. Dupont, '"Filius meus es tu"; Interprétation de Ps. **2**.7 dans le N.T.', *RScR* 35 (1948), 522–43; id.: ΤΑ 'ΟΣΙΑ ΔΑΥΙΔ ΤΑ ΠΙΣΤΑ (Ac. **13**.34 = Is. **55**.3)', *RevBibl* 68 (1961), 91–114; E. E. Kellett, 'A Note on Acts **13**.42', *Exp.Tim.* 34 (1922–3), 188–9; J. Dupont, 'Le salut des gentils et la signification théologique du livre des Actes', *NTS* 6 (1960), 132–55; O. Glombitza, 'Acta **13**.15–41. Analyse einer lukanischen Predigt vor Juden', *NTS* 5 (1959), 306–17; G. Klein, *ZThK* 64 (1967), 281–7.

VERSE 13: ἀνάγομαι = 'go on the high seas', 'sail away' (cf. **16**.11, **18**.21, **27**.21 and **28**.11). οἱ περὶ Παύλου: Luke seizes this last opportunity, while the three men are still together, to single out Paul as the leader by use of the expression 'Paul and those about him'. Πέργη was about eight miles upriver from the mouth of the Cestros and five from the riverbank. As the stream was not navigable for larger boats, the travellers perhaps landed at Attalia (cf. **14**.25): *Beg.* IV, 147. Παμφυλία was an impoverished region, lying between the sea and Mount Taurus, which from 25 B.C. to A.D. 43 constituted a province in its own right (Dio Cassius **53**.26; *Beg.* IV, 147). Luke does not reveal why John Mark parted company with the others,[1] and speculation leaves us none the wiser.[2]

VERSE 14: From the (malaria-ridden) coast[3] the two men march by arduous and perilous paths[4] to 'Pisidian' Antioch,[5] about 100 miles away, which belonged to the Roman province of Galatia.[6] Nothing is divulged about a mission in Perga. The spareness of Luke's narration gives the impression that Paul and Barnabas walk into the synagogue as soon as they arrive.

VERSE 15: In the first century A.D. the synagogue service[7] comprised the Shᵉma, the prayer (of eighteen petitions) and priestly blessing, then reading (and vernacular translation) from the law (*parasha*) and—though not at every service—the prophets (*haphtarah*); next followed a free address, usually

---

[1] He returned to Jerusalem, but in **15**.37ff. his presence in Antioch is presupposed.

[2] See e.g. Wendt 205, Zahn 425, *Beg.* IV, 147f.

[3] According to Ramsay (*St. Paul*, 92ff.) Paul here contracted a fever (cf. Gal. **4**.13) and for that reason went to Pisidian Antioch, which lies at the altitude of 3,900 ft. Jacquier (391) asks whether someone stricken with malaria would be capable of so rigorous a journey (cf. also Harnack, *Beiträge* III, 84 n. 4; ET).

[4] Jacquier (392) conjectures that Paul is alluding to this journey in II Cor. **11**.25.

[5] This Antioch, situated on the southern slopes of the Sultan Dagh, was founded by Seleucus Nicator. The Seleucids settled large numbers of Jews in Phrygia (to which Antioch properly belonged: Strabo thus calls it 'Αντιόχεια ἡ πρὸς τῇ Πισιδίᾳ—on the Pisidian border) and in Lydia, in order to have a reliable population in their borderlands (Josephus *Ant.* XII, 147–53). After 25 B.C. it became a Roman colony: *Pisidarum Colonia Caesarea* (cf. Ramsay, *The Cities of St. Paul*, III—*Antioch*, 247–314; Wikenhauser 335; H. Metzger, *Les Routes de Saint Paul dans l'Orient grec*, 1954, 17f.).

[6] According to the so-called South Galatian theory, the epistle to the Galatians was addressed to the congregations of Antioch, Iconium, Lystra and Derbe.

[7] Cf. Billerbeck IV 1, Excursus 8: 'Der altjüdische Synagogengottesdienst' (153–88); 9: 'Das Schᵉma' (189–207); 10: 'Das Schᵉmone-Esre' (208–49). See also *Beg.* IV, 148.

exhortatory, which the leader[1] could invite any competent Jew to deliver. Naturally it must have been customary in the case of strangers to enquire of them beforehand, not during the service, whether they would like to speak.[2] The criterion for Luke, however, is what is effective for his story. On ἄνδρες ἀδελφοί see note to 2.29.

VERSE 16: ἀναστάς: the giver of a synagogue address (*darshan*) did not stand up but sat (Luke 4.20; Billerbeck IV 1, 185). But Luke probably, for his Hellenistic readers, presents Paul as a Hellenistic orator—hence also the orator's gesture, which would be superfluous in a synagogue.[3] On ἄνδρες Ἰσραηλῖται see note to 2.22. On φοβούμενοι cf. explanation of 10.2.

VERSE 17: As in Stephen's speech, only more briefly, the orator begins by outlining the history of salvation from the time of the fathers. This must have been a favourite method with such sermons in Luke's time. Again LXX is all-pervasive.[4] παροικία here signifies 'abroad'. This time Luke omits the patriarchal and Mosaic periods, thus dividing his description of the *Heilsgeschichte* between Chapters 7 and 13.

VERSE 18: The Hellenistic expression τεσσαρακονταέτη χρόνον does not occur in LXX, although the sense does (e.g. Ex. 16.35). ἐτροποφόρησεν[5] is perhaps to be derived from τροφοφορέω, 'to nurture' (so also Holtzmann, 88; Loisy, 525; Zahn, 430). The Hebrew text speaks of 'bearing'.

VERSE 19: καθελών κτλ—see Deut. 7.1. κατεκληρονόμησεν τὴν γῆν see e.g. Jer. 3.18 LXX. B 81 do not have the καί.

VERSE 20: B ℵ A C sa bo syʰ vg[6] reckon the 450 years from the Exodus from Egypt to the acquisition of the promised land: 400 years in Egypt (cf. 7.6), 40 in the wilderness, 10 spent in conquering Canaan (Bauernfeind 173).

---

[1] Every synagogue had but one leader, who saw that the service of worship was conducted in due order. But the term ἀρχισυνάγωγος could also be bestowed as a title of honour. Since here (and in Mark 5.22) several leaders are implied, Billerbeck (op. cit. 146) conjectures that the members of the synagogue chapter were so styled. See Schürer II⁴, 509ff., and Juster, *Les Juifs dans l'Empire romain* I, 450ff.

[2] There is no discernible justification for Bauernfeind's conjecture that what is meant is a word of encouragement 'inspired from above' (172).

[3] However, Philo, *De spec. leg.* II § 62, 102 C.-W., describes the synagogue service rather as Luke does here: some sit quietly and listen, ἀναστὰς δέ τις τῶν ἐμπειρωτάτων ὑφηγεῖται τὰ ἄριστα καὶ συνοίσοντα, οἷς ἅπας ὁ βίος ἐπιδώσει πρὸς τὸ βέλτιον.

[4] ὁ θεὸς Ἰσραήλ recurs time without number in LXX, but the continuation τοῦ λαοῦ τούτου is not to be found there and is probably a Lucan expansion. B's τοῦ is surely a haplography; A C 81 D have τούτου. H L P S omit Ἰσραήλ. D's διὰ τὸν λαόν must be an ancient slip in the Western text (Ropes, *Beg.* III, 120 n. 17). ὕψωσεν: LXX Isa. 1.2 *et passim*. ἐν (not μετά—but Luke has just used two ἐν-phrases) βραχίονι ὑψηλῷ occurs in LXX Ex. 6.6 *et pass*. ἐξήγαγεν: see Deut. 5.15.

[5] Ropes, *Beg.* III, 120: 'nourished' (so II Macc. 7.27) makes better sense than 'bore'; Lake (*Beg.* IV, 149) points out that a verb combining the stem τροφ with φορέω would on grounds of euphony change the first φ into a π. Moreover, Hellenistic Greek inclines to replace simple forms (say ἔτρεφεν in this case) by sonorous compounds, even when the sense is not quite the same. A C E e d gig sa bo pesh syʰ give ἐτροφοφόρησεν.

[6] *Beg.* III, 121.

As this means harking right back beyond the wilderness period already reached, and counting over again the forty years in the wilderness already mentioned (verse 18), D d E e gig pesh and 𝔎 relate this note of time to the period of the Judges and modify accordingly.[1]

VERSE 21: Saul's[2] reign is estimated, as in Josephus *Ant.* VI, 378, at forty years (including 22 after the death of Samuel), whereas *Ant.* X, 143 (a dubious passage, however) speaks of only twenty years' rule.

VERSE 22: μεταστήσας, 'removing': I Sam. **15**.23. ἤγειρεν κτλ: I Sam. **16**.12f. The scriptural proof is in fact a conflation of different texts.[3] ἐγείρειν εἰς βασιλέα is not a Hebraism (Moulton 71f.).

VERSE 23: τούτου, which ought to stand after σπέρματος, is brought emphatically forward: the promise made to David is fulfilled in Jesus.[4]

VERSE 24: See comments on **10**.37 above. Before[5] Jesus' coming John preached only a baptism of repentance; no mention is made of his baptizing Jesus. Luke does not presuppose that Paul's audience know of John and Jesus, but he assumes that these are familiar to his readers.

VERSE 25: For ἐπλήρου τὸν δρόμον cf. II Tim. **4**.7: τὸν δρόμον τετέληκα (a peculiarly Christian (Hellenistic) language of devotion is in the making). John's disclaimer of Messianic pretensions is also reported by Luke **3**.15f., John **1**.19ff. and Justin *Dial.* **88**.7. As in Gen. **38**.25 LXX, τί is here Hellenistic for the relative pronoun (Moulton 93; Bl.-Debr. § 289, 4).

VERSE 26: The more familiar address ἄνδρες ἀδελφοί here as in **2**.29 replaces the more formal expression of the opening (**13**.16). Again the Jews and the Gentiles adhering to the synagogue are both addressed.[6] Cf. the

---

[1] In fact all the time-data of the Book of Judges, taken with the forty years of Eli (according to the Hebrew text of I Sam. 4 18—LXX says 'twenty'), yield 450 years. Thus the Western reviser presupposed the Hebrew text. But—as Lake asks in discussing the question, *Beg.* IV, 150—did one reckon so among the Jews? Josephus puts the time of the Judges at 'over 500 years' on one occasion (*Ant.* XI, 112f.), at '506 years' on another (*Ant.* XX, 230). On the other hand, *Ant.* VIII, 61 and X, 147f. give a period twenty years shorter. The OT synagogue (Seder Olam R. 15; Billerbeck II, 724f.) reckoned the time from the departure out of Egypt to the building of the Temple at 440½ years: this would mean that 396 years elapsed from the entry into Canaan to the death of Samuel.

[2] The conjecture in *Beg.* IV, 151 that Paul (himself a 'Saul') mentions Benjamin because he himself is of this tribe (Rom. **11**.1, Phil. **3**.5) both reads too much into the text, in a 'psychological' fashion, and wrongly takes the speech as a reproduction of the Pauline original.

[3] See Intro. § 1, 1 (c).

[4] Nestle refers in the margin to II Sam. **7**.12; *Beg.* IV, 152, to II Sam. **22**.51 LXX Δαυίδ καὶ τῷ σπέρματι αὐτοῦ. See on **2** 30.

[5] πρὸ προσώπου = 'before' in LXX Ex. **33** 2 *et pass. Beg.* IV, 152, refers to Mal. **3**.1 τὸν ἄγγελον . . . πρὸ προσώπου μου . . . ἡμέραν εἰσόδου αὐτοῦ.

[6] For οἱ ἐν ὑμῖν (B ℵ C), A 81 D d sy^hmg read ἡμῖν. The ἡμῖν (ὁ λόγος) of B ℵ A 81 D d is replaced in 𝔓45 C and the mass of late MSS by ὑμῖν, which was then no longer distinguished in pronunciation. —Lake (*Beg.* V, 86f.) affirms that if the context be disregarded the passage would not be enough to prove that φοβούμενος τὸν θεόν denotes a non-proselyte participant in the synagogue service. But here the only point is that these two groups, the Jews and the Gentiles associated with the synagogue, are clearly distinguished.

parallel **10**.36. 'The Word of this salvation' is the news of the redemption
manifested in Jesus. *Pace* Loisy (528) and Beyer (84), the 'to us' does not
mean the diaspora Jews as opposed to the Palestinian, but those now
living.

VERSES 27f.: 'For[1] the inhabitants of Jerusalem and their rulers, not
recognizing this' Jesus and failing to understand 'the voices of the prophets
read out every sabbath, fulfilled them by condemning' him, 'and though
they found no ground for death, they asked Pilate that he should be slain.'[2]
As in **3**.17, the slaying of Jesus is excused by ἀγνοία, and as in **3**.18 it is at
the same time asserted that precisely in this way the will of God attested in
scripture was fulfilled. The agreement with **3**.17f. testifies not to the theological unity of the preaching of the real Peter and the real Paul, but to the
composition of both speeches by Luke, whose own theology here again becomes visible. In Luke **23**.4 and Acts **3**.13 the innocence of Jesus is recognized
by Pilate, here by the Jews. The responsibility for this alteration may be
placed, with Lake (*Beg.* IV, 153), not on some divergent tradition, but on
Luke's desire for condensation of expression and grammatical simplicity.

VERSE 29: Here apparently the lowering of Jesus from the Cross and his
burial are ascribed to the Jews; in reality Luke has only shortened the account
as much as possible.[3]

VERSE 30: Here begins a section on the Resurrection extending to v. 37.
First its factuality is declared in what has now become a fixed form of words
(cf. **3**.15 and **4**.10).

VERSE 31: Then comes the confirmation of this fact through the appearances of Jesus. I Cor. **15**.5 shows that a formula constructed with ὤφθη
existed from early times.[4] It is a favourite device to introduce religious
predications with this kind of relative clause (cf. I Tim. **3**.16, but also Acts
4.10).[5] 'For many days' takes up **1**.3: Luke likes to vary an expression

---

[1] 'Paul is demonstrating that, despite his rejection by the Jews of Jerusalem, Jesus is
the Messiah foretold by the prophets' (Jacquier, 400). But perhaps in the γάρ the really
conclusive proof offered by verses 31f. is already anticipated.

[2] Ropes, *Beg.* III, 261, reconstructs the Western text as follows: 'For the dwellers
in Jerusalem and their rulers, not understanding the words of the prophets that are read out
every sabbath, fulfilled them (=*the words of the prophets*), and though they found no ground
for a sentence of death they condemned him and delivered him to Pilate to be put to death.
And as they were fulfilling everything written about him, they asked Pilate, after he had
been crucified, that he be taken down from the Cross; and having obtained (*their request*)
they took him down and laid him in a tomb.' This is plainly an attempt at an (unsuccessful)
revision of the B text. —D shows here its peculiar weaknesses: παρέδωκαν ἵνα εἰς ἀναίρεσιν
arose in such a manner that the Latin *ut interficeretur* produced the ἵνα, whereas B's
ἀναιρεθῆναι αὐτόν was rendered by εἰς ἀναίρεσιν!

[3] D's καὶ καθελόντες ... καὶ ἔθηκαν is not an Aramaism but a mixture of B's καθελόντες ... ἔθηκαν and *deposuerunt ... et posuerunt*.

[4] d's text is mixed here: *hic qui visus est his* ... : B's ὃς ὤφθη is conflated with D's
οὗτος ὤφθη into οὗτος ὃς ὤφθη.

[5] Alongside participial construction; see Norden, *Agnostos Theos*, 166–76 and 201–7.

without altering its general meaning (*Beg.* IV, 154).[1] τοῖς συναναβᾶσιν κτλ. corresponds to the contents of **10**.39, 41. The real Paul would not have appealed to the Christophanies before the Twelve without referring to his own vision (I Cor. **15**.8!). But as Luke saw history, only the Twelve, who were with Jesus during his earthly life as well, were fully valid witnesses of his resurrection.[2]

VERSES 32f.: The proclamation of the Resurrection of Jesus[3] now follows, on the basis of the apostolic witness. Luke has changed the word-order for emphasis, and there is no need to see an Aramaism (so Black, *An Aramaic Approach* . . ., 3rd edn., 53: see pp. 78f. above) in the anticipation of the words 'the promise made to the fathers', which properly belong to the ὅτι-clause. Three ideas are here propounded: 1. Jesus is risen; 2. thus the promise to the fathers is fulfilled; 3. this is the burden of our message. The admirably attested τοῖς τέκνοις ἡμῶν is an extremely early error; it must run τοῖς τέκνοις, ἡμῖν ('to us, the children'; *Beg.* III, 124; IV, 154). From this every variant can be explained. Since the Resurrection is envisaged as a begetting to eternal life, it can be verified by Psalm **2**.7.[4] In the scriptural proof, which he was not the first to assemble but took over (v. 22), Luke presents Christological statements from different periods, some of great age.

VERSE 34: Jesus' resurrection has now been certified by eyewitnesses (verse 31) and scriptural proof. Through this ἀνάστασις he is once and for all preserved from corruption—in contrast to David, to whom the promise therefore did not refer. That Jesus was 'no more to return to corruption' is

---

[1] It is interesting to see how the advocates of a revision hypothesis for **1**.3 explain the present verse. For Beyer (84) it is clear that here we have an allusion to the forty days, which prompts him to wonder 'whether a strange hand, here as in Chapter 1, has not subsequently interfered with the text'. Bauernfeind, on the other hand, enlists this verse to discredit the 40 days: 'The "many" . . . should not, following **1**.3, be regarded as a general periphrasis for the number 40 . . . If Luke himself had written **1**.3, it would be frankly strange if he left out the number here'. (175). Bauernfeind overlooks the literary finesse which changes an expression on its repetition—a feature shown once more by the end of the sentence.

[2] The statement that the Twelve are the witnesses to the Jewish people does not imply that Paul is now the witness to the Gentiles. For one thing, Luke did not accept the agreement of Gal. **2**.9 into his presentation; secondly, Paul himself is here speaking to the λαός (**13**.17); the break does not come until later (**13**.45ff.)—and even then only so far as Pisidian Antioch is concerned. The 'we' of verse 32, Paul and Barnabas, are in Luke's eyes men who base their message solely on the testimony of the Twelve.

[3] In accordance with **3**.26, ἀναστήσας Ἰησοῦν could in itself mean the sending of Jesus into the world. But this would interrupt the line of thought (verse 30 ἤγειρεν ἐκ νεκρῶν; verse 34 ἀνέστησεν ἐκ νεκρῶν) with irrelevant considerations regarding Jesus' earthly life.

[4] Cf. Rom. **1**.4 (see Michel, *Der Römerbrief*, 30ff.); so B. Weiss I, 499; Holtzmann, 90; Harnack, *Beiträge* IV, 75 (ET); Loisy, 533f.; Bauernfeind 176.—D, in a show of erudition, calls the psalm 'the first' and also quotes its verse 8 (*pace* Ropes, *Beg.* III, 263–5); Billerbeck II, 725, gives Talmudic references.

attested by citation of Isaiah **55**.3 LXX.[1] The difficult τὰ ὅσια Δαυὶδ τὰ πιστά is elucidated by—

VERSE 35, with its citation of Ps. **16**.10 (already put to use in **2**.25ff.). Here we find not only ὅσιος but also a δώσεις apparently corresponding to the δώσω of Isa. **55**.3. Presumably the two quotations had already been paired in the tradition employed by Luke (was there already at the time a kind of 'testimony book'?), for the abridged version of Isa. **55**.3 would be incomprehensible in itself. In the light of verse 35 the Isaiah text implies: 'I will give you Christians the scion of David together with the immortal life of the Resurrection.'

VERSE 36: We now come to the conclusive statement—prepared by two biblical expressions:[2] 'David . . . saw corruption'. The rest of the sentence is disputed.[3] Probably 'fell asleep' belongs with 'by the will of God'. 'After he had served *his own generation*' shows that David's personal significance was limited. ἐκοιμήθη is practically synonymous with the scandalous 'he saw corruption', and so the sting is drawn in anticipation by the reference to God's will.

VERSE 37: In conclusion Jesus' imperishable resurrection life is contrasted once again with the transitory life of David. This gives Jesus his significance for us, which is unfolded in verses 38f.

VERSES 38f.: On γνωστὸν κτλ see note to **4**.10. Through the risen Lord remission of sins and 'justification'—scarcely to be distinguished here—are conferred on those who believe in him. The forgiveness of sins is also named as a gift of grace in **2**.38 (once and for all at baptism), **5**.31 (linked with the preceding μετάνοια—which D d sy^hmg add to **13**.38), **10**.43 and **26**.18. The words καὶ ἀπὸ πάντων κτλ are evidently intended to reproduce Pauline theology. Luke's contemporaries were still aware that Paul had preached 'justification through faith' and (says Bauernfeind, 177) 'that is all Luke is willing to say'.[4] Luke and his community also cherished the conviction that it was the Christians, and not the Jews before them, who were the first to

---

[1] According to the Hebrew wording the passage would not fit, for it speaks of 'the eternal covenant', 'the everlasting blessings of David'; hence also the omission here of LXX διαθήκη αἰώνιος.—τὰ ὅσια occurs twice in LXX: in Deut. **29**.19 (=שְׁלוֹם) and Isa. **55**.3 (=חַסְדֵי דָוִד); what is meant is thus 'peace' or 'sure mercies', but not in the Lucan sense. For to Luke it includes incorruptibility, the indestructible resurrection life, of which neither the Hebrew text nor LXX thought.

[2] Cf. e.g. I Kings **14**.31 and Judges **2**.10 respectively.

[3] Did David serve his generation or the will of God? Did David fall asleep in his generation (dative of time) or through God's will? Or did David in his generation serve the will of God?

[4] Anyone who, like H. J. Holtzmann, Harnack, Preuschen, Vielhauer, makes the author here develop a doctrine that an incomplete justification through the law is completed by a justification through faith imputes to him a venture into problems which were foreign to him.

obtain justification. [In view of the awkwardness of 'justify from' in English, the verb has been rendered 'exonerate' in the translation (cf. RSV); Tr.]

VERSES 40f.: the concluding admonition. βλέπετε μή = 'take care lest . . .'. ἐν τοῖς προφήταις, i.e. in the book of the minor prophets, from which Hab. 1.5 LXX is quoted (with inessential variants).[1] The unexpected 'work' which threatens the despisers is—as Luke's readers would understand—the rejection of the Jews and the acceptance of the Gentiles.[2]

VERSES 42f.: These two verses seem so hard to reconcile that Spitta, Jüngst and Hilgenfeld excise the first as an editorial insertion, while Wendt prefers to remove the second. Paul and Barnabas (not being modern concert-goers!) do not leave before the end of the service. The blame for the admittedly misleading expression rests once more with Luke's brevity. He indicates two scenes: 1. as they (all!) went out, Paul and Barnabas were asked to 'speak about these things (ῥήματα)[3] next (μεταξύ)[4] sabbath': this paves the way for verses 44f.; 2. *outside*—in modern terms, as the congregation disperses —many Jews (they are not all hostile from the outset!) and Godfearers[5] follow the pair, who exhort them to 'continue in the grace of God' (i.e. the gospel): this paves the way for the report of the founding of a congregation.[6]

VERSE 44: 'On the next[7] sabbath[8] almost the whole town gathered together to hear the Word of God,' i.e. the preaching of Christ: Luke abandons

---

[1] In the Hebrew text the verse introduces a prophecy concerning the coming of the Chaldeans. But the Christian proof from scripture uses only the words quoted, regardless of this context.

[2] D d sy^{hmg} add a transitional καὶ ἐσίγησαν. Whether this refers to Paul and Barnabas or their audience is not clear.

[3] Like דָּבָר ῥῆμα can mean both 'word' and 'thing' (Gen. 18.14 *et passim*).

[4] Same linguistic usage: Barn. 13.5, I Clem. 44.2 and in Josephus (*Beg.* IV, 158).

[5] σεβομένων προσηλύτων only makes sense if σεβόμενος denotes not, as in 13.50, 16.14, 17.4, 17.17 and 18.7, a Gentile frequenting the synagogue without accepting the whole of the law, but a devout person—in this case a proselyte—who has accepted circumcision and the whole of the law. It is a question, however, whether προσηλύτων is not here an ancient gloss which made proselytes of the σεβόμενοι because the ἔθνη do not seem to be addressed before verse 47. Lake reasons otherwise (*Beg.* V, 74–96).

[6] The *LPS* version of v. 42 (Luther-Bible) is quite erroneous: 'As the Jews left the synagogue, the Gentiles asked them . . .' In v. 43, 614 minn sy^{hmg} intercalate ἀξιοῦντες βαπτισθῆναι after Βαρναβᾶ in order to give a content to 'continue in the grace of God'. After θεοῦ, finally, D d sy^{hmg} add the following sentence in preparation of v. 44: ἐγένετο δὲ καθ' ὅλης τῆς πόλεως διελθεῖν τὸν λόγον τοῦ θεοῦ. Correspondingly in v. 44 'the Word of God' is replaced by 'and when Paul had made a long speech about the Lord' (!)

[7] B ℵ C 81 D read ἐρχομένῳ (*Beg.* III, 126 n. 44). The word also occurs in the sense of 'next' in Josephus *Ant.* VI, 174 and 235 (each time Niese puts ἐχόμενος in the text), Luke 13.33 (ℵ D) and Acts 20.15 (D). The ἐχομένῳ of the later MSS approximates to the normal usage (*pace* Preuschen 86).

[8] To explain the great throng, Wendt glosses that according to Luke's 'source' Paul and Barnabas had in the meantime been conducting an active mission among the Gentiles (217). This represents a modern, not a Lucan, way of thinking: the mission to the Gentiles does not begin until verses 47f.

all realism of presentation for the sake of depicting Paul as a great orator and successful missionary.[1]

VERSE 45: There was no real call for the Jews[2] to be jealous if they found the masses streaming into their synagogue. Their resentment against competition is indeed only possible when a new religious community rises outside the synagogue and draws away the σεβόμενοι. But this the author quite unconcernedly already presupposes.[3] It is against Jesus, not Paul, that Jews 'blaspheme' (cf. 26.11).

VERSE 46: Now Paul and Barnabas openly proclaim the Gentile mission, since the Jews consider themselves unworthy of eternal life—the indestructible resurrection life: cf. verse 37—and reject salvation. At first, however, this holds only for Antioch, as the sequel[4] shows. Acts has so far (apart from the solitary conversion of Sergius Paulus) said nothing of a Pauline mission directed to Gentiles. The idea that Paul in every case may only turn to the Gentiles when the Jews reject him makes a false theory out of the initial approach in the synagogue, which was of course the obvious procedure.

VERSE 47 offers as biblical justification Isa. 49.6, claiming it as the Lord's command to the missionaries.[5]—Not the LXX text.

VERSE 48: The rejoicing[6] of 'the Gentiles' epitomizes the joyful acceptance of the gospel by the Gentile world at large. However, not all the population believes, as Luke shows by the predestinarian expression 'as many as were ordained to eternal life'. Christians partake of the Resurrection life of Christ.

VERSE 49: The Christian preaching spreads throughout the region—it is not tied to the physical presence of the missionaries. Loisy (542) supposes it was this rapid extension which called forth the Jewish countermeasures. But this is to construct a context of which Luke probably did not think.

VERSE 50: The Jews turn to the ladies of rank[7]—proselytes, no doubt—and (through their mediation?) the leading men of the town. The persecution is described rather as an expulsion than a tumult of the mob.

---

[1] Loisy (540) raises the question whether the synagogue would have offered room enough for the huge concourse described in verse 44, but Bauernfeind (179) considers this beside the point. Preuschen (86) even thinks of a special rally . . .

[2] Bauernfeind's explanation, 'the entire nucleus of the synagogue community . . . sees that the way of the synagogue is being forsaken', does not do justice to the tenor of οἱ Ἰουδαῖοι. Loisy, commenting on the next verse, is much better: '*Ce sont des Juifs, ce sont* les *Juifs*' (540).

[3] Wendt (217) and Loisy (540) avail themselves of the explanation that the Jews begrudged the Gentiles salvation.

[4] Acts 14.1; 16.13; 17.1, 10, 17; 18.4–6; 19.8; 28.26–8.

[5] Luke 2.32 relates it to Jesus, but it does not follow that it must also refer to Jesus here (against Wendt 217).

[6] Only here do they 'glorify the Word of God'. D therefore 'emends' ἐδόξαζον into ἐδέξαντο on the lines of 8.14, 11.1 and 17.11. Verse 49 shows that here too 'the Word of God' should be taken to mean 'the Christian message', not the injunction of Isa. 49.6.

[7] εὐσχήμονας: Bauer (*Wb* 646f.) gives 'distinguished, highly placed, respected, of good family'; cf. *ThWb* II, 768–70.

VERSE 51: Luke presses into service the gesture known from his gospel (Luke 9.5 and 10.11), which signifies a complete break with the community.[1] It is however ill-fitting to the situation, inasmuch as a Christian community remains behind and will be revisited by the missionaries (14.21). The journey to Iconium[2] on which they have now set out is lengthy indeed—about 78 miles even as the crow flies. But time and space appear to shrink in the sight of Luke.

VERSE 52: An edifying Lucan conclusion,[3] which with the word μαθηταί reminds the reader that a Christian community has arisen in Pisidian Antioch.

Luke begins this section with a firm piece of information: John Mark returns to Jerusalem. Why, we are not told. Luke relates the incident only because later it is to separate Barnabas and Paul. Absolutely nothing is said concerning the whole journey from Perga to Pisidian Antioch, though it meant tramping over a third of Asia Minor! It would seem that Luke just did not possess those edifying details he likes to incorporate. That being so, he makes a virtue of necessity, sweeps the reader off to Antioch, and devotes all his space to what happened there. A few brush-strokes, and the scene of the synagogue serivce is set; invited to speak, Paul launches into discourse—while Barnabas is relegated to a walking on-part. This is not psychologically motivated. If Luke had here sensed any likely doubt (but nothing shows he had) he might have pointed to the words of verse 9: 'Paul, filled with the Holy Spirit'. At all events, here Paul with one stroke becomes that great missionary whose image survived in the Church so much more forcefully than his theology. Luke does not hesitate to invent a long speech and put it in his mouth. It is intended (as distinct from the Areopagus speech, addressed to pagans) to show how Paul spoke to a synagogue audience. And that, according to Luke, is how Paul's mission almost invariably began.

Paul's starting-point is the situation. He begins with a retrospect of sacred history, before coming to the decision required in the present and the hope for the future. As far as possible, Luke avoids repeating anything already said in Stephen's speech. Hence the patriarchs and Moses are not mentioned. The *reader* already knows their significance. Instead we have other scenes —the inheritance of the land, the time of the Judges, the first two kings . . . The name of David facilitates the transition to Jesus, his descendant, in whom the promise made to David has been fulfilled. The σωτήρ Jesus was proclaimed beforehand by John the Baptist—a short excursus makes it clear that

---

[1] Wendt 218, Preuschen 87, Loisy 543, Bauernfeind 179, Billerbeck I, 571; cf. Cadbury, 'Dust and Garments' in *Beg.* V, 269–77.

[2] Three ways were open to the missionary on leaving Pisidian Antioch: westward on a road meeting the great Euphrates-Ephesus trade-route at Metropolis, north to the Black Sea by a pass over the Sultan Dagh, or the *Via Sebaste*, which led to Iconium, the modern Konya (*Beg.* V, 225f.).

[3] Cf. I Thess. 1.6 (Holtzmann, 92).

John himself had waived all Messianic claims, affirming himself unworthy to perform even the slightest menial service for his successor. The disciples of John in Luke's day seem to have held other views on their master, and Luke seizes this opportunity of making the necessary corrections.

With the more intimate address of verse 26 he then returns to the theme of σωτηρία: the promise of salvation is to be fulfilled here and now! Only, how can the Jesus condemned and shamefully executed in Jerusalem be the saviour? Again and again the Christian mission must have had to face and remove this objection, one doubly sensible before a Jewish audience. Hence Luke here once again takes up this question, which he had already handled in the Petrine speeches of the first chapter; however, he repeats only briefly the answers given there. In the first place, what happened in Jerusalem was due to Jewish ἄγνοια (verse 27)—ἀγνοεῖν here means 'not to realize with whom one is dealing, and what one is actually doing in spurning him'. Anything done in such ἄγνοια was thus not a genuine and final decision. To this extent the Jews and their rulers are exculpated by their 'ignorance'. But what happened in Jerusalem is also considered from a second point of view. Whatever wrongful human choices there were, they exactly fulfilled what the prophets had foretold, and accordingly—of course unwittingly—realized the plan and will of God. This factor, too, is adduced as tending to exonerate the Jews. Nevertheless, and without any adequate psychological preparation, Luke couples with this excuse the accusation: that the Jews before Pilate forced through the condemnation and execution of Jesus, even though they could find no αἰτία θανάτου. This is a point which will later be repeated at the trial of Paul. In any case the emphasis lies not so much on the guilt of the Jews as on the innocence of Jesus.

All these human errors and faults have now been redressed by God, in that he has raised Jesus from the dead. This basic event for Christian preaching is certified in two ways. First by reference to the μάρτυρες who accompanied Jesus from Galilee to Jerusalem and were privileged to see the Risen Lord for a period of 'many days'—the tradition of the forty days shows its significance. The twelve Apostles are the actual eyewitnesses on whose testimony that of Barnabas and Paul is founded. Secondly comes an appeal to scriptural proof, expounded partly with new material. The content of this proof repeats an idea already developed in Peter's speech in Chapter 2: the promise given to David cannot apply to this king himself, for he—unlike Jesus—'has seen corruption'. The promise rather is fulfilled only in the person of Jesus. And now the possibility opens of obtaining forgiveness of sins and justification, which the law of Moses did not offer. At this point Luke was evidently concerned to give the sermon an expressly Pauline ring —normally he is silent about the νόμος Μωϋσέως. The speech ends with an Old Testament warning that rumbles with the menace of an earth-tremor and drives home the responsibility of the Jews: should they reject the message,

God has an unexpected and surprising work in store. What is meant is not said. But the reader knows: it is the mission to the Gentiles.

A short interlude divides this sermon from Paul's next public appearance a week later. It shows how the interest of both Jew and Gentile has been aroused. All are eager to hear more, and many are prepared to adhere to the grace of God, i.e., in concrete terms, the gospel that they have heard preached. Already the formation of a local community is in prospect.

And now Luke embarks on the great, passionately animated scene which brings the crisis of decision to a head. The masses flock together, practically the whole town is assembled to hear the Word of God. But the Jews prove unequal to the demands of the occasion: they are moved by petty spite, and out of envy for the successful preacher they contradict him and blaspheme against Christ. This is the moment of divorce between the gospel and Judaism: solemnly the missionaries declare that they will now turn to the Gentiles, who receive the word of God with jubilation. Only by devious methods can the Jews still cramp the success of the mission: pulling strings in influential circles, they succeed in having the missionaries expelled. Paul and Barnabas, with a biblical gesture, renounce fellowship with them. But Luke is unwilling to end on such a discord. Hence follows a further sentence, that the disciples were filled with joy and the Holy Spirit—even an edifying story is fond of the happy ending . . .

Scholars like Wendt and Zahn have endeavoured to fill out the picture and make the whole psychologically and historically more plausible and comprehensible. All this could not have been despatched in two sermons! Such efforts, touching in their naivety, overlook the fact that Luke neither wanted to nor was able to set down a historically authentic report. He was not able to, because when Paul got back to Syrian Antioch (14.27) he did not consign to the records, for the documentation of his future biographers, the main lines of his sermons. Luke did not want to, because he had something else in mind. Both the sermon and the resultant events are ideal or typical occurrences clothing in historical dress a host of similar crises constantly recurring. The whole Pauline mission—as Luke and his age saw it—is compressed and epitomized in this scene.

Once this is observed, a contradiction which the attentive reader notes in verse 46 is resolved: Paul and Barnabas declare that they will now turn to the Gentiles, yet in 14.1 they go again to the synagogue! One may say, not without reason, that the decision of 13.46 holds only for Pisidian Antioch. That is correct. But at the same time the reader senses that these happenings bear a significance which surpasses the immediate occasion. This crisis of decision is representative of all later instances. The Jews who in Pisidian Antioch grow envious of the Christians are at the same time the Jews in general, while the ἔθνη attending the synagogue of Antioch are more than their actually very modest number: they are τὰ ἔθνη—all those multitudes of Gentiles who stream into the Christian Church and arouse the jealous rancour of the Jews.

Of a popular tradition or of an itinerary, such as comes to light in later chapters, there is here no trace. Luke here has created, admittedly not *ex nihilo*; but on the basis of the Christian preaching of his own time and its experiences with Jews and Gentiles he has composed a kind of abridgement of Pauline missionary history. The characteristic foreshortening of times and distances in Acts is also connected with this. The vast plateaux and ranges of Asia Minor shrink; Perga, Antioch and Iconium seem to lie side by side in neighbourly fashion, and it appears as if all that happened in Antioch is compressed into a week.

There is, to be sure, still another element at work, but one which drove the author in the same direction. Missionary routine, the long, arduous journeys with their hardship and perils, pastoral discussions with converts, negotiations with the authorities and the like—none of this was edifying, as Luke and his generation saw it. For edification one required the dramatic moment, the tense incident, that rises above the daily routine and makes the great decision plain to see—often plainer than it was in reality, where it is sometimes effected without attracting notice. Only where a travel-diary was actually available and compelled the author's attention could anything survive of the daily routine of the Pauline mission which endows the epistles of Paul with the richness of life.

31
ACTS 14:1–7
CONGREGATION-FOUNDING IN ICONIUM, AND FLIGHT

[1] And it came to pass that in Iconium they entered together into the synagogue of the Jews, and so spoke that a great multitude both of Jews and Greeks believed. [2] But the Jews who were disobedient stirred up and poisoned the minds of the Gentiles against the brethren. [3] So for a long time they stayed, in confident reliance on the Lord, who bore witness to the Word of his grace, granting signs and wonders to be done by their hands. [4] But the multitude of the city was divided; and some held with the Jews, and some with the Apostles. [5] But when there was a movement among the Gentiles and the Jews, together with their rulers, to molest and stone them, [6] they took note of it and fled to the cities of Lycaonia, Lystra and Derbe, and the region round about: [7] and there they preached the gospel.

Bibliography:

Ramsay, § 28 bibl., esp. 42–4; Kragerud, § 29 bibl., 252.

D. S. Sharp, 'The Meaning of μὲν οὖν in Acts 14.3', *Exp.Tim.* 44 (1932–3), 528; A. Verheul, 'Kent sint Paulus buiten "de Twaalf" nog andere apostelen?', *Studia Cathol.* 22 (1947), 65–75; A. J. Festugière, 'Notules d'exégèse: Actes 14.7', *RSPT* 23 (1934), 359–62.

VERSE 1: The mission in Iconium,[1] begun once again within the synagogue, has great success with both Jews and σεβόμενοι.[2] The verse shows the hallmarks of Lucan language: on ἐγένετο + acc. and inf. see 4.5; κατὰ τὸ αὐτό = 'together',[3] but perhaps here, as elsewhere, = 'likewise, in the same way'; on 'entering the synagogue of the Jews' cf. 13.5, 14; πιστεῦσαι = 'become a Christian' (see 13.12).

[1] Ethnically Phrygian, politically part of the province of Galatia (see Wikenhauser, 336f.; V. Schultze, *Altchristliche Städte und Landschaften* II-2, 1926). Ramsay recounts the internal and external history of Iconium in *The Cities of St. Paul*, 317–82.

[2] Such are evidently meant by the 'Greeks' present in the synagogue. Luke consciously distinguishes them by this designation from the ἔθνη of verse 2.

[3] So Bauer *Wb.* 805. But why stress the obvious, that they go together into the synagogue? It was taken by d and gig ('*similiter*') as = κατὰ τὰ αὐτά, 'in the same way', and many exegetes (e.g. Loisy 544, Jacquier 416, Beyer 85, Bauernfeind 179, Bruce 277) translate it so despite inadequate attestation (LXX Gen. 45.23; I Macc. 8.27?).

VERSE 2: Those Jews who refuse to admit the Christian message[1] counter-attack: they spread anti-Christian propaganda among the Gentile population, since they can no longer rely on their σεβόμενοι. The aorists used to describe this incitement[2] are ingressive (Bl.-Debr. § 318), and do not mark the result as already achieved.[3]

VERSE 3: The scene painted in verses 3f. is set apart from that following in verse 5 by the use of μὲν οὖν (see note to 1.6). Despite the active hostility, the missionaries—expressed in a lamely ambiguous pronoun—stay[4] a long time[5] in Iconium, since they set their trust[6] in the Lord,[7] who bears witness[8] to the 'Word of his grace' (i.e. what they preach) by causing signs and wonders to be done by their hands: here Luke says of Paul and Barnabas, word for word, the same as he had said of the Twelve in 5.12!

VERSE 4: The anti-Christian propaganda on the one hand, the miracle-attested activity of Paul and Barnabas on the other, produce a cleavage[9] in the populace (τὸ πλῆθος τῆς πόλεως). Some side with 'the Jews'—who now emerge ever more clearly as the adversaries of the mission—the others with 'the Apostles', as—to our surprise—Paul and Barnabas are named here (and in verse 14).[10]

VERSE 5: ὁρμή[11] denotes an impulsive 'movement, not controlled by reason' (Bertram), whether physical or psychological. Things have not yet

---

[1] ἀπειθέω is the antithesis of πιστεύειν taken in the sense of 'obey' (see 6.7): *Beg.* IV, 161.

[2] ἐπεγείρω, 'stir up' (cf. 13.50), occurs quite often in LXX; διωγμός comes only thrice there, but κακόω ('make bad', 'embitter') is frequent. The expression κακόω τὴν ψυχήν occurs, but with another meaning, in LXX Num. 29.7 and 30.14.

[3] The Western text took it this way and attempted to make the assumed meaning more explicit: 'The rulers of the synagogue of the Jews and the leaders of the synagogues brought upon them a persecution against the righteous' (D sy^hms Ephr.); here αὐτοῖς and κατὰ τῶν δικαίων (formed on κατὰ τῶν ἀδελφῶν in the B text) are competitive readings (as also, for that matter, may be ἀρχισυνάγωγοι and ἄρχοντες κτλ) As the contradiction with verse 3 is now blatant, 'but the Lord soon restored peace' has to be interpolated (D sy^hms, but also it and E).

[4] Luke frequently uses διατρίβω, 'to tarry', (in LXX mostly in late books) for the missionary's sojourn with a congregation: 15.35, 16.12, 20.6, 25.6 and 25.14.

[5] ἱκανός is a favourite word of Luke's—see note to 8.11.

[6] Luke readily uses παρρησιάζομαι to describe the Christian missionaries' confidence in a dangerous situation: 9.27f., 13.46, 14.3, 18.26, 19.8 and 26.26.

[7] We cannot tell whether κύριος here means God or Christ.

[8] Luke usually constructs μαρτυρέω with the dative: 10.43, 13.22, 15.8 and 26.22. *Pace* Ropes (*Beg.* III, 130) the ἐπί (prompted by the preceding ἐπί) before τῷ λόγῳ in ℵ* A pesh bo should not be held authentic because abnormal.

[9] According to the D reading of verse 2, this split has already occurred there; hence D replaces the aorist with a perfect.

[10] The commentaries generally trace this usage back to the source employed by Luke; but as the passage contains no other trace of such a source it would perhaps be better to assume that Luke appropriated the expression from the following story (14.14). Loisy argues otherwise (546f).

[11] *ThWb* V, 468–72.

reached the point of an 'onset' by a howling mob,[1] but one can sense the ominous state of mind in which the tension for such an outbreak builds up. The pagan mob with the Jews and their leaders are on the verge of maltreating (ὑβρίζειν) and stoning the missionaries. This prepares the ground for verse 19.

VERSE 6: The missionaries take note of what is brewing (for συνιδόντες cf. 12.12)[2] and are still able to escape in good time to Lycaonia, which did indeed likewise belong to the province of Galatia but ethnically formed a different region.[3] Its most important towns were Lystra[4] (southwest of Iconium) and Derbe[5] (farther to the south-east). On this journey cf. Lake, *Beg.* V, 225–7. περίχωρος denotes either the 'outskirts' or 'vicinity' (which would correspond to the usage of LXX) or 'the countryside', where there are no towns or community organization (see Ramsay, *The Bearing of Recent Discoveries*, 39, referred to in *Beg.* IV, 163).

VERSE 7: 'And there they preached the gospel': here Dibelius (*Studies* 86), Bauernfeind (180) and others find the traces of an itinerary.[6] But Luke is probably only indicating the further continuance of the mission. The Western text expands.

Modern criticism has attacked this passage at exactly the same point as the old, which finds expression in the attempts at emendation in the Western

---

[1] So, alas, Zahn: 'But when there came an onset by the Gentiles and Jews with their (respective) leaders, and indeed in such sort that they insulted and stoned them, the Apostles in view thereof (i.e. seeing the intolerable situation) fled to the cities of Lycaonia' (463). This clumsily worded interpretation takes no note of the fact that συνιδόντες does not make sense unless the stones had not yet begun to fly.

[2] The words read by Buchanan in h, '*sicut dixerat ihs eis LX . . .*' (supposing they really stand there, for Berger could decipher nothing—*Beg.* III, 130) are not, as Zahn believes (463), the oldest Acts text but merely a scribal reference to Luke 10.1.—D reads συνιδόντες καὶ κατέφυγον. This is not an Aramaism (so Black, *Aramaic Approach*[3] 69) but a mixed reading, a hybrid of the B-text and the Latin (d and h): *intellexerunt et fugerunt*.

[3] Lycaonia is bounded on the south by the Taurus mountains, on the east by Cappadocia, on the north by Galatia proper, on the west by Phrygia and Pisidia.

[4] Lystra is the modern Zoldera on the north bank of the Kopri, opposite Khatyn Serai, from which it is about 1 mile distant (Ramsay, *The Cities of St. Paul* 407–19).

[5] Derbe seems now to be found near Kerti Hüyük, see M. Ballance, 'The Site of Derbe' (*Anatol. Stud.* 7, 1957, 147 ff.).

[6] Spitta (171) suggests as the text of the itinerary: κἀκεῖ ἦσαν εὐαγγελιζόμενοι. καὶ μαθητεύοντες ἱκανοὺς ὑπέστρεψαν. Let us disregard the fact that κἀκεῖ (cf. 17.13, 22.10, 25.20 and 27.6) and ἱκανός are Lucan vocabulary, and assume that Luke has such an itinerary before him. Why then does he deliberately report the Lystra episode only after he has already mentioned Derbe, the region round about and the missionary work there? He could easily have written: '. . . and they fled to a city of Lycaonia called Lystra. And there was a man who . . .'. Verse 20 could have remained as it was, and the περίχωρος could easily have been introduced into verse 21. None of these alterations required any literary genius; the merest hack could have brought them off. A source-theory which assumes that a journal and a separate tradition were here woven together does not really solve the riddle in the slightest. Lake is more probably correct: verses 6f. describe the missionaries' general field of action, while verses 8ff. give the details of what took place within that field (*Beg.* IV, 167). See also the conclusion of our general discussion.

text: the apparent incompatibility of verses 2 and 3. Criticism indeed no longer takes the form of tampering with the text. But the introduction of a redactor, to whom one may credit everything, serves much the same purpose. Sorof (85), Preuschen (87f.)[1] and Spitta (189) pronounce verse 3 to be later. Jüngst (129) observed that even then all was not yet in order, and accordingly snipped out verses 4f. too as redactional accretion. He left standing only the words λιθοβολῆσαι αὐτούς, which now became dependent on ἐκάκωσαν τὰς ψυχάς. Clemen on the other hand (*Paulus* I, 230f.) harboured suspicions against the whole persecution story; he assigned verses 2 and 4–6a to the redactor. Wendt contrived a less drastic solution (218f., n. 2): the source had verse 3 preceding verse 2, and the redactor only transposed these two verses —why, one may not ask, in view of the incalculable nature of such a being as the redactor is.

Three theologians of high repute have gone beyond such detailed criticism. The first, B. Weiss (*Einl.* 576; ET), laconically pronounced that **14**.1–7 could not possibly have been borrowed from a source. Loisy (545) in his own way agreed with this, inasmuch as he assigned the whole passage to the redactor; if there was an underlying source it was unrecognizable. Harnack finally (*Beiträge* III, 172; ET) did not indeed deny the account to Luke, but called it 'entirely schematic, and in addition confusedly stylized'.

All these various descriptions reflect the same impression, evidenced among more recent scholars by Bauernfeind (180). Nothing suggests the presence of a concrete popular tradition or a travel-journal: no first convert is presented to us, no host for the 'Apostles'. Instead, as we have shown in the detailed commentary, we encounter Lucanisms at every turn: the vocabulary, turns of phrase and LXX formulae which Luke so loves to employ. This suggests the conjecture that Luke was here trying to formulate some particular content, based on the overall picture of Paul's missionary experiences, with which to give body and substance to a stage of the journey that was known to him by name alone. If however this narrative was not to degenerate into mere romancing, he had to keep the tone general, subdued. But from the viewpoint of the whole composition that was scarcely to be regretted. This mission in Asia Minor contains three distinct units: Antioch, Iconium, Lystra. Antioch derives its importance from Paul's great discourse and the first deliberate transition to the Gentile mission. Lystra, with its story of the worship accorded the Apostles and the stoning of Paul, forms the undeniable highpoint of the whole. Between them lies the present episode in Iconium, a much less colourful affair. It presents the appearance of a void, a lacuna, in the history of the mission, and allows the dramatic events on either side to stand out the more sharply. The narrative about Lystra is much more impressive if it does not directly follow the great scene in Antioch, but the reader

---

[1] Preuschen's censure is particularly severe: verse 3 is an 'awkwardly inserted editorial addition'.

must, as it were, pass through a valley between these two peaks. This is not to maintain that Luke arrived at his method of presentation by reflection on what was required for dramatic effect; the question how far his great literary talent required reflection at any time may here be left out of consideration. It is enough to see what he has in fact accomplished: he has presented the mission in three cities in such a way that, while the incidents each time follow the same inner logic (success of the preaching, Jewish counter-attack, expulsion), the reader does not have set before him a tedious and arid pattern, but is led unerringly up hill, down dale—and up again to a most impressive climax.

But, quite apart from its literary and historical significance as a transition and preparation, the passage has a theological value of its own: the great number of Jews and Gentiles converted in Iconium certifies—which is why Luke mentions it—the power of the Lord. When the reader further hears of the many wonders, he must feel that they also are part of God's 'witness' to the Christian proclamation. But the mention of these miracles is important in another respect: when in what follows a special miracle is recounted, the reader knows that it is not an isolated event, an exceptional case, but a link in a long chain. The fact that the missionaries are unable to stay in Iconium, but are eventually obliged to flee, exemplifies the affliction inseparable from being or becoming a Christian. But—Paul and Barnabas are very soon preaching again in another region: thus the final outcome of every persecution is the founding of a new congregation!

Taking this into consideration, one requires little reflection to see that, far from being a clumsily retained page from a logbook, verses 6f. are an integral part of Luke's composition and the natural conclusion of his message.

32

ACTS 14:8–20
PAUL AND BARNABAS IN LYSTRA

[8] And at Lystra there sat a crippled man, lame from birth, who had never walked. [9] This man heard Paul speaking. Paul fastened his eyes upon him, and seeing that he had faith to be saved, [10] said with a loud voice: 'Stand upright on your feet!' And he sprang up and walked about. [11] And when the crowds saw what Paul had done, they lifted up their voices, saying in the speech of Lycaonia, 'The gods have come down to us in the likeness of men!' [12] And they called Barnabas 'Zeus', and Paul 'Hermes', because he was the chief speaker. [13] And the priest of the 'Zeus before the city' brought oxen and garlands to the gates, and would have done sacrifice with all the people. [14] But when the Apostles Barnabas and Paul heard of it, they rent their garments, and rushed out among the crowd, crying out [15] and saying: 'Men, why are you doing this? We also are men like you, proclaiming to you that you should turn from these vain things to the living God, who made the heaven and the earth and the sea, and all that is in them. [16] In bygone generations he allowed all the Gentiles to walk in their own ways. [17] And yet he did not leave himself without witness, in that he did good, and gave you rains from heaven and fruitful seasons, filling your hearts with food and gladness.' [18] And saying this they prevented the people with difficulty from doing sacrifice to them. [19] But there came Jews from Antioch and Iconium: and having persuaded the crowds, they stoned Paul, and dragged him out of the city, supposing that he was dead. [20] But as the disciples stood round about him, he rose up, and entered into the city: and on the following day he left with Barnabas for Derbe.

Bibliography:

Cadbury, § 30 bibl.; Kragerud, § 29 bibl., 252f.; Williams, 170ff.

W. M. Calder, 'Zeus and Hermes at Lystra', *Expositor* Ser. VII, vol. X (1910), 1–6; id., 'Acts **14**.12', *Exp.Tim.* 37 (1925–6), 528; id., 'The "Priest" of Zeus at Lystra', *Expositor* Ser. VII, Vol. X (1910), 148–55; C. R. Conder, 'The Speech of Lycaonia', *Palestine Explor. Fund* 2 (1888), 250f.; A. M. Williams, 'St. Paul's Speech at Lystra', *Exp.Tim.* 31 (1919–20), 189; T. W. Crafer, 'The Stoning of Paul at Lystra, and the Epistle to the Galatians', *Expositor* Ser. VIII, Vol. VI (1913), 375–84; S. Eitrem, 'De Paulo et

Barnaba deorum numero habitis (Acta XIV)', *Coniectanea Neotestamentica* 3 (1939), 9–12; Conzelmann 79–81.

VERSE 8: Here begins a healing-story, which is however only a preparation for the narrative beginning in verse 11. ἐν Λύστροις[1] separates ἀδύνατος from the τοῖς ποσίν which belongs to it.[2] The unusual word-order[3] may be attributed to Luke, as may also the threefold mention of the cripple's disability.[4]

VERSE 9: Paul is preaching to the crowd—there is no synagogue available! —in Greek, and is evidently understood by the cripple; but then certainly not by him alone.[5] This emerges also from the admonitions of verses 15–17, which did not fail of their effect, hence were understood. On ἀτενίσας cf. 1.10; here it has the meaning of 'to fix one's eyes upon'. ἰδών = 'observing'.[6] πίστιν τοῦ σωθῆναι = faith such as is necessary to be healed.[7]

VERSE 10: 'μεγάλη φωνῇ is a favourite phrase of the author' (who in this, however, only shares the taste of his contemporaries): '7.57, 7.60, 8.7, 14.10, 16.28, 26.24 and Luke 4.33, 8.28, 17.15, 19.37, 23.23 and 23.46' (Preuschen 88). The loud voice often betrays that the speaker is driven by the Spirit or a demon. The healing command[8] corresponds to Ezek. 2.1. ἥλατο

---

[1] Λύστρα is heteroclite—dat. Λύστροις, acc. Λύστραν (Bl.-Debr. § 57). The D text omits the name, already mentioned in verse 7 (where it had created an amplifying transition); A C and the later MSS place ἐν Λύστροις before ἀδύνατος. Bibliography on 'Paul in Lystra' may be found in A. Bludau's article of that name in *Der Katholik*, 3rd. ser., 36 (1907), 81–113 and 161–83, and in W. M. Calder's essay in *The Classical Review* 24 (1910) 67–81; *Expositor* Ser. VII, Vol. X (1910), 1–6 and 148–55.

[2] Loisy's conjecture (549) that the name of the place was later introduced into an unlocalized story overlooks the reference to Lycaonia in verse 11, and does not explain the peculiar word order.

[3] Grounds of euphony seem to have decided Luke that ἀνὴρ ἀδύνατος and Λύστροις τοῖς ought not to be separated. Cf. Radermacher,[2] 35. ἀδύνατος τοῖς ποσίν: 'a person who has no use in his legs' (Radermacher,[2] 122).

[4] Preuschen (88) strikes out 'a cripple from his mother's womb' as an interpolation modelled on 3.2. But stories of healing do like this feature as enhancing the greatness of the miracle. Just here this was of quite special consequence for Luke, which is why he dwells so heavily on the affliction (so also Bruce 280).

[5] Zahn expressly denies that the Lycaonians knew no Greek, 'so that Paul and Barnabas . . . would have preached to deaf ears' (470) without noticing what pitfalls he is thus digging for himself. Bauernfeind senses the danger and therefore has the audience 'apprehend the preaching to some extent', though 'without much grasp of its meaning' (182). But even so slight a comprehension would have sufficed to render the rest of Luke's account inconceivable.

[6] D justifies Paul's diagnosis by introducing the verse with ὑπάρχων ἐν φόβῳ. This means not 'despair' or 'dejection' (Zahn 467) but 'crainte réligieuse' (Loisy 549).

[7] Cf. Mark 9.23; Luke 5.20; 7.50, 8.48, 17.19, 18.42; Acts 3.16. The various agreements, stressed by Zeller (214) and others, with the healing of the cripple in Chapter 3 rest on purely typical features and do not justify speaking of a 'remodelling of the earlier Petrine miracle story'.

[8] D prefaces it with 'I say to you in the Name of the Lord Jesus Christ' by analogy with 3.6 (Zahn 468 goes so far as to consider the even more expanded wording of h to be the original, ignoring the point that the hearers' misapprehension becomes impossible if

P

καὶ περιεπάτει: thus every bystander can see the reality of the miracle. This too is a typical feature and not a modelling on 3.8.

VERSE 11: 'They spoke in Lycaonian'[1] explains why it nearly came to a sacrifice—neither Paul nor Barnabas (as Chrysostom already pointed out) understood the vernacular. Modern exegetes supply a psychological underpinning: the Apostles hear from all sides 'excited ejaculations . . . naturally in their mother tongue' (Bauernfeind 182; similarly Zahn 476). Cf. p. 428 n. 7 on v. 15 below. It is Paul's mighty work which leads the ὄχλοι[2] into this error.

VERSE 12: Barnabas is called 'Zeus', but Paul 'Hermes'—'because he was the chief speaker'.[3] According to Zahn and other commentators, however, the Lycaonians in reality took them for their domestic gods;[4] but this hypothesis leads to further difficulties for expositors.[5] As Paul presumably bore little resemblance to the radiantly youthful Hermes,[6] Zahn for instance follows Chrysostom in supposing 'that Barnabas was a man . . . of imposing figure and venerable carriage' (472); according to Bauernfeind (182) likewise, 'the idea of that pair of deities, Zeus and Hermes' was in the first place evoked by Barnabas, which the text of course does not suggest. Loisy (552) protests that we know nothing of either Barnabas' stature or his age, and believes that 'Even in Lycaonia two Jewish exorcists would not have been so easily taken

---

Jesus' name was thus pronounced: Loisy 551, Bauernfeind 182). D further adds 'and walk', corresponding to Luke 5.23, and describes the healing as occurring εὐθέως παραχρῆμα (!) in accordance with 3.7.

[1] See F. Müller, 'Der 20. Brief des Gregor von Nyssa', *Hermes* 74 (1939), 16–91, where (68) Jerome's introduction to his commentary on Galatians is cited: *Galatas excepto sermone Graeco, quo omnis Oriens loquitur* (!), *propriam linguam eandem paene habere quam Treviros* (Migne *PL* 26, 379). As Müller shows (70ff.), this information derives not from Varro, but from Lactantius, who was a teacher first in Bithynian Nicomedia, then later at Treves in Gaul. Müller refers to J. Sofer, 'Das Hieronymuszeugnis über die Sprache der Galater und Treverer', *W. St.* 55 (1937), 148–58. Thus the continuance of the vernaculars, such as Acts presupposes, is sufficiently attested even for a much later period. See also K. Holl in *Hermes* 43 (1908), 243ff.

[2] ὄχλοι is a favourite word of Luke's: see p. 302 n. 2 above.

[3] Cf. Iamblichus, *De mysteriis Aegypt.* 1, where Hermes is called θεὸς ὁ τῶν λόγων ἡγεμών. Cf. Zahn 471 n. 80. Preuschen (89) followed Blass and Ramsay in wishing to strike out ἐπειδὴ κτλ. because it is absent from h. But the editor of h had left this line out by an oversight (*Beg.* IV, 164). Ramsay (*St. Paul*, 116ff.) seeks to prove that D's expansions here represent the original text.

[4] Zahn (471 n. 80) understands Zeus as Pappas, Hermes as Men. This is erroneous, according to Ramsay (*The Cities of St. Paul*, 285ff.), for Men was the chief among the gods of Anatolia.

[5] See the general discussion below.

[6] *Acta Theclae* 3 has the following description: 'And he saw Paul coming, a short man with a bald head and crooked legs but of noble carriage; his two eyebrows were grown together into one, and his nose was very slightly protrusive'. This however is not an historically accurate portrait but the slightly individualized sketch of a Jew. The fact that the same text continues 'Sometimes he appeared a human being, but sometimes he had the face of an angel' (Acts 6.15) contributes nothing to the present enquiry.

for gods.' As this misgiving has visited other commentators also, as far back as Zahn, they explain the identification by the survival of the Phrygian legend of Philemon and Baucis, by whom Zeus and Hermes in human guise were entertained (Ovid, *Metam.* VIII, 611–724).[1] But, Loisy again protests (550), the miracle was not so tremendous that the people should immediately be put in mind of their highest gods.—Barnabas = Zeus is naturally named in first place.

VERSE 13: 'The priest of the Zeus before the city'[2] (=the temple of Zeus at the entrance of the town) 'brought oxen and garlands[3] to the gates.'[4] The choice of commentators wavers between the city gates and the temple gates. The details given can most easily be reconciled on the assumption that the temple of Zeus stood hard by the city gates, and the altar in front of the temple—sacrifices were not offered just anywhere[5] (Loisy 553). The

---

[1] See L. Malten, 'Motivgeschichtliche Untersuchungen zur Sagenforschung, I: Philemon und Baukis', *Hermes* 74 (1939), 176–206; 'II: Noch einmal Philemon und Baukis', ibid. 75 (1940), 168–76. Ovid's story has three main elements, (a) theoxeny combined with hospitality (a theme already found in Homer, later in Hesiod, Pindar and others—but also in Gen. 18.1ff), (b) the flood as a punishment ((a) and (b) had probably been combined before Ovid) and (c) tree-worship. The third motif need not detain us: that its introduction by Ovid is artificial is shown by the very fact that the aged couple did not need to toil up the mountainside if their hut remained undamaged and was transformed into a temple. The other elements—the offering of hospitality to unknown gods with deliverance from catastrophe as the reward—have their OT parallel in the story of Lot. Ovid's setting is *collibus in Phrygiis*; Calder thought it possible to locate it exactly—on Lake Trogitis. Roman officers who had fought here under Quirinius in the years 12–6 B.C. presumably talked about it in Rome. But it has been found that the 'miracle' of Lake Trogitis is no isolated case, so the hypothesis falls to the ground. At the origin of the flood theme there is probably an old Phrygian flood legend connected with the name of King Nannakos. All attempts to show Zeus and Hermes as σύνναοι have failed: there are Greek inscriptions from the Lystra region which couple their names, but they date from the third century A.D. at the earliest. But above all it must be borne in mind that (as Zahn and Lake both stress) the Lycaonians would have named two of their own national gods.

[2] D reads οἱ δὲ ἱερεῖς τοῦ ὄντος Διὸς πρὸ πόλεως. As πρὸ πόλεως is used like the adjective προάστιος, and Ζεὺς πρὸ πόλεως was a widely current designation (temples outside a city were by no means uncommon—see Wikenhauser 362ff.), the text must have been assimilated to the latter. On τοῦ ὄντος see note to 5.17 above. The plurality of the priests in D shows how the scene has 'grown' in the course of tradition. Large Greek temples possessed a college of priests (*Beg.* IV, 165). D's ἐπιθύειν is indistinguishable in sense from the simple verb: Zahn's inference of some extraordinary sacrifice is unwarranted.—Is 'Zeus before the walls' the Grecized designation of some Phrygian god? Zahn boldly asserts that the Temple was the sanctuary of the Phrygian gods designated by the names 'Zeus' and 'Hermes' (475); the text suggests none of this.

[3] στέμματα may also mean woollen fillets (*Beg.* IV, 165).

[4] It is not clear where Paul and Barnabas were and what they did until the priest—who could not have been 'standing by' with his oxen—appeared. *Beg.* IV, 165, surmises that the cripple must have been sitting at the city gates, hard by the temple. But it is also incomprehensible why the populace did not do obeisance at the very moment when they allegedly recognized their gods in the two missionaries. But then Paul and Barnabas would have realized the pagans' mistake 'prematurely'—i.e. there could have been no question of a sacrifice. Hence Luke hastens to bring the priest on the scene and prevent such contradictions from becoming apparent.

[5] Wendt, however, suggests that the priest simply wished to sacrifice at the gate of the city in which the gods were thought to be dwelling (221).

inscription adduced by S. Eitrem,[1] *Regibus Io(ve et Herma) iterum* etc. (*CIL* III, suppl. 7371), includes a reference to Hermes only in Domaszewski's conjectural reconstruction.

VERSE 14: Loisy (553) infers from ἀκούσαντες[2] that Barnabas and Paul[3] were not in the vicinity of the temple. But they could not have been very far away, for they spring out[4] into the crowd preparing for the sacrifice. The 'Apostles'[5] tear their clothes as a sign of horror at the blasphemy.[6]

VERSE 15: 'Men, what are you doing?'[7]—this is equivalent to a command to stop. ὁμοιοπαθεῖς, 'of similar nature',[8] hence 'just like you'. εὐαγγελιζόμενοι ὑμᾶς ἐπιστρέφειν: on this use of the infinitive (D substitutes ὅπως) see Bl.-Debr. § 392, 3. τὰ μάταια = heathen idols, LXX Jer. 2.5 *et passim*; θεὸς ζῶν is the living God contrasted with them (cf. I Thess. 1.9f.), who in a formula borrowed from LXX (e.g. Exodus 20.11) is proclaimed as the Creator of the universe. 𝔓[45] expands: ἀποστῆναι ἀπὸ ... καὶ ἐπιστρέφειν.

VERSE 16: As in 17.30, the fact that God in past generations has let the Gentiles go their own way, without—as now—vouchsafing them a revelation, is evidently intended to excuse them. There is no question here of the Gentiles' being, as in Rom. 1.20, without excuse.[9]

VERSE 17: 'And yet',[10] God did not leave himself unattested, 'in that he did good, and gave you rains from heaven and fruitful seasons', thus 'filling your hearts with food and gladness'.[11] Cf. Psalms 145.16 and 147.8.

---

[1] Op. cit., § 32 bibl., 12.

[2] As D offers only ἀκούσας, Preuschen (89) assumed that originally Barnabas alone was mentioned—one of P.'s hasty conjectures.

[3] Barnabas is named first—an after-effect of the precedence given Zeus-Barnabas in verse 12. Bauernfeind, on the other hand, conjectures that here an original Barnabas tradition peeps through (182).

[4] According to *Beg.* IV 165 ἐκ has no force in such compounds. But in the uncommonly close parallel of Judith 14.16f. (διέρρηξεν τὰ ἱμάτια αὐτοῦ ... ἐξεπήδησεν εἰς τὸν λαὸν ... κράζων) Bagoas springs *out* of the tent.

[5] The Western text (D h gig pesh) omits οἱ ἀπόστολοι; on the other hand h reads *apostolos* in verse 9 instead of *Paulum*.

[6] See Mark 14.63 and Matt. 26.65. Cf. Klostermann, *Das Markus-Evangelium*, 3rd edn., 156 and Billerbeck I, 1007ff.

[7] Cf. Luke 16.2 τί τοῦτο ἀκούω = 'What's this I hear?'; Bl.-Debr. § 299, 1. Cf. Lerle, 'Die Predigt in Lystra', *NTS* 1960/61, 46f.

[8] Thus also Wis. 7.3, IV Macc. 12.13, James 5.17 (Dibelius, *Der Brief des Jakobus*, 237: 'a man like us') and the translation of Irenaeus III 12.9 *nos similes vobis sumus homines*. We have already heard this theme in 10.26. There is no thought of an antithesis to God's ἀπάθεια.

[9] Bauernfeind (183) also admits this.

[10] καίτοι, 'and yet', is classical (Bl.-Debr. § 450, 3). In LXX: IV Macc. 2.6.

[11] In *ZNW* 31 (1932), 86f., O. Lagercrantz has shown that Luke here twice prefers a co-ordination to subordination: the rain makes the καιροί fruitful, and gladness over the nourishment thus brought to men fills their hearts. This construction is for one thing determined by considerations of sound and rhythm, for another it avoids strings of genitives dependent one on the other (Bl.-Debr. § 442, 16). οὐκ ἀμάρτυρον—another litotes.

In Chapter 17, verses 24f. correspond to this part of the speech.[1]

VERSE 18: 'Scarcely were they able with these words to dissuade the people from offering them sacrifice'—so profound was the impression the miracle had made. From early times this conclusion was felt to be inadequate: C 81 sy[hmg] supply the missing flourish (to the best of their incapability) by adding '... but to go home, every one'.[2] On τοῦ μὴ θύειν see Bl.-Debr. § 400, 4f.

VERSE 19: A new scene opens;[3] there is no indication that Luke meant it to be taken as occurring on the same day.[4] Jews from distant Antioch and the nearer Iconium (it seems there were no Jews in Lystra) foment the mob and stone Paul[5] who, as presumably dead, is dragged outside the city.

VERSE 20: It is assumed that the enemies of the victim have departed, thinking him dead, and that now his fellow-Christians are standing about him. Some manuscripts have elaborated the scene.[6] Paul recovers consciousness, contrives to re-enter the town, and next day, accompanied by Barnabas, pursues his way to Derbe.—𝔓[45] D E read μαθητῶν αὐτοῦ; cf. comment on 9.25.

At first sight the earlier critics seem to have little help to offer here. Hilgenfeld (*Acta Ap.*, 283f.), Clemen (*Paulus* I, 231f.), Jüngst (131f.) and later Loisy (548ff.) explained the whole passage as the work of the redactor; Spitta (169f.) limited the redactor's share to verses 15b–17, Sorof (83ff.) on the other hand to verses 8–11a. This seems once again to call in the source-critics' *deus ex machina*, the redactor, to efface whatever each particular scholar did not find to his liking. But this picture changes if we see the results

---

[1] Bauernfeind thinks that verses 15–17 are addressed only to individual members of the excited throng (183). But this is compatible neither with the formal, carefully chosen language nor with the precisely marked-out structure of the whole: 1. we are not gods, 2. but over against the idols we proclaim the true God, the creator, 3. who has indeed never before revealed himself to you, 4. but yet has always borne witness of himself in the blessings of nature. Loisy was wrong to suggest that this speech was a waste of breath (556), for it achieves the immediate end of preventing the sacrifice; Luke does not mean to expound the whole kerygma, for which Chapter 17 will offer a better occasion.

[2] Accepting this addition, Zahn interprets: 'that's enough of talking for the present' (479). But see Nestle in *ZNW* 7 (1906), 259f.

[3] The Western text effects a transition with διατριβόντων αὐτῶν καὶ διδασκόντων. Zahn (480) adopts not merely this but also the broad tableau inserted by C 81 sy[hmg].

[4] The scene has been prepared by 14.5. The stoning does of course not take place according to the procedure described in the Mishnah. Stones are just thrown at Paul, who doubtless speaks of the same incident in II Cor. 11.25—ἅπαξ ἐλιθάσθην.

[5] Some considerable time must have elapsed before 1. news reached Antioch that Paul was in Lystra, 2. Jews from Antioch came to Lystra and 3. they worked up the populace to the point where a stoning could be dared. But this secondary consideration does not interest the narrator, nor does he suggest any reason for the Christians' failure to protect Paul.

[6] Zahn puts them all together to produce the following text: 'And the disciples surrounded him' (when it is too late!) 'and when the multitude had departed and the day declined and it was evening, he stood up ...' (481).

of this criticism in the light of *Formgeschichte*. Then Spitta's judgement gives expression to the recognition that stylistically the address of **14**.15b–17 is an independent unit which clearly stands out from its surroundings and belongs in terms of literary genre with the other speeches in Acts, above all that on the Areopagus. Again, Sorof's discrimination of **14**.8–11a signifies that these verses contain the kind of miracle- or healing-story common in Acts, whereas the continuation is essentially different in character. In Sorof, moreover, we already find an idea which Bauernfeind will later revive, namely that **14**.11b–20 may derive from a tradition whose hero was Barnabas, not Paul. And, at bottom, Harnack's theory (*Beiträge* III, 153; ET) is also very modern: that the Antiochian source to which Chapters 13 and 14 belong contained no more than the missionary route together with a few anecdotes; all the rest is the work of Luke, who made of them a 'story'. This is little different from Dibelius' conviction (*Studies*, 20f.) that the section is based on a travel-report, supplemented by an isolated story.

Such insights, derived from consideration of the form, establish the plausibility of at least one conclusion (already demonstrated in our detailed commentary): the passage is one unit in the sense that it all came from Luke's pen, but this is not to deny that its raw material is of varied origin. To shed more light on these questions, and illuminate the composition as a whole, let us analyse the section more closely, noting especially whether the narrative shows internal contradictions. We are thus not yet concerned with the actual scene which took place during Paul's mission in Lystra, but with the report which Luke has supplied.

The narrative begins in verse 8 like one of the familiar healing-stories: the ailment of the sick person is described. It is even described three times— 'crippled', 'lame from birth', 'had never walked'. This has nothing to do with redactional growth; Luke is simply emphasizing the gravity of the disability to which the miracle puts an end, thus indirectly making it comprehensible why it exercised so strong an effect on the Lycaonians. The similarity of this miracle to that of **3**.2ff. has prompted Zeller and others to surmise that the author wished to create a 'pendant' to Peter's miracle. But the agreements consist simply of what is typical of such stories and do not derive from any tendentious purpose. At one point however the present story very significantly *differs* from the other: the healing is preceded by the cripple's faith τοῦ σωθῆναι, and this faith has been awakened by Paul's preaching. It is true that this preaching is but lightly denoted by 'he heard Paul speaking', and the reader may easily fail to take the point. But on Luke's presentation the miracle of the healing occurred only because that preaching had created the precondition for it. For this reason alone it is worth while to look into it more closely and ask why Luke placed so little stress upon it.

As verses 11ff. imply, Paul (like Barnabas) is unfamiliar with the Lycaonian vernacular, therefore he must speak Greek to the crowd. Luke nowhere implies that the Lycaonians did not understand Greek; the example of the cripple shows on the contrary, that Paul's words were understood. If it be objected that the cripple was just an exception, one need only point to verses 15–17, where the two missionaries' remonstrations in Greek succeed in dissuading the populace, hence have been understood. The μόλις κατέπαυσαν of verse 18 does not mean that the Lycaonians had difficulty in grasping the sense of the Greek; Luke is emphasizing once again the overwhelming impression created by the miracle, which makes them reluctant to abandon their plan of homage. Luke, then, presents the question of language exactly as our other knowledge would lead us to expect—the Lycaonians understand Greek like their contemporaries all over the Near East, whereas the two missionaries were unacquainted with Lycaonian. This is most important for the evaluation of what follows.

Paul is speaking to the populace—the ὄχλοι—apparently in some kind of open public space, perhaps at the city gates. There is no mention of a synagogue; the presence of Jews is not assumed at all in the Lystra story—the audience is Gentile! It is the Apostle's first sermon to Gentiles delivered without any connection with the synagogue and the facilities it offered to Gentile sympathizers. To meet such a case, the model sermon with which we are familiar from Peter's speeches, and also from Chapter 13, will no longer serve. There Luke had given *in extenso* Paul's first missionary sermon to the Jews; but he tells us nothing of the contents of Paul's first missionary sermon to the Gentiles. A reason at once suggests itself: understandably enough, he was saving up this theme for the great scene on the Areopagus. This, coupled with **14**.15–17, allows us to recognize the broad lines of Pauline preaching to the Gentiles, as Luke conceived it. The speaker takes pagan polytheism as his starting-point and urges his listeners to turn from vain idols (μάταια) to the living God who made heaven and earth, and who has proved his goodness in the bounties of nature. Having established this basic theology, the speaker may now pass on to the sending of Jesus and speak of this σωτήρ and his σωτηρία (cf. **2**.21, 40, 47; **4**.9, 12; **5**.31; **11**.14; **13**.23, 26, 47; **16**.17, 30; **27**.20, 31, 34; **28**.28). That in this assumption we are not departing from the Lucan text is proved by the formulation in verse 9: πίστιν τοῦ σωθῆναι. It presupposes that Paul has been speaking of Jesus as σωτήρ. The reason why Luke merely hints at this, and does not use the name of Jesus even in the word of healing, becomes immediately transparent when we realize the difficulty which he thus evades: a preacher who proclaims a new faith, inveighing against the old gods, could not be mistaken by his hearers for one of those very gods! But if the content of this sermon is virtually suppressed, and only the miracle put before the reader, it will not seem implausible that these pagans should take Paul and Barnabas to be (their own) gods. This of course does not really remove the contradiction in the narrative, but renders it invisible.

Now according to Luke the Lycaonians not only took the missionaries for gods, but called them Zeus and Hermes. Why did he choose this pair? Were these names given by a tradition, and if so, by which? Zahn boldly maintained (475) that Zeus and Hermes were worshipped together in the temple mentioned at verse 13. But the text says nothing of this, and Malten (see p. 427 n. 1 above) rightly points out that research has never discovered an instance of Zeus and Hermes as 'σύνναοι'. Hence reference has been made to that Phrygian legend which Ovid has preserved in a Hellenistic version in the eighth book of his *Metamorphoses*: Zeus and Hermes visiting, in human guise, Philemon and Baucis. Zahn, however, draws attention to the fact that in the original legend the divine pair bore other, Phrygian names; he thinks of Pappas (=Zeus) and Men (=Hermes). But Men—even if later equated with Selene because of the similarity to Greek μήν ('moon', 'month')—was in fact the paramount male deity of the Anatolians, who worshipped him in conjunction with the Near-Eastern mother goddess (Ramsay, *The Cities of St. Paul*, 285ff.). Thus the rendering of the Phrygian divine couple as Zeus and Hermes is solely due to the Hellenistic mythology preserved in Ovid's version. That Luke's story is Hellenistic in its affinities is moreover illustrated by the reason he gives for the identification of Paul with Hermes: 'because he did the speaking'. This idea admittedly has in Hellenism another meaning than in our story: Hermes is 'the one who does the talking' as the messenger of the gods, who conveys the orders, for example of Zeus their king. That Zeus quietly sits by and Hermes speaks for him is a conception alien to Hellenistic mythology. The identification of Paul with Hermes (and hence of Barnabas with Zeus) is thus strictly speaking not justified by reference to this particular trait of Hermes.

To Luke, however, these identifications are of extraordinary importance. For only if Barnabas is Zeus is the appearance of the priest of Zeus with the sacrificial oxen conceivable, and with this the deification of the Apostles reaches its climax. But is it really conceivable? It must be admitted that Loisy is right: that the priest of Zeus would immediately believe that the two wonder-workers were Zeus and Hermes, and hasten up with oxen and garlands, is highly improbable, quite apart from the fact that the animals had first to be brought from the pasture and the garlands woven. It is not only the priest's credulity, moreover, but that of the people which is unconvincing. The healing of the cripple was admittedly a great miracle. But surely not so great as to persuade the Lycaonians that their very gods stood in their midst. If two Jewish exorcists heal a cripple, they may reasonably be regarded as great magicians, but no more. Jacquier, it is true, suggests (425) that celestial visitations would have been nothing out of the ordinary to this ignorant, superstitious folk. But this is going too far. Even if the old Phrygian legend recounted such a visit, this was still not something ordinary, of which the healing of an invalid would immediately put one in mind.

With this the difficulties are by no means at an end. The speech now made by Paul and Barnabas does not—as we have seen—go beyond what Paul will already have said in his address *before* the miracle. If the arguments now adduced restrain the Lycaonians from the sacrifice, then had they been advanced before, it would never have come to the point of an attempt to sacrifice.

In the face of these difficulties it is all the more important to understand how Luke entangled himself in such toils. II Tim. 3.10f. ('you followed me in . . . the persecutions, the sufferings, which befell me in Antioch, Iconium, Lystra') proves that among the Pauline congregations there was current a tradition according to which Paul had had to endure persecution and suffering in the three towns (named according to the order of the first missionary journey). This tradition was also known to Luke, and probably formed the backbone for his account of the journey in Asia Minor. But he rightly judged that the underlying tone of suffering, which this tradition bears in II Tim., was out of key with his own general conception. For even if he foreshadows Paul's travail in the story of his call (9.16), even if he does not suppress the persecutions at Antioch and Iconium, the stoning at Lystra, yet it is not the power of Christ in the weakness of Paul that he portrays, but the power of the Lord in the power of his disciple. Accordingly Luke obviates the impression of negative subjection and weakness, which the flight and suffering of the missionaries might evoke, by the way in which he arranges these events. In the sojourn at Antioch the real emphasis falls on Paul's speech and his solemn parting from the hidebound Jews. When Paul and Barnabas are expelled it is they who, with a magnificent gesture, draw the line of division: it is they, not their opponents, who appear to have the initiative. As for the διωγμός in Iconium, its edge is blunted by the fact that, strengthened by miracles, the missionaries have already long been active there and are able in good time, evading the persecution, to seek out a new mission field. The real suffering remained to be reported at Lystra: the stoning. This time, by recounting how the 'Apostles' were taken for gods, Luke reaches a highpoint in the demonstration of apostolic powers which wholly eclipses the ensuing 'passion'. Luke has treated this story (see Intro. §6, p. 88) with loving care, lavishing on it all the arts of his literary culture to make it vivid, impressive. First in verse 8 he laid the greatest possible stress on the disability whose healing gives rise to the whole succeeding episode. Then he took pains to make the 'deification' as convincing as possible. The Hellenistic version of a Phrygian legend supplied him with a pair of divine visitants—who had, moreover, appeared in Phrygia, not far from the region of the story. Even so, it was no easy matter to present the identification of the missionaries with just these two gods convincingly. Luke did not follow the path of several modern commentators, adducing as the reason the majestic bearing of Barnabas. He chose to rely on the oratorical role of Paul. Nothing in the text supports the conjecture that

Barnabas stood at the centre of the original tradition. That the preacher Paul was taken for the 'spokesman' Hermes was a thoroughly risky assertion. But it enabled the silent Barnabas to be identified with Zeus, and thus allowed the priest of Zeus to be introduced. He is the professional representative of pagan religion. So long as only the crowd regard the missionaries as gods, this valuation lacks official sanction. The veneration of the Christians becomes a serious matter only at the moment when the priest of Zeus is prepared to set the seal of his sacrifice on the popular homage.

It is now high time for the narrator to swing the helm. Having shown that the messengers of Christ need fear no comparison with the θεῖοι ἄνθρωποι of paganism, he must show the humility with which they turn attention away from themselves to the God who made heaven and earth. That Jesus is not mentioned here is explained by the situation: the proclamation of the true God is meant in this context only to prevent the confusion of Paul and Barnabas with false ones, not to develop the whole kerygma. The missionaries succeed in their remonstrations, though in μόλις κατέπαυσαν the unprecedented effect of the miracle echoes once again.

The reader is now inwardly proof against being misled even by the story of the stoning of Paul. The machinations of his old enemies, the Jews of Antioch and Iconium, combined with the fickleness of the Gentiles (who, however, according to Luke's wording do not take part in the stoning), appear to have cost Paul his life. But suddenly he stands up, re-enters the town, and the morrow sees Paul and Barnabas once more take the road. It is a moot point whether Luke intended this rapid recovery to be seen as a special divine miracle. He has recounted the Apostle's sufferings with such brevity that the Western scribes—h especially—felt expansion was called for. Ephraem Syrus (*Beg.* III, 420) succumbed even more wholeheartedly to this temptation; but Zahn also (418f.) regarded a good part of these accretions as the 'original version' of Acts. All of them, however, run counter to Luke's intention of playing down these παθήματα. The sufferings are quickly overcome, but no special intervention of God is discernible in the fact. On the very next day Paul is capable of resuming his mission with full energy and vigour.

If Hilgenfeld, Clemen, Jüngst and Loisy ascribe the whole episode to the redactor, they are expressing in their own way their sense that here we have not a historical report, but a story devised for edification—Bauernfeind unreservedly writes in terms of a legend. It is indeed merely right to acknowledge that in applying to Luke the yardstick of the modern historian we do him an injustice. For he lived in the tranquil conviction that the history of the apostolic mission was essentially a triumphal procession (albeit interrupted by occasional reverses) and must therefore be recounted as such.

33
ACTS 14:21-28
BACK TO SYRIA

[21] And when they had preached the gospel to that city, and had made many disciples, they returned to Lystra and to Iconium and Antioch, [22] strengthening the souls of the disciples, exhorting them to continue in the faith, and that 'through many tribulations we must enter into the kingdom of God'. [23] And they appointed elders for them in every congregation, and when they had prayed with fasting they commended them to the Lord in whom they had believed. [24] And passing through Pisidia they came to Pamphylia; [25] and after they had spoken the word in Perga, they went down to Attalia, [26] and from thence they sailed to Antioch, whence they had been committed to the grace of God for the work which they had fulfilled. [27] And when they had arrived and had gathered the congregation together, they reported all that God had done with them, and that he had opened a door of faith for the Gentiles. [28] And they remained no little time with the disciples.

Bibliography:

H. Gebhardt, 'Die an die Heiden gerichtete Missionspredigt der Apostel . . .', *ZNW* 6 (1905), 236–49; H. J. Cadbury, 'Lexical Notes on Luke-Acts, IV', *JBL* 48 (1929), 412–25; J. M. Ross, 'The Appointment of Presbyters in Acts 14.23', *Exp.Tim.* 63 (1951), 288; H. Greeven, 'Propheten, Lehrer, Vorsteher bei Paulus', *ZNW* 44 (1952/3), 1–43; Kragerud, § 29 bibl., 253; Conzelmann 81.

VERSE 21 picks up v. 7 (κἀκεῖ εὐαγγελιζόμενοι ἦσαν) with εὐαγγελιζόμενοι. The present participle alongside the aorist μαθητεύσαντες thus becomes intelligible. Paul and Barnabas 'evangelize' Derbe—the unimportant περίχωρος is no longer mentioned—and a large[1] congregation is founded there (see on **20.**4). Thereupon the missionaries begin to retrace their steps by the same route.[2]

[1] On ἱκανός see note to **14.**3.
[2] Why did they not pursue their journey over the Taurus to Cilicia? Zahn (483 n. 3) argues that they did not shun the Taurus passes and 'rude Cilicia' (Strabo) because of the lateness of the season—the return via Perga was far more perilous. It was only concern for the communities that made them return by the same road.—Ramsay explains that the missionaries' expulsion by the municipal authorities (**14.**5) would only be valid for the latter's twelve months of office (*The Cities of St. Paul*, 372ff.).

VERSE 22 shows marked Lucan style, even in the transition to direct speech.[1] For ἐμμένω τῇ πίστει[2] cf. **11**.23 προσμένω τῷ κυρίῳ and **13**.43 προσμένω τῇ χάριτι: all three instances mean 'remain a Christian'. On παρακαλοῦντες ... ὅτι see Bl.-Debr. § 397, 6 and 479, 2. 'Through many tribulations': i.e. persecution is to be the lot not only of Apostles but of Christians in general. 'Enter the kingdom of God' seems to imply that for the Christians this is accomplished in their death (cf. Luke **16**.19ff. and **23**.43).[3]

VERSE 23: That Paul and Barnabas everywhere appointed elders[4] agrees indeed with Titus **1**.5, but not with the community organization which emerges from the genuine Paulines. Luke has simply taken for granted that the ecclesiastical constitution of his own day already existed in the time of Paul. χειροτονέω means not election by the congregation but selection by Paul and Barnabas. On the attendant prayer and fasting see notes to **13**.3.[5] Pluperfect πεπιστεύκεισαν is explained by Bl.-Debr. § 86 (cf. **4**.22 γεγόνει).

VERSE 24: διελθόντες obviously means in this instance a mere passing-through without further missionary activity (see comment on **13**.6). Πισιδία (χώρα understood): 'Pisidia is a mountainous country bounded on the North by Phrygia, on the South by Pamphylia, on the West by Lycia and on the East by Isauria' (Jacquier 435). The savage hill-tribes of Pisidia did not understand Greek.

VERSE 25: λαλέω τὸν λόγον of Christian missionary preaching: see comments on **4**.29. It is only now, on the return-journey, that any preaching in Perga[6] is reported, but of its outcome we are told nothing. D 614 min add a mission in Attalia, a port founded (Jacquier 436) by King Attalos II of Pergamum (159–138 B.C.).

VERSE 26: κἀκεῖθεν, 'thence', is one of Luke's favourite words (Acts **7**.4, **16**.12, **20**.15, **21**.1, **27**.4 and **28**.15). It is clear from **13**.4 that Luke knew Seleucia to be the port of Antioch. If he does not mention it here, but simply says 'they sailed to Antioch', we may conclude that at **13**.13

---

[1] See p. 142 n. 2 above on **1**.4; cf. also **17**.3.

[2] πίστις = *fides quae creditur* as in **13**.8 and **24**.24.

[3] According to *Beg.* IV, 168, the eschatological sense is meant: the persecutions in Iconium and Lystra are regarded as 'woes' of the last days. But for Luke these incidents already lay far back in the past, and hence could not have any eschatological meaning. Furthermore, Luke had abandoned expectation of the imminent end.

[4] According to Zahn (484) they had been prevented from making such appointments by the sudden persecution. Zahn combines this argument with another: so long as Paul and Barnabas were busy laying the foundation with their preaching, the occasion for them did not exist.

[5] The content of the prayer is indicated by 'they commended them to the Lord' (similarly **20**.32): cf. Ps. **31**.6.

[6] As the allegedly more difficult reading, many editors have put the εἰς Πέργην of ℵ* A gig in the text. In fact the substitution of εἰς for ἐν is frequent and anything but abnormal in Hellenism (Bl.-Debr. § 205).

Attalia was omitted for similar reasons of concision. 'Committed[1] to the grace of God' is part of the Christian vocabulary of devotion and probably originated in a prayer. The very cautious expression ὅθεν ἦσαν κτλ. avoids attributing to men the initiation of the missionary journey; εἰς ἔργον echoes **13.2**.

VERSE 27: Likewise for the sake of brevity Luke writes 'they gathered the congregation together': he does not by any means regard the community as subjects of their leaders (see on **15.22**). ὅσα ἐποίησεν κτλ: ποιεῖν μετά τινος (cf. **15**.4) for ποιεῖν τινι, 'to do something [good] to someone' occurs in later parts of LXX.[2] ὅτι ἤνοιξεν κτλ. is no chance reminiscence of **11.18** (Loisy 562): God has opened the door of faith to the Gentiles.[3] ἀναγγέλλω means to 'make report'.

VERSE 28: A considerable interval[4] accordingly elapsed between the first missionary journey and the journey to Jerusalem (**15.2**). Luke does not present the situation as if the news of the Gentile mission immediately brought the Jerusalemites into action.

The whole of this conclusion is in the style of edification so dear to Luke. Verse 26 announces the completion of the work spoken of at **13.2**, and verse 27 leaves no possible doubt as to whom the reader should regard as the real subject of this 'first missionary journey': not Barnabas and Paul, still less the congregation of Antioch, but God, who opens the door to faith for the Gentiles.

After Luke's account of the Apostles' 'deification' in Lystra, such a reminder may seem to us timely indeed. But Luke will scarcely have felt that he required a self-correction. He was moved—as is particularly evident from the preamble and the conclusion to his account of the journey—by an entirely different concern, namely to justify the Gentile mission by removing it out of the hands of men and making it an act of God. Seen from the viewpoint of composition, the first missionary journey is the necessary preparation for the vindication and official acknowledgement of the Gentile mission in Chapter 15: it is the Holy Spirit which sends out the messengers of God; it was the Holy Spirit which empowered Paul to punish Elymas with a miracle that converted the proconsul. Then Paul's sermon in Pisidian Antioch shows

---

[1] In LXX παραδίδωμι means 'deliver' in an unfavourable sense (into the hands of enemies etc.).

[2] Tob. **12**.6 and **13**.7 (6), Judith **8**.26 and I Macc. **10**.27. But the expression also occurs in Hermas *Sim*. V **1**.1, and the Papyri (*Beg*. IV, 169).

[3] Here πίστις again includes what we would now call Christianity. The expression has two implications: 1. God has given the Gentiles access to true piety (Bauer, *Wb* 1316), 2. thereby they also have access to God himself. θύρα—cf. I Cor. **16**.9, II Cor. **2**.12 and Col. **4**.3.

[4] Like the expressions from Chapters 13 and 14 adduced by Jacquier (438f.), the litotes οὐκ ὀλίγος (see **12**.18) betrays the hand of Luke.

the Jews how the God of Old Testament *Heilsgeschichte* has fulfilled his promises in Jesus, and granted the remission of sins. Separation from the blaspheming Jews and exultant acceptance by the Gentiles becomes typical for the Christian mission. In Lystra, the enthusiasm of the Gentiles—however blindly mistaken—builds up to an unsurpassable climax (an aspect of the story which should not be overlooked). Then comes a harmonious aftermath in Derbe, and the consolidation and organization of the local congregations crowns the whole. Soon our travellers have landed where they started. The circle is complete, the work accomplished.

How much of this composition rests on ancient sources? In regard to this question scholars divide into three groups. The situation is at its simplest for exegetes like Zahn: since he regards the 'we' in the Western text of **11**.28 as the original, he can assume that Luke himself, resident in Syrian Antioch, heard Paul and Barnabas give their own account of the voyage.

Alas, nothing that the text yields justifies this optimism. Neither the Bar-Jesus story nor that of the events at Lystra reproduces a first-hand account. Hence Dibelius considered another solution more probable: Chapters 13 and 14 are based on an itinerary, in which Luke has intercalated two or three anecdotes. As we have seen above (p. 40), Harnack had paved the way for this view of the chapter. Now the details about the journey certainly do recall those of the later chapters which are generally ascribed to an itinerary. But Bauernfeind is right to warn against allowing this resemblance to make us overlook the crucial difference: the details of the Cyprus mission are so sparse and vague, the tale of events in Pisidian Antioch so artificially constructed, that there can be no question of an old itinerary here. If Luke knew nothing about the first part of the journey beyond the blinding of Elymas and the conversion of the proconsul, he could easily have supplied the other details without the aid of any tradition. For the second part of the journey, again, acquaintance with some such tradition as is visible in II Tim. **3**.11 would have been basis enough. We could even understand the description of the return journey on the old roads to mean that the author had no information for the rest of the journey, and therefore concluded that the missionaries had not called at any towns previously unvisited, especially since he considered the consolidation of the communities by the appointment of elders as absolutely essential, and therefore actually to have taken place.

This describes the position adopted by a second group of expositors, who believe that only isolated details of the first missionary journey can be traced back to traditions.

The third group, represented by men like E. Schwartz and Loisy, believe that the first missionary journey *never took place*, but is a distorted reflection or fictive double of the second. The mission to Cyprus is a parallel to that related in **15**.39, while the real counterpart of the Asia Minor adventures is to be found in **16**.1ff.

In this radical criticism, of course, still other arguments enter into play: first the conjecture that John the son of Zebedee met his death at the same time as his brother James, with the consequences this entails; and secondly— and only this concerns us here—Paul's description in Gal. **1**.21 of his activities following his first visit to Jerusalem. Here Paul says merely that he went 'into the regions of Syria and Cilicia'. This detail would not in itself have sufficed to call the Acts account into question. But the peculiar thing is that, although Luke says nothing of any mission in Syria and Cilicia, he has the so-called 'Apostolic Decree' of **15**.23 addressed to the communities of 'Antioch and Syria and Cilicia', then in **15**.41 shows Paul 'confirming' those very communities of Syria and Cilicia of whose founding he had nothing to say.

This state of affairs has constrained scholars like Jeremias, who—with good reason—considers the radical conclusions unfounded, to assume that, misled by a duplicate account of Paul's journey to Jerusalem with Barnabas (**11**.30/**12**.25–**15**.2ff.), which he did not recognize as such, Luke put the first journey in the wrong place; Paul and Barnabas undertook it after, not before, the agreement at Jerusalem. If this hypothesis is to be sustained then one may not with Wellhausen and Ramsay assume that the first journey took years to complete. Actually the events of this journey can be accommodated between the early spring and the autumn of a single year. Further, it is not hard to see why Luke was inclined to put this journey before Chapter 15: he possessed no tradition about the mission to Syria and Cilicia which would have enabled him to show how Paul stepped to the fore and how God 'opened the door of faith' to the Gentiles.

Though scarcity of material prevents our establishing this thesis on the highest level of historical certainty, it may finally be said for it that a mission proceeding from Antioch precisely at this juncture would be particularly easy to understand. It was indeed natural that, once the parent community had recognized their mission, the Antiochians should no longer have rested content with the existing limitations of their work, and gave their most capable missionaries, Paul and Barnabas, a free hand for an advance into the latter's native Cyprus and into the region in the south of Galatia which, in consequence of strong Jewish settlement, offered fertile soil for the dissemination of the gospel. That this theory is preferable by far to the unrestrained reckoning with a redactor—which has meanwhile been fairly generally abandoned—is a matter of course.

Thus we obtain as the most probable conclusion: the account in Chapters 13 and 14 actually deals with a journey that did not take place until after the concordat at Jerusalem. The basis in tradition is slender, but enough to warrant that such a journey really did occur.

34

ACTS 15:1–35
GENTILE FREEDOM FROM THE LAW ADMITTED IN JERUSALEM

[1] Now some men came down from Judaea and taught the brethren: 'Unless you are circumcised after the custom of Moses, you cannot be saved.' [2] And when Paul and Barnabas began no small quarrel and disputation with them, it was resolved that Paul and Barnabas and some others should go up to Jerusalem to the Apostles and elders about this question. [3] So then, sent on their way by the congregation, they passed through Phoenicia and Samaria, recounting the conversion of the Gentiles: and they caused great joy to all the brethren. [4] When they came to Jerusalem, they were received by the congregation and the Apostles and the elders, and they related all that God had done with them. [5] But there rose up some of the sect of the Pharisees who believed, saying: 'It is necessary to circumcise them, and charge them to keep the law of Moses.' [6] And the Apostles and the elders gathered together to consider this matter. [7] And when there had been much disputation, Peter stood up and said to them: 'Brethren, you know how from early days God made choice among you that by my mouth the Gentiles should hear the word of the gospel and believe. [8] And God, the knower of hearts, bore them witness, giving them the Holy Spirit just as he did to us; [9] and he made no distinction between us and them, cleansing their hearts by faith. [10] Now therefore why do you tempt God, in that you wish to put a yoke upon the neck of the disciples which neither our fathers nor we were able to bear? [11] But we believe that we shall be saved through the grace of the Lord Jesus in the same manner as they.' [12] And all the congregation kept silence; and they listened to Barnabas and Paul rehearsing what signs and wonders God had wrought through them among the Gentiles. [13] And when they had finished speaking, James answered, saying: 'Brethren, listen to me: [14] Symeon has related how first God saw to the taking out from the Gentiles of a people for his name. [15] And with this the words of the prophets agree, as it is written: [16] "After these things I will return, and I will build again the tabernacle of David, which is fallen; and I will build anew the ruins thereof, and I will set it up, [17] that the rest of men may seek the Lord, and all the Gentiles, upon whom my Name is called, [18] saith the Lord who does these things, known (to him) from all eternity." [19] Wherefore my judgement is that we should not burden those among the Gentiles who turn to God, [20] but should charge

them to abstain from pollution by contact with idols, and from fornication, and from what is strangled, and from blood. [21] For Moses from generations of old has in every city those who preach him, for he is read in the synagogues every sabbath.' [22] Then the Apostles and the elders, with the whole congregation, resolved to choose men of their number, and send them to Antioch with Paul and Barnabas: Judas called Barnabas, and Silas, leading men among the brethren. [23] And they wrote by them: 'The Apostles and the elder brethren to the brethren of the Gentiles in Antioch and Syria and Cilicia, greeting. [24] Since we have heard that some from us have perplexed you, unsettling your minds with words, to whom we gave no commandment, [25] we have resolved with one accord to choose out men and send them to you with our beloved Barnabas and Paul, [26] men who have hazarded their lives for the Name of our Lord Jesus Christ. [27] We have therefore sent Judas and Silas, who will themselves tell you the same things by word of mouth. [28] For it seemed good to the Holy Spirit and to us to lay upon you no greater burden than these necessary things: [29] to abstain from things sacrificed to idols, and from blood, and from things strangled, and from fornication; from which if you keep yourselves, you will do right. Farewell!' [30] So when they had been sent off, they came down to Antioch; and having gathered the congregation together, they delivered the letter. [31] And when they had read it, they rejoiced at the encouragement. [32] And Judas and Silas—who were themselves prophets—encouraged the brethren with many words, and strengthened them. [33] And after they had spent some time, they were sent off in peace by the brethren to those who had sent them. [35] But Paul and Barnabas remained in Antioch, teaching and preaching the Word of the Lord, with many others also.

Bibliography:

E. Nestle, 'Zum Erstickten im Aposteldekret', *ZNW* 7 (1906), 254–6; W. Sanday, 'The Apostolic Decree', *Theol. Studien Th. Zahn dargebracht*, Leipzig 1908, 319–38; H. Diehl, 'Das sog. Aposteldekret', *ZNW* 10 (1909), 277–96; L. Coccolo, 'Il decreto apostolico di Gerusalemme', *Entaphia Pozzi*, Milan-Turin-Rome 1913, 159–89; E. Preuschen, 'Untersuchungen zur Apg. I', *ZNW* 14 (1913), 1–22; L. Venetianer, 'Die Beschlüsse zu Lydda und das Apostelkonzil in Jerusalem', *Festschrift Ad. Schwarz*, 1916, 417–23; L. Brun, *Apostelkonzil und Aposteldekret*, Giessen 1921; D. Plooij, 'The Apostolic Decree and its Problems', *Expositor* 49 (1923), 88–100 and 223–38; M. Goguel, *RHPhR* 3 (1923), 138–44; J. W. Hunkin, 'The Prohibitions of the Council at Jerusalem', *JTS* 26 (1925/6), 272–83; E. Hirsch, 'Petrus und Paulus', *ZNW* 29 (1930), 63–76; G. Kittel, § 28 bibl.; O. Roller, *Das Formular der paulin. Briefe* (BWANT 4, 6), 1933, 440 n. 251 and 441 n. 254; K. Lake, 'The Apostolic Council of Jerusalem', *Beg.* V, 195–212; H. Lietzmann, 'Der Sinn des Aposteldekrets und seine Textwandlung', *Amicitiae Corolla*, London 1933, 203–11; R. Eisler, 'The Meeting of Paul and the "Pillars"',

Bull. of the Bezan Club 12 (1937), 58–64; W. Foerster, ʽDie δοχοῦντες in Gal. 2ʼ, *ZNW* 36 (1937), 286–92; D. W. Riddle, 'The Cephas-Peter Problem and a Possible Solution', *JBL* 59 (1940), 169–80; L. Cerfaux, 'Le Chapitre XVᵉ du livre des Actes à la lumière de la littérature ancienne', *Studi e Testi* 121, 1946, 107–26; O. Linton, 'A Contradiction and its Fate', *SEÅ* XII, Uppsala 1947: id. 1950/51, 87ff. (§ 22 bibl.); S. Giet, 'L'Assemblée apostolique et le décret de Jérusalem: Qui était Simon?', *RScR* 39/40 (1951/52), 203–20; D. T. Rowlingson, 'The Jerusalem Conference and Jesus' Nazareth Visit', *JBL* 71 (1952), 69–74; K. Heussi, 'Gal. 2 und der Lebensgang der jer. Urapostel', *TLZ* 77 (1952), 67–72; F. Birkeli, 'De historiske problemer som knytter sig til beretningen om apostelkonsilet i Apostlenes gjerninger kap. 15', *Norsk Teol. Tidsskr.*, Oslo, 54 (1953), 144–64; A. S. Geyser, 'Paul, the Apostolic Decree and the Liberals in Corinth', *Stud. Paul.*, 1953, 122ff., esp. 134–8; E. R. Smothers S. J., 'Chrysostom and Symeon (Acts 15.14)', *HTR* 46 (1953), 203–15; B. Reicke, 'Der geschichtl. Hintergrund des Apostelkonzils und der Antiochia-Episode Gal. 2.1–14', *Stud. Paul.*, 1953, 172–87; J. Munck, § 1 bibl., 150–6; A. W. Argyle, § 6 bibl.; R. Annand, 'A Note on the Three "Pillars"', *Exp.Tim.* 67 (1956–7), 178; E. Molland, 'La Circoncision, le baptême et l'autorité du décret apostolique dans les milieux judéo-chrétiens des Pseudo-Clémentines', *Stud. Theol.* IX (1956), 1–39; Dom J. Dupont, 'ΛΑΟΣ ΕΞ ΕΘΝΩΝ', *NTS* 3 (1957), 41–50, and 'Pierre et Paul à Antioch et à Jérusalem', *RScR* 45 (1957), 42–60 and 225–9; I. Logan, 'The Decree of Acts 15', *Exp.Tim.* 39 (1927–8), 428.

K. Bornhäuser, 'Paulus und das Aposteldekret', *NkZ* 34 (1923), 391–438; P. Carrington, 'Peter in Antioch', *AngThR* 15 (1933), 1–15; J. N. Sanders, 'Peter and Paul in the Acts', NTS 2 (1956), 133–43; O. Bauernfeind, 'Die Begegnung zwischen Paulus und Kephas, Gal. 1, 18–20', *ZNW* 47 (1956), 268–76; W. M. Aldrich, 'The Interpretation of Acts 15.13–18', *Bibliotheca Sacra* 111 (1954), 317–23; N. A. Dahl, 'A People for His Name (Acts 15.14)', *NTS* 4 (1958), 319–27; C. H. Turner, 'Jewish Christianity: The Apostolic Decree of Acts XV and the Apostolic Church Order', *Theology* 20 (1930), 4–14; G. J. Streeder, 'Het gezag van de afzenders van het zo gezegd aposteldecreet', *Vox Theol.* 11 (1939–40), 14–18; B. Katzenmayer, 'Das sogenannte Apostelkonzil von Jerusalem', *Internat. kirchl. Zeitschr.* 31 (1941), 149–57; K. T. Schaefer, 'Aposteldekret (Apg. 15.23–9)', *RAC* I, 1950, 555–8; J. A. Montgomery, 'On the Interpolation in Acts 15.29', *JBL* 52 (1933), 261; E. Molland, 'Den antikke joedenchristendom og aposteldekretet', *Norsk Teol. Tidsskr.* 57 (1956), 65–83; E. Haenchen, 'Quellenanalyse und Kompositionsanalyse in Act. 15', *Festschr. für J. Jeremias*, 1960, 153–64; R. Bultmann, *Exegetica* (1967), 412–23.

VERSE 1: Once again Luke replaces Jerusalem (see verse 24!) by Judaea. He wishes to avoid creating the impression that the τινές[1] are a Jerusalem

---

[1] According to Loisy (565), they are the 'false brethren' of Gal. 2.4 who 'slipped in'. That these τινές are not identified with the Pharisee converts of verse 5 is attributed by Bauernfeind (188)—wrongly—to the use of different sources.

delegation. Jerusalemite Jewish Christians come to Antioch—some considerable time after the first missionary journey (**14**.28)[1]—and there insist that circumcision is necessary for salvation.[2]

VERSE 2: This demand provokes turmoil[3] within the community, whose claim to be truly Christian is thus called in question, and lively discussions[4] between Paul and Barnabas[5] and the Jerusalem Jewish Christians. In this situation it is resolved (ἔταξαν—the community)[6] to send Paul, Barnabas and some others[7] to lay the point at issue before the Apostles and the elders (who here appear beside the Apostles as members of the court of reference).

VERSE 3: μὲν οὖν (see note to **1**.6) marks off the preceding verses as an introduction from the episode which now follows (*Beg.* IV, 171). As a demonstration of solidarity, the envoys are 'solemnly escorted' (Wendt, 227) out of Antioch by their fellow-Christians.[8] The remainder of the verse, in which they delight the brethren of Phoenicia and Samaria[9] with the news of the Gentile mission, indirectly informs the reader that 1. Jewish Christian communities now exist in Phoenicia[10] also; according to Acts there are Gentile

---

[1] Their coming is thus, according to Luke, not a reaction to the first missionary journey.

[2] D sy[hmg] add 'and walk in the ways of Moses', because the reviser wishes to emphasize that it is not a question of a single commandment only.—The Syriac *Didascalia* (24) also mentions here the prescriptions regarding food.—Luke mentions only circumcision, because the conflict about the law was fought out on this particular terrain.

[3] For this sense of στάσις cf. Acts **19**.40, **23**.7, **23**.10 and **24**.5.

[4] ζήτησις = 'disputation': cf. I Tim. **6**.4, II Tim. **2**.23 and Titus **3**.9 (with, however, a pejorative secondary sense). ζήτημα = 'question at issue', 'subject of dispute', as in **18**.15, **23**.29, **25**.9 and **26**.3 (Preuschen, 93).

[5] According to Preuschen (93), Symeon Niger, Lucius of Cyrene and Manaen are perhaps the subject of ἔταξαν. But Luke does not indicate this. No exact tradition is discernible.

[6] D makes the men from Judaea the subject of ἔταξαν and expands the text with the aid of I Cor. **7**.24 (not Gal. **2**.5, as Loisy 566 thinks). The D text evidences the developing tendency to have ecclesiastical controversies settled by higher authority; this procedure is seen as justified by the example of Jerusalem. As Dibelius rightly stresses (*Studies* 93), the reviser is not prejudiced against Paul; the sting here is actually taken out of the controversy.

[7] Those who wish may find here a place for Titus (Gal. **2**.1, 3), about whom Acts is consistently silent. But Luke merely wants to describe a formal delegation, which cannot consist of two men only when it is a question of so important a matter.

[8] Cf. **20**.38 and **21**.5. Preuschen's contention (93) that the report beginning with verse 3 takes no notice of the deputation, and knows only of a journey, rests on misinterpretation.—According to *Beg.* IV 171, a new source begins with verse 3, although Lake notes the Lucan style of the verses.—The verse does not justify any source-critical operations.— On διήρχοντο see Bl.-Debr. § 327.

[9] When Schlatter writes that Paul and Barnabas did not 'go up to Jerusalem directly from Caesarea' but 'first headed into Samaria', probably to the congregation at Shechem (*Erl.* 4, 130), he unwarrantably supposes that Luke had the same idea of the geographical situation as a reader who looks at the map of Palestine in Nestle. Cf. H. Conzelmann, *Die Mitte der Zeit*, 31 n. 1, 51 n. 6 and 57 (ET *The Theology of St. Luke*, 1960).

[10] See on **11**.19.

Christians so far only in the Antiochian mission-field; and 2. the mission to the Gentiles is gladly welcomed by Christians everywhere. The opposition to it can thus come only from a small minority.

VERSE 4: The solemnity with which the delegates were sent off is matched by a similar reception: the delegation is received[1] in a gathering of the whole congregation,[2] in which the governing body[3] appear in person, and is immediately allowed to present its report.[4] Luke does not mechanically repeat the whole expression from **14**.27 (q.v.); but, as verses 3 and 5 show, what is meant is not only the miracles but also the great success of the mission, the conversion of numerous Gentiles (Loisy, 570).

VERSE 5: Thereupon Pharisees who have become believers demand that the Gentiles must submit to circumcision and keep the whole Mosaic law. In contrast to the Western text,[5] Luke does not make the same men press for circumcision in Antioch and in Jerusalem: only a small group in Jerusalem think—understandably, given their background—in strict legal terms.[6]

VERSE 6 does not depict a separate session of the governing body: verse 12 shows that the πλῆθος, the whole congregation, is present[7] and by no means a silent witness. Luke merely wants to show that at the protest of the former Pharisees[8] the Apostles and elders[9] immediately take charge of the situation. How they bring it under control—through their spokesmen, Peter, then James—is shown in the following verses.

VERSE 7, according to Bauernfeind (189), means 'But when—even in this circle—a sharp conflict arose,' Peter intervened. But this interpretation

---

[1] ℵ A D 33 81 𝔐 give the classical ὑπό. D d sy^hmg add μεγάλως to παρεδέχθησαν.

[2] According to the statements about the size of the Jerusalem congregation, such a gathering was of course no longer possible. But in reality Luke always imagines this congregation only so large that it can assemble in a sizeable hall.

[3] An expression justified by verse 6, though it should not be taken to imply that the congregation took no part in the framing of resolutions.

[4] Luke intentionally avoids having the question of **15**.1f. raised directly: see general discussion below.

[5] It identifies the representatives of legalistic piety in verses 1 and 5. This apparently makes the narrative tighter, but in fact it creates a difficulty not noticed by Zahn also (497ff.): the authoritative position of these men becomes unintelligible in the framework of the Jerusalem ecclesiastical organization, and stands in contradiction with **15**.24. According to Bruce they exceeded the terms of their commission (290).

[6] Since Luke in **26**.5 describes the Pharisees as the ἀκριβεστάτη αἵρεσις within Judaism, this detail fits his general characterization of this movement.

[7] Dibelius rightly resists the temptation to attribute this apparent discrepancy to the use of different sources (*Studies*, 95 n. 6). Luke was not in a position to present the minutes of the meeting, nor was it his ambition to do so. He wishes to depict an assembly of the congregation, at first vehemently agitated, then calmed by the intervention of the Apostles, represented by Peter. In this aim he succeeded.

[8] Here αἵρεσις means neither 'heresy' nor even 'sect', but 'party' or 'tendency' (*Beg.* IV 171; Bauer *Wb* 46).

[9] In designating Paul and Barnabas as 'Apostles', Schlatter departs from Luke's presentation of things (*Erl.* 4, 180 *et passim*).

does not fit Luke's intention.[1] By πολλῆς ζητήσεως γενομένης he indicates the situation prevailing when Peter rose to speak: speech and counter-speech alternate in the assembly. Now, when excitement and conflict have reached their peak, Peter intervenes and with one stroke clarifies the situation in his address: 'From the earliest days[2] God made choice among you[3] that by my mouth the Gentiles should hear the word of the gospel and believe.' In this way Peter reminds his audience of the conversion of Cornelius (10.1–11.18) through which God caused the Gentile mission to begin.[4]

VERSE 8: God the knower of hearts[5] has borne sure witness[6] to the Gentiles by giving them the Holy Spirit: this is a reminder of 10.44–7.

VERSE 9: The words 'and he has made no distinction between[7] us and them'[8] appear to add to the foregoing ideas only a comparison with the Jewish Christians. But the continuation, 'in that he cleansed their hearts by the faith' (which he gave them) introduces a new thought: however impure

---

[1] If πρὸς αὐτούς is taken to refer to the Apostles and elders, it would be these who were tempting God by seeking to lay an intolerable yoke upon the Gentiles. Luke, however, has already in 11.2 avoided presenting the Apostles themselves as in conflict with Peter, and he cannot wish to show the reverse here. The conflict is with the little group whose descent from Pharisaism prevents their comprehending Gentile freedom from the law. To suggest that the controversy raged even in the apostolic core of the Church is to distort Luke's picture. Verse 12, moreover, shows that πᾶν τὸ πλῆθος had been noisily disputing —and this does not mean the Apostles and elders.

[2] Bauernfeind explains the expression thus: 'Measured by the short length of time, spanning under two decades, during which the Christian Church had been in existence, the Cornelius episode already lay well in the past' (190). But Overbeck had already pointed out that this reflection on the short life of the congregation, etc., simply cannot be attributed to Peter (225). We ought quietly to admit that the expression exaggerates, but was chosen to show that the matter was decided long ago. Moreover, it seems also to explain why the Christians have (apparently) forgotten it—it happened so long ago! Bruce, however, differs: 'in the early days' (of the Church) (292).

[3] LXX frequently renders בָּחַר בְּ by ἐκλέγεσθαι ἐν (which Torrey—*Comp. and Date,* 21f.—did not observe): I Sam. 16.9f.; 1 Kings 8.16, 44; 11.32; I Chron. 28.4f.; II Chron. 6.5 (twice,), 6, 34 and 7.12; Neh. 9.7. Luke adopts this turn of phrase, felt to be especially solemn, but does not use it in the sense of the Hebrew text which LXX reproduces.— εὐαγγέλιον: again at 20.24.

[4] Dibelius rightly stresses that 'this . . . allusion to Acts 10.1ff. cannot be understood by Peter's hearers, though it can by readers of the book. For the latter the Cornelius story has a normative significance . . . and this is the work of the writer Luke, for he can be shown to have expanded the story of Cornelius and endowed it with fundamental importance' (*Studies* 94f.). Cf. *Studies* 109ff. and pp. 343ff. above on 10.1ff.

[5] On the Hellenistic concept καρδιογνώστης see n. 8 on 1.24. As the knower of hearts God knows the inner worthiness of persons (De Wette, 226). The expression corresponds to 10.34: God is not προσωπολήμπτης. He does not enquire to what people a man belongs (that would be consideration of a merely superficial characteristic) but whether he is worthy in his heart.

[6] See *ThWb* IV 501, 20ff.

[7] The LXX construction is διακρίνω ἀνὰ μέσον.

[8] There is no thought here of the difference between the Pentecostal miracle and the ecstatic 'speaking with tongues' in 10.46: indeed Luke makes 10.46, even as to wording, as reminiscent of 2.11 as possible.

the Gentile may be as such in Jewish eyes, God has now created in him an inward purity. The idea of the 'knower of hearts' denied the difference between a devout Jew and a devout Gentile, and seemed to credit man with the ability to place himself in a position pleasing to God. Now on the contrary God himself appears as the one who produces this situation. In view of verse 10, however, it is open to doubt whether in mentioning purity Luke had in mind that 'in Judaistic eyes it was bound up with observance of the law' (Overbeck, 226).

VERSE 10: οὖν introduces a deduction: since God has recognized the Gentiles, it would amount to defying him[1] if one were to lay on the neck of the disciples[2] the intolerable yoke[3] of the law. 'Strictly speaking', remarks Overbeck, 'this is arguing from Jewish Christian freedom from the law' (226). It would be more correct to say that the Gentile Christian Luke, who is speaking here, has lost sight of the continuing validity of the law for Jewish Christians (which he does not contest—cf. **21**.21), because all that matters to him is to demonstrate Gentile Christian freedom from the law.

VERSE 11: 'We believe that we shall be saved, just like them, by the grace of the Lord Jesus.' Peter speaks in terms familiar to us from Paul. This does not mean that Luke wishes to portray him as a Paulinist, or as one who has anticipated the Pauline theology. He is making evident the conformity of the Jerusalem congregation with the premises of the Pauline mission as he sees it.[4]

Verses 10f. are in a sense complementary to the story of Cornelius. There the mission to the Gentiles was justified, firstly, by the miracles with which God inaugurated it, and secondly by the postulate that what matters to God is merely whether a man fears him and does right. But here a third and fourth basis for the Gentile mission apart from law are made plain: God

---

[1] The locution is frequent in LXX; with dependent infin., Ps. **78**.18: ἐξεπείρασαν τὸν θεὸν ... τοῦ αἰτῆσαι βρώματα.

[2] 'To style Gentile converts thus as "disciples" is tantamount to prejudging the observances as useless' (Loisy, 579).

[3] This statement corresponds neither to Jewish nor to Pauline theology. The Jewish saw in the law a privilege and a help: the idea of 'the yoke (of the law)' denoted the religious duties and contained no complaint that the law was hard or intolerable (cf. Billerbeck I, 608ff.; *Beg.* IV, 173f.). The Pauline saw the law as a means by which man sought to attain his own glory, and which therefore turned him away from God. Here however we have the law seen through Hellenistic Gentile Christian eyes, as a mass of commandments and prohibitions which no man can fulfil. Luke here is obviously speaking for himself and transmitting the view of his age and milieu.

[4] Bauernfeind asks: '... does not Paul himself, in Gal. **2**.15f., imply as Peter's opinion what' the latter 'says here in verse 11?' (190). The answer must be No: the difference between trust in God's saving help and trust in one's own efforts, which is what Paul means in Galatians by justification through faith in Christ and not by works of the law, is not in view here. Paul can (in Phil. **3**.4ff.) describe himself, in his Pharisee past, as spotless by the righteousness of the law, yet he holds this as σκύβαλα.—Pauline concepts are taken over by Luke, but not the Pauline theology that puts them to use. πιστεύομεν σωθῆναι: cf. **3**.18; Bl.-Debr. §§ 397, 2; 350.

bestows on the Gentiles the necessary purity, and the law is in any case impossible of fulfilment.[1]

VERSE 12: Peter's speech puts an end to all conflict within the πλῆθος[2] —the assembly holds its peace[3] and allows Barnabas and Paul[4] to relate the signs and wonders God has wrought through them among the Gentiles. These experiences, in which God's will became visible, confirm the arguments of Peter. Dibelius (*Studies*, 96) correctly recognizes why Luke does not reveal what Paul and Barnabas actually said: the incidents are already familiar to the reader from Chapters 13 and 14, whose significance for this scene *qua* Lucan composition now becomes clear.[5]

VERSE 13: After Peter and his witnesses, James now steps forward. This prepares the reader for his later becoming the leader of the congregation. Here Luke assigns him two tasks: first, after Peter's fundamental address James presents the scriptural proof, and secondly he proposes the resolution which it is urgent that the assembly adopt. That Luke is not here reproducing any historical recollection is proved by verse 17.

VERSE 14: On ἄνδρες ἀδελφοί see note on 1.16. Luke employs the form Συμεών[6] to show that James, the Lord's brother, is speaking Aramaic. πρῶτον does not mean that what once happened goes back to God's initiative (so Bauernfeind, 191), but harks back to ἀφ' ἡμερῶν ἀρχαίων.[7] Luke makes

---

[1] But even now the miracles are not forgotten; see verse 12!

[2] 'All the congregation kept silent' does not mean that there was no applause (so Bauernfeind, 190). When he adds 'The minute after Peter's speech remained unforgettable to all who took part' Bauernfeind overlooks the fact that pious tradition readily preserves an enthusiastic 'It is God's will', but not a distinctly unedifying embarrassed silence. Neither, for that matter, are these words merely an 'innocuous transitional remark' (Dibelius, *Studies* 95); the Apostle has restored calm, the ζήτησις is past, and the governing body, now that its witnesses have successfully appeared, can move the decisive resolution.

[3] If 'Catholic expositors' have inferred 'from the oft-stressed *silentium*' that 'only the clergy were allowed to speak in the Council' (Holtzmann, 96), this would not be very flattering for the clergy, for it would mean that at least some of them spoke against the Gentile mission without the law. Luke allows this opposition to be audible only within the πλῆθος.

[4] The fact that sometimes Paul (15.2, 22, 35), sometimes Barnabas (15.12, 25) is named first is no reason for jumping to the conclusion of different sources: Luke is fond of variety. Whether Barnabas enjoyed greater confidence in Jerusalem is not established. This holds even for the Lucan presentation of history.

[5] Bauernfeind supplements Luke: Paul must not only have spoken of the miracles, but have pointed out that the *sola fide* belonged to the essence of the faith. For many present this was still not clear, while the argument from miracle in contrast was decisive, and it was the reminiscence of such witnesses which determined the Lucan presentation (191). But what Bauernfeind reasonably feels as a 'distressing truncation' on the part of Luke was not in fact one for the author himself, hence it is illegitimate to make the deficiency good with the aid of Galatians and one's own historical imagination.

[6] According to D. W. Riddle ('The Cephas Problem and a Possible Solution', *JBL* 59 (1940), 169–80) this Symeon is a Christian leader distinct from another by the name of Peter. Cf. p. 394 n. 4.

[7] *Beg.* IV 175 objects that the word should then read πρώτως. But Luke is not writing classical Greek.

James speak with a certain solemn formality: ἐπεσκέψατο λαβεῖν[1] 'he attended to the business of acquiring' a people from among the Gentiles (note the distinction between λαός and ἔθνη). Cf. Dupont, *NTS* 3 (1957), 41–50.

VERSE 15: This action of God is confirmed by his words reported in the scroll of the 'minor prophets' (*Beg.* IV 176); cf. 7.42 and 13.40f.

VERSES 16–18: The text here agrees entirely in meaning, and for the most part in wording, with LXX.[2] The Hebrew text would be useless for James's argument, and would even contradict it.[3] Nearly every expositor concedes that the Jewish Christian James would not in Jerusalem have used a Septuagint text, differing from the Hebrew original, as scriptural proof.[4] It is not James but Luke who is speaking here. When he speaks of the re-erection of the ruined tabernacle of David, he does not see this as the restoration of the Davidic kingdom, nor does he even see in it an image of the true Israel. He conceives it as adumbrating the story of Jesus, culminating in the Resurrection, in which the promise made to David has been fulfilled: the Jesus event that will cause the Gentiles to seek the Lord.[5]

VERSE 19: If the Gentiles are to seek God, they ought not to be deterred by the law. Given this understanding of the Amos quotation, the διό-clause is genuinely connected to what precedes it. παρενοχλεῖν[6] exactly corresponds

---

[1] Cf. ἐπεῖδεν ἀφελεῖν Luke 1.25 (Bl.-Debr. § 392, 3). For ἐπεσκέψατο cf. Luke 1.68, 78 and 7.16.

[2] LXX has misread יִדְרְשׁוּ for יִירְשׁוּ and אָדָם for אֱדֹם (*Beg.* IV 176.)

[3] 'that they may conquer the remnant of Edom and all the nations'.

[4] This refutes Torrey's thesis of a continuous Aramaic source (*Beg.* IV, 176). Zahn makes a desperate attempt to save the speech for James: the LXX text of Amos 9 is perhaps more original than the Massoretic, and perhaps a corresponding Aramaic text was used in Galilee in James's time, and familiar to James (521 n. 83). Or perhaps James had in course of the years grown familiar with LXX, and here—out of regard for Paul and his companions—spoke Greek, and even cited Amos in the LXX text (similarly Bruce, 298). It is a sorry business when a viewpoint has to be defended with such arguments.—J. Munck wrongly reads out of the text that according to James God will first raise up Israel anew, and that 'when that has happened, it will have an effect on the Gentiles' (*Paulus und die Heilsgeschichte*, 229; ET *Paul and the Salvation of Mankind*, 1959). Since, as Munck himself sees, this is counter to Luke's view of the *Heilsgeschichte* and moreover—as he likewise discerns—the LXX quotation does not suit in the mouth of James, it follows that we must seek for v. 16 a meaning corresponding to *Lucan* theology.

[5] According to B ℵ C 81 sa the addition γνωστὰ ἀπ' αἰῶνος, absent from both LXX and the Hebrew (cf. Isaiah 45.21, 'that they may know τίς ἀκουστὰ ἐποίησεν ταῦτα ἀπ' ἀρχῆς', and Acts 3.21), refers to ταῦτα, but the Western text (A d Iren vg sy^hmg) creates the separate sentence: γνωστὸν ἀπ' αἰῶνός ἐστιν τῷ κυρίῳ τὸ ἔργον αὐτοῦ; D offers a conflation: ποιήσει ταῦτα· γνωστὸν κτλ. (*Beg.* III, 144). Loisy conjectures that the B-text addition was found by the editor in a testimony book: that God knew (or made known) his action from all eternity could have been added in such a book in order to round off the quotation (585f.).

[6] LXX employs παρενοχλέω to render various Hebrew verbs. παρα merely reinforces ἐνοχλέω, 'to burden' (*Beg.* IV, 177). Lake's translation of the aorist, 'stop overburdening' instead of 'do not overburden', credits Luke with an uncommon Atticistic subtlety, and is not supported by reference to 1.4 and 15.38. Moreover the Gentiles have not yet been saddled with the law; this lies still in prospect.

to the ἐπιθεῖναι ζυγόν of verse 10: James is now speaking as forcefully of freedom from the law as Peter! κρίνω, 'my opinion is',[1] introduces the motion which James now lays before the plenary session.

VERSE 20: Strange as it may at first seem to us, the following four requirements are conceived not as a legalistic imposition on the Gentile Christians, but as a concession to them, a meeting halfway.[2] The 'burden of the law' from which the Gentiles are to be relieved comprises, firstly and above all, circumcision, then the countless other legal prescriptions and prohibitions. All this for them now falls away. The 'pollution by idols' comes about through eating flesh sacrificed to heathen gods;[3] 'fornication' here refers to marriage in prohibited degrees of relationship, which the rabbis designated as 'forbidden on account of unchastity' (Billerbeck II, 729);[4] 'what is strangled' denotes flesh slaughtered other than ritually;[5] 'blood' means partaking of blood.[6]

[1] *Beg.* IV 177 wants to translate 'I decree': 'It is the definite sentence of a judge, and the ἐγώ implies that he is acting by an authority which is personal' (177). But Lake himself admits that κρίνω can denote merely a recommendation, and that the real resolution is only formed in verse 22, by Apostles, elders and the whole congregation. Cf. 16.4 and 21.25.

[2] 'The content of the Apostolic decree is regarded throughout as a concession to the Gentile Christians on the part of the men of Jerusalem, not the reverse' (Dibelius, *Studies*, 97).

[3] ἀλισγημάτων τῶν εἰδώλων = εἰδωλοθύτων in verse 29: the more sonorous expression matches the formal style of the speech (see on verse 14). *Beg.* V 205 overlooks this. On εἰδωλόθυτον see *ThWb* II, 375f.; Lietzmann, *Handb. z. NT: Korintherbr.*, 4th edn., 48ff. and 181ff. on I Cor. 10.20ff.; Billerbeck III, 420f. This is a ban not only on participation in pagan cultic meals but on buying sacrificed meat in the market. Rev. 2.20–25 does not exhibit 'a distinct reference to the wording of the decree' (so Bauernfeind, 194) but alludes to Num. 25.1ff.

[4] Here πορνεία refers to the forbidden marriages of Lev. 18.6–18 (cf. Billerbeck II, 376 and 729; I, 694). Wikenhauser suggests that 𝔓⁴⁵ (without καὶ τῆς πορνείας) may be the authentic text (*Apg.* 141).

[5] πνικτόν: 'all flesh of beasts not slaughtered according to Jewish ritual' (Bauernfeind, 196). It is not superfluous to mention αἷμα as well: 'In practice the partaking of food consisting of or prepared with blood was so different from the eating of unritually slaughtered meat that it was certainly advisable to mention them separately' (Bauernfeind, 196f.).—Gen. 9.4 forbids the eating of πνικτόν, Lev. 3.17 the partaking of blood; Lev. 17.10–14 combines the two prohibitions. The prohibition is also found in Lev. 19.26; Deut. 12.16, 23f. and 15.23. Cf. Billerbeck II, 730 and 733ff. Billerbeck thinks the Gentile Christians were forbidden only the flesh of maimed or deceased animals, since prohibition of any meat not ritually slaughtered would have imposed on them the very burden from which they were to be free.—In this connection it must be considered that as a food of the masses meat then played a far smaller part than today.

[6] The Greek text has two versions: 1. mentioning 'what is strangled' but without the 'golden rule' (so all uncials save D), 2. without any mention of 'what is strangled' but with the 'golden rule' (so D d Iren Cypr).

The second, which understands the prohibitions in a 'moral' sense (idolatry, fornication, murder), was according to G. Resch (*Das Aposteldekret nach seiner ausserkanonischen Textgestalt*, *TU* N.S. 13, 3) defended as original by Harnack (*Beiträge* III, 188ff.; IV, 22f.; ET), A. C. Clark (*The Acts of the Apostles*, Oxford 1933, 360f.) and Feine-Behm (*Einl.*, 9th edn. 83f.). But a later reinterpretation in a 'ritual' sense, in which πνικτόν was added (so Harnack), may be considered out of the question. Readily understandable, on the other

VERSE 21: The ceremonious way of speaking continues, with the result that this verse, though 'linguistically and textually unobjectionable, is, so far as context and meaning are concerned, among the most difficult in the New Testament' (Dibelius, *Studies.* 97). It gives the justification[1] for the immediately preceding verse 20: from ancient times the law has been preached in the synagogues of every city, therefore the Gentiles must observe the four prohibitions which it imposes also on them.

---

hand, is a later reinterpretation in a 'moral' sense, in which πνικτόν had to be dropped and the 'golden rule' added: this removed the contradiction with Gal. 2.6 and furnished a welcome summary of Christian ethics. The fact that the uncials (except D) read καὶ (τοῦ) πνικτοῦ in 15.20, τῶν πνικτῶν in 15.29 and πνικτόν in 21.25 can be explained in the same way as the varying order of the prohibitions: Luke is fond of variety in expression. If πνικτόν had been inserted later as a gloss, it would not have given rise to such variation.

At this point Zahn buried his principle of explaining the Western text as original (523ff.). He could not have Luke record James's stipulations as ethical in the 'first edition' but ritual in the second.

The following are among the scholars who have maintained that the prohibitions were originally of a ritual nature: P. Wendland (*Urchr. Literaturformen*, 2nd and 3rd edns, 320), Wendt (232f.), Diehl (bibl.), Preuschen (bibl.), J. Weiss (*Das Urchristentum*, 235f.; ET *Earliest Christianity*, 1959), Goguel (*Intro.* III, 187ff.; *Naissance du Chr.*, 329; ET *The Birth of Christianity*, 1953), Loisy (589), E. Meyer (*Ursprung und Anfänge des Chr.* III, 187ff.), Ropes (*Beg.* III, 265ff.), Lietzmann (bibl.), Beyer (95f.), H. Waitz (*ZKG* 1936, 277ff.), Bauernfeind (195f.), Cerfaux (bibl.), Dibelius (*Studies* 98 n. 12), K. Schäfer (*R.A.C.* I, 555f.) and W. G. Kümmel ('Die älteste Form des Aposteldekrets' in *Spiritus et Veritas: Festschrift für K. Kundsin*, 1953, 83ff.).

The thesis of Ropes (loc. cit.), that in *De pudicitia* 12 Tertullian gives the original text (without either πνικτόν or the 'golden rule'), and the more recent one advanced by Menoud that the original text did not contain the prohibitions of πορνεία or πνικτόν ('The Western Text and the Theology of Acts' in *Stud. NT Soc.*, Bulletin II, 1951, 19ff.), have been refuted by Kümmel (see above).

[1] According to Ropes, verse 21 states the justification for the preceding exegesis of Amos 9.11f., against which it could be objected that the prophecy meant only the restoration of the Davidic kingdom. Against this possible objection James is stressing that the Jews have synagogues all over the world. Thus, 'the nations on whom my name is called' covers not only the old Davidic kingdom but the whole civilized world (*Beg.* IV, 177f.). But what reader would have hit upon this meaning? The same applies to Dibelius' similar interpretation (*Studies*, 98).

Furthermore, 'Moses' is not the same as the 'words of the prophets' (verse 15). Thus the γάρ-sentence cannot well refer to verses 16–18, but only to verses 19 or 20. It does not fit verse 19: the fact that the Mosaic law is preached everywhere cannot be held to justify *not* inflicting it on the Gentiles.

Therefore it must apply to the immediately preceding verse 20. The Gentiles must be enjoined to abstain from the four things mentioned, because the law preached everywhere requires this of them. Deliverance from the 'burden of the law' consists in exemption from circumcision, which was felt as the really oppressive burden, and from the immense number of other commandments and prohibitions. Cf. also Bauernfeind 189 and 194ff.

It is not merely the very refined style of the speech which makes the verse opaque, but also a second circumstance: Luke here is choosing his words with special care in order that the tension between Jewish and Gentile Christians may appear as small as possible. In 21.20 on the other hand it is clear that James demands consideration for the Jewish Christians, who—myriads strong—are all 'zealots for the law'! In the Cornelius story Luke admittedly could not have brought in the four prohibitions, but it is obvious that the centurion's piety could have accommodated them.

VERSE 22: James's proposal is accepted: Apostles, elders and congregation resolve[1] to draw up a letter accordingly and to entrust its transmission to two respected members,[2] who accompany Paul and Barnabas back to Antioch.

VERSE 23: The nominative absolute γράψαντες refers to the logical subject of ἔδοξε κτλ.; such a construction was known to classical Greek also (*Beg.* IV 179). διὰ χειρός = 'by', of the agent, as very frequently in LXX.[3] Judas and Silas are not the writers but the carriers of the letter. The placing of ἀδελφοί in apposition to (ἀπόστολοι καί) πρεσβύτεροι is most unusual.[4] τοῖς κατά[5] τὴν κτλ. = 'the Gentile Christians[6] in Antioch, Syria and Cilicia': this formula comes as a complete surprise, for though Paul, as we have seen, mentions his period in Syria and Cilicia (Gal. 1.21), Acts has not spoken of any mission in these areas. Yet 15.41 takes it for granted that the

---

The origin and validity of the 'decree' is dealt with in our general discussion. Here however it may be noted that OT itself imposes these commands on Gentiles also (in contrast with circumcision!) in so far as they live among Jews: use of πνικτόν and αἷμα is forbidden in Lev. 17. 10ff., πορνεία (in the sense of forbidden marriages) in Lev. 18.26 to 'the stranger who sojourns among you' as well.

[1] Here ἔδοξε denotes not, as in Luke 1.3, private decision but a public resolution with force of—holy—law. In this the whole congregation—not merely the governing body of Apostles and elders—is associated, though it obviously cannot stand at the head of the letter embodying the decision.

[2] The entrusting of the letter not merely to Paul and Barnabas (so B. Weiss), but to a special deputation, served both to honour the Antiochian congregation and to stress the authority of that of Jerusalem. This is so, whether the story be historically true or not.

The ἡγούμενοι (see *ThWb* II, 909f.) are distinct from the elders: they are not called συμπρεσβύτεροι. Here the title does not signify 'honourable' (Wendt 238) so much as 'leading, prominent' (Bauer, *Wb* 679). Nothing further is known of Judas Barsabbas. He could be a brother of the Joseph Barsabbas of 1.23, but the name Barsabbas is common (= the sabbath-born): *Beg.* IV, 178. Silas is Paul's travelling-companion of 15.40, and is generally identified (Barnikol, *Forschungen* III, 16, is a dissentient) with the Silvanus named in I and II Thess. 1.1 as one of the senders of the epistle and in II Cor. 1.19 as having preached with Paul and Timothy in Corinth. I Peter 5.12 makes him the scribe who wrote this epistle. Silas is the Greek version of שְׁאִילָא, which latinized gives 'Silvanus'. Cf. excursus in Windisch, *Kath. Briefe* (*Hdb. z. NT* 15, 3rd edn., 1951), 80f. By reading Σειλεα here and Σιλαια in 17.4, D presupposes a trisyllabic form of the name (Sileas) (*Beg.* III, 269f., and IV, 178f.).

[3] So also Acts 2.23, 7.25 and 11.30. In 5.12 and 14.3 (διὰ χειρῶν), on the other hand, the reference is actually to the hands which wrought the miracle (as in Mark 6.2).

[4] Later MSS slip in a simplifying καί before ἀδελφοί; this makes the congregation one of the senders of the message. Orig. and sa, also to facilitate matters, drop ἀδελφοί, Schwartz (*NGG* 1907, 271 n. 1) and Preuschen (96) wanted to strike out 'the Apostles and elders', but that would make it necessary to add 'in Jerusalem' after 'the brethren'. According to Loisy, the redactor smuggled in the elders, the original having read 'the Apostles and the brethren in Jerusalem' (597f.). But as Luke again and again uses the address ἄνδρες ἀδελφοί, it remains possible that he ventured the unusual locution οἱ πρεσβύτεροι ἀδελφοί, which is just as difficult to translate.

[5] Such constructions with κατά replace the genitive (Radermacher, 2nd edn., 139; Bl.-Debr. § 224, 1).

[6] This designation of course is no more to be found in Luke's text than 'Jewish Christian'.

congregations there were founded with Paul's assistance (**15**.36!). **16**.4 shows that Luke did not regard the decree as applicable solely to the congregations named in **15**.23 (the mention in **21**.25 is to remind the reader, not Paul!); according to **15**.19 it is intended for Gentile Christians in general.—The form of greeting χαίρειν[1] usual in antiquity occurs in NT also at Acts **23**.26 and James **1**.1; see Moulton, 179 and Bl.-Debr. § 389 and § 480, 5.

VERSE 24: The letter harks back to the situation depicted in **15**.1f., without specifically mentioning the enquiry from the Antiochians. τινὲς ἐξ ἡμῶν: the 'men come down from Judaea' were thus Jerusalemites, though admittedly without any mandate.[2] This implies that the Apostles could have sent out messengers with real authority.[3] As in Gal. **1**.7 and **5**.10, ταράσσω means 'perplex', 'throw into alarm or confusion'; ἀνασκευάζω, 'overthrow', 'destroy', is 'cultivated Greek' (Bauernfeind, 193) and ill-matched stylistically with τὰς ψυχὰς ὑμῶν, an expression derived from LXX.

VERSE 25 announces the first resolution solemnly taken by the assembly,[4] namely to send chosen[5] men with 'our beloved Paul and Barnabas'.[6]

VERSE 26: Paul and Barnabas receive the title of honour 'men who have hazarded their lives[7] for the Name of our Lord Jesus Christ', a formula resounding with ecclesiastical glory.

---

[1] 'The letter shows in its form no peculiarly Christian deviation from the standard ancient epistle' (Bauernfeind 193, who calls the address 'undoubtedly old').

[2] Munck (*Paulus und die Heilsgeschichte*, 227; ET *Paul and the Salvation of Mankind*, 1952) cannot find a place for such Jerusalem Judaists in his conception (according to him the Judaists are Gentile converts in the Pauline communities who constructed, on the basis of Paul's presentation, a false picture of Jewish Christianity): Luke probably 'transferred these itinerant Judaists from the Pauline mission-field to Jerusalem, since he concentrates everything, so far as possible, around the Christian centres'. This is highly improbable.

[3] As with the speeches, so in this letter Luke is constrained to the utmost brevity. Here this gives rise to a stylistic deficiency: according to the wording the community of Jerusalem could have commissioned people to subvert the souls of the Christians at Antioch. Naturally what is meant is just that the persons in question had no mandate and could not appeal to the Apostles.—The verse is linked with Luke **1**.1 by the fact that both have the construction ἐπειδή (περ) . . . ἔδοξε, but this does not justify Preuschen's conclusion that both derive from the same editor (96f.).

[4] γενομένοις ὁμοθυμαδόν; Bauernfeind translated this as 'after we had reached agreement' (192f.) and takes it as an indication that 'even in Jerusalem unity had to be struggled for'. But if the formula is anything more than a formal statement that a general assembly took place, it is certainly meant to convey not a disunity overcome but the unanimity of the decision—'nous étant mis d'accord unanimement', as Loisy translates (599).

[5] ἐκλεξαμένους πέμψαι is an acc. + infin. dependent on ἔδοξε ἡμῖν. Better (though probably already outmoded) Greek, and at the same time more intelligible, would have been (here and in verse 22) the ἐκλεξαμένοις offered by 𝔓⁴⁵ B A 81, which according to *Beg.* IV 180 is here (but not in verse 22) the original reading.

[6] ἀγαπητός is a technical term occurring in the Pauline and post-Pauline writings, an expression of respect and acknowledgement; in Luke only here.

[7] Probably a customary expression—cf. Rom. **16**.4. The Western text—for after all Paul and Barnabas are still alive—adds εἰς πάντα πειρασμόν (*Beg.* III, 147). Reminded by this verse of **14**.19, Loisy attributes it to the redactor (600). The parallels adduced by Billerbeck (II, 740) touch only the expression, not the matter.

VERSE 27: The praise of the delegates from Antioch has caused a diversion from the theme, but now the thought is carried to its conclusion. The tense of ἀπεστάλκαμεν is chosen from the recipients' viewpoint, and perhaps this is also true of ἀπαγγέλλοντας.[1] These men will confirm the contents of the letter by word of mouth. τὰ αὐτά: the reader already knows what the decree will contain, the recipients as yet do not. It is thus evident that the composition of the letter goes back to Luke.

VERSE 28: γάρ is here a mere conjunctive, and not genuinely causal (Jacquier, 464). To the mention of the oral communication of τὰ αὐτά the second resolution is now appended in written form. It is clearly fitting that the letter should conclude with this, the all-important message. 'It has pleased the Holy Spirit and ourselves'—the highest supernatural authority and the legal earthly authority derived from it stand side by side; cf. official decisions, e.g. of the Roman emperors, Josephus, *Ant.* XVI, 163; ἔδοξέ μοι καὶ τῷ ἐμῷ συμβουλίῳ (Bauer, *Wb* 366). Jacquier (464) cites from Dalman, *Aramäische Dialektproben* 3, an epistle of Rabban Gamaliel to his colleagues in the diaspora: 'It has pleased us and our colleagues . . .' In the light of this the expression 'Apostolic Decree' seems reasonable so far as its second term is concerned; but the 'Apostolic' is misleading since it attributes to the Apostles an autonomy which for Luke they did not possess. 'To lay upon you no greater burden than these necessary things'[2]: the adverb ἐπάναγκες with an article is quite abnormal.[3]

VERSE 29 repeats the four prohibitions in a slightly different order and formulation.[4] ἐξ ὧν κτλ.: 'in keeping from these you will do right.' εὖ πράξετε could admittedly also mean 'it will go well with you', which would

---

[1] Contrast Bl.-Debr. § 339, 2c: 'The present participle may also denote a relatively future action.' The corresponding Lucan relative clause would run οἳ καὶ αὐτοὶ διὰ λόγου ἀναγγελοῦσιν τὰ αὐτά.

[2] Once again compression makes for misunderstanding. As is evident from verse 19, Luke means to convey not that some burden (though none so great as circumcision) is to be laid on the Gentiles, but that *no* burden is to be imposed—only the few necessary things. Since he did not recognize this, Zahn (539f.) hit upon the singular expedient of construing πλέον . . . βάρος as 'overburdening' above and beyond the irreducible onus of exposure to temptations from the godless and unbelieving.

[3] Various attempts have been made to eliminate the abnormality. G. J. Moore suggested deleting τῶν as a dittography of τούτων. We could then put a colon after τούτων and translate 'it is necessary to abstain', etc.; but such a use of ἐπάναγκες would itself be abnormal. Or the colon could be put after βάρος and the continuation rendered: 'only from these things is it necessary to abstain'. Klostermann (*Probleme im Aposteltext*, 1883, 132ff.) offers another suggestion, making use of Irenaeus and Tertullian: τούτων τῶν are replaced by 'apart from the things from which it is necessary to abstain'. If ἀπέχεσθαι is taken as a mistranscription of the imperative ἀπέχεσθε (though on occasion the infinitive can do duty for the imperative), we obtain: 'apart from what is necessary; abstain . . .' (*Beg.* IV 180f.).

[4] The Western text omits καὶ πνικτῶν. ℵ in conformity with verse 20, alters it to πνικτοῦ (cf. *Beg.* III 148).

promise a blessing in return for obedience.[1] D understood it in the sense of 'do right', as is clear from its addition φερόμενοι ἐν τῷ ἁγίῳ πνεύματι. This sense is also attested by Ignatius, *Eph.* **4**.2, *Smyrn.* **11**.3, and Justin, *Apol.* **28**.3. The actual conclusion consists of the familiar ancient formula ἔρρωσθε, while elsewhere the conclusions of NT letters (apart from James) bear a specifically Christian character.

VERSE 30: μὲν οὖν again opens a new scene. ἀπολυθέντες:[2] the delegates, Antiochian and Jerusalemite, are sent off with official ceremony. Luke leaves it an open question which of the two groups called the Antiochian congregation together; nor does he say to whom the letter was presented; ἐπιδιδόναι is a late Greek technical term for handing over a letter (*Beg.* IV 182).

VERSE 31: The congregation rejoices at the παράκλησις: gig renders this word as *exhortationem*, d as *orationem*, whereas Jerome more fittingly puts *consolatione*. What is meant, at all events, is the comforting decision that one may remain uncircumcised and yet be accepted as a full Christian.

VERSE 32: The καί of καὶ αὐτοί should be taken as in verse 27.[3] The fact that Judas and Silas are prophets explains their capacity for παράκλησις: see I Cor. **14**.3. As in verse 41, ἐπιστηρίζειν denotes the spiritual reinforcement of the congregation.

VERSE 33: ποιήσαντες χρόνον: in late Greek χρόνος can also mean 'year', but here it implies no more than 'lapse of time'; χρόνον τινά would be the normal expression. On the other hand ποιεῖν, in the sense of 'spend', 'stay', is normal usage. ἀπελύθησαν μετ᾽ εἰρήνης (with the kiss of peace = fraternal blessing) indicates a farewell not merely peaceful but also ceremonious.[4] This brings the whole episode to a harmonious end.[5]

VERSE 34 is an interpolation of the Western text, obviously intended to mend the inconsistency with verse 40, where it is implied that Silas remained

---

[1] Zahn's exegesis is determined by the desire to avoid a conflict with Galatians. Hence he wants to see the 'decree' as only a 'recommendation'. With this εὖ πράττειν fits better in the sense of 'prosperity and success in all the affairs of your calling', as Zahn with unrivalled prosiness puts it (541). Classically, it can in fact do duty for ὑγιαίνω or χαίρω (Zahn, 536 n. 13; *Beg.* IV 181; Bauer, *Wb* 1386). But as there was also an ancient formula for ending letters which ran roughly 'If you do this, you will do right', we may suppose it here. This is, however, one of the rare occasions when Loisy (602) agrees with Zahn.

[2] Despite *Beg.* IV 181f., the word here naturally does not mean the release of the accused as in 3.13, 4.21, 4.23 and 5.40.

[3] Loisy renders as 'Judas and Silas, who were also prophets' (605). He and Bauernfeind (201) are prepared to see it as a counterpart of **13**.1, but what reader would hit upon the allusion (already suggested by earlier expositors)?

[4] '... avec toutes les salutations et voeux de bon voyage usités en pareille circonstance' (Loisy 605).

[5] Later MSS substitute ἀποστόλους for ἀποστείλαντας αὐτούς (*Beg.* III 148). Zahn refuses to understand the ἀπό in the sense of ὑπό (which was however supplanted by ἀπό in later Greek: Bl.-Debr. § 232, 2) and finds that 'the move for the envoys' return came from the men of Antioch; μετ᾽ εἰρήνης is an assurance that this took place in the friendliest spirit' (553 n. 46); one can but shake one's head over such incomprehension.

in Antioch; but instead the inconsistency with verse 33 now becomes serious.[1]

VERSE 35 is a typically Lucan concluding verse. Barnabas and Paul are shown once more bending their common efforts to the task in Antioch before their final separation. διδάσκοντες corresponds to the διδάσκαλοι of **13**.1 and denotes their teaching work in the congregation at Antioch.[2] 'With many others also'[3]—so they are not alone in this work: this makes it possible for both to leave the city and undertake a mission at a distance (Wendt, 239, following B. Weiss) without the risk of harm to the Antiochian congregation.[4]

1. *Analysis of the Text*

This chapter has been the subject of passionate debate among scholars. Nearly every one of them has hacked his own way through the jungle of problems, and often it was done in a thoroughly violent fashion. Space forbids the retracing of all these paths, and it would only be confusing. We therefore content ourselves with a few characteristic examples from just before and after the turn of the century, and from the present time. They enable us to recognize what methods—or lack of method—have been applied to the evaluation of this central chapter of Acts. We begin with the late nineteenth-century critics.

First, B. WEISS (*Einl.*[2], 1889; ET), who considered that (a) **15**.1 showed strife arising out of a dispute in Antioch whereas (b) **15**.5 showed the same process taking place in Jerusalem; further that in several verses the matter is

---

[1] Zahn fails to see this and surrenders only 'Judas departed alone' as a superfluous addition (553). Neither Zahn nor the Western reviser recognized that Luke's only concern is to make Silas and Paul acquainted, not to bring Silas to Antioch with a view to his subsequent departure with Paul. John Mark is in Jerusalem, yet suddenly sets out for Cyprus from Antioch, without Luke's feeling obliged to tell us how he came there.

[2] The same is said of the Apostles in **5**.42.

[3] μετὰ καί: cf. W. Schmid, *Der Attizismus*, Vol. 3, 1893, 337—καί between prep. and noun is a usage found in Herodotus after μετά and σύν. Schmid refers to K. Buresch, *Philologus* 51, 449 n. 2: the placing of καί after the prep. (esp. μέχρι, ἄχρι and σύν) remained common in Koine. Further NT instance: Phil. **4**.3; cf. also I Clem. **65**.1 (Bl.-Debr. § 442 speaks of a 'pleonastic use of καί').

[4] O. Cullmann, in his *Peter*[2], (1962), puts forward the view that Peter was at the head of the Jewish Christian mission, based on Jerusalem (44), and appeared at the conference of Acts 15 as 'a missionary, no longer as the leader of the congregation' (51), while it was James who stood at the head of the mother-congregation in Jerusalem. But once one has recognized Luke's method of composition in Chapter 15, it is evident that Cullmann has not caught the meaning of the Lucan presentation. Cf. Haenchen, 'Petrus-Probleme' (*Gott u. Mensch* 1965, 55–67). The same is true of H. J. Schoeps' contention that, in contrast to Peter, James 'assented only with reluctance to the formula of agreement—even though he proposed it himself' (*Theol. und Gesch. des Judenchr.*, 1949, 67 n. 3; ET *Jewish Christianity*, 1969).

thrashed out before (a) the Apostles and elders, but in others before (b) the assembled congregation. The explanation of this apparent conflict is that in each case (b) derives from 'the source' (i.e. the source Weiss sees feeding the whole first half of Acts) and (a) from the reviser, Luke. To Luke he ascribed also the differences in the formulation of the decree in verses 23–29 and in James's proposals, and finally he conjectured that Luke misunderstood the mission of Judas and Silas. As escorts of a letter, with nothing to say beyond its contents, they were superfluous. Here we may have—this was his bold hypothesis—a false reminiscence of the sending of the τινὲς ἀπὸ ᾿Ιακώβου, which came only later. Paul, in token of his agreement, must have accompanied the two across Syria and Cilicia, 'where it was their duty and desire to arrange matters in accordance with the Apostolic decree' (op. cit., 143 n. 3). B. Weiss held that the speeches of Peter and James were authentic: 'The words of Peter and James, so characteristically different, could not possibly have been conceived by the author' (575f.). This is not the only occasion on which B. Weiss allots an important role in his source-criticism to this alleged psychological impossibility, which he here imports as a third factor alongside the internal contradictions of Acts and its divergences from Galatians.

SPITTA (179ff.) proceeds from the assumption that **15**.1–33 was abruptly inserted into the account of a missionary journey, so that **15**.36 is a direct resumption of **14**.28. There is also this inconsistency, that Judas and Silas in **15**.33 return to Jerusalem and yet Silas a few days later leaves Antioch in the company of Paul. Finally Spitta makes the point that the whole section belongs not after the first journey but before it, since **15**.23 presupposes only a mission to Syria and Cilicia. In short, the story is a parallel to **11**.29f. deriving from the 'bad source' B. This implies, however, that within that source it came directly after **12**.24, and was only brought to its present position by the redactor. In the process he inserted Peter's speech (more exactly verses 5–12), prompted by the two meetings of which Gal. **2**.2 speaks and by Gal. **2**.4. And so Spitta too—though with very different results— starts out from alleged contradictions in the text of Acts itself, and regards as original the report which agrees with Galatians.

Twenty years later WENDT sensed the stylistic difference between the present section and the mission-report on either side. Thus **15**.1–33 was an 'episodic addition' to that source report, though itself based on a tradition rather than freely imagined. It was not possible to assert exactly which details Luke had changed, but 'the speeches of Peter and James must be essentially of his composing' (225 n. 2). So here we find a note of greater caution. The critic no longer offers to define the exact source of every word. But also confidence in the speeches of Acts declines; one begins to have an ear for the voice of Luke. And finally the 'psychological impossibility' with which B. Weiss made such play ceases to be a favourite argument: only too often it was the exegete's psychological inability to see anything.

Another quarter of a century and we come to BAUERNFEIND. He still indeed assumes that Luke probably had reason to complain of too much rather than too little in the way of oral or written sources, but he does not attempt to reconstruct these sources from the discrepancies—which struck him also—within the text or between it and Galatians. For he recognizes that Luke did not consider it his task 'to produce a kind of synoptic mosaic of the separate accounts: the Christians for whom his book was intended required just *one* lucid picture which portrayed the truth of the agreement in a form they could grasp' (187). 'In the mind's eye of Luke there is *one* great scene, where the leaders act in the presence of the assembled congregation; only this decisive act is important for his readers . . .' (191). It is true that Bauernfeind did not pursue this cardinal insight to its utmost conclusion. Here and there a word or turn of phrase (verse 12!) tempted him into seeing still some historical reminiscence in Luke's composition.

In 1947 MARTIN DIBELIUS tackled the problem of the Apostolic Council, sensing more strongly than all his predecessors the methodological necessity of appreciating the real character of Luke's account (*Studies*, 93ff.). Hence he gives an analysis of the chapter which surpasses all previous attempts in its precision. From it he extracts two conclusions—(a) literary: the text is comprehensible without discrimination of sources. Luke shows that in the conversion of Cornelius God has authorized the Gentile mission, then adds the decree which he had come across somewhere. (b) historical: there is only *one* record of the proceedings in Jerusalem, that of Paul in Galatians. It should not be corrected on the basis of Acts; the decree 'does not derive from this meeting' (100).

The foregoing should suffice to show how the exploration of this chapter has evolved. Criticism first regarded it as a conglomerate of sources. It was a question of sorting out the mixture and discovering from the most reliable source what actually happened. The author came into the picture only as a purveyor of more or less reliable reports. The further research advanced, the more the source-question receded. The author comes again into view, and not merely as a transmitter of sources. It becomes clear that he did not write for a history-obsessed twentieth-century generation, but meant his narrative to implant in his own generation the certainty that its Gentile Christianity was in order, authorized by God and by responsible men.

Dibelius took the analysis of the chapter a long way in this direction. But his real interest was in the speeches. Hence much remains to be said regarding the introduction to the story. Luke's narrative opens with a prelude showing how the conference in Jerusalem came to take place. The congregation of Antioch, unsettled by its Judaist visitors, sends Paul and Barnabas to the Apostles and elders for a ruling on circumcision (vv. 1f). It seems superfluous that Luke should describe the delegation's journey through Phoenicia and Samaria. But the rejoicing of the Jewish Christians there over the Gentile

Q

mission immediately shows that not the whole of Jewish Christendom insists on circumcision, but only a small minority.

Verse 4 is at first surprising. Instead of asking the Apostles and elders for their decision, Paul and Barnabas relate their missionary activities. But Luke has an important reason for not having them straightway perform the commission with which they are charged. Suppose they had immediately asked, 'Must Gentiles be circumcised to become Christians?', the Apostles —at least, as Luke depicts them—would no less promptly have replied: 'No. Circumcision is not needful for salvation!' And there would have been an end of the matter. But that is not Luke's way of telling a story. For he knows that his readers will retain only what he puts before them in grand, impressive, animated scenes. It is therefore vital for him to imprint on their minds, with an unforgettable scene, this crucial event: the final authorization of the Gentile mission free from the law. In this he has succeeded, and the very device of letting Paul and Barnabas open the debate by relating their adventures enables him to create tension and build his climax. For now the Apostles and elders have not yet expressed their decision, which means that the Judaistic protest from the floor of the assembly can be made with a dramatic forcefulness that would not have been possible had they already spoken. In the process Luke accepts without hesitation the minor difficulties, that the Judaistic demand is now put forward twice by different groups: the vague τινές in Antioch, and here the Pharisee converts whose rigour is understandable though misconceived.

Thus we see that the introduction, so taken to task by critical expositors, is no mere patchwork of source-remnants. It leads with conscious aim to the great conflict, men of Antioch *versus* Pharisees. What will happen now that they stand confronted? It is time for the Apostles and elders to move into action. For although Luke will only report the intervention of the two decisive figures, Peter and James, he does not want them misunderstood as isolated leaders. So, in a single sentence, he indicates that they belong to a wider circle and speak in its name: 'And the Apostles and elders gathered together to see what should be done.' The reader needs no more than this one allusion to the body of the Apostles and presbyters: he must not be distracted from the main scene. Meanwhile the disputation within the πλῆθος has boiled up to a passionate conflict: πολλῆς δὲ ζητήσεως γενομένης. The moment has come for Peter to take the floor. He is the qualified speaker, not only because he was the first whom the Lord called to discipleship, but also and above all because it was through him that God long ago inaugurated the Gentile mission in the conversion of Cornelius. As in Chapters 10 and 11, this story here also is raised to the level of a fundamental principle: through Peter 'the Gentiles' have come to the faith. God acknowledged them by giving them the Spirit, as he did the disciples in Jerusalem at Pentecost. It would be defying God, like faithless Israel in the wilderness, to disregard his decision.

These appeals to Chapters 10 and 11 are not all. Peter throws a new argument into the debate: neither the Jews of old nor the Jewish Christians themselves have been able to keep the law with which they would now burden the Gentiles! This clearly does not represent the historical Peter's way of thinking, for the strict Jew by no means regarded the law as an intolerable burden. Luke is rather portraying the image which Hellenistic Gentile Christians had of the law: a mass of commandments and prohibitions which no man can satisfy. It is also evident that Peter's next and final sentence likewise, with its Pauline ring, is not a historical report of Peter's attitude but in the first instance the creed of Luke and his community: belief in Jesus is the only thing which saves—Jew and Gentile alike.

The speech has imposed silence on the violent disputation within the assembly. Now the congregation listens as Paul and Barnabas tell of the miracles which God caused them to perform on their mission. Allusion is now enough: for the reader still has the story of the cripple in the previous chapter fresh in his mind—not for nothing did Luke recount the healing with such elaboration. The testimony of the two missionaries vindicates the doctrine which Peter has just proclaimed through the experience which it relates. Verse 12, which many critics would excise, thus has an important function in the framework of Luke's design; it also serves as a transition to the second great speech, that of James (verses 13–21).

James first refers approvingly to Peter's words concerning the story of Cornelius (verse 14), then produces scriptural proof (verses 16–18). The citation of LXX at a point where it fundamentally departs from the Hebrew makes it incontrovertibly clear that the James speech too is not a historical report but a composition of the Hellenistic Gentile Christian Luke.

Having thus consolidated the position, James moves that the Gentile converts be not overburdened (*scil.* by circumcision) *but* advised by official letter that they must abstain from the flesh of pagan offerings, forbidden marriages, strangled flesh and partaking of blood.

This '*but*' is no doubt for us surprising. We only understand the coherence of the narrative if we grasp the fact that the burdensome nature of the law lay in circumcision, and beyond that only in the sheer multiplicity of the legal prescriptions. From Luke's point of view these four requirements were thus not a burden: the Apostolic Council's edict is rather the final recognition of the mission free from the law, hence of Gentile Christianity free from the law.

Approving this motion, the governing body and assembly of the congregation decide that Judas Barsabbas and Silas shall carry to Antioch a letter to that effect. B. Weiss felt the sending of the two superfluous: the letter could have been entrusted to Paul and Barnabas. This is a typical example of modern misunderstanding, and overlooks both the honour shown the congregation of Antioch by the delegation of such highly-respected men and also the authority of Jerusalem which therein finds expression.

We may well wonder, however, at the text of the letter, which indeed runs quite differently from what we might suppose. The answer to the Antiochian question about the necessity of circumcision ought (after the usual greetings, which we should expect to find couched in Christian terms) to run somewhat as follows: 'In answer to your question we decide that circumcision is not essential for salvation. Those who teach otherwise act without our authority. We are charging Judas and Silas, who will accompany your most excellent delegates on their return, with the transmission of this answer.'

The letter does not contain this sequence. It first mentions the appearance of Judaists in Antioch and its effects, thus harking back to what was reported in **15.1**. Consequently it has been decided to send 'men' to Antioch with Paul and Barnabas, a eulogy of whom now interrupts the message. This is resumed in verse 27: 'we have sent Judas and Silas, who will tell you the same by word of mouth.' But what 'same'? Naturally, the same as is known to the reader from verse 19f.—but of which the letter has so far said not a word. Only now are its recipients informed that 'the Holy Spirit and we have decided', etc. The letter closes with the customary salutation of antiquity, without any Christian modification.

Why this peculiar arrangement of the sentences, which prompted Loisy again to speculation as to the use of sources? The answer is simple: the author wanted the most important statement, the 'decree', to come at the end. Then, after a statement of the occasion, the sending of the Jerusalem delegation had to be mentioned first. Room had also to be found somewhere for the official recognition of Paul and Barnabas—which was not by any means an empty form. The consequences of this transposition are most clearly evident in the words τὰ αὐτά of verse 27. It is to them that the γάρ of verse 28, at first sight so hard to understand, refers: 'They shall tell you the same' (as the decree which they bring), 'namely: the Holy Spirit and we have decided . . .'.

The structure of the letter has thus become transparent. The tampering of source-criticism can only do harm. Despite the difficulty mentioned, the letter is a uniform composition, of which—need we say?—Luke must be regarded as the author. On the question of the 'decree' we shall have more to say later.

The two delegations travel to Antioch, hand over the letter before the assembled congregation and—through the waiving of circumcision—evoke an outburst of joy. Judas and Silas, now characterized as prophets, make their oral contribution to the reassurance and comforting of the brethren, and then, after formal leave-taking, begin their journey home. A summary note about Paul and Barnabas creates an interval between the Apostolic Council and the second missionary journey. The two men have not yet come to the parting of the ways, and are still working together, with help of many others, as teachers and missionaries in Antioch.

2. *Role of this Episode in the Scheme of Acts*

The above analysis has revealed the structure and cohesion of the Lucan composition. But what *function within the grand design* is this composition meant to serve?

Its closest affinities are evidently with the story of Cornelius (**10**.1–**11**.18), the recollection of which suffices to silence opposition to the Gentile mission without the law, for was it not God himself who instigated this mission? Such missions, though not announced as a programme until **13**.46ff., are immediately presupposed in **11**.19ff. Chapter 16 begins the description of the Gentile mission proper, whose goal of course is Europe—not without reason is Asia Minor despatched in three verses (**16**.6–8) and the crossing from Troas to Macedonia so heavily underscored. Chapter 15 is the turning-point, 'centrepiece'[1] and 'watershed'[2] of the book, the episode which rounds off and justifies the past developments, and makes those to come intrinsically possible.

Up to Chapter 15 all roads lead to Jerusalem. Wherever Christianity is implanted, the town or region concerned is in one way or another subordinated to the capital of Judaea. Philip's mission-field, Samaria, is annexed for Jerusalem by Peter and John (**8**.14–25); Galilee is added (**9**.31). Peter's miracle in Lydda wins over the whole plain of Sharon (**9**.32–5); from Joppa he moves on to Caesarea, where he to all intents and purposes founds the first Gentile Christian community (**10**.1–**11**.18). The congregation at Antioch, founded by fugitive Hellenists, is recognized and cared for by the sending of the Jerusalemite Barnabas (**11**.22ff.), and immediately demonstrates the closeness of its ties with the parent congregation by its collection of relief-money (**11**.27–30). Even the Lycaonian congregations of the first missionary journey come under the authority of the Apostolic Decree (**16**.4). The Christendom whose evolution is portrayed in these chapters does not indeed form a tightly-organized Church in which everything happens at the behest of Jerusalem. The congregations are but loosely linked, and refer to Jerusalem only for special rulings. Jerusalem, nevertheless, is the spiritual head of this *corpus Christianum*, and that as the *sedes Apostolica* where the eyewitnesses of the Lord's earthly life and resurrection reside.

Now in this connection Chapter 15 marks the turning-point. Not only does Peter make his last appearance here, the Apostles also are mentioned for the last time in the reference to the decree at **16**.4. Both are henceforth replaced by James and the elders. This shows that Luke's design is much more comprehensive. He has already for a long time been preparing this changing of the guard. At **12**.17 the name of James was expressly stressed at the very

---

[1] Even literally: it is preceded by 47 of the 94 pages in Nestle.
[2] As was already seen in 1897 by J. Weiss ('Absicht und literarischer Charakter der Apg.'. 25).

moment when Peter had to leave Jerusalem, and now he stands beside Peter
as the second main speaker: the departing leader of the Jerusalem congregation and his successor stand forward one after the other in unanimity. The
elders too had already been introduced (**11**.30). In Chapter 15 they are always
named beside the Apostles. By **21**.18 the Apostles have disappeared and the
elders alone remain, with James the brother of the Lord at their head. The
new government of the Church at first functions under and alongside the old
(this is the impression the reader must get) until it steps into its place. The
installation of elders by Paul and Barnabas (**14**.23) and the existence of a
similar college ruling at Ephesus (**20**.17) show that Luke presupposes the
presbyterial constitution to have been set up everywhere. In this respect, too,
Chapter 15 marks the turning-point: before it lies the period of apostolic
rule; the later Church stands under the sign of the elders. That an exodus of
the Apostles for the world mission brought about this change is the fantasy
of a later age, and is nowhere hinted at by Luke. It is not the ageing Apostles
who will bear the weight of the world mission, but Paul.

So far Paul has been only one among many secondary figures in the
history of the primitive mission. From Chapter 15 onward he becomes the
dominant figure. This does not mean for Luke that he ranked as equal with
the holy circle of the Twelve—Chapter 15 makes that very clear. The Apostles
and elders are the supreme court of authority to which Antioch sends Paul
and Barnabas. They do not deal with the Apostles on an equal footing but
receive their commands. Luke did not intend this as a point against Paul.
Paul is for him a chosen instrument of Christ (**9**.15), at the Apostolic Council
he wins the verdict against his Judaist opponents, in the Apostolic Decree
—again in company with Barnabas—he is named with high praise. This
recognition legitimates the great work to which Paul now sets his hand: the
founding of the European Gentile Church.

Hence Chapter 15 is in yet another sense a turning-point. Not only has
the focus shifted from Jerusalem. Not even her daughter congregation in
Antioch will now be the stage or protagonist of the action. Macedonia,
Athens, Corinth, Ephesus: these will be the new landmarks in the history of
the mission. Admittedly, Jerusalem is once more the stage in Chapter 21, but
strictly within the context of the Pauline story: no sooner is Paul arrested
than the congregation of Jerusalem vanishes without trace. The only significance of Jerusalem for the further destiny of the Church is as a place
of sacred memories.

3. *Luke's Version of the Apostolic Council*

Now that we have a clear picture of Luke's presentation of the Apostolic
Council in Chapter 15, in both its narrower and its wider context, we must
ask ourselves if this account is *intrinsically* plausible or tenable. As Dibelius
rightly stresses, 'Peter's speech rests . . . on the literary work of the author

and is intelligible solely in that connection' (*Studies* 95). The form of presentation betrays the hand of Luke. But does the combination of the facts
itself derive from Luke? As he presents the situation, Peter had already in
Caesarea admitted a Gentile, his household and his friends into the Church
without circumcision. That this was an unheard-of action Luke repeatedly
emphasizes: only with reluctance, and constrained by divine miracles,
visions, directives, did Peter take the step. The Jewish Christians from Joppa
stood aghast, and the congregation at Jerusalem called Peter to account.
According to Luke this event thus did not take place, as it were, secretly and
in private. On the contrary, it created the greatest stir and was openly discussed. The result was the public acknowledgement that Gentiles could be
admitted uncircumcised into the Christian community—**10**.45 and **11**.18
can have no other meaning.

On the other hand, this incident is supposed to have remained without
sequel, so that it vanished completely from human ken. The men who come
preaching circumcision from Jerusalem to Antioch know nothing of it. The
Pharisees turned Christian, who—as we shall assume for the moment—only
entered the Church after the Cornelius episode, have never heard of it. The
congregation itself has completely forgotten it—otherwise it would never
have come to the πολλὴ ζήτησις of **15**.7.

That so fundamental a decision of God, so stirring and surprising,
should in so short a time have been entirely forgotten, is so contradictory
that one must bluntly insist: it is intrinsically impossible. The whole theory
with which Luke reconciles the legitimacy of the Gentile mission without the
law (i.e. its recognition by Jerusalem!) with Antioch's struggle for the recognition of its mission to the Gentiles is an imaginary construction answering
to no historical reality.

Many exegetes maintain that the Jerusalem congregation did indeed
regard the conversion of Cornelius and his house as a divine decision, but
saw in it no mandate for itself (cf. J. Munck, *Paulus und die Heilsgeschichte*,
1954, 224; ET *Paul and the Salvation of Mankind*, 1959). But even if it had
not seen the incident as a divine summons to begin the mission without the
law there and then, there could no longer have been any question of opposition to such a mission within this congregation when another—that of Antioch
—recognized this charge as its own and complied with it.

But for Luke there was no other choice. He was for one thing convinced
that God willed the Gentile mission without the law. And he was equally
convinced that this mission was only legitimate if set in motion by the representative of the Jerusalem community. This meant that the only explanation
he could give of the opposition aroused in Jerusalem was that incredible
forgetfulness—which he naturally takes care not to describe as such. That he
now drafted speeches on these lines for Peter and James was nothing that need
occasion surprise. He was only expressing the connection as he saw it. But

Luke's version of the Apostolic Council—in this Dibelius is correct—does not possess historical value.

4. *Paul's Version*

This does not of course relieve us from the duty of subjecting to exacting scrutiny the only real *record* we possess, that of Paul in Galatians. It forms part of Paul's demonstration that he was independent of the community at Jerusalem, and in particular of 'those who were Apostles before' him (Gal. **1**.17). This circumstance determines Paul's choice of material, in that he had in mind only what served his proof (cf. H. Schlier, *Der Galaterbrief*, 1939, 52 n. 1). He had no intention of setting down an exhaustive account of his visit to Jerusalem.

The way in which Paul presents this journey as his second to Jerusalem after his conversion (which it undoubtedly was) obscures an important difference between it and its predecessor. On the first occasion, so far as we know, he was free from connection with any congregation and visited— incognito, it would seem—only Peter. He did not make the acquaintance of the other Apostles (James apart), still less the Christian community of Jerusalem. Nor did he then expound 'his gospel' to Peter and James, securing their approval of it (*pace* Ramsay). Otherwise there would have been no need for him, on the second visit, to apprise 'those of repute' of 'the gospel' he 'preached among the Gentiles, so as not to run or have run in vain' (Gal. **2**.2). But now, on this second visit, the situation was entirely different— even if the reader cannot at first deduce it from Paul's words. Paul does not say in Gal. **2**.1ff. where he had actually come from on this visit. The name of Antioch does not occur throughout the account of **2**.1–10, but appears first in **2**.11 in another connection. Yet there can be no doubt that Paul really did 'go up' from Antioch to Jerusalem. This is indirectly shown by the fact that he was accompanied by Barnabas, with whom according to **2**.13 he worked in Antioch. The question here is one not merely of topology, but of knowing in what capacity Paul then visited Jerusalem. Some indication is given by his sparse allusions to his companions. Only of Titus, not of Barnabas, is it said (**2**.1) that Paul 'took him with him'—Barnabas did not, like Titus, stand lower than Paul but on a level with him (**2**.9!).

Probably Paul is already reckoning with the objection that he did not go to Jerusalem of his own free will, but was summoned by Jerusalem. Against this insinuation he defends himself by the statement 'I went up by reason of a revelation' (**2**.2). This gives the assurance that his journey was undertaken on divine instructions. But it does not preclude a human side to the business. It may well have been that this prophetic admonition coincided with the wishes of the Antiochian congregation. That—from the human aspect— there was some element of constraint is undeniable. Paul himself suggests as much with the words 'that I might not run, or have run, in vain' (**2**.2).

The Gentile mission which renounced circumcision ('the gospel I preach among the Gentiles') was in danger, and this danger lay in the possibility that Jerusalem might reject this gospel. Now Paul admittedly did not acknowledge the Apostles at Jerusalem as a final court of appeal. But on their decision in fact depended the fate of the mission without the law and its Gentile Church. Hence Paul laid before them the proclamation by which his mission and his Church were living. It was not however only a question of the Apostles (Peter and John alone are mentioned) and James, but also of the assent of the Jerusalem congregation itself, as we must probably conclude from the κατ' ἰδίαν (2.2). For Paul at any rate, his discussions with the leaders in this connection were particularly important. For when he reports them to the Galatians he appears the equal of the 'authorities' in Jerusalem. We shall see, though, that the congregation of Antioch was no stranger to the proceedings.

Where the 'might'—and, in a sense, probably also the 'right'—lay is at once evident from the fact that Paul and Barnabas went to Jerusalem, not the 'pillars' to Antioch.

At this point there is an important adjustment to be made. The words 'I went up', 'I laid before them', 'which I preach', 'that I might not run' all sound as if they refer to a mission which Paul was at least leading, if not running singlehanded. When he dictated them Paul naturally was preoccupied with his own work, his own preaching. However, it was not merely his own activity that was threatened on the occasion of his second visit to Jerusalem. This is shown at the moment when we come to the decisive agreement among the leaders: it is not merely with Paul that the 'pillars' conclude an agreement, but with Paul and Barnabas. It thus becomes obvious that here it was not a question of missionary work undertaken solely by Paul. Nor was it any 'private action' by the two men, however easy Paul's words would make this interpretation. The two travelled to Jerusalem as representatives of the community of Antioch.

This point is so willingly conceded by the majority of scholars that one must fear they have not clearly seen the consequences. For it means that Paul then occupied a very different position than might be expected from his words. Even if he had not been sent to Jerusalem as an agent, but (like Barnabas) as a trusted and fully accredited representative, the community of Antioch was also on the stage—even if for the moment, so to speak, in the background. Paul's words give the impression that he stood quite alone before the 'pillars', their equal and a match for them. This impression is deceptive. Paul indeed feels himself *the* representative of the Gentile mission, and from the beginning of the section there stands before his eyes that confrontation with which he illustrates the equal justification of the Jewish and Gentile missions and their representatives, the confrontation of Peter and Paul. It is from this standpoint that he says earlier, 'They imposed nothing on me.'

Interpreted in terms of fact, this means 'on *us*', the Gentile Christians for whom Paul—with Barnabas—is acting. No legal burden was imposed upon them. On the contrary, the Jerusalemites saw that 'Paul' was 'entrusted' with the gospel to the Gentiles (that is, with missionary preaching apart from the law and with the conversion of the Gentiles) just as much as 'Peter' with that to the Jews, 'for *he* who worked in Peter for the apostolate of the Jews was also working in me toward the Gentiles'. The contrast of Peter and Paul, Jews and Gentiles, is simple and vivid. But if it is not to be misunderstood we must clearly realize that it is a simplification. In reality Peter does not stand alone on one side as *the* missionary of the Jews, Paul on the other as *the* missionary of the Gentiles. In reality John and James stand beside Peter (in verse 9 James is even named first!), and at the side of Paul stands Barnabas. This already makes it clear that the confrontation was a simplification. But the simplification goes further. James, John and Cephas are the 'pillars'— those pillars on which the structure of the Jerusalem mother-congregation rests. Their role of pillars has meaning only in their association with the congregation. Even if they determine the course of action, they may not take arbitrary decisions: each decision must subserve the οἰκοδομή of the congregation. But just as these men and the Jerusalem congregation belong together, Barnabas and Paul were linked with the congregation of Antioch, whether they were there called 'pillars', 'Apostles' and the like or not.

If this is not clear in Paul's account, this is thoroughly understandable. When he writes Galatians, he is fighting for that missionary work which he began alone after his separation from Antioch: he is no longer answerable to or supported by any congregation, unless those of his own founding. From this situation and point of view he does not emerge even when he is speaking of the past, of that bygone period when he was not yet the great solitary bearing virtually unaided the whole burden of his mission,–yet nevertheless already felt himself to be *the* Apostle whom the Lord had charged with the winning of the pagan world. Hence the 'I' and the 'me'—which Paul however, out of respect for the truth, drops at the critical moment. For when we read the words 'recognizing the grace accorded me' we expect the continuation: 'they gave me their acknowledgement'. Paul must have been uncommonly tempted to continue thus. But he writes: 'they offered me and Barnabas the right hand of fellowship'. He writes thus at a time when he had already separated from Barnabas, yet reports faithfully about the agreement that it was concluded not between Paul and Jerusalem, but between Jerusalem and the two representatives of Antioch.

Paul thus summarizes the outcome of the negotiations in Jerusalem 'we to the Gentiles, they to the circumcision'. The exegetes have mostly seen in this formula the, so to speak, official text of the protocol, and have only quarrelled as to how it should be understood. For, oddly enough, neither of the two interpretations proposed gives a satisfying sense. The formula could be taken geographically. In this case Jerusalem would have claimed Palestine for itself. If we drew upon I Peter 5.13, we might add Babylonia with its large Jewish colony, while the address of I Peter would further add Pontus, Galatia, Cappadocia, Asia and Bithynia. But then one could scarcely avoid seeing the whole of Syria also—including Antioch!—as a Jewish Christian mission-field! And that would at the same time make plain the absurdity of such a geographical interpretation, which would close to Paul and Barnabas the Gentile Church of Antioch with its mission-field and the whole area of the Pauline mission in Asia Minor . . . not to mention that Jerusalem would surely not have delivered the whole Jewish diaspora of the West into the care of the Gentile mission.

So the geographical interpretation is untenable. There would appear to be only one other explanation, the distinction according to religion: all Jews are 'missionary objects' of Jerusalem, all Gentiles the same for Antioch. Unfortunately, this does not hold water either. It would have barred Paul from the synagogues, and thus denied him access to those very Gentiles who were best prepared for conversion—the σεβόμενοι. On the other hand, it would not have left these σεβόμενοι open to the Jewish mission—they were Gentiles!

In view of this we must make up our minds that Paul's formula does not give the official wording of the agreement reached in Jerusalem, and realize that it too was coined from the viewpoint which governs the whole of Gal. 2. It was Paul's concern to demonstrate that the gospel he preached to the Gentiles met with approval, i.e. that the mission without the law carried authority. The negotiations in Jerusalem had become necessary only because the Gentile Christians at Antioch were being badgered to accept circumcision. It is to this situation (as Loisy 565 saw long ago) that Paul's remark about 'false brethren' who 'slipped in' refers (2.4). These demands of the 'Judaists' had been rejected in Jerusalem. The parent congregation did not force the law on the Gentiles.

The question is therefore whether 'we to the Gentiles, they to the circumcision' can be interpreted in this sense. In fact it can. It then means 'You may waive circumcision in the mission to the Gentiles'—it need not be said that Jerusalem itself left the law intact in evangelizing Jews. This ruling embodies Paul's formula but gives it a different emphasis, shows it in another light. As Paul formulates the result, it makes him (and Barnabas) of equal rank and stature with the 'pillars' they confront—and this was important for Paul in this context. Mere permission for a Gentile mission apart from the law would have made Jerusalem appear still the superior authority, which had simply thought fit to make a gracious concession.

Actually this recognition of the Antiochian Gentile mission was something astounding, and does all honour to the men of Jerusalem. By admitting uncircumcised Gentiles to membership of the new people of God they in any case left Jewish thought behind them, however the theology may have looked with which they justified this verdict. Of the content of that theology we are ignorant. We can only make such conjectures as that they started from the premise: 'the law was given solely to Israel'. If they held fast to this presupposition—shared by every Jew—they could link with it apparently without rupture the freedom of Gentile Christians from this law. This of course raised the question what meaning the law still possessed in these new circumstances, and herein lay the temptation to erect the validity of the law into a norm binding on every Christian. On this basis all those Judaistic efforts which plagued the Pauline mission can be understood.

5. *The Apostolic Decree*

According to Luke's account the Apostolic Council adopted an authoritative resolution to which the criticism of the Tübingen school already took exception. Overbeck thus summarized its unanimous conclusion: 'Paul's account is itself sufficient to rule out the existence of the Apostolic decree (verses 23–29)' (221). It is true that not only has Catholic exegesis (e.g. Jacquier 803ff.) rejected this criticism, but such Protestants as Wendt (232ff.), Schlatter (*Erläut.* 4, 186ff.), Lyder Brun (bibl.), Zahn (539) and Michaelis (*Das NT verd. u. erläut.* II, 65ff.) have seen no reason not to attribute the decree to the Apostolic Council. The overwhelming majority of Protestant scholars, however, have followed the Tübingers on this point, and indeed the solution suggested by Weizsäcker in 1886 (*Das apostolische Zeitalter der Kirche*, 186ff.; ET *The Apostolic Age*) has won the most support: 'the men of position imposed nothing on me' (Gal. **2**.6) excludes the possibility that the decree derives from the Apostolic Council; it is much more likely to have been drafted later, without Paul's collaboration, by reason of the dispute in Antioch (Gal. **2**.11ff.) and in order to make fellowship between Jewish and Gentile Christians possible. Pronouncements in this or a similar sense have been made by Spitta (212), Bousset (*Schriften des NTs* II, 49), von Dobschütz (*Das apostolische Zeitalter*, 1917, 36), Knopf (598f.), Bultmann (*TLZ* 47 (1922), 273), Hirsch (bibl.), Beyer (91f.), Lietzmann (*Geschichte der alten Kirche* I, 107; ET *The Beginnings of the Christian Church*, 1953), Lake (*Beg.* V, 204ff.), Bauernfeind (200), Schlier (77), Goguel (*La Naissance du Christianisme*, 329; ET *The Birth of Christianity*, 1953), Cullman (*Petrus*, 1952, 47ff.; ET *Peter*, 1962, 49ff) and W. G. Kümmel ('Die älteste Form des Aposteldekrets' in *Spiritus et Veritas: Festschrift fur K. Kundsin*, 1953, 97).

Weizsäcker's argument is attractive, but suffers from a methodological defect which most of his adherents also have not avoided. On the basis of a scene recorded only in Galatians, it seeks to reconstruct the events behind the Lucan text without thorough enquiry into the exact import of Luke's account itself. Instead of first tackling the literary problem posed by Luke's report of the decree, it brushes this task aside and insists on solving the historical problem at once.

Methodologically a different procedure is required. We must first extricate the meaning of the decree in the Lucan context. Here we shall be aided by the two insights we have already acquired: 1. Peter's speech is a Lucan composition without value as a historical source; 2. James's scriptural proof cannot possibly derive from him, for it presupposes Hellenistic Gentile Christian interpretation of LXX. The true force of these insights is only appreciated, however, when they are completed by a third: the whole scene **15.4–18** is an integral essay on the part of Luke to depict and at the same time justify the ultimate acceptance of the Gentile mission without circumcision. It is then very reasonable to assume that the rest of the scene, **15.19ff.**, was meant to convey no other meaning.

The question now is whether the text itself justifies this supposition. First James proposes (**15.19**) that the Gentile Christians should not be over-burdened. This means, as the context shows, that circumcision and the great mass of legal prescriptions cannot be expected of them (cf. verse 10). But this is not to say that they have no legal obligations at all. And indeed these legal obligations do not concern 'morality' but are requirements from what we would nowadays call the 'ritual' sphere.

James does not state that these requirements are intended to enable Jewish and Gentile Christians to eat together. The decree in its 'official' form (verse 28) bases them rather on a reference to their necessity, without entering into detail as to why they are necessary. James himself, on the other hand, justifies them by reference to the preaching and reading of 'Moses' every sabbath everywhere (verse 21). This would suggest that these four requirements are generally known as 'Mosaic', hence can be found in the Pentateuch. And in fact they stand in Lev. 17 and 18. What is more—as H. Waitz pointed out in 'Das Problem des sogenannten Aposteldekrets' (*ZKG* 55 (1936), 227)—they stand in the same order as in the 'official' text of the decree (**15.29 = 21.25**). Lev. **17.8** contains the condemnation of heathen offerings, **17.10ff.** that of αἷμα, **17.13** that of πνικτόν and **18.6ff.** that of marriage to near relatives. What links these four prohibitions together, and at the same time distinguishes them from all other 'ritual' requirements of 'Moses', is that they—and they only—are given not only to Israel but also to strangers dwelling among the Jews. Whereas in other respects the law applies solely to the Jews, it imposes these four prohibitions on *Gentiles also*!

Luke has not specifically mentioned this fact. He contents himself with the general reference to 'Moses'. Nevertheless we may ask if Loisy was guilty of over-interpreting Luke's argument when he wrote: 'The Gentile converts . . . are in harmony with true Judaism, provided they observe those prescriptions of the law which are addressed to them' (595). For this interpretation is entirely consonant with the content of the chapter so far discussed.

Luke has justified the non-circumcising Gentile mission with a whole series of arguments: 1. God's will was unmistakably expressed in the conversion of Cornelius (**15**.7–9); 2. not even the Jews are able to keep the law (verse 10); 3. there are the miracles which Barnabas and Paul report (verse 12); 4. there is the scripture proof from Amos **9**.11f. (**15**. 15–17). In verses 20f. he is now removing a last objection against the mission: it is in full accord with Moses himself, who demanded just those abstinences of the Gentiles.

That this was indeed the sense in which Luke intended those solemnly stylized words of James is corroborated, it seems to us, by **21**.25. Scholars admittedly have practically all adduced precisely this verse in support of the Weizsäcker theory. Here, they say, Paul is being informed of the decree at some much later date. Hence it was drawn up in the meantime without his knowing. Here then there comes to light another source than in Chapter 15, and so forth. But, as Loisy realized (799f.), **21**.25 is in reality addressed not to Paul but to the reader of the book. Luke was no stranger to the technique of instructing the reader by way of a speech ostensibly addressed to a personage of Acts. Of this no better proof could be desired than **1**.18ff. There is no difference of method in Chapter 21. In the speech of James and the elders to Paul, Luke first makes clear that by taking Nazirite vows Paul shows himself a devout Jew (**21**.23f.), then he turns to the problem of the Gentile Christians converted by him: they have been directed to fulfil these four precepts, thus in this respect the Pauline mission also is without reproach.

There is, finally, one more point that can be adduced in support of the contention that Luke understood the four requirements in this theological sense. According to **15**.21 Luke knew that these requirements came from 'Moses'. Hence he could scarcely have been unaware that they, and only they, applied also to the Gentiles, and that is why in **15**.28 he describes them as 'necessary'.

This is by no means to contend that Luke was the first to discover the peculiarity of these four conditions, found them useful to his theology and therefore put them in the mouth of James. If Luke reports that it *pleased the Holy Spirit* to lay these four commandments on the Gentile Christians, they must still have been fully valid for the Gentile Christians of his own day. Hence we cannot assume with Hadorn (*Theol. Handkommentar zum NT* 18, 55) and Bauernfeind (195) that by Luke's time these prohibitions were already obsolete. This would mean that they were no longer observed as they had once been appointed; but then Luke would be characterizing the Gentile Christians of his day (i.e. the greater part of the Church) as disobedient to the Holy Spirit!

It follows that Luke did not, as has sometimes been imagined (cf. Dibelius, *Studies* 99), borrow the four prescriptions from some old document on which he chanced to light, but described a living tradition which was probably even then traced back to the Apostles. In fact, the introduction of these four conditions must have occurred at a time when it was hoped that they would cement the fellowship of Jewish and Gentile Christians. For this, Jerusalem does not come into consideration, and James cannot be thought of as the author. For, as the incident at Antioch proves, he regarded table fellowship of Jewish and Gentile Christians as inadmissible, thus proving himself a strict Jew who in regard to dealings with non-Jews, even if they were Christians, knew himself still bound by the law of his fathers. These prohibitions must have come into force in a strongly mixed community of the diaspora, where Jewish claims were more moderate and could be satisfied by the four commandments which Moses himself gave to the Gentiles.

Now there are two objections which can be made against the above line of argument. One is that Jewish Christianity rapidly declined in importance, especially after the murder of James the Lord's brother and the flight of the brethren to Pella; it is consequently improbable that the constantly growing majority of Gentile Christians should in the long run have made such great allowances for the Jewish Christians. The other is that the Western text proves for the middle of the second century that people no longer had any appreciation for 'ritual' prescriptions.

It is quite correct to say that the Jewish Christians rapidly lost ground and that the Gentile Church of Justin's day no longer understood the Jewish Christian 'ritual' commandments. But the inferences drawn are questionable. The Western text of the Apostolic Decree may not be explained solely by lack of understanding for the ritual requirements. It has long been recognized that the Western text seeks to remove tensions and contradictions from Acts (see Intro. § 3, 1, p. 51). The discordance between the decree and Gal. 2.6 can scarcely have remained undetected by the Fathers of the Western text. Transposition of the ritual into *moral* requirements removes this contradiction, and moreover gives a welcome opportunity for a kind of brief outline of Christian ethics (Loisy, 588). But even where people had become entirely estranged from the ritual commandments of the law, the Gentile Christians made certain 'ritual' observances their own, quite independently of the association with Jewish Christianity. The admittedly scant material reveals, for example, that Gentile Christianity in the second century had a horror of the flesh of pagan sacrifices. According to Justin, only gnostic Christians ate it: the others would sooner have been struck dead (*Dial. cum Tryph.* **34**.8). Somewhat later, *ca.* A.D. 161, Minucius Felix (**36**.6) combats the accusation that Christians ate children by pointing out that they even abstained from the blood of animals. The woman martyr Biblis says exactly the same during the persecution of A.D. 177: 'How could they eat children who are not even allowed to eat the blood of irrational animals?' (Eusebius, *H.E.* V 1.26). Finally Tertullian, at the end of the second century, writes of the Christians: *qui ne animalium . . . sanguinem in epulis esculentis habemus, qui propterea suffocatis quoque et morticinis abstinemus, ne quo modo sanguine contaminemur* *vel intra viscera sepulto* (*Apologia* **9**.13). It is thus evident that abhorrence of blood, and hence also of strangled meat, had survived into the second century independently of consideration for the Jewish Christians. Hence there is nothing against the view that the four requirements were still in force among Gentile Christians at the time when Acts was written.

The mention of Syria and Cilicia, and also of Silas and Judas, will be discussed in the next section, the question of the collection at **24**.17.

35
ACTS 15:36–41
PAUL AND BARNABAS PART COMPANY; DEPARTURE ON THE SECOND MISSIONARY JOURNEY

[36] And after some days Paul said to Barnabas: 'Let us return now and visit the brethren in every city where we proclaimed the Word of the Lord, and see how they fare.' [37] Barnabas wanted to take with them John also, who was called Mark. [38] But Paul insisted that they should not take with them the man who had deserted them in Pamphylia and had not gone with them to the work (of mission). [39] There was a sharp contention, so that they separated from one another, and Barnabas, taking Mark with him, sailed away to Cyprus. [40] But Paul chose Silas and departed, commended by the brethren to the grace of the Lord. [41] And he went through Syria and Cilicia, strengthening the communities.

Bibliography:

B. W. Bacon, 'Peter's Triumph at Antioch', *Journal of Religion* 9, Chicago 1929, 204–23; Cadbury, § 4 bibl., esp. 50f.; Kragerud, § 29 bibl., 253f.; Conzelmann 88.

VERSE 36: In the second half of Acts, μετά + time-datum marks the beginning of a new section (Bruce, *Acts* 305f.). εἶπεν . . . Παῦλος—hence it was Paul who took the initiative for the new journey (Knopf 600). ἐπιστρέψαντες: 'again'—LXX uses it to render שׁוב; ἐπισκέπτομαι (extremely common in LXX as the translation of various verbs, but Luke's readers may also perhaps have sensed an echo of ἐπίσκοπος): 'look them up' (Bauer, *Wb* 590f.); the dependent πῶς ἔχουσιν adds 'how they are'.[1] The δή is pressing = 'come now, let us . . .', cf. Luke 2.15 and Acts 13.2. ἐν αἷς links with the plural implied in κατὰ πόλιν πᾶσαν (note the alliteration). ὁ λόγος τοῦ κυρίου = the Christian message.

Paul now unfolds no new mission-plan: only the existing congregations are to be revisited. But out of this God will bring about the 'second missionary journey'. Luke does not say so, but that is how he presents the story.

[1] ἐπισκέπτεσθαι πῶς ἔχοι Josephus, *Ant.* IV 112; VII 166; IX 112.

VERSE 37: John Mark had returned to Jerusalem at **13**.13. How he now came to be in Antioch is a detail with which Luke does not concern himself. In Zahn's opinion (557) Luke concealed the fact that—according to Col. **4**.10—John Mark and Barnabas were cousins in order to protect the latter from suspicions of nepotism.[1]

VERSE 38: The infinitive in Hellenistic fashion (Bl.-Debr. § 392, 1c) depends (as in **28**.22) on the imperfect ἠξίου (='he insisted on', Bauer, *Wb* 155; according to Bl.-Debr. § 324 of unfulfilled desire); and τὸν ἀποστάντα (repeated for emphasis in τοῦτον) is its direct object.[2] τὸ ἔργον: as in **13**.2 and **14**.26 the work of mission. Luke formulates the reproach with such restraint in order that his intervention on Mark's behalf may not be held against Barnabas.[3]

VERSE 39: 'A sharp contention arose'—the expression is so neutral that it does not touch on the question of responsibility. Far from harming the mission, the parting thus occasioned actually doubles it: Barnabas sails off with John Mark to his homeland Cyprus (see **4**.36), and is not mentioned in Acts again.[4]—Classical usage would here demand the indicative after ὥστε: Moulton 209, citing Blass.

VERSE 40: ἐπιλέγομαι = 'choose for oneself'. Luke considers it superfluous to state how Paul reached Silas [5] ˥ ˎ e fact that Paul was accompanied by this highly-regarded Jerusalemite (**15**.22: ἀνὴρ ἡγούμενος) places the new mission from the outset under the aegis of Jerusalem; similarly, the companionship of John Mark symbolizes—albeit in less illustrious fashion—the recognition of Jerusalem for the mission of Barnabas. Correspondingly, it is only for Paul that an official leave-taking is mentioned (cf. **14**.26); Barnabas seems to steal away. This is Luke's way of underlining the supreme importance of the Pauline mission. 'C'est plutôt le départ de Barnabé qui a été ainsi favorisé' was Loisy's indignant remark (617). Luke mentioned Silas in verses

---

[1] But the Mark of Philemon 24 is not necessarily (as Col. **4**.10 presupposes) identical with John Mark. In II Tim. **4**.11 the identity is not actually expressed, but is probably assumed, just as in I Peter **5**.13. Here Silvanus and Mark are both imagined as assistants of Peter in 'Babylon' (= Rome), which gave rise to the tradition that Mark was Peter's ἑρμηνευτής.

[2] Cf. the construction in Acts **1**.23–25.

[3] According to Moulton (130) the present infin. συμπαραλαμβάνειν expresses the nuance: Paul refuses to have an unreliable man with them day after day, while Barnabas simply wanted to take him with them (aorist). D avoids the repetition of the verb, which he felt clumsy, but at the cost of stylistic impairment.

[4] At the time of I Cor. **9**.6 Barnabas was still alive, though Knopf (600) has no warrant there for supposing him still on his travels, nor has Zahn (556) for inferring that the old intimacy with Paul had been re-established. The two never worked together again.—That John Mark 'as a travelling missionary aide restored his reputation' (Zahn *ibid.*) is, to say the least, most questionably worded.

[5] According to Zahn, who maintains the originality of the words in the Western text 'but Silas decided to remain' (irreconcilable with **15**.33), Silas had perhaps even thought of settling permanently in Antioch . . . (553).

22, 27 and 32 solely in order to prepare the reader for his participation in Paul's missionary work.[1] Beside him he then had to name a second legate.

VERSE 41: Here Luke takes up the mention of Syria and Cilicia in the address of the decree (15.23). Strictly speaking, Judas and Silas should not have remained in Antioch but have gone on with the decree through Syria and Cilicia. Since Luke (in contrast to Gal. 1.21) has not so far mentioned a mission in these areas, many scholars conclude from verses 23 and 41 that Luke is here following a different source. But at 9.31 Luke introduces the evangelization of Galilee (concerning which he possessed as few concrete details as in the case of Syria and Cilicia) in the same supplementary fashion as that of Syria and Cilicia here. In showing the decree as addressed to Syria and Cilicia also, though only Antioch had sought the decision, Luke makes it clear to the reader that the decree was no mere local ordinance; once Paul has conveyed it to the congregations of Lycaonia[2] (16.4), it has been made known to all Gentile Christians so far (according to Acts) converted. From 21.25 it then follows that it holds for Gentile Christians generally. But Luke has taken care not to present the decree at once as an edict *urbi et orbi* addressed to existing Gentile converts and all those to come: he was too expert a writer and historian for that.

Hitherto Paul and Barnabas have worked together. From now on they will work apart. This change is explained by the incident described: Paul fell out with Barnabas over John Mark. So Barnabas went off with John to his native Cyprus while Paul, now accompanied by Silas, took formal leave of Antioch and set out through Syria and Cilicia for Lycaonia.

Whoever maintains that this account derives from an Antiochian Luke, a companion of Paul, must here find himself in difficulty—unless, with the nonchalance of a Schlatter (193–5), he simply ignores the problem. For Paul (Gal. 2.11ff) tells of a different conflict with Barnabas: together with Peter and the other Jewish Christians of Antioch, Barnabas broke off table fellowship (i.e. partaking of the eucharist) with the Gentile Christians on the arrival of 'men from James', thus provoking Paul to harsh and unconditional rebuke.

[1] According to Beyer (97) the decree arrived in Antioch only after Paul's departure; hence Beyer considers that Acts may be mistaken in the name Silas; or perhaps the decree only arrived during the third missionary journey, in which Silas did not take part. Lietzmann (*Gesch. d. Alten Kirche* I, 107; ET *The Beginnings of the Christian Church*, 1953) makes Judas and Silas the τινες ἀπὸ Ἰακώβου of Gal. 2.12, and has them bring the decree to Antioch; how Paul then set off on a mission with one of these men from Jerusalem remains incomprehensible. These and similar conjectures do not take the literary problem really into consideration.

[2] The Western text has the commands of the Apostles and elders already conveyed to the congregations in Syria and Cilicia; D, that is, has noted that the charge of 15.23ff. has not yet been fully implemented.

The expositor faithful to tradition, for whom both accounts are authentic, must show their compatibility. According to Acts the quarrel between Paul and Barnabas immediately precedes their separation. The clash with Peter and Barnabas therefore must have taken place earlier. This is scarcely credible.

According to Galatians Paul made the conflict one of principle, and we have no reason to doubt this. Was he the victor? His indictment of Peter merges into a self-justification vis-à-vis the Galatians, and Peter drops out of the picture. According to Schlatter Paul is silent about Peter's admission of error so as not to appear anxious to shame him. Now Paul has accused Peter before the Galatians of hypocrisy. This is incomparably more shaming to Peter than a confession of repentance would have been! And how triumphantly Paul would have shown the power of his gospel, had he been able to write: 'Peter, Barnabas and the other Jewish Christians confessed that I was right, and ate once again with their Gentile brethren'! Here the *argumentum e silentio* is justified for once, as everything urged Paul to speak if he could. And his silence shows that success was denied him. Here, alas, Loisy (609) and Goguel (*La Naissance du Christianisme*, 329–31; ET *The Birth of Christianity*, 1953) are right.

This however put Paul in an untenable position. He had publicly, before the congregation, defended 'his gospel' against Peter and Barnabas—and failed. The most important member of the Antiochian community, Barnabas, indeed the whole Jewish Christian part of the congregation (Gal. **2**.13, cf. Acts **13**.1), and the Apostle Peter himself were not persuaded. The authority of Paul, even though not formally contested, was shattered. We cannot, with Wendt (240), Beyer (96) and Bruce (306), simply add the conflicts together. How could Paul, after such a rebuff—a rejection of his gospel!—calmly stay on in Antioch as if nothing had happened, and invite Barnabas to join him on another tour?

This is however not the last of the difficulties confronting the scholar faithful to tradition. The companion of Paul must have known of his conflict with Peter and Barnabas. Why does he suppress it and recount a different and relatively harmless quarrel with Barnabas? Long ago that heir of the Tübingen school, Overbeck, roundly maintained that Acts **15**.36–41 was deliberately substituted for the unpalatable truth of the real dispute, and this thesis Loisy adopted fifty years later (613, referring to E. Schwartz, *NGG* 1907, 272).

Bauernfeind (203) hoped to evade this painful conclusion by assuming that for Luke the personal quarrel of Paul and Barnabas was more painful than the discussion of principle. Apart from the fact that this does not give Luke a very good testimonial, apart from the fact that Paul fought that fundamental battle with all his personal feelings passionately engaged, Bauernfeind's argument does not help. No Christian of Antioch could have doubted for a moment that the more painful break arose from the conflict with Peter and Barnabas. Even such scholars as Knabenbauer and Jacquier (471) implicitly admit this.

In short, we cannot get through in this passage with the traditional view of Luke. Yet one need not go so far as Overbeck, Schwartz, Loisy and Preuschen (98), for whom the author has tendentiously suppressed the truth, or freely invented the whole of the first missionary journey. It is a very real question whether the author knew anything at all about that conflict. For in the incident of which Paul speaks in Gal. **2.**11 the Christians could find nothing indispensable or edifying. Hence this painful conflict between men so worthy as Peter, Paul and Barnabas was not handed down to posterity, and was quickly forgotten.

How then did the story preserved in Acts **15.**36ff. come into being? Was it a local community tradition? This is suggested neither by its style nor by its content. Such tales as those of Ananias and Sapphira or the raising of Tabitha can easily be understood as pious anecdotes early in independent circulation, but not **15.**36ff. The episode has no place but in a chronicle such as Acts. For in an account of Paul's missionary journeys the reader must be told why he set out no more with Barnabas. Luke must have inferred the circumstances from the statements about the persons with whom Paul journeyed. Before, it was Barnabas; now it is Silas. This change must have had its cause, and since Barnabas had worked together with John Mark in Cyprus, the combination was really very natural: thus John Mark, who prematurely returned from the first journey, was the occasion of the separation. If it seems audacious to credit Luke with such an independent construction, we may recall the Barnabas incident of **9.**26f., which can also be controlled by the Pauline account: this too was the product of retrospective inference (see p. 334f. above).

Loisy, treating Paul's passionate defence of his doctrine of justification with the petulance of a humanist, identifies the moment of Paul's departure with the dawning of his estimate of himself (according to Loisy indeed his over-estimate) as *the* missionary to the Gentiles (614f.). But this, to say the least, is to overload the conflict with psychological significance. Perhaps however one may say that a decision was taken which was fraught with consequences. Paul did not indeed storm out of Antioch in blazing indignation, but his relationship with this community (which now probably came into somewhat closer connection with Jerusalem) now grew cooler. He therefore decided to begin a mission of his own, and so for the first time became 'the missionary to the Gentiles'. The congregations which he founded in Europe were not daughters of Antioch: Paul was their 'father in Christ'.

That Silas (= Silvanus) was not one of the notables of Jerusalem should in the circumstances be self-evident. He was one of the small number of Jewish Christians whose minds were fully open to the Apostle's preaching of Christ without the law.

36
ACTS 16:1–5
JOURNEY THROUGH LYCAONIA.
CIRCUMCISION OF TIMOTHY

[1] He reached Derbe and Lystra. And behold, there was a disciple there by the name of Timothy, the son of a Jewish-Christian woman and a heathen father, [2] who was held in good repute by the brethren in Lystra and Iconium. [3] This man Paul wanted to go with him, and he took and circumcised him, because of the Jews who were in that region; for they all knew that his father was a heathen. [4] As they moved through the cities, they delivered to them for observance the ordinances decided upon by the Apostles and elders in Jerusalem. [5] And so the communities were strengthened in the faith and grew daily in number.

Bibliography:

C. S. C. Williams, *A Commentary on the Acts of the Apostles*, London, 1957, 188; A. F. J. Klijn, 'De besnijdenis in Handelingen en bij Paulus', *Kerk en Theologie* 1956 (October issue); Conzelman 88f.; G. Stählin 212f.

VERSE 1: 'He reached[1] . . .': the following episode deals only with Paul; Silas, therefore, is not mentioned. καὶ ἰδού: see on 1.10. ἐκεῖ refers to Lystra: Timothy[2] was a μαθητής, that is, a Christian. According to I Cor. 4.17 Paul had probably already converted him on his first journey: H. J. Holtzmann, 104. Timothy was the son of a Jewish woman[3] who had joined the Christian congregation and a 'Greek', i.e. Gentile father.

[1] D d gig sy^hmg bring to the reader's notice, by the words they add, that the communities in Syria and Cilicia were Gentile Christian. The handing over of the decree to them in the text of 15.41 in these MSS is thus provided with a motivation.

[2] Acts mentions him further in 17.14f.; 18.5; 19.22; 20.4. Compare also I Thess. 1.1; 3.2, 6; II Thess. 1.1; I Cor. 4.17; 16.10f.; Romans 16.21; Phil. 1.1; 2.19; and Philemon 1.

[3] II Tim. 1.5 speaks of the sincere faith which dwelt in Timothy's grandmother Lois and his mother Eunice, and 3.15 of the early introduction of the child to the sacred Scriptures. That is, as W. L. Knox remarks (52, n. 2) Christian legend. 'The marriage of Timothy's non-Jewish father and Jewish mother was according to Jewish law illegal.' (Bill. II 741, with reference to Jebamoth 45b). 'The children of such a marriage . . . were considered Israelites' (loc. cit.). In spite of this Timothy was not circumcised. The marriage of a Jewish woman with a pagan and the uncircumcision of the son reveal not a devout but rather a lax Judaism.

VERSE 2: What Luke wants to say is that because Timothy was held in good repute by the Christians in Lystra and Iconium this recommended him for employment in the mission.

VERSE 3: According to the text Paul circumcised him not in consideration for his Jewish mother,[1] but rather on account of the Jews in that region. It makes no difference to Luke how Timothy himself felt about the matter. Luke is only concerned about the acts of Paul. To be sure he will have assumed that Timothy did not oppose Paul's will.

VERSE 4: τὰς πόλεις: they are the places mentioned in verse 1f., to which might be added Pisidian Antioch, although it is not mentioned here.[2] The decree does not mention them.[3] For δόγματα compare ἔδοξεν **15**.28.

VERSE 5: The scene closes with μὲν οὖν (see on **1**.6). The summary remark 'the communities were strengthened in the faith' employs a formulary phrase recurring in Col. **2**.5 and I Peter **5**.9. The statement about the growth of the communities corresponds to what we have heard in **2**.41; **2**.47; **4**.4; **5**.14; **6**.7; **9**.31, 35, 42; **11**.21, 24; **12**.24; **14**.1. The growth of the communities shows the divine blessing which rests upon them. No particular tradition is here evident.[4] For τῷ ἀριθμῷ compare LXX Num. **9**.20 and Ez. **12**.16.

The early critics in search of sources found in this section once again traces of the redactor, that is in reality parts which they considered unworthy of belief. According to Jüngst 154 and Hilgenfeld (*ZwTh* 1896, 184f.) the redactor added verses 2, 3bc and 4f. The source thus reported only the calling of Timothy to the mission, but not his circumcision nor the delivering of the decrees from Jerusalem. Sorof (18f.) saw verses 1–5 as an addition of Timothy to the source. Verses 4f. were assigned to the redactor by Spitta 214f. also (after the example of Jacobsen). The same thesis was advocated by Clemen (*Paulus* I 256) and Ed. Schwartz (*NGG* 1907, 271). Preuschen 99 assigns vv.

---

[1] That the father was no longer living is a reasonable conjecture. A few MSS (1838 gig p) take it into account by speaking of the mother as a widow.

[2] According to *Beg.* IV 185, v. 6 might pick up v. 4 again, with Luke simply changing the expression. Then these cities would also be meant by 'Phrygia and the Galatian country'. Lake himself, however, assumes (*Beg.* V 236) that 'these cities' refers to those previously mentioned.

[3] The decree is here communicated to congregations which were not mentioned in its address. Luke thus indicates that Paul conveyed it to all his congregations. Of any co-operation of the πλῆθος of the Jerusalem community in the process there is no further word. The expression δόγματα makes these decisions (κρίνω is here and in **21**.15 employed differently from **15**.19!) appear like imperial edicts (cf. G. Kittel, *ThWb* II, 234f.). This also supports the view that Luke attributes to them universal meaning.

[4] The inner and outer growth of the communities belongs to the Lucan portrayal of the Apostolic Age. Luke can, therefore, make such affirmations even without sources. From such verses, however, we should not attempt to project a historical sketch. See p. 215 n. 2, on **4**.4.

3–5 to the reviser. So also Wendt 241, note 2, who however found only v. 3b made unclear by the reviser and v. 4 inserted.

Does the text require such a judgement? It gives a progressive description: beyond the Cilician gates the journey proceeds to the Lycaonian communities. The arrival in Derbe and Lystra is briefly reported, then comes an episode recounted in 'biblical' style. In Lystra lived a Christian by the name of Timothy. He was the son of a Jewish woman (who had now become a member of the Christian community) and a Gentile father (who was evidently already dead). Timothy had a good reputation with the Christians in Lystra and in the next town, Iconium (see Ramsay, *St. Paul* 179), which explains Paul's wish to have him as a companion for the rest of the missionary journey. In order not to offend the Jews in the vicinity (of whom there is no further mention)—for they all knew that as a son of a Gentile Timothy was uncircumcised—Paul circumcised him. Now however the report of the journey is not yet continued, but rather a note is appended which because of the story about Timothy Luke could not mention earlier: in these cities the missionaries delivered to the congregations the δόγματα which were decided upon by the Apostles and elders in Jerusalem. Here the Apostles are mentioned for the last time. Paul does everything to protect his missionary efforts from any offence. There is no further mention of persecutions. The communities are strengthened in the faith and grow daily in number. With this description of prosperity—and therefore of the divine blessing which rests upon the mission—Luke harmoniously concludes the section.

Real tradition becomes visible only in the account of Timothy. Luke, who knows nothing of the uncircumcised Titus (Gal. **2**.1, 3), presents Paul's companion on the second and third missionary journeys to the reader as one rendered inoffensive to the Jews by his circumcision. Tübingen criticism vehemently disputed the truth of this report. It is, as F. C. Baur had already asserted, 'downright unbelievable' (Overbeck 248). Against this judgement, which seemed very seriously to discredit the author of Acts, the more conservative scholars understandably put up a fierce resistance. Here three points of view in particular were asserted.

1. It was pointed out that here the circumcision does not serve to achieve salvation, but only to shield the mission from difficulties. (It is in fact in this way that v. 3 provides the reason for the—alleged—circumcision of Timothy.) Against such an interpretation of the circumcision Overbeck (250) already correctly objected: 'Circumcision without religious significance would simply have made no sense anywhere in Judaism at the time of Paul and in reality could never be considered.' Paul himself was at one with Judaism of his time, that in circumcision one had to deal with God. Judaism, however, believed that circumcision fulfilled a fundamental commandment of the obedience required by God and allowed one to tread the path to God, while Paul was convinced that this way did not lead to χάρις but rather to

the ὀργὴ θεοῦ (Rom. **4**.15). Paul could not disregard the religious significance of circumcision. The idea that a man could allow himself to be circumcised in order to avoid any difficulties in the mission (in Gal. **5**.11 it is remotely touched on) would have been for him a lie and at the same time a blasphemy against God.

2. This recognition is also important for the assessment of a second idea introduced into the debate. If Paul became like a Jew to the Jews in order to win Jews (I Cor. **9**.20) why should Timothy not also be circumcised in order to win the circumcised, although as a Christian he is free from the law like Paul himself? Why should Timothy not take the whole law upon himself out of love for the Jewish brethren (since he who allows himself to be circumcised is obliged to keep the whole law: Gal. **5**.3) in order—although inwardly free from the law- -to overcome their mistrust of the Christian gospel? Against these thoughts Overbeck objected, 'The historical Paul recognizes over against the law only the Christian freedom *not* to fulfil it, and this conception of ἐλευθερία had in that time historical reality' (250), not the idea of a freedom for the law. That is correct. But in addition it is worth considering that Barnabas and Paul have just had the freedom of the Gentile mission guaranteed to them in Jerusalem. What sense would there be for Paul, in setting out on this mission, to have his companion circumcised? I Cor. **7**.17–20 shows that Paul wanted nothing to do with the supplementary circumcision of a Christian—it would inevitably awaken the fatal misunderstanding that the true Christian simply must be circumcised.

3. Bauernfeind has therefore sought to find a reason for the circumcision of Timothy which is not touched by these objections. He starts out from an idea which has been utilized in this connection since H. Thiersch (*Die Kirche im apostolischen Zeitalter*, 1852, 138, cited by Overbeck 248): as son of a Jewish woman Timothy according to rabbinical law ought to have been circumcised. That he was not betrays an 'emancipated Judaism'. Paul 'wanted Christian Jews and not uprooted Jews' (204). This antithesis is not clearly formulated. Actually it ought to read: Paul did not want to win for Christ emancipated Jews but law-abiding Jews—and in this form the thought is clearly very questionable. But further, Timothy is certainly no longer an 'emancipated Jew' (quite aside from the fact that he did not arbitrarily step out from the law but as the son of a heathen grew up in heathenism). He is, on the contrary, a Christian—perhaps even baptized by Paul himself (cf. I Cor. **4**.17) on his first visit to Lystra. With this he has, however, broken with his past. The word 'the old is past, see! it has become new' (II Cor. **5**.17) applies also to Timothy. It does not help, consequently, when Bauernfeind appeals to Timothy's attachment to Judaism " according to the law of creation" (205). The ensuing baptism neither permits nor tolerates any completion by a circumcision based upon an attachment "according to the law of creation". The text in v. 3 plainly shows that Paul held the alleged circumcision

necessary only because Timothy was now to serve him as a missionary companion (and here we come again to what was said in point 1. above), not because Paul wanted to have no emancipated Jews in the Church.

The reasons adduced for the circumcision of Timothy thus do not apply, as soon as one takes the thought of the real Paul into consideration. How then did Luke come to include this story? He took it over from tradition. Gal. 5.11 shows that already Paul himself had to fight against the slanderous rumour that he too (occasionally) preached circumcision. This rumour, evidently spread by his Judaistic opponents, stubbornly persisted (Bousset for example still believed it and so interpreted Gal. 5.11 on the basis of Acts 16.1ff.— Schriften d. NT II, 67), and reached Luke as a tradition. This tradition he readily took up: it seemed to speak in favour of his pet theory that the Pharisee Paul strictly observed the law, and came into conflict with Judaism only through his proclamation of the resurrection. Here then Luke has not, as the Tübingen school contend, tendentiously replaced the truth known to him by a patchwork of his own; rather was he the victim of an unreliable tradition.

With the story of Timothy and the report of the delivery of the δόγματα of the Apostles and elders, it is evident that the mission now beginning is undertaken in complete concord with the Jewish Christians of Jerusalem. Luke thus sees the Pauline mission, which from now on becomes his real theme, as harmoniously integrated into the total work of the Church.

37

ACTS 16:6-8
THE JOURNEY THROUGH ASIA MINOR

[6] They went through Phrygia and the Galatian country but were prevented by the Holy Spirit from speaking the word in Asia. [7] But when they came to Mysia they sought to go to Bithynia, and the Spirit of Jesus did not let them. [8] Then when they had marched through Mysia, they came down to Troas.

Bibliography:

Dornseiff, 1936, 137, see bibl. to § 1; Dibelius, *Studies* 200f.; Conzelmann 88ff.

VERSE 6: 'They went through Phrygia[1] and the Galatian country,[2]

[1] Preuschen 99 treats Φρυγία as an adjective of three terminations qualifying χώρα; in later Greek, however, it has only two. ἡ Φρυγία therefore is a noun: the country of Phrygia. **18**.23 describes the journey differently with the words: διερχόμενος . . . τὴν Γαλατικὴν χώραν καὶ Φρυγίαν where 'Φρυγίαν without the article is in any case a noun' (Zahn 560). The parallel Lake cites from Luke 3.1 (Excursus: 'Paul's route in Asia Minor', *Beg.* V, 231) τῆς 'Ιτουραίας καὶ Τραχωνίτιδος χώρας shows that the article does not need to be repeated in such a context.
[2] Γαλατικὴ χώρα is therefore a second country named beside Phrygia. The expression here and in **18**.23 probably describes the district inhabited by Galatians. Paul need not have gone as far as Pessinus or Ancyra; cities like Nakoleya or Dorylaeum lie in the region settled by Galatians (Dibelius, *Studies* 200 n. 18).—Ramsay (*St. Paul*, 102) had interpreted τὴν Φρυγίαν καὶ Γαλατικὴν χώραν as a rendering of *regio Phrygia Galatica*: χώρα (=*regio*) includes as an administrative unit the remains of one of the old kingdoms which were incorporated into the Roman province of Galatia. *Phrygia Galatica* is the part of Phrygia incorporated in this province. It comprised the territory of the cities of Antioch, Derbe, Lystra and Iconium, to which communities the letter to the Galatians was directed. Against this Lake has shown 1. The Roman regional disposition of Asia Minor was associated with the great cities. *Regio* denoted such a city together with its hinterland. 2. The expression *Pontus Galaticus* is attested, but not *Phrygia Galatica*. But if the Roman authorities had used it, it would have been rendered in Greek ἡ Γαλατικὴ Φρυγία. 3. But then τῆς Γαλατίας in Gal. **1**.2 also need not refer to the territory of the cities of Antioch, Derbe, Lystra and Iconium (the so-called south-Galatian hypothesis). Some official historical writers do indeed employ ἡ Γαλατία to designate the Roman province (Schlier, *Galaterbrief*, 5). That, however, is unusual. The expression Γαλάται (Gal. 3.1) describes only the inhabitants of the territory of Galatia, not of Lycaonia, Pisidia, etc. (Pauly-Wissowa XIII, 556).—The assertion that Paul always uses the Roman names for the provinces has, without foundation, wellnigh become a dogma. The use of Μακεδονία does not decide the issue because here the names of country and province are identical. 'Ασία in I Cor. **16**.19, II Cor. **1**.8 and Romans **16**.5 may indicate either the Roman province or the Greek cities of western Asia Minor with their hinterland. 'Αχαία (I Cor. **16**.15; II Cor. **1**.1; **9**.2; **11**.10;

prevented[1] by the Holy Spirit from speaking the word in Asia'.[2] For διέρχομαι see **8**.4; λαλεῖν τὸν λόγον see **4**.29 ('conduct a mission').

VERSE 7: 'When they came to Mysia[3] (cf. on κατά **27**.7) they sought to go to Bithynia, and the Spirit of Jesus did not let them.' This is clearly the same divine power which in v. 6 is called 'the Holy Spirit'.

VERSE 8: 'Then when they had marched[4] through Mysia, they came down to Troas.'

The section reports very briefly an immense journey (which however did not 'last a couple of years', as Wellhausen, 31, writes). It is not confined to that visit to the old communities which was mentioned in **15**.36, but Paul begins—and this for Luke's readers is a complete surprise—a new and great missionary endeavour. This journey is not described with the accuracy of an itinerary but (as in **18**.22f.) only in very general geographical terms. Before we attempt to investigate possible sources and the like, we should take note of the impression which Luke's reader receives from this section. Twice the plans of the missionaries are thrown to the winds because of the higher power, the 'Holy Spirit', the 'Spirit of Jesus'. The goal which Paul and his companions finally achieved was not the one Paul had in mind at the outset. In fact, he had not even considered it at all. Not by human calculation and planning was

---

I Thess. **1**.7f.) actually means the Peloponnese and not Greece (Schlier, 6), 'Ιουδαία (I Thess. **2**.14; II Cor. **1**.16; Gal. **1**.22; Romans **15**.31) does not denote a Roman province (Judaea first became such under Vespasian: Schlier) but the country of Judaea. The Συρία distinguished from Judaea in Gal. **1**.21 is consequently also not the Roman province but the country, and likewise Κιλικία. Pauline usage throughout allows the reference of Γαλατία to the country of Galatia.

[1] Ramsay supposed κωλυθέντες =καὶ ἐκωλύθησαν: the travellers first went through Phrygian Galatia and then were hindered by the Spirit. In reality κωλυθέντες gives the reason why the travellers moved through Phrygia and Galatia. Travel to the west was barred for them. Cf. Moulton 133, 134.

[2] According to Ramsay Paul was allowed to pass through Asia (=the Roman province) but not to preach there. What reader would hit upon this sense? Paul's original goal will have been the great cities on the west coast such as Ephesus. 'Ασία here means the same region as in the Revelation of John.

[3] Mysia reached, according to Strabo, from the coast of the Aegean to the eastern slopes of the Mysian Olympus (Lake, *Beg.* V, 230). In Kotiaion or Dorylaeum Paul was κατὰ τὴν Μυσίαν, and Bithynia lay directly north of him. What the οὐκ εἴασεν κτλ meant is not indicated. Zahn conjectures 'that it was Silas-Silvanus who heard the dissuading voice of the Spirit and communicated it to the travellers in a convincing manner' (561). That looks like a pretty little fiction, but has arisen out of sober reflection: the 'newcomer Timothy' does not come into the picture, and if Paul himself had had a divine communication, Luke would have said so. Nevertheless with these pseudo-historical conclusions Zahn has misjudged the character of these verses. Cf. the general discussion.

[4] Bauer, *Wb* 1241 refers to I Macc. **5**.48, where παρέρχομαι means: 'to go through and over'. Because D knew only the meaning 'to pass by', and Troas lies in Mysia, and accordingly a journey past Mysia was out of the question, it replaced παρελθόντες by διελθόντες.

the Pauline mission brought to Troas and then to Macedonia, but by the mysteriously intervening *providentia specialissima* of God.

This reminds us of the story of Cornelius. By the way in which Luke developed it, it was made clear to the reader that the turning of the Christian mission to the Gentiles did not originate in any human desire but solely in the divine resolution. Here we have another important turning point in the history of the Christian mission. Only this time it is not a new group of men but a new area which is opened up for the Christian mission.

Thus the question arises: has Luke's hand here also given to the event its special complexion, the aspect of divine guidance? The wealth of miracle stories and discourses from which in chapters 10f. we could discern Luke's work of composition is here lacking. It is not so much what Luke reports (concerning the intervention of the Spirit), but rather what he does not relate that causes us to ask what share his composition had in the whole.

One may safely assume that Paul and his companions did not simply travel back and forth across the whole of Asia Minor, but kept to the major routes. They must then have passed through various cities. Such cities, how-ever, are not here mentioned. Derbe and Lystra are the last stopping-places named as such. In addition Iconium also is mentioned, Pisidian Antioch not at all. Only with Troas do we again receive a concrete account. But a tradition does not report in the general fashion in which the journey between Lystra and Troas is indicated. We shall therefore have to consider the recapitulation of the journey in our section as the condensation of a more exact report. (There is also a point of detail in favour of this view, which will be discussed below.) Why has the author undertaken such a condensation? If this journey was to have the character of one divinely guided, if Paul (to use an expression from Luther) was to be shown going his way like a blinded horse, then any specific account of places or details of the journey would only have spoilt the effect. They would have distracted the reader's attention from the main point. The only human undertakings which required to be recounted were those which enabled the divine intervention to be recognized as such. This alone was important for the author and his readers (Dibelius, *Studies*, 201).

So we must reckon with the probability that the author has shortened a more detailed account for his purpose. Such an account we must expect from a companion of Paul. If we assume that in 16.10 an itinerary much used in the subsequent course of the book is recognizable, then there is nothing against the view that it was also used earlier. From which of the companions on the journey it may derive will be discussed in relation to v. 10.

The tenor of the account in 16.6–8 has led most scholars to assume that Paul was directed by inner voices, visions and dreams. Jülicher has even censured the Apostle for yielding too readily to his visions in the shaping of his plans of action (*Einl.*, 1931,[7] 50; ET of 1st edn. *An Introduction to the*

NT, 1904). The Pauline epistles evoke a different picture of Paul. With all his obedience to the will of God he yet did not neglect at each point to consider the situation exactly, and although he tenaciously stuck to his major goals, he nevertheless reacted to new turns of events. We may therefore assume that at the beginning of his new missionary effort he had given consideration to the possible mission fields. Lake has put forward (op. cit. 237) some very instructive considerations concerning what Paul needed for successful activity. Paul certainly need not have thought exactly as Lake, but there is nothing against the view that he also thought of the decisive points. As a point of contact for his preaching of Christ, he needed synagogues in which Greek was spoken and around which a circle of Greek-speaking 'God-fearers' had gathered. He was, therefore, directed to the larger cities in which lived a flourishing Jewish community—we may scarcely assume Jews in the country at that time—cities in which Greek was spoken or in which at least a considerable part of the populace understood Greek. Perhaps it was only in Macedonia and Greece that Paul acquired to the full the knowledge born of experience (about which Lake also speaks) that it was advantageous if the Jews were not dominant in a city and therefore in a case of conflict could not suppress the Christian missionaries.

When Paul and his companions had to pass from Lystra or Iconium or Pisidian Antioch to a new field of endeavour, such favourable conditions existed chiefly in the west, in the Greek cities of coastal Asia Minor. From the Lycaonian cities a road ran by Apamea and Laodicea through the Lycus and Meander valleys to Ephesus. Paul could also have travelled by Philadelphia and Sardis to Smyrna or Pergamum. According to the Lucan account he actually had such a goal at first in mind. Verse 6 does not reveal in what manner the Spirit of God hindered Paul and his companions from going to Asia to preach the gospel. We see only that Paul turned toward the north, journeyed through Phrygia and the Galatian country, and intended to go to Bithynia. This brings into view the second field of endeavour which, in the prevailing conditions, held promise of success: the Greek cities on the Bosporus. From Kotiaion and Dorylaeum roads led to Nicaea and Nicomedia. Perhaps Paul would also, reaching further to the north-east, have set about bringing the gospel to the Greek cities on the Black Sea. In either case the history of the Christian mission would have taken a very different course. The 'Spirit of Jesus' thwarted this plan also, without our learning any details of the 'how' of the matter.

If this direction also was barred, still a third mission opportunity on a large scale offered itself: the Greek cities in Macedonia and Greece itself. In case Paul and his companions decided upon this, they had to travel from 'the Galatian country'—we may think with Lake of cities like those just mentioned, of Kotiaion and Dorylaeum—through Mysia to the Aegean coast. One of the roads which come under consideration ends in Troas. This does not yet mean that Paul now set out for Macedonia—he could have waited for a ship which would bring him and his companions directly to Greece. The continuation of the narrative, to be discussed shortly, makes a dream bring about the decision for Macedonia.

Luke has indicated in vv. 6–8 no kind of missionary effort. Also we may not conclude from the fact that preaching was barred to Paul in Asia that he preached in the other places he passed through. If the above considerations come at all close to the truth, then it seemed commendable to Paul not to delay the work in the field in prospect through carrying out a mission along the road. It is, however, possible that there was nonetheless a mission on the way—in the Galatian country. According to the letter to the Galatians Paul had to remain there a considerable time because of an illness, but he was well enough to preach with great success. The communities which resulted are not mentioned here by Luke, but he does presuppose them in **18**.23. They would not have existed in cities (otherwise the address of the letter to the Galatians would probably read differently), but rather in villages where there were no Jews. Was the relationship of the Galatians to their northern neighbours such that Paul renounced the further journey into Bithynia (ἐνέκοψεν ἡμᾶς ὁ Σατανᾶς [I Thess. **2**.18] would be his assessment of such a situation)? It would be one possible way in which we would conceive of a reason for the hindering of a mission in Bithynia.

38

ACTS 16:9f.

THE VISION IN TROAS

[9] And a vision appeared to Paul in the night: a Macedonian standing there beseeching him and saying: 'Come over to Macedonia and help us!' [10] And when he had seen the vision, we sought immediately to go to Macedonia, concluding that God had called us to preach the gospel to them.

Bibliography:

James A. Blaisdell: 'The Authorship of the "we" sections of the Book of Acts', *HTR* 13 (1920), 136–58, esp. 157; William A. McDonald, 'Archaeology and St. Paul's Journeys in Greek Lands', *The Biblical Archaeologist* 3 (1940), 18–24; H. J. Cadbury, '"We" and "I" Passages in Luke/Acts', *NTS* 3 (1957), 128–32; see § 27; E. Haenchen, 'Das "wir" in d. Apg. usw.', *Gott u. Mensch* (1965), 227–64.

VERSE 9: For ὅραμα cf. *ThWb* V, 350f.[1] A vision[2] appeared to Paul, namely a Macedonian man[3] stood there, besought him and said, 'Come over to Macedonia and help us!' The possible psychological conditioning behind the vision—Paul and his companions probably engaged in lively discussion of the question whether they should go over to Macedonia—did not lie within Luke's horizon. 'The Macedonian represents his country and his people': Loisy (627).

[1] The attempt of W. Michaelis (*Die Erscheinungen des Auferstandenen*, 1944, 110 and *ThWb* V, 351, 1–8) to suppress the visual aspect in favour of verbal revelation is in our opinion misguided. He might as well eliminate the visual aspect from ὅραμα altogether. The sentence, 'It is clear that ὅραμα and in connection with it also ὤφθη 16.9 and εἶδεν 16.10 could refer to a purely verbal revelation' altogether distorts the true relationships. The appearance of the Macedonian, who was probably recognizable by his clothing (so Michaelis) cannot be dismissed without making the words 'Come over to Macedonia and help us!' uncertain as to their sense. We may not use this passage as proof of the alleged possibility that in a ὅραμα, ὀφθῆναι or ἰδεῖν there is nothing to be seen! Paul sees (v. 9) the Macedonian standing there!

[2] It is not actually said that Paul was asleep, but διὰ νυκτός suggests it.

[3] How the man was recognized as Macedonian is not stated. Scholars have thought of his language, but also of his clothing. Loisy however considers this a false question: Paul 'dreamed of a Macedonian; the dream furnished him at one and the same time with the picture of the man and his identity' (627).

VERSE 10: The logical connection between ὡς . . . εἶδεν, εὐθέως κτλ. is certainly clear. D however has made it even more lucid: 'Being awake he now told us the dream and we recognized . . .'. ἐζητήσαμεν κτλ.: it is a question of finding a ship to travel to Macedonia. With ἐζητήσαμεν the 'we' appears for the first time (but see **11**.28!) and confronts the commentator with very difficult questions.

The positive summons to Paul to go to Macedonia shows the reader that the proscriptions of the mission in vv. 6 and 7 are now revealed to have been the gracious guidance of the Lord.

A long list of investigators has concluded from this passage that Luke the physician met Paul in Troas. Overbeck (255) could already adduce Kuinoel, Olshausen, Meyer, Bisping, Neander, Lekebusch and Baumgarten, and this list can be continued with such well-known names as Renan, B. Weiss, H. J. Holtzmann, Ramsay, Knopf, Schlatter, W. Michaelis, Beyer, Bauernfeind and Bruce. Sometimes it has even been contended that one might draw out from the text still more about this event. B. Weiss (*Einl.*[2], 147) considers it possible that the aftermath of the sickness which occurred in Galatia occasioned Paul's acquaintance with Luke. Ramsay (*St. Paul*,[7] 205) was convinced that Paul sought out the physician Luke resident in Troas, where he enjoyed a good reputation. Schlatter thinks it probable that the physician came to the Apostle: 'A physician could easily have been drawn to him and brought to the faith by the manner in which Paul dealt with the sick in power and in faith' (*Erläut.* 4, 201). The seductive prospect of learning yet more from the text has winged fantasy even further. Ramsay deduced from the words ἀνήρ τις (Latin: *quidam*) in **16**.9 (in reality what appears here is of course ἀνὴρ Μακεδών τις) that the only Macedonian known to Paul, namely Luke, was the man Paul saw in the vision (202). Renan felt he could recognize even more clearly the psychological threads of the event: Luke sought 'to persuade Paul of the favourable prospects for missionary effort in Macedonia. His words made a strong impression upon the Apostle', who now in the dream experienced the Macedonian's cry for help' (*St. Paul*, 79, [vol. 3 of 7-vol. series, London 1887–9]). Even Dibelius has not shrunk from a similar conjecture (*Studies* 210 n 10; Dibelius-Kümmel, *Paulus* 70; ET), although he does not fail to note how rationalistic it appears.

This blissful certainty that the text discloses to us not only the deeds of the various *dramatis personae* but also the subconscious feelings inspiring their decisions has not motivated all scholars. Even the foundation for this construction defended by the *communis opinio* does not stand so firm as appears at first sight. 'When he had seen the vision we sought at once to leave for Macedonia, since we concluded that God had called us to bring the good news to them.' Can a novice who has only just joined the missionary group and possibly even the Christian faith speak in this way? So de Wette posed the question (256). Does such a manner of expression not fit much

R

better in the mouth of Timothy, who had already travelled with Paul a good while, than in the mouth of Luke? But it did not stop at this doubt of de Wette's. Is it permissible at all to conclude, simply because the first 'we' appears here, that the speaker has only met Paul in Troas? Luke is—so Loisy calls to mind (630)—according to tradition an Antiochian. Should he not already have accompanied the Apostle from Antioch? W. L. Knox (52) also conjectured that the 'we' source begins before **16**.10, and Schlatter (201) like Bauernfeind (8) held this possibility open. But do we actually have the right to speak of a 'we' source and to confine it to those parts in which the 'we' appears? Overbeck (256) gave a negative answer: the author of Acts here for the first time has taken up the diary of a companion of Paul 'to mark the significance of the moment and to identify himself with the narrator', while in other parts it did not agree with his picture of Paul. Dibelius has combated the idea of a 'we' source from still another side: 'The much discussed "we", in which was discerned formerly, under the influence of modern historical thinking, the most primitive element of the travel narrative, was perhaps first inserted during the re-editing by Luke in order to make known his own part in Paul's journey' (*Studies* 104f.). The itinerary (which Dibelius also sees utilized) and the 'we' have, therefore, nothing to do with one another.

At this point, where the 'we' first appears, we cannot yet enter fully into all the questions raised. One thing, however, can already be clarified. Why have all the above-mentioned scholars maintained with such self-assurance, on the basis of the 'we' inserted here, that Luke attached himself to Paul in Troas? It is not the text alone which leads to this conclusion but beside it the ecclesiastical tradition about the author of Acts, the information in the Pauline epistles about Luke, and finally that 'preoccupation with sources' which— as Dibelius correctly saw—was such a temptation for a time plagued by historicism. Before we bring all these quantities into connection with the text, one other question should be answered: How must our passage have been understood by one of those readers for whom Acts was written? He knew from **15**.40 that Paul had departed on a mission with Silas, from **16**.3f. that he had also taken Timothy with him. That other persons had joined this group of three is nowhere stated or even indicated. The third person plural, in which **16**.8 recounts the arrival in Troas, still suggests only these three. If now directly after this the narrative suddenly employs the first person plural, then the ancient reader would naturally have thought: here one of these three men is introduced in the 'we' style. From **16**.9f. it is soon evident that the narrator cannot be Paul but must be either Silas or Timothy, whose attachment to the Pauline mission was previously depicted in some detail (**16**.3f.). Whether this assumption was true or not, the reader had no way of knowing. We too shall therefore return to this later. On the other hand, a further question must now be at least noted. Whoever may here have spoken in the 'we', the answer does not absolve us from the further question: What did the ancient reader understand by the 'we'? Did it say to him that now an eyewitness is speaking, or did it suggest also the assumption that the eyewitness was also the author of the book? Or finally was it possible for such a reader to have considered this 'we' as merely a stylistic device to bring the reader into closer touch with the events related? We do not want to forget these questions in what follows.

All these questions in fact presuppose a reflectiveness and literary sophistication which were foreign to most of Luke's readers. When they read the 'we' in **16**.10 they quite instinctively felt drawn into the fellowship of this missionary group and experienced its destiny as their own.

But the 'we' does still more. The vision, which takes up and crowns the twofold mention of the divine guidance in vv. 6 and 7, is proven to be reality by the missionaries' reaction to it, described in the 'we' style. We can therefore say that the 'we' has the same effect in this instance as the chorus of admiration confirming a miracle elsewhere. Whether or not the 'we' may also have had another purpose, in any case it serves here as a very forceful stylistic device, and interpretation ought not to neglect the fact.

39

ACTS 16:11–40
PHILIPPI

[11] Putting to sea from Troas we travelled direct to Samothrace and on the following day to Neapolis, [12] and from there to Philippi which is a city of the first part of Macedonia and a colony. We remained in this city some days. [13] And on the Sabbath we went outside the gate along the river where we supposed there was a place of prayer, and we sat down and spoke with the women who had gathered there. [14] And a woman by the name of Lydia, who was a dealer in purple from the city of Thyatira and a 'God-fearer', was listening. The Lord opened her heart so that she attended to what Paul said. [15] When she and her entire house were baptized, she asked: 'If you are convinced that I believe in the Lord, then come into my house and stay there!' And she constrained us to do it. [16] It happened as we went to the place of prayer that a slave girl who had a spirit of divination met us, who brought much gain to her owners by soothsaying. [17] This girl followed Paul and us and cried: 'These men are the servants of the most high God, who proclaim to you the way of salvation!' [18] And she did this for many days. But Paul was annoyed and turning (to her) spoke to the spirit: 'I command you in the name of Jesus Christ to come out of her!' And it went out in the same hour. [19] But when her owners saw that the hope of their gain had disappeared, they grabbed Paul and Silas, dragged them to the market place before the rulers [20] and brought them to the magistrates, saying: 'These men are throwing our city into alarm; they are Jews, [21] and they proclaim customs which we as Romans may not accept or practise.' [22] And the crowd likewise turned against them, and the magistrates had their clothes torn off and commanded that they be whipped. [23] After they had had them given many blows, they threw them into prison and charged the gaoler to guard them carefully. [24] He threw them, after he had received such a command, into the innermost cell and secured their feet in the stocks. [25] About midnight Paul and Silas prayed and sang a hymn to God. The prisoners were listening to them. [26] Suddenly a great earthquake occurred so that the foundations of the gaol were shaken. Immediately all doors were opened and everyone's bonds were loosened. [27] When the gaoler awoke and saw the doors of the gaol open, he drew his sword and was about to kill himself, thinking that the prisoners had escaped. [28] But Paul shouted to him in a

loud voice, 'Do not do yourself any harm, for we are all here!' ²⁹ Then he called for a light and ran in and fell down trembling before Paul and Silas, ³⁰ and after he had brought them out he said, 'Sirs, what must I do in order to be saved?' ³¹ And they said, 'Believe in the Lord Jesus, and you and your house will be saved.' ³² And they spoke to him the Word of God together with all in his house. ³³ And he took them with him that hour of the night and washed their lashes, and he was baptized directly with all his family, ³⁴ and led them up to his house and set before them a meal, and rejoiced with his entire household that he had believed in God. ³⁵ At daybreak the magistrates sent the lictors with the instruction, 'Let these men go!' ³⁶ The gaoler reported these words to Paul: 'The magistrates have sent word for you to be set free! So come out now and go in peace!' ³⁷ Paul, however, said to them, 'They have whipped us publicly without trial, though we are Romans, and thrown us in prison, and now they want to send us secretly away? No, they shall come and lead us forth!' ³⁸ The lictors reported these words to the magistrates. They grew afraid when they heard that they were Romans, ³⁹ and they came and apologized, gave them good words, and led them out and asked them to leave the city. ⁴⁰ And they left the gaol and went to Lydia and saw and exhorted the brethren, then departed from there.

Bibliography:

S. Lönberg, 'En Dionysosmyt i Acta Apostolorum', *Eranos*, Acta Philol. Suec. vol. 24, Gotoburgi 1926, 73–80; Cadbury 272f., see § 30; Dornseiff, 1936, 138, see § 1; P. H. Menoud, 1952, 26f., see § 7; Kragerud, 1955, 254f., see § 29. W. P. Arndt, 'A Note concerning the Text and the Meaning of Acts **16**.12', *Concordia Theol. Monthly* 16, 1945, 697ff.; W. Rees, 'St. Paul's Visit to Philippi (Acts 16)', *Scripture* 7 (1955), 99–105; E. Zeller, 'Eine griechische Parallele zu der Erzählung AG **16**.19f.', *ZwissTheol.* 8 (1865), 103–8; W. K. L. Clarke, 'Parallels between Acts and the Testament of Joseph', *JTS* 15 (1913–14), 598ff.; W. Mallinckrodt, 'Het wij-bericht in de Handelingen etc.', *Geloov en frijheid* 35 (1901), 439–505; T. A. Burke, 'The "We" Sections of the Book of Acts' (Diss.), The Divinity School, University of Chicago 1930; Conzelmann 90–94; G. Schille, *Anfänge der Kirche* (1966), 43–53; A. Suhl, 'Paulus u. seine Briefe. Ein Beitrag zur paulin. Chronologie' (diss., unpublished).

VERSE 11: ἀναχθέντες: see above on **13**.13. εὐθυδρομέω = to travel a direct course,¹ as in **21**.1. The island of Samothrace lies halfway between Troas and Neapolis. They drop anchor at night as on the voyage in chapter 20f.

---

¹ With the freight or passenger ships of the time crossing was possible only in limited measure. One had to take full advantage of the land and sea winds and the currents, and often reckon with detours into the bargain (**18**.21f.!). Here the wind conditions were evidently for once especially favourable.

VERSE 12: Neapolis (today Kavalla): harbour city of Philippi.[1] κολωνία:[2] Augustus had resettled here the former supporters of Antony from Italy. πρωτη[3] τῆς will be a dittograph for πρωτης (cf. *Beg.* IV 167–90; III 153–5): a city in the first part of Macedonia.[4] ἡμέρας τινάς appears at first to describe the entire sojourn, but really denotes

VERSE 13 the time between the arrival and the first Sabbath. ἔξω . . . ποταμόν: the Gangites is about 1¼ miles distant. ἐνομίζομεν:[5] if the missionaries had resided with Jews, they would have known the way. προσευχή: either = συναγωγή, which Luke always employs elsewhere (usage of the source?) or = prayer (so Bruce 314). The rabbi sits while teaching,[6] but do the Christian missionaries take over the teacher's position one after the other? Or does Luke want to say that the missionaries sit down[7] at the place appointed for prayer and engage the women, apparently gathered there alone, in a conversation that turns at once to the Christian message?

VERSE 14: Λυδία becomes a personal name[8] through ὀνόματι. πορφυρό-πωλις:[9] purple materials were a markedly luxury item for rich people; Lydia will have been wealthy herself. The fact that she is not mentioned in Philippians gave rise to Zahn's conjectures (see note 8). σεβομένη κτλ: either 'a godly woman' or (more probably) 'belonging to the special class of non-Jewish synagogue worshippers' (*Beg.* V 87). ἤκουεν indicates (imperf.!)

---

[1] The full name of the city was Colonia Julia Augusta Philippensis.

[2] Its citizens possessed *libertas* (city self-government), *immunitas* (freedom from taxes and tariffs), *ius Italicum* (they had the same rights as the citizens in an Italian city): *Beg.* IV 189f., cf. von Premerstein, Pauly-Wiss. X, 1919, art. *ius Italicum*, 1238–53; Kornemann, Pauly-Wiss. IV, 1901, art. *coloniae*, 511–88; Joachim Marquardt, *Römische Staatsverwaltung* I, 2nd edn., 1881, 86ff., 118ff.

[3] D reads ἥτις ἐστὶν κεφαλὴ τῆς Μακεδονίας and so interprets πρώτη falsely as 'capital city' (Amphipolis was really the capital). Zahn's defence of this text 'more than one country has had more than one capital city' (568) shows his blind prejudice for the D text.—πρώτη was also an honourable title of cities, but not of Roman colonies: *Beg.* IV 188.

[4] Beyer's rendering 'the first city of its region in Macedonia' (100f.) is linguistically just as impossible as Wendt's (245) 'the first city of the region entered' which Bauernfeind (206) and similarly Schlatter (201) accept.—Aemilius Paulus had divided Macedonia into four completely separate zones in 167 B.C. in order to prevent a general revolt of the country against Rome.

[5] ℵ reads ἐνομίζομεν προσευχὴν εἶναι, E ℵ ἐνομίζετο (it was customary) προσευχὴ εἶναι. D represents the Latin *videbatur* with ἐδόκει. That synagogues usually stood near water is not proven; Bill. II 742 knows no rabbinical proof for this. *Beg.* IV 191: 'The author describes a local . . . usage.' Cf. *ThWb* VI 602f.

[6] Lk. 4.20, cf. also 5.3; Mk. 9.35; Mt. 5.1 and 26.55.

[7] This does not necessarily presuppose a building.

[8] This is frequently found in Horace, e.g. Odes I 8, 13 and 25. Since there courtesans are meant, but Lydia here is an honourable woman, Zahn conjectures that she was called 'the Lydian' to distinguish her from other merchants of purple (Thyatira lay in Lydia); actually her name was either Εὐοδία or Συντύχη (Phil. 4.2)! The other name Zahn reserves (582) for the wife of the gaoler who is the Clement of Phil. 4.3! Renan (I. 88) on the other hand concludes from γνήσιε σύζυγε (Phil. 4.3) that Paul married Lydia!

[9] The guild of purple dyers in Thessalonica erected a stele with an inscription honouring a certain Menippus from Thyatira. Cf. Wikenhauser, *Geschichtswert* § 69, p. 410f. Schille, *TLZ* 84 (1959), 171 has Lydia remain in Thyatira.

a repeated encounter in which finally 'the Lord opened her heart'.[1] προσέχειν: as in 8.6 = to believe. In spite of the ἐλαλοῦμεν the conversion is attributed to Paul.

VERSE 15: ὡς κτλ.: the narrative jumps quickly over the intervening steps. εἰ κεκρίκατε κτλ.:[2] oriental politeness; Lydia is already recognized as a Christian through her baptism. παρεβιάσατο ἡμᾶς (Gen. 33.11 LXX): the missionaries could not turn down her offer.[3] So the mission in Philippi now possessed a strong centre, as v. 40 confirms.

VERSE 16 goes back to the movement of the missionaries described in v. 13. The going to the προσευχή, which makes sense only on the Sabbath, is now strictly superfluous. The slave girl had a πνεῦμα Πύθωνα, a spirit of divination,[4] whose prophesying brought her owners[5] great profit (ἐργασία as in 19.24).

VERSE 17 καὶ ἡμῖν: with this the 'we' disappears until 20.5.[6] The screaming of the possessed girl recalls the shouting demons in the gospels;[7] except that the demon of our passage, where he is not threatened, does not accuse but rather announces the true character of the foreign preacher in a way understandable for Gentiles.[8]

VERSE 18: πολλὰς ἡμέρας: the scene is so set by Luke that immediately after the casting out of the demon Paul is dragged before the authorities. Accordingly Paul cannot silence the demon on the girl's first outcry. The advantage of this arrangement for the author is that it makes Paul's reaction even more intelligible—he was annoyed by the ceaseless shouts.[9] Moreover the demon, aware of the supernatural reality, now expressly attests the true meaning of the Christian mission.[10] Exorcism in the name of Jesus is immediately

---

[1] Lk. 24.45 and II Macc. 1.4.

[2] πιστός with dative: I Macc. 7.8.

[3] They had probably up to this time lived in an inn at their own expense.

[4] Luke calls the soothsaying demon 'Python', by way of explanation, in apposition to the biblical word πνεῦμα (Bl.-Debr. § 242); πνεῦμα Πύθωνος 𝔓⁴⁵ ℵ is a simplification. Cf. Wikenhauser, *Geschichtswert* 401–7; W. Foerster, *ThWb* VI, s.v. Πύθων. The slave girl is to be thought of neither as an impostor nor as sick (Beyer 100f.); she is regarded by others and by herself as possessed by a demon which (by her ventriloquism—Πύθων is equated in antiquity with ἐγγαστρίμυθος) speaks through her.

[5] According to *Beg.* IV 192 perhaps only the owner and his wife. But these two could scarcely have dragged Paul and Silas before the authorities; this scene presupposes the presence of some men.

[6] Cf. p. 36.

[7] Mk. 1.24, 3.11, 5.7; Lk. 4.34, 41 and 8.28. In Acts 16.17 and Mk. 5.7 Jesus is called the 'Son of the Most High God', since the scene is set in Gentile territory.

[8] Our passage has nothing to do with the syncretistic divinity Θεὸς ὕψιστος (bibliography: see Bauer, *Wb* 1681).

[9] We should not speak of a 'healing'—so Beyer 101. Luke neither considered the slave girl sick nor did the thought of help enter as a motive for the act. Modern psychology has no place here.

[10] According to Wendt 246 Paul was 'annoyed by the cry of the soothsayer because the sacred task in which he was engaged should not be witnessed to by an unclean spirit.' But then Paul should not have permitted the demon to carry on for those many days.

effective; the spirit leaves at once.[1] So ends the demon story utilized by Luke.

VERSE 19: The owners of the slave girl, angered by the loss of their profit,[2] grabbed Paul and Silas.[3] ἀγορά: here perhaps 'court' rather than 'market' (*Beg.* IV 194). ἄρχοντες: 'the authorities'; στρατηγοί (=praetors) is the exact title.[4]

VERSE 20: They are the *duumviri*, who exercised jurisdiction in Roman colonial cities. Their lictors (ῥαβδοῦχοι v. 35) carried only bundles of rods without axes in them. The plaintiff voiced the complaint of disturbing the peace (ἐκταράσσουσιν τὴν πόλιν), since they were disturbing the law and order of the place.[5]

VERSE 21: The ἔθη unacceptable to the Romans cannot be more closely defined.[6] A travel narrative seems to lie in the background in verse 20f., since Luke would not produce any such accusation on his own.

VERSE 22: The crowd is anti-semitic. The authorities had the clothes of both criminals torn off[7] and had them whipped (cf. II Cor. **11**.25). For the question why the Roman right of citizenship did not take effect, see the general discussion.

VERSE 23: Paul speaks in I Thess. **2**.2 of suffering and maltreatment.— ἐπιθέντες ἔβαλον: naturally through the police. After flogging comes incarceration: Mommsen, *ZNW* 2 (1901), 90. The fact that the gaoler is to guard them securely already prepares for the action which follows.

VERSE 24 ὅς: see above on **1**.3. In line with the command both are put in the innermost[8] cell (v. 29). In addition their feet are secured in the stocks.

---

[1] For αὐτῇ τῇ ὥρᾳ see Jeremias, *ZNW* 42 (1949), 217 n. 6.

[2] ἐξῆλθεν is intentionally repeated.

[3] What becomes of Timothy and the narrator who speaks in the 'we' is not told. Loisy (638) conjectures that in reality Paul alone had to suffer—the 'we' in I Thess. **2**.2 means indeed only him. But what we have here is not a realistic narrative: how are we to imagine the slave girl continually accompanied by her masters to the spot, whenever the missionaries go out, and proceeding together with her masters after Paul and Silas? And yet the narrative suggests just that—if one interprets it realistically. Only under these conditions could the masters immediately recognize that the spirit had left her and that Paul was to blame for it.

[4] This does not deny what Loisy (637) maintains: that here we may note the trace of re-editing.

[5] That the driving out of a spirit is not a legally punishable offence is clear. Consequently it seems as if the accusation is a pretence by the owners, who only want to take revenge on Paul. But probably this accusation was actually raised against Paul (against Wendt 247) and indeed against his missionary endeavours. Judaism (from which Christianity is here not yet distinguished) is certainly as it were a *religio licita*, but it is not allowed to make proselytes among Romans, and Philippi is a Roman *colonia*: *Beg.* IV 195. Loisy correctly remarks (639) that here a fairly long missionary effort in Philippi is presupposed.

[6] Paul certainly did not preach circumcision. But it could have been, for example, the custom of the φίλημα ἅγιον at the Lord's Supper which gave the semblance of an immoral oriental cult.

[7] There is no question here of the authorities tearing their own clothes, after the Jewish fashion, as a symbol of horror (against Ramsay, *St. Paul*, 217).

[8] The comparative takes the place of the superlative: *Beg.* IV, 196. Popular narrative loves the extreme.

So the loneliness and suffering of the two men came to a height.

VERSE 25: About midnight[1] they sing a hymn of prayer.[2] That the other prisoners heard them proves to the reader that the earthquake is God's answer.[3]

VERSE 26: The earthquake which shook the[4] foundations of the gaol[5] seems to have affected only this building. It is not unusual that doors should spring open but that the prisoners' fetters should fall away is possible only in a miracle. Both occurrences appear in Euripides' *Bacchae* 455ff.[6]

VERSE 27: That the open doors shocked the gaoler is conceivable (but in cases of an act of God he was not responsible!).[7] That the official did not first look around to see who had escaped belongs to the logic of edifying narration and is not to be explained on psychological grounds.

VERSE 28: Paul sees, from his cell down below, that the gaoler will take his life,[8] and he stops him with a loud shout. The description of the event does not go beyond what was important for Luke and his readers, and so does not permit any realistic reconstruction.

VERSE 29: The gaoler calls for torches: it is midnight, cf. v. 25. The trembling of the man and his falling down before Paul and Silas prove that he considered them the mighty messengers of the godhead.[9]

VERSE 30: While he is leading them out,[10] he asks immediately, addressing them as 'χύριοι', about his eternal salvation.[11]

VERSE 31: The answer fits the question exactly. Included in the salvation

---

[1] Joseph prays at night to God in gaol, and the prayer is heard: *Test. Jos.* 9.

[2] For ὑμνεῖν see Mt. 26.30 parallel to Mk. 14.26; Hebr. 2.12. ὕμνοι Col. 3.16 parallel to Eph. 5.19. A closer affinity with our text is found in *Test. Jos* 8.5; Joseph has been whipped and thrown into prison. 'And when I was in bonds,' the Egyptian woman heard 'how I praised the Lord in the house of darkness and glorified my God with a joyous voice.' The correspondence lies in the fact that the suffering religious man praises God in gaol.

[3] Cf. in regard to what follows Otto Weinreich, *Gebet und Wunder*, 1929, 320ff., 326ff.

[4] σαλευθῆναι as in the parallel 4.31; see details there.

[5] Cf. in regard to the expression θεμέλια Ps. 82(81).5.

[6] 'The bonds loosened themselves from their feet and the bolted doors opened themselves without mortal hands.' Origen witnesses in *c. Cels.* II 34 to the belief prevalent in his time that magicians loosened fetters by their spells and opened doors. This feature of folk belief has contributed to the development of our story.

[7] *Digest.* XII 48,3 cited by Clemen, *Paulus* I, 260 n. 3.

[8] The attempts to figure out how Paul could have seen through the opened door into the lighted bedroom of the gaoler are both pathetic and comical in their lack of understanding. How Paul knows that no prisoners have fled, it were also better not to ask.

[9] According to Zahn 584 n. 4, he really threw himself down before them only in order to 'ascertain if their feet were free from the stocks'. If it had been an act of *proskynesis*, 'Luke would have expressed it clearly, and would not have let it pass without a word of restraint from the Apostle.' Here Zahn's dogmatic prejudice is obvious and forces him into misrepresentation of the text. See also on 28.6.

[10] D noted that the gaoler did not bother about the other prisoners who were also at liberty, and therefore inserted τοὺς λοιποὺς ἀσφαλισάμενος.

[11] Since this for Zahn comes too quickly, he interprets the question as 'uneasy consideration' of 'what he should now begin to do, in order to ward off any possible evil consequences of the shattering occurrence from his person.' The cry requires no answer,

is the entire οἶκος, family and servants. **11**.14 uses the same expression.

VERSE 32: The instruction for baptism is annexed to the admonition (the narrative here condenses events in the extreme). Where it took place (the cell is left in verse 30 and the courtyard is reached in verse 33) is a question on which Luke does not reflect.

VERSE 33: Now the gaoler—grammatically—becomes the subject of the narrative: he takes the missionaries with him, washes their backs, bleeding from the flogging, and is baptized along with his household—perhaps in a spring or fountain in the courtyard.[1]

VERSE 34: Then he leads them up into his house, sets before them a much needed meal[2] (it is towards 1.0 a.m.) and rejoices together with his household over the new faith. In the face of this happy outcome there is no thought of what the authorities will say about the prisoners' release.

VERSE 35: The authorities consider the flogging and a night in prison, together with expulsion, an adequate punishment and order the prisoners to be set free by the police.[3]

VERSE 36: The gaoler imparts the good news to Paul (Silas is a silent character). In the expression 'go in peace'[4] Luke takes the man's conversion into account.

VERSE 37: Paul appeals to the Roman right of citizenship (which, probably for the sake of simplicity, is also accorded to Silas) and demands restitution: no secret dismissal, but an honourable escort. It is at the same time implied that the public scourging was carried out without any investigation or proof of guilt. Luke makes Paul (again for the sake of simplicity) speak to the police, whom according to verse 36 he certainly did not see.[5]

VERSE 38: The authorities have a troubled conscience on account of their maltreatment of the 'Romans': cf. **22**.29.

VERSE 39: Paul's demands are met, but the expulsion still takes place.[6]

---

and presupposes only 'the sympathy of the person addressed with the embarrassment and irresolution of the questioner' (580). In this grotesque misinterpretation Zahn overlooks the fact that the man is not threatened by any evil consequences, since all the prisoners are still there. The reason for this most singular of all Zahn's explanations is suggested in p.497 n. 9.

[1] Zahn has the baptism—like Paul's own baptism once; see on **9**.18—take place in the gaoler's bathroom.

[2] This is the meaning of παρατίθεσθαι τράπεζαν.

[3] D saw here an unwarranted change in the attitude of the authorities and sought to introduce the recollection of the earthquake as a motive for this change, without noticing that the authorities knew nothing of the connection between the hymn of faith and the earthquake (v. 25f.).

[4] D has struck out these Christian words 'in peace' because Paul declines the order to leave in v. 37.

[5] B. Weiss, *Die Apg.* 205, incorrectly concludes from v. 37 that the gaoler brought the police to Paul.

[6] D was **not** satisfied with that: it makes many friends of the authorities come with them and assure them that they have now recognized the two missionaries as law-abiding people. D bases the banishment on fear of a new uprising.

VERSE 40: The authorities accompany them only out of the gaol. The departure from Lydia is at the same time departure from the congregation.[1] We hear nothing about Timothy until 17.14—Luke mentions only persons important for the narrative, otherwise he could not have accommodated so much material. And besides, the reader is not distracted from the important matters.

What does Luke have to say to his listeners with this passage? God has led Paul and his companions to a new mission field. In a surprisingly short sea voyage of two days (later—20.6—on the return journey five days will be required for the 156 miles) the harbour city of Philippi, Neapolis, is reached. Some eight miles distant to the north-west lies Philippi itself. But one must climb up a steep hill and then down again in order to come to the fertile plateau of Macedonia on which Philippi lay. Malaria is the main reason why there are only a few ruins standing there today.

In this city with its Italian colonists the missionaries are foreigners. They do not appear to have met any Jews of whom they could have made enquiries. So they wait until the Sabbath to walk out to the Gangites where they think there is a place of prayer, and find it. But only a few women come to pray. The foreign messengers are not discouraged. They speak to the women and deliver the good news of the Lord Jesus. God makes the Word take root in one of the women. Lydia is not Jewish by birth. In Thyatira, a centre for the manufacture of purple dye which lies south-east of Pergamum in Asia Minor in the Lydian district, she has grown up as a pagan child. Now she lives here as a well-to-do lady known as 'Lydia' or 'the Lydian'. She has joined the small Jewish congregation as a listener. Now she dares to cross over into the new community and lets herself be baptized. Her 'house', relatives and slaves, follows her. Her faith is linked with action. She will not tolerate that the missionaries should stay in just any quarters. They must move to her house, and living there they now assemble the brethren who are gradually won.

While the missionaries are going to the house of prayer, a slave girl follows them. She belongs to a syndicate which makes good earnings from her. For she is possessed by a spirit of divination. This spirit makes her now shout: 'These men are the servants of the most high God, who proclaim to you the way of salvation!' Not just once did this happen, but for many days. Finally it becomes too much for Paul, and he commands the spirit: 'In the name of Jesus Christ I command you: leave her!' And it did that same hour.

The spirit of divination is gone, and with it the profit. The owners take their revenge. They seize Paul and Silas, drag them to the market-place before the authorities and accuse them before the 'praetors'. They do not accuse them of driving out a spirit—such an accusation would not hold up in any

---

[1] D represents Paul and Silas as reporting the events at Lydia's house, not out of any historical interest, but as an edifying proof of what the Lord has done for them.

court—but they had spread forbidden Jewish propaganda among them, the Romans! The crowd take sides against the foreigners, the authorities in short order command whipping and have them both safely locked away in gaol. The mission is at an end.

It is not to be the gaoler's fault if they escape: he brings them into the innermost cell, chains them, and puts their feet in the stocks. Meanwhile, night has fallen. But Paul and Silas do not sleep. They begin to sing a hymn, and the other prisoners hear the two new inmates singing. Then the earth quakes. The foundations of the gaol shake, the doors spring open, the chains fall from the prisoners. The gaoler wakes up with a start, sees the doors open, and thinks the prisoners have fled. In despair, he is just about to plunge the sword into his breast when Paul's shout reaches him: 'Don't do yourself any harm! We are all here.' He calls for light, dashes into their cell and falls down before the men who apparently are in league with God, 'Sirs, what must I do that I may be saved?' 'You and your house believe in the Lord Jesus, and you will all be saved!' He and those who have followed him hear and believe in the good news. In the courtyard he washes the bleeding backs of the two men, and the same spring furnishes the water for baptism. God has allowed the imprisoned missionaries to continue their mission successfully. They are now taken up into the gaoler's home and given something to eat after all these hours. They are, however, no happier than the converted Gentile.

In the morning their release is ordered. Now, however, Paul appeals to the Roman right of citizenship. The authorities, who had Roman citizens whipped, and that without a trial, must come and apologize. Of course, a further stay in the place is not possible. They can only go to Lydia, report what God has done for them, and admonish them to steadfastness. Then Philippi lies behind them.

The report must have sounded something like this to Luke's reader. From a happy beginning it leads into a situation of hopeless distress and danger. But God proves stronger than the afflictions and uses them to serve his own purposes—how could one then despair? Luke has recounted this narrative that his readers might gather strength from it.

The critical research of the nineteenth century was no longer disposed to take this story simply and credulously as it stands. It asked what actually happened and tested all the facts for their probability and inner congruity. Verses 25–34 particularly gave offence to scholars like Gfrörer, Overbeck, B. Weiss, Spitta, Jüngst, Hilgenfeld, H. J. Holtzmann and Clemen.

As in 4.31 the place where the congregation prays trembles ($\dot{\epsilon}\sigma\alpha\lambda\epsilon\dot{\upsilon}\theta\eta$) as a sign of the divine response, so here the foundations of the gaol shake ($\sigma\alpha\lambda\epsilon\upsilon\theta\tilde{\eta}\nu\alpha\iota$ v. 26). The fact that in this earthquake not only do all the doors open but the chains also fall off by themselves does not strengthen the credibility of the narrative. Even if the earthquake had loosened the fastenings of the chains in the wall, the prisoners would still not have been freed from the chains as is here clearly supposed. But the inconceivability continues. A gaoler who, seeing the doors open in an earthquake, at once wants to take his life, without so much as a glance at the cells, is a very unlikely sort of person. As if that were not enough, Paul in his cell knows what the gaoler is about to do—how? And how does the δεσμοφύλαξ know who is calling to him from the cell (even if such a shout were audible in his bedroom)? Above all, how does he know that the earthquake is the answer to Paul and Silas' hymn? To the reader it is obvious, but the gaoler was asleep (v. 27—he was the only one in the whole gaol who slept, remarks Wellhausen (32) with his usual sarcasm). One can certainly come to the aid of Luke with conjectures about how the gaps should be filled in: the gaoler might have heard something of the Christian preaching, enough even, that he and his household—who have all come with him into Paul's cell—might be baptized after some brief instruction—'as if an interpreter of Acts could hope to restore the connection of the events before us, which Acts itself does not divulge and about which we otherwise have absolutely no information! As if the difficulty which the interpreter has in translating the events related into reality, this constant necessity for groping in the air in the attempt to recover the natural sequence of what is presumed to have happened, did not itself rather disclose the unhistorical character of the narrative!' (Overbeck 265). In addition there is the fact that in the sequel the earthquake plays no further role. The misguided attempt of D to refer back to it shows how difficult it had become: how should the στρατηγοί know that the earthquake had been sent to oblige Paul and Silas? In short, the whole episode is such a nest of improbabilities that it must be struck out as unhistorical. Its absence does not produce any gap whatever.

One can indeed go further and point to particular features of the narrative which seem to be typical. Celsus already recalled the *Bacchae* of Euripides (443–8) where it is reported that the Bacchae, who were chained in the state prison, were freed by calling on the god Bromios: 'The chains dropped off their feet by themselves and the bolts on the doors were opened without mortal hands.' Origen himself attests the belief current in his time that γόητές τινες ἐπῳδαῖς δεσμοὺς λύουσιν καὶ θύρας ἀνοίγουσιν (*c. Cels.* II 34). Concerning the earthquake as a sign of God's granting a prayer we have already spoken (ancient documentary evidences for the quaking of the place of prayer are presented above in reference to 4.31). Singing is such a frequent feature in the hagiographical narratives that Reitzenstein speaks of a 'literary convention' (*Hellenistische Wundererzählungen*, 1906, 121).

But precisely when we take note of these various motifs the distinctiveness of our narrative appears: here is depicted no escape from gaol (therefore the appeal to chapters 5 and 12 is in vain). The free prisoners—the others as well as Paul and Silas!—remain quietly in their cells. The only purpose of the miracle is the conversion of the δεσμοφύλαξ. It follows, therefore, that our story cannot have circulated as an isolated independent narrative. It has meaning only in the context of the whole presentation. It is not a question of the adoption of Hellenistic material, but the story is told with the methods of Hellenistic narrative technique.

So we come to a new type of analysis as applied to Acts especially through the efforts of Dibelius: form-criticism. From this point of view our text is made up of something like this:

A first group of verses extends from vv. 11–15. They may be classified as a travel narrative, briefly indicating the stops, the duration of the journey, the name of the host and the important events in the founding of the congregation. The way in which the status of the colony of Philippi and the smallness of the Jewish community are spoken about reveals exact knowledge of the conditions. Nor does the story of Lydia give any cause to suspect that here pious imagination has simply conjured up a romance. The 'we' which dominates in this text can therefore be understood without difficulty as the eyewitness account of the reporter.

Secondly, vv. 16–18 form a literary unit of another sort. They narrate the exorcism of a demon which strongly reminds one of such stories as Mk. **1**.23ff. and **5**.1ff. In Mark, as here, the spirit by whom the person concerned is possessed reveals the real nature of Jesus and his messengers, and is on that account driven out. Of course over against this correspondence there are also some salient differences. The demons feel themselves threatened by Jesus and so set themselves to resist him. That is not the case here. Our narrative has the demon from its supernatural knowledge cry out the truth about Paul and Silas, without any hostile intent. It is therefore not immediately silenced, but only when, after a long while, it becomes annoying to Paul. (To import into the text the fantasies concerning the alleged evil intentions of Apollo, represented by the *python* [A. Abt in Wikenhauser, taken over and developed by Bauernfeind 209], is to falsify its character). The story shows the reader two things: first, that the truth of the gospel has been confirmed also by the supernatural acknowledgement of the spirit-world, and second, that Paul through the exorcism in the name of Jesus is plainly superior to the spirits. This narrative is dovetailed into the foregoing verses through the 'we' in 16f. The sentence 16b concerning the κύριοι and their ἐργασία links it with what follows. Both connections are not above suspicion, as will become apparent.

With verse 19 we step out of the world of miracle into everyday reality. Only by juxtaposition does the reporter indicate that the accusation against Paul and Silas is unjustly raised—the true motive is the wounded egoism of the deprived owners. Why the crowd sided against Paul and Silas is not further explained; it is just the crowd . . . It is not said that the authorities took measures against the accused under pressure from the street—an investigation at which Paul could appeal to the Roman right of citizenship simply does not take place. The whole could be a continuation of the narrative of 11-15, of course extensively re-worked. The exact wording cannot be ascertained either here or there.

Concerning the fourth section, vv. 25-34, we have already spoken. The miracle—which recalls various motifs of the miracle-literature—serves first to attest the rescuing power of God; it is not, however, fully utilized. But above all, it serves for the conversion of the gaoler and his 'house'. Thereby it fulfils a special purpose in the context of the whole narrative. Its omission would—and here the opinions of earlier critics must be held in check—leave a real gap. It is the miracle that discloses the true meaning of the maltreatment and imprisonment of Paul and Silas. The suffering of a Christian is not in vain, but rather is immediately justified for the reader. It proves itself forthwith to be a gracious dispensation. What is more, the suffering is both cut short and tempered. One might say that the *theologia crucis* begins to change into a *theologia gloriae*.

There is no connection between vv. 34 and 35. What recalls the conversion of the δεσμοφύλαξ in the fifth section, vv. 35-40, is only the formula πορεύεσθε ἐν εἰρήνῃ. The earthquake is forgotten. Instead, another theme is taken up from vv. 19-24: the injustice of the authorities and their proceedings. Previously they were thoughtless and overweening, now they are distressed and humble. That it was nevertheless a question of expulsion Mommsen quite correctly held, and expulsion it remains. The reason D was the first to seek to clarify, by alluding to the frame of mind of the people. Actually the investigation of Paul's case should now have been taken up afresh and legally conducted. But no thought of this is entertained.

Here the author has pieced together many different materials into a unified narrative. In the process he skilfully passes over from the 'we' of an eyewitness report to the 'he' style of ordinary narration: in v. 16 the 'we' still includes Paul and his companions; in v. 17 Paul is distinguished from the 'we' (they 'followed Paul and us'), and from v. 18 on it speaks only of Paul. This technique—it is also found in **21**.7ff.—allows Luke here to place the story of the demon as well under the authenticity of the 'we'. According to the source theory indicated in § 6 of the Introduction (see above pp. 86f.), Luke probably received the information concerning Philippi—directly or indirectly—from an eyewitness of the Pauline mission. Luke gives the reader to understand this valuable source of his material through the fact that he reports the history of the mission in Philippi whenever possible in the 'we' style. He may have received not only information about the founding of the community and the expulsion of the Apostle, but also stories which circulated about Paul in Philippi: the exorcism of a demon and the conversion of the gaoler by Paul. So far as the latter is concerned, it is perfectly possible that the gaoler who locked up Paul and Silas for a night himself later became a Christian, and that it was then related that Paul himself had converted him.

Luke has reported this story with the full array of Hellenistic narrative art, so that the glory of Paul beams brightly.

I Thess. **2**.2 supports this view of things. According to this passage Paul has experienced great difficulties in Philippi: προπαθόντες καὶ ὑβρισθέντες . . . ἐν Φιλίπποις corresponds exactly to **16**.19–24 and **16**.35–40, aside from the marks of Paul's rehabilitation (that a miraculous occurrence in the style of **16**.25–34 is incompatible with the tone of I Thess. **2**.2 is really self-evident). But thereby arose a problem very pressing for Luke. He depicts the Roman authorities elsewhere as just, tolerant, even friendly to Christians. But in the Roman colony of Philippi the Pauline mission came into severe conflict with them: the two Christian missionaries are punished—on account of forbidden Jewish propaganda—with lashing, prison and banishment. This painful impression Luke has erased as far as possible by coupling the accounts he has received with an indirect apology for his hero: the story of the exorcism of the spirit of divination allowed him to interpret mean self-interest as the motive for the accusation against Paul and so to take away the weight of the charge. It will be for this reason that he included the girl's κύριοι—had Paul really proved himself a great exorcizer of demons, then the slave girl's masters would have taken care not to quarrel with him! According to **16**.22f. a sentence in line with the principles of law was given and executed. During this proceeding it was entirely possible—to judge from Acts **22**.25—for Paul and Silas to call out to the lictor the *civis Romanus sum*. But if Paul had transgressed the prevailing law with his mission among the Roman colonists (cf. Mommsen, *ZNW* 2 (1901), 89f.), it was wise for him not to appeal to his Roman right of citizenship. It would indeed have spared him from the lashing, but the appeal would have entangled him in a protracted trial with an uncertain outcome, and during this time the possibility for a mission would be as good as gone. Hence his subsequent complaint (along with the apology of the authorities) is probably Luke's incorrect deduction from **25**.11.

The author's freedom, which we encounter here, is strange to the modern reader. But it did not occur to any of the great Roman historians simply to say 'how it actually happened'. They all wanted to inform, influence and motivate. Luke would not have broken the tradition of great Roman historical writing (how far he knew it and used it as a model is another question) when he narrated the history of the mission in Philippi in his own fashion. The difference between *facta* and *ficta* has not been the same in all ages.

40
ACTS 17:1–15
THESSALONICA AND BEROEA

[1] They travelled by way of Amphipolis and Apollonia and came to Thessalonica, where there was a synagogue of the Jews. [2] And Paul went in to them, as was his custom, and on three Sabbaths preached to them beginning from scripture, explaining and proving that the Messiah must suffer and rise again from the dead, and that this Jesus 'whom I proclaim' is the Messiah. [4] And some of them let themselves be convinced and joined Paul and Silas, and a great many of the godfearing Greeks and not a few of the noble women. [5] But the Jews became jealous, and they took some depraved men from the rabble and stirred up a riot and brought the city into an uproar. They advanced on Jason's house and sought to bring them out to the crowd. [6] And when they did not find them, they dragged Jason and some of the brethren to the city authorities, shouting, 'These people are bringing the entire empire into an uproar, and now they have come here, and Jason is sheltering them. [7] And all these men act in opposition to the decrees of Caesar, saying that there is another who is king, Jesus!' [8] And they brought the people into tumult, and the city authorities, when they heard this, and when they had taken surety from Jason and the others, let them go free. [10] But the brethren immediately, during the night, sent Paul and Silas to Beroea, and when they arrived they went into the synagogue of the Jews. [11] These Jews were more fair than those in Thessalonica. They received the word with all eagerness and searched daily in the scriptures to see if it were so. [12] Many of them became believers and not a few of the noble women and men. [13] But when the Jews in Thessalonica learned that the Word of God was being preached by Paul in Beroea also, they came and stirred up and incited the crowds there too. [14] Then the brethren at once sent Paul away to go to the sea, and Silas and Timothy remained there. [15] Those who conducted Paul brought him as far as Athens, and when they had received instructions for Silas and Timothy to come to him as quickly as possible, they went away.

Bibliography:

H. U. W. Stanton, 'Turned the world upside down', *Exp.Tim.* 44 (1932–3), 526f. (on 17.6); *Beg.* IV 201–8; Renié 238–42; H. J. Cadbury, *The Book of Acts in History*, 1955, 40f., 61f., 86; Kragerud (1955), 255f., see § 29; Williams,

1957, 197–9; G. Stählin (1962), 233–7; J. Dupont, *The Sources of Acts*, 1964, 152, 154; G. Schille, 1966, 76, 79ff., 95ff.

VERSE 1: διοδεύσαντες: to journey through—with or without a mission stopover.[1] The following verses indicate the second meaning: the mention of the Jewish synagogue[2] in Thessalonica seems to suggest that there was no such synagogue in Amphipolis[3] and in Apollonia.[4] Thessalonica, which was reached on the Via Egnatia, the great main highway to the west, was the capital city of the second district of the Roman province of Macedonia, and also the residence of the Proconsul, although a 'free city' with its own council and popular assembly. Five or six 'city heads' (Dobschütz, *Thessalonicher-Briefe*, 1909, 10) functioned as the magistracy to which the task of administration and police protection fell. There was a large Jewish community.[5]

VERSE 2f. κατὰ ... εἰσῆλθεν: colloquial Greek[6] and on that account 'improved' by D. That Paul actually sought out the synagogues at hand in order to get in touch with the σεβόμενοι should not have been contested. Only the idea that on principle he first offered salvation to the Jews and only

[1] Dobschütz 9 inclines toward the first conception, appealing to διοδεύω Luke 8.1, διέρχομαι Acts 9.32, 13.6, 16.8, 18.23 and διαπορεύομαι 16.4. But in Lk. 8.1; Acts 9.32, 16.4 and 18.23 accounts of missionary efforts are added. Where they are lacking we have no reason to supply them.—It would be thoroughly understandable if Paul after the difficult conflict in Philippi had first resumed his missionary efforts in a more distant place where that incident would not be so quickly known. At the same time Thessalonica because of its strong Jewish community and synagogue offered better missionary conditions than the Roman colony of Philippi.—Why the plural 'communities of Macedonia' in II Cor. 8.1 is not wholly covered 'by Philippi and Thessalonica and finally also Beroea' (so Dobschütz 9) is not evident. The situation required a strong expression in II Cor. 8.1. The plural was actually justified if two or even three Christian communities existed in Macedonia.

[2] The reading ἡ συναγωγή offered by the later Mss. (cf. *Beg.* III 160) makes the synagogue of Thessalonica the only one in the entire country as far as Amphipolis (so Zahn 586f. also presents the situation). That may possibly be the intention of the author, but it is not necessarily a description of the actual situation. Did the Macedonian Jews really have to travel several days in order to be able to participate in a synagogue service? The older text in actual fact says only that there was a synagogue in Thessalonica.

[3] The old itineraries do not exactly agree in the distance (cf. Zahn 586, n. 17; Dobschütz 9 n. 1). We may reckon from Philippi to Amphipolis about 30 miles, from there to Apollonia about 29½ miles and from there to Thessalonica about 35 miles (similarly Loisy 650f.). *Beg.* IV 202 concludes from the distances, which are too great for a day's journey on foot, that Paul was in a position to hire horses for himself and his companions. It is probably closer to the facts that Amphipolis and Apollonia are mentioned only as points which were passed through on the journey and indicate its course, but not the goal of either the first or second day's journey.—Amphipolis lay on the Strymon (Struma), Apollonia between this and the Wardar. Cf. *TLZ* 1960, 250.

[4] D presents a mixed text—the καί before κατῆλθον can only be understood as the remains of the 'neutral text'.

[5] The very great community of Jews in Thessalonica (= Salonike) in modern times goes back to the Spanish Jews 'who fled there in the sixteenth century'; Dobschütz 10, n. 1.

[6] Cf. Radermacher[2], 215. Luke 4.16 is less striking because of the different word-order.

turned to the Gentiles when they refused it, is false. ἐπὶ σάββατα τρία: 'on three Sabbaths'[1] one after the other Paul is allowed to speak in the context of the synagogue service of worship[2] 'explaining[3] from the scripture and proving that the Messiah must suffer[4] and rise from the dead, and that the Messiah is Jesus, whom I proclaim to you.'[5] The doctrine of the death and resurrection of the Messiah Jesus was before Jewish-Christian hearers the most important.

VERSE 4: I Thess. does not mention this Jewish-Christian minority.[6] προσκληροῦσθαι (Bauer, *Wb* 1419): adhere to, attach. γυναικῶν τῶν πρώτων cf. **17**.12.[7] Luke likes to mention conversions from the upper classes. But it is strange that neither here nor in Beroea could these influential women avert the persecution of Christians.

VERSE 5: The Jews are understandably jealous of this missionary success, which damages their own mission (as in **13**.45). The rabble is apparently summoned to make the attacks upon the Christians appear like a popular movement. ὀχλοποιεῖν, only here,[8] 'to incite a revolt of the people'. Luke does not present anything particular about Jason[9] to his readers: with such a secondary character it is not worthwhile.[10] προάγειν πρὸς τὸν δῆμον: according to the tenor of the words one should think with Ramsay *(St. Paul* 228) of an assembly of the people. But according to the context δῆμος here will be a synonym for ὄχλος; the words then mean: to lead out to the (raging, demonstrating) crowd.

VERSE 6: Instead of the missing missionaries, the Christians, accidentally met, are accused, and for them the words in v. 6b do not really fit. πολιτάρχαι

---

[1] Not 'three weeks', as Schürer ('Die siebentägige Woche', *ZNW* 6, 1ff.), Preuschen 105 and Zahn 587 think (according to Zahn Paul had also to work at night in Thessalonica (I Thess. **2**.9), because he preached in the synagogue on weekdays as well). To be sure on one occasion, Lk. **18**.12, σάββατον means 'week', but otherwise it means the Sabbath: *Beg.* IV 202f.—Acts **16**.18 ἐπὶ πολλὰς ἡμέρας = 'on many days' as here ἐπὶ σάββατα τρία = 'on three Sabbaths'. Even if two services of worship had been held there weekly, they would not have filled up the 'weeks' in Thessalonica.

[2] διαλέγεσθαι (also **17**.17; **18**.4, 19; **19**.8f.; **20**.7, 9; **24**.12 and 25) as denoting discourse on doctrinal matters already shows the transition to the later meaning 'to preach'.

[3] Cf. Lk. **24**.32, 46.

[4] Cf. above on **1**.3; πάσχειν means death here as in Acts **3**.18, Lk. **24**.26, 46 (see also Acts **26**.23).

[5] Transition to direct speech as **1**.4 and **14**.22; **17**.3; **23**.22; **25**.5.

[6] According to Harnack, *SAB* (1910), 560ff., II Thess. was addressed to them.

[7] D understands this expression to mean 'wives of the first citizens', γυναῖκες τῶν πρώτων, and makes a distinction between Gentiles (Greeks) and God-fearers.

[8] However, we do find in Hippocrates ὄχλον ἐποίει (Bauer, *Wb* 1190).—According to Plut., *Aem. Paulus* 38, ἄνθρωποι ἀγοραῖοι are agitators.

[9] Jason was a common name in Thessaly as well as elsewhere, sometimes borne by Jews as a Greek name matching Joshua (= Jesus): *Beg.* IV 205. That the host of the missionaries, at whose house the Christians quite openly congregated, is portrayed as a Christian *Beg.* should not have doubted. On the other hand, it rightly emphasizes that there are no grounds for identifying this Jason with the one in Romans **16**.21.

[10] Alexander also (**19**.33) is introduced without further explanation.

was the name, especially in Macedonia, for the non-Roman magistrates of a city: *Beg.* IV 205.[1] αἱ τὴν κτλ. fits badly here, for Christianity has only just made its appearance: Loisy 654.[2]

VERSE 7: 'Jason has received them': according to *Beg.* IV 205 Jason might have furnished the work about which Paul speaks in I Thess. **2**.9. Here nothing is said of it. ἀπέναντι here not 'over against' but rather 'in direct opposition to'. βασιλεύς means the Roman Caesar: John **19**.12; I Pet. **2**.13, 17; I Clem. **61**.1: Wikenhauser, *Apg.* 157.

VERSE 8: What is meant presumably is that the crowd present at the marketplace and the leaders of the city were shocked when they heard that. Only in this way is the contradiction to ὀχλοποιήσαντες in v. 5 avoided, to which Loisy (654) calls attention.

VERSE 9: Again, as in v. 2, the loose style of the Hellenistic age: the subject is not 'the Jews' but the leaders of the city. λαβόντες τὸ ἱκανόν (*satis accipere*): Jason and the others are freed on bail.[3]

VERSE 10: This time the brethren are not the freed Christians, but the community as a whole. Only because of the highly condensed narrative does it appear as if Paul and Silas went directly from the highway into the synagogue of Beroea.[4]

VERSE 11: εὐγενέστεροι: 'fair' (Bauer, *Wb* 631). καθ' ἡμέραν: Paul, therefore, preaches to them daily, without there being any question of daily worship services. οἵτινες practically begins a new sentence.

VERSE 12: In **20**.4 Sopatros, the son of Pyrrhus from Beroea, is named as a member of the Pauline travelling party. Beroea thus participated in the great Pauline collection, which shows that the community there had continuity. 'Not a few of the prominent Greek women and men': D has completely rewritten the verse.[5]

VERSE 13: How the Jews from Thessalonica—naturally the whole Jewish community there did not make the journey—succeeded in bringing the masses

---

[1] The pertinent Macedonian inscriptions are published in Demitsas, Μακεδονία, Athens, 1896 and E. D. Burton, *American Journal of Theology*, II (1898), 598ff.

[2] *Beg.* IV 205 notes that ἀναστατόω appears not only in the LXX, but also in the papyri.

[3] According to *Beg.* IV 206, Jason contests the fact that he sheltered suspicious persons; the bail would have been forfeited if anyone had found them at his house. On that account Paul was immediately led away by night. I Thess. **2**.14 shows that the case was later taken up again since the Thessalonian Christians were persecuted by their fellow-countrymen. But the text deals with the danger in which Paul found himself, and not with Jason or his bail. For further treatment see the general discussion.

[4] Beroea, away from the great highways, was reached by the missionaries probably by way of Pella, some 22 miles from Thessalonica and 12½ miles north of Beroea (today Verria). The journey, which took them into the third district of Macedonia, lasted at least two days.

[5] 'Some of them now believed, others however did not believe, and from the Greeks and the people of eminence many men and women became believers.' The emphasis on the noble women is here effaced.

into an uproar here also is not stated. Luke's readers will have thought of 17.5. The 'Word of God' is again the missionary preaching. 𝔓⁴⁵ omits καὶ ταράσσοντες.

VERSE 14: ἐξαποστέλλω 'to send away' is seldom followed by an infinitive. ἕως ἐπί or ὡς ἐπί (as in later Mss.) is one concept: 'in the direction of', 'towards'.[1] Similarly Lk. 24.50 ἕως πρός; Acts 21.5 ἕως ἔξω, 26.11 ἕως καὶ εἰς. On the relationship to I Thess. 3.1f. see the general discussion. Timothy is again mentioned here, since particulars about him are going to be reported: an example of how Luke simply does not name secondary characters, unimportant for the moment, and only mentions them when they have a particular part to play in the events.

VERSE 15: 'Those who conducted Paul brought him to Athens': since, according to Luke, he left behind his helpers Silas and Timothy in Beroea and so was alone, the Christians brought him to the next mission post where they probably had relatives or acquaintances. According to 18.5 Silas and Timothy, who are to follow at the earliest possible opportunity, first met Paul again in Corinth.

In the narrative of Philippi the supernatural help was particularly emphasized. Now everything goes well without any such miracle. After a journey of over 95 miles Paul and Silas (Timothy is not mentioned) come to Thessalonica. Here a synagogue presents them with the opportunity to begin mission preaching. The theme, as Luke presents it, is the doctrine of the resurrection of the Messiah (the Christian doctrine of resurrection is according to 23.6 and 26.6ff. specially linked with that of the Pharisees) who had appeared in Jesus. While the Christian message here wins only a few Jews, great success is achieved among the Gentile σεβόμενοι. That many women of good standing were also converted is emphasized here and in 17.12. Perhaps Luke saw in this a resemblance to the 'women who served' in Jesus' lifetime (Lk. 8.2f.). Or perhaps he drew his conclusions about the apostolic age from experiences of his own age. At any rate he took particular pains to show that Christianity from the beginning was no obscure and negligible affair.

The Jews, who have to see their own adherents (probably financially and politically influential) taken from them, become jealous (since Luke does not

---

[1] The interpretation offered earlier by scholars like Zahn (595) was: 'Luke . . . says they travelled at first in the direction of the coast, but only until the point where their way branched off from the route to the sea.' D seems already to have understood the text in this way. So D faced the question: why is nothing reported about this land journey of Paul's? D furnished the answer with a free use of 16.6f., thus: 'He moved on past Thessaly, for he was prevented from preaching the Word to them.' These sentences are very crudely inserted in v. 15.

'The land route would have led him by Larissa, Pharsalos, Lamia, Elatea, Orchomenos and Thebes', of which only Larissa and Elatea still had any importance: J. Weiss, R. E.³ vol. 7, 163. Boeotia and Attica may at that time still have been in a wretched condition (cf. Strabo IX), even if under Roman rule the situation slowly improved.

put himself in their shoes, this ζηλῶσαι represents for him only something reprehensible) and make a move to retaliate. Here two measures are combined. First, the rabble is called out in order to document the 'people's rage'—in the face of the authorities also—and to carry along the citizens or at least to frighten them. Secondly, the Christians are accused of high treason: instead of the βασιλεύς in Rome they acknowledge only the βασιλεὺς ᾽Ιησοῦς! The attack on the missionary quarters at the house of the citizen Jason (perhaps he was one of the few Jewish-Christians) fails insofar as they do not encounter the men they are looking for. They lay hold of Jason and a few harmless Christians gathered at his house instead, and drag them before the πολιτάρχαι. Here they are set free on bail. Paul and Silas (and naturally also Timothy, who is still not mentioned) are promptly brought out by the Christians by night and betake themselves to the remote town of Beroea, where initially a quiet missionary effort and the founding of a community (this time with the help of the Jews themselves) is in store for them. Only when the Jews in Thessalonica hear about Paul's efforts and in accordance with the well-tried formula begin to stir up the crowd in Beroea, does Paul have to withdraw. While Silas and Timothy remain in Beroea, Paul—probably by a sea route—is brought to Athens whence he sends a message back with the men who had escorted him, that his two companions should follow at the earliest possible moment.

This account reads so smoothly and sounds so probable that there would have been no objection to it if there were not contradictory statements in I Thess. and Phil. If we want to judge the account correctly, however, we must view it in a larger context.

If we look over the Lucan reports concerning the Pauline mission from Chapter 13 on, two common features strike us. What Luke recounts of the missionary efforts of Paul is essentially in each case the story of the founding of the community and then the persecution which forces the Apostle away to his next goal. Variations may be introduced by the fact that the preaching is described more extensively (e.g. **13**.15–41), that a miracle contributes to the founding of a community (e.g. **14**.8ff.), leads to the persecution (**16**.16ff.) or otherwise accompanies the missionary work (**16**.25ff.). Luke is silent about the day to day work of the missionaries between the founding of the community and the persecution. Thereby the false impression easily arises that Paul had to travel on when he had hardly had time to lay the first foundation of the congregation. If we follow this impression in estimating the duration of the various phases of Paul's missionary activity, we shall inevitably make the periods of time too short. So for example Zahn (597) believed **17**.1–9 must be understood to mean that Paul spent only three weeks in Thessalonica. Fortunately I Thess. **2**.9 and Phil. **4**.16 allow us to fill in the gaps in the Lucan description: Paul stayed much longer in Thessalonica and in spite of working 'day and night' for his livelihood, became so needy that the community of Philippi καὶ ἄπαξ καὶ δίς sent him money for his support. This expression means 'frequently' (and not merely 'twice', which would have been expressed by a simple δίς): Bauer, *Wb* 160 and 396. If we take into consideration the distance between Thessalonica and Philippi (95 miles), the messages which had to be carried in both directions by the messengers every time, and the fact that the congregation in Philippi could not arrange a collection overnight, then we shall estimate the duration of the sojourn in Thessalonica to have been several months. It might have been the same in Beroea, even if Paul perhaps did not spend so much time in this small town.

Did Luke not know about the paid employment which Paul combined with his missionary activity? Of course he did! From **18**.3 the reader learns that Paul worked as a σκηνοποιός, and from **20**.34 he gathers that Paul cared for his own and his companions' needs by the work of his hands. The second passage, the Apostle's farewell speech, in delineating his own life, offers at the same time a picture of the ideal missionary. The reader is thereby taught to envisage Paul as earning his daily bread himself throughout his missionary career. Luke gives out this information in a general way within a context in which it has a strong and edifying effect, and so spares himself all details of this sort in the description of the Pauline mission itself. The incorporation of such details in the account of the mission would have had an all too prosaic rather than edifying effect. The first passage which speaks about the Apostle's manual work mentions it by way of introducing Paul's acquaintance with Aquila and Priscilla, and at the same time accurately specifies Paul's trade for the reader. We have accordingly no reason to interpret Luke's silence concerning Paul's manual work in Thessalonica to mean that he did not know anything about it, or that he thought this work to have been confined to those three weeks. So the only way to avoid a false historical estimate of this section also is to keep in view Luke's particular genius as an edifying Christian writer.

Closely coupled with these questions is a problem that—probably because it is 'not theological'—has hitherto had rather casual treatment: how did Paul actually finance his mission? Even a missionary who had so few personal needs as Paul required money. If, like Paul, he renounced the apostolic privilege of allowing himself to be supported by his congregations, then he had to earn his daily bread by the work of his own hands. The way the 'first missionary journey' is portrayed by Luke (or better: the way we usually understand the Lucan presentation) would either force the supposition that the three missionaries had been supplied with the necessary means for some months by the Antiochian community or—since Paul and Barnabas according to I Cor. **9**.6 apparently refused such support—would compel the conclusion that the travellers frequently stopped for longer periods along the way in order to replenish their funds. For this the cities in which according to the account of Acts communities were then founded would be the most likely choices. In this case also, then, if we approach the Lucan account as historians, we should have to interpret it not in terms of its wording alone, but also in terms of the hints and allusions which Luke has given in **18**.3 and **20**.34. That Paul earned money for his companions (**20**.34) can indeed only come into question in the form that, when for example he had Timothy travel with a commission to a community, he had to raise the necessary money. Otherwise the Apostle's assistants likewise will have earned their keep, either by a trade they had learned or as casual labourers—it would have been quite senseless if the leader of the mission filled his time with manual labour in order to make it possible for his assistants to preach!

From this point of view the statements concerning the preaching on the Sabbath take on a special meaning. On the Sabbath, when the Jews were forbidden to work and Paul on the other hand could reach the Jews and σεβόμενοι in the synagogue, the real mission first took place. The weekdays on the contrary were taken up with labour until the Friday evening. Only if Paul was in a position to forgo his work, for example because of a gift from the Philippians, could he devote the entire day to the mission. But even then he would still prefer certain fixed hours. We must bear in mind that not only Paul himself had to work but his hearers as well. In this context the note of codex D in **19**.9 takes on a special meaning, whether it may rest on a tradition or on compilation. According to D, Paul in Ephesus taught in the auditorium of Tyrannos from the fifth to the tenth hour, that is, from 11 a.m. to 4 p.m. These are the hot midday hours in which so far as possible work was stopped. We ought to take note of all this too when we are thinking of the writing of the Pauline letters. Paul was not absolute master of his own time, and the amanuensis to whom he dictated presumably just as little. It was, therefore, under extremely difficult conditions that Paul had to carry on his mission. We can only take the true measure of the extraordinary accomplishment of this missionary when, to all the other difficulties which he had to combat, and which Luke mentions in part, we add the constant need for money. On the other hand—and this too we should not forget—such participation in the working community offered the missionary at the same time opportunity to witness to Christ among his fellow workers and with his master. So it would be entirely possible, for example, that Jason at first only gave the foreign σκηνοποιός Paul work and shelter, and then was won by him.

We come now to the last question which this section presents to us. Jason is introduced very suddenly; but in the same way Timothy, who has not been mentioned since **16**.3, abruptly appears again in v. 14, although it is to be presumed that he has travelled together with Paul and Silas the whole time. The abrupt manner in which Luke has his characters walk on and off the stage has frequently been censured. Actually Luke places certain specific demands upon the reader. Jason is not specially characterized for us. This is not because the reader had heard about him, as about James the brother of the Lord, but rather because the reader himself can derive all that is necessary from the following account of how the Christian missionaries had lived with him and how the brethren assembled in his house. Luke spends as little time as possible on such secondary persons, and for him Timothy also is a secondary person (he apparently took him for a 'young man', like the author of I Tim. [4.12], and did not know that he was a very successful, quite self-sufficient and trustworthy fellow-worker of the Apostle). To recount at each point what Timothy did or where he stayed (for instance during the time Paul and Silas lay in gaol) would have detained Luke unduly, without contributing anything for the edification of the reader. On the contrary, it would only have broken the concentration on the real subject of the narrative (insofar as a man is the subject), namely Paul himself. Quite clearly the spotlight of interest is directed in this chapter exclusively upon Paul. All other characters come into view only if they have something directly to do with him. When, therefore, Luke indirectly depicts the loneliness of Paul in the idolatrous city of Athens, in that Paul summons his companions to join him as quickly as possible, then Silas and Timothy must naturally be mentioned. If Luke knew that in reality Timothy first accompanied Paul to Athens and then was sent by him to Thessalonica (I Thess. 3.2), it plays no part here. If the complicated coming and going of the journeys, about which Luke in any case did not want to report so much, are simplified by 17.14f. and 18.5, so was Luke's reader better served than if unimportant details had been exactly adhered to with historical accuracy. It might then be quite misguided to concoct complicated theories for the reconciliation of Acts with the statements of I Thess., as Zahn for instance (597 n. 42, although he is on the track of the correct solution of the difficulty), Wendt (253f.) and Bauernfeind (213) have done.

One might go further and ask with Loisy (655f.) whether the Lucan statements concerning the persecution by the Jews in Thessalonica do not perhaps also arise from such a simplification. Anyone who reads I Thess. without knowing anything of Acts does not hit upon the idea that Jews unleashed the persecution of the Christians in Thessalonica. I Thess. 2.15 does, of course, say concerning the Jews, 'they have persecuted us violently … they hinder us from speaking to the Gentiles so that they might be saved.' But we must observe carefully that according to 2.14 the Thessalonians were persecuted by their own race just as the Jewish-Christian congregations of Judaea were persecuted by the Jews. With this mention of the Jews Paul breaks out in the accusation just cited, which—corresponding remarkably with Lk. 11.49—is certainly supported by his own experiences, but is not connected with the events in Thessalonica. 2.14, 17 and 3.2f. lead us rather to suppose that Paul was driven out of Thessalonica by a Gentile anti-Christian movement, which erupted later against the community also and perhaps cost the Christians of Thessalonica a good deal more than the price of bail, even though the cases of death mentioned in I Thess. 4.13 had evidently nothing to do with this persecution. But the texts are not sufficient for us to base more than a question on them, the question whether Luke did not consider it self-evident that this time also the Jews, these arch-enemies of the gospel, were really the ones who pulled the strings. In this case we should also have to assess the reports about Beroea correspondingly.

41

ACTS 17:16–34

PAUL IN ATHENS

[16] While Paul waited for them in Athens, his spirit was enraged within him as he saw that the city was full of idols. [17] He spoke now in the synagogue with the Jews and the godfearers, and in the market place each day with those who happened to be there. [18] Some of the Epicurean and Stoic philosophers talked with him and some said, 'What does this babbler want to say?' Others said, however, 'He seems to be a preacher of foreign deities,'— for he preached Jesus and the resurrection. [19] They took him and led him to the Areopagus and said, 'Can we learn what this new teaching which you are proclaiming is? [20] For you bring some strange things to our ears. We want to know what they mean.' [21] All the Athenians and the foreigners there had taste for nothing else than to say or hear something new. But Paul took his stand in the middle of the Areopagus and spoke: 'You Athenians, I see that you are highly religious in every way. [23] For as I went (through the city) and looked on your objects of worship, I found an altar with the inscription "to the unknown god". What you now unknowingly worship, I proclaim to you. [24] God who made the world and everything in it, this Lord of heaven and earth, does not dwell in temples made by human hands, [25] nor is he served with human hands as if he needed anything, since he himself gives life to all and breath and everything. [26] He made from a single one the entire human race to dwell upon the whole earth, determining the allotted periods and the boundaries of their habitation, [27] that they might seek God in order to comprehend and find him, and he is indeed really not far from any one of us. [28] For in him we live and move and are, as some also of your poets have said, "for we are also his offspring". [29] Since then we are God's offspring we may not think that divinity is like gold or silver or stone, like any product of human art or design. [30] Overlooking the times of ignorance, God proclaims now to mankind that they should all everywhere repent, [31] because he has fixed a day on which he will judge the world with righteousness by a man whom he has appointed, as he has given assurance to all by raising him from the dead.' [32] When they heard about the resurrection from the dead, some began to mock, but others said, 'We want to hear you concerning this another time.' [33] So Paul went out from their midst. [34] Some men, nevertheless, joined him and became believers, among them Dionysius the Areopagite and a woman by the name of Damaris, and others with them.

Bibliography:

A. Phillippi, *D. Areopag u. die Epheten*, Berlin 1874; E. Norden, *Agnostos Theos*, Berlin 1913; B. Keil, *Beiträge z. Geschichte d. Areopags*, Leipzig 1920; H. Bolkestein, *Theophrast's Charakter der Deisidaimonia als religions-gesch. Urkunde*, Giessen 1929; P. J. Koets, *Deisidaimonia. A Contribution to the Knowledge of the Religious Terminology in Greek*, Purmerend 1929; W. Judeich, *Topographie von Athen*, 1931; P. Graindor, *Athènes de Tibère à Trajan*, Cairo, 1931; K. Lake, '"Your own poets"', *Beg.* V, 1933, 246–51; id., 'The Unknown God', *Beg.* V, 1933, 240–6; M. Dibelius, 'Paulus auf d. Areopag' 1939 (*Studies* 26–77) with older literature; id., 'Paulus in Athen' 1939 (*Studies* 78–83); W. Schmid, 'Die Rede d. Apostels vor d. Philosophen u. Areopagiten, Acta 17', *Philologus* 95 (1942), 79–120; A. N. Wilder, 1943, 317f. (see § 1); R. Bultmann, 'Anknüpfung u. Widerspruch', *ThZ* 2 (1946), 410f.; M. Dibelius, 'Die Reden d. Apg. u. d. antike Geschichtsschreibung' *SHA* 1949 (*Studies* 138–85); K. Reinhardt, 'Poseidonius', Pauly-Wissowa XXII, 1953, 819; B. Gärtner, 'The Areopagus Speech and Natural Revelation' (*ASNU* 21), Uppsala 1955 (literature: 253–72); W. Eltester, 'Gott u. d. Natur i. d. Areopagrede', in *Ntl. Forschungen f. R. Bultmann*, 1954, 202–27 (Beiheft z. *ZNW* 21); 2nd edn, 1957; H. Hommel, 'Neue Forschungen z. Areopagrede Acta 17', *ZNW* 46 (1955), 145–78; A. Kragerud, 'Itinerariet i. Apostlenes gjerninger', *Norsk Teol. Tidsskrift* 56 (1955), 255f.; W. Nauck, 'Die Tradition u. Komposition d. Areopagrede', *ZThK* 53 (1956), 11–52; F. Mussner, 'Einige Parallelen z. Areopagrede aus d. Qumrantexten', *BZ*, N.F. 1 (1957), 125–30; W. Eltester, 'Schöpfungsoffenbarung u. natürl. Theologie im frühen Christentum', *NTS* 3 (1957), 93–114; N. B. Stonehouse, 'The Areopagus Address' (in *Paul before the Areopagus and other NT Studies*), London 1957, 1–40; H. Hommel, 'Platonisches bei Lukas. Zu Acta **17**.28', *ZNW* 48 (1957), 193–200; E. Schweizer, 'D, Reden d. Apg.' *TZ* 13 (1957), 1–11; H. Conzelmann, 'Die Rede des Paulus a. d. Areopag', *Gymnas. Helvet.* 12 (1958), 18–32; id., *Hbd.*, 1963, 96–105; E. Haenchen, 'Judentum u. Christentum i. d. Apg.', *ZNW* 54 (1963), 177f.

O. T. Broneer, 'Athens, City of Idol Worship', *Bibl. Archaeologist* 21 (1958), 2–28; J. H. Maclean, 'St. Paul at Athens', *Exp.Tim.* 44 (1932–3), 550–3; J. de Zwaan, 'Semitica semitice (Act. **17**.16–34)', *Nieuwe Theol. Stud.* 19 (1936), 73–80; P. P. Parente, 'St. Paul's Address before the Areopagus', *CBQ* 11 (1949), 144–50; H. P. Owen, 'The Scope of Natural Revelation in Rom. I and Acts 17', *NTS* 5 (1959), 133–43; R. S. Kinsey, 'Was Paul Thinking of a Statue? (Acts 17)', *Studies for D. M. Robinson*, ed. by G. E. Mylonas, St. Louis, 1951; F. Mussner, 'Anknüpfung u. Kerygma in der Areopagrede (Apg. **17**.22b–31)', *Trier. Theol. Zeitschr.* 67 (1958), 344–54 P. H. Menoud, 'Jésus et Anastasie', *Rev. Théol. et Phil.* 32 (1944), 141–5; G. van der Leeuw, 'On moeting van Christendom en Hellenisme. Paulus op den Areopagus', *Uitzicht*, June 1941, 1–12; M. Delage, 'Résonances grecques dans le discours de St. Paul à Athènes', *Bull. association Guillaume Budé*, 4 sér. (1956), no. 3, 49–69; Conzelman 96–104.

VERSE 16: This Lucan transition verse prepares for the statements about temples and idols in vv. 23ff.—Athens[1], at that time a quiet little city[2] of some 5,000 citizens,[3] lived on its great past. For Luke it represents Gentile culture. That Paul was disturbed about the many idols[4] reminds us that the Christians did not regard them as works of art. As I Thess. **3**.1 shows, Timothy had come to Athens with Paul, but Paul had sent[5] him back forthwith to Thessalonica.

VERSE 17: μὲν οὖν introduces a new scene. Paul speaks[6] in the synagogue (therefore on the Sabbath) and (on weekdays)[7] in the market place[8] to everyone. This feature, reminiscent of Socrates (Bauernfeind 216), already prepares for the Areopagus scene.

VERSE 18: Luke now introduces some Epicurean and Stoic philosophers detached from this general audience.[9] He is fond of contrasting two groups in the audience, one of which shows an interest while the other sharply denies the Christian proclamation.[10] συμβάλλω can mean 'to converse with' but also to 'engage in an argument' (Bauer, *Wb* 1539). This double meaning or lack of sharpness in the description continues all through and is part of the individual character of this scene (see the general discussion). καί τινες: Luke will be thinking of the Epicureans with their materialism and practical atheism; for them Paul is a 'babbler'.[11] The Stoics, the 'other ones'[12] (οἱ δέ) certainly

---

[1] See above E. Curtius, W. Judeich, Joh. Weiss, Ed. Norden, P. Graindor.

[2] Horace speaks about *vacuae Athenae* in Ep. II 2.81.

[3] A conclusion reached, from the result of a vote of the people (3461 yes, 155 no), by B. Keil 88 n. 135.

[4] κατείδωλον: κατά in such expressions = 'full of', for example κατάδενδρος: Wendt 254, *Beg.* IV 209. How many idols and temples Paul might have seen on a trip through the city (coming from the north toward the Areopagus) is described in *Beg.* IV 209f.—Livy **45**.27: *Athenas ... habentes ... simulacra deorum hominumque omni genere et materiae et artium insignia*. Cf. also Strabo IX **1**.16; Pausanias I **17**.1.

[5] Whether Luke had no exact information of this or was simplifying cannot be ascertained.

[6] διαλέγομαι includes address and reply. Plutarch *Cic.* 24, 5 uses it for the teaching methods of a peripatetic philosopher, see p. 507 n. 2 and p. 519 n. 1.

[7] κατὰ πᾶσαν ἡμέραν presupposes a lengthy activity.

[8] Probably the pottery market (Κεραμεικός) northwest of the Acropolis, 'centre of Athenian life and commerce' (Wendt 284). Only here does Luke report that Paul speaks directly to Gentiles (except **14**.8ff., which see).

[9] Zahn 602 inopportunely recalls that only one teacher was active in both schools, and misunderstands the 'philosophers' as students.

[10] Cf. **2**.12f., **14**.4, **23**.6, **28**.24. That is the core of truth in Loisy's presentation (662).

[11] σπερμολόγος is originally used of birds that pick up grain, then of the scrap collectors searching the marketplace for junk, and further of anyone who snapped up the ideas of others and spread them about as his own without understanding what they meant, and finally any ne'er-do-well: *Beg.* IV 211. Cf. Norden 333, Ed. Meyer, *Urspr.* III, 91.

[12] *Beg.* IV 211 with Blass and Ed. Meyer sees in the τινές and οἱ δέ the Athenians generally. This might be true to the extent that the two groups represent the two standpoints towards the gospel in Athens and in Greece generally—apart from those actually converted.

recognize that Paul is presenting a new religious message, but they do not comprehend this preaching either. Luke reflects this by representing them as considering Ἀνάστασις polytheistically as a goddess standing alongside Jesus.[1] The ξένα δαιμόνια remind the educated reader of the accusation against Socrates.[2] This accusation of ἀσέβεια was however not handled before the Areopagus, but brought to the ἄρχων βασιλεύς and dealt with before a jury.[3]

VERSE 19: ἐπιλαμβάνομαι has more than one meaning.[4] Scholars either find in it an arraignment before the authorities[5] or hold that Paul was brought out of the tumult of the marketplace to the quiet hill of Mars.[6] Both interpretations are doubtful: there was room for only a few men on the rugged, rocky summit and not for such a large audience as Luke presupposes for this speech,[7] and if the 'Council of the Areopagus' assembled in the Stoa Basileios, the public were kept out of earshot.[8] Moreover, it is here clearly presumed that Paul was led away from the marketplace where the Stoa

---

[1] This interpretation of the reference to the resurrection (Anastasis) was first given by Chrysostom (*hom. in Act.* 38.1) and later by F. C. Baur, Overbeck 276, Preuschen 118, Wendt 255, Loisy 663, Williams 201, Rieu 152. Contrast *Beg.* and Zahn 605, who thinks that what the philosophers do not understand is the proclamation of the Trinity (Jesus, the Father who raises him, and the Holy Spirit), and so misses the intention of Luke.—D gig have omitted these apparently incomprehensible words.

[2] Xen. *Mem.* I.1.1: καινὰ δαιμόνια εἰσφέρων—hence Luke chooses the word δαίμονες here. 'The similarity with the accusation against Socrates almost exactly 450 years before . . . can scarcely have been overlooked by the author': *Beg.* IV 212; so also Dupont 123, Rieu 152.—*Beg.* IV (as also J. H. Lipsius, *Das attische Recht und Rechtsverfahren*, Vol. II, Pt. 1, 1908, 364) refers to Jos. *Contra Apionem* II 37 § 267, where the Athenians νῦν 'have killed the priestess, since she had been accused of introducing foreign gods' (ὅτι ξένους ἐμύει θεούς). But the examples of Josephus in II.37 all derive from the past. The priestess to whose execution he alludes was Theoris. Demosthenes effected her condemnation because she (like the Delphic Oracle, against which Demosthenes angrily declared, 'Φιλιππίζει ὁ θεός') advocated a treaty with Philip of Macedon. The charge was actually one of poisoning: Dem. *Speech against Aristogeiton* I 79A, 793 (τὴν μιαρὰν Θεωρίδα . . . τὴν φαρμακίδα); cf. fragment 136 from Philochorus in Harpocration s.v. Θεωρίς (μάντις ἦν ἡ Θεωρὶς καὶ ἀσεβείας κριθεῖσα ἀπέθανεν) to which Arnold Schäfer, *Demosthenes u. s. Zeit* II², 1886, 555 refers; Plutarch *Dem.* 14 says concerning this, 'He accused also the priestess Theoris, since she committed other crimes and taught the slaves to lie, and with the motion for the death sentence he brought about her death.'

[3] At the time of Origen it was believed (*c. Celsum* IV 67; V 20f.), through the impression left by Acts 17, that Socrates had stood before the Areopagus (*Beg.* IV 214). From this Keil 60 wrongly concluded that the Areopagus at the time of Origen had taken cases of blasphemy under its jurisdiction.

[4] In 9.27 and 23.19 a friendly meeting, in 16.19, 18.17, 21.30 and 39, on the other hand, arrest.

[5] So Holtzmann 110, Overbeck 277, Preuschen 108, *Beg.* IV 213; Loisy 663, Gärtner 64f., Williams 202, Rieu 152.

[6] So Wendt 255, Zahn 608, Beyer 106, Bauernfeind 116.

[7] The highest place (in the east) of the Areopagus is 377 ft., the Acropolis on the other hand is 512 ft.: Judeich 43, 299. A ridge below the summit of the Areopagus offers a place for a greater number to gather; Dibelius, *Studies* 80.

[8] A. D. Nock, *Gnomon* 25 (1953) 506 n. 5, refers to Ps.-Dem. 25, 23.

Basileios lay, i.e. to Mars' hill. So the romantic picture which Curtius and Ramsay have painted collapses as unrealistic: that Paul stands in the semicircle of the assembly and speaks to the pressing crowd. The assembly, furthermore, did not deal with questions of doctrine.[1]—δυνάμεθα γνῶναι (like βουλόμεθα γνῶναι in v. 20) prepares the way for the speech concerning the ἄγνωστος θεός: the speakers confess that they do not understand the Pauline preaching, but they would like to do so. καινός is interchangeable with ξένος.[2] Paul shows in v. 23 that he proclaims no καινά.

[1] In the constitutional history of Athens the duties and rights of the court of the Areopagus underwent many changes. Rome confined the self-government of Athens to a minimum. The Romans were shrewd enough, however, to allow at least the name of the old institutions to remain, and the nimbus of the Areopagus continued, so that Cicero (*De natura deorum* II, 29 § 74) could venture the formulation that the Athenian state was governed by the assembly of the Areopagus. Over against the 'court of the 600' and the Demos, the 'assembly of the Areopagus' (which was now recruited from a small group of aristocrats devoted to Rome: Keil 89) was pushed into the foreground. But what competence did it still possess? In the pseudo-Platonic dialogue *Axiochus* 367A αἵρεσις ἐπὶ τοὺς νέους, an educational committee of the Areopagus, is mentioned (Keil 25f.), under which the children from fourteen years on have to groan—beside it directors of the Gymnasium are named. Keil has accordingly interpreted the passage in Plutarch, *Cicero* 24, 5 to mean that Cicero served on the 'university commission' of the Areopagus (76). This sub-commission Gärtner 64f. and Williams 202 have taken over in good faith. But that the Areopagus deliberated mainly in sub-commissions Keil has deduced simply from the fact that there is no mention of any executive committee of this board of some thirty men. This *argumentum e silentio* proves nothing by itself: the office of the κῆρυξ, the president of the assembly who wields the state seal, will have taken care of the conduct of business. The passage in Plutarch yields something quite different. Plutarch writes: 'He (Cicero) procured Roman citizenship for the Peripatetic Cratippus under Caesar's rule; but he contrived that the Council of the Areopagus made a decree and asked that he might remain in Athens καὶ διαλέγεσθαι τοῖς νέοις as an ornament of the city' (ὡς κοσμοῦντα τὴν πόλιν). This means that Cicero wished the teacher whom he held in such high esteem to remain in Athens and there—in the Old Heidelberg of ancient times!—he could be heard by his son Marcus (cf. *De officiis* I 1), who studied in Athens from 46 to 44. He first laid the philosopher under an obligation by securing for him the Roman citizenship which was then difficult to obtain. Then he moved the Areopagus to a request which did honour to the philosopher. Such a tribute by the highest Athenian authority (as Keil himself, 2ff., treated it in the case of the memorial tribute to Titus Statilius Lamprias!) neither bespeaks a supervision of teaching methods, nor is a university commission in evidence. That Paul was brought to an 'informal hearing' before the assembly (so probably first De Zwaan, *HTR* 17 (1924) 134) is an apologetic compromise between the two contrasting impressions that Paul was brought before a court of law and that the philosophers asked him for information. Thalheim (Pauly-Wissowa II, 1896, 632) makes Keil's description cruder: 'that it' (the Areopagus) 'further exercised control over the education of the youth may be deduced from the fact that it decided to keep the Peripatetic Cratippus in Athens' (!). L. Mitteis, *Reichsrecht und Volksrecht i. d. östl. Provinzen d. römischen Kaiserreichs*, 1891, 55f., concludes from Acts 17 that Paul as a Roman citizen was subject to the Areopagus! G. Busolt/H. Swoboda, *Griech. Staatskunde* (*Hdb. d. Altertumswiss.* IV, 1, 1), Pt. 2, 3rd edn. 1926, 937 ascribe to the Areopagus 'supervision of the education of the youth and student affairs'. But Acts 17.19 is again set beside Plutarch, *Cic.* 24, 5 as proof of this: real proofs are lacking. For the rest, Paul had begun no lecture activity which could be compared even remotely with a philosophical school. The Lucan description rather recalls an orator in Hyde Park.—See on verse 21.

[2] Norden 53 n. 3.

VERSE 20 combines three elements: 1. the reminiscence of the accusation against Socrates; εἰσφέρεις: see above, p. 518 n. 2 to verse 18; 2. the classical expression εἰς ὦτα φέρειν[1] and 3. the Hellenistic εἰς τὰς ἀκοάς used in Luke 7.1. The whole passage as it stands gives the impression that the philosophers expressed themselves in very refined language. Because the 'foreign things' (cf. ξένων δαιμονίων v. 18) are incomprehensible to the listeners, they wish γνῶναι what Paul means.[2]

VERSE 21: Luke seldom addresses himself directly in explanation to the reader as he does here: *Beg.* IV 214. The curiosity of the Athenians was proverbial.[3] That it appears here as a motive precludes any sort of court proceeding—even a 'merely informal' one. Luke gives no indication that the philosophers saw in Paul a—possibly dangerous—competitor. When Norden (333) called our verse 'the most polished' that stands in the NT, he lavished too much praise upon an expression taken up by Luke; it is of course true that Luke gathers up all the features which were known to be characteristic of Athens.[4] The comparative καινότερον ('the newest of all') corresponds to Hellenistic usage.

VERSE 22: σταθείς: Paul assumes the attitude of the orator[5] The words 'in the midst of the Areopagus' as well as vv. 19 and 30 suggest that the narrator is thinking about Mars' hill. ἄνδρες 'Αθηναῖοι: this address is so framed as to fit the speech directed to the educated Greeks (represented by the philosophers). The Athenians indeed ranked as particularly religious because of their many temples and idols.[6] But if Paul in his *captatio benevolentiae* calls them 'very religious',[7] it is for another reason.[8]

VERSE 23: Paul gives the reason (γάρ) for his judgement by referring to an altar (which he has seen while wandering through the city) with the

---

[1] Cf. Soph. *Ajax* 149.

[2] Vv. 19 and 20 are not parallel versions from two accounts; rather Luke here underlines the fact that the listeners do not understand the Christian preaching and ask for the clarification which Paul gives with the following speech.

[3] Preuschen 108 refers to Dem. *Orat.* IV, 10: ἢ βούλεσθε περιιόντες αὐτῶν πυνθάνεσθαι λέγεταί τι καινόν.

[4] A. D. Nock in *Gnomon* 25 (1953) 506, '. . . . brilliant as is the picture of Athens, it makes on me the impression of being based on literature, which was easy to find, rather than on personal observation.'

[5] Cf. 2.14, 5.20, 27.21.

[6] Soph. *Oed. Col.* 260: τὰς γ' 'Αθήνας φασι θεοσεβεστάτας εἶναι; Jos. *C. Ap.* II, 11 § 130: τοὺς εὐσεβεστάτους τῶν 'Ελλήνων πάντες λέγουσιν. Preuschen 109 refers further to Pausanias I 17.1 and Aelian V 17.

[7] δεισιδαίμων is, as Bolkestein and Koets have shown, by no means 'superstitious' —that is a very modern concept!—but may at most denote an excess of what is normally considered to be pious behaviour (attention to omens, etc.). What is involved here, however, is not this meaning (which always has a flavour of reproach), but the cautiously appreciative 'religious'. Cf. the use of δεισιδαιμονία in 25.19, where Festus certainly does not wish to censure the religion of the people to which his guest belongs, but only characterizes it as strange to him (against Williams 202).

[8] As against Loisy 667.

inscription: ἀγνώστῳ θεῷ.[1] An altar with such an inscription has not yet been discovered; nor does ancient literature know anything about it.[2] σέβασμα, 'object of religious devotion', is a carefully chosen word which contains no approbation of paganism; *Wisd.* **14**.20, **15**.17 refers thus to the pagan idols. ὁ οὖν κτλ.: just this God is the true and only one. Paul concludes from this devotion that the heathen live at one and the same time in a positive and negative relationship with the right God: they worship him and yet do not know him—they worship him indeed, but along with many other gods! Still, this altar shows that Paul introduces no 'new gods': the accusation raised against Socrates cannot validly be made against Christianity. Out of the ignorance of the Athenians concerning this God, it inevitably follows that Paul must proclaim him. So the following speech fits in naturally—ἀγνοοῦντες takes up δυνάμεθα (or βουλόμεθα) γνῶναι and ἀγνώστῳ θεῷ.

---

[1] For ἄγνωστος see Bultmann *ThWb* I, 120-2. E. Norden's book of the same name interprets the ἄγνωστος θεός as the unknown and unrecognizable god of Gnosis, 57ff. (cf. also 312ff.), a view now generally recognized as incorrect.

[2] An inscription (probably second-century) discovered by Hugo Hepding reads: θεοις αγ . . ., καπιτ [ων] δαδουχο[ς]; the supplement θεοῖς ἀγνώστοις is highly improbable, since Kapito, as a 'torchbearer' the second highest priest, would not have dedicated an inscription to 'unknown gods' in the temple area of his goddess. Perhaps θεοῖς ἁγιωτάτοις was the original.—Pausanias (about A.D. 170/180) mentions (I 1.4) on the road from Phaleron to Athens 'altars as well of the so-called (ὀνομαζομένων) unknown gods . . .'. But this very formulation shows that the altars did *not* carry the inscription 'of unknown gods'! In V 14.8 he reports that by the great Zeus altar in Olympia is 'an altar of unknown gods and after this . . .'. The *Vita Apollonii* of Philostratus (soon after A.D. 200!) has Apollonius say concerning Athens in VI 3.5 that there 'also were altars of unknown gods erected.' These passages do not indicate any altar inscription 'of unknown gods' (the dative is later and according to *Beg.* V 242 first appears in the second century A.D.; Acts 17.23 would then be the earliest proof). This form of expression could have arisen from an inscription like the one from Thespiae (Dittenb. *Syll.* no. 725: τοῖς δαιμόνεσσιν.) Here the names of the native gods were omitted as self-evident for the donors. A later age spoke in such a case of 'unknown gods'. Another possibility of an altar without a name results from the account in Diog. Laert. I. 110 concerning Athens' purification by the Cretan Epimenides in 595 B.C. (therefore 800 years earlier than Diogenes Laertius): 'He took black and white sheep and brought them to the Areopagus, and from there he let them run wherever they wanted, charging those who accompanied them to sacrifice to the appropriate god wherever each one lay down. So nameless altars (ἀνωνύμους βωμούς) can still be found in Athens, a reminder of the expiatory sacrifices of that time.' Diogenes is repeating an older tradition. But his account proves only that at that time altars existed without a dedication to any particular god.—The tradition that Athens possessed 'altars of unknown gods' Tertullian also knew: *adv. Marc.* I.9, 'I find altars erected to quite unknown gods, but that is Attic idolatry' (his understanding of Acts 17.22 is operative here!). The corrupt passage *Ad nat.* II.9 reads, 'For also in Athens there is an altar with the inscription "to unknown gods".' Jerome maintains (*Comm. in Tit.* I.12), 'The inscription on the altar was not as Paul affirmed, but rather: "To the gods of Asia and Europe and Africa, *diis ignotis et peregrinis*"', and this inscription Paul altered. How Jerome arrives at this conclusion is unknown.

Luke probably knew from some handbook like that of Pausanias that there were 'altars to unknown gods' in Athens, and concluded that the individual altars bore the inscription ἀγνώστῳ θεῷ.—Further literature in Wikenhauser, *Geschichtswert* 369–90, *Beg.* V 240–6, Gärtner 242–7. The conjecture occasionally advanced that the altar was dedicated to Yahweh, whose name certainly would not have been mentioned, has nothing to support it.

S

VERSE 24: The speaker uses Isa. **42**.5 freely.[1] He first extracts from it a statement embracing the whole creation account of Gen. **1**.1–23;[2] then he constructs out of the Isaiah material a formula which expresses God's continuing lordship—the point here is not the *conservatio* but the *gubernatio*—: κύριος ὑπάρχων. This turn of phrase and the addition of the word κόσμος makes the Old Testament statements sound Greek as well. Both predicates, 'Creator of the world' and 'Lord of heaven and earth' now make it clear that God does not dwell in temples made by the hands of men.[3]

VERSE 25: Again it follows from this that God refuses to be honoured with sacrifices by men's hands.[4] After the polemic against the temple comes the attack on sacrifices. It is further based upon the idea of the Greek enlightenment (borrowed from the Jewish Hellenistic mission) that God needs nothing.[5] But this negation is supplemented—and here again Isa. **42**.5 gains credit—without any loss of rapport with the enlightened Gentiles[6], by the postive sentence: God is the great provider who dispenses life, breath and everything.[7] Indirectly this polemic—which immediately follows the

---

[1] Isa. **42**.5: οὕτως λέγει κύριος ὁ θεὸς ὁ ποιήσας τὸν οὐρανὸν καὶ πήξας αὐτόν, ὁ στερεώσας τὴν γῆν καὶ τὰ ἐν αὐτῇ καὶ διδοὺς πνοὴν τῷ λαῷ τῷ ἐπ' αὐτῆς καὶ πνεῦμα τοῖς πατοῦσιν αὐτήν.

[2] ὁ ποιήσας makes the creation appear as a once-for-all act in the past.

[3] See above on **7**.48. Cf. Seneca *ep.* **41**.3: *specus . . . non manu factus . . . animum tuum religionis suspicione percutiet:* what stems from man's hand awakens no numinous feeling. Here the thought is of course used entirely in the subjective-anthropological sense.

[4] See above on **7**.42f.

[5] Dibelius, *Studies* 43ff. Gärtner (215–8) unsuccessfully seeks to remove these ideas: the Greek sense of God's freedom from want negatively characterizes his being; God is —we should say—self-sufficient. But there is another sense of the freedom from want, where a false attitude is adopted towards the cult, in the bringing to God of offerings instead of thanksgiving and prayer; cf. Ps. 50.—But this psalm does not speak about the θεῖον which is ἀπροσδεές. On the other hand this is the case in II Macc. **14**.35 and III Macc. **2**.9f. Here the Greek thought of the god who is free from want actually does penetrate: Dibelius, *Studies* 44f. That this thought (e.g. Jos. Ant. VIII 111) can be combined with that of the true worship of God does not make it an Old Testament idea; Josephus shows himself here influenced by Greek thought. The most familiar formulation of this thought stands in Eurip. *Herc. fur.* 1345f.: δεῖται γὰρ ὁ θεός, εἴπερ ἐστ' ὀρθῶς θεός, οὐδενός. The combination of God's freedom from want and correct worship is present also in the paganism of that day, for example Seneca *ep.* **95**.47, 50.

[6] To the διδούς of Isa. **42**.5 corresponds for example Seneca *ep.* **95**.47: *non quaerit ministros deus, quidni? Ipse humanae generi ministrat . . .'*

[7] So Luke alters Isa. **42**.5: (a) he cannot say that God gives everyone πνεῦμα without being misunderstood by Christians: God gives the spirit only to the believers! Therefore he exchanges πνεῦμα for ζωήν, a word that is understandable to pagans as to Christians and prepares the way for verse 28; (b) for τῷ λαῷ ,which in LXX means mostly the elect people, the inclusive word 'all' is introduced; (c) finally 'and everything' is emphatically added. It is only with this that the contrast between God's freedom from want and his giving of everything to everyone becomes understandable (Dibelius *Studies* 46).—Many exegetes (cf. also Gärtner 175ff.) find in διδούς the *conservatio* expressed after the *creatio*. But the text from Isaiah and our passage pass over into the present tense because this creative act of God continues into the present, in distinction from the act of creation previously mentioned.

first proclamation—negates the whole pagan belief in gods without the
speaker having to touch upon the ticklish theme of the pagan state gods.
So—by a way mapped out by Jewish propaganda (Nauck 33)—the uniqueness of the true God comes to recognition.

VERSE 26: The construction and sense of this sentence are debated.[1] But
ἐποίησεν can in our opinion, after the ποιήσας of verse 24, only be a recapitulation of the creation account, which now turns to mankind: God created out
of one man (naturally Adam is meant; but why burden the listeners with this
name?)[2] the entire race of men.[3] Over against the one man stands the whole
human race, which God allowed to proceed from him. To mankind God has
appointed a double task. The first consists—in accordance with Gen. 1.28—
in making themselves at home on the entire surface of the earth. The following
participial clause ὁρίσας . . . αὐτῶν completes the foregoing statement,[4]
suggesting the means by which God made possible this settlement of the
earth—the participial clause had to be postponed because this could only be
mentioned after the creation of man was recounted—: God has set definite
times, and the reader knows from 14.17 that the seasons of the year are
meant.[5] God has, furthermore, determined the boundaries[6] of their habitation, and the word κατοικία shows that the speaker is still proceeding in the
context introduced by κατοικεῖν. Behind the whole much discussed expression
stands Ps. 74 (73).17: 'You have made all the boundaries of the earth;
summer and winter you have made.'

---

[1] Either the infinitive κατοικεῖν depends on ἐποίησεν ('he made to dwell'); then
ζητεῖν is the infinitive of purpose dependent upon this whole clause and we shall of necessity
attach ὁρίσας . . . αὐτῶν to what follows, seeing in this word a proof for the existence of
God from history or from nature (so for example Pohlenz and Eltester); or the asyndetic
infinitives κατοικεῖν and ζητεῖν depend on ἐποίησεν ('he created'), and ὁρίσας . . . αὐτῶν
belongs to what precedes (so most recently Conzelmann 99). The attempt by Dibelius
(*Studies*, 27–37) to find in ὁρίσας κτλ the proof for the existence of God (rare in antiquity)
on the basis of the doctrine of the habitable zones miscarries because the text speaks of
dwelling on the entire surface of the earth and not merely in particular zones. In reality
there is here no proof for the existence of God at all.

[2] In Greek culture also, as the so-called Naassene sermon shows, various stories
were in circulation about the origin of mankind from a first man or first human couple.

[3] Schrenk 140, note 8, contends against this translation that πᾶν ἔθνος must mean
'every nation' because it is without an article. However, we should not suppose the classical
rules of grammar apply in Luke, as the directly following ἐπὶ παντὸς προσώπου τῆς γῆς
shows; for the translation 'on every face of the earth' B. Weiss will scarcely have
found supporters. Since τῷ λαῷ in the LXX is used preferably for the elect people, Luke
has used πᾶσιν. Cf. Gen. 11.9.

[4] Similar appended participial clauses which relate to what precedes can be found,
for example, in 12.25, 17.31, 18.28, 19.9, 22.4, 16, 23.22 and 25.13.

[5] Against this view, advocated among others by Dibelius and Eltester, Gärtner
147–152 contends that καιροί signifies historical epochs, the expression for seasons of the
year being ὧραι. But Eltester (206) correctly objected, 'In the Koine one speaks of καιροί
as seasons of the year; anyone with any self-respect will stand by the old word ὧραι. So
the Atticist Moeris (second century A.D.) also characterizes this usage as Hellenistic (p. 214,
19 Becker).' Dio Chrysostom accordingly speaks (*Orat.* 12.32) in the Attic way of ὧραι,

VERSE 27: ζητεῖν τὸν θεόν: the second task of mankind (which is to be accomplished during earthly life and first gives to man his own true meaning). How man shall seek God, the speaker does not here say.[1] εἰ . . . εὕροιεν indicates that the finding cannot be taken for granted: actually Paul's listeners are still in the position of not knowing God. However, the speaker declares at the same time that the discovery of God is not impossible: God is indeed (καί γε confirms) near to each one of us![2]

VERSE 28 clarifies (γάρ) the 'not far': in God we live, we move and are.[3]

---

as Gärtner (147, n. 2) stresses. But that proves nothing: Luke is no Atticist (see Introduction 75ff.).—'Some parallels between the Qumran texts and the Areopagus speech' are suggested by Franz Mussner in *Bibl. Zeitschr.* 1 (1957) 125–50. Mussner holds that passages such as 1 QH I 13f., 19, 26; 1 QM XII 7; X 12b–15; 1 QpHab VII 12 indicate that the rigid legalism of the Qumran sect dominated not only their festival calendar but also their view of all events of the process of nature and history. We have however no reason to presuppose that this line of thought holds also in the Areopagus speech, which is much more influenced (as Nauck and Conzelmann particularly have shown) by the Jewish-Hellenistic missionary practice.

[6] ὁροθεσία (actually: 'drawing of boundaries') means here: 'boundaries' (see Eltester 209–12). The simple explanation is still the allusion to Ps. 74 (73).17. We should not speak of a scheme *creatio-conservatio-salvatio* (cf. Nauck, *ZThK* 53 (1956), 11ff.); it is 'nowhere carried out as a strictly ordered schema' (Conzelmann 29), not even in the Areopagus speech whose wide arches stretch from Creation to Judgement.

[1] Gärtner (158) aligns this seeking with the 'seeking of Yahweh' which the OT so often requires of Israel and which consists in obedience to the Torah revealed to Israel. But this interpretation is not convincing. For this Torah was not revealed to the heathen; Paul's listeners still live in ignorance of God. On the other hand Hellenistic Judaism in its mission to the Gentiles suggested that the Creator should be sought in the work of creation. So for example says Philo (*De spec. leg.* I 36), 'Nothing is better than to seek the true God, even if his discovery eludes man's capacity.' The expression ψηλαφάω Philo used in *De mut. nom.* 126 in the figurative sense of the grasp of the divine; cf. I Jn. **1**.1 and *Corp. Herm.* V 2. That Luke here is using a 'topos' from Hellenistic Judaism is shown also by the connection between seeking and finding (wanting to find) in Wisdom **13**.6: 'But only a small reproach attaches to them (the Egyptian heathen with their gods in animal form), since perhaps they (only) go astray while they are seeking for God and desire to find him. For occupied with his works they search through these . . .'. Dibelius (*Studies* 32–5), in this connection, has understood this search for God to belong to the realm of the mind. But Luke could not have meant it in a purely intellectual sense. Since he so strongly emphasizes that God is near and related to us, the other possibility suggests itself: just as the child notices in relationship with his father that there is a relationship also to his mother, so should man, to whom God in his grace is continually close (cf. **14**.17f.), notice that he has a relationship with God.

[2] The expression οὐ μακρὰν κτλ seems in this context to reproduce a 'topos' of the Greek popular philosophy (Conzelmann 25f.). Thus Dio Chrysostom XII 28 says about the first men: 'Since they were neither far from nor outside of the divine, but by nature in the midst of it, or rather, with a like nature and in every way bound up with it, they could not long remain in ignorance.' Jos. *Ant.* VIII 108 says of God: 'Thou art present and not far away', and Seneca maintains (*ep.* **41**.1), *Prope est a te deus, tecum est, intus est*; and in *ep.* **120**.14: *ubique et praesto est*.

[3] This anticlimax has not yet been found elsewhere. That Luke himself constructed it is unlikely: he would himself have maintained no such immanence of man in God as the wording of the text asserts. It must be a matter of a received Stoic formulation. That it originates from Epimenides (Bruce 338) is not the case. Hommel (199) proposes a triadic Platonic formula.

As the continuation (ὡς καί τινες κτλ) shows, the speaker does not take these expressions to mean a spatial nearness of God (although it is not denied), but rather God's relationship to men = God's creation of mankind (notice the agreement of ζῶμεν with διδοὺς ζωήν verse 25!). Here also Hellenistic Judaism paved the way: Aristobulus already adopted the verse of Aratus.[1] καθ' ὑμᾶς is Hellenistic for the obsolete ὑμετέρων. τινες certainly seems to mean several poets. But in fact the educated person quoted in this manner even if he had only one particular poet in mind: Dibelius *Studies* 50, n. 76. The quotation (Aratus *Phaenomena* 5) stands as proof in the same way as biblical quotations in the other speeches of Acts. What Luke sees expressed in it may be deduced from Lk. 3.38: here God is denoted as the father of Adam, although nothing more is intended than that he created Adam.

VERSE 29: On the basis of this understanding of God pagan image worship is now assailed.[2] The speaker falls back on the Jewish polemic against idolatry.[3] χάραγμα here = man-made image. What originates in our artistic ability and consideration, and therefore stands under us, cannot portray the divine, which stands over us! To the philosophers who were being addressed this polemic would of course have offered nothing new: it hit only Greek popular religion and not the enlightened philosophical Hellenism.

VERSE 30: μὲν οὖν marks the beginning of a new train of thought: up to this time God has overlooked the 'times of ignorance', that is, he has not punished according to deserts.[4] Now, however, a decisive change occurs in God's behaviour.[5] He lets repentance[6] be proclaimed to all men everywhere. With this he ceases to be 'an unknown God': the mention of the ἄγνοια shows that this topic is not forgotten. Paul's proclamation is ultimately motivated by this ἀπαγγέλλει. Up to this point the speech has moved in the realm of the

[1] Aristobulus, Fragment 4 in Eusebius *Praeparatio Evangelica* XIII 12, 3ff. (II, p. 191ff. Mras) Berlin, 1954. As Conzelmann 26 has already seen, Aristobulus understands 'the pantheistic expression simply of the omnipresence and omnipotence of the creator': Aratus confirms the biblical creation story! See also Conzelman, *Handbuch*, 101 and 155.

[2] Greek culture is familiar with the concept of an essential relationship of man with God: Dibelius *Studies* 52–4 with references, for example Dion of Prusa, *Orat.* XII 27: 'Every rational being has by nature a perception of the being of the gods on account of his relationship with them'; XXX 26: 'The gods love us, since we are indeed their relatives.' For Seneca see p. 524 n. 2.—The argument in the text is risky insofar as it logically appears to follow that the divine must be represented in human form: Bonhöffer, *Epiktet und das NT* 182. According to Conzelmann (27) two motifs prevail: the Jewish, that the created cannot represent the creator; and the Greek philosophical, that the living can be represented only through the living.

[3] Cf. 19.26 and see Deut. 4.28, Isa. 40.18, 44.9–20; Wisdom 13.10, 14. 7ff., and 15.7–17.

[4] Quite otherwise Paul in Romans 1; see the general discussion. For ὑπεριδών D has substituted παριδών after Sir. 28.7 (παρίδε ἄγνοιαν): Zahn 626, note 99.

[5] The alliteration πάντας πανταχοῦ shows rhetorical influence.

[6] μετάνοια: one does not run after the false gods any more, but rather follows the true God.

first article of belief without letting specifically Christian elements appear. Now—with a very sudden shift indeed—the second article becomes briefly prominent.[1]

VERSE 31: The command to repent corresponds to the fact (καθότι) that God has set a judgement day—that this is close at hand the speaker does not of course assert. On this day he[2] will judge the world with retributive justice (cf. Ps. 9.5; 95.13; 97.9 LXX). The 'overlooking' therefore has an end. This judgement will be conducted 'by a man',[3] whose name the speaker does not designate. ᾧ is an assimilation for ὅν. πίστιν παρασχῶν πᾶσιν: alliteration. The proof (for God's election) the resurrection has provided.[4] With the announcement of the world's judgement (by Jesus) the speech ends.

VERSE 32: Once again the proclamation of the resurrection is incomprehensible to the Gentiles (see verse 18), and once again both groups (see v. 18) react differently: one with open scoffing (Luke is probably thinking of the Epicureans), the other courteously requesting a deferment of further instruction *ad Kalendas Graecas*. There is no hint that Paul is interrupted (so Zahn 628). But even if that be assumed, on the analogy of **22**.22, the speech would not become a fragment requiring to be supplemented; it is inherently quite complete (Dibelius, *Studies* 57).

VERSE 33: Luke does not portray a pitiful departure, but rather lets the reader feel that Paul has happily emerged from a difficult situation. Not he but the audience has failed. One should not (so Williams 206) credit Luke with deliberately choosing, for the only broadly developed sermon to Gentiles, just such a sermon as Paul from now on was to replace by the pure preaching of the Cross of Christ!

VERSE 34: πιστεῦσαι: to become a Christian. But a baptism is no more mentioned than in **13**.12. Luke might have interpreted a report about the congregation which existed later in Athens, in which Dionysius and Damaris were named, as the direct result of Paul's speech. Perhaps the mention of the Areopagite led him to the idea that Paul preached on the Areopagus.[5] The

---

[1] Paul speaks of a similar change to that in verse 30 in I Cor. **1**.21.

[2] D (gig) m (Iren. lat.), i.e. the early 'Western' text, leave out ἐν ᾗ μέλλει to simplify.

[3] 'This use of ἐν in the language of judgement is classical': Moulton (*Einl. in die Sprache des NT*, Heidelberg 1911, 168) referring to I Cor. **6**.2 and 'the Delphic inscription *Syll.* 850, 8 (third century B.C.) κριθέντω ἐν ἄνδροις τρίοις, have them heard before three judges.'—D adds Ιησου after ἀνδρί and so destroys the great restraint of this missionary sermon.—ἀνδρί does not allude to the Son of Man (against *Beg.* IV 219); what place would the Jewish Son of Man expectation have had in this speech directed entirely to pagan listeners?

[4] Dibelius, *Studies* 57. Bruce cites in addition Vettius Valens 277, 29f.; see also Jos. *Ant.* II 218.

[5] D d h read Διονυσιος τις Αρεοπαγιτης ευσχημων, E on the other hand και γυνη τιμια κτλ. Zahn 629, note 5 has probably correctly deduced that in D a line of some twenty letters is missing and ευσχημων referred originally to Damaris (perhaps instead of this the

conclusion has the appearance of being filled out;[1] Williams 207: 'The entire sentence ... shows a lack of finish out of keeping with the rest of the chapter and indicates an absence of final revision.'

Scholars do not agree on the Areopagus scene: some see Paul appearing here before the 'council of the Areopagus', others dispute any sort of legal procedure: the audience brought the Apostle to Mars' hill in order to listen to him in undisturbed peace.

Both groups advance arguments: an accusation or the sentence of a legally constituted authority does not follow. The polite question after Paul's teaching makes even a merely informal investigation unlikely, and the emphasis on the curiosity of the Athenians as a dominant feature completely precludes any sort of court scene. On the other side, ἐπιλαβόμενοι sounds unpleasantly like an arrest. That they wanted to avoid the din of the city is obvious to us modern city-dwellers; but Athens was a rather quiet provincial town. But above all we should not overlook the allusive references to Socrates: Paul speaks in the marketplace to every man—like Socrates. They think he is introducing new gods—like Socrates. And Socrates came before the court on that account and was sentenced to death.

All these observations are correct, and we may not suppress any one of them. But how to combine them? If we treat Luke as a modern realist, then we entangle ourselves in contradictions. This indicates that he is using a different narrative technique. Dibelius—just like his opponent Wilhelm Schmid—has spoken of 'motifs' which appear in the Areopagus scene. This recognition we must take seriously: Luke actually utilizes a 'motif technique'. The narrative framework is composed of a number of motifs which at that time every half-educated person recognized as specifically Athenian: the many temples and images, the special religiosity of the Athenians, their philosophical schools, the Areopagus (hill and court!), the Socratic dialogues in the market place, the introduction of new gods, the Athenian curiosity. Luke has let these motifs follow one another so closely that the impression of Athenian life and spirit grips the reader. That does not mean, however, that Luke here reproduces his own experience of Athens. A. D. Nock remarks: 'Brilliant as is the picture of Athens, it makes on me the impression of being based on literature, which was easy to find, rather than on personal

---

usual Δαμαλις is to be read). Pious fantasy became preoccupied with her. Since Chrysostom she has passed for the wife of Dionysius. According to Zahn (608f.) she could have been 'the wife or mother of one of the presumably young "philosophers"'.

[1] τινὲς δέ ἄνδρες, ἐν οἶς ... γυνή does not really fit. But the passage is probably one of those on the basis of which Harnack already established a certain carelessness and negligence on the part of the author.—The two names Dionysius and Damaris are not mentioned in I Cor. 16.15; instead the 'house of Stephanas' is there called 'the firstfruits of Achaea'. This supports the explanation proposed at verse 34.

observation.' (See above p. 520 n. 4). This is relatively easy to demonstrate: these motifs are not precisely attuned to one another; the reader should not indeed analyse the narrative, but rather surrender to its overall impression. So Luke conjures up the shadow of Socrates—without calling his name, we should note!—and the reader feels Paul is here entering upon a dangerous adventure, and begins to breathe freely again when Paul finally 'goes out of their midst'. But only so far does Luke go; he does not think to involve Paul here in a legal process before an Athenian court and with this to endanger the fair name of his hero. Accordingly the scene here, as is often the case, certainly remains somewhat unclear, and that is true not only of the Areopagus. What the speech attacks, with arguments from the philosophy of the Greek enlightenment, is the heathen popular belief and not the religion of the philosophers. If the speech is nonetheless directed to these philosophers, it is because Greek culture is to be exhibited in its highest representatives. Still another question arises: do the philosophers, among them Epicureans, who hold Paul to be a babbler, lead him to Mars' hill? D already has had some thought about this. The reaction of the listeners in verse 32 certainly recalls the philosophers of verse 18. But in fact Luke is not thinking of such a specialized audience: Paul speaks in a sense to the whole of Athens, and Athens again represents the whole of Greek culture and religiosity. What we see here is an 'ideal scene', which baffles every attempt to translate it into reality. The problem of the narrative framework is thus resolved, and we may now turn to the speech itself, which is far more important.

Scholars have been particularly interested in the question whether the Paul who speaks here is the Paul of the letters. The last stage of this controversy is the debate between Dibelius and his opponents. Dibelius maintains that we have here a Hellenistic speech concerning the true knowledge of God, which stands as a foreign body in the NT (*Studies* 45, 56f.). Wilhelm Schmid, who has most searchingly defended the Pauline authorship of the speech against Dibelius, had to resort to the contention that the Lucan account has omitted important parts; Schmid seeks to reconstruct them with the help of such late authorities as Clement of Alexandria and Origen. That Dibelius has underemphasized the Old Testament components of the Areopagus speech has in the meantime become clear; but it has also become clear that Schmid and Gärtner (who would like to discount the Stoic element in the speech altogether in favour of the OT) could not 'save' the Pauline authorship. Wolfgang Nauck has helped us substantially forward here. He has pointed out that the Areopagus speech is in line with the mild branch of Jewish-Hellenistic mission propaganda, as it is documented in Aristobulus (he had already made use of a new interpretation of the verse of Aratus!). Paul in his letters, on the other hand, represents the stricter attitude within the Jewish mission, which the Sibylline fragments reveal to us.

Now it is advisable to operate not only with isolated passages, be they from the letters of Paul or from the Areopagus speech, but to take into consideration as far as possible the basic trend of the theological thinking in each case. In regard to Paul the verses in Romans 1.19f. above all have stood in the forefront of interest. But we must first consult also the rest of this chapter. In it Paul reveals his conviction that, because the Gentiles by their idolatry have denied God the glory due to him, he has punished them, by giving them over to moral depravity. Paul works out this theme in three parallel lines of thought (Romans 1.21–4, 25–7, 28–31), and in each case the sequence from the archetypal religious crime to the punishment with moral ruin is marked by the phrase παρέδωκεν αὐτούς ('he gave them over'; 1.24, 26, 28). There can be no talk here of an 'overlooking the times of ignorance', such as Acts 17.30 mentions. But these statements of the Apostle, by which he unites himself with the stricter branch of the Jewish-Hellenistic mission propaganda, we must supplement with other passages in his letters where his own theology is expressed without influence. That the Gentiles also need the salvation in Christ he can here make comprehensible by the fact that they too stand under the law. They do not indeed possess the Torah revealed to Israel; but for them the law written in the heart steps into its place and makes them just as guilty as the Torah does the Jews (Romans 2.14ff.). Or more precisely, the Gentiles also fall into the basic legalistic attitude which leads men to self-assertion and thereby brings them into opposition to God.

This doctrine seems to have remained unknown to Luke; at least he does not reproduce it. On the other hand he develops in the Areopagus speech—that it is a Lucan creation and not the shortened report of a Pauline sermon becomes clear precisely here—a doctrine of the religious status of the Gentiles which with all its use of the Jewish-Hellenistic tradition shows features entirely of its own. The analysis of 17.16–34 in the commentary on the individual verses has shown how purposefully Luke steers for the theme of the ἄγνωστος θεός, and how faithfully he keeps to it. That the Gentiles (represented by the Athenian philosophers) honour the unknown God—beside their other gods—demonstrates the peculiar dialectical relationship in which paganism stands to the true and only God: it does not know him—yet it honours him! This simultaneous yes and no makes it possible for the speaker to proclaim the true God to the Gentiles who are sunk in ἄγνοια, and at the same time to appeal to the word of a poet belonging to these very Gentiles and to take it over,—in an *interpretatio christiana*, to be sure.

This surprising discovery gives food for thought. At the time when Acts originated, the Gentile-Christian Church was hardly any longer recruiting its members from the Gentile synagogue-visitors as in the days of Paul. The Jews stood alienated and hostile against the Christians—Acts again and again points out this fact. The Christian missionary preaching could no more expect in its Gentile hearers the same presuppositions as formerly for the proclamation of the gospel. The missionary could no longer begin with the scripture proof for the Messiahship and resurrection of Jesus, when he addressed himself to the Gentiles. Consequently, while in the speeches directed to Jews in Acts Luke has unfolded the primitive Christian scripture proof, which the Church guarded like a precious treasure, he has also, first in the episode at Lystra (**14.**15–17) and then in the Areopagus speech, presented a new type of missionary preaching which met the different situation. That he should confine himself, in Chapter 14, to just a few allusions, valuable indeed as they are, was stylistically necessary, if the Areopagus speech was to attain its full weight. In this speech Luke describes (here Conzelmann 30 is thoroughly correct) first a particular event: Paul's disputation with the paganism not yet influenced by the synagogue. Luke would not have presented the picture of this particular event to his reader if it had not possessed a very special meaning for him: it was so to speak a kind of programme for the mission (to this extent Dibelius' observation in *Studies* 165 seems to us to contain something of the truth: 'So one preaches—so one should preach!').

Luke has thus trodden a path on which Hellenistic Judaism had already gone a good way before him. He has shown with the introduction of the concept of κόσμος and the characterization of God as οὐκ προσδεόμενός τινος, even more clearly with the unmistakeably Stoic-sounding verses 27 and 28, and especially with the citation from Aratus, that Greek wisdom lends itself to Christian interpretation. But with this Christian interpretation (which in truth was frankly just as much a reinterpretation as the exegesis of many OT passages) Luke has not overstepped a certain limit. In other words the agreement between OT-Christian and pagan-Stoic theology does not extend to the proclamation of Christ in the narrower sense, to Christology. The doctrine of the resurrection (it is tagged on in a sudden transition in verse 31: the attitude of God has changed with and since the resurrection!) awakens again and again the opposition of paganism, and even in the Areopagus speech Luke has let the doctrine of the risen one stand as the stumbling-block.

The later theologians deemed it unsatisfactory that the work of reconciliation between the gospel and Greek thought should be confined to the province of the first article of the creed, and so they sought to tie up Christology with the concepts of Greek ontology. This certainly did not eradicate the problem for good and all: it confronted the Church again and again. It confronts us too, for example, when the modern mission asks itself how far the young churches must take over the past of the lands which have brought the gospel to them (ought the Indians, say, to take over the chorale melodies familiar to us, although they are quite alien to their own musical sense?), or when the French 'worker-priests' felt it a failure when the Church remains outside the social problems of the working class which has largely slipped away from her. The question is, how deep does the command to Abraham strike the Christian mission? 'Go out of your fatherland and out from your friends and out of your father's house into a land which I will show you!' This question already occupied Luke, and in the Areopagus speech received a provisional answer.

42

ACTS 18:1–17
PAUL IN CORINTH

[1] After that Paul departed from Athens and came to Corinth. [2] And he found a Jew by the name of Aquila (he was a native of Pontus) who had lately come from Italy, and his wife Priscilla, because Claudius had commanded all Jews to leave Rome. And he went to them, [3] and because they were of the same trade he remained with them and they worked. They were in fact tentmakers by trade. [4] He preached in the synagogue every Sabbath and sought to convince Jews and Greeks. [5] But when Silas and Timothy returned from Macedonia, Paul went over entirely to preaching, testifying to the Jews that Jesus is the Messiah. [6] But when they contradicted and blasphemed, he shook out his garments and said to them, 'May your blood come upon your heads! Innocent of any guilt, I will go from now on to the Gentiles!' [7] And he went away from there to the house of a 'godfearing' man by the name of Titius Justus, whose house adjoined the synagogue. [8] Crispus, however, the chief of the synagogue, became a believer in the Lord, and many Corinthians, when they heard that, became believers and let themselves be baptized. [9] But the Lord spoke at night in a vision to Paul, 'Fear not, but speak and do not be silent, [10] for I am with you and no one will lay hands on you to do evil to you, for I have a great many people in this city.' [11] And he stayed for a year and six months teaching the Word of God among them. [12] But when Gallio was proconsul of Achaea, the Jews arose united against Paul and led him to the tribunal, [13] saying, 'This man leads men astray to worship God contrary to the law.' [14] When Paul was about to open his mouth, Gallio said to the Jews, 'If a crime had occurred here or a misdemeanour, you Jews, so would I rightfully receive your accusation. [15] But if it is a question of arguments over doctrine and persons and law with you, see to it yourselves. I will not be a judge over these things.' [16] And he drove them away from the tribunal. [17] Then they all seized Sosthenes, the chief of the synagogue, and beat him in front of the tribunal; and Gallio did not bother himself in the least about it.

Bibliography:

G. Wohlenberg, 'Eine Klaudiusinschrift von Delphi in ihrer Bedeutung f. d. paulin. Chronologie', *NkZ* 23 (1912), 380–96; Adolph Deissmann, *Paulus*[2] 1925, Beilage 1: Das Prokonsulat des L. J. Gallio, 203–25 (ET *Paul*[2] 1926, Appendix I: The Proconsulate of L. Junius Gallio, 261–86); M. Goguel,

RHPhR 12 (1932), 321–3 (on vv. 9–11); Cadbury, 1933, 274f., see § 30; K. Lake, 'The Proconsulship of Gallio', *Beg.* V 1933, 460–4; D. Buzy, 'Un cas de syllepse historique (Act. **18**.5)', *Rev. Bibl.* 45, 1936; W. A. McDonald, *The Biblical Archaeologist* 5 (1942), 36–48; Edgar J. Goodspeed, 'Gajus Titius Justus', *JBL* 69 (1950), 382f.; H. J. Cadbury, *The Book of Acts in History*, 1954, 44; John Knox, *Exp.Tim.* 66 (1955), 130; Kragerud 1955, 256f.—see § 29; Conzelmann 104–7.

A. Pujole, 'Egressus ab Athenis venit Corinthum (Act. **18**.1)', *Verb. Domini* 12 (1932), 273–80, 305–8; E. Henschel, 'Zu Apg. **18**.5', *Theol. Viatorum*, Berlin 1950, 213–5; W. Gutbrod, 'Zur Predigt des Paulus in Korinth. Nach Apg. 18', *Ev. Th.* 3 (1936), 379–84; W. Mallinckrodt, 'Gallio (Hand. 18)', *Geloof en frijheid* 40 (1906), 456–71; T. Schlatter, 'Gallio und Paulus in Korinth', *NkZ* 36 (1925), 500–13; W. Rees, 'Gallio the Proconsul of Achaia (Acts **18**.12–17)', *Scripture* 4 (1949), 11–20; B. Katzenmayer, 'War Petrus in Korinth?', *Intern. kirchl. Zeitschrift* 33 (1943), 20–27.

VERSE 1: Corinth had been totally destroyed in 146 B.C. by Mummius. Caesar[1] started the complete rebuilding and settled it with freedmen.[2] From 27 B.C. it was the capital city of the Roman province of Achaea. As a city of commerce on two sea-fronts (to the west with the harbour Λέχαιον, to the east with Κεγχρεαί, see below on verse 18) it soon became wealthy again, but also notorious on account of its immorality.[3]

VERSE 2: Ἀκύλας[4] is a Greek form of Aquila. Ποντικός: originating from the Roman province of Pontus on the Black Sea. προσφάτως: properly 'freshly

---

[1] Hence the city was called *Laus Julia Corinthiensis.*

[2] Strabo VIII 6, 23.

[3] The proverb 'Not everyman's concern is a trip to Corinth' (Strabo VIII 20) is to be understood on this basis; cf. Preuschen 110f. J. Weiss offers a good description in 'Griechenland in der apostolischen Zeit', *RE*³, vol. 7, 165–8, used in his commentary on I Cor. (*Krit.-exeget. Kommentar über das NT*, founded by Meyer, vol. 5, 9th edn.), Göttingen 1910, vii-xi.

[4] Luke seems to have depicted Aquila as a Jew in order to explain how he was included in Claudius' decree of banishment. If he had been first converted by Paul, this would certainly have been handed down *ad maiorem Pauli gloriam*. Moreover it would fit poorly into the Lucan historical picture if he had to admit that there were Christians in Corinth before Paul. It is probable that Aquila and Priscilla had a house-church in Corinth (corresponding to that in I Cor. **16**.19). On the other hand, they had not begun a mission. To be sure Paul says in I Cor. **16**.15 that the 'house of Stephen' was the ἀπαρχὴ τῆς Ἀχαΐας. But if Aquila and Priscilla emigrated as Christians from Rome to Corinth, they could not also claim the honorary title of 'the firstfruits of Achaea', which rather belonged only to people converted there. This consideration speaks (along with some others) against the picture Zahn sketches: the couple had indeed already 'heard about Jesus and the spreading growth of his party' (!). 'But of any kind of knowledge of the evangelical preaching or even inclination towards the Christian faith . . . Luke could not have kept silent' (636). 'From the sharing of the Jewish couple's home there soon grew a complete community of faith which Luke . . . did not even find it necessary to mention as a new event' (634). Curious Luke! That a Jewish couple expelled because of the conflict with Christians in Rome deliberately gave a Christian missionary work and shelter is far more improbable than that Paul found lodgings with Christians who had fled from Rome.

slaughtered', then 'recently', 'not long ago' (Bauer, *Wb* 1426); perhaps 49/50.[1] Πρίσκιλλα: a diminutive of Πρίσκα (I Cor. **16**.19; Rom. **16**.3; II Tim. **4**.19; cf. Harnack, *ZNW* 1 (1900), 33ff.); the remark concerning Priscilla is unhappily placed.[2]

VERSE 3: ὁμότεχνον: 'practising the same trade' (Bauer, *Wb* 1127). Here we have the clue to the meaning of 'he found' in verse 2: Paul enquired in the strange city about a (Jewish) master tradesman with whom he could practise his trade, and so found Aquila.—σκηνοποιοί: not 'weaver' as was earlier[3] thought, but 'leatherworker'.

VERSE 4: Because Paul earned his bread as workman, he could only carry on mission work on the Sabbath in 'the'[4] synagogue. 'He sought to convince Jews and Greeks': he addressed himself to the Jews and to the σεβόμενοι, as in **17**.17.

VERSE 5: 'But when Silas and Timothy came from Macedonia, Paul went over entirely to preaching'[5] (cf. Bauer, *Wb* 1562) 'testifying to the Jews that the Messiah was Jesus.' Probably Timothy had brought with him a gift of money (from Philippi? cf. Phil. **4**.15f.) which allowed Paul to give up earning his living by hand labour.[6] The Western text has fundamentally altered vv. 4ff.[7]

---

[1] See Introduction §§ 4, 5, p. 65.

[2] 'And Priscilla, his wife': 'looks like an insertion', says Preuschen 111. The Western text of verse 2, reconstructed by Ropes (*Beg.* III, 170), seeks to accommodate these words better, and is clearly secondary. Zahn 631 n. 9 of course does not recognize that.

[3] So e.g. still Bill. II, 746f.: out of goat's hair, especially in Cilicia, a rough cloth, called *cilicium*, was produced which was also used for tents. It was a natural conjecture that Paul in his homeland had learned the weaving of *cilicium* as a trade. But *cilicium* served neither exclusively nor particularly for tents; they were rather made chiefly from leather: Zahn 633. We must with Jeremias (*ZNW* 30 (1931), 299) understand by σκηνοποιός a leather-worker. This was already the view of the ancients with their explanation σκυτοτόμος (Rufinus, probably after Origen) and σκηνοράφος (Chrysostom): Zahn 632, n. 10.—At this juncture it is usually pointed out (e.g. Bill. II 745f.) that the Rabbis were in the habit of learning a trade. But Paul was not a Rabbi and also did not want to imitate the Rabbis: Loisy 689. Cf. below on **22**.3.

[4] Zahn and others have concluded from verses 4 and 7 that there was only this one synagogue in Corinth at that time. An inscription published by Deissmann, *Licht vom Osten*[4], 12f.; ET *Light from the Ancient East*) ΓΩΓΗΕΒΡ = (συνα)γωγὴ Ἑβρ(αίων), could have originated from this synagogue; cf. *Beg.* V 62–5.—The addition in D d h sy[hmg] καὶ ἐντιθεὶς τὸ ὄνομα (τοῦ κυρίου Ἰησοῦ) could be a variant of the following καὶ ἔπιθεν (sic) δὲ οὐ μόνον (Ἰουδαίους).

[5] It was not worthwhile for Luke to recount how the two, ordered to Athens in **17**.15, found Paul in Corinth. According to I Thess. **3**.2 Timothy admittedly came from Thessalonica after he had previously already been with Paul in Athens. The plural in I Thess. **3**.1 may apply only to Paul (against *Beg.* IV 224).

[6] Wendt 263f. translates '. . . . Paul was wholly caught up with the preaching' and explains, following B. Weiss: Paul really wanted to return home with the awaited travellers, since the missionary charge relative to Macedonia was now finished (but why did he then go to Athens and Corinth at all?); the activity begun during the waiting in Corinth induced him to a further stay. Highly unlikely! The imperfect συνείχετο is inchoative: *Beg.* IV 224. Preuschen 112 follows the variant τῷ πνεύματι for τῷ λόγῳ because the Armenian highly treasured by him also reads thus. It has also inspired Schlatter in his history of the

VERSE 6: The words of Paul show what the shaking of the clothes[1] indicated for the author. Paul completely repudiates any fellowship with the Jews and so is exempted from any further responsibility concerning them. As in 13.46 and 28.28 this renunciation makes it clear to the reader that Israel by her own fault has forfeited salvation and made the proclamation to the Gentiles necessary, so that now Paul can go to them with a good conscience.

VERSE 7: ἐκεῖθεν means 'from the synagogue'.[2] In Titius Justus[3] scholars have frequently been disposed to find Paul's companion Titus, who is not named in Acts (!). Ramsay makes him the Gaius of Romans 16.23: C. Titius!

VERSE 8: Crispus: Paul himself baptized him according to I Cor. 1.14; otherwise in Corinth he baptized only the first converts, 'the house of Stephanas', and that Gaius at whose home Paul wrote the letter to the Romans (Rom. 16.23). The chief of the synagogue (see on 13.15) was certainly a very respected person. For this reason his conversion made a great impression upon the godfearers and further conversions followed.

VERSES 9–11: The appearance of Christ by night explains Paul's long stay in Corinth (Preuschen 112)—Luke has the idea that Paul otherwise hurries through the countries quickly—and lets the reader feel Paul's preservation in the scene before Gallio as the fulfilment of a divine promise.[4] The year

---

Corinthian community. But it only shows that at an early stage the original text was already no longer understood.—*Beg.* IV 224 also ponders the opinion that now Silvanus and Timothy alone earned the daily bread. In view of II Cor. 11.8f. this is completely superfluous.

[7] Especially if with Ropes, *Beg.* III 172, we remove from D the words from συνείχετο to 'Ιησοῦν as interpolated from the B text, it becomes clear that here also the words συνείχετο τῷ λόγῳ have been the reason for the alteration. They are reproduced by πολλοῦ δὲ λόγου γινομένου.—D writes for 'Jesus' 'the Lord Jesus', and thereby betrays itself as secondary.

[1] In an excursus 'Dust and Garments' (*Beg.* V 269–77) Cadbury has discussed our passage in detail (274f.). Acts 13.51 offers a Lucan, Neh. 5.13 an OT parallel. With this rite, and also with the OT turn of phrase, Luke has taken pains to express the repudiation of Judaism—cf. for this also 20.26—in solemn biblical style.—If at the bottom of the action there originally lay an apotropaic ritual against blasphemy, neither Luke nor his readers were aware of it, as Cadbury admits. For the shaking off of dust as an act of imprecation cf. A. Hoffmann, *Das Gottesbild Jesu*, Hamburg 1934, 150f.

[2] D has noticed that it is not merely a change of teaching location, but rather of living quarters. It has, therefore, replaced 'from there' by 'from Aquila'. The difficulty is however more deeply grounded, in the composition of the section; cf. the general discussion.

[3] Ropes (*Beg.* III 173 note) holds the reading 'Ιούστου for original, thus without a second name (so A D d and Antiochian Mss.). Τιτίου (and, in another reading, Τίτου) would have arisen by dittography of ΤΙΙΟΥ. But neither dittography nor haplography will help to explain this case.

[4] The words of Christ recall biblical passages, especially Isa. 43.5: 'Fear not, for I am with you.' For κακόω cf. the notes to 14.2. The 'great many people' are the many in Corinth predestined for the faith (Loisy 696).—*Beg.* IV 226 explains the change from present to aorist in the command of Christ precisely according to classical grammar: 'Stop being afraid, speak out and do not be silent!' Now of course according to the classical rules (cf. Bl.-Debr. §§ 335 to 337) the present in general, even in the imperative, emphasizes duration of time, the aorist the occurrence of the action. But it is very questionable whether we

and a half means the entire length of the sojourn (Zahn 654).

VERSE 12: ὄντος says only that the event took place during the proconsul-ship of Gallio.[1] The inference is indeed that the Jews tried their fortune with a new proconsul. τὸ βῆμα: judge's seat, court.

VERSE 13: Gallio's answer seems to imply that νόμος here means the Jewish law. But the conclusion is not quite certain: the Christians might have been accused of standing outside the *religio licita* and, therefore, of breaking the Roman law. Luke however is not so much concerned with the accusation as with Gallio's pronouncement and attitude.[2]

VERSE 14: Paul does not need to answer because the accusation is al-together rejected. Gallio draws from the accusation the conviction that Christianity contains no ἀδίκημα, no violent movement, or ῥᾳδιούργημα, no fraudulent trickery that would 'naturally' (κατὰ λόγον: *Beg.* IV 227) make him 'duty bound' to deal with the accusation. ἀνέχομαι: 'receive an accusation'.

VERSE 15: It was much rather a question of disputes about preaching[3] (λόγος), names (ὀνόματα) and the Jewish law. All such matters the Jews themselves should decide. Gallio refuses to be judge in such cases.

VERSE 16: ἀπήλασεν: 'he drove them away' (a very strong expression for 'he sent them away'). Luke makes it clear even to the slow-witted reader how the antisemitic high official made the Jews depart. According to Zahn he had the Jews driven away by his lictors (658); so also Wikenh., *Apg.* 170.

VERSE 17: πάντες = the crowd (not the Jews[4] disappointed by Sosthenes[5])

---

should credit Luke with such classical refinements, or whether he has not simply changed the tenses for the sake of variation. Radermacher correctly stresses (155): '... in Acts 13.15ff. λέγετε and ἀκούσατε stand next to each other where a distinction is certainly possible but artificial, in I Peter 2.17 τιμήσατε and τιμᾶτε; cf. Romans 6.13 μηδὲ παριστάνετε . . .— ἀλλὰ παραστήσατε. In II Tim. 4.5 νῆφε stands beside mere aorists. The selection of a present or aorist imperative depends in part on individual discretion' (Moulton 174: I Peter has in commands twenty-two aorists against six presents, Paul in Gal. nine presents to one aorist, and in Phil. twenty presents against two aorists).

[1] Gallio (properly Marcus Annaeus Novatus, son of the Spanish orator and financier M. Annaeus Seneca) was the elder brother of the philosopher Seneca, after whose death Gallio too was forced by Nero to commit suicide. He had been adopted by the rich Lucius Junius Gallio. On the chronology see Introduction §§ 4, 6.

[2] Zahn accepts the 'hostile shout' from D without noting that it is one of D's charac-teristic embellishments.

[3] According to *Beg.* IV 228 λόγος means 'speech' in distinction to 'deed', ὀνόματα on the other hand means 'words'. Loisy 701f. decides in favour of 'teaching' and 'names'; so also Zahn 658. νόμου τοῦ καθ' ὑμᾶς is identical in meaning to τοῦ ὑμετέρου νόμου, Bl.-Debr. § 224, 1 with reference to Acts 17.28 and 26.3.

[4] So B. Weiss and Spitta; Zahn (who wants to include the clarifying addition Ἕλληνες from D in the text) makes 'the loafers and loiterers' responsible for this (659), while Ephraem even regards the Gentile-Christians (πάντες οἱ πιστεύοντες Ἕλληνες) as the perpetrators (*Beg.* III 437)!

[5] Schlatter and others have rediscovered him in the Sosthenes of I Cor. But the name occurs often. The attempt to learn more about the persons named in the text has in the history of exegesis often led to the identification of persons with the same name.

seize[1] the leader of the rejected delegation and beat him before Gallio's eyes without his interference.[2] Luke gives no indication that he condemns the beating, since this feature reveals especially clearly the disinterestedness of the Roman authorities.

If we read this account with the letters to the Corinthians in mind, we find a great deal missing (Loisy 696f.). But the events and circumstances about which the first letter to the Corinthians speaks arose only after Paul had already left the city. Luke would in any case certainly not have mentioned them—they did not fit into the harmonious picture of the deeds of Paul in Corinth that he projected for the benefit of the Christians. Luke, however, must have drawn on some source or other. It would be senseless to pass off all details as a creation of the author's fantasy, as Loisy is most inclined to do. The question of what did not issue from this source has been much discussed by scholars previously.

The words 'and Priscilla, his wife' in verse 2 destroy the continuity between the two clauses: 'who had lately come from Italy' and 'because Claudius had decreed that all Jews leave Rome.' Preuschen (111) considers the four intrusive words an insertion; Loisy, 687ff., on the other hand, rejects the disjointed sentence, without either being able to explain why anyone inserted the words so awkwardly.

Verse 4 has also aroused suspicion. According to Preuschen (111) it fits poorly with verse 5 'where Paul's activity seems to have begun only after the arrival of Silas and Timothy'. Loisy (692) transposes the verse after verse 7. Even more suspect are verses 5b and 6, against which O. Holtzmann, Spitta, Jüngst, Hilgenfeld and Wendt have raised objections: the renewed mention of the Jews (after verse 4b) makes sense only in preparation for verse 6, which does not harmonize with verse 7. Wendt and his predecessors therefore speak of a 'redactional addition to the source'. Since, however, verse 7 joins poorly to verse 5a, Wellhausen (36) has rejected verses 4–6 as an addition.

Overbeck (293) already brought verses 9f. into relationship with the unhistorical accounts of the visions in **9**.10, **16**.9 and **22**.17, while Jüngst (165f.) takes vv. 12–17 to be a redactional addition.

In regard to Luke's method of composition, all these scholars have thought of him as making insertions between sentences taken over unaltered from his source, and on occasion omitting or transposing something. They have thus overlooked the fact that Luke by no means worked so mechanically. In reality he has constructed our passage with a very carefully calculated

---

[1] ἐπιλαβόμενοι again in a hostile sense; cf. above on **17**.19.

[2] Bauernfeind's consideration, 'But if today Sosthenes falls into the hands of the πάντες, tomorrow the same thing can happen to the Christians' (225), Luke neither entertained nor suggested to his readers.

gradation of events. We must take note of this peculiarity and characteristic of the Lucan presentation before making a quest for its historical worth.

With a transitional sentence Luke brings Paul from Athens to Corinth (v. 1). Here Paul meets the married couple Aquila and Priscilla, whose residence in Corinth is precisely explained, and works with them (2f.), teaching in the synagogue on the Sabbath (verse 4). That is the first part—a quiet beginning. Now begins a climax: when his companions arrive, Paul gives himself up completely to the work of the mission (verse 5). The action precipitates the reaction: the Jews reject him and he solemnly goes over to the Gentile mission (verse 6), for which he finds a room with the proselyte Justus (verse 7). Then again an increase in the action: the chief of the synagogue, Crispus, becomes a Christian, and this gives rise to a regular wave of conversions (verse 8). A Christophany during the night admonishes Paul to persevere dauntlessly: nothing will befall him! (v. 9f.) So the way is prepared not only for the notice of v. 11, but also for the story which forms the high point of the entire section: the proceedings before Gallio (vv. 12–17). That Paul does not travel on directly after this incident shows the reader that he leaves the scene not under compulsion but as a victor, and at the same time leads into the following narrative (v. 18).

It is worthwhile considering more closely the particular details of this episode. The statements about *the meeting with Aquila and Priscilla* sound as if they come from some travel memoirs. The interest in Paul's host suggests this. What is reported concerning the fortunes of the couple has a parallel in the information about the origins of Lydia in 16.14. If something of the sort underlies verses 2f., then we find here reports of the greatest historical reliability. They provide a fixed point of reference for the very uncertain Pauline chronology: Paul spent roughly the time from the winter of 49/50 to the summer of 51 in Corinth. We learn, moreover, important details concerning Aquila and Priscilla. They are no common labourers, but a well-to-do couple who later have their own house church in Ephesus (I Cor. 16.19). Paul worked for some weeks in their workshop, presumably together with other journeymen, and lived with them. What is indicated concerning their past in Rome leads to the conclusion that the proclamation of Jesus as the Messiah reached the Jewish community in Rome around the year 49 and caused vehement conflicts. That Claudius banished all Jews from Rome (not from Italy!) might be a simplification in Luke as in Suetonius and at the same time an exaggeration of the true state of affairs (Loisy): the banishment will have applied only to the leaders and activists. In that case we would have to assume that Aquila and Priscilla had already at that time been particularly active on the Christian side. Of their having begun missionary work in Corinth also nothing is reported. Paul undertook the first baptism in Achaea. That they participated in the Pauline mission in Corinth is no more recounted than any missionary efforts of Silas and Timothy. But that is not to deny it. Only all the light falls upon Paul. He is the central person. He is *the* missionary. We gather from **18**.26 that the couple too were busy with missionary effort. But there we are dealing with a scene in which Paul does not appear. On the other side the interest which the author obviously takes in Aquila and Priscilla (they are mentioned again in **18**.18) shows that they were so important for the history of the Christian mission that Luke could not overlook them. Such things Luke does not say outright but simply indicates by the manner of his presentation. Luke's reader received no exhaustive description of all the events but rather a selection which he could then fill out through his own reflection and imagination.

The second matter Luke learned and which could also have been transmitted from travel memoirs is *the extension of the Pauline mission* after the arrival of the travellers from Macedonia. It has long been recognized that what is involved in v. 5a, although it is only implied rather than expressly stated, is that Silas and Timothy brought a substantial financial contribution. Paul alludes to this in II Cor. **11**.8f. in reproaching the Corinthians: 'Other congregations I plundered, accepting support from them for my service to you, and when I was with you and ran short, I did not sponge on anyone, because the brethren who came from Macedonia compensated for my want.' Thereby he was relieved from the necessity to earn his daily bread by manual labour, and it became possible for him to do missionary work not only on the Sabbath but during the entire week. The result was that he had to look around for a room for this purpose. The synagogue did not stand at his disposal, nor was Aquila's workshop the right place for constant discussion with individual visitors or addresses to groups. So the report that Paul moved with his missionary preaching from there, namely from Aquila, into a suitable private house can be understood without more ado.

From this move to the home of Titius Justus Luke has of course inferred that here that dramatic breach with the Jews took place, without which he could not conceive of a Pauline mission to the Gentiles. The scene with Gallio finally proves that Paul has broken with the Jews of Corinth. Luke however has not connected it with the breach itself, but rather set this breach much earlier than the accusation. Scholars are seemingly at one in the view that the repudiations of Judaism in the congregations in Pisidian Antioch (**13**.45ff.), here in Corinth, in Ephesus (**19**.9) and in Rome (**28**.24ff.) are due to the Lucan conception of the legitimacy of the (Pauline) mission to the Gentiles. Paul in Luke is not in the first place a missionary to Gentiles. He always and everywhere turns to the Jews, and it is only the fact that they blaspheme the Lord which in each case drives him to the Gentiles. In those circumstances there cannot in Acts be any question of the Pauline theology which stood behind the Pauline Gentile mission. The repetition of these scenes is intended to impress upon the reader that it is not the fault of Christians or of Christianity that it has become a religion distinct from Judaism and standing hostile alongside it. So far as Paul was concerned (and he represents for Luke here Christianity in general!), the Christians had always remained within Judaism. It is exclusively the fault of the Jews if Christianity now appears as a separate community.

By making the separation from the synagogue ensue in a dramatic scene Luke at the same time actually heightens the suspense: open conflict with the Jews has broken out—how will it be resolved? The conversion of the chief of the synagogue, Crispus, and the many Corinthians who follow his example conveys the answer. But if we take the move to Titius Justus no longer as an indication that Paul wanted to compete with the synagogue, but set it even before the break with the synagogue, then not only the enlistment of Crispus, the chief of the synagogue, but also that of the many others who followed him is much more comprehensible. That just these successes on Paul's part occasioned alarm among the Jews and led to an open breach is likewise perfectly conceivable. But from all this it does not follow (as Wendt 294, n. 1 thinks) that verse 7 followed verse 5a. Luke has not slavishly taken over the text of the itinerary (assuming that such was his source) but has reworked it into a new whole.

To this transformation of the presumably very scanty factual details into a skilfully developed account belongs also the story of the night vision in which Christ encourages the Apostle, summons him to preach further and reassures him concerning the futility of hostile conspiracies. Paul will yet win many more for Christ in Corinth! The narrative then reports nothing more of this further missionary success; the reader can assume that, like the other promises, this also was fulfilled. Paul remains (in all) one-and-a-half years in Corinth. That is for Luke a surprisingly long time. Elsewhere he always allows Paul to remain only a few weeks in a newly founded congregation. Now it is certainly true that Paul wanted to convert the inhabited world in east and west, and it is also true that at this time the preparation for baptism did not claim such a long period of time as later. But all this does not mean that Paul could found a great and lasting community overnight.

The threat about which the words of Christ speak comes true in the accusation before Gallio. The fortunate preservation of the Apostle appears through verse 10 as the fulfilment of a divine promise. The reader recognizes that Paul stands under the care of the *providentia specialissima*. Luke was so firmly convinced of this that again and again he has represented what (as he felt) should have happened to Paul as an actual event. So he has the Lord warn his missionary on one of Paul's visits to Jerusalem (which in reality did not occur at all; see below on 22.17ff.), and so save him from the danger which threatens from the Jews. Also the words of Christ in the vision of Ananias (9.10ff.) and those of the angel (27.23f.) are not derived from old tradition, but reflect the ideas of Luke and his time about the constant communion with the heavenly world which the men of apostolic times enjoyed. Luke has kept all these dialogues in the biblical style, but has not shunned putting a pagan proverb in the mouth of the risen Lord where Paul's audience seemed to require something of the sort (**26.15**). Luke's attitude to his material is much more free than is congenial to our historical way of thinking.

How far this is true of the reproduction of the scene before Gallio is difficult to say. Luke has placed the scene just before Paul's departure from Corinth, and only ἡμέραι ἱκαναί separate them. In fact it forms the high point of the Corinthian stories and for that very reason had to be moved by the author to the end. Verse 13 gives the accusation of the Jews only briefly and imperfectly. Gallio however—did Luke know that his brother Seneca was anti-semitic?—acknowledges in verse 15 that it is not a matter of an offence against Roman law (although this expression is not used), but rather only against the Jewish law (cf. Conzelmann, *Hdb.* 107). On the other hand Luke makes Gallio occupy that standpoint which he himself considers as the correct one and which he passionately desires that Rome herself should take as her own: that Christianity is an inner-Jewish affair in which Rome does not meddle. 'Let the Jews and Christians themselves agree!'—that is the meaning of the words ὄψεσθε αὐτοί with which Gallio concludes his address. That Luke was happy to be able to report such a precedent is certain; how far in so doing he reproduced old tradition it is difficult to say. But that Gallio rejected a Jewish complaint and that afterwards the anti-Jewish crowd beat the Jewish speaker, without interference from Gallio, may very well have been an event which remained in the memory of the Christian community. On the other hand, it is difficult to conceive on what grounds Gallio rejected the complaint, other than those stated by Luke, namely that the issue belonged to the internal affairs of the contending parties. So although we may not regard the text as an exact reproduction of events, we can view the report as a whole with confidence.

43
ACTS 18:18–23
PAUL'S TRAVELS

[18] Paul remained there a considerable time longer. Then he departed from the brethren and sailed away for Syria—and with him Priscilla and Aquila—after having his hair cut in Cenchreae; for he had a vow. [19] And they landed in Ephesus and he left them there, but he himself went into the synagogue and preached to the Jews. [20] When they asked him to stay a longer time, he did not consent, [21] but departing with the words, 'I shall return to you, if God is willing', he left Ephesus [22] and landed in Caesarea, went up and greeted the community, went down to Antioch, [23] and after he had spent some time there he left and went through the Galatian country and Phrygia in turn strengthening all the brethren.

Bibliography:

Oscar Holtzmann, 1905, see § 27; K. Lake, 1933, 239f., see § 30; Renié, 1951, 257f.; Kragerud, 1955, 257, see § 29; Williams, 1957, 213f; W. Michaelis, 'Kenchreä', *ZNW* 25 (1926), 144–54; Conzelmann 107–9.

VERSE 18: Does 'Syria' here denote Palestine, which politically constituted at that time a subordinate part of the province of Syria (cf. **20**.3)?[1] Luke has probably himself added '... and with him Priscilla and Aquila'[2] as an incidental remark.[3] '... having his hair cut' applies to Paul.[4] Here we have

---

[1] So Loisy 704, who here finds a duplication by the redactor of the journey of **20**.3. Zahn 661 explains 'Syria' by referring to the fact that according to verse 23 Paul spent a long time in Antioch.—'Syria' is most easily explained if Antioch was the actual destination and in the source the only one.

[2] Priscilla is named first also in verse 26, in Romans **16**.3 and II Tim. **4**.19. We need not therefore assume that she is here named first in order that the 'cutting' might be attached directly to 'Aquila'.

[3] Wellhausen regarded the words as probably an addition to the Lucan text (37).

[4] Among the ancients, D and h already relate the words to Aquila, making v. 19 begin with κατανττήσας; among the moderns, Overbeck 297 and Preuschen 113 because of the word order, Wendt 267 because such an act is extraordinary for Paul. Bauernfeind 227 finds in it 'what is characteristic for Aquila'. Zahn 661 asks himself whether not only Aquila but also Priscilla has her hair cut, and denies this on the basis of I Cor. **11**.6 ... Holtzmann 115 already asserted, against the reference to Aquila, that there was not sufficient interest in him for Luke to have mentioned his vow.

(as in **16**.1–3) one of the traits with which Luke illustrates the fidelity of Paul's piety to the law.[1] He has thereby laid up for the commentators serious problems in connection with the (Nazirite) vow.[2]

VERSE 19: Ephesus was the capital city of the Roman province of Asia, residence of the proconsul and a commercial metropolis. The surprising sentence 'and he left them behind,[3] but he himself went into the synagogue' is explained in different ways.[4] Probably the text of the source, after αὐτὸς δέ, continued immediately with ἀνήχθη in verse 21. The insertion lets Paul execute the first missionary effort in Ephesus. For διαλέγομαι here clearly means 'to preach'.[5] D has expanded the text.[6]

VERSE 20: Although the missionary prospects are promising, Paul will not remain,[7] without any apparent reason for his hasty departure.[8]

VERSE 21: Some witnesses have inserted here the notice concerning Aquila's

---

[1] So already Overbeck 296. Beyer considers this Lucan picture genuine: Paul has not yet completely detached himself from Jewish customs . . . (111).

[2] Nazirite vows (with which Num. 6.1–21 deals) had to be discharged in Jerusalem (incidentally the passage of Josephus, *Bell*. II 15.1, which is quoted against this, is also in agreement with it); there the hair was shorn. There is nowhere any report of a hair-cutting at the beginning of the Nazirate: *Beg*. IV 230. From the moment when the vow was spoken, the hair might not be cut any more. From Bill. II 747–51 it follows that for a Nazirite oath sworn in a foreign country 'the ceremonies of absolution in the Temple could not be undertaken immediately subsequent to the return to the homeland, but only after the lapse of a certain period of waiting' which according to the more liberal interpretation of Shammai took thirty days. Reference should rather not have been made to heathen hair sacrifice as a prototype; private vows similar to the Nazirate have been conjectured for the special benefit of this passage. Cf. below on **21**.23f.—Luke appears to have possessed no exact idea of the Nazirite vow; with the source utilized in **21**.23 it is a different matter.

[3] According to Zahn (661), Paul had taken the Jewish couple with him because Aquila's house 'was to serve him in Ephesus, as during the first months in Corinth, as a place to live and work', of which the text knows nothing. Presumably the well-to-do couple took the Apostle with them when they moved their business from Corinth to Ephesus. This would be the easiest way to explain his route.

[4] Ephesus is not in contrast with the synagogue there, unless we suppose with Hilgenfeld (250f.) that Aquila and Priscilla had been excommunicated in Rome. But this supposition has rightly found no approval. Bauernfeind (227) puts it down to the carelessness of the narrator: Luke wanted to summarize very briefly and yet give a little colour. This may well happen in a narrative, but here we are dealing with a work of literature. De Wette (299) and following him Holtzmann (116) explain: Luke anticipated the two remaining behind in order to get rid of these secondary figures. Wendt (268) saw here the trace of a reworked source: it is intended to supply the reason for Paul's later return to Ephesus.

[5] This Loisy (706) overlooked when he scoffed: the redactor wanted to explain why Paul did not preach in Ephesus, and brought him into the synagogue in order to tell the Jews the cause of it (Loisy holds the Western text in v. 21 to be the original).

[6] It does not make Paul go directly from the ship into the synagogue, but only on the next Sabbath (according to Zahn: on the Sabbath which began on the day after the arrival)! The present text of D is a mixed text; instead of καταντήσας the sequel presupposes κατήντησαν.

[7] II Cor. 2.12 also speaks of such a case, which occurred in Troas. But there Paul had a reason compelling for him: he found no peace in the uncertainty concerning the Corinthian congregation.

[8] It has therefore been added in the next verse by the Western text.

staying behind,[1] which indicates how troublesome the words in verse 19 were found to be. The Western and Antiochene texts (*Beg.* III 176f.) add here, 'I absolutely must celebrate the coming feast in Jerusalem.'[2] 'If God is willing' the well-known *conditio Jacobaea*,[3] derives not from Judaism, but from paganism: *Beg.* IV 231.[4]

VERSE 22: It is a matter of debate whether Paul visited the Jerusalem congregation or the one in Caesarea.[5] Luke will have thought of a visit to Jerusalem. That the Apostolic Council took place only at this time is a mistaken hypothesis.[6]

---

[1] Accordingly Zahn (663) assumes as the text of the 'original edition': 'And he departed by ship from Ephesus. He left Aquila in Ephesus; he himself, however, succeeded in departing from Ephesus . . .', without being disturbed by the unnecessary repetitions.

[2] An explanation constructed on the model of 19.21 and 20.16. Scholars argue as to which feast is meant. Zahn (663) speaks for the Passover, but believes on account of 19.1 that Paul did not celebrate it in Jerusalem. For in the Western text of 19.1 the Jerusalem trip is only projected, but not accomplished: *Beg.* IV 230.

[3] So called because of James 4.15. Cf. Zahn 664 n. 71.

[4] Socrates already taught it (Plato *Alcib.* I 31, 135d): Dibelius, *Der Brief des Jakobus*, Göttingen 1921, 215 n. 2. ([11]1964, 278 n. 3).

[5] Against Jerusalem it is alleged: ἀναβαίνω, where Jerusalem is concerned, is not used without stating the name: Mt. 20.18; Mk. 10.32f.; Lk. 2.42 (see v. 41); 18.31, 19.28; John 2.13, 5.1, 7.8, 10 (evident from the context), 11.55, 12.20 (evident from the context); Acts 11.2, 15.2, 21.12, 15, 24.11, 25.1, 9 and Gal. 2.1. ἡ ἐκκλησία only refers to Jerusalem when that certainly emerges from the context: Acts 12.1, 13.1 (A), 15.22; Zahn 665. But it is just the question whether here the context did not make it self-evident for Luke that Jerusalem is meant.—Overbeck has urged for Jerusalem: Each of the three journeys Acts 13.1–14.28; 15.40–18.21; and 18.23–21.18 starts from Antioch and ends with a visit to Jerusalem; each one contained a speech—in each case where the emphasis lies—: the first at the beginning, the second in the middle and the third at the end (189f.).—Loisy 709 relegates the entire journey from Ephesus onwards to his redactor, after the example of Wellhausen (38) who gave out this (fourth) journey of Paul to Jerusalem as a variant of the fifth in 20.3ff.

[6] Jakob Cappellus, the son of the well-known professor in Saumur, was probably the first to see in Acts 18.22 Paul's journey to Jerusalem described in Gal. 2.1ff. Then this hypothesis appeared in William Whiston (see *RGG*[2] V, 1897f.). In Germany Köhler maintained it (*Die Abfassungszeit der epistolischen Schriften* 8: cited by Meyer, *Galaterbrief*[5], 58 n. 1); then Wieseler (*Die Chronologie des apostolischen Zeitalters*, 1848, 201ff.) advocated this thesis without finding many echoes. In 1887 Volkmar (*Paulus von Damaskus bis zum Galaterbrief*) accepted this identification. In 1905 Oscar Holtzmann (in the article 'Die Jerusalemreisen des Paulus und die Kollekte', *ZNW* 6, 102–4) touched on the theme. In 1936 John Knox ('Fourteen Years Later, a Note on the Pauline Chronology', *Journ. of Rel.* 16, 341ff.) took up his effort to prove the fourteen years of II Cor. 12.2 identical with those mentioned in Gal. 2.1, which meant that for him the Jerusalem journey of 18.22 coincided with the journey of Gal. 2.1. In 1939 he discussed his thesis afresh in the article 'The Pauline Chronology', *JBL* 58, 15–29: Paul, converted in the year 37, came in 51 to the Apostolic Council in Jerusalem, and 18.22 describes this visit. In his book *Chapters in a Life of Paul*—which ascribes great historical worth to Acts—in 1950 he defended his thesis anew, and found a supporter in Donald T. Rowlingson ('The Jerusalem Conference and Jesus' Nazareth Visit', *JBL* 71 (1952) 69–74), save that here the conversion is set in 35 and the 'Jerusalem conference' in 52. The insurmountable difficulties with which this identification of II Cor. 12.2 and Gal. 2.1 has to contend can be seen especially clearly from note 16, p. 24 of 'The Pauline Chronology': 'Perhaps I should make separate mention of the fact that Barnabas who according to Gal. 2.1 accompanied Paul on this visit had,

VERSE 23: For the indefinite note of time ποιήσας χρόνον τινά see **15**.33. The usage is a classical one: Jacquier 467. ἐξῆλθεν: this begins the so-called third missionary journey. καθεξῆς shows that 'the Galatian country' and 'Phrygia' represent two different districts (against Ramsay). But why Phrygia is named second here and first in **16**.6 remains unclear. For Luke's use of καθεξῆς (Lk. **1**.3!) see *Beg.* II, 504f.

These six verses have troubled research with two questions: 1. who had his hair cut? and 2. which congregation was greeted by Paul? Behind them stands the real great problem: what was the Lucan picture of Paul like, and how far did it reflect the real Paul?

Only a few scholars have maintained that it was Aquila who had his hair cut in Cenchreae. Overbeck cites (apart from the Vulgate) Hugo Grotius and among more recent scholars Kuinoel, Meyer, Wieseler and Oertel, who were later joined by Jüngst (167), Preuschen (113), Wendt (267), Knopf (615) and Greeven (*ThWb* II, 775 n. 11). The word order is regularly advanced as the basis for this exegesis. The author is manifestly thought to have been incapable of inserting here the phrase 'and with him Priscilla and Aquila' as an incidental comment. The overwhelming majority of commentators are however of another opinion. In his survey of 1870 Overbeck could already name a long list of representatives of this view, which he also advocated (296): Chrysostom, Theophylact, Augustine, Jerome, Isidore of Seville, Bede, Calvin, Beza, Calov, Olshausen, Neander, Ebrard, Bisping (Catholic), Lekebusch, Baumgarten, Baur, Zeller and Ewald. Among others since that time, Spitta (245), B. Weiss (*Einl.*[2] 154), H. J. Holtzmann (116), Harnack (*Beiträge* IV, 57 n. 1; ET), Schlatter (225), W. Michaelis (II, 78), Billerbeck (II, 80ff., 755ff.), Loisy (705), Beyer (111) and Lake (*Beg.* IV 229f.) have decided in favour. They rightly point out that it is far from Luke's intention to recount such a detail for a secondary person like Aquila. According to Luke it was Paul who had his hair cut. Did he really have it done?

This 'hair-cutting' is difficult to explain. Beyer and Greeven indeed speak of a Nazirite vow, but most scholars are as cautious as J. A. Bengel was once when he explained: *Votum hoc, cuiuscumque rei fuit, proprie non fuit naziraeatus, sed naziraeatui affine*, a solution which Jacquier (557) also thought the most probable. German scholars speak mostly of a Nazirite-like private vow, for a Nazirite could only be absolved from his vow in the Temple at Jerusalem (cf. Bill. II, 747ff.). A man who had taken on the Nazirate in a foreign country had, according to the most liberal tradition, to

---

according to Acts, broken with him before Paul entered Greece or Asia. I have not done so because in both Galatians and Acts the break with Barnabas occurs immediately after the 'conference', and the transposition of one event would involve transposition of the other also.'

spend at least thirty days (= shortest duration of a Nazirate) in Jerusalem before the hair that was offered could be burned and sacrifice accomplished—and of this in Paul's case, according to **18**.22, there can be no question in any case. A stricter regulation forbade the cutting of the hair before the presentation in the Temple, and the punishment for transgression was forty lashes (Bill. II, 750 below); this may be noted merely to illustrate the situation. No wonder that Lake fell back upon the idea that Paul had his hair cut in Cenchreae not for the completion of a vow, but rather for its inception. But εἶχεν γὰρ εὐχήν tells against this, and there is (as Lake himself informs us) not one single proof for this supposition. Although Luke here in **18**.18 employs the same word εὐχή as in **21**.23 (where he expressly speaks of the Nazirate), there can still be no question of a Nazirite vow in this instance. The 'private vow', to which exegetes since Spitta and B. Weiss have had recourse again and again, was invented for our passage only, in order to make the variations from the Nazirite vow more tolerable.

The readers of Acts will have possessed no more exact knowledge of the Nazirite vow than Luke himself. All the difficulties, about which we have just spoken, did not therefore exist for them. Accordingly, they could submit quietly to the impression which this communication made upon them, namely that Paul was still a Jew of exemplary devotion to the law, who had actually been unjustly suspected. If such a reader asked himself for what purpose Paul took this vow, the answer lay close at hand in his own environment: in order to avert danger, or in order that he might accomplish an undertaking successfully. If Paul now, where his missionary journey in Macedonia and Greece has successfully ended, has his hair cut, then he will before the start of his work, at the beginning of this journey, have taken the εὐχή upon himself. Thus the reader (like Luke himself) took no offence at such a vow—one vows something to God, that he for his part may give something in return—and did not suspect that such an attitude was diametrically opposed to the Pauline doctrine of grace. The case (certainly quite differently lodged!) of the Nazirite vow in **21**.24ff. appeared fully to justify Paul's conduct in **18**.18, and to permit Luke here to bring out Paul's piety with a corresponding action.

The second problem of our passage is Paul's journey. What Luke says about it is from start to finish very perplexing. Paul means to travel to Syria—and lands in Ephesus. Then he travels, bypassing Syria, to Caesarea, and visits—the exegetes are not in agreement here—either the community there or even the one in Jerusalem. He comes for a while to Antioch and travels through the Galatian country and Phrygia again to Ephesus (which nevertheless he reaches only in **19**.1).

It is however not inconceivable that Paul on a journey to Syria from Cenchreae came first to Ephesus: ancient sea travel remained well in sight of the mainland and the islands. Possibly Paul could nowhere find a ship which travelled directly from Corinth to Syria, especially in view of the prevailing winds, of which we shall have more to say. Besides, it is quite possible that Aquila and Priscilla helped out the Apostle's small travel fund by taking him with them to Ephesus when they moved their business there from Corinth.

The real difficulty begins in verse 19: Paul left Aquila and Priscilla 'there', namely in Ephesus, but went himself into the synagogue—did this synagogue then not also lie in Ephesus? Why did he not take the two with him? That they were excluded from the synagogue, as Hilgenfeld conjectured, is negated by **18.26**. Finally, why does Paul go into the synagogue, only to depart at once with unreasonable haste, without taking advantage of the favourable mission opportunity which offered itself? All these difficulties disappear (as Wendt already recognized, 268 n. 1) if we consider the words 'went into the synagogue . . . if God is willing' in vv. 19–21 as an insertion. Luke wanted the Apostle to have the honour of the first Christian sermon in Ephesus and so of initiating the founding of the congregation. In reality there already existed in Ephesus, when Paul actually came to the city—**18.26** is proof—, a Jewish-Christian community which however still lived in the fellowship of the synagogue with the other Jews. Only after the three-month effort of Paul did it come to the point of separation (**19.9**).

The riddle of Paul's mysterious journey in verse 22 is not so simply resolved. Most scholars have, if hesitantly, discovered here a visit to the congregation at Caesarea. Hesitantly—since why does Paul travel to Caesarea if he has to return directly all that long distance to Antioch (over 250 miles as the crow flies)? We can explain this great detour (for Paul had indeed nothing particular to take up with the community at Caesarea) only by the direction of the winds: in the summer a strong north-east wind prevailed (**14.26** alludes to the different wind conditions in late autumn!) which prevented a trip to Seleucia, the harbour of Antioch (*Beg.* IV 231), and forced a detour round by Caesarea.

The other possibility is that Luke means a visit to Jerusalem. For to take ἀναβαίνειν as signifying the few yards' ascent from the harbour, the unnamed Σεβαστὸς λιμήν, to the actual city of Caesarea (so Knopf 615, Bauernfeind 227) is really a desperate attempt to solve the problem, especially since this ἀναβαίνειν is paralleled by a καταβαίνειν of several hundred miles. Zahn (664) holds this explanation, advocated by Grotius and Bengel, to be indeed 'a remarkable error', because with ἀναβαίνω the name of Jerusalem is not given. But Zahn does not recognize that here we have one of those cases where, for Luke at least, the reference to Jerusalem could be deduced from the context. The word ἀναβαίνω does not therefore speak against but rather for a visit to Jerusalem, as Jacquier (559) also assumes, with Weizsäcker, B. Weiss, Ramsay, Belser and Clemen.

Here we may with advantage distinguish between two problems. 'Does the Lucan text indicate a journey by Paul to Jerusalem?' and 'Is a journey by Paul to Jerusalem at that time probable?' are two entirely different questions both important in their own right and independent of each other. That the first question should be answered affirmatively is quite evident. As an author Luke is thrifty; he wastes no space. Hence it is highly improbable that he should have reported a mere token visit to the upper city of Caesarea, especially in this section where he most severely abridges everything. The second question is quite another matter. The visit to Jerusalem involved the greatest danger for Paul. Paul had no great collection to deliver there, as is the case in Chapter 21. What should he be doing now in Jerusalem, where the encounter in Antioch had certainly not been forgotten? But Luke did not know anything about this encounter. That deadly danger threatened in Jerusalem is a motif which is first introduced in Chapter 20. According to Luke's conviction Paul was on excellent terms with the congregation of Jerusalem; he has indeed just undertaken a missionary journey in the company of Silas, an ἀνὴρ ἡγούμενος, a leading man of this congregation. Hence from the viewpoint of Acts a Pauline visit to Jerusalem is quite reasonable, while from our knowledge of the situation it would have been a senseless risk. We have therefore to reckon with the fact that Paul—on account of unfavourable winds—travelled to Caesarea, and that Luke regarded the choice of this harbour as a sign of a short visit to Jerusalem. Presumably Luke will have supposed that Paul wanted to celebrate a feast there (Jacquier 558, together with Renan (*St. Paul*, 166) and Ramsay (*St. Paul*[7], 265) identifies it as the Passover). In reality Paul will have wanted to go to Antioch in order, after his great missionary success, to bind relations with this congregation still closer.

The journey through the Cilician Gates will not have begun before the latter part of spring or the beginning of summer, because only then did they become passable. Paul may have entered Ephesus again in the autumn. The representatives of the 'north Galatian' hypothesis find mentioned in verse 23 Paul's second visit to Galatia (Gal. 4.13).

44

ACTS 18: 24-28
APOLLOS IN EPHESUS

[24] A Jew named Apollos, an Alexandrian by birth, an eloquent man and strong in the Scriptures, came to Ephesus. [25] He was instructed in the way of the Lord and spoke ardently in the Spirit and taught accurately about Jesus although he knew only the baptism of John. [26] He began to speak freely in the synagogue. When however Priscilla and Aquila heard him, they took him aside and expounded to him the way of God more precisely. [27] As he wanted to go to Achaea, the brethren, giving him their support, wrote to the disciples that they might receive him. He came and greatly helped those who had become believers by his (particular gift of) grace. [28] For he powerfully refuted the Jews by proving to them publicly from the Scripture that Jesus is the Messiah.

Bibliography:

R. Schütz, *Apostel u. Jünger*, Giessen 1921, 121f.; G. A. Barton, 'Some Influence of Apollos in the NT', *JBL* 43 (1924) 207-23; H. Preisker, 'Apollos u. d. Johannesjünger in Act. **18**.24-**19**.6', *ZNW* 30 (1931) 207-23; Käsemann, 'Die Johannesjünger von Ephesus' *ZThK* (1952) 144-54 (reprinted in *Exeg. Versuche u. Vorarbeiten*, 1960; ET *Essays on NT Themes*, 1964, 136-49) Kragerud 1955, 257f., see § 29; Trocmé 69, 73 n. 4; Williams 213-6; Conzelmann 109.

G. Zuntz, 'A Textual Criticism of Some Passages of the Acts of the Apostles (**18**.27-**19**.7)', *Classica et Mediaevalia* 3 (1940) 20-46; S. Bugge, 'Apollos og de efesinske discipler, vanndåp og ånsdåp (Acta **18**.24-**19**.7)', *Norsk Teol. Tidsskr.* 44 (1943) 83-97; E. Schweizer, 'Die Bekehrung des Apollos, Apg. **18**.24-6', *Ev.Th.* 15 (1955), 248-54; W. Grundmann, *Paulus in Ephesus*, 1964, 46-82.

VERSE 24: Paul also uses[1] the short form Ἀπολλῶς.[2] 'An Alexandrian by birth' indicates nothing about a Christian community in Alexandria.[3] λόγιος:

---

[1] I Cor. **1**.12; **3**.4ff., 22; **4**.6 and **16**.12.

[2] For Apollonius (so D d). 'Apelles' in ℵ, and in Didymus and Ammonius, is a learned attempt to identify him with the Apelles of Romans **16**.10: *Beg.* IV 232.

[3] Cf. the discussion of the reading of D in the following verse.

commentators vacillate between 'eloquent'[1] and 'learned', 'educated',[2] if they do not permit or combine both meanings.[3] The comparison with Philo (Bauernfeind 229) readily suggests itself, but fits only if one does not picture Apollos as an ecstatic spiritualist. '. . . strong in the Scriptures': denotes the gift of the Spirit by which the hidden Christian meaning of the Old Testament is uncovered.

VERSE 25: Where Apollos had been instructed[4] in the 'way of the Lord'[5] remains undisclosed.[6] ζέων τῷ πνεύματι: some scholars think what is described here is a fiery temperament,[7] others the gift of the divine Spirit.[8] Apollos taught[9] 'accurately about Jesus'—how consistent is that with 'he knew only the baptism of John'?[10]

VERSE 26: ἤρξατο, because Priscilla and Aquila[11] immediately interfered?

---

[1] *Beg.* IV 233.

[2] Overbeck 302, Holtzmann 118.

[3] Bauer, *Wb* 942; Wendt 270; Beyer 112 ('highly educated and eloquent'); Bauernfeind 229.

[4] Lake thinks that by 'instructed' is meant inaccurate information by hearsay (*Beg.* IV 233), but the following 'accurate' does not square well with this interpretation.

[5] For ὁδός see W. Michaelis in *ThWb* V 93–5. 'Way of the Lord' or 'God' is for Luke the Christian teaching.

[6] D (which interprets and replaces the unusual ὁδόν by the familiar λόγον; so also d) inferred Alexandria, about which Luke never speaks, probably from v. 24. According to Loisy 711, supporters of Stephen came during the persecution to their old home in Alexandria and there provided the impulse for a distinctive development of Christianity; cf. Walter Bauer, *Rechtgläubigkeit und Ketzerei im ältesten Christentum*, Tübingen 1934, (²1964), 49–64, especially 51.—Zahn 699f. on the other hand will hear only of some pilgrims who brought back 'a certain report' about John the Baptist and Jesus, and who nevertheless converted Apollos—highly unlikely.

[7] So Overbeck 304; Holtzmann 118; Preuschen 114; Wendt 270; Loisy 711; Zahn 699; Bruce 351. Such a use of 'pneuma' is certainly very unusual; most of the passages quoted in support can also be used for the opposite interpretation. But the possession of the Spirit by an evidently still imperfect Christian does not really seem conceivable.

[8] Dibelius (*Die urchristliche Überlieferung von Johannes dem Täufer*, 1911, 95 n. 1); *Beg.* IV 233; Bauernfeind 229; Käsemann ('The Disciples of John the Baptist in Ephesus', 143): '. . . the expression "fervent in the Spirit" is unambiguously defined by Rom. 12.21 as a phrase current in the language of Christian edification.' Käsemann refers also to J. Weiss, *Das Urchristentum* 239 (ET *Earliest Christianity*, 1959, I, 316) and Preisker, 'Apollos und die Johannesjünger in Ephesus', *ZNW* 1931, 301–4.

[9] The imperfects express habitual custom: Zahn 669.

[10] While Beyer (112) sees here the representative of an early Christian circle which celebrated a baptism of repentance with reference only to the coming Messiah but without invocation of the name of Jesus, Holtzmann (118) a man who still held the standpoint of the baptism of John, and Dibelius (op. cit. 88f.) discovered traces of a syncretistic half-Christian belief, Wendt (270 n. 3) distinguished between the source, which knew of an Alexandrian-Jewish teacher, and the additions of the author, for whom Apollos was a follower of the Baptist (who already recognized Jesus as the Messiah). Käsemann on the other hand, who here carries further the opinion of Loisy (711), holds Apollos for a Christian teacher independent of apostolic Christianity, whom Luke depicts as still imperfect only in order that he may be found to require and participate in the help and approval of the Church: 153. Bruce 351: Apollos knew only a Galilean Gospel.

[11] That Priscilla is again named first (not admittedly in D; cf. Harnack, *SAB* 1900, 2–13) allows Knopf (616) here also to conclude that she is particularly active.

They are not, therefore, excluded[1] from the synagogue, in which here apparently Jewish-Christians and Jews are still harmoniously gathered together.[2] To what extent they instructed Apollos 'more accurately'[3] about the 'way of God'[4] is not stated. Scholars think mostly of the Christian baptism of the Spirit.

VERSE 27: Here it is clear that there already existed in Ephesus a (Jewish Christian) congregation.[5] 'Offering encouragement'—to whom? To Apollos[6] or to the Corinthian Christians?[7] Paul alludes in II Cor. 3.1 to such letters of recommendation, but whether directly to this one (so Loisy 715) is questionable. The D text is again secondary.[8] συμβάλλομαι = to help. The phrase διὰ τῆς χάριτος is sometimes referred to Apollos,[9] and sometimes to those who had become believers.[10] In the second half of the verse also D is secondary.[11]

VERSE 28: διακατελέγχομαι only here: the worn-out simple form of the verb is reinforced. '. . . the Jews'[12]: not mentioned by Paul in I Cor. Luke has perhaps deduced this activity from the statement in verse 24 that Apollos was a 'powerful interpreter of Scripture'. 'Publicly': after the Corinthian congregation's breach with the synagogue (18.6) Apollos could no longer seek out the Jews there: Loisy 717.

[1] Cf. the discussion above on v. 19.
[2] Cf. below on 19.9.
[3] Lake (*Beg.* IV 234) prefers the elative sense of the comparative; Luke is only using variety of expression in comparison with v. 25. Still after v. 25 one expects a climax: Wendt 271.
[4] Ropes (*Beg.* III, 178) holds the absolute ὁδός in D for the original text. Cf. above on 9.2. It occurs elsewhere only in Pauline narratives: 9.2, 19.9, 22.4, 24.14 and 22.
[5] That Aquila and Priscilla 'for the sake of brevity' are here described as 'the brethren' (so Wendt 271) is a desperate expedient. Loisy (715) and Bauernfeind (229) think (like earlier scholars) of the Christians won by Aquila and Priscilla. That is not much better.
[6] So Holtzmann 119, Knopf 615, Wendt 271, Loisy 715, Zahn 670, Beyer 114, Bauernfeind 227.
[7] So Overbeck 306, Preuschen 114.
[8] It tries to explain more precisely why Apollos went to Corinth: Corinthian Christians dwelling in Ephesus asked him to go to Corinth, and the Ephesian Christians wrote a letter of recommendation.
[9] Holtzmann 119, Wendt 271, Loisy 715, Beyer 112, Bauernfeind 227.
[10] Overbeck 306, Preuschen 114, *Beg.* IV 234.
[11] D replaces the unusual 'those who had become believers' by 'communities'; he has in view a more extended Christian mission in Greece than the Corinthian letters allow us to suppose.
[12] Because here this activity among the Jews is mentioned, we need not with Harnack (*Beitr.* III, 104 n. 1; ET) 'conjecture that Luke esteemed Apollos a more successful converter of Jews than Paul himself, and that hence there were compelling reasons for him to mention him'.

45
ACTS 19:1–7
PAUL AND THE DISCIPLES OF JOHN IN EPHESUS

[1] It happened that Paul—while Apollos was in Corinth—passing through the upper regions, came to Ephesus and found some disciples, [2] and he said to them: 'Did you receive the Holy Spirit, when you became believers?' They said to him, 'We have never even heard if there is a Holy Spirit.' [3] And he said, 'Into what were you baptized?' They said, 'Into the baptism of John.' [4] Paul said, 'John baptized with a baptism of repentance, telling the people they should believe in the one coming after him, that is, in Jesus.' [5] When they heard that they had themselves baptized in the name of the Lord Jesus. [6] And when Paul laid his hands on them the Holy Spirit came upon them and they spoke in tongues and prophesied. [7] There were in all about twelve men.

Bibliography:

Behm, 1911, see § 16; Charles Picard, *Ephèse et Claros*, Paris 1922, 703f.; Alberto Pincherle, 'Paolo a Epheso', *Ricerche Religiose* 3, Rome 1927, 422–39; Fr. Raphael Tonneau O.P., 'Ephèse au temps de Saint Paul', *Rev. Bibl.* 38 (1929), 5–34; 321–69; T. R. S. Broughton, 'Roman Asia Minor' in *Economic Survey of Ancient Rome* IV (1938), 800, 813; F. V. Filson, 'Ephesus and the NT', *The Biblical Archaeologist* 8 (1945), 73–80; M. M. Parvis, 'Archaeology and St. Paul's Journeys in Greek Lands. Part IV: Ephesus.', *The Bibl. Archaeologist* 8 (1945) 66–73; E. Käsemann, 'The Disciples of John the Baptist in Ephesus', *Essays on NT Themes* 1964, 136–49; see § 44. Josef Keil, *Ephesos. Ein Führer durch die Ruinenstätte und ihre Geschichte*, Wien 1957, esp. XV and 68.

VERSE 1: '... while Apollos was in Corinth' unites this with the preceding. διελθόντα τὰ ἀνωτερικὰ μέρη = the Asia Minor uplands = 'the Galatian land and Phrygia' of 18.23.[1] '... and found': that Paul's synagogue visit is not

---

[1] Lake (*Beg.* IV 236f., V 240) rejects Ramsay's interpretation 'hill country'—Paul, according to Ramsay, did not come from Pisidian Antioch on the main highway but on a northern route which led over the mountains—and wants (like Holtzmann 119) to have it understood as the 'hinterland' (as seen from Ephesus). Beyer 115: the 'interior' (of Asia Minor); Wendt 272, Preuschen 114, Loisy 717, Zahn 672f., Bauernfeind 227 also relate

recounted first is due to the Lucan composition: the relationship of the Apostle to the synagogue is depicted later in connection with his activity in Ephesus.[1] μαθητής for Luke always signifies 'Christian'.[2]

VERSE 2: Paul's question comes suddenly (Bauernfeind 229). Luke does not deal with what is for him the side issue, why Paul came to doubt the genuineness of the disciples' Christianity. That Paul's question must clarify the situation is for him self-evident (Knopf 619). πιστεύσαντες: Luke could also have written 'when you were baptized'. Those who are questioned explain that they had not even heard whether there is a Holy Spirit.[3]

VERSE 3: If the twelve are in such a dire position in regard to the Spirit, then their baptism cannot be in order.[4] Paul, therefore, goes on to ask, εἰς τί have you been baptized? The natural question would be, εἰς τίνα. But it is not to be made apparent that here a baptism has been effected in some other name than that of Jesus; hence the peculiar question and the equally peculiar answer 'into the baptism of John'. Of course it ought properly to run 'in the name of John'. But that Luke cannot permit. The Baptist would then be dispossessed of the place assigned to him by the Church.

VERSE 4: Now follows the instruction concerning the relationship of the baptism of John to Christian baptism: John even with his baptism was only a preacher of repentance. He baptized with a baptism of repentance and exhorted people to believe in the one who was to come after him,[5] i.e. Jesus.

VERSE 5: The listeners are willing and submit to baptism, true baptism (to speak of a re-baptism would be incongruous with the Lucan point of view): in the name of the Lord Jesus.[6] According to Zahn 675 n. 92, Aquila was 'without question' the one who did the baptizing.

---

the expression to the Galatian country and Phrygia.—ἀνωτερικός occurs only in Luke and medical authors. Despite this we should not use it to support the thesis that Luke the physician wrote Acts. For in the medical literature the ἀνωτερικὰ φάρμακα are the emetics: Preuschen 115, *Beg.* IV 237.

[1] This may be the answer to Bauernfeind's question (229) why Paul met these disciples before he sought out the synagogue again.

[2] Stressed by Wellhausen 39, Knopf 618, Preuschen 115, Loisy 718, Zahn 673, *Beg.* IV 237, Käsemann 136.

[3] We may not weaken this answer like Wendt (272); 'whether there is a Holy Spirit on earth for men' and Beyer (114): they had not heard that the Spirit of the last times 'now "is here"'. The Holy Spirit of the Christians is completely unknown to them!

[4] On the connection between baptism and Spirit in Luke see above on 8.14ff. and the general discussion pp. 556f. Cf. Käsemann, op. cit. 143ff.

[5] This goes beyond the synoptic tradition, in which John only proclaims the Coming One but does not summon to belief in him (which in the framework of his proclamation would have been meaningless). Neither is the Johannine tradition reproduced, in which John and Jesus work side by side. It should be borne in mind that our passage gives the final result of the Baptist's activity and significance, and is not narrating a detail from his life.

[6] 𝔓38 and D have added the words 'Christ for the forgiveness of sins' and thus produced the baptismal formula of their time. We can see from this how the formulae became more and more liturgically developed.

T

VERSE 6: With the laying on of hands by Paul, which concludes the baptismal ceremony, the Holy Spirit comes: the baptized speak in tongues and prophesy.[1] Like Peter in Acts 10.44, 46 so here Paul dispenses the (ecstatic) Spirit (Holtzmann 120), only the Spirit in this case appears more directly related to the act of baptism than in the Cornelius narrative. Cf. the commentary on Chapter 10 above.

VERSE 7: The narrative closes with the statement of the number 'in all about twelve'[2] (cf. above 4.4). ὡσεί seems to contradict the exact number; but Luke places ὡς or ὡσεί before all numbers: 2.4, 4.4, 5.7, 36, 10.3, 13.18, 20, 19.7 and 34.

For the understanding of the first narrative there are three basic possibilities: when Apollos came to Ephesus he was either a Jew, a disciple of John or a Christian. W. L. Knox (88) spoke of a Jewish preacher of repentance, as also (according to Wendt 270 n. 3) did at least Luke's source. Knopf (616) saw in Apollos a disciple of John: he held John to be a prophet, and like him proclaimed the imminence of the Messiah (not Jesus!). E. Schweizer (252) has renewed this interpretation fifty years later. Most scholars, however, consider Apollos a Christian. They disagree only over what is lacking in his Christianity. According to Zahn 669f. it is simply precise information: Alexandrian pilgrims would have brought home only 'a certain report' of the Baptist and Jesus which to be sure won Apollos, but which still had to be completed. It remains inexplicable how such a report could make anyone a missionary. Hence W. Michaelis 735f. thinks it better to consider Apollos himself a pilgrim to Jordan who had left Palestine before Good Friday. But in that case it still needs to be explained how in the next twenty years he had met no 'perfect Christian' who could have taught him about Easter and Pentecost. Beyer (114), Schlatter (228) and Lake (*Beg.* IV 231) think of Apollos as knowing something about the resurrection, but as not yet possessing the correct—or later—understanding of baptism (baptism in the name of Jesus). Dibelius (*Johannes der Täufer* 92 [Göttingen 1911]) doubts the orthodoxy of Apollos: in his 'half-Christianity' faith in Jesus as σωτήρ was bound up with syncretistic elements, as with Paul who however did not hold the syncretistic elements to be essential (93). Paul through his own connection with the primitive Church made it possible for syncretistic groups to become members in the apostolic Church; this may be the kernel of truth in the Lucan presentation (94). With this we come to the last variation: Apollos was an independent Christian missionary, an outsider, who actually (Bauernfeind

---

[1] Loisy (723) doubts that Luke differentiated the two as Paul does in I Cor. 14.

[2] Frequently (Weizsäcker 341, Wendt 273, *Beg.* IV 238) the question has been asked whether the number twelve is not to be understood allegorically—one could think of the twelve Apostles or the twelve tribes. But Luke has only given a small round number, such as the story required, without having any such undertones in mind.

228f.) or in the redactor's opinion (Loisy 713) or Luke's (Käsemann 252) was made a member in the *Una sancta*.

What does the analysis indicate? Sixty years ago Jüngst (168f.) remarked that vv. 24, 25ab, 27 and 28 convey a report about the origin, merits and activity of the Christian missionary Apollos. These laudatory statements are interrupted in vv. 25c and 26, which exhibit a defect (now removed by Priscilla and Aquila) in his teaching. The contradiction between 'he was instructed concerning the way of the Lord and ... taught accurately concerning Jesus' (v. 25) and 'they expounded to him the way of God more precisely' (v. 26) is particularly striking. These declarations really cancel each other out. Either Apollos taught inaccurately, in which case further instruction was possible and meaningful; or he taught accurately, which means that further instruction was unnecessary.

The viewpoint expressed in vv. 25 and 26 shows Apollos first receiving the completion of his teaching from the fellow-workers of Paul. Within certain limits I Cor. allows us to verify that. Apollos appeared during the absence of Paul as a teacher in the Corinthian community (of which Paul considered himself the father: 4.15). He there, to be sure, won new members for the congregation, but they looked on Apollos rather than Paul as their spiritual father, the one whom they considered their leader and honoured authority. Thus the ἐγώ εἰμι 'Απολλῶ stood next to and over against the ἐγὼ Παύλου (I Cor. 1.12). Over against this Paul recalls first that it is not Paul and Apollos but God, who gives the growth of the community, who alone is important. But Paul goes beyond this statement with a further analogy: 'According to the grace of God granted to me I have, like a wise architect, laid the foundation.' That does not mean that Paul won the first Christians in Corinth, but rather that he laid that foundation which is the only one, Jesus Christ (3.11). This Pauline preaching of Christ provided the foundation upon which 'another builds' (3.10, 12). Paul expresses himself very cautiously here; he does not mention names any longer but speaks only of 'the one who builds upon it'. The last day will prove whether his work will have any permanence; perhaps this work will be consumed by the judgement fire, even though the 'one who builds upon it' may himself be saved, ὡς διὰ πυρός. While, therefore, the ἐποικοδομῶν and his work still await the test, Paul has laid the right foundation and is relieved of such cares. Apollos—for he according to the sense is the ἐποικοδομῶν and the ποτίζων—thus does not come into the picture here as one who brings the foundational preaching of Christ in Corinth to a wider circle (Paul says absolutely nothing about any such extensive successes), but rather as the bringer of a proclamation which goes beyond the foundational preaching of Christ. Again and again Paul in these chapters comes back to two things which people missed in him but apparently detected in someone else, the gift of edifying speech, which was denied to Paul himself (II Cor. 10.10; if Luke had any suspicion of that!) and

the gift of 'wisdom'. It is difficult not to think here of the man from Alexandria who was 'powerful in the Scriptures' and who there found secrets of
which the preacher Paul had said not a word. What will remain of all this
'wisdom' in the judgement fire? At the conclusion of his treatment of
'wisdom' Paul once again mentions some names: beside his own those of
Apollos and Cephas. The fact that in I Cor. 4.6 he asserts that he has exemplified the situation by referring to himself and Apollos for the sake of the
Corinthians takes the personal sharpness from what he says. But the undertones remain. If we seek to exclude the purely personal from the Apostle's
reaction, then one thing remains: he has found in the proclamation of
Apollos (to whom he does not deny a Christian status: σωθήσεται) a foreign
element which to him appears as chaff rather than gold. Apollos was, therefore, no Paulinist, but a missionary quite independent in his work and
thought, whom Paul faced with considerable reserve. It is clear from this that
Acts 18.26 has not the slightest support in I Cor.

This verse however affirms that Apollos had Paul's fellow-workers to
thank for the perfection of his teaching in the Apostle's absence. This idea,
which does not agree with the rest of the account in 18.24–8, we must
attribute to Luke, who thought to improve the tradition he received. What
Bauernfeind has cautiously and Käsemann bluntly asserted, is quite apposite,
namely the assumption that for Luke it was intrinsically impossible for a
missionary to have worked independently (as a 'freebooter', as Käsemann has
formulated it) alongside the apostolic Church (of which Paul was but an
extended arm in Luke's view). Therefore Luke considered it necessary to
incorporate Apollos into the apostolic Church.

But why by means of 'the baptism of John'? To answer this question we
must begin with the second narrative, Paul's conversation with the twelve
disciples. It is generally agreed today that events could not have occurred as
Luke records in his 'condensed' presentation. To that extent the Lucan
composition is here at least a contributory factor. But with this the story
does not yet lose its obscurity. These men must—as μαθηταί—be Christians,
and yet they have not even heard that there is a Holy Spirit, much less
received it! They could not have belonged to the congregation in Ephesus, for
there they would have received better instruction from Priscilla and Aquila.
Therefore Luke is quite correct in having Paul encounter them not in the
Ephesian congregation but in an unidentified place somewhere. It comes to
light as their real failing that they were not baptized with the right baptism, the
baptism in the name of Jesus, and when Paul now completes this baptism
with the accompanying laying on of hands, the ecstatic Spirit is immediately
present with the speaking of tongues and prophesying—Luke can make the
reality of the Spirit visible in no other way.

What was so valuable for Luke in this narrative that he included it in
his work? He wanted in Chapter 19 to give a total picture of the successful

work of Paul. To it this narrative contributes an important feature: Paul wins over the sects. Of course Luke could not bestow the glory on him in this form: his ideal picture of apostolic times had no room for sects and schisms. And a sect which made the Baptist the bearer of salvation did not rightly belong in the picture. So he could only represent the disciples of John, about whom his tradition reported, as incomplete Christians, who were baptized 'with the baptism of John'. Here Luke's complete disparity from the early times is apparent. John's eschatological sacrament of baptism which saves from the fiery judgement has become merely an expression of repentance and cannot give the baptized person the real gift of baptism, i.e. the Spirit. In this guise, the readers could easily recognize the Baptist sects of their own day. It was not only a power of the past: the polemic of the Fourth Gospel against a messianic valuation of the Baptist proves that at that time the defensive battle against the Baptist sects was urgently required.

This incomplete Christianity, however, which reveals itself as such for these twelve men, helped Luke now to depict the incompleteness of Apollos' Christianity more concretely. Of course Luke formulates this with extraordinary caution. He does not say, 'Apollos had received only the baptism of John'—in that case, Aquila would have had to baptize him again as Paul had to do with the twelve men. And that the well-known missionary Apollos had first received Christian baptism from Aquila would have been a falsification which Luke did not want to write. So he helped himself with the expression 'knowing only the baptism of John'—as if it dealt with a defect in the teaching, which could be corrected by instruction.

In 19.1–7 Paul is, as usual, the focal point of the scene. In 18.24–8 on the other hand it appears to be Apollos. But that is only partly correct. Apollos owes it to Paul's fellow-workers that he is given the stamp of the correct teaching and administration of the sacrament. So the absent Paul—though not visible—is still the centre of events.

46

ACTS 19:8–40

PAUL'S WORK IN EPHESUS

We can estimate Chapter 19 aright only when we understand it in the total design of Luke's work. It is the last chapter in which Paul can freely pursue his missionary efforts. Over Chapter 20 already lie the shadows of departure, not merely from missionary work but also from life. Accordingly, before he depicts Paul in retrospect, in the farewell speech at Miletus, as the model missionary, Luke in Chapter 19 once more shows his reader the Apostle at work, and indeed at the zenith of his labours. For the uproar caused by Demetrius reveals how hard hit paganism as a cult religion was: the entire devotional handicraft of the temple of Artemis faces ruin! The burning of the books of magic in Ephesus, the home of the Ἐφέσια γράμματα, bespeaks that the hour has struck also for this more private side of pagan religion, magic. Before that stands the report about Paul's activity in Ephesus, which reached all Jews and Greeks in the province of Asia, and about the Pauline miracles, the proof of the Spirit and of power—as Luke understood it. Between these two sections, however, we find as a parenthesis the anecdote of the sons of Sceva which presents Paul as the one who cannot be imitated and at the same time serves to provide the motive for the renunciation of magic. Thus understood the chapter is a unity, which makes the reader feel that if now the prison gates close behind Paul, his work is still done.

To attain this goal, Luke has utilized very varied means. General summary reports alternate with colourful scenes. As the rules of such a composition demand, the most extensively developed episode ('Great is Artemis of the Ephesians!') stands at the end. Everything else which precedes it must be kept short. This has done perceptible damage to the story of the sons of Sceva if we measure it by the standards of a transparent tale *en miniature*. But that would be wrong. What Luke wants to say with this story is clear, and that suffices.

How far the individual features of this picture are historically authentic we shall also ask in each sub-section; but this is not the most important question. We do not have here a photograph of Paul taken by a fellow-worker, but the picture which stood before the eyes of the sub-apostolic Church of that Paul whom the early Church recognized and honoured and who down to Augustine and Luther stood before the Paul of the letters.

46a. 19:8–10: Paul separates the Congregation from the Synagogue

[8] Going into the synagogue he taught boldly for three months and sought to convince about the kingdom of God. [9] When, however, some hardened themselves and refused to obey, speaking evil of the 'way' before the whole congregation, he withdrew from them and separated the disciples, preaching daily in the lecture hall of Tyrannus. [10] This went on for two years, so that all the inhabitants of the province of Asia heard the word of the Lord, Jews as well as Greeks.

Bibliography:

Kragerud, 1955, 257f., see § 29; G. S. Duncan, 'Paul's Ministry in Asia— the Last Phase', *NTS* 3 (1957), 211–18; Williams, 1957, 219ff.

W. Aalders, *De oerchristelijke gemeente (Act. 19)*, Groningen, 1946.

VERSE 8 begins anew. '. . . going into the synagogue' was anticipated in **18, 19**. For παρρησία see above **9.27**. διαλέγομαι is best translated as 'preach' and πείθω as 'seek to convince' (cf. Wendt 273).

VERSE 9: '. . . some hardened themselves': cf. **13.45, 14.2, 18.6, 28.24f**. '. . . the way'—see above, **9.2**. πλῆθος (cf. **4.32**): the congregation. '. . . daily'[1] in the hall[2] of Tyrannus[3].[4]

VERSE 10: 'Two years': the 'three months' of verse 8 and perhaps the χρόνος of verse 22 should apparently be added to it; **20.31** speaks roundly of a τριετία. '. . . and all the inhabitants of (the province of) Asia' (therefore Mysians, Lydians and Carians: Bauernfeind 230) is according to Overbeck (314) an overstatement, according to Zahn (680) a 'grateful optimism'.[5] From

---

[1] According to Zahn (679) 'daily' is to be taken *cum grano salis*. But Luke really wants to indicate an unbroken activity of Paul.

[2] The earlier assumption that this σχολή may have been a private synagogue has been given up, although such a place could just as well be called σχολή as the gathering places of heathen cult associations (Bill. II 751, Holtzmann 121). Here we must rather think of a lecture hall (Preuschen 115).

[3] Whether Tyrannus was a teacher ('a schoolmaster': Zahn 678) or the owner of the hall, or whether it is a building well known as the 'hall of Tyrannus' can no longer be determined.

[4] D d sy^hms read Τυράννου τινός (and thus presuppose the first or the second of the above-mentioned possibilities) and add: 'from the fifth to the tenth hour', that is from 11 to 4 o'clock. That was the middle of the day and the midday rest. According to *Beg.* IV 239 this inconvenient time speaks for the genuineness of the report; according to Clemen, *Paulus* I, 285 the writer of these words recognized only the usual times of work and instruction (from the early morning to 11 o'clock). If Paul had preached during working hours, his listeners would have been prevented from attending.—The addition of D d E e pesh sy^hms (πλήθους τῶν ἐθνῶν) is a gloss due to misunderstanding: Ropes (*Beg.* III 182).

[5] Zahn 677 note 98 reads with D 'the words of the Lord' and explains this (secondary: Ropes, *Beg.* III 182) variant: 'Jesus is the proclaimer of this word. Jesus is the original evangelist.'

Ephesus further congregations of Pauline character were founded: Colossae, Laodicea, Hierapolis; cf. W. Bauer, *Rechtgläubigkeit und Ketzerei im ältesten Christentum*, 237.

The statements of time and place (three months, two years, the hall of Tyrannus) Luke must have taken over from tradition. But what creates life out of this chronological-topographical skeleton goes back to Luke himself, whose style is here unmistakable. Again follow, on this occasion after an amazingly long interval, the break with the Jews, the independent establishment of the Christian congregation and its missionary preaching in its own accommodation, rented though it was. In all this Paul is the sole agent: *he* 'separated the disciples'.

Such a presentation, which for Luke develops the fundamental lines of the Pauline history up till now, naturally leaves unanswered many questions which the historian must ask if he wants to achieve a living picture of that time: why does the break with the Jews actually come just now? Why did they not blaspheme during the time Apollos preached there in the synagogue and Aquila and Priscilla belonged to it? Why also did they not blaspheme during the first three months of the Pauline proclamation? Was it Paul—we may suggest this as a possible answer—who first proclaimed the doctrine of the emancipation of the Gentiles from the Law, revealing this secret of the divine guidance only as gradually as possible? Or another question: Paul separated the disciples—did the Christian community there (Luke could not be too outspoken about it because he wanted to let the Ephesian community appear so far as possible the work of Paul) not already have its own meetings previously, at which they celebrated the Lord's Supper? Or still another question: did Paul after a three-month effort so sovereignly rule the community (which he had not founded!) that he could order their separation from the synagogue? The abolition of fellowship with the synagogue would have been a difficult decision for the community, to which they must have agreed because it was not just individual Jews who blasphemed. Ephesian Judaism was filled with a deadly animosity toward the Apostle which can still be divined from Acts, but to present which was not to Luke's mind.

This separation from the synagogue and the missionary discourses in the hall of Tyrannus are two different though related matters. The Christians would not have held the Lord's Supper during the daytime in the hall of Tyrannus but in the evening in house congregations. We do not know how the teaching activity proceeded in the hall of Tyrannus. The time which the Western text suggests was decidedly unfavourable: on this Lake remarks, 'at 1.0 p.m. there were probably more people sound asleep than at 1.0 a.m.' (*Beg.* IV 239). Nevertheless this D text and the verse 20.34 have determined the picture which Ambrosiaster (on II Cor. 11.23, cited by Zahn 678) has sketched of the life of the Apostle here: *hic enim a mane usque ad quintam horam victum manibus quaerebat et ita exinde usque ad decimam horam disputabat publice tanto labore, ut contradicentibus suaderet.* That was too much even for Zahn. He wanted to understand 'the division of time in the Apostle's twofold work not of course as if Paul first worked in leather from 6.0 in the morning to 4.0 in the afternoon without rest or bodily refreshment, and afterwards talked for almost as many hours'. 'Also the statement that Paul held these discussions daily is to be taken *cum grano salis*', thinks Zahn (679). Paul would have found it 'difficult without offering a rent' to procure a reservation from Tyrannus which would allow him the use of his lecture hall daily from 11.0 a.m. to 4.0 p.m. With this supposition Zahn has touched upon a problem, for an answer to which Luke has left us no material. Even if Paul 'worked in leather' from early morning to 11.0 a.m. and as far as possible from 4.0 p.m. on, the wages would not have been sufficient to furnish a livelihood for him and his companions and to meet the cost of the rent. The congregation must have contributed substantially—Aquila and Priscilla were indeed not without means, and also we must not underestimate the liberality of a young community. But here again Luke lets all the limelight fall upon Paul. The picture of the missionary who earns everything with his own hands may have been introduced into the tradition from certain assertions in II Cor.

Luke has also kept silent about many other things that we would gladly know more precisely. According to his portrayal the reader has to believe that Paul in these two years remained in Ephesus and from the hall of Tyrannus reached the entire Roman province of Asia. Luke does not seem to know that Paul visited Corinth during this time. But even if he had known the history of the changing relationships between Paul and the Corinthian community, how much of it could he have admitted into his work without bursting it open? The case is very similar with the incident alluded to in I Cor. **15**.32.

46b. Acts 19:11–12: Paul's Miracles

[11] And God accomplished extraordinary deeds of power by the hands of Paul, [12] so that people brought to the sick scarves and handkerchiefs which had touched his skin, and the sicknesses left them and the evil spirits departed.

VERSE 11: 'Extraordinary'[1] deeds of power, healings, 'God did by the hands[2] of Paul': miracles are added to supplement the preaching. According

---

[1] The litotes οὐ τὰς τυχούσας (cf. **28**.2) is a Hellenistic idiom. The consideration attached by Bauernfeind 230 to this expression, that it deals with exceptions which never recur, thus loses its basis in the text.

[2] 'By the hands' is here as in **5**.12 no Semitism. The power is conveyed by direct contact (laying-on of hands): *Beg.* IV 239.

to *Beg*. IV 239, vv.11f. are a summary composed by Luke like 5.15. Wendt (274 n. 2) holds vv. 11–20 to be an addition of the author's derived from the oral tradition.

VERSE 12: The mighty deeds of Paul prompt the believers to lay scarves and handkerchiefs[1] of Paul's upon the sick to heal them. In this they are completely successful.

Luke speaks here first of those miracles (healings and exorcisms) which Paul personally accomplished, probably by laying on of hands, and then of those in which his scarves and handkerchiefs played the role of the miracle worker. Scholars have advanced different explanations of how this second type of miracle came about. But whether they were 'liberal' like Wellhausen or 'conservative' like Zahn, one perceives in most of them a certain uneasiness and the attempt to excuse the Apostle. Wellhausen (40) imagines the credulous or superstitious crowd which presses around the Apostle: 'The *sudaria* are taken away from him . . . or torn from him.' There is no such violence according to Zahn (681f.), but the crowd is civil, restrained and well-behaved: 'The relatives of the sick will have contrived to acquire some scarf or handkerchief for quite transitory use from Priscilla, Paul's hostess.' Had Paul anything against this, his opposition must have 'been silenced . . . by the immediate and repeated success'. Bauernfeind (231) feels no need for the intercalation of Priscilla: 'The idea that Paul knew nothing whatsoever about the use of the cloths has to be read into the narrative; rather the text suggests that people asked Paul for the cloths, received them, and took them still warm to the sick.' So we have come from the artless naïveté of Zahn to a surprisingly realistic theosophy which imagines decisions 'in the highest sphere' analogous to the precedents on the lower level. No less modern is the scepticism which cautiously ventures forth in Beyer (118): Paul performs healings of the sick 'which on this superstitious soil are exploited with a vengeance and made more crude by the crowd'. Paul gains 'the reputation that healing powers proceed from the very cloths and working-aprons which had come into contact with his skin'. Preuschen's formulation betrays a repugnance clothed in a scientific statement (117): 'The miraculous healings through the paraphernalia of the Apostolic toilette show the idea which lies at the basis of ancient belief in miracles, namely that the effect of a particular person can also be indirectly communicated'. But we might well ask whether the man of late antiquity really did see here a 'personal efficacy' in Preuschen's sense: if anyone is considered to be actively filled with miraculous power, it does not

---

[1] Overbeck (315) explains the σιμικίνθια (= *semicinctia*) as aprons which Paul wore in his work; *Beg*. IV 240 considers that possible. The usual explanation goes back to Ammonius: cloths of linen which persons held in the hand in order to dry off moisture from the face. A long garment without pockets did not permit the use of a handkerchief. We can safely translate 'handkerchief' if we want to awaken the correct image of the σιμικίνθια.

make much difference whether he transmits it by a laying-on of hands himself or with the cloth which has touched his body.

How can we test the historical worth of this information, without making one or the other hypothesis? Obviously only if we can, independently of Acts, establish how Paul himself and his contemporaries thought about his miracles. Concerning this Ernst Käsemann in his article 'Die Legitimät des Apostels' (*ZNW* 1942–3, 33–71) has already spoken definitively. He shows (35 and 61ff.) how Paul indeed affirms—without reference to concrete events—that he has accomplished the 'signs of the Apostle' (healings and exorcisms are meant) in Corinth. These mighty works, however, have so little reached the level of the unusual or extraordinary that his opponents have roundly denied that he possesses the ability to work wonders. So in those years—the controversy with these Corinthian opponents occurs at the very time about which verses 11f. speak!—the news cannot have got around that the very cloths which had lain on Paul's skin drove out sicknesses and demons. In other words vv. 11f. sketch the picture of Paul as it may have appeared according to the requirements of early Christian πνευματικοί. The Apostle is *eo ipso* the Mighty, the Triumphant. But that flatly contradicts, as Käsemann has irrefutably proven, the Pauline conception of the Apostle. The Apostle has no such objectively controllable characteristics (op. cit. 59). He can and must glorify himself only in his weakness. That the power of Christ works in him, only the Christian mind sees (58). Whosoever wants to see the Apostle distinguished by extraordinary miracles fails to recognize that in him is reflected the form of Jesus the crucified (55). Of this Pauline teaching about the apostolate there is in Luke not a word. He could view Paul (vv. 11f. make this clear) only with the eyes of his own time: the Paul, already transfigured by legend, who so overflowed with divine power that even the cloths on his body are drenched with it. Such an Apostle is already delivered from weakness. He lives no longer in the sphere of the cross but in that of glory.

46c. Acts 19:13–17: The Seven Sons of Sceva and the Demon

[13] Some of the wandering Jewish exorcists also attempted to call the name of the Lord Jesus over those who had evil spirits, saying 'I adjure you by Jesus whom Paul preaches!' [14] The seven sons of a certain Sceva, a Jewish High Priest, did this. [15] But the evil spirit answered and said to them, 'Jesus I know, and Paul I know; but who are you?' [16] And the man in whom the evil spirit was sprang upon them, mastered all of them and overpowered them, so that they had to flee out of that house naked and wounded. [17] And this became known to all Jews and Greeks who lived in Ephesus, and fear fell upon them all, and the name of the Lord Jesus was extolled.

Bibliography:

B. E. Taylor, 'Acts **19**.14', *Exp.Tim.* 57 (1945–6), 222; C. Lattey, 'A Suggestion on Acts **19**.16', *Exp.Tim.* 36 (1924–5), 381f.; H. G. Meecham, 'Acts **19**.16', *Exp.Tim.* 36 (1924–5), 477f; G. Klein, *ZNW* 64 (1967), 50–60.

VERSE 13: Not only Paul exorcises with the name of Jesus; some of the itinerant Jewish exorcists[1] also make use of it. At Mk. **9**.38f. and Luke **9**.49f. this is already presupposed[2] and allowed! The exact specification is necessary for the success of the exorcism; the demons are crafty and use the slightest opportunity to keep the magic formula from working. The famous expression from a magic papyrus, 'I adjure you by Jesus, the God of the Hebrews',[3] shows, like that in v. 13, that the magician has no personal relationship to the power invoked. The surprising plural ὑμᾶς with ὁρκίζω refers back to the preceding words τὰ πνεύματα τὰ πονηρά.

VERSE 14: A High Priest Sceva is not known (cf. Schürer II[4], 269ff.); the name will be the Latin Scaeva. Perhaps D already wanted to mitigate the improbability of this statement by making Sceva a mere ἱερεύς.[4] The commentaries have followed his example.

VERSE 15: The evil spirit speaks through the sick person, and indeed (Loisy 730) very wittily. γινώσκω and ἐπίσταμαι are not to be differentiated here; the demons know Jesus and his missionary perfectly. That the sick person sensed the lack of inner power in the psychotherapists (Bauernfeind 232) is an altogether too modern concept. Such a translation into psychological terms takes from the story what is essential—namely the conflict with supernatural powers.—Jesus' name works only if he is called upon by a Christian: Overbeck 316.

VERSE 16: The man possessed by the spirit springs upon the seven exorcists, masters them all[5] and gets the upper hand, so that they run naked[6] and bloody out of the house.[7]

[1] For this use of the 'name' cf. above on **5**.41 and **16**.18.—The Jews enjoyed a special reputation as exorcists with their magic formulae allegedly going back to Solomon; cf. for example Josephus *Ant.* VIII 45–9 (Bill. IV 534 in the very instructive excursus 21 'Zur altjüdischen Dämonologie').

[2] Zahn (682) refers to Mt. **12**.27, Lk. **11**.19 and falsely concludes, from the fact that this saying in Mt. stands in a discourse directed against the Pharisees, that these exorcists belonged to the Pharisaic party.—Bauernfeind wants to distinguish reputable Jewish exorcists from the Jews who were not serious; the former were possibly granted (by God) the expulsion of demons. That this distinction (231 below) is not Luke's meaning may be seen from the summary statement.

[3] Cf. Deissmann, *Licht vom Osten*, 1901, 180–9, 4th edn., 216ff. (ET *Light from the Ancient East*).

[4] Perhaps there is also influence from the Old Latin, which translates ἀρχιερεύς by *sacerdos: Beg.* IV 241.

[5] Eberhard Nestle (*Berliner Phil. Wochenschrift* 18 (1898), col. 254) was the first to point out that in later Greek ἀμφότεροι can mean not merely 'both' but 'all'. The papyrus Gen. I 67, 5; 69, 4 and papyrus Lond. 336 speak of more than two persons as ἀμφότεροι: *Beg.* IV 242. Acts **23**.8 offers a further example. Cf. A. C. Clark, *Acts*, 370–3.

VERSE 17: '. . . this became known': as in **1**.19 and **9**.42[1] a typical Lucan expression in this redactional transition verse: *Beg.* IV 242. The feeling of wonder plays a potent role in Acts.[2] Above all our passage recalls **1**.19, **4**.16 and **9**.12. For φόβος cf. **2**.43. The recognition of Jesus by the demon permits the Christians now in turn to make a complete break with magic.

The words at the end of verse 12 'and the evil spirits left' form the transition to the following story. It has caused the commentators a great deal of trouble, for it is indeed very strange. Elsewhere exorcists are not in the habit of appearing in groups—it would diminish not only their earnings and their authority but also their effectiveness. A High Priest by the name of Sceva (this is probably the Latin Scaeva) did not exist. Naturally we can avail ourselves (like Zahn 682) of the solution that Sceva was simply a man of high-priestly family and that his sons—who wanted better advertisement: Lake—made him 'the' High Priest. While in the seven Zahn thus sees degenerate sons of the high aristocracy, 'who after the manner of such people aspired for preference to introduce themselves into the most respected circles', Loisy sees in them people of a lower class, downright liars (729), and Lake speaks of Levantine rascals (*Beg.* IV 241). All these attempts to evade the 'High Priest' and thereby make the Lucan account more credible for us suffer from the fact that they do not properly separate the historical question and the question of Lucan composition. Luke has not signified any doubt about the authenticity of this High Priest. He would have defeated his own purpose and the story would be worthless if only a few rogues had been beaten up by a demon. If on the other hand highly respected Jewish exorcists, sons of an actual High Priest, had experienced such a fiasco, then what Luke wanted to bring before the eyes of his readers with this story would be palpably clear: so powerful was the success of Paul that the great Jewish exorcists had themselves to take over the ὄνομα which he invoked if—as Bauernfeind expresses it (231)—they wanted to remain 'competitive'. But even more, this attempt now reveals that no one is able to imitate Paul. Whoever attempts to copy him must learn very painfully that Paul—and he does not stand here, as Bauernfeind thinks (230), as an exception, but as the representative of the legitimate Christian Church!—is unrivalled. Out of the mouth of demons not only Jesus but also Paul is confirmed as having complete power, even if only in a peculiarly reserved way. Luke cannot very well let the demon say directly,

---

[6] *Beg.* IV 242 understands γυμνός as 'clothed only with the undergarment', the χιτών, without ἱμάτιον or σινδών, and refers for this to Gen. **39**.12, Amos **2**.16 and Mk. **14**.51f.

[7] That the house is first named here at the end is no justification for suspecting the expression: *Beg.* IV 242.

[1] Cf. also **2**.14, **4**.10 (**4**.16), **13**.28, **19**.17 and **28**.28.

[2] Cf. **2**.43, **3**.10, **4**.16, 21, **5**.12, 15, **6**.8, **8**.6, **9**.35, 42, **13**.12, **15**.12, **16**.30, **19**.11, **20**.12 and **28**.6.

'I let myself be driven out by Jesus and Paul, but not by you!' (although that is the final meaning of his words) without the reader asking, 'Yes, but why does this demon remain undisturbed? Why has Paul not driven him out?' With this the inner difficulty of this narrative has come to light: in this incident the demon remains the victor. However, as the last verse shows, what is aroused among all the Jews and Gentiles of Ephesus is not fear of the demon, but that holy awe which attends the appearance of the divine (as in 2.43 and 5.5, 11). That the name of the Lord Jesus is extolled, moreover, may be established only very indirectly by this story. So it appears that Luke has here made use of material alien to his purpose, which he could not quite mould together in spite of all his vigorous efforts to do so. Verse 13 still speaks of wandering Jewish exorcists who attempted to pronounce the name of Jesus over the possessed. In spite of this word 'attempted' (which might sound like a first frustrated attempt), what is involved here is a number of sick people and of separate 'cases'—for we do not find ourselves in an asylum whose inmates are all to be healed in one swift stroke. That means that here an ingredient of the tradition which Luke has employed is visible: the report contained also in Lk. 9.49 that even Jewish exorcists used the name of Jesus. These exorcists naturally did not appear as a closed group. But now they are identified with such a group, namely the seven sons of Sceva, who had gone out seven men strong to subdue a possessed man, and all seven had been quickly beaten into retreat. Whether these seven functioned already in the received tradition as sons of a Jewish ἀρχιερεύς is not so certain. Should that not have been the case, then it would be even more apparent that Luke here has reconciled different traditions. The demon's word, formulated with a thoroughly diplomatic adroitness, might bespeak Luke's own genius.

46d. Acts 19:18-20: The Burning of the Books of Magic

[18] And many of those who had become believers came, confessing and admitting their practice (of magic). [19] A number of those who had practised witchcraft brought their books of magic together and burnt them before everyone. And they estimated their worth, and it came to fifty thousand silver drachmae. [20] So the Word of the Lord grew with power and became mighty.

Bibliography:

A. S. Peake, 'Notes on Book-Burning', *Munera Studiosa*, Cambridge, Mass., 1946, 145-60; G. Klein, *ZNW* 64 (1967), 77-80.

VERSE 18: πεπιστευκότων: not only people just converted (against Wendt 276). ἐξομολογοῦμαι: to make a confession of sins before the congregation.[1] πρᾶξις: magic spells (*Beg.* IV 242). According to Bauernfeind (231), vv. 18ff. were fashioned by Luke from his own factual knowledge, and not already shaped in a source.

VERSE 19: ἱκανοί (see on 8.11): 'a whole multitude'. τὰ περίεργα πράσσειν (literally: play the busybody): euphemism for 'magic'. Βίβλος means here 'book of magic' (according to *Beg.* IV 243, however, to be thought of as parchment or papyrus leaves).[2] συνεψήφισαν: 'people calculated' the value to be *c.* 36,000 gold marks. Clemen, on the other hand (*Paulus* I, 285 n. 2): 'the quire' cost about 20pf. in Rome.—But for books of magic one had to pay more! ἐνώπιον πάντων: a public book-burning.[3]

VERSE 20: κατὰ κράτος: powerful (Bauer, *Wb* 888 with references). τοῦ Κυρίου belongs to the following.[4] The imperfects express duration of time: Wendt 276.

The adventure of the sons of Sceva has its effects (without the 'how' of the effects being entirely clear) upon the Christians also. Many of them now confess (probably publicly before the congregation) that they have earlier practised magic. It is somewhat peculiar that they only now decide on this confession. But one cannot very well infer from the perfect πεπιστευκότων a revival movement which—occasioned by the Sceva incident—had only just led great masses newly into the congregation. When Beyer (118) maintains that Paul required the Christians to renounce their concern with magic arts, he has freely altered the Lucan text, because to him evidently the Lucan motive for the sudden ἐξομολογεῖσθαι was not sufficient. Of these many one-time magicians who have become Christians a large number now bring their books of magic for public burning, and it is calculated that in the process a value equivalent to 50,000 days' wages goes up in flames. These Christians—they are only a portion of those 'many' who have meddled with magic—must have had astonishing resources at their disposal—if we could trust the report historically. Only this is precisely what we may not do. In reality Luke only wants to show how magic lost ground through the activity of Paul (= of Christianity), and according to his technique of narration he clothes this statement in the garb of an impressive scene. But even this scene

---

[1] So Preuschen 116, referring to Didache 4.14 ('In the congregation you shall confess your sins'); II Clem. **8**.3 (where the confession of sins in the service of worship is meant: Knopf, *Die apost. Väter*, I, 165); Barnabas **19**.12 ('Make confession concerning your sins').

[2] Zahn 684: 'These were the famed Ἐφέσια γράμματα of old.' Their chief centre of production at that time however was in Egypt: Preuschen 116.

[3] Livy XL 29, Suetonius *Aug.* 31, Diog. Laert. IX 52 and Lucian *Alex.* 47 report public book-burnings: *Beg.* IV 243.

[4] B A ℵ read τοῦ κυρίου ὁ λόγος: *Beg.* III 184. D (here a mixed text) offers ἡ πίστις τοῦ θεοῦ. Both expressions mean essentially the same thing: Christianity.

is overplayed when Beyer (118) writes, 'It is one of the most impressive pictures of Acts, as the great preacher of Jesus stands before the flaming pyre upon which the valuable treasures of Hellenistic sorcery burn.' The books of magic are for Acts anything but 'valuable treasures of Hellenistic sorcery'. Rather one might say with Bauernfeind (232), 'The . . . demons have lost a fight.' Luke however expresses it positively: 'So the Word of the Lord grew powerful and became stronger and stronger.' The Word 'of the Lord' is none other than the mission church itself, for which an abstraction like 'Christianity' had not yet been invented.

46e. Acts 19:21–22: Plans and Preparations for Paul's Journey

[21] When this had taken place, Paul resolved in the Spirit to travel through Macedonia and Achaea and to go to Jerusalem, saying, 'After I have been there, I must also see Rome!' [22] And after sending to Macedonia two of those who served him, Timothy and Erastus, he himself remained for a time in (the province of) Asia.

Bibliography:

G. S. Duncan, 'Paul's Ministry in Asia', *NTS* 3 (1957), 211–8; W. Miller, 'Who was Erastus?' *Bibl. Sacra* 88 (1931), 342–6.

VERSE 21: ταῦτα refers to the preceding events.[1] τίθεσθαι ἐν πνεύματι = resolve.[2] Since Luke does not want to mention the collection here (cf. however **24**.17) he does not give any further reason for the travel plans.[3] Yet the δεῖ of the journey to Rome can be understood as a reference to the divine will.

VERSE 22: Timothy went[4] by Macedonia to Corinth, but returned with bad news, so that Paul himself decided on his own futile trip to Corinth (see v. 21 note 3). The confused situation in Corinth was brought to order by

---

[1] On the other hand, scholars like Wendt 276 and Loisy 733 have conjectured that in the source used by Luke it referred to δύο ἔτη in v. 10.

[2] So for example Zahn 688, Bauer *Wb* 1616. Lake on the other hand (*Beg.* IV 244) finds it doubtful here as in **18**.25 and **20**.22 whether the Holy Spirit or the human spirit is meant.

[3] According to I Cor. **16**.5ff. Paul wanted to remain until Pentecost in Ephesus, then go by way of Macedonia to Corinth, perhaps stay there during the winter and in the following spring travel on (to Jerusalem). II Cor. **1**.15 intimates an altered plan: first to Corinth, then to Macedonia and again back to Corinth with the Jerusalem journey following. Actually Paul (after making one fruitless visit to Corinth in the meantime) came by Macedonia to Corinth and again travelled by Macedonia to Jerusalem: II Cor. **2**.12f.; Acts **20**.1ff.

[4] I Cor. **4**.17, **16**.10; if Philippians was written from Ephesus, then Phil. **2**.19–23 would also come into question.

Titus, whom Paul sent to Corinth together with an unnamed Christian[1] before his own final departure from Ephesus.[2] When Paul met him again in Macedonia, he sent him afresh to Corinth.[3]—An Erastus is named in Romans **16**.23 as οἰκονόμος τῆς πόλεως;[4] II Tim. **4**.20 will also refer to him. In Luke (who indeed mentions Titus just as little as the disagreement of the Corinthian congregation with Paul) a journey of Timothy has taken the place of the journey of Titus.—The statement that Paul 'remained for a time in Asia'[5] has provided some scholars[6] with the occasion for making Paul travel around in Asia Minor. But by Ἀσία Luke probably means only Ephesus.

The words ὡς δὲ ἐπληρώθη ταῦτα of course invite one to relate them to the δύο ἔτη in v. 10 and conjecture that they directly followed this in a source which Luke copied. But they make good sense just as they are in Luke: Paul with the activity described has fulfilled his task in Ephesus. Luke feels it necessary to mention here this fact and the corresponding plans for Paul's journey, in order that the reader may not think that Paul was driven out of Ephesus through the riot of Demetrius. No, he wanted to inspect Macedonia and Achaea, to go to Jerusalem and finally even to Rome! Here the theme for the finale of this great symphony is sounded for the first time (cf. **23**.11). How far these travel plans have already prospered is demonstrated by the despatch of two of Paul's helpers, Timothy and Erastus, to Macedonia—since Luke says nothing about the collection and the difficulties connected with it, the reader must imagine that these men had only to prepare for Paul's trip to Macedonia. Timothy plays only a very minor role in Acts, but it is an entirely different matter in Paul himself (cf. Romans **16**.23; I Cor. **4**.17, **16**.10; II Cor. **1**.1; Phil. **1**.1, **2**.19ff.) and in the Pastorals. According to I Cor. **4**.17 Paul certainly sent Timothy to Corinth. But that was earlier than we must date the mission according to our passage. On the other hand it would have corresponded admirably with II Cor. **2**.13 if Luke here had

---

[1] II Cor. **12**.18.

[2] II Cor. **2**.12f., **7**.6.

[3] II Cor. **8**.16ff.

[4] Zahn 688 identifies him with the Erastus of our verse. But could a man in such a position be described as one of τῶν διακονούντων Παύλῳ? Luke has certainly so described Timothy also, to whom in general he ascribed a much smaller position than he actually took. Cf. Williams 222f.

[5] **20**.16 alternates Ἀσία with Ephesus. At **20**.4 Tychicus and Trophimus are described as Ἀσιανοί (D: Ἐφέσιοι), while Trophimus in **21**.29 is called Ἐφέσιος. The Jews who recognize these two and Paul are ἀπὸ τῆς Ἀσίας **21**.27, **24**.19: they can only be Ephesian Jews.—Cases such as **19**.26, where πάσης τῆς Ἀσίας is clearly distinguished from Ἐφέσου, are different.

[6] Zahn (687) has Paul remain some months after the sending of Timothy, and make 'excursions to other cities not far from Ephesus'; from v. 26 he concludes that Paul's preaching activity extended over the province of Asia.—Wendt 277 also wants to distinguish between Ἀσία and Ephesus in v. 22. But already in v. 23 Luke again presumes Paul's presence in Ephesus.

spoken not of Timothy but of Titus. But Acts is silent about Titus here as elsewhere, without our being able to say for certain why. For that with the person of Titus was connected the recollection of the grievous controversies in Jerusalem, of which Luke had made no mention, is only a conjecture—albeit a not improbable one. Erastus also, according to Romans **16**.23—if it should actually be a case of the same man and not merely of the same name—had as city treasurer an incomparably higher position than one would assume from v. 22. It is even questionable whether Paul could have asked Erastus to come to him in Ephesus (for discussion of the matter of the collection, as Zahn 688 suggests).

According to I Cor. **4**.17 Timothy appears to have travelled alone, while Titus was accompanied by an unnamed but very deserving brother. This circumstance also speaks for the view that Luke either did not know the details of these journeys or mentioned only one, representative so to speak of them all, without concern for historical accuracy. We certainly do not have any occasion here for thinking of the use of a source-document!

46f. Acts 19:23–40: The Riot of Demetrius

[23] There arose about that time no little agitation concerning the 'Way'. [24] For a silversmith by the name of Demetrius, who manufactured silver Artemis temples, brought no little business to the craftsmen. [25] He gathered them together, and the workers of like trade, and said: 'Men, you know that our prosperity comes from this business, [26] and you see and hear that not only at Ephesus, but in almost the whole (province) of Asia this Paul has persuasively turned away many people by saying that they are no gods who are made with hands. [27] But not only does this our branch of business threaten to fall into disrepute but also the temple of the great goddess Artemis may be accounted for nothing, and she may in the future be deprived of her majesty which all Asia and the entire world revere.' [28] When they heard this they became angry and cried, 'Great is Artemis of the Ephesians!' [29] And the city was thrown into confusion, and they stormed as a body into the theatre dragging Paul's travelling companions, the Macedonians Gaius and Aristarchus, with them. [30] But when Paul wanted to go into the assembly, the disciples did not let him. [31] Also some of the Asiarchs, who were friendly with him, sent to him and warned him not to venture into the theatre. [32] Now one cried this, the other one that, for the assembly was in great confusion, and most of them did not know why they had come together. [33] Some of the crowd explained to Alexander as the Jews sent him forward; but Alexander motioned with his hand and wanted to make a defence to the people. [34] But when they recognized, 'He is a Jew!', then came a shout from them all which lasted about two hours, 'Great is Artemis of the Ephesians!' [35] The city clerk brought the crowd to silence with the words,

'You Ephesians, what man among you does not know that the city of the Ephesians is the temple-keeper of great Artemis and of the image which came from heaven? ³⁶ Since this is incontestable, you must contain yourselves peacefully and not do anything rash. ³⁷ For you have brought these men here, who are neither temple robbers nor have they blasphemed our goddess. ³⁸ If now Demetrius and those craftsmen associated with him have a complaint against anyone, there are days when court is held and there are governors—there they may accuse one another! ³⁹ If you seek anything further, it shall be settled in the regular assembly. ⁴⁰ For we stand in danger of being charged with rioting today since there is no reason at hand by which we can justify ourselves for this mob action.' And with these words he dismissed the assembly.

Bibliography:

Forschungen in Ephesos, published by Österreich. Archäol. Institut, Vol. 2 (*Das Theater in E.*, edited by R. Heberdey, G. Niemann, W. Wilberg), Wien 1912; Gunnar Rudberg, 'Hellenistik litteraturforskning och Nya Testamentet', *Eranos*, Acta Philol. Succ. vol. 23 (1925), 193–203, esp. 200f.; W. Michaelis, 'The Trial of St. Paul at Ephesus', *JTS* 29 (1928), 368–75; Lily Ross Taylor, 'Artemis of Ephesus', *Beg.* V (1933), 251–6 and 'The Asiarchs', *Beg.* V (1933), 256–62; Silva New, 'The Michigan Papyrus Fragment 1571', *Beg.* V (1933), 262–8; T. W. Manson, 'St. Paul in Ephesus. The Date of the Epistle to the Philippians', *BJRL* 23 (1939), 182–208; A. H. M. Jones, *The Greek City*, 1940, 239; G. S. Duncan, 'Were Paul's Imprisonment Epistles written from Ephesus?' *Exp.Tim.* 67 (1954–5), 163–6, and see §§ 46a–e; Kragerud 1955, 258, see § 29; Williams, 223–5; Conzelmann 113f.

E. L. Hicks, 'Demetrius the Silversmith', *Expositor* Ser. IV, vol. I (1890), 401–22; E. Ceroni, 'Grande Artemide degli Efesini! Il tumulto degli Efesini contro San Paolo alla luce delle recente scoperte archéologiche (Act. 19.28ff.)', *Scuola Cattol.* 60 (1932) 2, 121–42, 203–26; J. Bertrand, 'Het oproer der zilversmeden Hand. 19.23–40, een mesterstukje van reportage', *'t Helige Land* IV 10 (1951), 155–8; E. Lichtenecker, *Das Kultbild der Artemis von Ephesus*, Tübingen 1952.

VERSE 23: 'About that time': indefinite as in **12.1**. The following narrative depicts in reality no 'considerable unrest'; the situation will have been more dangerous than Luke presents it: *Beg.* IV 245. The absolute ὁδός[1] is used as in v. 9.

VERSE 24: A νεωποιός[2] ('vestryman', 'churchwarden': *Beg.* IV 246) by

---

[1] Sorof 33, Loisy 747 conjecture without sufficient evidence that in the source θεοῦ (= Artemis) stood for ὁδοῦ.

[2] The editor of the Ephesian inscription in the British museum, Hicks, in *Expositor* I (1890) 401ff. advanced the thesis, then contested by Ramsay, that Luke misunderstood the information of his source that Demetrius was a νεωποιός (or ναοποιός) and interpreted

the name of Demetrius is mentioned in an Ephesian inscription[1] about the middle of the first century A.D. 'Silver temples' (naturally in miniature): such have not yet been discovered nor are they mentioned in the ancient literature,[2] but rather little temples of terracotta which served as souvenirs, votive offerings and amulets; however, silver statuettes of Artemis are mentioned and have been found.[3] The τεχνῖται appear to be the craft-masters.[4] ἐργασία, 'business', here means 'good business', 'profit'.[5] Demetrius behaves like a guild master (Loisy 747) or the 'chief of a great industry, perhaps the only one of its kind' (Wendt 278).—Cf. Bo Reicke, *Diakonie, Festfreude und Zelos*, 313f.

VERSE 25: ἐργάται: the workers in the relevant trade workshops.[6] D has expanded the address ἄνδρες.[7]

VERSE 26: Ἐφέσου and πάσης τῆς Ἀσίας[8] (the entire Roman province) depend (emphatically brought forward) upon ἱκανὸν ὄχλον, which at the end of the clause is also strongly emphasized. μεθίστημι not: 'to bring out of control' (so Zahn 690) but 'to seduce' (Wendt 278), namely to apostasy from the old belief in the gods.[9] '... gods which are made with hands': this corresponds to heathen belief in its crassest form, as it had been touched on in 17.29 in the polemic of the Areopagus speech.

VERSE 27: All the following infinitives depend upon κινδυνεύει ('stands in danger'). μέρος = branch of business: Bauer, *Wb* 1000, i b η. εἰς ἀπελεγμὸν ἐλθεῖν only here: to come into disrepute (Latinism? cf. Bauer, *Wb* 165 and

---

it of the manufacture of silver miniature temples. The νεωποιοί, twelve in all, were named annually by the city and had supervision over the incoming votive offerings and necessary repairs in the temple (cf. Lily Ross Taylor: 'Artemis of Ephesos', Note XXI, 251–6 in *Beg.* V (1933)). According to Hicks, Demetrius was a silversmith by trade and manufactured silver Artemis statuettes.

[1] *Ancient Greek Inscriptions in the British Museum*, III 578 and p. 209: *Beg.* V 255. There is much in favour of the view that this inscription is of somewhat later date.

[2] *Beg.* IV 245. Chrysostom *hom.* 42, 1 (Armenian Catena 346): 'perhaps like little tabernacles': Preuschen 117. Wikenhauser *Apg.* 179 thinks of facsimiles of the cult image, placed in a niche; such a terracotta relief of Cybele is known.

[3] *Beg.* V 253; *Beg.* IV 246.

[4] Zahn (689) thought in much too modern fashion of artists who prepared for Demetrius sketches of the temple, from which the workers under his supervision produced the individual parts.

[5] *Beg.* IV 246.

[6] De Wette 322: 'the (other) workers involved in such a craft'; Bauernfeind 233: 'collectively the simple labourers of this branch of industry'; correspondingly Loisy 747; *Beg.* IV 246; Knopf 621.

[7] These words ἄνδρες συντεχνῖται may not with Zahn (690) be translated as 'fellow artists'; fellow craftsmen is more the meaning.

[8] Not genitive of place as is doubtfully conjectured in *Beg.* IV 246. Not 'strange Greek' (Lake, ibid.) but typical Lucan style of anticipating what is stressed. For the rest Demetrius speaks in an 'affected' manner (so Zahn 690 n. 18) only to our ears; Luke considers this a proper manner of speech for an address.

[9] According to Zahn 690 this sentence presupposes that 'Paul has let his voice and oratory be heard ... in other cities of the province also.' Apart from the fact that Paul was no great speaker (II Cor. 11.6; cf. Käsemann, 'Die Legitimät des Apostels', 35), 19.10 shows that Luke did not think of any such preaching tours.

Preuschen 118). μέγας is a rather common *epitheton ornans* with names of gods.[1] μέλλειν καθαιρεῖσθαι for the future infinitive, which has become defunct (Preuschen 118). καθαιρεῖσθαι = 'to incur the loss' with the genitive[2] like the *verba privationis*; cf. Bl.-Debr. § 180, 1 and Bauer, *Wb* 765.[3] ἦν refers to αὐτῆς. The worldwide reverence for Artemis of Ephesus was a fact.[4]

VERSE 28: After θυμοῦ ('rage'), D has inserted 'running into the street'. 'Great is Artemis of the Ephesians' is the usual form of the ceremonial acclamation of the deity, cf. Erik Peterson, Εἷς Θεός, 1926, 196ff.[5] Early examples in the LXX, Bel and the Dragon 18 ('Great are you, Bel') and 41 ('Great are you, Lord, God of Daniel'): Peterson, 207.

VERSE 29: Lake (*Beg.* IV 248) offers a good parallel in an inscription from Cnidus.[6] The Ephesus theatre with its almost 24,000 seating capacity was the right place for popular assemblies.—Aristarchus[7] according to 20.4 is from Thessalonica, Gaius from Derbe (but see on 20.4!). Lake (*Beg.* IV 248) reckons with the possibility that Μακεδόνα is to be read (dittography of the following); but Gaius is certainly a common name.[8]

VERSE 30: Zahn 694: Paul wanted to go into the theatre, 'since on the basis of his standing as a Roman citizen and his encouraging experiences in intercourse with high city and government officials he might hope' to free his companions. Bauernfeind 234 sees it differently: 'Paul regards remaining at home as almost equivalent to desertion.' 'But in such a case the control

---

[1] Cf. the Halle dissertation by B. Müller (1913): Μέγας Θεός: *Beg.* IV 247.

[2] The later reading τὴν μεγαλειότητα (H L P; *Beg.* III 186) is a simplification.

[3] Cf. for the whole theme the decree resolved in A.D. 160 for the revival of the Artemis cult, to extend the great festival of the goddess over the whole month of Artemision: *Beg.* V 255f.

[4] According to Wernicke (Pauly-Wissowa II, 1385) there is archaeological evidence for it at 32 places.

[5] Peterson 213: 'The wonder seen with one's own eyes elicited the cry of admiration, of astonishment and confession.' 199: the mention of the acclamations in Ephesus is explained stylistically from the model of the ancient romance, 'which in similar fashion interwove the mention of acclamations into the narrative'. 215 n. 1: 'The acclamation in the miracle narrative is an organic constituent . . .' 'The mention of the acclamation in the romance and in Acts' is 'a literary device to enliven the narrative.' 'If Wellhausen's hypothesis' (see below on v. 34) 'could be verified . . ., then we could assume that the acclamation of Acts 19 had stood in Luke's source, in which in terms of stylistic history it would have been conditioned by the connection with the ancient romance.' We may not therefore with Ramsay (*St. Paul* 279) hold as original the text of D (in which the articles are missing) because 'Great is . . .' is 'the quiet expression of worship', while 'Great Artemis!' on the other hand is a common formula of devotion and prayer (this indicative is anything but a 'quiet expression of worship'!). Nor may we with Holtzmann (123) hear in it only 'the watchword of the citizen's local megalomania . . . the spontaneous cry of an egoism clothed in piety, but feeling its ownership threatened'.

[6] Brit. Mus., Ins. 792, 4ff.: ὁ μὲν δᾶμος (cf. δῆμος vv. 30, 33) ἐν οὐ μετρίᾳ (cf. 20.12: οὐ μετρίως) συγχύσει γενόμενος . . . μετὰ πάσας προθυμίας (cf. 17.11: μετὰ πάσης προθυμίας) συνελθὼν εἰς τὸ θέατρον . . Cf. Jos. *Bell.* II, 489–93.

[7] Cf. 20.4, 27.2, Col. 4.10, Philemon 24. Aristarchus was a common name in Macedonia: *Beg.* IV 248.

[8] Romans 16.23; I Cor. 1.14; III John 1.

of his own conscience was entrusted to the reliable brethren' (loc. cit.).
—δῆμος: the assembled people; it was no ἔννομος ἐκκλησία (v. 39).

VERSE 31: The text presupposes that the Asiarchs,[1] and indeed every one of them, have no sooner heard about the riot than they immediately think about Paul and send him a warning note!

VERSE 32: The incident does not result in a trial: here, where the real decision ought to fall, the enterprising Demetrius has vanished, and his business friends also enigmatically abandon the campaign introduced with such promise of success.[2]

VERSE 33: An old *crux interpretum*![3] Alexander,[4] a Jew, sent forward by the Jews, wants to make a speech for the defence—naturally neither for Paul[5] nor the Jewish-Christians[6] but on behalf of the Jews.[7] ἐκ τοῦ ὄχλου is the subject.[8] Luke will have used συνεβίβασαν with the LXX in the sense of 'to instruct'.[9] κατεβίβασαν[10] and προεβίβασαν[11] are early attempts at improvement. According to Wendt 279f. the Jews send Alexander forward

---

[1] Cf. Lily Ross Taylor, 'The Asiarchs', Note XXII, *Beg.* V 256–62. The towns of the Roman province of Asia were bound together in a league which had essentially religious duties: to promote the cult of the ruling Caesar and the goddess Roma. The first temple of the league was built in Pergamum, others in Smyrna and Ephesus, which later also erected a second and third temple to Caesar. Every year an Asiarch was elected for the entire district of the league and another for each league city with a league temple; re-election was possible. At the time of Paul there will have been each year 3–4 Asiarchs who came from the noblest and richest families. Although the description ἀσιαρχήσας occurs for former Asiarchs, the title seems still to have been borne by former Asiarchs also. To what extent an Asiarch was also ἀρχιερεύς is debated.—In Lycia there was a corresponding Lyciarch, in Galatia a Galatarch etc.—The translation 'provincial diet' for such a town league (Zahn 695 and Wendt 279) is misleading to the extent that the modern reader will think in the first instance of a political authority. Actually 'the league of the cities of Asia, like other Greek leagues', was 'a religious organization with certain political functions': op. cit. 256. 'The league in Asia . . . became a valuable instrument of the provincial governors in securing loyalty to Roman rule': op. cit. 257. That these men elected for the promotion of the imperial cult were 'personally well disposed to the resolute enemy of the gods' (so Bauernfeind 234) is highly unlikely.

[2] Loisy conjectures (751) that v. 32 was originally attached to θέατρον in v. 29. From this word to θέατρον at the end of v. 31 the statements about Paul and his companions would then have been inserted (according to the sufficiently well-known technique).

[3] That the Jews considered the moment had arrived 'to pass from hate against Paul to an actual attack on his person' (so Zahn 695) is read into the text. Meyer's interpretation takes account of the reading προεβίβασαν: 'Those at the front dragged forward out of the crowd Alexander, whom the Jews had pushed forward from behind'!

[4] Fantasy can naturally establish a connection with the Alexander of I Tim. 1.20 and II Tim. 4.14.

[5] So Overbeck 324.

[6] This Lake considers impossible (*Beg.* IV 249).

[7] So most commentators (already Chrysostom). The usual interpretation is that the Jews wanted to distinguish themselves from the accused Christians.

[8] Cf. Luke 21.16; Acts 21.16; Jn. 7.40; 16.17. Bl.-Debr. § 164, 2; *Beg.* IV 249.

[9] Properly 'to bring together', then 'reconcile', 'establish' (Acts 9.22?), 'instruct' (LXX), 'presume' (Acts 16.10).

[10] Represented by D gig vulg; = he was dragged down from the rostrum?

[11] So most of the Koine MSS.

that he may ascertain 'the reason for the tumultuous gathering and uproar'. That may be partly correct—the situation (which according to Luke is confused) is itself unfortunately very indistinctly depicted. The position Luke has in mind appears to be roughly as follows: the crowd makes no distinction between Jews and Christians. The Jews then feel themselves threatened, and send Alexander forward. He is now informed about the real situation by some of the crowd, who know the facts, and on this basis wants to make a defence for the Jews. But he is not even allowed to speak!

VERSE 34: ἐπιγνόντες—φωνὴ μία—κράζοντες[1]: a construction according to sense. That Alexander is hindered from speaking by the crowd's shout of acclamation shows the reader how unpopular the Jews are in Ephesus.[2] The two-hour pandemonium of the crowd illustrates the—actually powerless—fanaticism of the heathens. 'Artemis of the Ephesians' was not the chaste huntress of the Greek myths, but essentially the Near Eastern mother-goddess, the symbol of fertility[3]: *Beg.* V 252.

VERSE 35: The γραμματεύς[4] (τοῦ δήμου) had to execute the decrees of the popular assembly: *Beg.* IV 249. νεωκόρος: 'guardian of the temple': later a title for cities which possessed and specially cared for a league temple of the imperial cult; here and *CIG* 2972 related to the Artemis cult: *Beg.* V 242 and IV 250. διοπετής[5]: 'come from heaven'; claimed for many images, but only here for the Ephesian Artemis: *Beg.* IV 250.

VERSE 36: The thought is: 'Ephesus is well known as the city of Artemis; thus there is no danger for the Artemis cult'. With this the claims of Demetrius are rejected, although admittedly he did not advance them here.

VERSE 37: 'These men': Aristarchus and Gaius (v. 29) are meant. Violation (strictly robbing) of temples and blasphemy of other gods seem to have been favourite accusations against the Jews.[6]

---

[1] The reading κραζόντων of most MSS is a simplification.

[2] On the basis of this verse Wellhausen (41) constructed his much-noticed thesis: 'It is . . . really the description of a witch-hunt against the Jews in Ephesus; this has been adapted by the author through the alteration of the introduction into a persecution of Christians.' The decisive point against this is that nothing happens to the Jewish speaker; he is only kept from saying a word.

[3] Hence she is portrayed with many breasts (πολύμαστος): Wendt 280. Her highest priest was a eunuch with the Persian title Megabyzos. Under him stood a countless number of men who held offices connected with the temple cult. Priestesses also are mentioned in inscriptions. Cf. Lily Ross Taylor, 'Artemis of Ephesus', Note XXI, *Beg.* V 251–6.

[4] Luther, Preuschen and Zahn; together with the στρατηγοί he controlled the administration of the city.

[5] Said of the Taurian Artemis in Euripides *Iph. Taur.* 87f., 1384f.: *Beg.* IV 250. Originally the 'fallen from the heavens' meant meteorites, which were worshipped as images, even if they possessed little or no similarity with a human form. That this διοπετές was an answer by the chancellor to Paul's polemic against the gods made with hands (*Beg.* IV 250 as a possibility) is a conjecture which by-passes the Lucan meaning of the scene.

[6] Cf. Romans 2.22 and Josephus *c. Ap.* II 237 (the lawgiver has forbidden blasphemy against those considered by others as gods) and *Ant.* IV 207 (similarly) where also the συλᾶν ἱερὰ ξενικά is forbidden.

VERSE 38: Now the chancellor mentions Demetrius and his associates, as if he had been present in their meeting: they are referred to the legal procedure in civil actions. The plurals ἀγοραῖοι and ἀνθύπατοι are generic.[1]

VERSE 39: περαιτέρω is original: *Beg.* III 189. According to Chrysostom (*hom.* XLII 2) the regular assembly of the people was held three times a month.

VERSE 40: οὐ (omitted by D e min gig vulg. sah boh: *Beg.* III 189) probably arose through dittography; 'since there is no reason in respect of which we can justify ourselves for this mob action'. Holtzmann, Wendt, Overbeck differ.

If we take the Demetrius story as an historical account and place this incident under close scrutiny, then we find a regular tangle of difficulties. Concerning Hicks' thesis that the little silver temples of Demetrius owe their existence merely to Luke's misunderstanding, we shall say nothing—it cannot be proven. Rather do we assume in the first place with Luke that Paul really threatened the existence of the Artemis cult by his missionary activity. But then we ought properly to expect all the circles interested in it to join in an action against Paul, and foremost of all the priesthood of the temple (which for that matter was at the same time a major bank with far-reaching connections and exercised the power of a large sum of capital!) and the city authorities. But no, Demetrius is allowed to make the running alone. He —yes, what does he really have in mind? Does he want to carry through an edict of expulsion against Paul or a lynching? It is not clear. Demetrius mobilizes his guild and leads a kind of popular assembly into the theatre. But then the inconceivable happens: nothing more is heard of him. How can a man who is presented as so good an organizer veil himself in silence at the very moment when—before an enthusiastic public—he ought to come out with a concrete proposal? Instead he lets the time expire unused, and not only he but his guild associates also.

Just as incomprehensible is the attitude of the Asiarchs. They have the duty of advancing the cult of Caesar (and the goddess Roma). In spite of this, when they hear about the riot, their first thought is Paul's safety. Here we must consider that these Asiarchs do not all live together. Do they all then react in the same manner? Or do they immediately call a council? Be that as it may: they are fortunate that this messenger still meets with Paul, because the disciples have restrained him! And Paul follows their advice.

Let us return to the theatre. The crowd is still gathered there, the greater part of it not knowing why it is here. That this situation of general confusion

---

[1] ἀγοραῖοι, elsewhere also always used without a noun—supply ἡμέραι or σύνοδοι—, corresponding to the Latin *conventus agere* (Cicero, Livy: Preuschen 120), is attested by inscriptions. At these sessions the proconsul or his representative presided: *Beg.* IV 251f. referring to Kornemann, article *conventus* in Pauly-Wissowa IV, 1900, esp. 1173ff.

is brought to an end is due to the Jews. They send forward one Alexander, who even appears to reach the speaker's rostrum and wants to make a speech in defence—up to this point not a word against the Jews has been reported. It is not surprising that Wellhausen came to the opinion that here the description of a Jew-hunt has been utilized—but not a thing happens to the Jewish speaker. He is merely not allowed to speak. For when he is recognized as a Jew a 'nearly two-hour long' outcry begins: 'Great is Artemis of the Ephesians!' What exactly is the point of this Jewish intermezzo, which has neither reasonable cause nor sensible conclusion?

Finally a respected person appears, the 'town clerk', who readily stills the crowd and makes a speech counter to that of Demetrius, at which however he was not present. With the statement that everyone knows Ephesus as νεωκόρος of Artemis the reproaches against the Christians are finished with —as if the success of the Christian mission were made good again by this vague assurance. But the crowd goes quietly home and at the same time has the anxious prospect of being prosecuted for στάσις. The Christians do not blaspheme the goddess—they only deny her divinity. But this the town clerk as well as his listeners has forgotten.

To all these difficulties must be added another and greater one. According to II Cor. 1.8ff. Paul ἐν τῇ ᾿Ασίᾳ, before he came to Macedonia, experienced a θλῖψις so severe that he considered death inevitable. We can still detect in his words the distress he has undergone not so very long ago. Of this experience Luke says nothing—why? Loisy (744) recognized the situation: escaping death by the skin of his teeth, Paul had to leave Ephesus. Even if Luke had known of this event, he would not have concluded his description of Paul's missionary activity with it. The harmonious development ought not to end on so shrill a dissonance. But probably in Luke's time there was no longer any exact knowledge of it. It was known only that a great θόρυβος had preceded Paul's departure from Ephesus. Luke could have told his readers about it briefly in a short sentence. But he did not want to evade the riot in this manner. It was to be vividly developed for his readers. For this not so very much material was necessary. The Artemis cult they knew and the temple in Ephesus, this seventh wonder of the world. He himself was educated enough to know also something about the Asiarchs and the constitution of the city. What else was needed? The names and figures of Demetrius and Alexander? Perhaps that Demetrius who appears on an inscription of that period as νεωποιὸς ἐπώνυμος (that means the first and highest of his year) had taken a leading part in the event in Asia and so lived on in the memory of the Christians. Of the Jew Alexander the stones admittedly do not speak. But in Christian legend an Alexander (a Jew?) played a part as an opponent of Paul, as I Tim. 1.20 and II Tim. 4.14 attest. Luke need not have appropriated the famous acclamation of the Ephesians from a romance. It will still have rung out at his time (only on a more fitting occasion).

All this is not much in the way of colour. But what a picture Luke has
created from it! The heathen Demetrius, wholesale manufacturer in devotional
goods, shows the reader through the speech to his guild: Paul with his preaching about a true God has brought a great crowd of people, far beyond
Ephesus, to apostasy from the old belief in the gods. The famed temple of
Artemis, and everything connected with it, threatens to fall into oblivion.
Paul's success can hardly be better described—and that from the mouth of an
enemy! That here the vested interests of the heathen craftsmen supply the
motive which impels Demetrius should not be denied (Bauernfeind 234
vouches for Demetrius' earnestness and ascribes to Luke a knowledge of the
fascination and tragedy of heathen art!): this very circumstance, that Demetrius cries out against Paul as a business man, proves to the reader how
genuinely the force of the Pauline mission makes itself felt, how deeply it
shook the whole of heathenism. Naturally the pagan belief in the gods is
itself summoned up by Demetrius—and this at the same time gives Luke
the transition to the shout 'Great is Artemis of the Ephesians!' which brings
the city into commotion. That such a popular movement is necessary to expel
Paul proves to the Christian reader again what a powerful position Paul had
acquired for himself. But it is also clear from another motif: Paul wanted to
venture bravely into the theatre, into which two of his travelling companions
had been dragged. But the disciples do not let him go, and the Asiarchs warn
him amicably. If these highly respected men from the first families of the
country, men who had the best connections with the Roman government,
intervened for him in such a way, then that was the best defence testimony
imaginable for Paul and Christianity. A sect whose leader has Asiarchs for
friends cannot be dangerous to the state! Do we understand now how well
founded Paul's position is in that respect?

But how is the scene in the theatre now to continue? Luke could not allow
the Apostle to appear there, for Paul would either have had to convert the
Ephesians—and that Luke could not report with a good conscience—or he
would have had to say the things which sound much more convincing from the
mouth of the town clerk. Luke also could not let Demetrius reappear, and
indeed not only on the literary grounds that he would simply have had to
repeat himself; no, a Demetrius stirring up the crowd in the theatre would
have incurably spoilt the entire scene. At this point the Jewish intermezzo
comes to the rescue: it shows besides how unpopular are the enemies of the
Christians, the Jews, and above all gives the signal for the two-hour long
repeated shout of acclamation. As the reaction to the appearance of a Jew
the shout does not indeed fit particularly well, but at the same time it reveals
that in final analysis the only thing heathenism can do against Paul is to
shout itself hoarse.

Moreover, the chancellor (as the representative of the secular authority)
makes his appearance (alongside the Asiarchs as the religious one), and gives

his support to the Christians: they have neither robbed nor affronted the goddess. Anyone who, like Demetrius, wants to accuse them ought to do so before the court: a tumultuous proceeding against the Christians is inadmissible. In this way it is indirectly admitted that the *nomen Christianum* as such is still no reason for an accusation. Indeed the roles are finally reversed: it is not Paul who (as maintained by his enemies in 24.5) stirs up στάσεις, but rather his enemies themselves! Anyone who calls to mind the apologies which fill the concluding part of Acts will hear all their motifs already sounding here.

So Paul is victorious, without himself setting foot on the field of battle. Politically exonerated, he can as victor leave the shattered paganism of Ephesus to itself.

47
ACTS 20:1–6
PAUL'S JOURNEY TO GREECE, MACEDONIA AND TROAS

[1] After the tumult had ceased, Paul sent for the disciples and admonished them, then taking leave of them departed to travel to Macedonia. [2] After he had journeyed through that region and admonished them with much preaching, he came to Greece, [3] and after a stay of three months, when a plot was made against him by the Jews as he was on the point of sailing for Syria, he decided to go back through Macedonia. [4] And there followed him Sopater, son of Pyrrhus, from Beroea; of the Thessalonians, Aristarchus and Secundus; Gaius from Derbe and Timothy; and from Asia Tychicus and Trophimus. [5] They went on ahead and waited for us in Troas. [6] But we sailed from Philippi after the days of Unleavened Bread, and within five days came to them at Troas, where we remained seven days.

Bibliography:

Clayton R. Bowen, 'Paul's Collection for the Saints', *HTR* 43 (1923), 49–58; E. B. Allo, 'La portée de la collecte pour Jérusalem dans les plans de St. Paul', *Rev. Bibl.* 45 (1936), 529–37; P. S. Minear, 'The Jerusalem Fund and Pauline Chronology', *AngThR* 25 (1943), 389–96; C. H. Buck,' The Collection for the Saints', *HTR* 43 (1950), 1–29; H. Conzelmann, 'Miszelle zu Act. **20**.4', *ZNW* 45 (1954), 266; Kragerud 1955, 258f., see § 29; Dieter Georgi, *Die Geschichte der Kollekte des Paulus für Jerusalem*, Theol. Forschungen vol. 38, Hamburg-Bergstedt 1965, 102pp; Conzelmann, 114f.; G. Stählin, 262–4.

VERSE 1: 'When the tumult had ceased': it was not the cause of Paul's departure![1] τοὺς μαθητάς: Paul takes leave of the congregation—whether in the lecture hall of Tyrannus or somewhere else is beside the point, and therefore is not indicated. παρακαλέσας:[2] the verb does not mean merely 'admonish', but also 'encourage', 'comfort' (Bauer, *Wb* 1224) and can

---

[1] When Jacquier (594) maintains on the basis of II Cor. **1**.8f. that Paul left Ephesus in order not to expose the community to persecution, and brought forward the time of his departure, he contradicts the report of Acts.

[2] D replaces παρακαλέσας by the παρακελεύσας popular in Hellenism, and adds πολλά. Conversely it omits the πορεύεσθαι, which seemed superfluous.

include the entire contents of a Christian sermon. πορεύεσθαι gives the expression a formal ring.

VERSE 2: διέρχομαι: see **8**.4. τὰ μέρη ἐκεῖνα: 'That country', namely Macedonia (see Bl.-Debr. § 141, 2). The communities of Philippi, Thessalonica and Beroea will have been visited. παρακαλέσας:[1] see v. 1. Ἑλλάς (only here in NT): actually = Achaea;[2] above all Paul was in Corinth (but the name of a town first appears again in v. 5!) where he wrote the letter to the Romans (Romans **15**.22–9).

VERSE 3: ποιήσας: see **15**.33. 'Three months': probably as in **19**.8 a round number, which relates to the autumn of 54 (so also Schlatter, *Erläut.* 4, 242 notes). γενομένης ἐπιβουλῆς κτλ: the Jewish conspiracy[3] compels Paul to change his plans –a sea voyage to Palestine—and to take the overland route via Macedonia. ἐγένετο γνώμης: choice Greek! (See Bl.-Debr. § 162, 7; cf. Thucydides 1, 113: ὅσοι τῆς αὐτῆς γνώμης ἦσαν). τοῦ ὑποστρέφειν: Bl.-Debr. § 400, 7: 'pleonastic' τοῦ.

VERSE 4: συνείπετο αὐτῷ[4] here describes Paul's retinue. Since Luke does not mention the collection here, the collection agents of the individual communities become mere companions. 'At the peak of his activity, surrounded by numerous attendants, the Apostle sets out on this last journey to Jerusalem': Overbeck 328. Σώπατρος = Σωσίπατρος Romans **16**.21? The Thessalonian Ἀρίσταρχος (mentioned also in **19**.29 and **27**.2) and the otherwise unknown Secundus constitute the first pair; the Lycaonians Gaius from Derbe[5] and Timothy (from Lystra: **16**.1; as already well known to the reader, he is here not described in any detail) the second pair; and the Ἀσιανοί[6] Tychicus and Trophimus the third pair. Luke is satisfied with seven names.

VERSE 5: This verse[7] admits of three interpretations: 1. 'We' = an

---

[1] D has again exchanged παρακαλέσας this time for χρησάμενος.

[2] Harnack (*Beiträge* III 94; ET): 'This exchange of Ἀχαΐα and Ἑλλάς is characteristic of Hellenistic authors': Zahn 700 on the contrary: 'Hellas . . . does not have the same meaning as Achaea . . . but describes Greece proper', without Thessaly.

[3] According to Ramsay (*St. Paul* 287) Paul originally wanted to use a pilgrim ship, which brought Jews from Achaea and Asia Minor to Jerusalem; there was a threat of murder on the voyage. So also Schlatter, *Erläut.* 4, 244. Zahn (701) on the contrary: the intention was to kill Paul on his embarkation at Cenchreae. According to Loisy (758) the redactor has invented the Jewish plot.

D has broken up the very condensed sentence and attempted to make it plain, but in the process has misunderstood: Paul, up to the Jewish plot, wanted to sail to Syria, but the Holy Spirit ordered the land route. Bauernfeind (235) justly remarks on this: 'This Western text does not go back to a revision by Luke.'

[4] The words ἄχρι (μέχρι) τῆς Ἀσίας in A D H L P S arise from the identification of the 'we' in vv. 5f. with that in v. 13. From this it follows that the seven accompanied Paul only to Troas (=Ἀσία). But since that identification is false this conclusion also is wrong.

[5] For the reading Δουβέριος in D d see Introduction § 3, pp. 52f.

[6] They are probably correctly identified by D as Ἐφέσιοι: cf. **21**.29; Eph. **6**.21; II Tim. **4**.12.

[7] Most early MSS. read προσελθόντες, D προελθόντες. The 'we' text which begins here could have as its basis the diary of a companion of Paul (see above pp. 86 f.), but Luke has reworked it.

indefinite number of Christians, among whom the narrator is included, from Philippi; Paul and the seven would then have travelled by-passing Philippi to Troas. That Paul did not visit his favourite congregation is, however, so unlikely that we do not consider this possibility any further. 2. 'We' = the narrator (Luke) and Paul. Then the seven would all have travelled ahead to Troas. But for what purpose? In addition, the Corinthian and Philippian delegates are not included in Luke's calculation; Paul would at least have gone with the latter to Philippi. That the Philippian delegation had not yet departed but was waiting here is excluded by the fact that Paul according to the original travel plans, changed at the last minute, would not have come to Philippi at all. 3. Only Tychicus and Trophimus, who were most familiar with the Asia Minor shipping, were sent ahead; all the others went with Paul to Philippi. In that case, in the 'we' a Christian who travelled with them from Philippi may be reporting (= Luke, on the usual interpretation, but also Timothy. Against Timothy is the fact that after the cessation of the 'we' in **16**.17 he is mentioned in the third person [**17**.14 and **18**.15]: *Beg.* IV 253). Lake has with reason advocated the third possibility (Tychicus and Trophimus alone travel ahead to Troas).

VERSE 6: 'After the days of Unleavened Bread': most exegetes find here a Passover feast which Paul, according to old Jewish custom, celebrated in his favourite congregation, allowing himself seven restful days;[1] but it can also be a simple indication of the date according to the Jewish calendar like **27**.9 (so Bauernfeind 235). Since it is not certain whether Paul departed from Philippi directly after the end of the Passover feast and in Neapolis immediately found a ship for Troas, calculations like those of Zahn 704f. are untenable. ἄχρι ἡμερῶν πέντε = 'within five days' (Bauer, *Wb* 256; overlooked by Bl.-Debr. § 216, 3), stylistically improved by D into πεμπταῖοι.

Prolixity and brevity surprisingly alternate here. V. 1 depicts at some length, although in general expressions, the departure from Ephesus: Paul does not steal away under cover of night, but takes his departure with proper ceremony in a meeting of the community. But then the style changes: until v. 5 no further city is mentioned; only the names of countries ring out: Macedonia, Hellas, afterwards Syria. The indefiniteness of this description is not explained by the view that Paul is inspecting only communities already known (in that case Corinth could have been named!). More pertinent is the second reason which Dibelius (211) adduces: everything points towards the journey to Jerusalem, imprisonment and the journey to Rome. So the reader is not told the place from which Paul sets out in the company of the seven. As participants in the fateful journey, they are precisely described.

---

[1] Zahn 704: 'seven days which for members of Jewish birth or upbringing were days of rest'. According to W. Michaelis, *Einleitung*[2] 165, Paul in these days wrote a letter directed to Ephesus, to which Romans **16**.3–23 belongs.

Since Luke is here again silent about the collection, the reader must consider these men as the retinue which befits so successful a missionary as Paul. In reality (if we disregard Timothy, whom Paul according to II Cor. 8.20 would not have wished for such a post) they are collection agents of the congregations. Since in Luke they are only companions, Luke can limit this retinue to the sacred number seven. His silence about the Corinthians (he had not indeed named Corinth) thus does not allow the conclusion that these at the last moment withdrew from the collection. The Philippians also are omitted.

Since Paul wanted to travel by ship from Corinth to Jerusalem (Romans 15.25f.) he had summoned all the delegates to Corinth, even those from Asia Minor. He wanted to by-pass Ephesus (see on v. 16). But now a Jewish plot was made known to him: on a pilgrim ship the fanaticism of the Jews could easily have been unleashed against Paul; in addition we may not forget that the group carried with it the entire collection in ready money (presumably exchanged into gold) (Jacquier 595). Hence Paul decided upon the land route. With the five first named (and the Corinthians and Philippians) Paul made his stay in Philippi over Easter. That he celebrated the Passover according to the Jewish ritual in a community with an overwhelming majority of Gentile Christians is unlikely. The two Ephesians however he sent on ahead to Troas, to find a ship which travelled to Palestine without a landing in Ephesus on the way. To judge from the long wait in Troas that did not occur very often.

So understood, the text admits both of the usual interpretation, that Luke joined Paul again in Philippi, and also of that according to which Timothy speaks in the 'we'. Up to this point there had been no occasion for the author to take over a 'we' occurring in an itinerary: Paul stood throughout commandingly in the centre of the scene (cf. the commentary to vv. 7ff.).

48

ACTS 20:7–12

THE RAISING OF EUTYCHUS

[7] When we were assembled on the Sunday to break bread, Paul spoke to them, and since he wanted to leave the following morning, he extended his address till midnight. [8] Now there were many lamps in the upper room where we were assembled. [9] A young man by the name of Eutychus, who sat on the window sill, was overcome by a deep sleep as Paul spoke still longer and (overcome by sleep) he fell from the third storey and was lifted up dead. [10] But Paul went down, lay upon him, and embraced him, then said, 'Do not raise a lament, for his soul is in him.' [11] Then he went up, broke bread and ate, and after he had spoken still longer, till daybreak, he departed. [12] But they brought the boy away alive, and were more than a little comforted.

Bibliography:

J. E. Roberts, 'The Story of Eutychus', *Exp.Tim.* 49 (1923), 376–82; Menoud, *RHPhR* 33, 1953, 27ff., see § 7. H. Riesenfeld, 'Sabbat et jour du Seigneur', *NTS* 1959, 210ff.; W. Rordorf, *Der Sonntag*, 1962, 193–9 (*ATLANT* 43; ET *Sunday*, 1968, 196-205); W. E. P. Cotter, 'St. Paul's Eucharist (Acts 20.6–12)', *Exp.Tim.* 39 (1927–8), 235; Conzelmann 115f.

VERSE 7: 'On the first day of the week'[1] (σάββατα) ranks—beside I Cor. **16**.2 (and Rev. **1**.10f.?)—as the first mention of the celebration of Sunday, but does not exclude daily celebration of the 'breaking of bread' (=Lord's Supper, cf. Behm, *ThWb* III 728f.). The author presupposes a Christian community in Troas, whose establishment (20.1f. by Paul?)[2] he has not recounted. συνηγμένων ἡμῶν: is repeated in v. 8. The story of Eutychus is inserted in the 'we' account here from another tradition and linked by the 'we' in vv. 7f. to what precedes (Dibelius, *Studies* 17).[3] διαλέγομαι: 'to preach' —only Paul speaks. μέλλων κτλ gives the reason why Paul preaches so long.

---

[1] According to whether one reckons the beginning of the day according to the Jewish manner or not, it is a question of the night from Saturday to Sunday or the following one.

[2] II Cor. **2**.12f. leads to such a conjecture.

[3] According to Dibelius, *Studies* 17 n. 37, Luke has inserted the story through vv. 7 and 11; the details of the service also belong in his view to the 'Christian embellishment'. According to G. Schille, *TLZ* 84 (1959), 172, it was the Passover night, the date of which Luke wanted for Philippi (!).

VERSE 8: ἦμεν συνηγμένοι:[1] the 'we' now disappears until v. 13. The mention of the many lamps is explained in very varied ways.[2] Perhaps here the aspersion, recorded later, against the Christian cult meal (promiscuity in the dark)[3] is already presupposed and combated.

VERSE 9: νεανίας is replaced by παῖς in v. 12, and thus means 'youth'.[4] Eutychus (no unusual name; not to be taken symbolically ['lucky fellow!']) had seated himself in the window (καθέζεσθαι ἐπὶ τῆς θυρίδος, Bauer, *Wb* 723). καταφερόμενος—κατενεχθείς: *sedentem somnus occupavit, somnio oppressus cecidit* (Bengel), while Preuschen 121 sees here two old variants. ἐπὶ πλεῖον: here temporal = 'long'.[5] τρίστεγον: the third storey if one reckons the ground floor as the first. A fall from such a height is not necessarily fatal (*Beg.* IV 256); here however death is presupposed.[6]

VERSE 10: ἐπέπεσεν: Paul lies upon the victim and embraces him, not to look for pulse and breath (for that ἐπέπεσεν would be highly inappropriate, especially as one had to think about broken bones), but rather the event is depicted after the model of the well-known stories of Elijah (I Kings 17.21f.) and Elisha (II Kings 4.34). The lamentation for the dead (θορυβεῖσθαι) is forbidden as in Mk. 5.39. Wendt (286), Zahn (708), Loisy (765) correctly emphasize that Paul does not say, 'His soul is *still* in him.'

VERSE 11: κλάσας τὸν ἄρτον: cf. v. 7. Naturally it is not Paul alone who partakes of the Lord's Supper, but everyone. Paul however stands in the centre of the narrative, and is consequently the only one mentioned. Thereafter Paul continues preaching (ὁμιλήσας)[7] until about five o'clock in the

---

[1] On the *coniug. periphrastica* see 1.10.

[2] Preuschen (121), Bauernfeind (236) explain like the text above. Dibelius, *Studies* (18 n. 38), considers this impossible and finds a humorous undertone: 'In spite of the burning lamps, he fell asleep.' Zahn (707): the vapour from the many lamps (and men) caused Eutychus to sit in the window and fall asleep. But how sleepy must the others have been who sat in the middle of the room! Knopf (625) concludes 'good recollection of the eye-witness', similarly Jacquier (599). Wendt (286) and Loisy (764) conclude from the mention of the many lamps that the accident was not caused by lack of light; Meyer (cited by Overbeck 334) on the other hand that thanks to the good lighting it was immediately noticed! Beyer (121) pictures a cosy scene: outside the dark night, the congregation with the guests in the lamplight ... D has removed the lamps, to him inexplicable, conjecturing ὑπολαμπάδες, 'little windows'.

[3] Minucius Felix, *Octavius* 9; Tertullian, *Apol.* 8f. Overbeck (334) admittedly contests this explanation (already given by Ewald) as a 'strange fancy'.

[4] νεανίας in 23.17 is replaced by νεανίσκος in 23.22. According to Hippocrates περὶ ἑβδομάδων § 5 (VIII 636 Littré), cited by Philo, *de opif. mundi* § 105 (37, 13ff. C.-W.), the life-span is divided as follows: 1–7 παιδίον; 8–14 παῖς; 15–22 μειράκιον; 23–28 νεανίσκος; 29–49 ἀνήρ; 50–56 πρεσβύτης (Philemon 9); beyond 56 γέρων. Luke at all events does not mean by νεανίας a 'man between 24 and 40 years old' (Bauer, *Wb* 1057).

[5] Acts 4.17 spatially: to a great distance.

[6] ἤρθη νεκρός as Test. Jud. 9.3. Overbeck (335) correctly emphasizes: 'as if dead' is not in the text.

[7] When Wellhausen 42 finds a proof of the reliability of the report in the fact that Paul's long speech is not recorded, it is overlooked that Luke inserts speeches only at notable points. This is immediately shown by the farewell speech in Miletus.

U

morning (ἕως αὐγῆς: daybreak before sunrise: *Beg.* IV 257). οὕτως (cf. 27.17): 'to sum up the contents of a preceding participial construction': Bl.-Debr. § 425, 6.

VERSE 12: The subject and destination of the carrying remain indefinite: some Christians or relatives bring the young man into the house or take him home.[1]

The commentators unanimously declare that so little stir is created by the miracle of raising the dead that we may doubt its occurrence and find in it only a miracle of preservation (so Beyer 121 and Bauernfeind 236). But the narrator intends to report a great miraculous act and not merely a correct diagnosis by Paul (Dibelius, *Studies* 18). If he nevertheless practises such reserve, it is not out of criticism: the story puts the heathen reader in a thoughtful frame of mind just with its very objectivity; the Christian recognized the association with Elijah and Elisha, and hence the miracle.

With a rare unanimity the earlier critics (also Zeller 269, Renan [*St. Paul* vol. ii, 119] and including even Wellhausen 42 and Preuschen 121) took the incident as historical and the story as a part of the 'we' account. But the narrative—bracketed by the 'we' in vv. 7f.—has been inserted into the itinerary (Dibelius, *Studies* 17f.). Its character is markedly secular: Zahn (708) without evidence has added a prayer by Paul. Luke has not quite succeeded in linking the miracle story with the departure scene: v. 12 still has the effect of the old conclusion to the miracle story. 'They' (not 'we') 'were comforted' shows the foreignness of the miracle story over against the itinerary. But it also remains unclear what now becomes of Eutychus. Zahn (710) makes him go up again with Paul to participate in the Lord's Supper and the other five hours of preaching, and then come hand in hand with Paul to the departure: an edifying correction and imaginative expansion of the traditional material, using the Western reading.

Once one sees how tradition and composition are here connected, one becomes careful in the historical evaluation of the story's details. It does not testify with certainty to a Christian celebration of Sunday by Paul, but in the first place to that usual in the time of Luke. This seems (v. 11) to have been only a Eucharist without the proper character of a meal (the congregation certainly did not wait until after midnight for their supper!), preceded by a sermon.

In the miracle story Luke did not—as the 'Tübingers' once thought and Zahn (707) astonishingly still assumes—have the intention of establishing a correspondence between Peter (Tabitha, Acts 9.36–43) and Paul, but rather here sketches once again, although with softened colours, the miraculous power of the Apostle departing from his work, who now hastens irresistibly toward the humiliation of his imprisonment.

---

[1] D felt the obscurity and wanted to remove it: 'When they had taken their leave, he (Paul) led the young man away alive' (cf. *Beg.* III 193).

49

ACTS 20:13–16

FROM TROAS TO MILETUS

[13] We however went ahead to the ship and departed for Assos, where we were to take Paul on board; for so he had arranged since he himself wanted to go on foot. [14] When he met us in Assos, we took him on board and came to Mitylene, [15] and departing from there we arrived opposite Chios the following day, on the next day we travelled over to Samos and finally we came to Miletus. [16] For Paul had decided to pass by Ephesus in order not to lose time in (the province of) Asia. For he was hurrying in order—if it should be possible for him—to be in Jerusalem on the day of Pentecost.

Bibliography:

Williams, 231f.; Conzelmann, 116; G. Stählin, 265f.

VERSE 13: 'We'[1], i.e. all Paul's companions, went to the ship.[2] Paul chose the shorter land route, according to Beyer 121, in order to be alone with God; according to Lake (*Beg.* IV 257f.) in order to avoid the difficult sea voyage from Troas to Assos, where a stormy northeaster blew five days out of seven. Further on Lesbos and the Asiatic coast gave protection from the wind. μέλλοντες ἀναλαμβάνειν: 'since we were to take in'; μέλλων πεζεύειν: 'since he wanted to go on foot'.

VERSE 14: To the travel-report may be ascribed the imperfect instead of the aorist, εἰς instead of ἐν (although this interchange is not foreign to Luke

---

[1] Preuschen had conjectured in his commentary on Acts (*Hdb.* 1912, vi and 121) that the text of the Armenian Catena was to to be altered to read: 'But I, Luke, and those with me'. Meanwhile the Armenian translation of Ephraem's Commentary in Codex 571 (*Beg.* III 442) disclosed that the conjecture was correct but the conclusion false. The text shows only that the writer, in accordance with tradition, considered Luke the author speaking in the 'we'.

[2] ΠΡΟΣΕΛΘΟΝΤΕΣ B A and ΠΡΟΕΛΘΟΝΤΕΣ ℵ C could easily have been confused with each other, whether misread or incorrectly written.—D has substituted κατελθόντες (= to go down to the ship lying in the harbour). Zahn adopts this text and draws from it the meaning 'boarding the ship': 'after the completely sleepless night, made very fatiguing through exciting experiences, the doctor considered it advisable to obtain for himself and his travelling companions, as well as the accommodation the ship's hold afforded, a substitute for their lost night's rest' (710f.). This fanciful justification of the Western text is characteristic of Zahn's commentary.

himself) and the later form of the name Μιτυλήνη. Dibelius (*Studies* 126) points out that Luke used a source here: 'The content' of these two verses 'was neither conceived in legend nor handed down as an anecdote; it can only be understood as a note taken from a list of stations, from an itinerary'. συμβάλλω occurs in the NT only in the Lucan writings. Mitylene was the capital city of the island of Lesbos, roughly 44 miles from Assos: Jacquier 602.

VERSE 15: B has the scribal error ἑσπέρᾳ (*Beg.* IV 258); the stretch from Mitylene to Samos is much too long for a day's voyage (here people evidently do not sail by night).[1]

VERSE 16 ought strictly to have come after the mention of Samos. Luke however first carried the itinerary through to Miletus, where he had in any case to interrupt with the speech. Paul avoided Ephesus (where the ship apparently did not put in at all) not for lack of time but (as Wellhausen 42 already conjectured) for the sake of security. So far as one can conclude from II Cor. 1.8–10 (and Romans 15.30f.) he had barely escaped from Ephesus with his life. That the pious Jew Paul wanted at all costs to spend Pentecost in Jerusalem[2] displaces for Luke the suppressed motive of the Pauline journey: the delivery of the collection.

---

[1] The Western text (D d gig pesh sy^hmg sa: *Beg.* III 195) has also the addition καὶ μείναντες ἐν Τρωγυλίῳ, which Ropes considered original. See Intro. § 3, p. 53.

[2] Since Chrysostom attempts have been made to calculate whether Paul came to Jerusalem in time for the feast. Since many statements of Acts concerning the journey are indefinite, this labour is vain. Luke himself drops the motif later, and does not even mention whether Paul arrived in Jerusalem before the feast.

50
ACTS 20:17–38
PAUL'S FAREWELL SPEECH IN MILETUS

17 From Miletus he sent to Ephesus and summoned the elders of the congregation. When they came to him, he said to them, 18 'You know how I was with you the entire time from the first day on which I set foot in Asia, 19 serving the Lord with all humility and tears and vexations, which beset me in the plots of the Jews, 20 how I did not hold back from proclaiming to you anything that is healthful and teaching you openly in the houses, 21 witnessing to the Jews and Greeks conversion to God and faith in our Lord Jesus. 22 And now, behold, I go bound by the Spirit to Jerusalem without knowing what is to happen to me there, 23 except that the Holy Spirit testifies to me in every city that imprisonment and afflictions await me. 24 But I account my life not worth mention, that I may fulfil my course and the service which I have received from the Lord Jesus, to witness to the Gospel of the grace of God. 25 And now behold, I know that you will see my face no more, you all, among whom I have gone about preaching the kingdom. 26 Therefore I testify to you this day that I am innocent of the blood of anyone. 27 For I have proclaimed to you the entire will of God without concealing anything. 28 So take heed to yourselves and the whole flock in which the Holy Spirit has set you as guardians to tend the community of God which he has obtained through the blood of his own (son). 29 I know that after my departure ravenous wolves will come to you which will not spare the flock, 30 and men will arise out of your midst who speak perversely in order to lead the disciples astray after them. 31 Stay alert, therefore, remembering that for three years, night and day, I have admonished every individual incessantly, with tears. 32 And now I commend you to the Lord and the word of his grace which is able to edify and to give you the inheritance among all the sanctified. 33 Silver or gold or garments I have not coveted. 34 You know yourselves that these hands have served the needs of myself and those with me. 35 In everything I have shown you that so working we should support the weak, and remember the words of the Lord Jesus, for he said, "It is more blessed to give than to receive".' 36 And after these words he kneeled down with them all and prayed. 37 They all broke out in loud crying and fell on Paul's neck and kissed him, 38 most of all disturbed over the word which he had spoken, that they would not see his face any more. And they brought him to the ship.

Bibliography:

H. Schulze, 'Die Unterlagen f.d. Abschiedsrede z. Milet i. Apg. **20**.18–38', *StKr* 1900, 119–25; Livingstone Porter, 'The Word ἐπίσκοπος in the pre-Christian Usage', *AngThR* 21 (1939), 103–12; J. Munck, 'Discours d'adieu dans le N.T. et dans la littérature biblique', *Mélanges Goguel*, 1950, 155–70; H. Schürmann, 'Es tut not, der Worte des Herrn Jesus zu gedenken', *Katechet. Blätter* 79 (1954), 254–61; J. L. d'Aragon, '"Il faut soutenir les faibles" (Actes **20**.35)', *Sciences ecclés.* 7 (1955), 5–22, 173–203; Kragerud 1955, 259f., see § 29; W. Nauck, 'Probleme des frühchristl. Amtsverständnisses (I Petr. **5**.2)', *ZNW* 48 (1957), 200–20; K. H. Rengstorf, "Geben ist seliger als Nehmen", Bemerkungen z.d. ausserevang. Herrenwort Apg. **20**.35, *Die Leibhaftigkeit des Wortes, Festschrift f. Adolf Köberle* 1958, 23–35.

H. Rosman, 'In omni humilitate (Act. **20**.19)', *Verb. Domini* 21 (1941), 272–80, 311–20; C. Claereboets, 'In quo vos spiritus sanctus, etc. (Actes **20**.28)', *Biblica* 24 (1943), 370–87; R. Balgarnie, 'Acts **20**.35', *Exp.Tim.* 19 (1907–8), 522f.; R. Roberts, 'The Beatitude of Giving and Receiving', *Exp.Tim.* 48 (1936–7), 438–41; U. Holzmeister, 'Beatum est dare, non accipere (Act. **20**.35)', *Verb. Domini* 27 (1949), 98–101; C. F. Vine, 'The "Blood of God" in Acts **20**.38', *CBQ* 9 (1947), 381–408; J. Dupont, 'Paulus an die Seelsorger. Das Vermächtnis von Milet (Apg. **20**.18–36)', 1966 [*KuBzAuNT*]; Williams, 232–5; Conzelmann, 116–120; G. Stählin, 266–72.

VERSE 17: Miletus is about 32 miles in a bee-line from Ephesus; the land route which had actually to be covered (with a crossing of the Meander) was much longer. Even if the messenger put it behind him in two days, that would have been impossible for the elders. If a ship stood immediately at their disposal for the journey in each direction, they still would not arrive within the three days which Jacquier (604) estimates as the duration of the trip. The author however has not thought about any of these problems, but has the elders 'sent for' in the same way as the disciples in **20**.1. Overbeck 399ff. already remarked that the itinerary here breaks off and the speech is drafted by the author, which Bauernfeind (239) also grants. Dibelius finally proved the speech to be Luke's work and evaluated it (*Studies* 155–8). 'Luke . . . may even have taken shorthand notes': Bruce 377 (!)

VERSE 18: The first part of the speech extends to v. 21 and looks back to the past, Paul's work in Ephesus. Ἀσία stands here as in v. 16 for Ephesus. The elders (see on v. 28) are here addressed as those first converted, who have been together with Paul from the first day. Construe 'You know how I from the first day on . . .': ἀπὸ πρώτης κτλ. is placed first for emphasis. πῶς ἐγενόμην: the Apostle's way of life and religious attitude.

VERSE 19: Humility, tears and Jewish persecution are its characteristic marks. The theme of tears is dealt with in detail in v. 31; that of humility (not 'humiliations' as many translate) is echoed in v. 29, that of persecution appears again in vv. 22f.

VERSE 20: Paul has publicly and in the house-churches proclaimed 'what is useful' without withholding anything[1] (this is repeated in v. 27). τὰ συμφέροντα means here that which is necessary for salvation.[2] J. Weiss (34) conjectures a concrete occasion—did the heretics mentioned in v. 30 appeal to Pauline secret tradition? Then v. 20 states positively: one must hold to the true apostolic tradition of the Church.—For ὑποστέλλομαι see Bauer *Wb* 1676, s.v. 2c.

VERSE 21 presents with extreme condensation the content of the Christian proclamation to Gentiles and Jews: Paul has witnessed to[3] the conversion to God in μετάνοια and belief in the Κύριος 'Ιησοῦς.[4]

VERSE 22f.: The second part which begins here (to v. 24) deals with Paul's present situation. καὶ νῦν ἰδού:[5] see on 13.11. Paul travels, bound by the (Holy) Spirit,[6] to Jerusalem. 'His journey lay upon him as a duty and a necessity: he could not do otherwise. It is commanded him by a clear and oft-confirmed order of the divine Spirit': Schlatter (250). What will happen to him[7] he does not know; he goes into the dark. Only[8] the Holy Spirit (by Christian prophets) proclaims to him in every city chains (prison, captivity) and hardships. Such prophetic admonitions Luke could not report up till now because in Chap. 20 he recounted nothing about Paul's visit to the congregations. He therefore adds something here. The details of what is to come, however, still remain in a darkness full of mystery.

---

[1] ὑποστέλλω also belongs to the 'biblical' concepts which Luke uses.

[2] Preuschen (123) is wrong when, appealing to Demosthenes I 16, he thinks of the profane sense.

[3] διαμαρτύρομαι, which occurs over twenty times in LXX, most often means 'to declare emphatically' or 'to affirm'; it has this meaning also in Acts (2.40; 8.25; 10.42; 18.5; 20.21, 23f.; 23.11; 28.23; *ThWb* IV 518f.).

[4] This construction of μετάνοια is singular (the frequent μετάνοια εἰς ἄφεσιν ἁμαρτιῶν leads in quite another direction). See Intro. § 7 A, p. 94.

[5] A LXX expression often used by Luke, which deals not with the future (Jacquier), but with Paul's present uncertain situation.

[6] Overbeck (344) explains τῷ πνεύματι δεδεμένος: 'The passage is . . . further nothing but a glance back to the resolution of 19.21.' Correspondingly Holtzmann (127): 'under inward compulsion'; Jacquier (608) supplies a Catholic-scholastic variant: τὸ πνεῦμα is 'la partie supérieure de l'homme', which stands under the influence of the divine Spirit. But Luke, who has struck out the real reason for Paul's journey, the collection, must put another in its place. A human resolution does not come into question; only a supernatural compulsion by the (divine!) Spirit explains the riddle, without however really clarifying it. Wendt's exegesis (290), already advocated by Hugo Grotius, is very shallow: Paul sees himself, in the Spirit, already chained.—We cannot require the author to use the full formula 'the Holy Spirit' twice in immediate succession.

[7] συναντήσοντα: one of the few cases of a future participle in the NT. The verb occurs in the NT (apart from quotations from LXX, in which it is very frequent) only in Luke.

[8] πλὴν ὅτι: Bl.-Debr. § 449, 1: 'other than that' (classical). At Phil. 1.18—Bl.-Debr. § 449, 2—it may rather mean 'only', 'in any case'. Dodd, *The Apostolic Preaching*, 18, finds in this speech 'so many echoes of the language of the Pauline epistles, that we must suppose . . . that he (Luke) worked upon actual reminiscence of Paul's speech upon this or some similar occasion'. Dodd in our opinion has overestimated the relationship with Paul's vocabulary.

VERSE 24 may be understood according to Bauer, *Wb* 943, as 'not worth mention' (cf. our 'not worth talking about') 'do I consider my life in order to fulfil . . .' = 'I readily give my life in order to . . .'. E H L P have simplified the text, D in another way. τελειώσω κτλ.: cf. II Tim. **4**.7; in Paul, Phil. **3**.14. τὴν διακονίαν κτλ: Paul's service is here described as testimony to the grace of God; in this Luke wants to let a specifically Pauline catchword ring out (cf. **13**.38f.).[1]

VERSE 25: καὶ νῦν ἰδού: see **13**.11. The third part of the speech, concerned with the future of Paul and the Church, extends from vv. 25–31. The interspersed references to Paul's past activity reveal him as an example for the future. Two thoughts run together: 'You Ephesians will not see me again' and 'All among whom I . . . went about preaching will not see me again'. In the transition from the first to the second the scene expands and reveals the true meaning of the section: Paul is taking leave not only of the Ephesian elders but of all congregations—they do not see him again! Anyone who writes thus knows nothing of Paul's deliverance and return to the East,[2] but rather of his death in Rome (see v. 38).

VERSE 26: διότι links with κηρύσσων: if anyone now goes astray, Paul is innocent; he has done his duty to the utmost.[3]

VERSE 27: Paul has proclaimed to the leaders of the communities (ὑμῖν!) the complete decree of God—there is therefore no Pauline teaching deviating from it and handed down alongside it. This repetition of v. 20 consequently underlines the integrity of the Church's preaching. Indirectly this already initiates the discussion of the heresy against which the leaders of the communities are warned to be on guard.—οὐ . . . ὑπεστειλάμην τοῦ μή: Bauer, *Wb* 1676 s.v. 2b.

VERSE 28 shows that the individual congregation is led by a presbytery (cf. **14**.23); its members are called ἐπίσκοποι. At the time of Luke, therefore, the presbyterian constitution after the Jewish model prevailed (for the early

---

[1] Wendt 291 n. 1 wants to reconstruct a source text: ὡς τελειῶσαι τὴν διακονίαν (= the collection!), ἣν παρέλαβον. In this way the refined style in which the author makes Paul deliver his farewell address is reinterpreted in favour of a source construction.

[2] According to Harnack (*Beitr*. IV 71f.; ET) this prediction was belied by the facts and therefore—since Luke could not have allowed Paul to pronounce a prophecy already recognized in his time to be false—Acts was published even before Paul's liberation from his first imprisonment. Since this early dating of the work cannot be sustained, it follows from the train of thought that Paul did not again come to the East.—Jacquier (610) makes Paul voice only what he knows 'par ses vues personnelles . . . et non par inspiration', in order not to endanger the inspiration of Acts. According to Zahn (718) Luke did not feel himself justified in altering the Pauline text, corrected by the later return. But Luke the author—if Paul really returned once again to the East—would have guarded against leading the reader, by the emphasis in v. 38, into the wrong view that Paul did not return. For the rest, prophecies refuted by history were not handed on—if they could not be interpreted.

[3] D with 'up to the present day I am innocent' has unsuccessfully sought to bring into order a meaningless sentence resulting from the omission of διότι μαρτύρομαι ὑμῖν.

period see the summary discussion on **1**.15–26, p. 163 f.). The OT image of pasturing the sheep (see esp. Ezek. **14**.11f.; Jer. **23**.2; Zech. **10**.3, **11**.16; in the NT esp. John. **10**.11, 14–16, **21**.15–17) describes the task of these congregational leaders.[1]

VERSE 29: With a new 'I know that . . .' the approaching misfortune is more closely described: 'after my departure[2] ravenous[3] wolves[4] will come to you, which will not spare the flock'—the heretics bring the congregation to ruin.

VERSE 30: But the community will be threatened not only through heretics intruding from without, but also from within: heretics will arise in the community itself,[5] who speak 'perversities';[6] the defection to the Gnostic heresy could not well be more clearly described in this prophecy. The reader moreover had it before his very eyes.

VERSE 31: The elders, therefore, are to 'stay alert', remembering Paul's exemplary conduct: 'that I three years, day and night,[7] incessantly admonished every single one with tears'. The single case in which Paul admonished

---

[1] The Church in the first century therefore did not take as its model the practice of the Dead Sea sect recognizable from CDC XIII 7–11 (otherwise Nauck 207). The passage adduced by Nauck, from Trad. Apost. III 4f. (prayer at the consecration of a bishop) does not belong to the oldest content of Hippolytus' Church Order, which rather likewise presupposes only a presbytery (see Franz Heinrich Kettler, *TLZ* 81 (1956), 446f.). "It has been suggested that the office of 'Bishop' in the Church has its origin in the Qumran 'overseer'" (Allegro, *The Dead Sea Scrolls* 1956, 144). But H. Braun (*Spätjüdisch-häretischer und frühchristlicher Radikalismus*, Vol. I, 1957, 104 n. 6) has established that in the (later) Damascus document, compared with the (older) community rule, the duties of the overseer', the Mebaqqer, are 'greatly increased'. If the young Christian community took this office as its model, in the form it showed at that time according to the Damascus document, then the monarchic episcopate must have stood at the beginning. Actually however the three 'pillars' Peter, James and John at first held the leadership in the Jerusalem congregation (Gal. **2**.6, 9). Paul's letters do not reveal any office comparable to the Mebaqqer. Acts **20**.23 clearly designates all the presbyters of Ephesus as 'overseers'. Thus as yet no individual (like Diotrephes, III John 9) had raised himself out of the group of the presbyters into 'monarchy'. We may accordingly agree with Bo Reicke ('The Constitution of the Church', in *The Scrolls and the NT*, ed. K. Stendahl, 1957, 154): we may speak of a certain parallelism in the development of the Church and of the Qumran community, since in both an office with almost monarchic authority gradually took shape.

[2] ἄφιξις strictly means 'arrival'; but in the passages named by Bauer, *Wb* 251 'departure' (so already Chrysostom). What is in mind is not Paul's departure from Ephesus or from the East but his departure from this world: according to Luke the heretics only penetrate into the Church after the apostolic age; cf. G. Bornkamm, *ThWb* IV 311f. The Latins have translated ἄφιξις by *discessio, discessum* and *abscessum*.

[3] Bauer, *Wb* 266 s.v. 2d: 'violent, pernicious, cruel, savage', with references.

[4] 'Wolves' as a description of heretics; Did. **16**.3; Ign. *Philad.* **2**.2; II Clem. **5**.2–4; Justin *Apol.* I 16, 13; *Dial.* **35**.3.

[5] Cf. I John **2**.19 and Mk. **13**.22 with the continuation πρὸς τὸ ἀποπλᾶν . . . τοὺς ἐκλεκτούς.

[6] Cf. **13**.10 διαστρέφων.

[7] νύκτα καὶ ἡμέραν as **26**.7 and Lk. **2**.37; Mk. **4**.27; genitive: Mk. **5**.5; I Thess. **2**.9; **3**.10; I Tim. **5**.5; II Tim. **1**.3. LXX almost always places the day first.—νύκτα δὲ ἡμέραν in D will be a mistake in hearing: καί was later pronounced as κε.

with tears a member of a community who threatened to go astray is portrayed in rhetorical generalization as his general attitude, as a constant pledging of himself for the preservation of the community.

VERSE 32: With καὶ τὰ νῦν begins the last part of the speech, which combines the blessing and the reminder to care for the needy. Paul commends the communities, which he has hitherto led himself, to the Lord[1]—this expresses the final departure just as sharply as vv. 25 and 38 . . . 'And to the word of his grace': cf. what was said on v. 24. (τῷ κυρίῳ) τῷ δυναμένῳ κτλ.. are expressions of edifying language, which refer to the earthly present (οἰκοδομή) and the heavenly future (κληρονομία) (Wendt 294).

VERSE 33f.: To this blessing Paul attaches a reference to his altruism, which is to be a model for Christian charity: he has coveted[2] no garment, gold or silver, but 'these hands have earned for my own and my companions' heeds'.[3] So Luke gives the reader to understand that Paul supported himself through his own labour, a trait for which the earlier description of the Pauline mission allowed only occasional space. It is thus now made a duty for Christian church leaders not to live at the expense of the community.

VERSE 35: 'In everything[4] I have shown you that so working we should support the weak'—the connection of thought with what precedes is not very close: care for companions and sparing of the community—care for the weak—'and remember the words of the Lord Jesus, for he said, "It is more blessed to give than to receive."' With this (ostensible) word of Jesus, unknown to the gospels, the speech concludes.[5]

---

[1] Cf. 14.23.

[2] Cf. 3.6; see also 'clothes, gold, silver' I Macc. 11.34; James 5.2; the wealth of Orientals consisted in large part of costly garments: Jacquier 619.

[3] This is admittedly an edifying exaggeration, as II Cor. 11.9 shows: Paul by his own work could not even keep himself from want, to say nothing of caring for his companions also. Cf. I Thess. 2.9; II Thess. 3.8; I Cor. 4.12; 9.15.

[4] The reading of D, πᾶσι . . . ὑμῖν, makes matters worse instead of better.

[5] A Jewish parallel to this saying is not known. Sir. 4.31 ('let not your hand be stretched out to take and closed at the time of giving back') describes with a double expression the greedy man who readily borrows and unwillingly repays. Did. 4.5 generalizes this: 'Do not become one who stretches out his hands for receiving, but clenches them when it comes to giving.' Here the distinction of giving and receiving does indeed appear, but both expressions depict only the greedy man. Did. 1.5 comes nearest to Acts 20.35: 'To everyone who asks you, give and do not require it back! For the Father wills that to all be given from one's own gifts of grace. Blessed is he who gives according to the commandment, for he is blameless. Woe to him who takes. To be sure, if anyone suffers want and so takes, then he will be blameless.' As comparison with Hermas *Mand.* IV 2, 4 shows, the passage deals with the problem bound up with the unconditional duty of a Christian to give to everyone who asks. But what if the provision is unscrupulously utilized? Answer: the giver acts in any case according to the commandment of God and therefore has honour (Hermas) or is μακάριος (Didache). Woe, however, to the receiver if he misuses the Christian duty to give! All this has nothing to do with Acts 20.35. For here it is a question of the support of the ἀσθενοῦντες.

Now Thucydides II 97, 4 shows that it was the rule in the Persian empire rather to give than to receive (διδόναι μᾶλλον ἢ λαμβάνειν). This applied in the first place to the relationship of the King to his φίλοι, but then to his subjects in general (cf. Xen. *Cyrop.*

VERSE 36: After the sermon follows a prayer at which the congregation also kneels—this will have been the usage in Luke's time.

VERSE 37: The departure of the elders is painted with biblical colours, cf. for example Gen. **33**.4. The kiss is here not the usual φίλημα ἅγιον of the Christians,[1] but induced by mingled sorrow and affection.[2]

VERSE 38: With the express reference back to v. 25 Luke emphasizes that the farewell is final. An author like Luke stresses such a sentence so expressly only 'if a negation by events was precluded, i.e. if the Apostle was already dead': Dibelius, *Studies*, 158 n. 46.

This speech also, despite its brevity, gives the reader the impression of a long address. This is partly due to the number of themes in it. They are in each case included in one of the sections which are separated from each other by definite introductory formulas: 1. 'you know' v. 18; 2. 'and now behold' v. 22; 3. 'and now I know' v. 25; 4. 'and now' v. 32. The first section deals with the past, Paul's activity in Ephesus; the second speaks of the present, his journey towards imprisonment. The third talks about the future: that of Paul (his death is indicated) and that of the Church (heresies will break in). The concluding section contains the blessing and the admonition for the care of the weak. That scholars like J. Weiss (33f.), Dibelius (*Studies* 157)

VIII 7, 14). *Beg.* IV 264 adduces τὸ προσθεῖναι τοῦ ἀφελεῖν βασιλικώτερόν ἐστιν (acc. to Plut. *Mor.* p. 173D a saying of King Artaxerxes) and ἄμεινον εἶναι πλουτίζειν ἢ πλουτεῖν (acc. Aelian, *Var. hist.* XIII 13); τοῦ εὖ πάσχειν τὸ εὖ ποιεῖν οὐ μόνον κάλλιον (= better), ἀλλὰ καὶ ἥδιον (Epicurus acc. to Plut. *Mor.* p. 778C): *errat . . . , si quis beneficium accipit libentius quam reddit* (Seneca *Ep.* 81, 17). I Clem. **2**.1 takes over the expression, subsequently naturalized in Greek: ὑποτασσόμενοι μᾶλλον ἢ ὑποτάσσοντες, ἥδιον διδόντες ἢ λαμβάνοντες.

If we now translate Acts **20**.35 as if μᾶλλον ἤ reproduced a Hebrew or Aramaic מן ('Giving is blessed, receiving not'), the contradiction results that the receiving ἀσθενής is characterized as 'not blessed'. It is less offensive if we translate μᾶλλον ἤ comparatively: 'Giving is more blessed than receiving!' Even so a small incongruity still remains: the receiving of the ἀσθενής ought not in any way to be defamed! Luke (as in **26**.14) has taken up a Greek proverb—this here becomes plain—into a section in other respects also very loosely composed, and placed it in the mouth of Jesus. It is Christianized by replacing the Hellenistic ἥδιον with the biblical μακάριον. The scribe of D has inserted the personal μακάριος after the model of the Sermon on the Mount, unfortunately without changing the infinitive to a participle.—K. H. Rengstorf, '"Geben ist seliger als Nehmen"', Bemerkungen z.d. ausserevang. Herrenwort Apg. **20**.35 '(*Die Leibhaftigkeit des Wortes, Festschrift f. A. Köberle* 1958, 23–35) considers it possible that the disciples of Jesus may have anticipated the opinion which later appears occasionally in rabbinical thought, that to receive alms is more deserving than to give alms (since the receiver makes it possible for the giver to fulfil the duty of love!); on the other hand Jesus could have spoken these words. But that the disciples of Jesus hovered in danger of a rabbinical intellectualism is extremely unlikely; hence we shall not reckon with this 'Sitz-im-Leben Jesu' at all. Rengstorf moreover overlooks the fact that in this saying we have a formula well known in the Graeco-Roman world.

[1] See I Thess. **5**.26; I Cor. **16**.20; II Cor. **13**.12; Romans **16**.16; cf. K. M. Hofmann, *Philema hagion*, 1938.

[2] καταφιλεῖν of a kiss of greeting or farewell is also used elsewhere: Bauer *Wb* 831. against Wendt 295.

and Bauernfeind (238) arrange the speech in different ways proves that it is more loosely constructed than one thinks at first sight.

When it was still regarded as the exact recapitulation of a speech by Paul, it presented the enigma that Paul here to an extraordinary degree presents himself as an exemplary model. Similar expressions are admittedly not lacking in the Pauline epistles: μιμηταί μου γίνεσθε he admonishes in I Cor. 4.16 and 11.1, γίνεσθε ὡς ἐγώ Gal. 4.12; and II Cor. 3.1. shows the reproach of his opponents—he commends himself. But was it necessary for Paul to extol himself in such a manner before the elders of the congregation of Ephesus, in which he had laboured now for years? The strangeness disappears if one recognizes with Dibelius (*Studies* 155–8) that this speech is not Paul's self-attestation at all, but only acquires its true meaning as Luke's witness about him.

Luke has it delivered at the moment when Paul is leaving his mission field (Miletus is the last station in ᾿Ασία) and for all practical purposes ending his free missionary activity. Here, where the reader takes leave of the Apostle's missionary labour proper, Luke supplies him in this speech with the portrait of Paul which he is to retain. He shows Paul as the ideal missionary and church leader, who is the exemplary model for later generations.

But the assurance that Paul has omitted nothing, that he bears no guilt if anyone goes astray, is repeated and delivered with such emphasis that we cannot make do with the information offered by Dibelius that this trait belongs to the style of such farewell speeches. Rather is J. Weiss correct: here there is a concrete motive. Only we may not seek it in reproaches which Paul had to counter in Ephesus. W. Bauer, in his still too little noticed book *Rechtgläubigkeit und Ketzerei im ältesten Christentum*[2] (Tübingen 1964, 235ff.), has called attention to the fact that the congregations founded by Paul in Asia Minor were largely lost to the Gnostic heresy. This Gnostic invasion did not first take place in the middle of the second century. The Revelation of John already reveals how strong was the Gnostic movement in the congregations of Asia Minor, which are here indeed no longer regarded as the heirs of the Pauline mission. The Lucan apology of Paul (that in this speech it is a case of such an apology was already recognized by J. Weiss, 34) corresponds to the situation at the end of the first century. Paul (whom Luke considers the representative of the apostolic, legitimate Church) bears no guilt for the catastrophe which after his death began to loom up in the Church of ᾿Ασία: he has done everything a man could possibly ask, indeed more. He has dedicated twenty-four hours a day to the work of the community, he has earned bread for himself and his companions with his own hands; a humble and modest man, who had proclaimed the whole saving teaching in household congregations and public sermons. What the Christian Gnostics teach may not appeal to the apostolic proclamation, and by that very fact pronounces judgement on itself.

Luke's concern here admittedly is not exhausted by such apologetic. As the ideal missionary and church leader Paul is the example which Luke holds before his own present age, which indeed—in contrast to the ostensibly heresy-free apostolic age—stood in battle with the Gnostic heresy (the Pastoral epistles show the same front). The community leaders, the elders, are summoned to risk themselves likewise to the utmost for the threatened communities, and thereby check the apostasy. This appeal of course does not have meaning only for this particular time of crisis. This is especially true of the call to care for the needy with which the speech concludes.

We shall not however do justice to the Lucan composition if we do not also take note of the 'prophecies of suffering' which it contains. Here also Dibelius (*Studies* 157f.) has already seen the decisive point: the public activity of Paul is at an end, 'and since the author does not intend to tell about his martyrdom, Luke does to some extent press the crown of martyrdom upon his head.' 'We can see that this speech could scarcely have been placed anywhere else.' This however does not have the result that everything further now breathes the air of martyrdom—on the contrary. Just because the martyrdom is here as it were anticipated, Luke can disregard it in what follows. Hence the narrative of Paul's imprisonment, despite all the hardships which Paul must bear, becomes a victorious saga. That the concluding chapters sound so confident has from Harnack on misled many readers into not taking the prophecies of suffering in our speech seriously. In reality the triumphant frame of the concluding chapters arises not out of knowledge of an earthly liberation of Paul but from the forestalling of his death.

If we keep all these themes in mind, we shall not demand of the speech that Pauline theology also be represented. Anyone who feels himself reminded sentence by sentence of the Pauline epistles (Bauernfeind 238f.) can nevertheless admit that 'Luke has paid attention to older preaching tradition and constructed from what he discovered an independent account' (239). The speech does not have the task of conveying theology at all—apart from the fact that Paul himself is presented to the clergy for imitation. For the speech is not merely directed to the Ephesian presbyters—that is the kernel of truth in the interpretation first advanced by Irenaeus (III 14): *In Mileto . . . convocatis episcopis et presbyteris, qui erant ab Epheso et a reliquis proximis civitatibus*. The speech is directed to the presbyters, to the clergy in general, which is summoned to zeal, humility and altruism. It is the only speech directed to the clergy in Acts and as such corresponds in its own way to the 'bishops' mirror' in I Tim. 3.1ff. and Titus 1.7ff.

The conclusion of the speech finally deserves special attention. It is a case of an (ostensible) saying of Jesus. Concerning Paul's relationship to the preaching of the Lord who walked the earth, Luke has up till now divulged nothing. Now the reader learns that Paul also knows this preaching (more precisely than the reader who has Luke's gospel in his mind) and obeys it. Paul is not only instructed by the exalted Lord, but follows faithfully the whole teaching of Jesus. He thereby proves himself a true Christian with the very last word which he speaks as a free man to his communities. This last word is not his own, but a word of his Lord.

51
ACTS 21:1–14
THE JOURNEY FROM MILETUS TO CAESAREA

[1] It now came about that we departed, after we had taken leave of them, and came by a straight voyage to Cos, on the following day to Rhodes and from there to Patara. [2] And when we had found a ship crossing directly to Phoenicia, we boarded it and set sail. [3] But when we had come in sight of Cyprus and had left it to port, we sailed to Syria and landed in Tyre. For there the ship was unloading its cargo. [4] And when we had sought out the disciples, we remained with them seven days; they told Paul through the Spirit that he should not go to Jerusalem. [5] When we had brought the days to an end, we went out and departed while everyone, with the women and children, escorted us outside the city. And after we had prayed, kneeling down on the beach, [6] we took leave of one another and boarded the ship, and they returned to their homes. [7] Completing the voyage, we came from Tyre to Ptolemais and after we had greeted the brethren we remained with them one day. [8] On the following day we set off and came to Caesarea and going into the house of Philip the evangelist, one of the seven, we stayed with him. [9] He had four virgin daughters who were prophetesses. [10] When we had spent several more days, there came from Judaea a prophet by the name of Agabus, [11] and coming to us and taking hold of Paul's girdle, he bound himself hand and foot and said, 'Thus says the Holy Spirit: "The man to whom this girdle belongs will the Jews thus bind in Jerusalem and deliver into the hands of the Gentiles!"' [12] When we heard this, we and the inhabitants there admonished him not to go up to Jerusalem. [13] Then Paul answered, 'Why do you weep and break my heart? For I am ready not only to let myself be bound but even to die in Jerusalem for the name of the Lord Jesus!' [14] When he would not be persuaded, then we became quiet and said, 'The will of the Lord be done!'

Bibliography:

Paul Corssen, 'Die Töchter des Philippus', *ZNW* 2 (1901), 289–99; Munck 1953, 159f., see § 1; Kragerud 1955, 259f., see § 29; Williams 235–8; Conzelmann 120f.; G. Stählin 272–5.

VERSE 1: ἐγένετο with acc. and inf., see **4**.5; Bl.-Debr. § 408. εὐθυδρο-μήσαντες: 'we travelled directly on and': Bauer, *Wb* 634. Jacquier (621) thinks that 'we' includes only Luke, Trophimus and Aristarchus, because the others are not mentioned any more; they would here have separated from Paul. Since they were the bearers of the collection, this thesis cannot be sustained, quite apart from the fact that Luke does not mention such a separation. ἀποσπασθέντας ἀπ' αὐτῶν links the narrative framework of the preceding speech with the itinerary which now continues.[1] The first day's journey leads to Cos, the second to Rhodes and the third to the Lycian harbour of Patara.

VERSE 2: Here the travellers transfer[2] to a ship sailing[3] direct to Phoenicia.

VERSE 3: ἀναφάναντες κτλ: 'sighting[4] Cyprus and leaving it to port we travelled to Syria and came to Tyre.' That required at least two days: Preuschen 125. 'For there[5] the ship was to unload its cargo.' ἦν ἀποφορτιζό-μενον probably = μέλλον ἀποφορτίζεσθαι.[6] It is thus clear that this ship is not going any further.

VERSE 4: ἀνευρόντες[7] δὲ τοὺς μαθητάς: Luke has not described the found-ing of this community.—Paul now had to wait the arrival of a ship with a suitable destination. Wendt (296), Ramsay (*St. Paul* 300) on the other hand assume, on account of τὸ πλοῖον in v. 6, that the unloading and re-loading of the ship lasted so long. The disciples' warning about Jerusalem will have been inserted in the itinerary by Luke.[8] Beyer (124) translates οἵτινες falsely by 'some', because to him the speech of all the disciples in the Spirit is questionable. Luke—οἵτινες corresponds to his usage—here once portrays what Paul (**20**.23) mentioned as happening everywhere. The simple πνεῦμα stands here as in **20**.22 for the Holy Spirit.

VERSE 5f.: ἐξαρτίσαι = 'complete' (Bauer, *Wb* 541) is in this use unusual. ἐγένετο with acc. and inf. speaks for Lucan redaction.[9] The entire community accompanies the travellers to the beach, and there takes leave—the model for **20**.35–8? Nothing can be deduced from τὸ πλοῖον; how else was Luke to relate it than 'we boarded the ship, but they went home'?

[1] D has further altered the Lucan report, according to which only Paul seems to have gone ashore (v. 38 προέπεμπον κτλ.), in favour of the 'we'.

[2] According to D 𝔓41 gig (21.1) the change took place only at Myra, 50 miles in a direct line further east (Zahn 729); see Intro. § 3, p. 53.

[3] διαπερῶν: the present participle here indicates a future action, Bl.-Debr. § 339, 2 and 323, 3.

[4] It is a case of a nautical term. techn.; see Bauer *Wb* 125; Bl.-Debr. § 309, 1.

[5] ἐκεῖσε here, as often in Hellenism, means the same as ἐκεῖ, 'there': Bauer, *Wb* 474.

[6] Bl-Debr. § 339, 2b: in § 353, 3 supplement on the other hand it is explained as a simple periphrastic imperfect. See against this Björck (47) on **1**.10.

[7] For ἀνευρεῖν = 'find by searching', cf. Luke **2**.16.

[8] So already Overbeck 356, Preuschen 125, Loisy 783.

[9] The periphrasis with ἐγένετο is not intended to reproduce either the longing to continue the journey or the gravity of the departure, but belongs to the elegant language which Luke here considers necessary. 'Complete the days' is a further example.

VERSE 7: διανύειν τὸν πλοῦν = 'to continue the journey' as Xen. Ephes. (second century A.D.). In Ptolemais also there already existed a community whose founding was not recorded; here the travellers remain one day. The land route from Ptolemais to Caesarea amounted to about 30–40 miles (Zahn 730 n. 93a), too far for a day's march, and moreover leading round Mt. Carmel. Perhaps a ship was used?

VERSE 8: Paul and those with him stay with Philip, the old companion of Stephen (6.5), who is here described as an 'evangelist' = 'proclaimer of the Gospel' (in contrast to the Apostle Philip) and as 'one of the seven'. In 8.40 it had been related that he came to Caesarea, whose community he probably founded (see above on 8.40).

VERSE 9: The four[1] prophesying daughters of Philip are mentioned, without their prophesying. This very fact indicates that this feature derived from the itinerary, which showed an especial interest in the various hosts, but knew nothing about warnings to Paul.[2]

VERSE 10: Τὸ ἐπιμενόντων (v. 4) supply ἡμῶν (Bl.-Debr. § 423, 6 supplement). ἡμέρας πλείους: 'several days'[3] (Bauer, *Wb* 1366f.). τις κτλ: Agabus is introduced as if he were unknown to the reader.[4] 'Ιουδαία again stands for Jerusalem; Caesarea also belonged to the administrative district of Judaea.

VERSE 11: Loisy complains (786) that Agabus does not first greet the Christians present, but goes directly for Paul—who was unknown to him? —, grabs his girdle[5] and ties himself up with it.[6] But it is exactly in this manner that Luke wanted the appearance of the prophet urged by the Spirit

---

[1] The *Prophetiae* (see above on 13.1) speaks of five daughters. Zahn accepts that as the Western text and wording of the Lucan 'original edition': 'That out of four maidens speaking prophetically in turns and serving the countless guests Luke erroneously made five, and later in B' (the alleged second edition of Acts with the text attested by B ℵ) '... corrected the oversight, no one will find surprising' (!): 731 n. 96.

[2] Spitta 231, Wendt 297 n. 2 conjecture that these virgins spoke weeping about Paul's fate (cf. v. 13), and that this feature of the source was omitted; an even more lively fantasy is developed by Jüngst 177 (see the general discussion, p. 603). The scholars who are intent only on the sources and what actually happened have no comprehension for the fact that Luke reports the weeping of Paul's friends indirectly, in Paul's words, where it has a much stronger effect.

[3] Zahn 730 (on v. 4): 'The nearer the goal, the less Paul is concerned with saving time.' In reality Luke no longer needs the motif of the feast (20.16).

[4] Wendt (297 n. 2), Jacquier (628), Beyer (126), Bauernfeind (241) conjecture that Luke has here taken over the wording of the 'we' source, in which Agabus was not yet named.

[5] This is not a leather girdle which Paul has just removed (Meyer); to bind himself hand and foot with such a girdle would have been an acrobatic performance. It is a question of a long cloth which was worn as a girdle, wound several times around the body. Money and other things could be kept there: see Mt. 10.9 and cf. Bill. I, 564f. Our passage has nothing to do with John 21.18 (against *ThWb* V, 306, 22ff.): it is not said of Paul that he will be girdled (= bound on the cross); there is no allusion to the manner of his martyrdom (although Luke can have known of his beheading), but rather to his arrest and delivery to the Romans.

[6] Cf. Bl.-Debr. § 284, 2.

to be understood. Agabus' symbolic act recalls the OT prophets, e.g. Isa.
20.2 and Jer. **13.**1ff. The accompanying word of interpretation 'Thus says
the Holy Spirit!' corresponds to the OT 'Thus says Yahweh!' The solemn-
sounding words recall the passion story of Jesus: here as there the Jews
appear as the really guilty ones, who deliver Jesus like Paul to the Gentiles.
Wendt 298 refers to Mk. **10.**33 and **15.**1; see also below on **28.**17.

VERSE 12: The plea of Paul's companions and the local Christians
strengthens the warning and underlines the danger. The pleading would of
course be meaningless if Agabus' prophecy were thought of as absolutely
bound to happen.[1]

VERSE 13: The warnings and entreaties allow Paul's readiness to suffer
to become plain: he is prepared 'for the name of the Lord Jesus' to suffer
not only imprisonment but also death in Jerusalem, which as once for Jesus
now becomes for his disciple also the city of destiny. κλαίοντες: the weeping
was not mentioned before: this trait increases the urgency of the supplication.
συνθρύπτω:[2] 'break into pieces', a rare word. Paul speaks even in this
gripping moment with a carefully chosen vocabulary.[3]

VERSE 14: Paul's companions submit to the inevitable and the reader
knows that now the disaster must come. Yet it is the will of the Lord
which is fulfilled here (cf. Luke **22.**42). ἡσυχάσαμεν: the aorist has a
punctiliar force: 'we became quiet.'[4]

At this section also critical scholars have not remained inactive. Three
things arouse their suspicion. 1. Overbeck (355–seconded by Hilgenfeld
(*ZwTh* 1896, 377), Preuschen 125 and Loisy 782f.) addressed himself to vv.
4f.: here all the disciples of Tyre are portrayed as prophesying in the Spirit,

---

[1] Overbeck 356 n. discusses a difficulty which lies in these warnings of the Spirit:
if the Spirit warned Paul against going to Jerusalem (v. 4b), then Paul acted against the
guidance of the Spirit when he nevertheless continued his journey. Olshausen sought to
help himself out of this difficulty with the information that the Spirit only announced the
imminent arrest; the plea was added by the disciples on their own. Similarly Baumgarten:
the Spirit proclaimed only the approaching danger . . . Against this Overbeck asks: what
sense then did the communication of the danger or imprisonment have, if it was not to warn
Paul? This consideration explodes not only v. 4b but also the entire Agabus scene.—That
Luke did not see the difficulty in which he has here entangled himself is true. For him the
warning of the Spirit which he relates was only the prophetic announcement of coming
events.—Overbeck further emphasizes that Paul had absolutely no motive for the journey
to Jerusalem. In reality that is the case only in Luke, because he keeps quiet about the
collection. This admittedly makes Paul's procedure enigmatic; but most readers do not
hit upon such questions.

[2] According to *Beg.* IV 269 συνθρύπτω originally means the pounding of clothes
with stones by the washerwomen, but then to crush, smash, shatter, so Jos. *Ant.* X 207.

[3] Cf. the classical ἑτοίμως ἔχω = 'to be ready': II Cor. **12.**14; I Peter **4.**5 and the
formula 'for the name of the Lord Jesus', which according to *Beg.* IV 269 is equivalent to
'for the sake of Jesus'. It is however a question whether the problem of the *nomen Chris-*
tianum does not already echo here.

[4] ἡσυχάζω Lk. **14.**4, **23.**56; Acts **11.**18; with Paul in I Thess. **4.**11 it has another
meaning.

without Paul reacting to their warning in vv. 5f. Does this not show that v. 4b is inserted? For Lake's explanation (*Beg.* IV 266), that Paul doubted the inspiration of the disciples, has rightly met with no approval. The fact that οἵτινες stands well apart from μαθητάς, that further, despite the prediction, nothing points to a departure overshadowed by dire forebodings, and that the warning is so meagre and insignificant, seals the fate of the unfortunate verse: it is secondary. 2. The daughters of Philip 'are indeed expressly introduced as προφητεύουσαι, but afterwards make no use at all of their talents, however much the occasion calls for it' (Wellhausen 43). That was at least the general impression (only Zahn 731f. and Bauernfeind 241 were so fortunate as to be able to deduce a prophecy by the four virgins); but does it not then appear that 'something has been omitted from the report in the source, namely the fact that it was these daughters of Philip who tearfully spoke of Paul's fate' (Wendt 298 n.)? Similarly, but without tears, Loisy (785). Jüngst (177) went still further: originally it was related that one of these daughters took Paul's girdle, bound herself with it and spoke the prophecy of v. 11; the scrupulous author found that unbecoming, and therefore has Agabus come from Judaea . . . 3. This however now brings Agabus himself also under suspicion—he had already aroused Wellhausen's displeasure (43): 'He copies the dramatic mime of the ancient seer, which belongs in the public market-place, and presents it before Paul as if he were a popular assembly.' A further observation condemns him even more strongly: that he binds himself hand and foot with the girdle is in Loisy's opinion (786) tolerable only as a thought, but in reality impracticable. And finally the Jews did not deliver Paul to the Gentiles fettered, as Agabus maintains (Overbeck 330, Loisy 786). In his favour there is of course the fact that despite **11**.28 he is introduced as someone quite unknown to the reader—does it not follow that Luke here has copied word for word the 'we' account, in which Agabus has not yet appeared? So Holtzmann 130, Wendt 298 and Beyer 126.

The observations of these scholars are important—as observations always are. But they are evaluated almost solely in historical terms: thus the Christians in Tyre did not give any warning, but probably the four prophetic daughters, and Agabus possibly did not come at all . . . This is to overlook the connections of the composition, which Luke carries through with great skill.

Up to the speech in Miletus the skies were bright, and even if on occasion thunder-clouds loomed menacingly, as in Ephesus, the storm was still graciously averted. With Paul's farewell speech the *peripeteia* begins. Here we hear to our surprise that the Holy Spirit in every city prophesies to Paul 'chains and sufferings' (**20**.23) and that he will return no more (**20**.25, 38). The travel narrative which begins with Chapter 21 allows Luke to bring the general and colourless hints of **20**.23 concretely before the eyes of the reader in a series of climaxing scenes. In v. 4b the community from which such a warning greets Paul is indeed named. But Luke has taken care not to name any particular prophet here, or allow Paul to answer the warning, or depict the sorrow of the community. All this would have deprived the great Agabus scene of its force and material, and with this scene now, as the final climax, the development culminates. That is why v. 4b of necessity remains so 'meagre and insignificant' (Overbeck): at this point Luke—if the author is not to destroy his own conception—cannot report any more. The allusion to the prophesying daughters of Philip prepares the reader for the real manifestation of the Holy Spirit, which richly compensates the reader by the force of its words and the clarity of its treatment. Now the imprisonment of Paul is not only proclaimed, but portrayed in action; and this occasions the impassioned plea of his companions and the local community that Paul should not go to Jerusalem! But now, when the danger has mounted to colossal proportions and concern for Paul has broken out in heart-rending supplications, now Paul testifies to his quite unshakeable willingness to suffer. As once Jesus himself, so now Paul also is not unexpectedly surprised by suffering, but rather has entered the gathering shadows with complete knowledge and firm resolve. This deliberate sustained intensification is the work of the author Luke, not a constituent of the tradition which came his way. For what the community retains in its memory is this or that impressive scene, not a gradually emergent development.

Our text is thus proven to be a composition; but its relationship to the tradition has also become transparent. The idea that the Spirit in every city prophesied Paul's imprisonment does not derive from the itinerary. Rom. **15.** 30ff. shows that Paul did not go to Jerusalem blind and with unburdened heart. Otherwise he would not have asked—one must almost say: implored—the Roman community to intercede with God, that the Jerusalem community might actually receive the collection from him (such an idea we naturally cannot expect in Acts), and he be delivered from the unbelieving Jews. On the other hand, Paul did not go to Jerusalem in the conviction that he would not leave it again as a free man, but he hoped after a happy settlement of the matter of the collection to be able to hurry on with the blessings of the Jerusalem community to Rome and Spain. The contested v. 4b is therefore actually a Lucan addition, but not because Paul does not answer this prophecy etc.; from the point of view of composition this is rather the given fact.

On the other hand, the information concerning Philip's four prophetic daughters is taken from the itinerary. Luke has not suppressed any prophecies by these girls or transferred them to Agabus. He has left standing these statements of the itinerary, which is always interested in Paul's hosts, because the προφητεύουσαι provides him with an introductory cue for the Agabus narrative.

This does not—as Loisy's sagacity correctly noted—derive from the itinerary, but—this possibility Loisy did not take into consideration—is grounded in another, oral tradition. Luke has assimilated this tradition into the itinerary by transposing it into the 'we' style—that the little word 'we' does not guarantee kinship with the itinerary, Dibelius has of course taught us. But by introducing the 'we' into this tradition, Luke has doubled its vivacity. Loisy (787) had considered Agabus a creation of the redactor. For this suspicion there is no occasion. Rather will stories have been told in the Christian communities about the great prophet Agabus, who foresaw the severe famine—he also predicted Paul's arrest to him! On the other hand, we need not close our eyes to the fact that the development of this scene in detail betrays the hand of Luke. Even one who does not want to ascribe the story of the girdle to Luke's inventiveness, guided by OT models, can yet agree with Overbeck: here the reader learns how he is to understand the forthcoming trial of Paul. Everything once again has happened as in the passion story of Jesus. The Jews have taken prisoner not only the Lord, but also his greatest missionary, and they have delivered both into the hands of the Gentiles. In Paul's case this is admittedly—in this respect the critics are correct —true only *cum grano salis*: the Jews wanted to kill Paul personally and the Romans saved his life. This Luke himself will admit at a later point. But if we do not adhere pedantically to the details of this prophecy of Agabus, but rather look at the essentials, we recognize also the relative correctness of this type of approach: the Jews by their assault on Paul caused the Romans to arrest him; by their continual accusations they prevented his release from custody, and are at least partly responsible for the fact that he finally had to appeal to Caesar, and travelled to Rome as one destined for death.

52
ACTS 21:15-26
THE RECEPTION IN JERUSALEM

[15] After these days we made ourselves ready and went up to Jerusalem. [16] And some of the disciples from Caesarea came with us; they brought us to a Cyprian Mnason, an early disciple, with whom we were to shelter. [17] When we came to Jerusalem, the brethren received us gladly. [18] On the following day Paul went with us to James; and all the elders were present. [19] And when he had greeted them he related in detail what God had done among the Gentiles through his service. [20] And when they heard it they praised God, and said to him, 'You see, brother, how many thousands there are among the Jews who have become believers, and all of them are zealous for the law. [21] They have been informed about you, that you teach all the Jews who live among the Gentiles to forsake Moses, telling them they should neither circumcise their children nor live according to the customs. [22] What is to happen now? They will in any case hear that you have come. [23] Do now what we say. We have four men who have taken an oath upon themselves. [24] Take these men and purify yourself with them and bear their expenses that they may have their heads shaved, and everyone will know that there is nothing to what has been said about you, but rather that you also live observing the law. [25] But as for the Gentiles who have believed, we have made a decision and sent it to them, that they keep themselves from meats offered to idols and from blood and from what has been strangled and from unchastity.' [26] Then Paul took the men and on the next day purified himself with them and went to the temple to report the fulfilment of the days of purification until the sacrifice had been presented for each one of them.

Bibliography:

T. Mommsen, 'Die Rechtsverhältnisse des Apostels Paulus', *ZNW* 2 (1901), 81–96; H. J. Cadbury, 'Roman Law and the Trial of Paul', *Beg.* V (1933), 297–306; A. N. Sherwin-White, 'The Early Persecutions and Roman Law Again', *JTS* 3 (1952), 199–213; Karl Becker, 'Tertullians Apologeticum', *Werden u. Leistung*, München 1954, Excursus 3: 'D. Apologeticum u. d. jurist. Grundlage d. Christenverfolgungen', 356–64; Von Campenhausen, 'D. Nachfolge des Jakobus', *ZKG* 63 (1950/51), 133ff.', Conzelmann 121–3.

E. Springer, 'D. Prozess des Apostels Paulus', *Preuss. Jahrbücher* 218, 1929; J. Lengle, 'Röm. Strafrecht bei Cicero und den Historikern', *Neue*

Wege zur Antike, 1 Reihe 11 (1934), 52f.; G. Jasper, 'Der Rat des Jakobus
. . . Apg. Kap. 21–28', *Saat und Hoffnung* 71 (1934), 89–105.

VERSE 15: 'After these days': see v. 10. ἐπισκευασάμενοι: 'we made
ourselves ready'; 'we prepared ourselves': Bauer, *Wb* 590.[1] The distance
from Caesarea via Lydda to Jerusalem was about 60 miles and could not be
covered in a day: Zahn 733.[2]

VERSE 16: συνῆλθον . . . σὺν ἡμῖν: 'there came with us'. τῶν μαθητῶν:
'some of the disciples'.[3] ἄγοντες: 'leading us' (not: leading Mnason). D
improves this accordingly. παρ' ᾧ[4] ξενισθῶμεν κτλ.: 'to Mnason . . . that we
might be with him as guests'. Mnason[5] (Attic Μνήσων, a common Greek
name: *Beg.* IV 270) originated (like Barnabas 4.36, cf. 11.20 and 15.39) from
Cyprus. Whether as an 'early disciple' (= Christian from the time of the
beginning of the community) he was an adherent of Stephen—who had later
returned to Jerusalem?—is not reported. Since however he received Paul and
his uncircumcised companions, that is probable. Mnason was important and
worth mention not as host for the night at an unnamed stopping-place, but as
host to Paul and his companions during their stay in Jerusalem: Loisy 791.[6]

VERSE 17: γενομένων ἡμῶν: gen. abs. despite the following ἡμᾶς: W. L.
Knox 5: 'very bad' (Bl.-Debr. § 423, 2). οἱ ἀδελφοί: Mnason and the Hellenistic Christians gathered with him (Wendt 300).[7]

---

[1] The word, little used in this sense, is replaced in C by παρασκευασάμενοι (to prepare
oneself), in D by ἀποταξάμενοι (to take leave), and in the later MSS by ἀποσκευασάμενοι
(to disarm, to strike the tents: Bauer, *Wb* 194).

[2] Ramsay (*St. Paul* 302) therefore assumed that the journey was not made on foot,
but on horseback: Luke as a physician may have urged that Paul should not begin his work
in Jerusalem weary and exhausted from a forced march! Hence Ramsay interprets ἐπισκευασάμενοι as the preparation and saddling of the horses.

[3] See Bl-Debr. § 164, 2 supplement.

[4] On the connection by the relative see Bl-Debr. § 294, 5 supplement, on the final
relative clause § 378.

[5] D latinizes to Νάσωνι.

[6] The participle ἄγοντες has a future sense (cf. 18.23): Bl.-Debr. § 339, 2. It does not
mean that they immediately arrived at Mnason's house, but that this is the destination of
the journey, which is reached in v. 17. Since this circumstance was not understood, and at
the same time people thought of the distance from Caesarea to Jerusalem, which could not
be traversed in a day, D (with sy^hmg) conjectured that Mnason lived in a village between
Caesarea and Jerusalem and altered the text accordingly. This produced the further advantage that v. 17 could now be taken to indicate the friendly reception by the Jerusalem congregation. That D in reality had no exact information of his own is shown by the fact that
he cannot give the name of the village. Zahn (734) makes Mnason a relatively well-to-do
landowner in the country, since 'no place name is given as his residence'! Cadbury, who
ascribes the interest in 'lodging' not to a 'we' source but to Luke, has discussed the question in *JBL* 45 (1926), 305ff.

[7] Now and then 'the disciples' are associated with the Jerusalem community:
Overbeck 380 ('the general acceptance which Paul found in Jerusalem'). But according to
v. 22 this community still knew nothing about Paul's arrival. Hence Lake avails himself
of the expedient: 'This was the unofficial reception' (*Beg.* IV 270). Jacquier 631; 'Il s'agit
ici d'une réunion privée, composée de frères et amis de Paul.' Beyer 129: but apparently
'not the entire community'. Knopf 632: 'first of all the Hellenists'.

VERSE 18: Here Overbeck (380) and others have the reproduction of the itinerary come to an end, even though it may still be utilized here and there in what follows. *Beg.* IV 270 recalls **16**.17; in both passages, as soon as the 'we' is discontinued, the distinction between 'Paul' and 'we' appears. πρὸς Ἰάκωβον: he is the real receptionist; admittedly 'all the elders' are present. On their significance the commentaries disagree: according to *Beg.* IV 270 they are 'only assessors'; similarly Zahn 735: James occupied an episcopal position. Loisy 793 on the contrary: 'James becomes a decorative figure in the present assembly and plays a silent role.'[1] The silence about Peter, in view of his mention in Chapter 15, compels the conclusion that he was no longer in Jerusalem. Luke did not name John (Gal. **2**.9) in Chapter 15.—The 'we' now ceases until **27**.1. This is no indication how far the itinerary ran. There could be purely literary reasons for the absence of the 'we': Paul stands dominant in the centre of the scene; Luke makes no further mention of the Christian community in Jerusalem after Paul's arrest.

VERSE 19 strongly recalls **15**.12, a verse which in a corresponding situation reports a similar incident: here we detect Luke, who again does not mention the collection.[2] Paul renders a detailed report. καθ' ἕνα ἕκαστον: 'one after the other = in detail': Bauer, *Wb* 469; Bl.-Debr. § 305.

VERSE 20: The praise of God[3] by the Jerusalem listeners passes immediately into the description of the delicate situation to elucidate which Luke is now solely concerned: it is indeed for his reader entirely new. There are 'many thousands' of Jews 'who have become believers', and that (as is evident from v. 22) in Jerusalem.[4] The exaggerations in ancient calculation

---

[1] That Luke says nothing about the 'older Apostles' Zahn (734) explains from his alleged intention to deal with them in a third volume (as if that justified their non-mention here!). Holtzmann (131) on the other hand thinks, 'The twelve Apostles, particularly Peter, seem to be no longer on the spot'; similarly Loisy 793. Wendt has them in part included among the elders (likewise Knopf 632), and in part travelling about doing missionary work in Palestine (300). H. v. Campenhausen, 'Die Nachfolge des Jakobus', *ZKG* 63 (1950/51), 133ff.

[2] Wendt 300 n. 2 conjectures that to it the word διακονία in the source referred; according to Spitta (262) and J. Weiss (35) Luke left out the source's statements about the collection. According to Bauernfeind (244) the delivery of the collection may have appeared to our narrator as a self-evident piece of ecclesiastical bureaucracy (!), and therefore not worth mentioning. But Luke has reported the delivery of a collection in Chapter 11, yet on the other hand said nothing about this second and larger collection. This shows that the idea of an aversion to ecclesiastical bureaucracy gets us nowhere.

[3] According to Zahn (735) James pronounces it; but Luke does not mention him any more. According to *Beg.* IV 270 the expression voices not only thankfulness but relief: it is not so terrible with Paul as was reported! This is read into the text.

[4] On the exaggeration of the numbers see above p. 215 n. 2. D gig p sa make things easier by substituting ἐν τῇ Ἰουδαίᾳ for ἐν τοῖς Ἰουδαίοις. Ed. Schwartz (*NGG* 1907, 290) and following him Preuschen 126f. (F. C. Baur had already advanced this idea in 1829) interpret the many myriads as referring to Jewish pilgrims to the feast (although there is no longer any mention of the feast), delete τῶν πεπιστευκότων and accept the late reading Ἰουδαίων, while Wellhausen (43) justly found all this doubtful.—Bo Reicke ('Der geschichtliche Hintergrund des Apostelkonzils und der Antiochia-Episode, Gal. **2**.1–14', *Studia*

are well known; all that is necessary for the meaning is: 'You see how strong the Jewish-Christian community is.' It consists purely of ζηλωταὶ τοῦ νόμου, who strictly hold to the law as the expression of the divine will.

VERSE 21: It is therefore understandable that the unfavourable reports about Paul made a very bad impression upon them: κατηχήθησαν[1] = 'it has been reported to them, communicated' (Bauer, *Wb* 838). By whom is not stated; only diaspora Jews come into question. Paul is accused of leading them to apostasy: they ought not to circumcise their children or live according to the 'customs' (= the legal prescriptions).[2] That the Jewish-Christian members of the Antiochian community felt themselves exempted from the regulations of the law concerning food is evident from Gal. 2.12f. That Paul advised against the circumcision of Jewish children is unlikely; if he had *not* circumcised Timothy, such conduct could have become the occasion for a rumour of this sort.

VERSE 22: τί οὖν ἐστιν: what is to be done to correct the false opinion about Paul? πάντως ἀκούσονται κτλ.: 'in any case they will learn', etc. The problem is not to be solved by simply keeping quiet: Paul's presence cannot be kept a secret very long.[3]

Paulina 172–87) has attempted to make the changing attitude of the Jerusalem community to the Pauline mission comprehensible on the basis of its position over against Jewish nationalism. In the fifties under Felix the Zealot terror increased: the ζηλωταὶ τοῦ νόμου are not to be thought of without reference to the Zealots.—Luke would have been careful not to show the Christians in alliance with Jewish Zealots. On the other hand it may be correct that the leaders of the community could not take any decision without consideration of the effects of their actions in Judaism.

[1] D: κατηκησαν for κατηχηθησαν (= people have reported); and τοὺς κατὰ ἔθνη εἰσὶν (!) Ἰουδαίους: this is clearly influenced by the Latin text *qui in gentibus sunt Judaeus* (d). The continuation in d *ne circumcidat filios neque gentes eius ambulant* betrays a confusion of ἔθνη and ἔθη. The τὰ after κατὰ has dropped out through haplography but also the words corresponding to *qui in gentibus* are missing.

[2] According to *Beg.* IV 271 this passage proves that at the time of the composition of Acts Jewish Christianity still flourished and that the Pauline Christians were concerned to make a compromise with it, in which each recognized the correctness of the other.—On the justification for the reproaches against Paul the exegetes are not in agreement: Beyer (127) maintains that Paul 'granted complete freedom from the law' to the Jewish-Christians in his mission territory, while Wendt (301) explains, 'The reproach was without doubt incorrect'; the Pauline doctrine of freedom from the law was misrepresented. According to Schlatter (259f). people complained 'about what the Christian Jews do in the communities of Paul'. 'Doubtless among the other Jews also that frequently occurred which Paul himself exercised as his right, that he lived with those who are without law as if he had no law.' But 'as the rule given to the Jews before Christ and the faith came, the law retained for him the full value of divine institution'.

[3] D d read πάντως δεῖ πλῆθος συνελθεῖν. This text is interpreted in different ways: 'excited mass scenes' Bauernfeind 243; 'a crowd'—of the curious—De Wette 382; 'there must be a meeting of the whole church' *Beg.* IV 272 (though the translation 'a mob will congregate' is considered possible). D wanted to establish a close relationship between the fact that the many Jewish Christians thought unfavourably of Paul and would hear about his coming, and the present situation. Despite the missing article he will have understood πλῆθος as the 'entire community', whose assembly cannot be evaded.

VERSE 23: What sort of unpleasantness can grow out of this is not stated; instead a positive proposal is submitted to Paul, the meaning of which first becomes clear at the end of v. 24. Its presupposition is: in the Jerusalem community there are four destitute Nazirites.[1]

VERSE 24 is difficult. ἁγνίσθητι σὺν αὐτοῖς does not fit either in the meaning 'to take on the Nazirate'[2] or in the other 'purify oneself from levitical impurity'.[3] The only thing clear is that Paul through the proposed action will prove himself a law-abiding Jew.

VERSE 25 seems to have no connection with what precedes and to relate the Apostolic Decree as something new. But neither of these is true. After James and the elders have spoken of the way in which Paul is to prove his conformity to the law, they pass to the question of Paul's converted Gentile-Christians: here there is no hesitation, since observance of these four commands has been imposed upon them. Formally these words are directed to Paul, but in reality (as 1.18f.) they are designed for the instruction of the reader.

VERSE 26: Here the difficulty of the ἁγνίζομαι returns. ἐκπλήρωσιν κτλ.:

---

[1] Cf. Num. 6.1–21. For εὐχή in the meaning 'Nazirite vow' see Greeven, *ThWb* II 775: εὐχὴν ἔχοντες ἐφ᾽ ἑαυτῶν 'leans on the usage of LXX'. The reading attested by B ℵ ἀφ᾽ ἑαυτῶν (= of their own accord) is probably a Greek interpretation for the strange-sounding LXX formula.

[2] 'Purify yourself with them'—'submit with them to the vows of the Nazirate (for the rest of the period of the Nazirate)' miscarries according to Bill. II 757 because 1. the simple ἁγνίζεσθαι 'nowhere describes the taking of the Nazirite vow'; 2. the four have already taken the vow and hence require no further vow; 3. the minimum duration of a Nazarate involved thirty days: Nazir 1.3; Siphre Num. 6, 2 § 22 (7a). Josephus speaks of it in *Bell.* II, 313. Only 3. is really important.

[3] Billerbeck interprets ἁγνίζεσθαι of the removal of a levitical impurity (LXX Num. 19.12 οὗτος ἁγνισθήσεται τῇ ἡμέρᾳ τῇ τρίτῃ καὶ τῇ ἡμέρᾳ τῇ ἑβδόμῃ καὶ καθαρὸς ἔσται; 31.19, 24; Jos. 3.5; II Chron. 29. 5, 34; 30.17) which Paul and the four Nazirites have contracted (although for different reasons). But this interpretation can hardly be substantiated. It contradicts 1. the Lucan account and 2. the event which we must assume behind it. 1. Billerbeck understands by the ἐκπλήρωσις τῶν ἡμερῶν τοῦ ἁγνισμοῦ the lapse of the days of the levitical purification. But Luke read in Num. 6.4 LXX of πάσας τὰς ἡμέρας τῆς εὐχῆς τοῦ ἁγνισμοῦ and ἕως ἂν πληρωθῶσιν αἱ ἡμέραι and could not well refer that to anything but the days of the Nazarate. Is it then probable that he referred ἁγνίζεσθαι to anything other than the Nazarate itself, even if the LXX reproduced this concept of the Nazarate by ἁγνίζεσθαι plus other definitions (ἁγνείαν, ἀπὸ οἴνου)? 2. It is readily comprehensible that Paul as a Jew coming from abroad was considered levitically unclean and therefore required the seven-day purification (it consisted of a sprinkling with the water of atonement on the third and seventh days). On the other hand it is scarcely conceivable that the four Nazirites should all together have become levitically unclean, and precisely at the moment when Paul entered Jerusalem (Luke says nothing about this). For if it had happened before, then—since this purification occasioned no expense, in contrast to the cleansing of a serious impurity which required sacrifices—they would of course immediately have had themselves purified. That the purification for the four had already begun (so Billerbeck understands v. 26: it is to be the third day of the atonement, when they are sprinkled for the first time with the water of atonement) contradicts the fact that Paul participates in it, for indeed he first had to present himself for the atonement. On a possible solution of the difficulty see the general discussion.

the days of the Nazirate are reported as fulfilled so that the sacrifices of atonement may be presented. The Nazirate is completed when the sacrifice is presented for each man: this seems to be the meaning of the passage.

1. First of all it is important to answer the question: what did Luke want to say in this narrative? Should his statements contradict what we know about the Nazirate of that time, we may not give them a new interpretation, although this does not mean that we should affirm with Zahn (741) that Luke is 'a better witness than the entire Rabbinic tradition'.

According to Luke, Paul and 'we' negotiated with James and the elders. As in 15.12, so here Paul first describes his missionary successes, which are indeed really God's successes. Despite the fact that the Jerusalemites praise God for these, they are distressed about what the numerous and zealous Jewish-Christians of Jerusalem have heard about Paul (apparently without rejecting it as slander): that he taught the diaspora Jews not to circumcise their children and no longer to live according to the old customs. That the elders do not believe this is clear: but it does not concern them alone. To convince the Jewish-Christians of his fidelity to the law, Paul is to redeem four poor Nazirites. (Luke seems to assume that for this Paul himself had to become a Nazirite until the time of their absolution.) Thereby the accusations against him will be proven groundless; there are no difficulties because of the Gentile Christians converted by Paul, since they have been directed to follow the Apostolic Decree, which here is communicated by way of reminder, apparently to Paul but in reality to the reader. Paul follows the advice, takes the four men, purifies himself with them and reports to the Temple the 'fulfilment of the days of purification', until the necessary sacrifice is presented for each of them. When the seven days were on the point of coming to an end . . .

This text contains two great difficulties. Verses 24 'purify yourself with them' and 26 'purifying himself with them' describe an action which Paul undertakes in association with the Nazirites and which is connected with his taking over of their expenses. Neither of the two meanings of ἁγνίζεσθαι fits here: Paul cannot have become a Nazirite with the others because the minimum time necessary was thirty days and not seven; but it is also not simply a question of deliverance from levitical impurity, since the 'days of consecration' (v. 26) indicate the absolution from the Nazirate and ἁγνισμός and ἁγνίζομαι must have the same meaning.

If however we take the Lucan text by itself, without consideration of the actual Jewish regulations, then it can be explained without any contradiction: Paul by an act of consecration or purification, undertaken in association with four Nazirites, enters into their Nazirate for the duration of seven days, hence for the minimum period within which the rites of absolution could be completed. This must be taken as Luke's understanding of the matter, and Luke will have taken it from the itinerary (and LXX). For that

Luke caught out of thin air the requirement that Paul should assume the expenses of the four Nazirites contradicts everything we have learned about his work so far. Also, the manner in which the seven days are mentioned as something familiar indicates (as long recognized) the utilization of a source. Finally it is not easy to see why the itinerary should cease with the entrance into Jerusalem, and should not also have described the crucial period up to the arrest.

This source lies before us in Luke's reproduction. We can however seek to reconstruct it by admitting only statements which do not contradict the Jewish regulations. Then the following picture results: at that time there were four poor Nazirites in the Jerusalem Christian community. The period of their Nazirate had already elapsed. The expense, which they could not afford, was to be assumed by Paul (the assumption of such expense counted as a pious deed); he had only to report this to the priest concerned and agree upon the time of absolution. Since Paul had come from abroad, he was however considered as levitically unclean. He had therefore first to regain levitical purity by a purification ritual. This consisted of being sprinkled with the water of atonement on the third and seventh day after reporting to the priest. Only when he was levitically clean could Paul be present at the absolution ceremony of the four, which took place in the 'holy place'. Paul accordingly, when he had accepted the proposal of the elders, went with the four Nazirites to the Temple and there reported first his own purification (ἁγνίζεσθαι) and secondly the ἐκπλήρωσις τῶν ἡμερῶν τοῦ ἁγνισμοῦ (of the Nazirate of the four). The date could then be fixed on which the appropriate sacrifices— for which Paul paid—were to be presented: it was the seventh day, on which he himself was to be cleared from guilt.

In this way all the difficulties hitherto presented are resolved: we need assume neither a— seven-day!—Nazirite vow for Paul, nor the improbability that the four men still lacked seven days of their Nazirate, or finally that all four had just at this point incurred levitical impurity.

It was not possible for Luke to envisage quite correctly these connections, which were reflected only in passing in the itinerary. In particular the distinction between ἁγνίζεσθαι = 'to have oneself purified' and ἁγνισμός = 'Nazirate' was not explained there. Hence Luke apparently identified the two; thus he came to the idea that Paul for the duration of seven days entered the Nazirate along with the four.

The Lucan presentation can thus be obtained without difficulty from what—using Jewish statements not available to Luke—we have put forward for the itinerary. The first great difficulty of our section (so far as it is at present possible) is thereby resolved.

2. The second difficulty is not so clear, but even more important. From the Apostolic Council on, Luke has not mentioned Paul's great collection. He is silent also about its delivery, which must have been mentioned in the

itinerary. Even in **24**.17 the word 'collection' does not occur; no reader who knew only Acts but not the Pauline epistles could deduce from this verse the great Pauline work of the collection. This silence of Luke's is extremely surprising. We ought to consider that Luke should have especially welcomed this intervention of Paul and his congregations on behalf of the mother community. He must have had a very important reason for keeping silent about it.

To discover this reason, let us begin with Romans **15**.31. Here Paul speaks of the two dangers which threaten him when he comes to Jerusalem with the collection. First, he has to fear the ἀπειθοῦντες ἐν τῇ ʼΙουδαίᾳ, the fanatical Jews themselves. Secondly, there is also the possibility that his collection may not be εὐπρόσδεκτος to the 'saints', i.e. that they may flatly refuse to accept it. Since Paul accepted responsibility for this collection, his quarrel with the Judaizers had flared up. If now, for example, what Paul had written to the Galatians in this quarrel had become known to the Palestinian church leaders—and why should they not have heard about it?—then it was difficult to predict whether people in Jerusalem would have anything to do with him at all. The Jerusalemites were not to be bought. But if James and the elders refused the Pauline collection, then the connection between the Pauline Gentile Church and the Church of Jerusalem would be severed. Paul would be disavowed before the representatives of his own congregations, and thereby morally most grievously stricken. The mission he planned in the western Mediterranean regions was then conceivable—if at all—only against the opposition of the mother community in Jerusalem and probably the fear he had already expressed in Gal. **2**.2 would then be realized: 'He would run in vain.'

We must however view the situation also from the standpoint of the leaders of the Jerusalem Church. If anyone taught that the law occasioned only wrath and was given only to multiply sins, they could strictly no longer recognize such a man as 'brother'. But even if they were prepared to regard such expressions as exaggerations, such as occur in the heat of debate, there was still the relationship to Jewry to consider. Paul's visit fell a few years before the murder of James the Lord's brother by the Jews. The Jerusalem community at that time was already striving for the last possibility of a mission in Israel. If they accepted the Pauline collection, then in the eyes of the Jews they would proclaim their solidarity with Paul. By so doing they threatened to destroy their own possibilities of mission. This is overlooked by every exegete who makes James and the elders accept the Pauline collection joyfully.

The leaders of the Jerusalem community wanted to avoid both the break with the Pauline mission Church and that with Palestinian Judaism. This could only be attained if Paul consented to an act which would take the wind out of the sails of the accusations against him. On the other hand Paul could not be expected to sacrifice the basic principles of his own mission. The Lucan account allows us to recognize in which direction the solution was sought. It was suggested to Paul that he assume the relatively considerable cost of redeeming the four poor Nazirites. If he agreed to this—and he had already earlier declared himself ready to support the poor saints—then the collection could be accepted, because such a redemption of Nazirites was considered as particularly pious by every Jew. Paul agreed to this proposal.

This also explains why Paul remained longer in Jerusalem. If his collection had been accepted without further ado, he could have left the dangerous area immediately. The unity of the Church was preserved, he himself recognized before the representatives of his congregations, his further mission threatened by no veto from Jerusalem. But the purification to which Paul had to submit in order to participate in the absolution of the four Nazirites held him fast in Jerusalem for a week, and compelled him on the third and seventh days to seek out the 'holy place'. On the second visit—immediately before the happy outcome—catastrophe struck.

Perhaps Luke knew about the collection. But that people hesitated to accept it must then have been for him a dark enigma which he did not know how to solve. His entire portrait of the relationship of Paul to the primitive community would have been destroyed had he taken up the negotiations about the collection in his work. So he decided not to mention the collection at all. For the apparently easy way out, to report only its reception, was likewise precluded: how was he to make it comprehensible to the reader that the primitive community further required Paul to pay for the four Nazirites, when Paul had just handed over a considerable gift of love from his congregations?

53
ACTS 21:27–36
PAUL'S ARREST

27 When the seven days were almost completed, the Jews from Asia, seeing him in the Temple, brought the whole people into an uproar and laid hands upon him 28 shouting, 'Israelites, help! This is the man who teaches everyone everywhere against the people and the law and this place. Moreover he has brought Greeks into the Temple and defiled this holy place!' 29 For they had seen the Ephesian Trophimus together with him in the city earlier; him, they supposed, Paul had led into the Temple. 30 And the whole city was aroused and the people ran together and they seized Paul and dragged him out of the Temple, and immediately the gates were closed. 31 And as they were attempting to kill him, word came to the tribune of the cohort: 'All Jerusalem is in riot!' 32 He at once took soldiers and centurions and ran down to them. But when they saw the tribune and the soldiers they stopped striking Paul. 33 Then the tribune came up, arrested him and ordered him to be bound with two chains, and asked who he was and what he had done. 34 The one shouted this, the other that in the crowd. Since he could learn nothing reliable on account of the tumult, he ordered him to be taken to the barracks. 35 But when he came to the steps, he had to be carried by the soldiers because of the violence of the mob. 36 For the mass of the people followed, shouting, 'Away with him!'

Bibliography:

Conzelmann, *Apg.* 123–5; G. Stählin 279–81.

VERSE 27: ὡς δὲ ἔμελλον κτλ.: 'when the seven days were almost completed', see above pp. 611 f. 'Ασία: again = Ephesus, since these Jews[1] know the Ephesian Trophimus (v. 29). It is not Jewish Christians who attack Paul— they are, like James and the elders, not mentioned again in Acts: *Beg.* IV 274—but rather the diaspora Jews. ἱερόν: the inner courtyard and the ten ell wide raised terrace in front, the so-called *chel*: Bill. II 761. But Luke himself did not know these details. συγχέω: Bauer, *Wb* 1535: 'to bring into confusion'; more clearly *Beg.* IV 275; 'to cause a riot'. ἐπέβαλαν[2] κτλ.: see on **12.1**.

[1] The presence of these Jews favours the view that Pentecost fell at this time.
[2] See Bl.-Debr. § 80f.

VERSE 28: ἄνδρες 'Ισραηλῖται: see on **2**.22 and *ThWb* III 389 n. 132. Paul allegedly teaches against λαός[1] (= Jews), νόμος and τόπος (Temple); cf. on **6**.13. πάντας πανταχῇ: 'everyone everywhere', a favourite paronomasia, cf. Bl.-Debr. § 488, 1; Acts **17**.30; **24**.3. Ἕλληνας κτλ.: entrance into the holy precinct (fenced off by a low barrier, called *Soreg*) was prohibited on pain of death for any non-Jew.[2] κεκοίνωκεν: the perfect shows the lasting effect which has begun; the holy place has become unclean: Bl-Debr. § 342, 4.[3]

VERSE 29: Luke explains how this error came about. According to J. Weiss 39f. 'something about Paul's association with Trophimus has dropped out', 'and indeed a report from which the accusation of v. 28 is better understood'.[4] But Luke's explanation is amply sufficient: these Jews credited Paul with any infringement of the law.

VERSE 30: That immediately the entire city was thrown into uproar is impossible;[5] but Luke thus explains the fact that the garrison is alarmed. Paul is dragged[6] out of the ἱερόν: 'Tumult and the spilling of blood must remain outside'—Wellhausen 46. The text speaks for the interpretation of θύραι given by Jeremias, *Jerusalem zur Zeit Jesu* II B 73 (ET *Jerusalem in the Time of Jesus*, 1969): the levitical Temple guards shut the gates which separated the ἱερόν from the court of the Gentiles; so also Jacquier 640 and Loisy 807.[7]

VERSE 31: At the moment Paul finds himself outside the ἱερόν, the Jews begin to beat him[8] and want to lynch him: ζητούντων ... ἀποκτεῖναι αὐτόν.[9] ἀνέβη φάσις: 'a report came'—Preuschen 128. χιλίαρχος (= *tribunus militum*) σπείρης, the commandant of the Roman garrison of Jerusalem:[10] ὅλη συγχύννεται (Bl.-Debr. § 73 supplement) κτλ.: 'all Jerusalem is in riot!'

---

[1] Cf. *ThWb* IV, 52, 18ff.; *Beg*. IV 274.
[2] Cf. Bill. II 761f.; Dittenberger *OGIS* 598. Josephus mentions this in *Bell*. V 193f., VI 124–6; *Ant*. XV 417.
[3] Zahn (745) conjectures that Paul may have taken Trophimus with him into the outer court which was accessible to non-Jews. That is very unlikely.
[4] Overbeck's allegorical interpretation of the accusation (387f.)—that Paul has opened the Messianic community to the Gentiles—is rightly rejected: Luke does not work with such allegories.
[5] Against *Beg*. IV 275; J. Weiss (40) considers it a strong redactional exaggeration.
[6] For the imperf. εἷλκον cf. Bl.-Debr. § 327.
[7] The gates in the walls round the outer limits of the Temple do not come into question.
[8] The self-evident subject is omitted: the Jews; cf. Bl.-Debr. § 423, 6 supplement.
[9] According to Zahn (745) also Temple police with clubs. But then Paul would not have come away without severe injury.
[10] It consisted of one cohort of auxiliary troops (nominally 760 infantrymen) with one squadron attached (240 men) and was stationed in the παρεμβολή, the citadel Antonia on the northwest corner of the Temple area, used as a barracks. The Antonia was connected with the Temple area by two staircases, the ἀναβαθμοί v. 35. On the two seventy-ell high towers at the south and east of the Antonia stood posts which overlooked the entire Temple area: Josephus *Bell*. V 242.

VERSE 32: ὅς: the relative pronoun as often in Luke actually introduces an independent clause. The classical λαβών B (the other MSS read παραλαβών 'taking with him') = 'with': Bl.-Debr. § 418, 5. στρατιώτας καὶ ἑκατοντάρχας: 'soldiers and officers'.[1]

VERSE 33: According to the wording the tribune himself, hurrying down at the head of his men, arrests Paul, and has him bound[2] with two hand-chains—the prophecy of **21**.11 is fulfilled: Holtzmann 134. The crowd, not the prisoner, is questioned.

VERSE 34: 'Since one in the crowd shouted this, the other that', the tribune is none the wiser and has[3] Paul brought into the barracks of the Antonia in order there γνῶναι τὸ ἀσφαλές: 'to learn the facts' or 'the truth'; cf. **22**.24, 30; **23**.28; **25**.26,[4] see Bauer, *Wb* 236.

VERSE 35: ὅτε δὲ ἐγένετο κτλ.: 'when he', Paul, 'came to the steps',[5] συνέβη[6] (classical for ἐγένετο = 'it happened', which had just been used with another meaning): 'he was in fact' or 'actually carried by the soldiers', ostensibly because of the fierce pressure of the mob.

VERSE 36: τὸ πλῆθος—κράζοντες: Bl.-Debr. § 134, 1. The crowd consisting of Jews shouted: αἶρε αὐτόν (*Beg.* IV 276 well translates with 'kill him!'): 'strike him dead!' This shout recurs again and again: Acts **22**.22; **28**.19 v.l.; Lk. **23**.18; John **19**.15; *Mart. Polyc.* **3**.2; **9**.2.

When Paul was in the Temple at the end of the time of purification, he was recognized by Jews from Ephesus who had seen him beforehand with Trophimus in the city. They presumed that he had taken his uncircumcised companion with him into the holy precinct, which was forbidden to the non-Jew on penalty of death, and with this accusation they stirred up the crowd. Paul is dragged out of the holy precinct—the temple guard immediately closed its doors—since it might not be defiled by an act of blood; then they began to beat him. The crowd would have killed him, if the alarmed Roman guard had not taken the captive from them. Since there was nothing to be learned from the wildly shouting crowd as to what the affair was all about, he was brought into the Antonia for interrogation.

In this sober report Luke after his fashion has set some guiding lights. He makes the Ephesian Jews recount the entire register of Paul's sins; his style is easily recognizable in the πάντας πανταχῇ. Then he intensifies the tumult in the Temple area, in which certainly a considerable crowd had taken part: the entire city is brought into commotion. 'Jerusalem is in riot!' is

---

[1] *Beg.* IV 275 concludes from the plural 'centurions' that 200 men were ordered out —as if Luke wanted to reproduce the scene with bureaucratic exactitude!

[2] Preuschen 129: Paul is chained to two soldiers, like Peter in **12**.6.

[3] Despite the same subject, a gen. abs.: Bl.-Debr. § 423, 4.

[4] γνῶναι τὸ ἀσφαλές, according to *Beg.* II 509; IV 276, appears often in the papyri.

[5] Josephus mentions these steps in *Bell.* V 243 as καταβάσεις.

[6] Bl.-Debr. § 393, 5; 408.

X

reported to the tribune. No wonder that he hurries down in person at the head of his soldiers and officers and personally undertakes the arrest; we shall see in the next section how indispensable for the progress of the Lucan narrative is the direction of the whole affair by the tribune himself.

The interpreters who were not satisfied with this general and yet so vivid picture, but wanted to establish with scientific thoroughness the city's share in the tumult, had to pay for it with their results. Zahn (745) makes the Asiatic Jews seize Paul, and then, when the rumour has spread into the city, receive a strong reinforcement from there and—seize Paul anew! B. Weiss avoids this duplication, which is contrary to both text and meaning, but at what a price! The seizing in v. 27 is to be only 'proleptic' (what does that mean here?), the Asiatic Jews put the city into uproar and then return with the mob to the Temple, where Paul has waited patiently for his capture. The failure of these two attempts to bring the city concretely into contact with the tumult in the Temple area shows us that frequently features apparently full of life and guaranteeing the witness in fact, when viewed closely, betray only the skill of the author.

Just as important for the recognition of Luke's manner of working is the second case, in which the traces of the work of composition are still more apparent. When Paul comes to the steps he is carried by the soldiers to keep him safe from the violence of the pressing mob. But if one carries an unpopular person on one's shoulders, one does not withdraw him from the assault of the mob: he is now completely exposed to every stone that is thrown. In reality a pressing crowd can be effectively blocked in other ways. Paul had to be carried because after the lynching attempt by the mob he was no longer able to climb the steps himself. But Luke could not report that—according to him indeed Paul will immediately deliver a speech from those very steps!

That the almost fainting Paul is yet bound with two chains we may also in these circumstances ascribe to the author, who often utilizes the motif of chains (see also **26.29**). For the author, other rules apply than for those who write police reports: the mention of the two ἀλύσεις awakens in the reader the feeling that Paul is from this moment on a prisoner. It is not as if Luke consciously used this artificial device—it was part of his talent to find artlessly such features of symbolic force.

54

ACTS 21:37-40
PAUL SPEAKS WITH THE TRIBUNE

[37] And as he was about to be brought into the barracks, Paul said to the tribune, 'Is it permissible for me to say something to you?' [38] He said, 'You understand Greek? You are not then the Egyptian who stirred up a revolt recently and led the four thousand Sicarii into the wilderness?' [39] But Paul said, 'I am a Jew, born in Tarsus, a citizen of a not inglorious city of Cilicia. I beg of you, let me speak to the people!' [40] When he had given him permission Paul, standing on the stairs, made a sign with his hand to the people. When there was a great hush, he spoke thus in Aramaic:

Bibliography:

J. Guillet, S.J.: 'Thème de la marche au désert dans l'Ancien et le Nouveau Testament', *RScR* 36 (1949), 161-81; Williams 241-3; Conzelmann 123-5; G. Stählin 281-3.

VERSE 37: μέλλων κτλ.: thus at the upper end of the steps. εἰ in a direct question[1] is Hellenistic Greek; cf. Lk. 13.23; 22.49. Paul speaks with elaborate politeness. Ἑλληνιστὶ γινώσκεις: 'do you speak Greek?'[2]

VERSE 38: οὐκ ἄρα: 'you are, therefore, not . . .'. ὁ Αἰγύπτιος: concerning him, the Sicarii and the march into the wilderness, Josephus has reported in detail (Schürer's description of these events is essentially a paraphrase of Josephus);[3] cf. also Krenkel, *Josephus und Lukas*, 1894, esp. 240ff. πρὸ

---

[1] Bl.-Debr. § 440, 3. In LXX: Gen. 17.17, I Sam. 10.24 and often.

[2] Cf. *Graece nescire* in Cicero *Pro Flacco* 4: Wendt 306.

[3] The decisive passage is *Bell.* II 254-65: 1. During the administration of Felix (from 52 on) nationalistic extremists began to appear who stabbed their enemies (especially at religious festivals) in crowds ('Sicarii' from *sica*, 'dagger'). Their first victim was the former High Priest Jonathan, who ranked as a friend of the Romans (see Intro. § 4). 2. From these Sicarii Josephus distinguishes the πλάνοι ἄνθρωποι or γόητες (Josephus will not describe them as prophets). They persuaded the people to follow them into the wilderness, where God would show them 'signs of freedom'. Felix (under him only *one* such case occurred) had the partisans cut down or dispersed. 3. Still more pernicious was the Αἰγύπτιος ψευδοπροφήτης (also called γόης or simply ὁ Αἰγύπτιος) who with 30,000 of those he had deceived marched from the wilderness (?) to the Mount of Olives to take possession of Jerusalem by force (according to *Beg.* IV 277 this number derives from a mis-reading of

τούτων κτλ.: see on **5.36**; ἀναστατόω: see on **17.6**; the real accusation against Paul seems to have been one of στάσις, disturbing the peace; see on **24.3**.

VERSE 39: ᾿Ιουδαῖος: in distinction to Αἰγύπτιος: see *ThWb* III, 360ff., esp. 382, 18ff. Ταρσεύς: see H. Böhlig, *Die Geisteskultur von Tarsus*, 1913; cf. however **22.3**, Schwartz, *RHPhR* 1957, 91ff. οὐκ ἀσήμου πόλεως πολίτης: the litotes and paronomasia (cf. Intro. § 5) characterize Paul as an educated person.[1] According to the later tradition in Jerome (*de vir. ill.* 5) Paul came to Tarsus with his parents as prisoners of war from Gischala in Galilee. Zahn (RE[3], 'Paulus' II) compromises: the parents originated from Gischala, Paul was born in Tarsus, where his father, liberated, became a Roman citizen. Paul does not mention his birthplace in his autobiography in Phil. **3.5**; we may conclude from this that he was not born in Palestine. μὲν . . . δέ makes only a linguistic and not a logical antithesis.

VERSE 40: ἑστώς . . . κατέσεισεν κτλ.: Paul 'with the familiar gesture' (Holtzmann 134) takes up the speaker's stance; cf. **12.17**; **13.16**; **26.1**. ῾Εβραΐδι διαλέκτῳ: Aramaic. J. P. Hyatt, *JBL* 76 (1957), 10 n. 25 thinks of Hebrew.

Directly before the barracks gate Paul speaks politely to the tribune. The latter, astonished that his prisoner speaks Greek, asks if he is not 'the Egyptian' who 'a short time ago' marched into the wilderness with four thousand Sicarii. Paul identifies himself in elegant Greek as a Jew and a citizen of the renowned city of Tarsus, then asks if he may speak to the people, which the tribune immediately allows. When the crowd see him assume the speaker's posture, they fall silent, and Paul begins an Aramaic address.

This description has made critical theologians like Zeller (280f.), Overbeck (389 and 364ff.), J. Weiss (40ff.), Wellhausen (46), Preuschen (129), Loisy (809ff.) very dubious. A man who has only just been beaten up by a fanatical mob is physically no longer capable of making such a speech. This

---

Δ = 4,000 (as Acts **21.38**) as Λ = 30,000). Clearer is *Ant.* XX 169–72: someone who passes himself off as a prophet comes to Jerusalem and advises the crowd to go with him to the Mount of Olives: there they will see how the walls of Jerusalem collapse. His adherents are killed or captured by Felix; he himself disappears.—Zahn, who discusses this text in 747–9 n. 26, falsely identifies the anonymous γόης of *Ant.* XX 188 (who appeared under Festus) with the Egyptian. That Josephus *Ant.* XX 170 parodies Jesus' promises in Lk. **6.20f.**, Mt. **12.28** and elsewhere is an assertion of Zahn's just as absurd as that Josephus ridicules Lk. **2.42–7** in *Vita* 2 or that he imitates the speech at Miletus in *Ant.* IV 315–24. Behind it probably stands unconsciously the wish to eliminate the unwelcome control of Luke by Josephus.

[1] οὐκ ἄσημος . . . πόλις e.g. Euripides, *Ion* 8 (Preuschen 129). D has 'improved' the free construction Ταρσεὺς κτλ into scholastic Greek.

reason suffices to prove that the speech and the dialogue preparing for it
are unhistorical. But there are also other reasons. How the tribune hits upon
the idea that his prisoner is precisely 'the Egyptian' is puzzling. It remains
just as enigmatic why he suddenly gives up this view when Paul speaks
Greek; the Egyptian Jews spoke Greek by preference. Further, it is incomprehensible that the tribune allows the man just arrested to speak to
the crowd, simply because he gives himself out as a Jew from Tarsus; whether
the tribune understands Aramaic is a problem by itself. Finally, the crowd
which had just been shouting, 'Kill him!' simply would not think of becoming
quiet just because the man was preparing himself to speak. From whatever
standpoint one examines this situation, in all the three factors which come
into consideration—Paul, who makes the speech, the tribune who allows it,
and the people who listen to it—the result is the same: this situation is
unhistorical.

But what does Luke want to say by this unhistorical composition? Let
us begin with the statement that the 'Egyptian' marched into the wilderness
with four thousand Sicarii. Here three different things are combined together.
Josephus frequently speaks of marches into the wilderness. The occurrence
under Felix (*Bell*. II 258–60) we have already mentioned at v. 38. But there
was a similar occurrence already under Fadus (44–46) (*Ant*. XX 97f.): the
march of the γόης Theudas mentioned in Acts 5.36. Another γόης called for
a march into the wilderness under Festus, the successor of Felix (*Ant*. XX
186). Astonishingly, something of the sort occurred also even outside Palestine;
in Cyrenaica a weaver named Jonathan led many of the poor into the desert
(see *Bell*. VII 437–40, 450). We can understand these movements best on
the basis of Mt. 24.26ff., the word of a Christian prophet who in the name of
the risen Lord restrained the Christian community from following these false
Messianic promises. For such is the case. Not that those men who called for a
march into the wilderness wanted themselves to be Messiah; they came
forward as prophets. But in the wilderness the Messiah would appear, and
then with his miraculous power destroy his enemies (cf. Rev. 19. 11–21). Since
they hoped for this heavenly intervention the bands who marched into the
wilderness were as good as unarmed, and could easily be annihilated by the
pursuing troops. Josephus has kept silent about these Messianic hopes and
spoken only allusively of 'signs of freedom' (one should perhaps translate
'miracles of liberation').

Something similar was the case with the 'Egyptian' (an Egyptian Jew).
Josephus (above all in the *Bellum*) has admittedly concealed so far as possible
the supernatural Messianic aspects of the expectation. The gathering on the
Mount of Olives had no military aspirations; it was rather expected that here
the Messiah would appear, and at his word the walls of Jerusalem would
come tumbling down and leave the way into the city open. (According to
Acts 1.11 the first Christians also appear to have hoped that the Messiah

(i.e. for them: Jesus) would come down from heaven on the Mount of Olives.)

Luke, however, has connected the Egyptian not only with the γόητες, but also with the Sicarii: he led four thousand Sicarii into the wilderness. Here those groups which in Josephus (*Bell.* II 254–6) are precisely distinguished are—historically incorrectly—moulded into one. The Sicarii at that time still appeared in Jerusalem as 'dagger men'. They thought of the liberation from the Roman yoke (like the λησταί, the 'Partisans') in quite different terms from those unarmed mobs who set all their hopes on a Messianic miracle. Only later did the γόητες and the λῃστρικοί unite (*Bell.* II 264).

But it was not Luke's purpose to give an historically accurate sketch of the Messianic and non-Messianic insurrection movements. Rather he has— and that was a stroke of the author's genius—unified the different groups into one single phenomenon and thereby awakened in his readers, whether or not they have already heard anything about the Sicarii or the Egyptian or the marches into the wilderness, the picture of that religious στάσις which was laid to Paul's account. That the tribune voices this suspicion and then lets it drop constitutes the first acquittal of Christendom: the suspicion that Paul belongs in this company is immediately abandoned. That the tribune expresses his suspicions about Paul thus does not reveal (as a psychological exegesis would assume) the naive frankness of this soldier, who in sudden confidence tells Paul what he thought about him, but rather instructs the reader, who from the beginning (and that from the mouth of the Roman commander himself) is taught that Christianity has nothing to do with political Messianism, and is also immediately recognized in this its non-political character. Bauernfeind (260) has the right idea that the tribune quickly took a liking to his strange prisoner, but it has been shifted to the private and psychological level: in the words of the tribune Luke reports the first alibi for Christianity accused in the person of Paul. Naturally he does this, author that he is, by making Paul and the tribune speak with one another. Anyone who takes this conversation historically embroils himself—as we have seen—in sheer impossibilities. Only one who understands it as a means of presentation which, in lively and graphic brevity, delivers the true nature of the Christian 'way' from a serious misunderstanding, appreciates Luke's presentation in the proper manner.

55
ACTS 22:1-21
PAUL'S SPEECH IN THE TEMPLE COURTYARD

[1] 'Brothers and fathers, hear my defence which I now direct to you!' [2] When they heard that he spoke to them in the Aramaic language, they became even quieter. [3] And he said, "I am a Jew, born in Tarsus in Cilicia, but brought up in this city, instructed carefully at the feet of Gamaliel according to the law of the fathers, a man zealous for God as you all are this day. [4] I persecuted this 'way' to the death, binding men and women and delivering them to prison, [5] as the High Priest and the whole council of elders bear me witness. When I had received letters from them to the brothers, I went to Damascus, in order to bind those who were there and bring them to Jerusalem that they might be punished. [6] It happened to me, however, as I was on the way and approaching Damascus, that suddenly about noon a great light from heaven shone about me, [7] and I fell to the ground and heard a voice saying to me, 'Saul, Saul, why do you persecute me?' [8] And I answered, 'Who are you, Lord?' And he said to me, 'I am Jesus of Nazareth, whom you are persecuting.' [9] Now those with me did indeed see the light, but the voice of him who spoke to me they did not hear. [10] Then I said, 'What shall I do, Lord?' And the Lord said to me, 'Get up, go to Damascus and there you will be told all that is appointed for you to do.' [11] Since I could not see because of the brightness of that light, I came guided by the hand by my companions to Damascus. [12] Ananias, however, a devout man according to the law who had a good reputation among all the Jews who were living there, [13] came to me and stood beside me and said, 'Brother Saul, receive your sight!' And that same hour I saw. [14] And he said, 'The God of our fathers has chosen you to know his will and to see the Just One and to hear the voice of his mouth. [15] For you will be a witness for him to all men of what you have seen and heard. [16] And now, why do you linger? Get up, have yourself baptized and wash away your sins, calling on his name.' [17] Now it happened to me, when I returned to Jerusalem and was praying in the Temple, that I fell into a trance [18] and saw him speaking to me: 'Hurry and go away quickly from Jerusalem, for they will not accept your witness about me.' [19] And I said, 'Lord, they know that I had those who believe in you taken to prison and beaten in the synagogues. [20] And when the blood of Stephen your witness was spilled, there I stood by and approved and watched over the clothes of

those who killed him!'   ²¹ And he said to me, 'Go, for I will send you far
away to the Gentiles!'"

Bibliography:

K. Erbes, 'Zeit und Ziel d. Grüsse Rö. **16**.3–5 u.d. Mitteilungen II Tim. **4**.
9–21', *ZNW* 10 (1909), 195–218; N. G. Veldhoen, *Het Proces van den Apostel
Paulus*, Leiden 1924; D. W. Riddle, 'The Occasion of Luke-Acts', *JRel.* 10
(1930), 545–61; A. Vitti, 'Notae in Act **22**.3, **26**.4–5', *Verb. Domini* 9 (1931),
331–4; Williams 243–5; Conzelmann 124–7; G. Stählin 283–7.

VERSE 1: ἄνδρες . . . πατέρες: as at **7**.2, although this time the High
Priest and the Sanhedrin are not present.¹ ἀκούσατε . . . ἀπολογίας: 'Hear
my present defence before you.'² With the word ἀπολογίας, standing emphatically at the end, the theme for the concluding part of Acts is announced.³

VERSE 2: Ἑβραΐδι διαλέκτῳ: see on **21**.40. In itself it is natural to speak
Aramaic to a Jewish crowd in Jerusalem. By this Luke emphasizes Paul's
adherence to Judaism, which has its effect in still greater attention from the
listeners.⁴

VERSE 3: First the information given to the tribune is repeated; then the
readers learn still more of the biography of Paul (Dibelius, *Studies* 159).
Luke would no doubt much rather have reported a Palestinian origin, in order to
prove Paul a Jew *par excellence;* but apparently he knew of no such tradition.
With γεγεννημένος, ἀνατεθραμμένος, πεπαιδευμένος Luke follows a fixed
biographical outline.⁵ ἀνατεθραμμένος . . . ταύτῃ: Paul has already spent

¹ Earlier commentators (Meyer, Bisping, Baumgarten, cited in Overbeck 391) admittedly conjectured that 'there were also members of the Sanhedrin in the crowd' or (so
Zahn 750) 'the Sagan and some priests'. If we wish to justify the formal address through
historical reflection at all, it is still better to have it directed to the younger and aged
members of the audience. But for Luke such points of content are not the only decisive
factors: at **23**.1 the Sanhedrin is addressed simply by ἄνδρες ἀδελφοί—because no great
speech follows. Luke has a keen ear for the balance between address and subsequent
speech.
² For the word order see Bl.-Debr. § 173, 1 supplement and § 473, 1.
³ Cf. ἀπολογεῖσθαι **24**.10; **25**.8; **26**.1f., 24.
⁴ μᾶλλον: 'more than ever': Bauer, *Wb* 966.
⁵ This W. C. van Unnik has proven in his excellent investigation *Tarsus or Jerusalem*
(London 1962). The triad of γέννησις, τροφή, παιδεία, or the corresponding verbs, was 'a
fixed literary unit' (9). 'It was the proper thing to describe the development of a man's
youth in this way' (28). The scheme is used also in Stephen's speech, Acts **7**.20ff., where it
is said of Moses ἐγεννήθη, ἀνετράφη, ἐπαιδεύθη. The ἀνατρέφειν takes place in the parents'
home, first of all through the mother. It falls according to Chrysippus in the first three years
of the child's life (39). The παιδεία—above all through the father and teacher—follows the
τροφή. With this Acts **26**.4 agrees. So it follows that 'at the feet of Gamaliel' belongs to
πεπαιδευμένος.—The reader must thus gather from the Lucan report that the family moved
to Jerusalem in Paul's earliest years, and that Paul spent his childhood and youth there.

his childhood in Jerusalem, παρά . . . πεπαιδευμένος: his youth at the feet of Gamaliel. παρὰ τοὺς πόδας assumes like Mt. **23**.2 that the rabbi sits in a chair, the pupils before him on the ground.[1] Γαμαλιήλ (see on **5**.34): flourished between A.D. 25 and 50.[2] That Paul studied under him 'is scarcely correct, since one must probably conclude from Gal. **1**.22 that before his conversion Paul did not stay very long in Jerusalem': Bultmann *RGG*[2] IV, 1020f. See above (p. 297) concerning Gal. **1**.22. The Pauline exegesis of scripture, which deals very freely with the OT text, does not correspond to the rabbinic, which observes the text with punctilious accuracy. His familiarity with the LXX betrays a lifelong association with the Greek OT. κατά . . . νόμου: 'according to careful observance of the law given to the fathers'.[3] ζηλωτής . . . σήμερον: 'being a man zealous for God[4] as you are all today.' Paul has expressed himself in Gal. **1**.14 and Phil. **3**.6ff. about his earlier attitude to the law. That in our verse he condemns his earlier zeal, like the present zeal of the Jews, as perverse, in conformity with Romans **10**.2 (Wendt 309, similarly Zahn 753) is introduced against the meaning of the text; Luke knows no break in Paul's attitude to the law.

VERSE 4: relative conjunction which actually introduces a main clause, as at **21**.32 (Zahn 753). 'This way': see on **9**.2. ἄχρι θανάτου: Luke has here and at **26**.10 generalized the single case described in **7**.54ff.: *Beg.* IV 279. δεσμεύων . . . φυλακάς: see on **8**.3 and **26**.10f.

VERSE 5: ὁ ἀρχιερεὺς κτλ.: as if High Priests and Sanhedrin were still the same as twenty years before![5] τὸ πρεσβυτέριον here as in Lk. **22**.66 = Sanhedrin. It is not mentioned in **9**.1 or in **26**.12. See above, pp. 320f. on **9**.2. ἀδελφοί are here the Jews; οἱ ἐκεῖσε (Hellenistic for ἐκεῖ) ὄντες on the other hand are the Christians.

VERSE 6: cf. **9**.3. The statement of time is new: noon. It is generally understood apologetically: the appearance was no 'night-time bugbear' (Bauernfeind 252). But people generally did not travel at night. Cf. **10**.9ff. (*TLZ* 1960, 250). It was precisely beside the noonday sun that the heavenly light

---

Anyone who considers this apposite must assume with van Unnik that the Hellenistic influence on Paul operated only after his conversion, when he went to Tarsus after the stay in Arabia and the short visit to Jerusalem (Gal. **1**.18).

[1] Bill. II 763ff. quotes from Pirqe Aboth 1, 4: 'Let yourself be dusted by the dust of their' (the scholars') 'feet'. Cf. Luke **8**.35; **10**.39 (II Kings **4**.38): 'late Jewish rather than Hellenistic': *Beg.* IV 278.

[2] His (alleged) Pharisaic-sounding motto, however, perhaps derives from his grandson Gamaliel II (around 90 A.D.): Bill II, 638.

[3] ἀκρίβεια is also in Josephus *Vita* 191, *Bell.* II 162 the catchword for Pharisaic legalism (cf. also Acts **26**.5).

[4] The Vulgate to simplify has replaced θεοῦ by νόμου, sy[h] by τῶν πατρικῶν μου παραδόσεων.

[5] 614 and sy[h] have introduced the ruling High Priest, Ananias (**23**.2; **24**.1) into the text.

appeared as ἱκανόν; **26**.13 is even clearer. For blindness at noon *Beg.* IV 280 refers to Deut. **28**.28f.

VERSE 7: cf. on **9**.4. ἔπεσα is Hellenistic for ἔπεσον. πίπτειν εἰς τὸ ἔδαφος: IV Macc. **6**.7. The word ἔδαφος occurs often in the LXX.

VERSE 8: cf. on **9**.5. The saying of Jesus is expanded by ὁ Ναζωραῖος (cf. *ThWb* IV, 879ff., esp. 883).

VERSE 9: a change from **9**.7; there they all hear but see nothing.[1]

VERSE 10: cf. on **9**.6. Holtzmann 135 finds it improper that ὁ κύριος is here said of Jesus before Jews; but Luke is thinking of his readers, not about Paul's listeners. ἀναστάς: *Beg.* IV 280 translates by 'at once'; see on **1**.13. ὧν attraction of the relative for ἅ (Bl.-Debr. § 294).

VERSE 11 corresponds to **9**.8 but is more detailed: blind from the[2] brightness. οὐκ ἐνέβλεπον is distinguished by only one letter from the reading in B οὐδὲν ἔβλεπον (= **9**.8), which is probably original. ἐμβλέπω = 'to look at' does not fit. Cf. ἀνέβλεψα v. 13. χειραγωγούμενος: the sure sign of blindness; see on **9**.8.

VERSE 12f.: corresponds to **9**.10–17; see there. Ananias, who is described as a μαθητής in **9**.10, appears here only as a man devout[3] before the law and in good reputation with all the Jews there.[4] Naturally he speaks Aramaic to Paul, which is indicated by Σαούλ. ἀναβλέπειν = 'to see again'. Most commentaries seek to retain beside this the meaning 'to look up', in order to do justice to the εἰς αὐτόν. This will however be a very old and false expansion, corresponding to the ἐνέβλεπον in v. 11. αὐτῇ τῇ ὥρᾳ: appears in the late parts of the LXX.[5]

VERSE 14: The Jewish flavour is strengthened by the expression 'the God of our fathers' and the description of Jesus (his name is avoided) with the old Messianic title of honour 'the Just One';[6] *ThWb* II, 188, 190f.: 'the attestation of the executed guiltless' (Schrenk). προχειρίζομαι, 'choose': said of Jesus in **3**.20 (see note there), in **26**.16 of Paul.[7] γνῶναι τὸ θέλημα αὐτοῦ: according to Romans **2**.18 and Col. **1**.9 apparently a common Jewish expression.[8]

VERSE 15: μάρτυς: here not = 'martyr'. 'To all men': in **9**.15 and **26**.17 universalism is still more clearly expressed through the naming of the Gentiles,

---

[1] D inserts a καὶ ἔμφοβοι ἐγένοντο after such Lucan passages as Lk. **24**.5, 37; Acts **10**.4; **24**.25.

[2] ἀπό: Hellenistic causal: Bl.-Debr. § 210, 1. Cf. Lk. **19**.3; Acts **11**.19; **12**.14; **20**.9.

[3] εὐλαβής occurs occasionally in LXX; on the other hand εὐλαβεῖσθαι is there very frequent.

[4] μαρτυρεῖσθαι as in **16**.2.

[5] I Esdras **8**.64; Esth. **8**.1 and **9**.2 v. l.; Dan. LXX **3**.6; **5**.5; Dan. Θ **3**.6, 15; **4**.33; **5**.5.

[6] See on **3**.14; cf. also **7**.52; I Peter **3**.18; I John **2**.1; **3**.7; *Beg.* IV 281.

[7] In LXX for לָקַח and שָׂם.

[8] In LXX only Ps. 102 (103).7: ἐγνώρισε . . . τὰ θελήματα αὐτοῦ; not on the other hand γινώσκω τὸ θέλημα τοῦ θεοῦ.

which is here reserved for v. 21. ὧν = τούτων ἅ (Bl.-Debr. § 294, 4). ἑώρακας καὶ ἤκουσας: the perfect stands here in a narrative sense as at Rev. **5**.7; II Cor. **12**.17; Bl.-Debr. § 343.[1] But euphony plays a part.

VERSE 16: τί μέλλεις: classical;[2] μέλλω only here = 'delay'. For ἀναστάς see v. 10. The accomplishment of the baptism (with invocation of the name of Jesus: see on **9**.14) and its meaning (washing away of sins) are indicated as in **2**.38. Cf. I Cor. **6**.11; Eph. **5**.26.

VERSE 17: ὑποστρέψαντι[3] presupposes (like **9**.26) Paul's speedy return to Jerusalem. In that case, as Wendt (310) maintains, the visit to the Temple and the vision would have taken place during the visit to Jerusalem described in Gal. **1**.18f. To this Knopf (638) objects: 'Revelations such as the one here described' do not fit 'in the days of his short and timid visit with Peter'. That Paul on this secret visit will not have sought out the Temple may be correct; but Luke knows nothing indeed of such a short and timid visit, but rather has Paul move about Jerusalem freely and openly; see on **9**.27f. By this feature Luke wants to show that in the Temple, God's holy place of revelation to which he remains loyal, Paul the devout Jew experiences the appearance of Jesus![4]

VERSE 18: Jesus (the name again does not occur) himself orders him out of Jerusalem, not because a Jewish plot threatens him, as in **9**.29, but rather because the Jews do not listen.[5] Luke is not bound by his presentation in **9**.29!

VERSE 19f.: Paul—in reality this verse is directed to the reader—emphasizes how he persecuted the Christians:[6] really (that is the meaning of this recollection) the Jews ought to listen to the one-time persecutor! That they do not reveals their stubbornness. The death of Stephen is mentioned only after the persecution, as its culmination. Stephen (like Jesus, Rev. **1**.5; **3**.14 and Antipas in Rev. **2**.13) is described as a 'martyr'.[7] καὶ αὐτός: see on **1**.3. συνευδοκῶν: see **8**.1.

---

[1] Against the interpretation of Bl.-Debr. § 342, 2 (perfect to describe the after-effect: 'that Paul has seen the Lord is what gives him lastingly his consecration as an Apostle, while the hearing is far less essential'): in Luke Paul simply does not possess the consecration of an Apostle. **26**.16 uses εἶδες in the same sense. The form ἀκήκοα was obsolete and therefore could not be used by Luke. Luke probably set store by the very assonance of ἑώρακας and ἤκουσας.

[2] For example Sophocles *Antig.* 449: τί δῆτα μέλλεις.

[3] The quite unclassical construction has a counterpart in Lk. **3**.21: J. Weiss 42 note.

[4] ἔκστασις **10**.10 and **11**.5 of Peter's vision.

[5] σπεῦσον καὶ e.g. LXX Gen. **18**.6; σπεύδειν in this use often in LXX: the speech of the exalted Lord is delivered in biblical style. ἐν τάχει also often occurs in LXX, so too διότι.

[6] For meaning of the conj. periphr. see on **1**.10, p. 149 n. 7

[7] So also Bauer *Wb* 977 with a wealth of references. H. F. v. Campenhausen, *Die Idee des Martyriums in der alten Kirche*, 1936, 31 n. 7: 'K. Holl, 'Die Vorstellung vom Märtyrer and die Märtyrerakte', *Ges. Aufsätze* II (1928) 71, understands the expression

VERSE 21: Jesus himself commands the Gentile mission as Paul's task; this is so expressed neither in Chapter 9 nor in Chapter 26. Only the heavenly command, as once with Peter at the baptism of Cornelius, has now led Paul (and thereby Christianity in general) to the Gentile mission. But at the same time it has been precipitated by the unbelief of the Jews themselves; there can thus, according to Luke, be no question of Christianity having separated itself from Judaism.

At Chapter 9 it has already been demonstrated that the repetition of the story of the call is not to be explained by a use of different sources, but rather by literary reasons (see above, pp. 325–9). But why Luke just at this point reports Paul's call for the second time is not visible at first glance. For the speech does not seem to fit the framework in which it is placed. Paul is in fact accused of having defiled the Temple by taking a Gentile into the ἱερόν with him. He does not however mention this accusation at all (Luke will go into it in Chapter 24), but rather depicts his Jewish past, his call, and finally his turning to the Gentile mission, to which he was ordered in the Temple itself. Why is he silent about what in this situation, as one would think, absolutely demanded mention?

Bauernfeind (251) answers: 'The primary question of the moment' was to be 'preceded by a fundamental clarification . . .; but this itself remains a torso on account of the interruption at v. 21, and to Luke's mind is to be understood as such.' In the interim however Dibelius (*Studies* 160) has shown that the interruption of the speaker by the listeners is a literary device peculiar to Luke: 'the speeches of Stephen and Demetrius and Paul's speeches on the Areopagus and before Agrippa are concluded in a similar way', and with the sermon after the healing of the lame man (**4**.1), Peter's speech in the house of Cornelius (**10**.44) and Paul's statement before the Sanhedrin (**23**.7) the situation is quite similar (Dibelius, *Studies* 161 n, 50). But Dibelius has further drawn attention to the fact that the interruptions always allow the speech 'to reach just that point which is important to the author' (op. cit. 160).

This opens up the understanding of the present speech in a completely new way. First of all negatively: it was not Luke's intention at all to describe Paul's trial in exact detail (Dibelius, *Studies* 133). What accusation was really raised against Paul we can only surmise; it is not conveyed to us with precision. It must have been a very serious charge, for Paul is involved in a capital proceeding, which is a matter of life and death. Luke did not have the slightest interest in reviving this accusation with complete historical accuracy. For

incorrectly as a technical term for the martyrs; neither Lucan usage nor the passage taken by itself points to this.' The reference to Luke's usage elsewhere is justified, but on the other hand the context—the αἷμα of μάρτυς Stephen is indeed emphasized—may show how μάρτυς obtains the sense of 'martyr'.

him it was actually not a matter of Paul's debates with his contemporary opponents, but rather—and here we come to the positive new understanding of the speech—of the debate between Christianity and Judaism and the problem of Luke's own present age. Between Judaism and Christianity there stood not some particular conflict such as the alleged defilement of the Temple, but rather the Christian mission to the Gentiles, the reception of Gentiles by Christian baptism into the people of God (Dibelius, *Studies* 160). Paul, however, was the great Gentile missionary. Hence it was—looking deeper— thoroughly appropriate that he should stand here as the accused who must defend himself. On this basis however the way in which he defends himself also proves appropriate: Luke does not have him go into the charge of defiling the Temple—which in the meantime had become unimportant—, but rather makes him speak to the decisive question of the validity of the Christian Gentile mission. It did not originate from human caprice (cf. Chapter 10), and the devout and strict Jew Paul would never have thought it up himself!

That Paul was such a devout Jew is now demonstrated as clearly as possible in this speech. Paul was not of course born in Jerusalem; but he grew up there from his earliest childhood. Then he studied there, at the feet of the most famous rabbi of his time, instructed in the exact fulfilment of the law, a man just as zealous for God as the Jews who have just sought to lynch him. As such a zealous man he persecuted 'the Way'—the name of Christ is avoided —with the most rigorous measures; what is indicated by the words 'until death' will be expressly stated at **26.10**. Then the journey to Damascus is recounted—with full authority from the High Priest and Sanhedrin!—and the event outside Damascus. It would have been a serious literary error if Luke had once again brought in the account of Chapter 9, merely changing the third person to the first. The reader now already knew what happened, and for the particular purpose of our scene the exalted Lord's conversation with Ananias offered nothing of significance. Hence Luke could avoid it. The source of Ananias' knowledge about the call of Paul and his charge to heal and baptize him was already known to the reader (and Luke here was thinking only of him, and not about Paul's listeners).

The figure of Ananias, on the other hand, Luke has not yet here abandoned—contrast Chapter 26. Ananias here appears altogether as a devout Jewish Christian: the circle represented by him, into which Paul came through his call, was precisely as devout in the law as Paul had been hitherto. The conversion accordingly does not signify any complete religious breach with Paul's past; it gives him a new relationship not with the law, but only to Jesus (who is named only by the OT-sounding Messianic title 'the Just One'). The universality of the Christian message entrusted to Paul is at first very cautiously expressed and therefore not noticed by the crowd: Paul is to witness to all men what he has seen and heard. Luke makes the decisive turn to the Gentile mission first emerge in a new scene. Paul returns from

Damascus to Jerusalem and there in the Temple, which as a devout Jew he seeks out as a matter of course, experiences an ἔκστασις in which Jesus (again he is not called by name) commands him immediately to leave Jerusalem because the Jews do not receive his witness. Paul objects: he has bitterly persecuted the Christians—this persecution and Paul's share in it appear even greater than in Chapter 9, in that a considerable number of death sentences is presupposed, although only the execution of Stephen is expressly mentioned. Chapter 26 will bring a final intensification. To this persecutor the Jews ought properly to give credence if now he bears witness to Jesus. But the Lord commands, 'Go, I send you far away to the Gentiles.' Thus in an entirely new way, quite independent of everything related before, the Pauline Gentile mission is traced back to a direct command to him from Jesus.

In this way, however, not only is the Gentile mission justified afresh, but at the same time the point is reached where Luke returns to the narrative framework: that Jesus—and of all things in a moment of rapture in the Temple!—should have sent Paul to the Gentiles, is enough to make the crowd break out anew in wild shouting: v. 22 corresponds exactly to **21.36**.

One thing still remains to be added. Luke in **21**.28 had not made the Jews from Ephesus accuse Paul merely on account of Trophimus—this reproach is only added with an ἔτι δὲ καί—but that he taught against the people, the law and the Temple was the real complaint. This accusation can be understood according to **21**.21 to mean that Paul alienated the Jews from the law and the Temple cult, the omission of circumcision being particularly mentioned. But the teaching against the λαός, that is the chosen Jewish people, the law and the Temple can also be understood to mean that the Gentile mission free from circumcision is intended: in it the precedence of the Jewish people is denied, the law no longer observed and the Temple cult consequently meaningless. Paul's defence of the Christian mission to the Gentiles in Chapter 22 in consequence formally corresponds to the Jewish accusation which Luke had named in Chapter 21. We see that the author in Chapter 21 already had in view the problem with which Chapter 22 is concerned: it is his own and that of his own time.

With this we come to a final peculiarity of this speech: it skilfully weaves together Paul's past and Luke's present. Paul defends himself against charges which are lodged against him; but fundamentally he does not speak of a past at that time already superseded—the Temple had long lain in ruins when Luke wrote Acts—, but of the burning question for Luke and the Christians of his time: can Christianity be understood in unbroken continuity with Judaism? If that is possible, then Christian doctrine can be recognized as an inner-Jewish αἵρεσις and hence as a religio quasi licita (Tertull. *Apol.* 21, 1). That Luke is basically concerned with this question is admittedly not yet plainly visible in this speech; the following chapters will prove it. Here in the first place it is only shown that the greatest Christian

Gentile missionary, 'the' Gentile missionary, was a devout and law-abiding Jew, who only on account of Jewish unbelief was sent by divine command to the Gentiles. If this is the case, then there is no fundamental gulf between Judaism and Christianity, the continuity between the two is unbroken, and Christianity can claim to be tolerated like Judaism. That history advanced far beyond this solution of Luke's ought not to mislead us now into interpreting the Lucan presentation ('historically') on the basis of the pre-Lucan period.

56

ACTS 22:22–29
PAUL APPEALS TO HIS ROMAN CITIZENSHIP

[22] They listened to him up to this word and then they raised their voices saying, 'Away from the earth with this man! For he ought not to live!' [23] And as they cried out and tore their clothes off and threw dust into the air, [24] the tribune ordered him to be brought into the barracks, and said he was to be interrogated under scourging, that he might learn why they shouted against him so. [25] But as they stretched him out for the lashing, Paul said to the centurion standing by, 'Is it permissible for you to lash a Roman, and that without a legal hearing?' [26] When the centurion heard that he went to the tribune, made his report and said, 'What are you about to do? For this man is a Roman!' [27] The tribune came down and spoke to him: 'Tell me, are you a Roman?' And he said, 'Yes.' [28] The tribune answered, 'I had to pay a large sum for this citizenship.' And Paul said, 'But I possess it by birth.' [29] Immediately those who were to interrogate him stood away from him. And the tribune was afraid when he learned, 'He is a Roman!', and because he had him chained.

Bibliography:

T. Mommsen, *ZNW* 2 (1901), 90; A. J. L. Wenger, *D. Quellen d. römisch. Rechts* 292; H. J. Cadbury, 'Dust and Garments', *Beg.* V, 1933, 269–77 (esp. 275–7); id., *The Book of Acts in History*, 1955, 71f. (the question of identification papers); H. Rosin, 'Civis Romanus sum', *Ned. Theol. Tijdschrift* 3 (1948/9), 16–27; J. M. Nap, 'Handelingen **22**.25', *Nieuwe Theol. Tijdschrift* 16 (1927), 245–58; A. N. Sherwin-White, *The Roman Citizenship*, 1939; Conzelmann 127.

VERSE 22: The command for the Gentile mission triggers a new outbreak of the people's rage[1] and thus leads back to the situation of **21**.36. Correspondingly the αἶρε κτλ. is repeated, but amplified and strengthened. καθῆκεν ('for he may not remain alive'): Bl.-Debr. § 358, 2.

---

[1] ἐπῆραν τὴν φωνήν: in the NT only Luke **11**.27; Acts **2**.14; (**4**.24); **14**.11; **22**.22; LXX Judges **2**.4 and often.

VERSE 23: κραυγάζω: 'to roar': II Esdras 3.13. ῥιπτέω τὰ ἱμάτια: 'to throw off the clothes' (Bauer, *Wb* 1460), like κονιορτὸν βάλλω 'to whirl the dust into the air' (Bauer, *Wb* 876), is intended to depict their furious indignation; Preuschen (131) thinks of preparation for stoning.[1]

VERSE 24: μάστιξιν ἀνετάζεσθαι αὐτόν: 'to interrogate with scourging', i.e. the form of torture usual for non-Romans and slaves; cf. T. Mommsen, *Römisches Strafrecht* 938f. That the tribune, a moment ago so friendly, orders the torture Bauernfeind (254) explains by saying 'as the next step there was simply nothing else to do'. But with this Luke again begins a scene loaded with suspense. ἵνα ἐπιγνῷ ... αὐτῷ: cf. on 21.34.

VERSE 25: προέτειναν αὐτὸν τοῖς ἱμᾶσι: either 'to bind with the leather thongs (ἱμᾶσι) a man stretched out', i.e. on a whipping post, or better 'to stretch out on a bench for the scourging' (οἱ ἱμάντες = *flagellum*): Bauer *Wb* 743. εἰ ἔξεστιν: as in 21.37 Hellenistic in direct questions: Bl.-Debr. § 440, 3. ἀκατάκριτον: has a double meaning as in 16.37: 'and moreover not yet legally sentenced' (Bauernfeind 253) or 'and that before the investigation' (Overbeck 397). The word can mean both: *Beg.* IV 283.[2]

VERSE 26f.: τί μέλλεις ποιεῖν: 'what are you about to do?' or 'what are you thinking of doing?' Ῥωμαῖος: Roman citizen. Did Paul carry a passport

---

[1] In the excursus 'Dust and Garments' (Beg. V 269-77) H. J. Cadbury discusses our passage also (275ff.). He mentions as parallels to the throwing off of garments Plato, *Republic* V 474 A; Dio Chrys. VII p.103M (Dindorf I 114), and refers to the laying aside of the clothes before Stephen's stoning: the dust-throwing could replace the throwing of stones, whether because such were not available, or out of fear of the soldiers. But the gestures could also be those of agitation and anger. Gregory of Nazianzus (*Or. in laudem Basilii* XV, Migne PG 36, 513f.) describes the conduct of the spectators at a chariot race: 'They jump up, shout, let dust rise to the heavens' (οὐρανῷ πέμπουσι κόνιν); but this does not describe a gesture. More important may be the reference to M. Jastrow, *The Book of Job*, 1922, 204 and M. Buttenwieser, *The Book of Job*, 1922, 44 on Job 2.12: when the three friends saw the divinely-afflicted Job, 'they raised their voices and wept, and each one of them tore his clothes and scattered dust on their heads to heaven'. These according to Buttenwieser are rites by which a man represented himself standing under the curse and thereby averted the curse. Cadbury considers whether Acts 13.51; 14.14; 16.22; 18.6 are also to be explained on this basis, but admits that neither the author nor his readers still knew the apotropaic origin of these gestures, which were executed on the occasion of blasphemy. The passages adduced by Buttenwieser, Jos. 7.6; I Sam. 4.12; II Sam. 1.2; 13.19; 15.32; I Macc. 3.47; 4.39; 11.71, say only that as a sign of mourning people tore their garments and placed earth or ashes upon their heads; Josephus alone (*Bell.* II 322) speaks of dust (κόνις) in this connection. Exod. 9.8, 10 speaks of flinging soot into the air (as a magical act) and uses the expression 'to the heavens', like Job 2.12. Considering Luke's biblicism it would not be impossible that he portrayed the conduct of the Jewish crowd on the model of such a passage as Job 2.12. But he could not have utilized LXX, which for 'they raised their voices' here does not use the normal ἐπῆραν τὴν φωνήν but translates βοήσαντες φωνῇ μεγάλῃ and renders וַיִּזְרְקוּ עָפָר by καταπασάμενοι γῆν instead of ἔβαλλον κονιορτόν or something similar; it omits the 'to the heavens'. Luke must have understood these gestures as expressions of horror at Paul's alleged blasphemy (his sending to the Gentiles). But ῥιπτούντων τὰ ἱμάτια creates difficulties.

[2] The tribune might neither interrogate a Roman under torture nor punish him by scourging; see p. 634 n. 4.

with him or was the mere declaration enough?[1] Here the latter seems to be the case; yet Luke may have chosen this presentation for its simplicity.

VERSE 28: πολλοῦ κεφαλαίου: 'for a large sum of money' (for the genitive see Bl.-Debr. § 179, 1). The point to be made is not doubt of Paul's word, but rather the value of Roman citizenship.[2] καί: emphasizes the following γεγέννημαι: 'I was actually born a Roman citizen': see on 1.3.

VERSE 29[3]: The interrogation under torture does not take place, but friendly questioning also stops. οἱ μέλλοντες: 'who stood ready ...' δέω: to put in chains. ἐφοβήθη: this expression is intended to show how greatly the tribune respects the law and Paul's status as a Roman citizen. καὶ ... δέ as also in 3.24. To explain the fear Cicero *In Verrem* 5, 26 is usually cited: *facinus est vincire civem Romanum; scelus verberari, parricidium necare,* Preuschen 132. But this is the pointed formulation of a lawyer. Roman governors were frequently little concerned with what legal prescriptions there were.[4]

---

[1] A false claim to Roman citizenship according to Epictetus III 24, 41 was punishable by death: Wellhausen 47; cf. Suetonius, *Claudius* 25.

[2] Preuschen 132 conjectures that the tribune Claudius Lysias bought his citizenship under the emperor Claudius, when the emperor's consort and favourites earned a great deal of money in this manner. But it is very questionable whether Luke knew anything at all about the tribune's citizenship, and did not merely want by this statement to emphasize Paul's inherited citizenship.

[3] In this verse D breaks off; the Latin text of this bilingual codex, d, had already stopped in the middle of v. 20: *Beg.* III 215.

[4] The legal situation, as shown by Cadbury's great excursus 26 'Roman Law and the Trial of Paul' (*Beg.* V 297–338; here also is listed the most important literature up to 1932), is unfortunately by no means clear. Paul had been arrested by Roman military police when a Jewish mob wanted to lynch him. Whether this was a case of protective custody or the arrest of a disturber of the public peace could only be decided when the reason for the lynch attempt was clarified—*inter alia* by an examination of Paul. The interrogation of a Roman citizen by means of torture was forbidden by the Lex Porcia and the Lex Julia. Concerning the Lex Porcia Cicero says, *Pro Rabirio* IV 12: *Porcia lex virgas ab omnium civium Romanorum corpore amovit ... Porcia lex libertatem civium lictori eripuit* (*Beg.* IV 201). Preuschen quotes from Livy X 9, 4: *Porcia tamen lex sola pro tergo civium lata videtur, quod gravi poena, si quis verberasset necassetve civem Romanum, sanxit.* The Lex Julia de vi publica et privata is described in the *Sententiae* of Paulus (V 26,1): *Lege Julia de vi publica damnatur, qui aliqua potestate praeditus civem Romanum antea ad populum, nunc imperatorem appellantem necaverit necarive iusserit, torserit, verberaverit, condemnaverit inve publica vincula duci iusserit. Cuius rei poena in humiliores capitis, in honestiores insulae deportatione coercetur.* While the Lex Julia indeed expressly names an appeal to Caesar as the condition of its application, the Lex Porcia at least according to the sense presupposes that the person threatened with *virgae* is known to be a Roman citizen.—Cf. p. 667 n. 2 to 25.11.—On the investigation of the legal situation in the early Christian persecutions see A. N. Sherwin-White: 'The Early Persecutions and Roman Law Again', *JTS* N.S. 3 (1952), 199–213; see esp. 205: normally the prosecution of Christians followed the forms of the *cognitio* system of penal jurisdiction in which proconsular *coercitio* finds its usual expression (*Digest*, Book 47, Sects. 11–22). It is not a question of offences against the *ordo* of the *leges publicae*, but of *crimina extra ordinem*, in which governors until the late second century had an entirely free hand. But there had to be a private charge against specific infringements of the law.

Again Luke depicts an extraordinarily vivid and changing scene. The crowd breaks out afresh in furious anger and behaves as if demented. Thereupon the tribune orders Paul to be brought into the barracks and there to be interrogated under torture. He is already fast bound for the scourging. At this moment of utmost suspense Paul asks the sergeant in charge of the execution whether here Roman citizens are treated in such a way, and that without investigation. Now a sudden change ensues: at one stroke Paul is once again a respected person, correctly and even politely treated. The tribune when he is informed hurries down himself, has the surprising fact that Paul is a Roman citizen verified, and underlines the value of this citizenship by recalling the large sum which he himself paid for it. But this remark allows Paul to appear yet again as superior: he is actually Roman by birth! No wonder that the tribune is now seized with anxiety because he has put this man in chains!

The story nevertheless appears in quite another light if we recall that Luke himself devised the speech and the scene preparing for it. It is astonishing how he has turned to account the narrow possibilities offered by the action once begun. The effective conclusion of the speech, the new outbreak of the crowd's fury, confirm the word of the Lord that the Jews would not accept Paul's witness. But at the same time it gives the tribune occasion to arrange the scourging of the prisoner in order to get the truth out of him. Luke has utilized this motif, that the Roman authorities cannot obtain any clear evidence concerning Paul's case, again and again (23.1, 28; 24.22; 25.20, 26). Here it serves to bring Paul's Roman rights of citizenship to light. As a good narrator, who allows the suspense to reach its highest point, Luke has his hero speak the liberating word only at the last moment.

Insofar as research took the Lucan narrative as the simple recapitulation of events, it became oppressed by all sorts of curious questions. Why did Paul not immediately divulge his Roman citizenship to the tribune when he asked about his identity? Lake (*Beg.* IV 278) conjectures that Paul was proud only of his citizenship of Tarsus and therefore named it in 21.39. This however made no impression on the tribune, but the Roman citizenship so little esteemed by Paul did! Bauernfeind 250, on the other hand, thinks that Paul in 21.39 preferred to appeal to the human kindness of the soldier . . . These psychological considerations become superfluous when we realize that for Luke the citizenship of Tarsus was enough to prove that Paul and the 'Egyptian' were not the same person. Hence he reserved the Roman citizenship for a later scene, in which he attests the correctness of the Roman authorities and at the same time creates a situation of unprecedented tension.

The question of the shackling will be discussed in connection with 22.30.

57
ACTS 22:30–23:11
PAUL BEFORE THE HIGH COUNCIL

[30] On the following day, since he wanted to learn exactly why he was accused by the Jews, he had him freed from his chains and commanded the High Priests and the entire Sanhedrin to assemble, and he brought Paul down and placed him in their midst. 23 [1] Paul, however, looked steadily at the Sanhedrin and said, 'Brethren, I have walked before God with all good conscience up to this day.' [2] The High Priest Ananias commanded those standing next to him to strike him on the mouth. [3] Then Paul said to him, 'God will strike you, you whitewashed wall! You sit there to judge me according to the law and against the law you order that I be struck?' [4] Those who stood by said, 'Do you revile the High Priest of God?' [5] And Paul said, 'I did not know, brethren, that he is the High Priest. For it stands written, "The ruler of your people you shall not revile!"' [6] Now when Paul recognized that one part consisted of Sadducees and the other of Pharisees, he cried out in the high council: 'Brethren, I am a Pharisee, a son of Pharisees. On account of the hope and resurrection of the dead I stand before the court.' [7] When he said this, an argument arose between the Pharisees and the Sadducees, and the crowd was divided. [8] For the Sadducees say there is no resurrection, nor angel, nor spirit; the Pharisees, however, acknowledge them all. [9] Then a great clamour arose and some scribes of the Pharisaic section rose up and said, strongly disputing, 'We find nothing wrong in this man. Now if a spirit has spoken with him or an angel—?' [10] And when a great uproar occurred, the tribune was afraid that Paul would be torn apart by them, and ordered the guard down to tear him away from their midst and bring him to the barracks. [11] And in the following night the Lord came to him and said, 'Have courage! For as you have borne witness for me in Jerusalem, so must you also bear witness in Rome!'

Bibliography:

O. Lagercrantz, *ZNW* 31 (1932) 86f.; G. Björck, *Coniect. Neot.* 4, 1940, 2f. Raymond R. Brewer, 'The Meaning of πολιτεύεσθαι in Phil. 1.27', *JBL* 73 (1954), 76–83 (esp. 78); J. Steckenberger, *Syneidesis im NT*, 1961, 49ff; Williams 247–9; Trocmé 104; Conzelmann 127–9.

VERSE 30: τῇ ἐπαύριον: supply ἡμέρᾳ. βουλόμενος . . . ἀσφαλές: see on 21.34. τὸ τί κατηγορεῖται: 'on what account he was accused by the Jews'; see on 4.21 (Bl.-Debr. § 267,2).[1] ἔλυσεν αὐτόν: from the chains mentioned in 21.33, as H L P also add.[2] ἐκέλευσεν . . . συνέδριον: Schürer II[3] 210 conceived this statement as a description of the tribune's actual authority. καταγαγὼν ἔστησεν: the tribune himself accompanies Paul to the session of the High Council summoned by him,[3] which is to inform him (see however on 23.3, 6), and finally (23.28) achieves this purpose.

VERSE 1: ἀτενίσας: 'looking steadily'—Paul has no anxiety before the judges: see on 1.10. ἄνδρες ἀδελφοί: see on 22.1.[4] ἐγὼ κτλ.: Paul has nothing to reproach himself for before God (24.16 repeats this). How this squares with the (alleged) participation in the killing of Stephen and other Christians, one may of course not ask. πολιτεύομαι in a religious sense: II Macc. 6.1 and often. The continuity of this devout life knows no break. This theology of the 'good conscience' is popular in the post-apostolic literature.[5]

VERSE 2: ἀρχιερεὺς Ἀνανίας:[6] that the High Priest presides, Paul himself presupposes in v. 3b. τοῖς παρεστῶσιν αὐτῷ: 'those standing next to him are servants present; cf. Lk. 19.24; John 18.22': Wendt 314. Whether it is the fact that Paul speaks out of turn or the content of his speech which supplies the reason for this punitive measure is not clear.

VERSE 3: τύπτειν . . . ὁ θεός: Bill. II 766: 'Shᶜbuoth 4.13 toward the end: (if anyone says) "God will strike you" . . . that is the curse written in the Torah (see Deut. 28.22)'. But this evidently customary malediction is

---

[1] H L P S read παρά (not classical) instead of ὑπό.

[2] ἔλυσεν: Jacquier (656) considers the chaining a constituent part of the *custodia militaris* and sees in it no inconsistency with the Lex Julia, probably because this speaks only of *in publica vincula duci*.

[3] Where this council at that time met we do not know: see Lake, 'Localities in and near Jerusalem mentioned in the Acts' (*Beg.* V 474–86), 'The Court-room of the Sanhedrin' (477f.): according to Josephus *Bell.* V 144; VI 354 the council assembled in a hall directly west of the Temple, between it and the Xystos; according to the Talmud in a room in the Temple on the south side of the courtyard.

[4] 'Does not correspond to the Jewish way of speaking': Bill. II 765. Overbeck 399: 'The lack of form nevertheless characterizes the dominant position of Paul over against his judges which is yielded by the narrative in general.'

[5] Cf. I Tim. 1.5, 19; 3.9; II Tim. 1.3; I Peter 3.16, 21; Hebr. 9.14; 13.18.

[6] According to *Beg.* I 32 and Loisy 827f., Agrippa II while Felix was procurator appointed as High Priest Jonathan, who was then murdered by the Sicarii (Josephus *Bell.* II 256; *Ant.* XX 162–4). But Jonathan had already in 37 A.D. been removed by Vitellius after only a year's term of office (*Ant.* XVIII 95, 123) and declined a re-election in the year 41 in favour of his brother Matthias. The designation ἀρχιερεύς he retained like all deposed High Priests. When Agrippa II according to *Ant.* XX 179 named Ishmael, the son of Phabi, as High Priest, his forerunner was thus not Jonathan but Ananias. Indeed Jonathan and Ananias were sent to Rome as prisoners for trial (*Bell.* II 243; *Ant.* XX 131) but they were released again (see Intro §§ 4, 8, pp. 69 ff.). According to *Ant.* III 320 Ishmael would already have been High Priest during the great famine, therefore 47/48. This may be an error; such is also the judgement of G. Hölscher (*Die Hohenpriesterliste bei Josephus und die evangelische Chronologie*, Heidelberg 1940, 17f.)

here understood as a prophecy (μέλλει of a divine decree) (Jacquier 658): Ananias was murdered in the year 66. τοῖχε κεκονιαμένε: probably a current term of abuse (Preuschen 132) which Luke felt to be a biblical expression (after Ez. **13**.10?).[1] καὶ σύ: καί only emphasizes the following pronoun, see on **1**.3. κάθη (Atticizing for κάθησαι: Bl.-Debr. § 100). κρίνων με; with this the court of enquiry changes into one of judgement. παρανομῶν κελεύεις: you offend against the law with your command: Bauer, *Wb* 1231; for the content reference is made to Lev. **19**.15: 'You shall do no injustice in judgement.'

VERSE 4: ἀρχιερέα τοῦ θεοῦ: the unusual expression is intended to emphasize the dignity of the man scolded by Paul.

VERSE 5: Since the High Priest presided over the Sanhedrin (Schürer II[3] 203), Zahn (763) assumed by way of explanation that Paul's words were meant ironically. But the tone (ἀδελφοί!) and the reference to Exodus **22**.27[2] presuppose that the words are meant seriously. Wendt (315) finds here a poor secondary source worked over. Correctly Overbeck (402): Luke takes the opportunity 'to set up Paul as the pattern of obedience to the law'.

VERSE 6: γνοὺς κτλ.: Preuschen (133) gives Paul credit for such a statement as an adroit chess-move: Knopf (641) also finds the Apostle's procedure 'very clever', and Nestle has referred to Mt. **10**.16 in the margin of the text: 'Be wise as serpents and without guile as doves.' On the other hand Wendt (316) correctly emphasizes: 'It would neither have been worthy of Paul' nor would 'the members of the Sanhedrin have allowed themselves to be led astray'. Paul does not maintain here that he *was* a Pharisee, but that he *is* and that for this reason alone he is accused; this is not compatible with Phil. **3**.5ff. ἐλπίδος (cf. **28**.20): what is meant is the Messianic hope (fulfilled in Jesus). ἀνάστασις νεκρῶν: for Paul/Luke naturally it is above all the resurrection of Jesus which is in mind.

VERSE 7: στάσις: Paul is reproached in **24**.5 with provoking στάσεις among all the Jews. But as here becomes clear, these are not riots, but only —even though vehement—theological disagreements![3]

VERSE 8f.: That the Sadducees (Luke omits the article before the name) deny resurrection, spirit and angel,[4] but the Pharisees recognize all[5] these, prepares for the Pharisaic acknowledgement that the appearance of Christ

---

[1] Wellhausen 47f. correctly rejects Smend's explanation (quoted by E. Schwartz, *NGG* 1907, 297) that here, following Ez. **13**.10–15, the imminent collapse of the theocracy is proclaimed—who could discover this meaning without a commentary? Reference to Mt. **23**.27 also does not fit.

[2] 'You shall not revile God, and a ruler of your people you shall not curse.' The Midrash interpreted אלהים of the judges; Bill. II 766f.

[3] Cf. v. 29.

[4] 'The denial of angels and spirits by the Sadducees cannot be substantiated from Jewish sources, but entirely corresponds to their this-worldly religion', Bill. II 767. But how could they deny the angels who appear in the Torah which they recognized?

[5] On ἀμφότερα = 'everything' see above on **19**.16.

outside Damascus (**22.**7ff.!) was a reality: a spirit or angel has spoken to Paul.[1] εἰ κτλ.: Bl.-Debr. § 482; the principal clause—e.g. 'what can one object to that?'—is omitted. ℵ supplies: μὴ θεομαχῶμεν.

VERSE 10: The tribune has the guard (= στράτευμα: *Beg.* IV 290) come down from the citadel to protect Paul from being torn to pieces: this pre-supposes that the tribune has at least one messenger with him.

VERSE 11: The appearance of Christ the following night is intended to give Paul new courage and the reader certainty that Paul actually did bear witness in Rome (before Caesar: **27.**24!). εἰς Hellenistic for ἐν: Bl.-Debr. p. 2, n. 1: § 205f., 218. The mention of Rome at the same time indicates the further course of affairs and makes Paul's appeal to Caesar appear as the given fact. 'The vision . . . resembles . . . those of **16.**9; **18.**9f.; **27.**23f.': Wendt 317. Tradition is not visible in these verses.[2]

This section shows Luke's manner of working and his point of view especially clearly. If we read it as an historical report then the persons act very strangely in an improbable and incomprehensible manner. This begins with the very fact that the tribune is afraid because he had had Paul bound and yet only releases him the next day. For we cannot with Schlatter (271) relate this 'binding' (**22.**29) to the binding for scourging: ἦν δεδεκώς un-doubtedly corresponds to ἐκέλευσεν δεθῆναι in **21.**33. Knopf (639) simply states the contradiction. Meyer and Baumgarten (quoted by Overbeck 397) have sought to understand it psychologically: the tribune first had to over-come a certain refractoriness within himself . . . Zahn has Paul released from the chains only the next morning, without any misgivings about the matter. Paul always wore chains, at the latest since his arrival in Caesarea, because now not only a murder attempt by the fanatical mob but also an attempt to free him by the Pharisaic party would have been possible (759f.)! That heightens the Lucan description of the Pharisees into the realm of the gro-tesque. Holtzmann (136f.) takes a way out used also elsewhere: he translates v. 30 'Because he had in mind to learn something more definite about the matter the next day . . .', he has the chains removed from Paul. But one cannot assign the two aorists ἔλυσεν and ἐκέλευσεν to two different days. Wendt (313f.) has only the heavy chains removed from Paul 'while the chaining to a soldier (see on **12.**6) which belongs to the *custodia militaris* remained in force'—an expedient which Overbeck (398) also accepts. But in **26.**29 it is presupposed that Paul is wearing chains and yet is not chained to a soldier! *Beg.* IV 285 interprets the passages in which Paul is described as δέσμιος (**23.**18; **25.**14; **28.**17) or δεδεμένος (**24.**27) to mean merely that he is in custody. From this Paul is released for interrogation before the High Council;

---

[1] On the pneuma concept cf. Luke **24.**39. According to Loisy (831) 'angel' here has the same meaning as in **12.**15.

[2] 'With the Sanhedrin trial . . . the vision of **23.**11 also falls': J. Weiss 43.

the Lex Julia forbids only chaining as a punishment but not handcuffing as a precaution during custody. But Luke was apparently of another opinion —the tribune indeed had not had Paul chained as a punishment. So research here is left stuck in an aporia.

But with this the difficulties of our section only begin. The tribune wants to know what the Jews have against Paul. He may indeed no longer interrogate the 'Roman' by torture but he could still question him. But he does not hit upon this idea. Instead he calls the Sanhedrin into session; according to Josephus *Ant.* XX 202 οὐκ ἐξὸν ἦν χωρὶς τῆς ἐκείνου (the governor's) γνώμης καθίσαι συνέδριον. But it would be naive to conclude from this on the basis of our passage that the commander of the Roman guard had authority to convene the Sanhedrin. There is, moreover, no point to this measure: the High Council was not present at the tumult in the Temple, with the exception perhaps of the Temple captain. If the tribune had conferred with him, that would have been useful. But he assembles the Sanhedrin and himself—unclean pagan that he is—attends the hearing. From v. 10 it appears that he had at least one messenger with him; Zahn (759 n. 46) even has the tribune accompanied by an appreciable number of soldiers, who stand guard before the place of assembly and then alarm the entire garrison of the Antonia!

The proceedings begin very strangely. Without being called upon by anyone, Paul begins to speak. Zahn (759 n. 46), it is true, concludes from **23**.1 that the tribune authorized and invited Paul to speak. The great scholar has overlooked the point that in that case the High Priest's procedure and the tribune's toleration of it become quite incomprehensible. Paul affirms that he has always had a good conscience. Thereupon the High Priest has him struck upon the mouth (according to Zahn by members of the court!) without the tribune protecting the Roman citizen. But perhaps that was not necessary, for Paul —he once wrote: λοιδορούμενοι εὐλογοῦμεν, I Cor. **4**.12—answers with a curse, which so takes the breath out of his opponents that they only weakly protest; he has the High Priest in front of him. Paul's answer, that he did not know that it was the High Priest, is so unbelievable that it has driven the theologians to desperate efforts: perhaps Paul was short-sighted and therefore did not recognize the High Priest (quoted by Jacquier 659) or in the confusion of voices he could not ascertain who gave the command to strike him on the mouth (so Jacquier's own explanation). A more elegant solution is offered by Zahn (763), who sees Paul here 'swinging the lash of irony'. Paul combines with his apology a proof of his learning in the scriptures. Entirely new and in contradiction to the beginning of the section is Paul's assertion, 'You sit here to judge me according to the law' and 'I stand before the court . . .' (v. 6). In this way the character of the scene has been transformed out of hand; it has become a trial, and Paul must defend himself. But on what account? Not because of the incident in the Temple, but—so he sees the situation and defends himself accordingly—because he is an arch-Pharisee and advocates the Pharisaic doctrine of the resurrection of the dead and the Messianic hope. This statement works like the apple of Discord: Pharisees and Sadducees begin immediately to dispute vehemently with one another, as if they had not already worked together for many years in the High Council and sufficiently knew their theological differences. Moreover both parties knew well enough that Paul's attitude to the law was unacceptable to them, and that it was precisely this which brought on him the deadly enmity of Judaism. Hence the way in which the Pharisees here appear as defenders of Paul and even justify the Christophany outside Damascus is an historical impossibility. The *pro et contra* takes on such a form that the tribune has to have the guard come down from the Antonia, for 'the excited taking of sides for or against Paul' (as Wendt 317 at once aptly and comically describes it) 'manifests itself in a tug-of-war in which he was in danger of being pulled apart'. Fortunately the troops still appear in time to snatch Paul away from the *rabies theologorum* and bring him back to the peace of the barracks. It is not surprising that F. C. Baur, Zeller, Overbeck, Spitta, Jüngst, Wendt, Preuschen and Loisy have refused to credit the author here and that for Beyer 'the obviously one-sided light and the mockery of this picture of the proceedings' is only 'fully comprehensible and tolerable' if Paul once 'with biting scorn narrated his appearance before the High Court' (138). We have not yet considered at all such details as that the tribune would perhaps have understood scarcely anything of the Aramaic proceedings (hence Zahn has them conducted in Greek: 759 n. 46). Wendt would delete the entire scene as an insertion; then v. 11f. also would fit better. For at the trial before the Sanhedrin Paul did not bear 'witness for the Lord before Jerusalem'. This was also the opinion of J. Weiss (43). But he preferred to ascribe v. 11f. also to 'the editor' . . .

But the perspective in which our section was here seen is not that of Luke. He does not mean to give any meticulous account of the proceedings. For him the charge against Paul is not a matter of the past, but the burning issue of contemporary Christianity. Hence he has already in **21.28** treated the charge of defiling the Temple as an afterthought and set the teaching against the Jewish people, the law and the Temple as the real accusation in the foreground. Hence in **22.22** he makes the crowd break out in furious indignation on account of the direction for the Gentile mission. That Christianity has separated from Judaism, from the true religion, this is the real accusation against which Luke wants to defend Christianity in the person of its πρωτοστάτης (**24.5**) Paul.

Luke the narrator does not advance this justification in a theological exposition, but in a series of lively and attractive pictures and scenes of which our section is the first or—if we reckon Paul's speech to the crowd in Chapter 22 as such—the second. As an author and narrator Luke knows about the laws of climax. Discussion on the highest level—i.e. before governors and kings—may **not** stand at the beginning; it can only form the crowning conclusion. The proceedings before the tribune can only be a curtain-raiser, which however already allows the reader to experience a dramatic conflict. If however it is to come to this, then the proceedings before the High Court cannot bear a merely informative character: here already it must be made clear that Paul—unlawfully!—stands as the accused before the representatives of Judaism. That in the process the character of this assembly becomes obscure is something Luke has to accept. To him the confusion which results is not at all unwelcome; it helps to illustrate his thesis that Judaism—at least theoretically—on this question does not form a unity.

The tribune, who indeed does not see to the bottom of the situation but is only seeking an explanation of it, naturally does not come into consideration as leader of the assembly. But neither does the High Priest—he and Judaism with him will strive in vain up to Chapter 25 to get the wheel in their hands. The central figure in the scene can only be Paul, and so Luke has him boldly begin with the statement that up to this day he has walked before God with a good conscience. Paul cannot here again recount the story of his life—Luke will in any case make use of it once again in Chapter 26. Hence in this one sentence he describes the continuity of Judaism and Christianity, as it comes to light unbroken with exemplary clarity in Paul himself. That as a result the High Priest has Paul struck upon the mouth is thus not so meaningless as at first appears: if Paul is correct in this sentence then the High Priest, and the whole Jewish charge which he represents, has lost his case. That this is actually the situation is made clear in Paul's answer: with a prophetic statement Paul proclaims to the proud Ananias the divine justice which the swords of the λῃσταί executed (Jos. *Bell.* II 441ff.). But at the same time this exchange makes clear the other point: from this tribunal Paul could never expect justice. He could never entrust his fate to it. So here the way is already prepared for that decision which will come in Chapter 26: the appeal to Caesar.

To develop the situation along these lines presented a difficult task for the author. The great conflict might not yet break out here, where the person of the High Priest was involved. Hence Luke lets the reaction of the 'bystanders' appear surprisingly tame, and Paul make an answer just as surprisingly pacific; in so doing he takes the opportunity to bring out in appropriate fashion Paul's biblical knowledge and obedience to its precepts. Luke's readers were not so critical as we and therefore did not feel Paul's answer 'meagre', as Bauernfeind (257) has called it, expressing the modern feeling. Now that this conflict is settled, Luke has made room for the really decisive action. Again Paul takes the initiative. He shouts only a single sentence to the assembly (**24.**21 proves that this sentence does not summarize longer statements): 'I am a Pharisee, from a strict Pharisaic family; I stand before the court on account of the (Messianic) hope and the resurrection of the dead.'

No proof should really be necessary that here it is not the historical Paul who speaks. That he 'was circumcised on the eighth day, from the γένος 'Ισραήλ, of the tribe of Benjamin, according to the law a Pharisee . . . and according to the righteousness of the law blameless', all that he 'considered as dung' that he might win Christ (Phil. 3.5–9). Just as little should there be need for proof that Luke does not here want to show a clever rabbinic trick by his hero. He is concerned about something much higher, namely the truth that the bridges between Jews and Christians have not been broken. It is Luke's honest conviction that fellowship between Pharisaism and Christianity is in the end possible: the Pharisees also hope for the Messiah, await the resurrection of the dead. In this they are at one with the Christians. Their mistake is only that in this hope and faith they are not consistent where Jesus is concerned. The resurrection of Jesus, and his Messiahship thereby attested, are not contrary to the Jewish faith.

This Luke does not express in a cool statement, but makes it visible in a stirring mob scene. Judaism affords room in itself for two movements: for the one, resurrection, spirit and angel are realities of faith, for the other they are not. The first group, then, of necessity stands on the side of the Christians, i.e. here Paul, and must speak up for him: 'We find nothing objectionable in this man!' Indeed the very appearance of Christ outside Damascus admits of a Pharisaic interpretation.

With this Paul's apology—in which he himself has spoken only a single sentence—comes to a happy end. The wild tumult between Pharisees and Sadducees shows that Christianity is a matter within Judaism, even if it gives rise to such strong passions. But at the same time it allows the author to break off the scene: the company of guards summoned from the Antonia—and therefore Rome!—saves Paul's life. The fact that Paul will not submit himself to the verdict of this Jewish court because there he would only be torn apart, has now been made clear even to the most imperceptive reader.

What understood as a historical report would be contradictory and improbable has thus as the illustrative composition of the author become a meaningful unity.

58

ACTS 23:12–35
CONSPIRACY AGAINST PAUL.
TRANSPORT TO CAESAREA

¹² When day came, the Jews hatched a plot and bound themselves by a sacred oath neither to eat nor drink until they had killed Paul. ¹³ Now there were more than forty who had made this oath together. ¹⁴ They went to the High Priests and elders and said, 'We have bound ourselves with a sacred oath to partake of nothing until we have killed Paul. ¹⁵ Do you now with the council present a petition to the tribune that he send him down to you, as if you wanted to investigate his case more exactly. But we are ready to kill him before he comes near (you).' ¹⁶ The son of Paul's sister heard about this ambush, went up and entered the barracks, and told Paul about it. ¹⁷ Paul called one of the centurions and said, 'Take this young man to the tribune, for he has something to tell him.' ¹⁸ The centurion took him, led him to the tribune and said, 'The prisoner Paul called me and asked me to bring to you this young man, who has something to say to you.' ¹⁹ The tribune took him by the hand and led him aside and asked, 'What is it that you have to tell me?' ²⁰ And he said, 'The Jews have agreed to ask you to send Paul down to the Council early in the morning in order to learn something more exact about him. ²¹ But do not listen to them! For more than forty men are lying in ambush for him and they have vowed neither to eat nor drink until they have killed him. Now they are ready, waiting for your consent.' ²² The tribune now dismissed the young man, commanding him to tell no one 'that you have related this to me'. ²³ And he called two centurions and said 'Get two hundred soldiers ready to march to Caesarea, along with seventy horsemen and two hundred lightly armed men, by 9 o'clock tonight', ²⁴ and to provide donkeys for Paul to ride and take him safely to Felix the governor. ²⁵ Meanwhile he wrote a letter with the following contents: ²⁶. 'Claudius Lysias to his Excellency the governor Felix, greetings! ²⁷ This man whom the Jews had seized and were about to kill I rescued, coming upon them with the guard, since I learned he is a Roman. ²⁸ And since I wanted to learn the reason for which they accused him, I brought him into their Council. ²⁹ I found him accused on account of controversial questions of their law, but no charge deserving of death or prison. ³⁰ When it was reported to me that there would be a plot against the man I

immediately sent him to you, and have asked his accusers to appear before you against him.' [31] The soldiers now took Paul according to orders and brought him to Antipatris by night. [32] On the following day they let the horsemen go on with him, and returned to the barracks. [33] These horsemen came to Caesarea and delivered the letter to the governor and presented Paul also to him. [34] When he had read the letter and had asked from what province he was, and learned that he came from Cilicia, he said, [35] 'I will hear you when your accusers have arrived.' He commanded him to be guarded in the praetorium of Herod.

Bibliography:

H. J. Cadbury, 'Roman Law and the Trial of Paul', *Beg.* V, 1933, 306–12; Trocmé 1957, 104; Williams 1957, 251f; Conzelmann 129–31; G. Stählin 289–93.

VERSE 12: 'The Jews[1] hatched a plot'[2] by binding[3] themselves with the oath 'I will be cursed if . . . '. ἕως οὖ with subjunctive: Bl.-Debr. § 383, 2.

VERSE 13: συνωμοσία[4]: a synonym of συστροφή. More than forty fanatics[5] are thus determined to kill Paul. But for this he has to be lured out from the barracks.

VERSE 14: οἵτινες (see Bl.-Debr. § 293, 3 also appendix) actually introduces a main sentence here. The fact that the scribes[6] are not mentioned does not prove that the conspirators turned only to the Sadducees.[7] μηδενὸς γεύσασθαι: thus fasting in the strictest form: a sign that for them it was completely serious.[8]

VERSE 15: ἐμφανίσατε: 'communicate officially' (Bauer, *Wb* 510f.).[9] μέλλοντας διαγινώσκειν ἀκριβέστερον: 'as people who wish to understand

---

[1] 𝔓48 L 𝔖 improve with 'some of the Jews'; v. 13 however explains the general statement.

[2] How *Beg.* IV 290 comes to the assertion that in LXX συστροφή ('meeting') appears to be synonymous with συνωμοσία (which does not occur in LXX at all) and ἐνέδρα is not evident. The meaning 'riot' or 'insurrection' will not be present here.

[3] See Bill. II 767; IV 293–333. Cf. Jerome *de vir. ill.* 2.

[4] 𝔓48 syh replace the expression by ἀναθεματίσαντες ἑαυτούς probably because they understood the text like Overbeck 406: 'the plot originated from Judaism in general, forty men pledged themselves to carry it out.'

[5] 'After πλείων . . . before numbers "than" is omitted': Bl.-Debr. § 185, 4.

[6] They are named in Lk. 22.52; Acts 4.23; 25.15; see also Mt. 21.23; 26.3, 47; 27.1, 3, 12, 20.

[7] According to Sanh. 82a the Sanhedrin ought not to support such zealots: Bill. II 767.

[8] The supposition that if the plot failed they would have to starve is in error: the rabbis knew how one gets out of such a vow.

[9] Also 23.22; 24.1; 25.1, 15; here = 'to render a report'.

his case more exactly'; this appears to agree with the wishes of the tribune.[1] πρὸ τοῦ κτλ.: thus the council will not be blamed. The awkward formulation is replaced by a more polished one in the Western text.[2]

VERSE 16: Where Paul's nephew learns about the ambush (which in one of the narrow streets of Jerusalem offered prospects of success) is not reported.[3] Schlatter conjectures, 'In their bold defiance the conspirators had not been sufficiently careful to keep their plan a secret' (280). Edersheim has a different conjecture (*Jewish Society and Life*, 227). Luke describes Paul's custody as so light that he can receive visitors without question. That he was fettered to a soldier with a chain (so Overbeck 407) is not here presumed: the nephew can indeed tell him the secret message.

VERSE 17: The narrative continues in the broadest style, increasing the suspense. The young man cannot go of himself directly to the commandant; a sergeant-major whom Paul—one might almost say—details for the duty, takes him there.

VERSE 18: The centurion carries out orders and reports. Luke easily varies his expressions: ἀπαγγεῖλαί τι in v. 17—τι λαλῆσαι here; in v. 19 again ἀπαγγεῖλαι.

VERSE 19: The tribune (Schlatter translates 'colonel' but our military ranks do not exactly correspond to the Roman) takes the young man[4] by the hand—'never was a tribune so amiable': Loisy 840. ἀναχωρήσας κατ' ἰδίαν: the tribune acts as if he already knew that it is a matter of strict secrecy.

VERSE 20: οἱ Ἰουδαῖοι (the young man himself is one: this shows it is really the author speaking [Loisy 841]) as in v. 12 is again at first general: here the conspirators and the Sanhedrin are meant.—Luke cannot simply repeat the whole story schematically. συνέθεντο: 'have come to an agreement', cf. Lk. 22.5. αὔριον: this is a new detail added. Luke thinks of the scene as occurring in the afternoon. μέλλων despite good evidence is to be rejected in favour of μέλλον;[5] the Sanhedrin allegedly wants to ascertain the facts exactly (ἀκριβέστερον for the positive).

---

[1] διαγινώσκειν is in itself a term. techn. of law (Bauer, *Wb* 362): the judicial decision. But Bauer's translation 'by careful investigation to bring his case to a decision' might not quite do justice to the Lucan expression, which contains echoes of the γνῶναι ἀκριβέστερον motif; moreover, the council does not have to decide the case at all.

[2] 'We pray you: (kindly) do this for us: assemble the Sanhedrin and inform the tribune.' The end of the verse is expanded in 614 sy^hmg by: 'even if we must die in the act'; *licet oporteat ad nos mori* (h). Wendt (318) correctly recognized the use of ἕτοιμοι τοῦ as LXX Greek.

[3] Zahn (751) conjectures that Paul's sister was considerably older than he, perhaps already born before the involuntary move to Tarsus, and had remained in Palestine. Paul might have grown up in her house in Jerusalem from his eighth or ninth birthday. This little romance has been involuntarily destroyed by van Unnik's work *Tarsus or Jerusalem* (see above on 22.3).

[4] B νεανίαν, ℵ A 81 νεανίσκον.

[5] μέλλων B A 81, μέλλον ℵ 33; confusion of the o-sounds frequently occurs: *Beg.* III 219.

VERSE 21: ἐνεδρεύω τινά: to lie in wait for someone. τὴν ἀπὸ σοῦ ἐπαγγε-λίαν: 'your consent'.[1]

VERSE 22: μὲν οὖν: transition to a new scene; see on 1.6, cf. 23.31. The tribune believes the information without question. ἐνεφάνισας κτλ.: transition to direct speech as at 1.4 and often, in order to enliven the scene (against Well-hausen 49, who sees an awkwardness here). V. 24 reverts to indirect speech.

VERSE 23: The text of B presupposes two hundred heavily armed infantry, seventy horsemen and the two hundred enigmatic δεξιολάβοι.[2] ἀπὸ τρίτης ὥρας τῆς νυκτός: the troops are ready to march from 9.0 p.m.

VERSE 24: κτήνη: riding animals (Bauer, *Wb* 900), see Lk. 10.34. Knopf (641) seems to assume that Paul marched with the infantry to Antipatris and can only here mount an ass. According to Zahn (769) Paul rides on an ass or mule, which had to be changed in Antipatris since it could no longer keep up the fast pace of the cavalry on the road from there to Caesarea, unless the plural is to be explained to mean that Lysias also provided Paul with a pack animal for his baggage . . .

VERSE 25: Zahn (770f. n. 66) vacillates as to whether the letter was com-posed in Greek or only the translation from the Latin preserved. Bauern-feind (260), less confidently, hopes the contents were made known to Paul. Wellhausen 48: Luke himself composed the letter 'and in the process took into consideration the Sanhedrin session of 22.30–23.10, which in reality scarcely took place'.[3]

VERSE 26: Κλαύδιος Λυσίας: 'the good old Greek name Lysias (. . . in v. 26 as a cognomen after the nomen gentile), and the circumstance that he had purchased his Roman citizenship, precludes a Latin origin' (Zahn 770 n. 66). κράτιστος = *egregius* corresponds more or less closely to our expression 'Excellency'.

VERSE 27: The commentaries commonly emphasize that the tribune has not entirely kept to the truth. But Luke had no reason to depict the tribune

---

[1] Jacquier 667: 'une périphrase du génitif'; the possessive pronoun σός is on the point of disappearing.

[2] According to Wendt (319) they are first mentioned in the seventh century in Theo-phylactus Simocatta 4, 1 and in the tenth century in Constantine VII Porphyrogennetos (*De themat.* 1, 1) beside bowmen and slingers, presumably as light-armed infantry. Schlatter (281) has the neighbourhood of the road covered by 'marksmen armed with slings' and any sudden attack thereby thwarted—as if these marksmen could have advanced in the pitch-dark night in the pathless country on either side of the road at the pace of the column! Lake conjectures that it means two hundred led horses (!): *Beg.* IV 293. The Western text seems to speak only of one hundred horsemen and two hundred δεξιολάβοι (h: *pedites*): *Beg.* III 221. Here the numbers are at least somewhat reduced. Beyer (137) however considers the high figure not entirely improbable, in view of the turbulent situation. But in this situa-tion of unrest the tribune would certainly not have sent half the garrison away to escort only one prisoner. For the rest, the Western text has undergone a novelistic expansion: Lysias provides the heavy protection out of anxiety that in the case of an attack on Paul he may be accused of having been bribed by the Jews.

[3] For the epistolary style cf. P. Wendland, *Urchr. Literaturformen*,[2] 411f.

handling the truth rather freely; that would have devalued his testimony. Luke rather in this recapitulation of events provides the reader with the image which he is to retain: the general impression that the Roman State respected Paul's Roman citizenship from the beginning.[1] In itself μαθὼν ὅτι 'Ρωμαῖός ἐστιν could even be related to what follows. But v. 27 corresponds to 21.31–22.29 (Paul's speech to the people is here naturally passed over), v. 28 in contrast to the period from 22.30 to the present moment.

VERSE 28f.: Astonishingly the tribune has gathered from the confusion of the Sanhedrin session that Paul is politically innocent and accused only because of theological differences of opinion (cf. 18.15!). δεσμοί = prison. ἔγκλημα κτλ.: 'accusation of a crime punishable by death or imprisonment' (Bauer, *Wb* 428).

VERSE 30: μηνυθείσης ... ἔσεσθαι: for construction see Bl.-Debr. § 424: 'When it was reported to me that an attempt would be made upon the man's life'.[2] The tribune would of course have had to send Paul to the governor in any case, as soon as the council claimed him for its jurisdiction. ἔπεμψα: epistolary aorist considered from the standpoint of the recipient. παραγγείλας κτλ: this instruction the tribune could only transmit to the accusers when Paul was safely out of Jerusalem; otherwise all the secrecy of the departure by night made no sense. Actually this detail is intended for the reader, who now knows how the action continues. Luke adds it in the letter for the sake of simplicity.[3]

VERSE 31f.: A night march of 40 miles brings all those undertaking it to Antipatris in the morning. The narrator makes great demands upon the poor infantry. Zahn (773 n. 70) accords them recognition and comfort: 'That was an excellent performance for the footsoldiers, but more easily accomplished in the cool night of early summer than during the day.' Unfortunately this overlooks the fact that Luke makes the infantry set out immediately from Antipatris on the return march ... Evidently he has only an inaccurate conception of the geography of Palestine. In reality infantry protection was requisite—if at all, for the conspirators were thinking of an attack in one of the narrow streets of Jerusalem on the following day—only in the vicinity of Jerusalem.

VERSE 33: The cavalry bring Paul along with the letter to Caesarea, after a further ride of 25 miles (Preuschen 136) and deliver both to the governor, who receives them in person.

---

[1] There is every reason not to forget Paul Wendland's sentence (329) while reading Acts: 'The popular narrator does not burden his memory with reminiscences, he produces new motifs which further the specific action of the moment, without harmonizing the details of the individual parts. The analysis of the plays of Sophocles has indeed taught us that the poet can vary the presuppositions and conditions of the action for different acts, according as they are effective for the characterization of the persons and for motivation.'

[2] According to Preuschen 136 (appealing to Buttmann and Blass) two constructions are blended together: μηνυθείσης μοι ἐπιβουλῆς ἐσομένης and μηνυθέντος μοι ἐπιβουλὴν μέλλειν ἔσεσθαι.

[3] Later MSS. have also added the usual salutation ἔρρωσο: *Beg.* III 222.

VERSE 34f.: Felix immediately arranges a short hearing: he enquires about the accused's home province,[1] hears that it is Cilicia, but decides to take the case himself when the plaintiffs are on the spot. The governor lives in the 'praetorium of Herod'. The fact that Paul is lodged there makes Knopf (644) conclude that he was under house arrest. Loisy (848) however makes the point that in this palace there were also rooms for the guard and cells for the prisoners (cf. Phil. 1.13 and 4.22, where however it is not a question of Caesarea).

Luke has developed this scene to extraordinary breadth. Its compass far surpasses its significance. The Jewish conspiracy is narrated precisely and with emphatic repetition (vv. 12f., 14 and 20f.). That the conspirators will not eat or drink until they have killed Paul shows the reader how desperate they are and hence how great is the danger for Paul. That they may have an opportunity for murder, the Sanhedrin is to ask the tribune to send Paul to the council for further investigation; on the way he is to be attacked. The Sanhedrin agrees to the murder plan, without the sympathy for Paul which the Pharisees had so lately shown asserting itself. Bauernfeind (259) speaks of the 'breaking away of a small Pharisaic group'; but in the Council the Pharisees were the leading group. In reality the contradiction to the previous scene is easily explained if we remember how independently the several scenes stand side by side in Luke. He and his readers set store by attractive single pictures; they had not the slightest inclination for their critical evaluation. Hence Luke can employ a technique which is denied the modern historian and which is shunned even by modern narrators. In Chapter 25 Luke has once again employed the motif of the attempted murder. In his eyes the Council was filled with such a blind rage —cf. the story of Stephen—that it did not shrink even from becoming accessory to a murder. That the tribune after the experience which he has just had with this board would scarcely have sent his prisoner back into this den of thieves (Wellhausen 48) is not considered; here again it is plain how loosely one scene is attached to another.

The plot becomes known to a nephew of Paul—how, we may not ask; Luke relates circumstantially and vividly how this information by way of Paul and a centurion finally reaches the tribune. This Roman officer is a man of exemplary friendliness and courtesy: he takes the young man by the hand and leads him aside, so that their conversation cannot be overheard. For the Jews must not learn that their purpose has been discovered; otherwise they will devise a new murder plan. Then the anonymous nephew disappears again. Bauernfeind (259) thinks that if he originated from Christian fantasy,

---

[1] A trial could be held in the accused's province, in the province of the crime, or in the one where he had been captured.—ποίας does not refer to the distinction between imperial and senatorial provinces (so Wendt 321) but = τίνος, which is usually used only substantively: Bl.-Debr. § 298, 2.

Y

he would have been made a Christian. But Luke has—rightly—avoided touching on the ticklish theme of the attitude of the Jerusalem community towards Paul's trial.

Luke skilfully makes the murder plan the occasion for the tribune to send his prisoner quickly and secretly to the governor. Loisy (839ff.) correctly pointed out that the tribune had to send the Roman citizen Paul to Caesarea in any case when the Jewish authorities claimed for themselves the right to pass sentence on the prisoner: for such questions he was not competent. But in that this transfer of the prisoner is coupled with the conspiracy, a dreary matter of routine is transformed into a narrative full of breathless suspense; at the same time Luke could thus present the intervention of the Roman authorities on Paul's behalf in the brightest light. For the transfer of the prisoner by night half the Roman garrison is detailed (many commentators consider this a realistic description!), and constrained to a forced march which is not made any more tolerable by Wendt's conjecture (321) that they would have marched on into the forenoon. In reality (as Preuschen 136 already saw) the distance from Jerusalem to Antipatris was not exactly known to the author. So he makes the infantry start their return march immediately. More important than such realistic corrections is the recognition of what Luke here brings before the reader's eyes: now Rome is saving the Apostle's life for the third time already (**21**.32f., in the Temple, **23**.10 in the Sanhedrin)! How favourably it judges him comes out in the tribune's accompanying letter: he explains the proceedings before the council exactly as Luke wants it: Paul—the Roman citizen!—has done nothing which merited death or prison. His conflict with the Jews is rooted solely in inner-Jewish differences such as those between the Pharisees and Sadducees. Accordingly Paul is exonerated by the highest representative of Rome who has as yet had anything to do with his trial.

The short hearing by Felix (preparation for the trial to come in **24**.1ff.) shows this governor as an impartial and correctly-acting official. Anyone who simply presupposes in Luke the portrait of Felix painted by Tacitus and Josephus misinterprets the scene. Felix has the prisoner immediately brought before him, takes cognizance of the documents, and after a brief cross-examination decides to take over the trial himself. Paul is shown to his quarters—in this situation he cannot ask for more.

But this scene fulfils yet another purpose. The highest Jewish authority —as here becomes evident—is not concerned with Paul on a merely informative level; it is bent on a regular accusation. Its nature will only become clear in the sequel. Thus all the characters in the action have taken their positions: Rome (represented by the tribune and Felix) as the benevolent protecting power, the council as the enemy resolved to stop at nothing. Between the two stands Paul. What will become of him?

59
ACTS 24:1–23
THE TRIAL BEFORE FELIX

[1] Now after five days the High Priest Ananias came down with some of the elders and an advocate Tertullus. They presented to the governor evidence against Paul. [2] When Paul had been called, Tertullus began the charge with the following words: 'Since we have achieved much peace through you and since reforms have been effected in favour of this people through your provision at all times and in all places, we recognize it, most excellent Felix, with all gratitude. [4] That I may not weary you further, I ask you to hear us briefly in your kindness. [5] For we have found this man to be a pestilent fellow and a provoker of riots against all Jews throughout the world and a ringleader of the sect of the Nazoreans. [6] He has also sought to defile the Temple. Him we arrested. [8] From him you will yourself, if you examine him concerning all these things, learn why we accuse him.' [9] The Jews also joined in the attack, saying that it was so. [10] Paul however answered when the governor nodded to him, 'Since I know that you have for many years been a judge for this people I begin my defence with good cheer. [11] You may ascertain that it is not more than twelve days since I came up to Jerusalem to worship. [12] And neither in the Temple did they find me disputing against anyone or instigating a riot of the people, nor in their synagogues, nor in the city. [13] Also they cannot prove to you that of which they now accuse me. [14] But this I admit to you: according to that "Way", which these persons call a sect, I serve the God of our fathers, believing everything written in the law and the prophets, [15] having the hope in God which these also themselves await, that there will be a resurrection of the righteous and the unrighteous. [16] On that account I also exercise myself to have a clear conscience toward God and man in all things. [17] After many years I have come here to bring alms for my people and offerings.[18] While I was so engaged they found me purified in the Temple, not with a mob or a tumult— [19] some Jews from (the province of) Asia, who ought to be before you and accuse me if they had anything against me. [20] Or let these men themselves say what crime they found when I stood before the council, [21] other than that one sentence which I shouted as I stood among them, "On account of the resurrection of the dead am I brought before you today for trial."' [22] But Felix, who was accurately informed about the 'Way', put them off, saying, 'When the tribune Lysias

comes down I will decide your case.' [23] He commanded the centurion to keep him in custody, but to permit him liberties and not prevent any of his friends from serving him.

Bibliography:

Williams 252–6; Conzelmann 131–3; G. Stählin 293–7; C. R. Bowen, 'Paul's Collection and the Book of Acts', *JBL* 42 (1923), 49–59; H. F. Folsom, 'Paul's Collection for the Jerusalem Christians' (diss.), Southern Baptist Theol. Seminary, 1949; C. H. Buck, Jr., 'The Collection for the Saints', *HTR* 43 (1950), 1–29.

VERSE 1: 'After five days': since Paul's arrival in Caesarea.[1] κατέβη means the arrival of the Jewish delegation in Caesarea.[2] ῥήτορος: a lawyer familiar with Roman and Jewish law.[3] οἵτινες refers to the entire Jewish delegation. ἐμφανίζω τινὶ κατά τινος: to lodge a complaint with somebody against someone.

VERSE 2: κληθέντος (without αὐτοῦ B; Bl.-Debr. § 423, 6): Paul is meant.[4] ἤρξατο κατηγορεῖν: both the speech of accusation and the defence keep to a customary outline (Preuschen 137).[5] πολλῆς: πολύς at the beginning of a speech (see v. 10) or a document similar to an address (Hebr. **1**.1) was particularly favoured.[6] εἰρήνης: Felix had indeed (Josephus, *Bell.* II 253–63) had many λησταί[7] crucified and had suppressed disorder. But only a *captatio benevolentiae*—common at the outset of an address—could assert that he had given the Jewish people peace (or: salvation) and reforms (διορθώματα [Bauer, *Wb* 394]; the later reading is κατορθώματα: ordered conditions) and applaud his concern (πρόνοια).[8] τῷ ἔθνει τούτῳ: the Jewish people which here, by and before a heathen, is not called λαός (cf. v. 17).

VERSE 3: πάντη . . . πανταχοῦ . . . πάσῃ: the paronomasia beloved of the orators (Bl.-Debr. § 488, 1) which Hebr. **1**.1 also shows, 'in every way and

---

[1] So Overbeck 410, Preuschen 137, Wendt 322, Loisy 848, Bauernfeind 261.

[2] Loisy doubts that the High Priest accompanied them (849); the later reading (H L P S) 'with the elders' makes the entire council appear.

[3] Loisy 849: evidence for this usage Bauer, *Wb* 1458.

[4] In the papyri the report of court cases often begins with a genitive absolute; P. Oxy. 1204. 13 κληθέντος Πλουτάρχου (the accused) . . . εἶπε Ἰσίδωρος (his lawyer): *Beg.* IV 297.

[5] On the other hand it is wrong when Preuschen calls them 'rhetorical exercises in style'; they are very ingeniously devised for the purposes in view.

[6] E. Schwartz, *NGG* 1907, 294 and *Beg.* II 492f. offer further examples.

[7] The λησταί mentioned by Josephus were originally religious freedom fighters; but with time it became ever more difficult to tell where the religious partisan ceased and the outright robber began.

[8] Stephan Lösch (*ThQ* 112 (1931), 306–14) has demonstrated that the mention of the εἰρήνη, διορθώματα ('re-establishment of law') and the (secularized) πρόνοια ('providence'!) belong to the rhetorical technique of such addresses; cf. II Macc. **4**.6 ἄνευ βασιλικῆς προνοίας ἀδύνατον εἶναι τυχεῖν εἰρήνης, quoted by W. K. L. Clarke, *Beg.* II 75.

every place', belongs to what precedes. ἀποδεχόμεθα 'we acknowledge' (without an object; what is meant is the efforts of Felix). κράτιστε: see on **23**.26. μετὰ πάσης εὐχαριστίας: translate for example: 'This we acknowledge with all thankfulness.'

VERSE 4: ἐγκόπτω in the sense of 'weary' points to LXX:[1] so sy and arm. συντόμως: Preuschen quotes Lucian, *bis accus*. 26: 'But in order not to make a long speech, since much time has already elapsed, I shall begin with the accusation.' The following is only the quintessence of an actual address. ἐπιεικείᾳ: the kindness—this expression also is only a polite phrase.

VERSE 5f.: εὑρόντες: cf. Lk. **23**.2 in the accusation against Jesus; the passion story of Jesus is often echoed. Luke shows that as it happened to the Master so too with the disciple. λοιμός as an abusive term for an evil man already in Demosthenes XXV.80.[2] στάσεις: 'riot'. The expression is intended to create in the governor the impression of a political *seditio* (Preuschen 137). Paul is the πρωτοστάτης –'instigator', 'ringleader'—of the Nazorean[3] 'faction', 'sect' (αἵρεσις here, v. 14 and **28**.22 with an unfavourable nuance).

VERSE 6: Properly the main sentence ought to come now: 'Him we have seized.' Instead of this Luke, breaking the construction, has added a further relative clause. ὃς καὶ ... ὃν καί: see **1**.3. The Jewish κοινόω is here replaced before Gentiles by βεβηλόω (*Beg*. IV 299). The reproach of (merely attempted) desecration of the Temple falls into the background; it is mentioned again only in **25**.8.

VERSE 8: If the governor questions Paul (ἀνακρίνω as at **4**.19; **12**.19; **28**.18), he will be able to learn from him everything about which the Jews accuse him.[4] The idea that Paul under questioning will have to confess everything allows the speech to come to a conclusion.

---

[1] *ThWb* III 855 n. 1: with reference to Job **19**.2, Isa. **43**.23. Strictly the verb means 'to restrain'. It could therefore also be translated 'in order not to delay you in your business of government'—see Preuschen 137.

[2] The word λοιμός occurs already in I Sam. **25**.25 LXX. A relationship to the interpolated decree of I Macc. **15**.21 (so Wendt 323) cannot be proven; see on **9**.2.

[3] See above on **22**.8.

[4] That the governor would learn everything about which the Jews accused Paul when he questioned him seemed to the Western text (found among others in (E) e gig p syʰ Chrys) so foolish that it referred παρ' οὗ to Lysias and accordingly rewrote vv. 6–8: 'whom we seized and wanted to judge according to our law' (use of Jn. **18**.31?). 'The tribune Lysias however interfered' (so παρελθών according to *Beg*. IV 299) 'and took him away with great force out of our hands (v. 8), commanding his accusers to come to you.' Holtzmann (141) considered this text genuine, because Lucan expressions are present; Loisy (854) because it contradicts the Lucan presentation and therefore betrays a source. Preuschen (138) read out of it not only an original arrest of Paul by the Temple police, but also a subsequent session of the council disrupted by Lysias! In reality κελεύσας κτλ refers to **23**.30 and the preceding 'with great force' to **23**.29 in the Western text (ἐξήγαγον αὐτὸν μόλις τῇ βίᾳ). That is, the Western text presupposes the same chain of events as the normal text. It has only falsely assumed (influenced by κρίνων με **23**.3 and κρίνομαι **23**.6) that Lysias brought Paul to the council not merely for information but rather for a trial. The idea that Tertullus appealed to Lysias as a witness derives from **24**.22. There is therefore no trace here of a special source. The usual text, correctly understood, is quite straightforward.

VERSE 9: συνεπέθεντο (cf. LXX Ps. 3.7; Deut. 32.27): 'they joined in the attack'. 'But also the Jews': Tertullus is not thought of as one (Loisy 849).

VERSE 10: νεύω τινί: to nod to someone. ἐκ πολλῶν (see on v. 2) ἐτῶν (cf. Tacitus *Ann.* XII 54): 'A conventional expression without historical value' (*Beg.* IV 300).[1] ἀπολογοῦμαι: cf. 26.1, 24. It is the real catchword of these last chapters.

VERSE 11: 'Since you can learn' alludes to 'you can learn for yourself' in v. 8. '. . . that for me no more than' ('after πλείων before numerals "than" is omitted': Bl.-Debr. § 185, 4) 'twelve days are (passed) from the (day) (on which)': Paul counts only the days spent in Jerusalem: Schlatter 285 n.[2] ἀνέβην of the arrival in Jerusalem, like κατέβη 24.1 of the arrival in Caesarea: Overbeck 415. Paul was only twelve days 'in the country'—how can he have created a revolution? That in addition he spent some of these days in custody is not here taken into consideration—Luke does not dwell upon such trifles. προσκυνήσων: Paul came only as a devout pilgrim to Jerusalem!

VERSE 12: εὗρόν με: is the verb presupposed as far as πόλιν. The real charge against which Paul defends himself is that of στάσεις. Paul neither spoke with anyone in the Temple—as an alleged agitator—nor led an insurrection, an ἐπίστασις (cf. II Macc. 6.3) ὄχλου, nor did he appear in the synagogues or in the city.

VERSE 13: The opponents cannot prove their accusations now advanced by Tertullus. Paul has accordingly answered the charge of v. 5. κινοῦντα στάσεις—admittedly only for Jerusalem.

---

[1] Zahn (777), comparing Acts 6.15, considers the addition in sy^hmg to be the Western text. That Paul answers '*statum divinum assumens*' is clearly an expansion which agrees with the later legendary picture of Paul. To the term κριτήν E Ψ 614 gig have further added δίκαιον, because to them the *captatio benevolentiae* seemed too meagre. Luke's *captatio benevolentiae*, contained in the εὐθύμως (cf. 27.22, 25f.), does not degenerate into such mendacious flattery. On the other hand we may not simply register here the image of Felix which Tacitus *Hist.* V 9 indicates with the words *per omnem saevitiam ac libidinem ius regium servili ingenio exercuit.* Felix was certainly a brutal and unscrupulous upstart. But Luke here had still no reason to characterize him unfavourably.

[2] First day: arrival in Jerusalem (21.17); second day: negotiation with James and the elders (21.18); third - ninth days: the seven days of purification (21.27); tenth day: Paul before the council (22.30); eleventh day: discovery of the plot (23.12); twelfth day: transfer to Caesarea (23.32). Since this transfer begins about 9 o'clock at night, but the beginning of the day is set after the Jewish manner at 6 o'clock in the evening, the day of the transfer is the twelfth, even if Paul did not spend all of it in Jerusalem.

This explanation of Schlatter's is in our opinion the best, and to be preferred to that of B. Weiss according to whom the author has simply added together the seven days in 21.27 and the five days in 24.1. Wendt (325) seeks to get out of difficulty by having Paul arrested on the fifth day of the Nazirate. But this does not fit 21.27 and the regulation requiring sprinkling with the water of purification on the third and seventh day. Paul certainly did not go into the Temple more often than was absolutely necessary. According to Zahn (778f.) Paul counts only the days which he has spent as a Jew among Jews (!). But since this produces too short a period, he must then count in two days of the journey from Caesarea. This is a tortuous apologetic. In reality only days come into the reckoning on which Paul was free and could do what his opponents averred. This however would yield only nine days.

VERSE 14: Now he takes up the accusation πρωτοστάτην . . . αἰρέσεως. He concedes his membership of the ὁδός (contemptuously called a 'sect' by his opponents). But in so doing he serves (λατρεύω as in **27**.23) the 'paternal God', i.e. 'God of the fathers' translated into Gentile Greek,[1] and believes everything κατὰ τὸν νόμον (κατά τι can in Hellenistic Greek replace the genitive: Bl.-Debr. § 224, 1)[2] καὶ . . . ἐν τοῖς προφήταις γεγραμμένα. The prepositions are readily interchanged: κατά . . . ἐν. Paul does not go into the πρωτοστάτης of v. 5 in any special way.

VERSE 15: ἐλπίδα; here the hope of the resurrection of the righteous and the unrighteous—before the governor there is no mention of that of the Messiah.[3] αὐτοὶ οὗτοι: 'these themselves'; Bauer, *Wb* 1183 s.v. οὗτος 1 a ζ.

VERSE 16: ἐν τούτῳ: usually explained as 'for this reason' (Bauer, *Wb* 1183).[4] καὶ αὐτός: see on **1**.3. Because judgement is bound up with the resurrection Paul strives to have a blameless conscience (cf. Phil. **1**.10). διὰ παντός stands emphatically at the end. For συνείδησις see p. 637 n. 5.

VERSE 17: δι' ἐτῶν πλειόνων: 'after many years'; this frankly does not square with a visit to Jerusalem at **18**.22.[5] ἐλεημοσύνας[6] ποιήσων: it is only because we know about Paul's great collection from his letters that we recognize an allusion to it here; for Luke's readers that was not possible. That the collection was intended only for the Christian community and not for 'his people' is likewise an obstacle which cannot be removed if we are looking here for absolutely reliable historical statements. The προσφοραί cannot properly be the Nazirite sacrifices, since Paul could not foresee these:[7] Holtzmann 142.

VERSE 18f.: But ἐν αἷς εὗρόν με ἡγνισμένον (cf. **21**.24, 26, in contrast to the alleged βεβηλοῦν of v. 6) proves that nevertheless they are meant. οὐ μετὰ ὄχλου καὶ θορύβου, 'not with a crowd and turmoil'—the expression στάσις is avoided. τινὲς δέ: the subject of εὗρον. The δέ expresses the antithesis which

---

[1] E.g. Sophocles, *Antigone* (Dindorf-Merkler) 838.

[2] Contrast Loisy 558: Paul is the perfect Jew, who regards even the Halakah according to the law as binding. But Luke always emphasizes the agreement with the Scriptures and not with the Halakah.

[3] According to Josephus *Bell.* II 163; *Ant.* XVIII 14 the Pharisees believed only in a resurrection of the righteous.

[4] Since ἀσκῶ is often combined with ἐν to indicate that in which a man 'exercises' himself, ἐν τούτῳ could anticipate the following infinitive, like εἰς τοῦτο in **26**.16.—Jacquier 684: 'dans cet état d'esprit' or (supplying χρόνῳ) 'in this interval till the resurrection'. Both interpretations are improbable.

[5] There is no indication in the text that many years have passed since the last collection journey—Nestle refers in the margin to **11**.29. See above pp. 68ff.

[6] Bill. IV 536–58 ('Die altjüdische Privatwohltätigkeit'); H. Bolkestein, *Wohltätigkeit und Armenpflege im vorchristlichen Altertum*, 1939.

[7] Spitta (270) finds 'in the words προσφοράς ἐν αἷς εὗρόν με ἡγνισμένον ἐν τῷ ἱερῷ at **24**.17, 18, which look back to **21**.24–6,' 'a very noteworthy addition of the redactor'. Jüngst 184f. has also rejected προσκυνήσων in vv. 11, 14c–16 and 20–21. So also J. Weiss 45f., for whom, as for O. Holtzmann, only the 'mention of the collection' inspires confidence! Hilgenfeld (*ZwTh* 1896, 536ff.) equally deletes vv. 17–21.

is not pursued (Zahn 781), that it was not Paul but the Jews from Asia Minor who fomented a θόρυβος. From the fact that these witnesses are not present Paul draws the conclusion that they could not give evidence: 'They ought to appear before you and make an accusation if they have anything against me.'[1] This deals with **21**.27–34—cf. θόρυβος there.

VERSE 20f.: Now Paul turns to **23**.2–10: 'or these here'—the Jerusalem delegation—'ought to say what crime they found when I stood before the council, other than . . .'[2] περὶ μιᾶς ταύτης φωνῆς: 'on account of this one sentence' (cf. Bl.-Debr. § 292). This confession of the Pharisaic belief (as Luke conceives it) was certainly no crime. With this demonstration of his Jewish orthodoxy Paul concludes his speech.

VERSE 22: ἀναβάλλω: legal term. techn., 'adjourn': Bauer *Wb* 92, who translates 'to intimate to them the decision to adjourn'. ἀκριβέστερον: 'very precisely' (*Beg* IV 304). ὁδός again = 'Christianity'. Whence Felix learned his precise information (cf. **25**.10) we are not informed. This knowledge is here mentioned as the motive for the adjournment. εἴπας Hellenistic for the classical εἰπών. ὅταν . . . καταβῇ, naturally from Jerusalem, which however is not named (cf. **18**.22).[3] διαγινώσκω: to give the decision.

VERSE 23: Paul remains in custody, but with ἄνεσις = 'with liberties';[4] moreover 'his friends' may serve him without restriction.[5]

The speeches of Tertullus and Paul do not offer any original text—they are much too short for that. Earlier scholars like Spitta (270,) Jüngst (184f.), Hilgenfeld (*ZwTh* 1896, 536ff.), Clemen (*Paulus* I, 315), J. Weiss (45f.), Wellhausen (50), Preuschen (137) and Loisy (854) assumed that here we have a source which has been worked over. Wendt (321f. n.), Bauernfeind (262) and Dibelius (*Studies* 7) went further and ascribed both speeches in form and content to the author of the book.

[1] The optative (classically incorrect: Bl.-Debr. § 385, 2) reduces the possibility latent in the conditional clause.—According to Jacquier 685 the δέ marks the contrast between the Jews of Asia Minor and the Jerusalem delegation, which did not find him etc.

[2] Here ἥ stands as if ἄλλο ἀδίκημα preceded it.

[3] Felix's knowledge of Christianity, which is here affirmed, does not betray any source (against Wendt 328), but is assumed by the author to explain the adjournment.— This is an adjournment *ad Kalendas Graecas*. Dibelius (*Studies* 7): 'The scene concludes in the same way as the similar argument between Antipater and Nicholaos before the emperor . . .: the matter is adjourned. The speeches are thus really intended for the reader.'

[4] ἄνεσις = *custodia liberior*, *Beg.* IV 304 against Jacquier. Here also οἱ ἴδιοι is explained with reference to **4**.23 as 'friends'. What is meant is not 'relatives', whom Ramsay and Zahn immediately bring on the scene, but rather the Christians.

[5] According to Zahn (783) Paul enjoyed visits from his friends, his sister and his nephew, his walks in a 'courtyard laid out with gardens', and if he wished, a bath, during which his chains were removed for half an hour . . . This description is modelled on Josephus *Ant.* XVIII 204 where Agrippa's imprisonment in Rome is described.—ἴδιος = 'a relative or friend': Moulton 89f. Felix cannot very well designate the Christians otherwise.

The detailed exposition (see notes to vv. 6–8, 17 and 22) has shown that references to sources in this section are either entirely questionable or simply do not remove the real difficulties because of which they were assumed. On the other hand all our troubles are removed if, with Wendt, Bauernfeind and Dibelius, we resolutely interpret the speeches as Lucan compositions.

The scene in Chapter 24 is distinguished from all the other 'apologies' in Acts by the fact that it makes Paul and his opponents engage in dialogue before the representative of Rome. First the plaintiffs, the Jews. The High Priest remains a silent figure. For the Jews the lawyer Tertullus is the sole spokesman. His speech is 'a masterpiece of . . . exquisite rhetorical artistry', as Stephan Lösch (*ThQ* 112 (1931) 317) has demonstrated. By its *captatio benevolentiae*, in proportion—three verses out of seven!—unusually broadly developed, it makes the reader immediately familiar with the atmosphere of such a trial (Dibelius, *Studies* 171). Through vv. 2–4 Luke allows us to detect that Tertullus knows his trade and is a dangerous opponent. Wellhausen's remark 'the orator makes no use of his eloquence' is ill-advised; Luke is much too clever to show the adroitness of the lawyer in the handling of the actual accusation. To bring the Apostle through to victory in the face of a detailed and finely structured accusation would have been possible (if at all) only in a much longer reply by Paul, and such a speech would have shattered the proportions of the chapter and required discussion of concrete details which in the course of the trial Luke more and more allows to disappear. Moreover the whole would have been love's labour lost, to the extent that the result would have appeared no different—adjournment of the trial for an indefinite period. Tertullus naturally flatters Felix—that every reader knew. But Luke would not have given so much space to it if he had wanted like Tacitus or Suetonius to depict Rome's representative as a degenerate and unscrupulous rascal. The accusation proper falls into two parts: 1. Paul is the champion of the Nazorean sect, who everywhere instigates riots among the diaspora Jews and thereby proves himself a 'pestilence' to society; 2. he has sought to defile the Temple. Such an accusation can in itself be verified by witnesses or by the confession of the accused. Tertullus makes use of both: he concludes by expressing the confidence that by an interrogation of Paul Felix will achieve a confession on all counts. The speech is thus quickly and elegantly ended. The witness motif is pushed through just as quickly: the members of the delegation step forward as the witnesses.

Now Paul gets the word from Felix. The mighty man—such a governor in his province was almost like an independent king, a demigod—does not speak: he only nods to the accused.

Paul too begins with a *captatio benevolentiae* (Luke was realistic enough not to exempt his hero from such a custom), but it is a very moderate one. Felix has already been 'for many years a judge for this people'; he therefore knows the circumstances. Paul consequently defends himself with confidence.

The Apostle first comes to grips with the accusation of στάσεις. Luke
has been very clever here. Paul demonstrates that in the few days of his
presence in Jerusalem he has nowhere appeared as a speaker, neither in the
Temple, nor in the synagogues nor in the city. His opponents cannot prove
their assertions to the contrary. Paul concedes—and with this he comes to
the next point—that he serves the 'paternal God' according to the 'Way'.
We see here why Luke so readily uses the concept of the 'Way'; this concept
describes the new religion of Jesus as an entity in itself and yet does not
divorce it from Judaism: indeed it is strongly reminiscent of such OT expressions as 'the ways of the Lord', which represented Judaism as the beloved
true religion. This way has not led Paul out of Judaism: he believes everything
in the law and the prophets (in **26**.22 this will become even clearer). For the
Christian Luke the death and resurrection of Jesus the Messiah are predicted
everywhere in the Scriptures (cf. Luke **24**.27!). Here also this thought stands
in the background. But as in **23**.6 only the general resurrection hope is
emphasized; its beginning in Christ is not specially mentioned. Hence Paul
can say he has the same hope as his opponents. Because Paul awaits the
resurrection of everyone (and with it the judgement!), he strives to have a good
conscience before God and man. With this sentence he prepares the way for
the third point about which he will speak: the alleged desecration of the
Temple. Paul the pilgrim came after many years to bring alms for his people
and offerings—the readers know of the Nazirate, and that is sufficient for
Luke. Engaged in this pious action he, a man just 'purified' (again only the
readers, who know **21**.24ff., understand this expression), was found in the
Temple by some Jews from Asia Minor, who are now not present and thus
cannot testify to anything. This point of accusation is consequently of no
account. The Jews present can only testify that Paul as a Pharisee confessed
the resurrection of the dead. Thus at the end there sounds once again the
theme which links Judaism and Christianity and emphasizes their essential
unity.

Both parties have spoken. Now comes the decision: Felix does not uphold the complaint, but announces his decision to adjourn. This he does
because he is very accurately informed about the 'Way'. Until he has heard
Lysias, the sentence is postponed. Paul goes into more lenient custody.
He has won a victory, although admittedly not a complete one. This is the
impression Luke wants the reader to carry away. For—and with this our
section takes its place in a larger context—this is the second of those four
appearances in which Paul after his apology has his innocence attested by the
judge concerned (cf. **23**.29; **25**.18f.; **26**.31f.). Luke could calmly allow the
tribune to proclaim the Apostle's political harmlessness, because his testimony
is effective only for the readers and not for the course of the trial. Festus and
Agrippa again can declare Paul innocent because he has already appealed to
Caesar and their decisions can have no further influence on the case—Paul

stands already before another judge. Here on the contrary such a declaration by Felix is not possible. If—as one would properly expect in view of his exact knowledge of Christianity!—he were to pronounce that Paul deserved neither death nor prison, then he would have to set him free. But Felix did not set him free. Hence Luke here had to be content with a compromise solution: adjournment and an alleviation of the imprisonment.

Paul does not speak to the charge that he is the leader of the Nazoreans —Luke has nothing against having Paul considered the representative of Christianity. For in these chapters it is not simply a matter of Paul the man but of the cause of Christ. The new faith—this is here again emphasized—is not a treason to the old. The hope of resurrection is the bond which holds the two together. That the Sadducees do not believe in the resurrection means only that it is a question within the Jewish faith in which Rome need not interfere, no matter where it breaks out. Thus—tacitly and indirectly—the question of the στάσεις in the diaspora is also dealt with.

What Luke actually learned about Paul's trial under Felix can only be conjectured. The most natural assumption is that a Jewish delegation with the lawyer Tertullus presented itself in Caesarea, but had to be satisfied with an adjournment. That Luke from such a notice could have created so colourful a story is the secret of his great art.

60
ACTS 24:24–27
FELIX AND PAUL

24 After some days Felix appeared with Drusilla his wife, a Jewess, and had Paul summoned, and he listened to him concerning the faith in Jesus Christ. 25 But when he spoke about righteousness and continence and the coming judgement, Felix became afraid and answered, 'For now you can go; at an opportune time I will have you called again.' 26 At the same time he was also hoping Paul would give him money. For this reason he frequently sent for him and conversed with him. 27 But when the two-year period was over, Felix was succeeded by Porcius Festus. Desiring to do the Jews a favour, Felix left Paul a prisoner.

Bibliography:

Lake, 'The Proconsulship of Festus', *Beg.* V, 1933, 464–7; Williams 250–2; Conzelmann 133; Stählin 292f.

VERSE 24: παραγενόμενος: Felix goes to that part of the praetorium where the prisoners lay (Wendt 329).[1] σὺν Δρουσίλλῃ: she was the youngest daughter of Agrippa I, born around A.D. 37.[2] τῇ ἰδίᾳ γυναικί: ἰδίᾳ is unemphatic and is not intended to allude to the questionable character of this marriage (Moulton 90). οὔσῃ Ἰουδαίᾳ: seems to provide the motive for Drusilla's interest in (the pious Jew!) Paul.[3] ἤκουσεν: this expresses a real interest in the Christian message, which Felix already knows well (v. 22).

VERSE 25: διαλεγομένου: 'preached' (see **17.2**). Righteousness, continence and the coming judgement are central themes in the post-apostolic

---

[1] According to Zahn (784) Felix had been temporarily away from Caesarea.

[2] She was the sister of Agrippa II and of Berenice (**25.**13), first engaged to Antiochus Epiphanes of Commagene (Josephus *Ant.* XIX 355), then married to King Aziz of Emesa, who complied with the condition of circumcision; Felix through the Jewish magician Atomos from Cyprus (see above on **13.**8) caused her to leave her husband and marry him, a Gentile (Jos. *Ant.* XX 141ff.). Her son Agrippa (and probably she herself) met his death in the eruption of Vesuvius in 79.—Cf. Schürer I⁴ 555, 557, 564, 577 (ET *History of the Jewish People in the Time of Jesus.*—Harnack, *Mission* II² 51 (ET *The Mission and Expansion of Christianity in the First Three Centuries*, 1908²). Achelis, *Das Christentum in den ersten drei Jahrhunderten* II, 366ff.

[3] The Western text explains this: 'who wished to see Paul and hear the word. Since he wanted to please her . . .': sy^hmg. See on v. 27.

preaching.[1] Here they are certainly very much to the point; moreover they are the reason why Felix's leaning towards Christianity comes to an end. ἔμφοβος γενόμενος: cf. the story of Herod Antipas and the Baptist (omitted in the Gospel of Luke) which with its striking parallels—the king and governor both won their wives in breach of a previous marriage—probably served as the model for our passage: ἐφοβεῖτο τὸν Ἰωάννην . . . καὶ ἡδέως αὐτοῦ ἤκουεν (Mk. **6**.20). τὸ νῦν ἔχον: 'for now', a Hellenistic expression which also appears in LXX: *Beg.* IV 305. καιρὸν μεταλαβών: 'to attain the favourable moment' = 'to find time': Bauer *Wb* 1011. μετακαλεῖσθαι like μεταπέμπεσθαι 'to have him brought', i.e. from prison into the room where Felix dealt with prisoners.

VERSE 26: χρήματα κτλ.: freeing prisoners for money was forbidden by the Lex Julia, but nonetheless took place (Josephus *Bell.* II 273; *Ant.* XX 215). Many commentators have concluded from this that Felix could assume Paul had ample funds at his disposal.[2] But the fact that this governor could be easily bribed was so well known that an author could use it as a motive without explanation. πυκνότερον: 'very often'; Bl.-Debr. § 244, 1 Appendix considers the meaning 'all the more frequently' also possible here. But Lucan usage suggests the elative sense.

VERSE 27: διετία = period of two years, cf. **28**.30. Here usually related to Paul's imprisonment and actually so intended by Luke, who is interested only in Paul's imprisonment: Harnack, *Beiträge* III 25f. (ET). But this does not exclude the possibility that a source spoke of a two-year term of office for Felix; see Intro. §§ 4, 8 pp. 70f. Πόρκιος Φῆστος: mentioned by Josephus *Bell.* II 271 and *Ant.* XX 182ff. Since no great scandals could be adduced from this able and honourable man's term of office, Josephus has very little to say about him. From this it has been concluded—in our opinion incorrectly—that he was in office only a short time (approximately a year); he died in Palestine. χάριτα (this form appears in the NT only here and in Jude 4): Hellenistic for χάριν. χάριτα καταθέσθαι (cf. **25**.9): 'to do a favour'. δεδεμένον: 'as a prisoner'.[3]

---

[1] Preuschen (140) refers to *Acta Pauli et Theclae* 5: Paul preached περὶ ἐγκρατείας καὶ ἀναστάσεως; *Actus Petri cum Simone* 2: abstinentiam, castitatem . . . iustitiam; *Acta Joh.* 84: Satan shall be far ἀπὸ ἐγκρατείας, ἀπὸ δικαιοσύνης.

[2] In this connection Zahn (786) and others bring in the great collection, of which Luke has never spoken in Acts (see on **24**.17). Bauernfeind (263), Bornhäuser (*Studien z. Apg.* 151), *Beg.* IV 305, Schlatter (290) likewise think that Felix has heard about the collection. Ramsay (*St. Paul* 312) considers it possible that Paul's family were reconciled with him and now supported him, so that he could appear as a well-to-do man (according to Ramsay Paul had two slaves to wait upon him!), or that Paul during the time in Caesarea came into an inheritance (!).

[3] Overbeck 425: 'The *custodia libera* (v. 23) was changed to the *militaris*'—but the text says nothing of this. Holtzmann 143: 'bound with a chain to the guard'. But Luke does not want to emphasize this feature; he is concerned to describe Paul's condition in general. It is senseless to take **26**.29 to mean that Paul was chained to a soldier during his speech.— The Western text replaces the consideration for the Jews (which Felix according to the

Even a critical scholar like Spitta (280ff.) considered this scene a constituent part of the 'source'—the good source A!—and that means he thought
to find in it an apposite tradition. Other scholars, like Jüngst, Clemen and
Hilgenfeld—to say nothing at all of Harnack (*Beiträge* III 181; ET)—have
followed him. But then the conduct of Felix—as Overbeck (422f.) already
proved—is anything but probable. That he himself appeared in order to
hear from Paul something about faith in the Messiah Jesus contradicts all
Tacitus and Josephus have reported about this man. If we try—with Bauernfeind (263)—to get round the difficulty by seeing in the Jewess Drusilla the
real driving force, we can indeed appeal to v. 24, also to the 'ladies of society'
in Acts 17.4, 12, and finally—with Zahn (787)—to the legend of Pilate's wife,
but scarcely to the real Drusilla. By the fact that she broke off her marriage
to King Aziz of Emesa and married the heathen Felix, who had a brilliant
career in prospect, she revealed how little the Jewish religion bound her. But
if we make curiosity the motive which impelled her, then we miss the tenor of
the narrative. This has often happened with this section in the history of
exegesis.

According to v. 24 Felix manifests a real interest in the Christian proclamation. He does not come to gather information for the further progress
of the trial or to put Paul in a generous frame of mind—anyone who assumes
with Bauernfeind that Felix had designs on Paul's money from the beginning
(263) does not do justice to the evidence of the text, as Overbeck (414 n. 2)
had already seen. But Felix's willingness to listen has its limits: the point at
which the sermon touched upon his own conscience. That is why he breaks
off his visit. So far the Lucan picture of Felix is not indeed compatible with
that presented by Tacitus and Josephus, but it is uniform. Now, however, it is
related that he returns very often because he hopes for a lucrative bribe.
Certainly many governors were open to bribery, and Felix probably more so
than others. But the man who visits Paul to hear about Jesus and the man who
visits Paul to see his money are not one and the same. The Felix who was
partial to Paul and Christianity has disappeared, and is replaced by the Felix
of Tacitus and Josephus (without Luke having read one line of them!). It is
consonant with this that on his departure he leaves Paul in prison, to make the
Jews well-disposed to himself.

This contradiction also can admittedly be resolved by a reference to the
unfathomable enigma of the human soul. But before we mount this heavy

---

evidence of Josephus did not have) by consideration for the Jewess Drusilla (614 sy^hmg:
Beg. III 227); here it seems to be assumed that Drusilla took amiss Paul's sermon on
righteousness and continence. Zahn (787) on the other hand is convinced that Drusilla 'did
not approve of her husband's unprincipled conduct'. When he speaks of her 'undenied
attachment to the Jewish faith', he forgets that she παραβῆναι ... τὰ πάτρια νόμιμα πείθεται
and married the Gentile Felix (Jos. *Ant.* XX 143), and if Zahn cannot but 'remember Pilate's
wife' that is still no proof.

artillery, which puts an end to all discussion, we ought to reflect that this contradictory portrayal becomes immediately comprehensible when we consider the major lines of Luke's presentation. Felix was the second of the four great witnesses for the Apostle's innocence. This witness was only of value if the governor at least to begin with was not described as the powerful but unscrupulous and cunning man which according to Tacitus and Josephus he was, but instead appeared as a correct official whose knowledge of the facts made him well-disposed. Hence Luke at first kept all the unfavourable features out of his picture, although he knew them (as v. 25 betrays and 26f. proves). Indeed he even ventured to go a step further and allow the Apostle to achieve a great success: Felix—together with his consort—is genuinely interested in Paul's preaching of Christ. Paul almost succeeded in converting the procurator Felix, as he converted the procurator Sergius Paulus and as he will almost succeed in converting King Agrippa II (**26**.28)!

With this however the point is reached at which the author has to swing the tiller over and take another tack if Paul's further destiny is not to become an incomprehensible riddle (this sudden change Overbeck 414 n. 2 did not understand). Probably the legend of King Herod's relationship with the Baptist here served him as a model. In that story also we find traits which meet us here: the king gladly listens to the prophet and returns again and again to him (notice the imperfect ἤκουεν Mk. **6**.20). But at the same time the preaching arouses his fear because it reveals his guilt. That Felix nevertheless still returns Luke explains not by a secret yearning for Christ, but by the prospect of money. Many commentators (cf. above, n. to v. 26) have honestly endeavoured to provide Paul with this money or at least find a reason for Felix's expectations. But for the motive of extortion Luke had no need to explain Paul's financial status. The governor was greedy for money, as governors are—that every reader understood. At the moment when Felix is recalled, however, this motive loses its force. The reader asks himself why Paul is not now finally set free, when the governor no longer has any advantage from his imprisonment and is convinced of his innocence. But Felix *had* a reason for not setting Paul free, the narrator answers: he wanted to put himself in good standing with the Jews and therefore sacrificed the man who was recognized as innocent. Paul would have been set free if the matter had gone according to law and justice and the base egoism of the judge had not held the upper hand.

We have referred in the Introduction (§ 4,8) to the possibility that in the tradition used by Luke what was meant by διετία was that after two years in office Felix was succeeded by Festus. Luke did not understand this statement in this way, but related it to Paul, in whose arrest alone he had any interest. He found an explanation for this long period of imprisonment on the assumption that Felix by delaying the trial wanted to extort a ransom.

61

ACTS 25:1–12
THE APPEAL TO CAESAR

[1] When Festus had arrived in the province, he went up after three days to Jerusalem from Caesarea, [2] and the chief priests and the leaders of the Jews laid before him denunciations against Paul and asked him [3] if he would do them a favour and have Paul summoned to Jerusalem, intending to lie in ambush in order to kill him on the way. [4] Festus answered that Paul was being held in custody in Caesarea, and he himself intended to go (there) in a short time. [5] 'Those in authority among you,' he said, 'let them go down with me and accuse him, if the man has anything bad on his conscience.' [6] After he had spent no more than eight or ten days among them, he went down to Caesarea and on the following morning he sat down on the judge's seat and ordered Paul to be brought. [7] When he had appeared, the Jews who had come down from Jerusalem surrounded him, bringing forward many serious charges which they could not prove, [8] while Paul defended himself: 'I have committed no crime either against the law of the Jews or against the Temple or against Caesar.' [9] Festus however wanted to do the Jews a favour and answered Paul and said, 'Will you go up to Jerusalem and submit to trial on these charges before me?' [10] But Paul said, 'I stand before the judgement seat of Caesar, where I must be tried. I have done no wrong in any way to the Jews, as you very well know. [11] If now I am guilty and have done something deserving death, I do not shrink from death. If however there is nothing to the matters of which they accuse me, then no one can surrender me to them: I appeal to Caesar!' [12] Festus then conferred with his advisers and answered, 'You have appealed to Caesar—to Caesar you shall go!'

Bibliography:

U. Holzmeister, 'Der heilige Paulus vor dem Richterstuhle des Festus', *ZkTh* 36 (1912), 489–511, 724–83; E. Täubler, 'Relatio ad principem (de appellatione St. Pauli ad Caesarem Act. 25.10–12)', *Klio* 17 (1920), 58–101; H. J. Cadbury, 'The Appeal to Caesar', *Beg.* V, 1933, 312–19; Williams 257f.; Conzelmann 133–5; Stählin 299–301.

VERSE 1: ἐπιβὰς τῇ ἐπαρχείᾳ: 'after he had arrived in the province.'[1]
'. . . after three days': the new governor visits Jerusalem at the earliest possible time, and Paul's trial is quickly set in motion again.

VERSE 2: ἐνεφάνισαν αὐτῷ: see on **24**.1. οἱ ἀρχιερεῖς: see on **4**.23. The High Priest then in office was Ishmael, son of Phabi (Jos. *Ant.* XX 179, 194, 196; III 320).[2] οἱ πρῶτοι τῶν Ἰουδαίων: 'the foremost, most respected' (Bauer, *Wb* 1439);[3] in **24**.1 'some of the elders', in **25**.15 'the elders' appear in their place. κατὰ τοῦ Παύλου: '(to bring a complaint) against Paul'.

VERSE 3: αἰτούμενοι κτλ: 'asking (it as) a favour against him'.[4] ἐνέδραν κτλ: see **23**.12ff. κατὰ τὴν ὁδόν: 'on the way'.[5]

VERSE 4: The governor politely declines: Paul is in Caesarea (εἰς Hellenistic for ἐν; Bl.-Debr. § 205f.) in prison. He himself will return to Caesarea very soon.[6] μὲν οὖν is here not the usual Lucan formula (see on **1**.6): the μέν, which properly ought to stand before Παῦλον, has a corresponding δέ, and also the change of scene does not fit in with this formula.

VERSE 5: The indirect speech passes into direct: cf. **23**.22. οἱ ἐν ὑμῖν δυνατοί: οἱ δυνατοί in Josephus often as a technical term.[7] The accusers are to travel with Festus to Caesarea—so no time is lost. εἰ τί ἐστιν κτλ: 'In case there is something wrong in the man'—the governor expresses himself very cautiously.[8] What is meant is: 'if Paul has actually committed a crime'.

VERSE 6: ἡμέρας οὐ πλείους (see note to **23**.13) ὀκτῷ: 'no more than eight days': the trial now comes very quickly to a decision. καταβάς: down from (high-lying) Jerusalem. τῇ ἐπαύριον: with Festus there is no delay. καθίσας . . . βήματος: when Festus sits on the elevated judge's seat, the court is in session. ἀχθῆναι: 'he commanded Paul to be brought forward'.

---

[1] ℵ A have ἐπαρχείῳ (supply χώρᾳ) in the same sense: the two forms alternate in the MSS. of Josephus and Eusebius also, without any recognizable rule: *Beg.* III 227.

[2] G. Hölscher, *Die Hohenpriesterliste des Josephus u. d. evangelische Chronologie* 18, assumed on the basis of Acts **23**.2, **24**.1 that Ananias was still in office in the year 59. But according to Josephus *Ant.* XX 179 it is established that Ishmael was nominated by Agrippa II already under Felix.

[3] Mk. **6**.21: πρῶτοι τῆς Γαλιλαίας; Acts **13**.50 οἱ πρῶτοι τῆς πόλεως: frequently in Josephus.

[4] According to *Beg.* IV 307, χάρις is a legal technical term (to translate *placitum*?).

[5] sy^hmg adds *illi qui votum fecerant, quomodo obtinuerunt, ut in manibus suis esset.* Ropes remarks that this reading overlooks the two years elapsed since **23**.12ff. (*Beg.* III 229).

[6] For construction see Bl.-Debr. § 406, 1.

[7] According to Overbeck 426 'the more general expression, which the author puts in the mouth of a Roman who has only just entered the country, instead of the local designations of vv. 1, 15'. Apart from the fact that the governor before receiving such a delegation would first be briefed by his experts, οἱ δυνατοί can be shown to be a political term. techn.: Jos. *Bell.* II 242f., together with ἀρχιερεῖς *Bell.* II 301, 316, 336 (here in addition the βουλή is also named), 422, 428. Cf. Schürer II⁴ 252 (ET *History of the Jewish People in the Time of Jesus*).

[8] Cf. Lk. **23**.41 where for reasons of reverence the formulation is just as cautious. In Acts **28**.6 μηδὲν ἄτοπον means only 'nothing bad'.

VERSE 7: παραγενομένου αὐτοῦ: 'when Paul had appeared (in the court room)'. περιέστησαν: the accusers surrounding Paul form a threatening group. πολλὰ καὶ βαρέα αἰτιώματα: 'many serious accusations'. The charge so generally described can be more precisely deduced from what follows. For the Jews however the responsibility of producing direct evidence remains outstanding.

VERSE 8: Again a transition to direct speech, as in v. 5, but without φησί and introduced by ὅτι;[1] see on 1.4. Paul has transgressed neither against the Jewish law (cf. 21.21) nor against the Temple (21.28) nor against Caesar. This third accusation—*laesa maiestas*—is a new one. τι ἥμαρτον: 'I have incurred some guilt, done something wrong'.[2]

VERSE 9: χάριν καταθέσθαι: see on 24.27; cf. χαρίζεσθαι 25.11, 16. περὶ τούτων: 'in regard to these accusations'. ἐπ' ἐμοῦ: 'under me', 'under my chairmanship, my direction'.[3] So also Wikenhauser *Apg.* 210. Freshly documented by Bauer *Einf.* 21.

VERSE 10: B places ἐστώς before οὗ also, ℵ only there. Bℵ thus both attest fundamentally the same text: 'I stand before the judgement seat of Caesar,[4] I stand where I ought to be tried.' Paul seems to presume that

---

[1] ὅτι *recitativum:* Bl.-Debr. § 470, 1.

[2] According to *Beg.* IV 308 Paul was charged with *seditio*.

[3] The commentaries vary greatly. Overbeck (427) finds here a complete change of front by Festus in comparison with v. 3, which however he judges a fiction. J. Weiss (49): the 'political denunciations however required clearing up, and Paul therefore puts himself under the imperial jurisdiction with all seriousness'. According to Preuschen (141) Festus' question is intended 'to offer the accused the opportunity of justifying himself completely by calling up a greater array of witnesses'. According to Wendt (333) Festus wants to have Paul judged 'in his presence' (but ἐπ' ἐμοῦ means 'under my direction'!). Wellhausen (52): Paul wants to remain 'where he belongs, namely before the imperial tribunal, by which he . . . can understand only the procurator's judgement. But how can he then . . . appeal from the procurator to Caesar, and that in the same breath . . .!' Wellhausen deletes v. 10a. Knopf (649): perhaps the procurator was inclined 'to have the Jewish council sit in judgement on Paul's religious offences', but probably he wanted only to change the place of trial to Jerusalem. Jacquier (694): Festus 's'était convaincu que l'accusation de lèse-majesté n'était pas fondée et qu'il ne restait contre Paul que les accusations d'ordre réligieux qui devaient être jugées par le Sanhédrin. Il pensa donc, qu'il avait lieu de renvoyer Paul devant ce tribunal.' Schlatter (293): Festus 'had already declared himself ready to surrender the decision to other judges, since he was not adequately informed. Hence Paul could now successfully make good his appeal to Caesar.' Loisy (876f.): Festus wanted to hand over the trial to the Jewish authorities, who in religious cases according to L. could pass and execute a death sentence (referring to Juster II 127–49). *Beg.* IV 308: 'Festus undertakes not to give up Paul to Jewish jurisdiction.' Cadbury, *Beg.* V 308 n. 5: 'It was natural for the governor to think it possible to get more information on the case in Jerusalem.' Beyer (144): when the governor wanted to transfer the trial to Jerusalem 'it appeared to the Apostle that the time had come to give the entire proceeding a different direction . . . Such an appeal to Caesar naturally had to be made before the judgement of another court was delivered' (unfortunately this is not at all natural). Bauernfeind (265): 'a court which takes such a proposal as v. 9 into consideration, will . . . finally surrender him entirely to the Jews. Hence he now briefly but firmly rejects the entire jurisdiction of Caesarea and demands judgement by Caesar.'

[4] Wendt (333) quotes Ulpian, *Digest* I, 19,1: '*quae acta gestaque sunt a procuratore Caesaris, sic ab eo comprobantur, atque si a Caesare ipso gesta sint.*'

here and here alone he stands before the judgement seat of Caesar (which is for him the only competent one), but not in Jerusalem. ὡς ... ἐπιγινώσκεις:[1] how does Festus know that?, asks Overbeck 428. But Luke tells the reader with these very words! κάλλιον, superlative: 'very well', see on **24.22**.

VERSE 11: μὲν οὖν: again not the Lucan formula as in **1**.6 and often, but as in v. 4 followed by δέ. ἀδικῶ 'I am in the wrong' (Bauer, *Wb* 33f.). οὐ παραιτοῦμαι τὸ ἀποθανεῖν: 'I do not wish to avoid death' (Bauer, *Wb* 1223, referring to Jos. *Vita* 141, where Josephus in a similar situation as the accused says: θανεῖν μέν, εἰ δίκαιόν ἐστιν, οὐ παραιτοῦμαι. It is thus a common expression, inserted here to say: Paul is concerned not about his life but about his rights). The real train of thought continues with εἰ δὲ κτλ: (If I have not transgressed against the Jews) 'no one can send me to them'—Paul thus considers Festus' proposal as an extradition to the Jews. Καίσαρα ἐπικαλοῦμαι: this appeal to Caesar raises many problems.[2]

---

[1] Cf. II Tim. **1**.18.

[2] The questions relating to the law of appeals have still not by any means been clarified since Mommsen's famous article in *ZNW* 2 (1901), 81–96, 'Die Rechtsverhältnisse des Apostels Paulus'. This is shown by Cadbury's survey of research, 'Roman Law and the Trial of Paul. III, The Appeal to Caesar' (*Beg.* V 312–9); J. Bleicken, *RE* 23,2 (1959), 2444f. The *provocatio*, originally the right of the Roman citizen to appeal in certain cases to the *comitia centuriata*, and the *appellatio*, originally the right of Roman citizens to appeal to colleagues of the official passing sentence or to a tribune of the people, were combined in the period of the Principate, when the *princeps* took the place of the sovereign people and as consul and tribune became the *maior collega* of the other consuls and tribunes.

According to Cadbury the following questions remain open: 1. Could only Roman citizens appeal, or all inhabitants of the Roman empire? (Acts does not mention Paul's Roman citizenship in this connection.) 2. How was the Roman citizenship authenticated? (In Acts **22**.27 Paul's word is enough.) 3. In what cases was an appeal to Rome allowed and which rule did the provincial governor follow in sanctioning the request? (According to Acts Festus first conferred with his *consilium*.) 4. Was an appeal permissible only after sentence was passed, or against a trial which a governor conducted, or (after the beginning of such a proceeding) against details, as in Acts **25**.11? 5. Could a governor no longer set the accused free after such an appeal (Acts **26**.32)? 6. Did the governor possess the *ius gladii* (cf. Mommsen *Strafr.* 243ff.) or was he incompetent in such cases? 7. Do the rights of a procurator differ from those of a legate in regard to the appeal?

As Mommsen already established with astonishment (93), Acts does not combine Paul's appeal with his citizenship (of which the reader nevertheless knows). But the author has by no means the intention of describing the trial with the accuracy of a minute. Hence conclusions about the legal situation are not to be drawn from this silence. Just as little had he any interest in depicting how Paul proved his Roman citizenship; he simplifies as much as possible and for that very reason lets Paul's word suffice. We may assume that appeal was allowed to Roman citizens only in capital cases (that on Luke's showing such was the case for Paul is clear from **25**.11a) and indeed according to the Lex Julia even after the provincial governor had given judgement. Whether the procurator had first to sanction the appeal or whether it was only not actually possible against his will, is not clear from the scanty material. The governor Florus (Jos. *Bell.* II 308) in the year A.D. 66 ordered the public scourging and crucifixion of Jews who held the rank of Roman *equites*; this shows that it was not a matter of course that the right of appeal would be observed. That is not to say, however, that behind v. 12 stands a source: it will describe the procedure generally followed. In general the psychological considerations quoted in p. 666 n. 3 are in view of this text superfluous; to the author the details of the juristic procedure are completely irrelevant

VERSE 12: συμβούλιον: the council of the *consiliarii* = *assessores*, the legal experts and advisers of the governor, is asked about the admissibility of the appeal in this case.[1] It is sanctioned. Jacquier (696) thinks that Festus may have conceded Paul's demand *avec un certain air moqueur*: 'Have you any idea what an appeal to Caesar means!' Jacquier was not conscious that this interpretation completely contradicts the Lucan portrait of Festus.

An author can tell the reader something directly or indirectly. Luke makes use of both means now. That Festus three days after his landing visits Jerusalem, and needs only eight days to finish the governmental business there, makes it just as clear as ἐν τάχει in v. 4 that the new master is a brisk and energetic worker. He will bring Paul's postponed trial to a swift conclusion.

The Jews, who renew the accusations against Paul without delay, wish the prisoner to be transferred to Jerusalem—in order to murder him on the way (cf. **23**.12). The reader thus knows what Paul has to expect from this quarter. Unwittingly Festus destroys this plan by inviting the accusers to come to Caesarea with him: there they can accuse him. How impartial Festus is, is revealed by the fact that he leaves the guilt of the accused an open question.

In this manner it comes to the trial in Caesarea, which Luke does not again describe in detail. Accusation and defence are no more than indicated. With this the court session which Festus announced in Jerusalem is really closed. It remains only for the procurator, having himself heard both parties, to pronounce the verdict.

But in reality, according to our narrative, something entirely different happens: the governor asks the accused whether he agrees to a removal of the trial to Jerusalem. Luke explains this surprising proposal of Festus as arising from the wish to please the Jews. But this explanation does not lighten the darkness. The procurator held court in Caesarea and Jerusalem. The removal of the trial to Jerusalem would therefore have been nothing irregular. But then it is not apparent why Festus wants Paul's consent. Moreover the proceedings are practically finished. Both parties have had their say and presented their arguments. The situation is thus now different from v. 3.

(and probably not known), as becomes clear above all in the summary in **28**.17ff. Only this much may be said, that Paul will have made use of the legal method of appeal only in the most extreme emergency. By so doing he set himself in opposition not only to the council but also to the procurator.

[1] Cf. Mommsen, *Röm. Staatsrecht*[3] I 307–9; II 245, 249; also *Hermes* XX, 287. H. Niedermeyer, *Über antike Protokoll-Literatur* (Diss. Göttingen 1918, 10–24. The conferences of the imperial *consilium*, the συγκαθήμενοι, were secret; also no minutes were kept.—The same is to be assumed for the governor's *consilium*. But in Acts **26**.31 the governor had indeed no other decision to take on which he could have consulted his *consilium*). Schürer I[4], 469 n. 82 (ET). Zahn (791) has Festus, in accordance with **26**.30f., go out with his assessors from the ἀκροατήριον into another room.

There no trial before Festus had yet taken place. What is really to be dealt with in Jerusalem? All that is wanting is Festus' decision.

The procurator's question thus remains fundamentally inexplicable in spite of Luke's explanation. It would be another matter if it was not only a question of changing the place of trial. Hence appeal has been made (cf. the quotations p. 666 n. 3)—and not without reason—to Paul's answer in vv. 10f. It is likewise very strange. Paul begins with the sentence, 'I stand before the judgement seat of Caesar; I stand where I must be tried.' This sounds as if in Jerusalem he would no longer stand before this judgement seat. It rather seems (although this is not expressed!) as if Festus wanted to charge τὸ συνέδριον with the further conduct of the trial. The train of thought is continued in v. 11b: if the Jewish accusation against Paul is unfounded no one may deliver him to the Jews as a favour—the word χαρίζεσθαι used here reminds the reader of the χάριν καταθέσθαι which has appeared twice before (24.27; 25.9), and of the expression αἰτούμενοι χάριν (25.3). Paul seems therefore to see in the removal of the trial to Jerusalem a surrender to the Jews.

If such is the situation, we can certainly understand that Paul does not agree to Festus' proposal. But it remains obscure why Paul does not simply decline and insist on a continuation of the trial in Caesarea, in accordance with v. 10. Instead of this Paul now appeals to Caesar. Zahn (790) has convinced himself that Paul goes further in v. 11 than in v. 10. But why Paul within two verses executes such an important change of position, Zahn does not explain. Here a hiatus remains.

Finally there is a third difficulty: if Paul had been accused only of transgression against the Jewish law and the Temple, then a reference of the trial to the council as the competent authority would have been possible, and perhaps even probable. But the fact that Paul was accused of a crime against Caesar also (25.8) changed the situation. Such an accusation belonged to the jurisdiction of the procurator; he could in no case let it out of his hands. In addition the Roman authorities in Judaea were then particularly on their guard because of the frequent uprisings against Rome. That Festus should not have tried a *crimen laesae maiestatis* himself or referred it to Rome is the height of improbability.

In sum: in Luke's account it remains incomprehensible: 1. why after the close of the proceedings no verdict follows, but a transference of the trial is proposed, 2. why Paul does not simply insist on the continuation of the trial in Caesarea, but appeals to Caesar, 3. why Festus does not himself want to try a man charged with *laesa maiestas* (or send him to Rome).

These contradictions are immediately resolved if we consider the Lucan narrative no longer as a court minute but rather as a suspense-laden narrative created by the author. Luke may have learned that Paul appealed to Caesar (at least this is still the simplest assumption; for the suspicion that the appeal is unhistorical—cf. Cadbury, *Beg.* V 319—there is no adequate foundation).

This was highly welcome to the dramatic narrator: it yielded a gripping scene full of suspense. But a great difficulty also presented itself. If Paul had appealed then it was against a decision (already given or expected) from the governor. That was, however, intolerable because Luke claimed the Roman officials as witnesses for the defence. Already with Felix this had not been accomplished without great pains. Here, however, the energetic and upright Festus threatened to desert to the ranks of Paul's enemies. This Luke could only prevent by depicting the decision in question as no real decision. He succeeded in this as well as might be expected. Festus only asks, and a question is not a decision. But Paul answers as if it were a decision, for one knows that a governor's question is as good as a decision. Hence Paul appeals to Caesar. So Luke can now go on to use Festus as a witness for the defence, indeed only now does this use become possible without restriction.

But how does it come to this decision, which is no decision at all? Luke has depicted Festus as an efficient official who tolerates no delay. He has further depicted the Jews as cold-blooded murderers. In the long run Luke cannot sustain this attitude of the parties if it should come to a decision. Festus must experience a moment of weakness. He too wants to do the Jews a favour. Thus Luke leaves undecided what the removal of the trial to Jerusalem really means. It is enough that in it a mortal danger for Paul appears to be imminent. Paul's appeal is therefore justifiable and understandable.

And now all is well, as well as it now could ever be. That Festus ratifies the appeal is the first indication of his goodwill which we encounter.

The nature of Festus' order, against which Paul appealed to Caesar, we do not know. Possibly Luke also did not know and therefore from the fact of the appeal, and his ideal picture of the Roman official, drew out that possibility which he has depicted with all his narrative skill.

62
ACTS 25:13–22
FESTUS AND AGRIPPA

[13] But when some days had passed, King Agrippa and Berenice came down to Caesarea and greeted Festus. [14] After they had spent several days there Festus brought Paul's case before the king and said, 'A man is here who was left a prisoner by Felix, [15] against whom, when I came to Jerusalem, the chief priests and elders of the Jews raised accusations, asking that he be sentenced. [16] To them I answered that it is not the custom for Romans to hand over a man before the accused has the accusers before him personally and receives an opportunity to defend himself against the charge. [17] So when they had come here I wasted no time and placed myself the following day on the judge's seat and commanded that the man be brought forward. [18] Placing themselves around him the accusers brought no charges of crimes as I had supposed; [19] they had however some points of dispute concerning their religion against him and concerning a certain dead Jesus whom Paul maintained to be alive. [20] Since I myself did not understand the investigation of such things I asked if he was willing to go to Jerusalem and there have himself tried. [21] But when Paul appealed to be kept for the decision of His Majesty I commanded him to be held until I can send him to Caesar.' [22] But Agrippa said to Festus, 'I should like also to hear the man!' 'Tomorrow,' he said, 'you shall hear him!'

Bibliography:

Conzelmann, *Apg.* 135–7; A. Wifstrand, 'Apg. **25**.13', *Eranos* 54 (1956), 123–37; Williams 258–60; Stählin 301–3.

VERSE 13: διαγίνομαι: (of time) 'to elapse'; cf. **27**.9; Mk. **16**.1. Ἀγρίππας: Marcus Julius Agrippa (II), great-grandson of Herod the Great, born A.D. 27, died 100.[1] Βερνίκη (correct Greek: Φερενίκη, Latin Veronica): Agrippa's

---

[1] Agrippa was brought up in Rome at the court of Claudius. He was first (around 50) King of Chalcis (in Lebanon); in 53 he obtained instead 'the Tetrarchy of Philip along with that of Lysanias of Abilene and the principality of the Arab Noarus in Lebanon. From Nero he received also a part of Galilee, with Tiberias and Tarichea, also the city of Julias in Perea and fourteen other villages belonging to it': Wellhausen, *Israelitische und jüdische Geschichte*[8] 1921, 337; in the year 55 Agrippa was 28, Berenice 27, Drusilla 18 years old.

sister, about a year younger.[1] ἀσπασάμενοι: greeting and visit coincide (Wendt 335, so also M. Zerwick, *Graecitas Biblica* 1949, 61 n. 3).[2]

VERSE 14: ἀνέθετο . . . Παῦλον: 'he presented Paul's case to him'. This not only prepares for the next great scene, but Luke also has the opportunity to present this case to the reader in brief retrospect, in such a way that the Roman official appears to be properly correct.

VERSE 15: καταλελειμμένος κτλ.: cf. **24**.27. δέσμιος: 'as a prisoner'. ἐνεφάνισαν: see **25**.2. αἰτούμενοι: see **25**.3. The scene in Jerusalem, previously only suggested, is now dramatically depicted. The Jews demand the condemnation (καταδίκην) of Paul from the outset; this is a sharpening, compared with the description in Chapter 25. That the entire council, chief priests and elders, present this demand is also an intensification.

VERSE 16: πρὸς οὓς ἀπεκρίθην κτλ.: Roman procedure is that of a constitutional state which does not hand over an accused man without protection (for χαρίζεσθαι see **25**.2): the defendant must be heard, and be able to defend himself personally (κατὰ πρόσωπον): Preuschen (143) quotes *Dig.* XLVIII **17**.1: *et hoc iure utimur, ne absentes damnentur. Neque enim inaudita causa quemquam damnari aequitatis ratio patitur.* τόπος: possibility, opportunity: cf. Jos. *Ant.* XVI 258 μήτε ἀπολογίας μήτ' ἐλέγχου τόπον ἕως ἀληθείας ἐχόντων.[3] J. Dupont, 'Aequitas Romana', *RScR* 49 (1961), 354ff.

VERSE 17: ἀναβολὴν μηδεμίαν ποιησάμενος: promptly (see **25**.6) in contrast to **24**.22. τῇ ἑξῆς... ἄνδρα: see v. 6: the prompt despatch is specially emphasized.

VERSE 18: περὶ οὗ σταθέντες: see v. 7. σταθέντες not 'in the formal speaker's position' (so Wendt 336)—the entire body of Jews does not speak at once! Rather the hostile attitude of the Jews is here described. οὐδεμίαν αἰτίαν . . . ὧν = τούτων (τῶν πονηρῶν, the crimes), ἅ. It is not a question of the contrast between political and religious offences, but of that between real offences and theological differences (Preuschen 143) which for the Romans are incomprehensible and pointless.

VERSE 19: περὶ τῆς ἰδίας (unemphatic = αὐτῶν) δεισιδαιμονίας (cf. on **17**.22): with this neutral expression—'religion'[4]—Festus speaks about

---

[1] Berenice was first engaged to Marcus, the nephew of the philosopher Philo. After the death of her first husband, her uncle Herod of Chalcis, she lived with her brother Agrippa. She deserted King Polemo of Cilicia, to whom she was married between 63 and 66, and returned to her brother; Juvenal (*Sat.* VI 156–60) accused her publicly of incest. After 70 she became the mistress of Titus, and already behaved like his consort (Dio Cass. LXVI 15). Suetonius (*Titus* 7) speaks of Titus' special love for her, *cui etiam nuptias pollicitus ferebatur.* But public opinion forced a separation, and when she came to Rome after Vespasian's death in 79 Titus sent her away, *invitam invitam*, as Suetonius remarks.

[2] Cf. Lk. **19**.6; Acts **1**.24, 30; **15**.8; **16**.6; **23**.25; **24**.22. Aorist participle of purpose: *Beg.* IV 310, in Ptolemaic papyri: see Mayser, *Grammatik* II, 1 (1926), 220.

[3] ἔχοι . . . λάβοι: optativus obliquus 'for the subjunctive (with ἄν) of indirect speech': Bl.-Debr. § 386, 4.

[4] So correctly Preuschen 144, referring to Jos. *Bell.* II 174; *Ant.* X 42. Holtzmann 144 wrongly '*superstitio*'; so also *Beg.* IV 311—the governor is not so impolite as to describe the Jewish religion before the Jewish king as superstition.

questions over which he admittedly shakes his head, but does not speak dis-respectfully. περί τινος . . . ζῆν: Luke thus describes the Roman's complete lack of understanding for the Christian message of the resurrection.

VERSE 20: ἀπορούμενος . . . ζήτησιν: with this Festus gives the reason for his polite (βούλοιτο) proposal to transfer the trial to Jerusalem. It is contrary to Luke's technique of a loose sequence of scenes if this reason is already introduced into Chapter 25.[1] The motif had already appeared in **22**.30 and **23**.28f.

VERSE 21: ἐπικαλεσαμένου: see **25**.11. The appeal is here treated as some-thing self-evident. τηρηθῆναι: a formal circumlocution, with which, however, Luke reproduces the official government style.[2] ὁ Σεβαστός: 'His Majesty', *Beg.* IV 312. ἀναπέμπω: to send to the proper authority: Bauer, *Wb* 118.

VERSE 22: Ἀγρίππας . . . Φῆστον: ellipse of the verb: see Bl.-Debr. § 480, 5.[3] καὶ αὐτός: the translation 'I too' is possible; but there was no talk of anyone else wanting to see him. Hence we should perhaps see in καὶ αὐτός only an emphatic 'I', analogous to **1**.6—Overbeck (431) points to the cor-respondence with the passion story: Jesus appears not only before the Roman governor but also before the Jewish king, who very much wants to see him. The Apostle's meeting with Agrippa however turns out far more harmonious. —αὔριον . . . ἀκούσῃ αὐτοῦ: at once laconically and politely Festus fulfils the wish of his honoured guest.

While J. C. Riehm (1821) and Kuinoel (1818, [2]1827) still assumed an eyewitness report for this conversation (quoted in Overbeck 431), later scholars have abandoned this claim. Spitta (280 ff.) admittedly incorporated our section into his good source A, and Zahn (792) presumed its reliability without touch-ing upon the questions; so also Schlatter (294). But this becomes the exception. Jüngst (186) already ascribed the scene to the editor and Clemen thought like-wise (*Paulus* I, 317), and of course Overbeck (431) and Loisy (882): 'un récit fictif'. Wellhausen expressed himself even more bluntly (53), speaking of a 'mere exuberance'. Wendt with greater soberness maintained that '**25**.14–22 in the nature of the case' is 'composed with literary licence' (334 n. 1), and Beyer also (144) has it originate from the author. Bauernfeind (226) admits that in this 'private conversation' we should naturally think of a 'reconstruction' by the author, but finds that it has turned out very 'genuine'. The formulation of *Beg.* IV 311 is classic: the account represents 'Luke's attempt to tell the story as he supposed that Roman officials would have told it'.

---

[1] ἀπορούμενος: only here with accusative; Bl.-Debr. § 148, 2 supplement.
[2] IG XIV 1072 translates the title of an office '*a cognitionibus Augusti*' by ἐπὶ διαγνώ-σεων τοῦ Σεβαστοῦ: *Beg.* IV 312. διάγνωσις = 'decision'.
[3] ἐβουλόμην represents a classical βουλοίμην ἄν as the expression for a wish capable of fulfilment: Radermacher[2] 160; Bl.-Debr. § 359, 2.

But this expresses only a judgement about the historical value of the section and does little or nothing for its understanding. Why did Luke tell the story thus and not otherwise? Why did he insert it here at all?

The preceding scene had made Paul appeal from the governor to Caesar. This introduced a wrong note—though toned down as far as possible—into the harmony which otherwise prevailed between Paul and the Roman officials. By the fact that our scene and the next still precede Paul's departure from Caesarea, Paul's relations do not end with a dissonance. Moreover, it was highly desirable that a high Jewish personality should express himself in favour of Paul. This was not to be expected of the Sanhedrin. So we may regard it as a particular stroke of genius that Luke makes Agrippa's visit serve this purpose. Wellhausen admittedly wondered why Luke here introduced 'the pretty couple who lived in incest' (53). But Luke intended to bring on not the degenerate Herodians whom we know from Josephus and Juvenal, but rather the last Jewish king there was! Agrippa of course did not rule over Judaea. But to him was entrusted the keeping of the High-Priestly vestments, and it was he who now could depose and nominate the High Priest. In this capacity he could be claimed as an authority on Jewish problems. That together with his sister he made an inaugural visit to the new procurator is not improbable.

Here Luke ties the threads together, and indeed very skilfully. He does not make Paul immediately come in touch with Agrippa but prepares for it in a special scene. When the government business has been discussed, Festus tells his guest about his interesting prisoner who is causing him so much trouble. Luke uses this opportunity to simplify the description of the trial and at the same time to exonerate Rome. For we cannot get away with the idea that Festus wanted to clear himself before Agrippa; there is no source relating their private conversation. Luke is thus here independently at work. It is no concern of his that the governor appears plagued with a bad conscience; no, Festus is an honourable man, thoroughly imbued with the fundamental principles of Roman constitutional law and, therefore, painfully correct. He has manfully resisted the Jewish demand for Paul's surrender and during the proceedings has discovered that no πονηρά whatever have been laid to his prisoner's charge, but only religious differences of the strange Jewish religion, which is completely foreign to the Roman. On this occasion however Luke now also shows that the Christian message of the resurrection is completely incomprehensible to the poor procurator—this will later (26.24) be dramatically expressed. Finally there betrays itself here his inability, bound up with that lack of understanding, to send to His Majesty a rational and factual report about this intricate affair—a motif which in the sequel will take on lasting significance.

This small section has thus accomplished a great deal: Festus is personally rehabilitated before the reader. He is ultimately only a poor heathen who cannot be blamed for his lack of understanding and who indeed was so well-meaning. A bright light falls on the Roman state, and suspense is awakened for what is to come: now final judgement must be passed upon Paul, this interesting man of whom King Agrippa says, 'Him I should like to hear!' 'Tomorrow you shall hear him,' his amiable host answers with Roman brevity.

63
ACTS 25:23–27
FESTUS SETS PAUL BEFORE THE ASSEMBLY

23 On the following day Agrippa and Berenice came and with great pomp went into the audience hall with the tribunes and the prominent men of the city, and at the command of Festus Paul was brought in. 24 And Festus said, 'King Agrippa and all you who are present, look on this man concerning whom the entire Jewish people appealed to me in Jerusalem and here, crying that he should no longer live. 25 But I gathered that he had done nothing worthy of death; and when he himself appealed to Caesar, I decided to send him (there). 26 But I have nothing definite to write about him to my lord. I have therefore brought him before you, and especially you, King Agrippa, so that I may have something to write after the investigation. 27 For it seems to me foolish if the one who sends a prisoner cannot also report the charges lodged against him.'

Bibliography:

Williams 260f.; Conzelmann 139f.; Stählin 303–6.

VERSE 23: μετὰ πολλῆς φαντασίας: 'pomp', 'pageantry' (Bauer *Wb* 1687); Radermacher[2] (12) conjectures the meaning 'stately procession'. The thought is then not only of the royal robes and Berenice's finery (Zahn 793 'princely finery and festive attire'), but also of the accompanying court. τὸ ἀκροατήριον: the audience hall in which court sessions also took place.[1] χιλιάρχοις—the omission of the article does not indicate that all (five) were present; against Jacquier 701—καὶ ἀνδράσιν τοῖς κατ' ἐξοχὴν (=τοῖς πρώτοις) τῆς πόλεως: the notables of the city of Caesarea:[2] Luke expresses himself very discriminately.

VERSE 24: ἄνδρες: only the men are addressed: Berenice—who is not described as a queen—is not. θεωρεῖτε τοῦτον: Paul stands at the centre of the entire assembly. ἅπαν τὸ πλῆθος: despite **25.2** not only the Jewish leaders

---

[1] Mommsen, *Römisches Strafrecht*, 1899, 362.
[2] Bauer, *Wb* 552 s.v. ἐξοχή refers to Philo, *Leg. All.* I 106, where Philo speaks of the 'individual and particular death of man': τὸν ἴδιον καὶ κατ' ἐξοχὴν θάνατον.—The Western text, represented by sy^hmg, has the notables of the entire province attend (*qui descendissent de provincia*): *Beg.* III 233.

(so *Beg.* IV 313), but 'the crowd'.[1] The narrator is thinking of mob scenes such as **21**.36. ἐνέτυχον:[2] to ask, beseech. καὶ ἐνθάδε: new as compared with **25**.7, and an intensification.[3] βοῶντες . . . ζῆν: cf. **22**.22; Paul—and with him Christianity—is assailed by Judaism with deadly enmity.

VERSE 25: To this Festus' own conviction is immediately opposed: that Paul has done nothing deserving death! The motif of **23**.29 and **25**.18 thus returns, an indication of its importance. καταλαμβάνομαι: to conceive, understand (Bauer, *Wb* 817). αὐτοῦ δὲ τούτου (cf. αὐτοὶ οὗτοι **24**.15, 20): this one himself; Bauer, *Wb* s.v. οὗτος 1 a ζ 1183.[4]

VERSE 26: 'About him I have nothing certain to write': this provides the motive for the present scene.[5] For ἀσφαλές see **21**.34; **22**.30. ὁ κύριος: the reference is to Nero, under whom the Kyrios title (first introduced in the East) began to find a place among the imperial titles.[6] The passage seems to be the earliest evidence for the absolute use of κύριος. Perhaps Luke however has projected the usage of the time of Domitian back into that of Nero. προάγω: to bring before. ἐφ'ὑμῶν: before you. Both are legal termini technici.[7] τῆς ἀνακρίσεως γενομένης: 'when the (present) investigation has taken place'— the scene is thus thought of as a judicial investigation.[8] γράψαι: Preuschen (144) and Jacquier (702) quote *Digest* XLIX 5.[9]

VERSE 27 is meant to explain the necessity for such an accompanying letter. ἄλογον . . . σημᾶναι: it would be foolish, if an accused person were sent to the emperor without an accusation.

For Zahn there was no historical problem in our section. According to his conviction Luke was in the position 'to hear from Paul's mouth the evening of the same day how it had gone in the forenoon with his defence

---

[1] Cf. I Macc. **8**.20, II Macc. **11**.16, 34.

[2] Constructio ad sensum: Bl.-Debr. § 134.

[3] Sy[hmg] amplifies considerably: *et in Hierosolymis et hic, ut traderem eum iis ad tormentum sine defensione*, in order to bring our story into agreement with **25**.4. Sy[hmg] continues, '*Non potui autem tradere eum, propter mandata quae habemus ab Augusto. Si autem quis eum accusaturus esset, dicebam ut sequeretur me in Caesaream, ubi custodiebatur; qui cum venissent, clamaverunt ut tolleretur e vita.*'

[4] According to Bauernfeind (267) Paul's appeal appears here 'as superfluous obstinacy'. But neither here nor in **26**.32 does Luke want to lay on Paul the blame for his not being set free.—Sy[hmg] continues: *quum autem hanc et alteram partem audivissem, comperi quod in nullo reus esset mortis. quum autem dicerem: Vis iudicari cum iis in Hierosolymam? Caesarem appellavit.* That this text is secondary is plain enough.

[5] Sy[hmg]: *de quo aliquid certum scribere domino meo non habeo.*

[6] ThWb III, 1053, 36f.: 'From Nero on a steady increase in this use of κύριος is to be observed.'

[7] Bauer, *Wb* s.v. προάγω 1, 1392 and ἐπί I 1a δ, 566.

[8] It is not a future investigation (so B. Weiss) which is meant, but 'the one which consists in the bringing forward of Paul for examination': Wendt 337.

[9] *Post appellationem interpositam litterae dandae sunt ab eo, a quo appellatum est, ad eum, qui de appellatione cogniturus est, sive principem sive alium; quas litteras dimissorias sive apostolos appellant.*

before the distinguished audience', or the officer of the guard had even
'allowed the physician Luke, whom he may many times have seen with Paul
in his cell, to enter the hall with him and attend the interesting proceedings'
(813f.). This confidence is today scarcely shared: 'How far the words of
Festus rest upon reminiscence . . . cannot be discovered' is Bauernfeind's
opinion (266). Wendt already ascribed the entire section to the author of
Acts (different from Luke) (334 n. 1); Loisy judges likewise (886).

Among those who still hold the scene to be historical, Beyer (146)
deserves special mention. He noticed that it has an individual quality all its
own. But since he regards the report as a true reflection of the events, he has
to put anything peculiar to the account of Festus; he calls the bringing
forward of Paul by Festus 'highly theatrical', without noticing what a mine
he is laying with these words.

In reality it is not only this 'theatrical bringing forward' which is remarkable, but the entire scene from beginning to end. Let us begin with the conclusion. Festus declares in v. 27 that it would be senseless to send a prisoner
to Rome without an accompanying report. But it was not foolish, it was a
dereliction of duty: the governor *had* to send such a report (Jacquier 702).
Hence the statement in v. 27 does not derive from the real Festus, who knew
very well that the sending of such a report was not within his discretion; it
comes from an author who was not so familiar with *litterae dimissoriae* as a
procurator.

But this still does not do away with the strangeness and unreality: it
is present also in the way and manner in which v. 26 speaks of the accompanying letter. Loisy coolly remarked on this (888), 'The procurator did not
have to formulate any accusation against Paul; he had only to describe the
state of the matter up to the appeal.' But for such a report there was evidence
at hand, even according to Acts itself: documents like the tribune's report
concerning Paul's arrest and the events up to Paul's removal to Caesarea, or
the accusation which the Jews had lodged under Felix, and the court record
about Paul's statements at his different hearings. Whether Festus himself
considered Paul guilty or innocent, or was not clear about it, makes no
difference. The judgement had been taken out of his hands; it was now Caesar's
task alone. Thus the same holds for v. 26 as earlier for v. 27: it is impossible
in the mouth of Festus and is comprehensible only as the word of an author
who had a false conception of such an accompanying letter, and began to
narrate on the basis of this conception.

Now if Festus did not need to have the question of guilt clarified for
the letter, the whole scene loses its point. For Agrippa was only to find out
for Festus what he had to write in the report to Caesar about the question of
guilt (cf. **26**.31f.).

Beyer's observation of the 'highly theatrical bringing forward' of Paul
has still however not yet been completely evaluated. If Agrippa was to

interrogate Paul, then it was natural to bring the Apostle before the king in the presence of Festus. Why did Luke also summon the—heathen!—staff officers of the Roman garrison and the—at least half of them—likewise heathen notables of Caesarea? Was it only the delight in lively mass scenes (which Luke certainly knew) which moved him to do this? Or was it only the author's feeling that Paul's innocence had to be once more publicly demonstrated for the reader before the Apostle departed from Caesarea as a transported prisoner? One expression which occurs later (**26.26**), and will be discussed there in its context, may throw some light upon our scene: 'for this was not done in a corner!' The way in which Luke makes Paul appear before the highest personalities—the governors Sergius Paulus, Gallio, Felix and Festus and now King Agrippa—is connected with the fact that in Acts he sought to reach the heights of ancient historical writing. Ancient literature however— as Eric Auerbach has shown in his work on realism in occidental literature *Mimesis* (Bern 1946)—allows 'everyday . . . reality to find its place in literature only in the framework of a lower or middle type of style, i.e. either as grotesquely comic or as agreeable . . . literature for entertainment' (494; ET 1957, 489). What is significant for world history demanded as its framework high society, the world of the high and mighty (mass scenes could be substitute for it, but are also combined with it)—and Luke was convinced that Christianity is of decisive significance for the whole world. But he could only express this conviction in the style of the literature of the period, and impart it to his own age, by making Paul again and again confront the statesmen and princes (even Caesar: **27.24**!) and converse on friendly terms with the Asiarchs as with men of equal standing, and thus raising him above the hole-in-corner existence in which great things cannot come about.

The scene of the hearing in Caesarea is thus anything but a realistic description—here where the accusation is not even voiced, but the accused alone dominates the field, an investigation as Loisy saw (888) promised even less success than in the preceding trials—but an attempt to justify the Christian mission in the lofty style of contemporary historical writing. Hence it is not without reason that the Σεβαστός is mentioned in **25.21**, 25 and the ruler spoken of as ὁ κύριος (**25.26**). With this the illustrious figure of the emperor himself appears in the background—that it was the terrible Nero must remain unnoticed in this context, as must the incestuous relationship between 'King' Agrippa and Berenice, of which every educated person knew —and doubtless Luke also. Anyone who does not notice the demands which a particular style imposes on an author—even in terms of content!—but conceives of such a presentation as a historically reliable report, like Beyer, must of necessity make a botch of his own correct insights.

64

ACTS 26:1–32
PAUL BEFORE AGRIPPA AND FESTUS

[1] Now Agrippa said to Paul, 'It is permitted for you to speak!' Then Paul stretched out his hand and defended himself, [2] 'Concerning all the charges of the Jews, King Agrippa, being about to defend myself today before you, I count myself fortunate, [3] especially since you are familiar with all the Jewish customs and controversies. I therefore beseech you to listen to me patiently. [4] My way of life from youth which was spent from the beginning among my people and in Jerusalem, all Jews know, [5] who knew me from the beginning—if they wanted to give a witness—that I lived according to the strictest direction of our religion as a Pharisee. [6] And now I stand here on trial by reason of the hope of the promise given to our fathers by God, [7] which our twelve tribes hope to attain by serving (God) fervently day and night. On account of this hope I am accused by the Jews, O King! [8] Why is it judged among you as unbelievable if God raises the dead? [9] Now I believed that I ought to do many hostile things against the name of Jesus of Nazareth. [10] This I did in Jerusalem, and many of the saints I locked in prisons with full authority from the chief priests, and if they were killed I voted against them, [11] and in all the synagogues I often sought to force them to blaspheme with punishment and, raging furiously against them, I persecuted them even to the cities outside. [12] When I went in this connection to Damascus with full authority and commission of the chief priests, [13] in the middle of the day I saw on the road, O King, a light from heaven beyond the brightness of the sun shining around me and those travelling with me. [14] And when we all fell to the earth, I heard a voice saying to me in Aramaic, "Saul, Saul, why do you persecute me? It is hard for you to kick against the goads." [15] Then I said, "Who are you, Lord?" And the Lord said, "I am Jesus whom you persecute. [16] Now then, rise up and stand upon your feet. For I have appeared to you in order to choose you as a servant and witness of what you have seen and what you will be shown, [17] rescuing you from the people and from the Gentiles to whom I send you, [18] to open their eyes, that they may turn from darkness to light and from the power of Satan to God, that they may receive forgiveness of sins and a lot among those who are sanctified by faith in me." [19] Wherefore, King Agrippa, I was not disobedient to the heavenly vision, [20] but I proclaimed to those in Damascus first, and

in Jerusalem [and the entire country of Judaea] and to the Gentiles, that they should repent and turn to God, doing deeds worthy of repentance. [21] Because of these things the Jews seized me in the Temple and sought to kill me. [22] Since I have now obtained help from God, I stand up to the present day as a witness for great and small, saying nothing other than what the prophets and Moses proclaimed would come to pass, [23] that the Messiah must die, that he as the first resurrected from the dead is to proclaim light to the people and to the Gentiles.' [24] When he said this for his defence, Festus shouted with a loud voice, 'You are out of your mind, Paul! Too much study has deprived you of your reason!' [25] But Paul answered, 'I am not out of my mind, illustrious Festus, but speak words of truth and prudence. [26] For concerning these things the king knows, to whom I speak with confidence, for I am convinced that to him none of these things is hidden; for this has not happened in a corner. [27] Do you believe the prophets, King Agrippa? I know that you believe.' [28] Then Agrippa to Paul, 'Soon you will convince me to play the Christian.' [29] But Paul, 'I would to God that sooner or later not only you but all my listeners today might become as I am—except for these chains!' [30] And the king stood up, and the governor and Berenice and those who sat by them, [31] and when they had withdrawn they spoke with one another and said, 'This man does nothing to deserve death or imprisonment!' [32] And Agrippa said to Festus, 'This man could have been set free if he had not appealed to Caesar.'

Bibliography:

F. Dornseiff, 'Lukas der Schriftsteller', *ZNW* 35 (1936), 129–54, esp. 138; A. Vögeli, 'Lukas und Euripides', *ThZ* 9 (1953), 415–38; Williams 261–6; Conzelmann 137–40; Stählin 306–13.

J. Hackett, 'Echoes of the Bacchae of Euripides in the Acts of the Apostles?', *Irish Theol. Quart.* 23 (1956), 218–27, 350–66; E. E. Kellett, 'A Note on Acts **26**.28', *Exp.Tim.* 34 (1922–3), 563f.; A. T. Robertson, 'The Meaning of Acts **26**.28', *Exp.Tim.* 35 (1923–4), 185f.; J. E. Harry, 'Almost Thou Persuadest Me to become a Christian (Acts **26**.28)', *AngThR* 12 (1929–30), 140–4; id., 'Almost Thou Persuadest Me . . . ', *AngThR* 28 (1946), 135f.

VERSE 1: ἐπιτρέπεταί σοι: Agrippa, who as the real expert (**25**.26) takes over the direction of the assembly,[1] gives Paul permission to speak. He politely avoids the 'I permit you'. ὑπὲρ σεαυτοῦ[2] λέγειν = ἀπολογεῖσθαι; the

---

[1] Preuschen (145) did not believe that Festus gave up the direction of the proceedings; in the 'source' Agrippa was the only listener. But there is no trace of a source here.—For ἐπιτρέπεται see Bl.-Debr. §§ 320 and 312, 2.

[2] Bl.-Debr. § 283, 1. Jacquier (705): perhaps Paul was chained only on the left hand, or the chains were light and long . . . There is naturally no thought of Paul appearing here chained to a soldier.

theme of the speech is thus generally indicated. ἐκτείνας τὴν χεῖρα: Paul
assumes—despite the chains![1]—the attitude of the orator.[2] ἀπελογεῖτο: for
the imperfect see Bl.-Debr. § 327.

VERSE 2: vv. 2f. contain the necessary *captatio benevolentiae.* περὶ πάντων
(alliteration) depends upon ἀπολογεῖσθαι; the unusual word order matches
the elegant language of this speech. ὑπὸ 'Ιουδαίων: for the omission of the
article see Bl.-Debr. § 262, 1.[3] ἥγημαι (classical with a present meaning:
Bl.-Debr. § 341) ἐμαυτὸν μακάριον: 'I consider myself fortunate'. μέλλων:
being about to . . .'.

VERSE 3: μάλιστα refers to 'I consider myself fortunate': 'especially since
you . . .'. The accusative γνώστην ὄντα σε 'stands in the air': Bl.-Debr.
§ 136, 2; 137, 3; such solecisms are often found, especially in the Revelation
of John.[4] κατὰ ('Ιουδαίους): Hellenistic replacement of the genitive: Bl.-Debr.
§ 224,1. Since Festus in 25.25 has already explained that Paul has committed
no crime deserving death, Paul defends himself here only against the charge
that he has transgressed against Judaism. Ostensibly Agrippa knows the
Jewish 'customs and controversies'.[5] μακροθύμως does not refer to an
interruption which ensued elsewhere (22.22; 23.7) (so Preuschen 145), but
is intended to produce the same favourable effect as συντόμως in 24.2: *Beg.*
IV 314.

VERSE 4: Paul speaks first (vv. 4f.) of his generally well-known Pharisaic
youth. μὲν οὖν: transition particle, see on 1.6. The controlling verb is the
classical ἴσασι (instead of οἴδασι). βίωσις (cf. Sir. Prol. line 14 τῆς ἐννόμου
βιώσεως): the way of life (Bauer, *Wb* 281). ἐκ νεότητος refers to βίωσιν: my
way of life from my youth. The addition τὴν ἀπ' ἀρχῆς γενομένην belongs to
what follows: his life from the beginning has been spent among his people[6]
and in Jerusalem: 22.3!

VERSE 5: προγινώσκοντές με ἄνωθεν: 'who know me from the beginning'.
The ὅτι-clause is again dependent upon ἴσασι: he amplifies the concept

---

[1] Cf. v. 29.
[2] Apul. *Metam.* 2, 21: *Porrigit dexteram et ad instar oratorum conformat articulum,
duobusque infimis conclusis digitis ceteros eminentes porrigit.*—sy[hmg] piously supplements the
secular description: *tunc ipse Paulus confidens et in spiritu sancto consolatus extendit manum.*
[3] The article is missing 'almost throughout with 'Ιουδαῖοι in Paul's defences against
the Jews, Acts 26.2, 3, 4, 7, 21; 25.10 (as with the name of the opponent in Attic court
speeches . . .)': Bl.-Debr. § 262, 1.
[4] A C 614 al have inserted ἐπιστάμενος (Bl.-Debr. § 416, 2) to improve the sentence,
other MSS. read εἰδώς.
[5] Otherwise Bengel: *consuetudinem in practicis, quaestionem in theoreticis.*
[6] Eger's interpretation of ἔθνος as 'province' (Judaea) is superseded (*Rechtsgeschichtliches zum NT*, 1919, n. 26); the same holds for the interpretation 'home province' (Cilicia)
in Zahn 797, *Beg.* IV 315. The connection with the Jewish people was recognized by H. J.
Cadbury, *The Making of Luke/Acts* 228, referring to Harnack, *Beiträge* III 54 (ET):
'speeches . . . in which the official usage, such as was customary before the heathen forum,
was to be followed' (cf. 24.17; 26.4; 28.19 as well as 24.3, 10).

βίωσιν.¹ αἵρεσις, 'direction', 'school' has no unfavourable connotations here, indeed it concerns the 'strictest'² in Judaism! τῆς ἡμετέρας θρησκείας: our religion.³ The expression is adapted to the heathen audience.

VERSE 6: From his Pharisaic past Paul passes over into the present. Although he is still the same believing Jew as before, indeed because he is, he stands now on trial. καὶ νῦν: cf. 20.25; but before this audience Paul does not continue with the biblical ἰδού. ἕστηκα... ἐλπίδι⁴ 'by reason of the hope of the promise given to our fathers'; what kind of hope it is, is not explained. But it can only concern the Messianic hope—brought to fulfilment in the resurrection of Jesus—which is inseparably bound up with the hope of resurrection; cf. 23.6.

VERSE 7: εἰς ἥν (the hoped-for fulfilment of the ἐπαγγελία⁵) καταντῆσαι:⁶ 'which our twelve tribes⁷ hope to obtain'. ἐν ἐκτενείᾳ: fervently, cf. 12.5 (as in LXX⁸). λατρεῦον (cf. 27.23) νύκτα καὶ ἡμέραν (cf. 20.31): said of Anna at Lk. 2.37. According to Preuschen (146) the Eighteen Benedictions are in mind here. According to the sense we should expect περὶ ταύτης τῆς ἐλπίδος (but Luke loves these appended relative clauses): because of this fundamental Jewish hope Paul is accused by the Jews—the absurdity of this accusation is thereby pilloried. Vv. 6f. are only comprehensible if the Jewish and the Christian hope are identified—as here in Luke by Paul. βασιλεῦ: for the vocative at the end of the sentence see Bl.-Debr. § 474, 6.

VERSE 8⁹ shows, however, that the Jews would have none of this unity, since they refused to believe in the resurrection of Jesus. τί ἄπιστον ... εἰ:

---

¹ Preuschen (145) incorrectly finds the juxtaposition of ἐκ νεότητος, ἀπ' ἀρχῆς and ἄνωθεν intolerable: Paul emphasizes to the utmost that he grew up from the beginning in Judaism (there is no thought here of his birth in Tarsus), and that as a Jew of the strictest order.
² Jos. *Vita* 191: Simon was τῆς ... Φαρισαίων αἱρέσεως, οἱ περὶ τὰ πάτρια νόμιμα δοκοῦσιν τῶν ἄλλων ἀκριβείᾳ διαφέρειν; similarly *Ant.* XVII 41; *Bell.* II 162. Cf. for the grammar Bl.-Debr. p. 3 n. 4; §§ 99, 2 and 60, 1.
³ θρησκεία means particularly cultic devotion, cf. Dibelius, *Der Brief des Jakobus* 114; *Beg.* IV 315; *ThWb* III 156 with reference to IV Macc. 5.7, 13, where a Gentile speaks about the Jewish religion with this concept.—ἀκριβεστάτη, a genuine superlative, is literary; Moulton 78 n. 1.
⁴ Cf. Bl.-Debr. § 14 supplement on the orthography; on the content, Acts 23.6.
⁵ On the concept of ἐπαγγελία see on 1.4.
⁶ B writes grammatically more correctly the fut. infin.; see Bl.-Debr. § 350.
⁷ Bl.-Debr. § 262, 3; Orac. Sibyl. III 249 solemnly speaks of δωδεκάφυλος λαός. Paul's carefully selected expression also is meant to sound solemn. That Paul wanted to recall the restoration of the twelve tribes in the Messianic kingdom (so Jacquier 707) is an over-interpretation; Paul is speaking only of the present and its expectations.
⁸ Judith 4.9 ἐν ἐκτενείᾳ μεγάλῃ; in II Macc. 14.38 it will mean rather 'persistent'; so Bauer *Wb* 486, for our passage also. But here the persistence is already expressed by 'day and night'.
⁹ E. Nestle, *Philologia sacra*, 1896, 54, wanted to place v. 8 after v. 22; Wendt (340 n. 1) accepted this transposition at least for 'the source'.

'why it is judged by you as unbelievable if God raises the dead?'[1] Actually Paul is speaking about the raising of Jesus. The Jews may not judge it unbelievable since they themselves believe in the (general) resurrection of the dead. εἰ = 'if in fact': here and in vv. 22f. it has almost the meaning of ὅτι.[2] Cf. Gen. 43.6 LXX: ἀναγγείλαντες . . . εἰ ἔστιν ὑμῖν ἀδελφός.

VERSE 9: Since at νεκρούς the speaker is thinking of Jesus, the transition to v. 9 is not so abrupt as Nestle (see p. 683 n. 9) assumed. Up to now Paul has been showing the unity of his conduct as a devout Jew and a devout Christian, which is misunderstood only by the foolish Jews. Now he continues with his life-story. The ultimate reason for the break which seems to lie between vv. 8 and 9 is that according to Luke's presentation it is really incomprehensible why Paul, the Pharisee who believes in the resurrection, himself persecuted those who confessed the risen Jesus. Luke does not explain this, but is content to mention the fact. ἐγὼ μὲν οὖν introduces a new paragraph: the thought turns from the attitude of the Jews back to Paul's former conduct. ἔδοξα ἐμαυτῷ:[3] By ἐμαυτῷ Luke means to strengthen the ἐγώ. δεῖν: dependent on 'I believed . . . I should': Bl.-Debr. § 405, 2. τὸ ὄνομα κτλ: the formal naming of the ὄνομα Ἰησοῦ proscribed among the Jews and—Romans? See on 4.7.

VERSE 10: ὅ (see on the relative ἧς in v. 7) καὶ ἐποίησα: the καὶ merely emphasizes the following word: 'this I did': *Beg.* IV 317; see on 1.3.[4] τῶν ἁγίων: expresses Paul's guilt: in the parallel passage 22.3ff., addressing the people, this expression is avoided. Paul's efforts are described by κατέκλεισα, κατήνεγκα, ἠνάγκαζον, ἐδίωκον: the aorist is relieved by the descriptive imperfect (Bl.-Debr. § 327). κατήνεγκα ψῆφον: to give one's vote against someone; Paul proves himself in the voting.[5] Here in contrast to 8.1 a series of executions of Christians is affirmed, in which Paul is said to have participated as judge: Paul's persecuting activity is enhanced as compared with 8.1, but in agreement with the allusions of 22.4.

VERSE 11: κατὰ πάσας τὰς συναγωγάς: in 9.2 only the synagogues of Damascus are mentioned; here the thought is first of those in Jerusalem. τιμωρῶν: the synagogue punishment of whipping will be meant here.

---

[1] Overbeck (437) explains, 'What do you think is unbelievable if God raises the dead? Answer: nothing.' Jacquier (707) ventured the translation, 'What? Does one judge it . . .' Neither of these explanations does justice to the passage, the difficulty of which lies not in grammar but in the idea presupposed.

[2] Advocated by H. J. Cadbury, *JBL* 48 (1929), 421f.

[3] According to Bl.-Debr. § 283, 1 ἔδοξά μοι would be classical, 'if as here no emphasis lies on the reflexive'.

[4] Usually translated 'this I also did'; cf. however *Beg.* IV 132. Jacquier (709) wants with Blass to distinguish the general ποιεῖν from πράττειν; actually ἐποίησα stands for πολλὰ ἐναντία ἔπραξα.

[5] Jacquier, to whom this judicial activity by the youthful Paul rightly appears incredible, attempts unsuccessfully to do away with the expression as a metaphor for συνευδοκέω (709). The council is here credited with the *ius gladii*.

ἠνάγκαζον is usually explained as a conative imperfect: so Bl.-Debr. § 326; Bauer, *Wb* 103; but see the following ἐδίωκον.[1] βλασφημεῖν: *maledicere Christo* in Pliny; cf. **13**.45. περισσῶς (popular substitute for μᾶλλον: Bl.-Debr. § 60, 3). ἐμμαινόμενος: raging furiously. ἕως καὶ εἰς τὰς ἔξω πόλεις: as far as outlying cities = outside Judaea. This also is an intensification compared with Chapters **9**.2 and **22**.5, where Paul goes from Jerusalem directly to Damascus.

VERSE 12: cf. **9**.2f.; **22**.5f. ἐν οἷς (Lk. **12**.1): 'at this time' (*Beg.* IV 318); 'under these conditions' (Bauer, *Wb* 1159 s.v. I 11c). ἐπιτροπή 'full authority'; beside ἐξουσία probably understood as 'commission'. ἀρχιερέων: in **9**.2 singular, in **22**.5 chief priests and Sanhedrin: Luke likes variation.

VERSE 13: ἡμέρας μέσης: **22**.6 περὶ μεσημβρίαν. κατὰ τὴν ὁδόν: **22**.6 ἐγγίζοντι τῇ Δαμασκῷ; 'I saw a light from heaven brighter than the sun shining about me': intensification compared with **9**.3 and **22**.6 (φῶς ἱκανόν). The light shone around his companions also.

VERSE 14: πάντων τε καταπεσόντων: in **9**.4 only Paul falls down, the others see no one; in **22**.6 also Paul alone is struck. But since in vv. 12ff. the figure of the disciple Ananias and the blinding and healing of Paul are omitted, the objectivity of the event can be demonstrated only by having all of them struck down.[2] τῇ Ἑβραΐδι διαλέκτῳ: that Jesus speaks Aramaic to Paul is indicated in **9**.4 and **22**.7 by the address Σαούλ, but here expressly noted. σκληρόν σοι πρὸς κέντρα λακτίζειν: a common Greek proverb, meaning 'opposition to me is senseless and impossible' (Bauernfeind 267). This for Paul's Hellenistic audience makes the significance of the call clear: Paul is completely in the power of Jesus. Cf. *Scholia vetera in Pindari Carmina* II 60f.: οὐ συμφέρει τῇ τύχῃ ἄνθρωπον ὄντα διαμάχεσθαι as the meaning of the quotation.[3]

---

[1] Jacquier 709: 'There is nothing unreasonable in the idea that some of those persecuted apostatized.' He and Preuschen 146 refer to Pliny *Ep.* X 96f.—Bl.-Debr. § 326 identifies ἠνάγκαζον as a conative imperfect and at the same time as an imperfect of repetition, while ἐδίωκον expresses only the latter. The imperfect could also however be understood as descriptive (Bl-.Debr. § 327).

[2] 614 gig sy^hmg amplify: διὰ τὸν φόβον. ἐγὼ μόνος ἤκουσα ...

[3] The question whether Luke is here dependent on Euripides (reference is particularly made to verse 794 of the *Bacchae*: θύοιμ' ἂν αὐτῷ μᾶλλον ἢ θυμούμενος/πρὸς κέντρα λακτίζοιμι θνητὸς ὢν θεῷ) has been much discussed: W. Nestle, 'Anklänge an Euripides in der Apg.', *Philologus* 59 (1900), 46ff.; F. Smend, 'Untersuchungen zu den Acta-Darstellungen von der Bekehrung des Paulus', *Angelos* 1 (1925), 34–5; W. G. Kümmel, *Römer 7 u. d. Bekehrung des Paulus*, 1929, 155–7, excursus on **26**.14; O. Weinreich, *Gebet und Wunder*, 1929, 282ff., 332ff.; H. Windisch, 'Die Christusepiphanie von Damascus und ihre religionsgeschichtlichen Parallelen', *ZNW* 31 (1932), 1ff.; A. Oepke, 'Probleme der vorchristlichen Zeit des Paulus', *ThStKr* 105 (1933), 387ff.; L. Schmid, *ThWb* III, 1938, 662–8; M. Dibelius, *Studies* 188–91 (1944); A. Vögeli, 'Lukas und Euripides', *ThZ* 9 (1953), 415–38. We agree with Vögeli's results: 'For the explanation of the epiphanies and miracles of deliverance or punishment in Acts recourse to Euripides is from a literary point of view superfluous, and the author's education does not extend beyond the popular philosophical standards of the Hellenistic age' (436f.), in which Euripides did not belong to school reading.

VERSE 15: cf. **9**.5 and **22**.8 (where ὁ Ναζωραῖος is further added). These are the words preserved in the old community tradition.

VERSE 16: ἀνάστηθι: cf. **9**.6 and **22**.10. στῆθι ἐπὶ τοὺς πόδας σου: Ez. **2**.1, 3. εἰς τοῦτο, 'thereto' is explained in προχειρίσασθαί (cf. **22**.14) σε ὑπηρέτην καὶ μάρτυρα (cf. **22**.15). Dibelius (*Studies* 92) assumes that the original text μάρτυρα ὧν τε εἶδες ὧν τε ὀφθήσεταί σοι has been distorted under the influence of the preceding ὤφθην. With this verse begins not a special source-report, but a Lucan narrative of the Christophany corresponding to the special situation.[1] Luke has shaped the words of the exalted Lord, the content of which was well established (sending of Paul to the Gentiles), with the aid of OT expressions and early Christian edificatory language. There is no mention here of blindness; see on v. 14. Paul is—corresponding to the conception in Acts (**16**.9f.; **18**.9; **22**.17ff.; **23**.11; **27**.23)—depicted as the constant recipient of heavenly visions.[2]

VERSE 17: ἐξαιρεῖσθαι can certainly also mean 'to choose'. But since in **7**.10, 34; **12**.10; **23**.27, it means 'to rescue', and further the choosing is already mentioned in v. 16, it means here 'to rescue', corresponding to Jer. **1**.7f. and I Chron. **16**.35: Paul will be rescued from the persecutions of the Jews and Gentiles. εἰς οὕς, in accordance with what follows, refers for preference to the Gentiles.

VERSE 18: '. . . to open their eyes': cf. Isa. **42**.7; '. . . to turn from darkness to light': cf. Isa. **42**.16. Now the biblical expressions are relieved by those of Christian edifying language: '(to turn) from the power of Satan to God': cf. Col. **1**.12f., where the concepts κλῆρος τῶν ἁγίων, ἐξουσία τοῦ σκότους, ἄφεσις ἁμαρτιῶν[3] occur.

VERSE 19: The address 'King Agrippa' shows that the words of Christ are ended. οὐκ ἐγενόμην ἀπειθής: an emphatic 'I obeyed'. τῇ οὐρανίῳ ὀπτασίᾳ: the 'heavenly appearance' here means the heavenly being who appeared. This is the decisive sentence: it was impossible for Paul (cf. σκληρὸν κτλ. v. 14!) to resist the heavenly command. The Christian mission is thereby justified.

VERSE 20: Paul preaches first to those in Damascus (**9**.19ff.!), then to those in Jerusalem (**9**.28f.). πᾶσάν τε χώραν τῆς Ἰουδαίας is formally and in

---

[1] That Paul was and is a pious Jew is a theme already dealt with in vv. 4ff. Hence it was no longer necessary to mention the devout Jew Ananias, by whom Paul was introduced into the new fellowship; mention of him was indeed prohibited, because the Gentile mission only appears as an absolute necessity when it is directly ordered by the heavenly ὀπτασία (cf. **22**.21; in Chapter 9 the Gentile mission is only mentioned quite unemphatically in **9**.15, a word of Christ to Ananias).

[2] Cf. **22**.15: 'Witness to what you have seen and heard.' μάρτυς is here not 'martyr'! It anticipates the μαρτυρόμενος of v. 22.

[3] The genitive of the infinitive, which occurs 'particularly in Luke', 'belongs to a higher level of the Koine': Bl.-Debr. § 400, especially in a final (and consecutive) sense: § 400, 5. —The expression ἄφεσις ἁμαρτιῶν does not occur in LXX; ἄφεσις stands for a whole series of Hebrew words among which 'release', דְּרוֹר comes closest to the NT sense of ἄφεσις.

content out of place.[1] Dibelius has sought to save the expression by the conjecture (*Studies* 92) that very early the word εἰς was omitted through haplography after Ἱεροσολύμοις;[2] but the whole is presumably an old and false gloss. For Acts, whose earlier account is here briefly repeated, knows nothing of a mission of Paul in Judaea, such as an early reader might conjecture on the basis of Rom. **15**.19. The content of the preaching is the summons to μετανοεῖν . . . θεόν,[3] as in earlier speeches of Acts. The one new addition recalls Lk. **3**.8: 'doing the works which reflect repentance'.

VERSE 21: ἕνεκα (Attic instead of the favourite εἵνεκεν) τούτων: on account of this missionary activity. There is no further mention of the alleged profanation of the Temple of **21**.28ff. διαχειρίζεσθαι (see **5**.30): to kill. For συλλαβόμενοι: cf. **1**.16; **12**.3; **23**.27. Since ἐπειρῶντο itself means 'they sought' we cannot explain the imperfect (with Wendt 344, Jacquier 713) as a conative imperfect, but must consider it as descriptive (Bl.-Debr. § 327).

VERSE 22: ἐπικουρία[4] . . . ταύτης: when Paul speaks of the Jewish attack upon him in the Temple, he has come to the end of the presentation of his missionary work. During this he has experienced God's help—thereby the promise of v. 17 is fulfilled, as it is also in relation to this last attack. Thus preserved alive by God he stands there as a witness to 'small and great', i.e. for everyone (not testifying to his rescue, but to the fulfilment of the OT promise!). That is his attitude at the present moment, but at the same time also throughout all his missionary work, and it is in this attitude that he is to remain in the memories of the readers of Acts. As such a witness Paul has fulfilled the call of v. 16.—He has said in this testimony nothing beyond what Moses and the prophets have said would take place.

VERSE 23 goes into detail: that[5] the Messiah must die,[6] that as the first one resurrected from the dead he preaches light to the Jewish people and the

---

[1] The accusative between the two datives is incomprehensible. Jacquier (713) sees in it an accusative of place describing the extent of Paul's activity; it is not—because of Gal. **1**.22—a question of preaching in Judaea. But it is methodologically inadmissible to draw conclusions from Galatians here. A sermon during Paul's visit to Jerusalem—so many exegetes—Luke has never mentioned. Ropes (*Beg.* III 237) assumes a Semitism, following Deut. **1**.19 (ἐπορεύθημεν πᾶσαν τὴν ἔρημον). But here a verb like 'to go' is lacking.

[2] The εἰς in E H L P S is a later correction and conjecture. 614 offers καὶ τοῖς ἐν; gig reads *et his qui in . . .*

[3] Cf. **3**.19.

[4] ἐπικουρία only here in the NT; in LXX only in Wisdom **13**.18. Hobart wanted to prove it a medical technical term (*The Medical Language of St. Luke*, 1881, 266). But in the physicians it is usually construed with δέομαι (requiring assistance); in the historians on the other hand it occurs as here with τυγχάνω: *Beg.* IV 320. Luke is thus to be seen here not as a physician, but as a historian!

[5] εἰ: here really = ὅτι; see above on v. 8. For παθητός see above on **1**.3; by παθεῖν is meant once again 'to die'. For Luke it is established fact (Lk. **24**.44-6) that the death of the Messiah is predicted everywhere in the OT.

[6] A Jewish tradition of the 'suffering Messiah' is not visible here, but only the Christian doctrine of his suffering death.

Gentile nations, and thus to the whole world of men. He proclaims light (cf. Isa. **9**.1) not only by the fact that through his resurrection he 'brings life and immortality to light'[1]—hitherto the resurrection was only a matter of hope and faith—but by mediating as Son (**13**.33) the forgiveness of sins (**13**.38; **26**.18).

VERSE 24: Again the artistic device of interruption after the decisive thing has been said (see on **22**.20), and indeed to emphasize this decisive point—the message of the resurrection. Festus (as already indicated at **25**.19) considers the resurrection impossible—he must however have grasped the difficult words of vv. 16ff. astonishingly well to be able to deny the doctrine of the resurrection as he does.[2] This teaching is madness, and Paul must have taken leave of his senses if he maintains it. Festus also indicates immediately in what manner this may have come about: the fault lay with too much study![3] Luke does not mean to draw an individual portrait of Festus here, but to show that the Roman official and the Roman state which he represents are not capable of dealing with these theological questions—as the Jew Agrippa was; 'the author is concerned only to characterize the parties in the assembly and the attitude they adopt to Paul's speech', as Overbeck already recognized (445). The psychological considerations of the commentators are superfluous. εἰς μανίαν περιτρέπει: Lucian, *Abdicatus* 30 shows that it is a current expression: *Beg.* IV 321.

VERSE 25: The μανία is the opposite of the Greek virtue σωφροσύνη,[4] which Paul possesses. He speaks 'words of truth and prudence', which therefore express the objective truth.

VERSE 26: For the truth and reasonableness of Paul's speech Agrippa is now called upon as an informed witness; ἐπίσταται . . . τούτων: he knows about it! πρὸς ὃν καί (the καί is again to be judged according to **1**.6; hence it is omitted in B) παρρησιαζόμενος: Paul speaks to Agrippa with complete freedom and confidence, 'for I am convinced that none of these things is hidden from him'. ἐν . . . γωνίᾳ: the death and resurrection of Jesus and the other

---

[1] Cf. II Tim. **1**.10—in our passage Luke has used two old Christological formulae: ἀνάστασις νεκρῶν, ἐγερθῆναι ἐκ νεκρῶν; cf. I Cor. **15**.20 and Col. **1**.18.

[2] μαίνῃ is difficult to translate: Luther's 'you rave' is today incomprehensible. 'You are out of your mind' is better, but does not capture the full meaning of μαίνῃ.

[3] τὰ γράμματα does not indicate here elementary knowledge but rather advanced knowledge (as in Plato *Apol.* 26D, where it concerns the writings of Anaxagoras: Bauer, *Wb* 328). But it is not really knowledge as such which has deprived Paul of his reason (although Bill. II 770 has cited in favour of this Targ. Jerus. I Nu. **22**.5: Balaam 'had become insane as a result of his great erudition'), but the study necessary to it: *Beg.* IV 321; Bauernfeind 268. Wendt 346 (similarly Knopf 655, Jacquier 716, Beyer 147): 'Paul must have discussed the problems only thematically indicated in v. 23 with an erudition imposing even to the procurator.' But this is to misunderstand Festus' words, which do not marvel at a great erudition but assume much study as the reason for Paul's insanity.

[4] Xen. *Memor.* I, **1**.16: διελέγετο τί σωφροσύνη, τί μανία: Bauer, *Wb* 1588.

miracles have happened in full publicity:[1] 'tout s'était passé publiquement: la prédication, la mort et la résurrection de Jésus, la prédication apostolique, le fait de Pentecôte . . . en un mot, la naissance du christianisme' (Jacquier 717). ἐν γωνίᾳ, 'in a corner' is a favourite Greek expression without Semitic parallel. οὐκ ἐν γωνίᾳ shows the rhetorical device of litotes.

VERSE 27: Agrippa as a devout Jew—he is assumed to be such here— must believe the prophets and hence also their prophecy of the death and resurrection of the Messiah, and this again means that he must believe in the Christian teaching.

VERSE 28: 'in short' = soon—Agrippa does not burden himself with a 'crash course' in theology but in an answer which deviates only at the last moment accords Paul the highest assent possible for him: 'Soon you will convince me to play the Christian'[2]—the statement really expected and fundamentally also intended 'to be a Christian' (so H L P S) he avoids, as one ought strictly to comprehend.[3] ποιεῖν in this sense is a technical term of the theatre.

VERSE 29: Paul takes up the king's word: 'I could wish'[4]—it is formulated as a wish capable of fulfilment!—'that sooner or later not only you but all my present listeners could be as I[5] am—except for these chains.' This

---

[1] Ἐνταῦθα περὶ τοῦ σταυροῦ λέγει τοῦτο, περὶ τῆς ἀναστάσεως, καὶ ὅτι πανταχοῦ τῆς οἰκουμένης γέγονε τὸ δόγμα, Chrysostom *hom.* 52, 4 quoted by Jacquier 717.

[2] As Overbeck 446f. already claimed, we may not take Agrippa's words ironically. If the king appealed to as a witness by Paul were to answer sarcastically (so for example Bauernfeind 268 interprets: 'You open your mouth—and the apparatus of conversion has to function; it cannot be otherwise. That is your whole concept of life.'), then the point of the scene would be blunted. Of course we may not with *Beg.* IV 323 translate the expression χριστιανὸν ποιῆσαι: 'You make short work of turning me into a missionary'—it is a question of becoming a Christian, not becoming a missionary. Yet *Beg.* IV 323 also mentions our interpretation as 'neater and easier, though insufficiently documented', referring to A. Nairne, *JTS* 21 (1920), 171f.; cf. also Schmiedel, *Encycl. Bibl.* I 754. A. Fridrichsen (*Coniect. Neotest.* III, 1938, 15) interprets, 'You want to make me believe that you have made me a Christian in the twinkling of an eye' (in this he assumes that the object—here: με—can be omitted if the infinitive has the same object as the main verb). This explanation also contradicts the requirements of the scene. —If Agrippa uses the word χριστιανός, then there is nothing contemptible in it: Luke makes the king employ the expression with which Hellenistic non-Christians according to 11.27 described the Christians.—χριστιανὸν ποιῆσαι is not (so Loisy 904 following Schmiedel, *Encycl. Bibl.* I, 751 n. 1) a Latinism (*Christianum agere*) without a Greek counterpart. The usage is already found in LXX: III Kingd. 20.7 (B); also in Joh. Climacus, Migne P. G. 88, 693 D ('My father loves me when I play the monk', ἐὰν ποιῶ μοναχόν) and Joh. Malalas 338 ('No one plays the King of the Romans like this one', οὐδεὶς ποιεῖ βασιλέα).

[3] The text χριστιανὸν γενέσθαι offered by the later MSS. is despite Zahn 809f. an early correction; Ephraem already read thus (against Preuschen 147; see *Beg.* III 450f.). πείθῃ also is a simplifying correction which presupposes Bachmann's solution 'Next you think to make me a Christian.'

[4] εὐξαίμην ἄν: a potential optative, which had become very rare: Bl.-Debr. § 359, 2; 385, 1.

[5] καὶ again only reinforces ἐγώ; see on 1.3.

answer shows that Agrippa in terms of sense has expressed the idea of becoming a Christian, only not so bluntly as the reading γενέσθαι makes it. The mention of the chains (which are not only symbolic for imprisonment!) shows how senseless it is that this man must stand in chains before his illustrious audience.

VERSE 30f.: Paul has had the last word. The assembly is ended. King and procurator rise with the other συγκαθήμενοι[1]—Zahn makes them regular legal advisers who now hold a session with the great lords in another room and come to a decision of 'not guilty'. Luke simply does not press the idea of the judicial assembly to that extent. Those present leave in lively conversation, which the reader can overhear: 'This man does nothing to deserve death or chains.' That is the general conviction. But why then is Paul not set free? V. 32 gives the answer.

VERSE 32: Agrippa, the authority here, explains to the governor, 'Paul could be free if he had not withdrawn himself from the jurisdiction of the procurator by the appeal to Caesar.' This imaginary acquittal is the highest recognition of Paul and his innocence (and hence that of Christianity!) which is possible in these circumstances. It is really only a technical or formal obstacle which makes his release impossible. Luke of course does not want to have Agrippa express the thought that Paul himself is to blame if he is not released. With that the entire scene would be ruined. For ἀπολελύσθαι κτλ, see Bl.-Debr. § 358, 1 supplement.

The third narrative of Paul's call (see above 325ff. and 628ff.) was a special favourite of the critical scholars. For since here the mediator Ananias is missing it appeared to fit best with Gal. 1.1 ('and not through a man'). Outright critics like Overbeck (430f.), Wellhausen (56) and E. Schwartz (*NGG* 1907, 299) admittedly considered the whole scene unhistorical. But that made no impression. In this regard they were this time correct: Paul by the appeal **was** withdrawn from the jurisdiction of Festus; therefore the latter no longer had to judge the question of Paul's guilt. Hence there was no occasion to trouble King Agrippa—who in reality was not the proper person.

But not only the basis but also the execution of this scene speaks against a historical core. It was indeed to be a legal investigation: 26.26 speaks of an ἀνάκρισις, 26.2,24 of the ἀπολογεῖσθαι of Paul, and the Roman staff officers and the notables of Caesarea are treated by Luke as regular assessors, συγκαθήμενοι, who confer together after the trial in an adjacent room and bring in a verdict of 'Not guilty!' But Luke does not speak of an actual sentence; he knows (v. 32) that the case has been taken out of Festus' hands.

---

[1] οἱ συγκαθήμενοι is the technical term for the advisers forming the consilium (see Hans Niedermeyer: 'Über antike Protokoll-Literatur' (Diss. Göttingen 1918) who on p. 20 also compares *cum consilio collocutus* CJT 26, 6: *Acta Cypr.* IV; Bruns, *Fontes* No. 180, 18, 188 with Acts 25.12).

So there remains a trial without prosecutor or witnesses; only the defendant speaks. The concrete crime (the defilement of the Temple!) is forgotten, to say nothing at all of **21.21** (Paul the apostate!). Beginning without an accusation, this remarkable scene ends with an unofficial discussion—admittedly favourable for Paul.

This alleged result also has an unreal effect. Certainly Agrippa was a worldly man and the law of Moses was irrelevant to him where his relationship with Berenice was concerned. But that he should so have exonerated Paul does not necessarily follow. At any rate he knew enough about the new teaching to prevent him advocating the release of a man whose handing over the Sanhedrin demanded.

But here it is not a matter of the historical trial of Paul, but of the conflict of Judaism against the Christian mission, which Paul represents as its victorious agent. Luke has designed his speech carefully, and turned it exactly for the audience. Hence the classical form ἴσασι (v. 4), expressions like ἔδοξα ἐμαυτῷ (v. 9) and οὐκ ἐγενόμην ἀπειθής (v. 19), the antithesis of μανία and σωφροσύνη (v. 23). Even the word of Jesus in v. 14 has to incorporate a Greek proverb.

Paul's life story, which the reader knows from Chapter 22, is therefore only hinted at in vv. 4f. Paul's diaspora Judaism is obliterated; he who does not remember **23.3** must think that Paul was in Jerusalem from his birth on. Then follows the old Lucan argument that Paul advocates only the Pharisaic hope (which here admittedly becomes the hope of the whole Jewish people). Without troubling himself about the inner tensions of this construction, Luke adds in still more glaring colours a picture of the Pauline persecution of the Christians—without such an intensification the speech would be an anticlimax in comparison with the earlier ones. Ananias has to be omitted: only if the heavenly command comes directly to Paul himself is it evident that he 'was not disobedient to the heavenly vision' (v. 19). Festus' objection against the Christian teaching of the resurrection shows only that the Roman authorities do not understand these questions of faith and therefore are not competent.

New and important is the fact that 'not one of these things has happened in a corner' (v. 26). These words light up Luke's presentation in Acts from beginning to end: the risen Lord was forty days with his disciples and went to heaven before many witnesses. At Pentecost thousands (2.41) experienced the mighty coming of the Spirit and its effect. The Apostles worked miracles before all the people (3.9; 5.15; 19.11f.), and spoke to thousands of listeners (4.4). They dealt with the High Council itself. Paul performs a miracle of punishment before the Proconsul Sergius Paulus, appears before the Proconsul Gallio, works in Ephesus in such a way that the Asiarchs concern themselves with his safety and the Chancellor speaks in favour of the Christians. The entire history of Christianity—it is no secret society!—is enacted publicly and before high and exalted personages. Christianity is not an inconspicuous event any longer, but a factor in world history. What Paul had written in I Cor. **1**.26ff. was superseded by the time of Luke. Luke does not launch a polemic against it; he is indeed not acquainted with the Pauline letters. In contrast, a new self-consciousness among the Christians makes its appearance in him. They are preparing themselves—Paul is the model!—to step out of their corner into the world of history and culture. Christianity finds an audience on the Areopagus and in the governor's court, and according to **27**.24 Paul even spoke before Caesar. And the men of high rank are not inaccessible: Paul brought the governor Sergius Paulus to the faith, made a deep impression upon the Proconsuls Felix and Festus, and almost converted King Agrippa.

On Luke's presupposition that the Christians proclaim only the same message as Moses and the prophets, namely the Messiah and his resurrection, such a conversion is by no means inconceivable: Agrippa as a devout Jew believed the prophets, and the prophets are at one with the Christians—must not Agrippa then become a Christian? That he really did become a Christian Luke could not maintain (the king, still alive, would not have accepted that: Loisy 903); but just as little could Agrippa give Paul a refusal. Luke's solution is so good that J. Weiss (51) declared Agrippa's words (v. 28) 'incomprehensible'. 'You almost make me a Christian' would have been too much. Hence Luke allows the king to turn aside at the last minute: 'You almost bring me to the point of playing the Christian.' These words which vacillate between yes and no, seriousness and humour, Paul adroitly takes up and answers with the same combination of seriousness and humour: 'May you all sooner or later be as I am '—the king, Berenice, Festus and the entire illustrious assembly –'except for these chains.' This Paul knows how one must speak in order to be popular at court. His complete guiltlessness is therefore recognized—*post festum* and *post* Festum—and but for the unfortunate appeal he would now be free!

This however almost bends the bow too far. An innocent exegete has read out of **25**.25 that Festus attributes the fact that he was not set free to Paul's thick-headedness. Luke naturally does not mean to say that Paul himself by an over-hasty appeal has caused the opening prison doors to slam shut again. The reader is only to carry away the impression that Paul was completely innocent, although he was not freed!

Now that we have experienced the last great apologetic scene, it is worth while to consider them all together. Fundamentally from **21**.27–**26**.32 Luke is ringing the changes on one and the same theme: the relationship between Rome, the Jews and the Christians. This triangular relationship seems at first to appear thus; the Jews accuse the Christians and Rome is appealed to as judge. But in reality—Luke convinces not by argument but by narration —it is different: Christianity (represented by Paul) has committed no πονηρά, no crimes against Roman law. The theological differences of Jews and Christians ultimately remain the only point of accusation. But on this the Roman authorities prove to be not competent; the question of the resurrection is to them incomprehensible.

Why has Luke devoted six chapters to this problem? Not for the sake of explaining Paul's trial: in the course of these chapters the image of it becomes more and more opaque. Does Luke handle the matter so because he is bent on a great reconciliation of Jews, Jewish Christians and Gentile Christians? Jewish Christianity after 70 had become unimportant, and the Gentile Christians were not Paulinists who had to contend with Judaizers for recognition. Luke no longer hoped for the conversion of the Jews. They had not used the hour of conversion granted them in God's plan of salvation, and now it is—according to God's same plan of salvation—too late: they will no longer change. Thus although Paul speaks in Chapter 22 to the Jewish people, in 23 to the Sanhedrin and in 26 to King Agrippa, Luke with all this is not canvassing for a last-minute conversion. Dibelius (*Studies* 213) therefore conjectures another reason: Luke wanted to help the Christians of his own age with their defence. 'These themes are intended to emphasize the fact that Christians have not rebelled against the emperor, nor against the temple, nor against the law' (Acts 25.8), 'but that the essential matter of dispute between them and the Jews is the question of the resurrection.' But when Luke wrote, the Temple lay in ruins, and no Christian was accused any longer because of his attitude to the Temple. This historical detail fits only Paul and not later Christianity. The same holds for Paul's Pharisaic past. The idea that Luke wanted to advise the Christians in their conduct before Roman courts cannot be substantiated. Why then this ever-renewed *apologia* of Paul? Luke had portrayed him, the most successful missionary, as the real driving force of the Christian mission. Then it was unfortunate that he was arrested, held prisoner, brought to Rome and finally executed. To that extent it was absolutely necessary to bring the proof of his innocence convincingly to light. But it was important not only to overcome this past. One had also to think about the future. Unlike his great contemporary, the seer of the Apocalypse, Luke did not see in Rome the great whore, whom God will soon annihilate in the judgement of this world. The end does not stand at the gates; before that a mighty missionary task still awaits the Christians. Hence Luke sees his task not in equipping the Church for martyrdom immediately before the end, but in securing for it the possibility of life within the Roman Empire. But with this very task Paul could help the Christians. How he, the Roman citizen, had been able to get along with the Romans—even in situations of conflict!—and to win their respect and trust. Why should Rome not tolerate the Christian 'Way'? Because the Jews up and down the country accused the Christians? They could be countered with the proof that precisely the strictest movement in Judaism, Pharisaism, agreed with Christianity in its belief in the resurrection. Luke emphatically presented this, especially in Chapters 23 and 26.

Luke no longer lives in the world of Paul. The Temple in Jerusalem stands no more, and everything in the law of Moses which is connected with the Temple cult has been rendered useless. The reception of uncircumcised Gentiles into the Christian Church God himself brought about; the OT demand for circumcision no longer applies to non-Jews. The Gentile Christians fulfil the requirements appointed for them in the law; hence no reproach can be brought against them (21.25). The ethical commandments of the law are valid among the Christians as a matter of course. That the law occasions only wrath, and awakens not obedience but rather disobedience—such and similar statements Luke would have relegated to what II Peter 3.16 calls δυσνόητα, things difficult to understand, 'which the ignorant and unstable distort . . .'. The Lucan Paul lacks much that the real Paul possessed, perhaps the best. But again the Lucan Paul also possesses much that was lacking from the real Paul, and yet was necessary if he was to be portrayed as *the* Christian witness to the truth in his time.

65

ACTS 27:1–44
SEA VOYAGE AND SHIPWRECK

[1] Now when it was decided that we should sail for Italy, Paul and some other prisoners were handed over to a centurion by the name of Julius of the Cohort Augusta. [2] Boarding a ship from Adramyttium which was to visit the ports of (the province of) Asia, we departed, the Macedonian Aristarchus from Thessalonica being with us. [3] The next day we landed in Sidon, and Julius treated Paul kindly and allowed him to go to his friends and have himself cared for. [4] Putting to sea from there we sailed under the lee of Cyprus because the winds were against us, [5] and when we had sailed through the Cilician and Pamphylian seas we came to Myra in Lycia. [6] There the centurion found an Alexandrian ship sailing for Italy and had us embark on it. [7] Making little headway in many days and arriving with difficulty at Cnidus, since the wind did not let us proceed, we sailed round Crete by Salmone, [8] and sailing by there only with difficulty we came to a place with the name 'Good Harbour', which was near the city of Lasea. [9] Since much time had been lost and the sea voyage was already dangerous, because the fast had already gone by, Paul gave warning, [10] saying to them, 'Men, I see that the voyage is going to involve hardship and much loss not only of the cargo and the ship but also of our lives.' [11] The centurion however followed the captain and the owner of the ship rather than Paul's advice. [12] Since the harbour was unsuitable for wintering, the majority decided to depart from there, in the hope that they might reach Phoenix, a harbour of Crete open to the southwest and northwest, and winter there. [13] But when a light southerly breeze set in, they thought they had achieved their purpose, and weighed anchor and sailed along Crete. [14] After a short time, however, the stormy wind called the north-easter struck them. [15] Since the ship was carried away and could not be brought about to face the wind, we gave way (to the wind) and let (the wind) carry us. [16] Sailing in the lee of an island called Clauda, we managed with difficulty to get control of the lifeboat; [17] when they had hoisted it up, they began emergency measures, undergirding the ship. And fearing they would strike on the Syrtis, they lowered the drift-anchor and so drove on. [18] Because we suffered greatly from the storm, on the next day they jettisoned cargo, [19] and on the third day with their own hands threw the ship's tackle overboard. [20] Since neither sun nor stars appeared for many days and no small tempest set upon us, finally all hope of our being

saved disappeared.   [21] And when no one would eat any longer, Paul then stepped forward in their midst and said, 'You should have listened to me and not departed from Crete, and avoided this hardship and loss.   [22] And now I advise you to be of good courage. For there will be no loss of life among you, only of the ship.   [23] For there came to me this night an angel of the God to whom I belong and whom I serve,   [24] saying, "Fear not, Paul! You must stand before Caesar, and behold, God has granted to you all those travelling with you!"   [25] Therefore be of good courage, men! For I trust God that it will be as it has been told me.   [26] But we must run upon an island.'
[27] Now when the fourteenth night came, while we drifted in the Adriatic, the sailors noticed about midnight that land was drawing near.   [28] And sounding they found twenty fathoms, but when they had travelled a little further and sounded again, they found fifteen fathoms.   [29] And afraid that we would run on the rocks, they threw four anchors out from the stern and prayed for day.   [30] But when the sailors sought to flee from the ship and lowered the lifeboat into the sea on the pretext that they wanted to lay out anchors from the bow,   [31] Paul said to the centurion and the soldiers, 'If these do not remain in the ship, you cannot be saved!'   [32] Then the soldiers cut the lines of the lifeboat and set it adrift.   [33] Until day was about to dawn, Paul admonished everyone to take something to eat, saying, 'Today you are awaiting the fourteenth day that you have gone without food and have taken nothing to yourselves.   [34] Therefore I beseech you to take something to eat, for this will help to save you. For not one of you will lose a hair from his head.'   [35] Saying this and taking bread, he thanked God before them all, and breaking it began to eat.   [36] Then all were of good courage and themselves took something to eat.   [37] We were in all two hundred and seventy-six souls on the ship.   [38] When they had satisfied themselves, they lightened the ship by throwing the grain into the sea.   [39] When it became daylight, they did not recognize the land but they noticed a bay with a beach, upon which they wanted to run the ship aground if possible.   [40] And casting off the anchors, they left them in the sea, at the same time loosening the lines which held the tiller, and hoisting the foresail they ran before the wind to the beach.   [41] Striking a shoal, they let the ship run aground and the bow struck and remained immovable, but the stern broke off at the impact.   [42] The soldiers decided to kill the prisoners so that no one could escape by swimming. [43] The centurion, however, who wanted to save Paul, kept them from their purpose and ordered those who could swim to jump first and make for land, [44] and then the rest, some on planks, others on some part of the ship. And so it happened that all reached land safely.

Bibliography:

A. Breusing, *Die Nautik der Alten*, Bremen 1886; H. Michaelsen, 'Riesenschiffe im Altertum' (*Zeitschr. f. Meereskunde* 8, Heft 87), Berlin 1914;

A. Köster, *Schiffahrt u. Handelsverkehr d. östl. Mittelmeeres im 3 u. 2. Jrtsd. v. Chr.* (*Beiheft z. Alten Orient* 1), Leipzig, 1924; id., *Studien z. Geschichte d. antiken Seewesens*, Leipzig, 1934; H. J. Cadbury, 'Lexical Notes on Luke-Acts V: Luke and the Horse-Doctors', *JBL* 52 (1933), 55–65 (esp. 63); Bo Reicke, 'Die Mahlzeit d. Paulus a.d. Wellen d. Mittelmeeres', *ThZ* 4 (1948), 401–10; L. Casson, 'The Isis and her Voyage', *TAPA* 81 (1950), 43–56; Menoud 1952, 33–6, see § 7; Renié 332–45; J. Vars, *L'art nautique dans l'antiquité*, Paris 1887, esp. 172–259; Haenchen, 'Acta 27', *Zeit u. Geschichte*, Dankesgabe an Rudolf Bultmann zum 80. Geburtstag, Tübingen 1964, 235–54; Williams 266–73; Conzelmann 140–7; Stählin 313–22.

J. Ronge, 'Act. **27.** 1–10', *Vig. Christ.* 14 (1960), 193ff.; W. K. L. Clarke, 'Acts **27.** 17', *Exp.Tim.* 26 (1914–5), 377f.; J. Renié, 'Summisso vase (Act 27.17)', *RScR* 35 (1948), 272–5; J. R. Madan, 'The ἀσιτία on St. Paul's Voyage', *JTS* 4 (1904), 116–21; G. A. Sim, 'Acts **27.** 39', *Exp.Tim.* 28 (1916–7), 187f.; W. Cowan, 'Acts **27.** 39', *Exp.Tim.* 27 (1915–6), 472f.; 28 (1916–7), 330f.; F. Zorell, 'Sprachliche Randnoten zum N.T. (Apg. **27.** 44)', *BZ* 9 (1911), 159f.; F. Brannigan, 'Nautisches über die Seefahrt des hl. Apostels Paulus Acta 27', *Theologie u. Glaube* 25 (1933), 170 86; W. Burridge, *Seeking the Site of St. Paul's Shipwreck*, La Valetta, Malta, 1952; F. Lallemand, *Das Logbuch des Maarkos Sestios*, Stuttgart 1958; E. Zinn, ''Άπορος Σωτηρία. Horaz im Rettungsboot', *Eranion.* Festschrift f. H. Hommel, Tübingen, 1961, 185–212.

VERSE 1: 'And so the governor decided to send him to Caesar': this 'Western' reading (97 h sy[hmg]) seems to have sprung from the recognition that the 'we' in the B text does not fit. Only Paul indeed is sent to Rome, but not his friends who of their own free will accompany him.[1] παρεδίδουν[2]: a circumlocution for the Roman authorities ('they handed him over'). ἑτέρους δεσμώτας: Paul is included in a transport of prisoners.[3] 'Ιούλιος: only the *nomen gentile* is given.[4] σπεῖρα Σεβαστή: Cohors Augusta; 'Augusta' is often an honorary title for auxiliary cohorts.[5]

[1] This admittedly required special permission from the procurator: Loisy 908. That for this purpose they had to become formally Paul's slaves is a quite unfounded assertion.

[2] The imperfect here breaks the classical rules: *Beg.* IV 325: cf. Bl.-Debr. § 327 and Bruce 452. But the imperfects in vv. 9, 11, 13, 15, 17f., 20, 27, 33, 39f. also give the impression that here (in Luke's source?) the imperfect is the tense of narrative: Radermacher[2] 153.

[3] Luke does not distinguish ἄλλος and ἕτερος: that the other prisoners are of a different kind (e.g. destined to fight the animals in the arena) is not indicated. Finally Paul has been accused of a crime which carried the death penalty (25.11!).

[4] He is mentioned only here and in v. 3, where A reads 'Ιουλιανός.

[5] See T. R. S. Broughton, 'The Roman Army', *Beg.* V 427–45, esp. 443f. A Cohors Augusta I is documented for the time of Agrippa II in Caesarea (Dittenberger OGIS 421, cf. Zahn 819 n. 55)—perhaps Luke transferred the troop distributions of his own time to the time of Paul. Since such an important prisoner was scarcely delivered to the centurion of a Syrian auxiliary troop, W. Ramsay conjectured (*St. Paul* 314f.) that the centurion was one of those *frumentarii* (admittedly attested only from the time of Trajan) who as officials with the rank of centurion not only cared for the provisioning of troops but were also employed as a kind of secret police of the emperor, and for the transference of prisoners.

VERSE 2: πλοῖον 'Αδραμυττηνόν: a ship with its home port Adramyttium (south-east of Troas).[1] κατά replaces a genitive;[2] see on **27.5**. The Asia Minor harbours are meant. In addition to the narrator Paul is accompanied by Aristarchus: see on **19.29, 20.4**; Philemon 24. Col. **4.10** calls him συναιχμάλωτος.[3]

VERSE 3: On the Syrian coast a current runs north; Nile water can be traced by edulcoration as far as Carmel: Köster, *Schiffahrt* 14. At only three knots the ship made the sixty-nine nautical miles in twenty-three hours: Breusing 149f. φιλανθρώπως (cf. **28.**2); here and in v. 43 the special friendliness of the centurion is emphasized: he allows Paul to go to his 'friends'[4] in order to have himself cared for. Luke avoids the name 'Christian'; cf. **24.23** ἰδίων. Perhaps the discharge and loading of merchandise made a somewhat longer stay necessary. Julius could of course allow Paul to go to the Christian community only in the company of a soldier.[5]

VERSE 4: ὑπεπλεύσαμεν: 'under', i.e. here sailing east of Cyprus, which protected them against the west wind which normally blows in late summer in the eastern Mediterranean. It did not allow any direct voyage to Italy. Probably indeed it came out of the west-north-west.

VERSE 5: τὸ πέλαγος . . . Παμφυλίαν: = the sea along the coasts of Cilicia and Pamphylia: Bauer, *Wb* 1271. This voyage was possible for one thing owing to a strong westerly current on the south coast of Asia Minor,[6] and for another through the wind blowing (particularly at night) seawards from the land. Only one had to keep close to the coast (*Beg.* IV 326). So the ship came to Myra.[7]

To sustain this hypothesis Ramsay had not only to declare the 'Western' text of **28.16** (see Mommsen-Harnack *SBA* 1895, 492ff.) to be original, but also to assume that Luke did not use the technical terminology and as a Greek did not bother about the Roman names. So Ramsay makes of the σπεῖρα Σεβαστη a 'troop of the emperor', and the centurion a *frumentarius*.—Balmer (271) affirms that 'part of an Augustan cohort must have been relieved' (= the soldiers mentioned in Chapter 27). But the Syrian Cohors Augusta **I** was recruited from Syrians, not Romans!—Voigt (727) has one of the five cohorts stationed in Caesarea ordered back to Rome!—See also on **28.16**.

[1] Cf. R. Harris, 'Adramyttium', *Contemp. Rev.* (1925), 194–202; Bauer, *Wb* 36.
[2] The marginal note in a 'Western' text Θεσσαλονικέων δὲ 'Αρίσταρχος καὶ Σέκουνδος, which refers back to **20.4**, is in 614 sy[h] among others incorporated into the text itself.
[3] Cf. Acts **2.10**; **17.28**: G. Rudberg, *Eranos* 19, 173ff.
[4] According to Harnack, *Miss. u. Ausbr.*[4], 1923, 435ff. (ET *The Mission and Expansion of Christianity*, 1908[2], 624), a classical designation of the Christians: cf. III John 15 (John **15.14**; Lk. **12.4**). Later however it occurs only in Gnostic-Christian circles: *Beg.* IV 326.
[5] This difficulty is removed by the text of h: *ille centurio permisit amicis, qui veniebant (ad eum), uti curam eius agerent.*
[6] It travels up to three sea-miles per hour: Balmer 294.
[7] B reads: Μυρρα. The reading Λύστραν (א* A vulg bo) Breusing (150) explains from the subsidiary form of the name: Λίμυρα. The 'fourteen days' of the 'Western' text (614 sy[hmg]) are the average duration of the voyage. Lucian, *Navig.* 7, gives ten days for the

VERSE 6: Since the grain-traffic from Egypt to Rome, because of wind conditions, regularly came to Myra, the centurion found a ship here bound for Italy.[1] ἐνεβίβασεν ἡμᾶς creates the same difficulties as the 'we' in v. 1. By it Luke again indicates that the reader has an eyewitness report before him (which however has been not a little reworked).

VERSE 7: ἱκανός here and v. 9: a favourite Lucan word. βραδυπλοοῦντες: Bauer, *Wb* 291: 'to make little headway'.[2] μόλις: 'only with difficulty'. κατὰ τὴν Κνίδον: up to the tip of Cnidos. μὴ προσεῶντος κτλ.; the narrator seems to assume that the course had to be changed on account of special wind conditions. But the normal route, up to Nelson's time, went by Myra, Rhodes and then south to Crete.[3] ὑπεπλεύσαμεν κτλ: 'we sailed in the lee of Crete by (Cape) Salmone', on the northeast tip of the island.

VERSE 8: μόλις . . . αὐτήν: 'only with difficulty sailing by that'. Balmer thinks of dangerous cross-winds in the lee of the coast which bring the ship dangerously close to the rocks. Καλοιλιμένες: in spite of its fine name 'Good Harbour', only a bay open to the east near the city of Lasaia.[4]

VERSE 9: ἱκανός see on v. 7; on the whole journey so far much time has elapsed. Renié thinks however of a long stay in 'Good Harbour'. ὄντος . . . πλοός: according to Vegetius, *De re militari* IV 39, sea voyages were

---

voyage from Sidon to the Lycian coast (*Beg.* IV 327). The 'Western' addition is not original: L. Casson, 'Speed under Sail of Ancient Ships', *TAPA* 82 (1951) 145 calculates for the voyage Alexandria-Myra-Crete 11–14 days' time, for Alexandria-Puteoli 50–70 days.

[1] Ramsay (*St. Paul* 324f.) maintains that a ship assigned to Rome's grain supply belonged to the 'imperial merchant marine', the ναύκληρος was the captain and the κυβερνήτης the first officer. He refers for this to *Archiv f. Papyrusforsch.* 5, 1913, 298. But here it is a matter of an entirely different case from the Ptolemaic period: Cleopatra had leased some ships which belonged to her for the transport of corn. The grain traffic from Egypt to Rome, however, was managed by private firms. When Claudius during a famine had to have grain brought from Egypt at the time of the dangerous winter storms, he promised the merchants a safe profit and accepted responsibility in the event of damage: Suetonius *Claudius* 18. Moreover, the inscriptions (Dittenberger *OGIS* 140, 7; 591, 3) show that the ναύκληρος is the owner and the κυβερνήτης is the 'ship's master' (the skipper); the merchant who finances the voyage, the *negotiator*, is called the ἐγδοχεύς. Renié (332) is thus incorrect in following Ramsay.

[2] *Beg.* IV 327 considers the meaning 'beating' possible. But ancient cargo ships (see Breusing 152) could only sail with a wind which came directly from the side ('to sail with half a wind'): Pliny *N.H.* II, 47. Real tacking was unknown to them and could not be carried out on the unwieldy cargo ships with their one large sail. Paul's ship is rated at over 1,200 tons laden weight (cf. Casson, *TAPA* 81 (1950), 55; Breusing's estimate (157) is probably too high). The average speed in a favourable wind will have amounted to 5 knots = 6 m.p.h.: Breusing 12.

[3] References in Casson, *TAPA* 81, 43ff.; only one usually sailed to the west past Cyprus, which was possible with a plain west wind. See also *Sailing Directions for the Mediterranean* IV, U.S. Hydrogr. Office No. 154 A, Washington 1942, 32f.

[4] B 69 al Λασεα is only a difference in transcription: αι was spoken as ε and often written correspondingly. The modern name Calolomonia may have arisen only at a later date on the basis of Acts; the ancient authors know nothing of it. Pliny *N.H.* IV 12 gives for Lasaia the two forms Lasos and Alos; A sy^hmg "Αλασσα, which is corrupted in the Vulgate to *thalassa*.

dangerous after the 15th of September and completely ceased between the 11th of November and the 10th of March. διὰ τὸ ... παρεληλυθέναι: the great fast five days before the festival of atonement (10th Tishri: see Billerbeck II 771f.).[1] παρήνει: according to Bl.-Debr. § 328 literary language.

VERSE 10: ὅτι: Hellenistic, only as an introductory sign; hence the acc. and infin.[2] can follow. ὕβρις: here the hardship inflicted by the elements (Bauer, *Wb* 1646). πολλὴ ζημία: great loss.[3] ψυχῶν (LXX!): 'our lives'.[4] The entire expression is typically Lucan. The prediction is moderated in vv. 22ff.

VERSE 11: Luke assumes that the centurion can decide on the ship's course (see above p. 697 n. 5). But in reality he could only claim places for the transport of his prisoners; he would also have been incapable of deciding technical nautical problems. On the question how Luke came to his presentation, see the general discussion. κυβερνήτης = the skipper who has responsibility for the navigation of the ship, not the man at the tiller, the helmsman. The ναυκληρός = the owner of the ship usually accompanied it on the voyage, as the inscriptions show. τοῖς ... λεγομένοις: Paul's words.[5]

VERSE 12 has no true connection with v. 11; on the other hand there is no lacuna if vv. 9b–11 are omitted (from παρήνει on).[6] ὑπάρχων for ὧν occurs often in Luke. Since 'Good Harbour' was 'unsuitable' for wintering, the majority decided to continue in order to reach the harbour of Phoenix which was favourable for a winter stay.[7]

---

[1] The fast fell in the year 59 on the 5th October, but in the preceding years before the Equinox; see Workman, *Exp.Tim.* 11 (1899/1900), 316–9.

[2] Since μέλλω with the present infin. takes the place of the future infin., the expression (like **11**.28; **23**.30 v.l.; **24**.5) combines two constructions. See also Bl.-Debr. § 397, 6 and Radermacher² 195.

[3] Since ὕβρις occurs in II Cor. **12**.10 and ζημία in Phil. **3**.7f., Renié 336 thinks he hears here the *ipsissima vox Pauli*. But Paul like the author here simply speaks the Hellenistic Greek of their time.

[4] Cf. for ψυχή Mt. **6**.25ff.; Lk. **12**.22ff.; for ζημιόω: Mt. **16**.26.

[5] Since Paul was assigned to the transport as a highly suspect prisoner (*crimen laesae majestatis?*), he in no way played the role with which Luke credits him; C.S.C. Williams' appeal to 'Paul's personality' (277) changes nothing. It would be thoroughly perverse to appeal to Paul's experience of sea voyages (which he certainly possessed): apart from the fact that he had not travelled this route before, while the owner and captain had, we must consider that Luke does not want to praise Paul as an experienced and weather-wise traveller, but as a man gifted by God with prophetic foresight. That God later changes the fate here foretold does not diminish the truth of this prophecy.

[6] Wellhausen (53) concluded from this that vv. 9–11 are interpolated. Preuschen (150) and Loisy (911) have followed him. Dibelius (*Studies* 205) had the insight and the courage to take up this critical tradition again.

[7] No one voices the intention 'possibly to attempt to get to Italy' (Williams 270). —The πλείονες are the majority of the seamen competent in these questions. Luke however thinks of Paul, the centurion, the owner and the navigation officer as deliberating. Phoenix was earlier usually identified with Lutro, which however is open towards the east, so that a gale blowing from that direction would have shattered a ship mooring in Lutro. Phoenix was βλέπων κατὰ λίβα κτλ. This expression according to the usage of LXX (II Chron. **4**.4; Ez. **8**.3ff.; **9**.2; **11**.1; **40**.6ff.; **43**.1ff.; **44**.1ff.) means to be open towards the south-west

VERSE 13: A light south wind seems to provide the opportunity for the change of harbours—a day's voyage. δόξαντες . . . κεκρατηκέναι: a very elegant, not to say affected expression. With ἄραντες supply according to the sense 'the anchors'. Presumably the ship was towed out of 'Good Harbour' by means of the lifeboat: Balmer 332. ἆσσον . . . Κρήτην: they sail close in along Crete (Bl.-Debr. § 244, 2).[1]

VERSE 14: Soon, as they sail round Cape Matala, the storm wind from Crete called Euraquilo (north-easter) strikes[2] the ship. That is, the Bora coming from Mt. Ida drove the ship out into the open sea, where in the meantime the strong north-easter had set in: *Beg.* IV 331.

VERSE 15: The ship is carried along with the storm and it is no longer possible ἀντοφθαλμεῖν – to bring the bow into the wind and anchor in this position.[3] So 'we abandoned' (ourselves or the ship) 'to the wind and let ourselves drive (ἐφερόμεθα) before the wind' (Voigt 728).[4]

VERSE 16: ὑποδραμόντες: sailing[5] 'under' = screened from the wind by

---

and north-west (Bauer, *Wb* 940). Therefore Phoenix is to be identified with the modern Phincka—in this name the old 'Phoenix' still lives on—, which opens towards the west. R. M. Ogilvie (in his excellent article 'Phoenix', *JTS* N.S. 9, 1958, 308ff.) has irrefutably shown that all this is right, and that the ground near Phineka has risen about 5m. since the days of Paul.—For the meaning of the names of the winds we follow Lake/Cadbury, 'The Winds', *Beg.* V, 1933, 338–44; cf. Pauly-Wissowa 20, 1950, 431–5.—In 'Anonymi Stadiasmus maris magni' (*Geographi Graeci minores*, Vol. I rec. C. Mullerus, Parisiis 1855, 506–8, §§ 323–8) we read concerning Phoenix and its vicinity: 'From Halai to Matala ρ′ (= 300) stadia (in reality π′ = 80); it is a city and has a harbour. From Matala to Sulia 65 stadia. It is a harbour, has good water. From Sulena (sic) to Psycheus 12 stadia . . . From Psycheus to Lamona 150 stadia, is a harbour and has a city and water. From Lamona to Apollonia 30 stadia. From Apollonia to Phoenix 100 stadia. It is a city, has a harbour and an island. From Claudia to Phoenix 300 stadia' (in reality 220), 'has a city and a harbour.'

[1] The ancient versions sometimes saw in ἆσσον a name; vulg. *de Asson*, bo: 'from Assos', sa: 'from Alasos' (= the other form of the name Lasaia, see v. 8).

[2] βάλλω intransitive: Radermacher[2] 23, 28f.; otherwise only of persons. The wind is conceived as a living being. The wind name εὐρακύλων (ℵ: εὐροκλυδών = εὖρος, east wind + κλυδών, surging waves) only here. Since εὖρος properly means 'east-south-east wind' and Aquilo 'north wind', perhaps a north-east wind is meant.

[3] C. Voigt 728: 'The attempt to bring the ship's head into the wind in order to heave to failed . . . or could no longer be accomplished because of the high sea, which would have struck the ship broadside and sunk it.' Otherwise the ship in this position—with its bow into the waves—would have weathered the storm at anchor.

[4] This does not mean that they simply gave up to the wind and waves. If a ship has no headway it can no longer be steered. But then it would soon be struck athwart by the waves and be battered to pieces. Thus, since they could not think of sailing before the wind with the 66-foot broad mainsail, they will have given the ship enough headway with the small sail on the foremast (see v. 40) to allow it to be steered and keep it from broaching.

[5] Κλαῦδα is probably the Alexandrian, Καῦδα B ℵ³ vulg pesh the Latin form of the name: *Beg.* IV 332. We can hardly think of their anchoring off Clauda (so Balmer 350f.), for then they could also have run for its harbour. It was only that for the time being they had relatively calm water in the lee of the island.

'an island'. νησίον 'island': the Hellenistic language is fond of diminutives; see for example Jn. **18**.10. ἰσχύσαμεν μόλις: 'we succeeded only with difficulty'. περικρατεῖς γενέσθαι has a literary ring. There was danger that the lifeboat, which up to this time had been in tow, would be dashed by a wave against the ship's stern.

The way in which Acts reports Paul's journeys allows many readers to overlook the fact that it speaks of numerous sea voyages by Paul. Luke was generally not concerned to give exactly the distances which Paul put behind him in the process. We wish to make this good, but for simplicity to measure the distances covered as the crow flies. The actual distances were thus even greater. (1) That the journey from Caesarea to Tarsus, mentioned in Acts **9**.30, was a sea voyage is not indicated at all. But it is extremely improbable that instead of this sea voyage of about 280 miles the land route was used. (2) Also the journey of Barnabas from Antioch to Tarsus and Paul's return trip with Barnabas to Antioch—in each case over 60 miles—will have been by sea (Acts **11**.25f.) although Luke says nothing of it. (3) On the other hand in **13**.4 by using the word ἀπέπλευσαν he gives us to understand that a ship was used for the journey—otherwise not possible—from Seleucia, the harbour of Antioch to Salamis on Cyprus; it could have covered the more than 125 miles in two days. (4) The journey from New Paphos in Cyprus to Perga or Attaleia also (Acts **13**.13), with its over 180 miles, is characterized as a sea voyage only by ἀναχθέντες. (5) In the journey from Attaleia to Antioch **14**.26—it was over 300 miles—Luke indicates that it was a sea voyage by κἀκεῖθεν ἀπέπλευσαν. (6) The journey from Troas by Samothrace to Neapolis **16**.1f.—something over 125 miles—is described in relative detail, since the composition suggested it: the beginning of the Pauline mission proper is described thus exactly and in the 'we' style in order that the reader may recognize that this important section of the history of the mission rests upon an eyewitness account. (7) It has often been assumed that Paul took the land route from Beroea to Athens. The words ἕως ἐπὶ τὴν θάλασσαν **17**.14 are taken to mean that Paul and his companions only seemed to take the road to the sea, but then chose the land route. But ἕως ἐπί, just like ὡς (= ἕως) εἰς in the Periplus Maris Erythraei (*Geographi Graeci minores*, Vol. 1, 259, § 4), means in the Koine Greek of that time 'up to' the sea. Paul thus chose the water route for this journey also. (8) That Paul with Aquila and Priscilla used a sailing vessel from Cenchreae to Ephesus—a sea voyage of over 250 miles —is apparent from κατήντησαν (κατήντησεν 𝔓74 ℵ, puts Paul in the foreground and matches the following κατέλιπεν). (9) The journey to Caesarea, characterized as a sea voyage by ἀνήχθη ἀπὸ τῆς Ἐφέσου **18**.21, will presumably have stretched over more than 650 miles. The bold line from Cnidus straight across the sea to Caesarea on the maps of Paul's journeys is perhaps a result of Luke's brevity in this report, 'he departed from Ephesus, and landed in Caesarea . . .' (10) Also from Caesarea to Antioch—it is about 280 miles—

Paul will rather have travelled aboard ship than on Shanks's mare. (11) Luke has presented only two of Paul's sea voyages in detail: the one from Philippi **20.6** to Caesarea **21.8** is described with all the ports of call in between: Troas, Assos, Mitylene, Samos, Miletus, Rhodes, Patara (where they changed ships), Tyre, Ptolemais. At a guess over 940 miles were covered in this voyage. The detail of the presentation and the 'we' indicate here also the use of an eyewitness account. Here too compositional grounds ultimately govern the colourful portrayal of a journey not in its details important. (12) The journey to Rome which goes from Caesarea **27.1** by Sidon, Myra (ship change), Caloi Limenes, Malta (**28.1**), Syracuse, Rhegium to Puteoli is the longest of all Paul's sea voyages in Acts. But Paul has weathered even more sea voyages than these; this emerges from his statement in II Cor. **11.25**: before the voyage to Rome he suffered shipwreck three times, and on one of these drifted νυχθήμερον in the sea—on some piece of wreckage or a plank—until some ship or other picked him up. Josephus narrates something similar of his own journey to Rome, *Vita* 15.

VERSE 17 continues in the third person, perhaps to indicate that the sailors carried out the manoeuvre. The lifeboat is hoisted and brought on deck. βοηθείαις ἐχρῶντο and ὑποζωννύντες τὸ πλοῖον are variously explained.[1] Σύρτις: the great Syrtis whose sandbanks were especially feared. χαλάσαντες τὸ σκεῦος: lowering the drift-anchor.[2]

---

[1] Either 'they applied means of protection' (use of ropes or something similar: cf. Aristot. *Rhetorica* II 5 = 1383a 'as in the dangers of the sea some look confidently to the future, because they are not used to the storm, others who have means of help on account of their experience') or βοήθεια means the object employed itself, e.g. the cable. But it could also mean, combined with ἄραντες: 'using a pulley'. Or: 'they employed rescue measures, "undergirding" the ship.' Of the four theories developed in regard to these last measures that depicted in old Egyptian pictures (*Beg.* V 351) does not fit: bow and stern were bound together by lines which ran along the deck on props (so Frank Brewster, *Harv. Stud. in Class. Philol.* 23 (1912) 63–77). Egyptian ships without keel and ribs—the trees of Egypt, acacia and sycamore, did not yield large beams and planks—threatened to break up if they were lifted amidships on the crest of a wave, with their bow and stern in the air. Hence the need for braces. But the ships which crossed the Mediterranean had keels and ribs. The second theory: the lines transversely secure the main ribs in the hold of the ship (so E. G. Schauroth, *Harv. Stud. in Class. Philol.* 22 (1911), 173–9), suffers like number 3—according to which the lines were run vertically round the ship (so J. Smith 210–5, Ramsay 329, Balmer 344ff., Preuschen 1430)—from the fact that the bracing held together only individual parts of the ship. The most likely theory in our opinion is the fourth: the lines were laid longitudinally round the ship, i.e. lengthwise, and braced with a winch (so Breusing 170ff., Cecil Torr in Daremberg-Saglio, Art. Navis IV, 32f., von Goerne, *NkZ* 1898, 364).—On the other hand, R. Hartmann thinks of repairing internal damages, Pauly-Wissowa Suppl. vol. IV, 1921, 776–82. 'Undergirding' is elsewhere mentioned only in reference to ancient warships.

[2] Ramsay (329) and Holtzmann (131) understand it of reefing of sails. But this had doubtless already been done when they ran into the storm. Zahn (831) thinks σκεῦος means all the equipment upon which the course and speed of the vessel depended: rudder, tackle, anchor. How Zahn would combine this with χαλάσαντες remains obscure. Renié (appealing to the former marine officer P. Ricard) translates 'drift-anchor' and explains: 'a broad piece of wood held vertical in the water by a weight on the lower end and an empty barrel on top,

VERSE 18 again shows the 'we' style. ἐκβολὴν ἐποιοῦντο: cf. Jonah 1.5 LXX.[1] Breusing (183–5) thinks of the jettisoning of part of the heavy grain cargo in order to lighten the ship, which was certainly weighed down by the water breaking into it. Renié (339) objects: they could not open the hatches to the holds, otherwise the water really would have poured in. He thinks of the baggage and goods which lay on the deck.[2]

VERSE 19: On the third day they (the sailors) with their own hands throw τὴν σκευὴν τοῦ πλοίου into the sea: the heavy mainyard with the mainsail (?), the spare yard, spars, tackle: Breusing 186, Voigt 729, Preuschen 152, Jacquier 734, Renié 340.[3]

VERSE 20 gives in the gen. abs. the reason why all hope was abandoned: with cloudy skies there was no way to plot a course. The imperfect here also serves as the narrative tense: 'and so all hope of rescue disappeared'.

VERSE 21: πολλῆς ἀσιτίας: they had no desire to eat at all. σταθεὶς . . . εἶπεν: the author has no real idea of the situation: with the howl of the gale and the pitch of the ship Paul could not deliver an address as on the Areopagus (cf. 17.22!). The speech shows many specific Lucan traits.[4]

VERSE 22: Here we expect a νῦν δέ. But at 20.25 and 20.32 also Luke wrote καὶ (τὰ) νῦν. The summons to εὐθυμεῖν is only obeyed in v. 36. 'None of you will lose his life, only the ship will be lost' is expressed with a very choice turn of phrase. πλήν with genitive = 'except' as 8.1; 15.28.

VERSE 23: The peculiar word order also—θεοῦ and ἄγγελος are widely separated—is specifically Lucan (see Intro. pp. 78f.), like καί after the relative

---

is dragged astern on a rope in such a way that every time the ship plunges down from a crest the drift-anchor offers great resistance.' The rope had to be half as long as the distance from crest to crest.—Cf. similarly Breusing 177–82 with reference to Lucian *Toxaris* 19. —The use of such a board in primitive form is described by Herodotus II 96. A. Köster has unravelled the passage: the drift-anchor kept the ship from coming broadside in the turbulent Nile water; with it one can hold on course a drifting ship (which had no movement of its own in the downward plunge). Thus according to Renié the anchor was intended to slow down the speed of the ship for a time—but was it so great if Paul's ship used only the foresail?—; according to Köster the anchor helped to hold the ship on course. It remains however questionable whether Luke understood the report before him in every detail.

[1] οἱ ναυτικοὶ . . . ἐκβολὴν ἐποιήσαντο τῶν σκευῶν τῶν ἐν τῷ πλοίῳ εἰς τὴν θάλασσαν τοῦ κουφισθῆναι ἀπ' αὐτῶν.

[2] It is a question whether the grain—as on the sailing ship Pamir—was simply heaped in the hold and covered above with planks (so Breusing 45; cf. σανίδες v. 44) or whether the wheat was transported in sacks. The actual jettisoning of the cargo seems to be described only in v. 38. It is not impossible that Luke has simply found room for the biblical trait from the book of Jonah.

[3] But Renié's sentence, 'The ship was only a pontoon, a derelict thrown on the mercy of the elements' may not be correct. With the storm-sail on the small slanting foremast (ἀρτεμών) and the drift-anchor the ship could hold its course. The real difficulty lay in the fact that the weather did not allow an accurate course to be fixed.

[4] ἔδει as 1.16; μέν solitarium as 1.1; πειθαρχεῖν as 5.29. The word-play κερδῆσαι ζημίαν is one of those choice expressions (Bauer *Wb* 849 recalls κερδαίνω ζημίαν Eurip. *Cycl.* 312) which are strewn throughout this chapter. ὕβρις and ζημία take up v. 10 again.

(see above on **1**.3). The appearance of an angel was an occurrence intelligible to Gentile and Jewish listeners alike; an appearance of Christ, on the other hand, would have required a long explanation. οὗ εἰμι is biblical: Gen. **50**.19 LXX. Elevated language here also!

VERSE 24 tells the reader indirectly that Paul witnessed to Christ before Nero. Since God has destined him for that, he must now stay alive. But the others also are to be saved because of him—so Luke explains the rescue of the whole ship's company. καὶ ἰδοῦ: the angel speaks the language of the (Greek) Bible.

VERSE 25: Paul's summons to be of good courage because of this revelation at first falls on deaf ears (see however v. 36). Here Luke makes plain above all Paul's trust in God's faithfulness, which the sequel so manifestly justifies.

VERSE 26 does not report a private conjecture by Paul, but rather the δεῖ introduces a prophetic prediction: they will soon strike an island—the only one which lies in the 250 miles of open sea between Tunisia and Sicily.[1]

VERSE 27 continues the narrative of v. 20: on the fourteenth[2] day of drifting in the Adriatic,[3] it becomes apparent[4] that land is near.[5]

VERSE 28: The first sounding gives twenty fathoms, around 120 feet, the second only 90 feet. It is thus certain that they are rapidly nearing the shore and in danger of running aground.

VERSE 29: 'Out of fear that we would drive[6] against cliffs' is probably what is meant by κατὰ . . . ἐκπέσωμεν (Bauer, *Wb* 483): again an unusual expression. ἐκ πρύμνης: exceptionally the anchors are cast out not from the bow but from the stern, so that the ship does not veer through 180°. For in the process it would have presented a broadside to the waves and that would have been fatal.[7]

---

[1] This prediction is by no means self-evident, as E. Meyer (*Urspr.* III, 29 n. 1) thinks: 'What then should . . . solid land be, on which one strikes, but an island?' Paul indeed does not say, 'The land, which we shall strike, will be an island', but 'we will strike an island' —and the chance of that was fairly close to zero.

[2] Since Clauda 324 hours have passed. If we reckon one-and-a-half nautical miles per hour we get 482 nautical miles covered. The distance from Clauda to Malta amounts to 474 nautical miles. The ship thus drifted in a very shallow curve direct for Malta: Breusing 189.

[3] Josephus *Vita* 15 recounts his shipwreck on the voyage from Palestine to Rome κατὰ μέσον τὸν Ἀδρίαν. Ptol. III 4,1: 15,1 includes the sea between Sicily and Crete in the Adriatic: H. Treidler, 'Das Ionische Meer im Altertum', *Klio* 22 (1928), esp. 86–91.

[4] According to Breusing (193) the nearness of land was recognized by the fact that the drift-anchor hit bottom. But that it was dragged at a depth of 120 feet is unlikely. On the other hand the breakers of Point Koura on Malta are audible for a mile and a half from a ship coming from the east: *Beg.* IV 338.

[5] So with the (later) reading προσάγειν. B προσαχειν (= gig; *resonare*) could be a corrupted (Doric?) form of προσηχεῖν 'to resound': *Beg.* IV 335.

[6] Cf. ἐκπέσωσιν v. 17.

[7] This W. Stammler (31) has not noticed. Bruce (463) lists cases of anchoring from the stern. It was possible if the foresail was struck and the drift-anchor further slowed the ship. Breusing (193) thinks of four anchors, two each on a cable. Ancient anchors weighed only 55 lbs.

VERSE 30: Breusing already recognized (193) that this presentation is unrealistic—would the owner and captain not have noticed what the sailors were about? Moreover, no seaman would think of leaving the safety of the ship in a boat to get to an unknown and rocky coast at night. The explanation of many commentators, that the sailors in the fight for survival had forgotten their duty, overlooks the fact that if they remained on the ship there was no danger to their lives. Luke and his source will be reproducing here a rumour which cropped up among the mistrustful passengers, above all among the soldiers. That is: when the sailors lowered the lifeboat in order to cast bow anchors from it, the soldiers suspected an escape attempt and cut through the lines in the blocks.[1]

VERSE 31: This Lucan verse makes Paul the saviour of the ship's company who even at midnight keeps his faithful watch. In reality however Paul by this course of action would have doomed the ship to run aground.[2]

VERSE 32: The soldiers (and the narrator whom Luke follows) do not think of the consequences of their action: with the lifeboat they could bring the passengers comfortably ashore; now however they had to make the risky attempt—it fails of course—to put the ship on the beach.[3] εἴασαν . . . ἐκπεσεῖν: 'they set the lifeboat adrift' (see vv. 17 and 29).

VERSE 33: ἄχρι οὗ (see Bl.-Debr. § 383, 1; cf. the beginning of v. 39): 'until it became daylight' = before daybreak. μεταλαβεῖν τροφῆς like 2.46 'to eat something'. That the ship's company have not eaten anything at all for fourteen days is admittedly impossible but is asserted by μηδὲν προσλαβόμενοι (= to take nothing): the author exaggerates somewhat in order to make the situation clear.[4]

VERSE 34: Paul urges them to eat, that they may have strength for the

---

[1] If as a precaution they wanted to anchor the ship from the bow as well, they could not simply throw out the anchor: since the ship no longer had headway, it would not have taken hold in the sea-bottom. They had therefore to drop it some distance ahead of the bow from the lifeboat and then from the ship pull on the anchor-rope for it to dig into the bottom.

[2] W. Stammler was the first to venture to state this: 'Paul the layman, suspicious of foul play, does not understand the seamen's purpose and through the military commander thwarts that purpose; the captain will not have been happy over such arbitrary interference by the armed forces, who were indeed travelling only as passengers' (13f.). Stammler, however, overlooks the contribution of Lucan redaction to the story.—But Breusing 193f. already had assumed that the seamen acted on the skipper's orders and with the agreement of the owner, otherwise the latter would have prevented the undertaking with the help of the centurion. The Lucan account thus becomes for Breusing an insoluble riddle: 'I openly declare that I do not venture any solution' (193/4). But he will not rule out the possibility of an honourable intention, although he recalls also the fight for survival described by Achilles Tatius 3, 3 where everyone wants to get in the boat.

[3] Bruce (464) seeks to exculpate Paul by assuming that he was misunderstood. But what could he have said that could thus have been misunderstood?

[4] Jacquier (740) and Wikenhauser (*Apg.* 225) weaken the statement: 'They have had no real meal.' That will fit what actually happened, but is at the same time a criticism of the report in Acts.

coming exertions.[1] οὐδενὸς . . . ἀπολεῖται: the logion transmitted as a saying of the Lord in Lk. 21.18 appears here as a saying of Paul; it is an OT proverb: Jacquier 740.[2]

VERSE 35: εἴπας Hellenistic for εἰπών. εὐχαρίστησεν τῷ θεῷ κτλ: Luke describes only the blessing before the meal, which for Jews and Christians was a matter of course: a eucharistic distribution of the bread finds mention only in the addition of the 'Western' text (614 sy^hmg).[3]

VERSE 36 signifies rather only that the others, under the influence of Paul's words and actions, also take courage again and begin to eat. Cf. for the usage 9.19.

VERSE 37: ἤμεθα Hellenistic for ἦμεν (Bl.-Debr. § 98). αἱ πᾶσαι ψυχαί (Bl.-Debr. § 275, 7): 'We were altogether 276 persons in the ship.'[4]

VERSE 38: κορεσθέντες κτλ: 'when they had satisfied themselves' (Bauer, *Wb* 979). The ship is lightened by throwing the heavy cargo of wheat overboard. The storm must have abated considerably, so that they could open the hatches.[5]

VERSE 39 would attach without hiatus to v. 32. τὴν . . . ἐγίγνωσκον: this is not surprising, because the normal shipping route did not go by Malta. Breusing 200. κόλπον: now called St. Paul's Bay; see map. αἰγιαλός: a level beach. εἰ δύναιντο: 'if possible'; only Luke in the NT employs the rare *optativus obliquus* (Bl.-Debr. § 386). It shows the author's concern to give his account a literary status. ἐξωθέω: to run it on the beach.[6]

VERSE 40: The anchor cable was simply allowed to fall into the sea. At the same time the lines (ζευκτήρια) which held the two tillers (πηδάλια)

[1] πρός with the genitive is literary: Moulton 106; cf. Thucydides III 59, 1: πρὸς τῆς ὑμετέρας δόξης. σωτηρία means earthly deliverance only here and Hebr. 11.7; the verb has this meaning as at least part of its force in Acts 14.9.

[2] I Sam. 14.45; II Sam. 14.11; I Kings 1.52 ℵ following LXX reads πεσεῖται.

[3] Belser, Blass, Olshausen, Ewald earlier thought of the eucharist: Bo Reicke (*ThZ* 1948, 409) and Menoud (*RHPhR* 1953, 33) have Paul here perform a prefiguration of the eucharist: Paul allowed his fellow-travellers 'to participate in a prefiguration of the Christian Lord's Supper as a potential preparation for later discipleship.' But Luke does not indicate anything of the sort. After Paul has spoken the benediction over the meal like any devout Jew or Christian, he breaks the bread and begins to eat, and the others follow his example and eat until they are satisfied.

[4] The number attaches to πᾶσαι. The reading of B sa ὡς ἑβδομήκοντα ἕξ is occasioned by dittography, πλοιωωσος from πλοιω σος (the digamma ς is 6, omikron 70 and sigma 200). Since Luke usually puts ὡς before numbers (see on 1.15) this error in B is very natural. The ship on which Josephus experienced shipwreck on his voyage to Rome had about 600 persons on board (*Vita* 15).

[5] See above on v. 18. The foremast could be used as a derrick (for launching the life-boat and) for loading and unloading the goods: Breusing 82. But that would only come into question here if the wheat were in sacks. If that was not the case, then the unloading of the wheat—with baskets or empty tubs, conjectures Balmer 365—was very difficult and required much more time than the twilight hours. Naber (*Mnemosyne* 1895, 267ff.) for σῖτον proposed ἱστόν, the mast. This raises the question how it was that the main mast did not break on impact and fall on deck. Balmer (402) assumes that it had already been removed earlier. But the main mast could only be lowered on very small boats: Breusing 55.

[6] ἐκσῶσαι for ἐξῶσαι in B* C sa bo rests upon an old error of hearing.

while the ship was anchored were loosed and the small foresail on the fore-mast (ἀρτεμών) hoisted (see Bauer, *Wb* 218). The ship thus again gains headway and can be steered, so that they can make for the beach.[1]

VERSE 41: The ship hits a τόπος διθάλασσος, a shoal; Breusing (205) thinks, probably correctly, of a bank of soft clay in the middle of the entrance to St. Paul's Bay. It lies today 39 feet under water, but in Paul's time probably only about 13 feet. To right and left of it the water is deeper.[2] ἐπέκειλαν τὴν ναῦν is again a literary expression.[3] The after-part breaks up.[4] ὑπὸ τῆς βίας is ambiguous.[5]

VERSE 42: Perhaps the rumour spread among the prisoners that the soldiers wanted to kill them. But in Luke's account this feature is rather surprising because in the first place—before the centurion's intervention—there is no possibility of escape for any of the passengers, least of all for prisoners probably bound with chains. For the rest, the centurion carried responsibility for his prisoners.[6]

VERSES 43f.: To save Paul, the centurion forbids the slaughter of the prisoners and orders those who can swim to head for land first and then the others to paddle to land on boards[7] or wreckage from the ship.[8] καὶ οὕτως κτλ: the promise of v. 24 is fulfilled.

For the readers those episodes in Chapter 27 which deal with Paul were especially edifying. Scarcely has he escaped being delivered over to the Jews when a storm on the voyage to Rome threatens to destroy him and the entire

---

[1] κατεῖχον is a nautical technical expression. Does this narrative imperfect not belong to Luke's source?

[2] Balmer (413ff. following Smith 143) conceives of the τόπος διθάλασσος as a channel between two large bodies of water and sees it in the 250-foot wide 'channel' or strait between Malta and the island of Salmonetta which lies in front of the bay. Then the ship would have run upon the beach in ten feet of water and would not have permitted any direct debarkation on land.

[3] Homer, *Odyssey* IX 546 'arriving there, we let the ship run up on the beach' (νῆα μὲν ἔνθ' ἐλθόντες ἐκέλσαμεν ἐν ψαμαθοῖσιν). Elsewhere in this chapter the ship is always named πλοῖον. ἐρείσασα = ramming itself: ἐρείδω also in Homer!

[4] Again the narrative imperfect: or 'it broke up gradually'?

[5] Either: by the force of the impact, which threw the bow high; or: by the force of the waves. Actually h reads τῶν κυμάτων, gig on the other hand supplies *maris*. But the first possibility is more likely. For the stern, curved like the bow, was quite equal to the battering of the waves.

[6] Renié (344) advances Justinian's stipulation that every soldier is responsible with his life for his prisoner. But escape only becomes possible at all—according to Luke's account—when the centurion allows individuals to reach land by swimming or paddling on boards.

[7] The cargo was probably covered with such; see above p. 704 n. 2.

[8] It remains a riddle why ἐπί is construed first with a dative and then with the genitive. If we take ἐπί τινων κτλ. = 'on the shoulders of some from the ship,' i.e. the sailors, then the water must have been shallow enough to wade through. In that case swimming was unnecessary. How were women and children rescued?—Cf. on this section E. Haenchen, 'Tradition u. Komposition in der Apg.', *ZThK* 52 (1955), 221 n. 1.

ship. Paul alone sees the danger beforehand and gives warning; for his sake God rescues also those who are travelling with him. Certainly Paul makes his contribution: like a faithful Eckhart he watches day and night; he stops the flight of the sailors and fills them all with confidence before the landing on Malta. When finally the soldiers want to kill the prisoners so that they will not flee, God has them all brought safely to land through the centurion, and thus fulfils his own promise (vv. 22, 34). In this way Chapter 27 is fitted into the final section of the book, which again shows Paul the prisoner as the focal point of the action: he, the prisoner, saves them all!

Scholars like Zahn, Ramsay and E. Meyer think they hear in this the eyewitness Luke's own account of his experiences. They do not observe with what a constructive imagination the author achieves his goal. He certainly possessed a journal of this voyage (see Intro. pp. 86f.). Yet Paul was no noble traveller with special authority, but a prisoner accused of inciting to riot. He therefore had no say in any of the decisions. Just those edifying supplements which extol Paul are additions by the author to a journal of reminiscences which could not report anything special about Paul, but only described the voyage, the danger and the rescue. The author's share and merits have been brought out precisely by such critical scholars as Schwegler and Zeller, Overbeck, Paul Wendland and Wellhausen. This 'dynamite hypothesis' Dibelius also has made his own (*Studies* 205f.).

The unreality of the scene is most easily seen at vv. 21–6: Paul delivers a speech on a pounding ship in a howling storm as if he stood on the Areopagus (see **17.**22!). How did Luke come to recount this scene? Paul refers to his earlier speech (in v. 10: the words ζημία and ὕβρις are repeated). Here in fact lies the key to the whole problem.

The reminiscences taken over by Luke (and in part stylistically reworked) went from v. 9a direct to v. 12. Verse 12 spoke of a majority which wanted to go on to Phoenix and winter there. Luke has pondered these words carefully. He gathers from them that there was a deliberation. Naturally only the important men took part. For Luke these were Paul, the centurion, the owner and the captain. The majority was for the fateful continuation of the voyage —thus Paul was against it, because he foresaw the outcome; not as a meteorologist or thanks to his great experience as a traveller (he had never travelled this stretch of water before!), but from prophetic alliance with God. He thus gave warning: The ship will sink with all hands!

In so doing the author deliberately shot somewhat beyond the mark: now Paul could correct himself in a second speech (vv. 21–6), to the effect that God for his sake—since he was to bear witness before Caesar (v. 24)— would save all his travelling companions. The cue for this second speech Luke found in the mood of doubt and indifference which expressed itself in their unwillingness to eat. Paul could base the summons to be of good courage (v. 22) on the fact that in the meantime the deliverance had been revealed to him (vv. 23f.). The prophetic statement that they would strike on an island linked this speech with what follows.

In reality the sailors did not think about escaping: to leave a safely anchored ship at night in a lifeboat on a rough sea to get to an unknown shoreline, whose breakers could be heard, would have been outright stupidity. Only landlubbers could conceive such a suspicion. Probably the minds of the passengers were haunted by a form of the sensational story, later narrated by Achilles Tatius, of how the captain and sailors abandoned the lost ship in the lifeboat. The legionaries possessed the resolve and in their swords the implements to chop the lines of the lifeboat. Luke could not imagine that the soldiers themselves deserved credit for this supposed rescue—Paul drew their attention to it! (v. 31). Actually the beaching of the ship was now unavoidable. In the lifeboat they could have brought everyone safely to shore next day, and the ship would not have had to be beached. If Paul awakened suspicion against the sailors, then he was responsible not for the rescue but rather for the shipwreck! This makes it particularly clear that v. 31 is an addition.

Paul's next speech (vv. 33f.) takes up the ἀσιτία motif again and carries the encouragement to a successful conclusion, but is subject to the same technical difficulties as vv. 21ff. (see p. 704). Paul, moreover, was probably chained like the other prisoners and not in a position to make a speech when he chose.

The last adventure Luke again took from the travel-journal: he interprets the rescue measures as dispositions by the centurion, who was accustomed to command. That this very method of rescue would have provided individual prisoners with the possibility of escape shows the loose construction of this scene.

According to Dibelius (*Studies* 205f.) Luke has not reported his own recollections of the voyage, but wanted as an historian to give a typical account of a sea voyage. Such adventures and shipwrecks (cf. II Cor. **11**.25 and Josephus *Vita* 15) of course often occurred. Frogmen have begun to recover the remains of individual ships and even entire ships' graveyards near the harbours and coasts of the Mediterranean. In the Hellenistic novels these catastrophes are reflected: Conzelmann in his commentary (*Hdb*[2] 151ff.) has printed suitable specimens as examples. From this it is clear: there was not a standard account of sea voyages by which one could prove himself an historian. In the novels the threatened or actual shipwreck is only one of the hundred adventures which the lovers have to undergo. That a travel report like this voyage to Rome leads with uncanny consistency to catastrophe is not the case.

Chapter 27 certainly has a highly literary effect. But it is precisely the Pauline speeches inserted by Luke which give this section its literary character, and not a 'profane' model. In the narrative of the voyage itself Luke has only here and there (e.g. in v. 13) shown his literary culture; further details are to be found in the article 'Acta 27' in the Festschrift for R. Bultmann's 80th birthday.

The scenes inserted correspond exactly to the Lucan image of Paul. Paul always stands in the limelight. He is never at a loss for advice. He never despairs. He plays 'the part of the true Roman in a Roman ship, looked up to even by the centurion, and in his single self the saviour of the lives of all', enthusiastically wrote W. Ramsay (*St. Paul*, 339), repeating the errors of the Lucan portrait of Paul. Luke did not suspect—and did not let the readers suspect—that Paul could despair of life (II Cor. **1**.8) and in that very fact experienced the miracle of God who awakens the dead (II Cor. **1**.9f.). He knows only the strong, unshaken favourite of God who strides from triumph to triumph.

66
ACTS 28:1-10
PAUL ON MALTA

[1] When we had reached safety, we learned that the island was called Malta. [2] And the barbarians treated us with unusual friendliness. For, lighting a fire, they brought us all around it on account of the rain which had set in and the cold. [3] But when Paul gathered a bundle of sticks and threw them on the fire, a snake came out because of the heat and fastened on his hand. [4] When the barbarians saw the creature hanging from his hand, they said to one another, 'This man is certainly a murderer whom, rescued from the sea, justice would not permit to live.' [5] But he shook off the creature into the fire and suffered no harm. [6] Now they were expecting him to swell up or suddenly drop dead. When they had waited a long time and saw that nothing bad happened to him, they changed their opinion and said he was a god. [7] In the neighbourhood of that place were lands which belonged to the 'chief of the island', (a man) by the name of Publius, who received us and treated us kindly for three days. [8] Now it happened that Publius' father lay in bed gripped with fever and dysentery. Paul went in to him and healed him by laying his hands on him and praying. [9] When that happened the others on the island who had diseases came and were healed. They honoured us with many praises, and on our departure they gave us what was necessary.

Bibliography:

H. J. Cadbury, 'Lexical Notes on Luke-Acts III: Luke's Interest in Lodging', *JBL* 45 (1926), 305–22 (esp. 319ff.); Williams 274ff.; Conzelmann 14f.; Stählin 322f.

    A. Barb, 'Der Heilige und die Schlange (Paul; Malta)', *Mitteilungen der Anthrop. Gesellschaft Wien* 82 (1953), 1–21; W. P. Gillieson, 'Acts **28.3**', *Exp.Tim.* 42 (1930–1), 192.

    VERSE 1: διασωθέντες links up with **27**.44 (διασωθῆναι). ἐπέγνωμεν (see **27**.39): 'we recognized that the island' on which we had landed 'was called Malta'.[1] Thus the prediction of **27**.26 has been fulfilled: Loisy 923. 'The

---

[1] On Malta see Zahn 841–4. The island possessed many harbours, from which a lively trade was conducted. Of its industries Diod. Sic. V 12 singles out especially the weaving of linen.

non-Christian "we" (Chapter 27) passes over into the Christian': Wellhausen 54, who asks with exaggerated scepticism whether in the source it was not a case of some anonymous barbaric island in the Mediterranean (55). In the following the 'we' describes the small Christian group whose strength is not disclosed.

VERSE 2: οἱ βάρβαροι: the inscriptions prove 'that . . . the common man, the worker and porter, gardener and dog-trainer on Malta could only understand, speak and read their Punic mother tongue': Zahn 842. Yet there were also Roman citizens and veterans of Caesar settled there,[1] who spoke Latin, and people enough who could understand Greek. The Lucan style of the passage is clear.[2] παρεῖχον: again the imperfect of narration. προσλαμβάνω will mean, like προσαναλαμβάνω ‭א‬* 614, 'to bring close, take in'. 'All of us': the 276 persons on the ship could not have gathered around one fire; consequently the narrator is thinking of the small group of Christians. There is no mention of the prisoners, the centurion and his soldiers. Because of the rain 'setting in' or 'imminent' (actually they must all have been completely soaked during the landing and for that reason alone needed the warmth of the fire) and the cold,[3] they gathered round the fire, which now becomes the occasion for the following story.

VERSE 3: Paul cannot stand idly by: he gathers a bundle of brushwood and throws it into the flames. Then a poisonous snake,[4] shooting out because of the heat, bites him on the hand (καθάπτω: see Bl.-Debr. § 310, 1): so it is apparent to everyone that he is really bitten.

VERSE 4: The barbarians conclude that Paul is definitely (πάντως) a murderer, since justice[5] does not allow the man rescued from the sea to live.

---

[1] Strabo XVII p. 833.

[2] For οὐ τὴν τυχοῦσαν cf. **19**.11, for φιλανθρωπία **27**.3 and **28**.7.

[3] Zahn (845) speaks of a 'cold winter's day'. But 'the average temperature for the month of October' on Malta 'is 22° Celsius'; in a north-east storm as here it can on occasion fall to 12° Celsius. But anyone coming to land in the wind soaked to the skin freezes: Balmer 423–7. The stormy south-east wind, which is more frequent in late autumn than in summer, brings according to Balmer 'an almost unbearable, oppressive heat'.

[4] This is what ἔχιδνα means, see Bauer, *Wb* 655. 'According to Spratt, *Travels and Researches in Crete* II 7, there are no poisonous snakes on Malta': Preuschen 155, who recalls by way of compensation that among us the country-folk consider the ring-snake poisonous. The scene, as Loisy (924) has shown, is not very easily conceivable; hence Zahn interprets: 'When . . . as a result of the increasing heat of the burning sticks an adder from the vicinity slithered out and bit Paul on the hand . . .'—this is even more difficult to imagine.

[5] The commentators point out that the barbarians spoke of a Punic deity (according to Zahn (845) Paul is the only one of the ship's company who understood these words), without asking themselves if there was among the Punic deities one corresponding to Δίκη. Luke has put a Greek idea in the mouths of the barbarians. Cf. the parallel cited by Wettstein (*Anthol. Pal.* VII 290), an epitaph by Statyllius Flaccus on a shipwrecked seaman killed by snakebite: 'O, he escaped the storm and the raging of the murderous seas/ but as he lay stranded in the Libyan sand/ not far from the beach and heavy with sleep, at last,/ naked and destitute, weary as he was from the terrible shipwreck,/ the viper struck him dead. Why did he struggle against the waves?/ He did not escape the lot which was destined for him on land.'

διασωθῆναι, occurring for the third time, provides the catchword for the narrative.

VERSE 5: ὁ μὲν οὖν—οἱ δέ stand in antithesis; it is not a case of the specifically Lucan μὲν οὖν. Paul shakes the creature[1] off so that it falls into the fire without anything happening to the Apostle.

VERSE 6: The Maltese wait[2] for him to swell up or suddenly fall dead, according to whether the poison takes effect slowly or quickly. 'But when they had waited a long time and saw that nothing bad[3] happened to him, they changed their opinion and said that he was a god'—a more natural expression would be that he was a favourite of the gods.[4] But the antithesis 'murderer' -'god' has a stronger effect.—Luke did not consider a reprimand corresponding to 14.15ff. necessary.

VERSE 7: A second story, whose focal point is again Paul, is now appended. τὰ περὶ τὸν τόπον ἐκεῖνον: the surroundings of that place. There lay the lands of the πρῶτος τῆς νήσου,[5] 'who[6] received us' (the Christians or all the shipwrecked?) 'and cordially[7] entertained us for three days'. Πόπλιος is the normal transcription of Publius. Since the naming with the first name only is remarkable, Ramsay (343) thinks it a transcription of Popilius. According to Zahn (846) on the other hand the mere mention of the first name reveals the friendly relationship which developed between him, Paul and Luke during the three months (note 5)!

VERSE 8: ἐγένετο elsewhere introduces an event, not a condition. For πυρετοῖς (attacks of fever) συνεχόμενον (gripped, tormented) cf. Luke 4.38. δυσεντέριον: diarrhoea, dysentery (Attic δυσεντερία). The medical terms present here were generally known, and therefore do not prove that a physician is reporting (against Harnack *Beitr.* I 11; ET). πρὸς ὅν: again a 'false' relative clause, see 1.3. The healing is accomplished not by medical means but by prayer and laying on of hands.[8]

---

[1] θηρίον, used for dangerous animals and especially of snakes, is documented in Bauer, *Wb* 713. For a similar incident see Williams 275.

[2] After προσδοκάω stands the acc.c. inf. fut.; this is here replaced by μέλλειν: Bl.-Debr. § 356.—According to Zahn 845 the Maltese 'certainly ... waited quite a few hours in suspense without result' (!).

[3] οὐδὲν ἄτοπον: see 25.5. The construction is unclassical: Bl.-Debr. § 423,4.

[4] So in Plutarch *Cleom.* 39, p. 823, it is said of Cleomenes, miraculously protected by a snake, that he was θεοφιλής or ἥρως καὶ θεῶν παῖς: *Beg.* IV 342.

[5] An official title: CIL X 7495: [*munic*]*ipi Mel*(*itensium*) *primus omni*[*um*]': IG XIV 601 '. . . Προυδὴνς ἱππεὺς 'Ρωμ(αίων) πρῶτος Μελιταίων . . .', who was *patronus*, *duumvir* (ἄρχων) and *flamen Augustalis*: *Beg.* IV 342, referring to A. Mayr, *Die Insel Malta im Altertum*, 1909, 106.

[6] ὅς : see on 1.3.   [7] φιλοφρόνως; cf. 27.44, 28.2.

[8] Beyer 153: 'How far the physician Luke played a part in this we do not in this case learn, but might suspect from the following verses. But if Paul is present, Luke in his great modesty ascribes every success to the Apostle's prayer.' This psychological explanation destroys the intention of the author, who wants precisely to show Paul as the mighty miracle worker. Here Harnack's influence is still at work. See H. J. Cadbury, *JBL* (1926) 196 n. 20.

VERSE 9: We may not with Harnack read out of ἐθεραπεύοντο that the sick received medical care from Luke:[1] it is intended to emphasize the very greatness of the miracles which Paul accomplishes. Cf. **19**.11f. Where Paul heals 'all the island's sick'—Zahn (847) considers this expression a popular hyperbole, but the narrator is in earnest—is unimportant and consequently not related.

VERSE 10: οἳ καί: see on **1**.3. τιμή can indeed describe the physician's fee (Bauer, *Wb* 1618 s.v. 2e),[2] but the exegetes decide correctly upon the translation 'honour', Jacquier (750) referring to Mt. **10**.8. He considers it possible 'que καί désigne aussi tous les habitants de l'île' (749). It is of course difficult to imagine that all the sick healed were present at Paul's departure, to say nothing of the whole populace making an appearance. ἐπέθεντο: 'they gave us what we needed'.

Luke links up with miracle stories the narrative of the events on landing and that of the stay on Malta; the first (vv. 2–6) is given in some detail. Paul again stands in the centre. The narrator avails himself throughout of the 'we', without our being able to state for certain who are meant by it. At any rate he is always speaking of himself and Paul. The description of the Maltese as 'barbarians'—Balmer (427f.) is not the only one to hear it from Luke's lips with regret—stands in deliberate antithesis to the great φιλανθρωπία which they show to the shipwrecked. At the same time the author thus makes comprehensible the superstition on the basis of which they account for Paul's destiny. Perhaps also their foreign language is hinted at, although in contrast to **14**.11 it is not particularly emphasized.

In the scene around the fire, Paul alone stands in the foreground; Luke has no interest in unnecessary secondary persons. So we do not learn what becomes of the other prisoners and the centurion with his soldiers. That the centurion is no longer mentioned is further due to the fact that Luke from now to the end of the book plays down Paul's imprisonment as much as possible. Because Paul himself gathers sticks for the fire—Jacquier indeed affirms that there was no forest near the bay, but consoles himself with the thought that Paul could find small shrubs among the rocks (746)—, it comes to that incident with the snake whose poisonous bite does not harm Paul (cf. Mt. **16**.18; Lk. **10**.19). The author wants to depict the surprising miracle reflected in the suddenly shifting opinion of the Maltese: at first they consider him a murderer who is being punished by the deity, then as a god. Dibelius (*Studies* 8 n. 16) remarks, 'The narrative **28**.1ff. is tailored to fit a personal glorification of Paul. Any religious point which might correspond in some way to the pious interest of the legend is completely lacking. The idea that the

[1] Harnack considers him a 'spiritual miracle-doctor': *Beitr.* III 119; ET.
[2] Cf. Dibelius, *Hdb. z. NT* 13³, 61 on I Tim. **5**.17.

man apparently punished by Δίκη is finally considered by the barbarians as a god governs everything. This idea is however non-Christian (and non-Jewish), because it presents a deification of the man concerned; there is not a word here to suggest the Christian point of Acts **14**.15.' So he forms his judgement on 'the completely secular' anecdote (*Studies* 204 n. 27): 'There is no reason to consider it a foreign story transferred to Paul. On the other hand, it does not sound like Christian tradition concerning Paul.' But in that case Dibelius can have considered it only a free Lucan construction—in *Studies* 8 he speaks of the 'literary purpose'—which of course would throw a remarkable light on the narrator. Nothing of this however would be altered if Luke had transferred a foreign anecdote to Paul, or even reported an actual experience. That the story closes 'triumphantly' with the sentence 'They said he was a god' is 'a pagan point of view, not Christian' (*Studies* 214) and remains astounding. It is characteristic for Luke how consistently he can portray Paul as a θεῖος ἄνθρωπος.

The same attitude, although somewhat weakened, likewise dominates the second scene (and series of scenes). The most probable view may be that Publius sheltered the whole shipwrecked company for three days before they were finally accommodated—probably in different parts of the island. But the narrator has eyes only for Paul, who heals the high official's fevered father by prayer and the laying-on of hands—and afterwards the entire sick population of the island. That there is no report of Christian preaching gave Bauernfeind (276) and others pause: 'Luke says nothing . . . of a proclamation of the Gospel; but however that may have been, at any rate the fact remains (!) that Paul did not find what he would most have liked to find.' Only nothing of the sort is indicated. For Luke the only important thing is the number of healing miracles which Paul accomplished—we may recall **19**.11. The many honours and the gifts lavished on their departure take the place of the chorus which elsewhere in miracle stories attests the reality of the miracle. In all this Paul no longer acts like a prisoner, but only as a mighty superman, who spreads blessings around him.

67
ACTS 28:11-16
FROM MALTA TO ROME

[11] After three months we departed in an Alexandrian ship which had spent the winter on the island, with the Twin Brothers as its figurehead. [12] Landing at Syracuse we remained three days, [13] and from there we sailed along (the coast) and came to Rhegium. And after a day, when the south wind set in, we came in two days to Puteoli. [14] There we found brethren and were invited to stay with them seven days. And so we came to Rome. [15] The brethren there, when they had heard about us, came to meet us as far as Forum Appii and the Three Taverns. When Paul saw them, he thanked God and took courage. [16] And when we came to Rome Paul was allowed to live privately with the soldier who guarded him.

Bibliography:

T. R. S. Broughton 1933, 444f., see § 25; E. D. St. Denis, 'Marc clausum (Act. 28.11)', *Revue des études latines* 25 (1947), 196-214; Williams 277; Conzelmann 147f.; Stählin 324f.

VERSE 11: 'After three months[1] we departed': according to Pliny, *N.H.* II, 47 sailing began on the seventh of February. That would put the shipwreck at the beginning of November. In contrast to 27.6 the 'we' appear to travel as free men. They use an Alexandrian ship which has spent the winter in a harbour on Malta. παράσημος Διοσκούροις: 'distinguished by the Twin Brothers' (Bauer, *Wb* 1233f.) who were fixed as figureheads—not surprising on an Egyptian ship.[2]

---

[1] This corresponds exactly to the statement of Jos. *Bell.* II 203 that messengers from Rome to Caesarea were delayed three months during the winter break in sailing.

[2] The cult of the Dioscuroi was especially widespread in Egypt; cf. R. Harris, *The Cult of the Heavenly Twins*; F. J. Dölger, 'Dioskuroi. Das Reiseschiff des Apostels Paulus und seine Schutzgötter', *Antike und Christentum* 6 (1950) 276-85. Dölger shows that παράσημον can also be a picture (painted on port and starboard bows), under which stood the name of those portrayed; often παράσημον, the ship's figurehead, is also used for 'ship's name'.—παρασήμῳ is in *Beg.* IV 344 considered as a substantive (a figurehead) in the dative of description like ὀνόματι (Bl.-Debr. § 197); Bl.-Debr. § 198, 7 appendix explains: 'either dativus abs. "with the Twins as the ship's figurehead" (Ramsay, *Luke* 36f., as correctly used according to inscriptions) or better a mechanical declension of a registry-like (πλοῖον) παράσημον Διόσκουροι "a ship, figurehead the Twins"; παράσημον subst. "armorial bearings on the bow" often in Papyri, also Plutarch.'

VERSE 12: The long stay of three days in Syracuse is either connected with wind conditions or cargo had to be unloaded and a new one taken on board.

VERSE 13: περιελόντες B ℵ* is explained, with τὰς ἀγκύρας understood, as 'to weigh anchor'. περιελθόντες in the other MSS. ('to sail around') could be an old correction, which does not fit—the coast runs almost in a straight line; cf. Ropes III, 251. παρελθόντες 'sailing along (the coast)' might be considered.—In Rhegium after a day's wait in the harbour a south wind comes up, which brings the travellers at the exceptional average speed of five knots (Bauernfeind 278) to Puteoli, on the Gulf of Naples, in two days. A vigorous walker required five days on the Appian Way from there to Rome: Zahn 849 n. 13.

VERSE 14: οὗ εὑρόντες ἀδελφούς sounds as if the travellers were at liberty, and sought out the Christians there. παρεκλήθημεν: the congregation invites them to stay for seven days.[1] '. . . and so we came to Rome' is surprising in view of v. 16.[2]

VERSE 15: 'From there', i.e. from Rome, 'came the brethren[3] to greet us, as far as Forum Appii and Tres Tabernae':[4] this is the only mention of the Roman Christians in Acts. Of an organized ἐκκλησία there is no mention. 'When Paul saw them, he thanked God and took courage'—the sentence does not mean that he was in despair before; it contains rather an indirect praise of the Roman Christians.—The military escort is again not mentioned.

VERSE 16: On arrival in Rome—with εἰσήλθομεν the 'we' finally falls silent—Paul is permitted to live in private quarters with his soldier guard.[5] καθ' ἑαυτόν is made clearer by the Western text with 'outside the (Praetorian)

---

[1] The Western text, which Ropes (III, 251) reconstructs according to gig sy^hmg and considers original, reads, 'We were comforted, remaining with them seven days.' This apparently removes the difficulty that the prisoners are invited as free men.

[2] Ramsay (*St. Paul* 346f.) relates 'Rome' in v. 14 to the *ager Romanus*, so to speak the 'administrative district of Rome'. But the following κἀκεῖθεν shows that the city is meant: *Beg.* IV 345. Moreover non-Roman readers would not have understood this.

[3] οἱ ἀδελφοί designates the Christians, not just some personal acquaintances of Paul.

[4] Forum Appii is 43 Roman miles = 65 km. and Three Taverns still 33 Roman miles = 49 km. distant from Rome: Preuschen 157. Wendt 364 credits the Roman Christians with the 65 km. = 40 miles as a day's march. According to Horace *Sat.* I 5, 3 *inde Forum Appi/ differtum nautis cauponibus atque malignis* the inns there were not to be recommended.

[5] The Roman authorities are intentionally not named; they remain discreetly in the background. This the Western text has failed to recognize and, in keeping with the circumstances of its time, it makes the centurion turn his prisoner over to the στρατοπέδαρχος. Mommsen conjectures that by this is meant the *princeps peregrinorum*, first traceable during the time of Trajan, who commanded the headquarters of the *frumentarii*, the *castra peregrinorum* (see n. 5 to 27.1). One can however, appealing to Pliny *Ep.* X 57 *ad Traj.*, defend the counter-theory that persons like Paul were delivered to the prefect of the Praetorian guard—who from 52–61 was Burrus (see Zahn 852)—and that στρατοπέδαρχος means the latter. What Zahn sets forth about Festus' accompanying letter, favourable to Paul, is a fantasy based on Luke's presentation in Chapter 26.

barracks'. According to Mommsen, *Röm. Strafrecht* 317 n. 5, *militi tradere* is a more lenient custody in contrast to *carcer* or *vincula*.

The section begins in the form of a travel journal. Paul and his companions travel like free people. Only at v. 16b are we reminded that Paul is still in custody, even if a lenient one. Zahn (853) completely misjudges the description of the situation intended by Luke (and the real situation) when he has the Apostle continually wearing chains on 'hand and foot'. On the five-day march from Puteoli to Rome the ankle chains would in any case be senseless. But Luke has done nothing to awaken such an impression in the reader; on the contrary, his report of the journey is so similar as to be interchangeable with that of the journey to Jerusalem.

The first difficulty has been found by scholars in the seven days during which 'we' were invited by the Christians in Puteoli. For the suggestion that the centurion himself waited here a week in order to receive instructions from Rome as to where he was to bring his prisoners was already rightly rejected by Loisy (928): the centurion required no other instructions than those he had received in Caesarea. Luke has rather inserted v. 14a so that during this week Paul's arrival could be made known to the Roman Christians; they did not of themselves know that Paul had arrived in Italy. Since Luke from 27.43 on consistently ignores Captain Julius, it was not difficult for him to introduce this delay.

The second and greater difficulty is that Paul arrives in Rome twice over. Ramsay's attempt at a solution (see note on 28.14) is a failure. The same however holds for Bauernfeind's very original interpretation, that the congregation in Puteoli 'could not quite find' in Paul 'the joyous echo which the Roman community would find at once' (278); hence Luke at the end of v. 14 once again expressly emphasized that it was they who 'with their attention prepared the entrance into Rome'. The text contains nothing about such an express emphasis. Luke has rather attached v. 15, of which there was nothing in the source, to the word 'Rome', which he found in the journal used. The reference in this verse to both Forum Appii and Tres Tabernae is usually interpreted to mean that the younger and particularly zealous Christians went 40 miles to meet Paul, while the others with 30 miles still show an astonishing readiness to welcome him. But perhaps Luke had no such detailed picture in view when he named the two best-known stopping-places on the Via Appia between Rome and Naples. By the fact that Luke makes Paul thank God and take courage at the sight of these Christians (one may not ask: at the sight of the first or the second group?), he has set up for the Roman Christians an honourable though modest monument. With v. 16a he has then returned to his source.

Bauernfeind has indeed gathered much more from v. 15 (278): 'In Rome a community was awaiting him which knew very well how to support its shepherds ... The bonds of love which unite the hearts with steadfastness and strength now already embraced a great part of the οἰκουμένη. "Afterwards I looked, and behold a great company which no man can number from all nations and peoples and tongues".' But Zinzendorf and the Apocalypse are very remote here. Luke is much more reserved in his description of Paul's welcome. One could interpret his silence about the community in Rome critically—he speaks only of Christians from Rome, but not of an organized ἐκκλησία there!—and say that the relations between it and Paul were by no means cordial (if we allow the epistle to the Philippians to originate from a Roman imprisonment): so Loisy 946. But Luke has avoided even hinting at such a tension. That he practically eliminates the Roman community by his silence has another and deeper reason: he wants Paul to proclaim in Rome the gospel up to that point unknown. Although Paul comes as prisoner to Rome, he there makes a beginning with the Christ-proclamation and so in the world's capital city crowns his work as the great missionary of Christianity. This Lucan representation of history is so daring that at first we react against it and seek another possibility for the understanding of the text. But the exegesis of the next section will show us that we have no other choice: Luke has consistently carried through his portrait of the Pauline world mission.

68
ACTS 28:17–31
PAUL IN ROME

[17] Now it happened after three days that he called together the leaders of the Jews. When they had come together, he said to them; 'I, brethren, having done nothing in any way against the people or the customs of our fathers, was delivered as a prisoner from Jerusalem into the hands of the Romans. [18] They wanted to set me free after investigation, because they found no reason to sentence me to death. [19] But when the Jews objected I was forced to appeal to Caesar, though not as if I wanted to accuse my people in any way. [20] For this reason I prayed to see you and be able to speak to you, for on account of Israel's hope do I wear these chains.' [21] But they said to him, 'We have neither received a letter concerning you from Judaea nor has any of the brethren come here and reported either officially or privately anything damaging against you. [22] So we request you to let us hear your point of view. For concerning this movement it is known to us that it is everywhere spoken against.' [23] After they had appointed a day for him, they came to him in his lodging in still greater numbers; he explained to them from morning till evening, witnessing to the kingdom of God and seeking to convince them about Jesus from the law of Moses and the prophets. [24] And some were convinced by his words, while others remained unbelieving. [25] Being at variance with one another, they departed, while Paul made one statement: 'Rightly did the Holy Spirit speak to your fathers through the prophet Isaiah: [56] "Go to this people and say: You will hear and shall not understand, and see indeed but not perceive. [27] For the heart of this people has grown dull and their ears are heavy of hearing and their eyes they have closed, lest they should see with their eyes and hear with their ears and understand with their hearts and turn, and I heal them." [28] Be it known to you now that this salvation of God has been sent to the Gentiles; they will listen.' [30] And he remained two whole years in his own rented quarters, and received all who came to him, [31] proclaiming the kingdom of God and teaching about the Lord Jesus Christ openly and unhindered.

Bibliography:

Beg. V 336f., 495; Williams 276–82; Stählin 325–9; Cadbury, *JBL* 45 (1926), 305–22; Dornseiff 1936, see § 1; L. P. Pherigo, 'Paul's Life after the Close of Acts', *JBL* 70 (1951), 277–84.

A. Charue, 'De duplici congressu S. Pauli et judaeorum romanorum iuxta Act. **28**.17–27'; *Collationes Namurenses* 23 (1929), 3–10; Conzelmann, 148–50 Trocmé 34ff.; F. Pfister, *ZNW* 14 (1913), 216ff.; *Beg. V* 296.

VERSE 17: ἐγένετο with acc. c. inf. (Bl-Debr. § 408) is a common Lucan introductory formula; Lucan also is the address ἄνδρες ἀδελφοί (see **2**.29). —Paul after three days calls together the 'first of the Jews'.[1] In these Wendt (365) sees 'presbyters, rulers, synagogue leaders, patrons' of the individual Jewish communities in Rome, who apparently had not been allowed to unite into a large corporation (Schürer III[3], 44ff.; perhaps that is the meaning of ἐκέλευσεν μή συναθροίζεσθαι in Dio Cassius 406, 6; cp. introd. § 4 (5), p. 65). Loisy (932) conjectures that here 'originally' the report was of Paul's discussion with the leaders of the Christian community; but this 'original' report of Loisy's is an illusion. Paul delivers to the assembly an address, whose first word—ἐγώ—forms the theme of his speech. He has done[2] nothing against the (Jewish) people or the customs of the fathers.[3] In spite of this he has been 'delivered from Jerusalem into the hands of the Romans': over against the first presentation (**21**.32f.), according to which Paul was rescued by the Romans from the Jews who wanted to lynch him, this is an astonishing change, through which Paul's fate becomes similar to that of Jesus (cf. **3**.13).

VERSE 18: οἵτινες instead of οἵ: see Bl.-Debr. § 293, 3 and n. 5 on **5**.16. ἀνακρίναντες: as in **4**.9; **12**.19; **24**.8; **25**.16 of a legal investigation, not as in Attic Greek for preliminary enquiry.—That the Romans wanted to set Paul free since they found in him nothing deserving of death is a very great change from the account up to this point; according to **25**.11 Festus wanted to 'present' him to the Jews! In **26**.12 it is not Festus who speaks but the Jew Agrippa and that after the appeal.

VERSE 19: That it was the opposition of the Jews which compelled Paul's appeal is different from **25**.11. οὐχ (Bl.-Debr. § 430, 2; Moulton 231) ὡς κτλ: Paul only defends himself and remains as friendly as ever towards his people. That he desperately resisted being judged by the Sanhedrin is not mentioned.

VERSE 20: 'For this reason', namely to inform the Roman Jews correctly, 'I have summoned you, to see and speak to you' or 'I have requested to see you and to be allowed to speak (to you)': the construction is in both cases difficult.—Now Paul divulges the true situation (thereby **23**.6; **24**.15; **26**.7 are again taken up): Paul bears 'these chains' which the Jews see on account of[4] the (Messianic) hope of Israel.

VERSE 21: εἶπαν Hellenistic for εἶπον. ἡμεῖς is brought forward since it is the subject of the entire sentence: 'We have been informed neither in writing

---

[1] Cf. **25**.2 and Lk. **19**.47 (Bl.-Debr. §§ 271 and 413, 3 Appendix; see also above on Acts **13**.50).—According to Wikenhauser *Apg.* 231 Paul with this continues his mission.

[2] For ἐναντίον ποιήσας cf. **26**.9 (in a speech inserted by Luke).

[3] Cf. **21**.21, 28; **24**.5f.

[4] εἵνεκεν Ionic-Hellenistic for the Attic ἕνεκα: Bl.-Debr. § 35, 3.

nor by word of mouth.' ἀπήγγειλεν describes an official, ἐλάλησεν a private communication: Loisy 934. The Roman Jews have ostensibly received no damaging report (πονηρόν) concerning Paul.

VERSE 22: The Jews politely[1] ask that Paul tell them his views: 'for concerning this "way" it is known to us[2] that it is everywhere spoken against.'[3] Otherwise the Jews appear still to know nothing about Christianity.

VERSE 23: ταξάμενοι: 'After they had appointed him a day', they came in even greater numbers (πλείονας). εἰς τὴν ξενίαν: into the inn in which Paul has rented a room.[4] οἷς: again the relative attachment of a principal clause, frequent in Luke. Grammatically ἐξετίθετο[5] is the main verb upon which the two participles διαμαρτυρόμενος[6] and πείθων[7] depend. But since the object of ἐξετίθετο and διαμαρτυρόμενος is the βασιλεία τοῦ θεοῦ, but the object of πείθων is τὰ περὶ τοῦ Ἰησοῦ, the 'kingdom of God' and 'the things about Jesus' properly stand side by side. The second expression refers to the facts of the death and resurrection attested in the Holy Scriptures, and therefore the Messiahship of Jesus. βασιλεία τοῦ θεοῦ can itself describe the entire Christian proclamation: so **19**.8 and **20**.25; at **1**.3 also it has this meaning (cf. *ThWb* I, 584, 22ff.). If on the other hand, as here and in **8**.12 and **28**.31, it is mentioned along with the events of Jesus, then it has the 'futuristic' meaning of which **14**.22[8] speaks. At the Parousia the future kingdom will come with the returning Jesus: Lk. **21**.31.—Paul's efforts to win the Jews last throughout the day: this shows how intent he was on winning them.

VERSE 24: In ἐπείθοντο there is no thought of a real conversion any more than in the similar scene at **23**.9. Theoretically the Jews are not at one as

---

[1] Bauernfeind's translation 'demand' is too sharp.

[2] γνωστόν ἐστιν is Lucan: see on **1**.19.—According to Bornhäuser (66) Christianity is here described by the Roman Jews as 'heresy'. This is to misinterpret αἵρεσις; the Roman Jews would not have eagerly (πλείονες!) allowed the teaching of a heresy to be expounded to them.

[3] E. Meyer's translation (III 62) 'it is everywhere judged adversely' is in our opinion linguistically impossible.

[4] *Beg.* IV 346 translates ξενία by 'hospitality'. But even if καλεῖν ἐπὶ ξενίαν is a common formula of invitation, 'hospitality' does not fit here: Paul does not invite the Jewish leaders to dinner, but they come to the inn where he lives. When Zahn (852) suggests that 'he must have succeeded in finding very spacious accommodation for city conditions, for the number of different persons who could visit him there undisturbed was from the first considerable, and must have grown from day to day', he has allowed his fantasy free rein at the wrong place. Luke did not, as Jacquier (758) thinks ('Le logement du Paul a du être assez spacieux pour les recevoir tous'), worry as to how the πλείονες all found room.

[5] Cf. **11**.4: ἐξετίθετο λέγων; **18**.26: ἐξέθεντο τὴν ὁδὸν τοῦ κυρίου.

[6] διαμαρτύρομαι (cf. Strathmann *ThWb* IV 518f.) is in Acts one of the words which describe the Christian proclamation; cf. **2**.40; **8**.25; **10**.42; **18**.5; **20**.21; **20**.24; **23**.11.

[7] πείθω (**13**.43; **18**.4; **19**.8, 26) reflects the efforts of the Christian missionary to convince his hearers of the truth of the Christian proclamation.

[8] See further the saying Lk. **23**.42, exactly matching Acts **14**.22, where the βασιλεία in heaven is designated as the 'kingdom of Jesus' as in Lk. **22**.30. Cf. Bent Noack, *Das Gottesreich bei Lukas*, Symb. Bibl. Upps. 10, 1948; H. Conzelmann, *Die Mitte der Zeit*, 1954, esp. 96ff. (ET *The Theology of Luke*, 1960, 117ff).

regards the Christian doctrine; but in practice neither of the two groups decides for Christianity: Loisy 937.

VERSE 25: The Jews are ἀσύμφωνοι, at variance as in **23**.10. In view of this position Paul speaks the 'one word', which is introduced by ὅτι *recitativum* (Bl.-Debr. § 410, 1). καλῶς κτλ (cf. Mk. **7**.6): 'has correctly . . . spoken'—'it is true, what the Holy Spirit said to your fathers by the prophet Isaiah', it is fulfilled in you. 'Spoken to the fathers', although Isa. **6**.9 is directed to the prophet; for the emphasis lies on the prophecy directed to Israel.[1] As such a prophecy of obduracy the Isaiah passage prepares for v. 28.

VERSE 26f.: πρὸς τὸν λαὸν τοῦτον against LXX and the Hebrew text is related to 'go' instead of to 'speak'; otherwise the quotation agrees with LXX. This had already made finite verbs out of the imperative 'harden', etc., so that the entire guilt falls upon the people whose stubbornness the prophet now already confirms as a fact. μήποτε cannot in this context have the meaning 'unless perhaps' assumed by Jeremias (*Die Gleichnisse Jesu*,[4] 11; ET *The Parables of Jesus* 1963[2], 17) for the conjectural saying of Jesus. The prophecy describes here only the actual stubbornness and not its possible cessation.

VERSE 28: γνωστόν: see on **1**.19. 'This salvation of God was sent to the Gentiles'—with this (as in **13**.48, **18**.6) the reason is given for the transfer of the saving proclamation from the Jews to the Gentiles. In Asia Minor, Greece and now Italy the same rejection by the Jews brings about the Gentile mission. αὐτοὶ καὶ ἀκούσονται: 'they will listen'. For καί see **1**.3; *Beg.* IV 348.[2]

VERSE 30: 'He remained two whole years[3] in his own rented quarters': anyone who writes thus knows (1) that a change then occurred, and (2) in

---

[1] As is clear from our passage, but also from Mk. **4**.12 par. and John **12**.40, Isa. **6**.9f. was understood in the Hellenistic community purely as God's judgement of rejection. We may not confound this theological interpretation with Rom. **11**.26.

[2] The Western text, which has left its traces in L P S, has inserted as v. 29: 'And when he said this the Jews went away disputing much among themselves': gig p sy^hmg vg codd (*Beg.* III 255).

[3] The question raised by the expression διετίαν ὅλην has been answered in different ways by scholars.

1. Harnack: *Beiträge* IV 81 (ET) advanced the thesis that 'Acts, viewed by itself, demands composition before the destruction of Jerusalem and before the death of Paul'. Ibid., 69: 'The closing verses of Acts . . . make it in the highest degree probable that the work was written when Paul's trial in Rome was not yet at an end.' So also A. C. Clark 389f., and Wikenhauser *Apg.* 233 as a possibility.

2. Bauernfeind 279: 'The moment the powerful community in Rome greets the Apostle to the Gentiles as one of its own, the ecclesiastical situation is created which speaks directly to the reader; here your service begins.' But this would have been no reason to break off before a favourable decision in the trial—if it occurred.

3. Ramsay (*St. Paul* 308f.) gathered from the conclusion of Acts: Paul's trial was important for Luke only if it ended with an acquittal; thus the introduction of the trial already shows that Paul was acquitted. This was effected through a decision from the highest

Roman court that it was permissible 'to preach Christianity'. The judgement which set Paul free was thus a Magna Carta of religious freedom! It was only annulled by later decisions from the same high court. Luke must have planned to relate in a third book of this freedom of Paul, the use which he made of this new-found freedom, and his second arrest and martyrdom.—Such a verdict by the highest court would actually have been of the very greatest importance to the Christians. They would by all means have appealed to it, even when Rome later altered her position. But Christian apologetic knows nothing of such a favourable verdict, and from this it follows that it was not issued. Moreover such a verdict would have formed the natural conclusion to Acts. The assumption that Luke broke off before it is simply meaningless.

4. Eger (*Rechtsgeschichtliches zum Neuen Testament*, Rektoratsrede Basel 1919, 20ff.) referred to an imperial edict (BGU 628 recto, printed in *Beg.* V 333f.) which was earlier (Mommsen) ascribed to the third century and is now credited to Nero (cf. Mitteis, *Grundzüge der Papyruskunde* II 1, 281). It concerns criminal cases which come before Caesar by *provocatio* or *remissio*. That they may not be delayed by a belated appearance of the parties, the *divus parens* (probably Claudius) had already appointed a period within which the parties had to appear in Rome. This period is now fixed for capital cases in which the parties have to travel across the sea at one and a half years. If both parties do not come, the case is dismissed. What happens if the accuser is absent is not stated. Lake (who develops this thesis in *Beg.* V 326ff.) now conjectures that the period was fixed by Claudius at two years and that after the expiry of this period, if the accuser did not appear, the accused was automatically set free. Paul's case was still dealt with under the conditions laid down by Claudius. The readers understood without any more ado from the wording of Acts **28**.30 that Paul was released after these years. But such a δίκη ἐρήμη, a trial ended through the non-appearance of the opposition, does not prove Paul's innocence. Hence Luke did not emphasize the release but rather the unrestricted freedom of preaching which Paul enjoyed in the two preceding years.

This hypothesis is well worked out. But—to disregard other factors—the decisive statement about the διετία remains unfounded and unproved. What can be adduced in its favour?

(a) Philo (*In Flacc.* 128f.; C.-W. Bd. 6, 143, 24ff.) reports about a certain Lampo who was accused in Alexandria of ἀσέβεια against the emperor Tiberius and whose trial the malevolent Prefect of Egypt protracted ἐπὶ διετίαν 'in order to make life more miserable for him than death by keeping the fear of an uncertain future suspended over him πρὸς μήκιστον χρόνον'. But are the two years 'the longest admissible time'? Moreover it is the governor who drags out the trial, not a plaintiff who does not appear, and an appeal to Caesar does not come into question.

Thus we cannot speak of a real parallel to Paul's case: this Ramsay (*Teaching of St. Paul in Terms of the Present Day*, 1913, 365, 378f.) and Cadbury (*Beg.* V 332) have conceded.

(b) Pliny (*Ep.* X 56) reports to Trajan: The Proconsul of Bithynia, Julius Bassus, had among other things exiled a man for life in the year 98. The sentences passed by Bassus were later lifted. The Senate granted all those sentenced a new trial before the new governor, if they proposed it within two years. The exile made no use of this possibility. To Pliny's question what should be done with him, Trajan answers (*Ep.* X 57) that the man has had a *biennium*, if he felt himself unjustly treated, to propose a new trial. Pliny was to send him now (more than ten years after the first verdict!) to Trajan's *praefecti praetorii* in Rome.—The text, as Cadbury emphasizes, does not speak of an appeal, but rather of a new trial before a new governor. The period of two years was appointed by the Senate for this exceptional case. A real parallel to Paul's trial thus does not exist here either.

The hypothesis that an accused was set free after two years if the plaintiff did not appear in Rome is therefore not supported by these cases. We even know of a case where several Jews sent as prisoners to Rome by the procurator Felix were in the year 66, hence after a much longer time than a biennium, still in custody: Josephus *Vita* 13f.

A further misgiving against this hypothesis remains unallayed: why should the plaintiffs not have appeared in Rome? Cadbury considers the costs which the journey and the trial would have brought on the Jewish accusers. But he himself points out that the Roman

what it consisted. But Luke does not divulge a thing.—That Paul 'received all visitors' does not mean—as the Western text understood it: 614 gig p—'Jews and Greeks', but rather (Wendt 369) the unrestricted reception of all visitors, who are now to be considered as Gentiles.

VERSE 31: κηρύσσων . . . Χριστοῦ: see on v. 23. μετὰ πάσης παρρησίας (alliteration!) 'freely and openly'.[1] ἀκωλύτως: this 'unhindered' shows the tolerance of Rome at that time towards the Christian message. That Rome should continue this policy is Luke's passionate desire, the fulfilment of which he wished to promote precisely in these last chapters.

The history of interpretation shows that anyone who interprets this section as a documentary report falls immediately into difficulties.

Paul has scarcely arrived in Rome and found his own quarters[2] when he calls the 'first of the Jews' together. It was certainly important for Paul to learn whether the High Council in Jerusalem had already made an agreement with the Roman Jews against him, and how Roman Judaism generally stood in relation to Christianity and to Paul himself. For the Roman Jews were in a position to support an accusation not only financially, but even more by their connections with the imperial court. In the case related by Josephus *Vita* 13–16 they could successfully appeal to Nero's Jewish favourite actor, Aliturus, and Nero's consort Poppaea Sabina. In view of this situation it would have been most natural for Paul first to discuss these questions with the leaders of the Christian community (or communities) in Rome: they must know best of all how the Roman Jews stood in relation to Christianity and which steps had the best prospects of success. But the Christian community in Rome is not mentioned at all. Instead of these Paul calls the leaders of the Jews together. Many commentators (Schlatter, Beyer, Bauernfeind, among others) have taken no offence at this. But one may not forget: Paul was a highly suspect prisoner implicated by Jews in a trial of life and

---

Jews could have made their great influence felt against Paul. Moreover the Sanhedrin, as is well known, had rich financial resources at its disposal.—In view of this situation we have no reason to count upon an automatic release of Paul after two years.

Finally it is not once stated that the trial against Paul rested at all during this period. If on the part of the Jews Paul was accused of *seditio* and the charge was not confined merely to the time in Jerusalem, about which Paul speaks in Acts 24.11ff., but was extended to the preceding period as Tertullus does in v. 5, then extensive and time-consuming investigations were necessary to procure the evidence requisite for a verdict. Admittedly we do not know whether the proceedings were conducted with such care.

5. On the attempts at a solution by Pfister and James, see above Intro. § 1, p. 12 n. 2. They are extremely improbable.

[1] παρρησία in Acts, as H. Schlier (*ThWb* V 880f.) has shown, contains the three motifs of public, candid and forceful speech. In our passage the emphasis is upon the first two.

[2] Since μίσθωμα is not elsewhere attested in this meaning, but only as 'house-rent' —Liddell-Scott 1137 adduce only this passage for the sense 'hired house'—Lake (*Beg.* IV 348) proposed the translation 'at his own cost'. What is meant is in any case the same as by καθ' ἑαυτόν in **28.16** and ξενία in **28.23**.

death, and for the Roman Jews anything but a respectable person whose invitation was immediately accepted. This difficulty, however, is not the only one.

Paul first of all reports about his trial. The reader of the book can understand this report; for Paul's listeners it would have been incomprehensible. Luke admittedly could not allow Paul to develop yet again the whole course of the proceedings up to this point; he had to be brief. But even this already shows that here the writer and not the historian determines the presentation. It turns out uniquely enough: only the accusation of a crime against the Jewish people and the 'customs of the fathers' comes into consideration. Against them Paul has not transgressed. In spite of this he has been delivered 'from Jerusalem' as a prisoner to the Romans; when they wanted to release him, he had to appeal to Caesar because of the Jewish opposition. That is, simply that view of the trial is suggested which Luke wants to impress on the reader as the definitive one. In reality the Romans—to mention only this— never wanted to release Paul, but the Jew Agrippa affirmed in a scene drafted by Luke—after the appeal!—that Paul could have been set free if he had not appealed to Caesar! Then Paul affirms again that he stands before them in these chains only because of Israel's hope—this too is a Lucan construction whose unreality is apparent. And thus the incomprehensible situation results: really no one is at fault—for Paul does not want to blame his people—and yet Paul stands under judgement charged with a capital crime!

Just as incomprehensible is the answer of the Jews. That since the appeal they have still heard nothing about Paul is perfectly understandable— the news could hardly travel faster than Paul himself. But the Roman Jews have apparently still heard nothing unfavourable about Paul at all, and that is unbelievable. What Luke has mentioned in Acts 21.21 about Jewish charges against Paul will have found its way not only to Jerusalem but also to Rome, and the detail with which Paul in Romans discusses the Jewish problem is conditioned not only by his personal interest in this question but betrays also his endeavour to prevent or correct misrepresentations of his teaching and conduct. The Roman Jews appear nevertheless—and that is even more surprising—to have heard scarcely anything so far not only about Paul but about the entire Christian αἵρεσις, and actually to know only that it everywhere meets with opposition. Hence they now want to obtain information from Paul himself. Such an ignorance on the part of the Roman Jews is impossible. The Epistle to the Romans proves that in Rome there was a substantial Christian community (how it was organized is here beside the point), and we have every reason for the assumption that the Christian message came to Rome at the end of the 40's, and as a Messianic preaching led to the sharpest controversies in the Jewish community.

In view of these arguments Schneckenburger (86) once asserted that in reality the Roman Jews had very precise information concerning Christianity.

But they concealed their knowledge, to give themselves the appearance of greater impartiality. Against this, Zeller (293) rightly pointed out that the Jews had no reason at all for such behaviour, and that Luke himself simply does not suggest such a Jewish falsehood. Lake (*Beg.* IV 346) wanted to explain 'the anxiety of the Roman Jews to dissociate themselves from the case' by the fact that 'the Romans had severe laws against prosecutors who failed to make good their accusations'. Only here the Roman Jews were simply not to appear as prosecutors before the court. If they had heard anything unfavourable about Christianity, they could have said it to Paul quietly without coming into conflict with those laws. Luke's presentation moreover does not suggest by a single syllable that the Jews held back their better knowledge. Luke presupposes that they earnestly desire instruction, show great interest (not only the 'leaders' come to Paul, but many others!), and that Paul himself takes them seriously.

Most exegetes have therefore assumed that the Jews spoke the truth. How then was their ignorance about Christianity possible in view of the Christian congregation and the proceedings under Claudius? Neander (496) dealt with the difficulty very simply: in the large city of Rome the rich Jews had other things to think about than the small Christian congregation and its religious questions. As if there were only rich and worldly Jews in Rome, and as if the Messianic proclamation of the Christians could have been a matter of indifference to the Jews! In view of the proceedings under Claudius, B. Weiss conceded that Christians and Jews once came into conflict in Rome—but this conflict now lay far in the past and was forgotten. Once accepted, the relationship between Christians and Jews in Rome had improved. But this does not mean that the Jews now knew no more about the Christians! Olshausen (*StKr* 1838, 925) grasps at another consideration: Claudius had once exiled the Jews. When later new Jews moved in, these no longer knew anything about the Christians . . . If nothing could be made of this all too naive explanation, what remained but Bleek's despairing assertion (*Einleitung in das NT* 412): in Rome there was still no close-knit Christian congregation at all! The Epistle to the Romans of course proves the contrary. But one thing can be said for Bleek: he reflects the impression which Luke's account makes upon readers who do not have Paul's letters at hand and critically compare them, but only read Acts scene by scene. This was the judgement not only of Hilgenfeld (*ZwTh* 1898, 595) and Holtzmann (156) but also of E. Meyer (III, 63). Luke as a matter of fact here ignores the Christian community in Rome (we shall soon see why). That in so doing he leaves the realm of history is clear.

This unhistorical presupposition, that the Roman Jews know about Christianity only from hearsay, also marks the second scene—and at the same time weakens it. Paul speaks for a whole day about the kingdom of God and the event of Jesus, and presents the scriptural proof for it. Some of the Jews are convinced, the others are not, and the two groups finally depart at odds with one another, while Paul sees the prophecy of Isa. 6.9f. fulfilled: God has hardened the Jews' hearts; salvation is now for the Gentiles, and 'they will listen'! That is Paul's last word in Acts. The road is finally open for the Gentile mission.

It is first of all very noteworthy that Paul in this manner describes all Jews as obdurate, even though some—as it is expressly said—'were convinced'. This difficulty arises from the fact that Luke here of necessity has to unite two conflicting ideas. For one thing the Christian message, according to his account, is essentially in agreement with Judaism. Luke had illustrated this in the fictitious scene before the Sanhedrin in 23.7ff., through the assent which the Pharisees accord to Paul. Here Luke has not taken the trouble to introduce again the opposition between the Pharisees and Sadducees; it is also out of place for Rome. Then the only possibility left to him was simply to make one group of Jews agree with Paul. On the other hand, however, it was by no means his intention to portray a Jewish conversion here; on the contrary, he wanted to present the Jewish reserve against the Christian message, that obduracy which compelled the mission to the Gentiles. The two together necessarily produced the tension in our text, that many Jews ἐπείθοντο and yet all are treated as obdurate.

But why now did Luke present Paul's activity in Rome in this unhistorical manner? A first hint is given us by the observation that the last scene of the book agrees exactly with that in Pisidian Antioch (13.46) and with the one in Corinth (18.6). Three times in Acts Luke has depicted in detail the experience—certainly often encountered by Paul—that the Jews closed their minds and hearts to the Gospel. The first of these cases occurred on the first missionary journey in Asia Minor, the second in the midst of Paul's activity in Greece, the third here at the end in Italy. Dibelius (*Studies* 150) correctly emphasizes that this is no accident, but the 'work of an author who is consciously creating, and not renouncing literary devices'. These three scenes, representative of all corresponding incidents, make visible the fundamental experience of Paul and the Christian mission generally. Against the will of the Christian missionaries their proclamation, through its rejection by the Jews, is forcibly directed to the Gentiles, among whom Luke will also have included Paul's visitors (v. 30).

But by the fact that Luke here presents Paul's missionary experience, it is now open for him to make Paul appear in Rome also conducting a mission to the Jews. Yet this situation is now no longer so easily brought about. Paul in Rome is no longer a free man. He cannot, as he had in Antioch and Corinth, seek out the synagogues and preach there. He must therefore have the Jews come to his quarters—the beginning of our section is thus clearly shown to be a necessary part of the Lucan composition. On the other hand, Paul cannot simply call the Jews together to preach to them. So instruction regarding his position is introduced as the reason for the invitation, and Luke uses the opportunity now to present Paul's trial with extreme brevity. That nothing more is reported about the concrete accusation and that it is really inconceivable how Paul was arrested at all and kept in custody, does not disturb Luke. For him it is actually a contradiction that the Apostle was not released. There is also another historical offence which does not exist for Luke: Paul is for him a person of such repute that at his request the 'first of the Jews' as a matter of course immediately put in an appearance. Luke always has his own picture of Paul before his eyes and not the picture which for example the Apostle's opponents possessed according to II Cor. **10**.10.

But the situation in which Paul speaks to the Roman Jews as a missionary can again be introduced only if the Roman Jews have not yet been informed of the accusations made against Paul in Jerusalem. Indeed, Paul must not have been discredited at all. Now we understand why Luke has the Jews assert in v. 21 that they have neither officially nor unofficially received anything detrimental from Judaea. But the situation presupposed involves even more: the Roman Jews may not even know anything very exact about Christianity. Verse 22 corresponds to this: they know only that this movement everywhere meets with opposition. Hence Paul, since he belongs to this αἵρεσις, has to speak his mind about it. This produces the missionary situation: ignorance of the Christian message, combined with the desire to learn something about it.

Now however a final difficulty presented itself. If Paul brings the Christian message to the uninformed Jews in Rome, how does it stand with the Christian community in Rome? Luke could not strike it out, and yet he could not presuppose its existence here. He helped himself out of this cul-de-sac as well as was conceivably possible. He gave the Roman Christians brief recognition in the preceding section, at Paul's arrival in Rome; they hasten to meet Paul at the Tres Tabernae and Forum Appii, and he is encouraged at the sight of them. With this Luke has bestowed on the Roman congregation—outside Rome!—the honourable mention which is its due. When he depicts Paul's Roman sojourn, he no longer needs to mention the Roman community. This silence about it is the price Luke has to pay for making Paul work in Rome as a missionary.

We have seen so far that, since Luke allows the missionary experience of Paul (and of Christianity) to repeat itself in Rome, the conclusion of the entire book agrees internally with the preceding description of the Pauline mission. The last chapter also is thus completely integrated into the total work in that it bases the justification of the Gentile mission on the refusal of the Jews. But that is not all. Luke had succeeded in transforming Paul's journey from Caesarea to Rome into a triumph of the witness of God. Imprisonment does not compel Paul to passivity, but must rather serve to show his activity in the brightest light. But with this the author had now set himself the task of maintaining this level in the last scene of the book. We may not deny to Luke the recognition that here yet again Paul has become the active centre of the whole. The reader closes the book with the conviction that Paul in the two years of this stay in his quarters learned by experience that 'the Gentiles listen'.

Correct as all this is, and certain as it is that the author has here discharged his task of carrying through the unity of his work to the last, and making Paul, the hero of the second part, remain the dominant central figure to the very margin of the presentation—for Luke even more was at stake. He had reported at the beginning of the book the missionary command of the exalted Lord (1.8): 'You will be my witnesses . . . to the ends of the earth.' But then this book cannot close with the great co-worker of the twelve Apostles, who has brought the gospel to the entire East, coming to Rome condemned to inactivity, and a congregation there not founded and fostered by any apostle forestalling him in the crowning achievement of his labours. Such a conclusion, to the mind of Luke and his readers, would have made a torso not only of Luke's work but of the apostolic mission itself.

But yet another major concern of Luke's would have received short measure with such a solution. In Rome Paul works 'unhindered'. With this Luke brings to its final destination that endeavour which we have observed again and again from Chapter 21 on, the effort to prove that the Roman government was favourably disposed to early Christianity and permitted its proclamation. Most readers of Acts may scarcely have realized what great pains Luke took to make it understandable why the innocent Paul was not released from custody. For the event which alone would have given telling force to the thesis of the favourable disposition and tolerance of Rome, Paul's liberation, Luke evidently could not report. Nowhere has he prepared his reader for a happy conclusion to the trial; he has always emphasized only that Paul deserved neither death nor imprisonment—and that is something different. On the other hand, Luke has told his readers through the mouth of an angel that Paul will yet give his witness before Caesar (27.24), and he has emphatically assured them in the farewell speech at Miletus that all 'among whom Paul travelled preaching the kingdom of God, will not see his face again' (20.25, 38). Of Paul's plan to go to Spain, the reader of Acts has heard not a word. Exegetes, misled by their knowledge of this plan and by the desire to make room for the Pastoral Epistles, have been remarkably hard of hearing where these hints are concerned. According to Zahn (718) it is proof of the fidelity of Luke's reporting that it has not altered even an unfulfilled prophecy. But the case here is quite different. Luke has not only had Paul make that prediction (in the final analysis one may not forget that the speech in Miletus derives from him and not from Paul) but in the concluding verse of this scene he has once again referred quite emphatically to this prophecy. We really ought to give Luke the author credit for not wishing expressly to characterize this 'I know' of **20**.25 as an error, and thereby to weaken all the other prophecies of Paul introduced by the same 'I know'.

Luke thus presupposes Paul's martyrdom. That he did not recount it (and also did not intend to recount it in a third book) can really be understood of itself. He did not see it as his task to enhance devotion to the martyrs. The only martyr of whom he speaks in detail is Stephen, the first martyr of the Christian Church. Luke could not ignore him, and he did not need to, for Stephen had been a victim of the godless Sadducees. On the other hand, the death of James the son of Zebedee, who had been executed by the government, by King Agrippa I, Luke mentions without emphasis and almost in passing (**12**.2), and he has remained completely silent about the martyrdom of James the Lord's brother. He did not desire, in the manner of the Revelation of John, to equip the Christians for martyrdom, but rather to spare the Church martyrdom so far as possible. Hence he did not allow Acts to end with the martyrdom of Paul, but rather with the good advice which, if followed, would have spared much blood and tears: ἀκωλύτως.

But was this apologetic attempt not hopeless from the beginning, since everyone knew that Paul was not released but executed, and that Christians had been burnt as living torches? These events frankly were a sore hindrance for Luke. But they did not make his attempt impossible. Paul and the other Christians had been done to death by Nero, and Nero's memory was proscribed. A Neronic judgement did not bind the Roman state. Hence the attempt to win peace for the Church, but also for the state, by referring to the state's earlier conduct and the Church's own past, was not in any way meaningless; it had to be undertaken, even if the probability of success was none too great. Through the history of the apostolic age, which sets up an edifying model for the Christian community, Luke endeavours to accomplish this task also. He found many an apologist to succeed him, but they followed other routes. The idea that the history of the Church can also be its *apologia* has remained the special preserve of the historical writer Luke.

INDEX

The index gives references of historical, literary and theological importance, but is not intended as a concordance.